CANADIAN

MANAGERIAL FINANCE

The Dryden Series in Finance

FOURTH EDITION

CANADIAN
MANAGERIAL FINANCE

PAUL HALPERN
University of Toronto

J. FRED WESTON
University of California, Los Angeles

EUGENE F. BRIGHAM
University of Florida

DRYDEN

Harcourt Brace & Company, Canada

Toronto   Montreal   Fort Worth   New York   Orlando   Philadelphia
San Diego   London   Sydney   Tokyo

Canadian Cataloguing in Publication Data

Halpern, Paul
    Canadian managerial finance

4th ed.
First ed. published under title: Essentials of
Canadian managerial finance.
Includes index.
ISBN 0-03-922909-2

1. Corporations – Canada – Finance. I. Weston,
J. Fred (John Fred) – 1916–   .   II. Brigham,
Eugene F., 1930–   .   III. Title.

HG4090.W48 1994   658.15'0971   C93-094222-1

Publisher: Scott Duncan
Senior Editor and Marketing Manager: Ronald Fitzgerald
Developmental Editor: Cheryl Teelucksingh
Marketing Co-ordinator: Lisa Whyatt
Director of Publishing Services: Jean Davies
Editorial Manager: Marcel Chiera
Supervising Editor: Carol Tong
Production Editor: Theresa Fitzgerald
Production Manager: Sue-Ann Becker
Manufacturing Co-ordinator: Denise Wake
Copy Editor: Lenore d'Anjou
Interior Design: Rob McPhail
Cover Design: Dave Peters
Typesetting and Assembly: Black Dot Graphics
Printing and Binding: Best Gagné Book Manufacturers
Cover Photo: Gary Buss/Masterfile

∞ This book was printed in Canada on acid-free paper.

3 4 5

To Irene, Marni, and Adam.

PREFACE

The central focus of modern corporate finance is the maximization of the value of the firm, and *Canadian Managerial Finance* investigates the role of financial management in attaining this value maximization. Corporations must operate in all kinds of economic environments, and changes in economic conditions can be rapid. For example, in the late 1980s the economy was booming but by 1990 a severe recession had begun. Different environments present different problems—and solutions—to the financial manager. Mergers and takeovers were predominant in the expansionary period; divestitures and restructurings are a major tool of financial managers today. Fortunately, the overall role of value maximization and the associated decision criteria will lead financial managers to correct decisions regardless of the economic environment.

Intended Market and Use

Canadian Managerial Finance is intended for use as an introductory text. The main parts can be covered in a one-term course, and, supplemented with cases and some outside readings, the book can also be used in a two-term course. If the book is used in a one-term course, the instructor will probably want to cover only selected chapters, leaving the others for students to examine on their own or to use as references in conjunction with work in later courses. In our classes, we normally cover Chapters 1 through 19, and finance majors then cover the remaining topics in the next course. Also, we have made every effort to write the chapters in a modular form, which makes it easy for instructors to cover the material in a sequence different from the one in the book.

Major Changes in the Fourth Edition

The theory and practice of finance are dynamic, and, as important new developments occur, they must be incorporated into a textbook such as this one. Also, we and a team of reviewers are constantly on the lookout for ways to improve the book in terms of clarity and understanding. As a result, we have made several important changes in this edition, including the following:

1. All sections have been updated to reflect the latest tax laws, interest rates, and other financial developments.
2. Additional "real world" examples have been added to the chapter openings entitled "A Managerial Perspective" to illustrate the importance of financial management.
3. A new section on business ethics has been added to Chapter 1, and attention is given to ethical issues throughout the remainder of the book.

4. A discussion of the nominal risk-free rate of interest, k_{RF}, called the "risk-free rate" throughout the text, has been added to Chapter 3.

5. The explanation of the time value of money has been moved from the first part of the book to Chapter 12, just before the discussion of capital budgeting. Although time value is a fundamental concept, it is not used until much later in the text. Its new position makes the flow from interest rate mathematics to its application in capital budgeting smooth and timely.

6. The capital budgeting chapter has been divided into two chapters, 13 and 14. The former presents the conceptual framework for capital budgeting, whereas the latter demonstrates the application of the concepts to actual examples. This change makes the capital budgeting area more digestible for students.

7. Sections on the modified internal rate of return (MIRR) and multiple IRRs have been added to Chapter 13. The modified IRR is more useful than the traditional IRR in capital budgeting, hence it is essential in any presentation of capital budgeting techniques.

8. Part of the discussion of capital structure theory, including the MM model and asymmetric information effects, has been moved from the body of Chapter 18 to a chapter appendix. This change was suggested by several reviewers who regarded the material as too theoretical for inclusion in many introductory courses. Now instructors have more flexibility in choosing to cover or to skip the material.

9. A discussion of putable bonds has been added to Chapter 21, and the coverage of bond indentures has been updated to include material on the impact of LBOs and similar events on the bond ratings of firms such as RJR Nabisco.

10. Several changes have been made to Chapter 24, including the addition of a section on corporate alliances. Also, new examples were added to illustrate information presented in the chapter—these examples concerned acquisitions made by Federated Department Stores and the leveraged buyout of RJR Nabisco by KKR. In addition, divestitures such as spinoffs and selloffs are described and evaluated.

11. The chapter on bankruptcy and reorganization has been rewritten to reflect the changes arising in the new *Bankruptcy and Insolvency Act* and to include a discussion of the *Companies' Creditors Arrangement Act*, under which many of the very largest firms have reorganized their operations.

12. Concept review questions have been added to the major sections within each chapter. These questions ask the students about key concepts in the section they have just read, and if they cannot answer the questions, then students should reread the section. Our own students call these questions "attention joggers," and they find them most useful.

13. The old chapter summaries have been replaced with new ones in which the main ideas covered in each chapter appear in a list of key concepts. This new format makes it much easier for students to review the chapter.

14. We have added to most sets of end-of-chapter problems an integrative problem that covers, in a comprehensive manner, all of the major concepts discussed in the chapter. These problems can be used as a basis for a lecture, or they can be used by students as comprehensive study problems.

15. The number of end-of-chapter problems has been increased, and the range of difficulty expanded.

Ancillary Materials

A number of additional items are available to students and instructors.

Instructor's Manual. A comprehensive manual is available to instructors who adopt the book. The manual contains (1) answers to all text questions and problems, (2) sample exam questions, (3) suggested course outlines, (4) a detailed set of lecture notes (including suggestions for use of the acetate transparencies described in the next section), and (5) detailed solutions to the integrative lecture problems, with transparency masters to illustrate them.

Study Guide. This supplement outlines the key sections of each chapter, and provides students with self-test questions and with a set of problems and solutions similar to those in the text and in the *Instructor's Manual.*

Casebook. A casebook, *Cases in Financial Management* First Canadian Edition (Dryden Press, 1992) by Eugene F. Brigham, Leo T. Gallant, and Louis C. Gapenski, provides a set of 23 cases that illustrate applications of the methodologies and concepts developed in the text.

Readings Books. A readings book, *Issues in Managerial Finance*, 3rd edition (Dryden Press, 1987), edited by Ramon E. Johnson, provides an excellent mix of theoretical and practical articles that can be used to supplement the text. Another supplemental reader is *Advances in Business Financial Management: A Collection of Readings* (Dryden Press, 1989), edited by Philip L. Cooley, which provides a broader selection of articles from which to choose.

Finance with Lotus 1-2-3®: Text, Cases, and Models. This text by Eugene F. Brigham, Dana A. Aberwald, and Susan E. Ball (Dryden Press, 1988) enables students to learn, on their own, how to use *Lotus 1-2-3*, and it explains how many commonly encountered problems in managerial finance can be analyzed with electronic spreadsheets.

PROFIT +. This software supplement by James Pettijohn contains 18 user-friendly programs that include the time value of money, forecasting, and capital budgeting. The program includes a user's manual, and it is available for the IBM PC.

Acknowledgements

I gratefully acknowledge the comments and suggestions from the following people who reviewed the manuscript of this fourth edition at various stages: Margaret Martin, University of New Brunswick; John Herzog, Simon Fraser University; Shelley MacDougall, Acadia University; A.J. Saaltink, Mohawk College; and Harold Musson, University of Windsor.

In addition, I have benefited from discussions with my colleagues at the Faculty of Management and Faculty of Law, University of Toronto. In particular, I would like to acknowledge the assistance provided by L. Booth, R. Daniels, R. Elitzur, V. Jog, J. MacIntosh, J. Mintz, M. Puffer, W. Rotenberg, A. White, and J. Ziegel.

I would also like to thank the following individuals and companies who provided access to data and reviewed chapters relevant to their experience: F. Bennie, of Canadian Bank Note Company Limited; A. Filipiuk, of Richardson Greenshields; K. Hawkins, of ScotiaMcLeod; P. Kidnie, of the Bank of Montreal; N. Nicholas, of Levesque Beaubien; the Canadian Bond Rating Service; and the Royal Bank of Canada.

Scott Allerston at the Business Information Centre of the Faculty of Management, University of Toronto displayed remarkable skill in finding data sources that at first blush appeared not to exist. Finally, a very special thanks to Madeline Stead who not only prepared solutions for the Solutions Manual and made valuable suggestions on the ordering of the chapters and the contents of a number of them, but also was instrumental in responding to editorial queries while I was out of the country. We both learned how international communications can be made easy through the use of the fax machine. Thanks go to the staff of Harcourt Brace & Company, Canada not only for their fine editorial work but also for their continued patience. Special thanks are due to Cheryl Teelucksingh, who, using gentle prodding was able to obtain the manuscript and revisions with some dispatch. This book reflects the talents of Ron Fitzgerald, Senior Editor and Marketing Manager; Theresa Fitzgerald, Production Editor; Carol Tong, Supervising Editor; and Lenore d'Anjou, Copy Editor.

Conclusion

Finance is, in a real sense, the cornerstone of the enterprise system—good financial management is vitally important to the economic health of business firms, and, hence, to the nation and the world. Because of its importance, finance should be widely and thoroughly understood, but this is easier said than done. The field is relatively complex, and it is undergoing constant change in response to shifts in economic conditions. All of this makes finance stimulating and exciting, but also challenging and sometimes perplexing. We sincerely hope that *Canadian Managerial Finance* will meet its own challenge by contributing to a better understanding of our financial system.

Paul Halpern
University of Toronto

A Note from the Publisher

Thank you for selecting *Canadian Managerial Finance*, fourth edition. The authors and publisher have devoted considerable time to the careful development of this book. We appreciate your recognition of this effort and accomplishment.

We want to hear what you think about *Canadian Managerial Finance*. Please take a few minutes to fill in the stamped reply card that you find at the back of the book. Your comments, suggestions, and criticisms will be valuable to us as we prepare new editions and other books.

BRIEF CONTENTS

CONTENTS

I

INTRODUCTION TO MANAGERIAL FINANCE

1

▲▲▲

The Finance Function

A Managerial Perspective

Managements of large firms with widely held equity are being attacked on many sides. Investors, especially institutional investors, such as pension and mutual funds, which own approximately 30 percent of the shares of Canadian companies, are no longer passive. They sell their shares when they disagree with management decisions. Even companies in which a strong control block owns superior voting shares have found their decisions under attack by institutional investors. Takeovers or potential takeovers also threaten the continued stewardship of many managements.

This struggle for control raises questions about the very nature of corporations. The theory behind the corporate form of organization is that managers are hired by shareholders for the express purpose of maximizing shareholder wealth. But is this theory really valid? Should managers focus primarily on shareholder interests, or should they have broader concerns?

Executives themselves are split on these issues. Some acknowledge that they view their primary goal as maximizing shareholder wealth, but others contend that they must look beyond the firm's shareholders to its other *stakeholders*—to its workers, suppliers, customers, and communities—and that only they, the managers, can balance the conflicts between these groups. Investors, on the other hand, often argue that managers hide behind ''social responsibility'' to deflect criticism of poor performance and to protect their jobs. These investors are simply fed up with entrenched managers' inefficient use of corporate resources and with their attempts to stop others from taking control and bringing in new ideas for improving efficiency and enhancing profits. It is also argued that if a competitive market is allowed to exist for firms and managers, then the best management teams will eventually run companies, and overall efficiency will be improved.

In this chapter we explore the control issue in more depth. We also outline the changing role and increasing importance of managerial finance, and we introduce the major types of financial decisions. The remainder of the book covers how these decisions should be made.

An Overview of Managerial Finance

What role does "finance" play within the firm? What specific tasks are assigned to the financial staff, and what tools and techniques are available to it for improving the firm's performance? On a broader scale, what is the role of finance in the Canadian economy, and how can financial management be used to further national goals? As we shall see, proper financial management within the firm will help any business provide better products to its customers at lower prices, pay higher wages and salaries to its workers and managers, and still provide greater returns to the investors who put up the capital needed to form and then operate the business. Since the economy—both national and global—consists of customers, employees, and investors (sometimes referred to as **stakeholders** of the company), sound financial management contributes to both individual well-being and the well-being of the general population.

The Changing Role of Financial Management

Finance consists of three interrelated areas: (1) *money and capital markets*, or macro finance, which deals with many of the topics covered in macroeconomics; (2) *investment*, which focusses on the decisions of individuals and financial institutions, such as mutual funds and pension funds, as they choose securities for their investment portfolios; and (3) *managerial finance*, or corporate finance, which involves the management of the firm. Each of these areas interacts with the others, so a corporate financial manager must have a good knowledge of capital market operations and of the way investors appraise securities, as well as of his or her own area.

The study of managerial finance has undergone significant changes over the years. When finance first emerged as a separate field of study in the early 1900s, the emphasis was on legalistic matters such as mergers, consolidations, the formation of new firms, and the different types of securities issued by firms. Industrialization was sweeping the country, and the critical problem faced by firms was obtaining capital for expansion. Capital markets were relatively primitive, and transfers of funds from individual savers to businesses were quite difficult. The earnings and assets values reported in accounting statements were unreliable, and trading in shares by insiders and manipulators caused prices to fluctuate wildly; both these factors made investors reluctant to purchase shares and bonds. In this environment, finance concentrated heavily on legal issues relating to the issuance of securities.

Radical changes occurred during the Depression of the 1930s. Business failures during that period shifted the focus to bankruptcy and reorganization, corporate liquidity, and government regulation of securities markets. Finance was still a descriptive, legalistic subject, but the emphasis moved from expansion to survival.

During the 1940s and early 1950s, finance continued to be taught as a descriptive, institutional subject, viewed from the outside rather than from the perspective of management. However, financial management techniques designed to help firms maximize their profits and increase the wealth of shareholders were beginning to receive attention.

A movement toward rigorous analysis developed during the late 1950s. Also, the major emphasis began to shift from the right-hand side of the balance sheet (liabilities and equity) to asset analysis. Computers were beginning to be used, and models were developed to help manage inventories, cash, accounts receivable, and fixed assets. Increasingly, the focus of finance shifted from the outsider's to the insider's point of view, and financial decision making within the firm was recognized as the critical issue in corporate finance. Descriptive, institutional materials on capital markets and financing instruments were still studied, but these topics were considered in terms of their effects on corporate financial decisions.

The 1960s and 1970s witnessed a renewed interest in the liabilities and equity side of the balance sheet, with a focus on the optimal mix of securities and the way in which individual investors make investment decisions—*portfolio theory*—and the implications of both topics for corporate finance. The study of corporate financial management was redesigned to help general management take actions that would maximize the value of the firm and the wealth of its shareholders. This was in the context that the results of corporate financial decisions depend upon how investors react to them. This recognition produced a blending of investment theory into the theory of corporate finance.

In the 1980s, four issues received emphasis: (1) inflation and its effects on interest rates; (2) deregulation of financial institutions and the accompanying trend away from specialized institutions toward broadly diversified financial service corporations; (3) a dramatic increase in the use of telecommunications for transmitting information and of computers for analyzing financial decisions; and (4) new and innovative methods for financing long-term investments. Ways to combat inflation and to deal with it when it heats up were worked into the fabric of both financial theories and financial decision processes. New financial institutions and products, such as money market funds and interest rate futures, were created. Older institutions made major structural changes: chartered banks now own brokerage firms. Technological developments in the computer hardware and telecommunications areas and the availability of software packages that make otherwise very difficult numerical analyses relatively easy began to bring about fundamental changes in the way managers manage. Data storage, transmittal, and retrieval techniques are sharpening the "judgemental" aspects of management, as financial managers can now obtain relatively precise estimates of the effects of alternative courses of action.

Several innovative financing techniques emerged in the 1980s in response to changing economic conditions. For example, a market for high-risk, high-yield bonds known as *junk bonds* was developed to finance mergers and managements' buyouts of their own firms. *Floating rate debt*, in which the interest rate is changed periodically to reflect current market conditions, was introduced to protect investors from the adverse effects of high inflation and fluctuating interest rates.

In the late 1980s and early 1990s, the economy moved into a recession, and companies re-evaluated their corporate and financial structures, employing current financial theory. Some companies determined that refocussing on fewer activities would create shareholder value. A frequent result was the sale of divisions or subsidiaries, generating funds often used to reduce the firm's debt ratio. In addition, the recession had associated with it a number of bankruptcies. Managers of some major companies had to learn how to negotiate with creditors to save their firms from liquidation.

Concept Review

► Identify three interrelated areas of finance and discuss the focus of each.
► Briefly outline the significant changes that the subject of managerial finance has undergone from the early 1900s to the early 1990s.
► What financial issues have received emphasis in the 1980s and 1990s?
► Identify several innovative financing techniques that emerged in the 1980s. What were the reasons for their development?

The Increasing Importance of Managerial Finance

The events discussed in the previous section have greatly increased the importance of managerial finance. In earlier times, the marketing manager would project sales, the engineering and production staffs would determine the assets necessary to meet those demands, and the financial manager's job was simply to raise the money needed to purchase the required plant, equipment, and inventories. This mode of operation is no longer prevalent; decisions are now made in a much more co-ordinated manner, and the financial manager generally has direct responsibility for the control process.

Surveys have found that the role of top corporate officers with legal and financial backgrounds has been increasing over time. The expanding size and complexity of corporate organizations, coupled with continuing international expansion, have increased the importance of financial planning and controls. The growth of government regulation and the obligations companies face under the law has heightened the need for legal advice. The engineer and the production expert have become less important in management than the financial executive and the lawyer.

The same shifts are also evident at lower levels of firms of all sizes, as well as in nonprofit and governmental organizations. Thus, it is becoming increasingly important for people in marketing, accounting, production, personnel, and other areas to understand finance in order to do a good job in their own fields. Marketing people, for instance, must understand how marketing decisions affect and are affected by the availability of funds, by inventory levels, by excess plant capacity, and so on. Similarly, accountants must understand how accounting data are used in corporate planning and reviewed by investors. The function of accounting is to provide quantitative financial information for use in making economic decisions, whereas the main functions of financial management are to plan for, acquire, and utilize funds in order to maximize the efficiency and value of the enterprise.

In brief, virtually all business decisions have financial implications, and nonfinancial executives simply must know enough finance to work these implications into their own specialized analyses. This point should make every student of business, regardless of major, concerned with finance.

Concept Review

► Explain why an understanding of financial planning and controls are important to today's chief executives.

The Financial Manager's Responsibilities

The financial manager must plan for the acquisition and use of funds so as to maximize the value of the firm. To put it another way, the financial manager makes decisions about alternative sources and uses of funds. Here are some of the specific activities involved.

1. *Forecasting and planning.*   The financial manager must interact with the other executives as they jointly look ahead and put in place the plans that will shape the future position of the firm.

2. *Major investment and financing decisions.*   On the basis of long-run plans, the financial manager must raise the capital needed to support growth. A successful firm usually achieves a high rate of growth in sales, which requires increased investments by the firm in the plant, equipment, and current assets necessary to produce goods and services. The financial manager must help determine the optimal rate of sales growth and decide on the specific investments to be made as well as on the types of funds to be used to finance these investments. Decisions must be made about the use of internal versus external funds, the use of debt versus equity, and the use of long-term versus short-term debt.

3. *Co-ordination and control.*   The financial manager must interact with executives in other parts of the business if the firm is to operate as efficiently as possible. All business decisions have financial implications, and all managers—financial and otherwise—need to take this into account. For example, marketing decisions affect sales growth, which in turn changes investment requirements. Thus, marketing decision-makers must take into account how their actions affect (and are affected by) such factors as the availability of funds, inventory policies, and plant capacity utilization.

4. *Interaction with capital markets.*   The financial manager must deal with the money and capital markets. As we shall see in Chapter 3, each firm affects and is affected by the general financial markets, where funds are raised, the firm's securities are traded, and its investors are either rewarded or penalized.

In sum, the central responsibilities of financial managers involve decisions such as which investments the firm should make, how these projects should be financed, and how the firm can manage its existing resources most effectively. If these responsibilities are performed optimally, financial managers will help to maximize the value of the firm as well as the long-run welfare of all those who interact with it.

Concept Review

▶ What is the financial manager's primary responsibility? What are some of the specific actions involved in carrying out that responsibility?

Finance in the Organizational Structure of the Firm

Organizational structures vary from firm to firm, but Figure 1-1 presents a fairly typical picture of the role of finance within a corporation. The *chief financial officer (CFO)*—who has the title of vice president: finance—reports to the president. Specific finance functions are typically divided between two senior financial officers: the *treasurer* and the *comptroller*, both of whom report to the CFO. The treasurer has direct responsibility for managing the firm's cash and marketable securities, for planning its capital structure, for selling equity and debt to raise capital, and for overseeing the corporate pension fund. Under the treasurer (in some firms under the comptroller) are the credit manager, the inventory manager, and the director of capital budgeting (who analyzes decisions related to investments in fixed assets). The comptroller is responsible for the activities of the accounting and tax departments.

As noted in Figure 1-1, the finance function is typically at the top of the organizational structure of the firm because optimum financial decisions are crucial to its survival and success. All important episodes in the lives of business firms raise questions that have major financial implications. Such choices include adding new product lines or eliminating old ones, expanding or adding plants or changing locations, and retaining earnings or raising external

Figure 1-1
The Place of Finance in a Typical
Business Organization

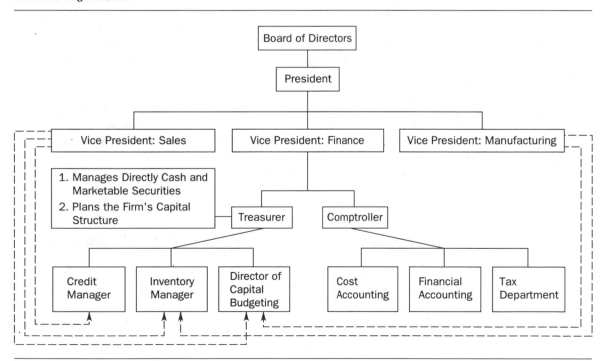

capital to support expansion. These decisions have a long-run effect on the profitability of the firm and therefore require top management consideration.

Concept Review

► Identify the two subordinates directly under a firm's chief financial officer, and indicate the responsibilities of each.

The Goals of the Corporation

Decisions are not made in a vacuum but, rather, with some objective in mind. Throughout this book we shall operate on the assumption that management's primary goal is **shareholder wealth maximization**. As we shall see, this goal translates into **maximizing the price of the common shares** as a result of the decisions undertaken. Managements are assumed to want to enhance value for the existing shareholders. For example, although a firm can increase the overall value of its equity by issuing new common shares, this will affect the wealth of existing shareholders—the shareholders before the equity issue—only if management uses the funds properly.

Firms do, of course, have other objectives. Managers, who make the actual decisions, are interested in their own personal satisfaction, in their employees' welfare, and in the good of the community and of society at large. Still, for the reasons set forth in the sections that follow, share price maximization is the most important goal of most corporations, and it is a reasonable operating objective on which to build decision rules.

To understand why share price maximization has become generally accepted as the basic goal of the firm, consider a company financed half from the owner's equity and half from debt borrowed at a fixed interest rate—say, 10 percent. If the company does very well, the value of its common equity will increase; the value of its debt, however, will not be materially affected because the bondholders will still receive only their 10 percent return. On the other hand, if the firm does not prosper, then the claims of the creditors, which by contract have to be honoured first, will reduce the return to equity holders. This will result in a decline in the value of the common equity. Thus, the ups and downs in the value of the common shares provide a good index for measuring a company's performance. It is partly for this reason that the goal of financial management is generally expressed in terms of maximizing the value of the firm's common shares.

Managerial Incentives To Maximize Shareholder Wealth

Shareholders own the firm and elect the management team. Management, in turn, is supposed to operate in the best interests of the shareholders. We know, however, that for some large firms, the common equity is widely held, and the managers have a great deal of autonomy. This being the case, might not these managers pursue goals other than share wealth maximization? For example, some have argued that the managers of a large, well-entrenched corporation might work just enough to keep shareholders' returns at a "fair" or "reasonable" level and then devote the remainder of their efforts and resources to public service activities, to employee benefits, to higher executive salaries, or to golf.

Similarly, an established, self-satisfied, and well-compensated management might avoid risky ventures, even when the possible gains to shareholders were high enough to warrant taking the gamble. The theory behind this argument is that since shareholders are generally well diversified in the sense that they hold portfolios of many different equity securities, if a company takes a chance and loses, then the shareholders lose only a small part of their wealth. Managers, on the other hand, are not diversified, since their human capital and cash flows depend on the firm, so setbacks affect them more seriously. Accordingly, some maintain that old-line corporate managers tend to "play it safe" rather than aggressively seeking to maximize the prices of their firms' equity.

It is almost impossible to determine whether a particular management team is trying to maximize shareholder wealth or is merely attempting to keep shareholders satisfied while pursuing other goals. For example, how can we tell whether employee or community benefit programs are in the long-run best interests of the shareholders? Are relatively high executive salaries really necessary to attract and retain excellent managers, who in turn will keep the firm ahead of its competition, or are they just another example of managers' taking advantage of shareholders? When a risky venture is turned down, does this reflect management conservatism, or is it a correct judgement regarding the risks of the venture versus its potential rewards?

It is impossible to give definitive answers to these questions. However, we do know that the managers of a firm operating in a competitive market will be forced to undertake actions that are reasonably consistent with shareholder wealth maximization. If they depart from this goal, they run the risk of being removed from their jobs through a hostile takeover or to a lesser extent a proxy fight. A **hostile takeover** is the purchase by one company of the equity of another over the opposition of the latter's management, whereas a **proxy fight** involves an attempt to gain control by getting shareholders to vote a new management group into office. Both actions are facilitated by low share prices, so for the sake of self-preservation management will try to keep its share price as high as possible. The dominant view is that takeovers rarely present a serious threat to a well-entrenched management team if that team has succeeded in maximizing the firm's value; people attempt to take over undervalued, bargain companies, not fully valued ones. So, although it may be true that some managers are more interested in their own personal positions than in maximizing shareholder wealth per se, the threat of losing their jobs still motivates them to try to maximize share prices.

At the other extreme are companies in which shares are not widely held and there is a controlling block of shares (usually, but not always, held by the members of the founding family). Here management is entrenched, and it is very difficult to have any discipline through the takeover market. In this situation, noncontrolling shareholders must rely on the controlling managers' desire to maximize share price and so maximize their own wealth. Unfortunately, there are situations in which the entrenched management undertakes decisions that, although in the best interests of the controlling shareholder, are not consistent with shareholder wealth maximization. Although there is no short-run mechanism with which to discipline this management, these non-wealth-maximizing decisions will lead to financial problems for the firm in the long run, and a sale of the controlling position may occur. This will result in a wider distribution of share ownership and the introduction of a more effective management dedicated to the goal of share price maximization.

Social Responsibility

Another issue that deserves consideration is **social responsibility**. Should businesses operate strictly in their shareholders' best interests, or are firms also partly responsible for the welfare of their employees, customers, and the communities in which they operate? Certainly firms have an ethical responsibility to provide a safe working environment for their employees, to ensure that their production processes are not endangering the environment, to engage in fair hiring practices, and to produce products that are safe for consumers.

Socially responsible actions such as these have costs, and it is questionable whether businesses would incur them voluntarily. It is clear, however, that if some firms do act in a socially responsible manner while others do not, then the socially responsible firms will be at a disadvantage in attracting capital. To see why this is so, consider first those firms that make *normal profits* and *rates of return on investment*: that is, the profits and rates of return are close to the average for all firms and just sufficient to attract capital. If one company attempts to exercise social responsibility, its product prices will have to increase to cover the costs of these actions. If the other businesses in the industry do not follow suit, their costs and prices will remain constant. The socially responsible firm will not be able to compete and so will be forced to abandon its efforts. Thus, any voluntary socially responsible acts that raise costs will be difficult, it not impossible, in industries that are subject to keen competition.

What about oligopolistic firms with profits above normal levels—cannot such firms devote resources to social projects? Undoubtedly they can, and many large, successful firms do engage in community projects, employee benefit programs, and the like to a greater degree than would appear to be called for by pure profit or wealth maximization goals.[1] Still, publicly owned firms are constrained in such actions by capital market factors. To illustrate, suppose a saver who has funds to invest is considering two alternative firms. One firm devotes a substantial part of its resources to social actions, while the other concentrates on profits and share prices. Most investors are likely to shun the socially oriented firm, thus putting it at a disadvantage in the capital market. After all, why should the shareholders of one corporation subsidize society to a greater extent than those of other businesses? For this reason, even highly profitable firms (unless they are closely held rather than publicly

---

[1]Even firms like these often find it necessary to justify such projects at shareholder meetings by stating that they will contribute to long-run profit maximization.

owned) are generally constrained against taking unilateral cost-increasing social actions.

Does all this mean that firms should not exercise social responsibility? Not at all, but it does mean that most significant cost-increasing actions have to be put on a *mandatory* rather than a voluntary basis, at least initially, to ensure that their burdens fall uniformly across all businesses. Thus, such social benefit programs as fair hiring practices, minority training, product safety, and pollution abatement are most likely to be effective if realistic rules are established initially and then enforced by government agencies. Of course, it is critical that industry and government co-operate in establishing the rules of corporate behaviour, that the costs as well as the benefits of such actions be accurately estimated and taken into account, and that firms follow the spirit as well as the letter of the law in their actions. Throughout this book, we shall assume that managers are share price maximizers who operate subject to a set of socially imposed constraints.

Business Ethics

Related to the issue of social responsibility is the question of business ethics. Ethics can be defined as "standards of conduct or moral judgement." *Business ethics* can be thought of as a company's attitude and conduct toward its employees, customers, community, and shareholders. High standards of ethical behaviour demand that a firm treat each of these constituents in a fair and honest manner. A firm's commitment to business ethics can be measured by its own tendency and that of its employees to adhere to laws and regulations relating to product safety and quality, fair employment practices, fair marketing and selling practices, the use of confidential information for personal gain, community involvement, bribery, and illegal payments to foreign governments to obtain business.

There are many instances of individual employees of firms' engaging in unethical behaviour. For example, a broker in Nesbitt Thomson Deacon Inc. lost $156 000 of a client's money that was invested in the stock market. The broker was accused of having churned the client's accounts to generate commissions and of making trades that were inappropriate for the client. In April 1991, the Ontario Securities Commission (OSC) found the broker guilty of the latter offence and suspended him from trading for 3 months. Just 3 days after this decision, new allegations were made that, between November 1989 and October 1990, the broker had misappropriated clients' money and engaged in unauthorized trades on a client's account. These irregularities occurred while he was working under the strict supervision of Nesbitt following prior problems with the OSC. The OSC once again found the broker guilty and banned him from the business of selling securities.

Again in the securities business, the OSC banned three principals and major shareholders of Osler Inc. for life from trading in Ontario's securities markets after concluding that they had operated a widespread coverup to deceive auditors and regulators. The principals generated substantial losses on bond trading for the firm's account as well as from the unauthorized use of clients' funds. The individuals decided to try to trade their way out of the problem but succeeded in compounding the losses. In 1988, the OSC and the Toronto Stock Exchange put Osler into receivership after it could not make a payment on a loan. The individuals were subsequently charged with 22 criminal charges of fraud, theft, and possession of stolen property by the Ontario Provincial Police.

Increasingly, firms are introducing strong codes of ethical behaviour and conducting training programs designed to ensure that all employees understand the correct behaviour in various business situations. However, it is imperative that top management—the chairperson, president, and vice presidents—be openly committed to ethical behaviour and that they communicate this commitment through their own personal actions as well as through company policies, directives, and punishment/reward systems.

An indication of the importance of corporate social responsibility and ethical behaviour is the introduction of mutual funds that invest in the equity of companies that meet certain criteria. These criteria are designed to identify companies that operate responsibly and ethically or do not have an exposure to the potentially large environmental costs associated with the products they produce. These mutual funds, sometimes called "green funds," have achieved strong rates of return relative to the overall market.

Share Price Maximization and Social Welfare

If a firm attempts to maximize its share price, is this good or bad for society? In general, it is good. Aside from such illegal actions as attempting to form monopolies, violating safety codes, and failing to meet pollution control requirements—all of which are constrained by the government—the same actions that maximize share prices also benefit society. First, share price maximization requires efficient, low-cost operations that produce the desired quality and quantity of output at the lowest possible cost. Second, share price maximization requires the development of products that consumers want and need, so the profit motive leads to new technology, to new products, and to new jobs. Finally, share price maximization necessitates efficient and courteous service, adequate stocks of merchandise, and well-located business establishments—these factors are all necessary to make sales, and sales are necessary for profits. Therefore, the types of actions that help a firm increase the price of its stock are also directly beneficial to society at large. This is why profit-motivated, free enterprise economies have been so much more successful than socialistic and other types of economic systems. Since financial management plays a crucial role in the operation of successful firms and since successful firms are absolutely necessary for a healthy, productive economy, it is easy to see why finance is important from a social standpoint.[2]

---

[2]People sometimes argue that firms, in their efforts to raise profits and share prices, increase product prices and gouge the public. In a reasonably competitive economy, which we have, prices are constrained by competition and consumer resistance. If a firm raises its prices beyond reasonable levels, it will simply lose its market share. Even giant firms like General Motors lose business to the Japanese and Germans, as well as to Ford and Chrysler, if they set prices over what will cover production costs plus a "normal" profit. Of course, firms *want* to earn more, and they constantly try to cut costs, to develop new products, and so on, and thereby to earn above-normal profits. Note, though, that if they are successful and do earn above-normal profits, those very profits will attract competition and eventually drive prices down, so again the long-term beneficiary is the consumer.

> ### *Concept Review*
>
> ▶ What is management's primary goal?
> ▶ What actions can be taken to remove the management of a firm operating in a competitive market if it has departed from the goal of maximizing shareholder wealth?
> ▶ Explain the difference between a hostile takeover and a proxy fight. How does the firm's share price influence those actions?
> ▶ What will happen if one competitive firm attempts to exercise social responsibility while another competitive firm in the same industry does not?
> ▶ Why must most significantly cost-increasing, socially beneficial actions be put on a mandatory rather than a voluntary basis?
> ▶ How would you define the term "business ethics"? How can a firm's commitment to business ethics be measured?
> ▶ How does the goal of share price maximization benefit society at large?

The Agency Problem

In a very important article, Michael Jensen and William Meckling defined an *agency relationship* as a contract under which one or more people (the principals) hire another person (the agent) to perform some service and delegate decision-making authority to that agent.[3] Within the financial management framework, agency relationships exist (1) between shareholders and managers and (2) between shareholders and creditors (debtholders). These relationships are discussed in the following sections.

Shareholders versus Managers

A potential **agency problem** arises whenever the manager of a firm owns less than 100 percent of the firm's common equity. If the firm is a proprietorship managed by the owner, we can assume that the owner-manager will take every possible action to improve his or her own welfare, with welfare measured primarily in the form of increased personal wealth but also in more leisure or perquisites.[4] However, if the owner-manager relinquishes a portion of the ownership by incorporating and selling some of the firm's shares to outsiders, a potential conflict of interests immediately arises. For example, the owner-manager may now decide not to work as strenuously to maximize shareholder wealth, because less of this wealth will go to him or her, or to take a higher salary or to consume more perquisites, because part of these costs will now fall on the outside shareholders. The smaller the proportion of shares owned by the manager, the greater is this potential problem since any cost of perquisite

---

[3]See Michael C. Jensen and William H. Meckling, "Theory of the Firm: Managerial Behavior, Agency Costs, and Ownership Structure," *Journal of Financial Economics*, October 1976: 305–60. The discussion of agency theory that follows draws heavily from their work.

[4]*Perquisites* are executive fringe benefits, such as luxurious offices, use of corporate planes and yachts, personal assistants, and so on.

consumption is borne to a greater degree by the outside shareholders. The smallest proportionate holdings by managers are found in large companies with professional management. This potential conflict between two parties, the principals (outside shareholders) and the agent (manager), is one type of agency problem.

Investors in the capital market are aware of the potential problem of perquisite consumption and increased leisure by management, so the share price is lowered to reflect the expected cost of such behaviour. This reduction in share price is a kind of *agency cost*, and its size will depend upon the proportion of the common shares owned by the management. The greater this proportion, the smaller is the agency cost.

Another potential conflict between management and shareholders arises in a **leveraged buyout**, a term used to describe the situation in which management itself (1) arranges a line of credit, (2) makes an offer, called a **tender offer**, to the shareholders to buy the shares not already owned by the management group, and (3) "takes the company private" after it has bought the outstanding shares.

To ensure that its managers act in the best interests of the outside shareholders, the firm must incur **agency costs**, which may take several forms: (1) expenditures to monitor managerial actions, or (2) expenditures to structure the organization so that the possibility of undesirable managerial behaviour will be limited.

There are two extreme positions regarding how to deal with the agency problem. At one extreme, which entails a firm's managers' being compensated only with shares of the firm's equity, agency costs would be low because the managers would have less incentive to take excessive leisure, salaries, or perquisites. However, it would be difficult to hire managers under these terms. At the opposite extreme, owners could closely monitor every managerial activity, but this solution would be extremely costly and inefficient. The optimal solution lies somewhere between the extremes, with executive compensation tied to performance and some monitoring also being done.

Several mechanisms that tend to force managers to act in the shareholders' best interests are discussed next.

The Threat of Firing.   Until recently, the probability of a large firm's management being ousted by its shareholders was so remote that it posed little threat. This situation existed for one of two reasons: (1) ownership was so widely distributed and management's control over the proxy mechanism was so strong that it was almost impossible for dissident shareholders to gain enough votes to overthrow the managers; or (2) the control of the firm was concentrated in a significant block of shares held by management, and it was impossible to remove the management. However, share ownership is being increasingly concentrated in the hands of large institutions, rather than individuals, and the institutional money managers have the clout, if they choose to use it, to exercise considerable influence over a firm's operations. Examples of major corporations whose managements have been ousted, forced to change their operating philosophy, or made to rescind proposed changes include Southam, Crownx, Donohue, and Inco.

The Threat of Takeover.   Hostile takeovers are most likely to occur when a firm's equity is undervalued relative to its potential because of poor managerial decisions. In a hostile takeover, the managers of the acquired firm are generally fired, and any who are able to stay on lose the autonomy they had prior to the acquisition. Thus, managers have a strong incentive to take actions that maximize share price.

Actions to increase the firm's share price and to keep it from being a bargain are obviously good from the standpoint of the shareholders, but other tactics that managers can take to ward off a hostile takeover may not be. An example of a questionable tactic is the poison pill. A *poison pill* is an action that practically kills a firm and thus makes it unattractive to potential suitors. An example was Inco's plan to sell large blocks of its shares at low prices to all shareholders except the party wishing to buy the firm. Some companies in the United States have provided for managers to receive huge retirement bonuses, which represent a large part of the company's wealth, if the firm is taken over (such payments are called *golden parachutes*).

Structured Managerial Incentives.   More and more, firms are tying managers' compensation to the company's performance. Research suggests that this motivates managers to operate in a manner consistent with share price maximization.[5]

Performance-based incentive plans have become an accepted management tool. In the 1950s and 1960s, most of these plans involved **executive stock options**, which allowed managers to purchase shares at some time in the future at a given price; the options would be valuable if the market price of the equity rose above the option purchase price. The firms that used these plans believed that allowing managers to purchase equity at a fixed price would provide an incentive for them to take actions that would maximize the share price. This type of managerial incentive lost favour in the 1970s, however, because the options generally did not pay off. The general stock market declined, and share prices did not necessarily reflect companies' earnings growth. Incentive plans ought to be based on factors over which managers have control, and since they cannot control the general stock market, such plans have proved to be weak incentive devices.

Another incentive plan is **performance shares**, which are shares of stock given to executives on the basis of performance as measured by earnings per share, return on assets, return on equity, and so on. Since share price is related to these variables, improving the earnings performance will improve the share price. For example, Honeywell uses growth in earnings per share as its primary performance measure. The firm has established overlapping four-year performance periods, beginning two years apart. At the start of each period, the participating executives are allocated a certain number of performance shares, say 10 000 shares for the president down to 1000 for a lower-ranking manager. If the company achieves, say, a targeted 13 percent annual average growth in earnings per share, the managers will earn 100 percent of their shares. If the corporate performance surpasses the target, they can earn even more shares, up to a maximum of 130 percent, which requires a 16 percent growth rate.

---

[5]See Wilbur G. Lewellen, "Management and Ownership in the Large Firm," *Journal of Finance*, May 1969: 299–322. Lewellen concluded that managers seem to make decisions that are largely oriented toward stock price maximization. Economic events since his study was published suggest that the incentives for stock price maximization are even stronger today than they were during the period his data covered.

However, if growth is less than the targeted 13 percent, they get less than 100 percent of the shares, and if it has fallen below, say, 9 percent, they get zero. Executives must remain with Honeywell through the performance period (four years) in order to receive the bonus shares.

Performance shares have a value even if the company's share price remains constant because of a poor general stock market, whereas, under similar conditions, stock options might have no value even though managers had been successful in boosting earnings. Of course, the *value* of the shares received depends on market price performance; 1000 shares of Honeywell equity are a lot more valuable if the share sells for $200 than if it sells for only $100.

All incentive compensation plans—executive stock options, performance shares, profit-based bonuses, and so forth—are supposed to accomplish two things. First, they offer executives incentives to act on those factors under their control in a manner that will contribute to share price maximization. Second, the existence of such performance plans helps companies attract and retain top-level executives. Well-designed plans can accomplish both goals.

Shareholders versus Creditors

The second agency problem involves potential conflicts between shareholders and creditors (debtholders). Creditors lend funds to the firm at rates that are based on (1) the riskiness of the firm's existing assets, (2) expectations concerning the riskiness of future asset additions, (3) the firm's existing capital structure (that is, the amount of debt financing it uses), and (4) expectations concerning future capital structure changes. These are the factors that determine the riskiness of the firm's cash flows and hence the safety of its debt, so creditors set their required rates of return, and hence the cost of debt to the firm, on expectations regarding these factors.

Now suppose the shareholders, acting through management, cause the firm to take on new projects that have greater risks than were anticipated by the creditors. This increased risk will cause the required rate of return on the firm's debt to increase, which in turn will cause the value of the outstanding debt to fall.[6] If the riskier capital investments turn out to be successful, all of the benefits will go to the shareholders because the creditors get only a fixed return, but if things go sour, the bondholders will have to share the losses. What we would have, from the shareholders' point of view, is a game of "heads I win, tails you lose," which is obviously not a good game from the bondholders' standpoint. Similarly, if the firm increases its level of debt in an effort to boost profits, the value of the old debt will decrease because the old debt's bankruptcy protection will be lessened by the new debt. In both of these situations, the shareholders will gain at the expense of the firm's creditors.

Can and should shareholders, through their manager-agents, try to expropriate wealth from the firm's creditors? In general, the answer is no. First, because such attempts have been made in the past, creditors today protect themselves reasonably well against such shareholder actions through restrictions in credit agreements. Second, if creditors perceive that the firm is trying

---

[6]In general, the higher the required rate of return on an existing debt issue, the lower its value. In Chapter 16 we will prove this point.

to take advantage of them in unethical ways, they will either refuse to deal further with the firm or require a much higher than normal rate of interest to compensate for the risks involved. Thus, firms that try to deal unfairly with creditors either lose access to the debt markets or are saddled with higher interest rates, which can lead to a decrease in the long-run share value.

In view of these constraints, the goal of maximizing shareholder wealth requires fair play with creditors. Shareholder wealth depends on continued access to capital markets, and access depends on fair play and abiding with both the letter and the spirit of credit agreements. Therefore, the managers, as agents of both the creditors and the shareholders, must act in a manner that is fairly balanced between the interests of these two classes of security holders. Similarly, because of other constraints and sanctions, management actions that would expropriate wealth from the firm's employees, customers, suppliers, or community will ultimately be to the detriment of shareholders. We conclude that in our society the goal of shareholder wealth maximization requires the fair treatment of other groups.

Concept Review

▶ What is an agency relationship? Within the financial management framework, what agency relationships exist?

▶ Identify some situations in which there are potential agency problems between shareholders and managers.

▶ What are agency costs? Explain what costs firms must incur to reduce them. Briefly outline several mechanisms that tend to cause managers to act in the shareholders' best interests.

▶ How might an agency problem arise between shareholders and creditors?

Managerial Actions To Maximize Shareholder Wealth

To maximize the long-run value of a firm's equity, what types of actions should its management take? First, consider the question of share prices versus profits: Will **profit maximization**—maximization of the firm's net income—result in share price maximization? In answering this question, we must analyze the matter of total corporate profits versus **earnings per share (EPS)**.

For example, suppose Nortel has 100 million shares outstanding and earns $400 million, or $4.00 per share, and you own 100 shares of the common equity, so your share of the total profits is $400. Now suppose Nortel sells another 100 million shares and invests the funds received in assets that produce $100 million of income. Total income rises to $500 million, but earnings per share decline to $500/200 = $2.50. Now your share of the firm's earnings is only $250, down from $400. You (and other current shareholders) have suffered an earnings dilution, even though total corporate profits have risen. Therefore, other things held constant, if management is interested in the well-being of its current shareholders, it should concentrate on earnings per share rather than on total corporate profits.

Will maximization of expected earnings per share always maximize shareholder welfare, or should other factors be considered? Think about the *timing of the earnings*. Suppose Nortel is considering one project that will cause earnings per share to rise by $0.20 per year for 5 years, or $1.00 in total, while another project will have no effect on earnings for 4 years but will increase earnings by $1.25 in the fifth year. Which project is better? In other words, is $0.20 per year for 5 years better or worse than $1.25 in Year 5? The answer depends on which project adds the most to the value of the equity, which in turn depends on the *time value of money* to investors. Thus, timing is an important reason to concentrate on wealth as measured by the share price rather than on earnings alone.

Still another issue relates to *risk*. Suppose the firm can choose between two projects. The first is not very risky; if it is undertaken, earnings will almost certainly rise by about $1.00 per share. The other project is quite risky; although our best guess is that it will raise earnings by $1.20 per share, we must recognize the possibility that there may be no increase whatsoever or even a loss. Depending on how averse shareholders are to risk, the first project may be preferable to the second.

The riskiness inherent in projected earnings per share (EPS) also depends on how the firm is financed. As we shall see, many firms go bankrupt every year, and the greater the use of debt, the greater the threat of bankruptcy. Consequently, although the use of debt financing may increase projected EPS, debt also increases the riskiness of projected future earnings.

Still another issue is the matter of paying dividends to shareholders versus retaining earnings and reinvesting them in the firm, thereby causing the earnings stream to grow over time. Shareholders like cash dividends, but they also like the growth in EPS that results from ploughing earnings back into the business. The financial manager must decide exactly how much of the current earnings to pay out as dividends rather than to retain and to reinvest—this is called the **dividend policy decision**. The optimal dividend policy is the one that maximizes the firm's share price.

We see, then, that the firm's share price is dependent on the following factors:

1. Projected earnings per share.
2. Timing of the earnings stream.
3. Riskiness of these projected earnings.
4. The firm's use of debt.
5. Dividend policy.

Every significant corporate decision should be analyzed in terms of its effect on these factors and hence on the price per share of the firm's equity. For example, suppose Pegasus is considering opening a new gold mine. If this is done, can it be expected to increase the firm's EPS? Is there a chance that costs will exceed estimates, that prices and output will fall below projections, and that EPS will be reduced because the new mine was opened? How long will it take for the new mine to start showing a profit? How should the capital required to open the mine be raised? If debt is used, how much will this increase Pegasus' riskiness? Should Pegasus reduce its current dividends and use the cash thus saved to finance the project, or should it maintain its dividends and finance the mine with external capital? Financial management is designed to help answer questions like these, plus many more.

> ### Concept Review
>
> ▶ Will profit maximization also result in share price maximization?
> ▶ Identify five factors that affect the firm's share price.

The Economic Environment

Although managers can take actions that affect the values of their firms' equity, there are additional factors that influence share prices. Among them are external constraints, the general level of economic activity, taxes, and conditions in the stock market. Figure 1-2 diagrams these general relationships. Working within the set of external constraints shown in the box at the extreme left, management makes a set of long-run strategic policy decisions that chart a future course for the firm. These policy decisions, along with the general level of economic activity and the level of corporate income taxes, influence the firm's expected profitability, the timing of its earnings, the eventual transfer of earnings to shareholders in the form of dividends, and the degree of uncertainty (or risk) inherent in projected earnings and dividends. Profitability, timing, and risk all affect the price of the firm's stock, but so does the state of the stock market as a whole because all share prices tend to move up and down together to some extent.

> ### Concept Review
>
> ▶ Identify some factors beyond the firm's control that influence its share price.

Figure 1-2
Summary of Major Factors Affecting Share Prices

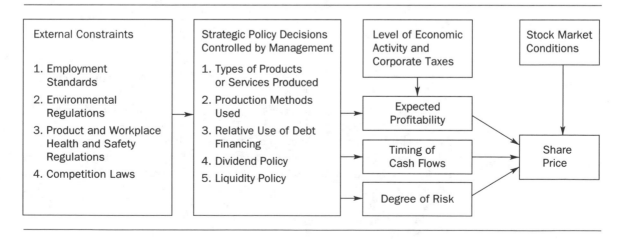

Organization of the Book

Part I contains fundamental background materials upon which the book builds. Finance cannot be studied in a vacuum—financial decisions are profoundly influenced by the economic and social environment in which they are made. Therefore, an introduction to the economic side of this environment, especially taxes and interest rates, is presented in Part I.

Part II, which includes Chapters 4 through 6, examines financial statements and financial forecasting. Because both long- and short-run plans are analyzed in terms of future financial statements, it is important to understand how these statements are developed and used by both managers and investors. We shall concentrate first on analyzing reports of past operations and then on projecting financial statements into the future under different strategic plans and operating conditions.

In Part III (Chapters 7 through 11), we examine current, ongoing operations. From accounting, we know that assets that are expected to be converted to cash within a year, such as inventories and accounts receivable, are called *current assets* and that liabilities that must be paid off within a year are called *current liabilities*. The management of current assets and current liabilities is known as *working capital management*, and Part III deals with that topic.

In Part IV (Chapters 12 through 15), we move into the vital subject of long-term investment decisions, or *capital budgeting*. Since major capital expenditures take years to plan and execute and since decisions in this area are generally not reversible and hence affect operations for many years, their effect on the value of the firm is obvious. One important element in this analysis is the time value of money, which introduces an adjustment for both futurity of cash flows and their risk.

Parts V and VI focus on long-term financial decisions. What are the principal sources and forms of long-term capital, and how are they valued? How much does each type of capital cost, and how does the method of financing affect the value of the firm? These sections apply valuation concepts, and we analyze key issues such as optimal debt-equity mix and dividend policy.

Part VIII investigates some of the long-term strategic decisions undertaken by the firm, such as mergers, acquisitions, and restructurings. In addition, we look at the financial decisions that must be made when a company is in financial distress.

Summary

This chapter has provided an overview of financial management. The key concepts covered are listed below.

☐ Finance consists of three interrelated areas: (1) *money and capital markets*, (2) *investments*, and (3) *managerial finance*.

☐ Managerial finance has undergone significant changes over the years. Since the 1980s, four issues have received emphasis: (1) *inflation* and its effects on interest rates; (2) *deregulation of financial institutions*; (3) a dramatic increase in the use of *telecommunications* for transmitting information and of *computers* for analyzing financial decisions; and (4) new and innovative methods for financing long-term investments.

☐ *Financial managers* are responsible for *obtaining and using funds* in a way that will *maximize the value of the firm.*

☐ The primary goal of management should be to **maximize shareholders' wealth**, and this means **maximizing the firm's share price**. Actions that maximize share prices also increase social welfare.

☐ An **agency problem** is a potential conflict of interest that can arise between (1) the owners of the firm and its management or (2) the shareholders and the creditors (debtholders).

☐ There are a number of ways to motivate managers to act in the best interests of shareholders. They include (1) the threat of firing, (2) the threat of takeovers, and (3) properly structured *managerial compensation packages.*

☐ The firm's share price depends on the firm's projected **earnings per share (EPS)**, the *timing of earnings*, the *riskiness of projected earnings*, the firm's *use of debt*, and its *dividend policy.*

☐ **International operations** are becoming increasingly important to individual firms and to the national economy.

Questions

1-1   What is the difference between share price maximization and profit maximization? Why is share price maximization a better operating goal than profit maximization?

1-2   Is the "normal" rate of return on investment the same in all industries? Do "normal" rates of return change over time? Explain.

1-3   Is the role of the financial manager likely to increase or decrease in importance relative to that of other executives if the rate of inflation increases? Explain.

1-4   Should shareholder wealth maximization be thought of as a long-run or a short-run goal? For example, if one action would probably increase the firm's share price from a current level of $20 to $25 in 6 months and then to $30 in 5 years, but another action would probably keep the price at $20 for several years but then increase it to $40 in 5 years, which action would be better? Can you think of some corporate actions that might have these general tendencies?

1-5   Drawing on your background in accounting, can you think of any differences in accounting procedures that might make it difficult to compare the relative performance of different firms?

1-6   Would the management of a firm in an oligopolistic or in a competitive industry be more likely to engage in what might be called "socially conscious" practices? Explain your reasoning.

1-7   Under what conditions might profit maximization not lead to share price maximization?

1-8   If you were the president of a large, publicly owned corporation, would you make decisions to maximize shareholders' welfare or your own personal interests? What are some actions shareholders can take to ensure that management's interests and their own coincide? What are some other factors that might influence management's actions?

1-9   The president of United Semiconductor Ltd. made this statement in the company's annual report: "United's primary goal is to increase the value of the common shareholders' equity over time." Later pages of the report made the following announcements. Discuss how United's major stockholders are likely to react to each of these actions and then how each might affect United's share price.

a. The company contributed $1.5 million to the symphony orchestra in its home office city.

b. The company is spending $500 million to open a new plant in South America. This plant will produce no revenues for 4 years, so earnings will be depressed during this period versus what they would have been had the decision been made not to open the new plant.

c. The company is increasing its relative use of debt. Whereas assets were formerly financed with 35 percent debt and 65 percent equity, henceforth the financing mix will be 50:50.

d. The company's manufacturing operations use a great deal of electricity, most of which it generates itself. Plans are to use nuclear fuel rather than coal to produce electricity in the future.

e. The company has been paying out half of its earnings as dividends and retaining the other half. Henceforth, it will pay out only 30 percent as dividends.

Self-Test Problem

ST-1   **Key terms.**   Define each of the following terms:
   a. Shareholder wealth maximization
   b. Hostile takeover; proxy fight; tender offer
   c. Social responsibility; business ethics
   d. Normal profits; normal rate of return
   e. Agency problem; agency costs
   f. Leveraged buyout
   g. Poison pill
   h. Performance shares; executive stock option
   i. Profit maximization
   j. Earnings per share
   k. Dividend policy decision

Solution to Self-Test Problem

ST-1   Refer to the relevant sections in this chapter to check your responses.

2

Business Organization and
the Tax Environment

A Managerial Perspective

With the Canadian economy in a recession in 1992, the federal government
introduced a budget intended to stimulate the economy without increasing the
deficit. Federal and provincial government budgets have important impacts on the
after-tax income of tax-paying participants in the economy. Financial executives
typically are busy either trying to anticipate tax law changes and the effects on their
firms' profits and cash flows or adjusting to announced changes in tax provisions.
Tax effects on long-term investments can be especially complicated. In one year, a
long-term investment in, say, the construction of a new plant, may appear to
promise profit, but a subsequent change in the tax laws can turn the good
investment into a bad one.

Financial management cannot be studied in isolation. If the value of a firm is to
be maximized, the financial manager must understand the legal and economic
environment in which decisions must be made. Further, the value of any asset—be
it a *financial asset*, such as a share of common equity or a bond, or a *real* (physical)
asset, such as land, buildings, equipment, or inventories—depends on the usable,
or *after-tax cash flows* that asset produces. Accordingly, this chapter identifies
relevant Canadian income tax provisions and their impact on the cash flows to
investors.

Alternative Forms of Business Organization

There are three main forms of business organization: the sole proprietorship,
the partnership, and the corporation. In terms of numbers, most businesses are
structured as sole proprietorships. In terms of dollar value of sales, however,
the bulk of business is conducted by corporations. Therefore, we shall
concentrate on them in this book. Still, it is important to understand the
differences among the three forms as well as their advantages and disadvantages.

Sole Proprietorship

A **sole proprietorship** is a business owned by one individual. Going into
business as a sole proprietor is very simple—one merely begins business

operations. However, most cities require even the smallest establishments to be licensed.

The proprietorship has two important advantages for small operations: (1) it is easily and inexpensively formed, as no formal charter is required, and it is subject to few government regulations; and (2) the business pays no corporate income taxes, although all of the firm's earnings are counted in the owner's income and thus are subject to personal income taxes, whether they are reinvested in the business or withdrawn.

The proprietorship also has four important limitations: (1) it is difficult for a proprietorship to obtain large sums of capital; (2) the proprietor has unlimited personal liability for the business's debts, which can result in losses greater than the money invested in the firm; (3) the life of a proprietorship is limited to the life of the individual who created it; and (4) the transfer of ownership is difficult. For all of these reasons, the individual proprietorship is restricted primarily to small business operations. However, businesses are frequently started as proprietorships and then converted to corporations if and when their growth causes the disadvantages of the proprietorship form to outweigh its advantages.

Partnership

A **partnership** exists whenever two or more persons associate to conduct a noncorporate business. Partnerships operate under different degrees of formality, ranging from informal, oral understandings to formal agreements. The major advantage of a partnership is its low cost and ease of formation. The disadvantages are similar to those associated with proprietorships: (1) the difficulty of raising large amounts of capital, (2) unlimited liability, (3) the limited life of the organization, and (4) the difficulty of transferring ownership. The tax treatment of a partnership is similar to that for proprietorships, which, when compared to the treatment of a corporation, can be either an advantage or a disadvantage, depending on the situation (a point illustrated later in this chapter).

Regarding liability, the partners must all risk their personal assets, even those not invested in the business, for under partnership law, they are jointly and severally liable for the business's debts. This means that if the partnership goes bankrupt and any partner is unable to meet his or her pro rata claim, the remaining partners must take over the unsatisfied claims, drawing on their personal assets if necessary.[1]

The first disadvantage—difficulty in raising large amounts of capital—is a result of the other disadvantages with the partnership, as well as the proprietorship, form of business organization. Although it may not be a problem for a slow-growing business, it can become a severe constraint if the company's products or services really catch on and the firm needs to raise large

---

[1] It is possible to limit the liabilities of certain partners by establishing a *limited partnership*, wherein certain partners are designated general partners and others limited partners. The *general partner* has all the rights and financial responsibilities of the partners in a regular partnership. The *limited partners*, however, have limited risk exposure; they are not personally responsible for any unsatisfied claims of the creditors, but they must remain passive with respect to the operations of the company.

amounts of capital to expand and thus capitalize on its opportunities. Many companies begin life as proprietorships or partnerships but at some point find it necessary to convert into corporations.

Corporation

A **corporation** is a legal entity, or "person," that can enter contracts and own property. It is separate and distinct from its owners and managers. This separateness gives the corporation three major advantages: (1) it has an *unlimited life*—it can continue after its original owners and managers are dead; (2) ownership interests can be divided into shares of common equity, which can be *transferred far more easily* than can partnership interests; and (3) it provides *limited liability*. To illustrate the concept of limited liability: suppose you invested $10 000 in a partnership, and it went bankrupt owing $1 million. Because the owners are liable for the debts of a partnership, you could be assessed for a share of the company's debt. You could even be held liable for the entire $1 million if your partners could not pay their shares. Thus, an investor in a partnership is exposed to unlimited liability. On the other hand, if you invested $10 000 in the common shares of a corporation that then went bankrupt, your potential loss on the investment would be $10 000—your liability would be limited to the amount of your investment in the business.[2]

A proprietorship or a partnership can commence operations without much paperwork, but setting up a corporation is a bit more involved. The incorporators must prepare incorporating documents and a set of bylaws. The incorporating documents—referred to as *articles of incorporation* or *letters patent*—include the following information: (1) name of the proposed corporation, (2) type of activities it will pursue, (3) amount of capital shares, (4) number of directors, and (5) names and addresses of directors. The incorporating documents are filed with the Ministry of Consumer and Corporate Affairs if the company is incorporated federally, or with the equivalent provincial department; when they are approved, the corporation is officially in existence.

The *bylaws* are a set of rules drawn up by the founders of the corporation to aid in governing the internal management of the company. Included are such points as (1) how directors are to be elected (say, all elected each year or one-third each year); (2) whether the existing shareholders will have the first right to buy any new common equity the firm issues; and (3) any provisions for management committees, such as an executive committee or a finance committee, and their duties. Also included is the procedure for changing the bylaws should conditions require it. Lawyers have standard forms for articles of incorporation and bylaws in their word processors and can set up a corporation with very little effort and cost.

The value of any business other than a very small one will probably be maximized if it is organized as a corporation. The reasons are as follows:

1. Limited liability reduces risk to equity investors, and the lower the risk, other things held constant, the higher the value of an asset.

---

[2]In the case of small corporations, the limited liability feature is often a fiction, as bankers and credit managers frequently require personal guarantees from the shareholders of small, weak businesses. The personal guarantee, in effect, converts limited liability to unlimited liability.

2. A firm's value is dependent on growth opportunities, which in turn are dependent on the firm's ability to attract capital. Since corporations can attract capital more easily than can unincorporated businesses, they have superior growth opportunities.

3. The value of an asset also depends on its *liquidity*, which means the ease of selling the asset and converting it to cash. Since an investment in the common equity of a corporation is much more liquid than a similar investment in a proprietorship or partnership, this too means that the corporate form of organization can enhance the value of a business.

4. Corporations are taxed differently than proprietorships and partnerships, and under certain circumstances, the tax laws favour corporations. (This point is discussed in detail later in the chapter.)

Since most firms are indeed managed with value maximization in mind, it is easy to see why most business is conducted by corporations.

Concept Review

▶ Briefly explain the differences among a sole proprietorship, a partnership, and a corporation.

▶ Explain why the value of any business other than a very small one will probably be maximized if it is organized as a corporation.

Financial Securities

Regardless of its form or organization, any business must have *assets* if it is to operate, and, in order to acquire assets, the firm must raise *capital*. Firms obtain capital by issuing financial securities, which fall into two categories: **debt** and **equity**. There are many different types of debt — long term and short term, secured and unsecured, and so on. Similarly, there are different types of equity. For example, the equity of a proprietorship is called *proprietor's interest* or *proprietor's net worth*, whereas for a partnership the word *partner* is inserted in lieu of *proprietor*. For a corporation, equity is represented by *preferred shares* and *common shareholders' equity*. Common equity, in turn, includes *common shares*, *contributed surplus*, and *retained earnings*.

The characteristics of the various types of capital are illustrated in Table 2-1, which presents the balance sheet of Business Securities, Ltd. (BSL) as of December 31, 1991. BSL began life in the 1940s as a proprietorship, then became a partnership, and finally was converted to a corporation in 1968. Its 1991 sales were $413 million, and the $285 million of assets shown in Table 2-1 were necessary to support these sales. BSL, like other companies, obtains the bulk of the funds used to buy assets by (1) buying on credit from its suppliers (accounts payable); (2) issuing debt securities — which means borrowing — that are bought by banks, insurance companies, pension funds, and other institutions; (3) selling preferred and common shares to investors; and (4) "saving money" by retaining some proportion of the income of the firm. This retention is reflected in the retained earnings account. (Recall from your accounting courses that a corporation saves whenever the company pays dividends that

Table 2-1
Business Securities, Ltd.
Balance Sheet as of December 31, 1991
(millions of dollars)

Assets		Claims on Assets	
Cash and marketable		Accounts payable	$ 24.2
securities	$ 12.1	Notes payable to banks	30.0
Accounts receivable	50.3	Accrued wages and taxes	5.8
Inventories	94.3	Total current liabilities	$ 60.0
Prepaid expenses	1.6	Long-term bonds	113.3
Total current assets	$158.3	Shareholders' equity	
Net fixed assets	126.8	Preferred shares (111 500	
		shares)	11.2
		Common shares and	
		contributed surplus	
		(1 706 351 shares)	10.4
		Retained earnings	90.2
		Total equity	$111.8
Total assets	$285.1	Total liabilities and capital	$285.1

are less than its net income, and that the savings that have been accumulated since the company began are reported as retained earnings on its balance sheet). Also, because wages and taxes are not paid on a daily basis, BSL obtains some "credit" from its labour force and the government in the form of accrued wages and taxes.

The first claim against BSL's income and assets is by its creditors—all those claims listed on the balance sheet above the shareholders' equity section. However, the creditors' claims are limited to fixed amounts. For example, most of BSL's long-term debt bears interest at a rate of about 8.5 percent per year, so its bondholders, in total, get interest of about $0.085 \times \$113.3$ million = $9.6 million per year. If BSL did extremely well and had profits of, say, $80 million, the bondholders would still get only $9.6 million. However, if BSL lost money, the bondholders would nevertheless get their $9.6 million; assets would be sold, the cash raised would be used to pay the bond interest, and the value of the common equity would decline. Further, if the company's situation became so bad that it simply could not generate the cash needed to make the required payments to the bondholders and other creditors (if this occurs, the firm is said to have *defaulted* on its debt), (1) the company would be forced into bankruptcy, (2) the assets would be sold off (generally at less than the values stated on the balance sheet), (3) the creditors would have first claim on the proceeds from the bankruptcy liquidation, and (4) the claims of the common equityholders would probably be wiped out.[3]

---

[3]The status of the different types of investors, as well as bankruptcy proceedings in general, is discussed in more detail in Chapters 20, 21, and 25. The point to remember here is that debtholders have a claim on a company's income and assets that is prior to that of shareholders.

The preferred shareholders stand next in line, after the creditors, for the firm's income and assets. BSL has 111 500 shares of preferred equity, each with a par value of $100. Each preferred share pays a dividend of $7.75 per year, or 7.75 percent on its $100 par value. The preferred dividends must be paid before any dividends can be paid on the common shares, and in the event of bankruptcy, the preferred must be paid off in full before anything goes to the common shareholders.

After all other claims have been paid, the remaining income, often called *residual income*, belongs to the common shareholders. This income may be retained for reinvestment in the firm, or it may be paid out as dividends to the common shareholders. Firms like BSL typically retain some earnings to support growth and then pay the rest out as dividends. The earnings retained still belong to the common shareholders. BSL has 1 706 351 shares of common equity outstanding. Investors actually paid about $6.08, on the average, for these shares ($10 375 000/1 706 351 = $6.08), but the company has saved (retained) $90 200 000/1 706 351 = $52.86 per share since 1968. Therefore, the common shareholders, on the average, have a total investment of $6.08 + $52.86 = $58.94 per share in the company; this is the common equity's *book value.*

BSL's debt and preferred shares are held primarily by its suppliers, some banks, and some institutions, such as life insurance companies and pension funds. The debt is rarely if ever traded, as this set of investors tends to hold debt until it matures. BSL's common equity, on the other hand, is listed on the stock exchange and is traded fairly actively. Individuals own about 65 percent of the shares, while institutions own the remaining 35 percent. In the summer of 1992, the stock traded in the general range of $40 to $47 per share; it has ranged from a high of $59 to a low of $10 over the past 10 years. The price rises and falls depending on (1) how the company is doing at a given point in time, (2) what is happening to other share prices, and (3) most important, how investors expect the company to do in the future. The market value (or price) does not depend directly on and is usually different from the book value. Book value, or the firm's common equity per share, is determined by accountants as the sum of assets valued at their original costs minus accumulated depreciation, minus all borrowed capital, minus preferred shareholders' claims, all divided by common shares outstanding. Market value, on the other hand, is a function of the cash expected to flow to shareholders in the future. It is easy to imagine a situation in which assets that were purchased years ago are worth far more today, and hence it is easy to see why market values can be above (or below) book values. We shall return to the issue of share price valuation in Chapter 16.

Concept Review

▶ What are the two basic forms of capital?
▶ What is a share's book value? What is its market value? Why do the two values generally differ?

The Income Tax System

Governments have available a number of techniques to generate tax revenues. These include sales, property, and excise taxes; customs duties; and income taxes. In this section, our interest is in the taxation of income of incorporated businesses (both private and public),[4] unincorporated businesses, and individuals. Our concern is with the basic elements of corporate and individual taxation as they affect the financing and investment decisions of corporations. (Since there is no intention of presenting a comprehensive introduction to taxation, the intricacies of tax law are not covered.)

Specific provisions in the *Income Tax Act* play an important role in the investment and financing decisions of both corporate and individual taxpayers. For example, the decision whether to use debt or common equity—referred to as the financing decision—is influenced by the fact that interest payments are a tax-deductible expense. The dividends paid by firms may be affected by the dividend tax credit given to shareholders. In addition, the tax environment will influence the decision to lease or to buy assets, to undertake an investment decision, to merge or not to merge, and whether or not to refund an outstanding bond or a preferred share issue.

The capacity to influence these decisions through provisions in the tax structure is one important ingredient in government fiscal policy. (*Fiscal policy* is that set of government decisions that attempts to influence the level of economic activity by altering the receipts and expenditures of the federal and provincial governments.)

Through the taxation system, the government can influence real corporate investment. First, the tax rates applied to taxable income can be changed. For example, a reduction in corporate tax rates will increase the after-tax profitability of investment projects and thereby increase the probability of their acceptance by firms. Second, the depreciation charge allowed for tax purposes—called *capital cost allowance*—can be changed. For example, the government may permit a higher capital cost allowance deduction through the use of an accelerated writeoff. This will lower the tax liability in the early years of a project and thus enhance the after-tax profitability of the investment. Third, the government can permit an investment tax credit for the purchase of new depreciable assets, allowing a given proportion of the cost of an asset to be deducted from taxes payable in the year of acquisition. The investment tax credit increases the after-tax profitability of the investment. Finally, the government can exempt certain income from taxation. A good example of this type of provision is the $100 000 lifetime exemption of capital gains from income taxation. By altering certain tax regulations, the government can have an important impact on the real investment activity of corporations and the personal investment choices of individuals.

---

[4]A corporation that is resident in Canada is considered a *public corporation* when at least one class of its shares is listed on a Canadian stock exchange. A *private corporation*, on the other hand, does not have listed common equity although there are equity holders of the firm.

We now turn to the determination of the *after-tax income* for any taxpayer, corporate or individual, by considering the determination of taxes payable. Although these two groups of taxpayers are considered separately, there is an important similarity in the calculation of taxes payable. For any taxpayer, the derivation of taxes payable requires the determination of

- The base on which the tax is to be calculated.
- The tax rates to be used.
- Any credits that provide a direct offset to taxes payable.

Table 2-2 provides a schematic description of the calculation of taxes payable. It outlines the components in the calculation and provides examples for both individuals and corporations. The base on which taxes are calculated is called *taxable income* and is shown in line 5. It is calculated as net income (line 3) less permissible deductions (line 4). Taxes payable (line 6) are calculated by applying the appropriate tax rate to taxable income. The final component is the

Table 2-2
Schematic Representation of Calculation of Taxes Payable

	Components in Calculating Taxes Payable	Entries for Each Component	
		Corporate	Individual
Line 1	Income accruing to taxpayer	Sum of all sources of income	Sum of all sources of income
Line 2	*Less:* Deductions of acceptable expenses	Expenses generally deducted in calculating net income on an accounting statement	Described in *Income Tax Act*
Line 3	Net income		
Line 4	*Less:* Permissible deductions	Examples: charitable donations, deduction for taxable dividends received	Examples: pension and RRSP contributions, union or professional dues
Line 5	Taxable income		
Line 6	Taxes payable before any credits	Adjustment in rates for manufacturing and small business operations	
Line 7	*Less:* Tax credits	Investment tax credit	Investment tax credit, dividend tax credit, medical deduction, credits for charitable donations, tuition fees, etc.
Line 8	Final taxes payable		

tax credit (line 7), which is applied directly to taxes payable to obtain the value of final taxes payable (line 8).[5]

For a simple example of the calculation of taxes, consider a corporation involved in a manufacturing business in British Columbia. The firm has taxable income (line 5) of $750 000 and the applicable corporate tax rate is 39.8 percent. The amount of taxes payable before any tax credits (line 6) is

$$\text{Taxes payable} = \$750\,000 \times 0.398 = \$298\,500.$$

The after-tax income for the corporation equals taxable income minus taxes payable. In this example, the amount is calculated as:

$$\text{After-tax income} = \$750\,000 - \$298\,500 = \$451\,500.$$

In the discussion that follows, we shall investigate each of the components highlighted in Table 2-2, first for corporations and then for individuals. Our major interest is in corporate taxation; the area of individual taxation, however, will be investigated—especially where it has an impact on financial variables, and thus on corporate decision making.

Corporate Taxation: Components of Income

One component of corporate income is business income derived from the operations of the company.[6] Another component is the full value of intercorporate dividends (whether or not the dividend-paying corporation is resident in Canada). A third component of income is net capital gains. The sale of any capital property at a price that differs from the purchase price of the asset results in a **capital gain** or **loss**. *Capital property* is defined to include not only depreciable property but also financial assets, such as shares and bonds, and land. In calculating the tax liability for a capital gain or loss, the sale price of the asset is compared to the *adjusted cost-base* of that asset. This base reflects either the actual price paid for the asset (if purchased during or after 1972) or an imputed value of the asset on valuation day, December 31, 1971 (if the asset was purchased prior to 1972). In calculating the capital gain or loss, the expenses incurred in the disposition of the asset are deducted from the

---

[5]In Table 2-2, the taxpayer appears to calculate net income as the sum of income from all sources (line 1) less the sum of all expenses (line 2). This is not strictly correct, as the *Income Tax Act* requires the taxpayer to calculate the difference between income and expenses for each source of income. Net income is then calculated as the sum of these differences over all sources. The results of the two approaches can be different if, for example, the taxpayer has a loss on one source of income that cannot be applied to positive net income from another source. We feel that the categories presented in lines 1 and 2 are useful from a descriptive and logical point of view, but the caveat about various sources of income should be kept in mind.

[6]For the purposes of determining applicable tax rates, a distinction is made between active and passive income. The former includes income derived from the activities of the company; the latter relates to income derived from the property of the corporation, such as rent or interest paid to it on loans. If virtually all of a firm's income is derived from royalties, rent, interest, or dividends, it is not considered to be an "active" business.

proceeds of sale. If there is a capital gain on the sale of the asset, the taxable capital gain, which for 1992 is equal to three-quarters of the capital gain, is included in income and taxed at regular rates. Capital losses are netted against capital gains. If gains exceed losses, three-quarters of the net gain is included in income and taxed at the corporate rate. There can be no capital losses on depreciable assets. The tax treatment of a sale of an asset at less than its initial value is considered in a subsequent section.

Deductions from Income

Generally, expenses can be deducted in calculating taxable income as long as they were incurred to earn income. Several important categories of expense will be discussed at this point, and others will be considered in subsequent chapters. For example, the tax treatment of bond discount and underwriting expenses for both share and bond issues is considered in Chapter 20, and lease payments are considered in Chapter 23. The deductions considered here are:

- Interest expenses.
- Dividend deductions.
- Application of losses, capital and noncapital.
- Capital cost allowances.

Interest and Dividends Paid by a Corporation

Interest payments on debt issued for business purposes are a tax-deductible expense. Common and preferred dividends, however, and interest charges on income bonds are generally not tax deductible.[7] Interest charges, therefore, generate a tax savings that is not available from the other conventional financing methods. For example, to pay $1.00 in interest requires that the corporation earn $1.00 before taxes; to pay $1.00 in taxable dividends, however, the corporation with a 45 percent tax rate must earn $1.82 before taxes. This amount is calculated as

$$\text{Pretax income} = \frac{\$1.00}{\$1.00 - \text{Tax rate}} = \frac{\$1.00}{0.55} = \$1.82.$$

Intercorporate Dividend Deductions.   In calculating net income, dividends received from other corporations are included. If the dividends are from taxable Canadian corporations, the full amount of the dividend may be deducted in the calculation of taxable income.

There are, however, certain exceptions to the tax-free status accorded Canadian intercorporate dividends. An important one is the treatment of dividends on term preferred shares, short-term preferreds, and guaranteed and collateralized preferred shares. The interest payoff patterns of these securities

---

[7]An *income bond* is a debt instrument on which interest is paid only if it is earned by the company. If the income bonds were issued in a reorganization of the company in default, the interest payments may be deductible in the calculation of taxable income.

are more similar to those of debt than to those of equity. In many cases, the payments are called dividends and not interest payments. Frequently, the lender has advanced funds to an entity that invested them to earn interest rather than active business income. In other cases, the shares are guaranteed by a financial institution. We shall consider some of these securities in Chapter 21. At this point, it is sufficient to establish that these preferred shares have a fixed term to maturity and may have a dividend rate that fluctuates with movements in a specified interest rate series. In essence, these securities are similar to debt, and hence their dividend payments are *not* tax free.

There are some exceptions to this provision. For example, if the recipient does not deal at arm's length with the payer or if the shares are issued by a corporation in financial difficulty, the dividends are tax free.

Application of Losses

Noncapital (Operating) Losses.   Noncapital losses can be **carried back**—applied to reduce taxable income—for the previous 3 years. In addition, these losses can be **carried forward** for 7 years. Any tax loss not completely used up within those 7 years cannot be applied in the eighth or subsequent years. Noncapital losses can be deducted from the taxable income in a year that includes either a capital gain component or noncapital income.

Net Capital Losses.   If the allowable capital losses exceed the taxable capital gains in any particular year, then the differences, called *net capital losses*, can be applied only against the taxable capital gains included in taxable income and not against noncapital income. These losses can be carried back 3 years and can be carried forward indefinitely.

An Example.   Table 2-3 illustrates the application of the carryback of operating losses. Suppose Apex Co. Ltd. had a $2 million pretax profit (*taxable income*) in 1990, 1991, and 1992, and then, in 1993, it lost $8 million. Also, assume that Apex's tax rate is 40 percent. The company can use the carryback feature to recompute its taxes for 1990, using $2 million of the 1993 operating losses to reduce the 1990 pretax profit to zero. This permits it to recover the taxes it paid in 1990. (It will receive a refund for that amount in 1994.) Because $6 million of the unrecovered losses are still available, Apex can repeat the procedure for 1991 and 1992. Thus, in 1994 the company will pay zero taxes for 1993 and also will receive a refund for taxes paid from 1990 through 1992. Apex will still have $2 million of unrecovered losses to carry forward, subject to the 7-year limit, until the entire $8 million loss has been used to offset taxable income.

The purpose of permitting this loss treatment is, of course, to avoid penalizing corporations whose incomes fluctuate substantially from year to year.

Capital Cost Allowance (CCA)

In the determination of accounting income (income for financial statement purposes), a portion of the cost of an asset is charged to income each year by means of depreciation. In other words, the depreciation expense is a method of

Table 2-3
Apex Co. Ltd.
Calculation of Loss Carryback and Carryforward
for 1990–1992 Using $8 Million 1993 Loss

	1990	1991	1992
Original taxable income	$ 2 000 000	$2 000 000	$2 000 000
Carryback credit	− 2 000 000	− 2 000 000	− 2 000 000
Adjusted profit	$ 0	$ 0	$ 0
Taxes previously paid (40%)	800 000	800 000	800 000
Difference = tax refund	$ 800 000	$ 800 000	$ 800 000

Total refund check received in 1994: $800 000 + $800 000 + $800 000 = $2 400 000.

Amount of loss carryforward available for use in 1994–2000
1993 loss	$ 8 000 000
Carryback losses used	6 000 000
Carryforward losses still available	$ 2 000 000

allocating the cost of an asset over its useful life. In computing taxable income *for income tax purposes*, the analogous expense is **capital cost allowance (CCA)**. Unlike the depreciation charge, the CCA deduction is not based on an estimate of the useful life of an asset. It is calculated by applying a fixed capital cost rate to a declining capital cost balance based on a formula to be described shortly. Since the base declines by the annual CCA charge and this charge is a percentage of the base, the asset will *never* be fully depreciated unless the CCA rate is 100 percent. The *undepreciated capital cost (UCC)* in any year is the base upon which the CCA charge is calculated for the year.

Each depreciable asset fits into one of the many asset classes available. The maximum CCA rate applicable to a particular class is specified in the *Income Tax Regulations*. The taxpayer may use a rate lower than that specified—in fact, no CCA need be claimed in any particular year.

When a taxpayer has a number of assets in a particular class, the costs of these assets generally are grouped into one unit, called an *asset pool*, for CCA calculations. Even if assets are scrapped (but not sold) or become obsolete, their cost still remains in the pool for CCA calculations. But when assets of a particular class are purchased or sold, the value of the undepreciated capital cost of the pool is affected.

In general, the costs of assets acquired are added to the undepreciated capital cost of a pool. The UCC in a pool is reduced by the application of CCA deductions and by the proceeds of disposal of assets in the pool. The CCA expense for a particular year is based on the value of UCC of the pool at the end of the previous year.

Examples of the assets that belong in the various pools and the maximum CCA rate applicable to these classes are listed in Table 2-4.

Table 2-4
CCA Rates for Asset Pools

Class	Asset	Maximum CCA Rate
1	Buildings bought after 1987	4%
10	Computer equipment and systems software; automotive equipment	30%
12	Computer application software; rental costumes; video cassettes	100%
16	Pinball machines; rental cars	40%
34	Solar heating equipment	50%

As already noted, the CCA calculations for most asset classes must use the declining balance method, but there are a few exceptions, such as a copyright provided over a limited time period. In these cases, the income tax expense can be set as equal annual amounts over the lifetime of the asset; the sum of these annual amounts must equal the original cost of the asset. This is equivalent to straight line depreciation. For water and air pollution control equipment, accelerated CCA is permitted. In this case, a maximum of 25 percent of the original cost of the asset is used in the year of acquisition, 50 percent in Year 2, and 25 percent in Year 3.

The Half-Year Rule. A provision concerning the calculation of CCA charges is the half-year rule. In the year of acquisition only one-half of the net amount of current additions less disposals is added to the pool. The CCA rate is applied to the resulting balance in the pool. The half of the net additions disallowed in the CCA calculation of the current year is added back to the asset pool to be included in the calculations for subsequent years. Thus, the CCA is calculated as if the asset was owned for half of the year, whether it was purchased at year end or in early January. For assets acquired after December 1989, CCA can be claimed only when the asset is put in use.

Table 2-5, in which an asset with a capital cost rate of 30 percent is acquired for $1000, illustrates application of the half-year rule. In this example, there is only one asset in the pool.[8] In the first year, the net increment to the pool is $1000,[9] but only one-half of this value is available for CCA calculation. Therefore, the base for the first year's CCA calculation is $500 (see column 3). The CCA charge for this year is the capital cost rate of 30 percent times the UCC available for CCA. Column 5 is equal to the UCC balance after the deduction of the first CCA charge plus the addition of the amount of the original cost of the asset not included in the UCC base for the calculation of the

---

[8]For an example of a purchase and sale of assets in the same class, see Problem 2-5.

[9]To be exact, the UCC at the start of Year 1 is zero, and the acquisition occurs sometime during that year.

CCA. Thus the $850 is obtained as the UCC amount after subtracting the CCA charge ($350) and adding back the disallowed amount ($500). The UCC can also be calculated directly as the original cost of the asset less the CCA charge in the first year. For all subsequent years, the UCC at the start of the year (column 2) and the UCC available for CCA (column 3) are equivalent.

Notice that our calculations stop at Year 5. If the asset is not sold, however, the UCC balance never reaches zero. Thus, there is always a CCA deduction, although its value becomes very small.

Calculating CCA.   Fortunately, in most applications of CCA calculations, the tedious approach displayed in Table 2-5 need not be utilized. The declining balance, fixed-rate CCA technique is amenable to mathematical modelling. Without presenting their derivations, formulas for the undepreciated capital cost (UCC) and the capital cost allowance (CCA) for any year can be given as

$$UCC_t = \begin{cases} C_o & \text{for } t = 1 \\ C_o(1 - (d/2))(1 - d)^{t-2} & \text{for } t \geq 2 \end{cases} \qquad (2\text{-}1)$$

$$CCA_t = \begin{cases} d/2 \times UCC_1 & \text{for } t = 1 \\ d \times UCC_t & \text{for } t \geq 2 \end{cases} \qquad (2\text{-}2)$$

where

UCC_t is the undepreciated capital cost applicable for the CCA charge in year t,
CCA_t is the capital cost allowance expense for year t,
C_o is the original cost of the asset,
d   is the capital cost rate of the class,
and t   is the year in question.

Equation 2-1 is used to calculate the appropriate base for the CCA charge, and Equation 2-2 provides the CCA value.

To understand the use of these formulas, consider the example used in Table 2-5. For the first year, UCC_t is $1000. Instead of adjusting the base by

Table 2-5
Calculation of CCA and UCC for an Asset with
Original Cost of $1000 and Capital Cost Rate of 30%

Year (1)	UCC Start of Year (2)	UCC Applicable for CCA (3)	CCA Charge = 0.3 × UCC (4)	UCC End of Year (5) = (2) − (4)
1	1000	500	150	850
2	850	850	255	595
3	595	595	179	416
4	416	416	125	291
5	291	291	87	204

removing one-half of the cost, an equivalent technique is to utilize one-half of the CCA rate. Thus, $CCA_1 = d/2 \times UCC_1 = 30/2 \times 1000 = \$150$. In all future periods, the full CCA rate is used.

In Year 2,

$$
\begin{aligned}
UCC_2 &= C_0(1 - (d/2)(1 - d)^{t-2} \\
&= C_0(1 - (d/2)) \text{ since } (1 - d)^0 = 1 \\
&= \$1000\,(1 - 0.30/2) \\
&= \$850, \\
\text{and } CCA_2 &= d \times UCC_2 = 0.30\,(\$850) \\
&= \$255.00
\end{aligned}
$$

If we wanted the CCA charge in the fifteenth year, the formula would result in a value of $2.47:

$$
\begin{aligned}
CCA_{15} &= d \times UCC_{15} \\
&= d \times C_0(1 - (d/2))(1 - d)^{13} \\
&= 0.3 \times \$1000\,(1 - 0.15)(0.7)^{13} \\
&= \$2.47
\end{aligned}
$$

It is important to stress that the corporation is not forced to take the CCA deduction in a particular year. It may decide to forgo the CCA charges in a particular year and use them in future years when they are of more benefit. The interaction of this flexibility of taking CCA charges and operating loss carryforwards effectively eliminates the constraint of the 7-year carryforward provision. For example, suppose the firm has $2 million remaining of a tax loss and it is the seventh and last year to use the loss. Also suppose that the taxable income after deducting $2 million for CCA would be zero, giving the firm no taxable income to which the remaining tax loss can be applied. But if the firm does not need to claim the CCA for this year, it can keep taxable income at $2 million and apply the tax loss to reduce this amount to zero. The CCA charges not used in this year are not lost; they can be applied to a future year.

Sale of Assets.   If there is a sale of any assets in the pool, the impact on the undepreciated capital cost is determined first, and then the capital cost allowance is calculated by applying the capital cost rate to the undepreciated capital cost adjusted for dispositions.

When a taxpayer has a number of assets in the same class, the costs of the assets are grouped together in a pool, and the pool is treated as a unit for the purposes of CCA calculations. When assets are sold from a pool, the *proceeds of sale* (if not in excess of the original cost) are subtracted from the pool as a whole, in the year of sale, to obtain the UCC value. As long as the resulting UCC of the pool is positive, there are no important tax problems to be considered. There may be, however, instances in which the subtraction of the proceeds of sale results in a negative UCC balance. This negative balance is referred to as *recaptured depreciation*, and it is considered as income and taxed at regular corporate income tax rates. For example, suppose the UCC pool is $1000 and you sell the asset for $1500. In essence, the government has allowed you to depreciate the asset for tax purposes at too high a rate; you have depreciated the asset down to $1000 when in fact it is worth $1500. In this case, the government expects you to pay tax on the $500 that you were allowed to overdeduct in the past.

Recapture occurs only if the proceeds of sale are in excess of the undepreciated capital cost of the *pool*, not of the asset sold.

There is one important exception to the statement that there are no tax problems to be considered when the resulting UCC of the pool is positive. This occurs if there are no assets remaining in the pool after the asset is sold—that is, if the asset that was sold was the last or only asset in the class. If no further assets are brought into the pool by year-end, then there is a *terminal loss* equal to the remaining UCC in the pool. This amount must be deducted from taxable income. In essence, the asset has been depreciated at too low a rate, and the government allows the remaining depreciation as a deduction from taxable income in that year.

Table 2-6 presents five examples to illustrate the calculation of the UCC of the pool after the sale of an asset. In the first example, the proceeds of sale are less than the UCC value of the pool before the sale. Therefore, the resulting UCC balance is $5000. In the second example, the proceeds of sale are less than the original cost of the asset but exceed the UCC before the sale. The subtraction of the proceeds from the before-sale UCC value gives an after-sale balance of $5000. This $5000 is recaptured depreciation and is included in regular income. The UCC of the pool after the sale is thus zero.

A further complication enters the analysis when the proceeds from the sale of an asset exceed the original cost of the asset. This excess is treated as a capital gain in computing the tax liability. Example 3 shows the capital gain impact. The proceeds of sale ($35 000) exceed the original cost of the asset and the UCC of the pool. The capital gain is equal to $5000 (the excess of the sale proceeds of $35 000 over the original cost of $30 000). As the capital gain accounts for $5000 of the $35 000 proceeds, we are now interested in the remaining proceeds of $30 000 (line 5). This value is subtracted from the UCC balance before the sale to determine the amount of the recapture. In the

Table 2-6
Calculation of UCC Balance after the Sale of Various Assets

	UCC Calculation Columns	Example 1	2	3	4	5
UCC balance before sale	(1)	$20 000	$20 000	$20 000	$50 000	$10 240
Assets sold						
Proceeds from sale	(2)	$15 000	$25 000	$35 000	$25 000	$ 8 000
Original cost	(3)	$30 000	$30 000	$30 000	$10 000	$20 000
Capital gain	(4) = (2) − (3)			$ 5 000	$15 000	
Proceeds net of capital gain	(5) = (2) − (4)	$15 000	$25 000	$30 000	$10 000	$ 8 000
Recaptured taxable income or (terminal loss)	(6) = (5) − (1)		$ 5 000	$10 000		($ 2 240)
Net proceeds	(7) = (5) − (6)	$15 000	$20 000	$20 000	$10 000	$10 240
UCC pool after sale	(8) = (1) − (7)	$ 5 000	—	—	$40 000	—

example considered here, the amount of recapture is $10 000 and is calculated as the difference between the proceeds of sale after removing the capital gain equal to $30 000 and the presale UCC balance of $20 000. The recapture amount is shown in line 6. The UCC balance after the sale is zero, and there is a $10 000 recapture to be included in income.

The fourth example also illustrates the impact of a capital gain. The capital gain, calculated as the difference between the sale price ($25 000) and the original cost ($10 000) of the asset, equals $15 000 (line 4). To calculate the recapture (if any), we compare the sale proceeds, after removing the impact of the capital gain, to the presale UCC balance. The former is equal to $10 000 (that is, $25 000 − $15 000), whereas the latter is $50 000. In this case there is no recapture to be taken into regular income. The UCC balance after the sale is $40 000; this equals the presale UCC balance minus the sale proceeds after removing the capital gain. In the fifth example, there is only a single asset in the pool. It is sold for $8000. Since its original cost was $20 000, there is no capital gain. After deducting the $8000 proceeds from the UCC value of $10 240, a terminal loss of $2240 remains. This amount is deducted from income.

To summarize the discussion, one-half of the capital cost of the purchased assets less the proceeds of disposition (up to the capital cost of the asset) is added to the undepreciated capital cost of the class. At the end of the year, after all the purchases and sales are taken into account, if the UCC of the pool is positive and there are still assets in the pool, then the capital cost rate is applied to the UCC. If the UCC is positive and there are no assets in the pool, the taxpayer takes a terminal loss. If the UCC of the pool is negative, the taxpayer takes recapture. If the proceeds of sale exceed the original capital cost of the asset, the taxpayer must take three-quarters of the capital gain into net income.

Computation of Tax

Up to this point we have described the major components in the calculation of taxable income. Now we consider the basic tax rates applied to the taxable income base and adjustments to taxes payable through tax credits.

The basic marginal federal tax rate for Canadian corporations applicable for 1992 is 28 percent. There is also a 3 percent surtax on the corporate income tax, which results in a combined effective rate of 28.8 percent calculated as

$$28\% \times 1.03 = 28.8\%.$$

A special incentive provision relating to the manufacturing and processing components of a company's business reduces the basic federal rate plus surtax to 23.8 percent. These special rates, which are applicable only to taxable income earned in these specific areas, will be further reduced to 22.8 percent in 1993 and to 21.8 percent in 1994.

The provinces also levy corporate income taxes; hence the total marginal tax rate faced by the corporation is the sum of the marginal federal rate and the provincial corporate rate. The combined federal and provincial tax rates for manufacturing and nonmanufacturing income, including the 3 percent corporate surtax, are presented in Table 2-7.

Table 2-7
Corporate Income Tax Rates, 1992
(including surtax on income)

	Manufacturing Profits	Nonmanufacturing Profits
Federal rate	23.8%	28.8%
Combined federal and provincial tax rates		
Alberta	38.8	44.3
British Columbia	39.8	44.8
Manitoba	40.8	45.8
New Brunswick	40.8	45.8
Newfoundland	40.8	45.8
Nova Scotia	39.8	44.8
Ontario	38.3	44.3
Prince Edward Island	38.8	43.8
Quebec	32.7	37.7
Saskatchewan	40.8	45.8

Source: Reprinted from *The Practitioner's Income Tax Act*, October 1992, page xxiv, by permission of Carswell, a division of Thomson Canada Limited, Scarborough, Ontario.

Provisions for Small Business

To encourage the formation of business, both the federal and provincial governments have provisions that reduce the effective corporate tax rate on small business. At the federal level, there is a federal small business tax rate reduction.[10] The basic federal tax rate is 12.8 percent, including the surtax. At the provincial level, a wide array of corporate income tax deductions are available on active business income for a small business. Some provinces apply a different corporate tax rate to manufacturing and to nonmanufacturing profits. In Table 2-8, the combined federal and provincial tax rates are presented for both manufacturing and nonmanufacturing profits.

In 1992, the Ontario government began to apply a surtax of 3.7 percent to the portion of a company's income over $200 000. The effect is to tax back the benefits the company gets on the federal government's lower, small business rate on its first $200 000 of income. Thus we see that any province, by setting its own tax policy and rates, can neutralize the effects of federal policy.

Tax Credits

The final component in determining the actual taxes payable is the tax credit. The application of the tax rate to the taxable income provides the federal taxes

[10]This deduction is applicable only to Canadian-controlled private corporations as defined by the *Income Tax Act*. Also, it is applicable only to the first $200 000 of income.

Table 2-8
Tax Rates for Small, Canadian-Controlled Private Corporations, 1992
(including surtax on income)

	Manufacturing Income	Nonmanufacturing Income
Federal rates	12.8%	12.8%
Combined federal and provincial tax rates		
Alberta	18.8	18.8
British Columbia	22.8	22.8
Manitoba	22.8	22.8
New Brunswick	21.8	21.8
Newfoundland	22.8	22.8
Nova Scotia	17.8	17.8
Ontario	22.3	22.3
Prince Edward Island	22.8	22.8
Quebec	18.55	18.55
Saskatchewan	21.8	21.8

Source: Reprinted from *The Practitioner's Income Tax Act*, October 1992, page xxiv, by permission of Carswell, a division of Thomson Canada Limited, Scarborough, Ontario.

payable. There are certain provisions, however, that permit a credit against income taxes payable, and this reduces the actual amount of federal taxes payable. These provisions include tax credits for political donations and the investment tax credit; we will consider only the investment tax credit, which can be used by individuals as well as by corporate taxpayers.

The *investment tax credit* is allowed only on qualified expenditures and only on expenditures made in certain regions of the country. The applicable regions are the Atlantic provinces, the Gaspé, and Cape Breton. The applicable investments include new buildings and equipment used for specific purposes such as logging, processing minerals, and manufacturing; expenditures for scientific research and experimental development may also qualify. The investment tax credit is designated as a percentage of the capital cost of the assets, and it varies across the regions. For example, for expenditures for scientific research, the rates range from 30 percent in Atlantic Canada to 20 percent in other regions. In the Cape Breton region, the current investment tax rate is 45 percent. Whenever the investment tax credit is utilized, the undepreciated capital cost of the asset must be reduced by the value of the investment tax credit used each year. In addition, there may be a limit on the amount of the investment tax credit that can be claimed in any one year. (The limit is stated as a certain percentage of the federal tax payable.)

The investment tax credit is a tool used by the federal government to stimulate regional development. The larger the investment tax credit rate, the greater the incentive to undertake expenditures that qualify for the tax credit. Thus, it is made available for new manufacturing investment in specially designated areas of the country characterized by high unemployment and low income.

Payment of Taxes

The actual payment pattern for corporate taxes has an impact on cash flows for investment decisions. Incorporated businesses must make installment payments over a 14- or 15-month period. An installment payment is due on the last day of each month of the corporation's tax year, and the balance of the tax payable, if any, is due 2 months after the end of the taxation year. If the company has claimed the small business deduction in the preceding year, the final installment payment is due at the end of the third month after the end of the taxation year. Finally, an unincorporated business is required to make installment payments on its tax liability on the fifteenth of the last month of each calendar quarter. Any balance remaining is due by April 30 of the following year.[11]

Large Corporations Capital Tax

A tax that is unrelated to the income earned by a corporation is the **large corporations capital tax**. This tax, which is levied by both federal and provincial governments, is based on the capital the firm employs in Canada. At the federal level, the tax is 0.2 percent annually of the capital employed in excess of $10 million. The tax is payable monthly. A separate capital tax is levied on financial institutions; the rates are 1 percent for capital between $200 and $300 million and 1.25 percent on capital in excess of $300 million.

All the provinces also apply a capital tax to financial institutions, although the rates and threshold values differ among provinces. For example, British Columbia applies a rate of 2 percent to financial institutions with assets in excess of $500 million and a permanent establishment in the province. Manitoba, Ontario, Quebec, and Saskatchewan also have a large corporations tax on nonfinancial intermediaries. Some of them have a size threshold and others do not. Quebec, for example, applies a 0.56 percent rate to all nonfinancial corporations.

The definition of capital can depend on the jurisdiction levying the tax. At the federal level, the assets are defined by accounting rules, but in Ontario, the assets are based on the rules underlying the calculation of income taxes. The main difference is the use of accounting depreciation for the former and CCA for the latter.

Goods and Services Tax (GST)

In 1991, the federal government introduced a tax of 7 percent on most goods and services. Companies may apply on a quarterly basis for a rebate of the tax they have paid. Therefore, the net effect of this tax on companies should be neutral. There is, however, a timing effect since the tax is paid throughout the

---

[11]Installment payments for individuals and corporations are based on taxes paid for the preceding period or an estimate of taxes payable for the current year.

quarter, but the rebate is paid after the end of the quarter. As well, there is increased paper work for the company because of the necessity to keep records of the tax paid.

> ### *Concept Review*
>
> ► What are the four general categories of deductions from income in the computation of corporate tax payable?
> ► How are dividends received by incorporated companies treated for corporate tax purposes?
> ► Describe two types of losses and the time periods for carrying forward and carrying back for each.
> ► Describe the concept of capital cost allowance (CCA) deductions for income tax purposes, the asset pool, and situations under which the pool is increased, reduced, or eliminated.
> ► What is recaptured depreciation? How does it arise? Is it different from a capital gain on the sale of an asset?
> ► What is the large corporations capital tax? How is it assessed?

Personal Taxation

As described in Table 2-2, the computation of both corporate and individual taxes payable follows the same basic logic. Since this text is not intended to cover personal finance, the coverage of the tax environment for individuals is limited. Our interest is in those income tax provisions that have an indirect impact on a corporation's actions. These include the taxation of capital gains and dividends.

Calculation of Taxable Income

In addition to income from an unincorporated business or partnership, income from employment, capital gains, and property (including dividends and rent) is included in the individual's income. We consider here the taxation of capital gains and interest; the discussion of the taxation of dividends is presented in a subsequent section.

   The full amount of interest income is included in the net income calculation, but the same is not true for capital gains. Just as in the calculation of capital gains in corporate taxable income, capital gains for individuals can be netted against capital losses. When the resulting value is positive—that is, when there is a net capital gain—a portion of this capital gain is included in income. For individuals, there is a lifetime capital gains exemption of $100 000.[12] For capital gains that exceed this limit or in situations in which the exemption is not applicable, a portion of the capital gain must be included in

---

[12]For capital gains on qualified farm property or shares of small business corporations, the exemption is $500 000.

income and taxed at regular income rates. In 1992, three-quarters of the capital gain is included in income.

The impact of the tax treatment of capital gains can be demonstrated with the example of an Ontario investor who has a marginal tax rate of 44.8 percent on regular income. In 1992, the effective rate on taxable capital gains was 33.6 percent ($0.75 \times 0.448 \times 100$).

When there is a net capital loss, it can be applied forward until it is absorbed or carried back for 3 years. Capital losses cannot, however, be applied against noncapital income.

An individual's taxable income also reflects the application of allowable deductions, such as those for pension contributions and child care expenses. The Canadian income tax system used to allow for more kinds of deductions. Now the tax allowances for many of these items—personal deductions, postsecondary tuition, and charitable donations, to name a few—have been converted from exemptions to tax credits.

There is an important distinction between an exemption and a tax credit. A *tax exemption* is a reduction of taxable income, so it is of more value to an individual with a high marginal tax rate than to a taxpayer with a lower marginal tax rate. For example, under a system using exemptions, each $1000 of exemption is worth $170 of federal tax saving to a taxpayer in the lowest tax bracket (with a tax rate of 17 percent) and $290 to an individual in the highest tax bracket (with a tax rate of 29 percent). A *tax credit*, however, reduces the tax payable independent of the individual's tax rate. The argument behind the movement to tax credits is that it is fairer to provide the same tax saving to individuals in identical situations, independent of their income.

Tax Rates: Individuals

As with corporate taxation, both the federal and provincial governments levy personal income taxes. The federal tax system is *progressive*—that is, the higher one's income, the larger the percentage paid in taxes. Each province imposes a tax on income earned in the province at whatever level it chooses. For all provinces except Quebec, this tax is expressed as a percentage of the basic federal income tax payable. Quebec is the only province that has its own progressive tax rate scheme. However, since the federal system is progressive, the *effective* tax rates in all provinces are progressive. The percentage rates vary among provinces. The amount of these percentage rates by province for 1992 are presented in Table 2-9. For all provinces except Quebec, the provincial tax is collected by the federal government and transferred to the province.[13]

The federal and provincial tax rates applicable to individuals on their employment income are also used for unincorporated businesses such as sole proprietorships and partnerships.

---

[13]There is a federal surtax—4.5 percent in 1992. It is applied after various tax credits, including those for charitable deductions and the dividend tax credit, are taken. The total federal tax rate can therefore vary by individual. Most of the provinces also impose a surtax on high incomes; some provide reduced rates for low incomes. These provincial surtaxes and reductions are not included in Table 2-9.

Table 2-9
Provincial Tax Rates for 1992 (excluding any surtaxes)

Province	Rate (% of federal tax)
Alberta	46.0%
British Columbia	52.0
Manitoba	52.0
New Brunswick	60.0
Newfoundland	64.5
Nova Scotia	59.5
Ontario	54.5
Prince Edward Island	59.5
Saskatchewan	50.0
Yukon	45.0

Table 2-10 presents the federal income tax rate structure for the 1992 taxation year. There are three tax brackets, and each bracket has a tax rate associated with it. This rate is the *marginal* federal tax rate that is applied to every dollar of taxable income in that bracket. For example, in the first bracket, the marginal federal tax rate is 17 percent. For the second bracket, the marginal rate is 26 percent; it is applied to the dollars of taxable income of more than $29 590 and less than or equal to $59 180. For the third bracket, the marginal rates increases to 29 percent; it is applied to the dollars of taxable income that exceed $59 181.

The calculation of the total federal tax liability can result in an effective tax rate that is different from the marginal rate. For example, consider an individual with taxable income equal to $59 180. This individual has a tax liability equal to $12 724.[14] This is equal to the tax paid on the first $29 590 at 17 percent and tax on the next $29 590 at 26 percent. The *average* federal tax rate, found in Column 3, is 21.5 percent. It equals the total tax paid divided by the total taxable income, as measured at the upper end of the income bracket. In the first bracket, since there is no fixed amount of tax to be paid, the average and the marginal tax rates are equal. In the third bracket, the average federal tax rate increases as income increases. For example, an individual with $100 000 in taxable income has a federal tax liability excluding surtaxes of $24 562. This translates to an average federal tax rate of 24.6 percent.

The combined federal and Ontario provincial tax rates are presented in columns 4 and 5 of Table 2-10. Column 4 presents the average total rate, while column 5 gives the total incremental, or marginal, tax paid on an additional dollar of income within the tax bracket. For example, when taxable income is in excess of $59 180, the amount of tax paid for each additional dollar of taxable income is 44.8 cents.

[14]Calculations in this example do not consider any personal tax credits. If these were included, the tax liability would be lower.

Table 2-10
Rates of Federal Income Tax, 1992
Including Impact of Ontario Tax at 54.5% (excluding surtaxes)

Taxable Income (1)	Tax (2)	Average Tax Rates at Upper End of Bracket		Total Marginal Rate (5)
		Federal (3)	Total[a] (4)	
Up to $29 590	17% of amount	17.0%	26.3%	26.3%
$29 591−$59 180	$5030 + 26% on next $29 590	21.5%	33.2%	40.2%
Over $59 180	$12 724 + 29% on remainder	—	—	44.8%

[a]Includes Province of Ontario tax of 54.5 percent of the federal tax payable. In Column 4, the average total tax rate is calculated as total tax payable divided by taxable income at the upper end of the bracket. Total tax payable is calculated as:

$$\text{Total tax payable} = \text{federal tax} + \text{provincial tax}$$
$$= \text{federal tax} + 0.545 \, (\text{federal tax})$$
$$= \text{federal tax} \, (1.545)$$

and the average total tax rate is

$$\frac{\text{Total tax payable}}{\text{Income at upper level}} = \frac{\text{Federal tax}}{\text{Income at upper level}} \times (1.545).$$
$$= \text{Average federal tax} \times 1.545$$
$$(\text{Column 3})$$

In column 5 the total marginal tax rate is defined as the increase in total tax paid for a $1 increase in taxable income within the specified bracket. This is calculated as:

$$\text{Total marginal tax rate} = \text{Federal marginal tax rate} \times 1.545.$$
$$(\text{column 5}) \qquad (\text{column 2})$$

Dividend Taxation

An example of a provision that has an impact on both taxable income and tax credits is the taxation of dividends from a company resident in Canada. Shareholders are subject to taxation on these dividends, but there is an adjustment to some preferred and all common share dividends received from Canadian sources that reduces the effective taxation at the personal level. This adjustment is the **dividend tax credit**, which reduces the amount of federal, and hence provincial, tax payable.

The amount of gross federal tax payable before the dividend tax credit is applied is found by applying the appropriate marginal federal tax rate to adjusted dividends received. To obtain the adjusted dividends, a gross-up is added to the actual dividends received. The gross-up is 25 percent of the dividends received. The tax credit, which is equal to two-thirds of the gross-up, is then deducted from federal tax payable to obtain the net federal tax payable. The provincial tax payable is found by applying the provincial percentage rate to net federal tax payable.

For example, consider two shareholders, each of whom receives $1000 in cash dividends. These shareholders live in Ontario and are in different tax brackets. The first investor is in the bracket with a 17 percent marginal federal rate. The second investor is in the top bracket and has a 29 percent marginal federal tax rate.

The calculation of the tax on dividends and the effective tax rate on dividend income is presented in Table 2-11; this example does *not* include the federal surcharge on income.

The total marginal tax rate for Investor 1 on regular income is 26.3 percent (that is, $0.17 \times 1.545 \times 100$), and for Investor 2 the rate is 44.8 percent (that is, $0.29 \times 1.545 \times 100$). For the first investor, the effective tax rate on dividends is 7.1 percent;[15] the presence of the dividend tax credit has reduced the effective tax rate from 26.13 percent on regular income to 7.1 percent. At the highest marginal tax rate, the dividend tax credit still reduces the effective tax rate on dividend income, from 44.8 percent to 30.3 percent. To give an example that is not calculated in the table, if the investor were in the middle tax bracket, the regular income tax rate would be 40.8 percent and the effective tax rate on dividend income, 24.5 percent.

The benefit of the dividend tax credit declines as the marginal tax rate on regular income increases. This falloff occurs because the gross federal tax

Table 2-11
Calculation of After-Tax Dividends

		Investor 1		Investor 2
1. Dividends received		$1000		$1000
2. Gross-up: 1/4 of dividend received		250		250
3. Total subject to tax (1 + 2)		$1250		$1250
4. Federal tax (gross)	@17%	213	@29%	363
5. Dividend tax credit: 2/3 of gross-up[a]		167		167
6. Net federal tax payable		$ 46		$ 196
7. Provincial tax: 54.5% of net federal tax		25		107
8. Total tax payable (6 + 7)		$ 71		$ 303
9. Dividend after tax (1 − 8)		929		697
10. Effective overall tax rate on dividends (8 ÷ 1)		7.1%		30.3%

[a]The dividend tax credit is also equal to 1/6 of the dividends received. In this example, it can be calculated as $1/6 \times 1000 = 167$.

---

[15]A formula to calculate the effective tax rate is

$$T_E = [T_F(1 + G) - (2/3)G] \times (1 + T_P)$$

where T_F is the marginal federal tax rate
T_P is the provincial percentage rate = 0.545 for Ontario
G is gross-up proportion = 0.25.
The dividend tax credit per dollar of dividends is equal to $(2/3) \times G$ or 0.1667.

increases with an increase in the federal marginal tax rate, but the tax credit is a constant, independent of the investor's marginal federal tax rate. At low marginal rates, the dividend tax credit is a bigger proportion of the gross federal tax payable.

Concept Review

► Describe the difference between a deduction and a tax credit.
► What are the tax consequences of selling a partially depreciated asset, if there are other assets in the pool?
► What are the tax consequences of owning a partially depreciated asset that becomes obsolete?
► From an individual's viewpoint, which of salary, interest, capital gains, and dividend income is taxed most heavily? Which most lightly?
► Describe the difference between marginal tax rates and average tax rates.
► Briefly explain how tax loss carryback and carryforward procedures work.

Summary

This chapter presented some background information on forms of business organization, financial securities, and income tax. The key concepts covered are listed below:

▢ Firms may be organized as **sole proprietorships**, **partnerships**, or **corporations**. The decision as to the form of organization to choose will depend upon the costs of set-up, the need for risk reduction and access to capital, and tax rates.

▢ Firms need capital to acquire assets. They raise this capital by issuing **debt** and **equity** securities and by **retaining earnings**.

▢ **Debtholders**, or **creditors**, have first claim to the firm's earnings and assets, whereas *common equity holders* (the firm's owners) are last in line to be paid. Shareholders' rewards can be high, but they can also be low.

▢ The value of any asset depends on the *after-tax cash flow* it produces. Tax rates and other aspects of our tax system are changed by federal and provincial governments frequently.

▢ Income tax rates for individuals are **progressive**—the higher one's income, the larger the percentage paid in taxes.

▢ Assets such as shares of common equity, bonds, and real estate are defined as **capital** assets. If a capital asset is sold for more than its purchase price, the profit is called a **capital gain**. If the capital asset is sold for a loss, it is called a **capital loss**.

▢ Interest income received by a corporation is taxed as ordinary income; however, most intercorporate dividends are, in effect, excluded from *taxable income*.

▢ Because interest paid by a corporation is a **deductible** expense but dividends are not, our tax system induces a preference for debt over equity financing.

☐ Ordinary corporate operating losses can be **carried back** to each of the preceding 3 years and **carried forward** for the next 7 years to offset taxable income in those years.

☐ **Capital Cost Allowance (CCA)** is the deductible expense for tax purposes that reflects the decrease in value of an asset. The higher the CCA, the lower the taxes paid by the firm. CCA is determined by applying a percentage CCA rate to a declining balance based on the original cost of the asset.

☐ The sale of assets can have consequences on the firm's taxable income through *recapture* of CCA, *terminal loss*, or *capital gains*.

☐ Both federal and provincial authorities levy a **large corporations tax** on the capital of both corporations and financial institutions. The tax rates and threshold asset sizes vary among the jurisdictions.

Questions

2-1 What are the three principal forms of business organizations? What are the advantages and disadvantages of each?

2-2 How can the federal government influence the level of business investment by adjusting the ITC?

2-3 For someone planning to start a new business, is the average or the marginal tax rate more relevant?

2-4 For tax purposes, how does the treatment of interest expense compare with that of common equity dividends from each of the following standpoints?
   a. A firm paying the interest or dividends.
   b. An individual recipient.
   c. A corporate recipient.

2-5 Why is personal income tax information important for a study of business finance?

2-6 Under what circumstances does it become advantageous for the small business to incorporate?

2-7 In what sense is a corporation a "person"?

2-8 Would it be practical for General Motors to be organized as a partnership?

2-9 Explain how the federal income tax structure affects the choice of financing (the use of debt versus equity) of Canadian business firms.

Self-Test Problems   (solutions appear on page 53)

ST-1 **Key terms.** Define each of the following terms:
   a. Proprietorship; partnership; corporation
   b. Retained earnings
   c. Equity

    d. Progressive tax system

    e. Marginal tax rate; average tax rate

    f. Capital gain

    g. Tax loss carryforward

    h. Capital cost allowance (CCA)

    i. Half-year rule

    j. Investment tax credit

    k. Dividend tax credit

ST-2 CCA calculations. A manufacturing firm acquires an asset for $1 million on January 1, 1992. It is added to a pool of assets that has an UCC balance of $3 million as of the same date. The firm has taxable income of $30 million as of December 31, 1992 before the deduction of CCA. The capital cost rate applicable to this pool of assets is 10 percent. If the firm operates in Ontario, calculate the total corporate tax payable.

ST-3 Impact of sale of assets. The current undepreciated capital cost of a specific pool of assets is $400 000. The firm decides to sell from the pool an asset that originally cost $500 000. Calculate the amount of recaptured depreciation and capital gains, if any, and the value of the undepreciated capital cost of the pool after the sale under the following assumed proceeds from sale:

    a. $200 000   **b.** $400 000

    c. $500 000   **d.** $700 000

    e. $300 000 when the asset is the only asset in the class.

Problems

2-1 Loss carryback, carryforward. The projected taxable income of the Carver Corporation Ltd., formed in 1992, is indicated in the following table. (Losses are shown in parentheses.) What is the projected corporate tax liability for each year? Use tax rates as shown in the text. Assume Carver is a small, Canadian-controlled private corporation in Manitoba.

Year	Taxable Income
1992	$(95 000)
1993	70 000
1994	55 000
1995	80 000
1996	(150 000)

2-2 CCA calculations.

    a. If a depreciable asset's original cost is $100 000, what will be the undepreciated capital cost (UCC) that should be used for calculating the CCA in the eighth year when the capital cost rates are 5 percent, 20 percent, and 30 percent?

    b. What is the maximum CCA for the eighth year of this asset for each of the capital cost rates in part a?

2-3 CCA calculation. An asset is acquired on June 30, 1990, for $10 000, and it is introduced to a pool with a UCC value applicable for CCA of $100 000. The CCA rate is 20 percent. For the years 1990, 1991, and 1992, identify the UCC applicable for CCA and the CCA charge on the pool of assets.

2-4 Impact of sale of assets. The Maple Creek Mining Company Limited has an asset pool consisting of a group of assets that all belong to a single class. These assets have an original cost of $6.0 million. The accumulated capital cost allowance on the pool is $2.8 million. The company sold assets that originally cost $5 million for $7.5 million. Describe the effect on company taxes. How would the recapture and/or capital gains be treated for tax purposes? Assume the company has a marginal tax rate of 42 percent.

2-5 Corporate tax liability. The Oak Leaf Snowplow Co. Ltd. had earnings before tax-deductible expenses of $1 million in 1993. Expenses, other than the CCA expense, were $500 000 during the year. The company's assets all fall into a single capital pool that had an UCC of $500 000 in that year. These assets were all in their fifth year of use during 1993, and the capital cost rate for that asset class was 30 percent. On the last day of 1993, the company sold some of its assets, which had an original cost of $250 000, to the Big A Snow Plow Co. Ltd. for $280 000. The company then used the funds to buy new, smaller equipment for $280 000. The corporate income tax rate is 42 percent, and the capital gains will be treated in the usual way. Calculate the company's 1993 income after taxes if it had no carryback losses to take advantage of. What would be the impact on Oak Leaf's tax liability if, instead of purchasing new snowplows, the company paid out the $280 000 proceeds from the sale of the old equipment as a dividend to shareholders?

2-6 Individual tax—dividend income. Assume that an investor residing in Vancouver receives $1000 in dividend income and is subject to a 26 percent marginal federal tax rate. Calculate the tax on the dividend income for this investor.

2-7 Tax payable, different sources of income. If an individual is subject to a 29 percent marginal federal tax rate, what is the total tax payable on $1000 income from (a) dividends, (b) bond interest, and (c) capital gains? Assume the capital gains exemption has been used up and the investor resides in Manitoba.

2-8 Corporate tax liability. The Teletron Electronics Company Ltd. has 1992 income of $365 000 from operations after the deduction of all operating costs but before any adjustment for (a) interest charges of $50 000, (b) dividends paid of $25 000, (c) dividends received from a taxable Canadian corporation of $15 000, or (d) income taxes. Teletron is a manufacturing firm located in Alberta and does not qualify as a small Canadian business. What are its income tax liability and its after-tax income?

2-9 Personal taxes. Carol Stanton has the following situation for the year 1992: salary of $47 500; dividend income of $12 000 on BCE shares; interest on Ontario Hydro bonds of $10 000; proceeds of $15 000 from the sale of 100 shares of Canadian Barrick stock purchased in 1982 at a cost of $9000; and proceeds of $15 000 from the sale of 100 shares of Canadian Barrick stock purchased in October 1990 at a cost of $12 500. Stanton has the personal exemption and tuition costs totalling $7000 eligible for nonrefundable tax credits. She has used none of her lifetime capital gains exemption to date. She is a resident of Nova Scotia.

a. What is Stanton's tax liability for 1992?

b. What are her marginal and average tax rates on taxable income?

c. If she has $100 000 to invest and was offered a choice of either BCE preferred shares, yielding 7 percent, or more Ontario Hydro bonds with a yield of 9 percent, which should she choose, and why? Assume the two investments are equally risky.

Integrative Problem

2-10 **Cash flow analysis.** After graduating with a degree in computer science and spending several years with a large computer company, Jan Berger has decided to go into business for herself. Initially, she will be the only employee of Berger's Computer Repair Service, and she plans to pay herself a salary of $30 000 per year. She must purchase $10 000 of equipment to get started; although this equipment should last at least 7 years, it will be depreciated in CCA class 10 at 30 percent per year. Berger estimates that her first-year revenues will be $60 000 and that her customer base, and hence her revenues, will grow by 10 percent a year thereafter. Berger also estimates that her operating expenses (for parts and so forth) will equal 30 percent of annual revenues. If her business grows as expected, she will hire additional employees after 3 years.

Berger believes that for liability reasons the business should be incorporated after 3 years, when she brings in additional employees, but she is not certain whether she should incorporate it now. Consequently, she has hired you to develop her projected income statements and to advise her on the form of organization that will minimize her taxes and maximize her cash flows over the first 3 years of operation. She estimates that her tax credits will be $1200 during each of the next three years. She is a resident of Ontario. Since this is Berger's first experience in running her own business, she has asked you to help her understand the reasons behind your recommendations. Consequently, you have developed the following list of questions, which, when answered, will give Berger the information she needs to make her decision.

a. What is depreciation? How is depreciation calculated? Why must depreciation be included in the income statement? What effect does depreciation have on the firm's cash flows?

b. Calculate the depreciation expense for the first three years of operation. Will the tax savings resulting from depreciation be the same or different under a proprietorship versus a corporation?

c. If Berger incorporates, what will the corporation's tax bill, after-tax income, and cash flow be for each of the first 3 years? Assume that the company's only income will be from computer repair services, and that its only expenses will be Berger's salary, the company's operating expenses, and depreciation. Use a tax rate of 22 percent.

d. Assume that Berger incorporates and pays herself a salary of $30 000 per year, that this is her only income, and that she can take tax credits of $1200 per year. Under these assumptions, what will her personal taxes be in each of the next three years?

e. What will Berger's total corporate and personal taxes be if she incorporates now?

f. Now assume that Berger does not incorporate, and she operates the business as a sole proprietorship. What will her tax bill be in each of the next three years?

g. Strictly on the basis of minimizing taxes during Years 1 to 3, should Berger incorporate?

Solutions to Self-Test Problems

ST-1 Refer to the appropriate sections of the text to check your responses.

ST-2 The CCA for the newly acquired asset is subject to the half-year rule; it is

$$0.5 \times d \times C_0 = 0.5 \times 0.10 \times \$1m = \$50\,000$$

The CCA for the assets in the existing pool is not subject to the half-year rule; it is

$$d \times UCC = 0.10 \times \$3m = \$300\,000$$

Total CCA is $350 000:

$$CCA = 0.10\,(\$3M) + 0.5(0.10)(\$1\,000\,000) = \$350\,000$$

Thus taxes can be calculated as

Taxable income	$30 000 000
CCA	350 000
Taxable income after CCA	$29 650 000
Taxes payable at 38.8%	$11 504 200

ST-3 The first step is to determine if there is a capital gain. In case d, where the proceeds exceed the original cost, there is capital gain. In the other cases, there is not.

The second step is to determine if there is any recapture of income; this will occur if the proceeds net of capital gain exceed the existing UCC pool. This is the case for c and d. In case e the proceeds are less than the existing pool, but no assets remain. Therefore, there is a terminal loss.

The third step is to determine the value of the undepreciated capital cost of the pool after the sale. Only in case a is there any UCC remaining;

in the other cases, the proceeds are so large that the pool is wiped out. In case e, the UCC is also wiped out; since no assets remain in the pool, the balance is eliminated by the terminal loss.

In case d, then, the $700 000 sale proceeds lead to the following tax implications:

- The UCC pool is wiped out.
- There is $100 000 of recapture, taxable as ordinary income.
- There is a $200 000 capital gain, taxable at the capital gains rate.

In case e, the $300 000 sale proceeds lead to the following tax implications:

- The UCC pool is wiped out.
- There is a $100 000 terminal loss, deductible against ordinary income.

Note that this can occur only if no assets remain in the pool. If other assets remained, the UCC pool after the sale would be $100 000.

Overall, in thousands of dollars:

	a	b	c	d	e
UCC balance before sale (1)	$400	$400	$400	$400	$400
Asset sold					
Proceeds from sale (2)	200	400	500	700	300
Original cost (3)	500	500	500	500	500
Capital gain (4) = (2) − (3)				200	
Proceeds net of capital gain (5) = (2) − (4)	200	400	500	500	300
Recaptured depreciation (terminal loss) (6) = (5) − (1)			100	100	(100)
Net proceeds (7) = (5) − (6)	200	400	400	400	400
UCC pool after sale (8) = (1) − (7)	200	—	—	—	—

3

Financial Markets, Institutions, and Interest Rates

A Managerial Perspective

Not many years ago, most Canadian citizens were farmers, craftspeople, or small business owners, and when they saved, they did so by investing in their own farms or businesses. Equity and debt markets did exist, but they touched the lives of relatively few people, primarily speculators and the very wealthy. Today, however, all that has changed. As a result of increasing industrialization, most people work for corporations, and most savings are channelled through such institutions as pension funds, insurance companies, and mutual funds. These institutions own more than 90 percent of all corporate bonds and about 60 percent of all equities not held by control blocks or parent companies, and these percentages are increasing steadily. Further, since individual investors tend to buy and hold while institutions manage their funds more actively, institutional investors account for about 90 percent of the trading activity in the bond market and about 60 percent in the stock market.

Since institutions handle most investment capital, it is critical that financial managers understand the environment and markets within which they operate. Therefore, in this chapter we examine the markets in which capital is raised, securities are traded, and share prices are established, as well as the institutions through which such transactions are conducted. In the process, we see how money costs are determined and explore the principal factors that determine the level of interest rates in the economy.

The Financial Markets

Business firms, as well as individuals and government units, often need to raise capital. For example, suppose Ontario Hydro forecasts an increase in the demand for power in its service area and decides to build a new power plant. It almost certainly will not have the approximately $1 billion necessary to pay for the plant, so it will have to raise this capital in the market. Or suppose Mr. Jones, the proprietor of a local hardware store, decides to expand into appliances. Where will he get the money to buy the initial inventory of TV sets, washers, and freezers? Similarly, if the Smith family wants to buy a home that costs $60 000 but has only $20 000 in savings, how can it raise the additional

$40 000? And if the City of Hamilton wants to borrow $20 million to finance a new sewer plant while the federal government needs some $35 billion to cover its projected 1991 deficit, they each need sources for raising this capital.

On the other hand, some individuals and firms have incomes that are greater than their current expenditures, so they have funds available to invest. For example, Edgar Rice has an income of $60 000, but his expenses are only $40 000; Ford Motor Company has accumulated more than $262 million that it holds in cash or has invested temporarily in marketable securities.

Entities wanting to borrow money are brought together with those having surplus funds in the **financial markets**. Note that "markets" is plural—there are a great many different financial markets in a developed economy. Each market deals with a somewhat different type of security, serves a different set of customers, or operates in a different part of the country. Some of the major types of markets follow.

1. *Physical asset markets* and *financial asset markets* must be distinguished. *Physical assets* (also called "tangible" or "real" assets) are those for such products as wheat, autos, real estate, computers, and machinery. *Financial assets* are shares, bonds, notes, mortgages, and other claims on real assets.

2. *Spot markets* and *futures markets* differ in whether the assets are being bought or sold for "on the spot" delivery (literally, within a few days) or for delivery at some future date such as six months or a year in the future. The futures markets (which could include the *options markets*) are growing in importance, but we defer discussion of them until much later in the text.

3. *Money markets* are financial markets for short-term (maturity less than 1 year) debt securities. The New York money market is the world's largest; it is dominated by the major U.S., Japanese, and European banks. London, Tokyo, and Paris are other major money market centres. The major money market in Canada is Toronto.

4. *Capital markets* are financial markets for long-term debt and corporate shares. The Toronto Stock Exchange, which handles the common shares of many of the largest corporations, is an example of a capital market. Bonds and shares of smaller corporations are handled in other segments of the capital market.

5. *Mortgage markets* deal with loans on residential, commercial, and industrial real estate and on farmland, while *consumer credit markets* involve loans on autos and appliances as well as loans for education, vacations, and so on.

6. *World*, *national*, *regional*, and *local markets* also exist. Thus, depending on an organization's size and scope of operations, it may be able to borrow all around the world, or it may be confined to a strictly local, even neighbourhood, market.

7. *Primary markets* are the markets in which corporations raise new capital and in which newly issued securities are involved. If Canadian Pacific sells a new issue of common equity to raise capital, this is a primary market transaction. The corporation selling the equity receives the proceeds from the sale in a primary market transaction.

8. *Secondary markets* are the markets in which existing, already outstanding securities are traded among investors. Thus, if Edgar Rice decides to

buy 1000 shares of CP common equity that is not a new issue, the purchase will occur in the secondary market. The Toronto Stock Exchange is a secondary market, since it deals in outstanding shares and bonds as opposed to newly issued ones. Secondary markets also exist for mortgages and other financial assets. The corporation whose securities are being traded is not involved in a secondary market transaction and thus does not receive any funds from such a sale.

Other classifications could be made, but this breakdown is sufficient to show that there are many types of financial markets.

A healthy economy is vitally dependent on efficient transfers of funds from savers to firms and individuals that need capital—that is, the economy depends on *efficient financial markets*. Without efficient transfers, corporations, both Crown corporations and those operating in the private sector, either could not raise capital or would have to pay excessive rates to obtain it. There would be an impact on the availability of goods and services to citizens, the Smith family would not have adequate housing, Edgar Rice would have no place to invest his savings, and so on. Obviously, the level of productivity and hence our standard of living would be much lower, so it is absolutely essential that our financial markets function efficiently—not only quickly, but also at a low cost.[1]

Concept Review

▶ Distinguish between physical asset markets and financial asset markets.
▶ Distinguish between spot and futures markets.
▶ Distinguish between money and capital markets.
▶ Distinguish between primary and secondary markets.

Financial Institutions

Transfers of capital between savers and those who need capital take place in the three different ways diagrammed in Figure 3-1:

1. **Direct transfers** of money and securities, as shown in the top section, occur when a business sells its common equity and bonds directly to savers, without going through any type of intermediary. The business delivers its securities to savers, who in turn give the firm the money it needs.
2. As shown in the middle section, transfers may also go through an **investment dealer**, or investment house, such as Burns Fry or Scotia-McLeod, which serves as an intermediary and facilitates the issuance of securities. The company sells its common equity and bonds to the

---

[1]When organizations such as the United Nations design plans to aid developing nations, just as much attention must be paid to the establishment of efficient financial markets as to electrical power, transportation, communications, and other infrastructure systems. Economic efficiency is simply impossible without a good system for allocating capital within the economy.

Figure 3-1
Diagram of the Capital Formation Process

1. Direct Transfers

2. Indirect Transfers through an Investment Dealer

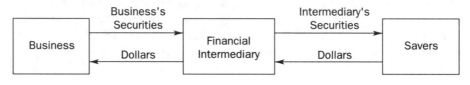

3. Indirect Transfers through a Financial Intermediary

investment dealer, which in turn sells these same securities to ultimate savers. The business's securities and the savers' money merely "pass through" the investment dealer. However, the investment dealer does buy and hold the securities for a period of time, so it is taking a chance—it may be able to resell them to savers only for an amount less than or equal to what it paid. Because the corporation receives money from the sale, this is a primary market transaction.

3.   Transfers can also be made through a **financial intermediary**, such as a bank or mutual fund. Here the intermediary obtains funds from savers, issuing its own securities in exchange, and then uses the money to purchase businesses' securities. For example, a saver might give dollars to a bank, receiving from it an investment certificate or a term deposit certificate, and then the bank might channel the money to a small business in the form of a mortgage loan. Thus, intermediaries literally create new forms of capital—in this case, investment or term deposit certificates, which are more liquid than mortgages and hence are better securities for most savers to hold. The existence of intermediaries greatly increases the amount of money in the economy and capital market efficiency.

In this chapter, we assume that the entity that needs capital is a business, specifically a corporation, although it is easy enough to visualize the demander of capital as a potential home purchaser, a government unit, and so on.

Direct transfers of funds from savers to businesses are possible and do occur on occasion, but it is generally more efficient for a business to obtain the services of a specialized financial institution called an *investment house*. ScotiaMcLeod, Burns Fry, and RBC Dominion are examples of investment houses. Such organizations (1) help corporations design securities with the features that will be most attractive to investors, (2) buy these securities from the corporation, and then (3) resell them to savers. Although the securities are sold twice, this process is really one primary market transaction, with the investment house acting as an intermediary in the process of transferring capital from savers to businesses.[2]

The financial intermediaries shown in the third section of Figure 3-1 do more than simply transfer money and securities between firms and savers—they literally create new financial products. Since the intermediaries are generally large, they gain economies of scale in analyzing the creditworthiness of potential borrowers, in processing and collecting loans, and in pooling risks and thus helping individual savers diversify, which means "not putting all their financial eggs in one borrower's basket." Further, a system of specialized intermediaries can enable savings to do more than just draw interest. For example, people can put money into banks and get both interest and a convenient way of making payments (chequing), put money in life insurance companies and get both interest and protection for their beneficiaries, and so on.

In Canada and other developed nations, a large set of specialized, highly efficient financial intermediaries has evolved. The situation is changing rapidly, and different types of institutions are performing services that were formerly reserved for other institutions, so institutional distinctions are becoming blurred. Still, there is a degree of institutional identity. Here are the major classes of intermediaries:

1. *Chartered banks*, which are the traditional financial "department stores," serve a wide variety of savers and those with needs for funds. Historically, the chartered banks have been the major institutions that handled chequing accounts and through which the Bank of Canada expanded or contracted the money supply. Today, however, some of the other institutions discussed below also provide chequing services and significantly influence the effective money supply. Conversely, commercial banks now provide an ever-widening range of financial services either directly or through financial subsidiaries. An example is the stock brokerage services provided by the Toronto-Dominion Bank. Note that commercial banks do not directly engage in the functions of investment dealers in the primary market. Their participation is through the ownership of investment dealers.

2. *Trust and mortgage loan companies* historically served individual savers and residential mortgage borrowers. The trust and mortgage loan companies take the funds of many small savers and lend the money to home buyers and other types of borrowers. In addition, the trust companies

---

[2]An investment dealer must be distinguished from an investment banker or merchant banker. The former does take a risk position in underwriting shares, but it does not intend to hold on to them. A merchant banker, on the other hand, takes a longer-term view of its investment. For example, Hees International Bancorp is a merchant banker that will invest funds in a firm in financial distress and manage it in the expectation of a turnaround.

provide financial services to businesses and individuals in what is called estate, trust, and agency (ETA) business.

ETA business reflects many diverse types of financial activities including, but not limited to, management of pension funds, administration of estates and personal trust funds, and administration of funds set aside by corporations for the repayment of debt. Trust companies act as agents in their ETA function, and their compensation is based on a set fee.

3. *Credit unions* and *caisses populaires* are co-operative associations whose members have a common bond, such as being employees of the same firm. Members' savings are loaned only to other members, generally for auto purchases, home improvements, and the like. Credit unions and caisses populaires may specialize as savings banks or as mortgage and consumer lenders, or they may combine the two functions.

4. *Pension funds* are retirement plans funded by corporations or government agencies for their workers and administered primarily by the trust departments of trust companies or by life insurance companies. Pension funds invest primarily in bonds, shares, mortgages, and real estate.

5. *Life insurance companies* take savings in the form of annual premiums, then invest these funds in shares, bonds, real estate, and mortgages, and, finally, upon the deaths of the insured parties, make payments to their beneficiaries.

6. *Mutual funds* are corporations that accept dollars from savers and then use these dollars to buy shares, long-term bonds, or short-term debt instruments issued by businesses or government units. These organizations pool funds and thus reduce risks by diversification. They also gain economies of scale, which lower the costs of analyzing securities, managing portfolios, and trading in shares and bonds. Different funds are designed to meet the objectives of different types of savers. Hence, we have bond funds for those who desire safety, equity funds for savers who are willing to accept significant risks in the hope of very high returns, and still other funds that are used as interest-bearing chequing accounts (money market funds). There are literally hundreds of different mutual funds, with dozens of different goals and purposes.

Financial institutions have historically been heavily regulated, with the major purpose of the regulation being to ensure the safety of the institutions for the protection of their savers. Until recently, the regulations were also intended to restrict competition among the four key financial industry groups (called the four pillars): investment dealers, insurance companies, trust companies, and chartered banks. Competition among these groups, if it existed, was at the interface between them and not in their core businesses. Under the current reform of Canadian financial legislation and regulation occurring at the federal and provincial levels, the four pillars have eroded significantly. There will no longer be any restrictions on the entry of a company from one pillar into the business traditionally undertaken by companies in another pillar, although some of the functions will have to be undertaken through subsidiaries.

In Ontario, the investment dealer business has been opened up to foreign competition; non-Canadians can now own 100 percent of a Canadian registered investment dealer. An investment dealer can now be acquired by any of the other financial institutions or any foreign dealer. Currently, most of the major Canadian banks own and operate an investment dealer; for instance the Bank of Nova Scotia purchased McLeod, Young, Weir and now operates it under the name ScotiaMcLeod, and the Toronto-Dominion Bank started its own discount broker, Greenline Investment Services. Banks are now also applying for licences to operate trust companies and to sell insurance policies.

With the removal of the four-pillar restrictions, it is very likely that American-style financial supermarkets will develop in Canada. The archetypal example of the financial supermarket is Sears, Roebuck in the United States; it owns Allstate Insurance, Dean Witter (a brokerage investment banking firm), Coldwell Banker (a real estate brokerage firm), a huge credit card business, and a host of other related businesses. A similar phenomenon in Canada is Trilon Financial Corp., which owns or controls, directly or indirectly, London Life Insurance, Wellington Insurance, Trilon Bancorp (a merchant banker), Royal LePage Ltd. (a real estate broker), and a number of international interests.

Concept Review

▸ Identify the three ways capital is transferred from savers to borrowers
▸ What is the difference between a commercial bank and an investment dealer?
▸ Distinguish between investment dealers and financial intermediaries
▸ What are the major classes of financial intermediaries in Canada? What are the primary functions of each?

The Stock Market

As noted earlier, secondary markets are the markets in which outstanding, previously issued securities are traded. By far the most active market—and the most important one to financial managers—is the **stock market**. It is here that the price of each share, and hence the value of a business firm, is established. Since the primary goal of financial management is to contribute to the maximization of the firm's share price, a knowledge of the market in which this price is established is essential for anyone involved in managing a firm.

The Stock Exchanges

There are two basic types of security markets: the organized exchanges, typified by the Toronto Stock Exchange (TSE), and the less formal over-the-counter markets.[3] As the organized exchanges have actual market locations and are easier to describe and understand, we consider them first.

---

[3]Some stocks are sold through organized exchanges whereas others are traded over the counter. Bonds are typically traded in over-the-counter markets by investment dealers, who may hold an inventory of the bonds. There is also a "private placement" market in which debt and equity issues are issued privately, usually to institutional investors. This process is contrasted to a public issue of securities, for which the information requirements are more onerous and in which the securities are made available to a large number of investors. The public issue process is described in Chapter 20.

The **organized security exchanges** are tangible, physical entities that conduct auction markets in securities listed with them. Each of the larger ones occupies its own building, has specifically designated members, and has an elected governing body—its board of governors. Members are said to have "seats" on the exchange, although everybody stands up. These seats, which are bought and sold, represent the right to trade on the exchange. The value of a seat on the TSE has fluctuated widely in the past.

For example, in November 1977 a seat traded for $17 000. At the beginning of April 1987, a TSE member sold a seat for $300 000, a record price at that time. The demand for seats was so great (because of the liberalization of entry and ownership into the Canadian securities business) that the TSE did not believe a sufficient number of seats would be made available from existing members. Never one to overlook a profitable opportunity, the TSE, in April 1987, decided to offer five new seats for sale at a fixed price of $360 000. This in effect put a ceiling on the value of a seat.[4] A trade in March 1992 was at $55 000.

Most of the larger investment dealers operate *brokerage departments*, which own seats on the exchanges and designate one of the officers of the firm as a member of the exchange. The exchanges are open on all normal working days, with the members meeting in a large room equipped with telephones and other electronic equipment that enables each brokerage house member to communicate with the firm's offices throughout the country.

Like other markets, a security exchange facilitates communication between buyers and sellers. For example, ScotiaMcLeod may receive an order to buy 100 shares of Royal Bank equity from a customer in its Vancouver office. Simultaneously, a brokerage house in Montreal may receive an order from a customer wishing to sell 100 shares of the Royal Bank. Each broker communicates the order to its firm's representative on the TSE. Other brokers throughout the country would also communicate their buy and sell orders to their representatives on the exchange. The exchange members with *sell orders* offer the shares for sale, and the shares are bid for by the members with *buy orders*. Thus, the exchanges operate as *auction markets*.[5]

Canada has four organized stock exchanges: Toronto, Montreal, Vancouver, and Alberta. The largest of these exchanges, by any measure of size, is the Toronto Stock Exchange, and for this reason we refer to its operations in our discussions. Many brokerage firms have seats on more than one stock exchange. In addition, a particular security that requires a wide distribution will be listed on more than one exchange. Therefore, in the example above, the broker in Montreal could trade the Royal Bank shares on The Montreal Exchange (ME) so long as the stock is listed on this exchange and the broker is a

---

[4]The fact that the TSE decided to sell new seats to provide funds to the exchange is consistent with a view that it believed the seat prices were too high and wanted to "cash in" on the euphoria surrounding deregulation.

[5]This discussion is not intended to describe the trading process of the TSE or other organized exchanges. One important point to note, however, is that the brokerage houses buy and sell securities as agents for their customers. The specialist, as found on the NYSE, attempts to provide a market for the securities in which he or she specializes by dealing as a principal from the specialist's own inventory of shares. The equivalent of the specialist on the TSE is the Registered Trader.

member of it. If the stock is listed in more than one market, brokers will check these markets to ensure that their clients receive the best price. Some Canadian companies, attempting to open up new sources for equity capital, list their shares on the New York Stock Exchange (NYSE) or the American Exchange (AMEX).

Since the shares of a company are sometimes listed on more than one stock exchange (domestic and/or international),[6] is it possible for the prices of the firm's shares to differ from one exchange to another? Any price differential must be transitory; a share of common equity is a claim on the earnings of a company regardless of where the shares are traded, and two assets with identical attributes must ultimately sell for the same price. Consider the case of a multiple Canadian listing in which the price of a share of Bell Canada Enterprises (BCE) on the ME is greater than the price per share of BCE on the TSE. In this case, an investor (or broker) could buy 100 shares of BCE on the TSE, sell the 100 shares at a higher price on the ME, and make a profit equal to the price differential less the transaction costs. As there is no risk in this operation and no money need be invested, the process (called *arbitrage*) of buying in one market and selling in another will continue as long as there is a profit to be made after transaction costs. But the purchase of shares in the lower-priced market will place upward pressure on the share price in that market, and the sale of the same shares in the higher-priced market will place downward pressure on the share price in that market; the differential thus tends to be equalized. There are brokerage firms that specialize in this arbitrage function.

The process of international arbitrage is identical and results in the share prices of a company's equity tending to be identical in the Canadian and foreign markets after adjustment for exchange rates. For example, suppose the share price of a particular company on the NYSE is $10.00 U.S.; the exchange rate on that day is $1.00 U.S. to $1.20 Canadian; and the price of the same share on the TSE is $13.00. An arbitrageur could buy the share on the NYSE for $10.00 U.S. and sell it on the TSE for $13.00 Canadian, or an equivalent of $10.83 U.S. The arbitrageur gets back the original $10.00 U.S. and has made a profit of $0.83 U.S. This arbitrage activity will continue as long as the process results in profits for the arbitrageur, after consideration of transaction costs in exchange rates and brokerage fees.

There are special procedures available for handling large blocks of securities. For example, if BCE, whose shares are already listed on the TSE, plans to sell a new issue of equity, the exchange has facilities that make it easier for the market to absorb the new issue. Similarly, if a large mutual fund or pension fund wants to sell a large block of a listed security, procedures are available that facilitate the sale without putting undue pressures on the share price.

---

[6]For the year ending December 31, 1991, there were 139 equity securities interlisted on the TSE and other exchanges. In terms of the total market value of interlisted shares traded, 60.4 percent was traded on Canadian exchanges with the major amount being traded on the TSE (48.6 percent of the total value traded). Of the 39.6 percent traded on U.S. exchanges, the bulk was on the New York Stock Exchange (at 29.3 percent of the total traded value) and the remainder on the American Exchange and the NASDAQ, an automated trading system (respectively, at 4.2 and 6.0 percent of the traded value).

Over-the-Counter Security Markets

In contrast to the organized security exchanges, the over-the-counter market for securities is an intangible organization. An explanation of the term "over-the-counter" will help clarify what this market is. The exchanges operate as auction markets—buy and sell orders come in more or less simultaneously, and the exchanges are used to match these orders. But if the shares of a company are traded less frequently, perhaps because they are the shares of a new or a small firm, few buy and sell orders come in, and matching them within a reasonable length of time would be difficult. To avoid this problem, some brokerage firms maintain an inventory of the shares. They buy when individual investors wish to sell, and sell when investors want to buy. At one time the inventory of securities was kept in a safe, and the shares, when bought and sold, were literally passed over the counter.

Today, **over-the-counter markets** are defined as all facilities that provide for any security transactions not conducted on the organized exchanges. These facilities consist of (1) the relatively few brokers who hold inventories of over-the-counter securities and who are said to "make a market" in these securities; (2) a large number of other brokers who act as agents in bringing these dealers together with investors; (3) the computers, terminals, and electronic networks that provide for communications between brokers. The dealers who make a market in a particular security will, upon request, quote a price at which they are willing to buy the shares (the *bid price*) and a price at which they will sell shares (the *asked price*). The spread between bid and asked prices represents the dealer's markup, or profit.

Bond transactions take place in the over-the-counter market. The reason is that bonds typically are traded among the large financial institutions—life insurance companies and pension funds—that deal in very large blocks of securities. It is relatively easy for the over-the-counter bond dealers to arrange the transfer of large blocks of bonds among the relatively few holders of the bonds. It would be impossible to conduct similar operations in the stock market among the many thousands of large and small shareholders.

The Investment Dealers Association of Canada (IDA) provides daily high and low prices and volumes in unlisted mines and industrials. For listed industrials that do not trade on a particular day, bid and ask prices are supplied to the IDA by a brokerage firm.

Some Trends in Securities Markets

The pervasive changes occurring in the securities markets will have an impact on the structure and functioning of those markets. Two of the more important changes are globalization of the industry and computerized trading.

1. *Globalization.*   The capital markets have become international in scope, and to compete at this level requires significant amounts of financial capital. Capital in the required amounts is difficult to generate from internal sources exclusively. In addition, competition on commission rates charged for brokerage services arose when these rates were deregulated. Both of these influences led to the creation of larger investment dealers/

brokers, usually through mergers. Creating a larger entity makes more capital available for firms to enter new markets and provide new services. Also, with an increase in the scale of brokerage operations, economies of scale can be realized and costs will fall.

A new wrinkle is the ongoing deregulation of the securities industry. This had led to mergers of banks and investment dealers, to mergers of foreign and Canadian dealers, and to the entry of foreign dealers through new operations. The mergers are providing capital and international expertise.

2. *Computerized trading.*   With the increased power of computer systems, it is now possible to introduce automated trading for common shares. Major strides have taken place in Canada and throughout the world to introduce computer systems that will completely replace the trading floor. However, there are some exchanges (among them the New York Stock Exchange and The Montreal Exchange) that have resisted the move to a "floorless" stock market.

The Vancouver Stock Exchange (VSE) was completely computerized by the end of 1990. The benefits of the full automation of the trading include rapid order execution—less than one second—and improved surveillance of the market for regulatory purposes. The VSE is the country's second largest in terms of volume and third biggest in terms of dollar volume (behind Toronto and Montreal). The TSE has had a computerized system in operation since 1977. CATS (Computer Assisted Trading System), which has the capability of handling all trading, has been used exclusively for the less frequently traded securities; the more active securities continue to trade on the floor of the exchange. However, in February 1992, the members voted to move to a completely automated trading system. It is anticipated that the system will be operational in the first quarter of 1994. The reason for the switch is the force of competition. Many of the securities that are listed on the TSE are also traded on U.S. exchanges and in over-the-counter markets. It is anticipated that the computerized trading will provide faster trades, more accurate execution, and lower transaction costs, thereby attracting trading to the TSE.

When the automated market arrives in Toronto, trading will be completely electronic with entry from terminals located in the TSE members' offices. Orders will be entered electronically, and transactions will occur in a pure auction without the intervention of humans. (Under the current system, trading is of the auction type, but traders are physically present on the exchange floor.) The market-making function will be undertaken by Registered Traders who are affiliated with TSE member firms and risk their capital by buying and selling securities to ensure that a liquid market exists.

Concept Review

▶ What are the two basic types of equity markets? How do they differ?

The Cost of Money

Capital in a free economy is allocated through the price system. **Interest** is the price paid for borrowed *debt capital*; in the case of *equity capital*, investors expect compensation in the form of *dividends* and *capital gains*. The factors that affect the supply of and the demand for investment capital, and hence the level of interest rates, are discussed in this section. In Chapters 16 and 21, we shall examine the precise way that bond and common share prices are established, given the level of interest rates in the economy.

The four fundamental factors affecting the cost of money are (1) *production opportunities*, (2) *time preferences for consumption*, (3) *risk*, and (4) *inflation*. To understand how these factors interact to affect interest rates, consider first an isolated island community where the people live on fish. They have a given stock of fishing gear that permits them to survive reasonably well, but they would like to have more fish. Now suppose Mr. Crusoe has a bright idea for a new type of fishnet that will enable him to double his daily catch. However, it will take him a year to perfect his design, build his net, and learn how to use it efficiently, and Mr. Crusoe would probably starve before he could put his new net into operation. Therefore, he may suggest to Ms. Robinson, Mr. Friday, and several others that if they give him one fish each day for a year, he will return two fish a day during all of the next year. If someone accepts the offer, then the fish that Ms. Robinson or one of the others give him will constitute *savings*. These savings will be *invested* in the fishnet, and the extra fish caught will constitute a *return on the investment*.

Obviously, the more productive Mr. Crusoe thinks the new fishnet will be, the higher his expected return on the investment and the more he can offer to pay Ms. Robinson, Mr. Friday, and other investors for their savings. We assumed above that Mr. Crusoe thinks he will be able to pay a 100 percent rate of return—he offered to give back two fish for every one he receives. He might try to attract savings for less—for example, he might try one and a half fish next year for every one he receives this year, which would represent a 50 percent rate of return to Ms. Robinson and the other potential savers.

How attractive this offer will be to potential investors depends in large part on their *time preferences for consumption*. For example, Ms. Robinson may be thinking of retirement and be willing to trade fish today for fish in the future on a one-for-one basis, that is, with a *zero* rate of return. On the other hand, Mr. Friday may have a wife and several children and need his current fish and may therefore be unwilling to "lend" a fish today except in exchange for three fish next year. In this case, Mr. Friday is said to have a high time preference for consumption, Ms. Robinson a low time preference.

Note also that if the entire population were living right at the subsistence level, time preferences for current consumption would necessarily be high, aggregate savings would be low, interest rates would be high, and capital formation would be difficult.

The *risk* inherent in the fishnet project, and thus in Mr. Crusoe's ability to repay the loan, also affects the return investors require. The higher the perceived risk, the higher the required rate of return.

In a more complex society, there are many businesses like Mr. Crusoe's, many products, and many savers like Ms. Robinson and Mr. Friday. Further, people use money as a medium of exchange rather than barter with fish. When money is used, rather than fish, its value in the future, which is affected by *inflation*, comes into play. The higher the expected rate of inflation, the larger the required return.

Thus, we see that the interest rate paid to savers depends in a basic way on (1) the *rate of return* producers can expect to earn on invested capital, (2) consumers' and savers' *time preferences for current versus future consumption*, (3) the *riskiness* of the loan, and (4) the *expected rate of inflation*. Producers' expected returns on their business investments set an upper limit on how much they can pay for savings, while consumers' time preferences for consumption establish how much consumption they are willing to defer and hence to save at different levels of interest offered by producers.[7] Higher risk and higher inflation also lead to higher interest rates.

Concept Review

▶ What is the price paid to borrow debt capital?
▶ What is the "price" of equity capital?
▶ What four fundamental factors affect the cost of money?

Interest Rate Levels

Capital is allocated among firms by interest rates. Firms with the most profitable investment opportunities are willing and able to pay the most for capital, so they tend to attract it away from inefficient firms and those whose products are not in demand. Of course, our economy is not completely free in the sense of being influenced only by market forces. Thus, the Canadian and provincial governments have agencies that help individuals or groups to obtain capital on favourable terms. Still, most capital in the Canadian economy is allocated through the price system.

Figure 3-2 shows how supply and demand interact to determine interest rates in two capital markets. Markets A and B represent two of the many capital markets in existence. The going interest rate, k, is initially 10 percent for the low-risk securities in Market A. Borrowers whose credit is strong enough to qualify for this market can obtain funds at a cost of 10 percent, and investors who want to put their money to work at low risk can obtain a 10 percent return. Riskier borrowers must obtain higher-cost funds in Market B. Investors who are more willing to take risks invest in Market B with the promise of receiving a 12 percent return but also with the realization that they might receive much less.

If the demand for funds in a market declines, as it typically does during a business recession, the demand curves will shift to the left, as shown in curve

---

[7]The term "producers" is really too narrow. A better word might be "borrowers," which would include corporations, home purchasers, people borrowing to go to college, and even people borrowing to buy autos or to pay for vacations. Also, the wealth of a society influences its people's ability to save and hence their time preferences for current versus future consumption.

Figure 3-2
Interest Rates as a Function of
the Supply of and Demand for Funds

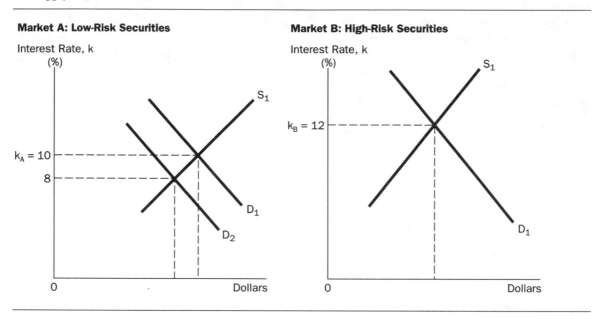

Market A: Low-Risk Securities

Interest Rate, k
(%)

$k_A = 10$

8

0   Dollars

S_1

D_1

D_2

Market B: High-Risk Securities

Interest Rate, k
(%)

$k_B = 12$

0   Dollars

S_1

D_1

D_2 in Market A. The market-clearing, or equilibrium, interest rate in this example declines to 8 percent. A similar shift occurs if the supply of funds decreases—say, because the Bank of Canada tightens credit. You should be able to visualize what will happen: the supply curve, S_1, will shift to the left, raising interest rates and lowering the level of borrowing in the economy.

Capital markets are interdependent. For example, if Markets A and B were in equilibrium before the demand shift to D_2 in Market A, then investors were willing to accept the higher risk in Market B in exchange for a *risk premium* of $12\% - 10\% = 2\%$. After the shift to D_2, the risk premium will initially increase to $12\% - 8\% = 4\%$. In all likelihood, this much larger premium will induce some of the lenders in Market A to shift to Market B; this, in turn, will cause the supply curve in Market A to shift to the left (or upward) and that in Market B to shift to the right. This transfer of capital between markets will raise the interest rate in Market A and lower it in Market B, thus bringing the risk premium back closer to the original level of 2 percent.

There are many capital markets in Canada. Canadian firms also invest and raise capital throughout the world, and foreigners both borrow and lend capital in Canada. There are markets for mortgages; farm loans; business loans; federal, provincial, and local government loans; and consumer loans. Within each category, there are regional markets as well as various types of submarkets. For example, in real estate there are separate markets for first and second mortgages, and for loans on owner-occupied homes, apartments, office buildings, shopping centres, vacant land, and so on. Within the business sector, there are dozens of types of debt and also several sharply differentiated markets for common equity.

There is a price for each type of capital, and these prices change over time as shifts occur in supply and demand conditions. Figure 3-3 shows how long-

and short-term interest rates to business borrowers have varied since 1968. Notice that short-term interest rates are especially prone to rise during booms and then fall during recessions. (The shaded areas of the chart indicate recessions.) When the economy is expanding, firms need capital, and this demand for capital pushes rates up. Also, inflationary pressures are strongest during business booms, and that also exerts upward pressure on rates. Conditions are reversed during recessions: slack business reduces the demand for credit, the rate of inflation falls, and the result is a drop in interest rates.[8]

Figure 3-3
Long- and Short-Term Interest Rates 1968–1991

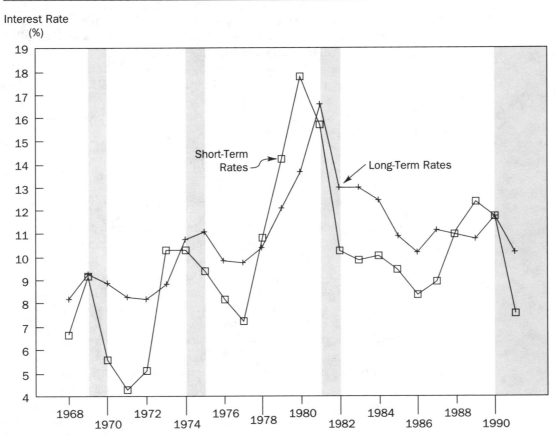

Note: Short-term rates are for 90-day prime commercial paper. Long-term rates are for an index of high-grade, long-term corporate bonds, compiled by McLeod, Young, Weir and a successor company, ScotiaMcLeod, and reported in the *Bank of Canada Review*.

Source: *Bank of Canada Review*, various issues.

---

[8]Short-term rates are responsive to current economic conditions, whereas long-term rates primarily reflect long-run expectations for inflation. As a result, short-term rates are sometimes above and sometimes below long-term rates. The relationship between long-term and short-term rates is called the *term structure of interest rates*. This topic is discussed later in the chapter.

Concept Review

▶ How are interest rates used to allocate capital among firms?
▶ What happens to market-clearing, or equilibrium, interest rates in a capital market when the demand for funds declines? What happens when inflation increases or decreases?
▶ Briefly explain why prices for capital change during booms and recessions.

The Determinants of Market Interest Rates

In general, the nominal (or stated) interest rate on a debt security, k, is composed of a real risk-free rate of interest, k*, plus several premiums that reflect inflation, the riskiness of the security, and the security's marketability (or liquidity). This relationship can be expressed as

$$\text{Market rate} = k = k^* + IP + DRP + LP + MRP, \tag{3-1}$$

and if we combine k* + IP and let this sum equal k_{RF}, then we have this expression:

$$k = k_{RF} + DRP + LP + MRP. \tag{3-2}$$

Here

k = the nominal, or stated, rate of interest on a given security.[9] There are many different securities, hence many different stated interest rates.

k^* = the real risk-free rate of interest, k*, which is pronounced "k-star," is the rate that would exist on a riskless security if zero inflation were expected.

k_{RF} = the nominal risk-free rate of interest. This is the stated interest rate on a security, such as a Government of Canada treasury bill, that is free of default risk. k_{RF} does include a premium for expected inflation, so k_{RF} = k* + IP.

IP = inflation premium. IP is equal to the average expected inflation rate over the life of the security.

DRP = default risk premium. This premium reflects the possibility that the issuer will not pay interest or principal on a security at the stated time and in the stated amount.

LP = liquidity premium. This is a premium charged by lenders to reflect the fact that some securities cannot be converted to cash on short notice at a "reasonable" price.

---

[9]The term *nominal* as it is used here means the *stated* rate as opposed to the *real* rate, where the real rate is adjusted for inflation. If you bought a 10-year Government of Canada bond in February 1992, the stated, or nominal, rate would be about 8.32 percent, but if inflation averages 5 percent over the next 10 years, the actual real rate would be about 8.32% − 5% = 3.32%. In Chapter 12, we will use the term *nominal* in yet another way: to distinguish between stated rates and effective annual rates when compounding occurs more frequently than once a year.

MRP = maturity risk premium. As we explain later, longer-term bonds are exposed to a significant risk of price declines, and a maturity premium is charged by lenders to reflect this risk.

We discuss the components whose sum makes up the stated, or nominal, rate on a given security in the following sections.

The Real Risk-Free Rate of Interest, k*

The **real risk-free rate of interest**, **k***, is defined as the interest rate that would exist on a riskless security if no inflation were expected, and it may be thought of as the rate of interest that would exist on short-term Government of Canada treasury bills in an inflation-free world. The real risk-free rate is not static—it changes over time depending on economic conditions, especially (1) on the rate of return corporations and other borrowers can expect to earn on productive assets, and (2) on people's time preferences for current versus future consumption. Borrowers' expected returns on real asset investments set an upper limit on how much they can afford to pay for borrowed funds, whereas savers' time preferences for consumption establish how much consumption they are willing to defer, and hence the amount of funds they will lend at different levels of interest. It is difficult to measure k* precisely, but most experts think that in Canada it has fluctuated in the range of 3 to 5 percent in recent years.

The Nominal Risk-Free Rate of Interest, k_{RF}

The **nominal risk-free rate**, **k_{RF}**, is the real risk-free rate plus a premium for expected inflation: $k_{RF} = k^* + IP$. To be strictly correct, the risk-free rate should mean the interest rate on a totally risk-free security—one that has no risk of default, no maturity risk, no liquidity risk, and no risk of loss if inflation increases. There is no such security, and hence there is no observable truly risk-free rate. However, there is one security that is free of most risks: a Government of Canada treasury bill (T-bill), which is a short-term security issued by the Canadian government. Longer-term government bonds ("long Canadas") are free of default and liquidity risks but are exposed to some risk from changes in the general level of interest rates.

If the term "risk-free rate" is used without either the modifier "real" or the modifier "nominal," people generally mean the nominal rate, and we shall follow that convention in this book. Therefore, when we use the term "risk-free rate, k_{RF}," we mean the *nominal* risk-free rate, which includes an inflation premium equal to the average expected inflation rate over the life of the security. In general, we use the T-bill rate to approximate the short-term risk-free rate, and a long-term Government of Canada bond rate to approximate the long-term risk-free rate. So whenever you see the term "risk-free rate," assume that we are referring either to the T-bill rate or to the long-term Government of Canada bond rate.

Inflation Premium, IP

Inflation has a major impact on interest rates because it erodes the purchasing power of the dollar and thus lowers the real rate of return on investments. To illustrate: suppose you save $1000 and invest it in a Government of Canada bond that matures in 1 year and pays 5 percent interest. At the end of the year you will receive $1050—your original $1000 plus $50 of interest. Now suppose the rate of inflation during the year is 10 percent, and it affects all items equally. If beer cost $1.00 per bottle at the beginning of the year, it will cost $1.10 at the end of the year. Therefore, your $1000 buys $1000/$1 = 1000 bottles at the beginning of the year but only $1050/$1.10 = 955 bottles at the end. Thus, in *real terms*, you will be worse off—you will receive $50 of interest, but it will not be sufficient to offset inflation. You would thus be better off buying 1000 bottles of beer (or some other storable asset, such as land, timber, apartment buildings, wheat, or gold) than buying the bond.

Investors are well aware of all this, so when they lend money, they seek to protect *purchasing power* by building in an **inflation premium**, **IP**, equal to the *expected inflation rate* over the life of the security. As discussed previously, for a short-term, default-free treasury bill, the actual interest rate charged, $k_{T\text{-bill}}$, is the real risk-free rate, k^*, plus the inflation premium, IP:

$$k_{T\text{-bill}} = k_{RF} = k^* + IP.$$

Therefore, if the real risk-free rate of interest is $k^* = 3\%$, and if inflation is expected to be 4 percent (and hence IP = 4%) during the next year, then the rate of interest on 1-year T-bills will be 7 percent. In January 1992, the expected 1-year inflation rate was about 3 percent, and the yield on 1-year T-bills was about 7.5 percent. This implies that the real risk-free rate at that time was about 4.5 percent.[10] The real risk-free rate is not observable, but on the basis of observed yields on Government of Canada securities and reported expected inflation rates, we know that the real risk-free rate varies over time and that it is generally in the range of 3 to 5 percentage points.

It is important to note that the rate of inflation built into interest rates is the rate of inflation *expected in the future*, not the rate experienced in the past. Thus, the latest reported figures might show an annual inflation rate of 5 percent, but that is for a past period. If people on the average expect a 2 percent inflation rate in the future, then 2 percent will be built into the current rate of interest. Note also that the inflation rate reflected in the interest rate on any security is the *average* rate of inflation *expected over the security's life*. Thus, the inflation rate built into a 1-year bond is the expected inflation rate for the next year, but the inflation rate built into a 30-year bond is the average rate of inflation expected over the next 30 years.[11]

---

[10]To be theoretically precise, we should use a geometric average. Also, since a large number of investors, both domestic and foreign, are active in the market, it is impossible to determine exactly the consensus on the expected inflation rate.

[11]In the calculation of the real rate, we assumed that the Government of Canada security was risk free and hence no risk premium is observed in the estimated real rate. However, during 1992, even with very low expected inflation rates (approximately 1.0 to 1.5 percent), the real rates of interest appeared to be very high (more than 5.0 percent). One explanation is that constitutional issues and the risk of a Quebec exit from Canada made investors, especially international ones, require a risk premium, even on government securities. The risk is not that the Government of Canada would default (it can always print enough money to pay the obligation), but that in the event of the separation of Quebec from the rest of Canada, there would be significant disruption in the country and delays in making bond payments. International investors will also be concerned about foreign exchange risk, which would be exacerbated by political problems.

Expectations for future inflation are closely related to, although not perfectly correlated with, rates experienced in the recent past. Therefore, if the inflation rate reported for last month is an increase, people tend to raise their expectations for future inflation, and this change in expectations causes an increase in interest rates.

Default Risk Premium, DRP

The risk that a borrower will **default** on a loan, which means not to pay the interest or the principal, also affects the market interest rate on a security: the greater the default risk, the higher the interest rate lenders charge. Government of Canada securities have no default risk, and hence they carry the lowest interest rates on taxable securities in Canada. For corporate bonds, the higher the bond's rating, the lower its default risk, and, consequently, the lower its interest rate.[12] Noted below are the average yields on medium-term (approximately 8 years to maturity) bond indexes as of June 30, 1992.

Long Canadas	8.13%
Long municipal bonds	8.85
AAAs	8.63
AAs	9.02
As	10.07
BBBs	10.30

The difference between the interest rate on a Government of Canada bond and that on a corporate bond with similar maturity, liquidity, and other features is the **default risk premium**, **DRP**. Therefore, if the bonds listed above are otherwise similar, the default risk premium is DRP = 8.63% − 8.13% = 0.5 percentage points (also referred to as 50 **basis points**) for AAA corporate bonds, 9.02% − 8.13% = 0.89 percentage points for AA, and 10.30% − 8.13% = 2.17 percentage points for BBB corporate bonds. Default risk premiums vary somewhat over time depending upon the risk aversion of investors and the economic climate. The risk premiums observed at June 30, 1992 were high, especially for the more risky BBB bonds, because of the recession and the large number of companies that had defaulted on their debt obligations.

Liquidity Premium, LP

An asset that is highly **liquid** is one that can be sold at a predictable price and thus can be converted to spendable cash on short notice. Active markets, which provide liquidity, exist for government bonds and for the equities and some bonds of larger corporations. Real estate and securities issued by small companies that are not known by many investors are *illiquid*—they can be sold to raise cash, but not quickly and not at a predictable price. If a security is not liquid, investors will add a **liquidity premium**, **LP**, when they establish the market rate on the security. It is very difficult to measure liquidity premiums with precision, but a differential of at least 2 and probably 4 percentage points

---

[12]Bond ratings and bonds' riskiness in general will be discussed in Chapter 21. For now, merely note that bonds rated AAA (or A++) are judged to have less default risk than bonds rated AA (or A+), AA bonds are less risky than A bonds, and so on.

is thought to exist between the least liquid and the most liquid financial assets of similar default risk and maturity.

Maturity Risk Premium, MRP

Government of Canada securities are free of default risk in the sense that one can be virtually certain that the federal government will pay interest on its bonds and will also pay them off when they mature. Therefore, the default risk premium on them is essentially zero. Further, active markets exist for many Government of Canada securities, so their liquidity premiums are also close to zero. Thus, as a first approximation, the rate of interest on a Government of Canada bond should be the risk-free rate, k_{RF}, which is equal to the real risk-free rate, k^*, plus an inflation premium, IP. However, an adjustment is needed for long Canadas. The prices of long-term bonds decline sharply whenever interest rates rise, and since interest rates can and do occasionally rise, all long-term bonds, even Canadas, have an element of risk called **interest rate risk**. As a general rule, the bonds of any organization, from the Canadian government to Molson Breweries, have more interest rate risk the longer the maturity of the bond. Therefore, a **maturity risk premium**, **MRP**, also called a **term premium**, which is higher the longer the years to maturity, must be included in the required interest rate.

The effect of maturity risk premiums is to raise interest rates on long-term bonds relative to those on short-term bonds. This premium, like the others, is extremely difficult to measure, but (1) it seems to vary over time, rising when interest rates are more volatile and uncertain and falling when they are more stable, and (2) since 1981, the maturity risk premium on 10-year and over Canadas appears to have generally been in the range of -3.3 to $+2.5$ percentage points.[13]

We should mention that although long-term bonds are heavily exposed to interest rate risk, short-term bonds are heavily exposed to **reinvestment rate risk**. When short-term bonds mature and the funds are reinvested, or "rolled over," any decline in interest rates results in reinvestment at a lower rate and hence leads to a decline in interest income. To illustrate: suppose you had $100 000 invested in 1-year Government of Canada bonds, and you lived on the income. In 1981, short-term rates were about 17 percent, so your income was about $17 000. However, your income declined to about $10 000 by 1985 and to little more than $6000 by the middle of 1992. Had you invested your money in long-term bonds, your income (but not the value of the principal) would have been stable.[14] Thus, although "investing short" preserves one's principal, the interest income provided by short-term bonds varies from year to year, depending on reinvestment rates.

---

[13]The MRP averaged 1.51 percentage points from 1926 to 1990. See *Canadian Economic Tables*, Towers, Perrin.

[14]Long-term bonds also have some reinvestment rate risk. To actually earn the stated rate on a long-term bond, the interest payments must be reinvested at the stated rate. However, if interest rates fall, the interest payments will be reinvested at a lower rate, and hence the realized return will be less than the stated rate. Note, though, that the premium added for reinvestment rate risk is lower on a long-term bond than on a short-term bond because only the interest payments (rather than interest plus principal) on the long-term bond are exposed to reinvestment rate risk.

Concept Review

▶ Write out the two equations for the nominal interest rate on a debt security.

▶ Distinguish between the real risk-free rate of interest, k*, and the nominal risk-free rate of interest, k$_{RF}$.

▶ What inflation rate is built into the interest rate on a security?

▶ Does the interest rate on a Government of Canada bond include a default risk premium? Explain.

▶ Distinguish between liquid and illiquid assets, and identify some assets that are liquid and some that are illiquid.

▶ Briefly explain the following statement: "Although long-term bonds are heavily exposed to interest rate risk, short-term bonds are heavily exposed to reinvestment rate risk."

The Term Structure of Interest Rates

A study of Figure 3-3 reveals that at certain times, such as 1983, short-term interest rates are lower than long-term rates, whereas at other times, such as 1980 and 1989, short-term rates are higher than long-term rates. The relationship between long- and short-term rates, which is known as the **term structure of interest rates**, is important to corporate treasurers, who must decide whether to borrow by issuing long- or short-term debt, and to investors, who must decide whether to buy long- or short-term bonds. Thus, it is important to understand (1) how long- and short-term rates are related to each other and (2) what causes shifts in their relative positions.

To begin, we can look up, in a source such as the *Bank of Canada Review* or the *Financial Post*, the interest rates on bonds of various maturities at a given point in time. For example, the tabular section of Figure 3-4 presents interest rates for issues of different maturities on two dates. The set of data for a given date, when plotted on a graph such as that in Figure 3-4, is called the **yield curve** for that date. The yield curve changes both position and slope over time. In December 1989, all rates were relatively high, and short-term rates were higher than long-term rates, so the yield curve was *downward sloping*. However, in December 1991, all rates had fallen, and short-term rates were lower than long-term rates, so the yield curve was *upward sloping*.

Figure 3-4 shows yield curves for Government of Canada securities, but we could have constructed them for corporate bonds. For example, we could have developed yield curves for risk classes, such as AAA or BBB. Or we could have drawn them for a specific company if we used data from a firm that issues across the maturity spectrum. (Examples of companies with a large number of bonds outstanding in different maturity categories are BCE and other regulated utilities that rely on long-term debt.) Had we constructed such curves and plotted them on Figure 3-4, the corporate yield curves would have been above those for Government of Canada securities on the same date because the corporate yields would include default risk premiums, but they would have had the same general shape as the federal government curves. Also, the riskier the corporation, the higher its yield curve. A corporation such as Olympia and

Figure 3-4
Yield Curves, December 1989 and December 1991

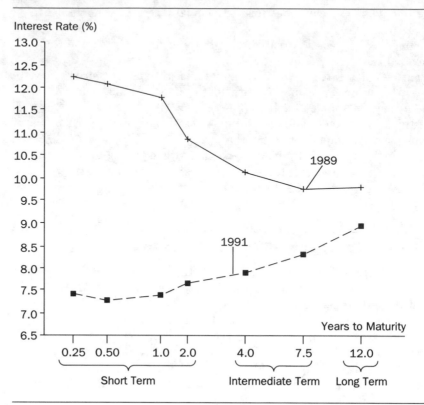

| | Interest Rate | |
Term to Maturity	December 1989	December 1991
3 months	12.22	7.43
6 months	12.04	7.28
1.0 year	11.74	7.39
2.0 years	10.84	7.65
4.0 years	10.19	7.95
7.5 years	9.68	8.37
12 years	9.69	8.97

Source: *Bank of Canada Review*, various issues.

York, which declared bankruptcy and, unable to obtain creditor approval of its business plan in March 1993 and was taken over by its creditors, would have had a yield curve substantially higher than that of BCE, which is an extremely strong company.

Historically, long-term rates are above short-term rates in most years, so usually the yield curve is upward sloping. For this reason, people often call an upward-sloping yield curve a *"normal" yield curve* and a yield curve that slopes downward an *inverted*, or *"abnormal," yield curve.* Thus, in Figure 3-4 the yield curve for December 1989 was inverted, but the one for December 1991 was normal. We explain in the next section why an upward slope is the normal situation; briefly, the reason is that short-term securities are less risky than longer-term securities, so short-term rates are normally lower than long-term rates.

Term Structure Theories

Several theories have been used to explain the shape of the yield curve. The three major ones are (1) the market segmentation theory, (2) the liquidity preference theory, and (3) the expectations theory.

Market Segmentation Theory.   Briefly, the **market segmentation theory** states that each lender and each borrower has a preferred maturity. For example, a person borrowing to buy a long-term asset, such as a house, or a hydro company borrowing to build a power plant, wants a long-term loan. However, a retailer borrowing in September to build its inventory for Christmas prefers a short-term loan. Similar differences exist among savers. A person saving up to take a vacation next summer wants to lend in the short-term market, but someone saving for retirement 20 years hence will probably buy long-term securities.

The thrust of the market segmentation theory is that the slope of the yield curve depends on supply-demand conditions in the long-term and short-term markets. Thus, according to this theory, the yield curve can at any given time be either upward sloping or downward sloping. An upward-sloping yield curve occurs when there is a large supply of funds relative to demand in the short-term market but a relative shortage of funds in the long-term market. Similarly, a downward-sloping curve indicates strong demand in the short-term market compared to that in the long-term market.

Liquidity Preference Theory.   The **liquidity preference theory** states that long-term bonds normally yield more than short-term bonds for two reasons. (1) Investors generally prefer to hold short-term securities because such securities are more liquid in the sense that they can be converted to cash with little danger of loss of principal. Investors will, therefore, accept lower yields on short-term securities. (2) At the same time, borrowers react in exactly the opposite way: they generally prefer long-term debt because short-term debt exposes them to the risk of having to repay the debt under adverse conditions. Accordingly, borrowers are willing to pay a higher rate, other things held constant, for long-term funds than for short-term funds. Taken together, these two sets of preferences—and hence the liquidity preference theory—imply that under normal conditions, the maturity risk premium, MRP, is positive and increases with maturity, and, hence, that the yield curve should be upward sloping.

Expectations Theory.   The **expectations theory** states that the yield curve depends on expectations about future inflation rates. Specifically, k_t, the nominal interest rate on a Government of Canada bond that matures in t years, is found as follows:

$$k_t = k^* + IP_t.$$

Here k^* is the real default-free interest rate, and IP_t is an inflation premium equal to the average expected rate of inflation over the t years before the bond matures. Under the pure expectations theory, the maturity risk premium (MRP) is assumed to be zero.

To illustrate: suppose that in late December 1991 the real default-free rate of interest was $k^* = 5\%$ and expected inflation rates for the next 3 years were as follows:[15]

	Expected Annual (1-Year) Inflation Rate	Expected Average Inflation Rate from 1991 to Indicated Year
1992	3%	3%/1 = 3.0%
1993	2%	(3% + 2%)/2 = 2.5%
1994	1%	(3% + 2% + 1%)/3 = 2.0%

Given these expectations, the following pattern of interest rates should exist:

	Real Default-Free Rate (k^*)		Inflation Premium, Which Is Equal to the Average Expected Inflation Rate (IP_t)		Government of Canada Bond Rate for Each Maturity (k)
1-year bond	5%	+	3.0%	=	8.0%
2-year bond	5%	+	2.5%	=	7.5%
3-year bond	5%	+	2.0%	=	7.0%

Had the pattern of expected inflation rates been reversed, with inflation expected to fall from 8 percent to 6 percent and then to 4 percent, the following situation would have existed:

	Real Default-Free Rate		Average Expected Inflation Rate		Government of Canada Rate for Each Maturity
1-year bond	5%	+	1.0%	=	6.0%
2-year bond	5%	+	1.5%	=	6.5%
3-year bond	5%	+	2.0%	=	7.0%

These hypothetical data are plotted in Figure 3-5. According to the expectations theory, whenever the annual rate of inflation is expected to decline, the

---

[15]Technically, we should be using geometric averages rather than arithmetic averages, but the differences are not material in this example. For a discussion of this point, see Robert C. Radcliffe, *Investment: Concepts, Analysis, and Strategy*, 2d ed. (Glenview, Ill.: Scott, Foresman, 1987), chap. 6.

Figure 3-5
Hypothetical Example of the Term
Structure of Interest Rates

a. Yield Curve When the Inflation
Rate Is Expected To Decline

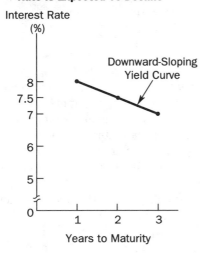

b. Yield Curve When the Inflation
Rate Is Expected To Increase

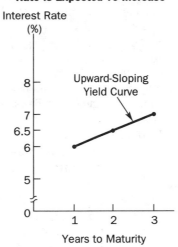

yield curve must be downward sloping, whereas it must be upward sloping if inflation is expected to increase.[16]

Various tests of the theories have been conducted. They indicate that all three theories have some validity. Thus, the shape of the yield curve at any given time is affected (1) by supply-demand conditions in long- and short-term markets, (2) by liquidity preferences, and (3) by expectations about future inflation. One factor may dominate at one time, another at another time, but all three affect the structure of interest rates.

Concept Review

▸ What is a yield curve? What information would you need to draw this curve?
▸ Distinguish among the following theories: (1) market segmentation theory, (2) liquidity preference theory, and (3) expectations theory.
▸ Distinguish between the shapes of a "normal" yield curve and an "abnormal" yield curve, and explain why each might exist.

---

[16]In the discussion, we have assumed that the risk-free real rate of interest is constant and the shape of the yield curve depends only upon expectations of the future rates of inflation. However, it is possible that there are expectations that the real rate will decrease; then, even with constant expected inflation, the yield curve can be downward sloping.

Other Factors That Influence Interest Rate Levels

In addition to inflationary expectations, liquidity preferences, and the supply-demand situation, other factors also influence the general level of interest rates and the shape of the yield curve. The four most important ones are (1) Bank of Canada policy, (2) the level of the federal budget deficit, (3) exchange rate considerations, and (4) the level of business activity.

Bank of Canada Policy

As you probably learned in your economics classes, the growth in the money supply has a major effect on both the level of economic activity and the rate of inflation. In Canada, the Bank of Canada controls the money supply. If the Bank wants to stimulate the economy, it increases the money supply. The initial effect of such an action is to cause interest rates to decline, but the action may also lead to an increase in the expected rate of inflation, which in turn pushes interest rates up. The reverse holds if the Bank tightens the money supply.

During periods when the Bank is actively intervening in the markets, the yield curve will be distorted. Short-term rates will temporarily be "too high" if the Bank is tightening credit and "too low" if it is easing credit. The yield curve will be flatter if short-term rates are "too high" and steeper if they are "too low." Long-term rates are not affected as much by the Bank's intervention, except to the extent that such intervention affects expectations for long-term inflation.

Exchange Rate Considerations

The Government of Canada can and does influence the exchange rate by its policy with respect to interest rate levels in Canada compared to those in other countries. For example, if the Government wants the exchange rate between the U.S. and the Canadian dollar to be high—that is, it wants a high value for a Canadian dollar in terms of a U.S. dollar—then interest rates in Canada have to be set above those in the United States. This will encourage U.S. and other foreign investors to sell their U.S. holdings and purchase Canadian bonds. The result will be an increased demand for the Canadian dollar by investors who need Canadian currency in order to purchase Canadian debt. This will put upward pressure on the Canadian dollar relative to the U.S. dollar and increase or maintain the exchange rate. Of course, there will be pressure on the interest rate differential between the two countries to decline. Conversely, if a reduction in the exchange rate is desired, the Canadian government can reduce domestic interest rates relative to those in the United States; investors will move funds out of Canada to the United States, where higher interest rates can be obtained. The result will be a reduction in the exchange rate—the Canadian dollar will be worth less in U.S. dollars.

Government Deficits

The federal and many provincial governments have been running large deficits for many years; as a result, they need to borrow heavily. This requirement for ongoing borrowing keeps interest rates high. The government can choose to fund its debt through short-term debt or long-term debt or a combination. Depending on how the debt is financed, there may be more influence at the short end of the yield curve or at longer maturities.

Business Conditions

Figure 3-3, presented earlier, can be examined to see how business conditions influence interest rates. Here are the key points revealed by the graph:

1. Because inflation has generally been increasing, the general tendency has been toward higher interest rates.
2. Until 1979, short-term rates were almost always below long-term rates. Thus, in those years the yield curve was almost always "normal" in the sense that it was upward sloping.
3. The shaded areas in the graph represent recessions, during which both the demand for money and the rate of inflation tend to fall and, at the same time, the Bank of Canada tends to increase the money supply in an effort to stimulate the economy. As a result, there is a tendency for interest rates to decline during recessions.
4. During recessions, short-term rates experience sharper declines than long-term rates. This occurs because (1) the Bank of Canada operates mainly in the short-term sector and hence its intervention has a major effect here, and (2) long-term rates reflect the average expected inflation rate over the next 20 to 30 years, and this expectation generally does not change much, even when the current rate of inflation is low because of a recession.

Concept Review

▶ Name four factors, in addition to inflationary expectations, liquidity preferences, and normal supply-demand fluctuations, that influence interest rates. Explain their effects.
▶ How does the Bank of Canada stimulate the economy? What are the effects of this action on interest rates?

Interest Rate Levels and Equity Prices

Interest rates have two effects on corporate profits: (1) because interest is a cost, the higher the rate of interest, the lower a firm's profits, other things held constant; and (2) interest rates affect the level of economic activity and, hence, corporate profits. Interest rates obviously affect share prices because of their effects on profits, but, perhaps even more important, they have an effect due to competition in the marketplace between equity securities and bonds. If interest rates rise sharply, investors can get higher returns in the bond market, which induces them to sell equity and to transfer funds from the stock market to the bond market. Such transfers in response to rising interest rates obviously depress share prices. Of course, the reverse occurs if interest rates decline. Indeed, the bull market of 1985–87 was caused almost entirely by the sharp drop in long-term interest rates.

Concept Review

▶ In what two ways do changes in interest rates affect share prices?

Interest Rates and Business Decisions

The yield curve for December 1991, shown earlier in Figure 3-4, indicates how much the Canadian government had to pay in 1991 to borrow money for 1 year, 5 years, 10 years, and so on. A business borrower would have had to pay somewhat more, but assume for the moment that we are back in 1991 and that the yield curve shown for that year also applies to your company. Now suppose your company has decided (1) to build a new plant with a 10-year life that will cost $1 million and (2) to raise the $1 million by selling an issue of debt (or borrowing) rather than by selling equity. If you borrowed in 1991 on a short-term basis—say for 1 year—your interest cost for that year would be only 7.39 percent, or $73 900, whereas if you used long-term (12-year) financing, your cost would be 8.97 percent, or $89 700. Therefore, at first glance, it would seem that you should use short-term debt.

However, this could prove to be a horrible mistake. If you use short-term debt, you will have to renew your loan every year, and the rate charged on each new loan will reflect the then-current short-term rate. Interest rates could return to their 1981 levels, so by 1995 you could be paying 19 percent, or $190 000, per year. These high interest payments would cut into and perhaps eliminate your profits. Your reduced profitability could easily increase your firm's risk to the point at which its bond rating would be lowered, causing lenders to increase the risk premium built into the interest rate they charge, which in turn would force you to pay even higher rates. These very high interest rates would further reduce your profitability, worrying lenders even more and making them reluctant to renew your loan. If your lenders refused to renew the loan and demanded payment, as they have every right to do, you might have trouble raising the cash. If you had to make price cuts to convert physical assets to cash, you might incur heavy operating losses, or even bankruptcy.

On the other hand, if you use long-term financing in 1991, your interest costs will remain constant at $89 700 per year, so an increase in interest rates in the economy would not hurt you. You might even be able to buy up some of your bankrupt competitors at bargain prices—bankruptcies increase dramatically when interest rates rise, primarily because many firms do use short-term debt.

Does all this suggest that firms should always avoid short-term debt? Not necessarily. If inflation remains low in the next few years, so will interest rates. If you had borrowed on a long-term basis, your company would be at a major disadvantage if its debt were locked in at high rates while its competitors (who used short-term debt and thus rode interest rates down in subsequent years) had a substantially lower borrowing cost. On the other hand, inflation may re-emerge and interest rates could rise up to new record levels. In that case, you would wish you had borrowed on a long-term basis.

Financing decisions would be easy if we could develop accurate forecasts of future interest rates. Unfortunately, predicting future interest rates with consistent accuracy is somewhere between difficult and impossible—people who make a living by selling interest rate forecasts say it is difficult, but many others say it is impossible.

Even if it is difficult to predict future interest rate *levels*, it is easy to predict that interest rates will *fluctuate*—they always have, and they always will. This being the case, sound financial policy calls for using a mix of long- and short-term debt, as well as equity, in such a manner that the firm can survive in most interest rate environments. Further, the optimal financial policy depends in an important way on the nature of the firm's assets—the easier it is to sell off assets and thus to pay off debts, the more feasible it is to use large amounts of short-term debt. This makes it more feasible to finance current assets than fixed assets with short-term debt. We shall return to this issue later in the book, when we discuss working capital management.

Interest Rate Futures

A fairly recent development in financial markets, which arose largely because of the fluctuations in interest rates, is the introduction of a market in *interest rate futures*. A *futures contract* is a contract in which two parties agree to exchange an asset for cash on a specified future date at a specified price, called the *futures price*. The futures price reflects the market's expectations regarding the cash price of the commodity that will prevail on the given date. Futures trading in commodities has been conducted for many years—farmers sell wheat futures in the spring at a specified price and then deliver when the crop comes in the fall, thus locking in the price early, while millers buy futures in the spring for fall delivery and lock in their costs. However, futures markets for financial instruments (financial futures) are a fairly recent innovation. A *financial futures contract* is simply a contract that involves a financial security rather than a commodity. The interest rate futures market has grown considerably in size, and it involves varied assets, such as 13-week T-bills, 15-year government bonds, 90-day commercial paper, foreign currencies, and so on. There are also stock index futures.

Financial futures can be used by conservative investors to provide a measure of protection against changes in future interest rates (*hedging*) and also by speculators hoping to make a profit from changes in interest rates. If short-term interest rates are expected to rise, a futures contract can be sold on, say, 1-year T-bill futures. If interest rates do rise, that will cause the price of the security to fall, so when the contract is closed, the seller will realize a profit equal to the difference between the futures price and the lower spot price. A futures contract can be bought if rates are expected to decline.

To illustrate: suppose a company knows it will need $1 million of new debt capital next year to finance the purchase of machinery for a new plant. It can borrow now at a 10 percent rate, but it does not need the money yet. However, if it waits until next year to borrow, rates may be up to 15 percent. A conservative company might sell a futures contract now and then, if rates do rise, make a profit on the futures contract that will offset the higher interest rates it must pay when it borrows. There will, of course, be a commission involved in the transaction, but the commission may be thought of as an insurance policy premium against rising future interest rates.

Concept Review

► If short-term interest rates are lower than long-term rates, why might a firm still choose to finance with long-term debt?
► Explain the following statement: "The optimal financial policy depends in an important way on the nature of the firm's assets."
► How can an interest rate futures contract reduce a company's exposure to interest rate risk?

Summary

In this chapter we discussed the nature of financial markets, the types of institutions that operate in these markets, how interest rates are determined, and some of the ways in which interest rates affect business decisions. The key concepts covered are listed below.

□ There are many different types of **financial markets**. Each market serves a different set of customers or deals with a different type of security.

□ Transfers of capital between borrowers and savers take place (1) by **direct transfers** of money and securities, (2) by transfers through **investment dealers**, which act as intermediaries, and (3) by transfers through **financial intermediaries**, which create new securities.

□ The **stock market** is an especially important market because this is where share prices (which are used to "grade" managers' performances) are established.

□ There are two basic types of stock markets: the **organized exchanges** and the **over-the-counter markets**.

□ Capital is allocated through the price system—a price is charged to "rent" money. Lenders charge **interest** on funds they lend, while equity investors receive *dividends* and *capital gains* in return for letting the firm use their money.

□ Four fundamental factors affect the cost of money: (1) *production opportunities*, (2) *time preferences for consumption*, (3) *risk*, and (4) *inflation*.

□ The **risk-free rate of interest**, k_{RF}, is defined as the **real risk-free rate**, k^*, plus an inflation premium, IP. $k_{RF} = k^* + IP$.

□ The **nominal interest rate** on a debt security, **k**, is composed of the real risk-free rate, k^*, plus **premiums** that reflect **inflation**, IP, **default risk**, DRP, **liquidity**, LP, and **maturity risk**, MRP. $k = k^* + IP + DRP + LP + MRP$.

□ If the real risk-free rate of interest and the various premiums were constant over time, interest rates in the economy would be stable. However, the *premiums*—especially the premium for expected inflation—*do change over time*, causing market interest rates to change. Also, Bank of Canada intervention to increase or decrease the money supply, as well as international currency flows, lead to fluctuations in interest rates.

☐ The relationship between the yields on securities and the securities' maturities is known as the **term structure of interest rates**, and the **yield curve** is a graph of this relationship.

☐ The yield curve is normally upward sloping—this is called *a normal yield curve*—but the curve can slope downward (an *inverted yield curve*) if the demand for short-term funds is relatively strong or if the rate of inflation is expected to decline.

☐ Interest rate levels have a profound effect on share prices. Higher interest rates (1) depress the economy, (2) increase interest expenses and thus lower corporate profits, and (3) cause investors to sell equities and transfer funds to the bond market. Each of these factors tends to depress equity prices.

☐ Interest rate levels have a significant influence on corporate financial policy. Because interest rate levels are difficult if not impossible to predict, sound financial policy calls for using a mix of short- and long-term debt and also for positioning the firm to survive in any future interest rate environment.

Questions

3-1   What are financial intermediaries, and what economic functions do they perform?

3-2   Suppose the Bank of Canada decided to greatly expand the money supply. What effect would this have
   a.   On the yield curve at the present time?
   b.   On the yield curve that would probably exist two or three years in the future?

3-3   If your firm needs more long-term capital, can you think of a situation in which you might want to use a short-term source of funds?

3-4   What would happen to the standard of living in Canada if people lost faith in the safety of our financial institutions?

3-5   How does a cost-efficient capital market help reduce the prices of goods and services?

3-6   Which fluctuate more, long-term or short-term interest rates? Why?

3-7   Suppose you believe that the economy is just entering a recession. Your firm must raise capital immediately, and debt will be used. Should you borrow on a long-term or a short-term basis?

3-8   Suppose a new type of computer-controlled industrial robot is developed that is quite expensive but that will, in time, triple the productivity of the labour force. What effect will this have on interest rates?

3-9   Suppose interest rates on Government of Canada bonds rise from 10 to 15 percent. Other things held constant, what do you think will happen to the price of an average company's common equity?

Self-Test Problems   (solutions appear on page 87)

ST-1   **Key terms.**   Define each of the following terms:
  a. Money market; capital market
  b. Primary market; secondary market
  c. Investment banker; financial service corporation
  d. Financial intermediary
  e. Mutual fund; money market fund
  f. Organized security exchanges; over-the-counter market
  g. Production opportunities; time preferences for consumption
  h. Real risk-free rate of interest, k*
  i. Nominal risk-free rate of interest, k_{RF}
  j. Inflation premium, IP
  k. Default risk premium, DRP
  l. Liquid asset; liquidity premium, LP
  m. Interest rate risk; maturity risk premium, MRP
  n. Reinvestment rate risk
  o. Term structure of interest rates; yield curve
  p. "Normal" yield curve; inverted ("abnormal") yield curve
  q. Market segmentation theory; liquidity preference theory
  r. Expectations theory
  s. Basis point

ST-2   **Inflation and interest rates.**   Assume that it is now January 1, 1993. The rate of inflation is expected to average 6 percent throughout 1993. However, increased government deficits and renewed vigour in the economy are then expected to push inflation rates higher. Investors expect the inflation rate to be 7 percent in 1994, 8 percent in 1995, and 9 percent in 1996. The real risk-free rate, k*, is currently 3 percent. Assume that no maturity risk premiums are required on bonds with 5 years or less to maturity. The current interest rate on 5-year Government of Canada bonds is 11 percent. Disregard maturity premiums.
  a. What is the average expected inflation rate over the period 1993-96?
  b. What should be the prevailing interest rate on 4-year Government of Canada bonds?
  c. What is the implied expected inflation rate in 1997 (Year 5), given that bonds maturing in that year yield 11 percent?

Problems

3-1   **Yield curves.**   Suppose you and most other investors expect the rate of inflation to be 7 percent next year, to fall to 5 percent during the following year, and to run at a rate of 3 percent thereafter. Assume that the real risk-free rate, k*, is 2 percent and that maturity risk premiums on Government of Canada securities rise from zero on very short-term bonds (those that mature in a few days) by 0.2 percentage points for each year to maturity, up to a limit of 1.0 percentage points on 5-year or longer bonds.
  a. Calculate the interest rate on 1-, 2-, 3-, 4-, 5-, 10-, and 20-year Government of Canada bonds, and plot the yield curve.

    b. Now suppose an AAA-rated company has bonds with the same maturities as the Government of Canada bonds. As an approximation, plot a yield curve on the same graph with the Canadas' yield curve. (Hint: Think about the default risk premium on the company's long-term versus its short-term bonds.)

    c. Now plot the approximate yield curve of Dofasco, a troubled steel company.

3-2 **Expected rate of interest.** Suppose the annual yield on a 2-year Government of Canada bond is 11.5 percent, while that on a 1-year bond is 10 percent. k* is 3 percent, and the maturity risk premium is zero.

    a. Using the expectations theory, forecast the interest rate on a 1-year bond during the second year. (Hint: Under the expectations theory, the yield on a 2-year bond is equal to the average yield on 1-year bonds in Years 1 and 2.)

    b. What is the expected inflation rate in Years 1 and 2?

3-3 **Expected interest rates.** Assume that the real risk-free rate is 4 percent and that the maturity risk premium is zero. If the nominal rate of interest on 1-year bonds is 11 percent and that on comparable-risk 2-year bonds is 13 percent, what is the 1-year interest rate that is expected for Year 2? What inflation rate is expected during Year 2? Comment on why the average interest rate during the 2-year period differs from the 1-year interest rate expected for Year 2.

Solutions to Self-Test Problems

ST-1 Refer to the relevant chapter sections to check your responses.

ST-2 **a.** Average = (6.0% + 7.0% + 8.0% + 9.0%)/4 = 30%/4 = 7.5%.

    b. $k_{T\text{-bill}} = k^* + IP = 3.0\% + 7.5\% = 10.5\%$.

    c. If the 5-year rate is 11 percent, the inflation rate is expected to average approximately 11% − 3% = 8% during the next 5 years. Thus, the implied Year 5 inflation rate is 10 percent:

$$8\% = (6\% + 7\% + 8\% + 9\% + I_5)/5$$
$$40\% = 30\% + I_5$$
$$I_5 = 10\%.$$

II

FINANCIAL ANALYSIS, PLANNING, AND CONTROL

4

Financial Analysis

A MANAGERIAL PERSPECTIVE

The "bottom line" in a company's income statement is its net income, or reported profits. This figure is the basis for dividends, and it is used to determine managers' bonuses. Further, accountants are paid high salaries to make sure income is reported "correctly." One would think, then, that the profit figure a company reports would be unambiguous and trustworthy. However, that is not always the case—companies can and do "play games" so as to influence the numbers they report. To illustrate, an article in the April 24, 1989, issue of *Fortune*, "Cute Tricks on the Bottom Line," made these points:

1. The figures reported in annual reports generally meet the accounting industry's guidelines. However, managers view accounting guidelines not as standards to be met but as obstacles to be overcome, and they are always on the alert for new ways of getting around the guidelines. To put it another way, companies often obey the letter but not the spirit of the law.

2. The temptation to stretch the truth hits companies of all sizes, even giant blue chips such as General Motors. For example, GM reported record earnings in 1988, enabling its managers to realize huge bonuses. However, almost 40 percent of its reported "profits" resulted not from operations but from "financial wizardry." One such piece of wizardry was an increase from 35 to 45 years in the life over which GM's plants are depreciated; this added $790 million to GM's reported profits, but nothing to its true income or cash flows.

3. Managers know that investors like a steady upward trend in earnings and that they dislike negative surprises, so what happens if a company gets lucky some year and has a huge one-time gain? It may report a sharp increase in this year's profits, which will be hard to top next year, or it may "bank" the windfall in a special reserve for later use.

Are accounting tricks such as these "good" or "bad"? On the one hand, if the underlying trend in reported earnings is really stable, then managers' attempts to report stabilized profits could provide more meaningful information than would "pure" numbers. On the other hand, actions such as those of GM could be obscuring the true picture. In any event, be aware that accounting numbers should always be viewed with at least some scepticism.

90

In this chapter, we examine the basic financial data available to managers and investors, and we then look at some analytical techniques used to appraise firms' riskiness, profit potential, and general performance.

If management is to maximize the firm's value, it must take advantage of the firm's strengths and correct its weaknesses. Financial statement analysis involves a comparison of the firm's performance with that of other firms in the same industry. This helps management identify deficiencies and then take actions to improve performance. In this chapter, we discuss how financial managers (and investors) evaluate the firm's current position. Then, in the next chapter, we shall see how managers forecast the firm's future position and how they use these forecasts to determine the effect of specific decisions on the firm's share price.

As you go through this chapter, it is important to remember that security values are based on *cash flows*, yet accounting statements concentrate primarily on *reported profits*. There can be major differences between profits as reported by accountants and actual cash flows. This makes it necessary to "look behind the accounting numbers" when appraising performance and when setting a value for the firm. For the most part, accounting numbers are valid—high accounting profits generally signify high cash flows and the ability to pay high dividends. However, there are enough exceptions to this rule to warrant a critical examination of all accounting data.

Financial Statements and Reports

Of the various reports corporations issue to their shareholders, the **annual report** is by far the most important. Two types of information are given in this report. First, there is a verbal section, often presented as a letter from the president, that describes the firm's operating results during the past year and discusses new developments that will affect future operations. Second, the annual report presents four basic financial statements—the *income statement*, the *balance sheet*, the *statement of retained earnings*, and the *statement of changes in financial position* (or *cash flow*). Taken together, these statements give an accounting picture of the firm's operations and financial position. Detailed data are provided for the 2 most recent years, along with historical summaries of key operating statistics for the past 5 or 10 years.

The quantitative and verbal information are equally important. The financial statements report *what has actually happened* to earnings and dividends over the past few years, whereas the verbal statements attempt to explain why things turned out the way they did. If the firm had serious problems, management will often identify the changes that are being made to correct the problems and its expectations for the future including a return to more normal profitability. Of course, the expected increase in profitability may not occur, and analysts should compare management's past statements with subsequent results. In any event, the information contained in an annual report is used by investors *to form expectations about future earnings and dividends, and about the riskiness of these expected values*. Therefore, the annual report is obviously of great interest to investors.

To illustrate the usefulness of the data in these reports, we will use the financial statements of the Surrey Company Limited. The company is an established retailing operation in Canada with stores in eight of the ten provinces and is a respected merchandiser of car, home, and office products. Originally a family business, the firm has grown to become a popular and widely held company with annual sales close to a billion dollars.

In order for Surrey to remain competitive in its industry, it is necessary for the financial officer of the company to analyze the financial accounts and review any changes in these accounts over time. The purpose of this review is to ensure that the firm's financial health is maintained. At this point, we present the basic components of the financial statements and explain their purpose. In the next section, we examine certain ratios, which will assist in the diagnosis of the health of the firm.

Income Statement

Table 4-1 presents the **income statement** for Surrey Company Limited for the year 1993. Net sales are shown at the top of the statement after which various costs, including income taxes, are deducted to arrive at the net income available to common shareholders.[1] The figure on the last line represents **earnings per share (EPS)**, calculated as net income divided by number of shares outstanding, at year end.

Table 4-1
Surrey Company Limited
Illustrative Income Statement for Year Ended December 31, 1993
(thousands of dollars)

Total revenue		$920 000
Cost of goods sold		710 000
Gross profit		$210 000
Less: Operating expenses		
Selling	$52 000	
General administrative	26 000	
Lease payment on buildings	20 000	98 000
Gross operating income		$112 000
Depreciation		9 000
Net operating income (NOI)		$103 000
Less: Other expenses		
Interest on notes payable	4 000	
Interest on mortgage	15 000	
Interest on debentures	24 000	43 000
Net income before taxes		$ 60 000
Income taxes (at 50%)		30 000
Net income for year available to shareholders		$ 30 000
Earnings per share (EPS)		$ 2.52

[1]Note that net operating income (NOI) is adjusted for other nonoperating income and expense to obtain earnings before interest and taxes (EBIT). If other income and expenses are small, NOI and EBIT are approximately the same; we shall usually assume this condition in subsequent chapters.

Balance Sheet

Surrey's **balance sheet**, given in Table 4-2, shows the value of the firm's assets and of the claims on these assets on December 31, 1992 and on December 31, 1993. The assets are arranged from top to bottom in order of decreasing liquidity; that is, assets toward the top of the column will be converted to cash *sooner* than those toward the bottom of the column. The top group of assets—cash, marketable securities, accounts receivable, and inventories, which are expected to be converted into cash within one year—is defined as *current assets*. Assets in the lower part of the statement—plant and equipment —are not expected to be converted to cash within one year; these are defined as *fixed assets*.

The right-hand side, or claims section, of the balance sheet is arranged similarly. Those items toward the top of the liabilities column mature, and must be paid off, relatively soon; those farther down the column are due in the more distant future.[2] Current liabilities must be paid within one year: since the firm never has to "pay off" common shareholders, common shares and retained earnings represent "permanent" capital.

Generally speaking, the right-hand side of the balance sheet displays the sources of funding for the assets employed on the left-hand side. The liabilities represent claims by the creditors, and common shares and retained earnings reflect the investment by the owners of the firm. Notice that the values of the liabilities and shareholders' equity do *not* represent market values.

Some additional points about the balance sheet are worth stressing.

1. *Cash versus other assets.*   Although the assets are all stated in terms of dollars, only cash represents actual money. Receivables are bills others owe Surrey; inventories show the dollars the company has invested in raw

---

[2]In Chapter 2 we noted that, for tax purposes, the depreciation expense is the capital cost allowance (CCA) charge. For accounting and reporting in financial statements, however, depreciation may be calculated on a different basis—for example, by the straight line method.

During the early years of the asset's life, the CCA charge may exceed the accounting depreciation expense used for reporting purposes. For a variety of reasons, the Canadian Institute of Chartered Accountants suggests that, for reporting purposes, the tax expense should be calculated on the basis of the depreciation technique used for reporting purposes. This tax charge or expense is presented on the income statement and is composed of two parts: the first taxes currently payable, based on the CCA charge, and the second the difference between the tax expense and the taxes currently payable, which is referred to as deferred taxes. In the early years of an asset's life, the taxes currently payable will be less than the tax expense on the income statement, and the deferred tax will be applied to a deferred-tax account on the liability side of the balance sheet; this positive deferred tax occurs because the CCA expense exceeds the reported depreciation expense. In future years, taxes payable will exceed the tax expense, and the deferred-tax account will be reduced.

A simple example may be useful. Suppose a company has $500 in net income before taxes and depreciaiton. The depreciation charge for reporting purposes is $100. Based on a 40 percent tax rate, the income tax expense is $160 (= $400 before-tax income × 40%). For tax purposes, the CCA charge is $200 and the taxes payable are $120 (= $300 taxable income × 40%). The tax expense of $160 is composed of taxes currently payable of $120 plus deferred taxes of $40. This $40 will be added to the deferred-tax account on the balance sheet.

The deferred-tax account can be thought of as an interest-free loan from the government. In our illustration, deferred taxes are excluded because they would present an unnecessary complication.

Table 4-2
Surrey Company Limited
Illustrative Balance Sheet
(thousands of dollars)

Assets	Dec. 31, 1992	Dec. 31, 1993	*Liabilities and Equity*	Dec. 31, 1992	Dec. 31, 1993
Current assets			*Current liabilities*		
Cash	$ 30 000	$ 15 000	Accounts payable	$ 45 000	$ 50 000
Receivables	250 000	230 000	Loans, notes payable	32 000	39 000
Inventories	100 000	170 000	Income taxes payable	2 000	2 000
Total current assets	$380 000	$415 000	Total current liabilities	$ 79 000	$ 91 000
Property and equipment			*Long-term debt*		
Leasehold			Mortgage bonds	90 000	107 000
Improvements	10 000	12 000	Sinking-fund debentures	220 000	220 000
Equipment	48 000	50 000	Total long-term debt	$310 000	$327 000
Building	110 000	130 000			
Less Depreciation	(33 000)	(42 000)	*Shareholders' equity*		
Land	37 000	41 000	Capital stock	50 000	50 000
Net property and equipment	$172 000	$191 000	Retained earnings	113 000	138 000
			Total net worth	$163 000	$188 000
Total assets	$552 000	$606 000	Total claim on assets	$552 000	$606 000

materials, work-in-process, and finished goods available for sales; and fixed assets reflect the amount of money Surrey paid for its plant and equipment when it acquired those assets at some time in the past. Surrey can write cheques at present for a total of $15 000 000 (versus current liabilities of $91 000 000 due within a year). The noncash assets should produce cash flows eventually, but they do not represent cash in hand, and the amount of cash they will eventually produce could be higher or lower than the values at which they are carried on the books.

2. *Liabilities versus shareholders' equity.*   The claims against assets are of two types: liabilities (or money the company owes) and the shareholders' ownership position.[3] The **shareholders' equity**, or **net worth**, is a residual:

$$\text{Assets} - \text{Liabilities} = \text{Shareholders' equity}$$
$$\$606 \text{ million} - \$418 \text{ million} = \$188 \text{ million}.$$

Suppose assets decline in value—for example, suppose some of the accounts receivable are written off as bad debts or some fixed assets turn out to be worthless and are written down to a value of zero. Since liabilities remain

---

[3]Firms occasionally set up reserves for certain contingencies, such as the potential costs involved in a lawsuit currently in the courts. These reserves represent an accounting transfer from retained earnings to the reserve account. If the company wins the suit, retained earnings will be credited and the reserve will be eliminated. If it loses, a loss will be recorded, cash will be reduced, and the reserve will be eliminated.

constant, the value of the shareholders' equity must decline. Note that if asset values rise (perhaps because of the impact of inflation), these benefits will accrue exclusively to the shareholders.

3. *Breakdown of the shareholders' common equity account.* A detailed discussion of the common equity account is provided in Chapter 20, "Capital Markets, Common Equity Financing, and the Underwriting Process" but a brief preview of that discussion is useful here. The equity section can be divided into four accounts—preferred shares, common shares, contributed surplus, and retained earnings. The first two accounts are referred to as **capital stock**. The last three accounts represent common equity. The retained earnings account is built up over time by the firm's "saving" a part of its earnings for the shareholders rather than paying all earnings out as dividends. The other two common equity accounts arise from the sale of shares by the firm to raise capital. The breakdown of the common equity accounts is important for some purposes but not for others. For example, a potential shareholder would want to know whether the company actually earned the funds reported in its equity accounts or whether the funds came mainly from selling shares. A potential creditor, on the other hand, would be more interested in the amount of money the owners put up than in the form in which money was put up. In the remainder of the chapter, we generally aggregate the three common equity accounts and call this sum *common equity* or *net worth*.

4. *The time dimension.* The balance sheet may be thought of as a snapshot of the firm's financial position *at a point in time*—for example, on December 31, 1993. Thus, on December 31, 1992, Surrey had $100 million of inventories, but this account had been increased to $170 million by the end of 1993. The income statement, on the other hand, reports on operations *over a period of time*—for example, during the calendar year 1993. Surrey had sales of $920 million and its net income available to common shareholders was $30 million. The balance sheet changes every day as inventories are increased or decreased, as fixed assets are added or retired, as bank loans are increased or decreased, and so on. Companies whose businesses are seasonal have especially large changes in their balance sheets. For example, most retailers have large inventories just before Christmas but low inventories and high accounts receivable after Christmas. Therefore, their balance sheets will look materially different, depending on the date chosen to construct the statement.

Statement of Retained Earnings

Earnings can be paid out to shareholders as dividends or retained and reinvested in the business. Shareholders like to receive dividends, of course, but if earnings are ploughed back into profitable projects, the value of the shareholders' position in the company increases. Later in the book we shall consider the pros and cons of retaining earnings versus paying them out in dividends; for now we are simply interested in the effects of dividends and retained earnings on the balance sheet. For this purpose, accountants use the **statement of retained earnings**, which identifies the changes in the common equity accounts between balance sheet dates. Surrey's statement is presented in Table 4-3. The company earned $30 million during 1993, it paid out $5 million in dividends, and it ploughed $25 million back into the business. Thus the balance sheet item "retained earnings" increased from $113 million at the end of 1992 to $138 million at the end of 1993.

Note that the balance sheet account "retained earnings" represents a *claim against assets*, not assets per se. Further, firms retain earnings primarily to expand the business—this means investing in plant and equipment, in inventories, and so on, *not* in a bank account. Thus, retained earnings as reported on the balance sheet do *not* represent cash and are *not* available for the payment of dividends or anything else.

The Cash Flow Cycle

Although all assets and liabilities on the balance sheet and revenues, expenses, and profits on the income statement are shown in dollar amounts, only the balance sheet asset "cash" represents real money. The ongoing activities of the business should result in the other assets generating cash. As a company like Surrey goes about its business, it makes sales, which lead (1) to a reduction of inventories, (2) to an increase in cash, and (3) if the sales price exceeds the cost of the item sold, to a profit. These transactions cause the balance sheet to change, and they also are reflected in the income statement. It is critical that you understand (1) that businesses deal with *physical* units such as autos, computers, or aluminum, (2) that physical transactions are translated into dollar terms through the accounting system, and (3) that the purpose of financial analysis is to examine the accounting numbers in order to determine how efficient the firm is at making and selling physical goods and services.

Several factors make financial analysis difficult. One of them is variations in accounting methods among firms. For example, different methods of inventory valuation[4] can lead to differences in reported profits for otherwise identical firms; good financial analysts must be able to adjust for these

---

Table 4-3
Surrey Company Limited
Statement of Retained Earnings for Year Ended December 31, 1993
(thousands of dollars)

Balance of retained earnings, December 31, 1992	$113 000
Add: net income, 1993	30 000
	$143 000
Less: dividends to shareholders	5 000
Balance of retained earnings, December 31, 1993	$138 000

---

[4]During periods of rising prices, the FIFO (first-in, first-out) method of inventory accounting shows a higher value for reported inventories than the LIFO (last-in, first-out) method. For example, if costs are rising at an annual rate of 10 percent, inventory items just acquired (or made) cost 10 percent more than identical items acquired (made) a year ago. Also, gross profits (sales revenues less the cost of goods) will be higher under FIFO than LIFO.

differences if they are to make valid comparisons among companies. Another factor involves timing—an action is taken at one point in time, but its full effects cannot be accurately measured until some later period.

To understand how timing influences the financial statements, one must understand the **cash flow** cycle within a firm, as set forth in Figure 4-1. The rectangles there represent balance sheet accounts—assets and claims against assets—whereas the circles represent actions taken by the firm. Each rectangle may be thought of as a reservoir, and the wavy lines designate the amount of the asset or liability in the reservoir (account) on a balance sheet date. Various transactions cause changes in the accounts, just as adding or

Figure 4-1
Cash and Materials Flows within the Firm

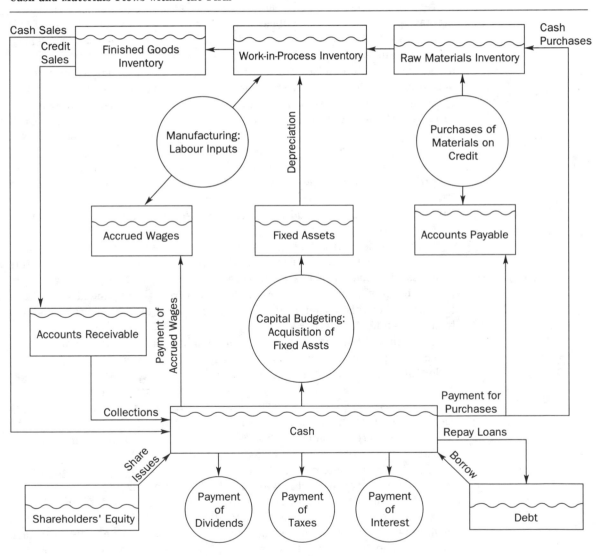

subtracting oil changes the level in an oil reservoir. For example, collecting an account receivable reduces the receivables reservoir but increases the cash reservoir.

The cash account is the focal point of the figure. Certain events, such as collecting accounts receivable or borrowing money from the bank, will cause the cash account to increase, while the payment of taxes, interest, dividends, and accounts payable will cause it to decline. Similar comments could be made about all the balance sheet accounts—their balances rise, fall, or remain constant depending on events that occur during the period under study, which for Surrey is January 1 through December 31, 1993.

Projected sales increases may require the firm to raise cash by borrowing from its bank or selling new equity. For example, if Surrey anticipates an increase in sales, (1) it will expend cash to buy or build fixed assets through the capital budgeting process; (2) it will step up purchases of raw materials, thereby increasing both raw materials and accounts payable; (3) it will increase production, which will cause an increase in work-in-process; and (4) it will eventually build up its finished goods inventory. Some cash will have been expended and hence removed from the cash account, and the firm will have obligated itself to expend still more cash within a few weeks to pay off its accounts payable and its accrued wages. These events will have occurred *before* any new cash has been generated from sales. Even when the expected sales do occur, there will still be a lag in the generation of cash until receivables are collected—because Surrey grants credit for 30 days, it will have to wait 30 days after a sale is made before cash comes in. Depending on how much cash the firm had at the beginning of the buildup, on the length of its production-sales-collection cycle, and on how long it can delay payment of its own payables and accrued wages, the company may have to obtain substantial amounts of additional cash by selling shares or bonds or by borrowing from the bank.

If the firm is profitable, its sales revenues will exceed its costs, and its cash inflows will eventually exceed its cash outlays. However, even a profitable business can experience a cash shortage if it is growing rapidly. It may have to pay for plant, materials, and labour before cash from the expanded sales starts flowing in. For this reason, rapidly growing firms generally require large bank loans or capital from other sources.

An unprofitable firm, such as Canadian Airlines International Ltd. in recent years, will have larger cash outlays than inflows. This, in turn, will lower the cash account, can cause a slowdown in the payment of accrued wages and accounts payable, and may also lead to heavy borrowings. Accordingly, liabilities rise to excessive levels in unprofitable firms. Similarly, an overly ambitious expansion plan will result in excessive inventories and fixed assets, while a poor credit–collection policy will result in bad debts and reduced profits that will first show up as high accounts receivable.

If a firm runs out of cash and cannot obtain enough to meet its obligations, then it cannot operate, and it will have to declare bankruptcy. Therefore, an accurate cash flow forecast is a critical element in a good financial plan. Financial analysts are well aware of all this, and they use the analytical techniques discussed in the remainder of this chapter to help discover cash flow problems before they become serious. In Chapter 5, "Financial Forecasting," we shall examine the techniques financial analysts use to estimate future capital requirements.

Statement of Changes in Financial Position

The graphic cash flow analysis set forth in Figure 4-1 is converted into numerical form and reported in annual reports as the **statement of changes in financial position**, or the **statement of cash flows**. This statement is designed (1) to show how the firm's operations have affected its liquidity, as measured by its cash flows, and (2) to show the relationships among cash flows from operating, investing, and financing activities. It helps to answer questions such as: is the firm generating the cash needed to purchase additional fixed assets for growth? is growth so rapid that external financing is required both for maintaining operations and for investing in new fixed assets? does the firm have excess cash flows that can be used to repay financing from earlier periods or to invest in new products? This information is useful both for investment analysis and for corporate planning, so the statement of changes in financial position is an important part of the annual report.

The Structure of the Statement.   The statement of changes in financial position has three major segments, each of which corresponds to an activity that has an impact on the source or use of cash. These segments refer to operating activities, investing activities, and financing activities. We consider the impact of each of these activities on the cash position of the firm.

Operating Activities.   Cash from operations generally is associated with the income statement. However, the net income figure at the bottom of the income statement does not give the full impact on the cash flows of the operating decisions for two reasons: (1) net income includes the deduction of noncash expenses such as depreciation and amortization of intangible assets; and (2) noncash working capital items such as receivables, inventories, and accounts payable are related directly to the operating decisions of a firm and changes in their balances will affect the cash position of the firm. Thus, if noncash working capital increases, there is a reduction in cash. In each of these cases, adjustments to the income statement must be made to reflect cash consequences of operating activities.

1. *Depreciation[5] and other noncash expenses.*   As we saw in Chapter 2, *depreciation* is an annual charge against income. For example, suppose a machine with an expected useful life of 10 years and an expected salvage value of zero was purchased in 1990 for $150 000. This $150 000 cost must be charged against production during those 10 years; otherwise, income will be overstated. If the machine is depreciated by the straight line method, the annual charge is $15 000. This amount is deducted from sales revenues, with such other costs as labour and raw materials, to determine income. Depreciation is *not a cash outlay*, however. Funds were expended back in 1990, so the depreciation charged against income in future years is not a cash outlay, as are labour or charges for raw materials.

---

[5]In this section we consider depreciation and the resulting cash flow as reported in the annual report. In Chapter 2, however, we noted that capital cost allowance is the depreciation expense used in calculating the actual tax liability. In our discussion of capital budgeting, we shall argue that the appropriate cash flow to use is based on the capital cost allowance and not on reported depreciation.

To illustrate the significance of depreciation in cash flow analysis, consider Surrey, which has the following income statement for 1993 ($ million).

Sales	$920
Costs excluding depreciation	$851
Depreciation	9
Income before tax	$ 60
Taxes @ 50%	30
Income after tax	$ 30

Assuming that sales are for cash[6] and that all costs, except depreciation, are paid during 1993, how much cash was available from operations to pay dividends, retire debt, or make investments in assets? The answer is $39 million, the sum of profit after tax plus depreciation. The firm received $920 million in cash from sales. Its costs other than depreciation were $851 million, and these were paid in cash, leaving $69 million. Depreciation is not a cash charge—the firm does not pay out the $9 million of depreciation expense—so $69 million in cash is still left after depreciation. Taxes, on the other hand are paid in cash, so $30 million for taxes must be deducted from the $69 million gross operating cash flow, leaving a net cash flow from operations of $39 million. This $39 million is, of course, exactly equal to income after tax plus depreciation: $30 million + $9 million = $39 million.

2. *Noncash working capital.* The net change in noncash working capital must be calculated. If there is a net increase in noncash working capital, then there is an equivalent reduction in the cash from operations. The actual calculation will be presented in a subsequent section.

Investing Activities. When noncurrent assets are purchased or sold, there are cash flow consequences. These cash flows are allocated to the "investing activities" section of the statement. Examples of these activities include purchases or sales of fixed assets or shares of another company.

Financing Activities. Firms finance their investing activities by the issuance of financial securities. These securities provide a cash flow to the firm. Thus, issues of debt and preferred or common equity provide an inflow of cash. Analogously, a retirement of a debt issue or repurchase of shares results in a reduction in cash.

The servicing costs of financial instruments *excluding* debt are financing activities for the purpose of this statement. Thus, common and preferred dividends are covered in this section. Interest payments are considered an expense and are already deducted in the calculation of net income.

Preparing the Statement. Several steps are involved in constructing a cash flow statement. The first step is to identify which balance sheet items provided

---

[6]In fact, Surrey makes most of its sales on credit, so when a sale is entered on the books, it represents a customer's promise to pay, or account receivable, rather than cash. Nevertheless, it is customary in preparing a statement of cash flows to consider income to be cash.

cash and which used cash during the year. This is done through a sources and uses of funds analysis. The change in each balance sheet account is determined, and this change is recorded as either a source (increase) or use (decrease) of cash in accordance with the following rules:

Sources

1. *Any increase in a liability or equity account.*   Borrowing from the bank is an example of a source of funds.

2. *Any decrease in an asset account.*   Selling some fixed assets and reducing inventories are other examples of sources of funds.

Uses

1. *Any decrease in a liability or equity account.*   Paying off a loan is an example of a use of funds.

2. *Any increase in an asset account.*   Buying fixed assets and building up inventories are other examples of uses of funds.

Thus sources of funds include bank loans and retained earnings, as well as money generated by selling assets, by collecting receivables, and even by drawing down the cash account. Uses include acquiring fixed assets, building up receivables or inventories, and paying off debts.

   Table 4-4 shows the changes that occurred in Surrey's balance sheet accounts during 1993, with each change designated as a source or a use. Note

Table 4-4
Surrey Company Limited
Changes in Balance Sheet Accounts during 1993
(millions of dollars)

		1992		1993	Change Source	Use
Assets						
Cash		$ 30		$ 15	$15	
Accounts receivable		250		230	20	
Inventories		100		170		$70
Gross fixed assets	$205		$233			28
Less: accumulated depreciation	(33)		(42)		9	
Net fixed assets		172		191		
Total assets		$552		$606		
Liabilities						
Accounts payable		$ 45		$ 50	$ 5	
Other current liabilities		34		41	7	
Long-term debt		310		327	17	
Common equity		50		50		
Retained earnings		113		138	25	
Total claims		$552		$606	$98	$98

that total sources of funds must equal total uses of funds; for Surrey this amount is $98 million.

The next step is to use the sources and uses information to construct the formal statement of cash flows. Each balance sheet change in Table 4-4 is classified as resulting from (1) operations, (2) long-term investments, or (3) financing activities. A completed statement is presented in Table 4-5. Note that every item in the "change" columns of Table 4-4 is carried over to Table 4-5 except retained earnings. Table 4-5 shows net income as the first line item under the operations section, while dividends paid are shown as a negative cash flow in the financing activities section, rather than netting the two items out and simply reporting the increase in retained earnings.

Under the operating activities segment, the cash from operations is equal to $1 million. This is composed of two amounts: $39 million from adjusted net income, and an increase in noncash working capital of $38 million (that is, a use of cash). This latter amount is equal to a use of cash of $70 million from the increase in inventories and a source of cash from the increase in accounts

Table 4-5
Surrey Company Limited
Statement of Changes in Financial Position (Cash Flows)
(millions of dollars)

	1993
Cash provided by (used for)	
Operating activities	
Income before extraordinary items	$ 30
Charges to income not involving cash	
—depreciation and amortization	9
Changes in noncash working capital (1)	(38)
	1
Financing activities	
Proceeds from debt issue	17
Dividends to shareholders	(5)
	12
Investing activities	
Acquisition of property, plant, and equipment	(28)
Decrease in cash	(15)
Cash at beginning of year	30
Cash at end of year	$ 15
(1) Changes in noncash working capital	
Cash provided by (used for)	
Accounts payable	$ 5
Other current liabilities	7
Accounts receivable	20
Inventories	(70)
(a)	$(38)

payable and other current liabilities and from the decrease in accounts receivable.

The financing activity source of cash of $12 million reflects proceeds from a debt issue and a dividend payment to shareholders. Finally, investing activities used $28 million for an increase in gross fixed assets.

The change in cash during the year reflects a use of $15 million; this is the sum of the cash consequences of each activity. In 1992, cash was equal to $30 million; in 1993, it was equal to $15 million. This is a use of cash of $15 million during the year.

The statement of changes in financial position tells the financial manager that funds were used for investment purposes; a source of funds came from financing. The operating activities, although generating cash inflows, were not sufficient to finance the activities. In fact, the cash balance was reduced over the period. The change in the noncash working capital position was negative, leading to a use of cash. This reflected an increase in inventories that was not offset by the increase in accounts payable and other current liabilities and the decrease in accounts receivable.

The cash flow statement suggests that Surrey has some problems to consider. First, the decrease in cash reflects both a major acquisition in fixed assets and a significant buildup in inventories. Operating activities appear strong, but unless sales grow sufficiently to compensate for the increased fixed assets, the company may be in for some serious problems.

Concept Review

▶ Identify the two types of information given in the annual report.

▶ Describe the four basic financial statements: (1) the income statement, (2) balance sheet, (3) the statement of retained earnings, and (4) the statement of changes in financial position (cash flow statement).

▶ List several aspects of accounting that make financial analysis difficult.

▶ Explain the following statement: "Retained earnings as reported on the balance sheet do not represent cash and are not 'available' for the payment of dividends or anything else."

▶ List the rules that determine whether a change in a balance sheet item is recorded as a source or use of funds.

Ratio Analysis

Financial statements report both on a firm's position at a point in time and on its operations over some past period. However, the real value of financial statements lies in the fact that they can be used to help predict the firm's future earnings and dividends. From an investor's standpoint, predicting the future is what financial statement analysis is all about, while from management's standpoint, financial statement analysis is useful both as a way to anticipate future conditions and, more important, as a starting point for planning actions that will influence the future course of events.

An analysis of the firm's ratios is generally the first step in a financial analysis. The ratios are designed to show relationships between financial statement accounts. For example, Firm A may have debt of $5 248 760 and interest charges of $419 900, while Firm B has debt of $52 647 980 and interest charges of $3 948 600. Which company is stronger? The true burden of these debts, and the companies' ability to repay them, can be ascertained (1) by comparing each firm's debt to its assets and (2) by comparing the interest it must pay to the income it has available for payment of interest. Such comparisons are made by **ratio analysis**.

Basic Types of Financial Ratios

Each type of financial analysis has a purpose, or use, that determines the different relationships emphasized. The analyst may, for example, be a banker considering whether or not to grant a short-term loan to a firm. Bankers are primarily concerned with the firm's near-term, or liquidity, position, so they stress ratios that measure liquidity. In contrast, long-term creditors place far more emphasis on earning power and on operating efficiency. They know that unprofitable operations will erode asset values and that a strong current position is no guarantee that funds will be available to repay a 20-year bond issue. Equity investors are similarly interested in long-term profitability and efficiency. Management is, of course, concerned with all those aspects of financial analysis—it must be able to repay its debts to long- and short-term creditors as well as to earn profits for shareholders.

It is useful to classify ratios into six fundamental types:

1. *Liquidity ratios*, which measure the firm's ability to meet its maturing short-term obligations.
2. *Debt management ratios*, which measure the extent to which the firm has been financed by debt.
3. *Asset management ratios*, which measure how effectively the firm is using its resources.
4. *Profitability ratios*, which measure management's overall effectiveness as shown by the returns generated on sales and investment.
5. *Growth ratios*, which measure the firm's ability to maintain its economic position in the growth of the economy and industry.
6. *Market value ratios*, which measure the ability of management to create market values in excess of investment-cost outlays. These valuation ratios are the most complete measure of performance in that they reflect the risk ratios (the first two) and the return ratios (the following three). Market value ratios are of great importance because they relate directly to the goals of maximizing the value of the firm and the wealth of shareholders.

Specific examples of each ratio are given in the following sections, where the Surrey case history illustrates their calculation and use.

Liquidity Ratios

Usually, the first concern of most financial analysts is liquidity: will the firm be able to meet its maturing obligations? Surrey has debts totalling $91 million that must be paid within the coming year. Can these obligations be satisfied?

Although a full liquidity analysis requires the use of cash budgets (described in Chapter 6), ratio analysis, by relating the amount of cash and other current assets to the current obligations, provides a quick and easy-to-use measure of liquidity. Two commonly used **liquidity ratios** are presented here.

Current Ratio.   The **current ratio** is computed by dividing current assets by current liabilities. Current assets normally include cash, marketable securities, accounts receivable, and inventories; current liabilities consist of accounts payable, short-term notes payable, current maturities of long-term debt, accrued income taxes, and other accrued expenses (principally wages). If a company is getting into financial difficulty, it begins paying its bills (accounts payable) more slowly, building up bank loans, and so on. If these current liabilities are rising faster than current assets, the current ratio will fall, which could signal trouble. The current ratio is the most commonly used measure of short-term solvency because it indicates the extent to which the claims of short-term creditors are covered by assets that are expected to be converted to cash in a period roughly corresponding to the maturity of the claims.

The calculation of the current ratio for Surrey at year-end 1993 is

$$\text{Current ratio} = \frac{\text{Current assets}}{\text{Current liabilities}} = \frac{\$415\,000\,000}{\$91\,000\,000} = 4.6 \text{ times.}$$

$$\text{Industry average} = 1.8 \text{ times.}$$

Surrey's current ratio is well above the average for the industry, 1.8 times, and this may be of concern to the management. Because current assets are near maturity, it is quite likely that they could be liquidated at 22 percent of book value in order to satisfy current creditors.[7]

Although industry average figures are discussed later in this chapter, it should be stated at this point that the industry average is not a magic number that all firms should strive to maintain. In fact, some very well-managed firms will be above it, and other good firms will be below it. However, if a firm's ratios are very far removed from the averages for its industry, the analyst must be concerned about why this variance occurs; that is, a deviation from the industry average should alert the analyst to check further.

Surrey's substantial discrepancy from the industry average could be a result of the combination of different types of companies in the merchandising industry category. Within this industry, there is a wide variation in current ratios for individual companies. Alternatively, Surrey's large current ratio may suggest that the firm should reduce its accounts receivable by reducing the credit sales to customers or increase its accounts payable by taking greater advantage of credit offered by its suppliers.

Quick or Acid Test Ratio.   The **quick** or **acid test ratio** is calculated by deducting inventories from current assets and dividing the remainder by current liabilities. Inventories are typically the least liquid of a firm's current

---

[7] $(1/4.6) = 0.22$ or 22 percent. Note that $(0.22)(\$415\,000\,000) \approx \$91\,000\,000$, the amount of current liabilities.

assets and the assets on which losses are most likely to occur in the event of liquidation. Therefore, this is an "acid test" measure of the firm's ability to pay off short-term obligations.

$$\text{Quick or acid test ratio} = \frac{\text{Current assets} - \text{Inventory}}{\text{Current liabilities}}$$

$$= \frac{\$245\,000\,000}{\$91\,000\,000} = 2.7 \text{ times.}$$

$$\text{Industry average} = 0.8 \text{ times.}$$

The average quick ratio for the industry is 0.8, and consistent with the observation of the current ratio, Surrey is well above the industry average. It is clear from these two ratios that Surrey is in a highly liquid short-term position. All short-term liabilities can be paid off easily if the receivables can be liquidated at more than 33 percent of their book value. This is calculated by the following formula:[8]

$$\frac{\text{Current liabilities} - \text{Cash}}{\text{Receivables}} = \frac{\$76\,000\,000}{\$230\,000\,000} = 0.33 \text{ or } 33\%.$$

Debt Management Ratios

The extent to which a firm uses debt financing, or **financial leverage**, has three important implications. First, creditors look to the equity, or owner-supplied funds, to provide a margin of safety. If owners have provided only a small proportion of total financing, the risks of the enterprise are borne mainly by the creditors. Second, by raising funds through debt, the owners gain the benefits of maintaining control of the firm with a limited investment. Third, if the firm earns more on the borrowed funds than it pays in interest, the return to the owners is magnified. For example, if assets earn 10 percent and debt costs only 8 percent, there is a 2 percent differential accruing to the shareholders. Leverage cuts both ways, however. If the return on assets falls to 3 percent, the differential between that figure and the interest cost of debt must be made up from equity's share of total profits. In the first instance, where assets earn more than the interest cost of debt, leverage provides a favourable result; in the second, it is unfavourable.

Firms with low debt leverage ratios have less risk of loss when the economy is in a recession, but they also have lower expected returns when the economy booms. Conversely, firms with higher debt ratios run the risk of large losses but also have a chance of gaining high profits. The prospects of high returns are desirable, but investors are averse to risk. Decisions about the use of leverage, then, must balance higher expected returns against increased risk.

Determining the optimal amount of debt for a given firm is a complicated process and we defer a discussion of this topic until Chapter 18. For now, we look at two **debt management ratios** used to examine the firm's debt in a

---

[8]In other words, cash on hand plus 33 percent of receivables provides funds equal to short-term liabilities.

$$\text{Cash} + 0.33 \times \text{receivables} = \$15\,000 + 0.33\,(\$230\,000\,000)$$
$$= \$91\,000\,000 = \text{current liabilities.}$$

financial statement analysis: (1) they check balance sheet ratios to determine the extent to which borrowed funds have been used to finance assets, and (2) they review income statement ratios to determine the number of times fixed charges such as interest payments are covered by operating profits. These two sets of ratios are complementary, and most analysts use both types.

Debt Ratio.   The ratio of total debt to total assets, generally called the **debt ratio**, measures the percentage of total funds provided by creditors. Debt includes current liabilities and all bonds. Creditors prefer moderate debt ratios because the lower the ratio, the greater the cushion against creditors' losses in the event of liquidation. In contrast to the creditors' preference for a low debt ratio, the owners may seek high leverage either to magnify earnings or because raising new equity means giving up some degree of control. If the debt ratio is too high, there is a danger of encouraging irresponsibility on the part of the owners. The stake of the owners can become so small that speculative activity, if it is successful, will yield a substantial percentage return to the owners. If the venture is unsuccessful, however, only a moderate loss is incurred by the owners because their investment is small and limited.

$$\text{Debt ratio} = \frac{\text{Total debt}}{\text{Total assets}} = \frac{\$418\,000\,000}{\$606\,000\,000} = 0.69 \text{ or } 69\%.$$

$$\text{Industry average} = 68\%.$$

Surrey's debt ratio of 68 percent means that the creditors have supplied that proportion of the company's total financing. As Surrey's ratio is slightly greater than the industry average, Surrey's financial officer could consider the possibility of future financing problems, but the difference is so small that it should not cause Surrey's management any serious problems. If new debt is issued to finance the acquisition of new assets, the debt ratio will increase, and this could result in substantially higher interest rates; in fact, the higher ratio might cause a hardship for the existing shareholders.[9] Finally, Surrey may have to determine if it is approaching its debt capacity level for the given level of equity in the company. If so, future financing will require an equity component as well as debt.

Times Interest Earned.   The **times-interest-earned (TIE) ratio** is determined by dividing earnings before interest and taxes (EBIT) by the interest charges. Since there are no additional income or expense items except interest, EBIT and net operating income (NOI) are identical. This ratio measures the extent to which earnings can decline without resultant financial embarrassment to the firm because of inability to meet annual interest costs. Failure to meet interest obligations can bring legal action by the creditors, possibly resulting in bankruptcy. Note that the before-tax profit figure is used in the numerator.

---

[9]The ratio of debt to equity is also used in financial analysis. The debt-to-assets (D/A) and debt-to-equity (D/E) ratios are simply transformations of one another:

$$\text{D/E} = \frac{\text{D/A}}{1 - \text{D/A}} \text{ and D/A} = \frac{\text{D/E}}{1 + \text{D/E}}.$$

Both ratios increase as a firm of a given size (total assets) uses a greater proportion of debt, but D/A rises linearly and approaches a limit of 100 percent, whereas D/E rises exponentially and approaches infinity.

Because income taxes are computed after interest expense is deducted, the ability to pay current interest is not affected by income taxes.

$$\text{Times interest earned} = \frac{\text{Earnings before interest and taxes}}{\text{Interest charges}}$$

$$= \frac{\text{Profit before taxes} + \text{Interest charges}}{\text{Interest charges}}$$

$$= \frac{\$103\,000\,000}{\$43\,000\,000}$$

$$= 2.4 \text{ times.}$$

$$\text{Industry average} = 2.4 \text{ times.}$$

Surrey's interest charges consist of three payments totalling $43 million (see Table 4-1). The firm's NOI available for servicing these charges is $103 million, so the interest is covered 2.4 times. Comparing this figure to the industry average indicates that Surrey, like the industry, has a small margin of safety in covering its interest payments. This ratio reinforces the conclusion, based on the debt ratio, that the company is likely to face some difficulties if it attempts to borrow additional funds. Surrey should not try to finance a greater part of the company with debt than it has up to this time.

Fixed-Charge Coverage.   The **fixed-charge coverage ratio** is similar to the times-interest-earned ratio, but it is somewhat more inclusive in that it recognizes that many firms lease assets and incur long-term obligations under lease contracts.[10] As we shall show in Chapter 23, leasing has become quite widespread in recent years, making this ratio preferable to the times-interest-earned ratio for most financial analyses. "Fixed charges" are defined as interest plus annual long-term lease obligations, and the fixed-charge coverage ratio is defined as follows:

$$\text{Fixed-charge coverage ratio} = \frac{\begin{array}{c}\text{Net income} \\ \text{before taxes}\end{array} + \begin{array}{c}\text{Interest} \\ \text{charges}\end{array} + \begin{array}{c}\text{Lease} \\ \text{obligations}\end{array}}{\text{Interest charges} + \text{Lease obligations}}$$

$$= \frac{\$60\,000\,000 + \$43\,000\,000 + \$20\,000\,000}{\$43\,000\,000 + \$20\,000\,000}$$

$$= \frac{\$123\,000\,000}{\$63\,000\,000}$$

$$= 2.0 \text{ times.}$$

$$\text{Industry average} = 2.0 \text{ times.}$$

---

[10]Generally, a long-term lease is defined as one that is at least 3 years long. Thus, rent incurred under a 1-year lease would not be included in the fixed-charge coverage ratio, but rental payments under a 3-year or longer lease are fixed charges and would be included. For certain types of leases, called *capital leases*, the lessee has in effect acquired the leased property through a financing method called a lease. The accounting profession has decided that a capital lease should be recorded on the books as an acquired asset and placed in the fixed assets section of the balance sheet under "capitalized leases." The asset is recorded at its fair market value, and the liability is recorded as the present value of future lease payments.

Surrey's fixed-charge coverage of 2.0 times is equal to the industry average. Just as with the debt and times-interest-earned ratios, the company seems to be maintaining a reasonable ratio with respect to the industry norm.

Considering that the debt ratio is slightly on the high side, if leases are considered as a form of debt, then Surrey, along with the industry, may be close to its borrowing capacity.

Cash Flow Coverage. Suppose Surrey issued preferred shares that required payment of $5 million in dividends per year and had to make annual payments of principal (sinking fund payments) on its various debt obligations of $15 million per year. To the numerator of the previous ratio, we add depreciation, which is a noncash charge, and to the denominator, we add the two additional items on a before-tax basis.[11] These adjustments produce the **cash flow coverage** ratio, which shows the margin by which operating cash flows cover financial requirements.

$$\text{Cash flow coverage ratio} = \frac{\text{Cash inflows}}{\text{Interest plus lease payments} + \dfrac{\text{Preferred share dividends}}{(1 - T)} + \dfrac{\text{Debt repayment}}{(1 - T)}}$$

$$= \frac{\$123\,000\,000 + 9\,000\,000}{\$63\,000\,000 + \dfrac{\$5\,000\,000}{1 - 0.50} + \dfrac{15\,000\,000}{1 - 0.50}} = \frac{\$132\,000\,000}{\$103\,000\,000}$$

$$= 1.3 \text{ times.}$$

Although industry standards on this ratio are not generally published, logic suggests that a cash coverage ratio of at least 2 times should be achieved in normal times, allowing for a substantial decline in cash inflows before a cash solvency problem is encountered. Surrey does not meet this standard.

Asset Management Ratios

Asset management ratios measure how effectively the firm employs the resources at its command. These ratios all involve comparisons between the level of sales and the investment in various asset accounts. The ratios presume that a "proper" balance exists between sales and the various asset accounts — inventories, accounts receivable, fixed assets, and others. As we shall see in the following chapters, this is generally a good assumption.

Inventory Turnover. The **inventory turnover ratio**, defined as sales divided by inventories, is calculated as follows:

$$\text{Inventory turnover ratio} = \frac{\text{Sales}}{\text{Inventory}} = \frac{\$920\,000\,000}{\$170\,000\,000} = 5.4 \text{ times.}$$

$$\text{Industry average} = 8.0 \text{ times.}$$

---

[11]Because preferred dividends and sinking fund payments must be made from the income remaining after payment of income taxes, dividing by $(1 - T)$ "grosses up" the payments and shows the before-tax amounts necessary to produce a given after-tax amount.

Surrey's turnover of 5.4 times is significantly less than the industry average of 8.0 times. This suggests that Surrey is holding greater inventories than necessary; the excess inventory is, of course, unproductive and represents an investment with a low or zero rate of return. Surrey must also be concerned with the possibility that its inventory contains damaged or obsolete materials not actually worth their stated value. With the combination of the very high current ratio, low quick ratio, and lower-than-average inventory turnover, there is a distinct possibility that some of the inventories are damaged or obsolete.

Three problems arise in calculating and interpreting the inventory turnover ratio. First, sales are at *market prices*; if inventories are carried at *historical cost*, as they generally are, it would be more appropriate to use cost of goods sold in place of sales in the numerator of the formula. However, most compilers of financial ratio statistics measure inventory turnover ratios based on sales. Thus, to permit comparison of the individual company and industry ratios, it is necessary to measure inventory turnover with sales in the numerator.

Second, the valuation of inventories may not be the same across firms in the same industry. Generally, the *FIFO valuation method* (first in, first out) is used. If, however, the *LIFO method* (last in, first out) is used, then older, lower-valued stocks may be included in the inventory, which could lead to a higher inventory turnover ratio.

The final problem lies in the fact that sales occur over the entire year, whereas the inventory figure is for one point in time. This makes it better to use an average inventory for the year, computed by adding the 12 end-of-month inventory figures and dividing by 12, or by adding the beginning and ending inventories and dividing by 2. If it is determined that the firm's business is highly seasonal or if there has been a strong upward or downward sales trend during the year, it becomes essential to make some such adjustment. Because Surrey is in a highly seasonal type of business, management would need more information than is provided here to determine if inventory turnover is an important problem.

Days Sales Outstanding.   **Days sales outstanding (DSO)**[12] is used to appraise accounts receivable; it is a measure of the accounts receivable turnover and is computed in two steps: (1) annual sales are divided by 365 to get the average daily sales;[13] (2) daily sales are divided into accounts receivable to find the number of days' sales tied up in receivables. This figure is called *days sales outstanding (DSO)* since it represents the number of days that the firm must wait after making a sale before receiving cash. Changes in this ratio will have an impact on the liquidity ratios, too. The calculations for Surrey show an

---

[12]In prior editions of this text, days sales outstanding (DSO) was referred to as "average collection period (ACP)." We have changed the terminology from ACP to DSO to conform to the more accepted business nomenclature. Therefore, wherever we previously used the term ACP, we now use DSO.

[13]Because information on credit sales is usually unavailable, total sales must be used. Since all firms do not have the same percentage of credit sales, there is a good chance that the average collection period will be somewhat in error.

average collection period of 91.25 days. This is well above the industry average of 30 days.

Step 1. Sales per day $= \dfrac{\$920\,000\,000}{365} = \$2\,520\,548.$

Step 2. DSO $= \dfrac{\text{Days sales}}{\text{outstanding}} = \dfrac{\text{Receivables}}{\text{Sales per day}} = \dfrac{\$230\,000\,000}{\$2\,520\,548} = 91.25$ days.

$$\text{Industry average} = 30 \text{ days.}$$

The calculations for Surrey show an average collection period of 91 days, which is well above the 30-day industry average. This comparison indicates that customers are not paying their bills promptly. One mitigating factor is that this ratio does not take into consideration the fact that some of the company's sales are on installment plans and the payments will be drawn out over several months. For simplification, however, the total revenue in the income statement includes interest earned on the delayed payments. The industry ratio includes some firms that deal mostly in cash sales. Even with these qualifications in the interpretation of the average collection period, it appears that the 91-day period for Surrey should be reduced.

For companies without installment sales, the days sales outstanding can be evaluated by comparison with the terms on which the firm sells its goods. For example, since Surrey sells on terms that require payment within 30 days and the average collection period is 91 days, then it is clear that customers, on average, are not paying their bills on time. If the trend in the collection period over the past few years has been rising while the credit policy has not changed, this would be even stronger evidence that steps should be taken to expedite the collection of accounts receivable.

One additional financial tool should be mentioned in connection with accounts receivable analysis—the *aging schedule*, which breaks down accounts receivable according to how long they have been outstanding. For Surrey, the aging schedule is as follows:

Age of Accounts (days)	Percentage of Total Accounts Receivable
0–20	12%
21–40	11
41–60	13
61–80	10
81–100	19
> 100	35
Total	100%

It is still difficult, based on this information, to determine just how many of the company's customers are delaying their payments. We can see that the more-than-100-days category has a large percentage of the total accounts receivable. Management should give serious attention to determining whether or not the 91-day collection period is because of installment sales. This potential problem for Surrey is emphasized by the industry collection period of 30 days.

Fixed-Assets Turnover.   The **fixed-assets turnover ratio**, also called the *fixed-assets utilization ratio*, measures how effectively the firm uses its plant and equipment. It is the ratio of sales to net fixed assets.

$$\text{Fixed-assets turnover ratio} = \frac{\text{Sales}}{\text{Net fixed assets}} = \frac{\$920\ 000\ 000}{\$191\ 000\ 000}$$
$$= 4.8 \text{ times.}$$
$$\text{Industry average} = 7.5 \text{ times.}$$

The Surrey turnover of 4.8 times compares poorly with the industry average of 7.5 times. This indicates that the firm is not using its fixed assets to as high a percentage of capacity as are the other firms in the industry. This figure could be misleading if Surrey leases fewer of its buildings than other firms in the industry, because, for the same level of sales as the average firm in the industry, the net fixed assets would be higher and the fixed-asset turnover lower.

A major potential problem exists when the fixed-assets turnover ratio is used to compare different firms. Recall that all assets except cash and accounts receivable reflect the historical cost of the assets. Inflation has caused the value of many assets that were purchased in the past to be seriously understated. Therefore, if we are comparing an old firm that acquired many of its fixed assets years ago at low prices with a new company that acquired its fixed assets only recently, we will probably find that the old firm reports a higher turnover. However, this is more reflective of the inability of accountants to deal with inflation than of any inefficiency on the part of the new firm. The accounting profession is trying to devise ways of making financial statements reflect current values rather than historical values. If balance sheets were stated on a current value basis, this would eliminate the problem of comparisons, but at the moment the problem still exists. Since financial analysts typically do not have the data necessary to make adjustments, they must simply recognize that a problem may exist and use their judgement to deal with it.

Total-Assets Turnover.   The final asset management ratio, the **total-assets turnover ratio**, measures the turnover of all the firm's assets; it is calculated by dividing sales by total assets.

$$\text{Total-assets turnover ratio} = \frac{\text{Sales}}{\text{Total assets}} = \frac{\$920\ 000\ 000}{\$606\ 000\ 000} = 1.5 \text{ times.}$$
$$\text{Industry average} = 2.5 \text{ times.}$$

Again, the poor turnover figure, as compared to the industry average, implies that Surrey is not generating sufficient sales for the amount of assets employed. This problem is related to the poor turnover experienced with inventory. Sales should be increased, or some inefficient assets should be disposed of, or both.

Profitability Ratios

Profitability is the net result of a large number of policies and decisions. The ratios examined thus far provide some information about the way the firm is operating, but the **profitability ratios** show the combined effects of liquidity, asset management, and debt management on operating results.

Profit Margin on Sales. The **profit margin on sales**, computed by dividing net income after taxes by sales, gives the profit per dollar of sales.

$$\text{Profit margin on sales} = \frac{\text{Net income after taxes}}{\text{Sales}} = \frac{\$30\,000\,000}{\$920\,000\,000} = 3.3\%.$$

$$\text{Industry average} = 1.2\%.$$

Surrey's profit margin is considerably above the industry average, indicating that the company's prices are relatively high or that its operating costs are relatively low or both.

Basic Earnings Power. The **basic earnings power ratio** is calculated by dividing the earnings before interest and taxes (EBIT) by total assets.

$$\text{Basic earnings power} = \frac{\text{EBIT}}{\text{Total assets}} = \frac{\$103\,000\,000}{\$606\,000\,000} = 17\%.$$

$$\text{Industry average} = 13\%.$$

Return on Total Assets. The ratio of net income after taxes to total assets measures the return on all capital invested in the firm; it is called the **return on total assets (ROA)** or **return on investment (ROI)**.[14]

$$\text{Return on total assets (ROA)} = \frac{\text{Net income after taxes}}{\text{Total assets}}$$

$$= \frac{\$30\,000\,000}{\$606\,000\,000} = 5.0\%.$$

$$\text{Industry average} = 3.0\%.$$

Surrey's return on assets is significantly above the industry average. This results from the high profit margin on sales that more than offsets the low turnover of total assets.

---

[14]In calculating the return on total assets, it is sometimes desirable to add interest to net income after taxes when forming the numerator of the ratio. The theory here is that since assets are financed by both shareholders and creditors, the ratio should measure the returns provided to both classes of investors. We have not done so at this point because the published averages we use for comparative purposes exclude interest. Later in the book, however, when we deal with leverage decisions, we will add back interest. This addition has a material bearing on the value of the ratio for utilities (which have large amounts of fixed assets financed by debt), and the technically correct ratio is the one normally used by utility analysts.

Return on Common Equity.   The ratio of net income after taxes to common equity, often called **return on common equity (ROE)**, measures the rate of return on the shareholders' investment.

$$\text{Return on common equity (ROE)} = \frac{\text{Net income after taxes}}{\text{Net worth}}$$

$$= \frac{\$30\ 000\ 000}{\$188\ 000\ 000} = 16.0\%.$$

$$\text{Industry average} = \ 9.2\%.$$

The 16 percent return on book equity is well above the industry average. This return must be considered superior as Surrey's debt ratio is equal to the debt ratio for the industry.

Growth Ratios

Growth ratios measure how well the firm is maintaining its economic position in the economy as a whole and within its own industry. During periods of inflation, the interpretation of growth ratios becomes more difficult. During inflationary periods, nominal growth rates increase greatly. The growth of the economy as well as of industries and firms reflects the inflation factor as well as the underlying (real) growth. Since reported figures are generally stated in nominal terms, the growth-rate reference standards that are employed will include the inflation factor. However, as a part of the further internal analysis by business firms, distinction needs to be made between inflation-related growth, which reflects changes in the measuring stick, and underlying real growth, which reflects the basic productivity of the economy and the firm.

The annual reports of business firms usually include a section of historical data on selected financial items. These may be used to develop the growth and valuation ratios. The data for Surrey are presented in Table 4-6.

From the basic data in Table 4-6, we have calculated the 5-year growth rates for six items for Surrey covering the years 1988 to 1993; the growth rates are presented in Table 4-7. The growth rates are obtained by dividing the last-period figure by the first-period figure, which gives a future value interest factor. Then, by referring to the future value interest tables, the growth rate represented by the ratio can be determined.[15]

We observe that the growth rate in sales for Surrey is above that for the industry. Moreover, the growth in net income is well above the industry average.

Next we consider the per-share growth analysis. First, we consider earnings per share (EPS), which reflect the methods by which the firm has financed its

---

[15]Future value interest factors are discussed in Chapter 12. Table A-3 on the insert card gives future values for interest rates from 1 to 36 percent, for periods from 1 to 60 years. Surrey's 5-year sales growth is calculated by dividing the sales level in 1993 by the sales level in 1988. 920/345 = 2.667. Looking at Table A-3, row 5, we see that this corresponds to an annual growth of between 20 and 24 percent. That is, $(1.20)^5 = 2.4883$, and $(1.24)^5 = 2.9316$. The rate we are looking for, k, would give $(1 + k)^5 = 2.667 = 21.7\%$. This is the annual growth rate that applied to the base value of 345 for 5 years results in a value of 920.

Table 4-6
Selected Historical Data for
Surrey Company Limited

	1988	1989	1990	1991	1992	1993
Firm (thousands of dollars)						
Sales	$345 000	$368 000	$460 000	$575 000	$713 000	$920 000
Net income	14 000	18 500	22 000	20 000	26 000	30 000
Per share						
Earnings	$1.18	$1.55	$1.85	$1.68	$2.23	$2.52
Dividends	0.19	0.23	0.27	0.27	0.34	0.42
Market price—common shares						
High	$11.00	$15.00	$16.00	$14.25	$20.50	$19.50
Low	8.00	12.00	13.00	11.25	17.50	16.50
Average	9.50	13.50	14.50	12.75	19.00	18.00
Book value per share of common equity, year-end	$7.30	$9.80	$10.90	$11.60	$13.70	$15.80

overall growth. Here again the growth rate is greater than the industry average. The dividend and earnings growth rates for Surrey are approximately equal, and each is in excess of the value for the industry.

Market price represents the results of investors' valuation of the expected earnings of a firm given the risk of these earnings. Market price growth for the industry as a whole has been strong (8.2 percent), and the results for Surrey are even stronger (13.6 percent). The average price for Surrey, however, did not display a stable growth pattern. The average price increased rapidly over 1988 and 1992 and actually declined in 1993.

Book value of equity per share indicates the resources in the company per share of investment in common equity. This grew at 16.7 percent for Surrey, which was in excess of the 10.3 percent growth of the industry. This could reflect the substantial growth in Surrey that was financed out of retained earnings. Overall, the growth performance of Surrey has been very strong, and this should have some implications for the valuation ratios considered next.

Table 4-7
Growth Rates, 1988–1993, Surrey and Industry Averages

	Surrey	Industry
Sales	21.7%	17.0%
Net income	16.5	10.3
Earnings per share	16.4	13.5
Dividends per share	17.2	12.1
Market price; average	13.6	8.2
Book value per share	16.7	10.3

Market Value Ratios

Market value ratios are the most comprehensive measures of performance for the firm in that they reflect the combined influence of financial ratios, which reflect risk, and those that reflect return. Two valuation ratios are calculated, and their patterns are summarized in Table 4-8.

Price-to-Earnings Ratio.   The **price-to-earnings (P/E) ratio** shows how much investors are willing to pay per dollar of reported earnings. P/E ratios are higher for firms with high growth prospects, other things held constant, but they are lower for riskier firms. The price-to-earnings ratio is calculated as the price per share divided by the earnings per share. In 1993, using the average price of $18.00 per share and the earnings per share (EPS) of $2.52, we find that Surrey's P/E ratio is 7.1.

$$\text{Price-to-earnings (P/E) ratio} = \frac{\text{Price per share}}{\text{Earnings per share}} = \frac{\$18.00}{\$2.52} = 7.1 \text{ times.}$$

The average price was used in this example, but the closing price at December 31, 1993, could be used as well.

Consider the trends in the price-to-earnings ratios shown in Table 4-8. For every year except 1991, the ratios for Surrey were higher than those for the industry. This reflects the superior performance of Surrey and its high growth rate. Notice also that the downturn in the P/E ratio in 1993 for Surrey was an industrywide phenomenon.

Market-to-Book Ratio.   The **market-to-book ratio** is another important valuation ratio because it indicates the value that the financial markets attach to the management and to the organization of the company as a going concern. Book value represents the historical costs of brick and mortar—the physical assets of the company—that have been financed by common equity shareholders. A well-run company with strong management, an efficient organization, and reasonable growth opportunities should have a market value greater than or at least equal to the book value of its equity. If the economy is in recession and earnings opportunities for the firm are poor, the market-to-book ratio can be less than unity, even though the management is good. Therefore, market-to-

Table 4-8
Market Value Ratios, 1988–1993, Surrey and Industry Averages

		1988	1989	1990	1991	1992	1993
Price-to-earnings ratio:	Surrey	8.1	8.7	7.8	7.6	8.5	7.1
	Industry	7.0	8.0	7.5	7.8	8.0	7.0
Market-to-book ratio:	Surrey	1.3	1.4	1.3	1.1	1.4	1.1
	Industry	1.1	1.2	1.2	1.1	1.1	0.9

book ratios will depend both on industry (or economywide) factors as well as on individual firm influences.

Surrey's book value per share at December 31, 1993, was $15.80. Dividing this book value per share by the average price per share provides the market-to-book ratio of 1.1 times.

$$\text{Market-to-book ratio} = \frac{\text{Market price per share}}{\text{Book value per share}} = \frac{\$18.00}{\$15.80} = 1.1 \text{ times.}$$

As we see from Table 4-8, the market-to-book ratio of the company was always in excess of 1.0. In the early years it was in the 1.3 to 1.4 range. The industry, except for 1993, had a market-to-book ratio greater than 1.0 as well. The fall in market-to-book ratios over 1993 was more precipitous for the company than for the industry, but the firm still retained a market-to-book ratio in excess of 1.0.

Trend Analysis

While the preceding ratio analysis gives a reasonably good picture of Surrey's operations, it is incomplete in one important respect—it ignores the time dimension. The ratios are snapshots at one particular time, but there may be trends in motion that are in the process of eroding a relatively good present position. Conversely, **trend analysis**, an analysis of the ratios over the past few years, may suggest that a relatively weak present position is being improved.

The method of trend analysis is illustrated in Figure 4-2, where graphs of Surrey's sales, current ratio, debt ratio, fixed-asset turnover, and return on net worth are presented for 1987 to 1993. The figures are compared with industry averages over the same period. Surrey's sales are growing at a rate faster than the industry's, which indicates that Surrey is in a growth phase. Casual observation will show that the Surrey ratios have not always followed the industry trends. This suggests that the company trends are due to its own internal conditions, not to national influences affecting the firm. In general, these differences appear to be greatest in the two most recent years.

Surrey's liquidity position has become significantly out of line with the industry average. The firm should take action soon to improve the use of its assets, both liquid and long term. This does not mean, however, that the industry ratio is the right one for Surrey—some analysis of the composition of the industry averages may be required.

Surrey's debt ratio has followed the same trend as that of the industry. Surrey has remained within about 10 points of the industry, but again, it must be cautioned that the amount of leased assets for Surrey and the industry are not known, and this information could have an important bearing on any comparison. This caveat extends to the fixed-assets turnover ratio, where it appears that the Surrey position is deteriorating. This may be because of rapid expansion in assets while the use of the assets is still below capacity. It is important, however, that Surrey not expand its assets any further until the existing fixed assets are operating efficiently.

Surrey's return on equity has consistently been above the industry's average even though their debt ratios have been of a similar magnitude. The

Figure 4-2
Illustration of Trend Analysis, 1987–1993

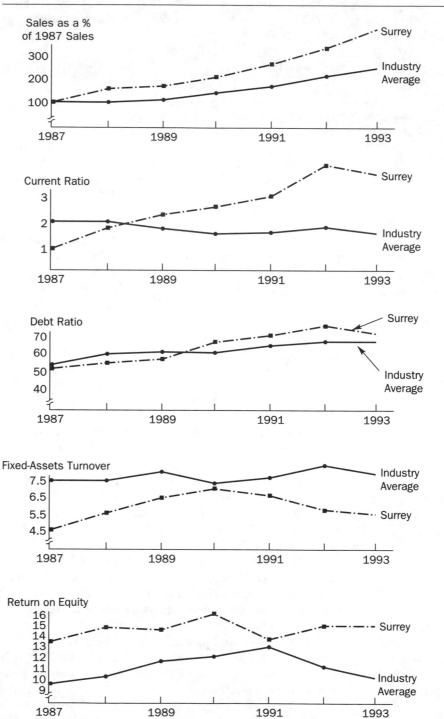

rate of return has been relatively stable, fluctuating between 14 and 16 percent. Only in 1990 did the return exceed 16 percent.

Common-Size and Index Analysis.   Trend analysis is often supplemented by expressing the financial statements items as percentages. The percentages can be related either to totals, such as total sales or total assets, in which case we produce a *common-size statement*, or to a base year, in which case the result is an *indexed* statement. With common-size statements, each balance sheet item is expressed as a percentage of total assets, and each income statement item is stated as a percentage of total sales. With indexed statements, the balance sheet and income statement items are indexed relative to an initial base year. Both types of statements can be used either to perform comparisons using data over different years relating to a given firm or to make intercompany comparisons within an industry.

Summary of Ratio Analysis: The Du Pont System

Table 4-9 summarizes Surrey's ratios, whereas Figure 4-3, from what is called the modified **Du Pont system** because that company's managers developed the general approach, shows the relationships between return on asset investment, asset turnover, and the profit margin. The left-hand side of the chart develops the *profit margin on sales*. The various expense items are listed and then summed to obtain Surrey's total costs. Subtracting costs from sales yields the company's net income. When we divide net income by sales, we find that 3.3 percent of each sales dollar is left over for the shareholders. If the profit margin is low or trending down, one can examine the individual expense items to identify and then correct the problem.

The right-hand side of Figure 4-3 lists the various categories of assets, totals them, and then divides sales by total assets to find the number of times Surrey "turns its assets over" each year. The company's total assets turnover ratio is 1.5 times.

The profit margin times the total assets turnover is called the *Du Pont equation*, and it gives the *rate of return on assets (ROA)*:

$$\text{ROA} = \text{Profit margin} \times \text{Total assets turnover}$$
$$= \frac{\text{Net income}}{\text{Sales}} \times \frac{\text{Sales}}{\text{Total assets}} \qquad (4\text{-}1)$$
$$= 3.3\% \times 1.5 = 5.0\%.$$

Surrey made 3.3 percent, or 3.3 cents, on each dollar of sales, and assets were "turned over" 1.5 times during the year, so the company earned a return of 5.0 percent on its assets.

If the company had used only equity, the rate of return on assets would have equalled the rate of return on equity. However, in the actual case, 69 percent of the firm's capital was supplied by creditors, and since the 5.0 percent return on total assets all goes to shareholders, who put up only 31 percent of the capital, the return on equity is higher than 5.0 percent.

Table 4-9
Summary of Financial Ratio Analysis

Ratio	Formula for Calculation	Value for Surrey	Industry Average	Evaluation
Liquidity				
Current	$\dfrac{\text{Current assets}}{\text{Current libilities}}$	4.6 times	1.8 times	Good, but should be investigated
Quick, or acid test	$\dfrac{\text{Current assets} - \text{Inventory}}{\text{Current liabilities}}$	2.7 times	0.8 times	Good, but should be investigated
Debt Management				
Debt	$\dfrac{\text{Total debt}}{\text{Total assets}}$	69 percent	68 percent	Satisfactory
Times interest earned (interest coverage)	$\dfrac{\text{Earnings before interest and taxes}}{\text{Interest charges}}$	2.4 times	2.4 times	Satisfactory
Fixed-charge coverage	$\dfrac{\text{Net income before taxes} + \text{Interest charges} + \text{Lease obligations}}{\text{Interest charges} + \text{Lease obligations}}$	2.0 times	2.0 times	Satisfactory
Cash flow coverage	$\dfrac{\text{Cash inflows}}{\text{Fixed charges} + \dfrac{\text{Preferred share dividends}}{(1 - T)} + \dfrac{\text{Debt repayment}}{(1 - T)}}$	1.3 times	n.a.	Poor
Asset Management				
Inventory turnover	$\dfrac{\text{Sales}}{\text{Inventory}}$	5.4 times	8.0 times	Poor
Days sales outstanding	$\dfrac{\text{Receivables}}{\text{Sales per day}}$	91 days	30 days	Poor
Fixed-assets turnover	$\dfrac{\text{Sales}}{\text{Fixed assets}}$	4.8 times	7.5 times	Poor
Total-assets turnover	$\dfrac{\text{Sales}}{\text{Total assets}}$	1.5 times	2.5 times	Poor

(continued)

Table 4-9 (*continued*)

Ratio	Formula for Calculation	Value for Surrey	Industry Average	Evaluation
Profitability				
Profit margin on sales	$\dfrac{\text{Net income after taxes}}{\text{Sales}}$	3.3 percent	1.2 percent	Good
Basic earnings power	$\dfrac{\text{Earnings before interest and taxes}}{\text{Total assets}}$	17.0 percent	13.0 percent	Good
Return on total assets	$\dfrac{\text{Net income after taxes}}{\text{Total assets}}$	5.0 percent	3.0 percent	Good
Return on common equity	$\dfrac{\text{Net income after taxes}}{\text{Net worth}}$	16.0 percent	9.2 percent	Good
Growth				
Sales	$\dfrac{\text{Ending value}}{\text{Beginning value}} = \text{FVIF}_{k,5}$	21.7 percent	17.0 percent	Satisfactory
Net income	$\dfrac{\text{Ending value}}{\text{Beginning value}} = \text{FVIF}_{k,5}$	16.5 percent	10.3 percent	Good
Earnings per share	$\dfrac{\text{Ending value}}{\text{Beginning value}} = \text{FVIF}_{k,5}$	16.4 percent	13.5 percent	Good
Dividends per share	$\dfrac{\text{Ending value}}{\text{Beginning value}} = \text{FVIF}_{k,5}$	17.2 percent	12.1 percent	Good
Valuation (1993)				
Price-to-earnings ratio	$\dfrac{\text{Price per share}}{\text{Earnings per share}}$	7.1 times	7.0 times	Satisfactory
Market-to-book ratio	$\dfrac{\text{Market value}}{\text{Book value}}$	1.1 times	0.9 times	Satisfactory

Figure 4-3
Modified Du Pont Chart Applied to
the Surrey Company (milions of dollars)

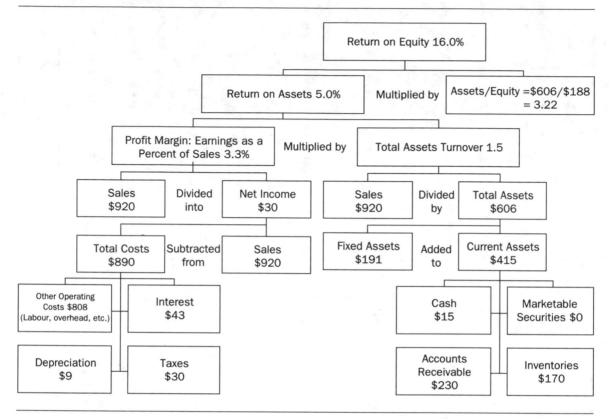

Specifically, the rate of return on assets (ROA) must be multiplied by the *equity multiplier*, which is the ratio of assets to common equity, to obtain the rate of *return on equity (ROE):*[16]

$$
\begin{aligned}
\text{ROE} \quad &= \text{ROA} \times \text{Equity multiplier} \\
&= \frac{\text{Net income}}{\text{Total assets}} \times \frac{\text{Total assets}}{\text{Common equity}} \qquad \textbf{(4-2)} \\
&= 5.0\% \times \frac{\$606}{\$188} \\
&= 5.0\% \times 3.22 \\
&= 16.0\%.
\end{aligned}
$$

We can combine Equations 4-1 and 4-2 to form the extended Du Pont equation:

---

[16]The equity multiplier can also be written as $\frac{1}{1-\text{D/A}}$, where D/A is the debt ratio. For convenience, we use the equation for the equity multiplier as given in Equation 4-2.

$$ROE = (\text{Profit margin})(\text{Total assets turnover})(\text{Equity multiplier})$$

$$= \frac{\text{Net income}}{\text{Sales}} \times \frac{\text{Sales}}{\text{Total assets}} \times \frac{\text{Total assets}}{\text{Common equity}} \qquad \text{(4-3)}$$

Thus, for Surrey, we have

$$ROE = (3.3\%)(1.5)(3.22)$$
$$= 16.0\%.$$

The 16.0 percent rate of return could, of course, be calculated directly: net income after taxes divided by common equity = \$30/\$188 = 16.0%. However, the Du Pont equation shows how the profit margin, the total assets turnover ratio, and the use of debt interact to determine the return on equity.[17]

Surrey can use the Du Pont system to analyze ways of improving the firm's performance. On the left, or "profit margin," side of its modified Du Pont chart, Surrey's marketing people can study the effects of raising sales prices (or lowering them to increase volume), of moving into new products or markets with higher margins, and so on. The company's cost accountants can study various expense items and, working with engineers, purchasing agents, and other operating personnel, seek ways of holding down costs. On the "turnover" side, Surrey's financial analysts, working with both production and marketing people, can investigate ways of minimizing investments in various types of assets. At the same time, the treasury staff can analyze the effects of alternative financing strategies, seeking to hold down interest expenses and the risks of debt while still using debt to increase the rate of return on equity.

Surrey does not have any liquidity problems; in fact, its level of liquidity may be higher than necessary. Liquid assets included in the liquidity ratios either do not earn any explicit rate of return (for example, inventories and accounts receivable) or earn a very low after-tax rate of return (for example, marketable securities). Surrey's large liquidity ratios indicate that, in the near term, the company is solvent, but this may be an error on the high side by management.

The debt ratio and the interest and fixed-charge coverage ratios all confirm that Surrey is adequately debt-financed without exposing the shareholders to unnecessary risk. Lease financing information is not provided at this point, but it should be recognized that this form of financing should be regarded as a substitute for debt financing because it generates a fixed claim on the earnings

---

[17]Another ratio that is frequently used is the following:

$$\text{Rate of return on investors' capital} = \frac{\text{Net income after taxes + Interest}}{\text{Debt + Equity}}.$$

The numerator shows the dollar returns to investors, the denominator shows the total amount of money investors have put up, and the ratio itself shows the rate of return on all investors' capital. This ratio is especially important in the public utility industries, where regulators are concerned about the companies' using their monopoly positions to earn excessive returns on investors' capital. In fact, regulators try to set utility prices (service rates) at levels that will force the return on investors' capital to equal a company's cost of capital as defined in Chapter 17.

of the firm. If lease obligations are considered, Surrey may be at its optimal capital structure.

The asset management ratios are Surrey's weakest point. As we have already cautioned, the comparisons with the industry may not be completely valid owing to the financing of fixed assets by lease contracts. Surrey should, however, consider rationalizing its fixed investments with a view to efficiency, as it appears that the firm is not making the best use of its buildings and equipment. This could also be a sign of the start of a growth phase, and the undercapacity may be only temporary. Investment occurs before returns, and in the long run this situation will improve if properly managed.

The profitability ratios all confirm that this is a basically healthy company. If the activity ratios suggest an underutilization of assets, the profitability ratios suggest that the firm has been able to make use of its large size across the country to spread fixed costs and to purchase goods in sufficient quantities to maintain a higher-than-average gross margin. Given the fact that the company has a level of financial risk similar to the industry as a whole, Surrey is earning a superior return.

Sales growth of Surrey is satisfactory in relation to the industry standard. Moreover, all of the profitability growth measures are strong and the valuation relationships are favourable. Additional perspective on the growth performance of Surrey is provided by trend analysis, which supplements the single measure provided by the growth percentage.

Industry-Specific Statistics

The above statistics are used in most industries, but there are statistics unique to specific industries. For instance, airlines use special activity ratios, such as passenger load factor and yield per revenue passenger mile. Retailers use sales per square metre to measure activity. Oil exploration and production companies use the finding cost per barrel (or cubic metre) and the lifting cost per barrel to measure the costs of finding and retrieving oil. Oil and gas exploration and production companies measure their inventory in millions of barrels of proven and probable reserves, as well as assigning a dollar value.

Concept Review

▶ Identify those ratios that are used to analyze a firm's liquidity, and write out their equations.
▶ Identify those ratios that are used to measure how effectively a firm is managing its assets, and write out their equations.
▶ Identify those ratios that are used to measure the extent to which a firm uses debt financing, and write out their equations.
▶ Identify those ratios that show the combined effects of liquidity, asset management, and debt management on operating results, and write out their equations.
▶ Identify those ratios that relate a firm's share price to its earnings and book value per share, and write out their equations.
▶ Explain how the modified Du Pont system combines ratios to reveal the basic determinants of ROE.

Sources of Comparative Ratios

The preceding analysis of Surrey pointed out the usefulness of *comparative ratio analysis*—comparing a company's financial ratios with those of other firms in its industry. Comparative ratios are available from a number of sources.

The industry averages used in Table 4-10 were obtained from The Financial Post investment databank of Toronto. This company provides its clients with an extensive database, access to a computer, and software packages to manipulate the data on approximately 500 Canadian publicly owned companies. The corporate database is derived from publicly available data.

Alternative sources of basic financial data and ratios are available. Dun and Bradstreet, Canada, Ltd. compiles financial ratios for a large number of industries. The publication is called *Key Business Ratios* and is derived from Revenue Canada data. Unfortunately, this taxation-based data source is not very current and the ratios may be dated. For example, the ratios presented in the 1990 Dun and Bradstreet report are based on 1987 tax statistics.

Statistics Canada gathers quarterly and annual data on all corporations in Canada. Balance sheet and income statement information is presented in aggregate form for all corporations as well as by industry sector and by size of firm. This data, however, is not very current. The TSE is now calculating and publishing book values for its composite index and all its subindexes and calculating price-to-book ratios for the indexes. The July 1990 composite price-to-book ratio was 1.37, down from 1.41 in 1989.

Instead of using the ratios as derived by the above-mentioned groups, the financial manager can derive the ratios from the basic firm data. This permits a definition of the industry that is satisfactory to the financial manager but differs from that used by the compilers of the financial ratios. This process of deriving ratios from basic data could be laborious and time-consuming were it not for the services of companies that provide access to financial information on a large number of companies through computer tapes.

External Use of Financial Ratios

We have analyzed a rather long list of ratios and indicated what each ratio is designed to measure. Sometimes it may be unnecessary to go beyond a few calculations to determine that a firm is in very good or very bad condition. Often, however, the analysis is equivalent to a detective-story investigation— what one ratio will not indicate, another may. Also, a relation vaguely suggested by one ratio may be corroborated by another. For these reasons, it is often useful to calculate a number of different ratios.

In certain situations, where the analyst's focus is narrow, a few ratios may tell the story. For example, a credit manager who has a great many invoices flowing across her desk each day may limit herself to three ratios as evidence of whether the prospective buyer of goods will pay promptly. She may use (1) either the current or the quick ratio to determine how burdened the prospective buyer is with current liabilities, (2) the debt ratio to determine how much of the prospective buyer's own funds are invested in the business, and (3) the profit margin to determine whether or not the firm has a favourable cost–price

Table 4-10
Financial Ratios by Industry, 1989

	Current Ratio	Cash Equivalent Ratio	Debt to Equity	Debt & Preferred to Equity	Sales to Total Assets	Collection Period	Inventory Turnover	Operating Income to Sales	Net Income to Sales	After-Tax Return on Capital	Return on Equity (Net)	Return on Equity (Cash Flow)
Communications	0.93	0.20	0.78	0.92	0.84	45.12	22.64	16.9	5.2	7.7	13.2	29.1
Consumer products	1.47	0.15	0.57	0.62	1.49	35.06	7.48	9.3	3.6	9.2	13.0	25.0
Electrical/ electronics	1.40	0.13	0.32	0.40	1.03	87.70	7.16	11.1	3.9	7.3	9.0	19.4
Gold and silver	2.48	1.42	0.20	0.22	0.32	32.62	9.79	29.9	11.4	4.6	6.0	16.3
Industrial products	1.62	0.18	0.66	0.78	0.97	61.04	5.68	13.8	4.6	7.7	11.4	23.9
Integrated mining	1.90	0.24	0.59	0.69	0.84	60.23	5.22	21.5	9.5	11.5	21.5	35.6
Merchandising industry	1.57	0.12	1.58	1.65	1.63	42.59	7.81	6.8	-2.1	-0.6	-21.4	26.7
Metal mining	2.77	1.91	0.38	0.50	0.23	72.13	8.07	15.9	22.0	6.9	8.6	9.1
Oil and gas production	1.49	0.46	0.53	0.63	0.33	66.61	22.58	38.8	7.3	4.1	4.5	23.9
Paper and forest products	1.69	0.12	0.79	0.86	0.92	45.17	6.71	15.3	5.3	7.4	12.8	28.8
Pipeline	1.0	0.50	1.47	1.62	0.48	41.20	36.77	27.8	8.1	7.0	11.0	35.9
Transportation	1.21	0.40	1.30	1.37	0.90	44.89	27.56	8.9	3.8	6.6	10.5	17.0
Utilities	0.89	0.04	1.65	1.80	0.50	64.49	15.96	28.7	5.7	5.0	9.3	29.2

Source: The Financial Post Investment database.

relationship. If the profit margin is high enough, this may justify the risk of dealing with a slow-paying customer since profitable companies are likely to grow and thus to become better customers in the future. However, if the profit margin is low in relation to other firms in the industry, the current ratio is low, and the debt ratio is high, a credit manager probably will not approve a sale involving an extension of credit.

Of necessity, the credit manager is more than a calculator and a reader of financial ratios. Qualitative factors may override quantitative analysis. For instance, oil companies, in selling to truckers, often find that the financial ratios are poor, and if they based their decisions solely on financial ratios, they would not make sales. Or, to take another example, a customer's profits may have been low for a period, but if that customer understands why and can remove the cause of the difficulty, a credit manager may be willing to approve a sale. The decision is also influenced by the seller's own profit margin. If the selling firm is making a large profit on sales, it is in a better position to take credit risks than if its own margin is low. Ultimately, the credit manager must judge a customer with regard to his or her character and management ability, and intelligent credit decisions must be based on careful consideration of conditions in the selling firm as well as in the buying firm. These points are discussed at length in Chapter 9, where we deal with credit policy.

Use of Financial Ratios in Security Analysis

We have emphasized the use of financial analysis by the financial manager and by outside credit analysts. However, ratio analysis is also useful in security valuation—the analysis of the investment merits of shares and bonds. When the emphasis is on security analysis, the principal focus is on judging the long-run profit potential of the firm. Profitability depends in large part on the efficiency with which the firm is run; since financial analysis provides insights into this factor, it is useful to the security analyst.[18]

In evaluating the risk of a bond, the analyst is interested in default risk; this risk includes not only the potential for bankruptcy, but also the chance that interest payments will be delayed. There are two agencies in Canada that assess this risk on bonds: the Canadian Bond Rating Service and the Dominion Bond Rating Service. Statistical techniques have been used to explain the ratings assigned by the rating services to the bonds of various companies. It has been determined that ratings are based on financial ratios that reflect the risk of the bonds and the profitability of the company. The ratios used include coverage, leverage, and return on investment. In an investigation of the bond ratings on long-term Canadian bonds, it was found that financial ratios were important in explaining the ratings. Of course, as in credit analysis, considerations other than the values of the financial ratios are important in determining a bond rating. In fact, the one variable found to be most important in determining the bond rating was the size of the issue. This result has been obtained in studies of both U.S. and Canadian ratings.

---

[18]A recent survey of 400 chartered financial analysts ranked ROE and P/E as the two most significant ratios, followed by EPS and net profit margin. See Charles Gibson, "How Chartered Financial Analysts View Financial Ratios," *Financial Analysts Journal*, May–June 1987.

Uses and Limitations of Ratio Analysis

Although ratio analysis can provide useful information concerning a company's operations and financial condition, it does have inherent problems and limitations that necessitate care and judgement. Some potential problems are listed here.

1. Many large firms operate a number of different divisions in quite different industries, and in such cases it is difficult to develop a meaningful set of industry averages for comparative purposes. This tends to make ratio analysis more useful for small, narrowly focussed firms than for large, multidivisional ones.

2. Most firms want to be better than average (although half will be above and half below the median), so merely attaining average performance is not necessarily good. For a target for high-level performance, it is best to look at the industry leaders' ratios.

3. Inflation has distorted firms' balance sheets—recorded values are often substantially different from "true" values. Further, since inflation affects both depreciation charges and inventory costs, profits are also affected. Thus, a ratio analysis for one firm over time, or a comparative analysis of firms of different ages, must be interpreted with care and judgement.

4. *Seasonal factors* can also distort ratio analysis. For example, the inventory turnover ratio for a food processor will be radically different if the balance sheet figure used for inventory is the one just before versus the one just after the close of the canning season. This problem can be minimized by using monthly averages for inventory (and receivables) when calculating ratios such as turnover.

5. Firms can employ *"window dressing"* techniques to make their financial statements look better to credit analysts. To illustrate, a Toronto builder borrowed on a 2-year basis on December 29, 1992, held the proceeds of the loan as cash for a few days, and then paid off the loan ahead of time on January 5, 1993. This improved his current and quick ratios and made his year-end 1992 balance sheet look good. However, the improvement was strictly window dressing; a week later the balance sheet was back at the old level.

6. Different operating and accounting practices can distort comparisons. For example, inventory valuation and depreciation methods can affect financial statements and thus distort comparisons among firms. Also, if one firm leases a substantial amount of its productive equipment, then its assets may appear low relative to sales, because leased assets may not appear on the balance sheet. At the same time, the lease liability may not be shown as a debt. Therefore, leasing can artificially improve both the turnover and the debt ratios. The accounting profession has recently reduced this problem, as we shall describe in Chapter 23.

7. It is difficult to generalize about whether a particular ratio is "good" or "bad." For example, a high current ratio may indicate a strong liquidity position, which is good, or excessive cash, which is bad (because excess cash in the bank is a nonearning asset). Similarly, a high fixed-assets

turnover ratio may denote either a firm that uses assets efficiently or one that is undercapitalized and simply cannot afford to buy enough assets.

8. A firm may have some ratios that look "good" and others that look "bad," making it difficult to tell whether the company is, on balance, in a strong or a weak position. However, statistical procedures can be used to analyze the *net effects* of a set of ratios. Many banks and other lending organizations use statistical procedures to analyze firms' financial ratios and, on the basis of their analyses, classify companies according to their probability of getting into financial distress.[19]

Concept Review

▶ What three groups use ratio analysis? What type of ratios does each group emphasize?

▶ List several potential problems with ratio analysis.

Summary

The primary purposes of this chapter were (1) to describe the basic financial statements and (2) to discuss techniques used by investors and managers to analyze them. The key concepts covered are listed below.

□ The four basic statements contained in the annual report are the **balance sheet**, the **income statement**, the **statement of retained earnings**, and the **statement of changes in financial position (statement of cash flows)**. Investors use the information contained in these statements to form expectations about the future levels of earnings and dividends, and about the riskiness of these expected values.

□ Financial statement analysis generally begins with **ratio analysis**: the calculation and examination of a set of financial ratios designed to reveal the relative strengths and weaknesses of a company compared to other companies in the same industry, and to show whether the firm's position has been improving or deteriorating over time.

□ **Liquidity ratios** show the relationship of a firm's current assets to its current obligations and thus indicate the firm's ability to meet its maturing debts.

□ **Asset management ratios** measure how effectively a firm is managing its assets.

□ **Debt management ratios** reveal (1) the extent to which the firm is financed with debt and (2) the firm's ability to meet its debt obligations.

□ **Profitability ratios** show the combined effects of liquidity, asset management, and debt management on operating results.

□ **Market value ratios** relate the firm's share price to its earnings and book value per share.

---

[19]The technique used is discriminant analysis. For a discussion, see Edward I. Altman, "Financial Ratios, Discriminant Analysis, and the Prediction of Corporate Bankruptcy," *Journal of Finance*, September 1968: 589–609; and Eugene F. Brigham and Louis C. Gapenski, *Intermediate Financial Management*, 3d ed. (Chicago: Dryden Press, 1990), chap. 20.

□ **Trend analysis** is important because it reveals whether the firm's ratios are improving or deteriorating over time.

□ The **Du Pont system** is designed to show how the profit margin on sales, the assets turnover ratio, and the use of debt interact to determine the rate of return on equity.

□ Ratio analysis has limitations, but used with care and judgement, it can be most helpful.

Questions

4-1   What four statements are contained in most annual reports?

4-2   Is it true that if a "typical" firm reports $20 million of retained earnings on its balance sheet, its directors could declare a $20 million cash dividend without any qualms whatsoever?

4-3   Financial ratio analysis is conducted by four groups of analysts: managers, equity investors, long-term creditors, and short-term creditors. What is the primary emphasis of each of these groups in evaluating ratios?

4-4   "A uniform system of accounts, including identical forms for balance sheets and income statements, would be a most reasonable requirement to impose on all publicly owned firms." Discuss this statement.

4-5   Profit margins and turnover ratios vary from one industry to another. What differences would you expect to find between a grocery chain such as Safeway and a steel company? Think particularly about the turnover ratios and the profit margin, and think about the Du Pont equation.

4-6   How does inflation distort ratio analysis comparisons, both for one company over time (trend analysis) and among different companies? Are only balance sheet items or both balance sheet and income statement items affected?

4-7   What factors would you, as a financial manager, want to examine if a firm's rate of return (a) on assets or (b) on equity were too low?

4-8   Suppose a firm used debt to leverage up its ROE, and in the process its EPS was also boosted. Would this necessarily lead to an increase in the price of the firm's shares? Assume the payout ratio remains constant.

4-9   How might (a) seasonal factors and (b) different growth rates distort a comparative ratio analysis? Give some examples. How might these problems be alleviated?

4-10   Indicate the effects of the transactions listed in the following table on total current assets, current ratio, and net profit. Use (+) to indicate an increase, (−) to indicate a decrease, and (0) to indicate either no effect or an indeterminate effect. Be prepared to state any necessary assumptions, and assume an initial current ratio of more than 1.0. (Note: A good accounting background is necessary to answer some of these questions; if yours is not strong, just answer the questions you can handle.)

	Total Current Assets	Current Ratio	Effect on Net Income
a. Cash is acquired through issuance of additional common shares.	+	+	0
b. Merchandise is sold for cash.	0	0	+
c. Corporate income tax due for the previous year is paid.	−	−	0
d. A fixed asset is sold for less than book value.	−	−	−
e. A fixed asset is sold for more than book value.	+	+	+
f. Merchandise is sold on credit.	0	0	+
g. Payment is made to trade creditors for previous purchases.	−	−	0
h. A cash dividend is declared and paid.	−	−	−
i. Cash is obtained through short-term bank loans.	+	0	0
j. Short-term notes receivable are sold at a discount.	+	+	0
k. Marketable securities are sold below cost.	−	−	0
l. Advances are made to employees.	−	0	−
m. Current operating expenses are paid.	−	−	0
n. Short-term promissory notes are issued to trade creditors for past due accounts payable.	0	0	0
o. Ten-year notes are issued to pay off accounts payable.	−	−	0
p. A fully depreciated asset is retired.	0	0	−
q. Accounts receivable are collected.	0	0	0
r. Equipment is purchased with short-term notes.	+	0	−
s. Merchandise is purchased on credit.	+	0	−
t. The estimated taxes payable are increased.	0	0	−

Self-Test Problems   (solutions appear on page 142)

ST-1   **Key terms.**   Define each of the following terms:

  a. Annual report; income statement; balance sheet
  b. Equity, or net worth; retained earnings
  c. Cash flow cycle
  d. Statement of retained earnings; statement of cash flows; statement of changes in financial position
  e. Depreciation; inventory valuation methods
  f. Liquidity ratios; current ratio; quick ratio, or acid test ratio
  g. Asset management ratios; inventory turnover ratio; days sales outstanding (DSO); fixed-assets turnover ratio; total-assets turnover ratio

h. Financial leverage; debt ratio; times-interest-earned (TIE) ratio; fixed-charge coverage ratio; cash flow coverage ratio

i. Profitability ratios; profit margin on sales; basic earnings power ratio; return on total assets (ROA); return on common equity (ROE)

j. Market value ratios; price-to-earnings (P/E) ratio; market-to-book ratio; dividend payout ratio; book value per share

k. Trend analysis; comparative ratio analysis

l. Du Pont chart; Du Pont equation

m. "Window dressing"; seasonal effects on ratios

ST-2 Debt ratio.   A.L. Kaiser & Co. Ltd. had earnings per share of $4 last year, and it paid a $2 dividend. Book value per share at year-end was $40, while total retained earnings increased by $12 million during the year. Kaiser has no preferred shares, and no new common shares were issued during the year. If Kaiser's year-end debt (which equals its total liabilities) was $120 million, what was the company's year-end debt ratio?

ST-3 Ratio analysis.   The following data apply to A.L. Kaiser & Company Ltd. (millions of dollars):

Cash and marketable securities	$100.00
Fixed assets	$283.50
Sales	$1 000.00
Net income	$50.00
Quick ratio	2.0 ×
Current ratio	3.0 ×
DSO	40 days
ROE	12%

Kaiser has no preferred stock—only common equity, current liabilities, and long-term debt.

a. Find Kaiser's
   i. Accounts receivable.
   ii. Current liabilities.
   iii. Current assets.
   iv. Total assets.
   v. ROA.
   vi. Common equity.
   vii. Long-term debt.

b. In Part a, you should have found Kaiser's accounts receivable = $109.6 million. If Kaiser could reduce its DSO from 40 days to 30 days while holding other things constant, how much cash would it generate? If this cash were used to buy back common shares (at book value) and thus reduced the amount of common equity, how would this affect
   i. The ROE?
   ii. The ROA?
   iii. The total debt ratio?

Problems

4-1   Ratio calculation.   Assume you are given the following relationships for The Berry Corporation:

Sales total assets	1.5 ×
Return on assets (ROA)	3%
Return on equity (ROE)	5%

Calculate Berry's profit margin and debt ratio.

 4-2   Ratio analysis.   Data for Cordell Computer Company and its industry averages follow.

Cordell Computer Company:
Balance Sheet as of December 31, 1993

Cash	$ 77 500	Accounts payable	$ 129 000
Receivables	336 000	Notes payable	84 000
Inventory	241 500	Other current liabilities	117 000
Total current assets	$ 655 000	Total current liabilities	$ 330 000
Net fixed assets	292 500	Long-term debt	256 500
		Common equity	361 000
Total assets	$ 947 500	Total liabilities and equity	$ 947 500

Cordell Computer Company:
Income Statement for Year Ended December 31, 1993

Sales		$1 607 500
Cost of goods sold		
Materials	$717 000	
Labour	453 000	
Heat, light, and hydro	68 000	
Indirect labour	113 000	
Depreciation	41 500	1 392 500
Gross Profit		$ 215 000
Selling expenses		115 000
General and administrative expenses		30 000
Earnings before interest and taxes		$ 70 000
Interest expense		24 500
Net income before taxes		45 500
Corporate income taxes (40%)		18 200
Net income		$ 27 300

(continued)

Cordell Computer Company *(continued)*

Ratio	Cordell	Industry Average
Current assets/current liabilities	_____	2.0 ×
Days sales outstanding	_____	35 days
Sales/inventories	_____	6.7 ×
Sales/total assets	_____	3 ×
Net income/sales	_____	1.2%
Net income/total assets	_____	3.6%
Net income/equity	_____	9%
Total debt/total assets	_____	60.0%

   a. Calculate the indicated ratios for Cordell.

   b. Construct the Du Pont equation for both Cordell and the industry.

   c. Outline Cordell's strengths and weaknesses as revealed by your analysis.

   d. Suppose Cordell had doubled its sales as well as its inventories, accounts receivable, and common equity during 1993. How would that information affect the validity of your ratio analysis? (Hint: Think about averages and the effects of rapid growth on ratios if averages are not used. No calculations are needed.)

4-3   **Liquidity ratios.**   The Porter Company Ltd. has $1 312 500 in current assets and $525 000 in current liabilities. Its initial inventory level is $375 000, and it will raise funds as additional notes payable and use them to increase inventory. How much can Porter's short-term debt (notes payable) increase without violating a current ratio of 2 to 1? What will be the firm's quick ratio after Porter has raised the maximum amount of short-term funds?

4-4   **Ratio calculations.**   The Watson Company had a quick ratio of 1.4, a current ratio of 3.0, and inventory turnover of 6 times, total current assets of $810 000, and cash and marketable securities of $120 000 in 1992. What were Watson's annual sales and its DSO for that year?

4-5   **Balance sheet analysis.**   Complete the balance sheet and sales information in the table that follows for Besley Industries using the following financial data:

Debt ratio	50%
Quick ratio	0.80 ×
Total assets turnover	1.5 ×
Days sales outstanding	36 days
Gross profit margin	25%
Inventory turnover ratio	5 ×

Balance Sheet

Cash	_____	Accounts payable	_____
Accounts receivable	_____	Long-term debt	60 000
Inventories	_____	Common equity	_____
Fixed assets	_____	Retained earnings	97 500
Total assets	$300 000	Total liabilities and equity	_____
Sales	_____	Cost of goods sold	_____

4-6 **Du Pont analysis.**   The Niendorf Furniture Company, a manufacturer and wholesaler of high-quality home furnishings, has been experiencing low profitability in recent years. As a result, the board of directors has replaced the president of the firm with a new president, Ronald Clay, who has asked you to make an analysis of the firm's financial position using the Du Pont system. The most recent industry average ratios and Niendorf's financial statements are as follows:

Industry Average Ratios

Current ratio	2 ×	Sales/fixed assets	6 ×
Debt/total assets	30%	Sales/total assets	3 ×
Times-interest-earned	7 ×	Net profit on sales	3%
Sales/Inventory	10 ×	Return on total assets	9%
Days sales outstanding	24 days	Return on common equity	12.9%

a. Calculate those ratios that you think would be useful in this analysis.

b. Construct an extended Du Pont equation for Niendorf, and compare the company's ratios to the composite ratios for the industry as a whole.

c. Do the balance sheet accounts or the income statement figures seem to be primarily responsible for the low profits?

d. Which specific accounts seem to be most out of line in relation to other firms in the industry?

e. If Niendorf had a pronounced seasonal sales pattern or if it grew rapidly during the year, how might that affect the validity of your ratio analysis? How might you correct the analysis for such potential problems?

Niendorf Furniture Company:
Balance Sheet as of December 31, 1993
(millions of dollars)

Cash	$ 45	Accounts payable	$ 45
Marketable securities	33	Notes payable	45
Net receivables	66	Other current liabilities	21
Inventories	159	Total current liabilities	$111
Total current assets	$303	Long-term debt	24
		Total liabilities	$135
Gross fixed assets	225		
Less depreciation	78	Common equity	114
Net fixed assets	$147	Retained earnings	201
		Total stockholders' equity	$315
Total assets	$450	Total liabilities and equity	$450

Niendorf Furniture Company:
Income Statement for Year Ended December 31, 1993
(millions of dollars)

Net sales	$795.0
Cost of goods sold	660.0
Gross profit	$135.0
Selling expenses	73.5
Depreciation expense	12.0
Interest expense	4.5
Total expenses	$ 90.0
Net income before tax	45.0
Taxes (40%)	18.0
Net income	$ 27.0

4-7   **Statement of cash flows.** The consolidated balance sheets for the Clouse Lumber Company at the beginning and end of 1993 follow. The company bought $50 million worth of fixed assets. The charge for depreciation in 1993 was $10 million. Earnings after taxes were $33 million, and the company paid out $5 million in dividends.

Clouse Lumber Company:
Balance Sheets at Beginning and End of 1993
(millions of dollars)

			Change	
	Jan. 1	Dec. 31	Source	Use
Cash	$ 7	$ 15	____	8
Marketable securities	0	11	____	11

(continued)

Clouse Lumber Company *(continued)*

	Jan. 1	Dec. 31	Change Source	Use
Net receivables	30	22		
Inventories	53	75		
Total current assets	$ 90	$123		
Gross fixed assets	75	125		
Less accumulated depreciation	25	35		
Net fixed assets	$ 50	$ 90		
Total assets	$140	$213		
Accounts payable	$ 18	$ 15		
Notes payable	3	15		
Other current liabilities	15	7		
Long-term debt	8	24		
Common equity	29	57		
Retained earnings	67	95		
Total liabilities and equity	$140	$213		

Note: Total sources must equal total uses.

a. Fill in the amount of source or use in the appropriate column.
b. Prepare a statement of changes in financial position.
c. Briefly summarize your findings.

4-8   Du Pont analysis.   The Nelson Electronic Corporation's (NEC) balance sheets for 1993 and 1992 are as follows (in millions of dollars):

	1993	1992
Cash	$ 21	$ 45
Marketable securities	0	33
Receivables	90	66
Inventories	225	159
Total current assets	$336	$303
Gross fixed assets	450	225
Less accumulated depreciation	123	78
Net fixed assets	$327	$147
Total assets	$663	$450
Accounts payable	$ 54	$ 45
Notes payable	9	45
Accruals	45	21
Total current liabilities	$108	$111
Long-term debt	78	24
Common equity	192	114
Retained earnings	285	201
Total long-term capital	$555	$339
Total liabilities and equity	$663	$450

Additionally, Nelson's 1993 income statement is as follows (in millions of dollars):

Sales	$1 365
Cost of goods sold	888
General expenses	300
EBIT	$ 177
Interest	10
EBT	$ 167
Taxes (40%)	67
Net income	$ 100

a. What was Nelson's dividend payout ratio in 1993?

b. The following extended Du Pont equation is the industry average for 1993:

$$\text{Profit margin} \times \text{Total assets turnover} \times \text{Equity multiplier} = \text{ROE}$$
$$6.52\% \times 1.82 \times 1.77 = 21.00\%.$$

Construct Nelson's 1993 extended Du Pont equation. What does the Du Pont analysis indicate about NEC's expense control, asset utilization, and debt utilization? What is the industry's debt-to-assets ratio?

c. Construct Nelson's 1993 statement of changes in financial position. What does it suggest about the company's operations?

4-9   Ratio trend analysis. The Tanner Corporation's forecasted 1993 financial statements follow, along with some industry average ratios.

Tanner Corporation:
Pro Forma Balance Sheet as of December 31, 1994

	1994
Cash	$ 72 000
Accounts receivable	439 000
Inventory	894 000
Total current assets	$1 405 000
Land and building	238 000
Machinery	132 000
Other fixed assets	61 000
Total assets	$1 836 000
Accounts and notes payable	$ 432 000
Accruals	170 000
Total current liabilities	$ 602 000
Long-term debt	404 290
Common equity	575 000
Retained earnings	254 710
Total liabilities and equity	$1 836 000

Tanner Corporation:
Pro Forma Income Statement for 1994

	1994
Sales	$4 290 000
Cost of goods sold	3 580 000
Gross operating profit	$ 710 000
General administrative and selling expenses	236 320
Depreciation	159 000
Miscellaneous	134 000
Taxable income	$ 180 680
Taxes (40%)	72 272
Net income	$ 108 408
Number of shares outstanding	23 000

Per-Share Data

EPS	$4.71
Cash dividends	$0.95
P/E ratio	5 ×
Market price (average)	$23.57

Industry Financial Ratios (1994)[a]

Quick ratio	1.0 ×
Current ratio	2.7 ×
Inventory turnover[b]	7.0 ×
Days sales outstanding	32 days
Fixed-assets turnover[b]	13.0 ×
Total assets turnover[b]	2.6 ×
Return on total assets	9.1%
Return on equity	18.2%
Debt ratio	50.0%
Profit margin on sales	3.5%
P/E ratio	6.0 ×

[a]Industry average ratios have been constant for the past four years.
[b]Based on year-end balance sheet figures.

a. Calculate Tanner's 1994 forecasted ratios, compare them with the industry average data, and comment briefly on Tanner's projected strengths and weaknesses.

b. What do you think would happen to Tanner's ratios if the company initiated cost-cutting measures that allowed it to hold lower levels of inventory and substantially decreased the cost of goods sold? No calculations are necessary. Think about which ratios would be affected by changes in these two accounts.

Integrative Problem

4-10   **Financial statement analysis.** Assume that you were recently hired as a financial analyst by Mainframe Industries, a manufacturer of computer components. Your first task is to conduct a financial statement analysis of the firm covering the last two years. Your boss has supplied you with the following financial data:

	1992	1993
Balance Sheets		
Cash	$ 69 120	$ 62 400
Accounts receivable	421 440	482 400
Inventory	858 240	1 003 200
Total current assets	$1 348 800	$1 548 000
Gross fixed assets	$ 589 200	$ 632 400
Less: Accumulated depreciation	175 440	199 440
Net fixed assets	$ 413 760	$ 432 960
Total assets	$1 762 560	$1 980 960
Accounts payable	$ 174 720	$ 210 240
Notes payable	240 000	270 000
Accruals	163 200	168 000
Total current liabilities	$ 577 920	$ 648 240
Long-term debt	$ 388 118	$ 509 534
Common equity	$ 552 000	$ 552 000
Retained earnings	244 522	271 186
Total equity	$ 796 522	$ 823 186
Total liabilities and equity	$1 762 560	$1 980 960
Income Statements		
Sales	$4 118 400	$4 620 000
Cost of goods sold	3 436 800	3 900 000
Other expenses	408 000	516 360
Depreciation	22 680	24 000
EBIT	$ 250 920	$ 179 640
Interest expense	75 000	91 200
EBT	$ 175 920	$ 88 440
Taxes (40%)	70 368	35 376
Net income	$ 105 552	$ 53 064
Other Data		
December 31 share price	$ 8.50	$ 6.00
Number of shares	120 000	120 000
Dividends per share	$ 0.22	$ 0.22
Lease payments	$ 48 000	$ 48 000

You were also given the following industry average data for 1993.

Ratio	Industry Average
Current	2.7 ×
Quick	1.0 ×
Inventory turnover	7.0 ×
Days sales outstanding (DSO)	32.0 days
Fixed-assets turnover	10.7 ×
Total assets turnover	2.6 ×
Debt	50.0%
TIE	2.5 ×
Fixed-charge coverage	2.1 ×
Profit margin	3.5%
Basic earning power	19.1%
ROA	9.1%
ROE	18.2%
P/E	14.2 ×
Market-to-book	1.4 ×

You were asked to structure your analysis by performing a set of tasks and then answering the following questions:

a. Use Mainframe's 1993 income statement and balance sheets to develop a statement of changes in financial position. (If it is done properly, the bottom line—net cash flow—should equal —$6720, the change in the cash account from 1992 to 1993.) Explain this statement.

b. Define liquidity within a financial statement analysis context. What are Mainframe's current and quick ratios? Assess Mainframe's liquidity position.

c. What are Mainframe's inventory turnover, days sales outstanding, fixed-assets turnover, and total assets turnover ratios? How does the firm's asset utilization stack up against that of the industry?

d. What are the firm's debt, times-interest-earned, and fixed-charge coverage ratios? How does Mainframe compare with the industry with respect to financial leverage? What conclusions can you draw?

e. Calculate and interpret the firm's profitability ratios—that is, profit margin, basic earning power, return on assets (ROA), and return on equity (ROE).

f. Analyze and discuss Mainframe's market value ratios—that is, its price-to-earnings ratio and market-to-book ratio.

g. Use the extended Du Pont equation (ROE = Profit margin × Total assets turnover × Equity multiplier) to obtain an overview of Mainframe's financial condition, and then discuss the firm's strengths and weaknesses.

h. Although financial statement analysis can provide useful information about a company's operations and financial condition, it does have some inherent problems and limitations that necessitate using care and judgement. Discuss these problems and limitations.

Solutions to Self-Test Problems

ST-1   Refer to the appropriate sections of the text to check your responses.

ST-2   Kaiser paid $2 in dividends and retained $2 per share. Since total retained earnings rose by $12 million, there must be 6 million shares outstanding. With a book value of $40 per share, total common equity must be $40(6 million) = $240 million. Since Kaiser has $120 million of debt, its debt ratio must be 33.3 percent:

$$\frac{\text{Debt}}{\text{Assets}} = \frac{\text{Debt}}{\text{Debt} + \text{Equity}} = \frac{\$120 \text{ million}}{\$120 \text{ million} + \$240 \text{ million}}$$

ST-3   **a.** In answering questions such as this, always begin by writing down the relevant definitional equations, then start filling in numbers.

   i.
$$\text{DSO} = \frac{\text{Accounts receivable}}{\text{Sales}/365}$$

$$40 = \frac{\text{A/R}}{\$1000/365}.$$

$$\text{A/R} = 40(\$2.740) = \$109.6 \text{ million}.$$

   ii.   Quick ratio
$$= \frac{\text{Current assets} - \text{Inventories}}{\text{Current liabilities}} = 2.0$$

$$= \frac{\text{Cash and marketable securities} + \text{A/R}}{\text{Current liabilities}} = 2.0.$$

$$2.0 = \frac{\$100 + \$109.6}{\text{Current liabilities}}$$

Current liabilities = ($100 + $109.6)/2 = $104.8 million.

   iii.
$$\text{Current ratio} = \frac{\text{Current assets}}{\text{Current liabilities}} = 3.0$$

$$= \frac{\text{Current assets}}{\$104.8} = 3.0.$$

Current assets = 3.0($104.8) = $314.4 million.

   iv.
$$\text{Total assets} = \text{Current assets} + \text{Fixed assets}$$
$$= \$314.4 + \$283.5 = \$597.9 \text{ million}.$$

   v.
$$\text{ROA} = \text{Profit margin} \times \text{Total assets utilization}$$

$$= \frac{\text{Net income}}{\text{Sales}} \times \frac{\text{Sales}}{\text{Total assets}}$$

$$= \frac{\$50}{\$1000} \times \frac{\$1000}{\$597.9}$$

$$= 0.05 \times 1.673 = 0.0836 = 8.36\%.$$

vi.
$$\text{ROE} = \text{ROA} \times \frac{\text{Assets}}{\text{Equity}}.$$

$$12.0\% = 8.36\% \times \frac{\$597.9}{\text{Equity}}.$$

$$\text{Equity} = \frac{(8.36\%)(\$597.9)}{12.0\%}$$

$$= \$416.5 \text{ million.}$$

vii.
$$\text{Total assets} = \text{Total claims} = \$597.9 \text{ million}$$
$$\text{Current liabilities} + \text{Long-term debt} + \text{Equity} = \$597.9 \text{ million}$$
$$\$597.9 + \text{Long-term debt} + \$416.5 = \$597.9 \text{ million}$$
$$\text{Long-term debt} = \$597.9 - \$104.8 - \$416.5 = \$76.6 \text{ million.}$$

Note: We could have found equity as follows:

$$\text{ROE} = \frac{\text{Net income}}{\text{Equity}}$$

$$12.0\% = \frac{\$50}{\text{Equity}}$$

$$\text{Equity} = \frac{\$50}{0.12}$$

$$= \$416.67 \text{ million (rounding error difference).}$$

Then we could have gone on to find current liabilities and long-term debt.

b. Kaiser's average sales per day were $\$1000/365 = \$2.739\,726$ million. Its DSO was 40, so $A/R = 40(\$2.739\,726) = \$109\,589\,041$. Its new DSO of 30 would cause $A/R = 30(\$2.739\,726) = \$82\,191\,781$. The reduction in receivables would be $\$109\,589\,041 - \$82\,191\,781 = \$27\,397\,260$, which would equal the amount of cash generated.

i.
$$\text{New equity} = \text{Old equity} - \text{Shares repurchased}$$
$$= \$416\,500\,000 - \$27\,397\,260$$
$$= \$389\,102\,740.$$

Thus,

$$\text{New ROE} = \frac{\text{Net income}}{\text{New equity}}$$

$$= \frac{\$50\,000\,000}{\$389\,102\,740}$$

$$= 12.85\% \text{ (versus old ROE of 12.0\%).}$$

ii.
$$\text{New ROA} = \frac{\text{Net income}}{\text{Total assets} - \text{Reduction in A/R}}$$

$$= \frac{\$50\,000\,000}{\$597\,888\,562 - \$27\,397\,260}$$

$$= 8.76\% \text{ (versus old ROA of 8.36\%).}$$

iii. The old debt is the same as the new debt:

$$\text{Debt} = \text{Total claims} - \text{Equity}$$
$$= \$597.9 - \$416.5 = \$181.4 \text{ million.}$$
$$\text{Old total assets} = \$597.9 \text{ million.}$$

$$\text{New total assets} = \text{Old total assets} - \text{Reduction in A/R}$$
$$= \$597.9 - \$27.4$$
$$= \$570.5 \text{ million.}$$

Therefore,

$$\frac{\text{Debt}}{\text{Old total assets}} = \frac{\$181.4}{\$597.9} = 30/3\%,$$

while

$$\frac{\text{New debt}}{\text{New total assets}} = \frac{\$181.4}{\$570.5} = 31.8\%.$$

5

▲▲

Financial Forecasting

A MANAGERIAL PERSPECTIVE

Financial forecasting is critical to both firms and investors. Consider the example of Campeau Corporation's acquisition of Federated Department Stores through a leveraged buyout (LBO). The interesting aspect of this transaction is that the acquisition of Federated's equity in the takeover was 97 percent financed by debt! In this LBO, as in most highly debt-financed transactions, a forecast of future cash flows was made, and then the amount of debt the company could carry was based on this forecast. Note that in this LBO, as in most, management planned to sell some of the company's assets and to use the proceeds from these asset sales to meet required principal payments as the debt matured. In fact, Campeau management sold off nine divisions that in aggregate amounted to approximately 50 percent of the assets at book value for approximately 90 percent of the pretransaction market value of Federated Department Stores. These transactions occurred within two years of the acquisition.

In an LBO, the acquiring company's management typically has two goals: (1) to borrow as much as possible so as to limit the amount of equity that must be put up, but (2) not to borrow so much that interest and maturity payments cannot be met from operating income plus the proceeds from planned asset sales. This whole approach to setting the capital structure is obviously risky, and the smaller the safety margins in the operating cash flows needed to service the debt, the riskier the operation. Further, the accuracy of the forecasts is clearly crucial—if the forecasts of operating income and asset sale proceeds are too high, then the company will be unable to service its debt, and it will be forced into bankruptcy.

The onset of the recession in 1990 had two important impacts on Campeau's cash flows. First, the operating cash flows from the remaining operating entities in Federated Stores were diminished. Second, with this reduced cash flow, the value obtained in any subsequent asset sales would be reduced as well. In fact, it became harder to sell the assets. This combination of effects led to the bankruptcy of Campeau and its rebirth in a reorganized entity called Camdev under new ownership and management. The reason for the failure of this takeover has been attributed to a number of factors, including paying too high a price for Federated and using too much debt to finance the acquisition.

Firms need assets to make sales, and if sales are to grow, assets must also increase. Growing firms require new investments; these include an immediate investment in current assets and, as full capacity is reached, investment in fixed assets. New investments must be financed, and new financing carries with it commitments and obligations to service the capital obtained.[1] Although some of the required capital can be obtained from retained earnings, if the growth rate is high, even a very profitable firm will need external capital.

This planning process is an integral part of the financial manager's job. As we shall see in subsequent chapters, long-term debt and equity funds are raised infrequently and in large amounts, primarily because of the fixed cost involved in selling securities. Thus, it is necessary for the firm to estimate its needs for funds for the next few years if it is to properly time its long-term security offerings. Also, because both managers and investors are concerned with *future* cash flows, financial managers should consider how alternative growth and financing actions will affect the firm's cash flows. To project cash flows, one needs projected financial statements. Therefore, in this chapter we discuss briefly how projected financial statements are constructed, after which we show how they are used to help estimate the need for different types of capital.

Sales Forecasts

The starting point for estimating cash requirements is a **forecast of sales**, an estimate of the firm's sales, in units and in dollars, for some specified future period. The sales forecast generally starts with a review of sales over the past 5 to 10 years, expressed in a graph like the one in Figure 5-1. The first part of the graph shows the actual sales for Interfaces Ltd. for the period of 1982 to 1992. Interfaces is a manufacturer of computer and telecommunications equipment with sales in both Canada and the United States.

During the 10-year period, Interfaces' sales grew from $175 million to $500 million, which represents a compound growth rate of 11.1 percent. However, the growth rate has accelerated sharply in recent years. This growth spurt has resulted primarily from changes in the telecommunications market in both Canada and the United States. The U.S. changes have forced the major telephone companies to buy products from companies such as Interfaces. Also, Interfaces' research and development program has been especially successful lately, so when the telecommunications/computer market opened the company was ready.

On the basis of the recent trend in sales, of new product innovations, and of a forecast by its economic staff that both economies will be quite strong during the coming year, Interfaces's planning group projects a 50 percent growth rate during 1993.

Of course, a great deal of work lies behind all good sales forecasts. A good planner looks at three areas of analysis: external, internal, and trends. Every company functions in a specific economic and competitive environment; an *external analysis* must be undertaken. Then, the company can draw on *internal sources*, such as what their own sales force says about customer requests, what prospects for sales there are, and so forth. *Trend analysis*, projecting growth

---

[1]"Servicing" capital refers to the payment of interest and principal on debt and of dividends on common and preferred shares.

Figure 5-1
Sales Forecast for Interfaces Ltd.

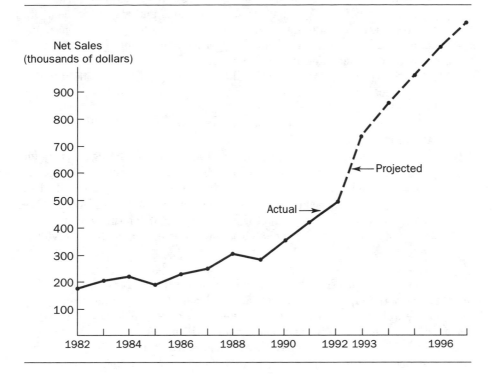

continuing at the same rate as in the past, may also be useful. However, the assumption that sales will continue to grow as they have in the past may not always be wise and may lead to unrealistic projections.

Specifically, Interfaces does the following:

1. To begin, Interfaces' sales are divided into three major product groups: (a) sales to telephone companies of equipment used in telephone networks; (b) sales of equipment such as PBXs used by hotels, motels, and businesses to route calls among rooms; and (c) sales of electronic components to computer manufacturers. Sales in each of these areas during the past 10 years are plotted, the trends are observed, and a "first approximation forecast," assuming a continuation of past trends, is made.

2. Next, the level of business activity for each of the company's market areas is forecasted—for example, what will be the level of hotel, motel, and office building construction in 1993? These forecasts are used as a basis for modifying the demand forecasts in each of Interfaces' business areas.

3. Interfaces' planning group next looks at the firm's probable shares of each major market. Consideration is given to such factors as the company's capacity, its competitors' capacity, and new products or product improvements that either Interfaces or its competitors may plan. Pricing strategies are also considered—for example, does the company

have plans to raise prices to boost profit margins, or to lower prices to increase market share and thus cut production costs as a result of gaining economies of scale? Such actions can greatly affect sales forecasts. In addition, since Interfaces has some export sales and also faces competition from Japanese and European firms in its Canadian and U.S. markets, changes in exchange rates and the value of the dollar can have an important influence on its market share.

4. Advertising campaigns, promotional discounts, credit terms, and the like also affect sales, so probable developments in these areas are also factored in.

5. Order backlogs and recent trends in new orders (or cancellations) are taken into account.

6. Forecasts are made for each product group, both in the aggregate (for example, sales to telephone companies) and on an individual product basis. The individual product sales forecasts are summed and then compared with the aggregate product group forecasts. Differences are reconciled, and the end product is a sales forecast for the company as a whole but with breakdowns by major divisions and for individual products.

If the sales forecast is off, the consequences can be serious. First, if the market expands *more* than Interfaces expects and has geared up for, then the company will not be able to meet its customers' needs. Orders will back up, delivery times will lengthen, repairs and installations will be harder to schedule, and customer dissatisfaction will increase. Customers will end up going elsewhere, and Interfaces will lose market share and will miss a major opportunity. On the other hand, if its projections are overly optimistic, Interfaces will end up with too much plant, equipment, and inventories. This will mean low turnover ratios, high costs and, possibly, writeoffs of obsolete inventory and equipment. All of this will result in a low rate of return on equity, which in turn will depress the company's share price. If Interfaces has financed the expansion with debt, its problems will, of course, be compounded. Thus, an accurate sales forecast is critical to the firm's long-run success.[2]

Concept Review

▶ What is normally the first step in a sales forecast?
▶ List additional items that are considered when developing the sales forecast.
▶ Briefly explain why sales forecasts are critical to the well-being of the firm.

---

[2] A sales forecast is actually the *expected value of a probability distribution* of possible levels of sales. Because any sales forecast is subject to a greater or lesser degree of uncertainty, for financial planning we are often just as interested in the degree of uncertainty inherent in the sales forecast (σ of sales) as we are in the expected value of sales.

Forecasting Financial Requirements

Several methods are used to develop **pro forma**, or forecasted, **financial statements**. In this chapter we focus on the *percentage-of-sales* and *regression methods*. We explain when each of the methods can and cannot be used. We also discuss the growing use of computerized models for forecasting financial statements.

Percentage-of-Sales Method

The simplest approach to forecasting financial requirements is the **percentage-of-sales method**. Two assumptions are necessary for this method to be effective: (1) most balance sheet accounts are related to sales, and (2) current levels of all assets are optimal for current levels of sales. For example, if there is unused plant capacity, sales can increase substantially before fixed assets need to be expanded, and there will not be a direct relationship between assets and sales. The method begins by expressing the balance sheet items as percentages of the firm's annual sales. As an example, consider again Interfaces Ltd., whose balance sheet and summary income statement as of December 31, 1992 are shown in Table 5-1. Interfaces operated its fixed assets at full capacity in 1992 to support its $500 million of sales, and it had no unnecessary current assets. Its profit margin on sales was 4 percent, and it paid out 50 percent of its net income to shareholders as dividends. If Interfaces' sales increase to $750 million in 1993, what will be its pro forma December 31, 1993 balance sheet? How much additional financing will the company require

Table 5-1
Interfaces Ltd.
Balance Sheet and Summary Income Statement
(millions of dollars)

I. Balance Sheet, December 31, 1992

Assets		Liabilities	
Cash	$ 10	Accounts payable	$ 50
Receivables	85	Accrued taxes and wages	25
Inventories	100	Mortgage bonds	70
Fixed assets (net)	150	Common equity	100
		Retained earnings	100
		Total liabilities	
Total assets	$345	and net worth	$345

II. Summary Income Statement, 1992

Sales	$500
Net income	20
Dividends	10

during 1993 to support the increased volume of sales? The percentage-of-sales method of calculating this figure is explained below.[3]

The first step in the percentage-of-sales forecast is to identify those balance sheet items that can be expected to vary directly with sales. Since Interfaces has been operating at full capacity, each asset item must increase if the higher level of sales is to be attained: more cash for transactions, more receivables, higher inventory levels, and additional fixed plant capacity.[4]

If Interfaces' assets are to increase, its liabilities and equity must likewise rise—the balance sheet must balance. Therefore, any increase in assets must be financed in some manner. **Spontaneously generated funds** will come from such sources as accounts payable and accruals, which rise spontaneously with sales; as sales increase, so will Interfaces' own purchases, and larger purchases will automatically result in higher levels of accounts payable. Thus, if sales double, accounts payable will also double. Similarly, a higher level of operations will require more labour, so accrued wages will increase, and assuming profit margins are maintained, an increase in profits will pull up accrued taxes. Retained earnings will also increase, but not in direct proportion to the increase in sales. Neither notes payable, mortgage bonds, nor common shares will rise spontaneously with sales; higher sales do not *automatically* trigger increases in these items.

We can construct a pro forma balance sheet for December 31, 1993 by proceeding as outlined in the following paragraphs.

Step 1. We start with Table 5-2, column 1, and divide each balance sheet item that varies directly with sales by sales to obtain the item's percentage of 1992 sales (column 2). An item such as notes payable that does not automatically vary with sales is designated "not applicable."

Step 2. We multiply these percentages (their fractions, really) by the $750 million projected 1993 sales to obtain the projected amounts as of December 31, 1993. These are shown in column 3 of Table 5-2.

Step 3. To obtain column 4, we simply insert figures for mortgage bonds and common equity from the December 31, 1992 balance sheet. At least one of these accounts will have to be changed later in the analysis.

Step 4. Also in column 4, we add the estimated addition to retained earnings for 1993 to the December 31, 1992 balance sheet figure for retained earnings to obtain the December 31, 1993 projected retained earnings. Recall that Interfaces expects to earn 4 percent on 1993 sales of $750 million, or $30 million, and to pay 50 percent of this out in dividends to shareholders. Thus, the **dividend payout ratio**—the percentage of earnings paid out in dividends—is 50 percent, and

---

[3]We recognize, of course, that as a practical matter, business firms plan their needs in terms of specific items of equipment, square metres of floor space, and other factors, and not as a percentage of sales. However, the outside analyst does not have access to this information; the manager, even though he or she has the information on specific items, needs to check forecasts in aggregate terms. The percentage-of-sales method serves both these needs surprisingly well.

[4]Some assets, such as marketable securities, are not tied directly to operations and hence do not vary directly with sales. Also, as we shall see later in the chapter, if some assets are not being fully utilized, sales can increase without increasing those assets.

Table 5-2
Interfaces Ltd.
Balance Sheets—1992 Actual and 1993 Projected
(millions of dollars)

	1992		1993 Projected		
	Actual (1)	% of Sales (2)	(3)	(4)	(5)
Cash	$ 10	2.0%	$ 15	$ 15	$ 15
Receivables	85	17.0	128	128	128
Inventories	100	20.0	150	150	150
Total current assets	$195	39.0%	$293	$293	$293
Net fixed assets	150	30.0	225	225	225
Total assets	$345	69.0%	$518	$518	$518
Accounts payable	$ 50	10.0%	$ 75	$ 75	$ 75
Accrued wages and taxes	25	5.0	38	38	38
Notes payable	0	0	0	0	4
Total current liabilities	$ 75	15.0%	$113	$113	$117
Mortgage bonds	$ 70	—ᵃ	—ᵃ	$ 70	$142
Common equity	100	—ᵃ	—ᵃ	100	144
Retained earnings	100	—ᵃ	—ᵃ	115	115
Funds available	$345		$113	$398	$518
Additional funds needed (AFN)	0		405ᵇ	120	0
Total liabilities and equity	$345		$518	$518	$518
Sales	$500		$750	$750	$750

ᵃNot applicable (item does not vary spontaneously and directly with sales).
ᵇif mortgage bonds, common shares, and retained earnings stay at their 1992 levels, they will contribute $270 million. Therefore, $405 − $270 = $135 million is still required.

dividends paid will be 0.5($30 million) = $15 million. Therefore, retained earnings for the year are projected to be $30 million − $15 million = $15 million. Adding this $15 million addition to the $100 million beginning retained earnings gives the $115 million projected retained earnings shown in column 4.

Step 5. Still in column 4, we sum the asset accounts, obtaining a total projected assets figure of $518 million for 1993. We also sum the projected liabilities and net worth items to obtain $398 million, the estimate of available financing. Since liabilities and equity must total $518 million, but only $398 million is projected, we have a shortfall of $120 million which we designate **additional funds needed (AFN)**. It will presumably be raised by bank borrowing, by issuing securities, or both. For simplicity, we disregard depreciation by assuming that cash flows equal to the amount of depreciation will be used to replace wornout fixed assets.

Step 6. Interfaces could use short-term bank loans (notes payable), mortgage bonds, common equity, or a combination of these securities to make up the shortfall. Ordinarily, it would make this choice on the basis of the relative costs of these different types of securities, subject to certain constraints. For example, in Interfaces' case, the company has a contractual agreement with its bondholders to keep total debt at or below 50 percent of total assets and also to keep the current ratio at a level of 2.5 or greater. These provisions restrict the financing choices as follows:[5]

1. Restriction on additional debt

Maximum debt permitted = (0.5)(Total assets)

= (0.5)($518 million) = $259 million

Less: Debt already projected for December 31, 1993

Current liabilities	$113 million	
Mortgage bonds	70 million =	183 million
Maximum additional debt	=	$ 76 million

2. Restriction on additional current liabilities

Maximum current liabilities = Projected current assets/2.5

= $293 million/2.5 = $117 million

Less: Current liabilities already projected	113 million
Maximum additional current liabilities	$ 4 million

3. Common equity requirements

Total additional funds needed (from Table 5-2)	$120 million
Maximum additional debt permitted	76 million
Common equity funds required	$ 44 million

We see, then, that Interfaces needs a total of $120 million from external sources. Its existing debt contract limits new debt to $76 million, and only $4 million of that amount can be short-term debt. Thus, since Interfaces wants to make maximum use of debt financing, it must plan to sell additional common equity in the amount of $44 million to cover its financial requirements. Here is a summary of its projected nonspontaneous external financings:

Short-term debt (notes payable)	$ 4 million
Long-term debt	72 million
New common equity	44 million
Total	$120 million

The impact of these financings is shown in column 5 of Table 5-2.

Step 7. Implicit in the above calculations is the absence of feedback from the additional sources of financing. That is, additional debt does not generate additional interest payments nor does additional common

---

[5]As we shall see in Chapter 21, restrictions like these are contained in virtually all long-term debt agreements. They are designed to protect bondholders against managerial decisions that would increase the risk the bondholders face.

equity generate additional dividends that impact the income statement. If the additional funds are all raised at the end of 1993, this will be true. More generally, however, a complete *cash budget* should be created. All cash flows, quarter by quarter (or month by month, week by week, day by day) are calculated. This will include additional interest payments required by new debt, and/or dividends paid to new shareholders. (Cash budgeting is discussed in more detail in Chapter 6.)

For example, assume that the additional $72 million in long-term debt is raised in midyear, and requires semiannual interest payments at 10 percent. That is, $3.5 million in interest must be paid in 1993. Also assume that the new common equity is sold at year-end, so that no additional dividends are required.

Table 5-3 shows the 1993 pro forma income statement with this additional charge. Now, net income is reduced to $27.84 million, and the addition to retained earnings is reduced to $13.92 million. This leaves $1.08 million still required.

This $1.08 million must be raised through additional equity, since the maximum amount of additional debt has already been raised.

Step 8. Steps 4 through 7 are repeated as often as required. In this simple example, a single iteration is sufficient.

Table 5-3
Interfaces Ltd.
Projected Financial Statements for 1993 with Financing Interactions
(millions of dollars)

I. Projected Income Statement, 1993

Sales	$750.00
Total Costs	703.60
Net income before taxes	$ 46.40
Taxes (40%)	18.56
Net income after taxes	$ 27.84
Dividends (50% payout)	13.92
Addition to retained earnings	$ 13.92

II. Projected Balance Sheet, December 31, 1993

Cash	$ 15.00	Accounts payable	$ 75.00
Receivables	127.50	Accrued wages and taxes	37.50
Inventories	150.00	Notes payable	4.00
Total current assets	$292.50	Total current liabilities	$116.50
Net fixed assets	225.00	Mortgage bonds	142.00
		Common equity	144.00
		Retained earnings	113.92
		Additional funds needed	1.08
Total assets	$517.50	Total liabilities and equity	$517.50

Projected Financial Statements and Ratios

Interfaces' financial staff can now construct a set of projected, or pro forma, financial statements and then analyze the ratios that are implied therein. Parts I and II of Table 5-4 give abbreviated versions of the final projected balance sheet and income statement; Part III provides the statement of cash flows; and Part IV gives a few key ratios. These statements can be used by the financial manager to show the other executives the implications of the planned sales increase. For example, the projected rate of return on equity is 11.6 percent. Is this a reasonable target, or can it be improved? The preliminary forecast also calls for the sale of $44 million of common equity, but does top management really want to sell any new equity? Suppose just over 50 percent

---

Table 5-4
Interfaces Ltd.:
Projected Financial Statements for 1993
(millions of dollars)

I. Projected Income Statement, 1993

Sales	$750
Total Costs	700
Net income before taxes	$ 50
Taxes (40%)	20
Net income after taxes	$ 30
Dividends (50% payout)	15
Addition to retained earnings	$ 15

II. Projected Balance Sheet, December 31, 1993

Cash	$ 15	Accounts payable	$ 75
Receivables	128	Accrued wages and taxes	38
Inventories	150	Notes payable	4
Total current assets	$293	Total current liabilities	$117
Net fixed assets	225	Mortgage bonds	142
		Common equity	144
		Retained earnings	115
Total assets	$518	Total liabilities and equity	$518

III. Projected Statement of Cash Flows, 1993

Cash Flows from Operations

Net income	$30	
Additions (sources of cash)[a]		
Increase in accounts payable	25	
Increase in accruals	13	
Subtractions (uses of cash)		
Increase in accounts receivables	(43)	
Increase in inventories	(50)	
Total cash flows from operations		($ 25)

(continued)

Table 5-4 *(continued)*

Cash Flows Associated with Long-Term Investments
    Increase in fixed assets (75)
Cash Flows from Financing Activities

Increase in notes payable	$ 4	
Proceeds from sale of bonds	72	
Proceeds from sale of common stock	44	
Dividends paid	(15)	
Net cash flows from financing activities		105
Net increase in cash		$ 5

IV. Key Ratios Projected for December 31, 1993[b]

1. Current ratio	2.5 times
2. Quick ratio	1.2 times
3. Total debt/total assets	50%
4. Return on equity	11.6%

[a]The figure for cash flows from operations normally includes depreciation. Here we have assumed that depreciation is reinvested in fixed assets; that is, we netted it out against fixed asset additions.
[b]Other ratios could be calculated, and we could analyze them by the Du Pont system.

of Interfaces' stock is owned by Jane Edwards, and she does not want the company to issue any shares and thereby cause her to lose her majority control. How then can the needed funds be raised, or what adjustments could be made? Later in the chapter, we look at approaches to answering questions such as these.

Relationship between Sales and Capital Requirements

Although the forecast of capital requirements can be made by constructing pro forma balance sheets as just described, under certain conditions it is easier to use a simple forecasting formula. The formula can also be used to highlight the relationship between sales growth and financial requirements:

$$\text{AFN} = \frac{A_s}{S}(\Delta S) + \frac{A_f}{S}(\Delta S) - \frac{L_s}{S}(\Delta S) - Mb(S_1), \tag{5-1}$$

where

AFN = additional funds needed.

$\frac{A_s}{S}$ = short-term assets that increase spontaneously with sales as a percentage of sales. Generally, all current assets are in this category.

$\frac{A_f}{S}$ = fixed assets that increase in "lumps," such as new manufacturing plants, and that consequently could have excess capacity at any point in time, as a percentage of sales. We assume that Interfaces' fixed assets are operated at full capacity and hence must be increased as sales rise.

$\frac{L_s}{S}$ = short-term liabilities that increase spontaneously with sales as a percentage of sales.

S_1 = total sales projected for next year; S_0 designates last year's sales.

ΔS = change in sales = $(S_1 - S_0)$.

M = profit margin on sales.

b = earnings retention ratio = (1.0 − dividend payout ratio).

$Mb(S_1)$ = the earnings that will be retained during the year and used to finance the sales increase.

Inserting values for Interfaces from Table 5-2 into Equation 5-1, we find the additional funds needed to be $120 million:

$$
\begin{aligned}
\text{AFN} &= 0.39(\Delta S) + 0.30\,(\Delta S) - 0.15(\Delta S) - 0.04(0.5)S_1 \\
&= 0.39(\$250.0 \text{ million}) + 0.30(\$250.0 \text{ million}) \\
&\quad - 0.15(\$250.0 \text{ million}) - 0.04(0.5)(\$750.0 \text{ million}) \\
&= 0.69(\$250.0 \text{ million}) - 0.15(\$250.0 \text{ million}) \\
&\quad - 0.04(0.5)(\$750.0 \text{ million}) \\
&= \$172.5 \text{ million} - \$37.5 \text{ million} - \$15.0 \text{ million} \\
&= \$120.0 \text{ million.}
\end{aligned}
$$

To increase sales by $250.0 million, Interfaces must increase assets by $172.5 million. This increase must be financed in some manner. Of the total, $37.5 million will come from a spontaneous increase in liabilities, while another $15.0 million will be obtained from retained earnings. The remaining $120.0 million must be raised from external sources. The value agrees with the amount developed in Table 5-2.

Notice what would have occurred if Interfaces' sales forecast for 1993 had been only $515 million, or a 3 percent increase. Applying the formula, we find the additional funds requirements as follows:

$$
\begin{aligned}
\text{AFN} &= 0.54(\$15 \text{ million}) - 0.02(\$515 \text{ million}) \\
&= \$8.1 \text{ million} - \$10.3 \text{ million} \\
&= -\$2.2 \text{ million.}
\end{aligned}
$$

In this case, no external funds are required. In fact, the company will have $2.2 million in excess of its requirements; it should therefore plan to increase dividends, retire debt, or seek additional investment opportunities. The example shows not only that higher levels of sales bring about a need for funds but also that larger increases cause the firm to go into the market for outside capital while small percentage increases can often be financed through retained earnings. In other words, a certain level of growth can be financed from internal sources, but higher levels of growth require external financing.

Dividend policy as reflected in the retention ratio (**b**, in Equation 5-1) also affects external capital requirements. By retaining a higher percentage of net income, Interfaces can lower its need for additional funds. However, since a reduction in dividend payout can lower share prices, this decision must be considered carefully by management. This issue is discussed in more detail in Chapter 19.

The AFN equation is also useful for financial planning purposes. Using the AFN equation, the firm can identify the rate of growth in sales that can be financed without recourse to the outside capital markets. This growth rate is known as the **sustainable growth rate**. Its value is determined by solving for the growth rate in sales in the AFN equation when the additional funds needed is set equal to zero. For Interfaces, the resulting growth rate is 3.9 percent. If its growth in sales is less than this amount—say, 3 percent as in the above example—the company generates excess cash. If the growth rate is greater than this sustainable value, the firm must raise capital from outside sources.[6] The *faster the growth rate, the greater the capital requirements*. If management foresees difficulties in raising the required capital, perhaps because Interfaces' shareholders do not want to sell additional equity, then management should reconsider the feasibility of the expansion plans.

Investments in fixed assets may occur in *lumpy* rather than smooth increments, and excess capacity may exist immediately after a new plant is opened and until volume has been built up to design capacity. In applications to individual companies, the relationship between fixed assets and sales is often linear and statistically significant—that is, the lumpiness does not normally create much of a problem. Therefore, we can combine A_f/S and A_s/S, and AFN becomes

$$\text{AFN} = \frac{A}{S}(\Delta S) - \frac{L_s}{S}(\Delta S) - Mb(S_1), \qquad \textbf{(5-2)}$$

where A stands for total assets.[7]

Here the ratio of assets to sales, A/S, is known as the **capital intensity ratio**. For firms such as utilities, which are capital intensive, a small growth in sales requires a large increase in outside capital.

Concept Review

▶ What are the key assumptions on which the percentage-of-sales method is based?

▶ Briefly explain the steps you would go through in developing a percentage-of-sales forecast.

▶ Under certain conditions it is easier to use a simple forecasting formula than to construct pro forma balance sheets. Give the formula and briefly explain it.

▶ How do each of the following affect external capital requirements:
   a.   Dividend policy?
   b.   Capital intensity?
   c.   Profit margin?

▶ Devine the sustainable growth rate, and describe how it can be used as a management planning tool.

---

[6]We found the 3.9 percent growth rate by setting AFN equal to zero, substituting g (S_0) for ΔS and S_0 + g(S_0) for S_1 in the AFN equation, and then solving the equation $0 = 0.39g(S_0) + 0.30(g)(S_0) - 0.15(g)(S_0) - 0.04(S_0 + gS_0)(0.5)$ for g. The g that solved this equation was 0.039, or 3.9 percent. Rearranging, the equation can be written as g = $Mb/(A_s/S + A_f/S - L/S - Mb)$.

[7]When using the percentage-of-sales method, we deal with net fixed assets. The assumption that depreciation cash flows are automatically reinvested in fixed assets is implicit in this treatment.

Forecasting Financial Requirements When the Balance Sheet Ratios Are Subject to Change

To this point we have been assuming that the balance sheet ratios of assets and liabilities to sales remain constant over time, which in turn requires the assumption that each "spontaneous" asset and liability item increases at the same rate as sales. In graph form, this implies the type of relationship shown in Panel a of Figure 5-2, a relationship that is (1) linear and (2) passes through the origin. Under those conditions, if the company's sales increase from $200 million to $400 million, inventory will increase proportionately, from $100 million to $200 million.

The assumption of constant ratios is appropriate at times, but there are times when it is incorrect. Three such conditions are described in the following sections.

Economies of Scale

There are economies of scale in the use of many kinds of assets, and when economies occur, the ratios are likely to change over time as the size of the firm increases. For example, firms often need to maintain base stocks of different inventory items, even if current sales levels are quite low. As sales expand, inventories grow less rapidly than sales, so the ratio of inventory to sales, I/S, declines. This situation is depicted in Panel b of Figure 5-2. Here we see that the inventory-to-sales ratio is 1.5, or 150 percent, when sales are $200 million but declines to 1.0 when sales climb to $400 million.

The relationship used to illustrate economies of scale is linear, but this is not necessarily the case. Indeed, as we shall see in Chapter 8, if the firm uses the most popular model for establishing inventory levels, the economic order quantity (EOQ) model, inventories will rise with the square root of sales. In this case, the graph in Figure 5-2b will be a curved line whose slope decreases at higher sales levels.

Lumpy Assets

In many industries, technological considerations dictate that if a firm is to be competitive, it must add fixed assets in large, discrete units; such assets are often referred to as **lumpy assets**. In the paper industry, for example, there are strong economies of scale in basic paper mill equipment, so when a paper company expands capacity, it must do so in large, lumpy, increments. This type of situation is depicted in Panel c of Figure 5-2. Here we assume that the minimum economically efficient plant has a cost of $75 million, and that such a plant can produce enough output to attain a sales level of $100 million. If the firm is to be competitive, it simply must have at least $75 million of fixed assets.

This situation has a major effect on the fixed-assets-to-sales (A_f/S) ratio at different sales levels, and consequently on financial requirements. At point A in Figure 5-2c, which represents a sales level of $50 million, the fixed assets are $75 million, so the ratio $A_f/S = \$75/\$50 = 1.5$. Sales can expand by $50 million, out to $100 million, with no additions to fixed assets. At that point, represented by point B, the ratio $A_f/S = \$75/\$100 = 0.75$. However, if the firm is operating

Figure 5-2
Three Possible Ratio Relationships
(millions of dollars)

a. Constant Ratios

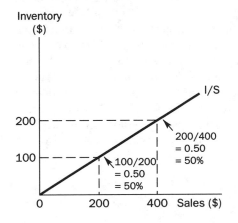

b. Economies of Scale, Declining Ratios

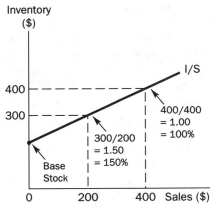

c. Lumpy Assets

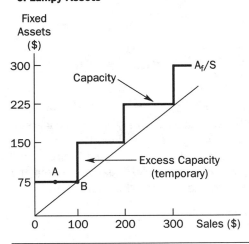

at capacity (sales of $100 million), even a small increase in sales would require a doubling of plant capacity, so a small projected sales increase would bring with it a very large financial requirement.[8]

---

[8]Several other points should be noted about Panel c of Figure 5-2. First, if the firm is operating at a sales level of $100 million or less, any expansion that calls for a sales increase of more than $100 million will require a *doubling* of the firm's fixed assets. A much smaller percentage increase would be involved if the firm were large enough to be operating a number of plants. Second, firms generally go to multiple shifts and take other actions to minimize the need for new fixed asset capacity as they approach point B. However, these efforts can go only so far, and eventually a fixed asset expansion will be required.

Cyclical Changes

Panels a, b, and c of Figure 5-2 all focus on target, or projected, relationships between sales and assets. Actual sales, however, are often different from projected sales, and the actual assets-to-sales ratio for a given period may thus be quite different from the planned ratio. To illustrate: the firm depicted in Panel b of Figure 5-2 might, when its sales are at $200 million and its inventories at $300 million, project a sales expansion to $400 million and then increase its inventories to $400 million in anticipation of the sales expansion. However, suppose an unforeseen economic downturn were to hold sales to only $300 million. Actual inventories would then be $400 million, but inventories of only $350 million would be needed to support actual sales of $300 million. In this situation, if the firm were making its forecast for the following year, it would have to recognize that sales could expand by $100 million with no increase whatever in inventories, but that any sales expansion of more than $100 million would require additional financing to build inventories.

Concept Review

▶ Identify and describe three conditions under which the assumption that each "spontaneous" asset and liability item increases at the same rate as sales is not correct.

Modifying the Forecast of Additional Funds Needed

If any of the conditions noted in the previous section apply (economies of scale, excess capacity, or lumpy assets), the asset-to-sales ratios will not be constant, and the simple percentage-of-sales forecasting method should not be used. Rather, other techniques must be used to forecast asset levels and the resulting external financing requirements. Two of these methods—linear regression and specific item forecasting—are discussed in the following sections.

Simple Linear Regression

If we assume that the relationship between a certain type of asset and sales is linear, then we can use simple linear regression techniques to estimate the requirements for that type of asset for any given sales increase. For example, Interfaces' levels of sales and inventories during the last 11 years are shown in Table 5-5, and its inventories, receivables, and net fixed assets are plotted as scatter diagrams versus sales in Figure 5-3. Estimated regression equations as found with a hand calculator are shown with each graph. The estimated relationship between inventories and sales (in millions of dollars) is

$$\text{Inventories} = \$20 + 0.16(\text{Sales}).$$

The plotted points are quite close to the regression line, which indicates a high degree of correlation. In fact, the correlation coefficient between inventories and sales is 0.98, indicating that there is a very strong linear relationship between these two variables.

Table 5-5
Inventory-to-Sales Relationships for
Interfaces Ltd., 1982–1992
(millions of dollars)

	Inventory (Y)	Sales (X)	Inventory to Sales Ratio (Y/X)
1982	$ 44	$175	0.251
1983	48	200	0.240
1984	53	215	0.247
1985	57	185	0.308
1986	60	235	0.255
1987	66	265	0.249
1988	73	300	0.243
1989	70	280	0.250
1990	78	350	0.223
1991	90	420	0.214
1992	100	500	0.200

We can use the estimated relationship between inventories and sales to forecast 1993 inventory levels. Since 1993 sales are projected at $750 million, 1993 inventories should be $140 million:

$$\text{Inventories} = \$20 + 0.16(\$750) = \$140 \text{ million.}$$

Figure 5-3
Investments and Sales: Interfaces Ltd., 1982–1992
(thousands of dollars)

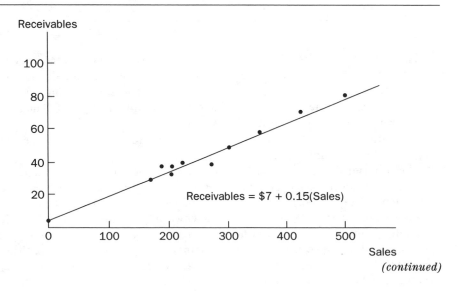

Receivables = $7 + 0.15(Sales)

(continued)

Figure 5-3 *(continued)*

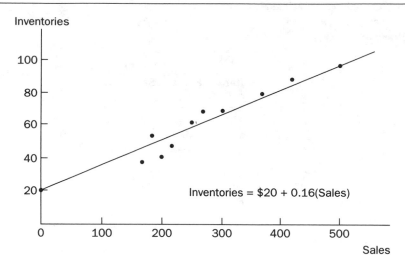

Inventories

Inventories = $20 + 0.16(Sales)

Sales

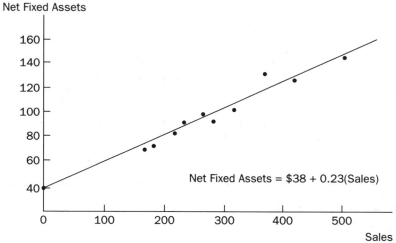

Net Fixed Assets

Net Fixed Assets = $38 + 0.23(Sales)

Sales

This is $10 million less than our earlier forecast based on the percentage-of-sales method. The difference occurs because the percentage-of-sales method assumes that the ratio of inventories to sales would remain constant, while in fact it will probably decline, because the regression line in Figure 5-3 does not pass through the origin. Note also that although our graphs show linear relationships, we could have easily used a nonlinear regression model had such a relationship been indicated.

The relationship appears to be a straight line because a number of offsetting influences are operating. First, as we shall see in Chapter 8 in our discussion of the EOQ formula, inventories often increase with the square root of sales, which causes the line to curve downward. Also, improved efficiencies in handling inventories, such as better transportation and inventory control systems, tend to cause the percentage of inventories to decrease over time. However, offsetting these two factors has been Interfaces' tendency to stock a greater variety of products, which has caused its inventories to rise relative to sales. These influences appear to be counterbalancing, since the actual data for Interfaces indicate that the straight line calculated is a very good fit to the data. However, for some other company this offset might not occur, which would require a more complicated type of analysis (curvilinear regression).

Specific-Item Forecasting

When the current level of some asset is not optimal for the current level of sales, the percentage of sales method must be modified. Consider again the Interfaces example set forth in Tables 5-1 and 5-2. Now suppose a ratio analysis along the lines described in Chapter 4 suggests that the ratios of cash, receivables, and inventories to sales as indicated in Table 5-2 are appropriate, as are the liability ratios and the retained earnings calculations, but that excess capacity exists in fixed assets. Specifically, fixed assets in 1992 were being utilized to only 80 percent of capacity. If fixed assets had been used to full capacity, 1993 sales could have been as high as \$625 million:

$$\begin{array}{c} \text{Full} \\ \text{capacity} \\ \text{sales} \end{array} = \frac{\text{Current sales}}{\begin{array}{c}\text{Percentage of capacity}\\\text{at which fixed assets}\\\text{were operated}\end{array}} = \frac{\$500\ \text{million}}{0.80} = \begin{array}{c}\$625\ \text{million sales}\\\text{at full capacity.}\end{array}$$

This suggests that Interfaces' target for the fixed-assets-to-sales ratio, A_f/S, should be

$$\begin{array}{c}\text{Target}\\A_f/S\\\text{ratio}\end{array} = \frac{\text{Fixed assets}}{\text{Full capacity sales}} = \frac{\$150\ \text{million}}{\$625\ \text{million}} = 0.24,$$

not the 0.30 that actually existed. Therefore, at the projected sales level of \$750 million, Interfaces would require fixed assets of only 0.24(\$750 million) = \$180 million rather than \$225 million. Therefore, the required increase in fixed assets would be up only \$30 million from the \$150 million currently on hand, rather than up \$75 million.[9]

We estimated earlier that Interfaces would need an additional \$120 million of capital. However, those estimates were based on the assumption that \$75 million of additional fixed assets would be required. If Interfaces could attain a sales level of \$750 million with an addition of only \$30 million of fixed assets, then the external funds needed would decline by \$75 − \$30 = \$45 million, to a total of \$125 million − \$45 = \$80 million.

Concept Review

▶ Identify two methods that can be used to forecast asset levels when the assets-to-sales ratio is not constant.

▶ Explain how one can adjust the formulas to calculate full capacity sales and the target fixed-assets-to-sales ratio when excess capacity exists in fixed assets.

---

[9]This \$30 million of required new fixed assets could also be determined by noting (1) that sales could grow from \$500 million to \$625 million without any increase in fixed assets but (2) that the sales increase from \$625 million to \$750 million would require new fixed assets of $(A_f/S)(\Delta S)$ = 0.24(\$125 million) = \$30 million.

Computerized Financial Planning Models

Although the type of financial forecasting described in this chapter can be done with a hand calculator, most well-managed firms with sales greater than a few million dollars use some type of computerized financial planning model. Such models can be programmed to show the effects of different sales levels, different ratios of sales to operating assets, and different assumptions about sales prices and input costs. Plans are then made regarding how financial requirements are to be met: by borrowing from banks, thus increasing short-term notes payable; by selling long-term bonds; or by selling new common shares. Pro forma balance sheets and income statements are generated under the different financing plans, and earnings per share are projected, along with such risk measures as the current ratio, the debt-to-assets assets ratio, and the times-interest-earned ratio.

Depending on how these projections look, management may modify its initial plans. For example, the firm may conclude that its sales forecast must be cut because the requirements for external capital exceed the firm's ability to raise money. Alternatively, management may decide to reduce dividends and thus generate more funds internally. The company also may decide to investigate production processes that require fewer fixed assets, or it may consider the possibility of buying rather than manufacturing certain components, thus eliminating raw materials and work-in-process inventories as well as certain manufacturing facilities. We discuss computerized forecasting models at greater length in Appendix 5A.

In subsequent chapters, we shall look in detail at ways to analyze potential changes in operations. In all such considerations, the basic issue is the effect that a specific action will have on future earnings and cash flows, on the firm's risk, and hence on the price of its shares. Since computerized planning models help management assess these effects, they are playing an increasingly important role in corporate management. An illustrative *Lotus 1-2-3* forecast-

---

[10]It is becoming increasingly easy for companies to develop planning models as a result of the dramatic improvements that have been made in computer hardware and software in recent years. *Lotus 1-2-3* is the most widely used system, although many companies also employ more complex and elaborate modelling systems, such as *IFPS (Interactive Financial Planning System)*. Increasingly, a knowledge of *Lotus 1-2-3* or some similar planning system is becoming a requirement for getting even an entry-level job in many corporations. Indeed, surveys indicate that the probability of a business student's getting an attractive job offer increases dramatically if he or she has a working knowledge of *Lotus 1-2-3*. In addition, starting salaries are materially higher for those students who have such a knowledge.

Note also that we have concentrated on long-run, or strategic, financial planning. Within the framework of the long-run strategic plan, firms also develop short-run financial plans. For example, in Table 5-2 we saw that Interfaces Corporation expects to need $120 million by the end of 1993, and that it plans to raise this capital by using short-term debt, long-term debt, and common shares. However, we do not know when during the year the need for funds will occur, or when Interfaces will obtain each of its different types of capital. To address these issues, the firm must develop a short-run financial plan, the centrepiece of which is the *cash budget*, which is a projection of cash inflows and outflows on a daily, weekly, or monthly basis during the coming year (or other budget period). We shall discuss cash budgeting in Chapter 6, where we consider the financial planning and control process.

ing model is described in Appendix 5A, and others are used to solve the computer-related problems for this chapter.[10]

> ### Concept Review
>
> ▶ Why are computerized planning models playing an increasingly important role in corporate management?

Summary

This chapter described in broad outline how firms project their financial statements and determine their capital requirements. The key concepts covered are listed below.

☐ Management establishes a *target balance sheet* on the basis of ratio analysis.

☐ Financial forecasting generally begins with a forecast of the firm's sales, in terms of both units and dollars, for some future time period.

☐ **Pro forma**, or projected, **financial statements** are developed to determine the firm's financial requirements.

☐ The **percentage of sales method** of forecasting financial statements is based on the assumptions (1) that most balance sheet accounts vary directly with sales and (2) that the firm's existing level of assets is optimum for its sales volume.

☐ A firm can determine the amount of **additional funds needed (AFN)** by estimating the amount of new assets necessary to support the forecasting level of sales and then subtracting from that amount the spontaneous funds that will be generated from operations. The firm can then plan to raise the AFN through bank borrowing, by issuing securities, or both.

☐ The *higher* a firm's sales growth rate, the *greater* will be its need for external financing. Similarly, the *larger* a firm's dividend payout ratio, the *greater* its need for external funds.

☐ The percentage of sales method cannot be used if *economies of scale* exist in the use of assets, if *excess capacity* exists, or if some assets must be added in **lumpy increments**.

☐ Linear regression and specific-item forecasting techniques can be used to forecast asset requirements in situations in which the percentage of sales method is not appropriate.

The type of forecasting described in this chapter is important for several reasons. First, if the projected operating results are unsatisfactory, management can "go back to the drawing board," reformulate its plans, and develop more reasonable targets for the coming year. Second, it is possible that the funds required to meet the sales forecast simply cannot be obtained; if so, it is obviously better to know this in advance and to scale back the projected level of operations than to suddenly run out of cash and have operations grind to a halt. Third, even if the required funds can be raised, it is desirable to plan for their acquisition well in advance. As we shall see in later chapters, raising capital takes time, and both time and money can be saved by careful forward planning.

Questions

5-1   Certain balance sheet items generally increase spontaneously with increases in sales. Put a check (√) by those items that typically increase spontaneously:

Cash   _____
Accounts receivable   _____
Inventory   _____
Marketable securities   _____
Fixed assets   _____
Accounts payable   ____√_____
Notes payable to banks   _____
Accrued wages   ____√_____
Accrued taxes   ____√_____
Mortgage bonds   _____
Common shares   _____
Retained earnings   _____

5-2   The following equation can, under certain assumptions, be used to forecast financial requirements:

$$\text{Additional funds needed} = \frac{A}{S}(\Delta S) - \frac{L_s}{S}(\Delta S) - Mb(S_1).$$

Under what conditions does the equation give satisfactory predictions, and when should it *not* be used?

5-3   Suppose a firm makes the following policy changes. If the change means that external, nonspontaneous financial requirements for any rate of growth will increase, indicate this by a (+); indicate decreases by a (−); and indicate indeterminant and/or no effect by a (0). Think in terms of the immediate, short-run effects on funds requirements, and assume all other things are held constant.

a.   The dividend payout ratio is decreased.   ___(−)___
b.   The firm contracts to buy rather than make certain   ___(+)___
     components used in its products.
c.   The firm decides to pay all suppliers on delivery,
     rather than after a 30-day delay, in order to take
     advantage of discounts for rapid payment.   ___(−)___
d.   The firm lengthens the credit period to its customers
     from 30 to 60 days.   ___0___
e.   Advertising expenditures are stepped up.   _____
f.   The firm's profit margin is eroded by increased compe-
     tition.   _____
g.   Notes payable are paid off by issuing preferred shares.   _____
h.   The firm begins to pay employees on a monthly basis
     rather than on a weekly basis.   ___0___

5-4   Is it true that computerized planning models were a fad during the 1970s but, because of a need for flexibility in corporate planning, they have been dropped by most firms?

5-5 Assume that an average firm in the office supply business has a 6 percent after-tax profit margin, a 40 percent debt-to-assets ratio, a total assets turnover of 2 times, and a dividend payout ratio of 40 percent. Is it true that if such a firm is to have *any* sales growth (g > 0), it will be forced either to borrow or to sell common shares (that is, it will need some nonspontaneous, external capital even if g is very small)?

Self-Test Problems (solutions appear on page 174)

ST-1 **Key terms.** Define each of the following terms:
  a. Sales forecast
  b. Percentage-of-sales method
  c. Spontaneously generated funds
  d. Dividend payout ratio; earnings retention ratio
  e. Pro forma financial statement
  f. Additional funds needed (AFN)
  g. Capital intensity ratio
  h. Sustainable growth rate
  i. Lumpy assets
  j. Excess capacity

ST-2 **Growth rate.** K. Billingsworth and Company Ltd. has the following ratios: A/S = 1.6; L/S = 0.4; profit margin = 0.10; and dividend payout ratio = 0.45, or 45 percent. Sales last year were $50 million. Assuming that these ratios will remain constant and that all liabilities increase spontaneously with increases in sales, what is the maximum sales growth rate, g, that Billingsworth can achieve without having to employ nonspontaneous external funds?

ST-3 **Additional funds needed.** Suppose Billingsworth's financial consultants report (a) that the inventory turnover ratio is sales/inventory = 3 times versus an industry average of 4 times and (b) that Billingsworth could raise its turnover to 4 without affecting sales, the profit margin, or the other asset turnover ratios. Under these conditions and using the data from the previous problem, what amount of external funds would Billingsworth require during each of the next 2 years if sales grew at a rate of 20 percent per year?

Problems

5-1 **Pro forma balance sheet.** A group of investors is planning to set up a new company, The Running Shoe, Ltd., to manufacture and distribute a novel type of running shoe. To help determine the new company's financial requirements, Janice Underwood, the president, has asked you to construct a pro forma balance sheet for December 31, 1992, the end of the first year of operations, and to estimate Running Shoe's external financing requirements for 1992. Sales for 1992 are projected at $5 million, and the following are industry average ratios for athletic shoe companies:

Sales to common equity	2.5×
Current debt to equity	40%
Total debt to equity	70%
Current ratio	2.75×
Net sales to inventory	5×
Accounts receivable to sales	20%
Fixed assets to equity	60%
Profit margin	6%
Dividend payout ratio	40%

a. Complete the pro forma balance sheet that follows, assuming that 1992 sales are $5 million and that the firm maintains industry average ratios. Round your answers to the nearest 0.1 million.

The Running Shoe, Ltd.
Pro Forma Balance Sheet, December 31, 1992
(millions of dollars)

Cash	$	Current debt	$
Accounts receivable		Long-term debt	
Inventories	_____	Total debt	_____
Total current assets		Equity	
Fixed assets	_____		_____
Total assets	$ _____	Total liabilities and equity	$ _____

---

b. If the investor group supplies all the equity, how much capital (exclusive of retained earnings) will it be required to put up during 1992?

5-2   Long-term financing needed.   At year-end 1991, total assets for Rothfield, Inc. were $1.2 million. Sales, which in 1991 were $2.5 million, are expected to increase by 25 percent in 1992. The 1991 ratio of assets to sales will be maintained in 1992. Accounts payable were 15 percent of sales in 1991, and this ratio will be maintained in 1992. Common equity amounted to $425 000 in 1991, and retained earnings were $295 000. Rothfield plans to sell new common shares in the amount of $75 000. Net income after taxes is expected to be 6 percent of sales; 40 percent of earnings will be paid out as dividends. If Rothfield has no current liabilities other than accounts payable, (a) what was Rothfield's total debt in 1991, and (b) how much new, long-term debt financing will be needed in 1992? (Hint: AFN − New stock = New long-term debt.)

5-3   Pro forma statements and ratios.   Hamsmith Computers makes bulk purchases of small computers, stocks them in conveniently located warehouses, and ships them to its chain of retail stores. Hamsmith's balance sheet as of December 31, 1991 is shown here (in millions of dollars):

Cash	$ 3.5	Accounts payable	$ 9.0
Receivables	26.0	Notes payable	17.5
Inventories	58.0	Accruals	9.0
Total current assets	$ 87.5	Total current liabilities	$ 35.5
Net fixed assets	35.0	Mortgage loan	6.0
		Common shares	15.0
		Retained earnings	66.0
Total assets	$122.5	Total liabilities and equity	$122.5

Sales for 1991 were $350 million, while net income after taxes for the year was $10.5 million. Hamsmith paid dividends of $4.2 million to common shareholders. The firm is operating at full capacity.

a. If sales are projected to increase by $70 million, or 20 percent, during 1992, what are Hamsmith's projected external capital requirements?

b. Construct Hamsmith's pro forma balance sheet for December 31, 1992. Assume that all external capital requirements are met by bank loans and are reflected in notes payable.

c. Now calculate the following ratios, based on your projected December 31, 1992, balance sheet. Hamsmith's 1991 ratios and industry average ratios are shown here for comparison:

	Hamsmith Computers		Industry Average
	12/31/92	12/31/91	12/31/91
Current ratio	_____	2.5×	3×
Debt/total assets	_____	33.9%	30%
Rate of return on equity	_____	13%	12%

d. Now assume that Hamsmith grows by the same $70 million but that the growth is spread over 5 years—that is, that sales grow by $14 million each year.

  i. Calculate total additional financial requirements over the 5-year period. (Hint: Use 1991 ratios, $\Delta S = \$70$, but *total* sales for the 5-year period.)

  ii. Construct a pro forma balance sheet as of December 31, 1996, using notes payable as the balancing item.

  iii. Calculate the current ratio, debt-to-assets ratio, and rate of return on net worth as of December 31, 1996. (Hint: Be sure to use *total sales*, which amount to $1960 million, to calculate retained earnings but 1996 profits to calculate the rate of return on equity—that is, ROE = (1996 profits)/(12/31/96 equity).)

e. Do the plans outlined in Parts c and d seem feasible to you? That is, do you think Hamsmith could borrow the required capital, and would the company be raising the odds on its going bankrupt to an excessive level in the event of some temporary misfortune?

5-4   Additional funds needed. Scampini Textile's 1991 sales were $36 million. The percentage of sales of each balance sheet item that varies directly with sales is as follows:

Cash	3%
Receivables	18
Inventories	25
Net fixed assets	35
Accounts payable	12
Accruals	8

The dividend payout ratio is 45 percent; the profit margin is 5 percent; the December 31, 1990 balance sheet account for retained earnings was $11.87 million; and both common shares and mortgage bonds are constant and equal to the amounts shown on the balance sheet that follows.

a. Complete the balance sheet below as of December 31, 1991:

Scampini Textile
Balance Sheet as of December 31, 1991
(thousands of dollars)

Cash	$	Accounts payable	$
Receivables		Accruals	
Inventories	____	Notes payable	2100
Total current assets		Total current liabilities	
Net fixed assets	____	Mortgage bonds	3500
		Common shares	3500
		Retained earnings	____
Total assets	$	Total liabilities and equity	$

b. Now suppose 1992 sales are projected to increase by 15 percent over 1991 sales. Determine the additional funds needed. Assume that the company was operating at full capacity in 1991, that it cannot sell off any of its fixed assets, and that any required financing will be borrowed as notes payable. Use Equation 5-1 to answer this question.

c. Develop a pro forma balance sheet for December 31, 1992. Assume that any required financing is borrowed as notes payable. Note that 12/31/91 retained earnings are $12.86 million.

5-5   Excess capacity. Chabut Lumber's 1991 sales were $36 million. The percentage of sales of each balance sheet item except notes payable, mortgage bonds, and common shares is given here:

Cash	5%
Receivables	30
Inventories	35

Net fixed assets	60
Accounts payable	20
Accruals	7
Profit margin (after taxes) on sales	7

The dividend payout ratio is 60 percent; the December 31, 1990 balance sheet account for retained earnings was $25.6 million; and both common shares and mortgage bonds are constant and equal to the amounts shown on the balance sheet that follows.

a. Complete the following balance sheet.

Chabut Lumber
Balance Sheet as of December 31, 1991
(thousands of dollars)

Cash	$	Accounts payable	$	
Receivables		Notes payable	3472	
Inventories		Accruals		
Total current assets	___	Total current liabilities		
Net fixed assets		Mortgage bonds	5000	
		Common shares	2000	
		Retained earnings	___	
Total assets	$ ___	Total liabilities and equity	$ ___	

b. Assume that the company was operating at full capacity in 1991 with regard to all items *except* fixed assets; had the fixed assets been used to full capacity, the fixed-assets-to-sales ratio would have been 45 percent in 1991. By what percentage could 1992 sales increase over 1991 sales without the need for an increase in fixed assets?

c. Now suppose that 1992 sales increase by 25 percent over 1991 sales. How much additional external capital will be required? Assume that Chabut Lumber cannot sell any fixed assets. (Hint: Equation 5-1 can no longer be used. You must develop a pro forma balance sheet as in Table 5-2.) Assume that any required financing is borrowed as notes payable. (Another hint: Notes payable = $6 082 000.)

d. Suppose that industry averages for receivables and inventories are 25 percent and 30 percent, respectively, and that Chabut Lumber matches these figures in 1992 and then uses the funds released to reduce equity. (It could pay a special dividend out of retained earnings.) What would this do to the rate of return on year-end 1992 equity?

5-6 **Additional funds needed.** The 1991 sales for Sirman Technologies, Inc., were $3.6 million. The dividend payout ratio is 60 percent. Retained earnings as shown on the December 31, 1990 balance sheet were $132 000. The percentage of sales in each balance sheet item that varies directly with sales is expected to be as follows:

Cash	5%
Receivables	10
Inventories	20
Net fixed assets	40
Accounts payable	10
Accruals	5
Profit margin (after taxes) on sales	5

a. Complete the balance sheet that follows, assuming that common shares and notes payable did not change during 1991.

Sirman Technologies, Inc.
Balance Sheet as of December 31, 1991

Cash	$ 180 000	Accounts payable	$ 360 000
Receivables	360 000	Notes payable	156 000
Inventories	720 000	Accruals	180 000
Total current assets	1 260 000	Total current liabilities	696 000
Fixed assets	1 440 000	Common shares	1 800 000
		Retained earnings	204 000
Total assets	$2 700 000	Total liabilities and equity	$2 700 000

---

b. Suppose that in 1992, sales will increase by 10 percent over 1991 sales. How much additional capital will be required? Assume the firm operated at full capacity in 1991.

c. Construct the year-end 1992 balance sheet. Assume 50 percent of the additional capital required will be financed by selling common shares and the remainder by borrowing as notes payable.

d. If the profit margin after taxes remains at 5 percent and the dividend payout rate remains at 60 percent, at what growth rate in sales will the additional financing requirements be exactly zero? (Hint: Set AFN equal to zero and solve for g.)

5-7 **External financing requirements.** The 1991 balance sheet for the Olsen Company is shown on page 173. Sales in 1991 totalled $8 million. The ratio of net profits to sales was 3 percent, while the dividend payout ratio was 65 percent of net income.

a. The firm operated at full capacity in 1991. It expects sales to increase by 20 percent during 1992. Use the percentage-of-sales method to determine how much outside financing is required. Then develop the firm's pro forma balance sheet using AFN as the balancing item.

b. If the firm must maintain a current ratio of 2.3 and a debt ratio of 40 percent, how much financing will be obtained using notes payable, long-term debt, and common shares?

c. Suppose that the Olsen Company expects sales to increase by 40 percent during 1992 and that its current ratio must be at least 2.3,

Olsen Company
Balance Sheet as of December 31, 1991
(thousands of dollars)

Cash	$ 80	Accounts payable	$ 160
Accounts receivable	240	Accruals	40
Inventory	720	Notes payable	252
Total current assets	$1040	Total current liabilities	$ 452
Fixed assets	3200	Long-term debt	1244
		Total debt	$1696
		Common shares	1605
		Retained earnings	939
Total assets	$4240	Total liabilities and equity	$4240

but its debt ratio could be as high as 50 percent. Under this situation, how much external financing would the firm require, and how would those funds be obtained?

Integrative Problem

5-8 **Financial forecasting.** Laura Evans, financial manager of Sorrell Laboratories, is currently working on her firm's financial forecast for the coming year. Sorrell's balance sheet for last year is as follows (in thousands of dollars):

Cash	$ 225	Accounts payable	$ 150
Receivables	375	Accruals	75
Inventory	750	Notes payable	188
Current assets	$1350	Current liabilities	$ 413
Net fixed assets	3000	Long-term debt	1800
		Total debt	$2213
		Common shares	1500
		Retained earnings	637
Total assets	$4350	Total liabilities and equity	$4350

Sorrell was operating at full capacity last year and had sales of $7.5 million. Sorrell's marketing department is forecasting a 20 percent sales increase for the coming year. Further, the firm has had a profit margin of 5 percent and a 60 percent payout ratio over the last several years, and these values are expected to continue in the near term. Your assignment is to assist Laura Evans by answering the following questions and completing the indicated tasks.

a. Use the percentage-of-sales method to prepare the coming year's pro forma balance sheet. What are the external funds requirements? What assumptions are necessary to use the percentage-of-sales approach?

b. For planning purposes, Evans assumes that the additional funds needed will be raised as 10 percent short-term debt (notes payable), 40 percent long-term debt, and 50 percent common shares. What dollar amounts are needed to cover Sorrell's forecasted deficiency? Recast the pro forma balance sheet to reflect the additional financing.

c. A simple forecasting formula can be used to estimate additional funds needed (AFN) when the percentage-of-sales method is used. Use this formula to forecast Sorrell's funds requirements.

d. Use the forecasting formula to estimate Sorrell's additional funds needed at sales growth rates of 10 percent and 30 percent. Repeat the analysis assuming zero sales growth. What effect does sales growth have on funds requirements?

e. What is the maximum sales growth rate Sorrell can achieve without using outside financing? (Hint: Use the forecasting formula and set AFN = $0.)

f. What effects do a firm's dividend policy, profitability, and capital intensity have on its external financing requirements?

g. Now assume that Sorrell is operating at only 80 percent of capacity with regard to fixed assets.
   i. What is the firm's additional financing requirement in this situation, assuming that sales are forecasted to increase to $9 million?
   ii. What would it be if Sorrell were operating at 90 percent of capacity?

Solutions to Self-Test Problems

ST-1 Refer to the appropriate sections of the text to check your responses.

ST-2 To solve this problem, we define ΔS as the change in sales and g as the growth rate in sales and then use the following three equations:

$$\Delta S = gS.$$
$$S_1 = S(1 + g).$$
$$AFN = (A/S)(\Delta S) - (L/S)(\Delta S) - Mb(S_1).$$

Set AFN = 0, substitute in known values for A/S, L/S, M, b, and S, and then solve for g:

$$0 = 1.6(\$50g) - 0.4(\$50g) - (0.10)(0.55)[\$50(1 + g)]$$
$$= \$80g - \$20g - 0.055(\$50 + 50g)$$
$$= \$80g - \$20g - \$2.75 - \$2.75g.$$
$$\$57.25g = \$2.75$$
$$g = \$2.75/\$57.25 = 0.048$$
$$= 4.8\%$$
$$= \text{Maximum growth rate without external financing.}$$

ST-3 Note that assets consist of cash, marketable securities, receivables, inventories, and fixed assets. Therefore, we can break the A/S ratio into its components: cash/sales, inventory/sales, and so forth. Then,

$$\frac{A}{S} = \frac{A - \text{Inventories}}{S} + \frac{\text{Inventories}}{S} = 1.6.$$

We know that the inventory turnover ratio is sales/inventories = 3 times, so inventories/sales = 1/3 = 0.3333. Further, if the inventory turnover ratio could be increased to 4 times, then the inventory/sales ratio would fall to 1/4 = 0.25, a difference of $0.333 - 0.2500 = 0.0833$. This, in turn, would cause the A/S ratio to fall from A/S = 1.6 to A/S = $1.6 - 0.0833 = 1.5167$.

This change would have two effects: (1) It would change the AFN equation, and (2) it would mean that Billingsworth currently has excessive inventories, so there could be some sales growth without any additional inventories. Therefore, we could set up the revised AFN equation, estimate the funds needed next year, and then subtract out the excessive inventories currently on hand:

Present conditions

$$\frac{\text{Sales}}{\text{Inventories}} = \frac{\$50}{\text{Inventories}} = 3,$$

so

Current level of inventories = $50/3 = $16.7 million.

New conditions

$$\frac{\text{Sales}}{\text{Inventories}} = \frac{\$50}{\text{Inventories}} = 4,$$

so

New level of inventories = $50/4 = $12.5 million.

Therefore,

Excess inventories = $16.7 − $12.5 = $4.2 million.

Forecast of funds needed, first year

ΔS in first year = gS = 0.2($50 million) = $10 million.
AFN = 1.5167($10) − 0.4($10) − (0.10)(0.55)($60) − $4.2
  = $15.2 − $4.0 − $3.3 − $4.2
  = $3.7 million.

Forecast of funds needed, second year

ΔS in second year = gS = 0.2($6 million) = $12 million.
AFN = 1.5167($12) − 0.4($12) − (0.10)(0.55)($72)
  = $18.2 − $4.8 − $4.0
  = $9.4 million.

Appendix 5A
Microcomputers and Financial Forecasting

In Chapter 5, we presented two methods of forecasting financial requirements, the percentage-of-sales method and the regression method, both of which required only paper, pencil, and a calculator. Although these simple procedures are useful to help gain an understanding of the basics of financial forecasting, pencil and paper computations are no longer used in the forecasting process by corporations—virtually all corporate forecasts are made with the aid of computerized forecasting models. Computerized financial models vary greatly in complexity, ranging from simple electronic spreadsheets that can be run on personal home computers to complex models that require mainframe computers. In this appendix we discuss computerized forecasting models in general, after which we illustrate the use of an electronic spreadsheet model that forecasts earnings and calculates key financial ratios for Interfaces Ltd.

Computerized Forecasting Models

The most simple computerized financial models are based on electronic spreadsheets. The user inputs both historical data and formulas, which the computer uses to calculate key relationships between sales and income statement and balance sheet items, and future sales levels or sales growth rates, with which the computer performs essentially the same calculations as the forecaster would have done using a calculator. The spreadsheet has two major advantages over pencil and paper calculations: (1) it is much faster to construct a spreadsheet model than to make a "by hand" forecast if the forecast period extends beyond 2 or 3 years, and (2) the spreadsheet model automatically recomputes all forecasts if one of the input variables is changed. As we shall see, this second feature is especially valuable.

Electronic spreadsheets, which are available for all personal computers, are simply computer programs that (1) set up an electronic matrix as a series of rows and columns—that is, like a sheet of accounting paper—and then (2) do arithmetic on the rows and columns automatically. For example, column 1 can be set up as last year's balance sheet, and then columns 2, 3, and so forth can be the balance sheets for Years 1, 2, and so forth, with each account programmed to increase at a specified rate. A "lower section" of the spreadsheet can be designated as a corresponding series of projected income statements, and a still lower section can calculate the projected ratios for each year. Some of the more popular spreadsheets are *Excel, Lotus 1-2-3*, and *Quattro Pro*.

Interactive financial forecasting models operate much like the spreadsheets, but they are more powerful. Some interactive models are available for use on large-memory personal computers; others require a mainframe computer. The most widely used interactive model is *Interactive Financial Planning System (IFPS)*, for which both mainframe and personal computer versions are available. Interactive models allow the forecaster to "work backwards" to find the value of a particular variable that will produce a desired outcome. For example, instead of determining the expected ROE that will result if sales grow at a specified rate, the model can determine the level of sales growth required to produce a desired ROE. This function helps financial managers plan their growth (and other variables) to maximize the value of the firm. Interactive systems can also be linked with other personal and mainframe computers within a firm, allowing many users to share data and programs.[11]

Interactive models also allow the user to specify variables as probability distributions rather than as discrete values. The model simulates real-world situations by randomly selecting a value from each probability distribution and then computing a set of outcomes associated with the values chosen. This process can be repeated several hundred times in a matter of minutes, and it results in a distribution of the possible outcomes. For example, sales growth can be specified as a random variable, and the distribution of possible net incomes and ROEs associated with the sales distribution can be generated by the forecasting model.

Among the most complex computerized forecasting models are integrated, data-based, financial planning systems. These systems link all areas of a corporation's operations in order to plan for the most efficient utilization of its financial and physical resources. Further, these models can use the firm's database of historic information to form probability distributions for use in the forecasting models. Oil companies, for example, use integrated planning models to forecast regional and worldwide demands for different types of petroleum products, to plan the best way to utilize their resources to meet this demand, and finally to forecast the financial conditions that will result under different operating plans. These models analyze a number of variables, including the company's own oil production, the cost of purchased crude oil, the capacity and operating costs of its plants, the type of fuel used by each, and so on. These input costs and output prices are then worked into financial statements and used to forecast the firm's future financial condition, need for outside capital, and so forth.

Even small firms, such as retail stores and auto repair shops, are finding that they cannot compete effectively if they do not use computers for planning and control purposes. Indeed, now that hardware and software costs have fallen so drastically, most businesses larger than shoeshine stands can use computers in a cost-effective way, and competing in business without a computer is almost like competing on a finance exam without a calculator. So, our advice is this—if you want to be a success (or even a nonfailure) in the business world, learn something about computers!

A Simplified Financial Forecasting Model

We can best demonstrate the usefulness of financial forecasting models by discussing one such model. In Table 5A-1, we use a simplified electronic spreadsheet model, which was developed using *Lotus 1-2-3*, to forecast a 5-year

---

[11]Electronic spreadsheets and interactive models can do many different types of things, such as (1) setting up a schedule for paying off a mortgage (amortization schedule); (2) figuring taxes; (3) managing security portfolios; (4) analyzing proposed capital budgeting projects; (5) analyzing bond refunding decisions; (6) analyzing lease proposals; (7) analyzing alternative capital structures for a firm; and an almost limitless list of other applications. Because of the power of spreadsheets and interactive models such as *IFPS* and the ease with which one can learn to use them, most business school programs, including MBA programs, are now having students learn how to use software packages rather than learn how to program in Fortran, Basic, or other languages (unless the student is interested in computer science per se).

Table 5A-1
Simplified Forecasting Model for Interfaces Ltd.

	A	B	C	D	E	F	G	H
			C	**D**	**E**	**F**	**G**	**H**
1	Year		1991	1992	1993	1994	1995	1996
2	Sales	+C2*1.2	500	600	720	884	1037	1244
3	FC	+C3*1.1	175	193	212	233	256	282
4	VC	+C4*1.22	288	351	429	523	638	778
5	EBT	+C2−C3−C4	37	56	80	108	143	184
6	Tax (46%)	+C5*0.46	17	26	37	50	66	85
7	Net income	+C5−C6	20	30	43	58	77	99
8	Dividend payout	+C8	0.50	0.50	0.50	0.50	0.50	0.50
9	Dividends	+C7*C8	10	15	21	29	38	50
10	Additions to RE	+C7−C9	10	15	21	29	38	50
11	Assets	+C11*1.2	345	414	497	596	715	858
12	Debt	+C11−C13−C14	145	199	280	330	411	504
13	Common shares	+C13	100	100	100	100	100	100
14	RE	+C14+D10	100	115	137	166	204	254
15	Profit margin	+C7/C2	0.04	0.05	0.06	0.07	0.07	0.08
16	ROE	+C7/(C13+C14)	0.10	0.14	0.18	0.22	0.25	0.28
17	ROI	+C7/C11	0.06	0.07	0.09	0.10	0.11	0.12
18	D/A	+C12/C11	0.42	0.48	0.52	0.55	0.57	0.59

Note: The formulas in column B would not appear on the printout of an actual *Lotus 1-2-3* model; they are presented here to show the relationships among items in the income statements and balance sheets from one year to the next.

financial forecast for Interfaces. The model was constructed under the following assumptions: (1) sales and assets will grow at 20 percent a year, (2) the external funds requirement will be met by using debt, (3) fixed costs will grow at 10 percent a year, (4) variable costs, including interest, will grow at 22 percent a year (variable costs will grow at a faster rate than sales because in this particular case the firm's debt level, and hence interest, will increase at a faster rate than sales), and (5) both the dividend payout ratio and the common equity account will remain constant. The model calculates net income, additions to retained earnings, and the forecasted level of assets, and it then solves for the level of debt needed to finance those assets. The model also computes the company's key financial ratios.

The *Lotus 1-2-3* spreadsheet designates columns A, B, C, . . . and rows as 1, 2, 3, . . . , and each cell in the matrix has a designation such as A1, A2, B1, B2, and so forth. Thus, in Table 5A-1 the years are in row 1, sales in row 2, fixed costs in row 3, and so forth. Column A provides labels; Column B the formulas used in the model; and columns C through H give data for the different years. Thus, cell C3 gives the 1991 value for fixed costs, cell C4 gives the 1991 value for variable costs, and so on. The 1992 value for sales is the 1991 value increased by 20 percent, and the electronic spreadsheet automatically computes this using the formula D2 = +C2*1.2, replicated for 1992 through 1996. Similarly, fixed costs, FC, variable costs, VC, and assets are increased in each year. The remainder of the income statement and balance sheet items are calculated, and then the ratios are developed.

We can see from Table 5A-1 that as Interfaces sales grow, its profit margin, ROE, and ROA also increase. This result occurs in part because a larger percentage of assets is being financed by debt rather than by equity—in fact, from 1991 until 1996, the firm's debt ratio will increase from 42 percent of assets to 59 percent.

The model allows us to examine the trends in the firm's profitability and debt ratios; however, it does not show us what is happening to the firm's liquidity and activity ratios. It would be easy enough to provide more detail on the income statement and balance sheet, and this might show us that Interfaces' current ratio was weak, that the firm was holding excess stocks of inventory, and so on. We could also build in constraints, such as requirements that the debt ratio not exceed 50 percent and that the current ratio be maintained at 2.0 times or higher. However, adding such constraints does increase the model's complexity, and if many constraints are involved, it pays to go from a spreadsheet to an interactive model such as *IFPS*.

We have illustrated computer modelling with a simple financial forecast. It should be noted that computerized models are used to analyze many of the financial decisions covered in this book, including cash budgeting, capital budgeting, capital structure analysis, lease analysis, and bond refunding decisions.

Finally, note that it is extremely easy to change the assumptions built into computer models to see the results under alternative scenarios. For example, if we wanted to see what would happen at a sales growth rate of 10 percent rather than 20 percent, we would simply move the cursor to cell B2, delete the "2" and replace it with a "1" (leaving the cell +C2*1.1), and the computer would immediately and automatically recalculate everything and produce a new Table 5A-1. Similar changes could be made with the profit margin, the tax rate, and so on. This type of analysis is called "what if" analysis—"what if the sales growth rate drops to 10 percent or the profit margin increases to 5 percent. Then what results would we get?" Being able to answer this type of question is extremely useful in all types of financial planning.

6

Financial Planning and Control

A MANAGERIAL PERSPECTIVE

Business is becoming increasingly competitive, and corporate profitability is increasingly dependent upon operating efficiency. This situation is desirable from a social standpoint, for consumers are getting higher quality goods at lower prices, but intense competition does make life tough on corporate managers. No longer can firms—even global giants—afford to sit back and assume that the strategies that got them where they are will work in the future. Thus, even an industry leader such as IBM has undergone major reorganizations in recent years, accompanied by massive layoffs and by forced job changes for many IBM employees.

Generally, corporate reorganizations result from studies showing that the old organizations were not optimal in terms of who had control over what or that the various divisions and subsidiaries did not fit together well. In this chapter, we examine the types of control systems that IBM and other successful Canadian companies use in their quest for operating efficiency.

In the last chapter we focussed on financial forecasting, emphasizing how growth in sales requires additional investments in assets, which in turn generally requires the firm to raise new external capital. We now go on to consider the planning and control systems used by management. First we look at the relationship between sales volume and profitability under different sets of operating conditions. Then we examine the control phase of the planning and control process, for a good control system is essential both to help ensure that plans are executed properly and to facilitate a timely modification of plans if the assumptions upon which the initial plans were based turn out to be incorrect.

Financial Planning and Control Processes

Financial planning involves making projections of sales, income, and assets based on alternative production and marketing strategies and then deciding how to meet these forecasted financial requirements. In the financial planning process, managers should also evaluate plans and identify changes in operations that will improve results. **Financial control** moves on to the implementational phase, and it deals with the feedback and adjustment process that is required (1) to ensure adherence to plans or (2) to modify existing plans in response to unanticipated changes in the operating environment. The process begins with the specification of the corporate goals, after which management lays out a series of forecasts and budgets for every significant area of the firm's activities, as shown in Figure 6-1.

Financial forecasting analysis begins with projections of sales revenues and production costs. In standard business terminology, a **budget** is a plan that sets forth the projected expenditures for a certain activity and explains where these funds will come from. Thus, the *production budget* presents a detailed analysis of the required investments in materials, labour, and plant facilities necessary to support the forecasted level of sales. Each of the major elements of the production budget is likely to have a subbudget of its own; thus, there will be a materials budget, a personnel budget, and a facilities budget. The marketing staff will also develop selling and advertising budgets. Typically, these budgets are set up on a monthly basis, and as time goes by, actual figures will be compared with projected figures, and differences must be explained or corrected, and projected figures for the remainder of the year will be adjusted if it appears that the original projections were unrealistic.

During the planning process, the projected levels of each of the different operating budgets will be combined, and from this set of data the firm's cash

Figure 6-1
Overview of the Financial Planning
and Control Process

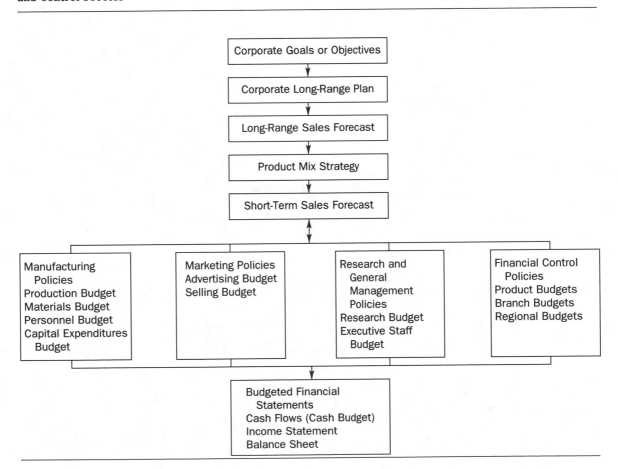

flows will be set forth in its *cash budget*. If a projected increase in sales leads to a projected cash shortage, management can make arrangements to obtain the required funds in a cost-efficient manner.

After all the cost and revenue elements have been forecasted, the firm's *pro forma*, or *projected*, income statement and balance sheet can be developed, as explained in Chapter 5. These pro forma statements are later compared with the actual statements; such comparisons can help the firm pinpoint reasons for deviations, correct operating problems, and adjust projections for the remainder of the budget period to reflect actual operating conditions. Through its financial planning and control processes, management seeks to increase profitability, avoid cash squeezes, and improve the performance of the individual divisions and thus the entire company.

Concept Review

▶ Briefly explain the relationship between the operating budget, the cash budget, and the pro forma income statement and balance sheet.

Breakeven Analysis

The relationship between sales volume and profitability is explored in cost-volume-profit planning, or breakeven analysis. **Breakeven analysis** is a method of determining the point at which sales will just cover costs—that is, the point at which the firm will break even—but it also shows the magnitude of the firm's profits or losses if sales are above or below that point. Breakeven analysis is important in the planning process, because the cost-volume-profit relationship can be greatly influenced by the proportion of the firm's investment in assets that is fixed, and changes in the ratio of fixed to variable assets are determined when financial plans are set. A sufficient volume of sales must be anticipated and achieved if fixed and variable costs are to be covered, or else the firm will incur losses. In other words, if a firm is to avoid accounting losses, its sales must cover all costs—those that vary directly with production and those that do not change as production levels change. Costs that fall into each of these categories are outlined in Table 6-1.

Table 6-1
Fixed and Variable Operating Costs

Fixed Operating Costs[a]	Variable (Direct) Operating Costs
Depreciation on plant and equipment	Factory labour
Rentals	Materials
Salaries of research staff	Sales commissions
Salaries of executive staff	
General office expenses	

[a]Some of these costs—for example, salaries and office expenses—could be varied to some degree; however, firms are reluctant to reduce these expenditures in response to temporary fluctuations in sales. Such costs are often called *semivariable costs*. In addition, costs that are fixed in the short run become variable as the time period of analysis is extended. Because breakeven analysis investigates the relationship between income and sales, given fixed and variable costs, it is a short-run analysis.

Note that interest charges are not listed in Table 6-1. Interest is a *financial* cost as opposed to an *operating* cost. Thus, breakeven analysis as we develop it in this chapter shows the breakeven point *before* interest charges. The reason for this emphasis is that, at this point, we are concerned with the firm's *operating plan* rather than its *financing plan*. We shall expand the analysis to include financial charges in Chapter 18, where we take up the issue of debt versus equity financing.

The essentials of breakeven analysis are depicted in Figure 6-2, the basic breakeven chart. Here units produced and sold are shown on the horizontal axis and costs and revenues measured on the vertical axis. We assume that the number of units sold is equal to the number of units produced. Fixed costs of $40 000 are represented by a horizontal line; they are the same (fixed) regardless of the number of units produced. Variable costs are assumed to be $1.20 a unit, so (1) total variable costs are found by multiplying $1.20 by the number of units sold, and (2) the total cost line rises at a rate of 1.2 dollars per

Figure 6-2
Breakeven Chart

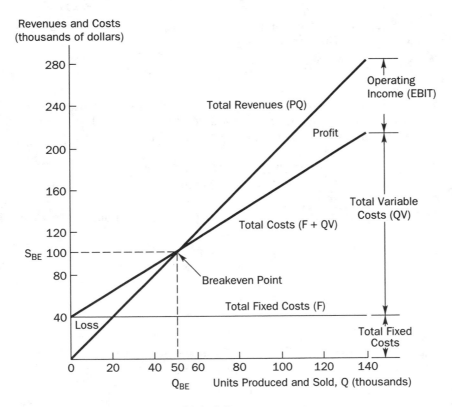

S = sales in dollars; S_{BE} = breakeven sales in dollars.
Q = sales in units; Q_{BE} = breakeven sales in units.
F = fixed costs = $40 000.
V = variable costs per unit = $1.20.
P = price per unit = $2.00.

1-unit increase in units produced and sold. Therefore, the total cost function, which is equal to fixed costs plus total variable costs, is shown on the graph as a straight line with an intercept of $40 000 and a slope of $1.20.

Each unit produced is assumed to be sold at $2.00 each. Therefore, a second straight line, with a slope of $2.00, is used to depict total revenues. The slope of the total revenue line is steeper than that of the total cost line, because the firm is gaining $2.00 of revenue for every $1.20 it pays out for labour and materials as each new unit is produced and sold. At the point where the steeper total revenue line cuts the total cost line, the firm's total revenues are just equal to its total costs, and at that volume the firm breaks even. Before the breakeven volume is reached, the firm suffers losses, but at sales levels above that point, it earns a larger and larger profit.

Breakeven Sales Volume

Figure 6-2 indicates that the breakeven sales volume is 50 000 units; at that volume, revenues and costs are both $100 000. We can calculate the breakeven point algebraically rather than graphically. From the data given, the firm's total revenue, or sales function, is

$$S = PQ = \$2.00Q, \tag{6-1}$$

where S is total sales in dollars, P is the sales price per unit, and Q is the volume in units. The total cost function is

$$TC = F + QV = \$40\,000 + \$1.20Q, \tag{6-2}$$

where F is total fixed costs and V is the variable cost per unit.

At the **breakeven point**, Q_{BE}, total revenues and total costs are equal. Therefore, equating the sales and total cost functions, we find

$$\$2.00Q_{BE} = \$40\,000 + \$1.20Q_{BE},$$
$$Q_{BE} = 50\,000 \text{ units.}$$

As a generalization, we can use this formula to find the breakeven volume in units, Q_{BE}:[1]

$$Q_{BE} = \frac{F}{P - V}. \tag{6-3}$$

---

[1]Equation 6-3 is derived as follows. At breakeven, total revenue, TR, is equal to total costs, TC:
$$TR = TC.$$
TR is equal to PQ, while TC is equal to fixed costs, F, plus variable costs, VQ, so
$$PQ = F + VQ.$$
Solving for $Q = Q_{BE}$, we obtain
$$Q_{BE} = \frac{F}{P - V}. \tag{6-3}$$

Thus, with our example,

$$Q_{BE} = \frac{\$40\,000}{\$2.00 - \$1.20} = \frac{\$40\,000}{\$0.80} = 50\,000 \text{ units.}$$

If we know both the breakeven volume in units and the sales price, then we can find the breakeven volume in dollars, S_{BE}:

$$S_{BE} = PQ_{BE} \qquad\qquad\qquad \textbf{(6-3a)}$$

Thus,

$$S_{BE} = \$2(50\,000) = \$100\,000.$$

Thus, the breakeven point in either units or in dollar sales can be calculated by use of Equation 6-3 or 6-3a.

Breakeven analysis based on dollar sales rather than on units of output is useful in determining the breakeven volume for a firm that sells many products at varying prices. This analysis requires knowing only total sales, total fixed costs, and total variable costs at the given sales level. The breakeven volume then is calculated as

$$S_{BE} = \frac{FC}{1 - VC/S}.$$

total sales

The Applications of Breakeven Analysis

When a project is being planned, it is relatively easy to estimate the fixed and variable costs associated with that project. These costs can be estimated by identifying and summing the major components of fixed expenses, such as rent, depreciation, and general and administrative expenses, and using this sum as total fixed costs. Total variable cost then can be calculated as total costs minus total fixed costs. Once a firm is operational, however, it is much more difficult to separate the firm's fixed and variable costs in order to calculate the firm's breakeven sales level.

Breakeven analysis can shed light on three important types of business decisions. (1) When one is making new product decisions, breakeven analysis can help determine how large the sales of a new product must be for the firm to achieve profitability. (2) Breakeven analysis can be used to study the effects of a general expansion in the level of the firm's operations; an expansion would cause the levels of both fixed and variable costs to rise, but it would also increase expected sales. (3) When the firm is considering modernization and automation projects, in which the fixed investment in equipment is increased in order to lower variable costs, particularly the cost of labour, breakeven analysis can help management analyze the consequences of these projects.

Limitations of Breakeven Analysis

When one attempts to apply breakeven analysis in practice, a number of issues immediately arise. Here are some examples:

1. The total revenue function as graphed in Figure 6-2 is based on the assumption that the price per unit is constant at $2 regardless of the

volume of sales and production. Is that realistic? For example, if demand is low, might the company not lower the sales price in an effort to boost sales? Conversely, if demand is high, might that not be a good time to boost the price and widen profit margins?

2. Is it realistic to expect variable cost per unit to be constant at all output levels? For example, at very low outputs, the cost per unit may be high because the labour force is not producing enough units to learn how to produce them efficiently, and because the firm cannot take advantage of quantity discounts in purchasing parts and materials. Similarly, at high volumes, the firm may have to employ labour on an overtime basis (at double-time wages) or to utilize its least efficient equipment, both of which lead to high unit costs. These considerations suggest that the cost curve will probably be nonlinear, rising at a declining rate over a range where economies of scale exist, then rising at constant rate, and finally rising at an increasing rate, indicating that diseconomies of scale had set in. If the cost curve is nonlinear, a situation might exist in which the firm has a loss at low sales levels, earns a profit over some range of sales volumes, and then has a loss at very high sales volumes. The appendix to this chapter presents a discussion of nonlinear breakeven analysis.

3. The firm might also want to consider changing its level of fixed costs. Higher fixed costs are not good, other things held constant, but they are generally associated with a more automated production process, which reduces variable costs per unit. Breakeven analysis as set forth in Figure 6-2 is not well suited to dealing with such changes.

These limitations make the use of a single breakeven chart as set forth in Figure 6-2 impractical—such a chart provides useful information, but the fact that it cannot deal with changes in the price of the product, with changing variable cost rates, and with changes in fixed cost levels suggests the need for a more flexible type of analysis. Today, such analysis is provided by computer simulation. Functions such as those expressed in Equations 6-1, 6-2, and 6-3 (or more complicated versions of them) are put into a *Lotus 1-2-3* or similar model, and then variables such as sales price, P, the variable cost rate, V, and the level of fixed costs, F, may be changed. The model can produce instantaneously new versions of Figure 6-2, or a whole set of such graphs, to show what the breakeven point would be under different production setups and price–cost situations. This point is discussed in the following section.

Concept Review

▶ Are interest payments considered in a breakeven analysis? Why or why not?

▶ Give the equations used to calculate the breakeven point in units and in dollar sales.

▶ Why might you want to use breakeven analysis based on dollar sales rather than on units of output? (Hint: Think of a multiproduct firm.)

▶ Give some examples of business decisions for which breakeven analysis might be useful.

▶ Identify some limitations to the use of a single breakeven chart.

Operating Leverage

If a high percentage of a firm's total costs are fixed, the firm is said to have a high degree of **operating leverage**. In physics, "leverage" implies the use of a lever to raise a heavy object with a small amount of force. In politics, people who have "leverage" can accomplish a great deal with their smallest word or action. In business terminology, a high degree of operating leverage, other things held constant, means that a *relatively small change in sales will result in a large change in operating income*. The concept of operating leverage is illustrated in Figure 6-3, where we compare three firms—A, B, and C—that use differing degrees of operating leverage.

Firm A uses the least amount of operating leverage, so it has a relatively small amount of fixed charges. It does not have much automated equipment, so its depreciation cost, maintenance expense, and property taxes are low. Note, however, that its variable cost line has a relatively steep slope, indicating that its variable costs per unit are higher than those of the other firms, which use more leverage.

Firm B is considered to have a normal amount of operating leverage and hence normal fixed costs. It uses automated equipment (with which one operator can turn out a few or many units at the same labour cost) to about the same extent as the average firm in the industry. Firm B breaks even at a higher level of operations (50 000 units) than does Firm A. At a production level of 40 000 units, B loses $8000 but A breaks even.

Firm C uses operating leverage to a greater extent than either Firm A or Firm B. It is highly automated, using expensive, high-speed machines that require very little labour per unit produced. With such an operation, Firm C has high fixed costs but its variable costs rise slowly. Because of the high overhead resulting from depreciation and maintenance expenses associated with the expensive machinery, Firm C's breakeven point is higher than that for either Firm A or Firm B. Once Firm C reaches its breakeven point, however, its profits rise faster than do those of the other firms.

Each firm's use of operating leverage can have a great impact on its average cost per unit. When only 40 000 units are sold, the average cost of production per unit for each firm (calculated by dividing total costs by the 40 000 units sold) is highest for Firm C and lowest for Firm A. The reverse holds true when output rises to 200 000 units.

	Average Cost per Unit	
	40 000 units	**200 000 units**
Firm A	$2.00	$1.60
Firm B	2.20	1.40
Firm C	2.50	1.30

These results have important implications. At a high volume of operations—say, 200 000 units per period—Firm C has a substantial cost savings over the other two firms and particularly over Firm A. Firm C could cut the price of its product to $1.50 per unit, which represents a level that would be unprofitable for Firm A, and still have a profit margin in excess of 13 percent ($0.20/$1.50).

The competitive advantage of high-volume, low-unit-cost operations may be made clear by an actual example. IBM introduced its personal computer (the

Figure 6-3
Operating Leverage

Revenues and Costs
(thousands of dollars)

Firm A

Selling price = $2
Fixed costs = $20 000
Variable costs = $1.50 Q

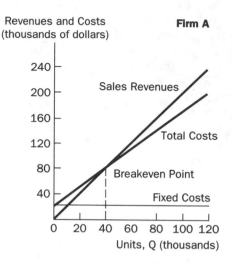

Units Sold (Q)	Sales	Costs	Operating Income (EBIT)
20 000	$ 40 000	$ 50 000	($10 000)
40 000	80 000	80 000	0
60 000	120 000	110 000	10 000
80 000	160 000	140 000	20 000
100 000	200 000	170 000	30 000
120 000	240 000	200 000	40 000
200 000	400 000	320 000	80 000

Revenues and Costs
(thousands of dollars)

Firm B

Selling price = $2
Fixed costs = $40 000
Variable costs = $1.20 Q

Units Sold (Q)	Sales	Costs	Operating Income (EBIT)
20 000	$ 40 000	$ 64 000	($24 000)
40 000	80 000	88 000	(8 000)
60 000	120 000	112 000	8 000
80 000	160 000	136 000	24 000
100 000	200 000	160 000	40 000
120 000	240 000	184 000	56 000
200 000	400 000	280 000	120 000

Revenue and Costs
(thousands of dollars)

Firm C

Selling price = $2
Fixed costs = $60 000
Variable costs = $1 Q

Units Sold (Q)	Sales	Costs	Operating Income (EBIT)
20 000	$ 40 000	$ 80 000	($40 000)
40 000	80 000	100 000	(20 000)
60 000	120 000	120 000	0
80 000	160 000	140 000	20 000
100 000	200 000	160 000	40 000
120 000	240 000	180 000	60 000
200 000	400 000	260 000	140 000

PC) in 1981. By 1989, volume was up to 9 million units per year. Because of the lower costs associated with higher volume, IBM had been able to cut PC prices by 70 percent, in spite of continued general inflation. Those price cuts put great pressure on IBM's low-volume, high-cost competitors, driving some of them out of business, and further expanding IBM's market position, sales volume, and total profits. This example demonstrates the extreme importance of the relationships among market position, volume, costs, and profits and the need to take this relationship into account in strategic planning. High-cost, low-volume producers have a hard time surviving against low-cost, high-volume competitors. The irony of the IBM example is that in 1991 and 1992, IBM was forced to reduce prices further in response to competition from producers with lower costs and high volumes.

mass production

Degree of Operating Leverage

Operating leverage can be defined more precisely in terms of the way a given change in volume affects earnings before interest and taxes (EBIT). To measure the effect of a change in volume on profitability, we calculate the **degree of operating leverage (DOL)**, defined as the ratio of the percentage change in EBIT to the percentage change in sales:

$$\text{Degree of operating leverage} = \frac{\text{Percentage change in EBIT}}{\text{Percentage change in sales}},$$

$$\text{DOL} = \frac{\Delta \text{EBIT}/\text{EBIT}}{\Delta Q/Q}, \qquad (6\text{-}4)$$

where Q is the quantity of output in units and ΔQ is the increase in output. For Firm B in Figure 6-3, the degree of operating leverage, DOL_B, for a change in units of output from 100 000 to 120 000 is

$$\text{DOL}_B = \frac{\Delta \text{EBIT}/\text{EBIT}}{\Delta Q/Q}. \qquad (6\text{-}4)$$

$$= \frac{(\$56\,000 - \$40\,000)/\$40\,000}{(120\,000 - 100\,000)/100\,000} = \frac{\$16\,000/\$40\,000}{20\,000/100\,000} = \frac{40\%}{20\%} = 2.0.$$

For this calculation, we assume an increase in volume from 100 000 to 120 000 units, but the calculated DOL_B would have been the same for any other increase from 100 000 units.

The degree of operating leverage can also be calculated as:[2]

---

[2]Equation 6-4a is developed as follows:

The change in output is defined as ΔQ. Fixed costs are constant, so the change in profits is $\Delta Q(P - V)$, where P = price per unit and V = variable cost per unit. The initial EBIT is $Q(P - V) - F$; so, the percentage change in EBIT is

$$\frac{\Delta Q(P - V)}{Q(P - V) - F}.$$

The percentage change in output is $\Delta Q/Q$; so, the ratio of the change in EBIT to the change in output is:

$$\frac{\Delta Q(P - V)/Q(P - V) - F}{\Delta Q/Q} = \frac{\Delta Q(P - V)}{Q(P - V) - F} \cdot \frac{Q}{\Delta Q} = \frac{Q(P - V)}{Q(P - V) - F}.$$

$$DOL = \frac{Q(P - V)}{Q(P - V) - F}. \tag{6-4a}$$

For Firm B we can calculate the degree of operating leverage at 100 000 units of output using Equation 6-4a, as 2.0:

$$
\begin{aligned}
DOL_B &= \frac{100\,000(\$2.00 - \$1.20)}{100\,000(\$2.00 - \$1.20) - \$40\,000} \\[6pt]
&= \frac{\$200\,000 - \$120\,000}{\$200\,000 - \$120\,000 - \$40\,000} \\[6pt]
&= \frac{\$80\,000}{\$40\,000} = 2.0,
\end{aligned}
$$

which is the same as the value found using Equation 6-4.

The DOL of 2.0 indicates that if units sold increase by, say, 20 percent, from 100 000 to 120 000 units, operating profits will increase by 2.0 × 20% = 40%. This can be confirmed by reference to the tabular data in Figure 6-3 and noting that (1 + 40%) × \$40 000 = 1.40 × \$40 000 = \$56 000.

It should also be noted that the degree of operating leverage for a given firm depends on the base level used in the DOL calculation. In our example, we calculated DOL for Firm B at a sales level of 100 000 units. Had we used a sale level of 60 000 units, DOL_B would have been 6.0:

$$DOL_B = \frac{60\,000(\$2.00 - \$1.20)}{60\,000(\$2.00 - \$1.20) - \$40\,000} = 6.0.$$

Thus, from a base of 60 000 units, a 33.3 percent increase in sales, from 60 000 to 80 000 units, would have led to a 6 × 33.3% = 200% increase in operating profits, or from \$8000 to \$8000 + 2.0(\$8000) = \$24 000.

Using Equation 6-4, we find that the degree of operating leverage at 100 000 units is 1.67 for Firm A and 2.5 for Firm C. Thus, for a 10 percent change in volume, Firm A, the company with the least operating leverage, will experience a profit gain of only 16.7 percent, while Firm C, the one with the most leverage, will enjoy a 25 percent profit gain. Clearly, the profits of Firm C, which has higher fixed costs and a higher degree of operating leverage, are more sensitive to changes in sales volume than are those of Firm A, with its lower fixed costs and lower DOL. Thus, the higher the degree of operating leverage, the more profits will fluctuate, in both an upward and a downward direction, in response to changes in sales volume.

A firm's degree of operating leverage has a number of important implications. First, Firm C's high degree of operating leverage suggests that it could make gains from increasing its sales volume even if it had to lower its price to do so. Suppose Firm C could increase its quantity sold from 100 000 units to 120 000 units by cutting the price per unit from \$2.00 to \$1.90. Its EBIT would then be \$48 000.

$$
\begin{aligned}
EBIT &= PQ - VQ - F \tag{6-5} \\
&= \$1.90(120\,000) - \$1(120\,000) - \$60\,000 \\
&= \$228\,000 - \$120\,000 - \$60\,000 \\
&= \$48\,000.
\end{aligned}
$$

Thus, Firm C could increase its profits from $40 000 at a volume of 100 000 to $48 000 at a volume of 120 000 by lowering its price from $2.00 to $1.90. This demonstrates that a firm with a high degree of operating leverage and consequently low variable costs per unit will be inclined to follow an aggressive price policy, particularly if its competitors have higher costs and thus cannot respond to price cuts.

At the same time, however, Firm C's high degree of operating leverage also indicates that the company is subject to large swings in profits as its volume fluctuates. Thus, if Firm C's industry is one whose sales are greatly affected by changes in the overall level of economic activity (as, for example, such durable goods industries as machine tools, steel, and autos), then its profits will be subject to wide fluctuations. Hence, while Firm C's profit potential is increased by its greater use of operating leverage, the riskiness of its earnings stream is also high.

The degree of operating leverage is an important ingredient in determining the business risk of a firm. *Business risk* is defined as the basic risk inherent in a firm's operations and is manifest in the variability of net operating income. Clearly, a company can influence the degree of business risk by its choice of the degree of operating leverage. Holding all other influences constant, the larger the degree of operating leverage, the greater will be the business risk. The underlying variability in sales volume, however, is another component in assessing business risk. The larger the degree of operating leverage, the greater will be the amplification of a change in sales on the net operating income. A regulated utility in the communications area, such as Bell Canada, may have a large degree of operating leverage, but owing to the stability of sales, the business risk is not substantial. Conversely, a company with a small fixed-cost component can still have high business risk if the basic sales volume has high variability.

Concept Review

► What does the term "high degree of operating leverage" imply, and what are some implications of having a high degree of operating leverage?

► Give the general equation used to calculate the degree of operating leverage.

► How is business risk related to operating leverage?

Cash Breakeven Analysis

Since some of the firm's fixed costs are noncash outlays, it is often useful for management to know what the **cash breakeven point** is. The cash breakeven chart for Firm B is shown in Figure 6-4. This figure is constructed on the assumption that $30 000 of the fixed costs from the previous illustration are depreciation charges and, therefore, a noncash outlay. Fixed cash outlays, then, are only $10 000, resulting in a cash breakeven point of 12 500 units rather than the 50 000-unit EBIT breakeven point.

An equation for the cash breakeven point can be derived from the equation for the EBIT breakeven point. The only change is to reduce fixed costs by the amount of noncash outlays:

$$Q_{BE} = \frac{F - \text{Noncash outlays}}{P - V}. \qquad\qquad \textbf{(6-6)}$$

For Firm B,

$$Q_{BE} = \frac{\$40\,000 - \$30\,000}{\$0.80}$$

$$= 12\,500 \text{ units.}$$

If noncash outlays are a large percentage of total fixed costs, the cash breakeven point will be quite low.

Cash breakeven analysis does not fully represent cash flows—for this a cash budget is required. However, cash breakeven analysis is useful in providing a general picture of the flow of funds from operations. A firm may incur a level of fixed costs that will result in losses during business downturns but in large profits during upswings. If cash outlays are small, then even during periods of loss, the firm might still be able to operate above the cash breakeven point. If the risk of insolvency (in the sense of inability to meet cash obligations) is small, a firm may be willing to increase its use of operating

Figure 6-4
Cash Breakeven Analysis

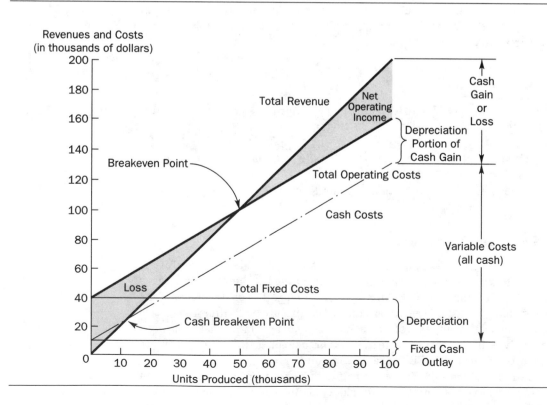

leverage in the hopes of earning higher profits. A firm with a high cash breakeven point, however, could not risk using a high degree of operating leverage without seriously exposing the firm to the possibility of bankruptcy.

The Cash Budget

A firm normally determines its needs for cash as a part of its general budgeting, or forecasting, process. First, it forecasts sales. Next, it forecasts the fixed assets and inventories that will be required to meet the forecasted sales levels and the timing of payments, along with the actual timing of sales and the timing of its own collections for sales. For example, the typical firm makes a 5-year sales forecast, and this forecast is used to help plan for fixed asset acquisitions (capital budgeting). Then the firm develops an annual forecast, in which sales and inventory purchases are forecasted on a monthly basis, along with the times when payments for both fixed assets and inventory purchases must be made. These forecasts are combined with projections about the timing of the collection of accounts receivable, the schedule for payment of taxes, the dates when dividend and interest payments will be made, and so on. Finally, all of this information is summarized in the **cash budget**, which shows the firm's projected cash inflows and outflows over some specified period of time.

Cash budgets can be constructed on a monthly, weekly, or even daily basis. Generally, firms use a monthly cash budget forecasted over the next 6 to 12 months, plus a daily cash budget for the coming month. The longer-term budget is used for general planning purposes, and the shorter term one for actual cash control.

Constructing the Cash Budget

We shall illustrate the process with a monthly cash budget covering the last 6 months of 1993 for the Marvel Toy Company, a leading producer of games, dolls, stuffed animals, and other toys. Its games and toys are sold year round, but the bulk of sales are made during September, when retailers are stocking up for Christmas.

All sales are made on terms that allow a cash discount for payments made within 10 days, but if the discount is not taken, the full amount must be paid in 40 days. However, Marvel, like most other companies, finds that some of its customers delay payment up to 70 days. Indeed, its experience shows that on 20 percent of its sales, payment is made during the month in which the sale is made; on 70 percent of the sales, payment is made during the first month after the month of the sale; and on 10 percent of the sales, payment is made during the second month after the month of the sale. Marvel offers a 2 percent discount for payments received within 10 days of sales. Typically, payments received in the month of sale are on discount sales.

Rather than produce at a uniform rate throughout the year, Marvel manufactures its games and toys immediately before they are required for delivery. Plastic, cloth, paint, and other materials amount to 70 percent of sales and are bought the month before the company expects to sell the finished products. Its own purchase terms permit Marvel to delay payment on its purchases for 1 month. Accordingly, if July sales are forecasted at $10.0 million, purchases during June will amount to $7.0 million, and this amount will actually be paid in July.

Such other cash expenditures as wages and rent are also built into the cash budget. Further, Marvel must make tax payments of $2.0 million on September 15 and December 15, as well as a $5.0 million payment for a new plant in October. Assuming that it needs to keep a target cash balance of $2.5 million at all times, and that it will have $3.0 million on July 1, what are Marvel's financial requirements for the period July through December?[3]

The monthly cash flow forecasts are worked out in Table 6-2. Section I of the table provides a worksheet for calculating collections on sales and

Table 6-2
Marvel Toy Company: Cash Budget
(thousands of dollars)

	May[a]	June[a]	July	Aug.	Sept.	Oct.	Nov.	Dec.
I. Collections and Payments								
(1) Sales (gross)	$5 000	$5 000	$10 000	$15 000	$20 000	$10 000	$10 000	$5 000
Collections								
(2) During month of sales: 20% minus 2% discount, or (0.2)(0.98)(month's sales)	980	980	1 960	2 940	3 920	1 960	1 960	980
(3) During first month after sale month: 70%, or (0.7) (previous month's sales)		3 500	3 500	7 000	10 500	14 000	7 000	7 000
(4) During second month after sale month: 10%, or (0.1)(sales 2 months ago)			500	500	1 000	1 500	2 000	1 000
(5) Total collections	$ 980	$4 480	$ 5 960	$10 440	$15 420	$17 460	$10 960	$8 980
(6) Purchases (70% of next month's sales)	$3 500	$7 000	$10 500	$14 000	$ 7 000	$ 7 000	$ 3 500	
(7) Payments (1-month lag)		$3 500	$ 7 000	$10 500	$14 000	$ 7 000	$ 7 000	$3 500

(continued)

---

[3]Setting the target cash balance is an important part of cash management. We shall discuss this topic in Chapter 10.

Table 6-2 *(continued)*

	May[a]	June[a]	July	Aug.	Sept.	Oct.	Nov.	Dec.
II. Cash Gain (Loss) for Month								
(8) Collections (from line 5)			$ 5 960	$10 440	$15 420	$17 460	$10 960	$8 980
Payments								
(9) Purchases (from line 7)			$ 7 000	$10 500	$14 000	$ 7 000	$ 7 000	$3 500
(10) Wages and salaries			750	1 000	1 250	750	750	500
(11) Rent			250	250	250	250	250	250
(12) Other expenses			100	150	200	100	100	50
(13) Taxes					2 000			2 000
(14) Payment for plant construction						5 000		
(15) Total payments			$ 8 100	$11 900	$17 700	$13 100	$ 8 100	$6 300
(16) Net cash gain (loss) during month (line 8 − line 15)			($ 2 140)	($ 1 460)	($ 2 280)	$ 4 360	$ 2 860	$2 680
III. Cash Surplus or Loan Requirements								
(17) Cash at start of month if no borrowing is done[b]			3 000	860	(600)	(2 880)	1 480	4 340
(18) Cumulative cash (cash at start + gain or − loss = line 16 + line 17)			$ 860	($ 600)	($ 2 880)	$ 1 480	$ 4 340	$7 020
(19) *Less:* Target cash balance			2 500	2 500	2 500	2 500	2 500	2 500
(20) Surplus cash or total loans outstanding required to maintain $2 500 target cash balance (line 18 − line 19)[c]			($ 1 640)	($ 3 100)	($ 5 380)	($ 1 020)	$ 1 840	$4 520

[a]Although the budget period is July through December, sales and purchases data for May and June are needed to determine collections and payments during July and August.

[b]The amount shown on line 17 for the first budget period month, the $3000 balance on July 1, is assumed to be on hand initially. The values shown for each of the following months on line 17 are equal to the cumulative cash as shown on line 18 for the preceding month; for example, the $860 shown on line 17 for August is taken from line 18 in the July column.

[c]When the target cash balance of $2500 (line 19) is deducted from the cumulative cash balance (line 18), a resulting negative figure on line 20 represents a required loan, whereas a positive figure represents surplus cash. Loans are required from July through October, and surpluses are expected during November and December. Note also that firms can borrow or pay off loans on a daily basis, so the $1640 borrowed during July would be borrowed on a daily basis, as needed, and during October the $5380 loan that existed at the beginning of the month would be reduced daily to the $1020 ending balance, which in turn would be completely paid off during November.

payments on purchases. Line 1 gives the sales forecast for the period May through December; May and June sales are necessary to determine collections for July and August. Next, on lines 2 through 5, cash collections are given. Line 2 shows that 20 percent of the sales during any given month are collected during that month. Customers who pay in the first month, however, typically take the discount, so the cash collected in the month of sale is reduced by 2 percent; for example, collections during July for the $10 000 000 of sales in that month will be 20 percent of total sales less the 2 percent discount = $(0.2)(\$10\,000\,000)(0.98) = \$1\,960\,000$. Line 3 shows the collections on the previous month's sales, or 70 percent of sales in the preceding month; thus, July collections for June sales are $(0.70)(\$5\,000\,000) = \$3\,500\,000$. Line 4 gives collections from sales two months earlier, or 10 percent of sales in that month;

for example, the July collections for May sales are $(0.10)(\$5\,000\,000) = \$500\,000$. The collections during each month are summed and shown on line 5; thus, the July collections represent 20 percent of July sales (minus the discount) plus 70 percent of June sales plus 10 percent of May sales, or $\$5\,960\,000$ in total.

Next, payments for purchases of raw materials are shown. July sales are forecasted at $10 million, so Marvel will purchase $7 million of materials in June (line 6) and pay for these purchases in July (line 7). Similarly, Marvel will purchase $10.5 million of materials in July to manufacture toys and games to meet August's forecasted sales of $15 million.

With Section I completed, Section II can be constructed. Cash from collections is shown on line 8. Lines 9 through 14 list payments made during each month, and these payments are summed on line 15. The difference between cash receipts and cash payments (line 8 minus line 15) is the net cash gain or loss during the month; for July there is a net cash loss of $\$2\,140\,000$, as shown on line 16.

In Section III, we first determine Marvel's cumulative cash balance at the end of each month, assuming no borrowing is done. Then we determine the company's forecasted cash surplus or the loan balance, if any, that is needed to force Marvel's cash balance to equal the target cash balance. The cash on hand at the beginning of the month is shown on line 17. We assume that Marvel will have $3 million on hand on July 1, but thereafter the beginning cash balance is taken as the cumulative cash balance (line 18) from the previous month. The beginning cash balance (line 17) is added to the net cash gain or loss during the month (line 16) to obtain the cumulative cash that would be on hand if no financing were done (line 18); at the end of July, Marvel forecasts a cumulative cash balance of $860 000 in the absence of borrowing.

The target cash balance, $2.5 million, is then subtracted from the cumulative cash balance to determine the firm's borrowing requirements or surplus cash. Because Marvel expects to have cumulative cash, as shown on line 18, of $\$860\,000$ in July, it will have to borrow $\$1\,640\,000$ to bring the cash account up to the target balance of $\$2\,500\,000$. Assuming that this amount is indeed borrowed, loans outstanding will total $\$1\,640\,000$ at the end of July. (We assume that Marvel did not have any loans outstanding on July 1, because its beginning cash balance exceeded the target balance.) The cash surplus or required loan balance is given on line 20; a positive value indicates a cash surplus, whereas a negative value indicates a loan requirement. Note that the surplus cash or loan requirement shown on Line 20 is a *cumulative* amount. Thus, Marvel must borrow $\$1\,640\,000$ in July; it has a cash shortfall during August of $\$1\,460\,000$ as reported on line 16; and, therefore, its total loan requirement at the end of August is $\$1\,640\,000 + \$1\,460\,000 = \$3\,100\,000$, as reported on line 20. Marvel's arrangement with the bank permits it to increase its outstanding loans on a daily basis, up to a prearranged maximum, just as you could increase the amount you owe on a credit card. Marvel will use any surplus funds it generates to pay off its loans, and because the loan can be paid down at any time, Marvel will never have both a cash surplus and an outstanding loan balance.

This same procedure is used in the following months. Sales will peak in September, accompanied by increased payments for purchases, wages, and other items. Receipts from sales will also go up, but the firm will still be left with a $2 280 000 net cash outflow during the month. The total loan requirement at the end of September will be $5 380 000, the cumulative cash deficit plus the target cash balance. This amount is also equal to the $3 100 000 needed at the end of August plus the $2 280 000 cash deficit for September. Thus, loans outstanding will hit a high of $5 380 000 at the end of September.

Sales, purchases, and payments for past purchases will fall sharply in October, and collections will be the highest of any month because they will reflect the high September sales. As a result, Marvel will enjoy a healthy $4 360 000 net cash gain during October. This net gain will be used to pay off borrowings, so loans outstanding will decline by $4 360 000, to $1 020 000.

Marvel will have another cash surplus in November, which will permit it to pay off all of its loans. In fact, the company is expected to have $1 840 000 in surplus cash by the month's end, and another cash surplus in December will swell the extra cash to $4 520 000. With such a large amount of unneeded funds, Marvel's treasurer will certainly want to invest in interest-bearing securities, or to put the funds to use in some other way. Various types of investments into which Marvel might put its excess funds are discussed in Chapter 10.

Before concluding our discussion of the cash budget, we should make some additional points:

1. Our cash budget example does not reflect interest on loans or income from the investment of surplus cash. These refinements could easily be added.
2. If cash inflows and outflows are not uniform during the month, we could be seriously understating the firm's peak financing requirements. The data in Table 6-2 show the situation expected on the last day of each month, but on any given day during the month it could be quite different. For example, if all payments had to be made on the fifth of each month, but collections came in uniformly throughout the month, the firm would need to borrow much larger amounts than those shown in Table 6-2. In this case, we would want to prepare a cash budget that showed requirements on a daily basis.
3. Since depreciation is a noncash charge, it does not appear on the cash budget other than through its effect on taxes paid.
4. Since the cash budget represents a forecast, all the values in the table are *expected* values. If actual sales, purchases, and so on, differ from their forecasted levels, then the projected cash deficits and surpluses will also be incorrect. Thus, Marvel might end up needing to borrow larger amounts than are indicated on line 20, so it should arrange a line of credit in excess of that amount.
5. Computerized spreadsheet programs such as *Lotus 1-2-3* are particularly well suited for constructing and analyzing cash budgets, especially with respect to the sensitivity of cash flows to changes in sales levels, collection periods, and the like. We could change any assumption—say, the projected monthly sales or the time when customers pay—and the cash budget would automatically and instantly be recalculated. This would show us exactly how the firm's borrowing requirements would change if various other things changed. Also, with a computer model, it is easy to add features like interest on loans, bad debts, and so on.

6. Finally, we should note that the target cash balance probably will be adjusted over time, rising and falling with seasonal patterns and with long-term changes in the scale of the firm's operations. Thus, Marvel will probably plan to maintain larger cash balances during August and September than at other times, and as the company grows, so will its required cash balance. Factors that influence the target cash balance are discussed in Chapter 10.

Concept Review

▶ What is done in each of the three sections of the cash budget?

▶ Why is depreciation not included in the cash budget?

▶ What would happen to the monthly cash budget if cash inflows and outflows were not uniform during the month? What type of analysis should be done in this situation?

Control in Multidivisional Companies

The concepts, techniques, and procedures described thus far in the chapter must be extended when applied to large national or multinational firms, which have plants and sales offices across the country or throughout the world. To permit faster decisions and to increase operating efficiency, large firms are generally set up on a decentralized or divisional basis. Each division is defined as a *profit centre*, and each has its plant, equipment, and working capital, as well as a share of such general corporate assets as research labs and headquarters buildings. Further, each division is expected to earn an appropriate return on its operating assets. Corporate headquarters, through its central staff, typically uses a form of the Du Pont system to control the various divisions. The Du Pont system was introduced in Chapter 4; here we expand our discussion to show how this system can be used in controlling the firm.

Du Pont System of Financial Analysis

As noted in Chapter 4, the *Du Pont system* facilitates integrated analysis of the turnover ratios and the profit margin on sales, and it shows how the various ratios interact to determine the rate of return on assets.

When the Du Pont system is used for divisional control, the process is often called **return on assets (ROA) control** where return is measured by operating income or earnings before interest and taxes, EBIT. Target levels for ROA are established, and actual ROAs are compared with target levels to see just how well each division is operating. If problems arise, corporate headquarters will investigate and take corrective action, including removing the managers of poorly performing divisions. Superior performers are rewarded with bonuses and other incentives. However, for meaningful comparisons, a corporation that uses ROA control must take into account any differences among divisions and adjust for them. For example, some divisions may have older fixed assets that were acquired at preinflation prices, and much of their equipment may have been depreciated down to a low book value yet still be serviceable. Such a division may well have a higher rate of return than another division with newer assets, even though both divisions are equally managed. If management believes the differences in asset book values are great enough to warrant an adjustment, earnings figures may be calculated on the basis of replacement cost depreciation, and assets may be written up on a current cost basis to put the divisions on a comparable basis.[4]

If a particular division's ROA falls below a target figure, the centralized corporate staff helps the division's own financial staff trace back through the Du Pont system to determine the cause of the substandard performance. Each division manager is judged by his or her division's ROA and rewarded or penalized accordingly. Division managers are thus motivated to keep their ROAs up to the target level. Their individual actions should, in turn, maintain the firm's ROA at an appropriate level.

In addition to its use in managerial control, ROA can be used to allocate funds to the various divisions. The firm as a whole has financial resources—cash flows from retained earnings, from depreciation, and from external financing. The available capital can be allocated on the basis of the divisional ROAs, with those divisions having highest ROAs receiving more funds than those with lower ROAs. However, capital budgeting analysis as discussed in Chapter 13 is better for allocating capital than is the use of divisional ROAs.

Pitfalls in the Use of ROA Control

Increasingly, managers are being compensated on some type of performance-based system: They receive a relatively low base salary, but they then receive bonuses or stock options that depend upon how well their divisions meet certain stated objectives. One of the most important of those objectives is, generally, their divisions' ROAs. This is quite logical, because the firm's ROA has a major effect on the value of its equity, and the firm's ROA obviously depends upon the ROAs of its different divisions.

However, any such control-by-incentive system runs the risk that executives will devise methods for "beating the system," so safeguards are required. Also, since the divisional managers are rewarded on the basis of their ROA performance, maintaining morale makes it essential that managers feel their divisional ROA targets are reasonable and that earned ROAs do indeed provide an accurate measure of relative performance. But ROA is dependent on a number of factors in addition to managerial competence, and these factors must be considered when judging performance on an ROA standard. Some of the key factors are listed below.

1. *Depreciation.*   ROA is very sensitive to depreciation policy. A division that is currently writing off assets at a relatively rapid rate will have high current depreciation expenses, a relatively low profit, and hence a lower ROA than a division using a slower depreciation method.

---

[4]*Replacement cost depreciation* is depreciation calculated by dividing the cost that would have to be incurred to replace an asset by the life of the asset. This type of depreciation is not used for taxes or for shareholder reporting, but it is occasionally used for internal management purposes.

2. *Book value of assets.*   If an older division is using assets that were acquired before the period of rapid inflation in the late 1970s and early 1980s and these assets have been largely written off, then both its current depreciation charges and its investment base will be low. This will make its ROA high in relation to the ROAs of rapidly growing divisions with newer assets.

3. *Transfer pricing.*   In most corporations, some divisions sell to other divisions. In the Ford Motor Company of Canada, for example, the assembly divisions purchase engines from other divisions. In such cases the prices at which goods are transferred between divisions, called the **transfer price**, has a fundamental effect on divisional profits and divisional ROA. If the transfer price of engines is set relatively high, then the assembly division will have a relatively low ROA and the engine division a relatively high ROA. If divisional managers are rewarded on the basis of ROA, it is easy to see how internal competition could become destructive.

4. *Time periods.*   Many projects have long gestation periods during which expenditures must be made for research and development, for plant construction, for market development, and so on. Such expenditures may add to the asset base without a commensurate increase in profits for several years. During this period, a division's ROA can be seriously reduced, and without proper adjustments, its division manager may be improperly penalized. This, in turn, may lead division managers to seek short-term, fast-payback projects. Given the frequency of personnel transfers in larger corporations, it is easy to see how the timing problem, if it is not recognized and corrected for, could make managers resist taking on long-term projects even when such investments are in the best interests of the firm.

5. *Industry conditions.*   If one division is operating in an industry in which conditions are favourable and rates of return are high, whereas another is in an industry suffering from excessive competition, the environmental differences may cause the favoured division to look good and the unfavoured division to look bad, quite apart from any differences in the abilities of their respective managers. Therefore, external conditions must be taken into consideration when appraising ROA performance.

Because of these problems, divisional ROAs must be supplemented with other criteria for evaluating performance. For example, a division's growth rate in sales, its profit margins, and its ROA should be compared with those of other firms in its own industry, as well as with those of divisions in the same firm. Like most other tools, ROA control can be helpful if used properly, but it can also be destructive if misused.

Concept Review

▶ Identify and explain some key factors that must be considered when judging performance on an ROA standard.

Summary

In this chapter we considered several planning and control systems used by financial managers. The key concepts covered are listed below.

□ **Financial planning** involves making projections of sales, income, and assets based on alternative production and marketing strategies and then deciding how to meet the forecasted financial requirements.

□ **Financial control** deals with the feedback and adjustment process that is required (1) to ensure that plans are followed or (2) to modify existing plans in response to changes in the operating environment.

□ **Breakeven analysis** is a method of determining the point at which sales will just cover costs, and it shows the magnitude of the firm's profits or losses if sales exceed or fall below that point.

□ The **breakeven point** is the sales volume at which total costs equal total revenues, and profits equal zero. The equation used to calculate the breakeven point is

$$Q_{BE} = \frac{F}{P - V}.$$

□ **Operating leverage** is a measure of the extent to which fixed costs are used in a firm's operations. A firm with a high percentage of fixed costs is said to have a high *degree of operating leverage.*

□ The **degree of operating leverage (DOL)** shows how a change in sales will affect operating income. Whereas breakeven analysis emphasizes the volume of sales the firm needs to be profitable, the degree of operating leverage measures how sensitive the firm's profits are to changes in the volume of sales. The equation used to calculate the DOL is

$$DOL = \frac{Q(P - V)}{Q(P - V) - F}.$$

□ A **cash breakeven point** can be calculated; it is the breakeven point when noncash items are subtracted from fixed costs. The equation is

$$Q_{BE} = \frac{F - \text{Noncash outlays}}{P - V}.$$

□ The *budgeting process* provides a detailed plan of how funds will be spent. A **budget** is a plan stated in terms of specific expenditures for specific purposes, and it is used for both planning and control.

□ A **cash budget** is a schedule showing projected cash inflows and outflows over a specified period. The cash budget is used to determine when the firm will have cash surpluses and shortfalls and thus to help management plan to invest surpluses or to cover shortages.

□ **Return on assets (ROA) control** refers to the use of the Du Pont system for divisional control.

Although the entire budget system is vital to corporate management, the cash budget is especially important to the financial manager. The cash budget is, in fact, the single most important tool for making short-run financial forecasts. If used properly, it can pinpoint the amount of funds that will be needed, when they will be needed, and when cash flows will be available to retire any loans the company has taken out.

As a firm becomes larger, it becomes necessary to decentralize operations. However, decentralized operations still require some degree of centralized control, and the principal tool used for such control is the ROA method. There are potential pitfalls with ROA control, but if it is used properly, then overall operations can be improved.

Questions

6-1   What benefits can be derived from breakeven analysis? What are some problems with breakeven analysis?

6-2   Explain how profits or losses will be magnified for a firm with high operating leverage as opposed to a firm with lower operating leverage.

6-3   What data are necessary to construct a breakeven chart?

6-4   What is the effect of each of the following changes on a firm's breakeven point?
     a. An increase in selling price with no change in units sold.
     b. A change from the leasing of a machine for $5000 a year to the purchase of the machine for $100 000. The useful life of this machine will be 20 years with no salvage value. Assume straight line depreciation.
     c. A reduction in variable labour costs.

6-5   Why is a cash budget important even when a firm has plenty of cash in the bank?

6-6   What is the difference between the percentage-of-sales method for forecasting financial requirements and the cash budget? How might they be used together?

6-7   Assume that a firm is developing its long-run financial plan. What period should this plan cover—1 month, 6 months, 1 year, 3 years, 5 years, or some other period? Justify your answer.

6-8   Would a detailed budget be more important to a large, multidivisional firm or to a small, single-product, owner-managed firm? Why?

6-9   Assume that your uncle is a major shareholder in a multidivisional firm that uses a naïve ROA criterion for evaluating divisional managers and that bases managers' salaries in large part on this evaluation. You can have the job of division manager in any division you choose. If you are a salary maximizer, what divisional characteristics would you seek? If, because of your good performance, you became president of the firm, what changes would you make?

Self-Test Problems (solutions appear on page 209)

ST-1 Key terms. Define each of the following terms:
  a. Financial planning; financial control
  b. Breakeven analysis; breakeven point; cash breakeven point
  c. Operating leverage; degree of operating leverage (DOL)
  d. Budget; cash budget
  e. Du Pont system; ROA control
  f. Transfer price

ST-2 Operating leverage. Olinde Electronics Ltd., produces stereo components that sell for P = $100. Olinde's fixed costs are $200 000; it produces and sells 5 000 components each year; EBIT is currently $50 000; and Olinde's assets (all equity financed) are $500 000. Olinde estimates that it can change its production process, adding $400 000 to investment and $50 000 to fixed operating costs. This change will reduce variable costs per unit by $10 and increase output by 2000 units, but the sales price on all units will have to be lowered to $95 to permit sales of the additional output. Olinde has tax loss carryforwards that cause its tax rate to be zero. Olinde uses no debt, and its average cost of capital is 10 percent.
  a. Should Olinde make the change?
  b. Would Olinde's degree of operating leverage increase or decrease if it made the change? What about its breakeven point?
  c. Suppose Olinde is unable to raise additional equity financing and would have to borrow the $400 000 at an interest rate of 10 percent. Use the Du Pont equation to find the expected ROA of the investment. Should Olinde make the change if debt financing must be used?

Problems

6-1 Operating leverage. The Berry Corporation produces tea kettles, which it sells for $15 each. Fixed costs are $700 000 for up to 400 000 units of output. Variable costs are $10 per kettle.
  a. What is the firm's gain or loss at sales of 125 000 units? Of 175 000 units?
  b. What is the breakeven point? Illustrate by means of a chart.
  c. What is Berry's degree of operating leverage at sales of 125 000 units? Of 150 000 units? Of 175 000 units? (Hint: You may use either Equation 6-4 or 6-4a to solve this problem.)

6-2 Breakeven analysis. The Conway Watch Company manufactures a line of ladies' watches that are sold through discount houses. Each watch is sold for $25; the fixed costs are $140 000 for 30 watches or less; variable costs are $15 per watch.
  a. What is the firm's gain or loss at sales of 8000 watches? Of 18 000 watches?
  b. What is the breakeven point? Illustrate by means of a chart.

   c. What is Conway's degree of operating leverage at sales of 8000 units? Of 18 000 units? (Hint: Use Equation 6-4a to solve this problem.)
   d. What happens to the breakeven point if the selling price rises to $31? What is the significance of the change to the financial manager?
   e. What happens to the breakeven point if the selling price rises to $31 but variable costs rise to $23 a unit?

6-3 **Breakeven analysis.** The following relationships exist for Denning Industries, a manufacturer of electronic components. Each unit of output is sold for $45; the fixed costs are $175 000, of which $110 000 are annual depreciation charges; variable costs are $20 per unit.
   a. What is the firm's gain or loss at sales of 5000 units? Of 12 000 units?
   b. What is the profit breakeven point?
   c. What is the cash breakeven point?
   d. Assume Denning is operating at a level of 4000 units. Are creditors likely to seek the liquidation of the company if it is slow in paying its bills?

6-4 **Degree of operating leverage.**
   a. Given the following graphs, calculate the total fixed costs, variable costs per unit, and sales price for Firm A. Firm B's fixed costs are $120 000, its variable costs per unit are $4, and its sales price is $8 per unit.

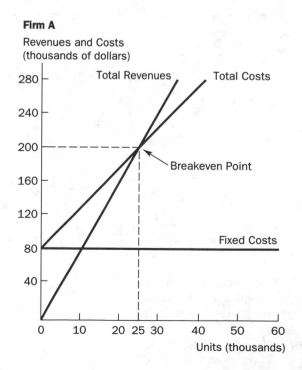

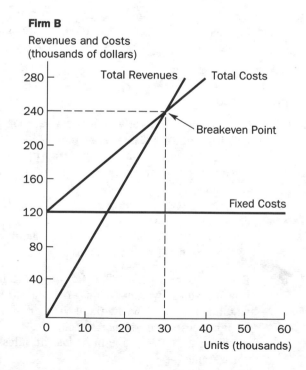

   b. Which firm has the higher degree of operating leverage? Explain.
   c. At what *sales level*, in units, do both firms earn the same profit?

6-5   **Cash budgeting.**   Don Sorenson recently leased space in the Southside Mall and opened a new business, Sorenson's Coin Shop. Business has been good, but Sorenson has frequently run out of cash. This has necessitated late payment on certain orders, which in turn is beginning to cause a problem with suppliers. Sorenson plans to borrow from the bank to have cash ready as needed, but first he needs a forecast of just how much he must borrow. Accordingly, he has asked you to prepare a cash budget for the critical period around Christmas, when needs will be especially high.

Sales are made on a cash basis only. Sorenson's purchases must be paid for during the following month. Sorenson pays himself a salary of $4800 per month, and the rent is $2000 per month. In addition, he must make a tax payment of $12 000 in December. The current cash on hand (on December 1) is $400, but Sorenson has agreed to maintain an average bank balance of $6000—this is his target cash balance. (Disregard till cash, which is insignificant because Sorenson keeps only a small amount on hand in order to lessen the chances of robbery.)

The estimated sales and purchases for December, January, and February are shown below. Purchases during November amounted to $140 000.

	Sales	Purchases
December	$160 000	$40 000
January	40 000	40 000
February	60 000	40 000

a. Prepare a cash budget for December, January, and February.
b. Now suppose Sorenson starts selling on a credit basis on December 1, giving customers 30 days to pay. All customers accept these terms, and all other facts in the problem are unchanged. What would the company's loan requirements be at the end of December in this case? (Hint: The calculations required to answer this question are minimal.)

6-6   **Cash budgeting.**   Monique Couture, owner of Monique's Fashion Designs, Inc., is planning to request a line of credit from her bank. She has estimated the following sales forecasts for the firm for parts of 1993 and 1994:

May 1993	$180 000
June	180 000
July	360 000
August	540 000
September	720 000
October	360 000
November	360 000
December	90 000
January 1994	180 000

Collection estimates obtained from the credit and collection department are as follows: collections within the month of sale, 10 percent;

collections the month following the sale, 75 percent; collections the second month following the sale, 15 percent. Payments for labour and raw materials are typically made during the month following the one in which these costs have been incurred. Total labour and raw materials costs are estimated for each month as follows:

May 1993	$ 90 000
June	90 000
July	126 000
August	882 000
September	306 000
October	234 000
November	162 000
December	90 000

General and administrative salaries amount to approximately $27 000 a month; lease payments under long-term lease contracts are $9000 a month; depreciation charges are $36 000 a month; miscellaneous expenses average $2700 a month; income tax payments of $63 000 will be due in both September and December; and a progress payment of $180 000 on a new design studio must be paid in October. Cash on hand on July 1 will amount to $132 000, and a minimum cash balance of $90 000 is to be maintained throughout the cash budget period.

a. Prepare a monthly cash budget for the last six months of 1993.

b. Prepare an estimate of the required financing (or excess funds)—that is, the amount of money Monique will need to borrow (or to have available to invest)—for each month during that period.

c. Assume that receipts from sales come in uniformly during the month (that is, cash receipts come in at the rate of 1/30 each day), but all outflows are paid on the fifth of the month. Will this have an effect on the cash budget—in other words, would the cash budget you have prepared be valid under these assumptions? If not, what can be done to make a valid estimate of peak financing requirements? No calculations are required, although calculations can be used to illustrate the effects.

d. Monique produces on a seasonal basis, just ahead of sales. Without making any calculations, discuss how the company's current ratio and debt ratio will vary during the year assuming all financial requirements are met by short-term bank loans. Could changes in these ratios affect the firm's ability to obtain bank credit?

e. If Monique went to a cash-only sales policy, how would that affect requirements, all other things held constant? No calculations are required.

6-7   **Return on assets control.**   Tambe & Co. is a diversified multinational corporation that produces a wide variety of goods and services, including rubber, soaps, tobacco products, toys, plastics, pollution control equipment, canned food, sugar, motion pictures, and computer software. The corporation's major divisions were brought together in the early 1970s under a decentralized form of management; each division was evaluated in terms of its profitability, efficiency, and return on investments. This decentralized organization was used for 17 years, during which Tambe experienced a high average growth rate in total assets, earnings, and stock prices.

Toward the end of 1991, however, those trends were reversed. The organization was faced with declining earnings, unstable share prices, and a generally uncertain future. This situation persisted into 1992, but during that year a new president, Kent Fairchild, was appointed by the board of directors. Fairchild, who had served for a time on the financial staff of E.I. Du Pont, used the Du Pont system to evaluate the various divisions. All showed definite weaknesses.

Fairchild reported to the board that a principal reason for the poor overall performance was a lack of control by central management over each division's activities. He was particularly disturbed by the consistently poor results of the corporation's budgeting procedures. Under those procedures, each division manager drew up a projected budget for the next quarter, along with estimated sales, revenues, and profit; funds were then allocated to the divisions, basically in proportion to their budget requests. However, actual budgets seldom matched the projections and wide discrepancies occurred; this, of course, resulted in a highly inefficient use of capital.

In an attempt to correct the situation, Fairchild asked the firm's chief financial officer to draw up a plan to improve the budgeting, planning, and control processes. When the plan was submitted, its basic provisions included the following:

- To improve the quality of the divisional budgets, the division managers should be informed that the continuance of wide variation between their projected and actual budgets would result in dismissal.
- A system should be instituted under which funds would be allocated to divisions on the basis of their average return on assets (ROA) during the last four quarters. Since funds are short, divisions with high ROAs would get most of the available money.
- About half of each division manager's present compensation should be received as salary; the rest should be in the form of a bonus related to the division's average ROA for the quarter.
- Each division should submit to the central office for approval all capital expenditure requests, production schedules, and price changes. Thus, the company would be recentralized.

a. i. Is it reasonable to expect the new procedures to improve the accuracy of the budget forecast?

   ii. Should all divisions be expected to maintain the same degree of accuracy?

   iii. In what other ways might the budgets be made?

b. i. What problems would be associated with the use of the ROA criterion in allocating funds among the divisions?

   ii. What effect would the period used in computing ROA (that is, 1 quarter, 4 quarters, 2 years, and so on) have on the effectiveness of this method?

   iii. What problems might occur in evaluating the ROA in the crude rubber and the auto tires divisions? What problems would occur

between the sugar products and the pollution control
equipment divisions?

c. What problems would be associated with rewarding each manager
on the basis of the division's ROA?

Integrative Problem

6-8   **Cash budget and breakeven analysis.**   Jill Triffs, financial manager
of Swimwear, Ltd., is currently forecasting the company's cash needs
for the first half of next year. Swimwear's sales are highly seasonal,
with most of its sales occurring in the spring, just prior to the summer
swimming season. The firm's marketing department forecasts sales as
follows:

November	$ 50 000
December	75 000
January	300 000
February	400 000
March	550 000
April	925 000
May	725 000
June	475 000
July	300 000

Collection estimates obtained from the credit and collection departments are as follows: 20 percent of dollar sales will be collected in the
month of sale; 60 percent will be collected the month following the sale;
and 20 percent will be collected two months following the sale.

Wages and material costs are related to production, and hence to
sales. The production department has estimated these costs as follows:

December	$175 000
January	175 000
February	250 000
March	275 000
April	425 000
May	175 000
June	75 000

Note, however, that payments for wages and materials are typically
paid during the month following the one in which the costs are incurred.

Administrative salaries are projected at $25 000 a month; lease
payments amount to $20 000 a month; depreciation expenses are $30 000
per month; and miscellaneous overhead expenses total $10 000 a month.
Quarterly tax payments of $125 000 must be made in March and June,
and $250 000 will be needed in April to purchase a new fabric-cutting
machine.

Jill expects the firm to have $50 000 on hand at the beginning of
January, and she wants to start each month with that amount on hand.
As Jill's assistant, you have been asked to help her by completing the
following tasks and answering the following questions:

a. What is financial planning? What is financial control, and what is its relationship to financial planning?

b. What is a budget, and where does it fit into the financial planning process?

c. What is breakeven analysis? Find the breakeven point in units and dollars for Swimwear, Ltd., if the company's fixed costs are $1 770 000 (including $360 000 of depreciation), the firm's variable costs are $16 per swimsuit, and the swimsuits will sell for $40 each.

d. What is meant by the term *cash breakeven point*? Find the cash breakeven point in units and dollars for Swimwear, Ltd., given the information in Part c.

e. Draw the breakeven chart for Swimwear, Ltd., as calculated in Part c.

f. Draw the cash breakeven chart for Swimwear, Ltd., as calculated in Part d.

g. What is operating leverage? Calculate Swimwear, Ltd.'s, degree of operating leverage at an output of 100 000 swimsuits, given the information in Part c. Use Equation 6-4a.

h. Construct the collections worksheet for the months of January through June.

i. Construct the remainder of the cash budget for the months of January through June. What is Swimwear's maximum loan requirement? What is the firm's maximum surplus balance?

j. i. Should depreciation expense be explicitly included in the cash budget?

 ii. Suppose the outflows all occur on the fifth day of each month, but the inflows all occur on the twenty-fifth day. How would this affect January's cash budget? What could Jill do to incorporate such nonuniform flows?

 iii. Swimwear's only receipts are collections. What are some other types of inflows that could occur?

k. The cash budget is a forecast, so many of the flows are *expected* values rather than amounts known with certainty. If actual sales, and hence collections and production, are different from the forecasted levels, then the projected surpluses and deficits will also be incorrect. What would you expect the impact on the cash budget to be if sales were 20 percent above those originally forecasted? What if sales were 20 percent below those originally forecasted? (Use the same assumptions as in Parts h and i.)

Solutions to Self-Test Problems

ST-1 Refer to the appropriate sections of the text to check your responses.

ST-2 a. i. Determine the variable cost per unit at present, using the following definitions and equations:

Q = units of output (sales) = 5000.

P = average sales price per unit of output = $100.

F = fixed operating costs = $200 000.

V = variable costs per unit.

$$EBIT = P(Q) - F - V(Q)$$
$$\$50\,000 = \$100(5000) - \$200\,000 - V(5000)$$
$$5000V = \$250\,000$$
$$V = \$50.$$

ii. Determine the new EBIT level if the change is made:

$$\begin{aligned} \text{New EBIT} &= P_2(Q_2) - F_2 - V_2(Q_2) \\ &= \$95(7000) - \$250\,000 - \$40(7000) \\ &= \$135\,000. \end{aligned}$$

iii. Determine the incremental EBIT:

$$\Delta EBIT = \$135\,000 - \$50\,000 = \$85\,000.$$

iv. Estimate the approximate rate of return on the new investment:

$$\Delta ROA = \frac{\Delta EBIT}{Investment} = \frac{\$85\,000}{\$400\,000} = 21.25\%.$$

Since the ROA exceeds Olinde's average cost of capital, this analysis suggests that Olinde should go ahead and make the investment.

b.

$$DOL = \frac{Q(P - V)}{Q(P - V) - F}.$$

$$DOL_{Old} = \frac{5000(\$100 - \$50)}{5000(\$100 - \$50) - \$200\,000} = 5.00.$$

$$DOL_{New} = \frac{7000(\$95 - \$40)}{7000(\$95 - \$40) - \$250\,000} = 2.85.$$

This indicates that operating income will be less sensitive to changes in sales if the production process is changed; thus the change would reduce risks. However, the change would increase the breakeven point. Still, with a lower sales price, it might be easier to achieve the higher new breakeven volume.

$$Old: Q_{BE} = \frac{F}{P - V} = \frac{\$200\,000}{\$100 - \$50} = 4000 \text{ units.}$$

$$New: Q_{BE} = \frac{F}{P_2 - V_2} = \frac{\$250\,000}{\$95 - \$40} = 4545 \text{ units.}$$

c. The incremental ROA is

$$ROA = \frac{\Delta Profit}{\Delta Sales} \times \frac{\Delta Sales}{\Delta Assets}.$$

With debt financing, the incremental profit associated with the investment is equal to the incremental profit found in Part a minus the interest expense incurred as a result of the investment:

$$\Delta\text{Profit} = \text{New profit} - \text{Old profit} - \text{Interest}$$
$$= \$135\,000 - \$50\,000 - 0.10(\$400\,000)$$
$$= \$45\,000.$$

The incremental sales is calculated as

$$\Delta\text{Sales} = P_2(Q_2) - P_1(Q_1)$$
$$= \$95(7000) - \$100(5000)$$
$$= \$665\,000 - \$500\,000$$
$$= \$165\,000.$$

$$\text{ROA} = \frac{\$45\,000}{\$165\,000} \times \frac{\$165\,000}{\$400\,000} = 11.25\%.$$

The return on the new equity investment still exceeds the average cost of capital, so Olinde should make the investment.

Appendix 6A
Nonlinear Breakeven Analysis

Our discussion of breakeven analysis and operating leverage earlier in the chapter relied on linear equations and straight line graphs, which implied (1) that price is a constant and (2) that once the fixed costs have been established, variable costs per unit are also constant. These assumptions are often reasonable for established firms in mature markets, but they are generally not valid for new, small businesses that have been set up to provide new products or services. In these instances, *nonlinear breakeven analysis* is required.

Waste Containers Incorporated (WCI), which was established in 1989 to develop and then to produce cylinders used for the disposal of biologically hazardous wastes from hospitals, clinics, and doctors' offices in the Toronto area, can be used to illustrate nonlinear breakeven. Mary Puffer, WCI's founder and president, realized in the early 1980s that the disposal of human tissues containing cancer cells, materials contaminated with infectious diseases, and other "hospital debris" was a growing problem. With the financial backing of several doctors affiliated with the University of Toronto and various hospitals, Puffer began experimenting with a disposal system consisting of a cylinder into which wastes would be placed, along with an acid solution, and then sealed. The acids would break down and render harmless the wastes, but it would take years for a complete breakdown to occur. Therefore, the cylinders themselves were disposable, but they were sturdy enough to permit burial in regular garbage dumps.

By 1991, Puffer had perfected the cylinders, tested them for leakage and effectiveness, obtained patents, and received approval for their use from provincial authorities. The issue facing her and her financial backers was to choose the best production plan and marketing strategy. Figure 6A-1 gives a picture of the type of analysis that was employed. First, Puffer noted that the waste disposal business is highly competitive, that the system would be more effective for some customers than others, and that any given customer would buy more of her cylinders at a lower price than at a higher price. She noted that in a linear breakeven analysis, TR = PQ, where TR = total revenue, P = price per unit, and Q = units sold. If P is a constant, then TR increases linearly with Q, and the straight line graph shown back in Figure 6-2 results. However, if a lower price is needed to sell more units, then P must decline as Q increases, and a nonlinear TR curve such as the one in Figure 6A-1 results.

Puffer also concluded that variable costs per unit would not be constant. First, if only a few units were produced, production workers would not be very efficient, quantity discounts could not be obtained on purchased materials, and so on. Therefore, as production increased from very low levels, unit production costs would decline. Put another way, there would be economies of scale. However, at very high production levels, it would be necessary to employ inefficient workers, to go to a second or even third shift, to pay overtime, and to run machinery to the point at which expensive breakdowns occurred frequently. Thus, beyond some output level, costs would begin to rise rapidly—there would be diseconomies of scale.

When Puffer graphed these factors, the result was the S-shaped total cost curves shown in Figure 6A-1.

**Figure 6A-1
Nonlinear Breakeven Analysis**

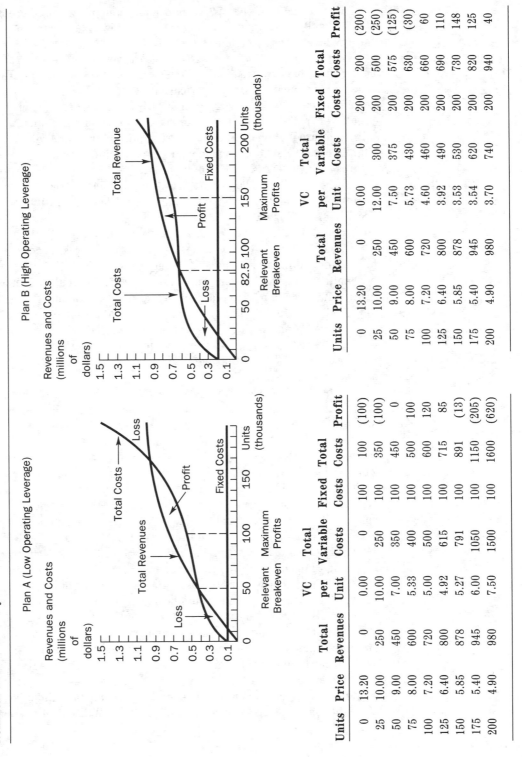

Plan B (High Operating Leverage)

Units	Price	Total Revenues	VC per Unit	Total Variable Costs	Fixed Costs	Total Costs	Profit
0	13.20	0	0.00	0	200	200	(200)
25	10.00	250	12.00	300	200	500	(250)
50	9.00	450	7.50	375	200	575	(125)
75	8.00	600	5.73	430	200	630	(30)
100	7.20	720	4.60	460	200	660	60
125	6.40	800	3.92	490	200	690	110
150	5.85	878	3.53	530	200	730	148
175	5.40	945	3.54	620	200	820	125
200	4.90	980	3.70	740	200	940	40

Plan A (Low Operating Leverage)

Units	Price	Total Revenues	VC per Unit	Total Variable Costs	Fixed Costs	Total Costs	Profit
0	13.20	0	0.00	0	100	100	(100)
25	10.00	250	10.00	250	100	350	(100)
50	9.00	450	7.00	350	100	450	0
75	8.00	600	5.33	400	100	500	100
100	7.20	720	5.00	500	100	600	120
125	6.40	800	4.92	615	100	715	85
150	5.85	878	5.27	791	100	891	(13)
175	5.40	945	6.00	1050	100	1150	(205)
200	4.90	980	7.50	1500	100	1600	(620)

Puffer concluded that WCI could adopt one of two production/marketing strategies. Plan A called for using relatively low fixed costs, but variable costs for any level of output would be relatively high. Plan B called for higher fixed costs but lower variable costs. The total revenue curve was the same under either plan, because customers do not care how the cylinders are produced as long as they meet quality specifications.

Which plan was better? Plan A, with low leverage, had a much lower breakeven point, 50 000 units versus 82 500 units for Plan B. Also, only $2 million of production capital would be required for Plan A versus $5 million for Plan B. (Note: Here a return on capital was included as a cost in the fixed cost figures.) However, Plan B would provide a higher level of profit than A, $148 000 versus $120 000, at the profit-maximizing output. The rate of return on invested capital for the two plans would be essentially the same at the profit-maximizing outputs.

When Puffer met with WCI's board, most members initially supported Plan A, primarily because they felt that it was less risky because of its low breakeven point. One member of the board asked if Puffer could assign probabilities to the various unit sales, for if she could, then the expected profits under each plan could be developed. It turned out, though, that Puffer did not believe a probability distribution would apply, because in the data, price varied along with units sales. It was agreed that the best estimates of profits at each sales level were the values shown in the profit columns of the data in Figure 6A-1. At that point, everyone agreed that Plan A was best and should be implemented.

As the meeting was breaking up, Puffer mentioned that Retort Industries (RI), a nationwide company and the largest factor in the medical waste disposal business, was rumoured to be considering entry into the cylinder business in the same area, but that once WCI began operations, RI would be frozen out. With this information, the board reconsidered the situation. If WCI went with Plan A, it would produce 100 000 cylinders and sell them at a price of $7.20. However, if WCI did that, then RI could enter the market, build a Plan B type plant, and set a price of $4.90. WCI would have to match RI's price. At that point, total demand would be 200 000 units, presumably shared equally between WCI and RI. WCI would then have total revenues of $100 000 \times \$4.90 = \$490 000$ versus total costs of $100 000 \times \$5 + \$100 000 = \$600 000$, so it would be losing $110 000. Note too that WCI would not even be covering its variable costs, so it would be better off closing down and losing only its $100 000 of fixed costs. RI, on the other hand, would be suffering losses, but it would be at least covering its variable costs, so it would continue to produce. But when WCI closed down, RI would then have the entire market, so it could both raise its price and increase output, and therefore earn a high profit.

It became clear that, under the circumstances, the greater danger lay in opting to build the smaller plant with high variable costs because that strategy would leave the door open for someone else to come in, build a larger and more efficient plant, charge a lower price, and drive WCI out of the market.

III

WORKING CAPITAL MANAGEMENT

7

▼▼

Working Capital Policy

A MANAGERIAL PERSPECTIVE

When Amory Jackson, president of Computer Enterprises Ltd., arrived at his office, he was shocked to learn that one of the company's principal suppliers had just served notice that it would no longer supply the firm with disk drives. Jackson was even more surprised to learn that the reason for this action was that Computer Enterprises had been slow in paying this supplier, and all of its other suppliers, for some time, and that the reason for the slow payments was a shortage of cash. Jackson practically screamed at the treasurer who brought the bad news, "Our growth has been terrific, and our profits are setting records. How can we possibly not have enough cash to pay our bills on time?"

Her response was short and sweet: "If you had been listening to what I've been telling you and if you had been reading our financial reports, you'd know that there's a big difference between profits and cash. We're making profits all right, but because of the growth you're so proud of, we've had to acquire more new assets than we could finance with retained earnings. We have lots of inventory, receivables, and fixed assets, but no cash. I've been telling you that we simply must change our operating policies. There are things we can do, but you're going to have to authorize a major change in our working capital policy right now or else watch the company go bankrupt."

This is not an unusual situation—it happens all the time. In this chapter and in the others that deal with working capital management, we examine the relationship between growth and the need for funds and consider ways to ensure that the funds necessary to support growth are always available.

Setting working capital policy involves answering two questions: (1) how much should we invest in each category of current assets, and (2) how should we finance that investment? About one-third to one-half of the typical firm's capital is invested in current assets, so providing correct answers to these questions is vital to the firm's profitability.

Two major types of current liabilities, trade credit and accruals, are extremely convenient, flexible, and inexpensive. Thus, virtually all firms, even the most conservative ones, will show some current liabilities on their books. Also, even conservative firms will utilize borrowing to meet a temporary need for funds, provided management is sure that funds will be available to pay off the debt at its maturity. Thus, working capital financing policy is a matter of degree: the more conservative the firm, the less it will rely on short-term credit, because the greater the use of such credit, the greater the firm's risk exposure. In this chapter we concentrate on financing policy decisions related to working capital.

Working capital management has recently received particular attention from corporate managers for two reasons. First, the very high interest rates in the early 1980s forced managers to examine more closely the funds invested in accounts receivable and inventory. Second, new computer and telecommunications technology now allows closer monitoring of levels of current assets and faster and more accurate communications with suppliers and customers.

Traditional measures of working capital and liquidity, such as *net working capital*, the *current ratio*, and the *quick ratio* are all static. Newer measures of liquidity, such as the *cash conversion cycle*, are dynamic, reflecting not only the level of short-term assets and liabilities but also the timing of cash inflows and outflows.

Working Capital Terminology

We begin our discussion by defining some basic terms and concepts:

1. **Working capital**, sometimes called *gross working capital*, simply means current assets.
2. **Net working capital** is defined as current assets minus current liabilities; the latter includes sources of funds such as overdrafts, bank loans, commercial paper issued by the firm, accrued wages, and taxes payable.
3. One key working capital ratio is the *current ratio*, which was defined in Chapter 4 as current assets divided by current liabilities. This ratio is intended to provide information about a firm's liquidity or its ability to meet obligations that will come due within a year. However, a high current ratio does not ensure that a firm will have the cash required to meet its needs. If inventories are not sold and receivables are not collected in a timely manner, then the apparent safety reflected in a high current ratio could prove illusory.
4. The *quick, or acid test ratio*, is defined as current assets minus inventories, divided by current liabilities. This ratio, which also measures **liquidity**, removes inventories (the least liquid current asset) from total current assets; it thus provides an "acid test" of a company's ability to meet its current obligations.
5. Although the current and quick ratios provide an indication of the firm's ability to satisfy its maturing obligations, they do not provide a complete picture of liquidity because they do not tell us anything about the *cash flows from operations*, which can also be used to meet obligations. For example, a fast food chain (in fact, any business) might show $20 million of current liabilities and only $5 million of current assets, but if its cash flows from operations are large enough, the company can have sufficient liquidity in spite of its low current ratio. Thus, to determine a firm's *effective liquidity*, it is useful to look both at its balance sheet ratios (current and quick) and at its cash flow position. We consider this point later in this chapter when we study the *cash flow cycle*.
6. **Working capital policy** refers to the firm's basic policies regarding (1) the target level for each category of current assets and (2) how current assets will be financed.
7. **Working capital management** involves all aspects of the administration of both current assets and current liabilities, a recognition of the

interrelationships between these quantities, and a recognition of the interrelationships between working capital and long-term capital and investments. Although not the subject of as much research as other areas of corporate finance, working capital management is crucial in terms of the survival of the company. As we shall see in Chapter 25, many bankruptcies are rooted in poor working capital decisions and policies.

We must distinguish between those current liabilities that are specifically used to finance current assets and those current liabilities that represent (1) current maturities of long-term debt; (2) financing associated with a construction program which will, after the project is completed, be funded with the proceeds of a long-term security issue; and (3) the financing of fixed assets. The current liabilities identified in the last three categories are not decision variables under working capital policy but arise from other decisions. Hence they will not be included in working capital decisions as we use the term.

Concept Review

▶ What is meant by the term "liquidity"?
▶ Why is the quick ratio also called the "acid test"?

Importance of Working Capital Management

Working capital management is an important topic for several reasons:

1. Surveys indicate that the largest portion of a financial manager's time is devoted to the day-by-day internal operations of the firm that fall under the heading of "working capital management."
2. Characteristically, current assets represent a substantial portion of the total assets of a business firm. (See Table 7-1 for a list of the ratios for firms in some Canadian industries. Notice, however, that the statistics are based on a broad definition of current assets.) Moreover, current assets fluctuate with sales, and sales vary over time.

   Thus, managing current assets is a dynamic process, and it requires the financial manager to monitor sales closely—indeed, to anticipate changing levels of sales—to ensure that assets are on hand in sufficient quantities to meet sales and production targets.
3. Working capital management is particularly important for small firms. Although small firms can minimize their investments in fixed assets by renting or leasing plant and equipment, they cannot avoid investments in cash, receivables, and inventories. Further, because small firms have relatively limited access to the long-term capital markets, they must necessarily rely heavily on trade credit and short-term bank loans, both of which affect net working capital by increasing current liabilities.
4. The relationship between sales growth and the need to finance current assets is close and direct. As sales grow, the firm must increase receivables and inventories, and it may need to increase its cash balance

Table 7-1
Balance Sheet Breakdown, 1990
(percentage of total assets)

	Cash and Equivalent	Accounts Receivable	Inventory	Total Current Assets[a]	Fixed Assets
Building Construction	12.8%	36.0%	27.1%	76.8%	18.4%
Printing, Publishing	8.5	28.3	13.7	50.8	40.0
Chemicals	13.2	24.1	22.6	60.4	31.8
Petroleum Refining	6.9	22.2	19.6	50.4	45.8
Primary Metal Industries	5.8	25.6	19.4	52.4	41.8
Machinery	10.7	26.0	26.5	63.7	30.1
Electronics	8.6	24.6	23.1	56.7	34.4
Retail-hardware, garden supp	6.5	21.6	40.6	69.4	23.0

[a]Includes other current assets not specifically noted in the first three columns.
Source: Dun and Bradstreet, *Industry Norms and Ratios*.

as well. For example, if the firm's days sales outstanding is 40 days and if its credit sales are $1000 a day, it will have an investment of $40 000 in accounts receivable. If sales rise to $2000 a day, the investment in accounts receivable will rise to $80 000. A sales increase will also produce an immediate need for additional inventories and, perhaps, for more cash. All such needs must be financed—any increase in an account on the left-hand side of the balance sheet must be matched by an increase on the right-hand side. Therefore, it is imperative that the financial manager be aware of sales trends and their effects on the firm's working capital needs.

Concept Review

▶ Why is working capital management important to a firm?

Cash Flow Cycle

An important aspect of working capital management is the provision for financing of increases in current assets required as the sales activity of the firm increases. Firms need assets to make sales; if sales are to be increased, assets must also be expanded. A growing firm is likely to need additional cash for immediate investment in receivables, inventories, and other current assets and, as full capacity is reached, for investment in fixed assets as well. New investments must be financed, and new financing carries with it the obligations and commitments to service the capital obtained. A growing firm can, therefore, have a cash flow problem. The nature of this problem, as well as the cause-and-effect relationship between assets and sales, is illustrated in the following discussion.

Effects on the Balance Sheet

Suppose that two partners invest a total of $50 000 to create the New Wave Dress Co. Ltd. The firm rents a plant; equipment and other fixed assets cost $30 000. The resulting financial situation is shown by Balance Sheet 1.

Balance Sheet 1

Assets		Liabilities	
Current assets		Common equity	$50 000
Cash	$20 000		
Fixed assets			
Plant and equipment	30 000	Total liabilities and	
Total assets	$50 000	net worth	$50 000

New Wave receives an order to manufacture 10 000 dresses. In itself, the receipt of an order has no effect on the balance sheet, but in preparation for the manufacturing activity, the firm buys $20 000 worth of cotton cloth on terms of net 30 days. Without additional investment by the owners, total assets decrease by $20 000, financed by the trade accounts payable to the supplier of the cloth.

After the purchase, the firm spends $20 000 on labour for cutting the cloth to the required pattern. Of the $20 000 total labour cost, $20 000 is paid in cash and $10 000 is owed in the form of accrued wages. These two transactions are reflected in Balance Sheet 2, which shows that total assets increase to $80 000. Current assets are increased; net working capital—total current assets minus total current liabilities—remains constant. The current ratio declines to 1.67, and the debt ratio rises to 38 percent. The financial position of the firm is weakening.

Balance Sheet 2

Assets		Liabilities	
Current assets		Accounts payable	$20 000
Cash	$10 000	Accrued wages payable	10 000
Inventories		Total current liabilities	$30 000
Work-in-process		Common equity	50 000
Materials	20 000		
Labour	20 000		
Total current assets	$50 000		
Fixed assets			
Plant and equipment	30 000	Total liabilities and	
Total assets	$80 000	net worth	$80 000

In order to complete the dresses, the firm incurs additional labour costs of $20 000 and pays $10 000 of accrued wages and $10 000 of additional labour cost, for a total cash outlay of $20 000. It is assumed that the firm desires to maintain a minimum cash balance of $5000. As the initial cash balance is $10 000, New Wave must borrow an additional $15 000 from its bank to meet the wage bill. The borrowing is reflected in notes payable in Balance Sheet 3. Total assets rise to $95 000, with a finished goods inventory of $60 000. The current ratio drops to 1.4, and the debt ratio rises to 47 percent. These ratios show a further weakening of the financial position.

Balance Sheet 3

Assets			Liabilities	
Current assets			Accounts payable	$20 000
Cash		$ 5 000	Notes payable	15 000
Inventory			Accrued wages payable	10 000
Finished goods		60 000		
Total current assets		$65 000	Total current liabilities	$45 000
Fixed assets			Common equity	50 000
Plant and equipment		30 000	Total liabilities and	
Total assets		$95 000	net worth	$95 000

New Wave ships the dresses on the basis of the original order, invoicing the purchaser for $100 000, payable within 30 days. Accrued wages and accounts payable have to be paid now, so New Wave must borrow an additional $30 000 in order to maintain the $5000 minimum cash balance. These transactions are shown in Balance Sheet 4.

Balance Sheet 4

Assets			Liabilities	
Current assets			Notes payable	$ 45 000
Cash		$ 5 000	Total current liabilities	$ 45 000
Accounts receivable		100 000	Common equity	50 000
Total current assets		$105 000	Retained earnings	40 000
Fixed assets			Total net worth	$ 90 000
Plant and equipment		30 000	Total liabilities and	
Total assets		$135 000	net worth	$135 000

Note that in Balance Sheet 4, finished goods inventory is replaced by receivables, with the markup reflected as retained earnings. This causes the debt ratio to drop to 33 percent. The receivables are carried at the sales price; therefore, current assets increase to $105 000 and the current ratio rises to 2.3. Compared with the conditions reflected in Balance Sheet 3, most of the financial ratios show improvement. However, the absolute amount of debt is large. Whether the firm's financial position is really improved depends upon the creditworthiness of the purchaser of the dresses. If the purchaser is a good credit risk, New Wave may be able to borrow further on the basis of the accounts receivable.

When the firm receives payment for the accounts receivable, it pays off the bank loan and is in the highly liquid position shown by Balance Sheet 5. If a new order for 10 000 dresses is received, it will have no effect on the balance sheet, but a cycle similar to the one we have been describing will begin.

Balance Sheet 5

Assets		Liabilities	
Current assets		Common equity	$50 000
Cash	$60 000	Retained earnings	40 000
Fixed assets			
Plant and equipment	30 000	Total liabilities and	
Total assets	$90 000	net worth	$90 000

The cash flow cycle can be generalized from this example. An order that requires the purchase of raw materials is placed with the firm. The purchase in turn generates an account payable. As labour is applied, work-in-process inventories build up. To the extent that wages are not fully paid at the time labour is used, accrued wages appear on the liability side of the balance sheet. As goods are completed, they move into finished goods inventories. The cash needed to pay for the labour to complete the goods may make it necessary for the firm to borrow.

Finished goods inventories are sold, usually on credit, which gives rise to accounts receivable. As the firm has not received cash, this point in the cycle represents the peak in financing requirements. If the firm did not borrow at the time finished goods inventories were at their maximum, it may do so as inventories are converted into receivables by credit sales. Income taxes, which were not considered in the example, can add to the problem. As accounts receivable become cash, short-term obligations can be paid off.

Managing the Cash Flow Cycle

Managing the cash flow cycle is the crux of working capital management. In analyzing the situation, it is useful to distinguish two separate factors, the *operating cycle* and the *payment cycle*, which combine to determine the *cash conversion cycle*.

The Operating Cycle

Briefly, the operating cycle takes into account the following two determinants of liquidity:

1. **Inventory conversion period**, defined as the length of time needed to convert raw materials into finished goods, and then to sell these products to customers. The inventory conversion period can be computed as 365 days divided by the inventory turnover ratio (sales/inventory). Assuming

that New Wave Dress Co. remains in business and produces $5 000 000 worth of dresses per year, with an average inventory of $274 000, the inventory conversions period will be

$$\text{Inventory conversion period} = \frac{365}{\text{Sales/Inventory}}$$
$$= \frac{365}{\$5\,000\,000/\$274\,000}$$
$$= 20.0 \text{ days.}$$

Thus, on average, 20 days elapses from the purchase of raw materials to the sales of finished goods.

2. **Receivables conversion period** is an indicator of the average time it takes a firm to convert its accounts receivable into cash. This cycle is measured by the days sales outstanding (DSO) or average collection period, and it was calculated in Chapter 4 as receivables/sales per day = receivables/(sales/365). If average accounts receivable are $205 000 and annual sales are $5 000 000, then DSO is

$$\text{DSO} = \text{Receivables conversion period} = \frac{\text{Accounts receivable}}{\text{Average sales per day}}$$
$$= \frac{\$205\,000}{\$5\,000\,000/365}$$
$$= 15.0 \text{ days.}$$

Thus it takes 15 days after a sale to convert an account receivable into cash.

The **operating cycle**, the sum of the inventory conversion period and receivables conversion period, is a measure of the amount of time that elapses between the purchase of raw materials to produce goods and the collection of cash in payment for those goods after they have been sold. The firm must finance the purchase of materials, the production of goods, and the carrying of both finished goods and receivables during the operating cycle.

The Payment Cycle

The operating cycle focusses on the timing of cash inflows, but it ignores the timing of outflows—*when* the firm must pay for purchases and labour. However, the firm's financing requirements will be influenced by its ability to delay payments by purchasing materials on extended credit terms or paying labour after work has been performed. Therefore, the firm should strive to manage outflows as well as inflows—the longer it can delay payments, the less severe will be any problems caused by the operating cycle. However, cash inflows and outflows are rarely, if ever, synchronized, so the cash flow cycle will as a general rule reveal periods when external funds are needed.

The **payables deferral period** is defined as the average length of time between the purchase of raw materials and labour and the payment of cash for them. It can be thought of as a measure of days payables outstanding, and is measured by

$$DPO = \text{Payables deferral period} = \frac{\text{Accounts payable}}{\text{Average cost of goods sold per day}}$$

$$= \frac{\$82\,500}{\$3\,000\,000/365}$$

$$= 10.0 \text{ days.}$$

The Cash Conversion Cycle

The **cash conversion cycle**[1] combines the three periods just defined and is equal to the length of time from the firm's actual cash expenditures on productive resources (raw materials and labour) to its own collection of cash from the sale of products. <u>The cash conversion cycle begins the day a bill for labour and/or suppliers is paid and runs to the day receivables are collected.</u> Thus, the cash conversion cycle measures the length of time the firm has funds tied up in working capital.

We can now use these definitions to analyze the cash conversion cycle. In general, the cash conversion cycle is written as follows:

Cash conversion cycle = Operating cycle − Payment cycle.

From the definitions of each of these cycles, we find that the cash conversion cycle is written as

(1)	(2)	(3)	(4)
Inventory conversion period	+ Receivables conversion period	− Payables deferral period	= Cash conversion cycle

This concept is diagrammed in Figure 7-1, for the New Wave Dress Co., where each component is given the number found in the above relationship.

1. It takes 20 days, on average, to convert purchased materials into sellable products and to sell these finished goods.
2. It takes another 15 days, on average, to collect accounts receivable and thus to convert sales into cash.
3. The firm is able to defer payments for purchase (goods, materials, and labour) for 10 days, on average.
4. Therefore, the cash conversion cycle (or period) is 20 days + 15 days − 10 days = 25 days.

Now consider the implications of all this. Suppose the firm buys goods (or materials plus labour) worth $1000. It will be able to defer payment for 10 days, but it will not receive cash from the sale of the final product until Day 35. Thus,

---

[1]Verlyn D. Richards and Eugene J. Laughlin, "A Cash Conversion Approach to Liquidity Analysis," *Financial Management* (Spring 1980), pp. 32–38.

Figure 7-1
The Cash Conversion Cycle

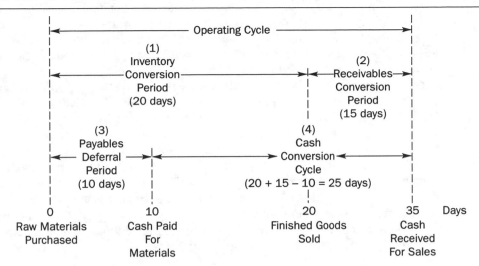

it will have to finance the $1000 for 25 days. If the firm is in a steady state, with purchases of $1000 per day, its working capital financing needs will be 25 × $1000 = $25 000.

Now notice these facts: (1) If the firm could manage to defer payments to, say, Day 15, this would reduce financing needs by $5000. Therefore, actions that lengthen the payment period also reduce financial requirements. Some firms, which do not monitor their due dates for bills and tax payments, pay unnecessarily early. Better controls can lead to a longer payables deferral period. However, actions such as deliberately paying late may be viewed as unethical and lead to poor relations with suppliers. (2) If the firm can shorten the inventory conversion period, perhaps by buying rather than manufacturing components, this too will reduce financial requirements. (3) Finally, if it can collect its receivables faster, perhaps by offering cash discounts, this will also reduce financial requirements. We see, then, that actions that affect the inventory conversion period, the receivables conversion period, and the payables deferrable period all, in turn, affect the cash conversion cycle and hence influence the firm's needs for capital. You should keep the cash conversion cycle in mind as you go through the remainder of this chapter and the other chapters on working capital.

Concept Review

▶ What is the cash conversion cycle?
▶ In what ways is the cash conversion cycle a more useful measure of liquidity than the current ratio? than net working capital?
▶ How can firms shorten their cash conversion cycle?

Current Asset Management

If a firm could forecast its cash inflows and outflows perfectly, it would hold exactly enough cash to make disbursements as required, exactly enough inventories to meet production and sales requirements, exactly the amount of accounts receivable called for by an optimal policy of extending credit to customers, and no marketable securities unless the interest on such assets exceeded the minimum return required on a firm's investments (an unlikely occurrence). The current asset holdings under the perfect foresight case would be the theoretical minimum for a profit-maximizing firm. Any larger holdings would increase the firm's assets without a proportionate increase in its returns, thus lowering its rate of return on investment. Any smaller holdings would mean the inability to pay bills on time, lost sales and/or production stoppages because of inventory shortages, and lost sales because of an overly restrictive credit policy. When uncertainty is introduced into the picture, current asset management involves (1) the determination of the minimum required balances for each type of asset and (2) the addition of a safety stock to account for the fact that forecasts are imperfect.

Risk–Return Tradeoff

If a firm follows a "*relaxed*" *working capital asset policy*, relatively large balances of cash and marketable securities will be maintained, large amounts of inventories will be kept on hand, and sales will be stimulated by the use of a credit policy that provides liberal financing and consequently results in a high level of accounts receivable. (The term "relaxed" as used here has no negative connotations.) If it follows a "*restricted*" *working capital asset policy*, the situation will be reversed, and inventories will be kept at minimal levels. The restricted policy generally produces the highest expected returns on investment, but it also involves the greatest risk. Examples of three alternatives are presented in Table 7-2. As one can observe in the table, the relaxed policy has the highest ratio of current assets to sales; the restricted approach minimizes the holdings of current assets and has the lowest ratio of current assets to sales.

In Part I of the table, it is assumed that the relaxed working capital asset investment policies stimulate sales to a slight degree because of greater inventory variety, fewer stockout problems, and more liberal credit. However, the indicated rate of return on assets is highest for the restricted working capital asset policy because here the required investment is much lower.

In Part II, an alternative set of assumptions is illustrated. It is assumed that the restricted current asset investment policy results in even greater stockouts and other problems, which lead to a larger adverse sales effect and which consequently lower the percentage of earnings before interest and taxes (EBIT) to sales. As a consequence, this policy now results in the lowest indicated return on assets. It is assumed that the moderate policy produces the same results as before, while the results of the relaxed policy are improved somewhat. Still, in Part II, the outcome for the moderate policy represents the highest return on assets for the relationships postulated.

Table 7-2
Effects of Alternative Working Capital Asset
Policies on Rates of Return

	Relaxed	Moderate	Restricted
Part I			
Sales	$110 000 000	$105 000 000	$100 000 000
EBIT @ 15% of sales	16 500 000	15 750 000	15 000 000
Current assets	70 000 000	55 000 000	40 000 000
Fixed assets	50 000 000	50 000 000	50 000 000
Total assets	$120 000 000	$105 000 000	$ 90 000 000
Rate of return on assets (EBIT/assets)	13.75%	15%	16.7%
Ratio of current assets to sales	0.64	0.52	0.40
Part II			
Sales	$115 000 000	$105 000 000	$ 80 000 000
EBIT as a percentage of sales	15%	15%	12%
EBIT amount	17 250 000	15 750 000	9 600 000
Total assets	$120 000 000	$105 000 000	$ 90 000 000
Rate of return on assets (EBIT/assets)	14.4%	15%	10.7%
Ratio of current assets to sales	0.61	0.52	0.50

This example illustrates the general idea that the kind of working capital asset policy a firm follows—restricted, relaxed, or moderate—may be a stimulus to sales and profitability or may negatively affect both the volume of sales and profitability. However, in the real world, things are considerably more complex than our simple example suggests. For one thing, different types of current assets affect both risk and returns differently. Increasing the holdings of cash does more to reduce the firm's risk exposure than would a similar dollar increase in receivables or inventories, but at the same time, idle cash penalizes earnings more severely than would the same investment in marketable securities.

Generalizations are difficult when we consider accounts receivable and inventories because it is difficult to measure either the earnings penalty or the risk effects from increasing the balance of these items beyond their theoretical minimum levels.

Alternative Working Capital Financing Policies

Working capital policies involve decisions with respect to both current asset investments and the maturity structure of the finance of these investments. The implications for the risk and expected return to the firm of the current asset investment decision has been analyzed in the previous section. Here, we consider the impact of the maturity structure on the financing of the current assets—that is, the firm's *working capital financing policy*.

Our analysis of the cash flow cycle has demonstrated that as sales increase, the investment in cash, receivables, and inventories must grow proportionately. As sales rise over the years, there will be associated permanent increases in current assets. Although individual receivables accounts are paid off and individual inventory items become embodied in completed products and are sold, the continuous operations of the firm will result in rising investments in receivables and inventories as sales increase. Temporary fluctuations in sales will be associated with similar fluctuations in current asset requirements. However, even when business is seasonally or cyclically low, current assets do not drop to zero, and this has led to the development of the idea of **permanent current assets** that are equal to the *permanent level of current assets*. This is distinguished from **temporary** or **fluctuating current assets**, which are seasonal and can fluctuate from zero to a significant level. The manner in which the permanent and temporary current assets are financed constitute the firm's *working capital financing policy*. The financing policy will affect the firm's risk posture.

Maturity Matching, or "Self-Liquidating" Approach.   One frequently used financing policy is that of matching the financing to the permanence of the assets; this represents the traditional notion of the *matching principle*, in which, to minimize both risk and financing costs, the firm matches the maturity of the liabilities to the length of time that the funds are needed. Therefore, short-term assets are financed with short-term liabilities and both long-term assets and permanent current assets are financed with long-term sources. This policy, which is also described as a moderate policy, is portrayed in Panel a of Figure 7-2. For example, suppose a firm borrows on a 1-year basis and uses the funds obtained to build and equip a plant that will last for 20 years. Cash flows from the plant are not sufficient to pay off the loan at the end of the year, so the loan must be refinanced. It is at this stage that the firm faces risk. First, there is the risk that the loan will have to be refinanced at interest rates higher than were expected to prevail when the borrowing occurred. Second, the lender may refuse to renew the loan. This would force the firm to search for new sources and to incur transaction costs. Had the plant been financed with long-term debt, however, the firm would face neither the risks noted above nor the added transaction costs, because cash flows would have been sufficient to retire the loan.

Alternatively, the firm could finance current assets with long-term sources of funds. In this instance, there will be periods when there is an excess of cash that will have to be invested in short-term securities. As the rates paid by the firm on the long-term sources usually exceed the investment in short-term securities, the firm will have lower profits than in instances in which the matching principle is applied.

Thus, if a firm finances long-term (permanent) assets with permanent sources of funds and fluctuating current assets with temporary sources, its financial risk is lower than it would be if permanent assets were financed with short-term debt or fluctuating current assets were financed with long-term debt. Further, the calculated net working capital—current assets minus current liabilities—will be positive.

Figure 7-2
Alternative Current Asset Financing Policies

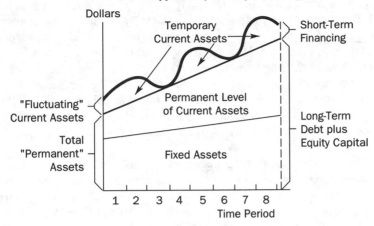

a. Moderate Approach (Maturity Matching)

Dollars

Temporary Current Assets

Short-Term Financing

"Fluctuating" Current Assets

Permanent Level of Current Assets

Long-Term Debt plus Equity Capital

Total "Permanent" Assets

Fixed Assets

1 2 3 4 5 6 7 8
Time Period

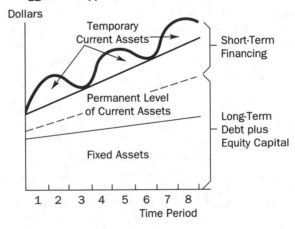

b. Aggressive Approach

Dollars

Temporary Current Assets

Short-Term Financing

Permanent Level of Current Assets

Long-Term Debt plus Equity Capital

Fixed Assets

1 2 3 4 5 6 7 8
Time Period

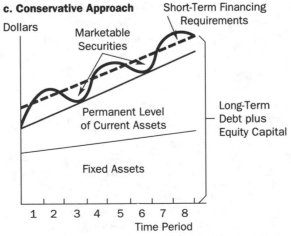

c. Conservative Approach

Short-Term Financing Requirements

Dollars

Marketable Securities

Permanent Level of Current Assets

Long-Term Debt plus Equity Capital

Fixed Assets

1 2 3 4 5 6 7 8
Time Period

At the limit, a firm can attempt to match exactly the maturity structures of its assets and liabilities. A machine expected to last for 5 years could be financed by a 5-year loan; a building lasting 20 years could be financed by a 20-year mortgage bond; inventory expected to be sold 20 days could be financed by a 20-day bank loan, and so forth. In effect, each loan would be paid off with the cash flows generated by the assets financed by the loan, so loans would be "self-liquidating." Actually, uncertainty about the lives of assets prevents this exact matching. For example, a firm may finance inventories with a 30-day loan, expecting to sell the inventories and to use the cash generated to retire the loan. If sales are slow, however, the cash will not be forthcoming, and the use of short-term credit may end up causing a problem. Still, if the firm attempts to match asset and liability maturities, we call this a *moderate (matching, or self-liquidating) working capital policy.*

Aggressive (Nonconservative) Approach.   Panel b of Figure 7-2 illustrates the situation for an aggressive firm that finances all of its fixed assets with long-term capital and part of its permanent current assets with short-term credit.[2] This results in a positive net working capital position for the firm but smaller than under the matching strategy.

Returning to Figure 7-2b, the dashed line could have been drawn *below* the line designating fixed assets, indicating that all of the current assets plus part of the fixed assets were financed with short-term credit. This would be a very risky position, and the firm would be very exposed to the danger of rising interest rates as well as to loan renewal problems. However, since short-term debt is often cheaper than long-term debt, some firms are willing to sacrifice safety for the chance of higher profits.

The financing choices made by Olympia & York and its slide into bankruptcy provide a good example of the potential benefits and costs of following the aggressive approach. Beginning in the early 1980s, O&Y broke with industry tradition of financing office buildings with 20- to 30-year mortgages and used 30- to 90-day commercial paper as part of the financing package along with 5- to 10-year bonds. By 1990, O&Y had borrowed more than $1 billion in each of commercial paper and 5- to 10-year bonds. Thus O&Y decided to move from a matching to an aggressive strategy.

The company's policy of borrowing short term began in the mid-1980s, when interest rates in general were high and short rates were higher than long rates. Generally, this implies that investors expect that interest rates will fall, and this is what O&Y hoped would happen. When rates fell, the company would lock in the lower long-term rates. Unfortunately, the fall in rates took longer than expected by the company. As the rates moved down, the economy moved into a recession that was particularly damaging to real estate investments. The cash flows from the properties were falling and interest expenses did not fall fast

---

[2]Firms usually have some short-term credit in the form of "spontaneous" funds—accounts payable and accruals. There are permanent levels of these spontaneous funds that constitute "free" capital; thus, virtually all firms employ at least some short-term credit at all times. In terms of the matching principle, the permanent spontaneous funds are considered long-term sources. We could modify the graphs to take these sources into account, but nothing is lost by simply abstracting from spontaneous funds, as we do.

enough. By the time short-term rates had completed their large decrease, cash flows and property values had fallen dramatically.

The decline in property values had a double impact: assets pledged as collateral for many loans were no longer providing sufficient protection, and the sale of properties to raise cash would be difficult and the funds obtained would reflect the low values. Investors were generally wary of all real estate investments and even more nervous about O&Y, given rumours about the company and its financial difficulties. However, O&Y still had to refinance its commercial paper frequently. Eventually, O&Y found it impossible to sell additional commercial paper and began to default on a variety of loans. In May 1992, the company filed for protection from its creditors and subsequently was declared bankrupt.

Conservative Approach.   As shown in Panel c of Figure 7-2, the dashed lines could also have been drawn *above* the line designating permanent current assets, indicating that long-term capital is being used to finance all permanent asset requirements and also to meet some or all of the seasonal demands. In the situation depicted in this graph, the firm uses a small amount of short-term credit to meet its peak requirements, but it also meets a part of its seasonal needs by "storing liquidity" in the form of marketable securities during the off season. The humps above the dashed line represent short-term financing; the troughs below the dashed line represent short-term security holdings. Panel c represents a very safe strategy in which the financing of the assets provides low levels of risk. The net working capital position is positive and large, reflecting the minimum use of short-term financing.

Alternative Financing Policies and Their Relationship to the Cash Conversion Cycle

The cash conversion cycle and the alternative financing policies interact with one another, and they should be considered jointly. For example, the firm might begin by tentatively adopting a working capital policy that it believes is reasonable. Then it could examine its cash conversion cycle and see if the tentatively approved financing policy is consistent with that cycle. Suppose the two are inconsistent—the cash conversion cycle is relatively long, so a relatively large amount of working capital is required, and that amount is above the level called for by the tentatively adopted working capital policy. At that point, the financial manager must develop a plan to shorten the cash conversion cycle, or modify the working capital financing policy, or take an action that involves both changes.

For example, if a firm has a restricted working capital asset policy, under which it holds a minimal level of cash, securities, inventories, and receivables, then one would expect the length of its cash conversion cycle to be short, because the inventory and receivables conversion periods would be relatively short. On the other hand, if it has a relaxed working capital asset policy, under which it holds relatively large amounts of cash, marketable securities, and inventories, then one would expect the length of its cash conversion cycle to be long, because higher levels of inventories and receivables automatically lengthen the inventory and receivables conversion periods. If a firm follows a policy between these two extremes, then one would expect the length of its cash conversion cycle to fall between the cycles of these other two policies.

Advantages and Disadvantages of Short-Term Credit

The three possible financing policies described above differ primarily in the relative amount of short-term debt financing each uses. An aggressive policy calls for the greatest amount of short-term debt, a conservative policy calls for the least, and the maturity matching (self-liquidating) approach falls in between. Although using short-term credit is generally riskier than using long-term credit, short-term credit does have some advantages. The advantages and disadvantages of short-term credit are considered in this section.

Flexibility

If the need for funds is seasonal or cyclical, a firm may not want to commit itself to long-term debt to finance current assets for the following reasons. (1) Issue costs are generally higher for long-term debts. (2) Although long-term debt can be repaid early provided the loan agreement includes a call or prepayment provision, prepayment penalties can be expensive if such provisions are not included. In addition, even if these prepayment provisions are included, they result in an increase in the yield that must be paid by the firm to obtain flexibility. Accordingly, if a firm expects its need for funds to diminish in the near future, or if it thinks there is a good chance that such a reduction will occur, it may choose short-term debt for the flexibility that it provides. (3) Long-term loan agreements usually require restrictive provisions or *covenants*, specifying, for example, that the current ratio be kept above a certain number, restrictions on additional debt that can be issued, and the requirement to provide financial statements to the bondholders. To a greater or lesser degree, these covenants constrain or restrict the ability of management to run the firm. Short-term debt credit arrangements are generally less restrictive.

Cost of Long-Term versus Short-Term Debt

In Chapter 3, we saw that the yield curve is normally upward sloping, indicating that interest rates are generally lower on short-term debt than on long-term debt. Thus, interest charges at the time the funds are obtained are normally lower if the firm borrows on a short-term rather than on a long-term basis. However, a borrower who uses long-term debt avoids the uncertainty of fluctuating short-term rates and the possibility of having to renew the debt under adverse money and capital market conditions.

Risk to the Borrowing Firm

Even though short-term debt is usually less expensive than long-term debt, the use of short-term debt subjects the firm to more risk than does financing with long-term debt. This added risk occurs for two reasons:

1. *Interest-rate risk.* If a firm borrows on a long-term basis, its interest costs will be fixed and therefore stable over time, but if it borrows on a

short-term basis, its interest expenses will fluctuate widely, at times going quite high. For example, from March to April of 1987, the interest rate on 90-day commercial paper—a short-term financial instrument issued by low-risk corporations—went from 6.80 percent to 8.15 percent, and it went to 9.55 percent by August of the same year. Even larger fluctuations occurred in the early 1980s, when 90-day commercial paper rates went from 10.9 percent in September 1980 to 12.35 percent in October and then to 22.2 percent in August 1981!

2. *Maturity risk.* If a firm borrows heavily on a short-term basis, and its sales then decline because of a recession or other economic changes that may be specific to the company, it may find itself unable to repay this debt, and it may be in such a weak financial position that the lender will not renew the loan; this could force the firm into bankruptcy.

Even if the cost of short-term debt is lower than that of long-term debt, its use is likely to entail greater risk. Thus, we are faced with a tradeoff between risk and rate of return. The nature of this tradeoff is illustrated in Table 7-3.

We assume that the firm has $100 million in assets, half held as fixed assets and half as current assets, and that it will earn 15 percent before interest and taxes on these assets; in other words, the firm's current asset investment policy is held constant. The debt ratio has been set at 50 percent, but the policy issue of whether to use short-term debt or long-term debt has not been determined.

In Part I of Table 7-3, short-term debt is assumed to cost 7 percent and long-term debt 9 percent. The greater the use of short-term debt—that is, the more aggressive financing policy—the higher the rate of return on equity (since short-term debt is assumed to have lower costs). However, if the firm uses short-term debt, it incurs additional risk from fluctuating interest rates—that is, interest rate risk.[3]

The impact of the variability of short-term interest rates is illustrated in Part II of this table, which portrays a situation the firm could face in the following year if the general level of interest rates rises. It is assumed that short-term rates increase to 21 percent (as they did in the early 1980s); long-term rates may rise also, but this would not affect the firm because it already has its debt in place at 9 percent. If the firm finances in Year 1 (Part I) entirely with long-term debt, then its interest expense will remain constant. However, if it uses only short-term debt in Year 1, it runs the risk of having to refinance this debt at substantially higher interest rates, and its rate of return would then be lower than if it were using long-term debt financing. If it uses a mix of long- and short-term debt in Year 1, its results come out between the two extremes. Thus, since short-term interest rates are subject to greater swings and volatility than is the cost of long-term debt, the rate of return on equity fluctuates most widely for the aggressive policy.

---

[3]This discussion assumes that the firm is not able to adjust its cash flows by adjusting prices as interest rates change. Although this may be the situation for most firms, a firm whose cash flows are positively correlated with interest rate levels would not be hurt as much by an increase in interest rates as a firm whose cash flows were negatively correlated with interest rate levels. Indeed, a firm whose cash flows are positively correlated with interest rate levels might regard the use of short-term debt as a risk-reducing strategy.

Table 7-3
The Effect of Maturity Structure of Debt
on Return on Equity (in millions of dollars)

	Conservative	Moderate	Aggressive
Part I: Normal Interest Rates			
Current assets	$ 50.00	$ 50.00	$ 50.00
Fixed assets	50.00	50.00	50.00
Total assets	$100.00	$100.00	$100.00
Short-term credit (@ 7%)	$ —	$ 25.00	$ 50.00
Long-term debt (@ 9%)	50.00	25.00	—
Total debt (debt/assets = 50%)	$ 50.00	$ 50.00	$ 50.00
Equity	50.00	50.00	50.00
Total liabilities and net worth	$100.00	$100.00	$100.00
Earnings before interest and taxes (EBIT)	$ 15.00	$ 15.00	$ 15.00
Less: Interest	4.50	4.00	3.50
Taxable income	$ 10.50	$ 11.00	$ 11.50
Less: Taxes (@ 40%)	4.20	4.40	4.60
Earnings on common shares	$ 6.30	$ 6.60	$ 6.90
Rate of return on equity	12.6%	13.2%	13.8%
Current ratio	∞	2:1	1:1
Times interest earned	3.33	3.75	4.29
Part II: Interest Rates Rise to 21%			
Current assets	$ 50.00	$ 50.00	$ 50.00
Fixed assets	50.00	50.00	50.00
Total assets	$100.00	$100.00	$100.00
Short-term credit (@ 21%)	$ —	$ 25.00	$ 50.00
Long-term debt (@ 9%)	50.00	25.00	—
Total debt (debt/assets = 50%)	$ 50.00	$ 50.00	$ 50.00
Equity	50.00	50.00	50.00
Total liabilities and net worth	$100.00	$100.00	$100.00
Earnings before interest and taxes (EBIT)	$ 15.00	$ 15.00	$ 15.00
Less: Interest	4.50	7.50	10.50
Taxable income	$ 10.50	$ 7.50	$ 4.50
Less: Taxes (@ 40%)	4.20	3.00	1.80
Earnings on common shares	$ 6.30	$ 4.50	$ 2.70
Rate of return on equity	12.6%	9.00%	5.4%
Current ratio	∞	2:1	1:1
Times interest earned	3.33	2.00	1.43

Fluctuations in earnings before interest and taxes (EBIT) can pose even more severe problems—if EBIT declines, lenders may simply refuse to renew short-term debt or agree to renew it only at very high rates of interest. To illustrate this, suppose the EBIT of $15 million in Table 7-3 declines to only $5 million. Because the firm's ability to repay has diminished, creditors will certainly be reluctant to lend to it. This will cause creditors to require a higher return on their investment and, thus, raise the interest expense, which will, of course, jeopardize the firm's future even more and, at the same time, compound the effects of the declining EBIT on shareholder returns. At the extreme, the debt may not be renewed. This refinancing risk is called *maturity risk*.

It is possible for the general level of interest rates to rise at the same time that a firm's EBIT is falling; the compound effects can cause the situation to deteriorate so much that the firm with the aggressive financing policy cannot renew its credit at any interest rate. The result is bankruptcy.

If the firm follows a conservative policy of using all long-term debt, it need not worry about short-term, *temporary* changes either in the term structure of interest rates or in its own financial position. Its only concern will be with its long-run performance, and its conservative financial structure may permit it to survive in the short run to enjoy better times in the long run.

On balance, many current liabilities arise because of the use of trade credit, which is both convenient and flexible, and other spontaneous current liabilities. Also, short-term bank borrowing may build up because it often provides the advantage of flexibility in meeting fluctuating needs for funds at a low cost. However, an excessive use of short-term debt does involve a considerable degree or risk. Finally, a single company may change its financing policy, moving from a conservative to aggressive policy or vice-versa. Companies that have been using a great deal of short-term financing may decide to switch to long-term debt to lock in favourable rates if they think interest rates are about to rise.

Concept Review

▶ What two considerations does uncertainty introduce into current asset management?

▶ Differentiate among the three alternative current asset management policies.

▶ What are the three criteria that financial managers should use to decide between long- and short-term credit?

Summary

This chapter examined (1) working capital management and (2) alternative ways of financing current assets. The key concepts covered are listed below:

☐ **Working capital** refers to current assets, and **net working capital** is defined as current assets minus current liabilities. **Working capital policy** refers to decisions relating to the target level and the financing of current assets.

☐ **Working capital management** involves the administration, within policy guidelines, of current assets and current liabilities.

☐ The **inventory conversion period** is the average length of time required to convert raw materials into finished goods and then to sell them.

☐ The **receivables conversion period** is the average length of time required to convert the firm's receivables into cash, and it is equal to the days sales outstanding.

□ The **payables deferral period** is the average length of time between the purchase of raw materials and labor and paying for them.

□ The **cash conversion cycle** is the length of time between paying for raw materials purchased and receiving cash from the sale of finished goods. The cash conversion cycle can be calculated as follows:

$$
\begin{array}{c}
\text{Inventory} \\
\text{conversion} \\
\text{period}
\end{array}
+
\begin{array}{c}
\text{Receivables} \\
\text{conversion} \\
\text{period}
\end{array}
-
\begin{array}{c}
\text{Payables} \\
\text{deferral} \\
\text{period}
\end{array}
=
\begin{array}{c}
\text{Cash} \\
\text{conversion} \\
\text{cycle}
\end{array}
$$

□ Under a *"relaxed" working capital asset policy,* a firm holds relatively large amounts of each type of current asset. A *"restricted" working capital asset policy* entails holding minimal amounts of these items.

□ **Permanent current assets** are those current assets that the firm holds even during slack times, whereas **temporary current assets** are the additional current assets that are needed during seasonal or cyclical peaks. The methods used to finance permanent and temporary current assets define the firm's *working capital financing policy.*

□ A *moderate,* or *self-liquidating,* approach to working capital financing involves *matching the maturities* of assets and liabilities, so that temporary current assets are financed with short-term debt and permanent current assets and fixed assets are financed with long-term debt or equity. Under an aggressive approach, some permanent current assets and perhaps even some fixed assets are financed with short-term debt. A conservative approach would be to use long-term capital to finance all fixed assets and some of the temporary current assets.

□ The advantages of short-term credit are (1) the speed with which short-term loans can be arranged, (2) increased flexibility, and (3) the fact that short-term interest rates are generally lower than long-term rates. The principal disadvantage of short-term credit is the extra risk that the borrower must bear because (1) the lender can demand payment on short notice and (2) the cost of the loan will increase if interest rates rise.

Questions

7-1 How does the seasonal nature of a firm's sales influence its decision regarding the amount of short-term credit in its financial structure?

7-2 Assuming a firm's volume of business remains constant, would you expect it to have higher cash balances (demand deposits) during a tight-money period or during an easy-money period?

7-3 What is the advantage of matching the maturities of assets and of liabilities? What are the disadvantages?

7-4 From the standpoint of the borrower, is long-term or short-term credit riskier? Explain. Would it ever make sense to borrow on a short-term basis if short-term rates were above long-term rates?

7-5 If long-term credit exposes a borrower to less risk, why do people or firms ever borrow on a short-term basis?

7-6   Considering the fact that increases in the inventory turnover and total assets turnover ratios correspond with a decrease in the cash conversion cycle, with what group of ratios would you classify the cash conversion cycle?

Self-Test Problems   (solutions appear on page 243)

ST-1   **Key terms.**   Define each of the following terms:
   a. Working capital; net working capital
   b. Working capital policy; working capital management
   c. Cash conversion cycle; operating cycle; inventory conversion period; receivables conversion period; payables deferral period
   d. Relaxed current asset policy; restricted current asset policy
   e. Conservative working capital financing policy; aggressive working capital financing policy
   f. Permanent current assets; temporary current assets
   g. Maturing matching, or "self-liquidating" approach to working capital finance
   h. Interest rate risk; maturity risk

ST-2   **Working capital financing.**   The Nelson Press, Ltd. and the Craig Book Company have the following balance sheets:

Balance Sheets
as of December 31, 1993
(thousands of dollars)

	Nelson Press, Ltd.	Craig Book Company
Current assets	$100 000	$100 000
Fixed assets (net)	100 000	100 000
Total assets	$200 000	$200 000
Current liabilities	$ 20 000	$ 80 000
Long-term debt	80 000	20 000
Common stock	50 000	50 000
Retained earnings	50 000	50 000
Total liabilities and equity	$200 000	$200 000

Earnings before interest and taxes for both firms are $30 million. The average tax rate is 40 percent.
   a. What is the return on equity for each firm if the interest rate on current liabilities is 10 percent and the rate on long-term debt is 13 percent?
   b. Assume the short-term rate rises to 20 percent. The rate on existing long-term debt remains unchanged, but the rate on new long-term debt rises to 16 percent. What would be the return on equity for Nelson and for Craig under these conditions?
   c. Which company is in a riskier position? Why?

ST-3   **Working capital policy.**   The Calgary Corporation is attempting to determine the optimal level of current assets for the coming year. Fixed assets are $600 000, and the firm wishes to maintain a 50 percent debt-to-assets ratio. The interest rate is 10 percent on all debt. Three alternative current asset policies are under consideration: 40, 50, and 60 percent of projected sales. The company expects to earn 15 percent before interest and taxes on sales of $3 million. Calgary's effective tax rate is 40 percent. What is the expected return on equity under each alternative?

Problems

7-1   **Cash conversion cycle.**   The Kelowna Company, Ltd. has an inventory conversion period of 75 days, a receivables conversion period of 38 days, and a payables deferral period of 30 days.
  a.   What is the length of the firm's cash conversion cycle?
  b.   If Kelowna's annual sales are $3 375 000 and all sales are on credit, what is the firm's investment in accounts receivable?
  c.   How many times per year does Kelowna turn over its inventory?

7-2   **Working capital policy.**   The Morgan Tile Corp. Ltd. is attempting to determine the optimal level of current assets for the coming year. Management expects sales to increase to approximately $2 million as a result of asset expansion presently being undertaken. Fixed assets total $1 million, and the firm wishes to maintain a 60 percent debt ratio. Morgan's interest cost is currently 10 percent on both short-term and long-term debt (which the firm uses in its permanent structure). Three alternatives regarding the projected current asset level are available to the firm: (1) a restricted policy requiring current assets of only 45 percent of projected sales; (2) a moderate policy of 50 percent to sales as current assets; and (3) a relaxed policy requiring current assets of 60 percent of sales. The firm expects to generate earnings before interest and taxes at a rate of 12 percent on total sales.
  a.   What is the expected return on equity under each current asset level? (Assume a 40 percent tax rate).
  b.   In this problem, we have assumed that interest rates and the level of expected sales are independent of current asset policy. Is this a valid assumption?
  c.   How would the overall riskiness of the firm vary under each policy? Discuss specifically the effect of current asset management on demand, expenses, fixed-charge coverage, risk of insolvency, and so on.
  d.   What would be the return on equity under each current asset level if actual sales were (i) $2.6 million or (ii) $1.4 million?
  e.   What would the return on equity be for each policy if the moderate policy generated sales at the $2.0 million level but the relaxed policy caused sales to rise to $2.6 million and the restricted policy caused sales to fall to $1.4 million?
  f.   Which current asset level is the least risky over the range of probable sales from $1.4 million to $2.6 million? Which current asset level do you recommend that Morgan maintain? Why?

7-3 **Working capital and financing.** Three companies—Aggressive, Moderate, and Conservative—have different working capital management policies as implied by their names. For example, Aggressive employs only minimal current assets, and it finances almost entirely with current liabilities plus equity. This restricted approach has a dual effect. It keeps total assets low, which tends to increase return on assets; but because of stockouts and credit rejections, total sales are reduced, and because inventory is ordered more frequently and in smaller quantities, variable costs are increased. Condensed balance sheets for the three companies follow.

	Aggressive	Moderate	Conservative
Current assets	$225 000	$300 000	$450 000
Fixed assets	300 000	300 000	300 000
Total assets	$525 000	$600 000	$750 000
Current liabilities (cost = 12%)	$300 000	$150 000	$ 75 000
Long-term debt (cost = 10%)	0	150 000	300 000
Total debt	$300 000	$300 000	$375 000
Equity	225 000	300 000	375 000
Total liabilities and equity	$525 000	$600 000	$750 000
Current ratio	0.75:1	2:1	6:1

The cost of goods sold functions for the three firms are as follows:

Cost of goods sold = Fixed costs + Variable costs.
Aggressive: Cost of goods sold = $300 000 + 0.70(Sales).
Moderate: Cost of goods sold = $405 000 + 0.65(Sales).
Conservative: Cost of goods sold = $577 500 + 0.60(Sales).

Because of the working capital differences, sales for the three firms under different economic conditions are expected to vary as follows:

	Aggressive	Moderate	Conservative
Strong economy	$1 800 000	$1 875 000	$1 950 000
Average economy	1 350 000	1 500 000	1 725 000
Weak economy	1 050 000	1 200 000	1 575 000

a. Construct income statements for each company for strong, average, and weak economies using the following format:

Sales
Less: Cost of goods sold
EBIT
Less: Interest expense
Taxable income
Less: Taxes (at 40%)
Net income

b. Compare the basic earning power (EBIT/assets) and return on equity for the companies. Which company is best in a strong economy? in an average economy? in a weak economy?

c. Suppose that, with sales at the average economy level, short-term interest rates rose to 20 percent. How would this affect the three firms?

d. Suppose that because of production slowdowns caused by inventory shortages, the aggressive company's variable cost ratio rose to 80 percent. What would happen to its ROE? Assume a short-term interest rate of 12 percent.

e. What considerations for management of working capital are indicated by this problem?

7-4   Working capital cash flow cycle.   The Belvedere Company is trying to determine the effect of its inventory turnover ratio and days sales outstanding (DSO) on its cash flow cycle. Belvedere's 1991 sales (all on credit) were $150 000, and it earned a net profit of 6 percent, or $9 000. It turned over its inventory 6 times during the year, and its DSO was 36 days. The firm had fixed assets totalling $40 000. Belvedere's payables deferral period is 40 days.

a. Calculate Belvedere's cash conversion cycle.

b. Assuming Belvedere holds negligible amounts of cash and marketable securities, calculate its total assets turnover and ROA.

c. Suppose Belvedere's managers believe that the inventory turnover can be raised to 8 times. What would Belvedere's cash conversion cycle, total assets turnover, and ROA have been if the inventory turnover had been 8 for 1991?

7-5   Working capital investment.   Magnum Inc. is a leading producer of automobile batteries. Magnum turns out 1500 batteries a day at a cost of $6 per battery for materials and labour. It takes the firm 22 days to convert raw materials into a battery. Magnum allows its customers 40 days in which to pay for the batteries, and the firm generally pays its suppliers in 30 days.

a. What is the length of Magnum's cash conversion cycle?

b. At a steady state in which Magnum produces 1500 batteries a day, what amount of working capital must it finance?

c. By what amount could Magnum reduce its working capital financing needs if it was able to stretch its payables deferral period to 35 days?

d. Magnum's management is trying to analyze the effect of a proposed new production process on the working capital investment. The new production process would allow Magnum to decrease its inventory conversion period to 20 days and to increase its daily production to 1800 batteries. However, the new process would cause the cost of materials and labour to increase to $7. Assuming the change would not affect the receivables conversion period (40 days) or the payables deferral period (30 days), what would be the length of the cash conversion cycle and the working capital financing requirement if the new production process were implemented?

Integrative Problem

7-6   **Working capital policy and financing.**   Ray Jones was recently hired as the financial manager of Bellemare Office Furnishings, Inc., a small manufacturer of metal office furniture. His first assignment is to develop a rational working capital policy.

Jones has identified three potential policies: (1) an aggressive policy that calls for a minimum amount of working capital and for substantial use of short-term debt, (2) a conservative policy that calls for a high working capital level and primary reliance on long-term as opposed to short-term debt, and (3) a moderate policy that falls between the two extremes. Jones estimates that the balance sheet would look like this under the three policies (in thousands of dollars):

	Balance Sheet		
	Aggressive	Moderate	Conservative
Current assets	$225	$300	$375
Net fixed assets	300	300	300
Total assets	$525	$600	$675
Short-term debt (8%)	$300	$150	$ 0
Long-term debt (10%)	0	150	300
Common equity	225	300	375
Total claims	$525	$600	$675

Short-term debt would have a cost of 8 percent, while long-term debt would cost 10 percent. Variable costs are expected to be 60 percent of sales regardless of which working capital policy is adopted, but fixed costs would increase if more current assets were held because of increased storage and insurance costs. Annual fixed costs would be $150 000 under an aggressive policy, $157 500 with a moderate policy, and $165 000 under a conservative policy.

Because its working capital policy would influence the firm's ability to respond to customers' needs, sales are expected to vary under different economic scenarios as follows (in thousands of dollars):

	Sales with Each Working Capital Policy		
Economy	Aggressive	Moderate	Conservative
Strong	$750	$788	$825
Average	600	675	750
Weak	450	563	675

As Jones's assistant, you have been asked to draft a report that answers the following questions:

a. What are the two basic decisions in formulating a working capital policy? Explain how a firm that is willing to take relatively high risks in the hope of earning high returns would make these two decisions, and then describe the policy decisions of a highly risk-averse (conservative) firm and of a moderate firm.

b. Why is working capital management important for the financial health of the firm?

c. Briefly explain Bellemare's working capital cash flow cycle.

d. What is meant by the term "cash conversion cycle"? Assume that if Bellemare followed the aggressive policy it would hold virtually no cash or marketable securities, so that current assets would be made up of only accounts receivable and inventories. Further, under this policy, accounts receivable would equal $100 000, inventories would equal $125 000, accounts payable would equal $60 000, sales would be $900 000, and purchases would total 75 percent of sales. Calculate the receivables conversion period, the inventory conversion period, the payables deferral period, and the cash conversion cycle for Bellemare if it follows an aggressive current assets policy.

e. Construct income statements for Bellemare for each working capital policy assuming an average economy. Also, calculate ROE. Use the following format:

	Income Statement with Each Policy		
	Aggressive	**Moderate**	**Conservative**
Sales			
Cost of goods sold	_____	_____	_____
EBIT			
Interest expense	_____	_____	_____
Taxable income			
Taxes (40%)	_____	_____	_____
Net income	_____	_____	_____
ROE	_____	_____	_____

f. Rework the income statements for weak and strong economies.

g. Assume that there is a 50 percent chance for an average economy and a 25 percent probability for both a strong and a weak economy. What is the expected ROE under each policy? Are the policies equally risky? Explain.

h. Now suppose that, after Bellemare has established its working capital policy, the Bank of Canada reacts to increasing inflationary expectations and begins to tighten monetary policy. As a result, interest rates increase. If Bellemare is following the conservative policy, it will have locked in its 10 percent long-term debt cost. However, if it is following an aggressive policy, and if short-term rates increase by 4 percentage points, then this will push Bellemare's short-term debt cost up to 12 percent. What impact will this have on the firm's profitability under each of the working capital policies, in an average economy, as measured by ROE?

Solutions to Self-Test Problems

ST-1   Refer to the appropriate sections of the text to check your responses.

ST-2

Income Statements
for Year Ended December 31, 1993

	Nelson Press Ltd.		Craig Book Company	
	a	b	a	b
EBIT	$ 30 000	$ 30 000	$ 30 000	$ 30 000
Interest	12 400	14 400	10 600	18 600
Taxable income	$ 17 600	$ 15 600	$ 19 400	$ 11 400
Taxes	7 040	6 240	7 760	4 560
Net Income	$ 10 560	$ 9 360	$ 11 640	$ 6 840
Equity	$100 000	$100 000	$100 000	$100 000
ROE	10.56%	9.36%	11.64%	6.84%

Nelson Press has a higher ROE than does Craig when short-term interest rates are high, while the Craig Book Company does better when rates are lower.

c. Craig's position is riskier. First, its profits and return on equity are much more volatile than are Nelson's. Second, Craig must renew its large short-term loan every year, and if the renewal comes up at a time when money is very tight or its business is depressed, or both, then it could be denied credit, which could put the company in serious trouble.

ST-3

The Calgary Corporation
Balance Sheets

	Restricted (40%)	Moderate (50%)	Relaxed (60%)
Current assets	$1 200 000	$1 500 000	$1 800 000
Fixed assets	600 000	600 000	600 000
Total assets	$1 800 000	$2 100 000	$2 400 000
Debt	$ 900 000	$1 050 000	$1 200 000
Equity	900 000	1 050 000	1 200 000
Total claims	$1 800 000	$2 100 000	$2 400 000

The Calgary Corporation
Income Statements

	Restricted	Moderate	Relaxed
Sales	$3 000 000	$3 000 000	$3 000 000
EBIT	$ 450 000	$ 450 000	$ 450 000
Interest (10%)	90 000	105 000	120 000
Earnings before taxes	$ 360 000	$ 345 000	$ 330 000
Taxes (40%)	144 000	138 000	132 000
Net income	$ 216 000	$ 207 000	$ 198 000
ROE	24.0%	19.7%	16.5%

8

▲▲

Inventory Management

A Managerial Perspective

In March 1992, Bargain Harold's Discount Ltd., a large chain of discount stores, was placed in receivership, the first step to bankruptcy. Only 18 months previously, the company had been purchased by the past president of Canadian Tire, who had a strong reputation as a successful retailer and an advocate for the use of management information systems. The real reasons for the demise of Bargain Harold's are yet to be determined, but there are some strong contenders. Prime among them is the inability of the firm's internal systems to provide correct information to management, which led to incorrect decisions. For example, the systems tended to produce overestimates of gross margins for some products and hence led to overinvestment in inventory in these products; also, forecasting methods for sales led to large inventory holdings for the Christmas season, which did not materialize. In both instances, inventories were larger than needed, and expensive financing had to be found during a period of slow growth in the economy. The company was unable to meet all of the conditions of its loan agreements and went into receivership. Erroneous inventory management was important in the failure of Bargain Harold's, but erroneous design and use of systems to provide management with the correct inputs to control inventory and make informed forecasts was really the crucial ingredient.

Inventories are essential for sales, and sales are necessary for profits. Actual inventory control is generally not under the direct control of the financial manager. Rather, in manufacturing companies, production people typically have control over inventories, whereas in retail concerns, merchandising people exercise this control. However, the financial manager is still concerned with inventory levels, for he or she has responsibility for tracking factors that affect the overall profitability of the firm; since inventories generally amount to some 10 to 15 percent of total assets, poor inventory control will hurt the firm's profitability. Also, you know from your study of the Du Pont system that ineffective inventory management can result in excessive inventories, which in turn can lead to a low rate of return on invested capital. Inventory management also has an effect on the cash conversion cycle, which was discussed in Chapter 7. Remember that one of the components of the cash conversion cycle is the inventory conversion period, the average length of time required to convert raw material into finished goods and then to sell these goods. Naturally, the larger the amount of inventories held, the longer the inventory conversion period, and the longer the cash conversion cycle, and the longer external financing will be needed.

The increasing use of computers and telecommunications has led to significant innovations in inventory management in the last decade. Production managers can plan production runs and predict raw materials requirements on a weekly or even daily basis using computers. Telecommunications allows the purchasing manager in one company to transmit instantly requirements to the order department of the supplier. In combination with prompt delivery of the goods, precise planning and rapid ordering have reduced the need for inventories, thus lowering carrying costs. These techniques are currently much used by large, multinational firms, and as they insist that their suppliers use these techniques, they are spreading throughout the corporate world. In this chapter we discuss in general terms the basics of inventory management and also consider briefly the newer approaches.

Inventory

A firm's **inventories** may be grouped into three classes: (1) raw materials, (2) work in process, and (3) finished goods (or merchandise for a retailer). The level of the *raw materials inventory* is influenced by anticipated production, seasonality of production, reliability of sources of supply, and efficiency of scheduling purchases and production operations. *Work-in-process inventory* is strongly influenced by the length of the production period, which is the time between placing raw material in production and completing the finished product. Work-in-process inventory turnover can be increased by decreasing the production period. One means of accomplishing this is to improve engineering techniques, thereby speeding up the manufacturing process. The level of the *finished goods inventory* is influenced by production and sales levels.

Whereas inventory levels depend upon sales, inventories must be acquired *ahead* of sales. The necessity of forecasting sales before establishing target inventory levels makes inventory management a difficult task. Because errors in establishing inventory levels can lead either to lost sales and profits or to excessive cost and hence profit problems, inventory management is as important as it is difficult. Inventory management is one area where co-ordination among sales, production, and financial managers is crucial.

A good example of this co-ordination is found in Canadian Tire Corporation, where information systems have been developed to provide the dealers, who own the individual stores, information on customers and buying patterns. This information assists the dealers in making informed decisions about inventory holdings by product line. For example, the system includes a forecasting model that permits each store to use its historical sales data, along with other relevant variables such as weather, to forecast sales and thus inventory requirements. The dealer can override the forecast, and this is usually done for products in which the dealer has particular expertise. Also a dealer can obtain a peer analysis report, which gives information at an aggregate level on the sales by product line of a group of dealers. This permits the dealer to look for exceptions and, after analyzing the reasons for the differences, take appropriate actions. Finally, information on buying patterns is used by the dealer and the Canadian Tire head office to develop programs to increase sales in certain product lines. These programs affect sales and inventory levels.

The above discussion indicates that managers can take specific actions to lower the firm's inventory investment. Any procedure that allows a firm to achieve a given sales volume with a lower investment in inventories will increase the firm's rate of return and, hence, the value of the firm. However, actions to reduce inventory investments can also increase risks because of a higher probability of sales lost due to stockouts or to costly production slowdowns. Managers must maintain inventories at levels that balance the benefits of holding down the level of investment against the costs associated with lower inventory holdings. Managers must establish three target quantities to achieve this balance by addressing the following questions: (1) what should be the level of inventory? (2) how much inventory should be ordered (or produced) at a given time? (3) at what level of inventory should new stock be ordered (or produced)? The remainder of this chapter is devoted to answering these questions.

Concept Review

▶ Into what three classifications can inventories be grouped?
▶ Identify the three basic questions on which inventory management focusses.
▶ Explain briefly why proper inventory management requires close co-ordination among the sales, purchasing, production, and finance departments.

Determinants of the Size of Inventories

The major determinants of investment in inventory are the following: (1) expected level of sales, (2) length of technical nature of the production processes, (3) durability versus perishability, or style factor, in the end products, (4) ease of replenishing stocks, and (5) the consequences of running short of an item.

Since these factors differ among different industries, there can be wide variation in the inventory-to-sales or inventory-to-assets ratios. For example, inventories in the tobacco industry are high because of the long curing process. Similarly, in the machine-manufacturing industries, inventories are large because of the long work-in-process period. Inventory ratios are low, however, in coal mining and in oil and gas production because no raw materials are used and the goods in process are small in relation to sales. Because of the seasonal nature of the raw materials, average inventories are large in the canning industry.

With respect to durability and perishability, large inventories are found in the hardware and the precious metals industries, where durability is great and the probability of obsolescence is small. Inventory ratios are low in the baking industry because of the perishability of the final product.

Within limits set by the economics of a firm's industry, there exists a potential for improvement in inventory control through the use of computers. A thorough description of these techniques—for example, materials requirements planning (MRP), electronic data interchange (EDI), and just-in-time delivery (JIT)—is outside the scope of this text, but it is important that financial managers, as well as production, sales, and accounts payable and receivable managers, be aware of them. Many Canadian companies, including General Motors of Canada and Provigo, now make all purchases through EDI. It is estimated that by 1995, 93 percent of all Canadian auto parts suppliers will be using JIT with *their* suppliers.[1] In order to sell to those firms, companies must have up-to-date inventory management techniques in place.

Determining the Inventory Investment

Managing assets of all kinds can be viewed as an inventory problem since the same principles apply to cash and fixed assets as to inventories themselves. First, a *working stock* must be on hand to meet expected needs for the items, with the size of the stock depending on the expected production and sales levels. Second, because demand may be greater than expected, it is necessary to have **safety stocks** on hand. The additional costs of holding the safety stock inventory must be balanced against the costs of sales lost because of inventory shortages (called *stockout costs*). The actual inventory level equals the sum of the working and safety stocks, although the inventory size will vary from this sum just before and just after an order has been received.

When borrowing money, buying raw materials for production, or purchasing plant and equipment, it is often cheaper to buy larger quantities than to buy small quantities on a weekly or daily basis. However, purchasing or producing more goods than are currently needed increases the firm's carrying costs and exposes it to the risks of being left with obsolete inventories if demand should fall. In the next section, we quantify the costs and benefits of changing the level of inventory investment, and we present a model, the *economic ordering quantity (EOQ) model*, which can help determine the optimal inventory level.

To make the discussion more concrete, let us consider as an example a firm that makes photographic film and requires silver as a raw material input. What are the important considerations in determining the amount of silver that this firm should have on hand in its inventory? At one extreme, the firm could hold a very small amount of silver and order on a day-to-day basis to cover what is actually used. This would be a wasteful policy, as the firm would incur substantial clerical and administrative costs (referred to as **ordering costs**). In addition, the firm would face a serious risk of not having enough raw materials if requirements on a particular day are greater than expected or if there is an unanticipated delay in receiving silver; this could result in lost current sales and, through a negative reputation effect, future sales as well.

To alleviate the ordering costs and the risks noted, the firm could make one very large order and always have enough silver on hand to meet its requirements. Although the large order size would permit the firm to take advantage of purchase discounts, this policy does have costs since the firm would incur substantial *holding* or *storage costs*. The direct or physical costs relate to the costs of storage space, handling insurance, and the prevention of theft. In addition, there are risks associated with deterioration, obsolescence, and adverse price fluctuations; the first two are not very important in our silver example, but the third can be substantial. Finally, there is a cost of tying up funds to finance the inventory—the cost is the foregone earnings on the money

---

[1] J. Lorinc, "Inventory: Taking Stock," *Canadian Business*, April 1991.

invested in the silver inventory; these costs will be referred to as **carrying costs**. The higher are interest rates, the greater is the carrying cost of inventory. When interest rates are high, there is significant pressure to lower inventory. In order to determine the optimal, or desired, inventory, a balance must be struck between the costs of holding a very large inventory—opportunity cost and storage costs—and the costs of having a small inventory—ordering costs. This tradeoff will be analyzed in some depth shortly. However, before determining the optimal inventory level, we shall look at some of the types of inventory decisions firms must make.

Typical Inventory Decisions

Three examples, one of a retail store and two of manufacturers, will illustrate the issues involved in inventory management and the problems poor inventory control can cause.

Retail Clothing Store.   Sunshine Sportswear Shops must order bathing suits in January for sales the following summer, and it must take delivery by April to be sure of having enough suits to meet the heavy May–June demand. Bathing suits come in many styles, colours, and sizes. If the buyer stocks incorrectly, either in total or in terms of the style-colour-size distribution, then the store will have trouble—it will lose potential sales if it stocks too few suits, and it will be forced to mark them down and take losses if it stocks either too many or the wrong types.

The effects of inventory changes on the balance sheet are important. For simplicity, assume that Sunshine has a $100 000 base stock of inventories, which is financed by common shares. Its initial balance sheet is as follows (in thousands of dollars):

Inventories (base stock)	$100	Common equity	$100
Total assets	$100	Total liabilities and equity	$100

Now the company anticipates a seasonal increase in sales of $300 000, and it takes on additional inventories in that amount, financing them with a bank loan:

Inventories	$400	Notes payable to bank	$300
		Common equity	100
Total assets	$400	Total liabilities and equity	$400

If everything works out as planned, sales will be made, inventories will be converted to cash, the bank loan will be retired, and the company will earn a profit. The balance sheet after a successful season might look like this:

Cash and marketable securities	$ 50	Notes payable to bank	$ 0
Inventories (base stock)	100	Common equity	100
		Retained earnings	50
Total assets	$150	Total liabilities and equity	$150

The company is now in a highly liquid position and is ready to begin a new season.

But what if the season has not gone well? Suppose sales have been slow, and as fall approaches, the balance sheet looks like this:

Inventories	$300	Notes payable to bank	$200
		Common equity	100
Total assets	$300	Total liabilities and equity	$300

Now suppose the bank insists on repayment of its loan, and it wants cash, not bathing suits. If the bathing suits did not sell well in the summer, how will out-of-style suits sell in the fall? Assume that Sunshine Sportswear is forced to mark the suits down to half price in order to sell them to raise cash to repay the bank loan. The result will be as follows:

Cash	$150	Notes payable to bank	$200
		Common equity	(50)
Total assets	$150	Total liabilities and equity	$150

At this point, Sunshine Sportswear goes bankrupt.[2] The bank gets the $150 000 of cash and takes a $50 000 loss on its loan. The shareholders are wiped out, and the company goes out of business.

Manufacturing Companies.   Now consider a different type of situation, that of General Appliance Ltd., a well-established appliance manufacturer, whose inventory position follows (in millions of dollars):

Raw materials	$ 200
Work-in-process	200
Finished goods	600
	$1000

Suppose General Appliance anticipates that the economy is about to get much stronger and that the demand for appliances is likely to rise sharply. If it is to share in the expected boom, General Appliance will have to increase production. This means it will have to increase inventories, and, since that increase will precede sales, additional financing will be required. The details are not shown here, but some liability account, probably notes payable, will have to be increased to support the inventory buildup.

Proper inventory management requires close co-ordination among the sales, purchasing, production, and finance departments. The sales/marketing department is generally the first to spot changes in demand. These changes must be worked into the company's purchasing and manufacturing schedules, and the financial manager must arrange any financing that will be needed to support the inventory buildup.

The importance of co-ordination between sales and production can be illustrated by Vanier Ltd., a manufacturer of home computers that was recently forced into bankruptcy because of a poor system of internal controls. The company set its production schedules for 1993 on the basis of 1992 sales.

[2]The term "go bankrupt" is used here in its colloquial meaning "to fail as a business." Bankruptcy is described more precisely in Chapter 25.

However, the introduction of new, improved computers by competitors caused sales to drop sharply during the first half of 1993. Production schedules were not adjusted downward, so both inventories and bank debt built up. By the time the situation had been properly assessed, inventories of now obsolete components had risen to $10 million. The situation was like this (in millions of dollars):

Cash	$ 1	Accounts payable	$ 3
Receivables	8	Notes payable to bank	15
Inventories: Useable	6		
Obsolete	10		
Total current assets	$25	Total current liabilities	$18
Fixed assets	10	Long-term debt	10
		Common equity	7
Total assets	$35	Total liabilities and equity	$35

The bank insisted upon payment of the note. Vanier simply could not generate the necessary cash, and it was thus forced into bankruptcy.[3] The company had some good products on the drawing board, but it did not survive to bring them to fruition.

Concept Review

▶ Define the terms *working stock* and *safety stock*.

▶ Briefly explain why proper inventory management requires close co-ordination among the sales, purchasing, production, and finance departments.

Inventory Costs

The goal of inventory management is to provide the inventories required to sustain operations at the minimum cost.[4] The first step is to identify all the costs involved in purchasing and maintaining inventories. Table 8-1 gives a listing of the typical costs associated with inventories, broken down into three categories: costs associated with carrying inventories, costs associated with ordering and receiving inventories, and stockout costs.

Although they may well be the most important element, we shall at this point disregard stockout costs; these are dealt with by adding safety stocks,

---

[3]As we shall see in Chapter 11, bank loans are generally written as 90-day notes. Thus, the loan must be repaid or renewed every 90 days. If the bank thinks a firm's situation has deteriorated, as Vanier's had, it will refuse to renew its loan. Then, if the firm cannot raise cash to repay the loan, it will become bankrupt.

[4]Since inventory control techniques are the subject of full courses in operations research programs, we cannot deal with the subject in a very complete fashion. However, the model that we illustrate is probably the most widely used and can be readily expanded to encompass many desired refinements.

Table 8-1
Costs Associated with Inventories

	Approximate Annual Percentage Cost
I Carrying Costs	
Cost of capital tied up	12.0%
Storage and handling costs	0.5
Insurance	0.5
Property taxes	1.0
Depreciation and obsolescence	12.0
Total	26.0%
II Ordering, Shipping, and Receiving Costs	
Cost of placing orders, including production setup	varies
Shipping and handling costs	2.5%
III Costs of Running Short (Stockout Costs)	
Loss of sales	varies
Loss of customer goodwill	varies
Disruption of production schedules	varies

Note: These costs vary from firm to firm, from item to item, and over time. The figures shown are estimates for an average manufacturing firm. Where costs vary so widely that no meaningful numbers can be assigned, we simply report "varies."

which are discussed later. The costs that remain for consideration at this stage, then, are carrying costs and ordering, shipping, and receiving costs.

Carrying Costs

Carrying costs generally rise in direct proportion to the average amount of inventory carried, which in turn depends on the frequency with which orders are placed. Consider Stead Company Ltd. which sells S units per year and places equal-sized orders of Q units N times per year. Assuming no safety stocks are carried, the average inventory, A, will be:

$$\text{Average inventory} = A = \frac{\text{Quantity ordered}}{2} = \frac{Q}{2}. \qquad \textbf{(8-1)}$$

Note also that the quantity ordered, Q, is equal to S divided by N, the number of orders placed per year, and substituting for Q in Equation 8-1, we obtain:

$$A = \frac{\text{Annual sales/Number of orders}}{2} = \frac{S/N}{2}. \qquad \textbf{(8-1a)}$$

For example, assume that Stead Company expects to achieve a sales volume, S, for the coming year equal to 3600 units and the sales are expected to be distributed evenly over the year. In this case, inventories will decline smoothly and gradually between the receipt of orders. The purchase price per unit of inventory, P, is equal to $40. No inventory is on hand at the beginning of the year, and none will be held at year's end.

One possible inventory strategy would be for Stead to place one order for Q = 3600 units at the beginning of the year. The initial inventory would be 3600 units, and the company would slowly reduce the inventory over the year. In this example, the number of times inventory is ordered, N, is 1 and the sales, S, are 3600, resulting in an average inventory of 1800 units:

$$A = \frac{Q}{2} = \frac{S/N}{2} = \frac{3600/1}{2} = 1800 \text{ units.}$$

With the purchase price of inventory of P = $40, the average inventory value is (P)(A) = ($40)(1800) = $72 000.

Alternatively, Stead could place two orders per year and the average inventory would be 900 units:

$$A = \frac{S/N}{2} = \frac{3600/2}{2} = 900 \text{ units.}$$

The average investment in inventory would be $(40)(900) = $36 000. As can be observed, by ordering more frequently, the average inventory level falls along with the investment in inventories.

How far should inventory reductions be carried? Smaller inventories result in lower carrying costs—cost of capital tied up in inventories, storage costs, insurance, and so on—but, since smaller average inventories imply more frequent orders, they also result in higher ordering costs. This is the tradeoff that the inventory model seeks to resolve.

Capital Costs

If Stead's cost of capital is 14 percent and it decides to order only once per year, it incurs $10 080 in capital costs to carry the average inventory investment of $72 000. Assume that each year Stead incurs $3100 of storage costs (for space, utilities, security, taxes, and so forth), $1020 of inventory insurance costs, and $3800 of depreciation and obsolescence costs. The firm's total cost of carrying the $72 000 average inventory is thus $10 080 + $3100 + $1020 + $3800 = $18 000 and its percentage cost of carrying inventory is $18 000/$72 000 = 0.25 = 25%. Defining the percentage cost as C, we can, in general, find the annual total carrying costs (TCC) as the percentage carrying cost, C, times the price per unit, P, times the average number of units, A:

$$\text{Total carrying costs} = \text{TCC} = (C)(P)(A) \qquad \textbf{(8-2)}$$

The cost of carrying the inventory for Stead will be

$$\text{TCC} = 0.25(\$40)(1800) = \$18\,000$$

If the company orders twice a year and, hence, has average inventories that are half as large (900 units), total carrying costs will fall to $9000. If orders are placed more frequently, carrying costs will continue to decline because of the decline in average inventories.

Ordering Costs

Although carrying costs are entirely variable and rise in direct proportion to the average size of inventories, ordering costs per order are assumed to be fixed. For example, the costs of placing and receiving an order, interoffice memos, long distance telephone calls, setting up a production run, taking delivery, and executive time are essentially a fixed amount for each order, so this part of total inventory cost is simply the fixed cost of placing and receiving orders times the number of orders placed. We call the fixed costs associated with ordering inventories, F, and if the firm places N orders per year, the annual total ordering costs (TOC) are

$$\text{Total ordering costs} = \text{TOC} = (F)(N). \tag{8-3}$$

Equation 8-1a can be solved for N to produce $N = S/2A$, and from Equation 8-1, we determine that $2A = Q$. Thus, $N = S/Q$ can be substituted for N in Equation 8-3:

$$\text{TOC} = \text{Total ordering costs} = (F)(N) = (F)(S/Q). \tag{8-4}$$

To evaluate Equation 8-4, suppose that for Stead, $F = \$125$, $S = 3600$ units, and $Q = 3600$. Then Stead's annual TOC will be $125:

$$\text{TOC} = (F)(S/Q) = (F)(N) = \$125(3600/3600) = \$125.$$

If Stead were to order 18 times per year, the ordering cost would be ($125)(18) = $2250.

Total Inventory Costs

Total carrying costs (TCC) as defined in Equation 8-2, and total ordering costs (TOC) as defined in Equation 8-3, may be combined to find total inventory costs (TIC) as follows:

$$\begin{aligned}\text{Total inventory costs} &= \text{TIC} \\ &= \text{TCC} + \text{TOC} \\ &= (C)(P)(A) + (F)(N). \end{aligned} \tag{8-5}$$

If Stead orders 200 units 18 times per year, its total inventory costs will be $3250:

$$\text{TIC} = \$1000 + \$2250 = \$3250.$$

Recalling from Equation 8-1 that the average inventory carried is $A = Q/2$, or one-half the size of each order quantity, and that $N = S/Q$, we can rewrite Equation 8-5 as follows:

$$\text{TIC} = (C)(P)(Q/2) + (F)(S/Q). \tag{8-6}$$

Using Equation 8-6, we calculate Stead's total inventory costs to be $3250:

$$TIC = (0.25)(\$40)(200/2) + (\$125)(3600/200)$$
$$= \$1000 + \$2250$$
$$= \$3250.$$

As you can observe in Equation 8-6, the total inventory cost depends upon the order quantity, Q. It is this relationship that will be used in the next section to identify the order quantity that results in the minimum total inventory cost.

Concept Review

▶ What is the goal of inventory management?
▶ What are carrying costs, and how are total carrying costs calculated?
▶ What are ordering costs, and how are total ordering costs calculated?
▶ How are total inventory costs calculated?

The Optimal Ordering Quantity

Inventories are obviously necessary, but it is equally obvious that a firm will suffer if it has too much or too little inventory. How can we determine the optimal inventory level? One commonly used approach utilizes the *economic ordering quantity (EOQ) model*, which is described in this section.

Figure 8-1 illustrates the basic premise on which inventory theory is built: namely, that some costs rise with larger inventories whereas other costs decline, and that there is an optimal order size that minimizes the total costs associated with inventories (TIC). First, as noted earlier, the average investment in inventories depends on how frequently orders are placed. If a firm places a small order every day, average inventories will be much smaller than if it places one large order once a year. Further, as Figure 8-1 shows, some of the firm's costs rise with larger orders. Larger orders mean larger average inventories, so warehousing costs, interest on funds tied up in inventory, insurance costs, and obsolescence costs all will increase. At the same time, ordering costs decline with larger orders and inventories, because the costs of placing orders, setting up production runs, and handling shipments will all decline if the firm orders infrequently and consequently holds larger quantities.

When the carrying and ordering cost curves in Figure 8-1 are added together, the sum represents the total cost of ordering and carrying inventories (TIC). The point at which the total cost curve is minimized represents the **economic ordering quantity, (EOQ)**, and this, in turn, determines the optimal average inventory level.

Figure 8-1
Determination of the Optimal Order
Quantity: Stead Company Ltd.

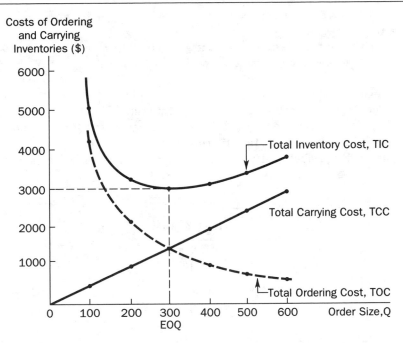

Q	Average inventory	TCC	TOC	TIC
100	50	$ 500	$4500	$5000
200	100	1000	2250	3250
300	150	1500	1500	3000
400	200	2000	1125	3125
500	250	2500	900	3400
600	300	3000	750	3750

It can be shown that under certain assumptions, the order quantity that minimizes the total cost curve in Figure 8-1 can be found by using the following formula, which is called the *EOQ model:*[5]

$$\text{EOQ} = \sqrt{\frac{2(F)(S)}{(C)(P)}}. \qquad (8\text{-}7)$$

---

[5]The total cost function as set forth in Equation 8-6 is differentiated with respect to Q, and the first derivative is set equal to zero to find the minimum point on the total cost curve in Figure 8-1. Equation 8-7 results from this operation.

Here

EOQ = the economic ordering quantity, or the optimum quantity to be ordered each time an order is placed.

F = fixed costs of placing and receiving an order.

S = annual sales in units.

C = carrying cost expressed as a percentage of inventory value.

P = purchase price the firm must pay per unit of inventory.

The assumptions of the EOQ model, which will be relaxed shortly, are: (1) sales can be forecasted perfectly; (2) sales are evenly distributed throughout the year; (3) orders are received with no delays whatsoever; and (4) F, C, and P are all fixed and independent of the ordering procedures.

Using the EOQ model, we find Stead Company's optimal ordering quantity to be 300 units:

$$
\begin{aligned}
EOQ &= \sqrt{\frac{2(\$125)(3600)}{(0.25)(\$40)}} \\
&= \sqrt{\frac{\$900\,000}{\$10}} \\
&= \sqrt{90\,000} \\
&= 300 \text{ units.}
\end{aligned}
$$

If this quantity is ordered 12 times a year (3600/300 = 12), or every 30 days, total costs of ordering and carrying inventories, calculated from Equation 8-5, will be $3000:

$$
\begin{aligned}
TIC &= CP(Q/2) + (F)(S/Q) \\
&= \$10(300/2) + \$125(3600/300) \\
&= \$1500 + \$1500 \\
&= \$3000.
\end{aligned}
$$

This is the lowest possible cost of ordering and carrying the required amount of inventories.

Equation 8-6 provides the optimal, or cost-minimizing, order quantity. Knowing the EOQ and continuing our assumption of zero beginning and ending inventory balances, the optimal average inventory is 150 units:

$$
A = EOQ/2 = 300/2 = 150.
$$

Stead will thus have an average inventory investment of 150 units at $40 each, or $6000.

Relationship between Sales and Inventories

Intuitively, we should suppose that the higher the ordering or processing costs, the less frequently orders should be placed. The higher the carrying costs of inventory, however, the more frequently stocks should be ordered. These two features are incorporated in the formula. Notice also that if Stead's sales had been estimated at 7200 units, the EOQ would have been 424, and the average inventory would have been 212 units instead of the 150 called for with sales of 3600 units. Thus, a doubling of sales leads to less than a doubling of inventories. That is, in fact, a general rule: the EOQ increases with the *square root* of sales, so any increase in sales calls for a less-than-proportionate increase in inventories and thus the inventory turnover ratio will increase as sales grow. The financial manager should keep this in mind when establishing standards for inventory control.[6]

Setting the Reorder Point

Stead's inventory situation is graphed in Figure 8-2. The company has an annual demand of 3600 units, and with an EOQ of 300 units, it needs to order 12 times each year, or once every 30 days. Immediately after an order is received, 300 units are in stock. The usage rate is 10 units per day (300/30 days), so inventories are drawn down by this amount each day, and this determines the slope of the line. If the sales rate increases, the line will become steeper.

The actual number of units held in inventory will vary from 300 units, just after an order is received, to zero, just before the next order arrives. On average, there will be 150 units held. At a cost of $40 per unit, the average investment in inventories will be $6000. If inventories are financed by a bank

Figure 8-2
Inventory Position without Safety Stock

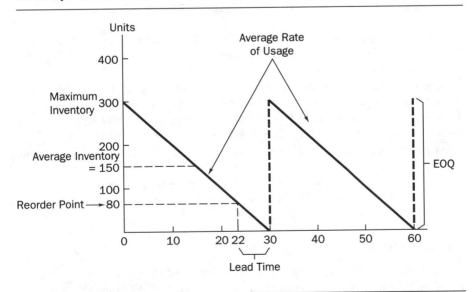

---

[6]Note, however, that these scale economies relate to the particular item, not to the entire firm. Thus, a large company with $500 million of sales may have a higher inventory/sales ratio than a much smaller company if the small company has only a few high-volume items whereas the large one sells a great many low-volume items.

loan, the loan will vary from a high of $12 000 to a low of $0, with the average amount outstanding over the course of a year at $6000.

Now let us relax the assumption of instantaneous order and delivery. Let us assume Stead requires 8 days to place an order and receive the delivery. In order not to interrupt its sales activities, Stead must keep an 8-day stock, or 80 units, on hand, whenever it places an order.

$$\text{Reorder point} = \text{Lead time} \times \text{Usage rate}$$
$$= 8 \text{ days} \times 10 \text{ units per day}$$
$$= 80 \text{ units.}$$

The stock that is required to be on hand at the time of ordering is defined as the *reorder point*; whenever inventory reaches this point, a new order will be placed. If Stead's inventory control process is automated, the computer will generate an order when the stock on hand falls to 80 units. At the end of the 8-day period, the inventory balance will be down to zero—but just at that time, the order of new units will arrive.

Goods in Transit.   If a new order must be placed before the previous order is received, a *goods-in-transit* inventory will build up. Goods in transit are goods that have been ordered but have not been received. A goods-in-transit inventory will exist if the normal delivery lead time is longer than the time between orders. This complicates matters somewhat; the simplest solution to the problem is to deduct goods in transit when calculating the reorder point. In other words, the reorder point is calculated as follows:

$$\text{Reorder point} = (\text{Lead time} \times \text{Usage rate}) - \text{Goods in transit.}$$

Note that lead time and usage rate must both be defined in terms of the same kind of time period. In other words, if lead time is specified in days, the usage rate must also be in days and not, for example, in weeks.

Goods in transit is not an issue for Stead because the firm orders 3600/300 = 12 times a year, or once every 4 to 5 weeks, and the delivery lead time is 8 days. However, suppose that Stead ordered 150 units every 14 days, and the delivery lead time was 21 days. Then, whenever an order was placed, another order of 150 units would be in transit. Therefore, Stead's reorder point would be

$$\text{Reorder point} = (21 \times 10) - 150$$
$$= 210 - 150$$
$$= 60.$$

Safety Stocks

To this point we have assumed that usage (demand) is known with certainty and is uniform throughout time, and that the order lead time never varies. Since either or both of these assumptions could be incorrect, it is necessary to modify the EOQ model to allow for this possibility. This modification usually takes the form of adding a *safety stock* to average inventories to account for uncertainties in demand and variations in production and shipping of inventories to the firm.

The concept of a safety stock is illustrated in Figure 8-3. First, note that the slope of the sales line measures the expected rate of sales. The company *expects* sales of 10 units per day, but let us assume that the maximum possible sales rate is twice that amount, or 20 units each day. Further, assume that Stead sets the safety stock at 80 units. Thus, it initially orders 380, which is the EOQ of 300 units plus the safety stock. Subsequently, it reorders the EOQ whenever the inventory level falls to 160 units, which is the safety stock of 80 units plus the 80 units expected to be used while awaiting delivery of the order. The company could, over the 8-day delivery period, sell 20 units a day, or double its normal expected sales; this maximum rate of sales is shown by the steep, dashed line labelled "Maximum rate of usage" in Figure 8-3. The condition that makes it possible to achieve this higher sales rate is the safety stock of 80 units; without it, the firm would run out of stock if the sales rate rose from 10 to 20 copies per day.

The safety stock is also useful for guarding against delays in receiving orders. The expected delivery time is 8 days, but with an 80-unit safety stock the company can maintain sales at the expected rate of 10 units per day for an additional 8 days if shipping delays hold up an order.

Safety stocks are obviously useful, but they do have a cost. For Stead Co., the average inventory is now EOQ/2 plus a safety stock of 80, or $300/2 + 80 = 150 + 80 = 230$ units, and the average inventory value is $(230)(\$40) = \$9200$. The increase in average inventory resulting from the safety stock causes an increase in inventory carrying costs.

The optimum safety stock varies from one situation to another, but in general it *increases* (1) with the uncertainty of sales forecasts, (2) with the costs (in terms of lost sales and lost goodwill) that would result from an inventory shortage, and (3) with the probability of delays in receiving

Figure 8-3
Inventory Position with Safety Stock Included

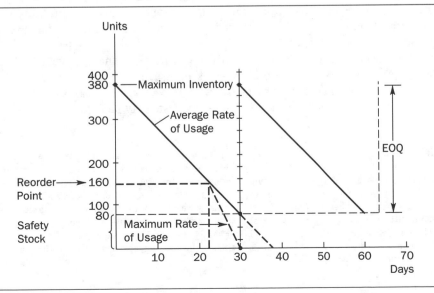

shipments. The optimum safety stock *decreases* as the cost of carrying it increases.[7]

Inventory Control Systems

The EOQ model, along with an analysis of safety stocks, can be used to establish the proper inventory level, but inventory management also involves an *inventory ordering and control system*. One simple control procedure is the *red-line method*. Here inventory items are stocked in a bin, a red line is drawn around the inside of the bin at the level of the reorder point, and the inventory clerk places an order when the red line shows. For the *two-bin method*, inventory items are stocked in two bins; when the working bin is empty, an order is placed and inventory is drawn from the second bin. These procedures work well for items such as bolts in a manufacturing process and for many items in retail businesses.

Companies are increasingly employing computerized inventory control systems. Canadian Tire and other firms use a computerized system called **electronic data interchange (EDI)** to help control their finished goods inventories. EDI systems allow specially formated documents, such as purchase orders, to be sent from one company's computer to another's. Most items sold by Canadian Tire have magnetic bar codes that are scanned by a reader when a customer checks out. While the register is processing the customer's payment, information about the items that have been sold (such as colour and size) is being transmitted to Canadian Tire's inventory control computers. The inventory control computers record the inventory reduction, and when the inventory level of an item falls to a specified amount, the computer automatically places an order with the manufacturer's computer through the EDI system.

A good inventory control system is dynamic. Companies such as IBM and General Motors stock hundreds of thousands of different items, and the sales (or use) of these items can rise or fall quite separately from fluctuating overall corporate sales. As the usage rate for an individual item begins to fall, the inventory manager must adjust this item's balance to avoid ending up with obsolete items—either finished goods or parts and materials for use in producing them.

The EOQ model is useful for establishing order sizes and average inventory levels given a *correctly forecasted* sales or usage rate, and assuming that purchase prices and ordering costs are *fixed*. However, usage rates change over time, and both purchase prices and ordering costs may be dependent upon the

---

[7]If we knew the probability distribution of usage rates and the probability distribution of order lead times, we could determine the joint probabilities of inventory shortages with various safety stock levels. With a safety stock of 80 units, for example, the probability of an inventory shortage might be 5 percent. If the safety stock was reduced to 40 units, the probability of a shortage might rise to 15 percent, whereas it might be reduced to 1 percent with a safety stock of 160 units. If we had additional information on the precise cost of running out of inventory, we could compare that potential cost with the cost of carrying larger safety stocks. The optimum safety stock would be determined at the point at which the marginal cost of a shortage was equal to the marginal inventory carrying cost.

buyer's arrangements with the seller, such as Canadian Tire's with its suppliers. Therefore, a good inventory management system must respond promptly to any change in these conditions. One system that is used to monitor inventory usage rates and in turn to modify EOQs and inventory item levels is the *ABC system*. Under this system, the firm analyzes each inventory item on the basis of its cost, frequency of usage, seriousness of a stockout, order lead time, and other criteria. Items that are expensive, are frequently used, and have long order lead times are put in the A category; less important items are put in the B category; and the least important items are designated C. Management reviews the A items' recent usage rates, stock positions, and delivery time situations quite frequently—say, monthly—and adjusts the EOQ as necessary. Category B items are reviewed and adjusted less frequently— say, every quarter—and C items are reviewed perhaps annually. Thus, the inventory control group's resources are concentrated where they will do the most good.

Efficient inventory management will result in a relatively high inventory turnover ratio, in low writeoffs of obsolete or deteriorated inventories, and in relatively few instances of work stoppages or lost sales because of stockouts. All this, in turn, will contribute to a high profit margin, a high total assets turnover, a high rate of return on investment, and a strong stock price.

Effects of Inflation on Inventory Management

Moderate inflation—say, 3 percent per year—can largely be ignored for purposes of inventory management, but at higher rates of inflation it becomes important to consider this factor. If the rate of inflation in the types of goods the firm stocks tends to be relatively constant, it can be dealt with easily; one simply deducts the expected annual rate of inflation from the carrying cost percentage, C, in Equation 8-7 and uses this modified version of the EOQ model to establish the working stock. The reason for making this deduction is that inflation causes the value of the inventory to rise, thus offsetting somewhat the effects of depreciation and other carrying cost factors. Since C will now be smaller, the calculated EOQ and hence the average inventory will increase. However, the higher the rate of inflation, the higher interest rates will be, and this will cause C to increase and thus lower the EOQ and average inventories.

On balance, there is no evidence that inflation either raises or lowers the optimal level of inventories of firms in the aggregate. It should still be thoroughly considered, however, for it will raise the individual firm's optimal holdings if the rate of inflation for its own inventories is above average (and is greater than the effects of inflation on interest rates), and vice versa.

Other Inventory Issues

Three other inventory-related issues should be mentioned. The first is the **just-in-time system**, **JIT**, in which a manufacturer co-ordinates production with suppliers so that raw materials or components arrive from suppliers just as they are needed in the production process. The primary focus of the just-in-time system is to reduce order costs and the purchase price of goods purchased. The Japanese have carried the just-in-time system to great lengths, and North American companies are increasingly adopting this system in their manufacturing plants. To some extent, the just-in-time system reduces the need for the purchaser to carry inventories by passing the problem back to its suppliers; however, with a co-ordinated production schedule, the supplier may also benefit (1) by being able to schedule production runs better and (2) by having to carry lower finished goods inventory safety stock. In any event, co-ordination between suppliers and users lessens total inventory requirements and also reduces total production costs.

Toyota provides a good example of the just-in-time system. Eight of Toyota's ten factories, along with most of Toyota's suppliers, dot the countryside around Toyota City. Delivery of components is tied to the speed of the assembly line, and parts are generally delivered no more than a few hours before they are used. Not surprisingly, automobile manufacturers were among the first North American firms to move toward just-in-time systems. General Motors of Canada has restructured its production system to increase its inventory turnover from twice a month in 1984 to once every 3 to 5 days.

Just-in-time systems are also being adopted by smaller firms. In fact, some production experts say that small companies are better positioned than large ones to use just-in-time methods, because it is easier to redefine job functions and to educate people in small firms. Fireplace Manufacturers, Inc., a producer of prefabricated metal fireplaces, was recently experiencing serious profit and cash flow problems. It discovered that its inventory control system was inadequate, and the JIT inventory control system was recommended. The JIT system allowed Fireplace to cut its inventories by 35 percent.

Another important development related to inventories is **out-sourcing**, which is the practice of purchasing components rather than making them in-house. Thus, if General Motors arranges to buy radiators, axles, and other parts from suppliers rather than making them itself, it has increased its use of out-sourcing. Out-sourcing is often combined with just-in-time systems to reduce inventory levels. However, one important reason for out-sourcing has nothing to do with inventory policy; because of wage rate differentials, a heavily unionized company like GM can often buy parts from a nonunionized supplier at a lower cost than it could make them.

A final point relating to inventory levels is the relationship between production scheduling and inventory levels. A firm with sales that are highly seasonal can choose to produce on a steady, year-round basis or can let production rise and fall with sales. If it establishes a level production schedule, its inventories will rise sharply during periods when sales are low and then decline during peak sales periods, but the average inventory held will be substantially higher than if production were geared to rise and fall with sales.

Computerized *materials requirements planning* systems, widely used in the manufacturing sector, enable firms to control which raw materials are ordered, and how much are ordered. This lowers the requirements for raw materials inventory. It is particularly effective when coupled with just-in-time delivery.

Our discussion of just-in-time systems, out-sourcing, and production scheduling all point out the necessity of co-ordinating inventory policy with manufacturing/procurement policies. Companies try to minimize *total production and distribution costs*, and inventory costs are just one part of total costs. Still, they are an important part, and financial managers should be aware of the determinants of inventory costs and how they can be minimized.

Concept Review

▶ What is the basic premise on which inventory theory is built?

▶ What is the EOQ model? Give its formula.

▶ How do you calculate the reorder point (1) when there are no goods in transit and (2) when there are goods in transit?

▶ Identify some conditions that would normally cause the safety stock to increase and some that would cause the safety stock to decrease.

▶ Identify and briefly explain some inventory control systems described in the text.

▶ Explain what just-in-time and out-sourcing mean, and discuss how they affect inventory levels and costs.

Summary

In this chapter the basics of inventory management were discussed, and an inventory model for helping the firm minimize its inventory investment was presented. The key concepts are listed below.

☐ **Inventory management** involves determining how much inventory to hold, when to place orders, and how many units to order at a time. Because the cost of holding inventory is high, inventory management is important.

☐ **Inventory** can be grouped into three categories: (1) raw materials, (2) work-in-process, and (3) finished goods.

☐ **Inventory costs** can also be divided into three types: **carrying costs, ordering costs**, and **stockout costs**. In general, carrying costs increase as the level of inventory rises, but ordering costs and stockout costs decline with larger inventory holdings.

☐ **Safety stocks** are held to avoid shortages (1) if demand becomes greater than expected or (2) if shipping delays are encountered.

☐ Total carrying costs (TCC) are equal to the percentage cost of carrying inventory, C, times the purchase price per unit of inventory, P, times the average number of units held, A:

$$TCC = (C)(P)(A).$$

☐ Total ordering costs (TOC) are equal to the fixed cost of placing an order, F, times the number of orders placed per year, N:

$$TOC = (F)(N).$$

☐ Total inventory costs (TIC) are equal to carrying costs plus ordering costs.

☐ The **economic ordering quantity (EOQ) model** is a formula for determining the order quantity that will minimize total inventory costs:

$$EOQ = \sqrt{\frac{2(F)(S)}{(C)(P)}}.$$

☐ Here F is the fixed cost per order, S is annual sales in units, C is the percentage cost of carrying inventory, and P is the purchase price per unit.

☐ *Reorder point* is the point at which stock on hand must be replenished.

☐ *Goods in transit* are goods that have been ordered but have not been received.

☐ The costs of running short of inventory include lost sales and lost customer goodwill. These costs can be avoided by carrying safety stocks. The cost of carrying safety stocks is equal to the percentage cost of carrying inventories times the purchase price per unit times the number of units held as the safety stock. These costs are separate from those used in the EOQ model.

☐ Firms use inventory control systems, such as the *red-line method* and the *two-bin method*, and the *ABC method*, as well as computerized inventory control systems to help them keep track of actual inventory levels and to ensure that inventory levels are adjusted as sales change. **Electronic data interchange (EDI)** is a computerized inventory system the helps the firm control its finished goods inventories. **Just-in-time (JIT) systems** are also used to hold down inventory costs and, simultaneously, to improve the production process.

Questions

8-1 A firm can reduce its investment in inventory by having its suppliers hold raw materials inventories and its customers hold finished goods inventories. Explain actions a firm can take that would result in larger inventories for its suppliers and customers and smaller inventories for itself. What are the limitations of such actions?

8-2 Indicate by a (+), (−), or (0) whether each of the following events would probably cause average annual inventories (the sum of the inventories held at the end of each month of the year divided by 12) to rise, fall, or change in an indeterminant manner and explain why.

a. We begin to manufacture a part formerly purchased from an outside supplier.   _____

b. Our suppliers switch from delivering by train to air freight.   _____

c. We double the number of styles we produce.   +

d. Large price reductions are offered to our firm from a manufacturer of bathing suits if the suits are purchased in December and January rather than in April.   +

e. The rate of general inflation increases.   _____

f. We change from producing just in time to meet seasonal sales to steady, year-round production (sales peak at Christmas).

+ during off season
- during peak season

g. Competition in the markets in which we sell increases.

(—) to become more competitive

h. Our major customer switches to a just-in-time ordering procedure.

_____

i. We adopt a more flexible plant design that reduces setup costs and makes small production runs more feasible.

(—) easier to produce

8-3 Explain how the managers of the following departments might be expected to differ in their views of inventory levels for raw materials, work in process, and finished goods.
   a. Production
   b. Purchasing
   c. Sales
   d. Finance

8-4 The toy business is subject to large seasonal demand fluctuations. What effect would this have on inventory decisions of toy manufacturers and toy retailers?

Self-Test Problems   (solutions appear on page 267)

ST-1 Key terms.   Define each of the following terms:
   a. EOQ; EOQ model
   b. Carrying costs; ordering costs
   c. Reorder point; stockout costs; goods in transit; safety stock
   d. Red-line method; two-bin method; ABC system; EDI
   e. Just-in-time system; out-sourcing; materials requirements planning

ST-2 EOQ and total inventory costs.   The Whole Grain Breads Company Limited buys 2.6 million bushels of wheat annually. The wheat must be purchased in multiples of 2000 bushels. Ordering costs, which include grain elevator removal charges, are $5000 per order. Annual carrying costs are 2 percent of the purchase price per bushel of $5.00. The company maintains a safety stock of 200 000 bushels. The delivery time is 6 weeks.
   a. What is the EOQ?
   b. At what inventory level should Whole Grain reorder to prevent its having to draw on the safety stock?
   c. What are the total inventory costs?
   d. The wheat processor agrees to pay the elevator removal charges, which amount to $3500 per order, if Whole Grain Breads will purchase wheat in quantities of 650 000 bushels. Would it be to Whole Grain's advantage to order under this alternative?

Problems

8-1 Inventory costs.   Computer Supplies, Ltd. must order floppy disks from its supplier in lots of one dozen boxes. Given the following information, complete the table below and determine the economic ordering quantity for floppy disks for Computer Supplies.

Annual demand: 2600 dozen
Cost per order placed: $7.00
Carrying cost: 15%
Price per dozen: $20

Order size (dozens)	26	50	100	130	200	2600
Number of orders	——	——	——	——	——	——
Average inventory	——	——	——	——	——	——
Carrying cost	——	——	——	——	——	——
Order cost	——	——	——	——	——	——
Total cost	——	——	——	——	——	——

8-2 Economic ordering quantity. The Rosecrans Garden Centre sells 24 000 bags of lawn fertilizer annually. Its optimal safety stock (on hand initially) is 1200 bags. Each bag costs Rosecrans $4, inventory carrying costs are 20 percent, and the cost of placing an order with its supplier is $25.

a. What is the economic ordering quantity?
b. What is the maximum inventory of fertilizer?
c. What is the average inventory?
d. How often must the company order?

8-3 EOQ and total ordering costs. The following cost relationships for purchase and storage of gyros have been established for the Kenyan Gyro Co. Ltd.:

• Orders must be placed in multiples of 100 gyros.
• Annual sales are 338 000 gyros.
• The purchase price per unit is $6 per gyro.
• The carrying cost is 20 percent of the purchase price of goods.
• The cost per order placed is $48.
• Desired safety stock is 12 000 units (on hand initially).
• Two weeks are required for delivery.

a. What is the most economical order quantity?
b. What is the optimal number of orders Kenyan should place per year?
c. At what inventory level should Kenyan reorder? (Hint: The inventory level should be sufficient to cover the amount used during delivery plus the safety stock.)
d. Calculate the total cost of ordering and carrying inventories if the order quantity is (i) 4000 units, (ii) 4800 units, and (iii) 6000 units. What are the total costs if the order quantity is the EOQ?

8-4 Changes in the EOQ. The following relationships for inventory costs have been established for the Bradley Tool Corporation:

• Annual sales are 560 000 units.
• The purchase price per unit is $1.50.
• The carrying cost is 15 percent of the purchase price of goods.
• The cost per order placed is $35.
• Desired safety stock is 10 000 units (on hand initially).
• One week is required for delivery.

    a. What is the most economical order quantity? (Round to the closest 100). What is the total cost of ordering and carrying inventories at the EOQ?

    b. What is the optimal number of orders to be placed?

    c. At what inventory level should Bradley reorder?

    d. If annual unit sales double, what is the percentage increase in the EOQ? What is the elasticity of EOQ with respect to sales (percentage change in EOQ/percentage change in sales)?

    e. If the cost per order doubles, what is the elasticity of EOQ with respect to the cost per order?

    f. If the carrying cost declines by 50 percent, what is the elasticity of EOQ with respect to that change?

    g. If purchase price declines by 50 percent, what is the elasticity of EOQ with respect to that change?

8-5 **EOQ and ordering discounts.** Benoit, a large manufacturer of toys and dolls, uses large quantities of cloth in its doll production process. Throughout the year, the firm uses 1 250 000 square metres of this cloth. The fixed costs of placing and receiving an order are $2000, including a $1500 set-up charge at the mill. The price of the cloth is $2.50 per square metre, and the annual cost of carrying this inventory item is 20 percent of the price. Benoit maintains a 12 500-square-metre safety stock. The cloth supplier requires a 2-week lead time from order to delivery.

    a. What is the EOQ for this cloth?

    b. What is the average inventory dollar value, including the safety stock?

    c. What is the total cost of ordering and carrying the inventory, including the safety stock? (Assume that the safety stock is on hand at the beginning of the year.)

    d. At what inventory unit level should an order be placed? (Use a 52-week year. Again, assume the 12 500 unit safety stock is on hand.)

    e. Suppose the mill offers to lower the set-up charge to $250 if Benoit will increase its order size from 100 000 to 183 500 square metres. Would it be to Benoit's advantage to order under this alternative?

    f. Now suppose the mill offers to lower the set-up charge to $750 if Benoit will order 140 000 metres at a time. Should Benoit accept this alternative?

Solutions to Self-Test Problems

ST-1 Refer to the appropriate sections of the text to check your responses.

ST-2 **a.**

$$EOQ = \sqrt{\frac{2(F)(S)}{(C)(P)}}$$

$$= \sqrt{\frac{(2)(\$5000)(2\,600\,000)}{(0.02)(5.00)}}$$

$$= 509\,902 \text{ bushels.}$$

Since the firm must order in multiples of 2000 bushels, it should order in quantities of 510 000 bushels.

b.

$$\text{Average weekly sales} = \frac{2\,600\,000}{52}$$
$$= 50\,000 \text{ bushels.}$$

$$\text{Reorder point} = 6 \text{ weeks' sales} + \text{safety stock}$$
$$= 6(50\,000) + 200\,000$$
$$= 300\,000 + 200\,000$$
$$= 500\,000.$$

c. Total inventory costs:

$$\text{TIC} = \text{CP}\left(\frac{Q}{2}\right) + F\left(\frac{S}{Q}\right) + \text{CP}(\text{safety stock})$$

$$= (0.02)(\$5.00)\left(\frac{510\,000}{2}\right) + (\$5000)\left(\frac{2\,600\,000}{510\,000}\right) + (\$5.00)(0.02)(200\,000)$$
$$= \$25\,500 + \$25\,490.20 + \$20\,000$$
$$= \$70\,990.20.$$

d. Ordering costs are reduced to $1500. By ordering 650 000 bushels at a time, total inventory costs are:

$$\text{TIC} = (0.02)(\$5.00)\left(\frac{650\,000}{2}\right) + (\$1500)\left(\frac{2\,600\,000}{650\,000}\right) + (0.02)(\$5.00)(200\,000)$$
$$= \$32\,500 + \$6000 + \$20\,000$$

$$= \$58\,500.$$

Therefore, the firm can minimize its total inventory costs by ordering 650 000 bushels at a time, and it would be to Whole Grain Breads' advantage to do so.

9

Credit Management and Policy

A MANAGERIAL PERSPECTIVE

After several years of slow growth and mediocre profits, White Automotive Supply's management decided to liberalize its credit terms to stimulate business. Previously, the company had required payment within 10 days and cut off sales to any customer who did not pay on time. Under the new policy, White gave customers the option of paying within 30 days without any interest, or within 3 months at an interest rate of 1 percent per month.

Sales exploded—after the new policy had been in effect for only 6 months, sales were up more than 40 percent from the previous year, and profits had risen even more sharply. White then began a major expansion program to meet its rising demand. However, the benefits of the new credit policy were just an illusion. Sales were up all right, but many of the sales ended up as bad debts, and the new credit policy led to a tremendous increase in accounts receivable, which had to be financed with bank debt. Further, the company's competitors responded by liberalizing their own credit terms, so some of White's initially higher sales later disappeared.

A year later, when the bad debts and the higher interest charges were hitting White's income statement with a vengeance, it was clear that the new credit policy had been a terrible mistake. At that point, management reverted to its old credit policy, but that abrupt change turned out to be another mistake—customers got mad, and sales dropped even faster than they had risen previously. At that point, White had a great deal of excess capacity, too much fixed cost, and substantial losses. White eventually had to declare bankruptcy, but after reading this chapter, you can help your firm avoid that fate.

Since the typical firm has about 20 percent of its assets in receivables, its effectiveness in managing receivables is important to its profitability and risk—and thus to its share price. Techniques for managing receivables are covered in this chapter. In general, firms would rather sell for cash than on credit, but competitive pressures force most companies to offer credit. When goods are shipped, inventories are reduced, and an account receivable is created.[1] Eventually, the

---

[1] Whenever goods are sold on credit, two accounts actually are created—an asset item entitled an *account receivable* appears on the books of the selling firm, and a liability item called an *account payable* appears on the books of the purchaser. At this point we are analyzing the transaction from the viewpoint of the seller, so we are concentrating on the variables under its control, in this case, the receivables. We shall examine the transaction from the viewpoint of the purchaser in Chapter 11, where we discuss accounts payable as a source of funds and consider their cost relative to the cost of funds obtained from other sources.

customer will pay the account, at which time receivables will decline and cash will increase.

Carrying accounts receivable is costly, but the costs involved can be offset by the fact that granting credit normally increases sales. The optimal credit policy is the one that balances the costs and benefits of receivables and thus maximizes the value of the firm.

The Accumulation of Receivables

An **account receivable** is a balance due from a customer. For any firm, the total amount of accounts receivable outstanding at any given time is determined by two factors: (1) the volume of credit sales and (2) the average length of time between sales and collections. For example, suppose you open a store on January 1 and, starting the first day, make sales of $100 each day. Customers are given 10 days in which to pay. At the end of the first day, accounts receivable will be $100; they will rise to $200 by the end of the second day; and by January 10 they will have risen to 10 × $100 = $1000. On January 11 another $100 will be added to receivables, but payments for sales made on January 1 will reduce receivables by $100; total accounts receivable will therefore remain constant at $1000. In general, once your firm's operations are stable, this situation will exist:

$$\frac{\text{Accounts}}{\text{receivable}} = \frac{\text{Credit sales}}{\text{per day}} \times \frac{\text{Length of}}{\text{collection period}}$$
$$= \$100 \times 10 \text{ days} = \$1000.$$

Note, however, that any change in either sales or the collection period will cause accounts receivable to change.

Notice also that the $1000 investment in receivables must be financed. To illustrate, suppose that when you started on January 1, you put up $100 as common equity and used the money to buy the goods sold the first day. Thus, your initial balance sheet would be as follows:

Inventories	$100	Common equity	$100
Total assets	$100	Total liabilities and equity	$100

We assume that the $100 of inventory is sold for $125, so, at the end of the first day, the balance sheet would look like this:[2]

Accounts receivable	$125	Common equity	$100
Inventories	0	Retained earnings	25
Total assets	$125	Total liabilities and equity	$125

In order to remain in business, you must replenish inventories. To do so requires that $100 of goods be purchased, and this requires $100 in cash.

---

[2]The firm would need other assets, such as cash, fixed assets, and a permanent stock of inventory. We abstract from these details so that we may focus on receivables.

Assuming that you borrow the $100 from the bank, the balance sheet at the start of the second day will be as follows:

Accounts receivable	$125	Notes payable to bank	$100
Inventories	100	Common equity	100
		Retained earnings	25
Total assets	$225	Total liabilities and equity	$225

At the end of the day, the inventories will have been converted to receivables, and you will have to borrow another $100 to restock for the third day.

This process will continue, provided the bank is willing to lend the necessary funds, until the eleventh day, when the balance sheet will read as follows:

Accounts receivable	$1250	Notes payable to bank	$1000
Inventories	100	Common equity	100
		Retained earnings	250
Total assets	$1350	Total liabilities and equity	$1350

From now on, $125 of receivables will be collected every day, and $100 of these funds will be used to finance the sales made that day. No more new bank funds will be required, and the bank loan can eventually be repaid out of profits.

Now suppose your sales double to $250 per day. After a brief transition period (10 days), your balance sheet would be as follows:

Accounts receivable	$2500	Notes payable to bank	$2100
Inventories	200	Common equity	100
		Retained earnings	500
Total assets	$2700	Total liabilities and equity	$2700

These examples should make it clear (1) that accounts receivable depend jointly on the level of sales and the collection period, (2) that any increase in receivables must be financed in some manner, but (3) that the entire amount of receivables does not have to be financed because the profit portion (here, $25 of each $125 of sales) does not represent a cash outflow. In this example, we assumed bank financing, but other possibilities include having the firm itself buy on credit (in which case financing would be done by accounts payable rather than notes payable), by selling bonds, or by selling more common equity.[3] Methods of financing accounts receivable (and other current assets) will be considered in Chapter 11.

Concept Review

▶ What two factors determine the total amount of accounts receivable outstanding at any given time?

---

[3]In time, profits will presumably be earned and reinvested in the business, but with normal profit margins, external funds will always be needed to support rapid growth.

Credit Policy

The success or failure of a business depends primarily on demand for its products—as a rule, the higher its sales, the healthier and more profitable the firm. Sales, in turn, depend on a number of factors, some exogenous but others controllable by the firm. The major controllable variables that affect sales are sales prices, product quality, advertising, and the firm's credit policy. **Credit policy**, in turn, consists of these four elements:

1. The *credit period*, which is the length of time buyers have before they must pay for their purchases.
2. *"Cash" discounts* given to encourage early payment.
3. *Credit standards*, which refers to the minimum financial strength of acceptable credit customers.
4. The *collection policy*, which reflects the firm's toughness or laxity in following up on slow-paying accounts.

The credit period and the discount allowed (if any), when combined, are called the **credit terms**. Thus, if a company allows its customers 30 days in which to pay but gives a 2 percent discount if payment is made within 10 days, it is said to offer credit terms of 2/10, net 30. The credit manager has the responsibility for enforcing the credit terms and administering the firm's credit policy. However, because of the pervasive importance of credit, the credit policy itself—both the setting of the credit terms and the specifying of the credit standards and collection policy—is established by the executive committee, which usually consists of the president and the vice presidents in charge of finance, marketing, and production.

Credit Period

The **credit period** is the length of time that a company gives its customers to pay; for example, credit might be extended for 30, 60, or 90 days. Generally, there is a relationship between the normal inventory holding period of the firm's customers and its credit period. Thus, fresh fruits and vegetables are normally sold on very short credit terms, whereas jewellery may involve a 90-day credit period. Lengthening the credit period stimulates sales, but there is a cost to tying up funds in receivables. Another problem associated with lengthening the credit period is the lower probability of collection. With a longer credit period, it takes longer for the selling firm to determine that its customer is in financial trouble. With a shorter credit period, this information is obtained earlier—when the customer has trouble paying the bill—and the firm can take some action before it is too late.

If sales are seasonal, a firm may use **seasonal datings** on discounts. For example, Lady Anne Knits Limited, a Toronto-based manufacturer of ladies' knitwear, produces a line of clothes for each season. The spring line, for example, is shipped in mid- to late December on terms of "net 30, February 1 dating." This means that the effective invoice date is February 1; therefore, the full amount of the invoice must be paid at the end of February regardless of when the shipment is made. The use of seasonal dating results in short-run financing of the retailer's inventories by Lady Anne, but there are some important benefits. As the merchandise is shipped to the retailer quickly, there is a reduction in Lady Anne's storage costs. In addition, the early shipment allows the retailer to provide a complete display of the merchandise earlier in the season; this should have a beneficial effect on sales.

Cash Discounts

The second element in the credit policy decision is the use of **cash discounts** designed to encourage early payment. Decisions on the size of the discount are analyzed by balancing the costs and benefits of different discount terms. For example, a change in credit terms from "net 30" to "2/10 net 30" should produce two benefits: (1) it should attract new customers who consider discounts a type of price reduction, thereby increasing gross sales; and (2) it should cause a reduction in the days sales outstanding, since some old customers will pay more promptly to take advantage of the discount. Offsetting these benefits is the dollar cost of the discounts taken. The optimal discount is established at the point at which costs and benefits are exactly offsetting. The methodology for analyzing changes in the discount is developed later in the chapter.

Changes in the terms on which the products are sold can be interpreted as changes in the *effective price* of the product paid by the buyer and hence changes in the per-unit revenue obtained by the seller. The effective price paid by the buyer reflects the combined impact of the actual price charged and the credit terms. With a cash sales policy, the price paid by the buyer is the invoiced price—say, for example, $100. Suppose credit terms are provided at net 30 *and* the price of the product remains at $100. The effective price has fallen; whereas under the cash sales policy, the buyer had to finance the cash purchase and incur the financial charges, now the financing costs are borne by the seller. The longer the credit terms given, the lower will be the effective price. Similarly, a change from a cash-only policy to credit terms of "2/10, net 30" is also a reduction in the effective price: the buyer now pays $98 if the discount is taken; if the discount is not taken, the effective price is still reduced. This reduction in the effective price may stimulate more sales.

On the other side of the transaction, changes in the credit terms keeping the invoice price of the product constant will reduce the firm's per-unit revenue. It is unlikely, however, that in the long run the selling firm will continue to provide "free" credit. The logical response by the selling company is to increase the invoice price of the product; the price can increase to make the effective price the same both before and after the change in credit terms.

Credit Standards

If a firm extends credit sales to only its strongest customers, it will have very few bad-debt losses, and it will not incur much in the way of expenses for a credit department. On the other hand, it will probably be losing sales, and the profit foregone on these lost sales may be far larger than the costs it has avoided. Determining the optimal credit standard involves equating the *incremental costs of credit* to the *incremental profits on the increased sales*. In addition to determining who will get credit, the credit policy must consider the size of the line of credit granted. The firm's credit standards policy should therefore not be focussed on minimizing bad-debt losses; the policy should be an optimizing strategy that looks at the tradeoff of credit terms that increases sales (and perhaps bad debts) but that provides a positive impact on profits.

Incremental costs include production and selling costs, as well as those costs associated with the "quality" of the marginal accounts, or *credit quality* costs. These credit costs include (1) default, or bad-debt losses, (2) higher investigation and collection costs, and (3) higher costs associated with the capital tied up in the receivables resulting from sales to customers who are less creditworthy, who pay their accounts more slowly, and who consequently cause the average collection period to be lengthened.

Because credit costs and credit quality are highly correlated, it is important to be able to judge the quality of an account. The best way to think about quality is in terms of the probability of default. Probability estimates are, for the most part, subjective, but credit rating is a well-established practice, and a good credit manager can make reasonably accurate judgements of the probability of default by different classes of customers.

The Five Cs System.   The traditional method of measuring credit quality is to investigate potential credit customers with respect to five factors called the **five Cs of credit**.

1. *Character* refers to the probability that a customer will *try* to honour obligations. This factor is of considerable importance, because every credit transaction implies a *promise* to pay. Will debtors make an honest effort to pay their debts, or are they likely to try to get away with something? Experienced credit managers frequently insist that the moral factor is the most important issue in a credit evaluation. Credit reports provide background information on people's and firms' past performances. Often credit analysis will seek this type of information from a firm's bankers, its other suppliers, its customers, and even its competitors.

2. *Capacity* is a subjective judgement of the customer's ability to pay. It is gauged by the customer's past records and business methods, supplemented by physical observation of the customer's plant, store, or other facilities. Again, credit analysts will obtain judgement-based information on this factor from a variety of sources.

3. *Capital* is measured by the general financial condition of the firm as indicated by an analysis of its financial statements, with special emphasis on the risk ratios—the debt-to-assets ratio, the current ratio, and the times-interest-earned ratio.

4. *Collateral* is represented by assets the customer may offer as security in order to obtain credit.

5. *Conditions* refers to both the impact of general economic trends on the firm and to special developments in certain geographic regions or sectors of the economy that may affect a customer's ability to meet its obligations.

Information on these five factors is obtained from a firm's previous experience with its customers, supplemented by a well-developed system of external information gathering. By analyzing the five Cs, credit managers try to formulate judgements as to the total expected costs of granting credit to a given customer. The decision is normally judgement-based, and credit managers must rely on their background knowledge and instincts.

Credit Risk Classes.   The selling firm can use its credit information to develop *customer risk classes*, or groups of customers ranked according to the probability of loss associated with sales to each group. The combination of credit rating and supplementary information might lead to the groupings shown in Table 9-1. If that selling firm has a 20 percent profit margin on goods sold and if it is producing at less than full capacity, it might adopt the following credit policies: sell on customary credit terms to Groups 1 to 5; sell to Groups 6 and 7 under more stringent credit terms, such as cash on delivery; and require advance payment on sales to Group 8 customers. As long as the bad-debt loss ratios are less than 20 percent—as is true for Groups 1 to 7—sales result in positive contributions to overhead and profit.

Modern credit managers often find that using such classification schemes permits them to concentrate time and attention on the customers judged the most likely to cause problems.

Credit Scoring.   The process of evaluating the five Cs of credit may be costly; for example, the clerical and outside credit bureau costs of investigating a suspected poor credit risk can be substantial. When a company sells to a large number of small customers, the standard credit evaluation costs can be prohibitive. An alternative technique, which reduces these costs, is the use of statistical procedures to determine the probability of a default of a particular customer. This technique provides a credit screen by generating a numerical evaluation of the credit risk of each applicant for credit. The numerical evaluation results in a score that is compared to a cutoff value, determined by the company, which leads to maximum profits. If the applicant's score is above the cutoff point, credit is granted; if it is below, credit is refused.

The numerical evaluation of risk is obtained by identifying a number of characteristics that are surrogates for the elements of the five Cs. These

Table 9-1
Probable Loss Ratios by Customer Class

Customer Risk Class	Probable Loss Ratio (%)
1	None
2	0–0.5
3	>0.5–1
4	>1–2
5	>2–5
6	>5–10
7	>10–20
8	>20

characteristics include factors such as bank reference, occupation, length of time on the job, whether the applicant owns a home or rents, income, amount of debt outstanding, marital status, and past credit experience. Using these factors and the firm's historical experience, the company can evaluate the percentages of good risks and of bad risks that have a specific characteristic. One characteristic may have very strong discriminating power; for example, it may be observed that, based on actual experience of the company, 93 percent of the good risks had a bank reference whereas only 60 percent of the bad risks had one. The statistical technique gives each characteristic a weight, or score, such that the sum of the scores on all characteristics equals 100. New applicants for credit are evaluated by determining their score based on their characteristics. Comparing this score to the cutoff value results in an accept or reject credit decision.

The cutoff value is also determined by reference to actual experience of the company. When the cutoff score is very high, the policy is very conservative and the company loses profits on good risks as well as averting losses on bad risks. If the cutoff score is very low, the policy is lenient and the firm, while gaining profits on good risks, incurs losses on bad risks. The optimal strategy is to choose the cutoff point that gives the best profit improvement over having no credit standards at all (providing credit for all).

Credit scoring systems are used extensively by credit card companies and by large retailers that grant credit to large numbers of customers and by manufacturers and wholesalers that sell to large numbers of customers such as builders or small retailers. Large numbers of customers are necessary to obtain statistical validity, and mechanically derived scores are useful because of the cost that would be entailed in obtaining good, consistent appraisals of the credit quality of thousands of individual customers "by hand."

Sources of Credit Information. Financial information necessary to undertake credit analyses can be gathered from a number of sources.

1. *Financial statements.* The first source of information is the set of financial statements each credit applicant is required to file. If the account is new, financial statements for the last three years may be requested. Typically, the applicant firm will provide audited financial statements, although some applicants may submit income tax returns in lieu of other statements. Of course, all such information will be kept confidential.

    The financial statement data allows the credit department to perform a financial ratio analysis. When evaluating requests for short-term credit, the emphasis is on liquidity. However, a good credit analyst will also be concerned with longer-term factors, such as financial stability, debt capacity, and profitability, for if the long-term outlook appears to have potential, it may pay for the seller to take a chance with a potential customer whose current liquidity position is weak. Current financial information is maintained on the account by having the firm submit updated financial statements regularly. Thus, with the aid of computer information systems, the financial trend of each customer, as well as its relationship to composites for the industry, can be analyzed.

2. *Information-Gathering Groups.*   Three major sources of external information are available. The first is the work of local credit associations. By periodic meetings of local groups and by correspondence, information about or experience with debtors is exchanged. For example, Credit Bureau, Inc. assembles and distributes information on debtors' past performance. The reports present the paying record of the debtors and the industries from which they have bought.

A more informal source of information sharing arises when credit managers of firms that sell to a particular industry meet periodically to exchange credit information. This activity may take place as a part of trade association meetings or on an informal basis.

The third major source of external information is the work of the credit reporting agencies, the best known of which is Dun & Bradstreet. Agencies that specialize in coverage of a limited number of industries also provide information. These agencies provide factual data that can be used by the credit manager in credit analysis; they also provide ratings similar to those on corporate bonds.

3. *Information from Banks.*   Another source of credit information is the customer's bank. Although a bank cannot disclose account and loan balances without the applicant's consent, some general information, such as the magnitude of the customer's account balance and number of "NSF" cheques written, can be provided. The extent to which the bank will disclose information depends in part on the information-seeking firm's past dealings with that bank and the personal relationships of the executives involved. Since bank loan officers want and need information from suppliers of trade credit, there is a basis for mutually beneficial exchanges.

Although a great deal of credit information is available, it must still be processed with human judgement. Computerized information systems do help managers make better credit decisions, but in the final analysis, credit determinations are exercises in informed judgement.

Collection Policy

Collection policy refers to the procedures a firm uses to collect receivables. If the account is overdue, there are a number of alternatives available. For example, a letter may be sent to an account holder who is 10 days past due; a more severe letter, followed by a telephone call, may be used if payment is not received within 30 days; and the account may be turned over to a collection agency after 90 days. If the amount is large, sometimes the credit manager will make a personal visit to the customer before the account is turned over to the collection agency. The collection process can be expensive in terms of both out-of-pocket expenditures and lost good will, but some firmness is needed to prevent an undue lengthening in the collection period and to minimize outright losses. A balance must be struck between the costs and benefits of different collection policies.

Integral to the collection policy is a monitoring technique to give the company information on the speed with which accounts receivable are being converted to cash. In addition, some mechanism must be established that evaluates the effectiveness of the collection policy. Aggregate measures such as days sales outstanding and the aging schedule are very useful. If deterioration in these measures is observed, the firm must re-evaluate its policy with an eye to reducing the time required to convert accounts receivable to cash. A number of techniques have been implemented to shorten this time period. For example, the terms of sale may require the receipt of payment at a particular place—say, Toronto—after 30 days. Or the selling firm sends out a deposit slip with the invoice; the buying firm goes to the bank, pays the bill, and funds are immediately entered in the selling company's bank account.

Changes in collection policy influence the level of sales, the collection period, the bad debt loss percentage, and the percentage of customers who take discounts. The effects of a change in collection policy, along with changes in the other credit policy variables, are analyzed later in the chapter.

Other Factors Influencing Credit Policy

In addition to the factors discussed previously, several other factors also influence a firm's overall credit policy.

Profit Potential.   Thus far we have emphasized the costs of granting credit. However, if it is possible to sell on credit and to assess a carrying charge on the receivables that are outstanding, then credit sales can actually be more profitable than cash sales. This is especially true for consumer durables (autos, appliances, clothing, and so on), but it is also true for certain types of industrial equipment. Thus, General Motors Acceptance Corporation (GMAC), which finances automobiles, is highly profitable.[4] Some encyclopedia companies even lose money on cash sales but more than make up these losses from the carrying charges on their credit sales; obviously, such firms would rather sell on credit than for cash.

The carrying charges on outstanding credit are generally about 18 percent on an annual interest rate basis (1.5 percent per month, so 1.5% × 12 = 18%).[5] Unless the bad debt percentage is quite high, having receivables outstanding that earn more than 18 percent is highly profitable.

Credit Instruments.   Most credit is offered on *open account*, which means that the only formal evidence of the credit is an invoice that accompanies the

---

[4]Companies that do a large volume of sales financing typically set up subsidiary companies called *captive finance companies* to do the actual financing. General Motors, Chrysler, and Ford all have captive finance companies, as does Eatons. The reason for this is that consumer finance companies, because their assets are highly liquid, tend to use far more debt—especially short-term debt—than manufacturers or retailers. Thus, if GM did not use a captive finance company, its balance sheet would show an exceptionally high debt ratio and a low current ratio. By having General Motors Acceptance Corporation (GMAC) as a separate but wholly owned corporation, GM avoids distorting its own balance sheet, which presumably helps it raise capital on more favourable terms.

[5]One could argue that 1.5 percent per month really represents an effective annual rate of 19.56%:

Effective annual rate = $(1.015)^{12} - 1.0 = 19.56\%$.

This point will be discussed further in Chapter 11.

shipment and that the buyer signs to indicate that goods have been received. The buyer and the seller then each record the purchase on their books. Under certain circumstances, the selling firm may require the buyer to sign a *promissory note* evidencing the credit obligation. Promissory notes are useful (1) if the order is very large; (2) if the seller anticipates the possibility of having trouble collecting (a note provides a stronger legal claim than a simple invoice); and (3) if the buyer wants a longer than usual time period in which to pay for the order (in that case, interest charges can be built into the promissory note).

Another instrument used in trade credit, especially in international trade, is the *commercial draft*. Here the selling firm draws up a draft, which looks like a cheque written by the buying firm and made payable to the seller but dated some time in the future. This draft is then sent to the buyer's bank, along with the shipping invoices the buyer will need to take possession of the goods. The bank forwards the draft to the buyer, who signs it and returns it to the bank. Only then will the bank deliver the shipping documents to the customer, who at this point can claim the goods. If the draft is a *sight draft*, then upon delivery of the shipping documents and acceptance of the draft by the buyer, the bank actually withdraws money from the buyer's account and forwards it to the selling firm. If the draft is a *time draft*, or *trade acceptance*, payable on a specified future date, the bank returns the draft to the selling firm, which can hold it for future payment, use it as collateral for a loan, or sell it on the open market to raise immediate cash. In each of these situations, the bank has served as an intermediary, making sure that the buyer does not receive the goods until the note (or draft) has been executed for the benefit of the seller.

A seller who lacks confidence in the ability or willingness of the buyer to pay off a time draft may refuse to ship without a guarantee of payment by the buyer's bank. Presumably the bank knows its customer, and, for a fee, it will guarantee payment of the draft. In this instance, the draft is called a *banker's acceptance*. Such instruments are widely used. They have a low degree of risk if guaranteed by a strong bank, and there is a ready market for them, making it easy for the seller of the goods to sell the acceptance to raise immediate cash. (Because banker's acceptances as well as trade acceptances are sold at a discount below face value and then paid off at face value when they mature, the discount amounts to interest on the acceptance. The effective interest rate on a strong banker's acceptance is a little above the Treasury bill rate of interest.)

A final type of credit instrument that should be mentioned is the *conditional sales contract*. Here the seller retains legal ownership of the goods until the buyer has completed payment. Conditional sales contracts are used primarily for sales of such items as machinery, dental equipment, and the like, which are often paid for on an installment basis over a period of two or three years. The significant advantage of a conditional sales contract is that it is easier for the seller to repossess the equipment in the event of default because title remains with the seller until payment has been completed. This feature makes possible some credit sales that otherwise would not be feasible. Conditional sales contracts generally carry an interest rate that is equivalent to what the buyer would have to pay on a bank loan.

Concept Review

▶ Identify and briefly explain the 5 Cs of credit.
▶ What is meant by the term "credit scoring"? Under what circumstances is it more likely to be used?
▶ Why would a firm classify its customers into "risk classes"? What differences in credit might be offered to each risk class?
▶ What is the purpose of a cash discount?
▶ What products are likely to be sold on very short credit periods? long credit periods? seasonal datings?
▶ Identify some procedures that a firm can use to collect overdue accounts.
▶ What are the primary instruments used to document trade credit transactions? When is each type of instrument likely to be used?

Monitoring the Receivables Position

The optimal credit policy, and hence the optimal level of accounts receivable, depends on the firm's own unique operating conditions. A firm with excess capacity and low variable production costs should extend credit more liberally, and thus carry a higher level of accounts receivable, than a firm operating at full capacity or having a slim profit margin. However, although optimal credit policies vary among firms, or even for a single firm over time, it is still useful to analyze—or monitor—the effectiveness of the firm's credit policy in an aggregate sense.

The two most commonly used indicators of the receivables position are (1) **days sales outstanding** (DSO), which is compared to the stated credit terms and tracked on a trend basis to detect any changes that might be occurring, and (2) the **aging schedule**, which breaks down accounts receivable according to how long they have been outstanding. However, as we will show later in this section, both the DSO and the aging schedule can, under certain conditions, give incorrect signals in the sense that they can suggest either an improving or a deteriorating situation when the reverse is actually true.

To facilitate the analysis, we assume that the firm has a fixed monthly collection pattern as determined by the credit sales paid in the month the sale is made and the proportions paid in subsequent months. In other words, a constant period of time elapses between a sale and the collection of cash from that sale, so the efficiency of the credit department is constant by definition. For our example, we assume that 10 percent of monthly sales are collected at the time of the sale, and 30 percent, 40 percent, and 20 percent are collected on the first day of each following month, respectively. An example of such a payment pattern for $60 000 sales in January, along with its graphic representation, is shown in Figure 9-1. In the graphic representation, the white rectangles represent the accounts receivable still outstanding at the end of each month, while the shaded rectangles represent the accumulated paid proportions of the January sales.

Figure 9-1
Collection Pattern of $60 000 Sales in January

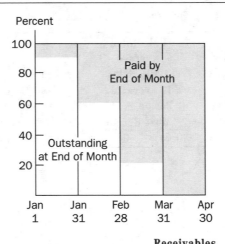

Month	Collection Pattern (%)	Collections from January Sales during Each Month (in $ thousands)	Receivables Outstanding from January Sales at the End of Each Month (in $ thousands)	Receivables Pattern: Original Sales Divided by Remaining Receivables (%)
January	10%	$ 6	$54	90%
February	30	18	36	60
March	40	24	12	20
April	20	12	0	0

Having specified a fixed collection schedule, let us further assume that the first quarter (January–March) is one of constant sales, the second quarter (April–June) is one of increasing sales, and that in the third quarter (July–September) sales decline in each of the three months. These assumptions, along with the corresponding days sales outstanding (DSO) schedule and the aging schedule (AS), which are explained in the following sections, are shown in Table 9-2.

As we go through Table 9-2, keep in mind that, since we have assumed a constant collection pattern (10%, 30%, 40%, and 20% at the time of sale and successive months, respectively), our customers by definition are continuing to make payments in the same manner throughout the period being analyzed. Thus, our credit manager's performance is constant. However, as we shall see, certain commonly used tools of analysis will show improvements and/or deterioration at times, even when the situation is perfectly stable. We use the example both to point out the pitfalls in judging the results of a credit policy and to show how to "do it right."

Table 9-2
Sales Pattern, Days Sales Outstanding,
and the Aging Schedule
(thousands of dollars)

Month	Sales	Receivables from Monthly Sales Still Outstanding at End of Quarter[a]	Calculated Average Daily Sales If Averaging Period Is the Most Recent		End-of-Quarter DSO (in days) If Averaging Period Is		Aging Schedule Receivables Age Groups (in days)	% of Total[f]
			30 days	90 days	30 days	90 days		
January	$60	$ 12					61–90	12%
February	60	36					31–60	35
March	60	54					0–30	53
Quarterly total		$102	$2	$2	51	51		100%
April	$30	$ 6					61–90	5%
May	60	36					31–60	29
June	90	81					0–30	66
Quarterly total		$123	$3[b]	$2[c]	41[d]	62[e]		100%
July	$90	$ 18					61–90	22%
August	60	36					31–60	45
September	30	27					0–30	33
Quarterly total		$ 81	$1	$2	81	41		100%

[a]Sales × receivables pattern percentage at the end of March for January sales = $60 000 × 0.2 = $12 000. Other values are found similarly.

[b]Second quarter average daily sales = $\frac{\$90\,000}{30\ \text{days}}$ = $3000 per day if the averaging period is the most recent 30 days.

[c]Second quarter average daily sales = $\frac{\$90\,000\,+\,\$60\,000\,+\,\$30\,000}{90\ \text{days}} = \frac{\$180\,000}{90\ \text{days}}$ = $2000 per day if the averaging period is the most recent 90 days.

[d]Second quarter average DSO = $\frac{\text{Total receivables}}{\text{Daily sales}} = \frac{\$123\,000}{\$3000\ \text{per day}}$ = 41 days, based on 30-day averaging.

[e]Second quarter average DSO = $\frac{\$123\,000}{\$2000\ \text{per day}}$ = 62 days, based on 90-day averaging.

[f]The aging schedule percentages (end-of-quarter receivables in different age groups) are found as follows for the second quarter:

$$\frac{\text{Receivables from relevant month}}{\text{End-of-quarter receivables}} = \frac{\$6000}{\$123\,000} = 5\%, \frac{\$36\,000}{\$123\,000} = 29\%, \text{and} \frac{\$81\,000}{\$123\,000} = 66\%, \text{respectively.}$$

Days Sales Outstanding

The average days sales outstanding (DSO) is often used to judge the effectiveness of a firm's credit policy. DSO is compared to the credit period and examined on a trend analysis basis to see whether or not customers are paying on schedule. The DSO at a given time, t, is calculated as the ratio of the total receivables at that time, AR_t, to daily sales:

$$DSO_t = \frac{\text{Total AR}_t}{\text{Daily sales}}.$$

The daily sales are obtained by averaging sales over some time period; this averaging period may be 30 days, 60 days, 90 days, or some other period. DSO using sales averaged over 30 days and 90 days are shown in Table 9-2. As of March 31, the DSO based on both 60 and 90 days is AR/Daily sales = $102/$2 = 51 days. However, as we move on to the second quarter, it is readily apparent that whenever monthly sales are changing, DSO is dependent on the averaging period chosen to calculate daily sales. Thus, we calculate a DSO of either 41 or 62 days, the first of which suggests an improvement over the first quarter's 51 days while the second suggests a deterioration. Yet we know, because we assumed a constant collection pattern, that in the second quarter customers' payments are exactly like first-quarter payments. From this example it is clear that the use of DSO for monitoring the effectiveness of the firm's credit policy must be handled with care.

The Aging Schedule

The aging schedule (AS) shows the percentage of end-of-quarter accounts receivable that are in different groups representing the period of time that receivables have been outstanding from the time of sales. The last two columns of Table 9-2 show the aging schedule for our firm at the three quarterly dates.

Since the firm's collection pattern is constant, the aging schedule, if it is to give consistent signals as to the firm's true accounts receivable situation, ought to be stable from quarter to quarter. However, this is not the case: In the second quarter, when sales are rising, the aging schedule shows a higher percentage of new receivables (66 percent versus 53 percent) and a lower percentage of old, past-due accounts (5 percent versus 12 percent) than in the first quarter. This suggests, incorrectly, that the credit department was doing better during the second quarter than during the first. The situation is reversed in the third quarter, when sales are declining, for declining sales artificially make the aging schedule look bad.

Despite the immense popularity of the DSO and aging schedules for monitoring accounts receivable, it is clear that the results should be carefully scrutinized before any conclusions are drawn.[6] These two procedures are valid if sales are stable, but they can be misleading if seasonal or cyclical variations are present. For this reason, firms are increasingly turning to the payments pattern approach, as described in the next section.

---

[6]For a more complete discussion of the problems with the DSO and the aging schedule, see Bernell K. Stone, "The Payments-Pattern Approach to the Forecasting and Control of Accounts Receivable," *Financial Management*, August 1976, pp. 65–82; and Wilbur G. Lewellen and Robert W. Johnson, "Better Way To Monitor Accounts Receivable," *Harvard Business Review*, May–June 1972, pp. 101–7.

The Payments Pattern Approach

The **payments pattern approach** seeks to overcome the difficulties encountered in using the DSO and aging schedule methods. To begin, note that a constant payment pattern implies that the same percentage of sales are collected in the various months. For example, the data in Table 9-2 reflect a constant payment pattern of 10 percent of sales paid in the month that they are made and 30, 40, and 20 percent in the three subsequent months respectively. Consequently, there must be a constant accounts receivable pattern (90, 60, and 20 percent) in the three subsequent months, as shown in Table 9-3.

In the payments pattern approach, accounts receivable are related to sales in the month of origin rather than to the average over some longer period. As a consequence, the payments pattern approach, in contrast to DSO and the aging schedule, is not affected by increasing or decreasing sales. No matter what the sales trend may be, the last column in Table 9-3 reflects the actual payment pattern. Of course, had any change in customers' payment behaviour occurred, this would have been immediately and correctly reflected in Table 9-3. Thus, the payments pattern approach provides an efficient and precise way to monitor the receivables position.

For example, assume that the firm's accounts receivable pattern has historically been 90 percent, 60 percent, and 20 percent—this is the situation we have been using. Now assume that in early March the report on actual payments for January and February credit sales shows a current balance

Table 9-3

**Accounts Receivable as Percentages
of Original Sales**

Month of Sale	Sales during that Month ($ thousands)	Receivables Still Outstanding at End of Quarter ($ thousands)	Percentage of Sales for the Month Still Outstanding at End of Quarter
January	$60	$ 12	$12/$60 = 20%
February	60	36	$36/$60 = 60%
March	60	54	$54/$60 = 90%
Quarterly total		$102	
April	$30	$ 6	$6/$30 = 20%
May	60	36	$36/$60 = 60%
June	90	81	$81/$90 = 90%
Quarterly total		$123	
July	$90	$ 18	$18/$90 = 20%
August	60	36	$36/$60 = 60%
September	30	27	$27/$30 = 90%
Quarterly total		$ 81	

fraction for January sales of 0.70 versus the historical value of 0.60, and a balance fraction for February sales of 0.95 versus the expected value of 0.90.

Obviously, customers have begun to pay more slowly, so the firm's investment in receivables is building up more rapidly than it should. Two such consecutive deviations from the normal pattern warrant inquiry. Has the credit department unconsciously lowered its credit standards and started permitting sales to substandard customers? Has the collection department slacked off in collecting past-due accounts? Or, perhaps, has a change in the economy (tighter money, or a recession) reduced our customers' ability to make on-time payments? The firm needs to know what is happening and why.

Accounts Receivable Analysis

In addition to using the DSO, aging schedule, and payments pattern methods to monitor overall accounts receivable, a credit manager can apply these techniques to individual accounts. If a deterioration in a customer's payment pattern is noted, the credit manager will want to investigate further.

Investors—both shareholders and bank loan officers—should pay close attention to accounts receivable management; otherwise, they can be misled by the firm's financial statements and later suffer serious losses on their investments. When a sale is made, the following events occur: (1) inventories are reduced by the cost of goods sold, (2) accounts receivable are increased by the sales price, and (3) the difference is recorded as a profit. If the sale is for cash, the profit is definitely earned, but if the sale is on credit, the profit is not actually earned unless and until the account is collected. Firms have been known to use credit policy to encourage "sales" to very weak customers in order to inflate reported profits. This may boost the share price, but only until credit losses begin to show up and to lower earnings, at which time the share price will fall. An analysis along the lines suggested previously will detect any such questionable practices as well as any unconscious deterioration in the quality of accounts receivable. Such early detection can help both investors and bankers avoid losses.

Concept Review

▶ Briefly explain the DSO and the aging schedule and how they are used to monitor the accounts receivable position.
▶ How can seasonal changes in sales impair the usefulness of the DSO and aging schedule for monitoring the firm's accounts receivable position?
▶ What is the payments pattern method? How does it overcome the problem mentioned above when sales grow or shrink?

The Role of the Credit Manager

The basic objective of credit management is to increase profitable sales and hence to add value to the firm by extending credit to worthy customers. In obtaining and analyzing credit information and in collecting receivables, credit managers perform an extremely important function. If the potential customer does not meet credit standards, one simple approach is to turn down the order. This might be justified by comparing the probable gain with the probable loss on the order.

Note, though, that the credit manager's larger objective is to help build a broad and increasing base of profitable sales. Therefore, a good credit manager will strive to learn the business of the firm's customers as well as, or better than, the executives of those firms. Such a credit manager will seek to keep current on sales trends, management performance, liquidity position, leverage, and profitability of existing and potential customers. In the process, he or she may be able to identify factors that have hurt a customer's financial position and ability to make credit payments. This information can be passed along to the customers, which in turn could help maintain the customer's health and consequently the sales of credit manager's own firm.

The creative credit manager keeps abreast of all external factors affecting his or her customers' businesses, serves as a valued sounding board for discussions of trends affecting the customers' industries as well as of important policy decisions in the individual firms, and provides a source of counsel on important policy and decision areas affecting the customers' future well-being. To be sure, such actions on the part of a credit manager reflect the ideal, and ideals must often be compromised by practical considerations of time and cost. Still, to the degree that these potentials are realized, a credit manager can make an important contribution to his or her own firm. If customers' businesses are profitable and expand, then the selling firm will also prosper. Thus, the credit function should be a major consideration in a firm's overall corporate strategy.

Concept Review

▶ What is the credit manager's basic objective?

Use of Computers in Credit Management

By its very nature, credit management lends itself to the use of computer controls. Credit management involves the collection, compilation, storage, analysis, and retrieval of information. Since accurate information about fund flows is critical to good management, an efficient information processing system is important.

All of the data relating to accounts receivable can be organized into a computer record system, which in turn can be used to provide the credit manager with current information on the status of accounts. Records may include the date the account was opened, the amount currently owed, the customer's maximum credit line, and a record of the customer's past payments. The credit rating assigned to the customer by Dun & Bradstreet or some other rating agency may also be noted. Periodically, the credit manager may analyze customer accounts, using one of the methods just described.

In addition, controls can be set up to monitor account delinquency. The computer can periodically flag past-due accounts and bring them to the credit manager's attention, or it can provide information as to how close an account balance is to the customer's maximum line of credit. Such information enables the credit manager to contact the customer on a timely basis.

At the extreme, the computer can be programmed to actually make selected credit decisions. Based on established criteria, potential sales can be screened, and the computer can accept or reject credit applications, establish maximum lines of credit for different customers, or flag accounts for further analysis. Aided by a computer, a relatively small staff can handle a large volume of credit activity.

In addition to producing information on individual accounts, the computer can provide the credit manager with information on groups of companies. Periodically, the credit manager may receive a summary of all accounts receivable, with information on each account individually and on all accounts in total. Information can be provided on billings, payments, discounts taken, and amounts owed. In addition, the computer can prepare special reports of analytical information that may be useful in making broad credit policy decisions. Data on individual companies may be used in a discriminant analysis to help set credit standards. Also, the payment history of companies in the same industry may be compared. Do companies in a particular industry tend to pay slowly during certain months of the year? If this appears to be the case, the credit manager should analyze the economic factors that cause firms in a particular industry to respond in similar ways. On the other hand, if a customer performs differently from most firms in the industry, the credit manager can examine the circumstances behind that firm's behaviour. The credit manager may also be able to identify management or operating problems that are developing in a firm and then take action to head off the problems before the account becomes a serious credit risk.

Computers increase both the amount and the frequency of information available to the credit manager. This information facilitates interaction with the customer, and it also enables the credit department to co-ordinate promptly and effectively with other departments of its own company as well as with general management. Thus, the effectiveness of the credit department has been greatly enhanced by computers, which make it feasible to obtain information on a timely basis that would otherwise be too expensive and time consuming to obtain.

Concept Review

▶ How can computers be used in credit management?

Analyzing Changes in the Credit Policy Variables

If a firm's credit policy is eased by such actions as lengthening the credit period, relaxing credit standards, following a less tough collection policy, or offering cash discounts, sales should increase. Easing the credit policy normally stimulates sales. However, if credit policy is eased and sales do rise, then costs will also rise because (1) more labour, materials, and so on will be required to produce the additional goods; (2) receivables outstanding will increase, which will raise carrying costs; and (3) bad-debt or discount expenses may also rise. Thus, the key question when deciding on a credit policy change is this: will sales revenues rise more than costs, causing net income to increase, or will the increase in sales revenues be more than offset by higher costs?

Table 9-4 illustrates the general idea behind credit policy analysis. Column 1 shows the projected 1993 income statement for Mitchell Office Furniture under the assumption that the firm's current credit policy is maintained throughout the year. Column 2 shows the expected effects of easing the credit policy by taking these actions: extending the credit period, offering larger discounts, relaxing credit standards, and easing collection efforts. Specifically, Mitchell is analyzing the effects of changing its credit terms from 1/10, net 30 to 2/10, net 40, of relaxing its credit standards, and of putting less pressure on slow-paying customers. Column 3 shows the projected 1993 income statement incorporating the expected effects of this easier credit policy. The change is expected to increase sales and lower credit analysis and collection costs, but discounts and several other types of costs would rise. The overall, bottom-line effect is an $8.8 million increase in projected profits. In the following paragraphs, we explain how the numbers in the table were calculated.

Mitchell's annual sales are currently projected at $400 million. Under its current credit policy, 50 percent of those customers who pay do so on Day 10 and take the discount; 40 percent pay on Day 30; and 10 percent pay late, on Day 40. Thus, Mitchell's days sales outstanding is $(0.50)(10) + (0.40)(30) + (0.10)(40) = 21$ days.

Table 9-4
Mitchell Office Furniture
Analysis of Credit Policy
(millions of dollars)

	Projected 1993 Income Statement under Current Credit Policy (1)	Effect of Credit Policy Change (2)	Projected 1993 Income Statement under New Credit Policy (3)
Gross sales	$400.0	+ $130.0	$530.0
Less: Discounts	2.0	+ 4.0	6.0
Net sales	$398.0	+ $126.0	$524.0
Production costs, including overhead	280.0	+ 91.0	371.0
Profit before credit costs and taxes	$118.0	+ $ 35.0	$153.0
Credit-related costs			
Cost of carrying receivables	3.2	+ 1.7	4.9
Credit analysis and collection expenses	5.0	(3.0)	2.0
Bad debt losses	10.0	+ 22.0	32.0
Profit before taxes	$ 99.6	+ $ 14.5	$114.1
Taxes (40%)	39.8	+ 5.8	45.6
Net income	$ 59.7	+ $ 8.8	$ 68.5

Even though Mitchell spends $5 million annually on analyzing accounts and on collections, 2.5 percent of sales will never be collected. Thus, bad debt losses amount to $(0.025)(\$400\,000\,000) = \$10$ million. In addition, Mitchell's cash collections are reduced by the amount of discounts taken. Fifty percent of the customers who pay (and 97.5 percent of all customers do pay) take the 1 percent discount, so discounts equal $(\$400\,000\,000)(0.975)(0.01)(0.50) = \$1\,950\,000 \approx \$2$ million. Notice that total sales are multiplied by $(1 - \text{Bad debt ratio})$ to obtain collected sales, and collected sales are then multiplied by the discount percentage times the percentage of paying customers who take the discount.

The annual cost of carrying receivables is equal to the average amount of receivables times the variable cost percentage, which gives the dollars of capital invested in receivables, times the cost of money used to carry receivables:

$$\begin{pmatrix}\text{Average} \\ \text{amount of} \\ \text{receivables}\end{pmatrix} \times \begin{pmatrix}\text{Variable} \\ \text{cost} \\ \text{ratio}\end{pmatrix} \times \begin{pmatrix}\text{Cost} \\ \text{of} \\ \text{funds}\end{pmatrix} = \begin{pmatrix}\text{Cost of} \\ \text{carrying} \\ \text{receivables}\end{pmatrix}$$

The average amount of receivables, in turn, is equal to the days sales outstanding times sales per day. Mitchell's DSO is 21 days, its variable cost ratio is 70 percent, and its cost of funds invested in receivables is 20 percent. Therefore, its annual cost of carrying receivables is approximately $3.2 million:

$$(\text{DSO})\begin{pmatrix}\text{Sales} \\ \text{per} \\ \text{day}\end{pmatrix}\begin{pmatrix}\text{Variable} \\ \text{cost} \\ \text{ratio}\end{pmatrix}\begin{pmatrix}\text{Cost} \\ \text{of} \\ \text{funds}\end{pmatrix} = \begin{pmatrix}\text{Cost of} \\ \text{carrying} \\ \text{receivables}\end{pmatrix}$$

$$(21)\left(\frac{\$400\,000\,000}{365}\right)(0.70)(0.20) = \$3\,221\,918 \approx \$3.2 \text{ million.}$$

Only variable cost enters this calculation, because this is the only cost element that must be financed as a result of a change in the credit policy. In other words, if a new customer buys goods worth $100, Mitchell will have to invest only $70 (in labour and materials); therefore, it will have to finance only $70, even though accounts receivable rise by $100. Variable cost thus represents the company's investment in the goods sold.

Mitchell's new credit policy calls for a larger discount, a longer payment period, a relaxed collection effort, and lower credit standards. The company believes that these changes will lead to a $130 million increase in sales, to $530 million per year. Under the new credit terms, management believes that 60 percent of the customers who pay will take the 2 percent discount and that bad debt losses will total 6 percent of sales, so discounts will increase to $(\$530\,000\,000)(0.94)(0.02)(0.60) = \$5\,978\,400 \approx \$6$ million. Half of the remaining paying customers (20 percent of total paying customers) will pay on Day 40, and the remainder on Day 50. The new DSO is thus estimated to be 24 days:

$$(0.6)(10) + (0.2)(40) + (0.2)(50) = 24 \text{ days.}$$

Also, the cost of carrying receivables will increase to $4.9 million:

$$(24)\left(\frac{\$530\ 000\ 000}{365}\right)(0.70)(0.20) = \$4\ 878\ 984 \approx \$4.9 \text{ million.}^{7}$$

Because the new policy will relax credit standards (hence reduce credit checking expenses) and also ease up on collections, the company expects to reduce its annual credit analysis and collection expenditures from $5 million to $2 million. However, the reduced credit standards and the relaxed collection effort are expected to raise bad debt losses from 2.5 percent to 6.0 percent of sales, or to $(0.06)(\$530\ 000\ 000) = \$32$ million.

The combined effect of all the changes in credit policy is a projected $8.8 million increase in net income. There will, of course, be corresponding changes on the projected balance sheet. The higher sales will necessitate somewhat larger cash balances and inventories and perhaps (depending on capacity conditions) more fixed assets. Accounts receivable will also increase. Since these asset increases will have to be financed, certain liability accounts or equity will also have to be increased.

The $8.8 million expected increase in net income is, of course, an estimate, and the actual effects of the change could be quite different. In the first place, there is uncertainty about the projected $130 million increase in sales. Conceivably, if Mitchell's competitors matched its changes, sales would not rise at all. Similar uncertainties must be attached to the number of customers who will take discounts, to production costs at higher or lower sales levels, to the costs of carrying additional receivables, and to the bad debt loss ratio. In the final analysis, the decision to make the change will be based on judgement, but the type of quantitative analysis set forth here is essential to making a good decision.

Analyzing changes in credit policy variables leads to a short discussion concerning sensitivity analysis. Sensitivity analysis involves looking at how changes in one or more variables affect some other variable. In the previous discussion we looked at how changes in a firm's credit policy variables—that is, extending the credit period, offering larger discounts, relaxing credit standards, and the like—affect the firm's net income. Sensitivity analysis is one type of analysis that is easily done on the computer, and indeed many

---

[7]Since the credit policy change will result in a higher DSO, Mitchell will have to wait longer to receive its profit on the goods it sells. Therefore, the firm will incur an opportunity cost as a result of not having the cash from these profits available for investment. The dollar amount of this opportunity cost is equal to the old sales per day times the change in DSO times the contribution margin, $(1 - v)$, times the cost of the funds invested in receivables:

$$
\begin{aligned}
\text{Opportunity cost} \quad &= \left(\frac{\text{Old sales}}{365}\right)(\Delta DSO)(1 - v)(k) \\
&= \left(\frac{\$400 \text{ million}}{365}\right)(3)(0.3)(0.20) \approx \$0.2 \text{ million.}
\end{aligned}
$$

Here v = variable cost ratio and k = cost of funds. For simplicity, we ignored opportunity costs in Table 9-4.

software packages, including *Lotus 1-2-3* and *Excel*, have specialized functions for this type of analysis.

The preceding paragraphs give an overview of the way changes in credit policy are analyzed. As noted, the most important considerations have to do with changes in sales and production costs. Specific estimates of these effects are handled by the marketing and production departments within the framework set forth here. The financial manager has the responsibility for the overall analysis, plus a primary role in estimating several specific factors, including discounts taken, the cost of carrying accounts receivable, and bad debt losses. To evaluate a proposed change in credit policy, one could compare projected income statements, such as column 1 versus column 3 in Table 9-4. Alternatively, one could simply analyze column 2, which shows the incremental effect, holding other things constant, of the proposed change. Of course, the two approaches are based on exactly the same data, so they must produce identical results. However, it is often preferable to focus on the incremental approach, because firms usually change their credit policies in specific divisions or on particular products and not across the board, so an analysis of complete income statements may not be feasible.

Concept Review

▶ Which costs rise, and why, when credit policy is eased?
▶ What is the key question when deciding on a credit policy change?
▶ What is the formula for calculating the cost of carrying receivables? Write it out.
▶ What are the costs and benefits of tightening credit policy?

Summary

This chapter has discussed how firms manage their accounts receivable. Because the typical manufacturing firm has about 20 percent of its assets invested in receivables, the management of receivables is obviously important. The key concepts covered are listed below.

☐ When a firm sells goods to a customer on credit, an **account receivable** is created.

☐ Firms can use an **aging schedule**, the **days sales outstanding (DSO)**, and/or the **payment patterns approach** to help keep track of their receivables position and to help avoid the buildup of possible bad debts.

☐ A firm's **credit policy** consists of four elements: (1) **credit period**, (2) **discounts** given for early payment, (3) **credit standards**, and (4) **collection policy**. The first two, when combined, are called the **credit terms**.

☐ The traditional method of measuring credit quality is to investigate potential credit customers with respect to five factors called the **five Cs of credit**. These factors are *character, capacity, capital, collateral,* and *conditions*.

☐ Three major sources of external credit information are available: (1) credit associations, which are local groups that meet frequently and correspond with one another to exchange information on credit customers; (2) credit managers' sharing of information on the creditworthiness of firms in a particular industry, which is done through trade associations or informally, and (3) credit reporting agencies, which collect credit information and sell it for a fee.

☐ Modern credit managers often use customer risk clauses. Under this system, statistical procedures are used to classify customers into several categories according to degree of risk. Credit terms can be differentiated so that the least risky customers are given the best terms, and the credit manager then concentrates time and attention on customers judged most likely to cause problems.

☐ Additional factors that influence a firm's overall credit policy are (1) profit potential and (2) the type of credit instruments offered.

☐ The basic objective of the credit manager is to increase profitable sales by extending credit to worthy customers and therefore adding value to the firm.

☐ If a firm eases its credit policy, its sales should increase. Actions that ease the credit policy include lengthening the credit period, relaxing credit standards and collection policy, and offering cash discounts. Each of these actions, however, increases costs. A firm should ease its credit policy only if the costs of doing so will be more than offset by higher sales revenues.

☐ A tightening of a firm's credit policy will reduce sales but also reduce costs. The credit policy should be tightened only if the reduction in sales revenue is more than offset by lower costs.

Questions

9-1   Is it true that when one firm sells to another on credit, the seller records the transaction as an account receivable while the buyer records it as an account payable and that, disregarding discounts, the receivable typically exceeds the payable by the amount of profit on the sale?

9-2   Evaluate this statement: "It is difficult to judge the performance of many of our employees but not that of the credit manager. If the credit manager is performing perfectly, credit losses are zero; the higher our losses (as a percentage of sales), the worse the credit manager's performance."

9-3   Explain how the credit terms offered by our firm's suppliers can affect the terms we offer to our own customers.

9-4   What are the four elements of a firm's credit policy? To what extent can firms set their own policies, as opposed to having to accept credit policies dictated by "the competition"?

9-5   Suppose a firm makes a purchase and receives the shipment on February 1. The terms of trade stated on the invoice read, "2/10, net 40, May 1 dating." What is the latest date on which payment can be made and the discount still be taken? What is the date on which payment must be made if the discount is not taken?

9-6   a.   What is the days sales outstanding (DSO) for a firm whose sales are $2 880 000 per year and whose accounts receivable are $312 000?

b. Is it true that if this firm sells on terms of 3/10, net 40, its customers probably all pay on time?

9-7 Indicate by a $(+)$, $(-)$, or (0) whether each of the following events would probably cause accounts receivable (A/R), sales, and profits to increase, decrease, or be affected in an indeterminant manner:

	A/R	Sales	Profits
a. The firm tightens its credit standards.	_____	_____	_____
b. The terms of trade are changed from 2/10, net 30, to 3/10, net 30.	_____	_____	_____
c. The terms are changed from 2/10, net 30, to 3/10, net 40.	_____	_____	_____
d. The credit manager gets tough with past-due accounts.	_____	_____	_____

Self-Test Problems   (solutions appear on page 297)

ST-1 **Key terms.**   Define each of the following terms:
   a. Accounts receivable
   b. Days sales outstanding; Aging schedule; Payments pattern approach
   c. Credit policy; credit period; credit standards; five Cs of credit; collection policy; credit terms
   d. Cash discounts
   e. Seasonal datings
   f. Open account; promissory note; commercial draft; banker's acceptance

ST-2 **Change in credit policy.**   The Ravin Company Ltd. expects to have sales of $10 million this year under its current operating policies. Its variable cost as a percentage of sales is 0.8, and its cost of capital is 16 percent. Currently, Ravin's credit policy is net 25 (no discount for early payment). However, its DSO is 30 days, and its bad debt loss percentage is 2 percent. Ravin currently spends $50 000 per year to collect bad debts, and its effective tax rate is 40 percent.

   The credit manager is considering two alternative proposals, given below, for changing Ravin's credit policy. Find (a) the expected incremental change in investment in accounts receivable, ΔI, and (b) the incremental change in profits, ΔP, taking into consideration the anticipated changes in carrying costs for accounts receivable, the probable bad debt losses, and the discounts likely to be taken, for each proposal. Should a change in credit policy be made?

   Proposal 1: Lengthen the credit period by going from net 25 to net 30. Anticipated effects follow:

ΔS = Incremental sales = $1 000 000.
B_N = Bad debt loss percentage on incremental sales = 4% on ΔS.
B_O = 2% on S_O (no change for old sales).
DSO_N = 45 days (on all sales).

Proposal 2: Shorten the credit period by going from net 25 to net 20. Anticipated effects follow:

$$\Delta S = -\$1\,000\,000.$$
$$B_N = 1.0\% \text{ (on all sales).}$$
$$DSO_N = 22 \text{ days.}$$

Problems

9-1   **Receivables investment.**   Weatherford Industries, Ltd. sells on terms of 3/10, net 30. Total sales for the year are $900 000. Forty percent of the customers pay on the tenth day and take discounts; the other 60 percent pay, on average, 40 days after their purchases.

  a.   What is the days sales outstanding?

  b.   What is the average amount of receivables?

  c.   What would happen to the average investment in receivables if Weatherford tightened its collection policy with the result that all nondiscount customers paid on Day 30?

9-2   **Easing credit terms.**   Milburn Auto Parts is considering changing its credit terms from 2/15, net 30 to 3/10, net 30 in order to speed collections. At present, 40 percent of Milburn's customers take the 2 percent discount. Under the new terms, this number is expected to rise to 50 percent. Regardless of the credit terms, half of the customers who do not take the discount are likely to pay on time, while the remainder pay 10 days late. The change would not involve a relaxation of credit standards; therefore, bad debt losses are not expected to rise above their present 2 percent level. However, the more generous cash discount terms are expected to increase sales from $2 000 000 to $2 600 000 per year. Milburn's variable cost ratio is 75 percent, and its cost of capital for investment in accounts receivable is 9 percent.

  a.   What is the days sales outstanding before and after the change?

  b.   Calculate the discount costs before and after the change.

  c.   Calculate the dollar cost of carrying receivables before and after the change.

  d.   Calculate the bad debt losses before and after the change.

  e.   What would be the incremental profit from the change in credit terms? Should Milburn change its credit terms?

  f.   Suppose that Milburn's customers did not change their payment pattern when Milburn adopted its new credit policy; that is, 40 percent still took the discount, 30 percent paid on time, and 30 percent paid late. How would this affect the decision, assuming that sales did increase to $2.6 million as forecasted?

9-3   **Credit analysis.**   Banff Distributors makes all sales on a credit basis. Once a year it routinely evaluates the creditworthiness of all its customers. The evaluation procedure ranks customers from 1 to 5, in order of increasing risk. Results of the ranking are as follows:

Category	Percentage of Bad Debts	Average Collection Period (days)	Credit Decision	Annual Sales Lost from Credit Restrictions
1	None	10	Unlimited credit	None
2	1.0	12	Unlimited credit	None
3	3.0	20	Limited credit	$375 000
4	9.0	60	Limited credit	$190 500
5	16.0	90	Limited credit	$220 000

The variable cost ratio is 70 percent. The cost of capital invested in receivables is 12 percent. What would be the effect on profitability of extending unlimited credit to each of categories 3, 4, and 5? Assume Banff's effective tax rate is 40 percent.

9-4   **Tightening credit terms.**   Daniel Richards, the new credit manager of Haskell Ltd., was alarmed to find that Haskell sells on credit terms of net 50 days when industrywide credit terms are net 30 days. On annual credit sales of $3 million, Haskell currently averages 60 days' sales in accounts receivable. Richards estimates that tightening the credit terms to 30 days would reduce annual sales to $2.6 million but that accounts receivable would drop to 35 days of sales, and the savings on investment in accounts receivable should more than overcome any loss in profit. Haskell's variable cost ratio is 70 percent, effective tax rate is 40 percent, and its cost of funds invested in receivables is 11 percent.

a. Should Haskell make the change in credit policy?

b. If sales declined to $2.8 million when credit terms were changed to net 30, would the change be profitable?

c. If credit terms were changed to net 45 days, Richards believes Haskell could pick up business from its competitors, and sales would increase to $3.3 million while DSO would fall to 50 days. Would this change be profitable?

d. If the credit policy is unchanged, sales are projected to be $3.4 million while the days sales outstanding will remain at 60 days. Which of the suggested credit policies (those suggested in Parts a, b, c, and d) would produce the greatest profit for Haskell?

9-5   **Calculating DSO and aging schedule.**   Kenwood Company Limited began doing business on July 1, 1993. Sales and end-of-quarter receivables for its first quarter are given below:

	Sales	End-of-Quarter Receivables
July	$30 000	$ 1 500
August	45 000	9 000
September	52 000	39 000
		$49 500

a. Calculate daily sales as of September 30, 1993, if the averaging period is the most recent 30 days or the most recent 90 days. (Assume 30 days per month.)

    b. Calculate the end-of-quarter DSO if the averaging period is the most recent 30 or 90 days. (Assume 30 days per month.)

    c. The payment pattern on Kenwood's accounts receivable is constant at 0.25, 0.55, 0.15, and 0.05. Prepare a schedule showing each month's collections and outstanding receivables through December 31, 1993, based on first quarter sales.

    d. What is Kenwood's accounts receivable pattern?

    e. Assuming that no sales are made after September 30, 1993, what would the accounts receivable balance be on October 31? on November 30?

    f. Prepare aging schedules as of August 31, September 30, and October 31.

9-6   **Relaxed collection efforts.** Continental Company Ltd. has annual credit sales of $2 million. Current expenses for the collection department are $30 000, bad debt losses are 1.2 percent, and the average collection period is 30 days. Continental is considering easing its collection efforts such that collection expenses will be reduced to $22 000 per year. The change is expected to increase bad debt losses to 3 percent and to increase the average collection period to 45 days. In addition, sales are expected to increase to $2.2 million per year.

    Should Continental relax collection efforts if the opportunity cost of funds is 12 percent, the variable cost ratio is 75 percent, and the tax rate is 40 percent?

Integrative Problem

9-7   **Credit policy.** Timothy Wong took over as financial manager for the Learning Aids Company Ltd., which supplies computer software to public and private schools, about a year ago. He questions the firm's credit policy, which has included credit terms of 2/10, net 30 for some time. Thus, customers buying from Learning Aids receive a 2 percent discount if they pay within 10 days of purchase, and they must pay the full amount in 30 days if they do not take the discount. If the current credit policy is maintained, next year's sales are expected to be $1 200 000. Currently, 40 percent of Learning Aid's paying customers normally take the discount and pay on Day 10, 40 percent pay the full amount on Day 30, and the remaining 20 percent of those who pay do so (on average) on Day 40. Two percent of Learning Aids sales end up as bad debt losses.

    Wong is thinking about tightening the firm's credit policy. His proposed new policy would entail changing the credit terms to 4/10, net 20 and enforcing stricter credit standards. Thus, customers who paid within 10 days would receive a 4 percent discount, but all others would have to pay the full amount after only 20 days. Wong believes that the increased discount would bring in more customers and would also encourage some existing customers to take the discount. The net result, he believes, would be to increase next year's sales to $1 350 000, with 60 percent of the paying customers taking the discount, 30 percent paying the full amount on Day 20, and 10 percent paying late on Day 30. Also, he believes that bad-debt losses would be reduced from 2 percent to 1 percent of gross sales. Learning Aid's operating cost ratio is 70 percent, and the cost of funds used to carry receivables is 11 percent; neither of these ratios would change under the new credit policy. Learning Aid's tax rate is 40 percent.

If Wong's assumptions are correct, should Learning Aid's credit policy be changed? To help him decide on this issue, complete the following tasks, and answer each of the following questions.

a. What are the four variables that make up a firm's credit policy? How would a change in each affect sales, the level of receivables held, and bad debt expenses? In what direction would each be changed, from its current level, if the credit policy were to be eased? tightened?

b. What are the 5 Cs of credit, which credit policy variable do they affect, and how are they used in carrying out the firm's credit policy?

c. What is the current level of the company's days sales outstanding (DSO), and what would the expected DSO be if Wong's proposed credit policy change were made?

d. What is the current level of bad debt losses, and what would the expected level be if the proposed change were made?

e. What is the current level of discount expenses, and what would the expected level be if the proposed change were made?

f. What is the current cost of carrying receivables, and what would the expected level be if the proposed change were made?

g. What is the expected incremental profit associated with the proposed change in credit policy? Based on the analysis thus far, should the change be made?

h. How certain could the company be that the proposed change, if implemented, would actually produce the expected results? Can you think of anything that the company could do to get more accurate, less uncertain estimates of the effects of the proposed changes?

i. Suppose the company makes the proposed change, but its competitors react by making similar changes in their own credit terms, with the net result being that Learning Aids' gross sales remain at the current $1 200 000 level. What would be the impact on the company's after-tax profits?

j. i. What does the term "monitoring accounts receivable" mean?
   ii. Why would a firm want to monitor its receivables?
   iii. How might the DSO and the aging schedule be used in this process?
   iv. How would seasonal fluctuations affect the validity of the DSO and the aging schedule for monitoring purposes?

Solutions to Self-Test Problems

ST-1 Refer to the appropriate sections of the text to check your responses.

ST-2 Under the current credit policy, the Ravin Company Ltd. has no discounts, has collection expenses of $50 000, has bad debt losses of

$(0.02)(\$10\,000\,000) = \$200\,000$, and has average accounts receivable of (DSO)(Average sales per day) = $(30)(\$10\,000\,000/365) = \$821\,918$. The firm's cost of carrying these receivables is (Variable cost ratio)(Accounts receivable)(Cost of capital) = $(0.80)(\$821\,918)(0.16) = \$105\,205$. It is necessary to multiply by the variable cost ratio because the actual *investment* in receivables is less than the dollar amount of the receivables.

a. *Proposal 1:* Lengthen the credit period to net 30 so that
- Sales increase by $1 million.
- Discounts = $0.
- Bad debt losses = $(0.02)(\$10\,000\,000) + (0.04)(\$1\,000\,000)$
$$= \$200\,000 + \$40\,000$$
$$= \$240\,000.$$
- DSO = 45 days on all sales.
- New average receivables = $(45)(\$11\,000\,000/365) = \$1\,356\,164$.
- Cost of carrying receivables = (Variable cost ratio)
$$\times \text{(Cost of capital)}$$
$$\times \text{(Average accounts receivable)}$$
$$= (0.80)(0.16)(\$1\,356\,164)$$
$$= \$173\,589.$$
- Collection expenses = $50 000.

Analysis of proposed change:

	Income Statement under Current Policy	Effect of Change	Income Statement under New Policy
Gross sales	$10 000 000	+ $1 000 000	$11 000 000
Less: Discounts	0	+ 0	0
Net Sales	$10 000 000	+ $1 000 000	$11 000 000
Production costs (80%)	8 000 000	+ 800 000	8 800 000
Profit before credit costs and taxes	$ 2 000 000	+ $ 200 000	$ 2 200 000
Credit-related costs			
Cost of carrying receivables	$ 105 205	+ $ 68 384	$ 173 589
Collection expenses	50 000	0	50 000
Bad debt losses	200 000	+ 40 000	240 000
Profit before taxes	$ 1 644 795	+ $ 91 616	$ 1 736 411
Taxes	657 918	+ 36 647	694 564
Net income	$ 986 877	+ $ 54 970	$ 1 041 847

The proposed change appears to be a good one, assuming the assumptions are correct.

b. *Proposal 2:* Shorten the credit period to net 20 so that
- Sales decrease by $1 million.
- Discount = $0.
- Bad debt losses = $(0.01)(\$9\,000\,000) = \$90\,000$.
- DSO = 22 days.

- New average receivables = (22)($9 000 000/365) = $542 466.
- Cost of carrying receivables = (Variable cost ratio)
    × (Cost of capital)
    × (Average accounts receivable)
  = (0.80)(0.16)($542 466)
  = $69 436.
- Collection expenses = $50 000.

  Analysis of proposed change:

	Income Statement under Current Policy	Effect of Change	Income Statement under New Policy
Gross sales	$10 000 000	($1 000 000)	$9 000 000
Less: Discounts	0	0	0
Net sales	$10 000 000	($1 000 000)	$9 000 000
Production costs (80%)	8 000 000	(800 000)	7 200 000
Profit before credit costs and taxes	$ 2 000 000	($ 200 000)	$1 800 000
Credit-related costs			
Cost of carrying receivables	$ 105 205	($ 35 770	$ 69 436
Collection expenses	50 000	0	50 000
Bad debt losses	200 000	110 000)	90 000
Profit before taxes	$ 1 644 795	($ 54 230)	$1 590 564
Taxes	657 918	(21 692)	636 226
Net income	$ 986 877	($ 32 538)	$ 954 339

This change reduces net income, so it should be rejected. Ravin will increase profits by accepting Proposal 1 to lengthen the credit period from 25 days to 30 days, assuming all assumptions are correct. This may or may not be the *optimal*, or profit-maximizing, credit policy, but it does appear to be a movement in the right direction.

Note that we have not included in our analysis the effects of increased (decreased) inventory, accounts payable, and other working capital components that would result from the increase (decrease) in sales. However, for a complete analysis of the business impact of a change in credit policy, these factors should also be considered.

10

Cash and Marketable Securities Management

A MANAGERIAL PERSPECTIVE

Efficiency in the use of assets is crucial to good corporate performance. The cash and marketable securities balance is no different. On the one hand, holding cash or other marketable securities incurs an opportunity cost since the assets could have been used to earn higher returns in the firm. However, this cost may be more than offset by the safety provided by the presence of liquid assets in uncertain times. In this chapter, we discuss the rationale for holding cash and near-cash marketable securities and describe two models that incorporate the tradeoff noted above.

At the end of 1991, approximately 4.0 percent of the average industrial firm's assets were held in the form of cash. In addition, sizable holdings of near-cash marketable securities are often reported on corporations' financial statements. However, cash balances vary widely both among industries and among the firms within a given industry, depending on the individual firms' specific conditions and on their owners' and managers' aversion to risk.

Efficient cash management is important to all firms. Financial managers, working with banks, have developed cash gathering and disbursing techniques that speed up the availability of funds and thus enable the firm to put its cash to work sooner. In this chapter, we examine these techniques, and we also analyze the factors that financial managers consider when they determine how much cash and marketable securities to hold. These same factors, incidentally, apply to the cash holdings of individuals and nonprofit organizations, including government agencies.

The Cash Management Function

Liquid assets generally provide low yields, but holdings of liquid assets reduce the firm's risk. Therefore, one issue in cash management involves a risk-return tradeoff. Another issue is the division of the holdings in liquid assets between **cash**, which is defined as the total of bank demand deposits plus currency, and marketable securities, such as Government of Canada Treasury bills (T-bills), commercial paper, and money market funds. These marketable securities are so easy to convert to cash as to be called **near-cash assets**. Cash provides the ultimate degree of liquidity, and it is essential for making payments, but near-cash assets serve many of the same functions as cash yet provide a return that cash per se does not. Therefore, the firm's financial manager must decide on the allocation of liquid assets between cash and near-cash assets. Other aspects of the cash management function include the use of efficient cash gathering and disbursement systems, the use of cash management models, the management of the marketable securities portfolio, and arrangements for backup borrowing capacity (lines of credit) in case a cash shortfall develops. Cash management functions have assumed more importance in recent years because of high and volatile interest rates and because of the greater globalization of business. This has led to greater emphasis on management of interest rate and foreign exchange rate risk through the use of hedging techniques such as futures, forwards, swaps, and options.

During every day of the business year the firm is faced with cash inflows and cash outflows. The important cash flows are noted in Table 10-1.

It is useful to classify these cash flows into two categories: those that are random and those that are controllable. In the former category are those cash flows that cannot be predicted; the actual value of any of these flows on a particular day will be equal to an expected value plus a random element. Included in this category are inflows from accounts receivable and cash sales. The controllable cash flows include payments for taxes, payroll, interest, cash dividends, and capital expenditures. (In fact, even cash outflows from payroll are not totally predictable. If employees are paid by cheque on Fridays, not all will cash their cheques on that day. Some will delay until Saturday or later. By looking at historical patterns, a statistical model can be developed to identify the lag between when a cheque is issued and when it is cashed. Of course, this problem can be minimized by having a direct deposit of employee cheques to the employee's bank.)

This distinction between random and controllable here is somewhat arbitrary as all the operational cash inflows and outflows—that is, all cash flows owing to normal operations—ultimately depend on sales that are random. Thus, the distinction is really based on the ability of the firm to plan for the substantial withdrawals that occur at specific times and that depend upon the time horizon in question. For example, the dollar outlay for controllable withdrawals such as dividends may not be known with certainty at the beginning of the year, but after the board of directors has passed the resolution declaring the dividend, the amount of the dividend outflow will be known with certainty. Similarly, extraordinary expenditures can be classified

Table 10-1
Cash Inflows and Outflows

Inflows	Outflows
1. Collections of accounts receivable	1. Payment of accounts payable
2. Cash sales receipts	2. Payroll
	3. Payment of taxes
	4. Interest payments
	5. Cash dividends
	6. Capital expenditures

as known, controllable withdrawals that should be planned for outside of the context of the desired cash balance. All withdrawals that are considered controllable are excluded from our discussion here of the operational cash balance. Payment will be made eventually, however, so the cash must ultimately be available. Provisions for these controllable expenditures are considered in the discussion of the investment in marketable securities in a subsequent section of this chapter.

Narrowing our focus to the "random" cash inflows and outflows, we consider the decision on the size of the cash balance. In addition, the linkage between the cash balance and investment in marketable securities is investigated.

Reasons for Holding Cash

Firms hold cash for the following four reasons:

1. *Transactions.*   Cash balances are necessary in business operations. Payments must be made in cash, and receipts are deposited in the cash account. Those cash balances associated with routine payments and collections are known as **transactions balances**.

2. *Precaution.*   Cash inflows and outflows are somewhat unpredictable (with the degree of predictability varying among firms and industries). Therefore, firms need to hold some cash in reserve for random, unforeseen fluctuations in inflows and outflows. These "safety stocks" are called **precautionary balances**, and the less predictable the firm's cash flows, the larger such balances should be. However, if the firm has easy access to borrowed funds—that is, it can borrow on short notice—its need to hold cash for precautionary purposes is reduced. This borrowing flexibility is not obtained without cost by the firm: the firm must decide whether the added cost of the flexibility is less than the added cost of higher precautionary cash balances. Firms that would otherwise need large precautionary balances tend to hold highly liquid, low-risk marketable securities rather than cash per se; marketable securities accomplish the same purposes as cash balances, but they provide greater interest income than bank operations.

3. *Speculation.*   Some cash balances may be held to enable the firm to take advantage of any bargain purchases that might arise; these funds are called **speculative balances**. Like the precautionary need, the speculative need for cash is normally met by reserve borrowing power and by marketable securities holdings rather than by actual cash balances.

4. *Compensation to banks.*   Commercial banks perform many functions for business firms, and firms pay for these services in part by direct fees and in part by maintaining compensating balances with their banks. A **compensating balance** represents the minimum level that a firm agrees to maintain in its chequing account with the bank. The bank, in turn, can lend these funds out and earn interest on them. This represents an indirect fee to the bank, which compensates it for services performed for the business firm. These requirements are discussed in more detail in a subsequent section.

Although the cash accounts of most firms can be thought of as consisting of transactions, precautionary, speculative, and compensating balances, we can-

not calculate the amount needed for each purpose, sum them, and produce a total desired cash balance, because the same money often serves more than one purpose. For instance, precautionary and speculative balances can also be used to satisfy compensating balance requirements. Firms do, however, consider these four factors when establishing their target cash positions.

The cash and marketable securities balances may rise to sizable levels on a temporary basis as funds are accumulated to meet specific future needs. These "financing balances" are built up to meet the controllable cash withdrawal requirements, such as dividend and interest payments, bond repayments, and investments in fixed assets.

Advantages of Holding Adequate Cash and Near-Cash Assets

In addition to the motives just discussed, sound working capital management requires maintenance of an ample supply of cash for several specific reasons:

1. It is essential that the firm have sufficient cash and near-cash assets to take **cash discounts** (also called *trade discounts*). A commonly encountered billing procedure, or credit term, allows a 2 percent discount if the bill is paid within 10 days, with full payment required in 30 days in any event. (This is usually stated as 2/10, net 30, as we saw in Chapter 9.) As the net amount is due in 30 days, failure to take the discount means paying this extra 2 percent for using the money an additional 20 days. The following equation is used to calculate the cost, on an annual basis, of not taking discounts.

$$\text{Cost} = \frac{\text{Discount percentage}}{(100 - \text{Discount percentage})} \times \frac{365}{(\text{Final due date} - \text{Discount period})}.$$

The numerator of the first term, discount percentage, is the cost per dollar of credit, while the denominator (100 − discount percentage), represents the funds made available by not taking the discount. The second term shows how many times a year this cost is incurred. To illustrate, the cost of not taking a discount when the terms are 2/10, net 30 is 37.24 percent:

$$\text{Cost} = \frac{2}{98} \times \frac{365}{20} = 0.0204 \times 18.25 = 37.24\%.$$

This represents an annual interest rate of more than 37 percent.[1] Most firms have a cost of debt that is substantially less than 37 percent, so not taking discounts is expensive.

---

[1]Notice that the calculated cost can be reduced by paying late. Thus, if the illustrative firm pays in 60 days rather than the specified 30, the credit period becomes 60 − 10 = 50, and the calculated cost becomes

$$\text{Cost} = \frac{2}{98} \times \frac{365}{50} = 0.0204 \times 7.3 = 14.9\%.$$

In periods of excess capacity, some firms may be able to get away with late payments, but such firms may suffer a variety of problems associated with being "slow payer" accounts.

2. Adequate holdings of cash and near-cash assets can help the firm maintain its credit rating by keeping its current and acid test ratios in line with those of other firms in the industry. A strong credit standing enables the firm to purchase goods from trade suppliers on favourable terms and to maintain its line of credit with banks and other sources of credit.

3. Ample cash is useful for taking advantage of favourable business opportunities, such as special offers from suppliers or the chance to acquire another firm, that may come along from time to time.

4. The firm should have sufficient liquidity to meet emergencies, such as strikes, fires, or marketing competitors' campaigns.

Concept Review

▶ Why is cash management important?

▶ What are the reasons firms hold cash? Which do you think are the most important?

Increasing the Efficiency of Cash Management

A cash budget prepared along the lines discussed in Chapter 6 is a necessary starting point for managing the firm's cash. Such a budget can be used to forecast when cash will be building up and when it will be declining, and, thus, the cash budget represents the starting point in the cash management system. However, as we discuss in this section, there are other elements of a good cash management program.

Cash Flow Synchronization

If you as an individual were to receive income once a year, you would probably put it in the bank, draw down your account periodically, and have an average balance during the year equal to about half your annual income. If you received income monthly, instead of once a year, you would operate with a lower average chequing account balance. If you could arrange to receive income daily and to pay rent, tuition, and other charges on a daily basis and if you were quite confident of your forecasts of inflows and outflows, you could hold a very small average cash balance. Exactly the same situation holds for business firms. By improving their forecasts and by arranging things so that cash receipts coincide with cash outflows, firms can hold their transactions balances to a minimum. Recognizing this point, utility companies, oil companies, department stores, and others arrange to bill customers and to pay their own bills on regular "billing cycles" throughout the month. Such **synchronized cash flows** reduce cash balances, decrease required bank loans, lower interest expenses, and boost profits.

Speeding Collections

Float refers to funds that are tied up in cheques that have been written but are still in process and not yet collected.

Firms encounter float in both collecting their receivables and paying their own bills. Float can come from several sources. In Canada, cheques encounter two major sources of delay: mail float and processing float. *Mail float*, also called *disbursement float*, is a result of the delay between putting the cheque in the mail and its receipt. It is equal to the dollar amount of funds associated with cheques written by the firm that have not yet been deducted from the firm's bank account. *Processing float*, also called *collection float*, is caused by delays within the firm such as not depositing cheques on the day they are received or not following up on late payments. It is equal to the dollar amount of the cheques written to the firm but not yet deposited and available for use.

In some other countries, float is also caused by delays within the banking system. However, there is virtually no float generated within the Canadian banking system, one of the, if not the, most efficient in the world. Since 1986 we have had same-day settlement of cheques. This means that when a firm deposits a cheque, it has access to the funds the same day. Most Canadian firms need to deal with only one bank, a large national bank with a national and international branch network. We also have automated clearing at several sites across the country. In the United States, in contrast, there are a multitude of banks, of varying credit standards, fragmented and geographically dispersed across the country. Many cash management techniques that originated in the United States are concerned with minimizing bank float and managing bank service. These are not particularly relevant in Canada.

Mail float is minimized by shortening or eliminating the amount of time payments spend in the postal system. Processing float is minimized by reducing the amount of time the cheque spends in the firm's office.

Preauthorized payments. Firms with large-volume, small-dollar-amount payments and a stable customer base, such as utilities, encourage customers to allow preauthorized payments. This allows the company to automatically debit the customer's account, typically monthly, usually for a fixed amount. A stable customer base reduces the clerical effort spent updating account information. Although preauthorized payments are efficient and appear to be the trend of the future, the pace of acceptance by payers has been much slower than was originally predicted, partly because a payer who uses a preauthorized payment system loses the use of disbursement float and partly because people like to be able to use cancelled cheques as receipts.

Lockbox. Firms may use a lockbox plan, which is a post office box located near the firm's customers and rented by the firm's bank. Since the post office box is near the customer, the time the payment spends in the postal system is minimized. The bank clears the box, on at least a daily basis, and processes the payments. Lockboxes are particularly effective at reducing float in the United States, where they are also useful in reducing bank float. Canadian companies with U.S. customers should consider using lockboxes in that country.

EFT. The Canadian Payments System has developed standards for an intercorporate *electronic funds transfer (EFT)* system that will include all the Canadian financial institutions. Canada will be one of the first countries in the world to implement such a system. A pilot project involving the Bank of Nova Scotia and the Toronto-Dominion Bank completed the first electronic payment in 1990. EFT is a companion to electronic data interchange, by which firms can send purchase orders and invoices electronically. EFT allows the payment to be sent electronically as well. Although the customer loses the benefit of float, the improved reliability and reduced clerical costs should make EFT more cost effective than paying by cheque. A good example of EFT is its use by companies such as General Motors and Chrysler to obtain direct access to dealer bank accounts and thereby collect their accounts immediately. This arrangement reduces the time between the delivery of the product and the collection of the account.

As well, EFT systems are being established in retail outlets to allow customers to use debit cards to make immediate payment. This system is referred to as *EFT/POS point of sale*. There are several pilot projects presently running in Canada. Customers will need to be motivated to use a debit card, with the associated immediate reduction of their bank balances, instead of a credit card or a cheque, which provides them with float.

Finally, EFT also refers to the payment of many bills at ATMs (automated teller machines) or over the telephone. Again, the firm benefits by the reduction of both mail and processing float.

Slowing Disbursements

Just as expediting the cash gathering process conserves cash, effective management of disbursements accomplishes similar results by keeping cash on hand for longer periods. A firm obviously can simply delay payments, but this involves equally obvious difficulties. Firms have, in the past, devised ingenious methods for "legitimately" lengthening the collection period on their own cheques. Since such practices are usually recognized for what they are, there are severe limits to their use.

Another procedure for delaying payouts is the use of *drafts*. Although used rarely, they are very effective in slowing down the expenditure of funds. Whereas a cheque is payable upon demand, a draft must be transmitted back to the issuer, who approves it and then deposits funds to cover it, after which it can be collected. Because there is a period of time required to clear the draft and transmit it to the issuer for approval, the company has extended the time that it has use of the funds before they must be paid out.

In the United States, insurance companies often use drafts. For instance, Aetna can pay a claim by draft on Friday. The recipient deposits the draft at a local bank, which sends it on to Aetna's Hartford bank. It may be Wednesday or Thursday before the draft arrives. The bank then sends it to the company's accounting department, which has until 3:00 P.M. that day to inspect and approve it. Not until then does Aetna deposit funds in its bank to pay the draft.

Net Float.   **Net float** is the difference between mail float and processing float. It is also equal to the difference between the balance in a firm's chequebook and the balance on the bank's records. In general, a firm wants to operate with a positive net float. This means that the firm is able to collect relatively rapidly the cheques written to it and thus to get the use of the money paid to it. Those to whom it writes cheques are relatively less efficient in clearing them, allowing the firm to use the funds for a while after it writes cheques.

Concept Review

▶ What are the causes of float?
▶ When does float work to the firm's advantage? To its disadvantage?
▶ How can float be reduced?
▶ Explain how a firm can have negative float.
▶ How can a firm speed up collections? Slow down disbursements?

Compensating Banks for Services

In addition to lending firms money, banks provide a great many services—clearing cheques, operating lockbox plans, supplying credit information, and the like. Because these services cost the bank money, the bank must be compensated for rendering them. During the 1980s and 1990s, banks have moved increasingly to charging on a fee-for-service basis. That is, they charge for each service rendered. However, compensating and maintenance balances are still required as well.

Maintenance Balances.   Banks earn most of their income by lending money at interest, and most of the funds they lend are obtained in the form of deposits. If a firm maintains a deposit account with an average balance of $100 000 and if the bank can lend these funds at a net return of $18 000, then the account is, in a sense, worth $18 000 to the bank. Thus, it is to the bank's advantage to provide services worth up to $18 000 to attract and hold the account.

Banks determine first the costs of the services rendered to their larger customers and then the average account balances necessary to provide enough income to compensate for these costs. Firms can make direct fee payments for these services, but they often find it more convenient to maintain *maintenance balances* than to pay monthly cash service charges to the bank.[2]

Compensating Balances.   Under some bank loan agreements, firms are required to maintain compensating balances. During periods when the supply of credit is restricted and interest rates are high, banks frequently insist that borrowers maintain accounts that average some percentage of the loan amount as a condition for granting the loan; 10 percent is a typical figure. If the required balance is larger than the firm would otherwise maintain, then the effective cost of the loan is increased. The excess balance presumably "compensates" the bank for making a loan at a rate below what it could earn on the funds if they were invested elsewhere.[3]

The *Bank Act* requires that the borrower must agree to the use of compensating balances or they cannot be stipulated in the loan agreement. Because the compensating balance is recognized by both the borrower and the

---

[2]Maintenance balance arrangements apply to individuals as well as to business firms. Thus, you might get "free" chequing services if you maintain a minimum balance of $500 but be charged 25 cents per cheque if your balance falls below that amount during the month.

[3]The effect of compensating balances on interest rates will be discussed further in Chapter 11.

lender as a method of increasing the interest rate, it is unlikely that a borrower would be able to remove a compensating balance provision while maintaining the stated rate on the loan.

Both maintenance and compensating balances can be established (1) as an *absolute minimum*—say, $100 000—below which the actual balance must never fall, or (2) as a *minimum average balance*—perhaps $100 000—over some period, usually a month. The absolute minimum is a much more restrictive requirement because the average amount of cash held during the month must be at least $100 000 more than the amount of the firm's transactions balances. The $100 000 in this case is "dead money" from the firm's standpoint. Under the minimum average, however, the balance can fall to zero one day provided it is $200 000 some other day, with the average working out to $100 000. Thus, the $100 000 in this case is available for transactions.

The minimum average balance technique is the one used to measure maintenance and compensating balances in Canada. In the United States, average balances are typical and absolute minimums rare for business accounts. U.S. bankers have indicated that during periods of very tight money, the absolute balance requirement is less rare.

Overdraft System.   Canada is one of a number of countries in which the banks use an *overdraft system*. In such a system, a depositor may write cheques in excess of the bank balance, and the bank automatically extends a loan to cover any shortage. The maximum amount of such loans and the interest cost of this line of credit must, of course, be established ahead of time. As there are no maintenance or compensating balances in the account, the bank will charge a higher rate on the overdraft loan than on an equivalent loan to a company that has these balances.

The cost of the overdraft must be considered net of the opportunity cost of keeping excess funds available. It is very unlikely that a company can forecast its cash flows so exactly that it obtains a zero balance in its chequing account every night. Therefore, if a company never has an overdraft, it must be keeping excess funds available in the bank and thus not invested in short-term marketable securities.

To identify the costs of not using overdrafts, assume that the interest rate on the overdraft is 10 percent per annum or 0.027 percent per day (10%/365 days) and that short-term investments (say, Treasury bills) pay 8.5 percent per annum or 0.023 percent per day. Every day that the company's forecast is wrong and it must go into an overdraft position costs 0.004 percentage points per day—the cost of 0.027 percent minus 0.023 percent. Every day that the forecast is correct, the firm gains 0.023 percent since it has its funds invested in T-bills. The percentage difference may be small, but with large dollar amounts invested, a few days' overdraft per month does not seem so costly.

Concept Review

► Why do firms maintain compensating balances?
► What is an overdraft system?
► Is it a sign of poor cash management to have an overdraft?

Matching the Costs and Benefits of Cash Management

Although a number of procedures may be used to hold down cash balance requirements, implementing these methods is not a costless operation. How far should a firm go in making its cash operations more efficient? As a general rule, the firm should incur these expenses as long as marginal returns exceed marginal expenses.

For example, suppose that by (1) establishing a lockbox system and (2) increasing the accuracy of its cash inflow and outflow forecasts, a firm can reduce its investment in cash by $1 million without increasing the risk of running short of cash. Further, suppose the firm borrows at a cost of 12 percent. The steps taken will release $1 million, which can be used to reduce bank loans and thus save $120 000 per year. If the costs of the procedures necessary to release the $1 million are less than $120 000, the move is a good one; if they exceed $120 000, the greater efficiency is not worth the cost.[4] Another example is a cash management or *treasury workstation* (a personal computer with specialized software), which may cost $5000. Its benefit is to provide more timely and accurate cash forecasts for the firm; this may enable the firm to reduce its uninvested cash balances. For example, if uninvested cash balances can be reduced by $20 000 per day when interest rates are 10 percent, the workstation will save $2000 per year. If the workstation has a life of 3 years, the purchase will not be worthwhile.[5] It is clear that larger firms, which have larger cash balances, can better afford to hire the personnel necessary to maintain tight control over their cash positions. Cash management is thus one element of business operations in which economies of scale are present.

Clearly, the value of careful cash management depends on the costs of funds invested in cash, which in turn depend on the current rate of interest. In the 1980s, when interest rates were often near historic highs, firms devoted a great deal of care to cash management.

Marketable Securities

Marketable securities are securities that can be sold on short notice for close to their quoted market price. As noted at the beginning of the chapter, sizable holdings of short-term marketable securities are often reported on corporations' financial statements. The reasons for such holdings, as well as the factors that influence the choice of securities held, are discussed in this section.

---

[4]This analysis of the investment in cash management is an application of capital budgeting techniques to be described in Chapter 13. In this simplified example, there is a level annual cost of cash management. In a more complicated example, the costs might not be the same each year and a somewhat more involved analysis would be necessary.

[5]The $5000 cost is equivalent to equal annuity payments of $2010 at 10 percent for 3 years. A complete analysis would have to include the time of a salaried employee to operate the computer, if one has to be hired.

Reasons for Holding Marketable Securities

Marketable securities typically provide much lower yields than operating assets. Why would any company want large holdings of low-yielding assets? There are two basic reasons for these holdings: (1) they serve as a substitute for cash balances, and (2) they are used as a temporary investment. These points are considered next.

Marketable Securities as a Substitute for Cash.   Some firms hold portfolios of marketable securities in lieu of larger cash balances. They sell some securities from the portfolios whenever they need to replenish the cash account.

Marketable Securities as a Temporary Investment.   Temporary investments in marketable securities generally occur in one of the three following situations:

1. When the firm must finance seasonal or cyclical operations. Firms that are engaged in seasonal operations frequently have surplus cash flows during one part of the year and deficit cash flows during the other. For example, retailers such as Sears often purchase marketable securities during their surplus periods and then liquidate them when cash deficits occur. Other firms, however, choose to use bank financings to cover such shortages.
2. When the firm must meet some known financial requirements. If, say, a major plant construction program is planned for the near future or if a bond issue is about to mature, a firm may build up its marketable securities portfolio to provide the required funds. Furthermore, marketable securities holdings are frequently built up immediately preceding quarterly corporate tax payment dates.
3. When the firm has just sold long-term securities. Expanding firms generally have to sell long-term securities (shares or bonds) periodically. The proceeds from such sales are often invested in marketable securities, which are then sold off to provide cash as it is needed to pay for operating assets.

Holding Marketable Securities versus Borrowing

Actually, each of the needs listed above can be met either by taking out short-term loans or by holding marketable securities. Consider Chum Perfume Company, whose sales are growing over time but fluctuate on a seasonal basis. The firm plans to borrow to meet seasonal needs. As an alternative financial policy, Chum could hold a portfolio of marketable securities and then liquidate these securities to meet its peak cash needs.

A firm's marketable securities policy is an integral part of its overall working capital policy. If the firm has a conservative working capital financing policy, its long-term capital will exceed its permanent assets, and it will hold marketable securities when inventories and receivables are low. With an aggressive policy, it will never carry any securities and will borrow heavily to meet peak needs. With a moderate policy, under which maturities are matched, the firm will match permanent assets with long-term financing; it will meet most seasonal increases in inventories and receivables with short-term loans, but it will also carry marketable securities at certain times.

Figure 10-1 illustrates three alternative strategies for a firm such as Chum. Under Plan A, which represents a relatively aggressive financing policy, Chum would hold no marketable securities, relying completely on bank loans to meet seasonal peaks. Under the conservative Plan B, Chum would stockpile marketable securities during slack periods and then sell them to raise funds for peak needs. Plan C is a compromise; the company would hold some securities but not enough to meet all of its peak needs.

There are advantages and disadvantages to each of these strategies. Plan A is clearly the most risky; the firm's current ratio is always lower than under the other plans, indicating that it might encounter difficulties either in borrowing the funds needed or in repaying the loan. On the other hand, Plan A requires no holdings of low-yielding marketable securities, and this will probably lead to a relatively high expected rate of return on both total assets and equity.

Plan B is the more conservative, less risky one. First, the company is minimizing its liquidity problems because it has no short-term debt hanging over its head. Second, it is sure of having the funds available to meet payments as they come due. On the other hand, when firms borrow, they generally have to pay interest rates that are higher than the return they receive on marketable securities; therefore, following the less risky strategy does have a cost. Again, the firm faces a risk–return tradeoff.

It is difficult to prove that one financing strategy is better than another. In principle, the practice of holding marketable securities reduces the firm's expected rate of return, but it also reduces k_s, the required rate of return on its common equity. Although we can quantify the cost of following a more conservative policy—it is the average differential between the percentage

---

Figure 10-1
Alternative Strategies for Meeting Seasonal Cash Needs

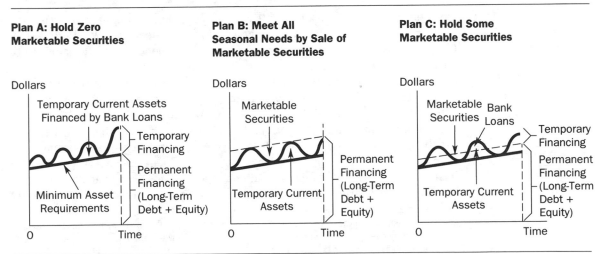

Plan A: Hold Zero Marketable Securities

Plan B: Meet All Seasonal Needs by Sale of Marketable Securities

Plan C: Hold Some Marketable Securities

return received on marketable securities and the interest rate paid on the long-term debt—it is almost impossible to quantify the benefits in terms of how much such a policy reduces risk and how this risk reduction affects k_s. Further, it is impossible to measure the higher sales and profits, if any, that a liquid asset portfolio might make possible should a credit crunch occur. Accordingly, the basic policies with regard to securities holdings are generally set on the basis of judgement or, in some instances, by circumstances beyond the company's control.

Criteria for Selecting Marketable Securities

A wide variety of securities, differing in terms of default risk, interest rate risk, liquidity risk, and expected rate of return, are available to firms that choose to hold marketable securities. In this section, we first consider the characteristics of different securities, and then we show how the financial manager selects the specific instruments to be held in the portfolio.

Default Risk.   The risk that the issuer will be unable to make interest or principal payments as they come due is known as **default risk**. All securities except those issued by the Canadian government are subject to some degree of default risk for Canadian investors.[6] The risk of default is one of the factors that influence rating agencies such as the Canadian Bond Rating Service when quality ratings are assigned to securities. Quality assessments can and do change over time.

   Since the firm's liquidity portfolio is often held for a specific need, if it should depreciate in value because of overall market changes of the default experience of securities in the portfolio, the firm would have trouble meeting its obligations. Further, most nonfinancial corporations do not have investment departments specializing in appraising securities and determining the probability of their going into default. Accordingly, the marketable securities portfolio is generally confined to securities with a minimal risk of default. However, the lowest-risk securities also provide the lowest returns, so safety is bought at the expense of yield.

Interest Rate Risk.   *Interest rate risk*, as described in Chapter 3, is the risk that interest rates will change over the life of a security. We shall see in Chapter 16 that in general the price of a long-term bond fluctuates much more with changes in interest rates than does the price of a short-term bond with the same default risk. Further, interest rates fluctuate widely over time, and short-term rates fluctuate more than long-term rates. A recent example demonstrates the variability of short rates. Late in September 1992, the Canadian dollar declined dramatically and short-term rates increased significantly over a very short period. Over one day, interest rates on Government of Canada treasury bills increased by approximately 2 percentage points (200 basis points). These two factors combine to make long-term bonds riskier than short-term securities for a firm's marketable securities portfolio. Partly

[6]Securities issued by other governments, such as the Swiss or the British, may be regarded as default-free by their citizens, but a Canadian company that owned such securities would have to worry about both currency transfer blockages and exchange rate fluctuations.

because of this risk differential, however, higher yields are more frequently available on long-term than on short-term securities; again risk–return tradeoffs must be recognized.

Time Horizon.   Looking only at the maturities of the securities held in the firm's marketable securities portfolio is not sufficient to determine the risk exposure. The other element of relevance is the length of time that the funds will be invested. Typically, funds are invested in marketable securities when they are temporarily not required for company operations. If the securities purchased have a maturity that is shorter than the time period over which the funds will be idle, the firm is incurring the risk that the funds may have to be reinvested at lower interest rates. Conversely, if the maturities of the securities are longer than this time period, there is the risk that interest rates may increase and, in order to obtain the required cash, the securities will have to be liquidated at reduced market values. These risks will be minimized only when the maturities of the securities purchased are equal to the time period for which the funds are surplus—this is known as a *hedging* or *matching* strategy. Because these funds are surplus for the short term, the portfolios are usually composed of short-term securities. Securities with less than 1 year to maturity are often referred to as *money market instruments*.

Purchasing Power Risk.   Another type of risk is **purchasing power risk**, or the risk that *inflation* will reduce the purchasing power of a given sum of money. Purchasing power risk, which is important both to firms and to individual investors during times of inflation, is lower on assets whose returns tend to rise during inflation than on assets whose returns are fixed. Thus, real estate, short-term debt, and common shares are generally better hedges against inflation than are bonds and other long-term fixed-income securities.

Liquidity, or Marketability, Risk.   Some assets can be sold at the current market price on very short notice, while for other assets no ready market exists, and they can be disposed of quickly only if the price is cut sharply. Real estate is a good example—a building might bring $100 000 if it can be sold over a 6-month period but only $80 000 if the owner has to sell it within a week. The difference between the "steady state" value of an asset and its probable price if disposed of quickly is a measure of the asset's *liquidity*. For securities, liquidity risk is related to the size and activity of the market relative to the number of shares in the transaction. BCE equity, with its large number of shareholders and frequent transactions, is more liquid than the shares of Willowbunch Printing Company Ltd. Similarly, short-term T-bills can be disposed of quickly at close to the quoted market price and thus have little **liquidity**, or **marketability**, risk.

Taxability.   The tax position of a firm's marketable securities portfolio is influenced by the overall tax position of that firm. A firm with prior years' losses to carry forward can ignore taxability, but a firm that pays the full marginal corporate tax rate must take taxability into account. The market yields on a security will reflect tax considerations, yet the tax position of an individual firm may differ from that of the market as a whole. To the extent that a firm's tax position differs from that of the overall market, it may find that investment in marketable securities is enhanced.

Returns on Securities.   The higher the risk of a financial instrument, the higher is its expected and required return. Therefore, corporate treasurers must make a tradeoff between risk and return when choosing investments for their marketable securities portfolio. The motive for holding marketable securities is protection against uncertain and fluctuating inflows and outflows; thus, the dominant strategy calls for relatively less risky alternatives at the sacrifice of some return. Accordingly, corporate treasurers emphasize relatively short-term, highly liquid money market assets in assembling the marketable securities portfolio.

Types of Marketable Securities

Table 10-2 provides a listing of the major types of securities available for investment, along with yields as of December 31, 1987 and 1991. After giving careful consideration to how long the surplus funds will probably be held, the financial manager will decide upon a suitable maturity pattern for the firm's holdings. The numerous alternatives can be selected and balanced in such a way that the manager obtains the maturities and risks appropriate to the financial situation of the firm. Commercial bankers, investment dealers, and brokers provide the financial manager with detailed information on each of the forms of investments in the list. Because the characteristics of these investment outlets change with shifts in financial market conditions, it would be misleading to attempt to give detailed descriptions of them here. The financial manager must keep up to date on these characteristics and should follow the principle of making investment selections that offer maturities, yields, and risks appropriate to the firm.

Smaller and medium-sized corporations often invest their liquid assets in money market mutual funds; the funds provide instant liquidity and their assets are invested in T-bills, bank certificates of deposit, bankers' acceptances, or high-quality commercial paper. Larger companies bypass the money funds by investing directly and avoiding the funds' fees.

Concept Review

▶ What are the major reasons for a firm to hold marketable securities?
▶ List three situations in which a firm would hold marketable securities as a temporary investment.
▶ As identified in Figure 10-1, what are the three alternative strategies for meeting seasonal cash needs? Which one is an aggressive policy and which one is conservative?
▶ What risks do financial managers consider when developing their marketable securities portfolio?

Table 10-2
Securities Available for Investment of Surplus Cash

Security	Typical Maturity at Time of Issue	Approximate Yield to Maturity (Dec. 31)	
		1987	1991
Suitable To Hold as Near-Cash Reserve			
Overnight money market financing	Overnight	8.16%	7.40%
Government of Canada Treasury bills	90 days	8.24	7.43
Government of Canada Treasury bills	180 days	8.48	7.28
Government of Canada bonds	1–3 years	8.63	7.31
Commercial paper[a]	30–90 days	8.30	7.57
Bankers' acceptances[b]	30 days	8.23	7.48
Not Suitable To Hold as Near-Cash Reserve			
Government of Canada bonds	3–6 years	8.81	8.18
Government of Canada bonds	> 10 years	9.23	9.00
Long-term provincial bonds	> 10 years	9.82	9.69
Mid-term corporate bonds	< 10 years	10.02	9.48
Long-term corporate bonds	> 10 years	10.13	10.17
Common shares of other corporations	Unlimited	Variable	Variable

[a]Commercial paper is a short-term note issued by a financially secure company. These securities are discussed in Chapter 11.

[b]Bankers acceptances are short-term notes similar to commercial paper except that redemption is guaranteed by a bank. See Chapter 11 for a complete description of this money market security.

Source: *Bank of Canada Review*, April 1988, 1992.

Models of Cash Management

Interest in cash management increased dramatically in the 1980s in response to high inflation rates, which threatened to devalue any idle or unaccounted-for cash. With the recent reduction in inflation, cash management has still remained an important consideration for financial managers who are attempting to increase shareholder value by improving the efficiency with which their firms use all assets, including cash. There are a number of models available that are of assistance to the management of the firm in the determination of the optimal cash balance. These models range from the very simple to the very sophisticated. In this section we will consider two general types of models. The first type considers the risk of cash inflows and outflows but does not explicitly encompass the costs of cash management; these models are referred to as *subjective risk* models. The second type considers explicitly the costs of cash management and evaluates the cash balance problem within an *inventory framework*.

Subjective Risk Models

The firm is interested in determining the daily desired cash balance that covers both transactions and precautionary motives. One way of doing this is to consider the daily changes in the firm's cash balances for those cash inflows and outflows that are not controllable. Because we are interested in the daily cash flow changes from the normal operations of the company, some form of seasonal adjustment is necessary. For example, if there are specific seasonal influences, the daily change in the firm's cash balance for different seasons can be considered. The result is different desired cash balances for each season.

For a given season, a frequency distribution of daily changes in the cash balance is constructed. This distribution, shown in Figure 10-2, will be characterized by an expected or average daily change and a standard deviation. (For purposes of exposition, we have presented the frequency distribution based on continuous observations; in reality, it will be discrete.)

How does the firm use this information to determine its desired opening cash balance? In a risk context, because the firm is concerned only with random events that will reduce the cash balance and perhaps result in a stockout, it is interested only in the negative changes. Suppose the company management has decided that the cash balance should be sufficiently large so that the probability of not having enough cash on any given day is 5 percent. Therefore, the desired opening cash balance must be sufficiently large that only 5 percent of the negative dollar changes will be greater than the desired opening balance. In our illustration in the figure, 5 percent of the observations are larger than −$13.2 million. Thus, the desired opening balance is $13.2 million.

As an example, suppose a company estimates the frequency distribution in Figure 10-2; the mean or average daily change is zero and the standard deviation is $8 million. Assuming a normal distribution, what is the desired

Figure 10-2
Distribution of Daily Changes in Cash Balance

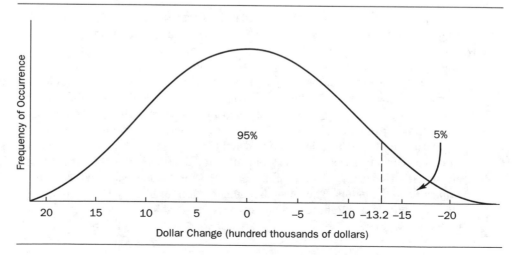

opening cash balance if the firm wishes a 1 percent and a 5 percent probability of a stockout?

For a probability of 1 percent, the opening cash balance is $18.56 million. This figure is obtained by adding to the average daily change (which in this case is zero) a value equal to 2.32 times the standard deviation. When the probability is 5 percent, the opening cash balance is equal to $13.2 million = 0 + 1.65 × ($8 million).[7] To the extent that the average daily change in the cash balance is negative, the desired opening cash balance will be higher by the amount of this average value.

This approach directly captures management's degree of risk aversion. The more risk the management is willing to accept, the smaller is the desired opening balance. If an automatic overdraft system is available, the desired opening balance can also be lowered. Alternatively, the firm can hold a stock of marketable securities that may be liquidated.

The benefit of this approach is that it combines decisions based on the transactions and precautionary motives into a single decision; the resulting desired opening cash balance reflects the risk of the cash flows and management's attitude toward risk. Unfortunately, this approach is deficient in a number of ways. First, it implies that each day the actual cash balance is compared to the desired balance, and either the purchase or sale of securities is undertaken to obtain the desired value. This will generate substantial transactions costs. Second, the larger the opening cash balance, the greater is the loss of interest income that could be obtained by investing the cash in marketable securities. This leads directly to consideration of the risk–return tradeoff: the smaller the desired cash balance, the less the investment in cash and the funds can be released into more profitable investments. The lower cash balance, however, also results in a greater risk of a cash shortage, which results in monetary and nonmonetary losses. (The latter loss refers to the loss of good will by the firm's suppliers and bank.) A complete model must consider the risk–return tradeoff more explicitly.

---

[7]Let Z be a random variable defined as:

$$Z = \frac{x - \mu}{\sigma}. \tag{10-1}$$

where μ and σ are the mean and standard deviation of the probability distribution of daily cash balance charts and x is the value of the cash balance.

Based on Equation 10-1, Z is a normal distribution with a mean of zero and a standard deviation equal to 1. Suppose a cash balance is required with a 1 percent probability of stockout. To find the cash balance, obtain that value of Z from the normal probability tables for which the probability of observing a value in excess is 1 percent. The value of Z is 2.32. Rearranging Equation 10-1 as:

$$x = \mu + Z\sigma$$

and substituting the values $\mu = 0$, $\sigma = \$8$ million, and Z = 2.32, the resulting value of x is $18.56 million.

If a 5 percent probability level is required, the Z value is 1.65 and x = 0 + 1.65 ($8 million) = $13.20 million.

Inventory-Type Models

It should not be surprising that cash can be viewed as a raw material; hence, if there are ordering and carrying costs that have the same relationship to the size of inventory as discussed in Chapter 8, there is an optimal cash balance or cash inventory. If a small cash balance is used, then, as cash is used up, frequent replenishment will be required. This can be achieved by selling off some securities, and there will be an order cost. This cost includes clerical, decision-making, and brokerage costs. In fact, if the target cash balance is small, the firm will have to invest any excess cash in securities, thereby incurring order costs as well. On the other hand, if a large cash balance is held, the firm incurs a carrying cost in the form of interest foregone on the cash tied up. Therefore, the relationships of carrying and ordering costs with the size of the inventory are as portrayed in Figure 10-3, and that analysis can be used.

This view of cash balance decision as an inventory problem has led to a number of models. We shall consider two: the first, presented by W. Baumol,[8] is a simple model that assumes no uncertainty in the cash flows and hence deals with the transactions demand for cash; the second, developed by M. Miller and D. Orr,[9] is a more sophisticated model that includes uncertainty. The models are presented to provide a better understanding of how certain variables influence the optimal inventory of cash.

Baumol Model.   The **Baumol model** balances the opportunity cost of holding cash against the transactions costs of obtaining it. Suppose the firm has determined that the level of cash disbursements during the year will be T;

Figure 10-3
The Baumol Model of the Demand for Cash

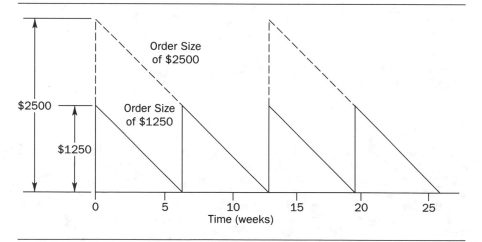

[8]W. Baumol, "The Transactions Demand for Cash: An Inventory Theoretic Approach," *Quarterly Journal of Economics*, November 1952: 545–56.

[9]M. Miller and D. Orr, "Model of the Demand for Money by Firms," *Quarterly Journal of Economics*, August 1966: 413–35.

these expenditures are known with certainty and are to be paid out in a steady stream over the year. The firm must make a decision as to the amount of cash to be "ordered" and hence how often this order must be placed. The cash order is obtained either by borrowing that is to be repaid with some future receipt, by an issue of securities (likely short-term), or by selling marketable securities held by the firm. Let the size of this cash order be C.

For example, suppose the firm has determined that its cash disbursements will be $10 000 per year: that is, T = $10 000. If the cash order is $1250, then the firm will make a new order 8 times per year, or every 6.5 weeks. If the cash order is $2500, a new order will be made 4 times per year, or every 13 weeks. This sequence—order, pay expenses, reorder—results in the sawtoothed pattern in Figure 10-3. Notice that the opening balance is depleted steadily over the order period, and when the balance reaches zero a new order is made.

How does the firm decide on the optimal size of the cash order? First, the order costs must be identified. Each time the firm makes a cash order it must incur a cost of F for making a security trade or obtaining a loan; these "brokerage costs" include not only the payment to the broker to execute the order (if securities have to be issued or liquidated) or service charges to the bank (if borrowing is used) but also clerical and administrative costs associated with making and receiving the order. On the other hand, there is an opportunity cost of having cash tied up in the cash inventory: over the year the average cash balance is C/2; therefore, the annual opportunity cost is the earnings that could have been obtained if the cash were invested in a riskless asset. If the interest rate is k percent per annum, the interest cost of having an order of C is kC/2.

Notice that there is a tradeoff between order and holding costs. As the cash order becomes larger, fewer orders are necessary and the annual order costs fall. However, the average inventory increases and the holding cost increases. It is the combination of these costs that determines the optimal cash order and hence the average cash balance.

The result of the Baumol model is Equation 10-2, which determines the optimal cash order, C^*.

$$C^* = \sqrt{\frac{2FT}{k}}. \qquad\qquad (10\text{-}2)$$

The cash order size depends on the brokerage costs, F, and the amount of cash expenditures, T. As these increase, the cash order, C, and hence the average cash balance, increases. In addition, the cash order depends on the interest rate—as interest rates increase, the cash order (and the average cash balance) decreases. The impacts of these variables F, T, and k on the cash order certainly are consistent with our intuition. The final value for the average cash balance actually held by the company will depend on the results of the model *and* on any bank requirements regarding compensating and minimum balances.[10]

---

[10]The costs in the inventory model can be expressed on either a before-tax or an after-tax basis. Both methods lead to the same conclusions regarding target cash balances and comparative costs. We present the model here on a before-tax basis.

To illustrate the use of this model, consider a company facing the following values for the variables in Equation 10-2:

$$T = \$1\ 800\ 000.$$
$$F = \$25 \text{ per order.}$$
$$k = 10 \text{ percent per annum.}$$

The cash order is determined as follows:

$$C^* = \sqrt{\frac{2FT}{k}} = \sqrt{\frac{2(\$25)(\$1\ 800\ 000)}{0.10}} = \$30\ 000.$$

Assuming a zero safety stock, the average cash balances for the period will be \$15 000:

$$\frac{C^*}{2} = \frac{\$30\ 000}{2} = \$15\ 000.$$

The total number of transactions or transfers required, per year, will be \$1 800 000/\$30 000 = 60, or just over 1 transaction per week. Finally, the total cost per year of maintaining cash balances, TC, can be calculated:

$$\text{Total cost} = \text{Ordering cost} + \text{Carrying cost}$$

$$TC = F\left(\frac{T}{C^*}\right) + k\left(\frac{C^*}{2}\right)$$

$$= \$25\left(\frac{1\ 800\ 000}{30\ 000}\right) + 0.10\left(\frac{\$30\ 000}{2}\right)$$

$$= \$1500 + \$1500 = \$3000.$$

On the basis of the data in the example, the total cost of "inventorying" cash is \$3000 per year, and this is the minimum cost attainable.

Although this model presents the determinants of the optimal cash order and average cash balance, it is subject to some serious reservations. These include its assumptions of perfect certainty and a steady stream of cash disbursements. In the next paragraphs, these assumptions are relaxed and a more realistic model is presented.

Miller-Orr Model.   The assumptions in the Baumol model require that the firm make specific orders of cash when the cash balance reaches zero. This solution, however, is not appropriate when the cash balance moves up and down in part in an unpredictable manner. A model is required that reviews the daily cash balance of the firm and signals the management either that the opening balance is too low and needs to be replenished or that the opening balance is too high and the excess needs to be invested in marketable securities. The **Miller-Orr model** provides a solution to this problem. The model is basically an inventory model; it evaluates both order costs and holding costs.

Consider a company that has decided that the cash balances it holds will reflect noncontrollable cash expenditures (controllable cash outlays, such as dividends and interest payments, are evaluated separately). The cash balance at the beginning of any particular day will reflect the values of the cash receipts and disbursements during the previous day. In Figure 10-4 the path of the daily cash balance for a hypothetical company is presented. The initial cash balance is noted on the left side of the diagram as m_0.

As time passes, the cash balance appears to wander randomly until time t_0, when there appears to be an upward trend in the cash balance. The firm permits the cash balance to increase in size until the day at which the cash balance reaches or breaks through the upper limit, h. At this point, t_1, the firm purchases enough securities (or repays enough bank loans) to reduce the cash balance to the return point, z. The firm then permits the cash balance to wander. At t_2, the cash balance reaches the lower limit, l, and enough securities are sold to replenish the cash balance to the return point z. The cash balance strategy permits the cash balance to wander until either the upper or lower limit is reached (or exceeded); at this time, the firm purchases or sells a sufficient amount of securities to restore the cash balance to the return point.

In order to implement the model, the financial manager must determine the values of the upper limit, h, the lower limit, l, and the return point, z. These are obtained in the solution to the model. The spread between the upper and lower limits will depend on the order costs, the variability of the cash flows, and the holding cost that is captured by the interest rate. The order cost reflects the costs of transferring funds from marketable securities to cash and vice versa.

The smaller the spread between the upper and lower limits, the more frequent will be these transfers. With substantial order costs, the more transfers that occur, the greater the total order costs faced by the firm. If the cash flows are extremely variable, a narrow spread will result in the cash

Figure 10-4
Daily Cash Changes

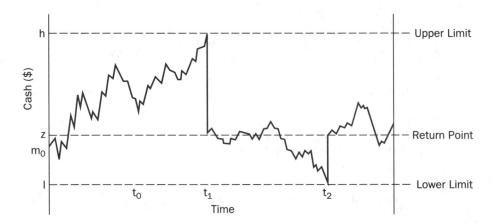

Source: M. Miller and D. Orr, "An Application of Control-Limit Models to the Management of Corporate Cash Balances," in *Financial Research and Management Decisions*, ed. by A. A. Robichek (New York: John Wiley & Sons, 1967). Copyright © 1967 John Wiley & Sons, Inc. Reprinted by permission of John Wiley & Sons, Inc.

balance reaching one or the other of the limits very frequently, which will generate large order costs. If cash flows are variable or transactions costs high, the spread will be wide. If the spread between the limits is wide, the firm may accumulate large cash balances before the upper limit is reached—this is a distinct possibility because the return level is not midway between the upper and lower limits but at one-third of the spread. With high interest rates, the firm with a high cash balance will incur substantial foregone earnings. Thus, when interest rates are high, the spread between the two limits will narrow.

The Miller-Orr solution is as follows. Let

F = Transfer or ordering costs, per order;
σ^2 = Daily transactions variance in the cash account;
v = Daily rate of interest;
z = Return point = $\left[\dfrac{3}{4} \times \dfrac{F\sigma^2}{v}\right]^{\frac{1}{3}}$.

In order to implement the Miller-Orr model the financial manager must start by specifying the lower limit control point. In the discussion, we assume that the lower limit is zero. To the extent that bank requirements determine a nonzero lower limit, a simple adjustment is required; this adjustment will be illustrated in an example.

To illustrate how the Miller-Orr model is implemented, consider the following example:

F = Order costs = \$100 per transaction.
v = 0.00038%, which is the daily equivalent of 15% per annum.
σ^2 = \$64 000 000.

The value of σ^2 is equivalent to a daily standard deviation of \$8000 based on the daily changes in the cash balance over a representative period. The return point is equal to

$$z = \left[\frac{3}{4} \times \frac{F\sigma^2}{v}\right]^{\frac{1}{3}} = \left[\frac{3}{4} \times \frac{\$100 \times \$64\,000\,000}{0.00038}\right]^{\frac{1}{3}} = \$23\,287 \approx \$23\,000.$$

The upper limit is $h = 3z = \$69\,000$, and the lower limit, by definition, is zero.
The decision rule then becomes:

1.   When the cash balance is equal to the upper limit of \$69 000, invest in marketable securities equal to 2z, or \$46 000. This restores the cash balance to the return point.
2.   When the cash balance is equal to zero, sell securities of \$23 000. This again restores the cash balance to the return point.

Now assume that bank requirements necessitate a minimum bank balance of \$20 000. In this case, all that is required is that both limits and the return point be increased by \$20 000; this will not affect the size of the spread between the upper and lower limits or the relationship of the return point to these limits. Therefore, in our numerical example we have the following results:

$$h = \$69\,000 + \$20\,000 = \$89\,000.$$
$$l = \$0 + \$20\,000 = \$20\,000.$$
$$z = \$23\,000 + \$20\,000 = \$43\,000.$$

When the cash balance rises to $89 000, buy $46 000 of marketable securities; when the cash balance falls to $20 000, sell $23 000 of securities to replenish the cash position.

The Miller-Orr control policy model is easy to use and appears to provide reasonable directions to management with respect to cash management. Notice that in our discussion of the model we have excluded a consideration of those cash outflows that are controllable; what is left is the net effect on the cash balance of those cash flows that are substantially unpredictable. Finally, the model rests on some assumptions that may appear untenable; for example, it is assumed that the fluctuations in the cash balance are entirely random and that there is no upward or downward trend in the cash balance over the period of analysis. Even if these assumptions are not met exactly, the model can still be of use to management. The model is not intended to replace management but to provide tools that can be used along with other managerial techniques to improve the company's performance.

Concept Review

▶ What is the Baumol model? What are the main assumptions underlying it? Write down the formula.
▶ What is the Miller-Orr model? What are the advantages of this model over the Baumol model?

Company Liquidity Policies in Practice

The liquidity policies of companies vary with their individual circumstances and needs. This is illustrated in Table 10-3, where data on the components of liquid assets is presented for several classifications of industries, along with the total for all nonfinancial industries, as of the end of the second quarter, 1992. The total liquid assets held by all nonfinancial industries was approximately 6 percent of total assets and 23 percent of revenues.

The lowest ratio of liquid assets to total assets was in the telecommunications sector, which includes regulated telephone utilities as well as cable companies. Since the telephone utilities receive payments every day from customers, the firms in this industry can hold very small balances of liquid assets. In addition, these firms typically have substantial lines of credit, which can be drawn upon if they find themselves in need of immediate cash. On the other hand, general services to business had high liquidity ratios with respect to assets and revenues. These firms have relatively low investment in fixed

Table 10-3
A Comparison of Liquidity Relationships, 1992
(millions of dollars)

	Total Nonfinancial Industries	Telecommunication	General Services to Businesses	Accommodation, Food and Beverage, Health and Recreation	Consumer Goods and Services
Cash	$27 391	$171	$1 458	$2 437	$2 592
Marketable securities	25 991	234	1 918	3 305	2 502
Liquid assets	$53 382	$405	$3 376	$5 742	$5 094
Percentage of total assets					
Cash	2.9%	0.5%	5.0%	6.1%	4.1%
Marketable securities	2.7	0.7	6.6	8.3	4.0
Liquid assets	5.6%	1.2%	11.6%	14.4%	8.1%
Percentage of revenues					
Cash	11.8%	4.3%	31.4%	24.8%	9.5%
Marketable securities	11.2	5.8	41.4	33.6	9.2
Liquid assets	23.0%	10.1%	72.8%	58.4%	18.7%

Source: Statistics Canada, *Quarterly Financial Statistics for Enterprises*, 1992Q2, cat. no. 61-008. Reproduced with the permission of the Minister of Industry, Science and Technology, 1993.

assets and hence relatively high investment in current assets. Also, they are often small firms, which find it difficult to obtain bank financing and must therefore provide their own liquidity.

Summary

This chapter discussed cash and marketable securities management. In it, we examined the motives for holding cash, several ways in which firms can minimize their cash holdings, the different types of marketable securities that can be used as substitutes for cash, and the Baumol and the Miller-Orr models for determining optimal cash balances. The key concepts covered are listed below.

□ The primary goal of cash management is to reduce the amount of cash held to the minimum necessary to conduct business. Sound working capital management requires an ample supply of cash so the firm can (1) take **trade discounts**, (2) maintain its credit rating, (3) take advantage of favourable business opportunities, and (4) meet emergencies.

□ The **transactions balance** is the cash necessary to conduct day-to-day business, whereas the **precautionary balance** is a cash reserve held to meet random, unforeseen needs. A **compensating balance** is a minimum chequing account balance that a bank requires as compensation either for services provided or as part of a loan agreement. Firms also hold **speculative balances**, which allow them to take advantage of bargain purchases. Note, though, that borrowing capacity and marketable securities reduce the need for both precautionary and speculative balances.

☐ A firm can lower its cash balances if it can **synchronize its cash outflows and inflows**.

☐ **Float** represents funds tied up in cheques that have been written but are still in process and not yet collected. *Mail float* is caused by the delay between the time that a cheque is placed in the mail and when it is received. It is equal to the dollar amount of funds associated with cheques written by the firm that have not yet been deducted from the firm's bank account. This is also called *disbursement float*. *Processing float* is caused by the delay within the firm between the time the cheque is received and deposited in the bank. It is equal to the dollar amounts of the cheques written to the firm but not yet deposited and available for use. This is also called *collection float*.

☐ Float can be reduced by the use of **pre-authorized payments**, which allow the company to automatically debit customers' accounts. This eliminates mail float and reduces processing float.

☐ Float is also reduced by the use of **electronic funds transfer**, which allows funds to be transferred electronically. The loss of float benefits the firm receiving the payment, but is a loss to the customer; both benefit by reduced clerical costs and improved reliability.

☐ Also, the use of **lock boxes** can speed collections and thus reduce a firm's required cash holdings.

☐ **Net float** is the difference between mail float and processing float. It is equal to the difference between the balance in a firm's chequebook and the balance on the bank's records. The larger the net float, the smaller the cash balances the firm must maintain, so a positive net float is good for the firm.

☐ Firms can reduce their cash balances by holding **marketable securities**, which are securities that can be sold on short notice at close to their quoted market values. Marketable securities serve both as a substitute for cash and as a temporary investment for funds that will be needed in the near future. Safety is the primary consideration when treasurers select marketable securities.

☐ The **Baumol model** is an economic model used to help determine the optimal cash balance. This model balances the opportunity cost of holding cash against the transactions costs associated with replenishing the cash account either by selling off marketable securities or by borrowing. The equation for determining the optimal cash transfer, C*, is

$$C^* = \sqrt{\frac{2(F)(T)}{k}}.$$

☐ The **Miller-Orr model** is an extension of the Baumol model and uses the inventory approach incorporating ordering and holding costs and uncertainty in the changes in the daily cash balance due to unpredictable transactions. The model determines the upper and lower limits of the cash balance, the reorder points, and the return point.

Questions

10-1 Would you expect a firm with a high growth rate to hold more or fewer precautionary and speculative cash balances than a firm with a low growth rate? Explain.

- I would expect a firm in high growth rate to hold more pr. + sp. cash b. b/c they are growing and have more unpredictable unforseen expenditures than a firm with low growth rate. They are more stable and less surprises

[handwritten note in margin: When it's upward sloping b/c you get a better yield]

10-2 Would a corporate treasurer be more tempted to invest the firm's liquidity portfolio in long-term as opposed to short-term securities when the yield curve was upward sloping or downward sloping?

10-3 Discuss the differences between default risk and interest rate risk. Which has the greater effect on the selection of marketable securities?

10-4 Explain the possible effects on a firm's cash balance of each of the following factors (other things held constant):
   a. The general level of interest rates rises. *—devalues it.*
   b. The cost of trading in marketable securities falls.
   c. The firm improves sales forecasts through the use of a more accurate forecasting technique.
   d. The firm's research department develops a new product with great market potential.
   e. The firm institutes a new billing procedure that better synchronizes its cash inflows and outflows.

10-5 What are the principal reasons for holding cash? Can a firm estimate its target cash balance by summing the cash held to satisfy each cash need?

10-6 What does the term *liquidity* mean? Would liquidity or the rate of return be more important to a firm that held a portfolio of marketable securities as a precautionary balance against the possibility of losing a major lawsuit? Explain.

10-7 Discuss the variables in the Miller-Orr cash model that are important in determining the spread between the upper and lower cash balance limits.

10-8 Firm A's management is very conservative, whereas Firm B's is more aggressive. Is it true that, other things the same, Firm B would probably have larger holdings or marketable securities? Explain.

10-9 When selecting securities for portfolio investments, corporate treasurers must trade off risk and expected returns. Is it true that most treasurers are willing to assume a fairly high exposure to risk to gain higher expected returns?

Self-Test Problems   (solutions appear on page 329)

ST-1 **Key terms.** Define each of the following terms:
   a. Transactions balance; compensating balance; precautionary balance; speculative balance
   b. Trade discounts
   c. Synchronized cash flows
   d. Float; net float; overdraft system
   e. Marketable securities; near-cash assets
   f. Default risk; interest rate risk; purchasing power risk; liquidity (marketability) risk

    g. Baumol model

    h. Miller-Orr model

ST-2   **Optimal cash transfer.** Warrior Industries projects that it will have cash outlays of $3 750 000 that occur uniformly throughout the forthcoming year. Warrior plans to meet these demands for cash by periodically selling marketable securities from its portfolio. The firm's marketable securities are invested to earn 12 percent, and the cost per transaction of converting funds to cash is $40.

    a. Use the Baumol model to determine the optimal transaction size for transfer from marketable securities to cash.

    b. What will be Warrior's average cash balance?

    c. How many transfers per year will be required?

Problems

10-1   **Cash Discounts.** Rutherford Associates is short on cash and is attempting to determine whether it would be advantageous for the firm to forego the discount on this month's purchases or to borrow funds to take advantage of the discount. The discount terms are 1/10, net 30.

    a. What is the maximum annual interest rate that Rutherford Associates should pay on borrowed funds? Why?

    b. What are some of the intangible disadvantages associated with foregoing the discount?

10-2   **Optimal Cash Transfer.** Oren Miller, the new treasurer of the Melody Novelty Company, is having a difficult time forecasting the firm's cash balance levels. A detailed study of daily cash balances over the past 3 years reveals apparently random fluctuations in the level of cash, precluding use of the inventory method of cash management. Miller decides to apply the Miller-Orr model to his situation in order to make transfers from marketable securities to cash and vice versa as automatic as possible.

    The standard deviation, σ, of daily net cash flows is $600. The interest rate on marketable securities is 10 percent, and the cost per transaction is $75. A clause in Melody Novelty's loan agreement with its bank requires a minimum compensating balance of $40 000.

    a. What is the cash return point?

    b. What are the upper and lower limits for the cash balance?

    c. In what lot sizes will marketable securities be purchased and sold?

10-3   **Optimal Cash Transfer.** Using the Miller-Orr model, find the level of cash at which a firm will buy and sell marketable securities and the sizes of the transactions. Assume that loan requirements necessitate a minimum bank balance of $30 000, order costs are $60 per transaction, the annual rate of interest is 20 percent, and the daily transactions variance in the cash account is $80 million.

10-4   **Optimal Cash Transfer.** Maury Industries Ltd. projects that cash outlays of $4.5 million will occur uniformly throughout the year. Maury plans to meet its cash requirements by periodically selling marketable securities from its portfolio. The firm's marketable securities are invested to earn 12 percent, and the cost per transaction of converting securities to cash is $27.

a. Use the Baumol model to determine the optimal transaction size for transfers from marketable securities to cash.

b. What will be Maury's average cash balance?

c. How many transfers per year will be required?

d. What will be Maury's total annual cost of maintaining cash balances? What would the total cost be if the company maintained an average cash balance of $50 000 or of $0 (it deposits funds daily to meet cash requirements)?

Integrative Problem

10-5 Cash and Marketable Securities Management.   Ray Smith, a retired librarian, recently opened a sports shop called Ray's Camping & Fishing Gear, Unlimited. Ray decided at the age of 62 that he wasn't quite ready to stay at home, living the life of leisure. It had always been a dream of his to open an outdoor sports shop, so his friends convinced him to go ahead. Because Ray's educational background was in literature and not in business, he has hired you, a finance expert, to help him with the store's cash management. Ray is very eager to learn, so he asked you to develop a set of questions to help him understand cash management. Now answer the following questions:

a. What is the goal of cash management?

b. For what reasons do firms hold cash?

c. What is meant by the terms *precautionary* and *speculative balances*?

d. What are some specific advantages for a firm's holding adequate cash balances?

e. How can a firm synchronize its cash flows? What good does this do?

f. How can a firm speed up collections and slow down disbursements?

g. Define *compensating balance* and *overdraft system*. Explain how each is used.

h. Why would a firm hold marketable securities?

i. What criteria should a firm use in building its marketable securities portfolio? What are some securities that should and should not be held?

j. What is the Baumol model, and what are its major assumptions? How might the firm use the Baumol model? Assume that Ray's opportunity cost of holding cash is 9.5 percent, the fixed cost of obtaining a loan is $75, and the total amount of cash needed for transactions during the year is $200 000. What is the optimal cash balance, and what is the total cost associated with the average cash balance? If Ray tries to use the Baumol model to determine his cash balances, what could go wrong? Should Ray hold a safety stock of cash?

Solutions to Self-Test Problems

ST-1   Refer to the appropriate sections of the text to check your responses.

ST-2   a.

$$C^* = \sqrt{\frac{2(F)(T)}{k}}.$$

$F = \$40.$
$T = \$3\,750\,000.$
$k = 12\%.$

$$C^* = \sqrt{\frac{2(40)(3\,750\,000)}{0.12}} = \$50\,000.$$

b.   Average cash balance = $\$50\,000/2 = \$25\,000$.

c.   Transfers per year = $\$3\,750\,000/\$50\,000 = 75$, or nearly every 5 days.

11

▲▲

Short-Term Financing

A Managerial Perspective

Companies have a variety of short-term financing instruments available, including trade credit, loans from financial institutions, accruals, banker's acceptances, and commercial paper. The availability of each source depends upon the company's size, risk, and profitability. The costs of short-term financing differ among the sources used and among funds obtained through the capital markets. Large companies may employ an individual with responsibility to ensure that short-term capital is being obtained at the best rate, but small companies do not. Thus the latter firms may borrow at rates that are greater than those used by the competition or use inappropriate borrowing instruments. After reading this chapter, you should be able to help such companies, or at least ensure that your firm is not one of them.

To this point in the text, we have considered the decisions the financial manager must make concerning alternative asset financing policies. We also showed that debt maturities can affect both risk and expected returns; although short-term debt is generally riskier to the firm than long-term debt, it is also generally less expensive, and it may be obtained faster and under more flexible terms. The primary purpose of this chapter is to examine the different types of short-term credit that are available to the financial manager. We also examine the issues the financial manager considers when selecting among the various types of short-term credit.

Short-term credit is defined as any liability originally scheduled for payment within one year. The major sources of short-term credit are (1) accrued wages and taxes, (2) trade credit among firms, (3) bank loans, (4) commercial paper, and (5) banker's acceptances. The first two sources are referred to as *spontaneous sources of funds* because they arise in the course of doing business. The last three sources are *nonspontaneous* because they are not generated by the operations of the firm.

Accruals

Firms generally pay employees on a weekly, biweekly, or monthly basis, so the balance sheet will typically show some accrued wages. Similarly, it will show accrued taxes, because firms' estimated income taxes, taxes withheld from employee payrolls, and sales taxes collected are generally paid on a weekly, monthly, or quarterly basis. These **accruals** increase spontaneously as a firm's operations expand. Accruals also represent a "free" source of credit since no explicit interest need be paid on these funds. However, a firm cannot ordinarily control its accruals; the timing of wage payments is set by economic forces and by industry custom, and tax payment dates are established by law. Thus, firms use all the accruals they can, but they have little control over the level of these accounts.

Concept Review

▶ Define short-term credit.

▶ What are the five major sources of short-term credit?

▶ Why are accruals considered "free" debt?

Accounts Payable, or Trade Credit

In the ordinary course of events, a firm buys its supplies and materials on credit from other firms, recording the debt as an *account payable*. *Accounts payable*, or **trade credit**, as it is commonly called, is the largest single category of short-term debt. It represents about 40 percent of the current liabilities of nonfinancial corporations. This percentage is somewhat larger for smaller firms; since small companies may not qualify for financing from other sources, they rely especially heavily on trade credit.

   Trade credit is a spontaneous source of financing in that it arises from ordinary business transactions. For example, suppose a firm makes average purchases of $2000 per day on terms of "net 30" which means that it must pay for goods 30 days after the invoice date. On average it will owe 30 times $2000, or $60 000, to its suppliers. If its sales, and consequently its purchases, double, accounts payable will also double to $120 000. Just by growing, the firm will have spontaneously generated an additional $60 000 of financing. Similarly, if the terms of credit are extended from 30 to 40 days, accounts payable will expand from $60 000 to $80 000; thus, lengthening the credit period also generates additional financing. To the extent that firms can *stretch* the credit period, they can increase the financing generated through accounts payable. The stretching can be accomplished by paying after the due date; for example, with credit terms of net 30, if the firm pays in 35 days, it has increased its financing through accounts payable. Of course, one firm's accounts payable is another's accounts receivable, and the latter company exerts pressure to prevent this stretching phenomenon.

The Cost of Trade Credit

As we saw in Chapter 9, firms that sell on credit have a *credit policy* that includes certain *credit terms*. For example, Porter Electronics sells on terms of "2/10, net 30," meaning it gives a 2 percent discount if payment is made within 10 days of the invoice date but the full invoice amount is due and payable within 30 days if the discount is not taken.

   Suppose Rourke Computers, Ltd., buys an average of $12 million of electronic components from Porter each year, minus a 2 percent discount, for net purchases of $11 760 000/365 = $32 219.18 per day. For simplicity, suppose Porter is Rourke's only supplier. If Rourke takes the discount, paying at the end of the tenth day, its payables will average (10)($32 219.18) = $322 192, so it will on average be receiving $322 192 of credit from its only supplier, Porter Electronics.

Now suppose Rourke decides *not* to take the discount—what happens? First, Rourke begins paying invoices after 30 days, so its accounts payable increases to (30)($32 219.18) = $966 575.[1] Porter Electronics is now supplying Rourke with an *additional* $966 575 − $322 192 = $644 383 of credit. Rourke can use this additional credit to pay off bank loans, to expand inventories, to increase fixed assets, to build up its cash account, or even to increase its own accounts receivable.

Rourke's new credit from Porter Electronics has a cost. Because Rourke is foregoing a 2 percent discount on its $12 million of gross purchases, its costs rise by $240 000 per year. Dividing this $240 000 by the additional credit, we find the implicit cost of the added trade credit as follows:

$$\text{Approximate percentage cost} = \frac{\$240\,000}{\$644\,383} = 0.372 = 37.2\%.$$

Assuming that Rourke can borrow from its bank (or from other sources) at an interest rate of less than 37.2 percent, it should not borrow the additional $644 383 by foregoing discounts.

The following equation can be used to calculate the approximate percentage cost, on an annual basis, of not taking discounts:

$$\begin{array}{c} \text{Approximate} \\ \text{percentage} \\ \text{cost} \end{array} = \frac{\text{Discount percentage}}{100 - \begin{array}{c} \text{Discount} \\ \text{percentage} \end{array}} \times \frac{365}{\begin{array}{c} \text{Days credit is} \\ \text{outstanding} \end{array} - \begin{array}{c} \text{Discount} \\ \text{period} \end{array}}. \qquad \textbf{(11-1)}$$

The numerator of the first term, the discount percentage, is the cost per dollar of credit, while the denominator (100 − discount percentage) represents the funds made available by not taking the discount. The second term shows how many times each year this cost is incurred. To illustrate the equation, the approximate cost of not taking a discount when the terms are 2/10, net 30 is computed as follows:[2]

---

[1]A question arises here: if a company does not plan to take discounts, should its accounts payable reflect gross purchases or purchases net of discounts? Although generally accepted accounting practices permit either treatment, most accountants prefer recording both inventories and payables net of discounts and then reporting the higher payments that result from not taking discounts as an additional expense, called "discounts lost." In this book, therefore, we show accounts payable *net* of discounts even when the company does not expect to take the discount.

[2]In terms of effective annual interest, the rate is even higher. In the case of trade discounts, the discount amounts to interest, and with terms of 2/10, net 30, the firm gains use of the funds for 30 − 10 = 20 days, so there are 365/20 = 18.25 "interest periods" per year. The first term in the equation is (Discount percentage)/(100 − Discount percentage) = 0.02/0.98 = 0.0204 = 2.04%. This "interest rate" is the periodic rate that is "paid" 18.25 times each year. Therefore, the effective annual rate cost of trade credit is

$$\text{Effective rate} = (1.0204)^{18.25} - 1.0 = 1.446 - 1.0 = 44.6\%.$$

Thus, the 37.2 percent cost calculated by the approximation formula, Equation 11-1, understates the true cost of trade credit. Equation 11-1 would be correct if the full cost of the discounts was incurred at the end of the year, but in actuality these costs are incurred all during the year. This point will be discussed in Chapter 12.

$$\text{Approximate percentage cost} = \frac{2}{98} \times \frac{365}{20}$$
$$= 0.0204(18.25)$$
$$= 0.372 = 37.2\%.$$

Notice, however, that the cost of trade credit is reduced by paying late. Thus, if Rourke can get away with paying in 60 days rather than in the specified 30, the effective credit period becomes $60 - 10 = 50$ days, and the approximate cost drops from 37.2 percent to $(2/98)(365/50) = 14.9\%$. If their suppliers have excess capacity, firms may be able to get away with late payments, but this is an unethical practice, and it will lead to a variety of problems associated with stretching accounts payable and being branded a slow-paying account. These problems are discussed later in the chapter.

The cost of the additional trade credit obtained by not taking discounts can be worked out for other purchase terms. Some illustrative costs are as follows:

Credit Terms	Approximate Cost
1/10, net 30	18%
1/10, net 20	37
2/10, net 30	37
2/10, net 20	74

As these figures show, the cost of not taking discounts can be substantial. Incidentally, throughout the chapter we assume that payments are made either on the *last day for taking discounts* or on the *last day of the credit period*. It would be foolish to pay, say, on the fifth or twentieth day if the credit terms were 2/10, net 30.

Effects of Trade Credit on the Financial Statements

A firm's policy with regard to taking or not taking discounts can have a significant effect on its financial statements. To illustrate, let us assume that Rourke Computers is just beginning its operations. On the first day, it makes net purchases of $32 219.18; this amount is recorded on its balance sheet under accounts payable.[3] The second day it buys another $32 219.18 of goods. The first day's purchases are not yet paid for, so at the end of the second day, accounts payable total $64 438.36. Accounts payable continue to increase and after 10 days they are up to $322 191.80.

If Rourke takes discounts, then on Day 11 it will have to pay for the $32 219.18 of purchases made on the first day, which will reduce accounts payable. However, it will buy another $32 219.18 of goods, which will increase payables. Thus, after the tenth day of operations, Rourke's balance sheet will level off, showing a balance of $322 191.80 in accounts payable, assuming it pays consistently on the tenth day in order to take discounts.

Now suppose Rourke decides not to take discounts. In this case, on Day 11 it will add another $32 219.18 to payables, but it will not pay for the purchases made on the first day. Thus, the balance sheet figure for accounts payable will rise to $(11)(\$32\,219.18) = \$354\,410.98$. This buildup will continue through Day

---

[3]Inventories also increase by $32 219.18, but we are not now concerned with this account.

30, at which point payables will total (30)($32 219.18) = $966 575. On Day 31, Rourke will buy another $32 219.18 of goods, thus increasing accounts payable, but it will also pay for the purchases made on Day 1, which will reduce payables. Thus, the balance sheet item "accounts payable" will stabilize at $966 575 after 30 days, assuming Rourke does not take discounts.

Part I of Table 11-1 shows Rourke's balance sheets after it reaches a steady state under the two trade credit policies. Total assets are unchanged by this policy decision, and we assume that accruals and the common equity account are also unchanged. The differences show up in accounts payable and notes payable. If Rourke elects to take discounts and thus gives up some of the trade credit it otherwise could have obtained, it has to raise $644 383 from some other source. It could sell more common equity or used long-term bonds, but we assume that it chooses to use bank credit, which has a 10 percent cost and is reflected in the notes payable account.

Part II of Table 11-1 shows Rourke's income statements under the two policies. If the company does not take discounts, its interest expense is zero, but it has a $240 000 expense for discounts lost. On the other hand, if it does take discounts, it incurs an interest expense of $64 438, but it avoids the cost of discounts lost. Because the discounts lost exceed the interest expense, the

Table 11-1
Rourke Computers' Financial Statements with
Different Trade Credit Policies

	Does Not Take Discounts; Uses Maxiumum Trade Credit	Takes Discounts; Borrows from Bank	Difference
I. Balance Sheets			
Cash	$ 486 575	$ 486 575	$ 0
Receivables	1 000 000	1 000 000	0
Inventories	2 000 000	2 000 000	0
Fixed Assets	2 980 000	2 980 000	0
Total Assets	$ 6 466 575	$ 6 466 575	0
Accounts payable	$ 966 575	$ 322 192	$ + 644 383
Notes payable	0	644 383	− 644 383
Accruals	500 000	500 000	0
Common equity	5 000 000	5 000 000	0
Total liabilities and equity	$ 6 466 575	$ 6 466 575	$ 0
II. Income Statements			
Sales	$15 000 000	$15 000 000	$ 0
Less: Purchases	11 760 000	11 760 000	0
Labour	2 000 000	2 000 000	0
Interest	0	64 438	− 64 438
Discounts lost	240 000	0	+ 240 000
Net income before tax	$ 1 000 000	$ 1 175 562	$ + 1 175 562
Taxes (40%)	400 000	470 225	+ 470 225
Net income	$ 600 000	$ 705 337	$ + 705 337

take-discounts policy results in a higher net income and thus in a higher share price.

Components of Trade Credit: Free versus Costly

On the basis of the preceding discussion, trade credit can be divided into two components: (1) *free trade credit*, which involves credit received during the discount period and which for Rourke amounts to 10 days' net purchases, or $322 192; and (2) *costly trade credit*, which involves credit in excess of the free credit and whose cost is the discounts lost. Rourke can obtain $644 383, or 20 days' net purchases, of nonfree trade credit at a cost of approximately 37 percent. Financial managers should always use the free component, but they should use the costly component only after analyzing the cost of this capital and determining that it is less than the cost of funds that could be obtained from other sources. Under the terms of trade found in most industries, the costly component will involve a relatively high percentage cost, so stronger firms will avoid using it.

Firms sometimes can and do deviate from the stated credit terms, thus altering the percentage cost figures just cited. To illustrate, a firm that buys on terms of 2/10, net 30 may pay in 15 days (rather than 10) and still take discounts. Its treasurer simply waits until 15 days after receipt of the goods to pay and then writes a cheque for the invoice amount less the 2 percent discount. The company's suppliers want its business, so they may tolerate this practice. As noted earlier, a firm that buys on terms of 2/10, net 30 may forego discounts, but it may pay in 60 rather than in 30 days, thus stretching its trade credit. Neither of these firms is "loved" by its suppliers, and neither could continue these practices in times when suppliers were operating at full capacity and had order backlogs. Provided such behaviour is not a common practice in the industry, both firms have bad reputations in their industries, and both will have a hard time getting deliveries when their suppliers are operating at full capacity.

Concept of "Net Credit"

Trade credit has a double-edged significance for the firm. It is a source of credit for financing purchases, and it is a use of funds to the extent that the firm finances credit sales to customers. For example, if, on the average, a firm sells $3000 of goods per day and has 40 days sales outstanding, it will have accounts receivable of approximately $120 000 at any given time. If the same firm buys $2000 worth of materials per day and the balance is outstanding for 20 days, accounts payable will average $40 000. The firm is extending net credit for $80 000, the difference between accounts receivable and accounts payable.

Large, well-financed firms tend to be net suppliers of trade credit; small firms and undercapitalized firms of all sizes tend to be net users of trade credit. Note, though, that whether a firm is a net supplier or a net user of trade credit is not a policy decision per se; rather, the firm's position is the result of its decisions with regard to granting credit and using available trade credit.

Importance of Trade Credit as a Source of Financing

Trade credit is an important and convenient source of financing, especially for weaker and smaller firms. A company that fails to qualify for bank financing may receive trade credit because previous experience has familiarized the seller with the creditworthiness of its customer. Because the seller knows the merchandising practices of the industry, it is usually in a good position to judge the capacity of its customer to pay and the risk of selling to the customer on credit. The amount of trade credit fluctuates with the buyer's purchases, subject to any credit limits that may be operative. Although trade credit may be the only alternative available to the buyer, some buyers that could obtain funds elsewhere use costly trade credit because they do not realize how expensive it is. In such circumstances, careful financial analysis may lead to the substitution of alternative forms of financing.

Trade credit may represent a virtual subsidy or a sales promotion device on the part of the seller. The authors know, for example, of instances in which manufacturers quite literally supplied *all* the financing for new firms by selling on credit terms substantially longer than those of the new company. In such instances, however, the buying firm must be careful that it is not really paying a hidden financing cost in the form of higher product prices than could be obtained elsewhere. Extending credit involves a cost to the selling firm, and this firm may well be raising its own prices to offset the "free" credit it extends.

Concept Review

► Give the equation used to calculate the approximate percentage cost, on an annual basis, of not taking discounts.
► Briefly explain the difference between free trade credit and costly trade credit.
► What is meant by the term "net credit"?

Short-Term Bank Financing

Commercial banks, whose loans appear on firms' balance sheets as notes payable,[4] are second in importance to trade credit as a source of short-term financing. Banks occupy a pivotal position in the short-term and intermediate-term money markets. Their influence is greater than is apparent from the dollar amounts they lend because the banks provide nonspontaneous funds. As the financing needs of the firm increase, it requests its bank to provide the additional funds. If the request is denied, either because the firm does not meet the bank's credit standards or because credit conditions are tight, the firm will be forced to slow down its rate of growth or to cut back operations.

Bank Loan Characteristics

In the following paragraphs, the main features of commercial bank loans are described briefly. The various types of interest charged by banks are presented in the next section.

---

[4]This item may appear on the firm's balance sheet as "due to bank."

A bank loan is either a self-liquidating loan, such as the financing of a seasonal buildup in inventory, or a loan needed for working capital; the latter loan must be repaid out of profits. A loan has the following characteristics: the interest rate is set at the *prime rate*, which is the rate of interest given to the bank's prime risks, plus an additional amount that reflects the risk of the particular company. Because the prime rate can fluctuate over time, the interest rates charged on loans are also flexible.

Forms of Loans.   Banks provide two basic types of short-term commercial loans: (1) operating loans and (2) bridge loans.

1. *Operating loans.*   Most businesses negotiate an operating loan—also referred to as a **revolving line of credit**, an *operating line of credit*, or more loosely a *line of credit*—for a period of 1 year. The negotiations occur shortly after the firm has received its year-end financial statements and has prepared a business plan for the next fiscal year. The loan arrangement —also called *facilities*—specifies a maximum amount that can be borrowed, and the borrower can use up the maximum without further reference to the bank provided certain conditions are met. These conditions are intended to limit the bank's risk if the financial health of the firm deteriorates over the term of the loan. The firm must supply monthly financial statements, an aging schedule for receivables, and statements of inventory. There is a limit on the amount of loans outstanding to a maximum of 75 percent of the good receivables and 50 percent of the inventories.[5] (This last restriction is referred to as "margining.") The loan balances fluctuate up to the maximum according to the borrower's need. The loan balances are also expected to fluctuate down to zero at some points during the year—hence the term "revolving." They are normally secured by inventory and receivables—hence the margin requirement.

   Most operating loans are **demand facilities**: that is, the bank can demand repaying at any time, provided "reasonable" time is given for the repayment. Repayment can be demanded even though the borrower has met all the conditions described above. However, banks are very cautious about demanding payment since they do not want to precipitate a failure of the company.

2. *Bridge loans.*   A **bridge loan** permits the use of funds from some source such as the sale of an asset, a bond issue, or a share issue before they are actually received. The loan "bridges" the period during which the funds are needed to be used and when they are received. The loan is normally outstanding for a very short term. Bridge loans are also called *interim financing.*

---

[5]Changes to the *Bankruptcy Act,* in effect since the beginning of December 1992, permit unpaid suppliers to reclaim goods if they were shipped within the 30 days prior to the buyer's declaring bankruptcy or going into receivership. Since this would reduce the stock of assets available for the bank to recover their loans, some banks reduced the amounts they were prepared to lend on the basis of inventories, even before the new act went into effect. To maintain the same line of credit, firms are being required to find additional collateral. Retailers are most seriously affected by this new provision since inventory is their main asset.

Commercial loans with maturities of more than a year are called **term loans** or *term facilities*. This type of loan is used to finance permanent working capital or acquisition of fixed assets. Unlike the case with a demand facility, repayment can be requested only if the borrower has not met some of the terms or conditions of the loan (called *covenants*) or at the review date of the loan.

Unconfirmed Line of Credit.   An **unconfirmed line of credit** is a formal understanding between the bank and the borrower concerning the maximum loan balance the bank will extend the borrower. These facilities are rare for small and mid-sized borrowers but are used mainly by larger firms or multinational companies, which have other credit facilities on which they can rely if necessary. Small and mid-sized companies use the operating loan (which is also, somewhat confusingly, referred to as a line of credit).

Under an unconfirmed line of credit, a bank loan officer may indicate to a financial manager that the bank regards the firm as "good" for up to $80 000 for the coming year. Subsequently, the manager signs a promissory note for $15 000 for 90 days—this is said to be "taking down" $15 000 of the total line of credit. This amount is credited to the firm's chequing account at the bank. Before repayment of the $15 000, the firm may borrow additional amounts up to a total outstanding at any one time of $80 000. There is no legal requirement for the bank to extend credit up to the maximum; however, each time the firm wants to draw down additional amounts, the bank must agree to extend the additional credit. This protects the bank from being forced to extend credit to the firm even if there has been a deterioration in the profitability of the firm. Interest is charged only on the amount of credit actually being used by the firm. If the firm has surplus cash, it can pay down the loan, which will both reduce its interest expense and increase its available credit.

Promissory Note.   When a bank loan is approved, the agreement is executed by signing a **promissory note**. The note specifies: (1) the amount borrowed; (2) the percentage interest rate; (3) the repayment schedule, which can involve either a lump sum or a series of installments; (4) any collateral that might be put up as security for the loan; and (5) any other terms and conditions to which the bank and the borrower have agreed.

When the note is signed, the bank credits the borrower's chequing account with the amount of the loan, so on the borrower's balance sheet, both the cash and the notes payable accounts increase.

Other Bank Fees.   Banks can levy additional fees for loans, which increase their return without increasing the stated interest rate. One such fee is called a **commitment fee**, and its size is independent of the amount of credit used. The commitment fee is set at one-half to three-quarters of 1 percent (that is, 50 to 75 *basis points*) and is compensation to the bank for its obligation to extend credit.

Another fee is a **standby fee**; it is not a common feature for other than very large (committed) operating lines of credit.[6] This fee is levied as a percentage of the unused portion of the credit. It is not levied on the unconfirmed line of

---

[6]A standby fee is more likely to be charged on a long-term credit facility because such a commitment is considered as a liability by regulators and, as such, has a capital requirement and an opportunity cost under regulatory guidelines.

credit since the bank has not guaranteed that the firm will obtain extra credit up to the maximum limit.

As an illustration: Evans Tile and Flooring has negotiated a revolving credit arrangement for $10 million for 2 years. The commitment fee is equal to $50 000, which is one-half of 1 percent on the total line of credit. In addition, a standby fee of one-quarter of 1 percent on the unused balance of the committed funds is charged. Of course, interest also has to be paid on the amount of money that Evans actually borrows. If $5 000 000 of the credit were taken down, the unused portion would be $5 000 000 and the standby fee would be $12 500 = 0.0025 × $5 000 000. For this credit arrangement, Evans paid interest of prime plus 2 percent.

Size of Customers.   Banks make loans to firms of all sizes. By dollar amount, the bulk of loans made by commercial banks is obtained by firms with total assets of $5 million and more. But by number of loans, firms with total assets of $100 000 or less account for more than 50 percent of bank loans.

Maturity.   Commercial banks concentrate on the short-term lending market, with the bulk of their loans, measured either by dollar volume or number of loans, in this maturity category. Loans with maturities longer than 1 year have not been very important in the past. Recently, the chartered banks have been providing these loans, however, to meet competitive pressures.

Security.   Almost all the short-term loans provided by the Canadian banking system are secured. The forms of security that are described later in this chapter relate to accounts receivable and inventories.

Compensating Balances.   On large accounts, banks typically require that a regular borrower maintain an average chequing account balance equal to approximately 10 percent of the monthly usage. These balances, which are called *compensating balances* and were described in Chapter 10, are a method of raising the effective interest rate on a loan. For example, if a firm raises $90 000 as a loan but must maintain a 10 percent compensating balance, it must borrow $100 000 to obtain the required $90 000. If the stated interest rate is 15.0 percent, the effective interest cost is actually 16.7 percent—the $15 000 annual interest cost divided by the amount of the loan, $90 000. Compensating balances are less common that they once were and are now rare in the market serving small and middle-size firms.

Cost of Bank Loans

The cost of a bank loan (including lines of credit and revolving credit) depends upon the riskiness of the borrower, the size of the loan (because of the fixed costs of making and servicing loans), the level of interest rates in the economy, and the maturity of the loan. The **prime rate** is the rate charged to the bank's most creditworthy customers on short-term loans.[7] The prime rate has ranged

---

[7]At times, banks will lend to their largest customers at rates below the published prime rate. Therefore, the prime rate is no longer the "true" rate a bank charges its strongest customers, although it is still described as such.

in recent years from 20.00 percent in 1981 to 5.75 percent on November 1, 1993. For loans to large, stable companies, the banks will charge the prime rate. A firm that does not qualify as a "prime risk" may be charged a rate of interest from a quarter to 1 percentage point up to 3 or more percentage points above the prime rate in gradations of 25 basis points.[8] The increment above the prime rate will reflect the risk of the loan; the upper end of the range is rarely used because banks prefer not to lend to very risky companies. There is little variation in the stated rates on unsecured loans as companies whose operations are risky do not obtain unsecured loans—the loans are either secured or the companies borrow from nonbank financial intermediaries.

The effective cost of unsecured loans is very difficult to calculate. The bank has a number of variables that it can manipulate to influence the true interest cost. For example, charging commitment fees and standby fees and requiring compensating balances can be used to alter the effective cost of a loan. Thus, a company may obtain a loan at prime, but the effective cost can be above prime when all of the other fees are considered.

Interest rates on bank loans are calculated in three ways: as simple interest, as discount interest, and as installment loan interest. These three methods are explained next.

Regular, or Simple, Interest.   Determination of the effective, or true, rate of interest on a loan depends on both the stated rate of interest and the method of charging interest used by the lender. **Simple interest** is interest charged on the amount borrowed and is paid at the maturity of the loan. In this case, the nominal, or stated, rate of interest is also the effective rate of interest. For example, on a $20 000 loan for 1 year at 10 percent, the borrower repays principal of $20 000 and interest of $2000 at the maturity date:

$$\text{Effective rate}_{\text{simple}} = \frac{\text{Interest}}{\text{Borrowed amount}}$$
$$= \frac{\$2000}{\$20\,000} = 10\%.$$

If the loan had been written for less than a year—say, for 91 days—then the interest charge would be calculated as follows (using a 365-day year):

$$\text{Interest charge} = (\text{Interest rate per day})(\text{Number of days})(\text{Amount borrowed})$$
$$= \left(\frac{\text{Annual rate}}{365}\right)(91)(\$20\,000)$$
$$= \left(\frac{0.10}{365}\right)(91)(\$20\,000)$$
$$= \$499.$$

If this loan was then "rolled over" 4 times—365 days divided by the 91 day maturity of the loan—the total interest paid would be (4)($499) = $1996,

<hr>

[8]The commercial loan business has become very competitive, and companies are very sensitive to interest rates charged. The banks have been known to quote yields on their loans in one-eighths in order to meet competitive yields from other lending sources.

which is approximately equal to the interest paid on the annual loan. However, with the 91-day loan, some of the interest would have to be paid every 91 days rather than at the end of the year. Thus, the effective cost to the borrower would be higher; to put the point another way, the bank is better off since it can get some funds earlier to reinvest.[9]

Discount Interest.   On a **discount interest** loan, the bank deducts the interest in advance. This is called *discounting* the loan, and it increases the effective rate of interest. For example, on the $20 000 loan for 1 year at 10 percent, the interest is $2000, and the borrower obtains the use of only $18 000.[10] The effective rate of interest is 11.1 percent versus 10 percent on the simple interest loan.[11]

$$\text{Effective rate}_{\text{discount}} = \frac{\text{Interest}}{\text{Borrowed amount} - \text{Interest}}$$
$$= \frac{\$2000}{\$18\,000} = 11.1\%.$$

---

[9]As you will see in Chapter 12, the effective or true rate of interest on this loan is equal to 10.38 percent. This is calculated as

$$\text{Effective rate}_{\text{simple}} = \left(1 + \frac{k_{\text{nom}}}{m}\right)^m - 10$$
$$= \left(1 + \frac{0.10}{4}\right)^4 - 1.0$$
$$= 0.1038 \text{ or } 10.38\%$$

where k_{NOM} is the nominal or stated rate of 10 percent and m is the number of times that the loan rolls over = 4.

[10]If the borrowing firm actually requires $20 000, it must borrow $22 222.22:

$$\text{Face value} = \frac{\text{Funds required}}{1.0 - \text{Nominal rate}}$$
$$= \frac{\$20\,000}{1.0 - 0.10} = \frac{\$20\,000}{0.9}$$
$$= \$22\,222.22.$$

The borrower signs a note for $22 222.22 but receives only $22 222.22 − 0.10($22 222.22) = $20 000. Increasing the face value of the loan does not change the effective rate of 11.1 percent on the $20 000 of usable funds.

[11]If the term of the loan is for 3 months, rather than for a year, the effective annualized interest rate is calculated as follows:

$$\text{Effective rate}_{\text{discount}} = \left[\frac{\text{Annualized interest}/4}{\text{Borrowed amount} - (\text{Interest}/4)} + 1\right]^4 - 1$$
$$= \left(\frac{\$500}{\$20\,000 - \$500} + 1\right)^4 - 1$$
$$= (1.0256)^4 - 1 = 0.107 = 10.7\%.$$

Note that the annualized interest rate is less for discounted loans with shorter maturities than for those with longer maturities because the firm, on average, obtains use of a larger amount of money. In this case, the firm has use of $19 500, rather than $18 000, by borrowing on a quarterly basis.

Alternatively,

$$\text{Effective rate}_{\text{discount}} = \frac{\text{Nominal interest rate}}{1.0 - \text{Nominal interest rate}}$$
$$= \frac{0.10}{1 - 0.10} = \frac{0.10}{0.90} = 11.1\%.$$

Discount interest is not common now on bank loans; however, it is used for some financial instruments such as banker's acceptances (BAs), which are sold at a discount to face value. (BAs are considered in a subsequent section of this chapter.)

Installment Loan Interest.   The effective rate of interest is even higher if the loan is repaid in 12 monthly installments but the interest is calculated on the original balance. With such a loan, which is called an **installment loan**, the borrower has the full amount of the money only during the first month and by the last month has already repaid eleven-twelfths of the loan. Thus, the borrower of $20 000 receives $20 000 and pays $2000 for the use of about half the amount received because the *average* amount outstanding during the year is $10 000. If interest is paid at maturity, the approximate effective rate on an installment loan is calculated as follows:

$$\text{Approximate effective rate}_{\text{installment loan}} = \frac{\$2000}{\$10\,000} = 20\%.$$

Under the discounting method, the effective cost of the installment loan is more than 22 percent:

$$\text{Approximate effective rate}_{\text{discounted installment loan}} = \frac{\$2000}{\$9000} = 22.2\%.$$

Here we see that interest is paid on the *original amount* of the loan, not on the amount actually outstanding (the declining balance). This causes the effective interest rate to be approximately double the stated rate. Interest is calculated by the installment method on most consumer loans (for example, automobile loans) but rarely on business loans larger than about $15 000.

Even though this method of calculating interest is used rarely for business loans, it is presented as an example of the impact the specific terms of the loan can have on its effective interest cost. Commitment fees and compensating balances have similar impacts.

Loans with Compensating Balances.   Compensating balances tend to raise the effective interest rates on loans in a manner similar to discount interest. The amount of funds that the firm must borrow, and pay interest on, is increased by the amount of the required compensating balance. To illustrate: suppose the bank offers to lend a firm $20 000 at a 10 percent simple interest rate but requires the firm to maintain a compensating balance equal to 20 percent of the amount of the loan.

Although the firm needs $20 000, it must borrow $20 000/(1 − 0.20) = $25 000. The interest paid will be 0.10($25 000) = $2500, but the firm will get the use of only $20 000. Therefore, the effective interest rate is

$$\text{Effective rate}_{\text{simple/CB}} = \frac{\text{Interest}}{\text{Borrowed amount}} = \frac{\$2500}{\$20\,000} = 12.5\%.$$

Alternatively,

$$\text{Effective rate}_{\text{simple/CB}} = \frac{\text{Nominal interest rate}}{1.0 - \text{Compensating balance fraction}}$$

$$= \frac{0.10}{1.0 - 0.20} = \frac{0.10}{0.80} = 0.125 = 12.50\%.$$

If both compensating balances and discounting are used, the rate is higher yet. The following formula can be used to determine the effective rate:

$$\text{Effective interest rate} = \frac{\text{Nominal interest rate}}{1.0 - \left(\begin{array}{c}\text{Compensating}\\\text{balance}\\\text{fraction}\end{array}\right) - \left(\begin{array}{c}\text{Nominal}\\\text{interest}\\\text{rate}\end{array}\right)}$$

$$= \frac{0.10}{1.0 - 0.20 - 0.10} = 14.3\%.$$

In this latter case, a firm that needed $20 000 would have to borrow

$$\frac{\$20\,000}{1.0 - 0.20 - 0.10} = \$28\,571.43.$$

It would pay 10 percent of this amount as interest, so its effective interest rate would be $2857.14/$20 000 = 14.3%, as we calculated above. The firm's balance sheet would, right after it borrowed the money, show a $20 000.00 increase in usable cash balances, $5714.29 of cash held for compensating balances, and $2857.14 as prepaid interest (an asset) for a total asset increase of $28 571.43. It would also show an offsetting increase of $28 571.43 in notes payable.

Concept Review

▶ Explain how a firm that expects to need funds during the coming year might be sure that the needed funds will be available, and discuss the cost of that assurance.

▶ Explain the difference between a regular, or simple, interest loan and a discount interest loan.

▶ Give the formula for approximating the effective rate for an installment loan.

▶ How does the formula for approximating the effective rate for a simple interest loan compare to that for a simple interest loan with compensating balances?

Commercial Paper

Commercial paper (CP) is the name given to the unsecured promissory notes of large, strong firms; they are sold primarily to other business firms, insurance companies, pension funds, money market mutual funds, and banks. Although the amounts of commercial paper outstanding are smaller than bank loans outstanding, this form of financing has grown rapidly in recent years. The major issuers of commercial paper are the sales finance and consumer loan companies; large nonfinancial corporations also make considerable use of this financing vehicle. From 1985 to the end of 1991, the total dollar amounts of commercial paper outstanding grew by 13.4 percent per annum. The growth was larger in the early period, slowed from 1988 to 1990, and actually was negative over 1991. However, the picture is somewhat different if we look separately at the two CP submarkets. For the sales finance and consumer loan paper segment, over the total period, there was a 7.4 percent per annum growth rate; for the period from 1989 to 1991, there was a negative 21.0 percent per annum growth. This falloff reflected the recession and its impact on demand for goods. In the nonfinancial category, the growth rate for the overall period was 15.5 percent; although the growth rate in every year was positive, it has been decreasing. For example, during 1988, the growth rate was 36.0 percent; this figure decreased steadily to 9.8 percent for 1991. This slowdown also reflects the recession and the increasing risk of the nonfinancial corporations. As at the end of December 1991, commercial paper outstanding for the sales finance and consumer loan segment was $6.2 billion and for the nonfinancial segment, $24 billion.

Commercial paper is traded in the money market by investment dealers, who purchase the paper at a discount and then sell it or hold it in inventory. The evolution of an active money market in which trading of a number of short-term negotiable notes takes place was an important condition for the existence of substantial activity in the commercial paper market.

Maturity and Cost

The maturities of commercial paper usually vary from 1 day to 1 year, but only a minimal amount is issued for more than 90 days. This may be due to corporate need. In addition, instead of using a fixed term to maturity, commercial paper can be issued on a demand basis.

The rates on prime commercial paper fluctuate with demand and supply. Their values are above the treasury bill rate and usually 25 to 125 basis points below the prime rate. For example, on October 16, 1992, the prime rate was 8.25 percent, the 91-day T-bill rate was 7.25 percent, and the 90-day commercial paper rate was 7.85 percent. Because compensating balances are not required for commercial paper, the effective cost differential from the prime rate is still wider.[12]

---

[12]This factor is offset to some extent by the fact that firms issuing commercial paper are generally required by investment dealers to have unused bank lines of credit to back up their outstanding commercial paper, and fees must be paid on these lines (often referred to as "standby" lines). Still, it is clear that the effective cost of commercial paper is far below the prime rate, and as a result (1) companies that are strong enough to use commercial paper are choosing it over bank loans at the prime rate, and (2) banks make loans to companies eligible to sell commercial paper at rates below prime.

Use of Commercial Paper

The use of commercial paper is restricted to a comparatively small number of concerns that are exceptionally good credit risks. A nonfinancial issuer uses the proceeds of the issue to finance short-term working capital needs. The paper is issued with a minimum denomination of $50 000, and interest is paid either at a stated rate or on a discount basis. Purchasers of commercial paper hold it in their temporary marketable securities portfolios as liquidity reserves, and for this purpose safety is a paramount concern.

A limitation of the commercial paper market is that the size of the funds available is limited to the excess liquidity that corporations—the main suppliers of funds—have at any particular time. Another disadvantage is that a company in temporary financial difficulty may receive little help. Commercial paper dealings are impersonal, and no weakness whatever is tolerated—a firm whose position deteriorates because of a strike or some other problem is simply cut off from the market. Banks are much more personal and much more likely to help a good customer weather a temporary storm. On the other hand, using commercial paper permits a corporation to tap a wide range of credit sources, including financial institutions outside its own area as well as industrial corporations across the country, and this can reduce interest costs.

Concept Review

▶ What types of firms use commercial paper?

▶ Why would commercial paper be purchased as an investment?

▶ List an advantage and a disadvantage of a firm's use of commercial paper.

Banker's Acceptances

In Canada, a **banker's acceptance (BA)** is a source of short-term funds, equivalent to commercial paper, that is issued by firms whose credit standing is not of the highest quality. The bank, by accepting the financial instrument, guarantees payment on it at the maturity date. The borrowing firm gets the funds from the bank, and the bank, in turn, sells the instrument on a discount basis to investors through its money market desk. The investor can hold the BA to maturity or sell it.[13] At maturity, the investor is paid by the bank, and the bank is paid by the issuing firm. The interest rate on the banker's acceptance should reflect the credit risk characteristics of the guaranteeing bank. Because a banker's acceptance is a loan or advance, the bank can request that the borrowing company provide the normal forms of security to ensure that there will be funds available in the company's account when the acceptance is presented for payment. In addition, the acceptance is considered as part of the line of credit used by the company. The growth rate for BAs over the period 1985 to 1991 was 14 percent per annum. Different parts of the period, however, displayed different patterns of growth. Up to 1988 the annual growth rates

---

[13]In some ways, a BA is like a negotiable, postdated, certified cheque. The bank, by guaranteeing payment, has certified that the BA (cheque) will be paid.

were very high. From that year on the growth rate fell; during 1991, it was a negative 15 percent. As at the end of 1991, there was $37 billion outstanding in banker's acceptances in Canada.

Maturity and Cost

Although the maximum maturity for a banker's acceptance is 180 days, the usual maturity is 30 to 90 days.[14] These bills are issued in multiples of $100 000, and a commission, called an *acceptance fee* or a *stamping fee*, is charged the customer. The fee arrangements vary among banks. For example, the Royal Bank of Canada has a prime-based stamping fee, which was 1 percent in October 1992. The spread over this prime acceptance fee matches the spread over the prime rate for the borrower and is based on the borrower's risk. Occasionally, for large, very good risks, the bank will stamp for an amount that is less than the prime acceptance fee. Companies that pay the low stamping fee are likely those that could issue commercial paper. The effective rate of interest is calculated as the sum of the costs of the issue (that is, the commission plus the discount on the sale to the investment dealer) divided by the proceeds obtained by the issuer from the investment dealer.

For example, suppose the acceptance fee on a $10 million issue is 50 basis points, so that the stamping fee is $50 000. If the interest rate on outstanding acceptances with 91 days to maturity is 8 percent, then the proceeds to the issuer are $9 800 000. The effective interest rate, including the stamping fee, is 8.67 percent.[15] The stated interest rate on outstanding banker's acceptances is usually 0.5 to 1.0 percentage points below the prime rate. As of November 1, 1993, the 90-day rate on banker's acceptances was 4.39 percent, which was below the prime rate of 5.75 percent and above the 91-day T-bill rate of 4.33 percent. However, when the stamping fee is factored in, the effective cost of the acceptance increases.

---

[14]Treasury bills are sold on one day of the week (currently Tuesdays) and always mature on the same day of the week, unless that day is a holiday. Thus, T-bills issued with 3-month maturity will almost always mature in 91 days (13 weeks $\times$ 7 days). Commercial paper and banker's acceptances, on the other hand, can be issued on any day of the week and mature on any day. Although we refer to those with approximately 3 months' maturity as 90 or 91-day paper, they can in fact mature in 88, 89, or 92 days.

[15]The effective rate is calculated as follows:

$$\text{Effective rate}_{BA} = \frac{\text{Interest cost} + \text{Stamping fee}}{\text{Net proceeds from investment dealer}}.$$

$$\text{Interest cost} = 8\% \times \frac{91}{365} \times \$10\,000\,000 = \$199\,452 \text{ for 91 days.}$$

$$\text{Stamping fee (commission)} = 0.0050 \times \frac{91}{365} \times \$10\,000\,000 = \$12\,466 \text{ (pro-rated basis).}$$

$$\text{Net proceeds} = \text{Face value} - \text{Interest}$$

$$\text{Effective rate}_{BA} = \frac{\$211\,918}{\$9\,800\,548} = 0.0216 \text{ per 91 days}$$

The annual effective rate is $0.0216 \times \left(\dfrac{365}{91}\right) = 0.0867$ or 8.67%.

Since banker's acceptances are similar to commercial paper, the net cost to the corporation from either instrument should be close. The interest rates on each of these instruments for three maturity categories are presented below. For each maturity category, the commercial paper rate is greater than the banker's acceptance rate. This reflects the higher probability of default on commercial paper compared to the guarantee provided by the commercial bank for a banker's acceptance.

Yields as of November 1, 1993

Term (days)	Banker's Acceptances	Commercial Paper
30	4.33%	4.49%
60	4.36	4.48
90	4.39	4.45

However, these yields do not reflect the associated costs of either a banker's acceptance or commercial paper to the issuer. To compare the costs of these issues, the cost differential for these instruments is compared in Table 11-2. These spreads are representative of a high-quality firm; at any point in time, the actual values may differ from those shown in Table 11-2.[16]

As noted in the table, the only charge on banker's acceptances is the stamping fee, which is 50 basis points. For commercial paper, there is an issuing fee and, if required, a standby fee paid to the bank, along with a higher base rate of 10 basis points above the T-bill. The costs of the two instruments are reasonably close (50 versus 48 basis points). If a company is very strong, a standby fee may not be needed; this would be an advantage of the use of commercial paper.

Table 11-2
Cost Differential (basis points)

	Banker's Acceptances	Commercial Paper
Base rate*	–	10
Issuing fees	–	13
Standby fees	–	25
Stamping fees	50	–
Total	50	48

*The base rate is the number of basis points over the T-bill rate.

[16]The base rates, or spreads over Treasury bills, on October 16, 1992, were 20 basis points for banker's acceptances and 60 basis points for commercial paper. These spreads vary over time, depending on general economic conditions. The base rates in Table 11-2 are lower and more typical.

The Use of Security in Short-Term Financing

A **secured loan** is one backed by collateral—the borrower pledges specific assets that will be forfeited to the lender in case of nonpayment.

Thus far we have not addressed in any depth the question of whether or not loans should be secured. Commercial paper and banker's acceptances are never secured by specific collateral, but all the other types of loans can be secured if this is deemed necessary or desirable. Given a choice, it is ordinarily better to borrow on an unsecured basis, as the bookkeeping costs of secured loans are often high. However, smaller or less-established firms may find that they can borrow only if they put up some type of collateral to protect the lender, and even strong firms may find that by using security they can borrow at a much lower rate. In fact, only the very best credit risks borrow on an unsecured basis. This is unlikely to be more than 5 percent of the borrowers of a bank.

Several different kinds of collateral can be employed, including marketable securities, land and buildings, equipment, inventory, and accounts receivable. Marketable securities make excellent collateral, but few firms hold usable portfolios of shares and bonds; the short-term marketable securities held by the firms are usually dedicated to meeting anticipated payments such as dividends or wages or are needed to replenish cash balances. Similarly, real property (land and buildings) and equipment are good forms of collateral, but they are generally used as security for long-term rather than working capital loans. Thus the bulk of secured short-term business borrowing involves the use of short-term assets—accounts receivable and inventories—as collateral.

In describing security for short-term, chartered bank financing, the *Bank Act* specifies the procedures to be followed and the forms of security that can be used. *Section 178* of the act specifies that banks may lend to manufacturing companies, wholesalers, and retailers on the security of inventories, both current and future. Although the company need not relinquish control of the inventory under a section 178 loan, the bank has the rights and powers identical to those it would have obtained had a direct form of security on the inventory, such as a warehouse receipt, been used.

Alternative methods of securing inventories (other than those specified in section 178) can also be used by the banks. In the case of companies not in the sectors noted above, these alternatives *must* be used.

Finally, accounts receivable can be used as security for bank loans. In fact, lending on the security of receivables is by far the most common form of lending.

For a long time, the simplicity and administrative ease with which security under section 178 is handled was not duplicated for nonbank use of personal property as security. This situation was improved by the passage of a *Personal*

Property Security Act (PPSA) in many provinces.[17] These acts replace a number of existing statutes that dealt with personal property as security and simplify the registration process through the use of a computerized registry. The result is that by far the most common security instrument is a *general securities agreement* (GSA), which gives a *floating charge* on all assets except real property. Under a floating charge, the bank, or other financial institution, has a claim on a security that is not specifically pledged on another loan. Section 178 security has only minor benefits over a GSA, so the use of the former is diminishing in provinces that have a PPSA.

Financing Accounts Receivable

Accounts receivable financing involves either the pledging (assignment) of receivables or the selling of receivables (factoring). The **pledging of accounts receivable** is characterized by the fact that the lender has not only a lien on the receivables but also recourse to the borrower (seller); if the person or the firm that bought the goods does not pay, the selling firm must take the loss. In other words, the risk of default on the assigned accounts receivable remains with the borrower. If the credit, bookkeeping, and collection functions remain with the borrower, this is referred to as "non-notification financing," as the buyer of the goods is not notified about the assignment of the receivables. "Notification financing" occurs if the lender assumes collection and bookkeeping responsibilities, as the buyer must be notified of the assignment. The financial institutions that lend on the security of accounts receivable are chartered banks, large industrial finance companies, and factoring companies.

Factoring accounts receivable involves the purchase of accounts receivable by the lender without recourse to the borrower (seller). The buyer of the goods is notified of the transfer and makes payment directly to the lender. Since the factoring firm assumes the risk of default on bad accounts, it must do the credit checking and the collection on slow accounts. Accordingly, factoring companies provide not only money but also a credit department for the borrower.

Most factoring companies began their operations servicing the textile industry; however, they are currently diversifying their activities into other areas such as footwear and data processing. A chartered bank can now act as a factor through a subsidiary operation.

Procedure for Pledging Accounts Receivable

The financing of accounts receivable through pledging is initiated by a legally binding agreement between the seller of the goods and the financing institution. The agreement sets forth in detail the procedures to be followed and the legal obligations of both parties. Once the working relation has been estab-

---

[17]This act was originally passed in Ontario, but similar legislation has now been enacted in most other provinces as well. Quebec has modified its Civil Code in a way similar to the PPSA; New Brunswick, as of mid-1993, was in the process of adopting a PPSA; only Nova Scotia, Prince Edward Island, and Newfoundland have not adopted such an act. Therefore, even though the legislation is provincial, comparable legislation is in effect throughout almost the entire country.

lished, the seller periodically takes a batch of invoices to the financing institution. The lender reviews the invoices and makes an appraisal of the buyers. Invoices of companies that do not meet the lender's credit standards are not accepted for pledging. The financial institution seeks to protect itself at every phase of the operation. First, selection of sound invoices is one way the lender safeguards itself. Second, if the buyer of the goods does not pay the invoice, the lender still has recourse against the seller. Third, additional protection is afforded the lender because the loan is generally made for less than 100 percent of the pledged receivables; for example, the lender may advance the selling firm only 75 percent of the amount of the pledged invoices.

Procedure for Factoring Accounts Receivable

The procedure for factoring is somewhat different from that for pledging. Again, an agreement between the seller and the factor is made to specify legal obligations and procedural arrangements. When the seller receives an order from a buyer, a credit approval slip is written and immediately sent to the factoring company for a credit check. If the factor approves the credit, shipment is made and the invoice is stamped to notify the buyer to make payment directly to the factoring company. If the factor does not approve the sale, the seller generally refuses to fill the order; if the sale is made anyway, the factor will not buy the account.

The factor performs three functions in carrying out the normal procedure outlined above: (1) credit checking, (2) lending, and (3) risk bearing. The seller can select various combinations of these functions by changing provisions in the factoring agreement. For example, a small or medium-sized firm may have the factor take on the risk bearing function and thus avoid establishing a credit department. The factor's charge for this service may well cost less than establishing a credit department that would have excess capacity because of the firm's small credit volume. At the same time, if the selling firm uses part of the time of a noncredit specialist to perform credit checking, lack of education, training, and experience may result in excessive losses.

The seller may have the factor perform the credit checking and risk taking functions, but not the lending function. The following procedure illustrates the handling of a $10 000 order under this arrangement. The factor checks and approves the invoices. The goods are shipped on terms of net 30. Payment is made to the factor, which remits to the seller. But assume that the factor has received only $5000 by the end of the credit period. The $10 000 must be remitted to the seller (less the fee, of course). If the remaining $5000 is never paid, the factor sustains a $5000 loss. Note that in this situation, the factor does not remit funds to the seller until either they are received from the buyer of the goods or the credit period has expired. Thus, the factor does not supply any credit.

Now consider the more typical situation in which the factor performs the lending, risk bearing, and credit checking functions. Upon proof of the shipment of goods, the factor immediately advances up to 90 percent of the invoice amount to the seller even though the payment is not due for 30 days. The 10 percent holdback is a reserve established by the factor to cover disputes between seller and buyer on such issues as damaged goods, goods returned to the seller by the buyer, and failure to make outright sale of goods. This holdback is paid to the selling firm when the factor collects on the account.

Factoring is normally a continuous process instead of the single cycle described above. The seller of the goods receives orders and transmits the purchase orders to the factor for approval; on approval, the goods are shipped; the factor advances the money to the seller; the buyers pay the factor when payment is due; and the factor periodically remits any excess reserve to the seller of the goods. Once a routine is established, a continuous circular flow of goods and funds takes place between the seller, the buyers of the goods, and the factor. Thus, once the factoring agreement is in force, funds from this source are spontaneous in the sense that an increase in sales will automatically generate additional credit.

Cost of Receivables Financing

Accounts receivables assignment and factoring services are convenient and advantageous, but they can be costly. For factoring, a fee of 0.875 to 1.5 percent of sales is charged for the credit checking and risk bearing functions. If a loan is made by the factor, the cost of money is 2 to 3 percentage points over prime.

Both factoring companies and banks will lend short term on the assignment of accounts receivable; in this case the lending institution does not accept any of the credit risk. For non-notification financing, the collection and credit checking is done by the selling company. Interest costs for this form of financing from factoring companies range from 6 to 8 percentage points over prime. This very high premium reflects the fact that the factor does not receive the funds from the accounts receivable and bears the risk of default on the loan.

For notification financing, the factoring company undertakes credit management and collections. There is a factoring commission (0.875 to 1.5 percent of sales) that covers the costs of collection and credit management. The interest cost on the loan is prime plus 1.5 to 2.5 percentage points. That the premium is lower than for non-notification financing reflects the control exercised by the factor on the credit granted and the collections; the loan is less risky.

Evaluation of Receivables Financing

It cannot be said categorically that accounts receivable financing is always either a good or a poor method of raising funds for an individual business. Among the advantages is, first, the flexibility of this source of financing; as the firm's sales expand, causing more financing to be needed, a larger volume of invoices and hence a larger amount of receivables is generated automatically. Second, a firm can use receivables as security for a loan that it might otherwise be unable to obtain. Third, factoring can provide the services of a credit department that might otherwise be available to the firm only under much more expensive conditions.

Accounts receivable financing also has disadvantages. First, when invoices are numerous and relatively small in dollar amount, the administrative costs involved may render this method of financing inconvenient and expensive. Second, since receivables are generally the firm's most liquid noncash assets, some suppliers may refuse to continue selling to the firm on credit because receivables financing weakens the position of trade creditors.

Future Use of Receivables Financing

Computer technology is at the point where credit records of individuals and firms can be kept on-line. Credit card systems have been devised whereby a retailer can have on hand a unit that, when an individual's magnetic credit card is inserted into a box, gives a signal that the person's credit is "good" and that an institution is willing to "buy" the receivable created when the store completes the sale. The cost of handling invoices is falling rapidly because of advances in technology. This is making it possible to use accounts receivable financing for very small sales, and it is reducing the cost of all receivables financing. The net result is a marked expansion of accounts receivable financing. It seems safe to predict that this trend will continue.

Inventory Financing

A large amount of short-term credit is secured by business inventories. For companies in eligible sectors, chartered banks have the option in most provinces of lending under section 178 of the *Bank Act* or using the provincial PPSA, and lending under a GSA. As already noted, lending under section 178 or a GSA are now equivalent, and the use of section 178 lending is diminishing. For provinces in which there is no PPSA and for companies in ineligible sectors, direct forms of inventory security are required. These include the floating charge debenture, the infrequently used trust receipts, and warehouse financing. These methods of using inventories as security are discussed below.

Floating Charge Debentures

A *floating charge debenture*, also known as a *blanket inventory lien*, provides a claim to all assets currently owned or subsequently acquired that are not already covered by a fixed charge. Because the bank does not have direct control of the assets under this debenture, it must protect its loan from an erosion of the security. Therefore, the debentures have trust indentures with specific covenants designed to protect the bank. Examples of these covenants include the submission of quarterly financial reports and restrictions on some financial decisions. If the borrower is in default, the floating charge "crystallizes" and becomes a fixed charge on any assets remaining at the time of the crystallization. Since the security at the point of default will depend on the assets under the floating charge, the debenture details the rights of the company to issue more fixed or floating charges to other lenders that would have a priority higher than the bank's floating charge.

Trust Receipts

A *trust receipt* is an instrument acknowledging that the borrower holds the goods in trust for the lender. When trust receipts are used, the borrowing firm, on receiving funds from the lender, conveys a trust receipt for the goods. The goods can be stored in a public warehouse or held on the premises of the borrower. The trust receipt provides that the goods are held in trust for the lender or are segregated in the borrower's premises on behalf of the lender, and proceeds from the sale of goods held under trust receipts are transmitted to the lender at the end of each day. Automobile dealer financing is the best example of trust receipt financing.

One defect of trust receipt financing is the requirement that a trust receipt must be issued for specific goods. For example, if the security is bags of coffee beans, the trust receipts must indicate the bags by number. In order to validate its trust receipts, the lending institution would have to send an employee to the premises of the borrower to see that the bag numbers are correctly listed. Furthermore, the complex legal requirements of trust receipts require the attention of a bank officer. These problems are compounded if borrowers are widely separated geographically from the lender. To offset these inconveniences, warehousing is coming into wider use as a method of securing loans with inventory.

Warehouse Financing

Like trust receipts, *warehouse financing* uses inventory as security. A public warehouse represents an independent third party engaged in the business of storing goods. Sometimes the use of a public warehouse is not practical because of the bulkiness of goods and the expense of transporting them to and from the borrower's premises. *Field warehouse* financing represents an economical method of inventory financing in which the warehouse is established at the place of the borrower. To provide inventory supervision, the lending institution employs a third party: the field warehousing company. This company acts as the control (or supervisory) agent for the lending institution.

Field warehousing is illustrated by a simple example. Suppose a potential borrower has stacked iron in an open yard on its premises. A field warehouse can be established if a field warehousing concern places a temporary fence around the iron, erects a sign stating "This is a field warehouse supervised and conducted by the Lawrence Warehousing Corporation," and assigns an employee to supervise and control the inventory.

The example illustrates the three elements in the establishment of a warehouse: (1) public notification of the field warehouse arrangement, (2) physical control of the inventory, and (3) supervision of the field warehouse by a custodian of the field warehouse concern. When the field warehousing operation is relatively small, the third condition is sometimes violated by hiring an employee of the borrower to supervise the inventory. This practice is viewed as undesirable by lending institutions, as it means there is no control over the collateral by a person independent of the borrowing concern.[18]

---

[18]This absence of independent control was the main cause of the breakdown that resulted in hundreds of millions of dollars in losses connected with loans to the Allied Crude Vegetable Oil Company. The people running Allied speculated in the commodities market, lost heavily, and then improperly sold products that were being used as collateral for loans. An American Express subsidiary, American Express Field Warehousing Company, was running the warehouse operation, and it had hired men from Allied's staff as custodians. Their dishonesty was not discovered because of another breakdown—the fact that the American Express touring inspector did not actually take a physical inventory of the warehouses. As a consequence, the swindle was not discovered until losses running into the hundreds of millions of dollars had been suffered. The banks that had made the secured loans sued American Express; eventually a settlement was worked out under which the losses were shared by American Express and the banks.

The field warehouse financing operation is described best by a specific illustration. Assume that a tomato canner is interested in financing its operations by bank borrowing. The canner has sufficient funds to finance 15 to 20 percent of its operations during the canning season. These funds are adequate to purchase and process an initial batch of tomatoes. As the cans are put into boxes and rolled into the storerooms, the canner needs additional funds for both raw materials and labour. Because of the canner's poor credit rating, the bank decides that a field warehousing operation is necessary to secure its loans. The field warehouse is established, and the custodian notifies the lending institution of the description, by number, of the boxes of canned tomatoes in storage and under his or her control. Thereupon the lending institution establishes for the canner a deposit on which it can draw.

From this point on, the bank finances the operations. The canner needs only enough cash to initiate the cycle. The farmers bring more tomatoes; the canner processes them; the cans are boxed, and the boxes are put into the field warehouse; field warehouse receipts are drawn up and sent to the bank; the bank establishes further deposits for the canner on the basis of the receipts; the canner can draw on the deposits to continue the cycle.

Of course, the canner's ultimate objective is to sell the canned tomatoes. As the canner receives purchase orders, it transmits them to the bank, and the bank directs the custodian to release the inventories. It is agreed that, as remittances are received by the canner, they will be turned over to the bank. These remittances by the canner pay off the loans.

Typically, a seasonal pattern exists. At the beginning of the tomato harvesting and canning season, the canner's cash needs and loan requirements begin to rise. They reach a maximum by the end of the canning season. It is hoped that, just before the new canning season begins, the canner has sold a sufficient volume to have paid off the loan completely. If for some reason the canner has had a bad year, the bank may carry the loan over another year to enable the firm to work off its inventory.

Acceptable Products.   In addition to canned foods, which account for about 17 percent of all field warehouse loans, many other product inventories provide a basis for field warehouse financing. Some of these are miscellaneous groceries, lumber products, and coal and coke.

These products are relatively nonperishable and are sold in well-developed, organized markets. Nonperishability protects the lender if it should have to take over the security. For this reason, a bank would not make a field warehousing loan on perishables such as fresh fish. However, frozen fish, which can be stored for a long time, can be field warehoused.

An organized market aids the lender in disposing of an inventory that it takes over. Lending institutions are not interested in going into the canning or the fish business. They want to be able to dispose of an inventory quickly and with a minimum of effort.

Cost of Financing.   The fixed costs of a field warehousing arrangement are relatively high; such financing is therefore not suitable for a very small firm. If a field warehouse company sets up the field warehouse itself, it will typically set a minimum charge of about $1000 a year, plus about 1 or 2 percent of the amount of credit extended to the borrower. Furthermore, the financing institution will charge 8 to 12 percent interest. The minimum size of an efficient field warehousing operation requires an inventory of about $100 000.

Appraisal.   The use of field warehouse financing as a source of funds for business firms has many advantages. First, the amount of funds available is flexible because the financing is tied to the growth of inventories, which in turn is related directly to financing needs. Second, the field warehousing arrangement increases the acceptability of inventories as loan collateral. Some inventories would not be accepted by a bank as security without a field warehousing arrangement. Third, the necessity for inventory control, safe-keeping, and the use of specialists in warehousing has resulted in improved warehouse practices. The services of the field warehouse companies have often saved firms money in spite of the costs of financing. The field warehouse company may suggest inventory practices that reduce the labour that the firm has to employ and reduce inventory damage and loss as well.

The major disadvantages of a field warehousing operation are (1) the fixed-cost element and (2) the additional administrative expenses, which reduce the feasibility of this form of financing for small firms and for firms whose inventory turns over rapidly.

Other Security

Personal Guarantee

Because of the limited liability of a corporation, a creditor is not able to attach personal property of the debtor if a corporate loan is in default. One way around this problem, especially for loans to small companies, is to have the principal shareholders (and perhaps their spouses if they have a direct interest in the company) sign a *personal guarantee* of the loan. This guarantees the repayment of the loan, both principal and interest, up to stated maximum amount.

Chattel Mortgage

A *chattel mortgage* is a mortgage of personal or movable property such as an automobile or machinery and equipment—but not real estate. The goods are left with the borrower until there is a default, at which point they become the property of the lender. Chartered banks are permitted to use this form of security.

Concept Review

► Differentiate between pledging accounts receivable and factoring accounts receivable.
► What is section 178 lending? What is a general securities assignment (GSA)?
► Describe three methods of inventory financing.

Summary

This chapter examined (1) different types of short-term credit available to firms, (2) the decisions the financial manager makes in selecting among the types of short-term credit, and (3) decisions regarding the use of security to obtain credit. The key concepts covered are listed below.

□ *Short-term credit* is any liability originally scheduled for payment within one year. The major sources of short-term credit are (1) accruals, (2) accounts payable, (3) loans from banks, (4) commercial paper, and (5) banker's acceptances.

□ **Accruals**, which are continually recurring short-term liabilities, represent free, spontaneous credit.

□ **Trade credit**—*accounts payable*—is the largest category of short-term debt. This credit arises spontaneously as a result of purchases on credit. Firms should use all the *free trade credit* they can obtain, but they should use *costly trade credit* only if it is less expensive than other forms of short-term debt. Suppliers often offer discounts to customers who pay within a stated discount period. The following equation may be used to calculate the approximate percentage cost, on an annual basis, of not taking discounts:

$$\begin{matrix} \text{Approximate} \\ \text{percentage} \\ \text{cost} \end{matrix} = \frac{\text{Discount percentage}}{100 - \begin{matrix} \text{Discount} \\ \text{percentage} \end{matrix}} \times \frac{365}{\begin{matrix} \text{Days credit} \\ \text{is outstanding} \end{matrix} - \begin{matrix} \text{Discount} \\ \text{period} \end{matrix}}.$$

□ Bank loans are an important source of short-term credit. Interest on bank loans is usually quoted as **simple interest**. In some instances **discount interest**, or **installment interest,** is used. The effective rate on a discount or installment loan always exceeds the stated nominal rate.

□ When a bank loan is approved, a **promissory note** is signed. It specifies: (1) the amount borrowed, (2) the percentage interest rate, (3) the repayment schedule, (4) the collateral, and (5) any other conditions to which the parties have agreed.

□ Banks often require larger borrowers to maintain *compensating balances*, which are deposit accounts set at a certain percent of the loan amount. Compensating balances raise the effective rate of interest on bank loans.

□ **Revolving lines of credit** are a loan facility indicating the maximum amount of credit the bank will extend to the borrower provided conditions are met.

□ Operating loans are of two types: **demand facilities** and **term facilities**. The former requires repayment to the bank "upon demand." For the latter, the bank can request repayment before maturity only if the borrower has not met some of the terms of the loan.

□ The bank can charge a **commitment fee,** which is independent of the amount of the credit used and is compensation to the bank for the obligation to extend credit. In addition it can charge a **standby fee**, which is levied on the unused portion of the credit; this fee is used normally for large lines of credit.

□ The **prime rate** is a published interest rate charged by banks to very large, strong corporations.

□ *Simple interest* is interest charged on the basis of the amount borrowed. The effective rate on a 1-year simple interest loan is calculated as follows:

$$\text{Effective rate}_{\text{simple}} = \frac{\text{Interest}}{\text{Amount received}}.$$

If compensating balances (CB) are added, the effective rate is calculated as follows:

$$\text{Effective rate}_{\text{simple/CB}} = \frac{\text{Nominal rate}}{1.0 - \text{CB}}.$$

□ *Discount interest* is interest calculated on the face amount of a loan, but it is deducted in advance. This method is not common for bank loans, but it is used for some financial instruments, including banker's acceptances. The effective rate on a 1-year discount interest loan is calculated as follows:

$$\text{Effective rate}_{\text{discount}} = \frac{\text{Interest}}{\text{Face value} - \text{interest}}.$$

If compensating balances are added, the effective rate is calculated as follows:

$$\text{Effective rate}_{\text{discount/CB}} = \frac{\text{Nominal rate}}{1.0 - \text{Nominal rate} - \text{CB}}.$$

□ *Installment interest* is interest calculated and added to funds received to determine the face amount of an installment loan; the effective rate on a one-year add-on interest loan is calculated as follows:

$$\text{Approximate effective rate}_{\text{installment}} = \frac{\text{Interest}}{(\text{Amount received})/2}.$$

□ **Commercial paper** is unsecured short-term debt issued by large, financially strong corporations. Although the cost of commercial paper is lower than the cost of bank loans, commercial paper's maturity is short, usually 90 days or less, and it can be used only by large firms with exceptionally strong credit ratings.

□ A **banker's acceptance (BA)** combines aspects of both the bank loan and commercial paper. Since the bank guarantees that the funds will be available when the acceptance is presented, it is like a loan. The bank receives added compensation for the guarantee through a *stamping fee*. BAs are sold and traded in the money market just as is commercial paper. The rate on a BA is usually slightly higher than that on commercial paper.

□ Sometimes a borrower will find it necessary to obtain a **secured loan**. In that case, the borrower pledges assets such as real estate, securities, equipment, inventories, or accounts receivable as collateral for the loan.

□ Accounts receivable financing involves either **pledging** or **factoring receivables.** Under a pledging arrangement, the lender not only gets a claim against the receivables but also has recourse to the borrower. Factoring receivables involves the purchase of accounts receivable by the lender, generally without recourse to the borrower.

☐ There are three primary methods of inventory financing: A *floating charge* debenture (inventory blanket lien) gives the lender a lien against all of the borrower's inventories. A *trust receipt* is an instrument that acknowledges that the goods are held in trust for the lender. *Warehouse financing* is an arrangement under which the lender employs a third party to exercise control over the borrower's inventory and to act as the lender's agent. The bank can lend under *section 178* of the federal *Bank Act* to companies that are in eligible sectors or under a *general security assignment* in provinces that have a *Personal Property Security Act.* If neither condition holds, then the bank will require direct forms of security.

☐ Pledging receivables is especially sensible for the small firm that has customers with better credit histories than the firm itself, as this allows the firm to take advantage of the strength of its customer base.

☐ For small firms with limited managerial resources and limited experience in monitoring and collecting credit accounts, factoring may be more than worth the cost. The small firm's comparative advantage is its ability to deliver a product; the factor's advantage is its ability to provide financial and credit services.

Questions

11-1 "Firms can control their accruals within fairly wide limits; depending on the cost of accruals, financing from this source will be increased or decreased." Discuss.

11-2 Is it true that both trade credit and accruals represent a spontaneous source of capital for financing growth? Explain.

11-3 It is inevitable that most firms will obtain a certain amount of their financing in the form of trade credit, which is, to some extent, a free source of funds. What are some other reasons for firms to use trade credit?

11-4 Trade credit has an explicit interest rate cost if discounts are available but not taken. What are the intangible costs associated with the failure to take discounts?

11-5 The availability of bank credit is often more important to small firms than to large ones. Why?

11-6 Given that commercial paper interest rates are always lower than bank loan rates to a given borrower, why might firms that are capable of selling commercial paper choose also to employ bank credit?

11-7 Indicate whether each of the following changes will raise or lower the cost of a firm's accounts receivable financing, and explain why.
   a. The firm eases up on its credit standards in order to increase sales.
   b. The firm institutes a policy to make credit sales if the amount of the purchase is less than $100. Before the change, about 40 percent of all invoices were less than $100.

    c. The firm agrees to give recourse to the finance company for all defaults.

    d. A firm that already has a recourse arrangement is merged into a larger, stronger company.

    e. A firm without a recourse arrangement changes its terms of trade from net 30 to net 90.

11-8 Would a firm that manufactures specialized machinery for a few large customers be more likely to use a form of inventory financing or a form of accounts receivable financing? Why?

11-9 Discuss this statement: "A firm that factors its accounts receivable will look better in a ratio analysis than one that pledges its receivables."

11-10 Why is it impractical for a typical retailer to use warehouse receipt financing? Would a field warehouse be feasible? Would a floating charge debenture be feasible?

11-11 Describe an industry that might be expected to use each of the following forms of credit, and explain your reasons for choosing each one:
    a. Field warehouse financing.
    b. Factoring.
    c. Accounts receivable pledging.
    d. Trust receipts.

Self-Test Problems   (solutions appear on page 366)

ST-1 **Key terms.**   Define each of the following terms:
    a. Accruals
    b. Trade credit; stretching accounts payable; free trade credit; costly trade credit
    c. Promissory note; revolving line of credit; unconfirmed line of credit
    d. Prime rate
    e. Simple interest; discount interest; installment loan interest
    f. Compensating balance
    g. Commercial paper; banker's acceptance
    h. Secured loan
    i. Section 178 lending; general securities assignment
    j. Pledging receivables; factoring
    k. Floating charge debenture; trust receipt; warehouse receipt financing; field warehouse

ST-2 **Receivables funding.**   The Naylor Company Ltd. is considering two methods of raising working capital. The first method is a commercial bank loan secured by accounts receivable; the second is to factor accounts receivable. Naylor's bank has agreed to lend the firm 75 percent of its average monthly accounts receivable balance of $250 000 at an annual interest rate of 9 percent. The loan would be discounted, and a 20 percent compensating balance would be required.

    A factor has agreed to purchase Naylor's accounts receivable and to advance 85 percent of the balance to the firm. The factor would charge a 3.5 percent factoring commission and annual interest of 9 percent on the invoice price less both the factoring commission and the reserve account. The monthly interest payment would be deducted from the advance. If Naylor chooses the factoring arrangement, it can eliminate its credit department and reduce operating expenses by $4000 per month. In addition, bad debt losses of 2 percent of the monthly receivables will be avoided.

a. What is the annual cost associated with each financing arrangement?

b. Discuss some considerations other than cost that may influence management's decision between factoring and a commercial bank loan.

Problems

11-1   Cost of trade credit.   What is the equivalent annual interest rate that would be lost if a firm failed to take the cash discount under each of the following terms?

a. 1/15, net 20.

b. 2/10, net 60.

c. 3/10, net 30.

d. 2/10, net 45.

e. 1/10, net 40.

11-2   Cost of credit.

a. A firm buys under terms of 3/15, net 45, but actually pays on Day 20 and still takes the discount. What is the cost of its nonfree trade credit?

b. Does it receive more or less credit than it would if it paid within 15 days?

11-3   Cash discounts.   Suppose a firm makes purchases of $3.6 million per year under terms of 2/10, net 30 and takes discounts.

a. What is the average amount of accounts payable net of discounts? Assume that the $3.6 million of purchases is net of discounts—that is, gross purchases are $3 673 469, discounts are $73 469, and net purchases are $3.6 million. Also, use 365 days in a year.

b. Is there a cost of the trade credit the firm uses?

c. If the firm did not take discounts, what would be its average payables and the cost of this nonfree trade credit?

d. What would the firm's cost of not taking discounts be if it could stretch its payments to 40 days?

11-4   Cost of bank loans.   Green Thumb Garden Shop is negotiating with Millstone Bank for a 1-year loan of $50 000. Millstone has offered Green Thumb the following alternatives:

- A 16 percent annual rate on a simple interest loan, with no compensating balance and interest due at the end of the year.

- A 9 percent annual rate on a simple interest loan with a 20 percent compensating balance requirement and interest due at the end of the year.

- An 11 percent annual rate on a discounted loan with a 10 percent compensating balance.
- A 10 percent annual interest rate, with the loan to be repaid in 12 monthly installments and interest calculated on the original balance due at the end of the year.

Which alternative has the lowest effective interest rate?

11-5   Trade credit versus bank credit. Wagner Industries projects an increase in sales from $1.5 million to $2 million, but it needs an additional $300 000 of current assets to support this expansion. The money can be obtained from the bank at an interest rate of 12 percent, discount interest; no compensating balance is required. Alternatively, Wagner can finance the expansion by no longer taking discounts, thus increasing its accounts payable. Wagner purchases under terms of 2/10, net 30, but it can delay payment for an additional 35 days—paying in 65 days and thus becoming 35 days past due—without a penalty because of its suppliers' current excess capacity problems.

   a. Based strictly on an interest rate comparison, how should Wagner finance its expansion?

   b. What additional, qualitative factors should Wagner consider before reaching a decision?

11-6   Banking financing. Shelby Saw Inc. has fallen behind in its accounts payable. Although its terms of purchase are net 30 days, the current accounts payable balance represents 60 days' purchases. Shelby is seeking to increase bank borrowings in order to become current in meeting its trade obligations (that is, to reduce accounts payable to 30 days' purchases). The company's balance sheet is shown below.

Shelby Saw Inc.
Balance Sheet

Assets		Liabilities	
Cash	$ 100 000	Accounts payable	$ 600 000
Accounts receivable	300 000	Bank loans	900 000
Inventory	1 400 000	Current Liabilities	$1 500 000
Current assets	$1 800 000	Long-term debt	700 000
Fixed assets	1 200 000	Net worth	800 000
Total assets	$3 000 000	Total liabilities	$3 000 000

   a. How much financing is required to eliminate past-due accounts payable?

   b. As a bank loan officer, would you make the loan? Explain.

11-7   Short-term financing analysis. Arva Feed and Supply Company buys on terms of 1/10, net 30, but it has not been taking discounts and has actually been paying in 60 rather than 30 days. Arva's balance sheet follows.

Arva Feed and Supply Company
Balance Sheet (thousands of dollars)

Assets		Liabilities	
Cash	$ 50	Accounts payable (net of discounts)	$ 500
Accounts receivable	450	Notes payable	50
Inventories	750	Accruals	50
Current assets	$1 250	Current liabilities	$ 600
		Long-term debt	150
Fixed assets	750	Common equity	1 250
Total assets	$2 000	Total liabilities and equity	$2 000

Now Arva's suppliers are threatening to stop shipments unless the company begins making prompt payments (that is, paying in 30 days or less). The firm can borrow on a 1-year note (call this a current liability) from its bank at a rate of 15 percent, discount interest, with a 20 percent compensating balance required. (Arva's $50 000 of cash is needed for transactions; it cannot be used as part of the compensating balance.)

a. Determine what action Arva should take by calculating (i) the costs of nonfree trade credit and (ii) the cost of the bank loan.

b. Assume that Arva forgoes discounts and then borrows the amount needed to become current on its payables from the bank. How large will the bank loan be?

c. Based on your conclusion in Part b, construct a pro forma balance sheet. (Hint: You will need to include an account entitled "prepaid interest" under current assets.)

11-8 **Alternative financing arrangements.** Sunlight Sailboats estimates that because of the seasonal nature of its business it will require an additional $350 000 of cash for the month of July. Sunlight has the following four options for obtaining the needed funds:

• Establish a 1-year line of credit for $350 000 with a commercial bank. The standby fee of 0.5 percent on the unused portion, and the interest charge on the used funds, will be 12.0 percent per annum. Assume that the funds are needed only in July and that there are 30 days in July.

• Forego the July trade discount of 3/10, net 40 on $350 000 of accounts payable.

• Issue $350 000 of 30-day commercial paper at a 11.4 percent per annum interest rate. The total transaction fee on using commercial paper is 0.5 percent of the fair value.

• Issue $350 000 of 60-day commercial paper at an 11.8 percent per annum interest rate. Since the funds are required for only 30 days, the excess funds ($350 000) can be invested in 10.8 percent per annum marketable securities for the month of August. The total transaction fee on purchasing and selling the marketable securities is 0.5 percent of the fair value.

a. What is the cost of each financing arrangement?

b. Is the source with the lowest expected cost necessarily the source to select? Why or why not?

11-9 **Factoring receivables.**   Wilkins Manufacturing Ltd. needs an additional $375 000, which it plans to obtain through a factoring arrangement. The factor would purchase Wilkins's accounts receivable and advance the invoice amount, less a 2 percent commission, on the invoices purchased each month. (Wilkins sells on terms of net 30 days.) In addition, the factor charges 13 percent annual interest on the total invoice amount, to be deducted in advance.

a. What amount of accounts receivable must be factored to net $375 000?

b. If Wilkins can reduce credit expenses by $1200 per month, and avoid bad-debt losses of 3 percent on the factored amount, what will be the total dollar cost of the factoring arrangement?

11-10 **Receivables financing.**   The Morton Plastics Company Limited manufactures plastic toys. It buys raw materials, manufactures the toys in the spring and summer, and ships them to a large number of department stores and toy stores by late summer or early autumn. The company factors its receivables. If it did not, Morton's last balance sheet would have appeared as follows:

Morton Plastics Company Limited
Pro Forma Balance Sheet
as of October 31, 1993

Assets		Liabilities	
Cash	$ 40 000	Accounts Payable	$1 200 000
Receivables	1 200 000	Notes payable	800 000
Inventory	800 000	Accruals	80 000
Total current assets	$2 040 000	Total current debt	$2 080 000
		Mortgages	200 000
		Common equity	400 000
Fixed assets	800 000	Retained earnings	160 000
Total assets	$2 840 000	Total claims	$2 840 000

Morton provides advanced dating on its sales; thus, its receivables are not due for payment until January 31, 1994. Also, the company would have been overdue on some $800 000 of its accounts payable if the above situation actually existed.

Morton has an agreement with a finance company to factor the receivables for a flat commission of 1.5 percent, plus interest at 3 percentage points over the prime rate (currently 10 percent) on the outstanding balance. It deducts a reserve of 15 percent for returns and damaged materials. Interest and commission are paid in advance. No interest is charged on the reserved funds or on the commission.

a. Show Morton's actual balance sheet on October 31, 1993, giving effect to the purchase of all the receivables by the factoring company and the use of the funds to pay accounts payable.

b. If the $1.2 million is the average level of outstanding receivables and if they turn over 4 times a year (hence the commission is paid 4 times a year), what are the total dollar costs of financing and the effective annual interest rate?

11-11 Inventory financing.   Because of crop failures last year, the Supreme Ketchup Co. Ltd. has no funds available to finance its canning operations over the next 6 months. It estimates that it will require $1 440 000 for inventory financing during the period. One alternative being considered is to establish a 6-month $1 800 000 line of credit with terms of 10 percent annual interest on the used portion, a 1 percent commitment fee, and a $250 000 compensating balance at all times.

Expected inventory levels to be financed are:

Month	Amount
July	$300 000
August	1 200 000
September	1 440 000
October	1 440 000
November	720 000
December	0

Calculate the cost of the line of credit, including interest charges and commitment fees. (Hint: Each month's borrowings will be $250 000 greater than the inventory level to be financed because of the compensating balance requirement.)

11-12 Field warehouse financing.   Because of the relative perishability of canned vegetables, field warehouse financing would also be appropriate for Supreme Ketchup in Problem 11-11. The costs of the field warehousing alternative in this case would be a flat fee of $2500 plus 9 percent annual interest on all outstanding credit and 1 percent of the maximum amount of credit extended.

a. Calculate the total cost of the field warehousing operation.

b. Compare the cost of the field warehousing to the line of credit in Problem 11-11. Which alternative should Supreme choose?

Integrative Problem

11-13 Short-term financing.   C. Charles Smith was recently hired as president of Dellvoe Office Equipment, Ltd., a small manufacturer of metal office equipment. As his assistant, you have been asked to review the company's short-term financing policies and to prepare a report for Smith and the board of directors. To help you get started, Smith has prepared some questions that, when answered, will give him a better idea of the company's short-term financing policies.

a. What is short-term credit? What are the four major sources of this credit?

b. Is there a cost to accruals? Do firms have much control over them?

c. What is trade credit?

d. Like most small companies, Dellvoe has two primary sources of short-term debt: trade credit and bank loans. One supplier, which supplies Dellvoe with $50 000 of materials a year, offers terms of 2/10, net 50.

i. What are Dellvoe's net daily purchases from this supplier?

ii. What is the average level of Dellvoe's accounts payable to this supplier if the discount is taken? What is the average level if the discount is not taken? What are the amounts of free credit and costly credit under both discount policies?

iii. What is the approximate cost of the costly trade credit? What is its effective annual cost?

e. In discussing a possible loan with the firm's banker, Smith has found that the bank is willing to lend Dellvoe up to $800 000 for 1 year at a 9 percent nominal, or stated, rate. However, he forgot to ask what the specific terms would be.

i. Assume the firm will borrow $800 000. What would be the effective interest rate if the loan were based on simple interest? If the loan had been an 8 percent simple interest loan for 6 months rather than for a year, would that have affected the effective annual rate?

ii. What would be the effective rate if the loan were a discount interest loan? What would be the face amount of a loan large enough to net the firm $800 000 of usable funds?

iii. Assume now that the terms call for an installment (or add-on) loan with equal monthly payments. The add-on loan is for a period of one year. What would be Dellvoe's monthly payment? What would be the approximate cost of the loan? What would be the effective annual rate?

iv. Now assume that the bank charges simple interest, but it requires the firm to maintain a 20 percent compensating balance. How much must Dellvoe borrow to obtain its needed $800 000 and to meet the compensating balance requirement? What is the effective annual rate on the loan?

v. Now assume that the bank charges discount interest and also requires a compensating balance. How much must Dellvoe borrow, and what is the effective annual rate under these terms?

f. Dellvoe is considering using secured short-term financing. What is a secured loan? What two types of current assets can be used to secure loans?

g. What are the differences between pledging receivables and factoring receivables? Is one of the two generally considered better?

h. What are the differences among the three forms of inventory financing? Is one type generally considered best?

i. Dellvoe had expected a really strong market for office equipment for the year just ended, and in anticipation of strong sales, the firm increased its inventory purchases. However, sales for the last quarter of the year did not meet its expectations, and now Dellvoe finds itself short on cash. The firm expects that its cash shortage will be temporary, only lasting 3 months. (The inventory has been paid for and cannot be returned to suppliers. The office equipment market is one in which designs change nearly every 2 years, and

Dellvoe's inventory reflects current design changes, so its inventory is not obsolete.) Dellvoe has decided to use inventory financing to meet its short-term cash needs. It estimates that it will require $800 000 for inventory financing during this 3-month period. Dellvoe has negotiated with the bank for a 3-month, $1 000 000 line of credit with terms of 10 percent annual interest on the used portion, a 1 percent standby fee on the unused portion, and a $125 000 compensating balance at all times.

Expected inventory levels to be financed are as follows:

Month	Amount
January	$800 000
February	500 000
March	300 000

Calculate the cost of funds from this source, including interest charges and standby fees. (Hint: Each month's borrowings will be $125 000 greater than the inventory level to be financed because of the compensating balance requirement.)

Solutions to Self-Test Problems

ST-1   Refer to the appropriate sections of the text to check your responses.

ST-2   **a.** *Commercial bank loan*

Amount loaned	= (0.75)($250 000)	= $187 500
Compensating balance	= (0.20)($187 500)	= (37 500)
Amount received		= $150 000
Interest expense	= (0.09)($187 500)	= $ 16 875
*Credit department	= ($4000)(12)	= 48 000
*Bad debts	= (0.02)($250 000)(12) =	60 000
Total annual costs		= $124 875

Factoring

Amount loaned	= (0.85)($250 000)	= $212 500
Commission for period	= (0.035)($250 000)	= (8 750)
Prepaid interest	= (0.09/12)($203 705) =	(1 528)
Amount received		= $202 222
Annual commission	= ($8750)(12)	= $105 000
Annual interest	= (0.09)($203 750)	= 18 338
Total annual costs		= $123 338

b. The factoring costs are slightly lower than the cost of the bank loan, and the factor is willing to advance a significantly greater amount. On the other hand, the elimination of the credit department could reduce the future adaptability of the firm.

IV

CAPITAL BUDGETING

12

▲▲

Time Value of Money

A MANAGERIAL PERSPECTIVE

Every year from the middle of January until the last week of February, it is impossible to escape articles and advertisements by financial institutions concerning contributions to registered retirement savings plans (RRSPs). With changes in the RRSP legislation in 1991, the RRSP information has become even more abundant than usual and focusses on ways for individuals to save on current taxes while building a portfolio to fund retirement over and above the contribution made by the government.

A number of these articles address the question of how much is needed for retirement and the importance of the rate of return earned by an RRSP fund over the preretirement period. For example, if the return is 8 percent, investing $5500 per year for 20 years will produce a fund of $271 826; at a 10 percent return, the fund will be $346 514.

What does an RRSP have to do with the time value of money? Actually, a great deal. The impact on the retirement pool and hence the annual income available in retirement from returns earned, the amount invested per year, and the time periods over which the RRSP contributions are made are all directly related to the time value of money. If you study this chapter carefully, you will recognize the importance of the contributions to RRSPs and perhaps help yourself or your parents in planning for retirement.

In Chapter 1, we saw that the primary goal of management is to maximize the wealth of existing shareholders. We also saw that share values depend, in part, on the timing of the cash flows investors expect to receive from an investment—a dollar expected soon is valued more highly than a dollar expected far in the future. Therefore, it is essential that financial managers have a clear understanding of discounted cash flows and its impact on the value of the firm. These concepts are discussed in this chapter, in which we show how the timing of cash flows affects asset values and rates of return.

The principles of the time value of money developed here have many other applications, ranging from setting up schedules for paying off loans to making decisions about whether to acquire new equipment. In fact, of all the techniques used in finance, none is more important than the time value of money, or discounted cash flow analysis (DCF). Since this concept is used throughout the remainder of the book, it is vital to understand the material in this chapter thoroughly before going on to other topics.[1]

Time Lines

One of the most important tools in time value of money analysis is the **time line**, which permits us to visualize the timing of what is happening in a particular problem and then helps us to set up the problem for solution. For an illustration of the time line concept, consider the following diagram:

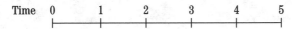

Time 0 is today; Time 1 is one period from today, or the end of Period 1; Time 2 is two periods from today, or the end of Period 2; and so on. Thus, the values written at the tick marks represent end-of-period values. Often the periods are years, but other time intervals, such as half years, quarters, months, or even days, are also used. If our time periods are years, the interval from 0 to 1 is Year 1, and Time 1 represents both the end of Year 1 and the beginning of Year 2.

Cash flows are placed directly below the tick marks, and the applicable interest rates are shown directly above the time line. Unknown cash flows, which we are trying to find in the analysis, are indicated by question marks. Now consider the following time line:

```
Time          0    5%   1      2      3
              |---------|------|------|
Cash Flows  −100                     ?
```

Here the interest rate for each of the three periods is 5 percent; a single-amount (or lump sum) cash *outflow* is made at Time 0; and the Time 3 value is an unknown *inflow*. Since the initial $100 is an outflow, it has a minus sign. Since the Period 3 amount is an inflow, it does not have a minus sign. Note that no cash flows occur at Times 1 and 2. Note also that, to reduce clutter, we do not show dollar signs on time lines.

Now consider the following situation, in which a $100 cash outflow is made today, and you will receive an unknown amount at the end of Time 2:

```
     0    5%   1   10%   2
     |---------|---------|
   −100                  ?
```

[1]This chapter—indeed the entire book—is written on the assumption that most students have access to financial calculators. The cost of these calculators is relatively small, and students who cannot use them run the risk of being deemed obsolete and hence uncompetitive before they even graduate. However, there is the risk that individuals will learn to use financial calculators in a "cookbook" fashion without understanding the logical processes that underlie financial mathematics. Then when faced with a new type of problem, they will not understand the process well enough to set it up. Recognizing this problem and the pervasiveness of financial calculators, we have decided to introduce financial calculator solutions in the footnotes to each of the major sections; our emphasis in the main text, however, remains on the logic behind the solutions, which is best observed through the use of regular calculators and tables.

Here the interest rate is 5 percent during the first period, but it rises to 10 percent during the second period. If the interest rate is constant in all periods, we show it only in the first period, but if it changes, we show all the relevant rates on the time line.

Time lines are essential when you are first learning time value of money concepts, but even experts use time lines to analyze complex problems. We use time lines throughout the book, and you should get into the habit of using them when you work problems.

Concept Review

▶ Why is understanding the time value of money essential for financial managers?

▶ What is a time line?

▶ Draw a time line that illustrates the following situation: (1) an outflow of $10 000 occurs at Time 0; (2) inflows of $5000 occur at the end of each of Years 1, 2, and 3; (3) and the interest rate during the 3 years is 10 percent.

Future Value

A dollar in hand today is worth more than a dollar to be received in the future because, if you had it now, you could invest it, earn interest, and end up with more than one dollar in the future. The process of going from today's values, or present values (PV), to future values (FV) is called **compounding**. To illustrate: suppose you deposited $100 in a bank savings account that paid 5 percent interest each year. How much would you have at the end of 1 year? To begin, we define the following terms:

PV = present value, or the beginning amount, of your account. Here PV = $100.

 k = interest rate the bank pays on the account per year. The interest earned is based on the balance at the beginning of the year, and we assume that it is paid at the end of the year. Here k = 5%, or expressed as a decimal, 0.05. On financial calculators, the term i is often used rather than k.

 I = dollars of interest you earn during the year = Beginning amount × k, or PV(k). Here I = $100(0.05) = $5.

FV_n = future value, compound value, or ending amount, of your account at the end of n years. Whereas PV is the value now, at the *present* time, FV_n is the value *n years into the future*, after interest has been added to your account.

 n = the number of periods involved in the analysis.

In our example, n = 1, so $FV_n = FV_1$, and it is calculated as follows:

$$FV_n = FV_1 = PV + I$$
$$= PV + PV(k)$$
$$= PV(1 + k)$$
$$= \$100(1 + 0.05) = \$100(1.05) = \$105.$$

(12-1)

Thus, the **future value (FV** at the end of one year, FV_1, equals the present value multiplied by 1.0 plus the interest rate, so you will have $105 after one year.

What would you end up with if you left your $100.00 in the account for 5 years? The answer is $127.63; this value is worked out in Table 12-1. Notice that the table value for FV_2, the value of the account at the end of Year 2, is equal to

$$FV_2 = FV_1(1 + k) = PV(1 + k)(1 + k) = PV(1 + k)^2.$$

Continuing, we see that FV_3, the balance after 3 years, is

$$FV_3 = FV_2(1 + k) = PV(1 + k)^3.$$

In general, FV_n, the future value at the end of n years, is found as follows:

$$FV_n = PV(1 + k)^n. \qquad\qquad \textbf{(12-2)}$$

Applying Equation 12-2 to our 5-year, 5 percent case, we obtain

$$
\begin{aligned}
FV_5 &= \$100(1.05)^5 \\
&= \$100.00(1.2763) \\
&= \$127.63,
\end{aligned}
$$

which is the same as the value worked out in Table 12-1.

Now let us analyze the same problem with a time line.

	0	5%	1	2	3	4	5
Initial Deposit	—100		FV_1 = ?	FV_2 = ?	FV_3 = ?	FV_4 = ?	FV_5 = ?
Interest Earned			5.00	5.25	5.51	5.79	6.08
Amount at End of Each Period			105.00	110.25	115.76	121.55	127.63

Note the following points:

1.   You start by depositing $100.00 in the account. This is shown as an outflow at t = 0.

Table 12-1
Compound Interest Calculations

Period (n)	Amount at Beginning of Period n	×	(1 + k)	=	Amount at End of Period n
1	$100.00		1.05		$105.00
2	105.00		1.05		110.25
3	110.25		1.05		115.76
4	115.76		1.05		121.55
5	121.55		1.05		127.63

2. You earn $100.00(0.05) = $5.00 of interest during the first year, so the amount at the end of Year 1 (t = 1) is $100.00 + $5.00 = $105.00.

3. You start the second year with $105.00, earn $5.25 on the now larger amount, and end the second year with $110.25. Your interest during Year 2, $5.25, is higher than the first year's interest, $5.00, because you earned $5(0.05) = $0.25 interest on the first year's interest.

4. The process continues, and because the beginning balance is higher in each succeeding year, the annual interest earned increases.

5. The total interest earned, $27.63, is reflected in the final balance at t = 5: $127.63.

Interest Tables

The *future value interest factor for k and n, FVIF$_{k, n}$*, is denoted as $(1 + k)^n$, and these factors can be found by using a calculator.[2] However, tables have been constructed for values of $(1 + k)^n$ for wide ranges of k and n. Table 12-2 is illustrative; a more complete table, with more years and more interest rates, is given in Table A-3 on the insert card. Notice that we have used the term *period* rather than *year* in Table 12-2. As we shall see later in the chapter, compounding can occur over periods of time other than 1 year. Thus, although compounding is often on an annual basis, it can be quarterly, semiannually, monthly, or for any other period.

Table 12-2
Future Value of $1 at the End of n Periods: FVIF$_{k,n}$ = $(1 + k)^n$

Period (n)	4%	5%	6%
1	1.0400	1.0500	1.0600
2	1.0816	1.1025	1.1236
3	1.1249	1.1576	1.1910
4	1.1699	1.2155	1.2625
5	1.2167	1.2763	1.3382
6	1.2653	1.3401	1.4185
7	1.3159	1.4071	1.5036
8	1.3686	1.4775	1.5938
9	1.4233	1.5513	1.6895
10	1.4802	1.6289	1.7908

---

[2]For example, to calculate $(1 + k)^n$ for k = 5% = 0.05 and n = 5 years, we multiply $(1 + k)$ = (1.05) by (1.05); multiply this product by (1.05); and so on:

$$(1 + k)^n = (1.05)(1.05)(1.05)(1.05)(1.05) = (1.05)^5 = 1.2763.$$

This same result is obtained using the exponential function of a calculator, y^x. Here y = (1.05), x = 5, and $(1.05)^5$ = 1.2763. If you have a financial calculator, simply punch in n = 5, k = i = 5, and PV = 1, and then punch the FV button to obtain the factor 1.2763. Alternatively, you could punch in n = 5, k = i = 5, and PV = 100 and then hit the FV button to find the final answer, $127.63.

Since $(1 + k)^n = \text{FVIF}_{k, n}$, Equation 12-2 can be rewritten as follows:

$$FV_n = PV(\text{FVIF}_{k, n}). \qquad \qquad \textbf{(12-2a)}$$

To illustrate: the FVIF for our 5-year, 5 percent example can be found in Table 12-2. We look down the first column to 5, then across this row to the 5 percent column to find the interest factor, 1.2763. Then, using this interest factor, we determine the value of $100.00 after 5 years as follows:

$$FV_5 = PV(\text{FVIF}_{k, n})$$
$$= \$100.00(1.2763) = \$127.63.$$

Graphic View of the Compounding Process: Growth

Figure 12-1 shows how $1.00 (or any other sum) grows over time at various rates of interest. The data used to plot the curves can be obtained from the appropriate columns of Table A-3 on the insert card. The greater the rate of interest, the faster the rate of growth. The interest rate is, in fact, a growth rate; if a sum is deposited and earns 5 percent, then the funds on deposit will grow at the rate of 5 percent per period. Note also that time value concepts can be applied to anything that is growing—sales, population, earnings or dividends per share, or whatever.

Concept Review

▶ Explain what is meant by the following statement: "A dollar in hand today is worth more than a dollar to be received next year."
▶ What is *compounding*?

(continued)

Figure 12-1
Relationships among Future Value, Interest Rates, and Time

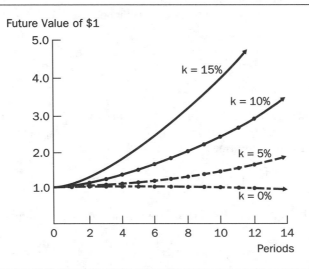

(continued)

▶ Explain the following equation: $FV_1 = PV + I$.
▶ Set up a time line that illustrates the following problem. You make an initial deposit of $100 to an account that pays 5 percent interest annually. You want to know how much money you will have at the end of 3 years.
▶ What equation can you use to solve the preceding problem?

Present Value

Suppose you have some extra cash, and you have a chance to buy a low-risk security that will pay $127.63 at the end of 5 years. Your local bank is currently offering 5 percent interest on 5-year investment certificates, and you regard them as being safe from default. The 5 percent rate is defined as being your **opportunity cost** rate, or the rate of return you could earn on next-best investments of equivalent risk. How much should you be willing to pay for the security?

In the future value example presented in the previous section, we saw that an initial amount of $100.00 growing at 5 percent per year yields $127.63 at the end of 5 years. Thus, you should be indifferent in your choice between $100 today and $127.63 at the end of 5 years. The $100 is defined as the present value of $127.63 due in 5 years when the opportunity cost rate is 5 percent. If the price of the security is anything less than $100.00, you should definitely buy it. If the price is greater than $100, you should turn it down. If the price is exactly $100, then you could buy it or turn it down. We can say that the security's "fair value" is $100.

In general, the **present value (PV)** of a cash flow due n years in the future is the amount that, if it were on hand today, would grow to equal the future amount. Since $100.00 would grow to $127.63 in 5 years at a 5 percent interest rate, $100 is the present value of $127.63 due 5 years in the future when the appropriate interest rate is 5 percent.

The time line for this problem is set out below:

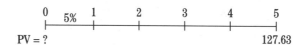

Finding the present value of a future cash flow—which is called **discounting**—is simply the reverse of compounding. To develop the discounting equation, we simply begin with Equations 12-2 and 12-2a,

$$FV_n = PV(1 + k)^n = PV(FVIF_{k, n}), \qquad \textbf{(12-2) (12-2a)}$$

which can be solved for PV and written in several equivalent forms:

$$PV = \frac{FV_n}{(1 + k)^n} = FV_n\left(\frac{1}{1 + k}\right)^n = FV_n(PVIF_{k, n}). \qquad \textbf{(12-3)}$$

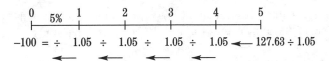

A numerical solution is obtained by dividing $127.63 by 1.05 five times, or by $(1.05)^5$, as shown below. The term in parentheses in Equation 12-3 is called the *present value interest factor for k and n, $PVIF_{k,n}$*. Table A-1 on the insert card contains present value interest factors for selected values of k and n. The value of $PVIF_{k,n}$ for k = 5% and n = 5 is 0.7835, so the present value of $127.63 to be received after 5 years when the opportunity cost rate is 5 percent equals $100:

$$PV = \$127.63(PVIF_{5\%, 5}) = \$127.63(0.7835) = \$100.00.$$

Graphic View of the Discounting Process

Figure 12-2 shows how the present value of $1 (or any other sum) decreases as the discounting period increases. The curves in the figure were plotted with data taken from Table A-1 of the insert card; they show that (1) the present value of a sum to be received at some future date decreases as the payment date is extended further into the future and (2) that the rate of decrease is greater the higher the interest (discount) rate. At relatively high discount rates, funds due in the future are worth very little today. Even at a relatively low discount rate, the present value of a sum due in the very distant future is quite small. For example, $1 due in 10 years is worth about 61 cents today if the discount rate is 5 percent, but it is worth only 25 cents today at a 15 percent

Figure 12-2
Relationships among Present Value, Interest Rates, and Time

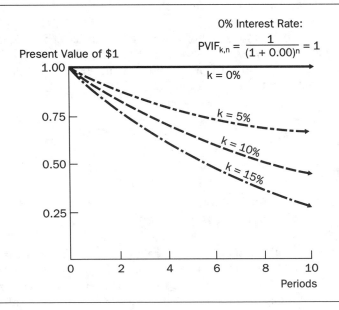

discount rate. Similarly, $1 due in 5 years at 10 percent is worth 62 cents today, but at the same discount rate, $1 due in 10 years is worth only 39 cents today.

Solving for Time and Interest Rates

At this point, you should realize that the compounding and discounting processes are reciprocals of one another, and that we have been dealing with one equation in two different forms:

FV Form:

$$FV_n = PV(1 + k)^n = PV(FVIF_{k, n}). \tag{12-2}$$

PV Form:

$$PV = \frac{FV_n}{(1 + k)^n} = FV_n\left(\frac{1}{1 + k}\right)^n = FV_n(PVIF_{k, n}). \tag{12-3}$$

There are four variables in these equations—PV, FV, k, and n—and if you know the values of any three, you (or your financial calculator) can find the value of the fourth. Thus far, we have always given you the interest rate, k, and the number of years, n, plus either the PV or the FV. In many situations, though, you need to solve for either k or n.

Solving for k.   Suppose you can buy a security at a price of $78.35, and it will pay you $100.00 after 5 years. Here we know PV, FV, and n, but we do not know k, the interest rate you will earn on your investment. Problems such as this one can be displayed on a time line as follows:

```
  0   i = ?  1       2       3       4       5
  |----------|-------|-------|-------|-------|
-78.35                                      100
```

In equation form:

$$FV_n = PV(1 + k)^n. \tag{12-2}$$
$$\$100.00 = \$78.35(1 + k)^5. \text{ Solve for k.}$$

To obtain a numerical solution, you can use a trial-and-error process in which you insert different values of k into Equation 12-2 until you find a value that "works" in the sense that the right-hand side of the equation becomes equal to $100.00. The solution value is k = 0.05, or 5 percent. The trial-and-error procedure is extremely tedious and inefficient for most time value problems, however, so no one in the "real world" uses it.

Alternatively, the future value table can be used.

$$FV_n = PV(1 + k)^n = PV(FVIF_{k, n})$$

$$\$100.00 = \$78.35(FVIF_{k, 5})$$

$$FVIF_{k, 5} = \frac{\$100.00}{\$78.35} = 1.2763.$$

Find the value of the FVIF as shown above, and then look across the period 5 row in Table A-3 on the insert card until you find FVIF = 1.2763. This value is in the 5 percent column, so the interest rate at which $78.35 grows to $100.00 over 5 years is 5.0 percent.[3] This procedure can be used only if the interest rate is in the table; therefore, it will not work for fractional interest rates or where n is not a whole number. Approximation procedures can be used, but they are laborious and inexact.[4]

Solving for n.   Suppose you know that a security will provide a return of 5 percent per year, that it will cost $78.35, and that you will receive $100.00 at maturity, but you do not know when the security matures. Thus, you know PV, FV, and k, but you do not know n, the number of periods. Here is how to set up this type of problem on a time line:

In equation form:

$$FV_n = PV(1 + k)^n \qquad\qquad \textbf{(12-2)}$$

$$\$100.00 = \$78.35(1.05)^n. \text{ Solve for } n.$$

Again, you can go through a trial-and-error process wherein you substitute different values for n into the equation. You will find (eventually) that n = 5 "works," so 5 is the number of years it takes for $78.35 to grow to $100.00 if the interest rate is 5 percent.

---

[3]The solution can also be set up in present value format:

$$PV = FV_n (PVIF_{k, n})$$
$$\$78.35 = \$100(PVIF_{k, 5})$$

$$PVIF_{k, 5} = \frac{\$78.35}{\$100} = 0.7835.$$

This value corresponds to k = 5.0 percent in Table A-1 on the insert card.

[4]With a financial calculator, enter n = 5, PV = −78.35, and FV = 100, and then press i to get i = k = 5. This procedure can be used for any interest rate or any value of n, including fractional values.

Alternatively, you can use the tabular approach:

$$FV_n = PV(1 + k)^n = PV(FVIF_{k,n})$$

$$\$100.00 = \$78.35(FVIF_{5\%,n})$$

$$FVIF_{5\%,n} = \frac{\$100.00}{\$78.35} = 1.2763.$$

Now look down the 5 percent column in Table A-3 on the insert card until you find FVIF = 1.2763. This value is in row 5, which indicates that it takes 5 years for $78.35 to grow to $100.00 at a 5 percent interest rate.[5]

> ### Concept Review
>
> ▶ Assuming that you are given PV, FV, and the interest rate, k, write out an equation that can be used to determine the time period, n.
> ▶ Assuming that you are given PV, FV, and the time period, n, write out an equation that can be used to determine the interest rate, k.

Future Value of an Annuity

An **annuity** is a series of payments of a fixed amount for a specified number of periods. For example: $100 at the end of each of the next three years is a 3-year annuity. The payments are given the symbol PMT, and they can occur at either the beginning or the end of each period. If the payments occur at the end of each period, as they typically do, then we have an **ordinary annuity**, or a *deferred payment annuity*, as it is sometimes called. If payments are made at the beginning of each period, then we have an **annuity due**. Since ordinary (or deferred) annuities are far more common in finance, when the word *annuity* is used in this book, you should assume that payments are received at the end of each period unless otherwise indicated.

Ordinary Annuities

An ordinary, or deferred, annuity consists of a series of equal payments made at the end of each period. If you receive $100 at the end of each year for 3 years

---

[5]The problem could also be solved as follows:

$$PV = FV_n(PVIF_{k,n})$$

$$\$78.35 = \$100(PVIF_{5\%,n})$$

$$PVIF_{5\%,n} = \frac{\$78.35}{\$100} = 0.7835.$$

This value corresponds to n = 5 years in Table A-1 on the insert card.

With a financial calculator, enter k = i = 5, PV = −78.35, and FV = 100, and then press n to get n = 5.

and deposit each annual payment in a savings account paying 5 percent interest per year, how much will you have at the end of 3 years? To answer this question, we must find the future value of an annuity, FVA_n. Each payment is compounded to the end of period n, and the sum of the compounded payments is the future value of the annuity, FVA_n.

The process undertaken to obtain this future value is shown in the following time line:

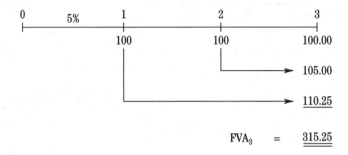

This procedure is represented in the equation below:

$$FVA_n = PMT + PMT(1 + k)^1 + PMT(1 + k)^2 + \ldots + PMT(1 + k)^{n-1}$$

$$= PMT \sum_{t=1}^{n} (1 + k)^{n-t} \qquad (12\text{-}4)$$

Using the time line approach requires the calculation of the future value of each cash flow and the summation of these future values; this is a tedious procedure for long annuities. An alternative approach utilizes the summation term in Equation 12-4. This term is called the *future value interest factor for an annuity, $FVIFA_{k,n}$*.[6]

$$FVIFA_{k,n} = \sum_{t=1}^{n} (1 + k)^{n-t} = \frac{(1 + k)^n - 1}{k}. \qquad (12\text{-}4a)$$

FVIFAs have been calculated for various combinations of k and n; Table A-4 on the insert card contains a set of interest factors. To find the answer to the 3-year, $100.00 annuity problem, first refer to Table A-4 and look down the 5 percent column to period 3: the FVIFA is 3.1525. Thus, the future value of the $100.00 annuity is $315.25:[7]

$$FVA_n = PMT(FVIFA_{k,n}) \qquad (12\text{-}5)$$

$$= \$100.00(FVIFA_{5\%, 3}) = \$100.00(3.1525) = \$315.25.$$

---

[6]The third term in Equation 12-4a is found by applying the algebra of geometric progressions. This equation is useful in situations in which the required values of k and n are not in the tables and no financial calculator is available.

[7]With a financial calculator, you can obtain FVA_n directly. Just enter n = 3, k = i = 5, and PMT = 1000. Press the FV button to obtain the answer. Alternatively, if the PV button is pushed, you obtain the present value of the annuity.

Annuity Due

Had the three $100.00 payments in the previous example each been made at the *beginning* of the year, the annuity would have been an *annuity due*. In the time line, each payment would be shifted one to the left. Thus, each payment would be compounded for one extra year.

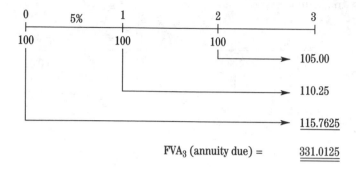

We can modify Equation 12-5 to handle annuities due as follows:

$$FVA_n(\text{Annuity due}) = PMT(FVIFA_{k,n})(1 + k).$$ **(12-5a)**

Each payment is compounded for an extra year, and multiplying $PMT(FVIFA_{k,n})$ by $(1 + k)$ takes care of this extra compounding. Applying Equation 12-5a to the previous example, we obtain

$$FVA_n(\text{Annuity due}) = \$100.00(3.1525)(1.05) = \$331.0125.$$

The payments occur earlier, so more interest is earned. Therefore, the future value of the annuity due is larger: $331.01 versus $315.25 for the ordinary annuity.

Concept Review

▶ What is the difference between an ordinary annuity and an annuity due?

▶ What is the equation for determining the value of an ordinary annuity? How do you modify this equation in order to determine the value of an annuity due?

▶ For all positive interest rates, is the $FVIFA_{k,n}$ larger, smaller, or equal to the number of periods of the annuity? Why must this relationship always hold?

▶ Which annuity has the greater future values: an ordinary annuity or an annuity due?

Present Value of an Annuity

Suppose you are offered the following alternatives: (1) a 3-year annuity with payments of $100 at the end of each year or (2) a lump sum payment today. You have no need for the money during the next 3 years, so if you accept the annuity you will simply deposit the payments in a savings account that pays 5 percent interest. How large must the lump sum payment today be to make it equivalent to the annuity? The time line for this problem is shown below with the numerical solution values at the left. The PV of the annuity, PVA_n, is $272.325. This is obtained by finding the present value of each of the payments and then summing them.

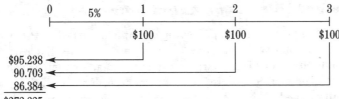

The general equation used to find the PV of an ordinary annuity is shown below:[8]

$$PVA_n = PMT\left(\frac{1}{1+k}\right)^1 + PMT\left(\frac{1}{1+k}\right)^2 + \ldots + PMT\left(\frac{1}{1+k}\right)^n$$

$$= PMT\left[\frac{1}{(1+k)} + \frac{1}{(1+k)^2} + \ldots + \frac{1}{(1+k)^n}\right]$$

$$= PMT\left[\sum_{t=1}^{n}\left(\frac{1}{1+k}\right)^t\right].$$

This equation can be restated as

$$PVA_n = PMT(PVIFA_{k,n}) \qquad\qquad \textbf{(12-6)}$$

The term in parentheses here is called the *present value interest factor for an annuity, PVIFA$_{k,n}$*. Values for this term at different values of k and n are shown in Table A-2 on the insert card. To find the answer to the 3-year annuity problem, simply refer to Table A-2 and look down the 5 percent column to the third period. The PVIFA is 2.7232, so the present value of the $100.00 annuity is $272.32:[9]

$$PVA_n = PMT(PVIFA_{k,n})$$

$$PVA_3 = \$100.00(PVIFA_{5\%,3}) = \$100.00(2.7232) = \$272.32$$

---

[8]The summation term is called the PVIFA. Using the geometric progression solution procedure, we find its value as

$$\sum_{t=1}^{n}\left(\frac{1}{1+k}\right)^t = \frac{1}{k} - \frac{1}{k(1+k)^n}.$$

This form of the equation is useful for dealing with annuities when the values for k and n are not in the tables and no financial calculator is available.

[9]Again, the problem can be solved directly with a financial calculator. Just punch in n = 3, k = i = 5, and PMT = 100, and then hit the PV button to find PVF_n = $272.325.

An especially important application of the annuity concept relates to loans with constant payments, such as mortgages and auto loans. With such loans, called *amortized loans*, the beginning amount is the present value of an ordinary annuity, and the payments constitute the annuity stream. We shall examine constant payment loans in more depth in a later section of this chapter.

Present Value of an Annuity Due

Had the payments in the preceding example occurred at the beginning of each year, the annuity would have been an *annuity due*. Each payment would be discounted for one less year; on a time line, each payment would be shifted to the left one period. With each payment occurring one period earlier, the annuity due should have a higher PV than the ordinary annuity. The following time line presents the procedure in which each cash flow is discounted and shows the PVA, which is the sum of the discounted cash flows.

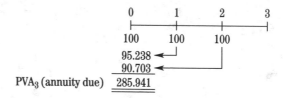

Since the payments come in faster, an annuity due is more valuable than an ordinary annuity. This higher value is found by multiplying the PV of an ordinary annuity by $(1 + k)$:

$$PVA_n(\text{Annuity due}) = PMT(PVIFA_{k,\,n})(1 + k). \qquad \text{(12-6a)}$$

In our example,

$$= \$100.00(2.7232)(1.05) = \$285.94.$$

Concept Review

▶ Which annuity has the greater present value: an ordinary annuity or an annuity due? Why?

Perpetuities

Most annuities call for payments to be made for some finite period of time—for example, $100 per year for 3 years. However, some annuities go on indefinitely, or perpetually. These annuities are called **perpetuities**.

The present value of a perpetuity is found by applying Equation 12-7:

$$PV(\text{Perpetuity}) = \frac{\text{Payment}}{\text{Interest rate}} = \frac{PMT}{k}. \qquad \text{(12-7)}$$

To illustrate; in 1815, after the Napoleonic Wars, the British government sold a huge bond issue and used the proceeds to pay off many smaller issues that had been floated in prior years to pay for the war. Since the purpose of the new bonds was to consolidate past debts, the bonds were called *consols*. Suppose each consol had promised to pay $100 interest per year in perpetuity (actually, interest was stated in pounds). What would each bond be worth if the opportunity cost rate, or the discount rate, was 5 percent? The answer is $2000:

$$\text{PV(Perpetuity)} = \frac{\$100}{0.05} = \$2000.$$

Suppose the interest rate rose to 10 percent; what would happen to the consol's value? The value would drop to $1000:

$$\text{PV(Perpetuity)} = \frac{\$1000}{0.10} = \$1000.$$

We observe that the value of a perpetuity changes dramatically when interest rates change.

Perpetuities are discussed in Chapter 16, where procedures for finding the values of various types of securities are discussed.

Concept Review

▶ What happens to the value of a perpetuity when interest rates increase?
▶ What happens when interest rates decrease? Why do these changes in value occur?
▶ What is the difference in value of a perpetuity if purchased today compared to its purchase one year from today?

Uneven Cash Flows

The definition of an annuity includes the words *constant amount*—in other words, annuities involve situations in which cash flows are *identical* in every period. Although many financial decisions do involve constant cash flows, some important decisions involve nonconstant or uneven cash flows. For example, common shares typically are expected to pay an increasing series of dividends over time, and fixed-asset investments, such as acquisitions of new equipment, normally do not generate constant cash flows. Consequently, it is necessary to extend our time value discussion to include *uneven cash flow streams*.

Throughout the book, we follow convention and reserve the term *payment (PMT)* for annuity situations in which the cash flows are constant, using the term *cash flow (CF)* to denote uneven cash flows. This is consistent with the convention used with financial calculators.

Present Value of an Uneven Stream

The PV of a stream of uneven cash flows is found as the sum of the PVs of the individual components of the stream. For example, suppose we must find the PV of the following cash flow stream, discounted at 6 percent:

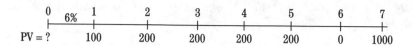

The PV can be found by applying the general present value equation:

$$PV = CF_1\left(\frac{1}{1+k}\right)^1 + CF_2\left(\frac{1}{1+k}\right)^2 + \ldots + CF_n\left(\frac{1}{1+k}\right)^n$$

$$= \sum_{t=1}^{n} CF_t\left(\frac{1}{1+k}\right)^t = \sum_{t=1}^{n} CF_t\,(PVIF_{k,\,n}) \qquad\qquad \textbf{(12-8)}$$

We can find the present value of each individual cash flow and sum these values to obtain the present value of the stream. Here is what the process looks like:

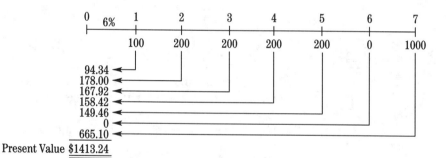

All we did was apply Equation 12-8, show the individual terms at the left of the diagram, and then sum the individual PVs to find the PV of the entire stream.

The present value of a cash flow stream can always be found by summing the present values of the individual cash flows, as shown above. However, cash flow regularities within the stream may allow the use of shortcuts. For example, notice that cash flows 2 through 5 represent an annuity. We can use that fact to solve the problem by using the annuity equations for some of the cash flows.

Step 1. Find the PV of $100.00 due in Year 1:

$$\$100.00(0.9434) = \$94.34.$$

Step 2. The Year 2–5 cash flows represent an ordinary annuity, so we find its PV at Year 1 (a year before the first payment). The PV is calculated as

$$PVA_3 = PMT(PVIFA_{6\%,\,4}) = \$200.00(3.4651) = \$693.02.$$

This present value must now be discounted back one more period to get its Year 0 value of $653.80. (This type of annuity is called a *delayed annuity* since the cash flows start at a time in the future.)

Step 3.   Find the PV of the $1000 due in Year 7:

$$\$1000.00(0.6651) = \$665.10.$$

Step 4.   Sum the components:

$$\$94.34 + \$653.80 + \$665.10 = \$1413.24.$$

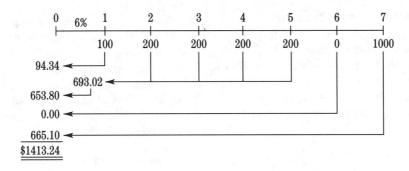

Future Value of an Uneven Stream

The future value of an uneven cash flow stream—sometimes called the *terminal value*—is found by compounding each payment to the end of the stream and then summing the future values:

$$FV_n = CF_1(1 + k)^{n-1} + CF_2(1 + k)^{n-2} + \ldots + CF_n(1 + k)^{n-t}$$

$$= \sum_{t=1}^{n} CF_t(1 + k)^{n-1} = \sum_{t=1}^{n} CF_t(FVIF_{k,\,n}). \qquad (12\text{-}9)$$

The future value of our illustrative uneven cash flow stream is $2124.92:

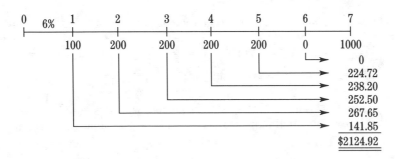

We are generally more interested in the present value of an asset's cash flow stream than in the future value, because the present value represents today's value, which we can compare to the price of the asset.

> ## Concept Review
>
> ▶ Give two examples of financial decisions that typically involve uneven cash flows.
> ▶ What is meant by the term *terminal value*?

Semiannual and Other Compounding Periods

In all of our examples thus far, we have assumed that interest is compounded once a year, or annually. This is called *annual compounding*. Suppose, however, that you put $100 in a bank that advertises that it pays 6 percent "compounded semiannually." *Semiannual compounding* means that interest is actually paid every six months. How much will you accumulate at the end of 1 year, 2 years, or some other period under semiannual compounding?

To illustrate semiannual compounding, assume that $100.00 is placed into an account at an interest rate of 6 percent and left there for 3 years. For annual compounding, the future value is calculated as follows:

$$FV_n = PV(1 + k)^3 = \$100.00(1.06)^3 = \$119.10.$$

Alternatively, the future value can be obtained by using the value for $FVIF_{6\%, 3}$, which is equal to 1.1910.

With semiannual compounding, there are $n = 2 \times 3 = 6$ semiannual periods, so every 6 months you will earn $k = 6/2 = 3$ percent. Note that on all types of contracts, interest is always quoted as an annual rate, and if compounding occurs more frequently than once a year, that fact is stated, along with the rate. In our example, the quoted rate is "6 percent, compounded semiannually." Here is how we find the FV after 3 years at 6 percent with semiannual compounding:

| | | 1 | | 2 | | 3 | Years |
|0|1|2|3|4|5|6|6-Month Periods|

3%
−100   FV = ?

Using the future value equation, we can calculate the value as equal to

$$FV_n = PV(1 + k)^n = \$100.00(1.03)^6$$
$$= \$100.00(1.1941) = \$119.41,$$

where k is the **periodic rate**, the rate per period, which is equal to the annual rate divided by compounding periods per year = 6/2 = 3 percent, and n is the total number of periods, which equals the number of years times the periods per year $= 3 \times 2 = 6$.

Alternatively, the future value can be calculated by using the FVIF as follows:

$$FV_6 = \$100.00(FVIF_{3\%, 6}) = \$100.00(1.1941) = \$119.41.$$

Notice that the FV is larger under semiannual compounding than under annual compounding because interest on interest is being earned more frequently.[10]

Throughout the world economy, different types of investments use different compounding periods. For example, bank and trust accounts may pay interest monthly or even daily, most bonds pay interest semiannually, and shares generally pay dividends quarterly. If we are to compare securities with different compounding periods, we need to put them on a common basis. This need has led to the development of the terms *nominal*, or *quoted*, *interest rate* versus the *effective annual rate (EAR).*[11] The nominal, or quoted rate in our example is 6 percent. The **effective annual rate (EAR)** is defined as that rate that would produce the same ending (future) value if annual compounding were used. In our example, the effective annual rate is the annual rate that would produce an FV of \$119.41 at the end of Year 3.

We can determine the effective annual rate, given the nominal rate and the number of compounding periods per year, by solving this equation:

$$\text{Effective annual rate (EAR)} = \left(1 + \frac{k_{nom}}{m}\right)^m - 1.0. \qquad \textbf{(12-10)}$$

Here k_{nom} is the nominal or quoted rate, and m is the number of compounding periods per year. For example, to find the effective annual rate if the nominal rate is 6 percent, compounded semiannually, we make the following calculations:

$$\begin{aligned}
\text{Effective annual rate (EAR)} &= \left(1 + \frac{0.06}{2}\right)^2 - 1.0 \\
&= (1.03)^2 - 1.0 \\
&= 1.0609 - 1.0 = 0.0609 = 6.09\%.
\end{aligned}$$

Semiannual compounding (or any nonannual compounding) can be handled in two ways:

1. State everything on a periodic basis rather than on an annual basis. For example, use n = 6 periods rather than n = 3 years, and use k = 3% per period rather than k = 6% per year.

---

[10]Semiannual compounding is handled easily with a financial calculator. We merely set i = 6, n = 3, and PV = 100, and then hit the FV button to get the solution, FV = \$119.10.

[11]The term *nominal* as it is used here has a different meaning from *nominal* as it was used in Chapter 3. There, "nominal interest rates" meant the stated rates as opposed to the real (inflation-adjusted) rates. In this chapter, the "nominal rate" means the stated rate as opposed to the *effective annual rate.*

2. Alternatively, find the effective annual rate by applying Equation 12-10, and then use this rate as an annual rate over the given number of years. In our example, use k = 6.09 percent and n = 3 years.

Of course, once you start dealing with noninteger interest rates, such as 6.09, the use of a calculator is essential.

The points made about semiannual compounding can be generalized as follows. When compounding periods are more frequent than once a year, we use a modified version of Equation 12-2 to find the future value of any sum.

$$\text{Annual compounding: } FV_n = PV(1 + k)^n \qquad \textbf{(12-2)}$$

$$\text{More frequent compounding: } FV_n = PV\left(1 + \frac{k_{nom}}{m}\right)^{mn}, \qquad \textbf{(12-2a)}$$

where m is the number of times per year compounding occurs, and n is the number of years. When banks compute daily interest, the value of m is set at 365, and Equation 12-2a is applied.

To illustrate the impact of more frequent compounding, the effective annual rates for different compounding periods per year for nominal annual interest rates of 6 and 12 percent are presented in Table 12-3. There are two important observations from this table. First, for a given nominal rate, the effective annual rate of interest increases as the number of compounding periods per year increases. Second, the effective rate increases at a decreasing rate. The largest impact is the change from annual to semiannual compounding. Increasing the number of compounding periods per year results in progressively smaller increases in the effective annual interest rate.

By letting m approach infinity, Equation 12-2a can be modified to the special case of *continuous compounding*. Continuous compounding is extremely useful in theoretical finance, but it has limited practical applications. Some banks in the United States pay interest on a continuous basis. (Continuous compounding is discussed in Appendix 12-A.)

To further understand the impact of compounding more frequently than annually, consider the interest rate charged on credit cards. For example, suppose a bank charges 1.5 percent per month and, in its advertising, it states that the *annual percentage rate (APR)* is 18.0 percent, calculated as the

Table 12-3
Effective Annual Rate (EAR)

Annual Nominal Rate, k_{nom}	Number of Compounding Periods per Year, m				
	1	2	3	6	Infinite[a]
6%	6%	6.09%	6.12%	6.15%	6.18%
12	12	12.36	12.49	12.62	12.75

[a]This is continuous compounding, and the effective rate is calculated as $e^{k_{nom}}$.

monthly rate times 12. The true rate, however, is the effective annual rate of 19.6 percent:

$$\text{Effective annual rate} = \text{EAR} = \left(1 + \frac{0.18}{12}\right)^{12} - 1.0$$

$$= (1.015)^{12} - 1.0$$

$$= 0.196 = 19.6\%.$$

Semiannual and other compounding periods can also be used for discounting and for calculating both lump sum and annuities. For example, what is the present value of an annuity that requires payments of $50.00 every 6 months if the interest rate is 8 percent compounded semiannually? The time line is:

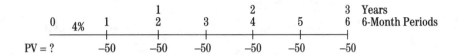

The present value of this annuity is calculated as:

$$\text{PVA}_n = \text{PMT}(\text{PVIFA}_{k, n})$$

$$= \$50.00(\text{PVIFA}_{4\%, 6})$$

$$= \$50.00(5.2421) = \$262.11.$$

If payments were made annually and there was annual compounding, the present value of the annuity would be $257.71. Since the payments come in sooner, the $50 semiannual annuity is more valuable than the $100 annuity.

Bond Values: A Special Case of Semiannual Compounding

Since most bonds pay interest semiannually, semiannual compounding procedures are appropriate for determining bond values. To illustrate: suppose a particular bond pays interest in the amount of $50 every 6 months, or $100 a year. The bond will mature in 10 years, paying $1000 (the principal) at that time. If you buy the bond, you will receive an annuity of $50 every 6 months, or 20 payments in total, *plus* $1000 at the end of 10 years, or twenty 6-month periods. What is the bond worth, assuming that the appropriate market discount, or interest, rate is 10 percent?

Since you are buying an annuity *and* a lump sum payment of $1000, each must be valued separately. For the annuity, the following procedure is used:

1. Use k/m = 10%/2 = 5% as the "interest rate."
2. In Table A-2 of the insert card, look up the PVIFA for 20 periods at 5 percent. It is 12.4622.

3.   Find the PV of the stream of interest payments:

$$PVA_{20} = \$50.00(PVIFA_{5\%,\,20})$$

$$= \$50.00(12.4622) = \$623.11.$$

To find the PV of the \$1000 maturity value:

1.   Use $k/m = 10\%/2 = 5\%$ as the "interest rate."
2.   In Table A-1 of the insert card, look up the PVIF for 20 periods at 5 percent. It is 0.3769.[12]
3.   Find the PV of that value at maturity:

$$PV = \$1000.00(PVIF_{5\%,\,20})$$

$$= \$1000(0.3769) = \$376.90.$$

The bond value that equals the sum of the values of the two components is:

$$\text{Bond value} = \$623.11 + \$376.90 = \$1000.00.$$

Concept Review

▶ What change must you make in your calculations to determine the future value of an amount that is compounded semiannually versus one that is compounded annually at the same quoted interest rate?

▶ Why is semiannual compounding better than annual compounding from a saver's standpoint?

▶ What is meant by the term *annual percentage rate*?

▶ How does the term *nominal rate* as used in this chapter differ from the term as it was used in Chapter 3?

▶ How is a bond like an annuity? What additional payment does a bond have?

Fractional Time Periods

In all of the examples thus far in the chapter, we have assumed that payments occur at either the beginning or the end of periods, not at some date *within* a period. However, we often encounter situations that require compounding or discounting over fractional periods. For example, suppose you deposit \$100.00 in a bank that pays 10 percent interest, compounded annually. If you leave your money in the bank for 9 months, or 0.75 year, how much will you have in your

---

[12]Students sometimes want to find the present value of the \$1000 due at the end of 10 years by discounting it back 10 periods at 10 percent rather than 20 periods at 5 percent. That would be incorrect, because all cash flows in a given contract must be discounted on a consistent basis—in this case, semiannually. If you found the value of the bond by the incorrect procedure, you would be out of step with actual bond valuation procedures in the financial community.

account? Problems such as this can be handled easily, but the tables generally cannot be used.

To solve the problem in the example, use the general future value equation, as follows:

$$FV_n = PV(1 + k)^n$$

$$FV_n = \$100.00(1.10)^{0.75} = \$100.00(1.0741) = \$107.41.$$

Concept Review

▶ What is the best way to deal with fractional time periods?

Amortized Loans

One of the most important applications of compound interest involves loans that are to be paid off in installments over time. Examples include automobile loans, home mortgage loans, and most business debt other than very short-term debt. If a loan is to be repaid in *equal* periodic amounts (monthly, quarterly, or annually), it is said to be an **amortized loan.**[13]

To illustrate: suppose a firm borrows $1000.00 to be repaid in three equal payments—one made at the end of each of the next 3 years. The lender is to receive 6 percent interest on the loan balance outstanding each year. The first task is to determine the amount the firm must repay each year, or the annual payment. To find this amount, recognize that the $1000.00 represents the present value of an annuity of PMT dollars per year for 3 years, discounted at 6 percent. The time line and the equation needed for this problem are presented below:

```
 0        6%       1           2           3
 +        |        +           +           +
-1000             PMT         PMT         PMT
```

$$PV = \frac{PMT}{(1 + k)^1} + \frac{PMT}{(1 + k)^2} + \frac{PMT}{(1 + k)^3} = \sum_{t=1}^{3} \frac{PMT}{(1 + k)^t}$$

$$\$1000 = \sum_{t=1}^{3} \frac{PMT}{(1 + k)^t}$$

Here we know everything except PMT, so we can solve the equation for PMT. We could use a trial and error process to find the value of PMT. This would be a tedious process, but we would eventually find PMT = $374.11. Alternatively,

---

[13]The word "amortized" comes from the Latin *mort*, meaning "dead," so an amortized loan is one that is "killed off" over time.

we could substitute known values and look up the value of PVIFA for 6 percent, 3 periods in Table A-2 of the insert card:

$$PVA_n = PMT(PVIFA_{k, n})$$

$$\$1000 = PMT(PVIFA_{6\%, 3}) = PMT(2.6730)$$

$$PMT = \frac{\$1000.00}{2.6730} = \$374.11$$

Therefore, the firm must pay the lender $374.11 at the end of each of the next 3 years, and the percentage cost to the borrower, which is also the rate of return to the lender, will be 6 percent.

Each payment consists partly of interest and partly of repayment of principal. This breakdown is given in the **amortization schedule** shown in Table 12-4. The interest component is largest in the first year, and it declines as the outstanding balance of the loan goes down. For tax purposes, a business borrower reports the interest payments in column 3 as a deductible cost each year, while the lender reports this same amount as taxable income.

Financial calculators are programmed to calculate amortization tables—you simply key in the inputs, and then press one button to get each entry in Table 12-4. If you have a financial calculator, it is worthwhile to read the appropriate section of the manual and learn how to use the amortization feature.

Concept Review

▶ To construct an amortization schedule, how do you determine the amount of the periodic payments?
▶ How do you determine the amount of each payment that goes to interest and to principal?

Table 12-4
Loan Amortization Schedule

Year	Beginning Amount (1)	Payment (2)	Interest[a] (3)	Repayment of Principal[b] (4)	Remaining Balance (1) − (4) = (5)
1	$1000.00	$ 374.11	$ 60.00	$ 314.11	$685.89
2	685.89	374.11	41.15	332.96	352.93
3	352.93	374.11	21.18	352.93	0
		$1122.33	$122.33	$1000.00	

[a]Interest is calculated by multiplying the loan balance at the beginning of the year by the interest rate. Therefore, interest in Year 1 is $1000(0.06) = $60; in Year 2, interest is $685.89(0.06) = $41.15; and in Year 3, interest is $352.03(0.06) = $21.18.
[b]Repayment of principal is equal to the payment of $374.11 minus the interest charge.

Comparison of Different Types of Interest Rates

Up to this point, we have discussed three different types of interest rates: nominal rates, periodic rates, and effective annual rates. To reduce confusion, it is useful to compare the three types and to show when each should be used.

Nominal, or Quoted, Rate.   The nominal, or quoted, rate is the rate that is quoted by borrowers and lenders. Practitioners in the equity, bond, mortgage, commercial loan, consumer loan, banking, and other markets express all financial contracts in terms of nominal rates. So, if you talk with a banker, broker, mortgage lender, auto finance company, or student loan officer about rates, the nominal rate is the one he or she will normally quote you. However, to be meaningful, the nominal rate quotation must also include the number of compounding periods per year. For example, a bank might offer 8.5 percent, compounded quarterly, on deposits, or a mutual fund might offer 8.0 percent, compounded monthly, on its money market account.

Nominal rates can be compared with one another, but *only* if the instruments being compared use the *same number of compounding periods* per year. Thus, to compare an 8.5 percent deposit with an 8.0 percent money market fund, you need to put both instruments on an *effective annual rate (EAR)* basis as discussed later in this section.

Note also that the nominal rate is never shown on a time line, and it is never used as an input in a financial calculator unless compounding occurs only once a year (in which case k_{nom} = periodic rate = EAR). If more frequent compounding occurs, you must use either the periodic rate or the effective annual rate as discussed below.

Finally, note that the nominal rate is called the *annual percentage rate (APR)* in situations in which interest is actually figured on a monthly basis:

$$k_{nom} = APR = \text{Monthly rate} \times 12.$$

The APR rate is never used in actual calculations; it is simply reported to borrowers.

Periodic Rate.   The periodic rate is the rate charged by a lender or paid by a borrower each period. It can be a rate per year, per 6-month period, per quarter, per month, per day, or per any other time interval (usually 1 year or less). For example, a bank may charge 1 percent per month on its credit card loans, and a finance company may charge 3 percent per quarter on consumer loans. We find the periodic rate as follows:

$$\text{Periodic rate} = \frac{k_{nom}}{m},$$

which implies that

$$k_{nom} = (\text{Periodic rate})(m) = APR,$$

where k_{nom} is the nominal annual rate and m is the number of compounding periods per year. To illustrate, consider a finance company loan at 3 percent per quarter:

Nominal annual rate $= k_{nom} =$ (Periodic rate)(m) $= (3\%)(4) = 12\%$,

and

$$\text{Periodic rate} = \frac{k_{nom}}{m} = \frac{12\%}{4} = 3\% \text{ per month.}$$

If there is one payment per year or if interest is added only once a year, then m = 1, and the periodic rate is equal to the nominal rate. But, in all cases in which interest is added or payments are made more frequently than annually, the periodic rate is *less* than the nominal rate.

The periodic rate is used for calculations in problems in which two conditions hold: (1) payments occur on a regular basis more frequently than once a year, and (2) a payment is made on each compounding (or discounting) date. Thus, if you are dealing with an auto loan that requires monthly payments, with a semiannual payment bond, or with an education loan that calls for quarterly payments, then on your time line and in your calculations you use the periodic rate, k_{nom}/m. The periodic rate is not be used to find the PV of an annuity that calls for annual payments, but it is used for an annuity for which discounting occurs quarterly because in the latter case the payments and discounting periods per year do not coincide.

Note that in each of the above examples, the interest compounding period is the same as the payment period. The periodic rate can be used directly in calculations only if the number of payments per year is consistent with the number of interest compounding periods.

To illustrate use of the periodic rate, suppose you make eight quarterly payments of $100.00 into an account that pays 12 percent, compounded quarterly. How much will you have after 2 years?

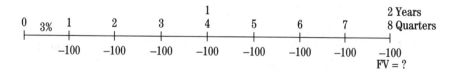

$$\text{FVA} = \sum_{t=1}^{n} \text{PMT}(1 + k)^{n-t} = \sum_{t=1}^{8} 100.00(1.03)^{8-t}.$$

By compounding each $100.00 payment at 12/4 = 3 percent for the appropriate number of periods and then summing these individual FVs, you obtain the FV of the payment stream, $889.23.

Alternatively, you can look up FVIFA for 3 percent, 8 periods, in Table A-4 of the insert card, and complete the arithmetic:

$$\text{FVA}_n = \text{PMT}(\text{FVIFA}_{k,\,n})$$
$$= \$100.00(\text{FVIFA}_{3\%,\,8}) = \$100.00(8.8923) = \$889.23.$$

Effective Annual Rate (EAR).   The effective annual rate is the rate with which, under annual compounding (m = 1), we would obtain the same results as if we had used a given periodic rate with m compounding periods per year. The EAR is found as follows:

$$\text{EAR} = \left(\frac{1 + k_{nom}}{m}\right)^m - 1.0. \qquad \textbf{(12-10)}$$

In the EAR equation, k_{nom}/m is the periodic rate and m is the number of periods per year. For example, suppose you could borrow using either a credit card with charges of 1 percent per month or a bank loan that costs 12 percent, quarterly compounding. Which should you choose? To answer this question, the cost rate of each alternative must be expressed as an EAR:

$$\text{Credit card loan: EAR} = (1 + 0.01)^{12} - 1.0 = (1.01)^{12} - 1.0$$
$$= 1.126825 - 1.0 = 0.126825 = 12.6825\%.$$

$$\text{Bank loan: EAR} = (1 + 0.03)^4 - 1.0 = (1.03)^4 - 1.0$$
$$= 1.125509 - 1.0 = 0.125509 = 12.5509\%.$$

Thus, the credit card loan is slightly more costly than the bank loan. This result should have been intuitive to you—both loans have the same 12 percent nominal rate, yet you would have to make monthly payments on the credit card versus quarterly payments under the bank loan.

Concept Review

▸ Define the nominal (or quoted) rate, the periodic rate, and the effective annual rate.

Summary

Financial decisions often involve situations in which someone pays money at one point in time and receives money at some later time. Dollars that are paid or received at two different points in time are different, and this difference is recognized and accounted for by time value of money analysis. The key concepts covered in this chapter are listed below, using the data shown in Figure 12-3 to illustrate the various points. Refer to the figure constantly, and try to find in it an example of the points covered as you go through this summary.

☐ **Compounding** is the process of determining the **future value (FV)** of a cash flow or a series of cash flows. The compounded amount, or future value, is equal to the beginning amount plus the interest earned.

☐ Future value (single payment):

$$FV_n = PV(1 + k)^n = PV(\text{FVIF}_{k, n}).$$

Figure 12-3
Illustration for Chapter Summary (k = 4%)

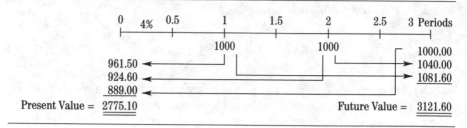

Example: $961.50 compounded for 1 year at 4 percent:

$$FV_1 = \$961.50(1.04)^1 = \$1000.$$

☐ **Discounting** is the process of finding the **present value (PV)** of a future cash flow or a series of cash flows; discounting is the reciprocal of compounding.
☐ Present value (single payment):

$$PV = \frac{FV_n}{(1 + k)^n} = FV_n \left(\frac{1}{1 + k}\right)^n = FV_n(PVIF_{k,\,n}).$$

Example: $1000 discounted back for 2 years at 4 percent:

$$PV = \frac{\$1000}{(1.04)^2} = \$1000(1/1.04)^2 = \$1000(0.9246) = \$924.60.$$

☐ An **annuity** is defined as a series of equal periodic payments (PMT) for a specified number of periods.
☐ Future value (annuity):

$$FVA_n = PMT + PMT(1 + k)^1 + PMT(1 + k)^2 + \ldots + PMT(1 + k)^{n-1}$$

$$= PMT \sum_{t=1}^{n} (1 + k)^{n-t}$$

$$= PMT \left[\frac{(1 + k)^n - 1}{k}\right] = PMT(FVIFA_{k,\,n}).$$

Example: FVA of 3 payments of $1000 when the interest rate is 4 percent:

$$FVA_3 = \$1000(3.1216) = \$3121.60.$$

☐ Present value (annuity):

$$PVA_n = \frac{PMT}{(1 + k)^1} + \frac{PMT}{(1 + k)^2} + \ldots + \frac{PMT}{(1 + k)^n}$$

$$= PMT \sum_{t=1}^{n} \left[\frac{1}{1 + k}\right]^t = PMT \left[\frac{1 - \frac{1}{(1 + k)^n}}{k}\right] = PMT(PVIFA_{k,\,n}).$$

Example: PVA of 3 payments of $1000 when the interest rate is 4 percent.

$$PVA_3 = \$1000(2.7751) = \$2775.10.$$

☐ An annuity whose payments occur at the end of each period is called an **ordinary** or **deferred annuity**. The formulas above are for ordinary annuities.

☐ If each payment occurs at the beginning of the period rather than at the end, then we have an **annuity due**. In Figure 12-3, assuming the periods are years, the payments would be shown at 0, 1, and 2 rather than at 1, 2, and 3. The PV of each payment would be larger, because each payment would be discounted back one year less and hence the PV of the annuity would also be larger. Similarly, the FV of the annuity due would also be larger, because each payment would be compounded for an extra year. The following formulas can be used to convert the PV and FV of an ordinary annuity to an annuity due:

PVA(annuity due) = PVA of an ordinary annuity × (1 + k).
FVA(annuity due) = FVA of an ordinary annuity × (1 + k).

☐ If the time line in Figure 12-3 were extended out forever, so that the $1000 payments went on forever, we would have a **perpetuity** whose value could be found as follows:

$$PV(\text{perpetuity}) = \frac{PMT}{k} = \frac{\$1000}{0.04} = \$25\,000.$$

☐ If the cash flows are unequal, you cannot use the annuity formulas. To find the PV or FV of an uneven series, find the PV or FV of each individual cash flow and then sum them. However, if some of the cash flows constitute an annuity, the annuity formula can be used to calculate the present value of that part of the cash flow stream.

☐ Calculations of the time value of money generally involve equations that have four variables, so if you know three of the values, you (or your calculator) can solve for the fourth.

☐ If you know the cash flows and the PV (or FV) of a cash flow stream, you can determine the interest rate. For example, in the Figure 12-3 illustration, if you were given the information that a loan called for 3 payments of $1000 each, and that the loan had a value today of PV = $2775.10, then you could find the interest rate that caused the sum of the PVs of the payments to equal $2775.10. Since you are dealing with an annuity, you could proceed as follows:

a. Recognize that $PVA_n = \$2775.10 = \$1000(PVIFA_{k,\,3})$.

b. Solve for $PVIFA_{k,\,3}$:

$$PVIFA_{k,\,3} = \frac{\$2775.10}{\$1000} = 2.7751.$$

c. Look up 2.7751 in Table A-2 on the insert card, on the third row. It is in the 4 percent column, so the interest rate must be 4 percent. If the factor did not appear in the table, this would indicate that the interest rate was not a whole number. In this case, you could not use this procedure to find the exact rate. In practice, though, this is not a problem, because most people use financial calculators to find interest rates.

☐ Thus far in the summary we have assumed that payments are made, and interest is earned, at the end of each year, or annually. However, many contracts call for more frequent payments; for example, mortgage and auto loans call for monthly payments, and most bonds pay interest semiannually. Similarly, most banks compute interest daily. When compounding occurs more frequently than once a year, this fact must be recognized. We can use the Figure 12-3 example to illustrate the procedures. First, the following formula is used to find an **effective annual rate (EAR)**:

$$\text{Effective annual rate} = \text{EAR} = \left(\frac{1 + k_{nom}}{m}\right)^m - 1.0.$$

For semiannual compounding, the effective annual rate is 4.04 percent:

$$\left(\frac{1 + 0.04}{2}\right)^2 - 1.0 = (1.02)^2 - 1.0 = 1.0404 - 1.0 = 0.0404 = 4.04\%.$$

This rate could then be used (with a calculator but not with the tables) to find the PV or FV of each payment in Figure 12-3.

If the $1000-per-year payments were actually payable as $500 each 6 months, you would simply redraw Figure 12-3 to show 6 payments of $500 each, but you would also need to use a **periodic interest rate** of 4%/2 = 2% for determining the PV or FV of the payments.

☐ The general equation for finding the future value for any number of compounding periods per year is:

$$FV_n = PV \left(\frac{1 + k_{nom}}{m}\right)^{mn},$$

where

k_{nom} = quoted interest rate,
m = number of compounding periods per year, and
n = number of years.

☐ An **amortized loan** is one that is paid off in equal payments over a specified period. An **amortization schedule** shows how much of each payment constitutes interest, how much is used to reduce the principal, and the remaining balance of the loan at each point in time.

☐ Financial calculators have built-in programs that perform all of the operations discussed in this chapter. It is useful for you to own such a calculator and to learn how to use it. Even if you do, though, it is essential that you understand the logical processes involved.

The concepts covered in this chapter will be used throughout the remainder of the book. For example, in Chapter 16 we apply present value concepts to the process of valuing stocks and bonds, and we see that the market prices of securities are established by determining the present values of the cash flows they are expected to provide. In later chapters, the same basic concepts are applied to corporate decisions involving both expenditures on capital assets and determination of the types of capital that should be used to pay for assets.

Questions

12-1 What is an *opportunity cost rate*? How is this rate used in time value analysis, and where is it shown on a time line? Is the opportunity rate a single number that is used in all situations?

12-2 An *annuity* is defined as a series of payments of a fixed amount for a specific number of periods. Thus, $100 a year for 10 years is an annuity, but $100 in Year 1, $200 in Year 2, and $400 in Years 3 through 10 does not constitute an annuity; however, the second series *contains* an annuity. Is this statement true or false?

12-3 If a firm's earnings per share grew from $1 to $2 over a 10-year period, the total growth would be 100 percent, but the annual growth rate would be less than 10 percent. Is this statement true or false? Explain your answer.

12-4 Would you rather have a savings account that pays 5 percent interest compounded semiannually or one that pays 5 percent interest compounded daily? Explain your choice.

12-5 To find the present value of an uneven series of cash flows, you must find the PVs of the individual cash flows and then sum them. Even if some of the cash flows constitute an annuity (for example, $100 each for Years 3, 4, 5, and 6), annuity procedures can never be of use because the entire series is not an annuity. Is this statement true or false? Explain your answer.

12-6 The present value of a perpetuity is equal to the payment on the annuity, PMT, divided by the interest rate, k: PV = PMT/k. What is the sum, or future value, of a perpetuity of PMT dollars per year? (Hint: The answer is infinity, but explain why.)

Self-Test Problems   (solutions appear on page 406)

ST-1 **Key terms.** Define each of the following terms:
   a. PV; k; I; FV_n; n; PVA_n; FVA_n
   b. $FVIF_{k, n}$; $PVIF_{k, n}$; $FVIFA_{k, n}$; $PVIFA_{k, n}$
   c. Opportunity cost; time line
   d. Annuity; lump sum payment; uneven payment stream
   e. Ordinary (deferred) annuity; annuity due
   f. Perpetuity; consol; terminal value
   g. Compounding; discounting

h. Annual, semiannual, quarterly, monthly, daily, and continuous compounding

i. Effective annual rate; nominal (stated) interest rate; periodic interest rate; APR;

j. Amortization schedule; principal component versus interest component of a payment; amortized loan

ST-2 **Future value.** Assume that it is now January 1, 1993. On January 1, 1994, you will deposit $1000 into a savings account that pays 8 percent.

a. If the bank compounds interest annually, how much will you have in your account on January 1, 1997?

b. What will your January 1, 1997 balance be if the bank uses quarterly compounding rather than annual compounding?

c. Suppose you deposit the $1000 in four payments of $250 each on January 1 of 1994, 1995, 1996, and 1997. How much will you have in your account on January 1, 1997, based on 8 percent annual compounding?

d. Suppose you deposit four equal payments in your account on January 1 of 1994, 1995, 1996, and 1997. How large would each of your payments have to be for you to obtain the ending balance you calculated in Part a?

ST-3 **Discounted cash flow analysis.** Assume that it is now January 1, 1993, and you will need $1000 on January 1, 1997. Your bank compounds deposits at an 8 percent rate annually.

a. How much must you deposit on January 1, 1994, to have a balance of $1000 on January 1, 1997?

b. If you want to make equal payments on each January 1 from 1994 through 1997 to accumulate the $1000, how large must each of the four payments be?

c. If your father were to offer either to make the payments calculated in Part b or to give you a lump sum of $750 on January 1, 1994, which would you choose?

d. If you have only $750 on January 1, 1994, what interest rate, compounded annually, would you have to earn to have the necessary $1000 on January 1, 1997?

e. Suppose you could deposit only $186.29 each January 1 from 1994 through 1997, but you still needed $1000 on January 1, 1997. What interest rate, with annual compounding, must you seek out to achieve your goal?

f. To help you reach your $1000 goal, your mother offers to give you $400 on January 1, 1994. You will get a part-time job and make 6 additional payments of equal amounts each 6 months thereafter. If all of this money is deposited in a bank that pays 8 percent, compounded semiannually, how large must each of the 6 payments be?

g. What is the effective annual rate being paid by the bank in Part f?

h. *Reinvestment rate risk* is defined as the risk that maturing securities (and coupon payments on bonds) will have to be reinvested at a lower rate of interest than they were previously earning. Is there a reinvestment rate risk involved in the preceding analysis? If so, how might this risk be eliminated?

ST-4   **Nominal and effective annual rates.**   Bank A pays 8 percent interest, compounded quarterly, on its premium rate savings account. The managers of Bank B want its money market account to equal Bank A's effective annual rate, but interest is to be compounded on a monthly basis. What nominal, or quoted, rate must Bank B set?

Problems

12-1   **Present and future values for different periods.**   Find the following values using the equations. Then work the problems using a financial calculator or the standard tables on the insert card to check your answers. Disregard rounding differences.
   a. An initial $500 compounded for 1 year at 6 percent.
   b. An initial $500 compounded for 2 years at 6 percent.
   c. The present value of $500 due in 1 year at a discount rate of 6 percent.
   d. The present value of $500 due in 2 years at a discount rate of 6 percent.

12-2   **Present and future values for different interest rates.**   Use the tables or a financial calculator to find the following values:
   a. An initial $500 compounded for 10 years at 6 percent.
   b. An initial $500 compounded for 10 years at 12 percent.
   c. The present value of $500 due in 10 years at a 6 percent discount rate.
   d. The present value of $1552.90 due in 10 years at a 12 percent discount rate and at a 6 percent rate. Why are the present values dependent upon interest rates?

12-3   **Future value of annuities.**   Find the future value of the following annuities. The first payment in these annuities is made at the end of Year 1—that is, they are ordinary annuities.
   a. $400 per year for 10 years at 10 percent.
   b. $200 per year for 5 years at 5 percent.
   c. $400 per year for 5 years at 0 percent.
   d. Now rework Parts a, b, and c assuming that payments are made at the beginning of each year—that is, that they are annuities due.

12-4   **Present value of annuities.**   Find the present value of the following ordinary annuities.
   a. $200 per year for 10 years at 10 percent.
   b. $200 per year for 5 years at 5 percent.
   c. $200 per year for 5 years at 0 percent.
   d. Now rework Parts a, b, and c assuming that payments are made at the beginning of each year—that is, that they are annuities due.

12-5   Uneven cash flow stream.

    a. Find the present values of the following cash flow streams. The appropriate interest rate is 8 percent.

Year	Cash Stream A	Cash Stream B
1	$100	$300
2	400	400
3	400	400
4	400	400
5	300	100

    b. What is the value of each cash flow stream at a 0 percent interest rate?

12-6   Uneven cash flow stream. Find the present value of the following cash flow stream, discounted at 7 percent: Year 1, $100; Year 2, $400; Years 3 through 20, $300.

12-7   Present value comparison. At 14 percent, which amount is worth more: $1000 today or $2000 after 6 years?

12-8   Future Value. The production target in the 5-year plan of the Logo Company calls for output to increase by 7 percent a year. If 1992 production is 8 million tonnes, what is the target production for 1997?

12-9   Time for a lump sum to double. To the closest year, how long does it take $200 to double if it is deposited and earns the following rates?
    a. 7 percent.
    b. 10 percent.
    c. 18 percent.
    d. 100 percent.

12-10   Effective rate of interest. You can buy a bond for $1000 that will pay no interest during its 7-year life but will have a value of $2502 when it matures. What rate of interest will you earn if you buy the bond and hold it to maturity?

12-11   Estimating growth rate. If the Carter Company's earnings in 1994 are $1.99 a share, while 8 years earlier (in 1986) they were $1, what has been the firm's rate of growth in earnings?

12-12   Required annuity payments. On December 31, Helen Ventor buys a building for $255 000, paying 20 percent down and agreeing to pay the balance in 20 equal annual installments that are to include principal plus 12 percent compound interest on the declining balance. What is the value of each installment?

12-13   Reaching a financial goal. You will need $138 500 at the end of 12 years. You know that the best you can do is make equal payments into a bank account on which you can earn 8 percent interest compounded annually. Your first payment is to be made at the end of the first year.
    a. What amount must you pay annually to achieve your objective?

    b. Instead of making annual payments, you decide to make one lump sum payment today. To achieve your objective of $138 500 at the end of the 12-year period, how large should this sum be? Assume you can still earn 8 percent interest compounded annually on your account.

12-14 Effective rate of interest. Your broker offers to sell you a note for $13 250.00 that will pay $2345.05 a year for 10 years. If you buy the note, what rate of interest will you be earning?

12-15 Effective rate of interest. A bank agrees to lend you $1000.00 today in return for your promise to pay back $1828.04 seven years from today. What rate of interest is the bank charging you?

12-16 Sales growth. The Lowell Company's sales last year were $1 million.
    a. Assuming that sales grow 18 percent a year, calculate sales for each of the next 6 years.
    b. Plot the sales projections on a graph.
    c. If your graph is correct, your projected sales curve is nonlinear. If it had been linear, would this have indicated a constant, increasing, or decreasing percentage growth rate? Explain.

12-17 Effective rate of interest. Find the interest rate or rate of return on each of the following:
    a. You borrow $700 and promise to pay back $749 at the end of 1 year.
    b. You lend $700, and you receive a promise of $749 at the end of 1 year.
    c. You borrow $85 000 and promise to pay back $201 229 at the end of 10 years.
    d. You borrow $9000.00 and promise to make payments of $2684.80 per year for 5 years.

12-18 Future value for various compounding periods. Find the amount to which $500 will grow under each of the following conditions:
    a. 12 percent compounded annually for 5 years.
    b. 12 percent compounded semiannually for 5 years.
    c. 12 percent compounded quarterly for 5 years.
    d. 12 percent compounded monthly for 1 year.

12-19 Present value for various compounding periods. Find the present values of $500 due in the future under each of the following conditions:
    a. 12 percent nominal rate, semiannual compounding, discounted back 5 years.
    b. 12 percent nominal rate, quarterly compounding, discounted back 5 years.
    c. 12 percent nominal rate, monthly compounding, discounted back 1 year.

12-20 Annuities. Find the indicated value of the following ordinary annuities:
    a. FV of $200 every 6 months for 4 years at a nominal rate of 12 percent.
    b. PV of $200 every 3 months for 4 years at a nominal rate of 12 percent.

12-21 Effective versus nominal interest rates. Bank A pays 7 percent interest compounded annually on time deposits. Bank B pays 6 percent interest compounded quarterly.

  a. In which bank would you prefer to deposit your money?

  b. Could your choice of banks be influenced by the fact that you might want to withdraw your funds during the year rather than at the end of the year? In answering this question, assume that funds must be left on deposit during the entire compounding period in order for you to receive any interest.

12-22 Bond values.

  a. What is the value of a $1000 par value 10-year bond that pays $30 interest semiannually ($60 per year) and that yields 10 percent, compounded semiannually?

  b. What is the bond's value if it is sold to yield 8 percent?

  c. What is the bond's value if the semiannual interest payments are $40 rather than $30 and it yields 6 percent?

12-23 Bond values. You have just purchased a newly issued $1000 5-year Malley Company bond at par. The bond (Bond A) pays $60 in interest semiannually ($120 a year). You are also negotiating the purchase of a $1000 6-year Malley Company bond (Bond B) that returns $30 in semiannual interest payments and has 6 years remaining before it matures.

  a. What is the going rate of return on bonds of the risk and maturing of Malley Company's Bond A?

  b. What should you be willing to pay for Bond B? (Assume the term structure in the medium-term range (5-10 years) is flat.)

  c. How will your answer to Part b change if Bond A pays $40 in semiannual interest instead of $60 but still sells for $1000? Bond B still pays $30 semiannually and $1000 at the end of 6 years.

12-24 Uneven cash flow stream. The Petite Printing Company Limited is considering the purchase of a new press that will provide the following stream of profits:

Year	
1	$20 000
2	30 000
3	40 000
4	50 000
5	60 000
6	70 000

  a. What is the present value of the profit stream, using a 15 percent discount rate?

  b. If the press costs $150 000, should Petite Printing purchase it?

Integrative Problem

12-25 Time value of money analysis.   Answer the following questions concerning the time value of money analysis.

a. Why are discounted cash flow (time value of money) concepts so important in financial analysis? What is a time line? What is a lump sum cash flow? An annuity? An uneven cash flow stream?

b. i. What is the future value of $500 after 3 years if it is invested in an account paying 8 percent annual interest?

ii. What is the present value of $500 to be received in 3 years if the appropriate interest rate is 8 percent?

c. What is the difference between an ordinary, or regular, annuity and an annuity due? What type of annuity is shown below? How would you change it to the other type of annuity?

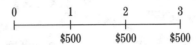

d. What is the future value of a 3-year ordinary annuity of $500 if the appropriate interest rate is 8 percent? What is the present value of the annuity? What would the future and present values be if the annuity were an annuity due?

e. What is the present value of the following cash flow stream? The appropriate interest rate is 8 percent.

Year	CF
0	$ 0
1	50
2	150
3	150
4	(25)

f. What annual interest rate will cause $500.00 to grow to $665.50 in 3 years?

g. What is the result of compounding more often than annually? What is the difference between the stated, or nominal, rate and the effective annual rate? What is the effective annual rate for a nominal rate of 8 percent, compounded semiannually? Compounded quarterly? Compounded daily? What is the future value of $500 after 3 years under 8 percent semiannual compounding? Quarterly compounding?

h. What is the value at the end of Year 3 of the following cash flow stream if the interest rate is 8 percent, compounded semiannually? What is the PV of the same stream? Is the stream an annuity?

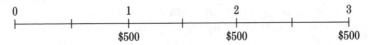

i. Construct an amortization schedule for a $1000 loan with an 8 percent annual rate, to be repaid in 3 equal installments. What is the annual interest expense for the borrower, and the annual interest income for the lender?

Solutions to Self-Test Problems

ST-1   Refer to the appropriate sections of the text to check your responses.

ST-2   a.

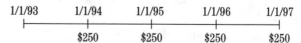

$1000.00 is being compounded for 3 years, so your balance on January 1, 1994, is $1259.71:

$$FV = PV(1 + k)^n = \$1000(1 + 0.08)^3 = \$1259.71.$$

b. The effective annual rate for 8 percent, compounded quarterly, is

$$\text{Effective annual rate} = \left(\frac{1 + 0.08}{4}\right)^4 - 1.0$$

$$= (1.02)^4 - 1.0 = 0.0824 = 8.24\%.$$

Therefore,

$$FV = \$1000(1.0824)^3 = \$1000(1.2681) = \$1268.10.$$

Alternatively, use FVIF for 2 percent $3 \times 4 = 12$ periods:

$$FV = \$1000(FVIF_{2\%, \text{ 12 periods}}) = \$1000(1.2682) = \$1268.20.$$

(Calculator solution = $1268.24.)

Note that since the interest factors are carried to only four decimal places, rounding differences occur. Rounding differences also occur between calculator and tabular solutions.

c.

As you work this problem, keep in mind that the tables assume that payments are made at the end of each period. Therefore, you can solve this problem by finding the future value of an annuity of $250 for 4 years at 8 percent:

$$PMT(FVIFA_{k, n}) = \$250(4.5061) = \$1126.53.$$

d.   FV = $1259.71; k = 8%; n = 4.

$$\text{PMT}(\text{FVIFA}_{8\%, \ 4 \ \text{years}}) = \text{FV}$$
$$\text{PMT}(4.5061) = \$1259.71$$
$$\text{PMT} = \frac{\$1259.71}{4.5061} = \$279.56.$$

Therefore, you would have to make 4 payments of $279.56 each to have a balance of $1259.71 on January 1, 1994.

ST-3   **a.**   Set up a time line like the one in the preceding problem:

1/1/93	1/1/94	1/1/95	1/1/96	1/1/97
0	?	0	0	$1000

Note that your deposit will grow for 3 years at 8 percent. The fact that it is now January 1, 1993, is irrelevant. The deposit on January 1, 1994, is the PV, and the FV is $1000. Here is the solution:

$$\text{FV} = \$1000; \ n = 3; \ k = 8\%.$$
$$\text{FV}(\text{PVIF}_{8\%, \ 3 \ \text{years}}) = \text{PV}$$
$$\text{PV} = \$1000(0.7938) = \$793.80$$
$$= \text{Initial deposit to accumulate } \$1000.$$

(Calculator solution = $793.83.)

b.   Here we are dealing with a 4-year annuity whose first payment occurs 1 year from today, on January 1, 1994 and whose future value must equal $1000. You should modify the time line to help visualize the situation. Here is the solution:

$$\text{FV} = \$1000; \ n = 4; \ k = 8\%.$$
$$\text{PMT}(\text{FVIFA}_{8\%, \ 4 \ \text{years}}) = \text{FVA}$$
$$\text{PMT} = \frac{\text{FVA}}{(\text{FVIFA}_{8\%, \ 4 \ \text{years}})}$$
$$= \frac{\$1000}{4.5061}$$
$$= \$221.92 = \begin{array}{l}\text{Payment necessary} \\ \text{to accumulate } \$1000.\end{array}$$

c.   This problem can be approached in several ways. Perhaps the simplest is to ask this question: "If I received $750 on January 1, 1994, and deposited it to earn 8 percent, would I have the required $1000 on January 1, 1997?" The answer is no:

$$\$750(1.08)(1.08)(1.08) = \$944.78.$$

This indicates that you should let your father make the payments rather than accept the lump sum of $750.

You could also compare the $750 with the PV of the payments:

$$PMT = \$221.92; \ k = 8\%; \ n = 4.$$

$$PMT(PVIFA_{8\%, \ 4 \ years}) = PV$$

$$\$221.92(3.3121) = \$735.02 = \text{Present value}$$
$$\text{of the required payments.}$$

This is less than the $750 lump sum offer, so your initial reaction might be to accept the lump sum of $750. However, this would be a mistake. As we saw before, if you were to deposit the $750 on January 1, 1994, at an 8 percent interest rate, to be withdrawn on January 1, 1997, interest would be compounded for only 3 years, from January 1, 1994, to December 31, 1996, and the future value would be only

$$PV(FVIF_{8\%, \ 3 \ years}) = \$750(1.2597) = \$944.78.$$

The problem is that when you found the $735.02 PV of the annuity, you were finding the value of the annuity *today*, on January 1, 1993. Now you are comparing $735.02 today with the lump sum of $750 one year from now. This is, of course, invalid. What you should have done was take the $735.02, recognize that this is the PV of an annuity as of January 1, 1993, multiply $735.02 by 1.08 to get $793.82, and compare $793.82 with the lump sum of $750. You would then take your father's offer to make the payments rather than take the lump sum on January 1, 1994.

d. $$PV = \$750; \ FV = \$1000; \ n = 3; \ k = ?$$

$$PV(FVIF_{k, \ 3 \ years}) = FV$$

$$FVIF_{k, \ 3 \ years} = \frac{FV}{PV}$$

$$= \frac{\$1000}{\$750} = 1.3333.$$

Use Table A-3 on the insert card to find the interest rate corresponding to an FVIF of 1.3333. Look across the period 3 row of the table, watching for 1.3333. The closest value is 1.3310, in the 10 percent column. Therefore, you would require an interest rate of approximately 10 percent to achieve your $1000 goal. The exact rate required, found with a financial calculator, is 10.0642 percent.

e. $$FV = \$1000; \ PMT = \$186.29; \ n = 4; \ k = ?$$

$$PMT(FVIFA_{k, \ 4 \ years}) = FV$$

$$\$186.29(FVIFA_{k, \ 4 \ years}) = \$1000$$

$$FVIFA_{k, \ 4 \ years} = \frac{\$1000}{\$186.29} = 5.3680.$$

Using Table A-4 of the insert card, we find that 5.3680 corresponds to a 20 percent interest rate. You might be able to find a borrower willing to offer you a 20 percent interest rate, but there would be some risk involved—he or she might not actually pay you your $1000!

(Calculator solution = 19.9997%.)

f.

1/1/93	1/1/94		1/1/95		1/1/96		1/1/97

$400 ? ? ? ? ? ?

Find the future value of the original $400 deposit:

$$FV = PV(FVIF_{4\%, 6}) = \$400(1.2653) = \$506.12.$$

This means that on January 1, 1997, you need an additional sum of $493.88:

$$\$1000.00 - \$506.12 = \$493.88.$$

This will be accumulated by making 6 equal payments which earn 8 percent compounded semiannually, or 4 percent each 6 months:

$$FV = \$493.88; n = 6; k = 4\%.$$

$$PMT(FVIFA_{4\%, 6}) = FV$$

$$PMT = \frac{FV}{(FVIA_{4\%, 6})}$$

$$= \frac{\$493.88}{6.6330} = \$74.46.$$

g. Effective annual rate $= \left(1 + \dfrac{k_{nom}}{m}\right)^m - 1.0$

$$= \left(1 + \frac{0.08}{2}\right)^2 - 1 = (1.04)^2 - 1$$

$$= 1.0816 - 1 = 0.0816 = 8.16\%.$$

h. There is a reinvestment rate risk here, because we assumed that funds will earn an 8 percent return in the bank. In fact, if interest rates in the economy fall, the bank will lower its deposit rate, because it will be earning less when it lends out the funds you deposited with it. If you buy investment certificates that mature on the date you need the money (January 1, 1997), you will avoid the reinvestment risk, but that would work only if you were making the deposit today. Other ways of reducing reinvestment rate risk will be discussed later in the text.

ST-4   Bank A's effective annual rate is 8.24 percent:

$$\text{Effective annual rate} = \left(1 + \frac{0.08}{4}\right)^4 - 1.0$$

$$= (1.02)^4 - 1 = 1.0824 - 1$$

$$= 0.0824 = 8.24\%.$$

Now Bank B must have the same effective annual rate:

$$\left(1 + \frac{k}{12}\right)^{12} - 1.0 = 0.0824$$

$$\left(1 + \frac{k}{12}\right)^{12} = 1.0824$$

$$1 + \frac{k}{12} = (1.0824)^{1/12}$$

$$1 + \frac{k}{12} = 1.00662$$

$$\frac{k}{12} = 0.00662$$

$$k = 0.07944 = 7.94\%.$$

Thus, the two banks have different stated rates—Bank A's stated rate is 8 percent, while Bank B's stated rate is 7.94 percent—but, both have the same effective annual rate of 8.24 percent. The difference in their stated rates is due to the difference in compounding frequency.

Appendix 12A
Continuous Compounding and Discounting

Continuous Compounding

In Chapter 12, we implicitly assumed that growth occurs at discrete intervals—annually, semiannually, and so forth. For some purposes, however, it is better to assume instantaneous, or *continuous*, growth. The relationship between discrete and continuous compounding is illustrated in Figure 12A-1. Panel a shows the annual compounding case, where interest is added once a year; in Panel b, compounding occurs twice a year; and in Panel c, interest is earned continuously. As the graph shows, the more frequent the compounding period, the larger the final compound amount, because interest is earned on interest more often.

In Chapter 12, Equation 12-2a was developed to allow for any number of compounding periods per year:

$$FV_n = PV\left(1 + \frac{k_{nom}}{m}\right)^{mn}, \qquad \textbf{(12-2a)}$$

Where

k_{nom} = the stated interest rate.
  m = the number of compounding periods per year.
  n = the number of years.

To illustrate: let PV = $100, k = 10%, and n = 5. At various compounding periods per year, we obtain the following future values at the end of 5 years:

Figure 12-A1
Annual, Semiannual, and Continuous
Compounding (25% Rate)

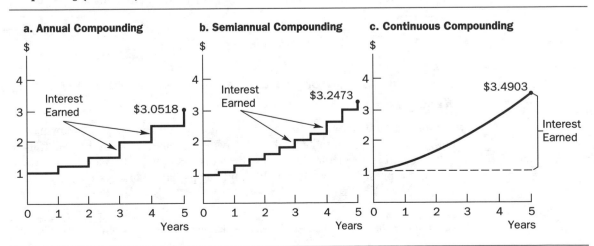

a. Annual Compounding   b. Semiannual Compounding   c. Continuous Compounding

$$\text{Annual: } FV_5 = \$100\left(1.0 + \frac{0.10}{1}\right)^{1(5)} = \$100(1.10)^5 = \$161.05.$$

$$\text{Semiannual: } FV_5 = \$100\left(1.0 + \frac{0.10}{2}\right)^{2(5)} = \$100(1.05)^{10} = \$162.89.$$

$$\text{Monthly: } FV_5 = \$100\left(1.0 + \frac{0.10}{12}\right)^{12(5)} = \$100(1.0083)^{60} = \$164.53.$$

$$\text{Daily: } FV_5 = \$100\left(1.0 + \frac{0.10}{365}\right)^{365(5)} = \$164.86.$$

$$\text{Hourly: } FV_5 = \$100\left(1.0 + \frac{0.10}{8760}\right)^{365(24)(5)} = \$164.87.$$

We could keep going, compounding every minute, every second, every one-thousands of a second, and so on. At the limit, we could compound every instant, or *continuously*. The equation for continuous compounding is

$$FV_n = PV(e^{kn}), \tag{12A-1}$$

where e is the value 2.7183 . . . [14] If $100 is invested for 5 years at 10 percent compounded continously, then FV^5 is computed as follows:

$$\text{Continuous: } FV_5 = \$100(e^{0.10(5)}) = \$100(2.7183 \ldots)^{0.5}$$
$$= \$164.87.$$

Continuous Discounting

Equation 12A-1 can be transformed into Equation 12A-2 and used to determine present values under continuous compounding:

$$PV = \frac{FV_n}{e^{kn}} = FV_n e^{-kn}. \tag{12A-2}$$

Thus, if $1649 is due in 10 years and if the appropriate *continuous* discount rate, k, is 5 percent, the present value of this future payment is

$$PV = \$1649\left[\frac{1}{(2.7183 \ldots)^{0.5}}\right] = \frac{\$1649}{1.649} = \$1000.$$

Some Further Applications of Compound Interest Relationships

A problem that arises in finance in a number of forms is the following. An obligation of $1000 is to be paid in 20 days. If payment is made immediately, a $20 discount is given and the payment required is only $980. What is the rate of interest represented by the $20 discount for payment 20 days early?

---

[14]Scientific or financial calculators with exponential functions can be used to evaluate Equation 12A-1.

The basic problems can be formulated as: what do I earn by being able to settle an obligation PV by a payment of 0.98 PV by paying in advance by (20/365) of a year? The answer depends upon the compounding period used. This is illustrated for several different compounding periods.

Annual Compounding.   The basic equation for annual compounding is

$$PV(0.98)(1 + k)^{20/365} = PV.$$

What is the value of k that satisfies the equation? Dividing through by 0.98PV, we obtain

$$(1 + k)^{20/365} = \frac{1}{0.98}.$$

Solving for k we find

$$k = (1.020408)^{365/20} - 1$$
$$k = 44.58\%.$$

Daily Compounding.   With daily compounding, the basic equation is

$$PV(0.98)1 + \frac{k^{(20/365)365}}{365} = PV.$$

Dividing by 0.98PV, we obtain

$$\left(\frac{1 + k}{365}\right)^{20} = 1.020408$$
$$\left(\frac{1 + k}{365}\right) = (1.020408)^{1/20}$$
$$k = 36.89\%.$$

Thus, with daily compounding rather than annual compounding, the interest rate to equate the two sides of the equation is lower. We can predict that the interest rate will therefore be somewhat lower for continuous compounding.

Continuous Compounding.   With continuous compounding, the basic equation is

$$PV(0.98)e^{k(20/365)} = PV$$
$$k = \left(\frac{365}{20}\right)\ln\left(\frac{1}{0.98}\right)$$
$$= 18.25(0.0202027)$$
$$k = 36.87\%.$$

The solution for k does decline as expected.

Simple Compounding.   A simple approximation formula gives results similar to those obtained for continuous, or daily, compounding. When k is small and n is large, a compound interest relation can be approximated by the following:

$$(1 + k)^n = (1 + kn).$$

Now the basic equation can be written as

$$0.98PV[1 + k(20/365)] = PV$$

Dividing both sides by 0.98 PV, we obtain

$$(20/365)k = (1/0.98) - 1$$

$$(20/365)k = \left(\frac{1 - 0.98}{0.98}\right)$$

$$k = \left(\frac{0.02}{0.98}\right)\left(\frac{365}{20}\right)$$

$$k = 37.24\%.$$

This is the standard simplified textbook formula for calculating the interest return from taking a cash discount, presented in Chapter 9. The answer is k = 0.020408 (18.25) = 37.24 percent. Thus, the standard simplified approximation method gives a result close to the answer obtained by daily, or continuous, compounding. The simple formula gives the same result as the more "complex" compounding methods.

The relationships set out above provide a perspective on interest rate problems encountered throughout this book as well as on the work of the practising financial manager.

13

Capital Budgeting Techniques

A MANAGERIAL PERSPECTIVE

Businesses invest hundreds of billions of dollars annually in fixed assets. By their very nature, such investments affect a firm's fortunes for many years. A good decision can boost earnings sharply and increase the price of a firm's shares, but a bad decision can lead to bankruptcy.

A classic example of a bad capital budgeting decision that could easily have been avoided involved Lockheed's production of the L-1011 Tri-Star commercial aircraft. When Lockheed made the final decision to go forward with Tri-Star production, it estimated the breakeven volume at about 200 planes. The company had orders for about 180 planes, and it was sure of getting at least 20 more orders. Consequently, it decided to commit $1 billion and to commence production.

However, Lockheed's analysis was flawed—it failed to account for the cost of the capital tied up in the project. Had its analysts appraised the project correctly, they would have found that the breakeven point was far above 200 planes—so far above that the Tri-Star program was almost certainly doomed to fail. This mistake contributed to a decline in Lockheed's share price from $73 per share to $3. Had Lockheed's managers read this chapter and heeded its advice, that loss might have been avoided.

Our treatment of capital budgeting is divided into three parts. First, Chapter 13 gives an overview and explains the basic techniques used in capital budgeting analysis. In Chapter 14, we consider how cash flows are estimated and we apply the techniques. Finally, in Chapter 15, we bring risk into the analysis.

Significance of Capital Budgeting

The term *capital* refers to fixed assets used in production, while a *budget* is a plan detailing projected inflows and outflows during some future period. Thus, the firm's *capital budget* outlines its planned expenditures on fixed assets, and **capital budgeting** is the whole process of analyzing projects and deciding which projects should be included in the capital budget. Obvious examples of capital outlays are expenditures for land, buildings, and equipment, and for permanent additions to working capital associated with plant extension. Advertising and promotion campaigns, as well as research and development programs, are also classified as capital budgeting expenditures. The capital budgeting process is of fundamental importance to the success or failure of the firm because capital budgeting decisions, probably more than anything else, determine the firm's future.

A number of factors combine to make capital budgeting decisions perhaps the most important ones managers must make. Further, all departments of a firm—production, marketing, and others—are vitally affected by capital budgeting decisions; thus, all executives, no matter what their primary responsibility, must be aware of how these decisions are made. In addition, the determination of the information required to use the capital budgeting techniques forces a careful analysis of the expected costs and benefits of the projects being considered.

First and foremost, the fact that the results of capital budgeting decisions continue over an extended period means that the decision-maker loses some flexibility. For example, the purchase of an asset with an economic life of 10 years requires a long waiting period before the final results of the action can be known. Further, because asset expansion is fundamentally related to expected future sales, a decision to buy or to construct a fixed asset that is expected to last 10 years involves an implicit 10-year sales forecast.

An erroneous forecast of asset requirements can have serious consequences. If the firm has invested too much in assets, it will incur unnecessarily heavy expenses. On the other hand, if it has not spent enough on fixed assets, two serious problems may arise. First, the firm's equipment may not be sufficiently modern to enable it to produce competitively. Second, if it lacks adequate capacity, it may lose a portion of its market share to rival firms, and regaining lost customers typically requires heavy selling expenses, price reductions, and product improvement, all of which are costly.

Another aspect of capital budgeting is timing: capital assets must be ready to come "on stream" at the time they are needed. The executive vice president of a decorative tile company gave the authors an illustration of the importance of capital budgeting. His firm tried to operate near capacity most of the time. During a 4-year period, the firm experienced intermittent spurts in the demand for its product, which forced it to turn away orders. After these sharp increases in demand, the firm would add capacity by renting an additional building and then purchasing and installing the appropriate equipment. It would take 6 to 8 months to have the additional capacity ready. At this point, the company frequently found that there was no demand for its increased output, since other firms had already expanded their operations and had taken an increased share of the market. If the firm had properly forecasted demand and planned its capacity increases 6 months to a year in advance, it would have been able to maintain and perhaps even increase its share of the market.

Effective capital budgeting can improve both the timing of asset acquisitions and the quality of assets purchased. A firm that correctly forecasts its needs for capital assets has the opportunity to purchase and install them before its sales exceed capacity. In practice, though, most firms do not order capital goods until they approach full capacity. If sales increase because of an increase in general market demand, all firms in the industry will tend to order capital goods at about the same time. This often results in backlogs, long waiting times for machinery, a deterioration in the quality of the capital goods, and an increase in their prices. The firm that foresees its needs and purchases capital assets early can avoid these problems. Note though, that if a firm forecasts an increase in demand and expands capacity to meet its anticipations but then does not see its sales increase, it will be saddled with excess capacity and abnormally high costs. This can lead to losses and even bankruptcy. Thus, the sales forecast is critical.

Finally, capital budgeting is important because asset expansion typically involves substantial expenditures, and before a firm spends a large amount of money, it must make the proper plans—large amounts of money are not available automatically. A firm contemplating a major capital expenditure program may need to arrange its financing several years in advance to be sure of having the funds required for the expansion.

Concept Review

▶ Why is a capital budget so important?

Generating Ideas for Capital Projects

Capital budgeting projects are *created* by the firm, rather than being presented like a set of securities that already exist in the securities market. For example, a sales representative may report that customers are asking for a particular product that the company does not now produce. The sales manager then discusses the idea with the marketing research group to determine the size of the market for the proposed product. If it appears likely that a significant market does exist, cost accountants and engineers will be asked to estimate production costs. If it appears that the product can be produced and sold to yield a sufficient profit, the project will be undertaken.

A firm's growth and development, even its ability to remain competitive and to survive, depend upon a constant flow of ideas for new products and for ways to make existing products better, or to produce them at a lower cost. Accordingly, a well-managed firm will go to great lengths to develop good capital budgeting proposals. For example, the executive vice president of one very successful corporation indicated that his company takes the following steps to generate projects:

> Our R&D department is constantly searching for new products and also for ways to improve existing products. In addition, our executive committee, which consists of senior executives in marketing, production, and finance, identifies the products and markets in which our company will compete, and the committee sets long-run targets for each division. These targets, which are spelled out in the corporation's strategic business plan, provide a general guide to the operating executives who must meet them. These executives then seek new products, set expansion plans for existing products, and look for ways to reduce production and distribution costs. Since bonuses and promotions are based in large part on each unit's ability to meet or exceed its targets, these economic incentives encourage our operating executives to seek out profitable investment opportunities.

While our senior executives are judged and rewarded on the basis of how well their units perform, people further down the line are given bonuses for specific suggestions, including ideas that lead to profitable investments. Additionally, a percentage of our corporate profit is set aside for distribution to nonexecutive employees, and we have an employees' stock ownership plan (ESOP) to provide further incentives. Our objective is to encourage employees at all levels to keep on the lookout for good ideas, including those that lead to capital investments.

If a firm has capable and imaginative executives and employees and if its incentive system is working properly, many ideas for capital investment will be advanced. Since some ideas will be good ones while others will not, procedures must be established for screening projects, as we discuss in the remainder of the chapter.

Concept Review

▶ How does a firm get ideas for capital projects?

Project Classification

Aside from the actual generation of ideas, the first step in the capital budgeting process is to assemble a list of the proposed projects together with the data necessary to appraise them. Analyzing capital expenditure proposals is not a costless operation—benefits can be gained from a careful analysis, but such an investigation does have a cost. For certain types of projects, a relatively refined analysis may be warranted; for others, cost-benefit studies may suggest that a simpler procedure should be used. Accordingly, firms frequently classify projects into the following categories, and they analyze projects in each category somewhat differently:

1. *Replacement: maintenance of business.* Category 1 consists of expenditures necessary to replace worn out or damaged equipment used to produce profitable products. These projects are necessary if the firm is to continue in its current businesses. The only issues here are should the firm continue to produce these products or services, and should the firm continue to use its existing plant and equipment? Usually, the answers are yes, so maintenance decisions are normally made without going through an elaborate decision process.

2. *Replacement: cost reduction.* This category includes expenditures to replace serviceable but obsolete equipment. The purpose of these expenditures is to lower the costs of labour, materials, or other items such as electricity. These decisions are somewhat more discretionary, so more detailed analysis is generally required to support expenditures.

3. *Expansion of existing products or markets.* Expenditures to increase output of existing products or to expand outlets or distribution facilities in markets now being served are included here. These decisions are more complex because they require an explicit consideration of future demand in

the firm's product markets. Mistakes are more likely, so still more detailed analysis is required, and the final decisions are made at a higher level within the firm.

4. *Expansion into new products or markets.* These are expenditures necessary to produce a new product or to expand into a geographic area not currently being served. These projects involve strategic decisions that could change the fundamental nature of the business, and they normally require the expenditure of large sums of money over long periods. Invariably, very detailed analysis is required, and final decisions are generally made by the board of directors as a part of the strategic plan. Mergers and acquisitions often are analyzed as a part of the capital budgeting process, and they are used to implement the strategic plan.

5. *Safety and environmental projects.* Expenditures necessary to comply with government orders, labour agreements, and insurance policy terms fall into this category. These expenditures are often called *mandatory investments*, or *non-revenue-producing projects*. How the decisions are handled depends on their size, with small ones being treated much like the Category 1 projects described previously.

6. *Other.* This catchall includes office buildings, parking lots, executive aircraft, and so on. How they are handled also depends on their size.

In general, relatively simple calculations and only a few supporting documents are required for replacement decisions, especially maintenance-type investments in profitable plants. More detailed analysis is required for cost-reduction replacements, for the expansion of existing product lines, and especially for investments in new products or areas. Also, within each category, projects are broken down by their dollar costs: the larger the required investment, the more detailed the analysis, and the higher the level of the officer who must authorize the expenditure. Thus, although a plant manager may be authorized to approve maintenance expenditures up to $10 000 on the basis of a relatively unsophisticated analysis, the full board of directors may have to approve decisions that involve either amounts over $1 million or expansions into new products or markets. Statistical data are generally lacking for new product decisions, so here judgements, as opposed to detailed cost data, are a key element in the decision process.

Administrative Aspects. After a capital budget has been adopted, payments must be scheduled. Characteristically, the finance department is responsible for scheduling payments and for acquiring funds to meet payment schedule requirements. The finance department is also primarily responsible for co-operating with the members of operating divisions to compile systematic records on the uses of funds and the uses of equipment purchased in capital budgeting programs. Effective capital budgeting programs require such information as the basis for periodic review and evaluation of capital expenditure decisions—the feedback and control phase of capital budgeting, often called the *post-audit review*.

In Canada, there are a number of companies that are subsidiaries of multinational companies. Because the multinational operates to maximize the market value of its equity, considerations of the tax laws and operating costs in each country in which it operates are important. Using these inputs, the multinational may make decisions for an operating subsidiary that are different from those that would be made if the company were independent. Thus, the parent organization may provide the operating subsidiaries with the funds for capital expenditures and the cost of capital that should be used. The capital budgeting analysis will still be important within the subsidiary, however, as cash flow information will still be required to make investment decisions.

Choosing among Alternative Proposals

In most firms, a large number of project proposals are generated. Some proposals are good, others are poor, and methods must be developed to distinguish between the good and the poor. Essentially, the end product is a ranking of the proposals and a cutoff point for determining how far down the ranked list to go.

Some projects are eliminated because they would exclude other projects. **Mutually exclusive projects** are alternative investments; if one alternative is accepted, the other must be rejected. For example, the installation of a conveyor belt system in a warehouse and the purchase of a fleet of fork trucks for the same warehouse are mutually exclusive projects—accepting one implies rejection of the other.

Independent projects are projects whose costs and revenues are independent of one another. For example, in addition to its warehouse investment, the firm may need equipment to package its products. The work requires a packaging machine, and the purchase of equipment for this purpose is independent of the equipment purchased for the warehouse.

Finally, projects can be **contingent** or **interdependent**. For these projects, the choice of one requires the choice of the other. For example, suppose a chemical company is considering the purchase of a machine to produce a new product. A specially designed packaging system is required if the new product project is to be accepted. It would be incorrect to consider the new product and the packaging system as independent projects. Instead, the two are interdependent and must be combined and evaluated as a single project. Projects may also be time contingent. For example, by undertaking a particular project today, the firm may place itself in a strategic position to be able to take other projects in the future that would not otherwise be available. A correct analysis of the original project involves an evaluation of the potential returns of these future projects.

Concept Review

► Identify and briefly explain how capital project classification categories are used.
► Describe the features of mutually exclusive, independent and contingent projects. How is each type considered in the capital budgeting process?

The Evaluation Process

There are six steps that are followed in the process of evaluating a particular project:

1. First, the cost of the project must be determined. This value should reflect all of the costs to be incurred in the initial period that will be a direct result of taking on the project.

2. Next, management estimates the expected cash flows resulting from the project, including the value of the asset at the end of the lifetime of the project. These cash flows will reflect the setup costs if they are spread over several years.

3. Third, the riskiness of the projected cash flows must be estimated. To do this, management needs information about the probability distributions of the cash flows.

4. Then, given the riskiness of the projected cash flows and the general level of money costs in the economy as reflected in the risk-free rate, k_{RF}, management determines the appropriate **cost of capital**, or discount rate, at which the project's cash flows are to be discounted.

5. Next, the expected cash flows are put on a present value basis to obtain an estimate of the asset's value to the firm as of the current period.

6. Finally, the present value of the expected cash inflows is compared with the required outlay, or cost, of the project; if the asset's present value exceeds its cost, the project should be accepted. Otherwise, the project should be rejected. (Alternatively, the expected rate of return on the project can be calculated, and if this rate exceeds the project's required rate of return—often called the *hurdle rate*—the project is acceptable.)

If the firm identifies or creates an investment project that has a present value greater than it costs, wealth is created in the firm and the share price will increase. Therefore, the more effective the firm's capital budgeting procedures, including their ability to create projects, the higher will be the firm's share price.

Importance of Good Data.   Most discussions of measuring the cash flows associated with capital projects are relatively brief. It is important to emphasize, however, that in the entire capital budgeting procedure, probably nothing is of greater importance than a reliable estimate of the cost savings or revenue increases that will be achieved from the prospective outlay of capital funds. The increased output and sales revenue resulting from expansion programs are obvious benefits. Cost-reduction benefits include changes in quality and quantity of required direct labour, in amount and cost of scrap and rework time, in fuel costs, and in maintenance expenses, down time, safety, flexibility and so on. So many variables are involved that it is obviously impossible to make neat generalizations. However, this should not minimize the crucial importance of analyzing the benefits to be derived from capital expenditures. Each capital equipment expenditure must be examined in detail for possible additional or incremental costs and savings and revenues.

All the subsequent procedures for ranking projects are no better than the data input—the old saying "garbage in, garbage out" is certainly applicable to capital budgeting analysis. Thus, the data assembly process is not a routine clerical task to be performed on a mechanical basis. It requires continuous monitoring and evaluation of estimates by those competent to make such evaluations—engineers, accountants, economists, and cost analysts.

Concept Review

► List the six steps of the evaluation process.

Capital Budgeting Ranking Criteria

The point of capital budgeting—indeed, the point of all financial analysis—is to make decisions that will maximize the current market price of the firm's common equity, or, equivalently, to make decisions that will maximize the market value of the equity of the shareholders outstanding before the investment decision was made. The capital budgeting process is designed to answer two questions: (1) which of several mutually exclusive investments should be selected? (2) how many projects, in total, should be accepted?

Four major methods are used to evaluate projects and to decide whether or not they should be accepted for inclusion in the capital budget. These *ranking methods* are (1) payback, (2) net present value (NPV), (3) regular internal rate of return (IRR), and (4) modified internal rate of return (MIRR). We first explain how each ranking criterion is calculated, and then we evaluate how well each performs in terms of identifying the set of projects that will maximize the firm's share price.[1]

We use the cash flow data shown in Table 13-1 for Projects A and B to illustrate each method, and throughout this chapter we assume that the projects are equally risky. The cash flows, CF_t, are expected values, and they include depreciation, salvage values, and tax effects. Also, since many projects require an investment in both fixed assets and working capital, the investment outlays shown as the initial cash flow, CF_0, include any necessary changes in net working capital.[2] Finally, we assume that all cash flows occur at the end of the designated year.

---

[1]Various types of "accounting rates of return" methods, such as return on assets (ROA), or return on investment (ROI), using the accounting definition of income, are occasionally used in project evaluation, but all of these methods have serious flaws, and hence we omit them from this text. Also, the *profitability index*, or *benefit–cost ratio*, which is found by dividing the PV of the inflows by the PV of the costs and shows the benefits per dollar of costs, is sometimes used, especially in government agencies. This method is a discounted cash flow method, like the NPV and MIRR methods, but it is not as good.

[2]The most difficult part of the capital budgeting process is the estimation of the relevant cash flows. For simplicity, the net cash flows are treated as a given in this chapter, thus allowing us to focus on the capital budgeting ranking criteria. However, in Chapter 14 we will discuss the cash flow estimation in detail. Also, note that *working capital* is defined as the firm's current assets and that *net working capital* is current assets minus current liabilities.

Table 13-1
Net Cash Flows for Projects A and B

Year (t)	Project A	Project B
0	($1000)[a]	($1000)
1	500	100
2	400	200
3	300	300
4	100	400
5	10	500
6	10	600

[a]Represents the net investment outlay, or initial cost.

Payback Period

The **payback period** is defined as the number of years it takes a firm to recover its original investment from net cash flows. The payback period was the first formal method used to evaluate capital budgeting projects. The easiest way to calculate the payback period is to accumulate the project's net cash flows and see when the cumulative total becomes positive. For example, the annual and cumulative net cash flows of Project A are shown in the following table:

Project A's Net Cash Flows

Year	Annual	Cumulative
0	($1000)	($1000)
1	500	(500)
2	400	(100)
3	300	200
4	100	300
5	10	310
6	10	320

Thus the investment is recovered by the end of Year 3. Assuming that cash flows occur evenly during the year, the recovery actually occurs one-third of the way into Year 3: $100 remains to be recovered at the end of Year 2, and since Year 3 produces $300 in net cash flows, the payback period for Project A is 2.33 years. Using the same procedure, we find that the payback of Project B is 4.00 years.

To use this technique, the company specifies a target payback period and compares the payback period of the project to the target. If the target is a 3-year payback period, Project A will be accepted, but Project B will be rejected. If the projects are mutually exclusive, A will be ranked over B since its payback is shorter.

Some firms use a variant of the regular payback, the discounted payback period, which is similar to the regular payback period except that the expected cash flows are discounted by the project's cost of capital, or the required rate of return for the project.[3] Thus, the **discounted payback period** is defined as the number of years required to recover the investment from *discounted* cash flows. Table 13-2 contains the discounted net cash flows for Projects A and B, assuming a 10 percent cost of capital. To construct Table 13-2, each cash inflow in Table 13-1 is divided by $(1 + k)^t = (1.10)^t$, where t is the year in which the cash flow occurs and k is the project's cost of capital. After 3 years, Project A will have generated $1011 in discounted cash inflows, as shown in Table 13-2 when the cash inflows for Years 1 through 3 are summed. Since the cost is $1000, the discounted payback is just under 3 years, or, to be precise, 2 + ($214/$225) = 2.95 years. Project B's discounted payback is 4.79 years. The comparison is:

Discounted payback A: 2.0 + $214/$225 = 2.95 years.
Discounted payback B: 4.0 + $246/$310 = 4.79 years.

For Projects A and B, the rankings are the same regardless of which payback method is used; that is, Project A is preferred to Project B, and Project A will still be selected if the firm's target payback is 3 years or less. However, it is possible for the regular and the discounted paybacks to produce conflicting rankings.

Although the payback period is very easy to calculate, it can lead to incorrect decisions. As the illustration demonstrates, it ignores cash flows beyond the payback period. If the project is one maturing in later years, the use of payback period can lead to the selection of less desirable investments. Projects with longer payback periods are characteristically those involved in

Table 13-2
Discounted Cash Flows for Projects A and B

| Year | Project A | | Project B | |
(t)	Annual	Cumulative	Annual	Cumulative
0	($1000)	($1000)	($1000)	($1000)
1	455	(545)	91	(909)
2	331	(214)	165	(744)
3	225	11	225	(518)
4	68	79	273	(246)
5	6	85	310	64
6	6	91	339	403

[3]The cost of capital can be viewed as the minimum acceptable rate of return required on a project of a given level of risk. The cost of capital is based on market data and reflects the opportunity cost of investors—both debt and equity. If the firm cannot earn this opportunity cost, it should not invest in the project. Thus, if investors require a 10 percent return on projects with a certain level of risk, the opportunity cost is 10 percent.

long-range planning—developing new products or tapping new markets. These strategic decisions often do not yield their highest returns for a number of years. This means that the payback method may be biassed against the very investments that are most important to a firm's long-run success.

The use of the payback period method is sometimes defended on the grounds that returns beyond 3 or 4 years are fraught with such uncertainty that it is best to disregard them altogether in a planning decision. This is clearly an unsound procedure, however. Some investments with the highest returns are those that may not come to fruition for 8 to 10 years. The new product cycle in industries involving advanced technologies may not have a payoff for 8 or 9 years. Furthermore, even though returns that occur after 3, 4, or 5 years may be highly uncertain, it is important to make a judgement about the likelihood of their occurring. To ignore them is to assign a zero probability to these distant receipts. This procedure can hardly produce the best results.

Another defence of the payback method is that a firm that is short of cash must necessarily give great emphasis to a quick return of its funds so that they may be put to use in other places or in meeting other needs. Although the payback approach does provide an indication of the *liquidity* of projects, it does not relieve the payback method of its many shortcomings; there are better methods for handling the cash shortage situation.[4]

A third reason for using the payback method is that projects with faster paybacks typically have more favourable short-run effects on earnings per share. Firms that use payback for this reason are sacrificing future growth for current accounting income; in general, such a practice will not maximize the value of the firm. The discounted cash flow techniques discussed in the next section, if used properly, automatically give consideration to the present earnings versus future growth tradeoff and strike the balance that will maximize the firm's value.

The payback method is sometimes used simply because it is so easy to apply. If a firm is making many small capital expenditure decisions, the costs of using more complex methods may outweigh the benefits of possibly "better" choices among competing projects. However, it is essential that the companies be aware of the shortcomings of the payback method and the costs that are imposed on shareholders by the use of the technique.

Net Present Value (NPV) Method

As the flaws in the payback method were recognized, people began to search for methods of evaluating projects that would recognize that a dollar received immediately is preferable to a dollar received at some future date. This led to the development of **discounted cash flow (DCF) techniques**, which incorporate the time value of money.

One DCF technique is called the **net present value (NPV) method**. This approach is implemented as follows.

---

[4] We interpret a cash shortage to mean that the firm has a high opportunity cost for its funds and a high cost of capital. We would consider this high cost of capital in the internal rate of return method or the net present value method, thus taking account of the cash shortage.

1. The analyst finds the present value of each cash flow, including both inflows and outflows, discounted at the project's cost of capital.
2. These discounted cash flows are added together; this sum is the project's NPV. (This process is equivalent to subtracting the present value of all future net cash flows from the cost in the initial period of the project.)
3. If the NPV is positive, the project is acceptable; if the NPV is negative, it should be rejected. If the two projects are mutually exclusive, the one with the higher net present value should be preferred.

The equation for NPV is as follows:

$$NPV = \frac{CF_0}{(1+k)^0} + \frac{CF_1}{(1+k)^1} + \cdots + \frac{CF_n}{(1+k)^n}$$

$$= \sum_{t=0}^{n} \frac{CF_t}{(1+k)^t} = \sum_{t=0}^{n} CF_t(PVIF_{k,t}). \tag{13-1}$$

Here CF_0, CF_1, and so forth represent the expected net cash flows; k is the project's marginal cost of capital; and n is the project's expected life. The cost of capital, k, depends upon the risk of the project, the level of interest rates in the economy, and several other factors. In this chapter, k is taken as given, but it is discussed in detail in Chapter 17. Cash outflows (expenditures on the project, such as the cost of buying equipment or building factories) are treated as *negative* cash flows. For Projects A and B, only CF_0 is negative, but for many large projects, such as the construction of pipelines, nuclear power generators, and even new computer hardware, outflows occur for several years before operations begin and cash flows turn positive; for these projects, the first few values of CF_t are negative.

At a 10 percent cost of capital, the NPV of Project A is $90.67. The NPV can be found using a time line approach, as shown in Figure 13-1. Alternatively, we can use Equation 13-1, as follows:

$$NPV_A = \frac{-\$1000}{(1.10)^0} + \frac{\$500}{(1.10)^1} + \frac{\$400}{(1.10)^2} + \frac{\$300}{(1.10)^3} + \frac{\$100}{(1.10)^4} + \frac{\$10}{(1.10)^5} + \frac{\$10}{(1.10)^6}$$

$$= -\$1000 + \$454.55 + \$330.58 + \$225.39 + \$68.30 + \$6.21 + \$5.64$$

$$= \$90.67.$$

By a similar process, we find $NPV_B = \$403.94$. On this basis, both projects should be accepted if they are independent, but B should be the one chosen if they are mutually exclusive.[5]

---

[5]In making a decision on mutually exclusive projects, it is best to compare projects of equal lives. If one project has cash flows that extend for a longer period, a comparison of the alternative requires an assumption of what will be done with the cash flows over the period between the cessation of the shorter and the longer projects. This time difference is not crucial if (1) the difference in the lifetime is small; (2) the difference will occur far in the future—for example, one project lasts 20 years, the other 25; or (3) it is assumed that the cash flows from the shorter-lived project are reinvested at the cost of the capital.

Figure 13-1
NPV of Project A at a 10% Cost of Capital

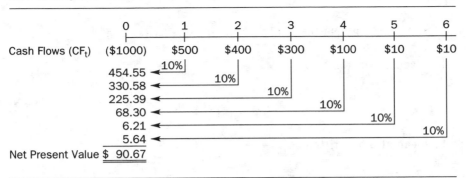

Rationale for the NPV Method. The rationale for the NPV method is straightforward. When a firm takes on a project financed by outside sources, the value of the firm will increase by an amount equal to the present value of the expected cash flows. Thus, if the NPV of a project is positive, the increase in the value of the firm is greater than the amount of outside funds needed to finance the investment. The NPV reflects the gain in wealth accruing to the firm's shareholders existing before the investment decision was undertaken. In our example, the value of the firm will increase by $1091 and the existing shareholders will gain $91 if Project A is undertaken; if Project B is accepted, the increase in the value of the firm is $1404 and $404 accrues to the existing shareholders. Viewing the alternatives in this manner, it is easy to see why B is preferred to A, and it is also easy to see the logic of the NPV approach.[6] In considering the capital budget, the increase in the wealth to existing shareholders will be equal to the sum of the NPVs of all accepted projects.[7]

Internal Rate of Return (IRR) Method

The **internal rate of return (IRR)** is defined as that discount rate that equates the present value of a project's expected net cash inflows to the present value of the project's expected costs.

---

[6]If the project is financed by retained earnings, the value of the firm increases by an amount equal to the NPV of the project. In this case, although the present value of the cash flows increases the value of the firm, the payment of the initial cost with internally financed funds reduces the value of the firm by the initial cost.

[7]This description of the process is somewhat oversimplified. Both analysts and investors anticipate that firms will identify and accept positive NPV projects, and share prices reflect these expectations. Thus, share prices react to announcements of new capital projects only to the extent that such projects were not already expected. In this sense, we may think of a firm's value as consisting of two parts: (1) the value of its existing assets and (2) the value of its "growth opportunities," or projects with positive NPVs. Security analysts (and investors) thus analyze companies based on a set of cash-producing assets plus a set of growth opportunities that will materialize if and only if it can come up with positive NPV projects through its capital budgeting process. Of course, the growth opportunities component may have a zero value if the firm invests in projects with zero NPVs.

$$PV \text{ (inflows)} = PV \text{ (investment costs)}$$

or

$$PV \text{ (inflows)} - PV \text{ (investments costs)} = 0,$$

which can be written as

$$\sum_{t=0}^{n} \frac{CF_t}{(1 + IRR)^t} = 0, \tag{13-2}$$

which can also be written as

$$\sum_{t=0}^{n} CF_t(PVIF_{IRR,\, t}) = 0. \tag{13-2a}$$

For our Project A, here is the set-up for finding the IRR:

$$\frac{-\$1000}{(1 + IRR)^0} + \frac{\$500}{(1 + IRR)^1} + \frac{\$400}{(1 + IRR)^2} + \frac{\$300}{(1 + IRR)^3}$$

$$+ \frac{\$100}{(1 + IRR)^4} + \frac{10}{(1 + IRR)^5} + \frac{10}{(1 + IRR)^6} = 0,$$

or

$$-\$1000 + \$500(PVIF_{IRR,1}) + \$400(PVIF_{IRR,2}) + \$300(PVIF_{IRR,3})$$

$$+ \$100(PVIF_{IRR,4}) + \$10(PVIF_{IRR,5}) + \$10(PVIF_{IRR,6}) = 0.$$

These cash flows can also be laid out on a time line, as shown in Figure 13-2. Here we know the value of each CF_t, but we do not know the value of IRR. Thus, we have an equation with one unknown, which we can solve for the value of IRR.

Notice that the IRR formula, Equation 13-2, is simply the NPV formula, Equation 13-1, solved for the particular discount rate that causes the NPV to equal zero. In other words, the same basic equation is used for both methods, but in the NPV method the discount rate, k, is specified and the NPV is found, whereas in the IRR method the NPV is specified to equal zero and the value of IRR that forces the NPV to equal zero is found.

Equation 13-2 (or 13-2a) can be solved to find the IRR in several ways:

1. *Trial and error.*   Substitute into the equation different values for the IRR until you find the value that forces the NPV to equal zero. This process is extremely tedious and inefficient.

2. *Financial calculators or computers.* Use one of the better financial calculators, or computer spreadsheet packages such as *Lotus 1-2-3* and *Excel*, which have IRR functions that will solve Equation 13-2 rapidly. Simply input the cash flows, and the computer or calculator finds the IRR.

Figure 13-2
IRR for Project A

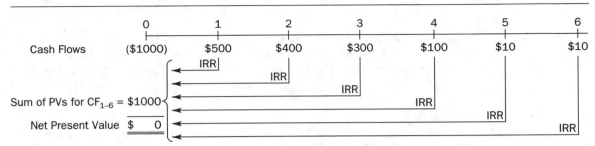

$IRR_A = 15.1\%$ = discount rate that forces the sum of the PVs
of CF_{1-6} to equal the project's cost, \$1000

Since internal rates of return can be calculated very easily with financial calculators or computers, most firms now have computerized their capital budgeting processes and automatically generate IRRs, NPVs, and paybacks for all projects. Thus, businesses have no difficulty whatsoever with the mechanical side of capital budgeting, and a serious business student should have a financial calculator capable of finding IRRs. All IRRs reported hereafter in this and the following chapter were obtained using a financial calculator (or a PC). By keying in the cash flows and then pressing the IRR button, we find that Project A has $IRR_A = 15.1\%$, whereas $IRR_B = 19.7\%$.

Let us assume that the required cost of capital is 10 percent. Then the IRR rule indicates that if Projects A and B are independent, both are acceptable — both of them are expected to earn more than the cost of the capital needed to finance them. If they are mutually exclusive, B ranks higher and should be accepted, whereas A should be rejected. If the cost of capital is more than 19.7 percent, both projects should be rejected.

IRR for Level Cash Flows. If the cash flows from a project are level, or equal in each year, then the project's internal rate of return can be found by a relatively simple process. In essence, such a project is an annuity in which the firm makes an initial outlay, C_0, and receives a stream of net cash flow benefits, CF, for a given number of years. The IRR for the project is found by applying Equation 12-6, discussed in Chapter 12.

To illustrate: suppose that a project costs \$10 000 and is expected to produce net cash flows of \$1627 a year for 10 years. The cost of the project, \$10 000, is equal to the present value of an annuity of \$1627 a year for 10 years at the internal rate of return. Therefore the relationship can be written as

$$C_0 = (CF)(PVIFA_{IRR, \, 10}),$$

which can be expressed as

$$PVIFA_{IRR, \, 10} = \frac{C_0}{CF}.$$

Substituting values into the example, we obtain

$$\text{PVIFA}_{\text{IRR, 10}} = \frac{\$10\,000}{\$1627} = 6.146.$$

Looking up PVIFA in Table A-4 of the insert card, we search across the 10-year row and find it (approximately) under the 10 percent column. Accordingly, 10 percent is the IRR on the project. In other words, 10 percent is the value of the IRR that will satisfy Equation 13-2 when CF is constant at $1627 for 10 years and C is $10 000. This procedure works only if the project has constant annual cash flows.

If the time period of the level cash flows is long, there is a relationship between the IRR and the payback period. For example, in the illustration above, assume that the expected net cash flows are perpetual. With a perpetuity, the present value of the net cash flows is written as CF/k. To find the IRR for the perpetuity, we set the present value of the perpetual cash flow evaluated at the IRR equal to the initial cost of the project:

$$\frac{CF}{IRR} = C_0 \quad \text{or} \quad IRR = \frac{CF}{C_0}.$$

When we substitute the values of the example, we find that the IRR equals

$$\frac{\$1627}{\$10\,000} = 0.1627 = 16.27\%$$

The payback period (PBP), which is the number of years needed to recover the initial cost of the investment, can be written as

$$\frac{C_0}{CF} = \frac{\$10\,000}{\$1627} = 6.146 \text{ years.}$$

But

$$\frac{1}{PBP} = \frac{1}{(C_0/CF)} = \frac{CF}{C_0} = IRR.$$

Therefore, if the project cash flows are expected to be level and the time period is very long, the reciprocal of the PBP is an estimate of the IRR.

Rationale and Use of the IRR Method.   Why is the particular discount rate that equates a project's cost with the present value of its receipts (the IRR) so special? We can answer this question by considering the effects of the internal rate of return on the firm's profitability. Let us assume that our firm obtains $1000 by borrowing from a bank at an interest rate of 14.5 percent. The firm will use the money to invest in Project C, which has cash flows of $500, $400, $300, and $100 in Years 1 through 4, respectively. This produces an internal rate of return of 14.5 percent. Since the internal rate of return on this particular project is 14.5 percent, the same as the cost of the bank loan, the firm can invest in the project, use the cash flows generated by the investment to pay off the principal and interest on the loan, and come out exactly even on the transaction. This point is demonstrated in the following tabulation, which shows that Project C provides cash flows that are just sufficient to pay 14.5 percent interest on the unpaid balance of the bank loan, retire the loan over the life of the project, and end up with a balance that differs from zero only by a rounding error of 32 cents:

Beginning Loan Balance (1)	Cash Flow (2)	Interest on the Loan at 14.5%: (3) = 0.145 × (1)	Repayment of Principal (4) = (2) − (3)	Ending Loan Balance (5) = (1) − (4)
$1000.00	$500	$145.00	$355.00	$645.00
645.00	400	93.53	306.47	338.53
338.53	300	49.09	250.91	87.62
87.62	100	12.70	87.30	0.32

If the internal rate of return exceeds the cost of the funds used to finance the project, a surplus is left over after paying for the capital, and this surplus accrues to the firm's shareholders. Thus, taking on the project increases the equity value of the firm. If the internal rate of return is less than the cost of capital, taking on the project imposes a cost on existing shareholders, and in this case accepting the project results in a reduction of shareholder value.

Although the previous example demonstrated the breakeven characteristic of a project with an internal rate of return equal to its cost of capital under an all-debt-financing assumption, the result is independent of the form of financing used. For example, if equity were issued and the cost of equity capital were 14.5 percent, the cash flows would be sufficient to pay dividends and repay to the equity investor the amount invested.

The investment decision rule for the internal rate of return approach is to accept all projects for which the internal rate of return exceeds the cost of capital and to reject all projects for which the internal rate of return is less than the cost of capital. It is easy to see why the cost of capital is often called the *hurdle rate*. The internal rate of return criterion states that, if projects are independent, the firm should accept all that have IRRs in excess of the cost of capital. If projects are mutually exclusive, the project with the higher IRR should be accepted.[8]

Concept Review

▶ List the four major methods used to rank capital projects.
▶ How is the payback period of a project calculated, and what information does it provide to the firm?

(continued)

---

[8]In this discussion we assume that the firm relies exclusively on the NPV or IRR approach and accepts or rejects projects using the rules described. There may be situations in which a firm accepts a project that does not meet the NPV or IRR criterion. This could reflect other influences that are not quantifiable from the data; an example would be a strategic project that provides entry to a market. Similarly, projects that appear to meet the criteria for acceptance may be rejected for other reasons. The analysis here uses only quantifiable information. Management may bring to bear other factors that it perceives to be important.

(continued)

- Identify the steps used in the net present value (NPV) method.
- What is the rationale behind the NPV method?
- How do you calculate the IRR of a project?
- What is the rationale behind the IRR method?

Consistency of NPV and IRR Methods

As noted above, the NPV method (1) accepts all independent projects whose NPV is greater than zero, and (2) ranks mutually exclusive projects by their NPVs, selecting the project with the higher NPV. The IRR method, on the other hand, finds the value of IRR that forces the NPV of Equation 13-1 to equal zero. The IRR method results in accepting independent projects whose IRR is greater than k, the cost of capital, and selecting among mutually exclusive projects depending on which has the highest IRR.

It is apparent that the only structural difference between the NPV and IRR methods lies in the discount rates used in the two equations—all the values in the equations are identical except for IRR and k. Further, we can see that if IRR > k, then NPV > 0.[9]

Accordingly, the two methods give the *same* accept-reject decisions for specific projects—if a project is acceptable under the NPV criterion, it is also acceptable if the IRR method is used.

This relationship between the NPV and IRR criteria is presented graphically in Figure 13-3, with data for Project A from the previous section. On the vertical axis, the net present value is plotted, and on the horizontal axis, the cost of capital. The relationship between the NPV and the cost of capital is called the *net present value (NPV) profile*. When the cost of capital is equal to zero, the net present value is the simple summation of the cash flows—$320 for Project A.

As the cost of capital increases, cash flows further in the future have reduced weight in the net present value. At a cost of capital of 5 percent, NPV is $195; at 10 percent, $92; at 15 percent, −$3; and at 20 percent, −$80. As the cost of capital increases, the NPV approaches a lower limit of −$1000 (the initial outlay for Project A). Notice that at approximately 15 percent, the NPV is zero and this is the IRR of the project.

If the cost of capital is 10 percent, the NPV is positive and the project should be accepted. The same accept decision is generated by the IRR criterion, since the IRR (15 percent) is greater than the cost of capital (10 percent). If the

---

[9]This can be seen by noting that NPV = 0 if and only if IRR = k:

$$NPV = \sum_{t=0}^{n} \frac{CF_t}{(1 + k)^t} = \sum_{t=0}^{n} \frac{CF_t}{(1 + IRR)^t} = 0.$$

If IRR > k, then NPV > 0, and if IRR < k, then NPV < 0. We should also note that, under certain conditions, there may be more than one solution to the IRR equation; hence, multiple IRRs can be found.

Figure 13-3
Relationships of NPV and IRR Criteria: Net Present Value Profile

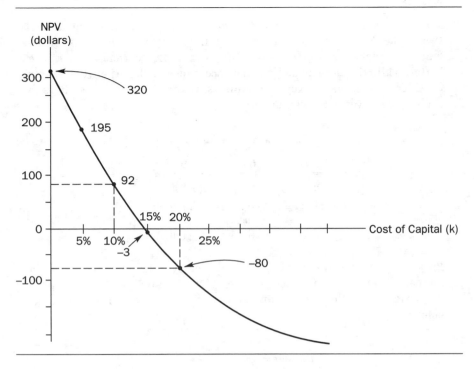

cost of capital is greater than the IRR, the IRR criterion says reject; this is consistent with the negative NPV, which requires a reject decision.

When firms select investment projects, they generally look at both the NPV and the IRR. However, each of these criterion gives a different view of the project, and they may yield conflicting results. The NPV focusses on how much a project will add to the value of the equity, assuming the cash flows materialize. The IRR indicates the rate of return the project will yield if things work out as expected.

1. *Basic focus.* The NPV focusses on how much a project will add to the value of the existing equity holders—the IRR focusses on a project's rate of return. Firms ought to try to maximize their equity value, not their rate of return, if the two are in conflict. To illustrate: it is far better to earn 50 percent on a $1 million investment (IRR = 50%, NPV = $500 000) than 200 percent on a 10-cent investment (IRR = 200%, NPV = 20 cents). The example is extreme, but it does illustrate the basic difference between the NPV and the IRR methods.

2. *Independent projects: no conflict.* The two methods always lead to the same decision regarding the acceptance or rejection of independent projects because if a project has a positive NPV, its IRR will be greater than the cost of capital. Thus, if one criterion signals acceptance, so must the other. The easiest way to see this is to look back at Figure 13-3 and note that if the cost

of capital is to the left of (or less than) a project's IRR, then the NPV must be greater than zero. Therefore, for independent projects, the NPV and IRR criteria always lead to the same accept–reject decisions.

3. *Mutually exclusive projects: potential conflicts.*   Conflict can arise between the NPV and the IRR methods if the firm is choosing between mutually exclusive projects—the NPV can indicate that one project is better, while the IRR can suggest the acceptance of the other. For example, consider two mutually exclusive projects, C and D, whose cash flows over their 3-year lives are given below:

	Net Cash Flow from Project	
Year	C	D
0	($1200)	($1200)
1	1000	100
2	500	600
3	100	1100

Project C's cash flows are higher in the early years, but D's cash flows increase over time and exceed those of C in later years. Each project costs $1200, and their NPVs, discounted at the specified rates, are shown below:

Discount	**NPV**	
Rate	C	D
0%	$400	$600
5	300	400
10	200	200
15	100	50
20	50	(85)
25	(25)	(175)
30	(100)	(250)

The net present value profiles of Projects C and D are plotted in Figure 13-4. As can be seen in this figure, the IRR for Project C is 22 percent and for D, 17 percent. Because Project D's largest cash flows come late in its life, when the discounting effects of time are most significant, its NPV falls rapidly as the discount rate rises. Because C's cash flows come early, when the impact of higher discount rates is not so severe, its NPV falls less rapidly as discount rates increase.

Notice that from the IRR rankings, Project C is preferred to Project D, since C has the higher internal rate of return. However, if the cost of capital is less than 10 percent, Project D has a higher NPV than C. In this case, the IRR and NPV rankings are inconsistent.

We can generalize these results: whenever the NPV profiles of two projects cross one another, a conflict will exist if the cost of capital is below the *crossover rate.* For our illustrative projects, no conflict exists if the

Figure 13-4
Net Present Value Profile

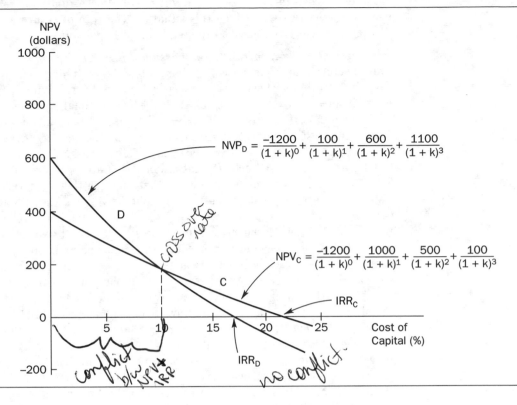

$$NVP_D = \frac{-1200}{(1+k)^0} + \frac{100}{(1+k)^1} + \frac{600}{(1+k)^2} + \frac{1100}{(1+k)^3}$$

$$NPV_C = \frac{-1200}{(1+k)^0} + \frac{1000}{(1+k)^1} + \frac{500}{(1+k)^2} + \frac{100}{(1+k)^3}$$

firm's cost of capital exceeds 10 percent (C is always preferred to D), but the two methods rank C and D differently if k is less than 10 percent. Which answer is correct? Logic suggests that the NPV method is better, because it selects that project that adds the most to shareholder wealth.

4. *Conflicts occur because of size and/or timing differences.* Conflicts between NPV and IRR for mutually exclusive projects can occur only if the projects' NPV profiles cross. Profiles can cross only under these conditions:
   a. One project is larger (has a greater investment cost) than the other. In this case, the larger project will have a higher vertical axis intercept than the smaller one in a graph such as Figure 13-4, so one NPV profile can cut the other.
   b. The time patterns of the cash flows differ such that the cash flows of one project come in earlier than the cash flows of the other project. This can occur in situations like the example of Projects C and D, in which the life of the projects is the same but the timing of the cash flows differs; it can also occur with projects that differ dramatically in terms of their maturity.

When either size or timing differences occur, the firm will have different amounts of funds to invest in the various years, depending on which of the two mutually exclusive projects it chooses. For example, if one project costs more than the other, the firm will have additional funds to invest at t = 0 if it selects the smaller project. Similarly, for projects of equal size, the one whose early cash inflows are larger will provide more funds for reinvestment in the early years. Given this situation, the rate of return at which differential cash flows can be invested is quite important.

5. *Reinvestment rate (opportunity cost) assumption.*   Conflicts between mutually exclusive projects arise as a result of scale- or timing-induced cash flow differentials. Therefore, the critical issue in resolving conflicts between mutually exclusive projects is this: how beneficial is it to have cash flows come in earlier rather than later? The answer depends on what the firm can do with the additional funds, or the *opportunity cost rate* at which it can invest differential early years' cash flows. The NPV and the IRR decision rules are based on different assumptions about the *reinvestment rate*. The NPV method implicitly assumes that the cash flows generated by a project can be reinvested at the cost of capital, whereas the IRR method assumes that the firm will reinvest at the IRR. These assumptions are inherent in the mathematics of the discounting processes for the two methods: (1) discounting is the reverse of compounding; (2) compounding implies reinvestment; and (3) the NPV method discounts cash flows at the cost of capital, whereas the IRR method discounts cash flows at the project's IRR.

   Which is the better assumption—that cash flows can be reinvested at the cost of capital, or that they will be reinvested at the project's IRR? It can be demonstrated that the best assumption is that projects' cash flows are reinvested at the cost of capital. Therefore, we conclude that the best reinvestment rate assumption is the cost of capital, which is implicit in the NPV method. This, in turn, leads us to prefer the NPV method, at least for firms willing and able to obtain capital at a cost reasonably close to their current cost of capital. We reiterate that when projects are independent, the NPV and IRR methods both lead to exactly the same accept–reject decision. However, for evaluating mutually exclusive projects, the NPV method is better.

   We should also note that there is one other situation in which the IRR approach may not be usable—this is when one is evaluating "nonnormal" projects. A *normal* capital project is one that has one or more cash outflows (costs) followed by a series of cash inflows. If, however, a project calls for a large cash outflow either sometime during or at the end of its life, it is defined as a *nonnormal* project. Nonnormal projects can present unique difficulties when evaluated by the IRR method. The most common problem encountered when evaluating nonnormal projects is multiple IRRs, which we discuss later in the chapter.

6. *Actual usage.*   Researchers have conducted a number of surveys designed to see which capital project evaluation methods firms actually use. Here is what these surveys have found:
   a. Most firms of significant size use either NPV or IRR or both when evaluating major projects.
   b. Firms also use the payback method, but primarily as an indicator of risk and liquidity. When payback is used, it is generally regarded as a secondary method, to be used along with NPV or IRR.
   c. More firms use IRR than NPV, in spite of the theoretical superiority of NPV. This usage seems to stem from the fact that the IRR method was

developed before the NPV: firms used IRR first, it became ingrained in their capital budgeting procedures manuals, and inertia is hard to overcome in large organizations. However, we should also note that the surveys generally show a trend toward NPV; that is, the more recent surveys show a higher percentage of NPV users than the earlier surveys. Also, the surveys show an increasing trend toward the use of multiple criteria. Most companies use computer programs to evaluate projects, and it is easy enough to program the computer to produce all three values: IRR, NPV, and payback.

Concept Review

▶ Why, at times, is a project with a lower IRR preferable to one with a higher IRR?

▶ How can we find the Y-axis intercept for an NPV profile? Also, what is the significance of the X-axis intercept?

▶ Why can there be no conflict between the NPV and IRR methods when projects are independent?

▶ What two conditions can cause NPV profiles to cross?

▶ Why can there be a conflict between the NPV and IRR methods when projects are mutually exclusive?

▶ What key assumption is different in the NPV and IRR methods?

Modified Internal Rate of Return (MIRR)

In spite of a strong academic preference for the NPV, surveys indicate that business executives prefer the IRR over the NPV by a margin of 3 to 1. Apparently, managers find it "more natural" to analyze investments in terms of percentage rates of return than dollars of NPV. Given this fact, can we devise a percentage evaluator that is better than the regular IRR? The answer is yes—we can modify the IRR to make it a better indicator of relative profitability and hence better for use in capital budgeting. The new measure is called the **modified IRR**, or **MIRR**, and it is defined as follows:[10]

$$\text{PV costs} = \text{PV terminal value.}$$

$$\sum_{t=0}^{n} \frac{COF_t}{(1 + k)^t} = \frac{\sum_{t=0}^{n} CIF_t(1 + k)^{n - t}}{(1 + MIRR)^n}.$$

$$\text{PV costs} = \frac{TV}{(1 + MIRR)^n}. \qquad \textbf{(13-2b)}$$

---

[10]Although MIRR is widely used by financial managers, the authors have never seen a discussion of it in the academic literature. However, such a discussion was presented by Samuel Weaver, director of financial analysis, Hershey Corporation, at the annual conference of the Financial Management Association in Las Vegas, October 1987. At the FMA conference a year later, every executive who spoke on capital budgeting indicated that his or her firm relied heavily upon MIRR.

Also, note that MIRR can be computed on some of the better financial calculators. For the exact procedure, see the Hewlett-Packard 12C or 17B owners' handbook.

Here COF refers to cash outflows, or the cost of the project, and CIF refers to cash inflows. In words, the term on the left is simply the PV of the investment outlays when discounted at the cost of capital, and the numerator of the term on the right is the sum of the future values of the inflows, assuming that the cash inflows are reinvested at the cost of capital. The numerator is also called the *terminal value (TV)*, and the discount rate that forces the PV of the costs to equal the PV of the TV is defined as the MIRR.

If the investment costs are all incurred at $t = 0$, and if the first operating inflow occurs at $t = 1$, as is true for our illustrative Projects A and B, then the following equation can be used:

$$\text{Cost} = \frac{\text{TV}}{(1 + \text{MIRR})^n} = \frac{\displaystyle\sum_{t=1}^{n} \text{CIF}_t(1 + k)^{n-t}}{(1 + \text{MIRR})^n}. \qquad \textbf{(13-2c)}$$

We can illustrate the calculation with Project A:

$$\$1000 = \frac{\$500(1.10)^{6-1} + \$400(1.10)^{6-2} + \$300(1.10)^{6-3} + \$100(1.10)^{6-4} + \$10(1.10)^{6-5} + \$10(1.1)^{6-6}}{(1 + \text{MRR})^6}$$

$$= \frac{\$805.26 + \$585.64 + \$399.30 + \$121.00 + \$11.00 + \$10.00}{(1 + \text{MIRR})^6} = \frac{\$1932.20}{(1 + \text{MRR})^6}.$$

Using a financial calculator, we enter PV = 1000, FV = 1932.20, and n = 6, and press the i button to find $\text{MIRR}_A = 11.6\%$. Similarly, we find $\text{MIRR}_B = 11.3\%$.

We can also illustrate this process with a time line. This is shown for Project A in Figure 13-5.

Figure 13-5
MIRR for Project A at a 10% Cost of Capital

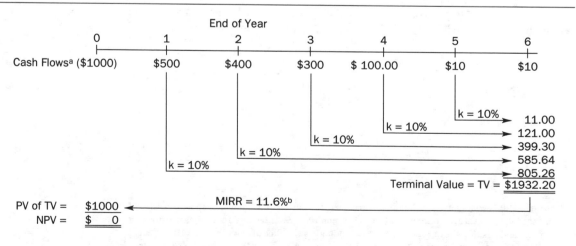

[a] The cash inflows are compounded to the terminal year at the cost of capital, k. It is assumed that the cash inflows are reinvested at k.
[b] The TV is discounted at a rate that causes the PV of the TV to equal the cost of the project; this equalizing discount rate is called MIRR.

The modified IRR has a significant advantage over the regular IRR. MIRR assumes that cash flows from all projects are reinvested at the cost of capital, whereas the regular IRR assumes that the cash flows from each project are reinvested at the project's own IRR. Since reinvestment at k is generally more correct, the modified IRR is a better indicator of a project's true profitability. Therefore, if managers want to choose from alternative projects the one with the highest rate of return, MIRR gives a better picture of the "true" rate of return. This is why the MIRR is rapidly becoming the method of choice among financial executives.

Is MIRR as good as NPV for selecting among competing (mutually exclusive) projects? If the two projects are of equal size, NPV and MIRR will always lead to the same project selection decision. Thus, for any two projects like our Project A and B, if $NPV_B > NPV_A$, then $MIRR_B > MIRR_A$, and the kinds of conflict we encountered between NPV and the regular IRR will not occur. However, if the projects differ in size, conflicts can still occur. Thus, if we were comparing a large project with a smaller, mutually exclusive one, we might find $NPV_B > NPV_A$, but $MIRR_A > MIRR_B$.

Our own conclusion is that MIRR is superior to the regular IRR as an indicator of a project's "true" rate of return or expected long-term rate of return, but that the NPV method is still best, especially for choosing among competing projects that differ in size, because it provides a better indicator of how much each project will cause the value of the firm to increase.

Concept Review

▶ How does the modified IRR method differ from the regular IRR method?

▶ What advantage does the modified IRR approach have over the regular IRR approach?

▶ Is MIRR as good as NPV for selecting among mutually exclusive projects? Why or why not?

Multiple IRRs

One problem is fairly common with the regular IRR method. If negative cash flows occur after a project has gone into operation—that is, if it is a *nonnormal* project—then when we solve for Equation 13-2,

$$\sum_{t=0}^{n} \frac{CF_t}{(1 + IRR)^t} = 0, \qquad (13\text{-}2)$$

it is possible to obtain more than one positive value of IRR, which means that there are multiple IRRs.

To illustrate this problem, suppose a firm is considering a \$1.6 million expenditure at Year 0 to develop a strip mine (Project M). The mine will produce a cash flow of \$10 million at the end of Year 1. Then, at the end of Year 2, \$10 million must be expended to restore the land to its original condition. Therefore, the project's expected net cash flows are as follows (in millions of dollars):

Year 0	End of Year 1	End of Year 2
−$1.6	+$10	−$10

These values can be substituted into Equation 13-2:

$$\frac{-\$1.6 \text{ million}}{(1 + IRR)^0} + \frac{\$10 \text{ million}}{(1 + IRR)^1} + \frac{-\$10 \text{ million}}{(1 + IRR)^2} = 0.$$

When this equation is solved, we find that NPV = 0 when IRR = 25% and also when IRR = 400%.[11] Therefore, the IRR of the investment is both 25 and 400 percent. This relationship is depicted graphically in Figure 13-6.[12]

Note that no dilemma would arise if either the NPV method or the MIRR method were used; we would simply find the NPV or the MIRR and use it to

Figure 13-6
NPV Profile for Project M

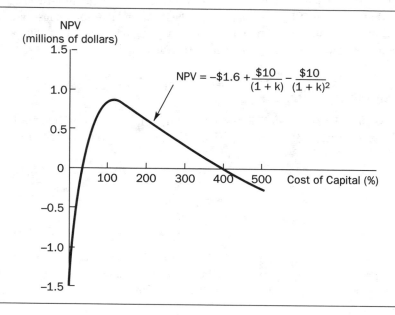

$$NPV = -\$1.6 + \frac{\$10}{(1 + k)} - \frac{\$10}{(1 + k)^2}$$

[11]If you attempt to find the IRR of this project with many financial calculators, you get an error message; this message occurs if a project has more than one IRR. We actually found our project's IRRs by using *Lotus 1-2-3* to calculate NPVs at a number of different values for k and then plotting the NPV profile. The intersections with the X-axis gave a good idea of the IRR values. We then could use either trial and error or the *Lotus 1-2-3* IRR function to find the exact value of k that forces the equation to zero.

[12]Does Figure 13-6 suggest that the firm should try to raise its cost of capital to about 100 percent in order to maximize the NPV of the project? Certainly not. Logically, the firm should seek to minimize its cost of capital; this will cause the price of its shares to be maximized. Actions taken to raise the cost of capital might make this particular project look good, but they would be terribly harmful to the firm's more numerous normal projects. Only if the firm's cost of capital is high in spite of efforts to keep it down, will this nonnormal project have a positive NPV.

evaluate the project. If Project M's cost of capital is 10 percent, its NPV is −$0.77 million, and the project should be rejected. The MIRR is 5.6 percent, which is less than the cost of capital, so the MIRR method also indicates that the project should be rejected.[13]

The Post-Audit

An important aspect of the capital budgeting process is the **post-audit**, which involves (1) comparing actual results with those predicted by the project's sponsors and (2) explaining why any differences occurred. For example, many firms require that the operating divisions send a monthly report for the first 6 months after a project goes into operation and a quarterly report thereafter until the project's results are up to expectations. From then on, reports on the project are handled like those of other operations:

The post-audit has several purposes, including the following:

1. *Improving forecasts.*   When decision-makers are forced to compare their projections to actual outcomes, there is a tendency for estimates to improve. Conscious or unconscious biases are observed and eliminated; new forecasting methods are sought as the need for them becomes apparent; and people simply tend to do everything better, including forecasting, if they know that their actions are being monitored.

2. *Improving operations.*   Businesses are run by people, and people can perform at higher or lower levels of efficiency. When a divisional team has made a forecast about an investment, its members are, in a sense, putting their reputations on the line. If costs are above predicted levels, sales below expectations, and so on, executives in production, sales, and other areas will strive to improve operations and to bring results into line with forecasts. In a discussion related to this point, an IBM executive made this statement: "You academicians worry only about making good decisions. In business, we also worry about making decisions good."

The post-audit is not a simple process. There are a number of factors that can cause complications. First, each element of the cash flow forecast is subject to uncertainty, so a percentage of all projects undertaken by any reasonably venturesome firm will necessarily go awry. This fact must be considered when appraising the performances of the operating executives who submit capital expenditure requests. Second, projects sometimes fail to meet expectations for reasons beyond the control of the operating executives and for reasons that no

---

[13]For additional insights into the multiple rate problem, see William H. Jean, "On Multiple Rates of Return," *Journal of Finance*, March 1968: 187–92.

one could realistically be expected to anticipate. For example, the decline in oil prices in the mid-1980s adversely affected many energy-related projects, as well as real estate projects in Alberta and other oil-producing areas. Third, it is often difficult to separate the operating results of one investment from those of a larger system. Although some projects stand alone and permit ready identification of costs and revenues, the actual cost savings that result from a new computer system, for example, may be very hard to measure. Fourth, it is often hard to hand out blame or praise because the executives who were actually responsible for a given decision may have moved on by the time the results of a long-term investment are known.

Because of these difficulties, some firms tend to play down the importance of the post-audit. However, observations of both businesses and governmental units suggest that the best-run and most successful organizations are the ones that put the greatest emphasis on post-audits. Accordingly, we regard the post-audit as being one of the most important elements in a good capital budgeting system.

Concept Review

- ▶ What is done in the post-audit?
- ▶ Identify at least two purposes of the post-audit.
- ▶ What factors can cause complications in the post-audit?

Capital Budgeting in the Small Firm

The allocation of capital in small firms is as important as it is in large ones. In fact, given their lack of access to the capital markets, it is often more important in small firms because the funds necessary to correct a mistake may not be available. Also, large firms allocate capital to numerous projects, so a mistake on one project can be offset by successes with others.

In spite of the importance of capital expenditures to small business, studies of the way capital budgeting decisions are made generally suggest that many small firms use "back-of-the-envelope" analysis, or perhaps even no analysis at all.

We are left with a puzzle. Capital budgeting is clearly important to small firms, yet they do not use the tools that have been developed to improve these decisions. Why does this situation exist? One argument is that managers of small firms are simply not well trained. This argument suggests that the managers would use the more sophisticated techniques if they understood them better.

Another argument states that management talent is a scarce resource in small firms, and even if managers are financially sophisticated, the demands on their time do not permit them to take the time to use elaborate techniques to analyze a proposed project.

A third argument relates to the cost of analyzing capital projects. To some extent, these costs are fixed; they may be larger for bigger projects, but not by much. To the extent that the costs of analysis are indeed fixed, it may not be economical to incur them if the project itself is relatively small. This argument suggests that small firms with projects that are comparatively small may in some cases be making the sensible decision when they rely upon management's "gut feeling."

Note also that a major part of the capital budgeting process in large firms involves lower level analysts' marshalling facts needed by higher-level decision-makers. This step is less necessary in the small firm. Thus, a cursory examination of a small firm's decision process might suggest that capital budgeting decisions are based on snap judgement, but if that judgement is exercised by someone with a total knowledge of the firm and its markets, the decision could be better than one based on an elaborate analysis by a lower-level analyst in a large firm.

Also, small firms tend to be cash oriented. They are concerned with basic survival, so they tend to look at expenditures from the standpoint of their near-term effects on cash. This cash and survival orientation leads the firm to focus on a relatively short time horizon, and this, in turn, leads to an emphasis on the payback period. The limitations of the payback approach are well known; nevertheless, the technique is popular in small business because it gives the firm a feel for when the cash committed to an investment will be recovered and thus available to repay loans or for new opportunities. Therefore, small firms that are cash oriented and have limited managerial resources may find the payback method an appealing compromise between the need for extensive analysis on the one hand and the high costs of analysis on the other.

Small firms also face greater uncertainty in the cash flows they might generate beyond the immediate future. Large firms have "staying power"—they can make an investment and then ride out business downturns or situations of excess capacity in an industry. Such periods are called "shake-outs," and it is the smaller firms that generally get shaken out. Therefore, most small business managers are uncomfortable making forecasts beyond a few years. Since discounted cash flow techniques require explicit estimates of cash flows through the life of the project, small business managers may not take seriously an analysis that hinges on "guesstimate" numbers, which, if wrong, could lead to bankruptcy.

The Value of the Firm and Capital Budgeting. The single most appealing argument for the use of net present value in capital expenditure decisions is that NPV gives an explicit measure of the effect of the investment on the value of the firm: if NPV is positive, the investment will increase the value of the firm and make its owners wealthier. In small firms, however, it is often the case that shares are not traded in public markets, so their value cannot be observed. Also, for reasons of control, many small business owners and managers do not want to broaden ownership by going public.

It is difficult to argue for value-based techniques when the value of the firm itself is unobservable. Furthermore, the objectives of the individual owner-manager of a closely held firm may extend beyond the firm's monetary value. For example, the owner-manager may value the firm's reputation for quality and service and therefore may make an investment that would be rejected on purely economic grounds. In addition, the owner-manager may not hold a well-diversified investment portfolio but may instead have all of his or her eggs in this one basket. In that case, the manager would logically be sensitive to the total risk of the firm, not just to its systematic or undiversifiable component. This would translate into the choice of an appropriate cost of capital.

Another problem faced by a firm that is not publicly traded is that its cost of equity capital is not easily determined. Since a cost of capital estimate is required to use either the NPV or the IRR method, a small firm in an industry of small firms may simply have no basis for estimating its cost of capital.

That small firms make less extensive use of DCF techniques than larger firms may be a rational decision resulting from a conscious or subconscious conclusion that the costs of sophisticated analyses outweigh their benefits; it may reflect nonmonetary goals of small business owner-managers; or it may reflect difficulties in estimating the cost of capital, which is required for DCF analyses but not for payback analysis. However, nonuse of DCF methods may also reflect a weakness in many small business organizations. We simply do not know. We do know that small businesses must do all they can to compete effectively with big business, and to the extent that a small business fails to use DCF methods because its manager is unsophisticated or uninformed, it may be putting itself at a serious competitive disadvantage.

Summary

This chapter discussed the capital budgeting process. The key concepts covered are listed below.

☐ **Capital budgeting** is the process of analyzing potential expenditures on fixed assets and deciding whether the firm should undertake those investments.

☐ The capital budgeting process requires the firm (1) to determine the cost of the project, (2) to estimate the expected cash flows from the project and the riskiness of those cash flows, (3) to determine the appropriate **cost of capital** at which to discount the cash flows, and (4) to determine the *present values* of the expected cash flows and of the project.

☐ The **payback period** is defined as the expected number of years required to recover the original investment. The payback method ignores cash flows beyond the payback period, and it does not consider the time value of money. The payback method does, however, provide an indication of a project's risk and liquidity because it shows how long the original capital will be "at risk."

☐ The **discounted payback method** is similar to the regular payback method except that it discounts cash flows at the project's cost of capital. Like the regular payback method, it ignores cash flows beyond the discounted payback period.

☐ The **net present value (NPV) method**, which is a **discounted cash flow (DCF) technique,** discounts all cash flows at the project's cost of capital and then sums those cash flows. The project is accepted if this sum, called the NPV, is positive.

☐ The **internal rate of return (IRR) method** is another DCF technique. The IRR is defined as the discount rate which forces the present value of the future cash inflows of an investment to equal the cost of the investment. The project is accepted if the IRR is greater than the project's cost of capital.

☐ The NPV and IRR methods make the same accept–reject decisions for **independent projects**, but if projects are **mutually exclusive**, then ranking conflicts can arise. If conflicts arise, the NPV method should be used. Both the NPV and IRR methods are superior to the payback, but NPV is better than IRR.

☐ The NPV method assumes that cash flows will be reinvested at the firm's cost of capital, while the IRR method assumes reinvestment at the project's IRR. Because reinvestment at the cost of capital is the better assumption, the NPV is superior to the IRR.

☐ The **modified IRR (MIRR) method** corrects some of the problems with the regular IRR. MIRR involves finding the *terminal value (TV)* of the cash inflows compounded at the firm's cost of capital and then determining the rate (the MIRR) that forces the TV to equal the present value of the outflows.

☐ The **post-audit** is a key element of capital budgeting. By comparing actual results with predicted results, and then determining why differences occurred, decision-makers can improve both their operations and their forecasts of projects' outcomes.

☐ Small firms tend to use the payback method rather than a discounted cash flow method. This may be a rational decision (1) if the cost of the DCF analysis outweighs the benefits for the project being considered; (2) if the firm's cost of capital cannot be estimated accurately; or (3) if the owner-manager is considering nonmonetary goals.

Although this chapter has presented the basic elements of the capital budgeting process, there are many other aspects of this crucial topic. Some of the more important ones are discussed in the following chapter.

Questions

13-1 How is a classification scheme for projects (replacement, expansion into new markets, product development, and so forth) used in the capital budgeting process?

13-2 Explain why the NPV of a relatively long-term project—defined as one for which a high percentage of cash flows are expected in the distant future—is more sensitive to changes in the cost of capital than is the NPV of a short-term project.

13-3 If two mutually exclusive projects are being compared, the shorter-term project may have the higher ranking under the NPV criterion if the cost of capital is high, but the longer-term project might rank higher if the cost of capital is low. Why? Would changes in the cost of capital ever cause a change in the IRR ranking of two such projects?

13-4 In what sense is a reinvestment rate assumption embodied in the NPV, IRR, and MIRR methods? What is the implicitly assumed reinvestment rate of each method?

13-5 "If a firm has no mutually exclusive projects, only independent ones and it also has a constant cost of capital and normal projects in the sense that each project has one or more outflows followed by a stream of inflows, then the NPV and IRR methods will always lead to identical capital budgeting decisions." Discuss this statement. What does it imply about using the IRR method in lieu of the NPV method? If each of the assumptions made in the statement were changed (one by one), how would these changes affect your answer?

13-6 Are there conditions under which a firm might be better off if it chose a machine with a rapid payback rather than one with a larger NPV?

13-7 A firm has $100 million available for capital expenditures. It is considering investing in one of two projects; each has a cost of $100 million. Project A has an IRR of 20 percent and an NPV of $9 million. It will be terminated at the end of 1 year at a profit of $20 million, resulting in an immediate increase in earnings per share (EPS). Project B, which cannot be postponed, has an IRR of 30 percent and an NPV of $50 million. However, the firm's short-run EPS will be reduced if it accepts Project B, because no revenues will be generated for several years.
a. Should the short-run effects on EPS influence the choice between the two projects?
b. How might situations like the one described here influence a firm's decision to use the payback method as a part of the capital budgeting process?

Self-Test Problems   (solutions appear on page 452)

ST-1 Key terms. Define each of the following terms:
a. Capital budget; capital budgeting; strategic business plan
b. Regular payback period; discounted payback period
c. DCF techniques; net present value (NPV) method
d. Internal rate of return (IRR) method; IRR
e. Modified internal rate of return (MIRR) method
f. NPV profile; crossover rate
g. Independent projects; mutually exclusive projects; contingent (interdependent) projects
h. Project cost of capital
i. Reinvestment rate assumption
j. Post-audit

ST-2 Project analysis. You are a financial analyst for Porter Electronics Ltd. The director of capital budgeting has asked you to analyze two proposed capital investments, Projects S and L. Each project has a cost of $10 000, and the cost of capital for each project is 12 percent. The projects' expected net cash flows are as follows:

Year	Project S	Project L
0	($10 000)	($10 000)
1	6 500	3 500
2	3 000	3 500
3	3 000	3 500
4	1 000	3 500

a. Calculate each project's payback period, net present value (NPV), internal rate of return (IRR), and modified internal rate of return (MIRR).

b. Which project or projects should be accepted if the two are independent?

c. Which project should be accepted if the two are mutually exclusive?

d. How might a change in the cost of capital produce a conflict between the NPV and IRR rankings of these two projects? Would this conflict exist if k were 5%? (Hint: Plot the NPV profiles.)

e. Why does the conflict exist?

Problems

13-1 Payback, NPV, and IRR calculations. Project L has a cost of $52 125, and its expected net cash inflows are $12 000 per year for 8 years.

a. What is the project's payback period (to the closest year)?

b. The cost of capital is 12 percent. What is the project's NPV?

c. What is the project's IRR? (Hint: Recognize that the project is an annuity.)

d. What is the project's discounted payback period, assuming a 12 percent cost of capital?

13-2 NPVs and IRRs for independent projects. Lancaster Engineering is considering including two pieces of equipment, a truck and an overhead pully system, in this year's capital budget. The projects are not mutually exclusive. The cash outlay for the truck would be $17 100, and that for the pulley system, $22 430. The firm's cost of capital is 14 percent. The anticipated after-tax cash flows, including depreciation, are as follows:

Year	Truck	Pulley
1	$5100	$7500
2	5100	7500
3	5100	7500
4	5100	7500
5	5100	7500

Calculate the IRR and NPV for each project, and indicate the correct accept–reject decision for each.

13-3 NPVs and IRRs for mutually exclusive projects. Prock Industries must choose between a gas-powered and an electric-powered forklift truck for moving materials in its factory. Since both forklifts perform the same function, the firm will choose only one. (The investments are mutually exclusive.) The electric-powered truck will cost more, but it will be less expensive to operate; it will cost $22 000, whereas the gas-powered truck will cost $17 500. The cost of capital that applies to both investments is 12 percent. The life for both types of truck is estimated to be 6 years, during which time the net cash flows for the electric-powered truck will be $6290 per year and those for the gas-powered truck will be $5000 per year. (These annual net cash flows include depreciation expenses.) Calculate the NPV and the IRR for each type of truck, and decide which to recommend for purchase.

13-4 Capital budgeting methods.   Project S costs $15 000 and is expected to produce benefits (cash flows) of $4500 per year for 5 years. Project L costs $37 500 and is expected to produce cash flows of $11 100 per year for 5 years. Calculate each project's NPV, IRR, and MIRR, assuming a cost of capital of 14 percent. Which project would be selected, assuming they are mutually exclusive, according to each ranking method? Which should actually be selected?

13-5 NPV and IRR analysis.   Gentry Fabrication is considering two mutually exclusive investments. The projects' expected net cash flows are as follows:

Year	Project A	Project B
0	($300)	($405)
1	(387)	134
2	(193)	134
3	(100)	134
4	600	134
5	600	134
6	850	134
7	(180)	0

a. Construct NPV profiles for Projects A and B.

b. What is each project's IRR?

c. If each project's cost of capital was 12 percent, which should be selected? If the cost of capital was 18 percent, what would the proper choice be?

d. What is each project's MIRR at a cost of capital of 12 percent? At k = 18%? (Hint: Consider Period 7 as the end of Project B.)

e. What is the crossover rate? What is its significance?

13-6 Timing differences.   The Black Rock Oil Exploration Company Ltd. is considering two mutually exclusive plans for extracting oil on property for which it has mineral rights. Both plans call for the expenditure of $12 000 000 to drill development wells. Under Plan A, all the oil will be extracted in 1 year, producing a cash flow at t = 1 of $14 400 000. Under Plan B, cash flows will be $2 100 000 per year for 20 years.

a. What are the annual incremental cash flows that will be available to Black Rock if it undertakes Plan B rather than Plan A? (Hint: Subtract Plan A's flows from B's.)

b. If Black Rock accepts Plan A and then invests the extra cash generated at the end of Year 1, what rate of return (reinvestment rate) would cause the cash flows from reinvestment to equal the cash flows from Plan B? (In other words, what is the crossover rate?)

c. Suppose a company has a cost of capital of 12 percent. Is it logical to assume that it will take on all available independent projects (of average risk) with returns greater than 12 percent? Now suppose that all available projects with returns greater than 12 percent have been taken on. Does this mean that cash flows from past investments have an opportunity cost of only 12 percent? All the firm can do with these cash flows is to replace money that has a cost of 12 percent. Finally, does this imply that the cost of capital is the correct rate to assume for the reinvestment of a project's cash flows?

d. Construct NPV profiles for Plans A and B, identify each project's IRR, and indicate the crossover rate of return.

13-7 Scale differences.   The Perkins Printing Company is considering two mutually exclusive expansion plans. Plan A calls for the expenditure of $40.00 million on a large-scale, integrated plant that will provide an expected cash flow stream of $6.40 million per year for 20 years. Plan B calls for the expenditure of $12.00 million to build a somewhat less efficient, more labour-intensive plant that has an expected cash flow stream of $2.72 million per year for 20 years. Perkins's cost of capital is 10 percent.

a. Calculate each project's NPV and IRR.

b. Set up a Project Δ that has cash flows equal to the difference between the cash flows for Plan A and for Plan B. What are the NPV and the IRR for this Project Δ? (Hint: If Perkins goes with the larger plant, Plan A, its investment will be $28.00 million larger than if it built the smaller plant and its annual cash flows will be $3.68 million larger.)

c. Graph the NPV profiles for Plan A, Plan B, and Project Δ.

d. Give a logical explanation, based on reinvestment rates and opportunity costs, as to why the NPV method is better than the IRR method for rating these projects when the firm's cost of capital is constant at some value, such as 10 percent.

13-8 Multiple rates of return.   Drake Uranium Ltd. is deciding whether or not it should open a strip mine, the net cost of which would be $3.300 million. Net cash inflows are expected to be $20.775 million, all coming at the end of Year 1. The land must be returned to its natural state at a cost of $18.750 million, payable at the end of Year 2.

a. Plot the project's NPV profile.

b. Should the project be accepted if k = 7%? If k = 12%? Explain your reasoning.

c. Can you think of some other capital budgeting situations in which negative cash flows during or at the end of the project's life might lead to multiple IRRs?

13-9 Multiple rates of return.   Rae Development Ltd. (RDL) has many excellent investment opportunities, but it has insufficient cash to undertake them all. RDL has been offered the chance to borrow $4 million from the Provincial Retirement Fund at 10 percent, with the loan to be repaid at the end of 1 year. Also, a "consulting fee" of $1 400 000 would be paid to Oreo City's mayor at the end of 1 year for helping to arrange the credit. Of the $4 million received, $2 million would be used immediately to buy an old city-owned hotel and to convert it to a gambling casino. The other $2 million would be invested in other lucrative RDL projects that otherwise would have to be foregone because of a lack of capital. For 2 years, all cash generated by the casino would be ploughed back into the casino project. At the end of 2 years, the casino would be sold for $4 million.

Assuming that the deal has been "worked out in the sunshine" and is completely legal and that cash from the other RDL operations would be available to make the required payments at the end of Year 1, under what rate-of-return conditions should RDL accept the offer? Disregard taxes.

13-10 Present value of costs. The Tanner Coffee Company is evaluating internal distribution systems for its new roasting, grinding, and packing plant. The two alternatives are a conveyor system with a high initial cost but low annual operating costs and several forklift trucks, which would cost less but have considerably higher operating costs. The decision to construct the plant has already been made, and the choice here will have no effect on the overall revenues of the project. The cost of capital for the plant is 9 percent, and the distribution systems expected net costs are as follows:

Year	Conveyor	Forklift
0	($300 000)	($120 000)
1	(66 000)	(96 000)
2	(66 000)	(96 000)
3	(66 000)	(96 000)
4	(66 000)	(96 000)
5	(66 000)	(96 000)

a. What is the IRR of each alternative?
b. What is the present value of the costs of each alternative? Which method should be chosen?

Integrative Problem

13-11 Basics of capital budgeting. Steven Johnson, director of capital budgeting for Sunshine Marine, has just completed estimating the cash flows of two projects that the firm is considering. Project L is the code name for an upgraded Loran navigation receiver, and Project S is a sonar-based depth sounder. Both projects involve the production and sale of these two new models of marine electronics equipment, but they differ significantly in their production and sales schedules. L's cash flows will increase over time, while S's will decline. The projects both would have 3-year lives, because Sunshine is expecting to market a new generation of devices at that time. The following is Johnson's net cash flow estimates (in thousands of dollars):

Year	Project L	Project S
0	($150)	($150)
1	15	105
2	90	75
3	120	30

Depreciation, salvage values, net working capital requirements, and tax effects are included in these cash flows.

Also, Johnson made a subjective risk assessment of both projects, and he concluded that they both have risk characteristics similar to those of Sunshine's other projects. The firm's overall cost of capital is 10 percent. Now Johnson must determine whether the projects should be accepted or rejected, and then make a presentation to the company's board of directors. Assume that you are Johnson's assistant and that he has asked you to help him prepare for the presentation by answering the following questions:

a. What is capital budgeting? What is the similarity between firms' capital budgeting decisions and individuals' investment decisions?

b. What is the difference between independent and mutually exclusive projects? between normal and nonnormal projects?

c. What is the payback period? Find the paybacks for Projects L and S. What is the rationale for using the payback evaluation method? According to the payback method, which project or projects should be accepted if Sunshine's maximum acceptable payback is 2 years and the projects are independent? mutually exclusive? What is the difference between payback and discounted payback? What is the main advantage of payback? Does the payback method provide any useful information when making a capital budgeting decision such as this one?

d. Define the term *net present value (NPV)*. What is each project's NPV? What is the rationale behind the NPV evaluation method? According to NPV, which project or projects should be accepted if they are independent? mutually exclusive? Would the NPV change if the cost of capital changed?

e. Define the term *internal rate of return (IRR)*. What is each project's IRR? What is the logic behind the IRR evaluation method? According to IRR, which project or projects should be accepted if they are independent? mutually exclusive? Would the projects' IRRs change if the cost of capital changed? Is it logical for the projects' rankings to remain constant even if there are large changes in capital costs? Explain.

f. What is the underlying cause of ranking conflicts between the NPV and the IRR methods? Under what conditions can conflicts occur? Which method is better? Why?

g. What are the three properties that a capital budgeting evaluation method must exhibit if it is to lead to correct capital budgeting decisions? Which of the methods we discussed have these properties?

h. Draw the NPV profiles for Projects L and S. At what cost of capital do the profiles cross? What are the implications of the NPV profiles regarding the acceptability of Projects L and S using NPV and IRR, assuming that the projects are independent? assuming that they are mutually exclusive? What condition could cause a ranking conflict?

i. Assume that Sunshine Marine is considering sponsoring a pavilion at the upcoming world's fair (Project F). The pavilion would cost $1.2 million, and it is expected to generate $7.5 million in cash flow during its 1 year of operation. However, it would then take another year and $7.5 million to demolish the building and return the site to its original condition. Thus, Project F's expected net cash flows look like this (in millions of dollars):

Year	Cash Flow
0	($1.2)
1	7.5
2	(7.5)

The project is estimated to have average risk, and its cost of capital is 10 percent. What is Project F's NPV? What is its IRR? Draw its NPV profile. Does Project F have normal or nonnormal cash flows? Should the project be accepted?

j. Define the *modified IRR (MIRR)*. Find the MIRRs for Projects L, S, and F. Why is MIRR better than IRR? Is MIRR as good as NPV?

Solutions to Self-Test Problems

ST-1   Refer to the appropriate sections of the text to check your responses.

ST-2   **a.** *Payback*

To determine the payback, construct the cumulative cash flows for each project:

Year	Project S	Project L
0	($10 000)	($10 000)
1	(3 500)	(6 500)
2	(500)	(3 000)
3	2 500	500
4	3 500	4 000

$$\text{Payback}_S = 2 + \frac{\$500}{\$3000} = 2.17 \text{ years.}$$

$$\text{Payback}_L = 2 + \frac{\$3000}{\$3500} = 2.86 \text{ years.}$$

Net Present Value (NPV)

$$NPV_s = -\$10\,000 + \frac{\$6500}{(1.12)^1} + \frac{\$3000}{(1.12)^2} + \frac{\$3000}{(1.12)^3} + \frac{\$1000}{(1.12)^4}$$

$$= \$966.01.$$

$$NPV_L = -\$10\,000 + \frac{\$3500}{(1.12)^1} + \frac{\$3500}{(1.12)^2} + \frac{\$3500}{(1.12)^3} + \frac{\$3500}{(1.12)^4}$$

$$= \$630.72.$$

Internal Rate of Return (IRR)
Find the discount rates that equate each NPV to zero:

$$IRR_s = 18.0\%.$$
$$IRR_L = 15.0\%.$$

Modified Internal Rate of Return (MIRR)
Begin by finding each project's terminal value (TV) of cash inflows:

$$TV_s = \$6500(1.12)^3 + \$3000(1.12)^2$$
$$+ \$3000(1.12)^1 + \$1000 = \$17\,255\,23.$$
$$TV_L = \$3500(1.12)^3 + \$3500(1.12)^2$$
$$+ \$3500(1.12)^1 + \$3500 = \$16\,727.65.$$

Each project's MIRR is the discount rate that equates the PV of the TV to each project's cost, $10 000. Thus,

$$MIRR_s = 14.61\%.$$
$$MIRR_L = 13.73\%.$$

b. The following table summarizes the project rankings by each method:

	Project That Ranks Higher
Payback	S
NPV	S
IRR	S
MIRR	S

Note that all the methods rank Project S over Project L. In addition, both projects are acceptable under the NPV, IRR, and MIRR criteria. Thus, both projects should be accepted if they are independent.

c. In this case, we would choose the project with the higher NPV at k = 12%, or Project S.

d. To determine the effects of changing the cost of capital, plot the NPV profiles of each project. The crossover rate occurs between 6 to 7 percent (more precisely, at 6.2 percent).

   If the firm's cost of capital is less than 6 percent, a conflict exists because $NPV_L > NPV_S$, but $IRR_S > IRR_L$. Therefore, if k is 5 percent, a conflict exists. Note, however, that when k = 5.00%, $MIRR_S$ = 10.64% and $MIRR_L$ = 10.83%; hence the modified IRR ranks the projects correctly, even if k is to the left of the crossover point.

e. The basic cause of the conflict is reinvestment rate assumptions that differ between NPV and IRR. NPV assumes that cash flows can be reinvested at the cost of capital, while IRR assumes reinvestment at the (generally) higher IRR. The high reinvestment rate assumption under IRR makes early cash flows especially valuable, and hence short-term projects look better under IRR.

NPV Profiles for Projects S and L

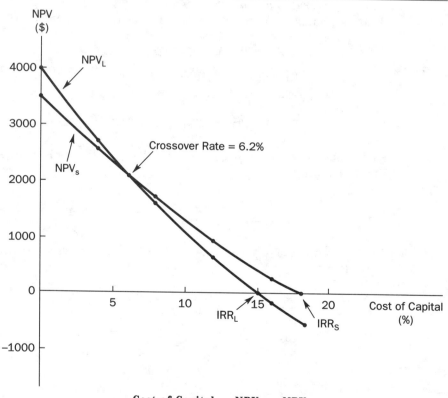

Cost of Capital	NPV$_S$	NPV$_L$
0%	$3500	$4000
4	2545	2705
8	1707	1592
12	966	631
16	307	(206)
18	5	(585)

14

▲▲▲

Project Cash Flows

A MANAGERIAL PERSPECTIVE

Capital budgeting involves the commitment of funds to a project for which the cash flows are expected to arise over a long time period. The essence of a successful application of the process is a good estimate of the cash inflows and outflows associated with the project. The problems that arise when cost controls and good forecasting are not applied can be seen in the difficulties of the SkyDome project in Toronto. The project, which started construction in 1986 with an expected price tag of approximately $235 million, ended up costing $585 million by 1990 when it opened. And although the building is very popular and draws enormous crowds for baseball games and blockbuster rock concerts, it does not appear to generate enough cash flow to cover the interest payments.

The cost increases of SkyDome arose from two sources. The first was the introduction, just after the project commenced, of a luxury hotel, six restaurants, and an entertainment centre, for an added cost of approximately $100 million. The second was the escalation of construction costs for the overall project. It appeared that cost controls were not in effect, and any cost overruns were to be covered by the province. The additions to the project were sold to the public as commercial propositions that would not cost a dime of taxpayers' money. This suggests that the revenue forecasts on which these additions were based were unrealistic.

The experience of SkyDome suggests that cost controls and realistic projections are crucial in capital budgeting decision-making.

The basic principles of capital budgeting were covered in Chapter 13. Now we examine some additional issues, including how cash flows are estimated, how expansion decisions are made, and how replacement decisions are made. In the following chapter, we shall show how risk is incorporated into capital budgeting decisions.

Cash Flow Estimation

The most important, but also the most difficult, step in the analysis of a capital budgeting project is the estimation of its **cash flows**—the investment outlays and the expected annual net cash inflows after the project goes into operation. The initial costs and the expected ongoing cash flows must be *directly related* to the acceptance of the project.

Many variables are involved in cash flow estimation, and many individuals and departments participate in the process. For example, the forecasts of unit sales and sales prices are normally made by the marketing group, based on their knowledge of price elasticity, advertising effects, the state of the economy, competitors' likely reactions, and trends in consumers' tastes. Similarly, the capital outlays associated with a new product are generally obtained from the engineering and product development staffs, while operating costs are estimated by cost accountants, production experts, personnel specialists, purchasing agents, and so forth.

Because it is difficult to make accurate forecasts of the cost and revenues associated with a large, complex project, forecast errors can be quite large. For example, the initial cost estimates underpinning the construction of large projects can be incorrect. Similar (or even worse) miscalculations are common in forecasts of production design costs, such as the costs to develop a new personal computer. Further, as difficult as plant and equipment costs are to estimate, sales revenues and operating costs over the life of the project are generally even more uncertain. The uncertainty may be larger the further into the future the forecast of cash flows is required.[1] Yet if cash flow estimates are not reasonably accurate, any analytical technique, no matter how sophisticated, can lead to poor decisions and hence to operating losses and reduced share prices. This does not suggest that firms will not make forecasting errors—only that the estimates of cash flows should be the best available at the time the project is evaluated.

The financial staff's role in the forecasting process includes (1) coordinating the efforts of the other departments, such as engineering and marketing, (2) ensuring that everyone involved with the forecast uses a consistent set of economic assumptions, and (3) making sure that no biases are inherent in the forecasts. This last point is extremely important, because division managers often become emotionally involved with pet projects or develop empire-building complexes, both of which tend to lead to cash flow forecasting biases that make bad projects look good—on paper.

It is almost impossible to overstate the difficulties that can be encountered in cash flow forecasts. It is also difficult to overstate the importance of these forecasts. Still, observing the principles discussed in the next several sections will help to minimize forecasting errors.

Concept Review

► What is the most important step in the analysis of a capital project?
► What is the financial staff's role in the capital projects forecasting process?

Identifying the Relevant Cash Flows

One important element in cash flow estimation is the identification of *relevant* cash flows, which are the specific set of cash flows that should be considered in

---

[1]One factor mitigating the impact of the time period over which the forecast is to be made is that the cash flow discounting process actually recognizes that risk increases with time.

the decision at hand. Two rules can help financial analysts avoid mistakes: (1) capital budgeting decisions must be based on cash flows, not accounting income, and (2) only *incremental* cash flows—those that would result from the acceptance of the project—are relevant to the accept–reject decision. These two rules are discussed in detail in the following sections.

Cash Flows versus Accounting Income

In capital budgeting analysis, annual *cash flows,* not *accounting income,* is utilized. Cash flows and accounting profits can be very different. In measuring cash flows, two issues must be resolved: (1) is the income being measured according to accounting or Revenue Canada requirements? and (2) how is the cash flow actually calculated?

Table 14-1 addresses the first of these issues. The firm's income statement as reported in its financial statements is presented in column 1. Column 2 has the income statement based on actual taxes payable. It is the latter financial statement that reflects the actual after-tax cash consequences of the operations of the firm. Note that the actual taxes payable by the firm are $6000. As reported to the shareholders, taxes of $10 000 represent the $6000 of taxes payable in the current period plus deferred taxes of $4000.[2]

The expected net cash flows or expected future returns of a particular capital investment must reflect its after-tax cash consequences to the firm. Hence, the relevant statement is that used for tax purposes. In any capital budgeting application, therefore, the actual taxes paid based on charges for capital cost allowance (CCA) are used in the cash flow calculation and not taxes that would be payable using the accounting depreciation expense.

Table 14-1
Illustrative Income Statements

	Income Statement as Reported to Shareholders (1)	Income Statement for Tax Reporting (2)
Sales	$145 000	$145 000
Operating costs	(100 000)	(100 000)
Operating income, before depreciation, interest, and taxes	$ 45 000	$ 45 000
Depreciation expense		
Per books	(15 000)	
CCA expense		(25 000)
Net operating income	$ 30 000	$ 20 000
Interest expense	(5 000)	(5 000)
Income before tax	$ 25 000	$ 15 000
Taxes (40 percent)	(10 000)	6 000
Net income	$ 15 000	$ 9 000

---

[2]Deferred taxes have been discussed in Chapter 4, footnote 2.

The second issue is the actual calculation of the net cash flow. This calculation, based on the income statement in column 1 of Table 14-1, is presented in Table 14-2. (Since the net cash flows are used to make payments on all financing sources used, there is no deduction for any payments to the financing sources.[3]) In column 1, the net cash flow is equal to after-tax net operating income ($12 000) plus the capital cost allowance charge. The latter is added back since it does not have any cash flow consequences apart from its impact on taxable income. In column 2, the net cash flow is calculated directly as operating income before tax of $45 000 minus the actual taxes paid of $8000.

In other words, after-tax net cash flow can be written as:

$$\frac{\text{After-tax}}{\text{net cash flow}} = \frac{\text{Net operating}}{\text{income after tax}} + \text{CCA} \qquad \qquad \textbf{(14-1)}$$

$$= \left[\text{sales} - \frac{\text{Operating expenses}}{\text{(including CCA)}} \right] (1 - T) + \text{CCA},$$

where T is the marginal corporate tax rate applicable to the firm. For the example in the table, the after-tax net cash flow equals:

$$(\$145\,000 - \$125\,000)\,(1 - 0.4) + \$25\,000 = \$37\,000.$$

Table 14-2
Calculations of Net Cash Flow

	(1)	(2)
Sales	$145 000	$145 000
Operating costs	(100 000)	(100 000)
Operating income	$ 45 000	$ 45 000
CCA expense	(25 000)	—
Net operating income	$ 20 000	$ 45 000
Taxes (40 percent)	(8 000)	(8 000)
Operating income after tax	$ 12 000	$ 37 000
Plus: CCA charges	25 000	—
Net cash flow	$ 37 000	$ 37 000

[3]Actually, net cash flow should be adjusted to reflect all noncash charges, not just CCA charges. However, for most firms, CCA is by far the largest noncash charge. Also note that Table 14-2 does not reflect a deduction for interest charges, which would be present if the firm used debt. Most firms use debt and hence finance part of their capital budgets with debt. Therefore, the question has been raised as to whether or not interest charges should be reflected in capital budgeting cash flow analysis. The consensus is that interest charges should not be dealt with explicitly in capital budgeting—rather, the effects of debt financing are reflected in the cost of capital which is used to discount the cash flows. The cost of capital is discussed in Chapter 17.

An equivalent formulation of after-tax net cash flow is obtained by considering operating income that does not reflect noncash expenses.[4] Then one can write:

$$\text{After-tax net cash flow} = (\text{Operating income})\,(1 - T) + T\,(\text{CCA}) \qquad \textbf{(14-2)}$$
$$= (45\,000)\,(1 - 0.4) + 0.4(\$25\,000)$$
$$= \$37\,000.$$

The first term equals the after-tax operating income before considering the taxable deduction for CCA, and the second term is the *tax shield*, or *tax saving*, generated by the CCA expense.

More generally, the after-tax net cash flow of the firm should represent the cash consequences of the firm's activities during the period, including any new investments undertaken. Therefore, the general expression for after-tax net cash flow is

$$\text{After-tax net cash flow} = \text{NOI}\,(1 - T) + \text{CCA} - \text{New investment,}$$

where NOI includes the tax depreciation expense.[5]

Incremental Cash Flows

In the previous section we reviewed the calculation of the after-tax net cash flow for the firm as a whole. But in evaluating a capital project, we are concerned only with those cash flows that result directly from the project. These cash flows, called **incremental cash flows**, represent the changes in the firm's total cash flows that will occur as a direct result of accepting or rejecting the project. Several special problems in determining incremental cash flows are discussed next.

---

[4]The equivalence of the two expressions is apparent when we break Equation 14-1 into its components:

$$\text{After-tax net cash flow} = \left\{ \begin{array}{c} \text{net operating} \\ \text{income} \end{array} \right\} (1 - T) + \text{CCA}$$

$$= \left\{ \left(\begin{array}{c} \text{operating} \\ \text{income} \end{array} \right) - \text{CCA} \right\} (1 - T) + \text{CCA}$$

$$= \left\{ \begin{array}{c} \text{operating} \\ \text{income} \end{array} \right\} (1 - T) + T(\text{CCA}),$$

which is Equation 14-2.

[5]In a number of theoretical studies, it is assumed that the firm is adding to its gross fixed assets an amount each year that is exactly equal to its depreciation expense in order to maintain the earning power of the assets. If the investment is equal to the tax depreciation expense, CCA, then the investment in new assets and the deduction for depreciation cancel out. The after-tax net cash flow would then be equal to NOI $(1 - T)$. In our example, the after-tax net cash flow would be \$20 000. If it is assumed that the new investment is equal to the depreciation expense reported on the income statement, then the after-tax net cash flow is written as:

$$\text{After-tax net cash flow} = \text{NOI}(1 - T) + \text{CCA} - \text{depreciation.}$$

Only if depreciation = CCA will the after-tax net cash flow be equal to NOI $(1 - T)$.

Sunk Costs.   Sunk costs are not incremental costs, and they should not be included in the analysis.[6] A **sunk cost** is an outlay that has already been committed or that has already occurred and hence is not affected by the accept-reject decision under consideration. To illustrate: in 1991, World Music was considering the establishment of a branch in a newly developed section of Vancouver. To help with its evaluation, World Music had, back in 1990, hired a consulting firm to perform a site analysis; the cost was $100 000, and this amount was expensed for tax purposes in 1990. Is this 1990 expenditure a cost that is relevant to the 1991 capital budgeting decision? The answer is no—the $100 000 is a sunk cost, and World Music cannot recover it regardless of whether or not the new branch is built. It often turns out that a particular project has a negative NPV when all the associated costs, including sunk costs, are considered. However, on an incremental basis the project may be a good one because the incremental cash flows are large enough to produce a positive NPV on the incremental investment.

Opportunity Costs.   The second potential problem relates to **opportunity costs**, defined here as the cash flows that could be generated from assets the firm already owns provided they are not used for the project in question. To illustrate: World Music already owns a piece of land that is suitable for the branch store. When evaluating the prospective branch, should the cost of the land be disregarded because no additional cash outlay would be required? The answer is no, because there is an opportunity cost inherent in the use of the property. In this case, the land could be sold to yield $150 000 after taxes. Use of the site for the branch would require foregoing this inflow, so the $150 000 must be charged as an opportunity cost against the project.

   Note that the proper land cost in this example is the $150 000 market-determined value, irrespective of whether World Music originally paid $50 000 or $500 000 for the property. (What the company paid would, of course, have an effect on taxes and hence on the after-tax opportunity cost.)

Effects on Other Parts of the Firm: Externalities.   The third potential problem involves the effects of a project on other parts of the firm, which economists call *externalities*. For example, some of World Music's customers who would shop at the new branch store are already customers of World Music's existing location. The sales, and hence profits, generated by these customers would not be new to the company; rather, they would represent a transfer from the downtown store to the branch. Thus, the net revenues produced by these customers should not be treated as incremental income in the capital budgeting decision. On the other hand, if having a suburban store would help the company attract new business to its existing store, the additional revenues that would actually flow to the downtown store should be attributed to the branch. Although often difficult to quantify, externalities such as these should be considered.

Shipping and Installation Costs.   When a firm acquires fixed assets, it often must incur substantial costs for shipping and installing the equipment. These

---

[6]For a classic example of the improper treatment of sunk costs by a major corporation, see U.E. Reinhardt, "Break-Even Analysis for Lockheed's TriStar: An Application of Financial Theory." *Journal of Finance*, September 1973: 821–38.

charges are added to the invoice price of the equipment when the cost of the project is being determined. Also, the full cost of the equipment, including shipping and installation costs, is used as the depreciable basis when CCA charges are being calculated. Thus, if World Music bought a computer with an invoice price of $100 000, and paid another $10 000 for shipping and installation, then the full cost of the computer—and its capital cost base for CCA charges—would be $110 000.

Salvage Value.   An asset's **salvage value** is its value at the end of a specified period of time. It is important in analyzing capital budgeting for two reasons. First, it may be foreseen that an asset that the firm acquires today will be sold in a given number of years for a given amount. Second, if the asset being considered would be a replacement, the firm may plan to sell the old asset. In this case, the salvage value of the old asset is its present market value.

Concept Review

▶ Briefly explain the difference between *accounting income* and *net cash flow*. Which should be used in capital budgeting? Why?
▶ Explain what the following terms mean, and assess the relevance of each concept in capital budgeting: *incremental cash flow*, *sunk cost*, *opportunity cost*, *salvage value*, *externality*, and *shipping plus installation costs*.

Changes in Net Working Capital

Normally, additional inventories are required to support a new operation, and expanded sales also lead to additional accounts receivable. Both of these asset increases must be financed. However, accounts payable and accruals will increase spontaneously as a result of the expansion, and this will reduce the net cash needed to finance inventories and receivables. The difference between the required increase in current assets and the spontaneous increase in current liabilities is the *change in net working capital (NWC)*. If this value is positive, as it generally is for projects that are intended to increase sales of the current product line, additional financing—over and above the cost of the fixed assets—will be needed to fund the increase in current assets.

As the project approaches termination, inventories are sold off and not replaced, and receivables also are converted to cash. As these changes occur, the firm receives an end-of-project cash flow that is equal but opposite to the net working capital requirement that occurred when the project was begun.

Concept Review

▶ How is an increase in net working capital dealt with in the capital budgeting analysis?
▶ Does the company get back the dollars it invests in working capital? How?

Capital Budgeting Project Evaluation

Up to this point, we have discussed several important aspects of cash flow analysis, but we have not seen how they affect the capital budgeting decision. In this section, we illustrate these effects by examining first an expansion project and then a replacement project. The latter is more complicated than the former since there are some tax implications that have to be incorporated.

Expansion Project

An *expansion project* is defined as one that requires the firm to invest in new facilities to increase sales. For example, suppose that Caligari Cabinets Limited anticipates an increase in demand for one of its products. In order to meet this demand, a new cutting and finishing machine costing $10 000 is needed. The necessary equipment will be purchased and installed late in the 1993 and paid for on December 31, 1993. The project will also require an initial investment of $2000 in net working capital. The initial working capital investment will be made on December 31, 1993. The machine will last 5 years, will be sold at the beginning of the sixth year,[7] and, based on forecasted sales levels, is expected to generate an increase in net operating income, before taxes, of $3500 per year for 5 years beginning at the end of 1994. It is anticipated that when the machine is sold for scrap, the CCA pool will still have assets in it. The capital cost rate applicable for CCA calculations is 20 percent. Taxes are at a 40 percent rate; the salvage value is expected to be equal to the undepreciated capital cost for the sixth year of $3686; and the firm's after-tax cost of capital for this project, which is considered to be of average risk for the firm, is 10 percent. Should Caligari Cabinets buy this new machine?

Analysis of Cash Flows. We start the cash flow part of the analysis by identifying the investment outlay required for the project. In an expansion decision, the estimation of this cash outlay is straightforward. As there is no replacement of existing equipment, there will be no tax complications caused by the sale of old equipment. The initial outlay is presented in Table 14-3 under the 1993 column. It is $12 000, which consists of the cost of the machine, including any installation costs, and the required investment in net working capital.

Having estimated the initial capital requirements, we must now identify the annual incremental cash flows that will occur once production begins; these are presented in the remaining columns of Table 14-3. The after-tax net cash flow is equal to the after-tax net operating income, $3500 in all 5 years; plus the amount deducted for capital cost allowance. The CCA allowances for the project must be based on the incremental impact of the purchase on the pool of assets. The incremental impact on the pool is equal to the acquisition cost of the asset of $10 000.[8] In the first year, the CCA deduction is $1000 (half the

---

[7]To obtain the CCA deduction for the fifth year, we assume that the machine is sold at the beginning of the sixth year.

[8]The original capital cost of the asset on which CCA deductions are based reflects the full cost to the company of acquiring the asset. These costs include legal, accounting, engineering, and other fees necessary to acquire the property. If the asset is purchased outside of Canada, the Canadian dollar equivalent as of the date of purchase is used as the original capital cost.

Table 14-3
Caligari Cabinets Expansion Project, Net Cash Flows, 1993–1998

	1993	1994	1995	1996	1997	1998
Equipment	$−10 000					
Increase in NWC	−2 000					
Sales		$10 000	$10 000	$10 000	$10 000	$10 000
Less: Cost of goods sold		6 500	6 500	6 500	6 500	6 500
Operating income before tax		3 500	3 500	3 500	3 500	3 500
Less: CCA charge		1 000	1 800	1 440	1 152	922
NOI before tax		2 500	1 700	2 060	2 348	2 578
Less: Tax (40 percent)		1 000	680	824	939	1 031
NOI after tax		1 500	1 020	1 236	1 409	1 547
Add back: CCA		1 000	1 800	1 440	1 152	922
Cash flow from operations		2 500	2 820	2 676	2 561	2 469
Return of NWC						2 000
Salvage value						3 686
Lost tax savings from sale						−983
Tax saving remaining						983
Net cash flow	$−12 000	$ 2 500	$ 2 820	$ 2 676	$ 2 561	$ 8 155
Net present value (10%)	$1 426					

regular charge because of the half-year rule), leaving after-tax net operating income of $1500. The net cash flow from operations for the year is $2500: that is, the sum of the after-tax net operating income plus the CCA charge. Table 14-4 provides the calculation of the CCA value for each year, along with the UCC balance before and after the deduction of the charge. Note that the investment in net working capital will be recovered in 1998.

However, the cash flow analysis is not complete: the Canadian tax system has some special features with respect to capital cost allowances. First, the

Table 14-4
Caligari Cabinets Expansion Project, CCA and UCC by Year

Year	UCC: Base for Calculation of CCA Charge	CCA	UCC: After Deduction of CCA
1	$10000	$1000	$9000
2	9000	1800	7200
3	7200	1440	5760
4	5760	1152	4608
5	4608	922	3686
6	3686		

benefits of CCA deductions for tax purposes continue forever. The tax shield from this continued charge for CCA is a value to the firm since it reduces future taxes, so its cash flow consequences must be considered. As of the end of 1998, the UCC in the pool associated with this asset will be $3686. The present value at the end of 1998 of the future tax savings beginning in 1999 is written as follows:

$$\text{Present value} = \frac{TC_0 d}{(k + d)},$$

where C_0 represents the value of the UCC in the pool associated with this asset and d is the maximum CCA rate applicable to this class of assets. This present value is equal to $(0.40 \times \$3686 \times 0.2)/(0.1 + 0.2) = \$983$ and is shown in Table 14-3 in the line marked "tax saving remaining."

So far, our consideration of these late tax savings assumes that the asset is not sold. When a sale occurs, there are two consequences. The first is the cash inflow for the salvage value; in this example, it is $3686, and this amount is entered directly in the table. The second is that under Canadian tax regulations, the sale of an asset reduces the size of the asset pool by the amount of the sale price; the result is lost tax savings. The present value of these lost tax savings, evaluated at the time of sale, is written as

$$PV_{lost} = \frac{TSd}{(k + d)},$$

where S is equal to the sale value. In our example, the lost tax savings are equal to $986, which is just equal to the present value of the remaining tax benefits. (This is a special case in which the salvage value was assumed equal to the UCC value.) The value of the lost tax savings is entered as a negative cash flow item in Table 14-3.[9]

The final element in the cash flow is the recovery of the net working capital amount of $2000, which is assumed to occur at the end of the life of the project.

With the net cash flows forecasted for each year, the net present value for the project can be calculated and the accept–reject decision made.

Making the Decision.   To summarize the data and get them ready for evaluation, it is useful to combine all of the net cash flows on a time line like the one shown in Figure 14-1, which uses data taken from Table 14-3. Figure 14-1 also shows the payback period, the internal rate of return (IRR), the

---

[9]In preparing the NPV calculations for the project, the analyst may want to determine the sensitivity of the NPV to the assumed value of the salvage. For short-lived projects, the salvage value may have a strong influence on the acceptability of the project. For example, in the Caligari Cabinets case, the reader can confirm that if the salvage value equals zero, the NPV is −$252 and the IRR is 9.3 percent. With a $5000 salvage value, the NPV rises to $2025 and the IRR to 15.2 percent. The actual value obtained for salvage may be highly variable, and the analyst should be very careful in accepting a project based on an aggressive assumption of the salvage value.

Figure 14-1
Caligari Cabinets Expansion Project, Time Line of Cash Flows, 1993–1998

1993	1994	1995	1996	1997	1998
($12000)	$2500	$2820	$2676	$2561	$8155

Payback period: 4.2 years
IRR: 13.9% vs. a 10% cost of capital
MIRR: 12.5% vs. a 10% cost of capital
NPV: $1426

modified internal rate of return (MIRR),[10] and the net present value (NPV). At the 10 percent cost of capital rate, the project appears to be acceptable using the NPV, IRR, or MIRR methods; it is also acceptable if Caligari requires a payback period of 4.2 years or less.

Note, however, that the analysis thus far has been based on the assumption that the project has the same degree of risk as the company's average project. If the project is considered to be riskier than an average project, it is necessary to increase the cost of capital, which in turn may cause the NPV to become negative and the IRR and MIRR to fall below the cost of capital. In the next chapter, we shall include a risk analysis.

An Alternative Approach to Evaluating an Expansion Project

If the analyst does not have to determine the IRR or MIRR for a project, then the calculation of its NPV can be simplified. In Table 14-3, we found the after-tax net cash flow for each year by determining the after-tax income and adding back the CCA deduction. As we demonstrated in a previous section, however, a project's after-tax cash flow in any year can be written as the sum of two components: its after-tax operating income (that is, revenues less operating expenses) calculated as if there were no deduction for CCA, and the tax saving resulting from the deduction of the CCA expense. The formula for the after-tax net cash flow in Year t is

$$\begin{pmatrix} \text{After-tax net} \\ \text{cash flow} \end{pmatrix}_t = \begin{pmatrix} \text{Operating} \\ \text{income} \end{pmatrix}_t (1 - T) + T(\text{CCA}_t) \qquad \textbf{(14-2a)}$$

---

[10]The calculations of the net cash flows as presented in Table 14-3 are necessary if an IRR or a MIRR is required. Note that with the possibility of values of the net tax savings, calculated as tax benefits less the tax losses when the asset is sold, that can arise in every year in perpetuity, the calculation of an IRR is impossible. By evaluating these cash flow consequences at the end of the project, calculations of the IRR and MIRR are possible.

Thus, the 1994 after-tax net cash flow can be calculated as

$$\left(\begin{array}{c}\text{After-tax net}\\\text{cash flow}\end{array}\right)_t = \$3500(1 - 0.4) + 0.4(\$1000)$$

$$= \$2100 + \$400 = \$2500,$$

which is the same value we found by the method used in Table 14-3.

The present value of the after-tax annual cash flow, as presented in Equation 14-2, is equal to the present value of the after-tax operating income plus the present value of the tax savings generated by the CCA tax shield. In calculating the first quantity, we note that the example says the after-tax operating income will be constant over the 5 years and equal to $2100 per year—that is, $3500 \times (1 - 0.4)$. Using the PVIF of 3.791 for a 5-year annuity at 10 percent, we find that the present value of the after-tax operating income is $7961.

The calculation of the present value of the tax saving can be simplified greatly by remembering how CCA charges are determined under Canadian tax regulations. If the project is undertaken with no expectation of selling the asset, CCA charges can be expected to continue forever. The present value of the tax saving is written as follows:

$$PV_{\text{tax saving}} = \sum_{t=1}^{\infty} \frac{T(CCA_t)}{(1 + k)^t},$$

where T is the tax rate and k is the cost of capital. This term can be simplified as follows:

$$PV_{\text{tax saving}} = \frac{TC_0 d/2}{1 + k} + \frac{TdC_0(1 - d/2)}{k + d} \times \frac{1}{1 + k}$$

$$= \frac{TC_0 d}{k + d} \times \frac{2 + k}{2(1 + k)},$$

where C_0 is the cost of the asset as originally included in the asset pool and d is the CCA rate.

In our example, assuming a zero salvage value would result in the present value of tax savings of $2545:

$$PV_{\text{tax saving}} = \frac{0.4 \times 10\,000 \times 0.2}{0.1 + 0.2} \times \frac{2 + 0.1}{2(1 + 0.1)}$$

$$= 2666.67 \times 0.9545$$

$$= \$2545.$$

The present value of the after-tax cash flow from operations would be $10\,506, which is the sum of the present values of the after-tax operating income, $7961, and the tax saving, $2545.

In our example, however, the asset is expected to be sold after 5 years for a positive salvage value, and the book value of the asset pool will be reduced by the proceeds of the sale. This sale will reduce the future tax saving; the amount of the lost tax saving depends upon the expected salvage value and upon the time at which the sale is expected to be made. The present value of the tax saving when there is a positive expected salvage value is written as

$$PV_{\text{tax saving}} = \frac{TC_0 d}{k + d} \times \frac{2 + k}{2(1 + k)} - \frac{TdS}{k + d} \times \frac{1}{(1 + k)^n}, \qquad \textbf{(14-3)}$$

where S is the salvage value, and n is the number of years into the future when the asset will be sold.

The first term of this equation reflects the present value of the tax savings based on a zero expected salvage value so that all possible future tax savings accrue to the project in question. The second term measures the present value of the tax savings lost because of the sale.

It is often easier to incorporate the full impact of the salvage value directly into the present value of tax savings equation. This is accomplished by adding to Equation 14-3 a term equal to the present value of the expected salvage value:

$$PV_{\text{tax saving, salvage}} = \left(\frac{TC_0 d}{k + d} \right) \times \left(\frac{2 + k}{2(1 + k)} \right) + \frac{S}{(1 + k)^n} \times \left(1 - \frac{Td}{k + d} \right). \quad \textbf{(14-4)}$$

The second term in Equation 14-4 reflects the net impact of the salvage value received for the machine at the end of its economic lifetime. This is composed of the present value of the inflow, which is equal to the salvage value, less the outflow resulting from the lost tax savings.[11] (Of course, when the salvage value is zero, this term is equal to zero, and the present value of the tax savings and salvage is equal to the full value of the tax savings.)

In our example, the variables in the equation have the following values:

$$C_0 = \$10\,000.$$
$$d = 0.2.$$
$$n = 5.$$
$$T = 0.4.$$
$$k = 10 \text{ percent} = \text{Cost of capital.}$$
$$S = \$3686.$$

Thus,

$$PV_{\text{tax saving, salvage}} = \$2545 + \frac{\$3686}{(1 + 0.1)^5} \left[1 - \frac{(0.4)(0.2)}{0.1 + 0.2} \right]$$

$$= \$2545 - \$1678 = \$4223.$$

The present value of the after-tax operating cash flow is \$12 184, which equals the present value of the after-tax operating income, \$7961, plus the present value of the tax saving, including salvage, of \$4223.

---

[11]The derivation of Equations 14-3 and 14-4 is presented in Appendix 14A.

Determining the Net Present Value.   The project's net present value is found as the sum of the present values of the inflows, or benefits, less the outflows, or costs. In equation form:

$$\text{NPV} = \text{PV}\left\{\begin{array}{c}\text{after-tax}\\\text{operating}\\\text{income}\end{array}\right\} + \text{PV}\left\{\begin{array}{c}\text{tax}\\\text{savings}\\\text{and salvage}\end{array}\right\} + \text{PV}\left\{\begin{array}{c}\text{net}\\\text{working}\\\text{capital}\end{array}\right\} - \text{initial cost.}$$

In tabular form, the net present value equals

Inflows
PV of after-tax operating income	$7 961
PV of tax savings and salvage	4 223
PV of net working capital	1 242
Less: Net cash outflow, or cost	12 000
Net present value (NPV)	$ 1 426

Since the NPV is positive, the project should be accepted.

Replacement Decision

All companies make replacement decisions. The analysis relating to these decisions is somewhat different from that for expansion decisions because the cash flows from the old asset must be considered. For example, the purchase of a new truck requires the sale of the existing asset. Thus, the cash inflows and outflows associated with accepting the new project must be *incremental*. For example, if the new truck will have operating costs of $3000 per year and the old has operating costs of $3500, the incremental savings in operating costs is $500. Further, the proceeds from the sale of the old asset will have an impact on the CCA pool that will be used to calculate the future incremental tax savings.

These problems are highlighted in the replacement example that follows. Since we have already presented calculations of the present values of the net cash flows and salvage values from the ultimate sale of the new machine, the analysis of these factors is brief.

The Widget Division of Casino Inc., a profitable, diversified manufacturing company, purchased a machine 5 years ago at a cost of $7500. The machine had an expected life of 15 years at the time of purchase and an expected salvage value of zero. The machine is included in an asset pool in which the maximum capital cost allowance rate is 20 percent and the company intends to use the maximum allowed. Currently (that is, at the beginning of the sixth year after purchase), the undepreciated capital cost is $2765.[12] The division manager reports that she can purchase a new type of machine for $12 000 (including

---

[12]The undepreciated capital cost is calculated as follows:

$$\begin{aligned}\text{UCC}_6 &= C_0(1 - d/2)(1 - d)^4\\&= 7500(1 - 0.1)(1 - 0.2)^4\\&= \$2765.\end{aligned}$$

installation) and that over its 10-year life, it will expand sales from $10 000 to $11 000 a year. Further, it will reduce labour and raw materials usage sufficiently to cut annual operating costs from $7000 to $5000. The new machine has a maximum capital cost allowance rate of 20 percent and an estimated salvage value at the end of Year 10 of $1300; the sale at that time will not eliminate the asset pool. The old machine's current market value is $1000. Taxes are at a 40 percent rate, and Casino's after-tax cost of capital is 10 percent. Should Casino purchase the new machine?

Using the simplified approach presented in the previous example, which does not require us to estimate the annual after-tax cash flows directly, we consider the replacement decision analysis.

The net initial cash outlay consists of two items: (1) payment to the manufacturer for the new machine, including installation costs, and (2) proceeds from the sale of the old machine. The amount paid for the asset is $12 000, and the sale proceeds from the old machine are $1000. The net result is that the purchase of the new machine will involve an immediate cash outlay of $11 000; this is the initial-period cash flow used for capital budgeting purposes.

The incremental cash flows from the project reflect the benefits to be derived from the investment. These benefits are composed of two components: (1) the incremental after-tax cash operating income, and (2) the present value of the tax savings from CCA deductions. Each of these elements is considered below.

1. *Incremental after-tax operating income.*   The calculations of the incremental cash flows are presented in Table 14-5. In column 1, Casino's estimated after-tax operating income is presented as it would be without the new machine. Column 2 provides after-tax operating income if the new investment is made. Column 3 shows the differences between the first two columns. The $1800 at the bottom of column 3 is the incremental after-tax operating income for each of the 10 years with the new machine.

2. *Present value of the tax savings from CCA.*   The tax savings are calculated by applying the capital cost rate to the appropriate base used for tax purposes (reflecting the half-year rule). The calculation of the base and the incremental impact is presented in Table 14-6. If the new machine is not purchased, the book value of the asset is equal to its UCC value of $2765, and

Table 14-5
Casino Inc., Replacement Project,
Calculation of After-Tax Operating Income

	Without New Machine (1)	With New Machine (2)	Difference (3) = (2) − (1)
Sales	$10 000	$11 000	$1000
Operating costs	(7 000)	(5 000)	−2000
Operating income	$ 3 000	$ 6 000	$3000
Taxes (40 percent)	(1 200)	(2 400)	1200
After-tax operating income	$ 1 800	$ 3 600	$1800

Table 14-6
Casino Inc., Replacement Project,
Calculation of Incremental Book Value of New Machine for Tax Purposes

	Old Machine (1)	New Machine (2)		Incremental Impact (3) = (2) − (1)
	UCC $2765	UCC—old machine	$ 2 765	$ 0
		Cost of new machine	12 000	12 000
			$14 765	$12 000
		Less: Sales proceeds	1 000	1 000
		UCC—new machine	$13 765	$11 000

the tax savings will be based on this value. If the new machine is purchased, the book value of the new machine for tax purposes will reflect the deduction of the sale proceeds of the old machine and the addition of the cost of the new machine. The calculation of the value in the CCA pool for tax purposes (assuming that the sale of the old machine will not eliminate the pool) is presented in column 2 of Table 14-6. The value of the new machine, $13 765, equals the book value of the old asset before the sale plus the cost of the new asset minus the proceeds of the sale of the old asset.

The incremental impact of buying the new machine compared to using the old machine is calculated in column 3. The incremental impact to the base on which CCA is calculated is equal to $11 000. This is equal to the cost of the new machine less the sale proceeds.

The approach we have used here is a direct method of calculating the appropriate base. It will be used in subsequent calculations of the present value of the tax savings.

Present Value of the Cash Flows.   As in the previous example, the present value of the net cash flows is composed of two components. The first is the present value of the after-tax operating income. For the old machine, the after-tax operating income is $1800 per year for 10 years. Using the annuity factor, we find the present value of that amount to be $11 061. For the new machine, the present value of the after-tax operating income of $3600 per year for 10 years is $22 122.

The second component is the present value of the tax savings from CCA charges, based on the incremental contribution to the capital base. When there is a net replacement (that is, when the replacement value increment to the pool exceeds the sale proceeds of the old machine), the tax savings are calculated on the net incremental value. The CCA charge for the first year is at one-half the regular rate, and for all subsequent years, it is at the full rate. The formula used to calculate the present value of the tax savings, including expected losses in tax savings due to the ultimate sale of the new asset, is Equation 14-4, where the initial value, C_0, is the net increment to the pool of $11 000.[13] In our example, the present value of the tax savings including salvage works out to $3167.[14]

Determining the Net Present Value.   Table 14-7 summarizes the present values of all the cash flows of the proposed project. The sum of the present values of the incremental inflows is $14 228.

Finally, the present value of the incremental inflows associated with accepting the new machine is compared to the incremental outflow if it is accepted. This comparison is presented in Table 14-8. The NPV of the project is positive, so the new machine should be accepted.

Summary of Cash Flows.   Table 14-9 summarizes the budgeting decision process used in the replacement example. The first step is to calculate the project cost, which reflects the investment in the new equipment, minus the receipts from the sale of the old machine. Next, the annual incremental benefits from taking the new machine are calculated and their present value is determined. The present value of the annual benefits is calculated as the sum of the present value of the after-tax operating income, which does not include a

Table 14-7
Casino Inc., Replacement Project,
Comparative Present Values with and without the New Investment

	With Old Machine (1)	With New Machine (2)	Difference (3) = (2) − (1)
Present Value of			
After-tax operating income	$11 061	$22 122	$11 061
Tax savings	n/a	n/a	3 167
Total present value of inflows			$14 228

[13]This method is equivalent to the half-year rule described in Chapter 2. This rule requires that the CCA charge for the first year be based on one-half the net increment to the pool. For all subsequent periods the full UCC is used.

[14]The calculation of the present value of the tax savings for the incremental impact of taking the new machine and selling the old is calculated as follows:

$$PV_{\text{tax saving}} = \frac{TC_0 d}{k + d} \times \frac{2 + k}{2(1 + k)} + \frac{S}{(1 + k)^n} \left[1 - \frac{Td}{k + d} \right]$$

$$= \frac{0.4 \,(\$11\,000)(0.2)}{0.1 + 0.2} \times \frac{2 + 0.1}{2(1 + 0.1)} + \frac{\$1300}{(1.1)^{10}} \left[1 - \frac{(0.4)(0.2)}{0.1 + 0.2} \right]$$

$$= \$2800 + \$367$$

$$= \$3167.$$

Table 14-8
Casino Inc., Replacement Project,
Calculation of Net Present Value

Present value of incremental inflows (from Table 14-7, column 3)	$14 228
Less: Net cash outflow, or cost	11 000
Net present value (NPV)	$ 3 228

deduction for CCA, plus the present value of the tax savings from CCA deductions including the impact of the salvage value at the end of the project's life. The present value of the tax savings incorporates the adjustment to the book value base for CCA charges because of the sale of the old machine at a price below the UCC value and the expected salvage value. The present value of the benefits is $14 228.

The final step is to sum the present values of the inflows and then deduct the project cost of $11 000 to determine the NPV of $3228 in the example. As the NPV is positive, the project should be accepted.

Table 14-9
Casino Inc., Worksheet for Capital Budgeting
Project Evaluation

1. *Project cost, or initial outflows required to undertake project*

Investment in new equipment	$12 000	
Less: Receipt from sale of old machine	1 000	
Total project cost		$11 000

2. *Calculation of annual benefits*

Change in sales	$ 1 000	
Plus: Reduction in costs	2 000	
Change in operating income	$ 3 000	
Less: Taxes (40 percent)	1 200	
Change in after-tax operating income	$ 1 800	
Present value of after-tax operating income Change in cash flow times interest factor $1800 × 6.145 =		$11 061
Present value of change in tax savings		3 167
Present value of benefits		$14 228

3. *Net Present Value*

PV of benefits	$14 228
Less: Project cost	11 000
NPV	$ 3 228

> *Concept Review*
>
> ► Explain and differentiate between the capital budgeting analyses
>   required for expansion and for replacement projects.

Capital Rationing

Capital budgeting decisions are typically made as described in this chapter—independent projects are accepted if their NPVs are positive, and choices among mutually exclusive projects are made by selecting the one with the highest NPV. This statement assumes, however, that if the firm has an especially large number of good projects in a particular year, management simply goes to the financial markets and raises whatever funds are required to finance all of the acceptable projects. But some firms do set limits on the amount of funds they are willing to raise. In such a case, the capital budget must also be limited. This situation is known as **capital rationing**.

Managers may be unwilling to engage in external financing for a number of reasons. Some have high levels of risk aversion and simply refuse to issue debt. Others have no objection to selling debt but do not want to sell equity capital for fear of losing some measure of voting control. Still others refuse to use any form of outside financing, considering safety and control to be more important than additional profits. Finally, some recognize their firms' limited management experience or human resources and want to constrain the size of the capital budget to the number of projects that management can control.[15]

Capital rationing results in limiting the rate of expansion to a slower pace than would be dictated by purely rational value-maximizing behaviour. It is important to recognize that capital rationing is very likely to be a short-run problem. If the management of a firm decides to limit its investment budget and hence not accept profitable projects, the firm will become a target for a takeover or the management will face opposition at the annual shareholders' meeting. From a competitive point of view, a company cannot arbitrarily limit its capital budget while its competitors do not since doing so would place the competitors in an advantageous position.

Project Selection under Capital Rationing

How should projects be selected under conditions of capital rationing? Under conditions of true capital rationing, the firm's value is not being maximized,

---

[15]Firms sometimes set a limit on capital expenditures not because of a shortage of funds but because of limitations on other resources, especially managerial talent. A firm may feel, for example, that its personnel development program is sufficient to handle an expansion of no more than 10 percent a year and set a limit on the capital budget to ensure that expansion is held to that rate. This is not *capital* rationing—rather, it involves a downward re-evaluation of project returns if growth exceeds some limit; that is, expected rates of return are, after some point, a decreasing function of the level of expenditure.

but the firm may choose to maximize value subject to the constraint that the capital ceiling is not exceeded. Following constrained maximization behaviour will, in general, result in a lower market value than following unconstrained maximization, but some type of constrained maximization may produce reasonably satisfactory results. Mathematical models have been developed to assist firms in making asset investment decisions in a long-run self-constrained environment.

If a financial manager faces short-run capital rationing and if the constraint cannot be lifted, what should be done? The manager's objective should be to choose, from all of the available projects, the subset of projects that maximizes the aggregate NPV subject to the capital constraint. Satisfactory results can be obtained by ranking projects by their net present value per dollar of initial cost.[16] Starting at the top of this list, the company takes projects of successively lower rank until the available funds have been exhausted. No investment with a negative NPV per dollar of initial cost (that is, a negative NPV) should be undertaken.

Why do we rank projects based on the NPV per dollar of initial cost instead of NPV? In a capital rationing situation, the manager is interested in obtaining the most effective use of limited capital available. The NPV per dollar of initial cost reflects the scarcity of investment funds by putting a premium on lower-cost projects. For example, in a no-rationing situation, two projects with the same NPV would have the same rank; this ranking would be independent of the initial cost. If the two projects are ranked in a capital rationing situation, however, the one with the lower initial cost is ranked higher since the same NPV is obtained with a smaller investment.

A firm might, for example, have the investment opportunities shown in Table 14-10 and only $6 million available for investment. In this situation, the firm has ranked the projects from highest to lowest NPV per dollar of project cost and takes each project in turn in order to meet the constraint. The firm would probably accept Projects 1 through 4 and Project 6; ending with a capital budget of $5.9 million and a cumulative NPV of $2.6 million. Under no circumstances should it accept Projects 8, 9, or 10, as they all have negative net present values.

Concept Review

▶ What is meant by the term *capital rationing*?
▶ Why do few sophisticated firms ration capital today?
▶ Why is the ranking procedure using NPV per dollar cost used in a short-run capital rationing situation?

---

[16]Alternatively, the rankings can be based on the IRR of the projects under consideration, beginning with the project with the highest internal rate of return. The profitability index is also used to rank projects. The profitability index (PI) is calculated as the present value of the future cash flows divided by the initial cost. Since the PI for each project is equal to one plus the ratio of NPV to initial cost, these two procedures provide identical rankings.

Table 14-10
The Prospective Projects Schedule

Nature of Proposal	Project's Initial Cost (1)	PV of Benefits (2)	Project's NPV (3)	Ratio of NPV to Project's Cost (4) = (3)/(1)
1. Purchase of leased space	$2 000 000	$3 200 000	$1 200 000	0.60
2. Mechanization of accounting system	1 200 000	1 740 000	540 000	0.45
3. Modernization of office building	1 500 000	2 070 000	570 000	0.38
4. Addition of power facilities	900 000	1 125 000	225 000	0.25
5. Purchase of affiliate	3 600 000	4 248 000	648 000	0.18
6. Purchase of loading docks	300 000	342 000	42 000	0.14
7. Purchase of tank trucks	500 000	540 000	40 000	0.08
8. Installation of conveyor system	200 000	186 000	− 14 000	− 0.07
9. Construction of new plant	2 300 000	2 093 000	− 207 000	− 0.09
10. Purchase of executive aircraft	200 000	128 000	− 72 000	− 0.36

Summary

This chapter discussed three issues in capital budgeting: cash flow estimation, expansion decisions, and replacement decisions. The key concepts covered are listed below.

☐ The most important, but also the most difficult, step in analyzing a capital budgeting project is estimating the **incremental after-tax cash flows** the project will produce.

☐ **Net cash flows** consist of (1) sales revenues minus cash operating costs reduced by taxes plus (2) cash flows based on CCA charges equal to the CCA charge times the tax rate of the firm.

☐ Adjustments of the cash flow must be made for the consequences of **salvage values** of assets at the beginning of the period of the project for replacement decisions and at the end of the project for both replacement and expansion decisions.

☐ In determining incremental cash flows, **opportunity costs** (the return on the next-best alternative investment of equal risk) must be included, but **sunk costs** (cash outlays that have been made and that cannot be recouped) are not included. Any *externalities* (effects of a project on other parts of the firm) should be included in the analysis.

☐ Capital projects often require an additional investment in *net working capital (NWC)*. An increase in NWC must be included in the initial cash outlay in Year 0 and then shown as a cash inflow in the final year of the project.

☐ **Capital rationing** occurs when management constrains the size of the firm's capital budget during a particular period. Project selection can be undertaken under capital rationing by ranking projects by net present value per dollar of investment and choosing a set of projects that (1) have positive NPVs and (2) utilize fully the constrained capital budget.

Questions

14-1   Cash flows rather than accounting profits are listed in Table 14-2. What is the basis for this emphasis on cash flows as opposed to net income?

14-2   **a.** In Equation 14-2, why is operating income reduced by multiplying it by $(1 - T)$, while the CCA (depreciation for tax purposes) is multiplied by T?
b. In Table 14-3, why is the salvage value shown in line 13 reduced in the next line by the tax savings lost by the sale?
c. In Table 14-3, why are "tax savings remaining" shown?
d. In Table 14-3, what would happen if the new machine permitted a reduction in net working capital?
e. In Table 14-6, why is the UCC with the old machine included in the calculation of the UCC with the new machine?
f. In Table 14-6, why are the proceeds of selling the old machine deducted from the UCC with the new machine?

14-3   Explain why sunk costs should not be included in a capital budgeting analysis but opportunity costs and externalities should be included.

14-4   Explain how net working capital is recovered at the end of a project's life, and why it is included in a capital budgeting analysis.

14-5   In general, is an explicit recognition of incremental cash flows more important in new project or replacement analysis? Explain your answer.

14-6   The James Corporation uses the payback method in evaluating investment proposals. It is now considering new equipment whose additional net after-tax earnings would be $300 a year. The equipment costs $1500. Its expected useful life is 10 years (assume straight line depreciation). The company uses a 3-year payback as its criterion. Should the equipment be purchased?

14-7   What are the most critical problems that arise in calculating a rate of return for a prospective investment?

14-8   In addition to rate of return analysis, what factors should be considered in determining capital expenditures?

Self-Test Problems   (solutions appear on page 481)

ST-1   **Key terms.**   Define each of the following terms:
a. Cash flow; accounting income
b. Incremental cash flow; sunk cost; opportunity cost
c. Change in net working capital
d. Salvage value

e. Expansion project analysis; replacement analysis

f. Capital rationing

ST-2   Replacement decision.   Rocky Mountain Ski Enterprise Ltd. (RMSE) is considering the replacement of its ski tow equipment with a more sophisticated chair-lift facility. The present equipment cost $200 000 5 years ago. It has a further life of 15 years, after which it would have a zero salvage value. The new installation would last for 15 years, after which it could be sold for $150 000. The capital cost of the new chair lift is $600 000; however, if the existing towing equipment is sold today, it would provide $50 000 toward the new outlay. Both kinds of equipment have a CCA rate of 8 percent.

   The management of RMSE foresees that the new chair lift would raise revenues from the current $700 000 per year to $1 200 000 per year. Operating costs would also increase from $350 000 to $400 000 per year. The corporate tax rate is 46 percent, and the cost of capital is 12 percent. Should RMSE install the new chair lift? Prepare a worksheet similar to those illustrated in Table 14-9.

ST-3   Replacement decision.   The Winfield Company Ltd. is using a machine whose original cost was $72 000. The machine is 2 years old and has a current market value of $16 000. The asset is being depreciated for book purposes over a 12-year original life. The salvage value is expected to be zero. The asset belongs in the pool that has a capital cost allowance rate of 30 percent. The tax rate is 50 percent, and the pool has a book value of $500 000.

   Management is contemplating the purchase of a replacement that would cost $75 000 and have an estimated salvage value of $10 000 after 10 years. The new machine would have a greater capacity, increasing annual sales from $1 million to $1.01 million, or by $10 000. Operating efficiencies with the new machine would produce expected savings of $10 000 a year. The cost of capital is 8 percent, a 50 percent tax rate is applicable, and the company's total annual operating costs are $800 000. The new asset would belong in the same CCA pool as the old machine.

a. Should the firm replace the machine?

b. Would your decision change if the capital cost allowance rate applicable to the pool were 15 percent?

c. How would your decision be affected if management locates a second new machine that costs $140 000, has a $20 000 estimated salvage value, and would provide $25 000 in annual savings over its 10-year life? It would also increases sales by $10 000 a year. (There are now three alternatives: (i) keep the old machine, (ii) replace it with a $75 000 machine, or (iii) replace it with a $140 000 machine.) This third asset falls in the same CCA pool as the other two, and the applicable CCA rate is 30 percent.

d. How would your decision be affected if a new generation of equipment, expected to be on the market in about 2 years, will provide increased annual savings and have the same cost, asset life, and salvage value? In giving your answer, disregard the changes in Parts b and c—that is, use under the original assumption that one $75 000 replacement machine is available now.

e. How would your decision be affected if the asset lives of the various alternatives were not the same?

ST-4   New project analysis.   You have been asked by the president of Ellis Construction Company to evaluate the proposed acquisition of a new earthmover. The mover's basic price is $50 000, and it will cost another $10 000 to modify it for special use by Ellis Construction. Assume that the mover falls into a CCA class with a rate of 30 percent and is the only asset in that class. It would be sold after 3 years for $20 000, and it would require an increase in net working capital of $2000 for spare parts inventory. The earthmover purchase would have no effect on revenues, but it is expected to save Ellis $20 000 per year in before-tax operating costs, mainly labour. Ellis's marginal tax rate is 40 percent.

a. Set up tables similar to Tables 14-3 and 14-4 showing Ellis's cash flows with the new machine for Years 0 to 3.

b. What is the NPV of buying the earthmover if the cost of capital is 10 percent?

c. What is the IRR of buying the earthmover? What is the MIRR?

d. Should Ellis acquire the earthmover?

Problems

14-1   NPV calculation.   Electronic Systems Ltd. expects to be able to realize sales of $140 000 per year and net cash operating costs of $100 000 per year on Project A. The investment outlay, C, on the project is $100 000; its life is 10 years; the tax rate, T, is 40 percent. The applicable cost of capital, k, is 12 percent. Assuming the project has a capital cost allowance rate of 25 percent and the expected salvage value is the undepreciated capital cost at the end of 10 years after the deduction of the CCA charge in year 10, calculate its NPV.

14-2   New project analysis.   You have been asked by the president of your company to evaluate the proposed acquisition of a new spectrometer for the firm's R&D department. The equipment's base price is $140 000, and it would cost another $30 000 to modify it for special use by your firm. Assume that the spectrometer falls into a CCA class with a rate of 30 percent and would be sold after 3 years for $60 000. Use of the equipment would require an increase in net working capital of $8000 (for spare parts inventory). The spectrometer would have no effect on revenues, but it is expected to save the firm $50 000 per year in before-tax operating costs, mainly labour. The firm's marginal tax rate is 40 percent.

a. Set up a table similar to Table 14-3 showing the expected cash flows for Years 0 to 3.

b. What is the NPV of buying the spectrometer if the cost of capital is 12 percent?

c. What is the IRR of buying the spectrometer? What is the MIRR?

d. Should your firm acquire the spectrometer?

14-3   New project analysis.   The McLaughlin Company is evaluating the proposed acquisition of a new milling machine. The machine's base price is $108 000, and it would cost another $12 500 to modify it for special use by the firm. Assume that the milling machine falls into a CCA class with a rate of 30 percent, is the only asset in that class, and would be sold after 3 years for $65 000. The machine would require an increase in net working capital of $5500 (for inventory). The milling machine would have no effect on revenues, but it is expected to save the firm $44 000 per year in before-tax operating costs, mainly labour. McLaughlin's marginal tax rate is 34 percent.

a. Set up a table similar to Table 14-3 showing the expected cash flows for Years 0 to 3.

b. What is the NPV of buying the machine if the cost of capital is 12 percent?

c. What is the IRR of buying the milling machine? What is the MIRR?

d. Should McLaughlin acquire the machine?

14-4   **Replacement analysis.**   The Elmwood Company Ltd. is considering the purchase of a new machine tool to replace an obsolete one. Assume that the machine being used for the operation has both a market value and a book value for capital cost purposes equal to zero, but it is in good working order and would last physically for at least an additional 15 years. The proposed new machine would perform the operation so much more efficiently, however, that Elmwood engineers estimate that labour, material, and other direct costs of the operation would be reduced by $4500 a year if it is installed. The proposed machine costs $24 000 delivered and installed, and its economic life is estimated to be 15 years with a zero salvage value. The company expects to earn 12 percent on its investment after taxes (12 percent is the firm's cost of capital). The tax rate is 50 percent and the capital cost allowance rate for tax purposes is 30 percent.

a. Should Elmwood buy the new machine?

b. Assume that the book value of the old machine for CCA purposes has been $6000 and that it has no sale value. How do these assumptions affect your answer?

c. Change Part b to give the old machine a market value of $4000. How does this affect your answer?

d. Change Part b to assume that the annual saving would be $6000. (Do not make the change in Part c: that is, do not assume the machine can be sold for $4000.)

e. Rework Part a assuming the relevant cost of capital is 6 percent. What is the significance of this change? What can be said about Parts b, c, and d under this assumption?

f. In general, how would each of the following factors affect the investment decision, and how should each be treated?

i. The expected life of the existing machine decreases.

ii. Capital rationing is imposed on the firm.

iii. The cost of capital is not constant but is rising.

iv. Improvements in the equipment to be purchased are expected to occur each year. Every year in the foreseeable future, industry experts expect an increase in the returns or expected savings from new machines over the saving expected with this year's model.

14-5   **Replacement analysis.**   Granger Shipyards is considering the replacement of an 8-year-old riveting machine with a new one that would increase earnings before depreciation from $30 000 per year to $58 000 per year. The new machine costs $60 000 and has an estimated life of 8 years with no salvage value. The machine has a CCA rate of 30 percent. The applicable corporate tax rate is 40 percent, and the firm's cost of capital is 12 percent. The old machine has been fully depreciated, and it has no salvage value. Calculate the net present value for the project. Should Granger replace the old riveting machine with the new one?

14-6   **Replacement analysis.**   Assume that Granger Shipyards (in Problem 14-5) could take an investment tax credit of 10 percent on the purchase of the new machine, and that this machine would have a salvage value of $8000 at the end of 8 years. Assume further that the old machine has a book value of $24 000 and a remaining life of 8 years. The old machine was purchased in 1987, and it is being depreciated using a CCA rate of 30 percent. If replaced, the old machine can be sold now for $15 000. Should the machine replacement be made? Assume that the investment tax credit is applied to reduce the cost of the asset. In addition, the base for CCA calculations is reduced by the dollar amount of the investment tax credit.

14-7   **New project analysis.**   J.V.P. Associates is a group of consulting financial analysts. They publish a monthly newsletter that reviews the current state of the Canadian economy, stock and bond market trends, and possible future market developments. Because of budget constraints, the funds available for investment this year are limited to $120 000. Three projects are being considered. Each is an investment in a printing press that would produce a good quality publication, but the capacities of each would be different. Management has projected that there would be some extra costs and some extra revenues from increasing distribution.

	Press A	Press B	Press C
Year 0	−$90 000	−$70 000	−$50 000
1	+ 50 000	+ 23 000	+ 15 000
2	+ 40 000	+ 23 000	+ 15 000
3	+ 20 000	+ 23 000	+ 15 000
4	+ 10 000	+ 23 000	+ 15 000
5	+ 5 000	+ 23 000	+ 15 000

a.   If the firm's cost of capital is 16 percent, which of the presses should be acquired? If presses B and C must be installed jointly, which of the presses should be acquired?

b.   Consider presses B and C together as one possible investment. Graph the net present value of press A and of presses B + C with the NPV on the Y axis and the cost of capital on the X axis. Which project would be preferred at a discount rate of 18 percent, A or B + C? Which would be preferred at a discount rate of 10 percent?

Integrative Problem

14-8 **Cash flow estimation.** South Niagara Ltd., a leading producer of fresh, frozen, and made-from-concentrate fruit juices, is currently evaluating a new product, fresh fruit punch. The new product would cost more, but it is superior to the competing reconstituted punches. As a recently hired financial analyst, you have been asked to analyze the project and to present your findings to the company's executive committee.

The production line would be set up in an unused section of South Niagara's main plant. The machinery is relatively inexpensive, costing an estimated $200 000, but shipping and installation would cost an additional $40 000. Further, South Niagara's inventories would have to be increased by $25 000 to handle the new line, but accounts payable would rise by $5000. The machinery falls into a 30-percent CCA class, is expected to be used for 4 years, and would have a salvage value of $25 000 at the end of this time.

The new product is expected to generate incremental net revenues (before taxes and excluding depreciation) of $125 000 in each of the next 4 years. South Niagara's tax rate is 40 percent, and its required rate of return is 10 percent.

You should perform the following tasks and answer the following questions in making your analysis.

a. Define *incremental cash flows*. Construct the project's incremental cash flow statement for its first year of operation. Does this cash flow statement include any financial flows, such as interest expense? Why or why not?

b. Suppose the firm spent $10 000 last year to rehabilitate the production line site in preparation for another project that was subsequently abandoned. Should this cost be included in the analysis? Further, assume that the plant space could be leased out to another firm at $5000 a year. Should this be included in the analysis? Finally, assume that the fresh fruit punch product is expected to decrease sales of the firm's frozen fruit punch by $20 000 per year. Should this be considered in the analysis? Be sure to explain your answers fully.

c. What would be the company's net investment outlay (t = 0 cost) on this project? What would be the net cash flow at the end of the project's operating life?

d. Set up a table similar to Table 14-3 to estimate the project's cash flows. What is its NPV? Should the project be undertaken?

e. Now assume that the project is a replacement project rather than a new, or expansion, project. Describe how the analysis would have to be changed to deal with a replacement project. (No calculations are necessary.)

Solutions to Self-Test Problems

ST-1 Refer to the appropriate sections of the text to check your responses.

ST-2 Worksheet—Rocky Mountain Ski Enterprises

a. Project cost

Investment in new equipment	$600 000
Less: Receipt from sale of old lift	(50 000)
Total project cost	$550 000

b. Calculation of annual benefits

Change in sales	$500 000
Less: Change in costs	(50 000)
Change in operating income	$450 000
Less: Taxes (46%)	207 000
Change in after-tax operating income	$243 000

  i. Present value of change in after-tax operating income
Change of $243 000 times interest factor for a 15-year annuity at
12 percent, i.e. $243 000 × 6.811 $1 655 073

  ii. Present value of tax savings if new equipment is purchased:
- Calculation of incremental book value of new machine: This is equal to cost of new machine less salvage from old or $600 000 − $50 000 = $550 000 = C_0.
- Calculating of present value of tax savings (including salvage):

$$PV_{\text{tax saving}} = \frac{TC_0 d}{k + d} \times \frac{2 + k}{2(1 + k)} + \frac{S}{(1 + k)^n}\left[1 - \frac{Td}{k + d}\right]$$

where S is salvage on new machine after 15 years or $150 000.
Substituting in the appropriate values, we obtain:

$$PV_{\text{tax saving}} = \frac{(0.46)(550\,000)(0.08)}{0.12 + 0.08} \times \frac{2 + 0.12}{2(1.12)} +$$

$$\frac{150\,000}{(1.12)^{15}}\left[1 - \frac{(0.46)(0.08)}{0.12 + 0.08}\right]$$

$$= \frac{20\,240}{0.20} \times 0.9464 + 27\,404 \times 0.816$$

$$= 95\,776 + 22\,362$$

$$= 118\,138.$$

c. Net Present Value

PV of inflows: After-tax operating income	$1 655 073
Tax saving (including salvage)	118 138
	$1 773 210
Less: Project cost	550 000
NPV	$1 223 210

Thus, the new chair lift should be installed.

ST-3 **a.** Replace if NPV is positive. Cost of replacement: Cost of new machine less salvage of old:

$$= \$75\,000 - \$16\,000$$
$$= \$59\,000.$$

Cash flows

i. From operations: the reduction in operating costs and the increase in revenues increases operating income by \$20 000 annually. After tax, this component of cash flow is \$20 000 $\times$ $(1 - 0.5) = \$10\,000$.

The present value of the cash flow is

$$\$10\,000 \times \text{PVIFA}_{8,10} = \$10\,000 \times 6.7101$$
$$= \$67\,101.$$

ii. Tax saving (including salvage):

$$PV_{\text{tax saving}} = \frac{TC_0 d}{k + d} \times \frac{2 + k}{2(1 + k)} + \frac{S}{(1 + k)^n} \left[1 - \frac{Td}{k + d} \right]$$

$$= \frac{(0.5)(59\,000)(0.3)}{0.08 + 0.3} \times \frac{2 + 0.08}{2(1.08)} +$$

$$\frac{10\,000}{(1.08)^{10}} \left[1 - \frac{(0.5)(0.3)}{0.08 + 0.3} \right]$$

$$= \frac{8850}{0.38} \times \frac{2.08}{2.16} + 4632 \times 0.6053$$

$$= 22\,427 + 2804$$

$$= 25\,231.$$

$$NPV = \$67\,101 + \$25\,231 - \$59\,000$$
$$= \$33\,332.$$

Therefore, the asset should be replaced.

b. This change affects the present value of tax savings. With a CCA rate of 15 percent, the present value of tax savings including salvage is \$21 648, a reduction from the value when the CCA rate was 30 percent. The NPV is \$29 750, so the asset still should be replaced.

c. $NPV_2 = -140\,000 + 16\,000 + 35\,000(1 - 0.5)\,\text{PVIFA}_{8,10} +$

$$\frac{(0.5)(124\,000)(0.30)}{0.08 + 0.3} \times \frac{2.08}{2.16} + \frac{20\,000}{(1.08)^{10}} \left[\frac{1 - (0.5)(0.3)}{0.08 + 0.3} \right]$$

$$= -124\,000 + 117\,427 + 47\,135 + 5607$$

$$= 46\,169.$$

This alternative should be selected since it has the greatest NPV.

d. Once the investment has been made, it should be regarded as a sunk cost. At that point, any new generation of equipment in which an investment would have a positive net present value should be adopted regardless of recent past investments. Before the initial new investment is made, prospects for new generations of equipment may affect estimates of (i) salvage value and (ii) life of the prospective equipment being considered for purchase.

    e. Different asset-life lengths must be handled by dealing explicitly with questions about the nature and timing of asset replacement. The generally followed practice is to assume that replacements extend the time horizon to the point at which unequal lives are rendered unimportant by the impact of compound discounting.

ST-4   **a.**   See the table below.

Answer Key for Question ST-4a

Part I. CCA and UCC Calculations

Year	UCC: Base for Calculation of CCA Charge	CCA	UCC: After Deduction of CCA
1	$60 000	$ 9 000	$51 000
2	51 000	15 300	35 700
3	35 700	10 710	24 990
4	24 990		

Part II. Project Cash Flows

	Year 0	Year 1	Year 2	Year 3
Equipment	($50 000)			
Modifications	(10 000)			
Increase in NWC	(2 000)			
Incremental operating income before tax		$20 000	$20 000	$20 000
Less: CCA		9 000	15 300	10 710
NOI: before tax		$11 000	$ 4 700	$ 9 290
Less: Tax @ 40%		4 400	1 880	3 716
NOI: after tax		$ 6 600	$ 2 820	$ 5 574
Add back: CCA		9 000	15 300	10 710
Cash flow from operations		$15 600	$18 120	$16 284
Return of NWC				2 000
Salvage				20 000
Less: Lost tax savings from sale				6 000
Tax saving, remaining				7 497
Net cash flows	($62 000)	$15 600	$18 120	$39 781
PV @ 10%	($62 000)	$14 182	$14 975	$29 888
FV @ 10%		$18 876	$19 932	$39 781

    b. The NPV at 10% is −$2955. Since the NPV is negative, the earthmover should not be purchased.

c. The IRR of buying the earthmover is 7.7 percent, versus a cost of capital of 10 percent.

   The terminal value is $78 589. The MIRR is 8.2 percent versus a cost of capital of 10 percent.

   Note that the IRR and MIRR are computed by calculating the PV of the remaining tax savings due to CCA at the end of Year 3, using a cost of capital of 10 percent. In reality, the tax savings due to CCA are not all realized in Year 3; they extend forever. However, it would be impossible to compute IRR or the terminal value for computation of the MIRR if the cash flows were allowed to extend to infinity.

d. Based on NPV, IRR, and MIRR decision criteria, the earthmover should not be purchased.

Appendix 14A
Derivation of the Present Value of Tax Savings

A crucial component in the capital budgeting analysis is the calculation of the present value of tax savings derived from capital cost allowances. Although the present value of the after-tax net cash flows can be calculated directly, problems that arise from expected salvage values are easier to handle by calculating the present value of the net cash flow as the sum of the present values of after-tax operating income and tax savings. Let

C_0 = the original capital cost of the asset.
 d = the maximum capital cost allowance rate for the class.
CCA_t = the capital cost allowances applied in year t.
UCC_t = the undepreciated capital cost on which the capital cost allowance for year
        t is calculated, i.e., the UCC at the beginning of year t.
 T = the company's tax rate.
 k = the opportunity cost of capital.

The tax savings from capital cost allowances is equal to the capital cost allowance taken in the year times the tax rate, $T(CCA_t)$. As the asset is never fully used up, the tax savings occur in perpetuity. The present value of the tax savings is presented in Equation 14A-1:

$$PV_{\text{tax saving}} = \frac{T(CCA_1)}{1 + k} + \frac{T(CCA)_2}{(1 + k)^2} + \frac{T(CCA_3)}{(1 + k)^3} + \ldots \qquad \textbf{(14A-1)}$$

$$= \frac{T}{1 + k} \left[CCA_1 + \frac{CCA_2}{1 + k} + \frac{CCA_3}{(1 + k)^2} + \ldots \right] \qquad \textbf{(14A-2)}$$

To solve for this present value, it is necessary to write the capital cost allowances in every year as a function of a set of fixed and given variables. In the first year, CCA_1 is equal to the original cost of the asset times one-half of the capital cost rate; that is,

$$CCA_1 = C_0 d/2.$$

The undepreciated capital cost at the beginning of the second year is the original value less the CCA charge for Year 1:

$$UCC_2 = C_0 - CCA_1 \qquad \textbf{(14A-3)}$$
$$= C_0 - C_0(d/2)$$
$$= C_0 - (1 - d/2).$$

In Year 2 and all subsequent years, the CCA charge is equal to the full capital cost rate times the undepreciated capital cost at the beginning of the year:

$$CCA_2 = d(UCC_2) \qquad \textbf{(14A-4)}$$
$$= dC_0(1 - d/2). \quad \text{From 14A-3.}$$

The undepreciated capital cost for Year 3 is the undepreciated capital cost for Year 2 less the CCA taken for the year:

$$UCC_3 = UCC_2 - CCA_2.$$

Substituting the expression from Equation 14A-3 for UCC_2 and from Equation 14A-4 for CCA_2, we obtain Equation 14A-5:

$$UCC_3 = C_0 (1 - d/2) - dC_0 (1 - d/2) \qquad \textbf{(14A-5)}$$
$$= C_0 (1 - d/2) (1 - d).$$

We are now in a position to generalize these expressions. For any year, t, the undepreciated capital cost at the beginning of the year, can be written as follows:

$$UCC_t = \begin{cases} C_0; \ t = 1 \\ C_0(1 - d/2)(1 - d)^{t-2}; \ t \geq 2. \end{cases} \qquad \textbf{(14A-6)}$$

This expression requires the input of C_0, d, and t, all of which are observable.

The generalization of the CCA charge is straightforward. The CCA in any year, t, where t is greater than 1, is equal to the full cost rate, times the undepreciated capital cost at the beginning of that year.

$$CCA_t = dUCC_t. \qquad \textbf{(14A-7)}$$

Substituting the expression for UCC_t from Equation 14A-6 into Equation 14A-7, we obtain the following expression:

$$CCA_t = \begin{cases} C_0d/2; \ t = 1 \\ dC_0(1 - d/2)(1 - d)^{t-2}; \ t \geq 2. \end{cases} \qquad \textbf{(14A-8)}$$

The groundwork has been set for the solution of the present value of the tax savings. Equation 14A-2 can be rewritten with the substitution of the appropriate expression for CCA_t from Equation 14A-8:

$$PV_{\text{tax saving}} = \frac{T}{1 + k} \left[C_0d/2 + \frac{dC_0(1 - d/2)}{1 + k} + \frac{dC_0(1 - d/2)(1 - d)}{(1 + k)^2} + \cdots \right.$$
$$\left. + \frac{dC_0(1 - d/2)(1 - d)^{N-2}}{(1 + k)^{N-3}} + \cdots \right] \qquad \textbf{(14A-9)}$$

$$= \frac{TC_0d/2}{1 + k} + \frac{TdC_0(1 - d/2)}{(1 + k)^2} \left[1 + \frac{1 - d}{(1 + k)} + \cdots \right.$$
$$\left. + \frac{(1 - d)^{N-2}}{(1 + k)^{N-2}} + \cdots \right].$$

The expression in the square brackets in Equation 14A-9 is the sum of an infinite geometric series beginning with the value 1. Each factor is obtained by multiplying the previous value by the fixed value $(1 - d)/(1 + k)$. The summation of this series is $(1 + k)/(k + d)$. Substituting this into Equation 14A-9, we obtain the following expression for the present value of the tax savings.

$$PV_{\text{tax saving}} = \frac{TC_0 d/2}{1 + k} + \frac{TdC_0(1 - d/2)}{k + d} \times \frac{1}{1 + k} \qquad \textbf{(14A-10)}$$

This present value in Equation 14A-10 is composed of two terms. The first term equals the present value of the tax saving in the first year when one-half the CCA rate is applied to the original cost. The second term is the present value of all subsequent tax savings when the full CCA rate is applied to the appropriate base $C_0 (1 - d/2)$. Notice that from Period 2 onward all CCA charges can be derived from the UCC at the beginning of the second year and the full cost rate applied to this base.

Equation 14A-10 can be rewritten as:

$$PV_{\text{tax saving}} = \frac{TC_0 d}{k + d} \times \frac{2 + k}{2(1 + k)}. \qquad \textbf{(14A-11)}$$

The above analysis has been presented under the assumption that the asset will never be sold. Suppose, however, that when the asset is purchased it is expected to be sold after n years for a salvage value of S dollars. If the asset were not sold, the present value of the tax savings would be equal to the expression in Equation 14A-10. With the sale of the asset, however, all the capital cost allowances from year $n + 1$ on will be lost. But, since the value of the pool will be reduced by the sale proceeds, the lost CCA charges will depend on the salvage value.

The present value of the lost tax savings is written as follows:

$$PV_{\text{lost}} = \frac{1}{(1 + k)^n} \left[\frac{T(CCA_{n+1})}{1 + k} + \frac{T(CCA_{n+2})}{(1 + k)^2} + \cdots \right]. \qquad \textbf{(14A-12)}$$

The expression in the square brackets is the sum of an infinite geometric progression beginning in period $n + 1$. The expression $1/(1 + k)^n$ converts this infinite sum to a present value as of the acquisition data. The CCA in period $n + 1$ is equal to the proceeds of sale times the cost rate, d. Hence, all the lost tax savings can be written in terms of the salvage value, S.

$$CCA_{n + 1} = dS.$$
$$CCA_{n + 2} = dS(1 - d).$$
$$CCA_{n + 3} = dS(1 - d)_2.$$

Substituting these expressions into Equation 14A-12 and solving for the sum of the infinite geometric series, we obtain the following expression for the present value of the lost tax savings:

$$PV_{\text{lost}} = \frac{TdS}{k + d} \times \frac{1}{(1 + k)^n} \qquad \textbf{(14A-13)}$$

The present value of the tax savings obtained from the purchase and eventual sale of this asset is equal to the present value of the tax savings, as if the asset were held forever, less the lost tax savings based on the salvage value of the asset plus the cash flow obtained from the sale of the asset at the end of the lifetime of the project. This expression is presented in Equation 14A-14, which is the same as Equation 14-4.

$$PV_{\text{tax saving}} = \frac{TC_0 d/2}{1 + k} + \frac{TdC_0(1 - d/2)}{k + d} \times \frac{1}{1 + k} - \left[\frac{TdS}{k + d} \times \frac{1}{(1 + k)^n} \right] + \frac{S}{(1 + k)^n}$$

$$\text{or} \quad \frac{TC_0 d}{k + d} \times \frac{2 + k}{2(1 + k)} + \frac{S}{(1 + k)^n} \left[1 - \frac{Td}{k + d} \right] \qquad \textbf{(14A-14)}$$

Since it is the salvage value that is deducted from the book value of the pool, this is the incremental impact that must be used in evaluating the lost tax savings.

15

▲▲▲

Risk Analysis in Capital Budgeting

A MANAGERIAL PERSPECTIVE

At the end of 1987, Robert Campeau made the first of many bids to acquire Federated Department Stores. Federated was a large company that had a number of divisions and operated 238 department stores, 76 mass merchandising stores, 129 supermarkets, and 232 other stores. Campeau finally made the winning bid in May 1988; the share price was $73.500, which was well above the Federated's share price of $32.875 prior to the takeover activity. At the end of 1989, Campeau filed for bankruptcy protection!

The acquisition of Federated can be viewed as the result of a capital budgeting decision in which the expected cash flows were composed of the expected dollar value of divisions that Campeau intended to sell off and the expected cash flows of the divisions that Campeau Corporation would operate. Presumably the initial price paid was set such that Campeau believed the net present value of these cash flows was greater than zero.

However, all of these cash flows were subject to risk. An understanding of their volatility and how they could be affected by the state of the economy would have—or should have—been important information in assessing the risk of the acquisition and the determination of the initial price.

The basic concepts and procedures of capital budgeting were discussed in the previous two chapters without any consideration of differential project riskiness. In this chapter, we add risk to capital budgeting analysis. The basic idea is that riskier projects must be expected to earn higher returns. Therefore, the discount rate used in the analysis of a project with an uncertain outcome must include a risk adjustment factor—the higher the risk, the higher the discount factor.

Risk in Financial Analysis

The **risk** of an asset is defined in terms of the likely variability of future returns from the asset. For example, if an investor buys $1 million of short-term government bonds expected to yield 7 percent, then the return on the investment, 7 percent, can be estimated quite precisely, and the investment is said to be risk free. If, however, the $1 million is invested in shares of a company just being organized to prospect for oil off the east coast of Canada, the investment's return cannot be estimated precisely. An analyst might review the possible outcomes and conclude that the rate of return *expected*, in a statistical sense, is 20 percent, but the investor should also recognize that the *actual* rate of return could range from, say, +1000 percent to −100 percent. Because there is a significant danger of earning an actual return considerably less than the expected return, the shares would be described as being relatively risky.

Risk, then, is related to the probability of earning a return less than the expected return—the greater the chance of low or negative returns, the riskier the investment. We can use statistical concepts to define risk more precisely.

Probability Distributions

Any investment decision—for that matter, almost *any* kind of business decision—requires that a forecast of future events be made. In capital budgeting decisions, the key forecast relates to the project's annual cash flows. Often, this forecast is made as a single figure, or *point estimate*, frequently called the "most likely" or "best" estimate. For example, one might forecast that the cash flows from a particular project will be $500 a year for 3 years.

How good is this point estimate? That is, how confident is the forecaster of the predicted return: very certain, very uncertain, or somewhere in between? This degree of uncertainty can be defined and measured in terms of the forecaster's **probability distribution**—the probability estimates associated with each possible outcome. In its simplest form, a probability distribution could consist of just a few potential outcomes. For example, in forecasting cash flows, we could make an optimistic estimate, a pessimistic estimate, and a most likely estimate; alternatively, we could make high, low, and "best guess" estimates. We might expect our high, or optimistic, estimate to be realized if the national economy booms, our pessimistic estimate to hold if the economy is depressed, and our best guess to occur if the economy runs at a normal level. Of course, the probabilities associated with each outcome must sum to one.

The traditional measure of risk applied to individual projects relates to the variability of outcomes and is stated in terms of probability distributions such as those presented in Figure 15-1. This illustration presents the probability distributions of Projects A and C in terms of rates of return. These returns are derived from the cash flows expected to prevail under alternative scenarios. A particular rate of return can be interpreted as the internal rate of return from the project based on the associated cash flow.[1] The tighter the probability distribution of expected future rates of return, the more likely the actual return is to be close to the expected return, and the smaller the risk of the

---

[1]For example, a project costs $1000 and has three possible cash flow outcomes: $210 per year for 3 years, $438 per year for 3 years, and $711 per year for 3 years. The internal rate of return, IRR, is obtained by solving the following equation for a specific sequence of cash flows:

$$\$1000 = \frac{CF_1}{1 + IRR} + \frac{CF_2}{(1 + IRR)^2} + \frac{CF_3}{(1 + IRR)^3}.$$

If the cash flow outcome is $210 per year, the internal rate of return is −20 percent. For annual cash flows of $438 or $711, the internal rate of return is 15 percent or 50 percent, respectively.

Figure 15-1
Graph of Two Probability Distributions

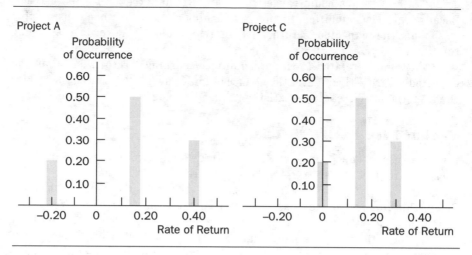

project. Accordingly, Project C is less risky than Project A; each of the possible returns for C is closer to its expected return than are the possible returns for A.

Consider the probability distribution of Project A as reformatted in Table 15-1. Here we observe that there is a 20 percent chance of a recession, and if this does occur, the project will yield a −20 percent rate of return (written as −0.20). There is a 50-percent chance of a normal period and a 30-percent probability of a boom during which the project will earn a high rate of return.

Expected Return

If we multiply each possible outcome by its probability of occurrence and then sum these products, as in Table 15-2, we have a *weighted average* of outcomes. The weights are the probabilities, and the weighted average is the **expected rate of return k̂**, called "k-hat." The expected rate of return of Project A is shown in Table 15-2 to be 0.185 or 18.5 percent.

The process followed in Table 15-2 can be set forth as an equation:

Table 15-1
Probability Distribution for Project A

State of the Economy	Probability of State Occurring	Rate of Return If State Occurs
Recession	0.20	−0.20
Normal	0.50	0.15
Boom	0.30	0.50
	1.00	

Table 15-2
Calculation of Expected Return: Project A

State of the Economy (1)	Probability of State Occurring (2)	Rate of Return (3)	Product (2) × (3) = (4)
Recession	0.20	−0.20	−0.04
Normal	0.50	0.15	0.075
Boom	0.30	0.50	0.15
		Expected return = $\hat{k}_A$ =	0.185

$$\text{Expected rate of return} = \hat{k}_A = \sum_{i=1}^{n} P_i k_i. \qquad (15\text{-}1)$$

Here k_i is the ith possible outcome, P_i is the probability of the ith outcome, and n is the number of possible outcomes. Thus $\hat{k}$ is a weighted average of the possible outcomes with each outcome's weight being equal to its probability of occurrence. Using the data in the table, we can calculate the expected rate of return for Project A as:

$$\hat{k} = P_1(k_1) + P_2(k_2) + P_3(k_3) \qquad (15\text{-}1a)$$

$$= 0.2(-0.20) + 0.5(0.15) + 0.3(0.50)$$

$$= -0.4 + 0.075 + 0.15 = 0.185 = 18.5\%.$$

Measuring Risk: The Standard Deviation

Risk is a difficult concept to grasp, and a great deal of controversy has surrounded attempts to define and measure it. However, a common definition—one that is satisfactory for many purposes—is stated in terms of probability distributions such as those presented in Figure 15-1: the tighter the probability distribution of expected future returns, the smaller the risk of a given investment. According to this definition, Project C is less risky than Project A since the chance that the actual return will end up far below the expected return is smaller for Project C than for Project A.

To be most useful, any measure of risk should have a definite value—we need a measure of the tightness of the probability distribution. One such measure is the **standard deviation**, the symbol for which is σ, called "sigma." The smaller the standard deviation, the tighter the probability distribution, and, accordingly, the lower the riskiness of the asset.[2] To calculate the

---

[2]Since we defined risk in terms of the chances of returns being less than expected, it would seem logical to measure risk in terms of the probability of returns below the expected return, rather than by the entire distribution. Measures of below-expected returns, which are known as *semivariance measures*, have been developed, but they are difficult to analyze. Additionally, if the distribution is reasonably symmetric, which is often the case for security returns, the standard deviation is as good a risk measure as the semivariance.

standard deviation, we proceed as shown in Table 15-3, taking the following steps:

1. We calculate the expected rate of return:

$$\text{Expected rate of return} = \hat{k} = \sum_{i=1}^{n} P_i k_i.$$

For Project A, we previously found $\hat{k} = 0.185$ or 18.5 percent.

2. In column 1 of Table 15-3, we subtract the expected rate of return, $\hat{k}$, from each possible outcome, k_i, to obtain a set of deviations about $\hat{k}$:

$$\text{Deviation}_i = k_i - \hat{k}.$$

3. Next we square each deviation (column 2) and multiply the result by the probability of occurrence for its related outcome (column 3). Then we sum these products to obtain the *variance* of the probability distribution:

$$\text{Variance} = \sigma^2 = \sum_{i=1}^{n} (k_i - \hat{k})^2 P_i. \tag{15-2}$$

4. Finally, we take the square root of the variance to obtain the standard deviation:

$$\text{Standard deviation} = \sigma = \sqrt{\sum_{i=1}^{n} (k_i - \hat{k})^2 P_i.} \tag{15-3}$$

Thus, the *standard deviation* is a probability-weighted average deviation from the expected value; it gives an idea of how far above or below the expected

---

Table 15-3
Calculating Project A's Standard Deviation

$k_i - \hat{k}$ (1)	$(k_i - \hat{k})^2$ (2)	$(k_i - \hat{k})^2 P_i$ (3)
$-0.20 - 0.185 = -0.385$	0.1482	$(0.1482)(0.2) = 0.0296$
$0.15 - 0.185 = -0.035$	0.0012	$(0.0012)(0.5) = 0.0006$
$0.50 - 0.185 = 0.315$	0.0992	$(0.0992)(0.3) = 0.0298$
		$\text{Variance} = \sigma^2 = 0.0600$

$$\text{Standard deviation} = \sigma = \sqrt{\sigma^2} = \sqrt{0.0600} = 0.2449 \text{ or } 24.49\%$$

value the actual value is likely to be. Project A's standard deviation is seen in Table 15-3 to be $\sigma = 0.2449$ or 24.49 percent.[3]

If we make the further assumption that the probability distribution is *continuous*, implying that a probability can be estimated for each possible outcome, then we can draw an unbroken curve through all the indicated rates of return. The distribution of returns for two projects, D and E, graphed in Figure 15-2, are examples of continuous probability distributions. The graph of Project D exhibits two features of a more favourable investment: (1) it has a higher expected return, and (2) its probability distribution is bunched closer together, indicating less dispersion and consequently less risk.

The Coefficient of Variation as a Measure of Risk

Certain problems can arise when the standard deviation is used as a measure of risk. To illustrate: consider Figure 15-3, which shows the probability distributions of annual net cash flows for Investments C and D. Investment C has an expected return of $1000 and a standard deviation of $300. Investment D also has a standard deviation of $300, but its expected return is $4000. The likely percentage deviation from the mean of Investment C is considerably higher than that for the mean of Investment D; put another way, C has more risk *per dollar of return* than D. On this basis, it is reasonable to assign a higher degree

---

[3]In the example, we described the procedure for finding the mean and standard deviation when the data are in the form of a known probability distribution. If the only data available are sample returns over some past period, the standard deviation of returns can be estimated using this formula:

$$\text{Estimated } \sigma = S = \sqrt{\frac{\sum_{t=1}^{n} (\bar{k}_t - \bar{k}_{Avg})^2}{n - 1}}. \tag{15-3a}$$

Here $\bar{k}_t$—"k bar t"—denotes the past realized rate of return in period t, and $\bar{k}_{Avg}$ is the average annual return earned during the last n years. Here is an example:

Year	$\bar{k}_t$
1990	15%
1991	−5
1992	20

$$\bar{k}_{Avg} = \frac{(15 - 5 + 20)}{3} = 10\%.$$

$$\text{Estimated } \sigma \text{ (or S)} = \sqrt{\frac{(15 - 10)^2 + (-5 - 10)^2 + (20 - 10)^2}{3 - 1}}$$

$$= \sqrt{\frac{350}{2}} = 13.2\%.$$

Figure 15-2
Graph of Continuous Probability Distributions

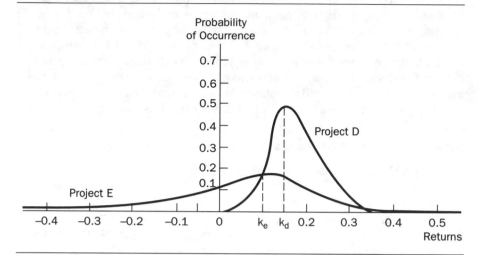

of risk to Investment C than to Investment D even though they have identical standard deviations.

The usual procedure for handling this problem is to divide the standard deviation (σ_J) by the mean, or expected value of the cash flows, ($\bar{CF}_J$), to obtain the **coefficient of variation** (CV_J) for project J:

$$CV_J = \frac{\sigma_J}{\bar{CF}_J} \qquad (15\text{-}3)$$

For Investment C, we divide the $300 standard deviation by the $1000 expected value, obtaining 0.300 as the coefficient of variation. Investment D's coefficient of variation is similarly calculated as 0.075. Since Investment D has a

Figure 15-3
Probability Distributions of Two Investments with Different Expected Returns

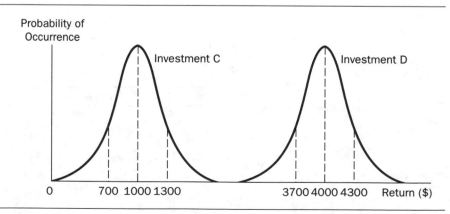

lower coefficient of variation, it has less risk per unit of expected return than does Investment C.

When assessing the risk for projects viewed in isolation, there may be instances in which it is preferable to use the coefficient of variation, rather than the standard deviation. In general, the coefficient of variation should be used when appraising returns stated in dollars, as there is a need to adjust the standard deviation by the size of the cash flow. When the probability distribution is based on rates of return, the use of the coefficient of variation is not necessary, since the rate of return is not in dollars and should be independent of the average size of the cash flows.

The Mean-Variance Criterion and Risk Aversion

In Figure 15-2, it appears that Project D is preferable to Project E because D has a higher expected return (mean) and a lower standard deviation (and hence variance) than does E. This illustrates the basis for a fundamental tenet of finance: the *mean-variance criterion*, which states that, holding risk constant, investors will prefer projects with a greater expected return (higher mean) to less expected return, and holding expected return constant, they will prefer less risk (less variance) to more risk. This preference by investors for less risk is called **risk aversion**. In the situation depicted in Figure 15-2, Project D is preferred to E since it provides both a lower variance and a higher mean. A preference for D over E would not arise if D had both a higher mean and higher variance than E.

The mean-variance criterion is based on the general notion that investors are, on average, averse to risk, so riskier securities require higher expected returns than less risky securities. However, we must extend our analysis of risk. As we shall see, there are times when an investment such as E can be logically regarded as being less risky than D.

Concept Review

▶ How do you calculate the standard deviation?
▶ Which is a better measure of risk: the standard deviation or the coefficient of variation? Explain your answer.
▶ Explain what is meant by the following statement: "Most investors are risk averse."
▶ What are the implications of risk aversion for security prices and rates of return?

Portfolio Risk and the Capital Asset Pricing Model

Thus far in the chapter, we have considered the riskiness of an asset or project in isolation. Now we analyze the riskiness of assets held in portfolios.[4] As we shall

[4] A *portfolio* is a collection of investment securities or a collection of investment projects. Using the security example, if you owned some BCE shares, some Magna shares, and some Abitibi shares, you would be holding a three-security portfolio. For reasons set forth in this section, the majority of all shares are held as parts of portfolios.

see, an asset held as part of a portfolio is generally less risky than the same asset held in isolation. This fact has been incorporated into a generalized framework for analyzing the relationship between risk and rates of return; this framework is called the **capital asset pricing model (CAPM)**. The CAPM framework is an extremely important analytical tool in both financial management and investment analysis. In the following pages, we discuss the elements of the CAPM.

Portfolio Risk and Return

Most financial assets are not held in isolation; rather, they are held as part of a *portfolio* (a combination of assets). Banks, pension funds, insurance companies, mutual funds, and other financial institutions are required by law to hold diversified portfolios. Even individual investors—at least those individuals whose security holdings constitute a significant part of their total wealth—generally hold portfolios, not just the shares of one firm. This being the case, the fact that a particular equity security goes up or down is not very important from an investor's standpoint; what is important is the return on the investor's portfolio and the portfolio's risk. Logically, then, the risk and return of an individual security should be analyzed in terms of *how the security affects the risk and return of the portfolio* in which it is held.

To illustrate the concepts of portfolio risk and return, we shall consider a portfolio made up of shares of Firms A and B. The pattern of returns for Firm B is indicated by Table 15-4. Firm A's only asset is Project A, whose returns distribution was presented in Table 15-1 above. Notice in column 2 of Table 15-4 that Firm B is assumed to have the same returns as Firm A, but their state pattern is exactly reversed; whereas A's highest returns occur during economic booms, B does best during recessions. (Firm A might be an auto manufacturer and B a recap tire producer, whose sales are strongest when many people cannot afford new cars or tires and have to settle for recaps.) We can see from Table 15-4 that the expected return for Firm B is 11.5 percent versus 18.5 percent for A, and B's variance of returns is 6 percent, the same as A's.

For our example, the shares of Firm B are combined with those of Firm A to form Portfolio AB. We assume that the shares of each firm are held in equal proportions in the portfolio.

Table 15-4
Calculation of Expected Return and
Standard Deviation of Firm B

State of the Economy	P_s	k_B	$P_s k_B$	$(k_B - \hat{k}_B)$	$(k_B - \hat{k}_B)^2$	$P_s(k_B - \hat{k}_B)^2$
Down	0.2	0.50	0.10	0.385	0.1482	0.0296
Average	0.5	0.15	0.075	0.035	0.0012	0.0006
Up	0.3	−0.20	−0.06	−0.315	0.0992	0.0298
	1.0		$\hat{k}_B =$ 0.115			$\sigma_B^2 =$ 0.0600
						$\sigma_B =$ 0.2449

Portfolio Returns. The *expected return on a portfolio*, $\hat{k}_p$, is simply the weighted average expected return on the individual equity securities in the portfolio, with the weights, w_J, being the fraction of the total portfolio invested in each security:

$$\hat{k}_p = w_1\hat{k}_1 + \ldots + w_n\hat{k}_n$$

$$= \sum_{J=1}^{n} w_J\hat{k}_J. \tag{15-5}$$

Note that the sum of the weights must equal unity.

Let us assume that in January 1994 a security analyst estimates that the expected return and standard deviation for the equity of Atlas Auto Parts (Firm A) and Bayview Recap Tires (Firm B) are as follows:

	Expected Return $\hat{k}$	Standard Deviation
Atlas (A)	0.185	0.2449
Bayview (B)	0.115	0.2449

If we form a \$100 000 portfolio, investing \$50 000 in shares of Firm A and \$50 000 in shares of Firm B, the expected return on the portfolio is 15 percent:

$$\hat{k}_p = w_A\hat{k}_A + w_B\hat{k}_B$$

$$= 0.5(0.185) + 0.5(0.115)$$

$$= 0.0925 + 0.0575 = 0.15 = 15\%.$$

Of course, after the fact and a year later, the actual *realized* rates of return on the individual securities—the k_J values—will almost certainly differ from their expected values so that the actual portfolio return k_p will be somewhat different from $\hat{k}_p = 15\%$.

If we put all of our money in the equity of Firm A, our one-security portfolio would have an expected return of 18.5 percent, while if we invested only in the equity of Firm B, we could expect a return of 11.5 percent. At this point, it looks as though we should invest only in A, but before reaching that conclusion, we must consider risk.

Portfolio Risk.   As we just saw, the expected return on a portfolio is simply a weighted average of the expected returns of the individual securities in that portfolio. However, unlike the return, the riskiness of a portfolio, σ_p, is generally *not* a weighted average of the standard deviations of the individual securities in it. Rather, the portfolio's risk is usually smaller than the weighted average of the securities' sigma. In fact, it may even be theoretically possible to combine two assets, such as the securities of Firms A and B, that are quite risky individually, and form a portfolio that is completely riskless, with $\sigma_p = 0$. Figure 15-4 graphs the rates of returns and the probability distributions of returns for Assets A and B and Portfolio AB. Although Assets A and B are both risky if held in isolation, when combined to form Portfolio AB, they are not risky at all.

Figure 15-4
Probability Distributions of Returns for Two Perfectly Negatively Correlated Assets (r = −1.0) and for Portfolio AB

Probability Distributions of Returns

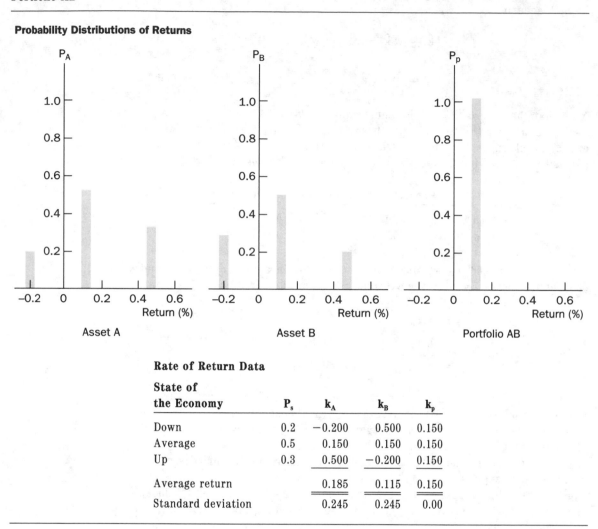

| Asset A | Asset B | Portfolio AB |

Rate of Return Data

State of the Economy	P_s	k_A	k_B	k_p
Down	0.2	−0.200	0.500	0.150
Average	0.5	0.150	0.150	0.150
Up	0.3	0.500	−0.200	0.150
Average return		0.185	0.115	0.150
Standard deviation		0.245	0.245	0.00

The reason Assets A and B can be combined to form a riskless portfolio is that their returns move *countercyclically* to one another—when A's returns fall, B's rise, and vice versa. In statistical terms, we say that the returns on Assets A and B are *perfectly negatively correlated*, with the **correlation coefficient** = r = −1.0. *Correlation* is defined as the tendency of two variables to move together.

The opposite of perfect negative correlation, with r = −1.0, is *perfect positive correlation*, with r = +1.0. Returns on two securities with perfect positive correlation would move up and down together, and a portfolio consisting of two such securities would be just as risky as the individual securities. This point is illustrated in Figure 15-5, a display of a portfolio of

Figure 15-5
Probability Distributions of Returns for Two Perfectly Positively Correlated Assets (r = +1.0) and for Portfolio AA′

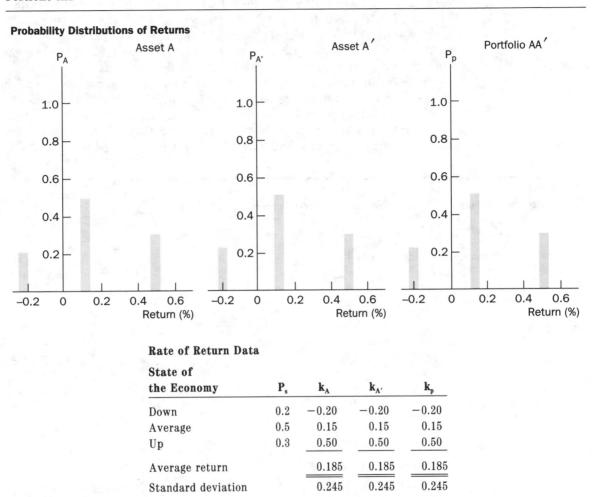

Probability Distributions of Returns

Rate of Return Data				
State of the Economy	P_s	k_A	$k_{A'}$	k_p
Down	0.2	−0.20	−0.20	−0.20
Average	0.5	0.15	0.15	0.15
Up	0.3	0.50	0.50	0.50
Average return		0.185	0.185	0.185
Standard deviation		0.245	0.245	0.245

Assets A and A′, which have identical probability distributions. We see that the portfolio's standard deviation is equal to that of the individual equity securities, indicating that diversification does nothing to reduce risk if the portfolio consists of perfectly positively correlated securities.

Figures 15-4 and 15-5 demonstrate (1) that when securities are perfectly negatively correlated (r = −1.0), all risk can be diversified away, but (2) that when they are perfectly positively correlated (r = +1.0), diversification does no good whatever in terms of reducing risk.

In reality, most common equity securities are positively correlated, but not perfectly so. On average, the correlation coefficient for the returns on two randomly selected equity securities is about +0.6, and for most pairs of equities, r lies in the range of +0.5 to +0.7. Under such conditions, combining equity securities into portfolios reduces risk but does not eliminate it completely. Figure 15-6 illustrates this point by combining Assets A and X, whose correlation coefficient is 0.57, into a portfolio. The probable returns for both assets are given in Figure 15-6. The portfolio's average return is 18.5 percent. The standard deviation of the portfolio, 16.1 percent, is less than the average standard deviation of the two equity securities, 19.0 percent. Thus, the portfolio's risk is less than the average of the risks of its individual elements—diversification has reduced but not eliminated risk.

In between these extremes of perfect positive and perfect negative correlation, combining two securities into a portfolio reduces but does not eliminate the riskiness inherent in the individual securities.

Another way of demonstrating the diversification effect of combining securities with different correlation coefficients is presented in Figure 15-7.

Figure 15-6

Probability Distributions of Returns for Two Positively Correlated Assets (r = +0.57) and for Portfolio AX

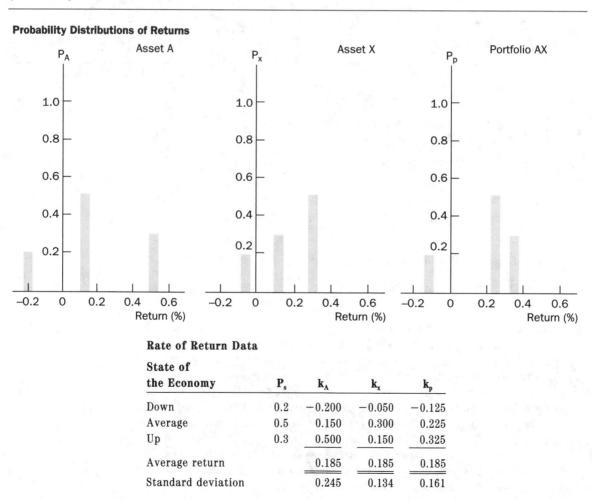

Probability Distributions of Returns

Rate of Return Data

State of the Economy	P_s	k_A	k_x	k_p
Down	0.2	−0.200	−0.050	−0.125
Average	0.5	0.150	0.300	0.225
Up	0.3	0.500	0.150	0.325
Average return		0.185	0.185	0.185
Standard deviation		0.245	0.134	0.161

Figure 15-7
Relationship of Expected Return and Risk on a Portfolio

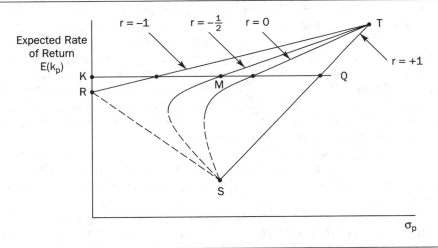

The expected rate of return on the portfolio, $E(k_p)$, is plotted on the vertical axis, and the standard deviation of portfolio return is plotted on the horizontal axis. A portfolio is constructed by investing a portion of the available funds into Asset S and the remainder in Asset T. Different portfolios are obtained from these two assets by altering the weights. When $r = +1$, there is a straight-line relationship between Assets S and T. As the correlation coefficient moves away from 1, the line joining S and T becomes more curved. At the extreme of $r = -1$, there is a set of proportions invested in Securities S and T whereby risk disappears entirely. This is shown as point R in Figure 15-7.

To demonstrate the importance of diversification, consider the expected portfolio return denoted by K. If $r = 1$, the risk-return point is Q. As the correlation moves away from $+1$, the same expected portfolio return is obtained (since the weights do not change) but the overall risk of the portfolio is reduced. In Figure 15-7, the measure of diversification is the difference between point Q and the portfolio standard deviation along line KQ for a given degree of correlation. For example, the diversification effect when $r = -1/2$ is equal to MQ.

What would happen if we included more than two securities in the portfolio? As a rule, *the riskiness of a portfolio is reduced as the number of securities in it increases.* If we added enough partially correlated securities, could we completely eliminate risk? In general, the answer is no, but the extent to which adding securities to a portfolio reduces its risk depends upon the degree of correlation among the securities. The smaller the correlation coefficient, the lower the remaining risk in a large portfolio. If we could find a set of securities whose correlation coefficients were zero or negative, all risk could be eliminated. In the typical case, in which the correlations among the individual securities are positive but less than $+1.0$, some but not all risk can be eliminated.

To test your understanding of the points made so far, consider the following questions. Would you expect to find higher correlations between the returns on two companies in the same or in different industries? For example, which correlation of returns would probably be higher: that of Shell Canada's and Petro-Canada's shares of common equity or that of BCE and either Shell or Petro-Canada? How would these correlations affect the risk of portfolios containing them? The answer is that the correlation coefficient of Shell and Petro-Canada is very high; it is much lower between either of them and BCE. The implication is that a two-security portfolio comprised of shares of firms in the same industry is riskier than a two-security portfolio in which the constituent components are from different industries. Thus to minimize risk, portfolios should be diversified across industries.

Figure 15-8 generalizes the two-asset case to a large number of assets, N, in a risk-return diagram. If we can assume that there are no assets with correlations equal to $+1$ or -1, the portfolio risk-return relationship is shown in Figure 15-8.

The hypothetical set of all possible portfolios—called the *attainable set*—is shown as the crosshatched area in Figure 15-8. Do all of these portfolios present portfolio opportunities from which an investor or firm would choose? To answer this question we need to introduce the concept of an efficient portfolio. An **efficient portfolio** is a portfolio that provides the highest possible expected return for any degree of risk or the lowest possible degree of risk for any expected return. In Figure 15-8, the boundary BCDE defines the efficient set of portfolios. Portfolios to the left of the efficient set are not possible, because they lie outside the attainable set—that is, there is no set of

Figure 15-8
N — Asset Portfolio Opportunities

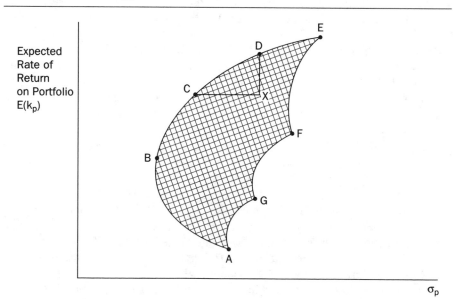

rate of return values that will yield a portfolio with an expected rate of return and risk represented by a point to the left of BCDE. Portfolios to the right of the efficient set are inefficient, because some other portfolio could provide either a higher return with the same degree of risk or a lower risk for the same rate of return. To illustrate: consider Portfolio (point) X. Portfolio C provides the same rate of return as Portfolio X, but C is less risky. At the same time, Portfolio D is as risky as Portfolio X, but D provides a higher expected rate of return. Points C and D (and other points on the boundary of the efficient set between C and D) are said to dominate point X.[5]

Company-Specific Risk versus Market Risk. As noted earlier, it is very difficult, if not impossible, to find securities whose expected returns are not positively correlated—most securities tend to do well when the national economy is strong and badly when it is weak.[6] According to data accumulated in recent years, σ_1, the standard deviation of a one-equity-security portfolio (or an average share) is approximately 28 percent. A portfolio consisting of all available equity securities, which is called *the market portfolio*, would have a standard deviation, σ_M, of about 15.1 percent. Thus, about half of the riskiness inherent in an average individual equity can be eliminated if the security is held in a reasonably well-diversified portfolio, one containing about 40 equity securities. Some risk always remains, however, so it is virtually impossible to diversify away the effects of broad declines in the equity market that affect almost all shares.

That part of the risk of a security that can be eliminated through diversification is called diversifiable, company-specific, or unsystematic risk. That part that cannot be eliminated is called nondiversifiable, market, or systematic risk. The name is not especially important, but the fact that a large part of the riskiness of any individual security can be eliminated is vitally important.

Company-specific risk is caused by such things as lawsuits, strikes, successful and unsuccessful marketing programs, winning or losing major contracts, and other events that are unique to a particular firm. Since these events are essentially random, their effects on a portfolio can be eliminated by diversification—bad events in one firm will be offset by good events in another. **Market risk**, on the other hand, stems from such things as war, inflation, recessions, and interest rate movements; these are factors which affect all firms simultaneously. Since all firms are affected in the same direction by these factors, this type of risk cannot be eliminated by diversification. An equity security's **total risk** is its company-specific risk plus its market risk.

We know that investors demand a premium for bearing risk; the higher the riskiness of a security, the higher the expected return required to induce

---

[5]Although the curve ABCDE presents the set of feasible portfolios, only the portion BCDE is the mean-variance efficient set of portfolios. The segment AB is inefficient, and an investor would not choose a portfolio from this segment. For example, for any portfolio on segment AB, an investor can get a higher expected rate of return for the same risk.

[6]It is not too hard to find a few securities that happened to rise because of a particular set of circumstances in the past while most other securities were declining. It is much harder to find securities that could logically be *expected* to go up in the future when other securities were falling.

investors to buy (or hold) it. But if investors are concerned primarily with *portfolio risk*, rather than the risk of the individual securities in the portfolio, how should the riskiness of the individual securities be measured? The answer, as provided by the capital asset pricing model (CAPM), is this: the relevant riskiness of an individual security is its contribution to the riskiness of a well-diversified portfolio. In other words, the riskiness of Moore Corp. to a doctor who has a portfolio of 40 securities, or to a trust officer managing a 150-security portfolio, is the contribution that Moore Corp. makes to the portfolio's riskiness. The security might be quite risky if held by itself, but if most of its risk can be eliminated by diversification, the security's **relevant risk**, which is its contribution to the portfolio's risk, may be small.

A simple example will help make this point clear. Suppose you can flip a coin once; if a head comes up, you win $20 000, but if it comes up tails, you lose $16 000. This is a good bet—the expected return is 0.5($20 000) + 0.5(−$16 000) = $2000. However, it is a highly risky proposition because you have a 50 percent chance of losing $16 000. Thus, you might well refuse to make the bet. Alternatively, suppose you are offered the chance to flip a coin 100 times, and you win $200 for each head but lose $160 for each tail. It is possible that you will flip all heads and win $20 000, and it is also possible that you will flip all tails and lose $16 000. But the chances are very high that you will actually flip about 50 heads and 50 tails, winning a net $2000. Although each individual flip is a risky bet, overall you have a low-risk proposition because you have diversified away most of the risk. This is the idea behind holding portfolios of equity securities rather than just one equity security, except that with equities all of the risk cannot be eliminated by diversification—those risks related to broad, systematic changes in the equity market will remain.

Are all securities equally risky in the sense that adding them to a well-diversified portfolio will have the same effect on the portfolio's riskiness? The answer is no. Different securities will affect the portfolio differently, so different securities have different degrees of relevant risk. How can the relevant risk of an individual security be measured? As we have seen, all risk except that related to broad market movements can, and presumably will, be diversified away. After all, why accept risk that can easily be eliminated? The risk that remains after diversifying is *market risk*, or risk that is inherent in the market, and it can be measured by the degree to which a given security tends to move up and down with the market. In the next section, we develop a measure of a security's market risk, and later we introduce an equation for determining the required rate of return on a security, given its market risk.

The Concept of Beta

The tendency of a security to move with the market is reflected in its **beta coefficient** β, which is a measure of the security's volatility relative to that of an average security. β is a key element of the CAPM.

An *average-risk equity security* is defined as a security that tends to move up and down in step with the general market as measured by some index such as the Toronto Stock Exchange 300 Index. Such a security will, by definition, have a beta of 1.0, which indicates that, in general, if the market moves up by 10 percent, the security will also move up by 10 percent, while if the market falls by 10 percent, the security will likewise fall by 10 percent. A portfolio of such $\beta = 1.0$ securities will move up and down with the broad market averages and will be just as risky as the averages. If $\beta = 0.5$, the security is only half as volatile as the market—it will rise or fall only half as much—and a portfolio of such securities is half as risky as a portfolio of $\beta = 1.0$ securities. On the other hand, if $\beta = 2.0$, the security is twice as volatile as an average security, so a portfolio of such securities will be twice as risky as an average portfolio.

Betas for many of the companies on the TSE and other exchanges are calculated and published by Value Line, ScotiaMcLeod, and many other organizations. The beta coefficients of some well-known companies are shown in Table 15-5. Most equity securities have betas in the range of 0.50 to 1.50, and the average beta for all equity securities is 1.0 by definition.[7]

The beta, hence the riskiness, of a *portfolio* is a *weighted average* of the betas of the securities of that portfolio:

$$\beta_p = w_1\beta_1 + w_2\beta_2 + \ldots + w_n\beta_n,$$
$$= \sum_{i=1}^{n} w_i\beta_i,$$

where β_p is the beta of the portfolio, w_i is the *i*th security's weight measured as the ratio of the amount invested in the security to the total amount invested in all securities in the portfolio, and β_i is the beta of security i. Therefore, if a higher-beta-than-average security ($\beta > 1.0$) is added to an average-risk ($\beta = 1.0$) portfolio, then the beta, and consequently the riskiness, of the portfolio will increase. Conversely, if a lower-beta-than-average security

Table 15-5
Illustrative List of Beta Coefficients

Inco Limited	1.50
Alcan Aluminum	1.45
Laidlaw Inc.	1.35
American Barrick Resources	1.20
Hees International Bancorp	1.05
Bank of Nova Scotia	1.00
Thomson Corp.	1.00
Gandalf Technologies	0.95
Shell Canada	0.95
Labatt(John)	0.85
Norcen Energy Resources	0.85
Provigo	0.70
British Columbia Tel	0.60
TransAlta Utilities	0.55

Source: Value Line Investment Survey, Canadian edition. © February 1992 Value Line Publishing, Inc.

---

[7]The betas we have been discussing are called *historic*, or *ex post* betas because they are based strictly on historic, or past, data. Another type of beta, the *fundamental beta*, which is based partly on past actions and partly on expected future conditions, can also be calculated.

($\beta < 1.0$) is added to an average-risk portfolio, the portfolio's beta and risk will decline. Thus, since a security's beta measures its contribution to the riskiness of the market portfolio, beta is the appropriate measure of the security's riskiness.

The preceding analysis of risk in a portfolio setting is called the capital asset pricing model. We can summarize our discussion to this point as follows:

1. A security's risk consists of two components, market risk and company-specific risk.
2. Company-specific risk can be eliminated by diversification, and most investors do indeed diversify directly, by purchasing shares in a mutual fund, or by investing for retirement in a pension fund. We are left, then, with market risk, which is caused by general movements in the stock market and which reflects the fact that all securities are systematically affected by certain overall economic events such as war, recessions, and inflation. Market risk is the only risk relevant to a rational, diversified investor because he or she should have already eliminated company-specific risk.
3. Investors expect to be compensated for bearing risk—the greater the riskiness of a security, the higher its required return. However, compensation is required only for risk that cannot be eliminated by diversification. If risk premiums existed for diversifiable risk, then well-diversified investors would buy these securities and bid up their prices, and their final (equilibrium) expected returns would reflect only nondiversifiable market risk.
4. The market risk of a security is measured by its beta coefficient, which is an index of the security's relative volatility. Some benchmark betas follow:

    $\beta = 0.5$: security is only half as volatile, or risky, as the average security.

    $\beta = 1.0$: security is of average risk.

    $\beta = 2.0$: security is twice as risky as the average security.

5. Since a security's beta coefficient determines how the security affects the riskiness of a diversified portfolio, beta is the most relevant measure of a security's risk.

We must stress that betas are supposed to reflect investors' expectations regarding future volatility, and we have no way of measuring exactly what those expectations are. Therefore, it is impossible to obtain precise estimates of true betas, even though *approximation betas*, based on past volatility, can be calculated.

Concept Review

▶ Explain the following statement: "A security held as part of a portfolio is generally less risky than the same security held in isolation."
▶ What is meant by *perfect positive correlation* and *perfect negative correlation?*

(continued)

(continued)
▸ In general, can the riskiness of a portfolio be reduced to zero by increasing the number of different securities in the portfolio? Explain.
▸ What is an *average-risk equity security*?
▸ Why is beta the theoretically correct measure of a security's riskiness?

The Security Market Line: The Relationship between Risk and Expected Rates of Return

In the preceding section we saw that under the CAPM theory, beta is the appropriate measure of a security's relevant risk. Now we must specify the relationship between risk and expected return. For a given level of beta, what expected rate of return will investors require on a security in order to compensate them for taking on the risk? Under the capital asset pricing model (CAPM) theory, the **security market line (SML)** expresses the required return on an investment as a risk-free rate plus a risk adjustment factor that investors require as compensation for bearing risk. This risk adjustment factor for a given security is obtained by multiplying the market risk premium required by the riskiness of the individual investment as measured by its beta. In equation form, the SML is expressed as follows:

$$k_i = k_{RF} + (k_M - k_{RF})\beta_i. \qquad (15\text{-}6)$$

Here

k_i = required rate of return on the ith security[8]

k_{RF} = risk-free rate of return. In this context, k_{RF} is generally measured by the rate of return on Government of Canada bonds. Depending on the use to be made of the estimated cost or equity, the security can be either short term or long term. For most applications in this section, the long-term bond rate is used.

β_i = beta coefficient of the ith equity security. The beta of an average equity security is $\beta_A = 1.0$.

k_M = required rate of return on a portfolio consisting of all equities, which is the market portfolio. k_M is also the required rate of return on an average ($\beta_A = 1.0$) equity security.

RP_M = ($k_M - k_{RF}$) = market risk premium. This is the additional return over the risk-free rate required to compensate an investor for assuming an average amount of risk. Average risk means $\beta_A = 1.0$.

[8]There is a distinction made between *expected* and *required* rates of return. The former reflects what the investor expects to earn on the security, while the latter is what the investor requires given the level of risk of the security or project. If the expected rate of return is less than the required level, the investor will not purchase the security, and if he or she already owned it, it would be sold. This will put pressure on the price of the security, and it will fall until the resulting expected rate of return is equal to the required return. In equilibrium, the two returns have to be identical. Here we can use the terms interchangeably since we assume equilibrium in the equity market.

$RP_i = (k_M - k_{RF})\beta_i$ = risk premium on the ith security. The security's risk premium is less than, equal to, or greater than the premium on an average security, depending on whether the security's beta is less than, equal to, or greater than 1.0. If $\beta_i = \beta_A = 1.0$, then $RP_i = RP_M$.

The **market risk premium, RP_M**, depends on the degree of aversion that investors in the aggregate have to risk.[9] Let us assume that at the current time, long-term Government of Canada bonds yield k_{RF} = 9 percent and an average share of common equity has a required return of k_M = 13 percent. Therefore, the market risk premium is 4 percent:

$$RP_M = k_M - k_{RF} = 13\% - 9\% = 4\%.$$

It follows that if one security is twice as risky as another, its risk premium is twice as high; conversely, if its risk is only half as much, its risk premium is half as large. Further, we can measure a security's relative riskiness by its beta coefficient. Therefore, if we know the market risk premium, RP_M, and the security's risk as measured by its beta coefficient, β_I, we can find its risk premium as the product, $(RP_M)\beta_I$. For example, if $\beta_I = 0.5$ and $RP_M = 4\%$, then RP_I is

$$
\begin{aligned}
\text{Risk premium for Security I} = RP_I &= (RP_M)\beta_I \qquad\qquad \textbf{(15-7)}\\
&= (4\%)(0.5)\\
&= 2.0\%.
\end{aligned}
$$

To summarize, given estimates of k_{RF}, k_M, and β_I, we can use the security market line (SML), equation 15-6, to find the required rate of return on Security I.

$$
\begin{aligned}
\text{SML equation: } k_i &= k_{RF} + (k_M - k_{RF})\beta_I\\
&= k_{RF} + (RP_M)\beta_I\\
&= 9\% + (13\% - 9\%)\,(0.5)\\
&= 9\% + 4\%(0.5)\\
&= 11\%
\end{aligned}
$$

If another security, J, is riskier than Security I and has $\beta_J = 2.0$, then its required rate of return is 17 percent:

$$k_J = 9\% + (4\%)2.0 = 17\%.$$

An average security, with $\beta = 1.0$, has a required return of 13 percent, the same as the market return:

---

[9]It should be noted that the risk premium of an average security, $k_M - k_{RF}$, cannot be measured with great precision because it is impossible to obtain precise values for k_M. However, empirical studies suggest that where long-term Government of Canada bonds are used to measure k_{RF} and where k_M is the actual return on the TSE 300 Index, the market risk premium varies from year to year, and it has generally ranged from 4 to 8 percent during the last 20 years.

The assumptions embodied in the CAPM framework are discussed in Eugene F. Brigham and Louis C. Gapenski, *Intermediate Financial Management*, 3d ed. (Chicago: The Dryden Press, 1990), chap. 2. Some of the assumptions of the CAPM theory are unrealistic, and, because of this, the theory does not hold exactly.

$$k_A = 9\% + (4\%)1.0 = 13\% = k_M.$$

The SML equation is often expressed in graph form, as in Figure 15-9, which shows the SML when k_{RF} = 9 percent and k_M = 13 percent. Note the following points:

1. Required rates of return are shown on the vertical axis, while risk as measured by β is shown on the horizontal axis.
2. Riskless securities have $\beta_i = 0$; therefore, k_{RF} appears as the vertical axis intercept in Figure 15-9.
3. The slope of the SML reflects the degree of risk aversion in the economy; the greater the average investor's aversion to risk, (a) the steeper the slope of the line, (b) the greater the risk premium for any security, and (c) the higher the required rate of return on securities.[10] These points are discussed further in a later section.

Figure 15-9
The Security Market Line (SML)

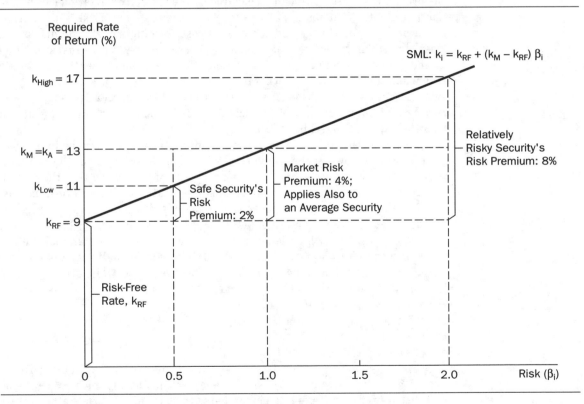

---

[10]Students sometimes confuse beta with the slope of the SML. This is a mistake. The slope of any line is equal to the "rise" divided by the "run," or $(Y_1 - Y_0)/(X_1 - X_0)$. Consider Figure 15-9. If we let Y = k and X = β, and we go from the origin to β = 1.0, we see that the slope is $(k_M - k_{RF})/(\beta_M - \beta_{RF}) = (13 - 9)/(1 - 0) = 4$. Thus, the slope of the SML is equal to $(k_M - k_{RF})$, the market risk premium. In Figure 15-9, $k_i = 9\% + 4\beta_i$, so a doubling of β (for example, from 1.0 to 2.0) would produce an increase of 4 percentage points in k_i.

4. The values we worked out for securities with $\beta_i = 0.5$, $\beta_i = 1.0$, and $\beta_i = 2.0$ agree with the values shown on the graph for k_{low}, k_A, and k_{high}.

Both the SML and a company's position on it change over time because of changes in interest rates, in investors' risk aversion, and in individual companies' betas. Such changes are discussed in the appendix to this chapter. Since all three elements in Equation 15-6 are subject to change, it is obvious that the required rate of return on a specific investment can also change over time.

Concept Review

▶ How do changes in risk affect required returns?

Risk Assessment

In the preceding sections, we have identified measures of risk relating either to the probability distribution and measured by the standard deviation (or, where appropriate, the coefficient of variation) or to the systematic risk of a security, based on portfolio theory and the capital asset pricing model. The discussion was primarily in the context of investment in securities with the investor being an individual or a mutual or pension fund. However, the concepts are equally true when the investor is a corporation and the investment is a capital project. In this section and the next, we discuss procedures for (1) measuring the riskiness of potential capital projects and (2) incorporating this information into the capital budgeting decision.

Three separate and distinct types of capital project risk can be identified: (1) the project's own **stand-alone risk**, which is its risk disregarding the facts that it is but one asset within the firm's portfolio of assets and that the firm in question is but one security in most investors' portfolios; (2) **within-firm risk**, which is the effect a project has on the company's risk without taking account of the effects of the shareholders' own personal diversification; and (3) *market*, or *beta*, *risk*, which is project risk assessed from the standpoint of an investor who holds a highly diversified portfolio. As we shall see, a particular project may have high stand-alone risk, yet because of portfolio effects, taking it on may not have much effect on either the firm's risk or that of its owners.

A project's stand-alone risk is measured by the variability of the project's expected returns; its within-firm risk is measured by the project's impact on the firm's earnings variability; and its market risk is measured by the project's effect on the firm's beta coefficient. Taking on a project with a high degree of either stand-alone or within-firm risk will not necessarily affect the firm's beta to any great extent. However, if the project has highly uncertain returns and if those returns are highly correlated with those of the firm's other assets and also with most other assets in the economy, the project will have a high degree of all types of risk. For example, suppose General Motors decides to undertake a major expansion to build solar-powered autos. GM is not sure how its technology will work on a mass production basis, so there are great risks in the venture—its stand-alone risk is high. Management also estimates that the project will have a higher probability of success if the economy is strong, for then people will have more money to spend on the new autos. This means that the project will tend to do well if GM's other divisions also do well and to do badly if other divisions do badly. This being the case, the project will also have high within-firm risk. Finally, since GM's prospects are highly correlated with those of most other firms, the project's beta coefficient will also be high. Thus, this project will be risky under all three definitions of risk.

Market risk is important because of its direct effect on a firm's share price: beta affects k, and k affects the share price. Within-firm risk, often called *corporate risk*, is important for three primary reasons:

1. Undiversified shareholders, including the owners of small businesses, are more concerned about corporate risk than about market risk.
2. Empirical studies of the determinants of required rates of return generally find that both market and corporate risk affect share prices. This suggests that investors, even those who are well diversified, consider factors other than market risk when they establish required returns.
3. The firm's stability is important to its managers, workers, customers, suppliers, and creditors, as well as to the community in which it operates. Firms that are in serious danger of bankruptcy, or even of suffering low profits and reduced output, have difficulty attracting and retaining good managers and workers. Also, both suppliers and customers are reluctant to depend on weak firms, and such firms have difficulty borrowing money at reasonable interest rates. These factors tend to reduce risky firms' profitability and hence share price, and thus, they also make corporate risk significant.

For these three reasons, corporate risk is important even if a firm's shareholders are well diversified.

Concept Review

▶ Describe the three types of project risk.
▶ How is a project's stand-alone risk measured?
▶ How is within-firm risk measured?
▶ How is market risk measured?
▶ List three reasons why corporate risk is important.

Techniques for Measuring Stand-Alone Risk

What about a project's stand-alone risk—is it of any importance to anyone? In theory, this type of risk should be of little or no concern. However, it is of great importance, for the following reasons:

1. It is much easier to estimate a project's stand-alone risk than its within-firm risk, and it is far easier to measure stand-alone risk than market risk.
2. In the vast majority of cases, all three types of risk are highly correlated—if the general economy does well, so will the firm, and if the

firm does well, so will most of its projects. Thus, stand-alone risk is generally a good proxy for hard-to-measure market risk.

3. Because of points 1 and 2, if management wants a reasonably accurate assessment of a project's riskiness, it ought to spend considerable effort on ascertaining the riskiness of the project's own cash flows—that is, its stand-alone risk.

The starting point for analyzing a project's stand-alone risk involves determining the uncertainty inherent in the project's cash flows. This analysis can be handled in a number of ways, ranging from informal judgements to complex economic and statistical analyses involving large-scale computer models. To illustrate what is involved, consider a project many of whose individual cash flows are subject to uncertainty. For example, sales for each year are projected at 20 000 units to be sold at a net price of $2000 per unit, or $40 million in total. Actual unit sales will almost certainly be somewhat higher or lower than 20 000, however, and the sales price will probably turn out to differ from the projected price. In effect, the sales quantity and the sales price estimates are expected values taken from probability distributions. The distributions could be relatively tight, reflecting small standard deviations and low risk, or they could be flat, reflecting a great deal of uncertainty about the final value of the variable in question and hence a high degree of stand-alone risk.

The nature of the individual cash flow distributions and their correlations with one another determines the nature of the NPV distribution and, thus, the project's stand-alone risk. Below we discuss three techniques for assessing a project's stand-alone risk: sensitivity analysis, scenario analysis, and Monte Carlo simulation.

Sensitivity Analysis.   Intuitively, we know that many of the variables that determine a project's estimated cash flows are based on some type of probability distribution, rather than being known with certainty. We also know that if a key input variable, such as units sold, changes, the project's NPV also will change. **Sensitivity analysis** is a technique that indicates exactly how much the NPV will change in response to a given change in an input variable, other things held constant.

Sensitivity analysis begins with a *base case* situation, which is developed using the *expected* values for each input. For example, relying on the base case assumptions, the NPV for the project is $7.0 million. Now the analyst asks a series of "what if" questions: "What if unit sales fall 20 percent below the most likely level?" "What if the sales price per unit falls?" "What if variable costs are 65 percent of dollar sales rather than the expected 60 percent?" Sensitivity analysis is designed to provide the decision-maker with answers to questions such as these.

In a sensitivity analysis, each variable is changed by several specific percentage points above and below the expected value, holding other things constant; then a new NPV is calculated for each of these values; and, finally, the set of NPVs is plotted against the variable that was changed. Figure 15-10 shows our project's sensitivity graphs for three of the key input variables. The table below the graphs gives the NPVs that were used to construct the graphs. The slopes of the lines in the graphs show how sensitive NPV is to changes in

Figure 15-10
Sensitivity Analysis (thousands of dollars)

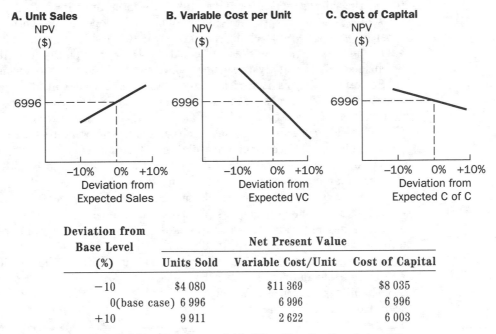

Deviation from Base Level (%)	Net Present Value		
	Units Sold	**Variable Cost/Unit**	**Cost of Capital**
−10	$4 080	$11 369	$8 035
0(base case)	6 996	6 996	6 996
+10	9 911	2 622	6 003

Note: This analysis performed using *Lotus 1-2-3*, so the values are slightly different from than those that would be obtained using interest factor tables because of rounding differences.

each of the inputs: the steeper the slope, the more sensitive the NPV is to a change in the variable. The figure makes it clear that the project's NPV is very sensitive to changes in variable costs, fairly sensitive to changes in unit sales, and not very sensitive to changes in the cost of capital.

If we were comparing two projects, the one with the steeper sensitivity lines would be regarded as riskier because for that project a relatively small error in estimating a variable such as the variable cost per unit would produce a large error in the project's expected NPV. Thus, sensitivity analysis can provide useful insights into the riskiness of a project.

Before we move on, three additional points about sensitivity analysis warrant attention. First, spreadsheet computer models are ideally suited for performing sensitivity analysis. We used a *Lotus 1-2-3* model to conduct the analyses represented in Figure 15-10; it generated the NPVs and then drew the graphs. Second, we could have plotted all of the sensitivity lines on one graph; this would have facilitated direct comparisons of the sensitivities among different input variables. Third, it is easy to vary more than one variable at a time, and thus to do *multivariable sensitivity analysis*, although one cannot easily construct graphs to illustrate each variable's effect.

Scenario Analysis.   Although sensitivity analysis is probably the most widely used risk analysis technique, it does have limitations. Consider, for example, a proposed coal mine project whose NPV is highly sensitive to changes in output, in variable costs, and in sales price. However, if a utility company has contracted to buy a fixed amount of coal at an inflation-adjusted price per tonne, the mining venture may be quite safe in spite of its steep sensitivity lines. In general, a project's stand-alone risk depends on both (1) the sensitivity of its NPV to changes in key variables and (2) the range in likely values of these variables as reflected in their probability distributions. Because sensitivity analysis considers only the first factor, it is incomplete.

Scenario analysis is a risk analysis technique that considers both the sensitivity of NPV to changes in key variables and the range of likely variable values. In a scenario analysis, the financial analyst asks operating managers to pick a "bad" or "worst case" set of circumstances (low unit sales, low sales price, high variable cost per unit, high construction cost, and so on) and a "good" or "best case" set. The NPVs under the bad and good conditions are then calculated and compared to the expected, or base case, NPV.

In our example, the company's managers are fairly confident of their estimates of all the project's cash flow variables except price and unit sales. Further, they regard a drop in sales below 15 000 units or a rise above 25 000 units as being extremely unlikely. Similarly, they expect the sales price as set in the marketplace to fall within the range of $1500 to $2500. Thus, 15 000 units at a price $1500 defines the lower bound, or the *worst case scenario*, whereas 25 000 units at a price of $2500 defines the upper bound, or the *best case scenario*. Remember that the base case values are 20 000 units and a price of $2000.

To carry out the scenario analysis, we use the variable values of the worst case to obtain the worst case NPV and the variable values of the best case to obtain the best case NPV.[11] We actually performed the analysis using a *Lotus* model; and Table 15-6 summarizes the results of this analysis. We see that the base case forecasts a positive NPV; the worst case produces a negative NPV; and the best case results in a very large positive NPV.

Table 15-6
Scenario Analysis

Scenario	Probability of Outcome (P_i)	Sales Volume (units)	Sales Price	NPV (thousands of dollars)
Worst case	0.25	15 000	$1500	($ 5761)
Base case	0.50	20 000	2000	6996
Best case	0.25	25 000	2500	23397
			Expected NPV =	$ 7907
			σ_{NPV} =	$10349
			CV_{NPV} =	1.3

[11]We could also have included worst and best case values for fixed and variable costs, income tax rates, salvage values, and so on. For illustrative purposes, we limited the changes to only two variables. Also, note that we are treating sales price and quantity as independent variables; that is, a low sales price could occur when unit sales were low, and a high sales price could be coupled with high unit sales, or vice versa. As we discuss in the next section, it is relatively easy to vary these assumptions if the facts of the situation suggest a different set of conditions.

We can use the results of the scenario analysis to determine the expected NPV, the standard deviation of NPV, and the coefficient of variation. To begin, we need an estimate of the probabilities of occurrence of the three scenarios, the P_i values. Suppose management estimates that there is a 25 percent probability of the worst case scenario occurring, a 50 percent probability of the base case, and a 25 percent probability of the best case. (Of course, it is *very* difficult to estimate scenario probabilities accurately.)

With the probabilities and the scenario NPVs, we have a discrete probability distribution of returns measured in dollars instead of in percentages (rates of return). The expected NPV (in thousands of dollars) is $7907.[12]

$$
\begin{aligned}
\text{Expected NPV} &= \sum_{i=1}^{n} P_i(\text{NPV}_i) \\
&= 0.25(-\$5761) + 0.50(\$6996) + 0.25(\$23\,397) \\
&= \$7907.
\end{aligned}
$$

The standard deviation of the NPV is $10 349 (in thousands of dollars):

$$
\begin{aligned}
\sigma_{\text{NPV}} &= \sqrt{\sum_{i=1}^{n} P_i(\text{NPV}_i - \text{Expected NPV})^2} \\
&= \sqrt{\begin{array}{l} 0.25(-\$5761 - \$7907)^2 + 0.50(\$6996 - \$7907)^2 \\ + 0.25(\$23\,397 - \$7907)^2 \end{array}} \\
&= \$10\,349.
\end{aligned}
$$

Finally, the project's coefficient of variation is 1.3:

$$
\text{CV}_{\text{NPV}} = \frac{\sigma_{\text{NPV}}}{E(\text{NPV})} = \frac{\$10\,349}{\$7907} = 1.3.
$$

Now that coefficient of variation can be compared with the coefficient of variation of the company's "average" project to get an idea of the relative riskiness of the specific project under consideration. The company's existing projects, on average, have a coefficient of variation of about 1.0, so, on the basis of this stand-alone risk measure, the managers would conclude that the project is 30 percent riskier than the firm's "average" project.

Scenario analysis provides useful information about a project's stand-alone risk. However, it is limited in that it only considers a few discrete outcomes (NPVs) for the project, although there really are an infinite number of

---

[12]Note that the expected NPV is *not* the same as the base case NPV, $6996 (in thousands). This is because the two uncertain variables, sales volume and sales price, are multiplied together to obtain dollar sales, and this process causes the NPV distribution to be skewed to the right. A big number times another big number produces a very big number, which in turn causes the average, or expected value, to be increased.

possibilities. In the next section, we describe a more rigorous method of assessing a project's stand-alone risk.

Monte Carlo Simulation.   Another analytical technique is **Monte Carlo simulation**, so named because it grew out of work on the mathematics of casino gambling.[13] It ties together sensitivities and input variable probability distributions. However, simulation requires a relatively powerful computer coupled with an efficient financial planning software package, whereas scenario analysis can be done using a PC with a spreadsheet program or even using a calculator.

The first step in a computer simulation is to specify the probability distribution of each uncertain cash flow variable. Once this has been done, the simulation proceeds as follows:

1. The computer chooses at random a value for each uncertain variable based on the variable's specified probability distribution. For example, a value for unit sales is chosen and used in the first model run.
2. The value selected for each uncertain variable, along with values for fixed factors such as the tax rate and depreciation charges, are then used in the model to determine the net cash flows for each year; these cash flows are then used to determine the project's NPV in the first run.
3. Steps 1 and 2 are repeated many times, say 500, resulting in 500 NPVs, which make up a probability distribution.

Using this procedure, we performed a simulation analysis on our project. As in the scenario analysis, we simplified the illustration by specifying a probability distribution for only one key variable: unit sales. For all of the other variables, we simply used their expected values. The resulting NPV distribution is graphed in Figure 15-11.

The primary advantage of simulation is that it shows the range of possible outcomes along with their attached probabilities, rather than merely a point estimate of the NPV. From Figure 15-11, we can see that our project's expected NPV is $7.3 million and that the standard deviation of the NPV is $10.2 million. Thus, the coefficient of variation is $10.2 million/$7.3 million = 1.40. These figures differ slightly from those developed in the scenario analysis because we used different assumptions in the two analyses. Simulation software packages can be used to estimate the probability of NPV > 0, or IRR > 0, and so on. This additional information can be quite helpful in assessing the riskiness of a project.

Limitations of Scenario and Simulation Analysis.   In spite of its obvious appeal, Monte Carlo simulation has not been widely used in industry. One of the major problems is specifying the correlations among the uncertain cash flow variables. Mechanically, it is easy to incorporate any type of correlation among variables into a simulation analysis; for example *@RISK*, a simulation software program, permits one to specify both intervariable and intertemporal correlations. However, it is not easy to specify what the correlations should be. Indeed,

---

[13]The use of simulation analysis in capital budgeting was first reported by David B. Hertz, "Risk Analysis in Capital Investments," *Harvard Business Review*, January–February 1964: 95–106.

Figure 15-11
NPV Probability Distribution (millions of dollars)

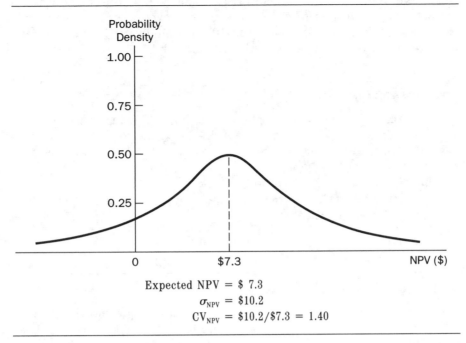

Expected NPV = $ 7.3
σ_{NPV} = $10.2
CV_{NPV} = $10.2/$7.3 = 1.40

people who have tried to obtain such relationships from the operating managers who must estimate them have eloquently emphasized the difficulties involved. Clearly, the problem is not insurmountable, as simulation is used in business. Still, it is important not to underestimate the difficulty of obtaining valid estimates of probability distributions and correlations among the variables.[14]

Another problem with both scenario and simulation analyses is that even when the analysis has been completed, no clear-cut decision rule emerges. One ends up with an expected NPV and a distribution about this expected value, which can be used to judge the project's stand-alone risk. However, the analysis provides no mechanism to indicate whether a project's profitability as measured by the expected NPV is sufficient to compensate for its risk as measured by σ_{NPV} or CV_{NPV}.

Finally, scenario and simulation analyses ignore the effects of diversification, both among projects within the firm and by investors in their personal investment portfolios. Thus, an individual project may have highly uncertain returns when evaluated on a stand-alone basis, but if those returns are not correlated with the returns on the firm's other assets, the project may not be very risky in terms of either within-firm or market risk. Indeed, if the project's

---

[14]For more insight into the difficulties involved in estimating probability distributions and correlations in practice, see K. Larry Hastie, "One Businessman's View of Capital Budgeting," *Financial Management*, Winter 1974: 36–43. Hastie was treasurer of Bendix Corporation.

returns are negatively correlated with the returns on the firm's other assets, it actually may decrease the firm's corporate risk, and the larger its σ_{NPV}, the more it will reduce the firm's overall risk. Similarly, if a project's returns are not positively correlated with the stock market, even a project with highly variable returns may not be regarded as risky by well-diversified shareholders, who are normally more concerned with market risk than with total risk.

Concept Review

▶ List three reasons why, in practice, a project's stand-alone risk is important.

▶ Differentiate between sensitivity and scenario analyses. Why might scenario analysis be preferable to sensitivity analysis?

▶ Briefly explain Monte Carlo simulation.

▶ Identify some problems with sensitivity analysis, scenario analysis, and Monte Carlo simulation.

Beta (or Market) Risk

The types of risk analysis discussed thus far in the chapter provide insights into projects' risks and thus help managers make better accept-reject decisions. However, these risk measures do not take account of portfolio risk, and they are subjective rather than objective in that they do not specify whether a project should be accepted or rejected. In this section, we show how the CAPM can be used to help overcome those shortcomings. Of course, the CAPM has shortcomings of its own, but it nevertheless offers useful insights into risk analysis in capital budgeting.

As an example, consider the case of G.L. Steel Company, an integrated steel producer operating in the Great Lakes region. G.L. Steel's beta = β = 1.1; k_{RF} = 8%; and k_M = 12%. Thus, based on the SML equation, G.L.'s cost of equity is 12.4 percent:

$$\begin{aligned} k_s &= 8\% + (12\% - 8\%)1.1 \\ &= 8\% + (4\%)1.1 \\ &= 12.4\%. \end{aligned}$$

This suggests that investors should be willing to give G.L. money to invest in average-risk projects if the company can earn 12.4 percent or more on this money. (Here again, by *average risk* we mean projects having risk similar to the firm's existing assets.) Therefore, as a first approximation, G.L. should invest in capital projects if and only if these projects have an expected return of 12.4 percent or more.[15] In other words, G.L. should use 12.4 percent as its

---

[15]To simplify things somewhat, we assume at this point that the firm uses only equity capital. If debt is used, the cost of capital used must be a weighted average of the costs of debt and equity. This point is discussed at length in Chapter 17.

discount rate to determine the NPVs of any average-risk project that it is considering.

Suppose, however, that taking on a particular project would cause a change in G.L.'s beta coefficient and hence change the company's cost of equity. For example, suppose the firm is considering the construction of a fleet of barges to haul iron ore, and barge operations have betas of 1.5 rather than 1.1. Since the firm itself can be regarded as a *portfolio of assets* and since the beta of any portfolio is a weighted average of the betas of its individual assets, taking on the barge project would cause G.L.'s overall corporate beta to rise to somewhere between its original beta of 1.1 and the barge project's beta of 1.5. The exact value of the new beta would depend on the relative size of the investment in barge operations versus G.L.'s other assets. If 80 percent of G.L.'s total funds ended up in basic steel operations with a beta of 1.1 and 20 percent in barge operations with a beta of 1.5, the new corporate beta would be 1.18:

$$\text{New beta} = 0.8(1.1) + 0.2(1.5)$$
$$= 1.18.$$

This increase in G.L.'s beta coefficient would cause its share price to decline unless the increased beta were offset by a higher expected rate of return. Specifically, taking on the new project would cause the overall corporate cost of capital to rise from the original 12.4 percent to 12.72 percent:

$$k_s = 8\% + (4\%)1.18$$
$$= 12.72\%.$$

Therefore, to keep the barge investment from lowering the value of the firm, G.L.'s overall expected rate of return must also rise from 12.4 to 12.72 percent.

If investments in basic steel must earn 12.4 percent, how much must the barge investment earn for the new overall rate of return to equal 12.72 percent? We know that if G.L. undertakes the barge investment, it will have 80 percent of its assets invested in basic steel projects earning 12.4 percent and 20 percent in barge operations earning X percent, and the average required rate of return will be 12.72 percent. Therefore,

$$0.80(12.40\%) + 0.20X = 12.72\%$$
$$0.2X = 2.8\%$$
$$X = 14.0\%.$$

Thus, we see that the barge project must have an expected return of at least 14 percent if the corporation is to earn its new cost of capital.

In summary, if G.L. takes on the barge project, its corporate beta will rise from 1.1 to 1.18; its overall required rate of return will rise from 12.4 to 12.72 percent; and the barge investment will have to earn 14 percent if the company is to earn its new overall cost of capital.

This line of reasoning leads to the conclusion that if the beta coefficient for each project, β_j, can be determined, then an individual project's cost of capital, k_j, can be found as follows:

$$k_j = k_{RF} + (k_M - k_{RF})\beta_j.$$

Thus, for basic steel projects with $\beta = 1.1$, G.L. should use 12.4 percent as the discount rate. The barge project, with $\beta = 1.5$, should be evaluated at a 14.0 percent discount rate:

$$\begin{aligned} k_{Barge} &= 8\% + (4\%)1.5 \\ &= 8\% + 6\% \\ &= 14\%. \end{aligned}$$

On the other hand, a low-risk project such as a new steel distribution centre with a beta of only 0.5 can have a cost of capital of 10 percent:

$$\begin{aligned} k_{Centre} &= 8\% + (4\%)0.5 \\ &= 10\%. \end{aligned}$$

Figure 15-12 gives a graphic summary of these concepts as applied to G.L. Steel. Note the following points:

1. The SML shows how investors are willing to make tradeoffs between risk, as measured by beta, and expected returns. The higher the beta risk, the higher the rate of return needed to compensate investors for bearing this risk. The SML specifies the nature of this relationship.
2. G.L. Steel initially has a beta of 1.1, so its required rate of return on average-risk investments is 12.4 percent.

Figure 15-12
Using the Security Market Line Concept in Capital Budgeting

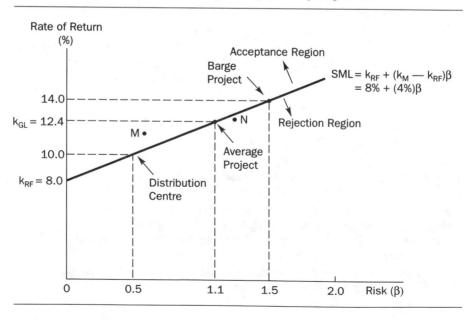

3. High-risk investments such as the barge line require higher rates of return, whereas low-risk investments such as the distribution centre require lower rates of return. It is not shown on the graph, but if G.L. makes relatively large investments in either high- or low-risk projects as opposed to average-risk ones, its corporate beta, and therefore the required rate of return on its common shares, k_s, will change.

4. If the expected rate of return on a given capital project lies *above* the SML, the expected rate of return on the project is more than enough to compensate for its risk, and the project should be accepted. Conversely, if the project's rate of return lies *below* the SML, it should be rejected. Thus, Project M in Figure 15-12 is acceptable, whereas Project N should be rejected. N has a higher expected return than M, but the differential is not enough to offset its much higher risk.

Concept Review

▶ What is meant by the term *average-risk project*? Explain how one finds the cost of capital for such a project, for a low-risk project, and for a high-risk project.

▶ Complete the following sentence: "An increase in a company's beta coefficient will cause the share price to decline unless _____."

▶ Explain why a firm should accept a given capital project if its expected rate of return lies above the SML. What if the expected rate of return lies on the SML? Below the SML?

Techniques for Measuring Beta Risk

The estimation of project betas is difficult and fraught with uncertainty. However, two approaches can be used to estimate individual assets' betas—the pure play method and the accounting beta method.

The Pure Play Method. In the *pure play method*, the company tries to find several single-product companies in the same line of business as the project being evaluated, and it then applies their betas to determine the cost of capital for its own project. For example, suppose that G.L. can find three existing single-product firms that operate barges and that G.L.'s management believes its barge project would be subject to the same risks as these firms. G.L. can then determine the betas of those firms, average them, and use this average beta as a proxy for the barge project's beta.[16] The pure play approach can only be used for major assets, such as whole divisions, and even then it is frequently difficult to implement because it is often impossible to find proxy firms.

The Accounting Beta Method. As noted above, it is often impossible to find single-product, publicly traded firms suitable for the pure play approach. If

[16]If the pure play firms employ different capital structures than that of G.L., this fact must be dealt with by adjusting the beta coefficients. See Brigham and Gapenski, chap. 9, for a discussion of this aspect of the pure play method.

that is the case, analysts may be able to use the *accounting beta method*. Betas normally are found by regressing the returns of a particular company's shares against returns on a stock market index. However, an analyst can run a regression of the company's rate of return on assets (EBIT/Total assets) over time against the average return on assets for a large sample of companies, such as those included in the TSE 300. Betas determined in this way (that is, by using accounting data rather than stock market data) are called *accounting betas*.

Accounting betas for projects can be calculated only after the project has been accepted, has been placed in operation, and has begun to generate output and accounting results. However, to the extent that management thinks a given project is similar to other projects, the firm has undertaken in the past, other projects' accounting betas can be used as proxies for that of the project in question. In practice, accounting betas are normally calculated for divisions or other large units, not for single assets, and divisional betas then are imputed to the asset. This point is discussed later in the chapter.

Concept Review

▶ Differentiate between the pure play method and the accounting beta method for estimating individual assets' betas.

Diversification to Reduce Risk

As we learned earlier in the chapter, a security may be quite risky if held in isolation but not very risky if held as part of a well-diversified portfolio. The same thing is true of capital budgeting; the returns on an individual project may be highly uncertain, but if the project is small relative to the total firm and if its returns are not highly correlated with the firm's other assets, the project may not be very risky in either the corporate or the beta sense.

Many firms do make serious efforts to diversify; often this is a specific objective of the long-run strategic plan. For example, real estate developers have diversified geographically to lessen the effect of a slowdown in one region. The major objectives of many such moves are to stabilize earnings, reduce corporate risk, and thereby raise the value of the firm's common equity.

The wisdom of corporate diversification designed to reduce risk has been questioned—why should a firm diversify when shareholders diversify on their own and without all the trouble and expense of a merger?

As you might suspect, the answer is not simple. Although shareholders can directly obtain some of the risk-reducing benefits through personal diversification, other benefits can be gained only by diversification at the corporate level. For example, a relatively stable corporation may be able to attract a better work force and also to use more low-cost debt than can two less stable firms. And, of course, there may also be spillover effects from mergers. Further, certain operations, such as research, may gain economies of scale from combined or otherwise expanded operations.

Project Risk Calculations

We have discussed the three types of risk normally considered in capital budgeting analysis—stand-alone risk, within-firm (or corporate) risk, and market risk—and we have discussed ways of assessing each. However, two important questions remain: (1) is it correct for a firm to be concerned with stand-alone and within-firm risk in its capital budgeting decisions, and (2) what should the firm do when the stand-alone or within-firm assessment and the market risk assessment lead to different conclusions?

These questions do not have easy answers. From a theoretical standpoint, well-diversified investors should be concerned only with market risk, managers should be concerned only with share price maximization, and these two factors should lead to the conclusion that market, or beta, risk ought to be given virtually all the weight in capital budgeting decisions. However, if investors are not well diversified, if the CAPM does not really operate as theory says it should, or if measurement problems keep managers from implementing the CAPM approach in capital budgeting, it may be appropriate to give stand-alone and within-firm risk more weight than financial theorists suggest. Note also that the CAPM ignores bankruptcy costs, even though such costs can be substantial, and that the probability of bankruptcy depends on a firm's corporate risk, not on its beta risk. Therefore, one can easily conclude that even well-diversified investors want a firm's management to give at least some consideration to a project's within-firm risk, instead of concentrating entirely on market risk.

Although it would be desirable to reconcile these problems and to measure project risk on some absolute scale, the best we can do in practice is to determine project risk in a somewhat nebulous, relative sense. For example, we can generally say with a fair degree of confidence that a particular project has more or less stand-alone risk than the firm's average project. Then, assuming that stand-alone and within-firm, or corporate, risk are highly correlated (which is typical), the project's stand-alone risk will be a good measure of its corporate risk. Finally, assuming that market risk and corporate risk are highly correlated (as studies suggest), a project with more corporate risk than average will also have more market risk and vice versa for projects with low corporate risk.[17]

---

[17]For example, see M. Chapman Findlay III, Arthur E. Gooding, and Wallace Q. Weaver, Jr., "On the Relevant Risk for Determining Capital Expenditure Hurdle Rates," *Financial Management*, Winter 1976: 9–16.

Incorporating Project Risk and Capital Structure into Capital Budgeting

Thus far, we have seen that capital budgeting can affect a firm's market risk, its corporate risk, or both. We have also seen that it is extremely difficult to quantify either type of risk. In other words, although it may be possible to reach the general conclusion that one project is riskier than another, it is difficult to develop a really good *measure* of project risk. This lack of precision in measuring project risk makes it difficult to incorporate differential risk into capital budgeting decisions.

There are two methods for incorporating project risk into the capital budgeting decision process. One is called the *certainty equivalent* approach. Under it, the expected cash flows in each year are adjusted to reflect project risk. All cash flows that are not known with certainty are scaled down, and the riskier the flows, the lower their certainty equivalent values.

The certainty equivalent approach is difficult to implement in practice, however, and hence we focus on the **risk-adjusted discount rate** approach, under which differential project risk is dealt with by changing the discount rate. Average risk projects are discounted at the firm's average cost of capital, above-average risk projects are discounted at a higher cost of capital, and below-average risk projects are discounted at a rate below the firm's average cost of capital. Unfortunately, because risk cannot be measured precisely, there is no good way of specifying exactly *how much* higher or lower these discount rates should be; given the present state of the art, risk adjustments are necessarily matters of judgement and somewhat arbitrary.

Capital structure also may be taken into account if a firm finances different assets in different ways. For example, one division may have a lot of real estate, which is well suited as collateral for loans, whereas some other division may have most of its capital tied up in special-purpose machinery, which is not good collateral. As a result, the division with the real estate may have a higher *debt capacity* than the division with the machinery and hence an optimal capital structure that contains a higher percentage of debt. In this case, the financial manager may calculate the cost of capital differently for the two divisions.[18]

Although the process is not exact, many companies use a two-step procedure to develop risk-adjusted discount rates for use in capital budgeting.

---

[18]We shall say much more about optimal capital structure and debt capacity in Chapters 17 and 18.

First, *divisional costs of capital* are established for each of the major operating divisions on the basis of each division's estimated average riskiness and its capital structure. Second, within each division, all projects are classified into three categories: high risk, average risk, and low risk. Then, each division uses its basic divisional cost of capital as the discount rate for average-risk projects, reduces the divisional cost of capital by one or two percentage points when evaluating low-risk projects, and raises the cost of capital by several percentage points for high-risk projects. For example, if a division's basic cost of capital is estimated to be 10 percent, a 12 percent discount rate may be used for a high-risk project and a 9 percent rate for a low-risk project. Average-risk projects, which constitute about 80 percent of most capital budgets, are evaluated at the 10 percent divisional cost of capital. This procedure is far from precise, but it does at least recognize that different divisions have different characteristics and hence different costs of capital, and it also acknowledges differential project riskiness within divisions.

Concept Review

- ► How are risk-adjusted discount rates used to incorporate project risk into the capital budget decision process?
- ► Briefly explain the two-step process many companies use to develop risk-adjusted discount rates for use in capital budgeting.

Summary

The primary goals of this chapter were to show how risk is measured in financial analysis, to explain how risk affects rates of return, and to apply risk adjustment procedures to the capital budgeting process. The key concepts covered are listed below.

- □ **Risk** can be defined as the chance that some unfavourable event will occur.
- □ Most rational investors hold *portfolios* of securities, and they are more concerned with the risks of their portfolios than with the risks of individual securities.
- □ The **expected return** on an investment is the mean value of the probability distribution of its possible returns.
- □ The *higher the probability* that the actual return will be far below the expected return, the *greater the risk* associated with owning an asset.
- □ The average investor is **risk averse**, which means that there must be compensation for holding risky securities; therefore, riskier securities must have higher expected returns than less risky securities.
- □ A security's risk consists of (1) **company-specific risk**, which can be eliminated by diversification, plus (2) **market risk**, which cannot be eliminated by diversification.
- □ The **Capital asset pricing model (CAPM)** is an important analytical tool for analyzing the relationship between risk and required rates of return. Since investors do not hold securities in isolation, but as part of a diversified portfolio, the **relevant risk** of an individual security is its contribution to the riskiness of a well-diversified portfolio, which is the security's market risk.

Since market risk cannot be eliminated by diversification, investors must be compensated for it.

☐ A security's **beta coefficient, β**, is a measure of its market risk. Beta measures the extent to which the security's returns move with the market.

☐ A high-beta security is more volatile than an average security, and a security with a low-beta is less volatile than average. An average security has $\beta = 1.0$ by definition.

☐ The beta of a portfolio is a *weighted average* of the betas of the individual securities in the portfolio.

☐ The **security market line (SML)** equation shows the relationship between securities' risks and rates of return. The return required for any security, i, is equal to the risk-free rate plus the **market risk premium** times the security's beta:

$$k_i = k_{RF} + (k_M - k_{RF})\beta_i.$$

☐ Even though expected rates of return on securities are generally equal to their required returns, a number of things can happen to cause required rates of return to change. (1) The risk-free rate can change because of changes in anticipated inflation. (2) A security's beta can change. (3) Investors' aversion to risk can change.

☐ **Within-firm risk (corporate risk)** reflects the effects of a project on the firm's risk. It is measured by the project's effect on the firm's earnings variability. Shareholder diversification is not taken into account.

☐ Corporate risk is important because it influences the firm's ability to use low-cost debt, to maintain smooth operations over time, and to avoid crises that might consume management's energy and disrupt employees, customers, suppliers, and the community.

☐ A project's **stand-alone risk** is the risk the project would have if it were the firm's only asset and if the firm's shareholders held only that one security. Stand-alone risk is measured by the variability of the asset's expected returns. Stand-alone risk is often used as a proxy for both market and corporate risk because (1) market and corporate risk are difficult to measure and (2) the three types of risk are usually highly correlated.

☐ **Sensitivity analysis** is a technique that shows how much an output variable, such as NPV, will change in response to a given change in an input variable such as sales, other things held constant.

☐ **Scenario analysis** is a risk analysis technique in which the best and worst case NPVs are compared with a most likely or base case NPV.

☐ **Monte Carlo simulation** is a risk analysis technique in which a computer is used to simulate probable future events and thus to estimate future rates of return and the riskiness of the project.

☐ Projects that are riskier than the firm's average project require higher rates of return, while low-risk projects require lower rates of return.

☐ The *pure play method* and the *accounting beta method* can be used to estimate betas for large projects.

☐ The **risk-adjusted discount rate** is the rate that is used to evaluate a particular project. The discount rate is increased for projects that are riskier than the firm's average project, and it is decreased for less risky projects.

Both the measurement of risk and its incorporation into capital budgeting involve judgement. It is possible to use a quantitative technique, such as simulation, as an aid to judgement, but in the final analysis the assessment of risk in capital budgeting is a subjective process.

Questions

15-1   The probability distribution of a less-risky expected return is more peaked than that of a riskier return. What shape would the probability distribution have for (a) completely certain returns and (b) completely uncertain returns?

15-2   Describe the mean-variance approach to risk and uncertainty.

15-3   Security A has an expected return of 7 percent, a standard deviation of expected returns of 35 percent, a correlation coefficient with the market of −0.3, and a beta coefficient of −0.5. Security B has an expected return of 12 percent, a standard deviation of returns of 10 percent, a correlation with the market of 0.7, and a beta coefficient of 1.0. Which security is more risky? Why?

15-4   Suppose you own a portfolio consisting of $250 000 worth of long-term Government of Canada bonds.
   a. Is your portfolio riskless?
   b. Now suppose you hold a portfolio consisting of $250 000 worth of 30-day treasury bills. Every 30 days your bills mature and you reinvest the principal ($250 000) in a new batch of bills. Assume that you live on the investment income from your portfolio and that you want to maintain a constant standard of living. Is your portfolio truly riskless?
   c. Can you think of any asset that would be completely riskless? Could someone develop such an asset? Explain.

15-5   How is risk measured when assets are viewed in a portfolio framework?

15-6   A life insurance policy is a financial asset. The premiums paid represent the investment's cost.
   a. How would you calculate the expected return on a life insurance policy?
   b. Suppose the owner of a life insurance policy has no other financial assets—the person's only other asset is "human capital" *or* (lifetime earnings capacity). What is the correlation coefficient between returns on the insurance policy and returns on the policyholder's human capital?
   c. Life insurance companies have to pay administrative costs and sales representatives' commissions; hence, the expected rate of return on insurance premiums is generally low, or even negative. Use the portfolio concept to explain why people buy life insurance in spite of negative expected returns.

15-7   Differentiate among (a) sensitivity analysis, (b) scenario analysis, and (c) simulation analysis. Suppose Bell Canada is considering two investments: one calling for expenditure of $100 million to develop a satellite communications system and the other involving the expenditure of $10 000 for a new truck. On which one is the company more likely to use simulation?

15-8   Distinguish between beta (or market) risk, within-firm (or corporate) risk, and stand-alone risk for a project being considered for inclusion in the capital budget. Which type of risk do you believe should be given the greatest weight in capital budgeting decisions? Explain your answer.

15-9   Suppose Reading Engine Company, which has a high beta as well as a great deal of corporate risk, merges with Simplicity Patterns, Ltd. Simplicity's sales rise during recessions, when people are more likely to make their own clothes, and, consequently, its beta is negative, but its corporate risk is relatively high. What will the merger do to the costs of capital in the consolidated company's locomotive engine division and in its patterns division?

15-10   Suppose a firm estimates its cost of capital for the coming year to be 10 percent. What are reasonable costs of capital for evaluating average-risk projects, high-risk projects, and low-risk projects?

Self-Test Problems   (solutions appear on page 539)

ST-1   **Key terms.**   Define the following terms. Use graphs or equations to illustrate your answers wherever feasible.

  a.   Risk; probability distribution
  b.   Expected rate of return, $\hat{k}$
  c.   Continuous probability distribution
  d.   Standard deviation, σ; variance, σ^2; coefficient of variation, CV; mean-variance criterion
  e.   Risk aversion
  f.   Risk premium for Stock i, RP_i; market risk premium, RP_M
  g.   Capital asset pricing model (CAPM)
  h.   Expected return on a portfolio, $\hat{k}_p$
  i.   Correlation coefficient, r; efficient portfolio
  j.   Market risk; company-specific risk; relevant risk
  k.   Beta coefficient, β; average stock's beta, β_A
  l.   Security market line (SML); SML equation
  m.   Slope of SML as a measure of risk aversion
  n.   Stand-alone risk; within-firm risk; market risk
  o.   Corporate risk
  p.   Sensitivity analysis; base case
  q.   Scenario analysis; worst case scenario; base case scenario
  r.   Monte Carlo simulation analysis
  s.   Project beta versus corporate beta
  t.   Pure play method of estimating project betas; accounting beta method
  u.   Corporate diversification versus shareholder diversification
  v.   Risk-adjusted discount rate; project cost of capital; certainty equivalent

ST-2   Returns on securities.   Securities A and B have the following historical rate of return:

	Security A's Returns, k_A	Security B's Returns, k_B
1988	-10.00%	-3.00%
1989	18.50	21.29
1990	38.67	44.25
1991	14.33	3.67
1992	33.00	28.30

a. Calculate the average rate of return for each security over the period 1988 to 1992. Assume that someone held a portfolio consisting of 50 percent of A and 50 percent of B. What was the realized rate of return on the portfolio in each year from 1988 through 1992? What were the average returns for the portfolio?

b. Now calculate the standard deviation of returns for each security and for the portfolio. Use the equation in Footnote 3.

c. Looking at the annual returns data on the two securities, would you guess that the correlation coefficient between their returns is closer to 0.9 or to -0.9?

d. If you added more securities at random to the portfolio, which of the following is the most accurate statement of what would happen to σ_p?

i. σ_p would remain constant.

ii. σ_p would decline to somewhere in the vicinity of 15 percent.

iii. σ_p would decline to zero if enough securities were included.

ST-3   Corporate risk analysis.   The staff of Scampini Manufacturing has estimated the following net cash flows and probabilities for a new manufacturing process:

	Net Cash Flow		
Year	'Worst Case' $P = 0.2$	'Base Case' $P = 0.6$	'Best Case' $P = 0.2$
0	($100 000)	($100 000)	($100 000)
1	20 000	30 000	40 000
2	20 000	30 000	40 000
3	20 000	30 000	40 000
4	20 000	30 000	40 000
5	20 000	30 000	40 000
5*	0	20 000	30 000

Line 0 gives the cost of the process, Lines 1 through 5 give operating cash flows for years 1 through 5, and Line 5* contains the estimated salvage values at the end of year 5. Scampini's cost of capital for an average-risk project is 10 percent.

a. Assume that the project has average risk. Find the project's expected NPV. (Hint: Use expected values for the net cash flow in each year.)

b. Find the best case and worst case NPVs. What is the probability of occurrence of the worst case (i) if the cash flows are perfectly dependent (perfectly positively correlated) over time? and (ii) if they are independent over time?

c. Assume that all the cash flows are perfectly positively correlated, that is, there are only three possible cash flow streams over time: (1) the worst case, (2) the most likely, or base, case, and (3) the best case, with probabilities of 0.2, 0.6, and 0.2, respectively. Each of these cases is represented by a column in the table. Find the expected NPV, its standard deviation, and its coefficient of variation.

d. The coefficient of variation of Scampini's average project is in the range 0.8 to 1.0. If the coefficient of variation of a project being evaluated is greater than 1.0, the firm adds percentage points to the firm's cost of capital. Similarly, if the coefficient of variation is less than 0.8, it deducts 1 percentage point from the cost of capital. What is the project's cost of capital? Should Scampini accept or reject the project?

Problems

15-1 Expected returns. The market and Security J have the following probability distributions:

Probability	k_M	k_J
0.3	15%	20%
0.4	9	5
0.3	18	12

a. Calculate the expected rate of return for the market and for Security J.
b. Calculate the standard deviation for the market and for Security J.
c. Calculate the coefficient of variation for the market and for Security J.

15-2 Expected returns. Securities X and Y have the following probability distributions of expected future returns:

Probability	X	Y
0.1	−10%	−35%
0.2	2	0
0.4	12	20
0.2	20	25
0.1	38	45

a. Calculate the expected rate of return, $\hat{k}$, for Security Y. ($\hat{k}_X = 12\%$.)
b. Calculate the standard deviation of expected returns for Security X. (That for Security Y is 20.35 percent.) Now calculate the coefficient of variation for Security Y.

15-3   **Required rate of return.**   Suppose k_{RF} = 8 percent, k_M = 11 percent, and k_A = 14 percent.
   a. Calculate Security A's beta.
   b. If Security A's beta were 1.5, what would be A's new required rate of return?

15-4   **Required rate of return.**   Suppose k_{RF} = 9 percent, k_M = 14 percent, and β_I = 1.3.
   a. What is k_I, the required rate of return on Security I?
   b. Now suppose k_{RF} (i) increases to 10 percent or (ii) decreases to 8 percent. The slope of the SML remains constant. How would the changes affect k_M and k_I?
   c. Now assume k_{RF} remains at 9 percent but k_M (i) increases to 16 percent or (ii) falls to 13 percent. The slope of the SML does not remain constant. How would these changes affect k_I?

15-5   **Portfolio beta.**   Suppose you hold a diversified portfolio consisting of a $7500 investment in the common shares of each of 20 different companies. The portfolio beta is equal to 1.12. Now, suppose you have decided to sell one of the securities in your portfolio with a beta equal to 1.0 for $7500, and to use these proceeds to buy common shares of a different company. Assume the new security's beta is equal to 1.75. Calculate your portfolio's new beta.

 15-6   **Portfolio required return.**   Suppose you are the money manager of a $4 million investment fund. The fund consists of four equity securities. The amounts invested and the betas are as follows:

Security	Investment	β
A	$ 400 000	1.50
B	600 000	(0.50)
C	1 000 000	1.25
D	2 000 000	0.75

If the market required rate of return is 14 percent and the risk-free rate is 6 percent, what is the fund's required rate of return?

15-7   **Security market line.**   The Edwards Investment Fund has total capital of $500 million invested in five equity securities:

Security	Investment	β
A	$160 million	0.5
B	120 million	2.0
C	80 million	4.0
D	80 million	1.0
E	60 million	3.0

The beta coefficient for a fund such as Edwards Investment can be found as a weighted average of its investments. The current risk-free rate is 8 percent, whereas market returns have the following estimated probability distribution for the next period:

Probability	Market Return
0.1	10%
0.2	12
0.4	13
0.2	16
0.1	17

a. What is the estimated equation for the security market line (SML)? (Hint: First determine the expected market return.)

b. Compute the fund's required rate of return for the next period.

c. Suppose Dan Edwards, the president, receives a proposal for a new equity security. The investment needed to take a position in the security is $50 million; it will have an expected return of 18 percent; and its estimated beta coefficient is 2.0. Should the new security be purchased? At what expected rate of return should Edwards be indifferent to purchasing the security?

15-8   Realized rates of return.   Securities A and B have the following historical returns:

	Security A, k_A	Security B, k_B
1988	(18.00%)	(14.50%)
1989	33.00	21.80
1990	15.00	30.50
1991	(0.50)	(7.60)
1992	27.00	26.30

a. Calculate the average rate of return for each security during the period 1988 through 1992.

b. Assume that someone held a portfolio consisting of 50 percent of Security A and 50 percent of Security B. What would have been the realized rate of return on the portfolio in each year from 1988 through 1992? What would have been the average return on the portfolio during this period?

c. Calculate the standard deviation of returns for each security and for the portfolio.

d. Calculate the coefficient of variation for each security and for the portfolio.

e. If you are a risk-averse investor, would you prefer to hold Security A, Security B, or the portfolio? Why?

15-9 **Risk adjustment.**   A firm is considering a project under the following circumstances. The risk-free rate of return is 9 percent, and the market risk premium is 5 percent. The beta of the project under analysis is 1.4. The expected net cash flows after taxes are estimated at $1500 per year for five years. The required investment outlay on the project is $4500.

a. What is the required risk-adjusted return on the project?

b. Should the project be accepted?

15-10   Risk of expected cash flows.   The Rowan Company is faced with two mutually exclusive investment projects. Each project would cost $6750, and each has an expected life of 3 years. Annual net cash flows from each project would begin one year after the initial investment is made and have the following probability distributions:

Project A		Project B	
Probability	**Cash Flow**	**Probability**	**Cash Flow**
0.2	$6000	0.2	$ 0
0.6	6750	0.6	6750
0.2	7500	0.2	18 000

Rowan has decided to evaluate the riskier project at a 12 percent rate and the less risky project at a 10 percent rate.

  a. What is the expected value of the annual net cash flows from each project? What is the coefficient of variation?
  b. What is the risk-adjusted NPV of each project?
  c. If it is known that Project B is negatively correlated with other cash flows of the firm while Project A is positively correlated, how should this knowledge affect the decision? If Project B's cash flows are negatively correlated with gross domestic product (GDP), would that influence your assessment of its risk?

15-11 Sensitivity analysis. Your firm is considering the purchase of a tractor. It has been established that this tractor will cost $36 000, will increase before-tax operating cash flows exclusive of depreciation effects by $12 000 per year, and will be depreciated via straight line to zero over 5 years. The board of directors is having a heated debate as to whether the tractor will last 5 years. Specifically, Wayne Brown insists that he knows of some that have lasted only 4 years. Tom Miller agrees with Wayne but argues that it is more likely that the tractor would give 5 years of service. Connie Liew says that she has seen some last as long as 8 years. Given this discussion, the board has asked you to prepare a scenario analysis to ascertain the importance of the uncertainty about the tractor life. Assume a 40 percent tax rate on both income and capital loss, a zero salvage value, and a cost of capital of 10 percent. For simplicity, also assume that the straight-line depreciation charge is the depreciation for tax purposes.

15-12 Divisional required rates of return. Hehre Computer Corporation, a producer of office equipment, currently has assets of $15 million and a beta of 1.4. The risk-free rate is 8 percent, and the market risk premium is 5 percent. Hehre would like to expand into the risky home computer market. If the expansion is undertaken, Hehre would create a new division with $3.75 million in assets. The new division would have a beta of 1.8.

  a. What is Hehre's current required rate of return?
  b. If the expansion is undertaken, what would be the firm's new beta? What would be the new overall required rate of return, and what rate of return would the home computer division have to produce to leave that overall rate unchanged?

15-13 CAPM approach to risk adjustment. Goodtread Rubber Company Ltd. has two divisions: the tire division, which manufactures tires for new autos, and the recap division, which manufactures recapping materials that are sold to independent tire recapping shops throughout Canada and the United States. Since auto manufacturing fluctuates with the general economy, the contribution of the tire division's earnings to Goodtread's share price is highly correlated with returns on most other shares. If the tire division were operated as a separate company, its beta coefficient would be about 1.50. The sales and profits of the recap division, on the other hand, tend to be countercyclical—recap sales boom when people cannot afford to buy new tires. The recap division's beta is estimated to be 0.5. Approximately 75 percent of Goodtread's corporate assets are invested in the tire division and 25 percent in the recap division.

Currently, the rate of interest on Government of Canada bonds is 9 percent, and the expected rate of return on an average share is 13 percent. Goodtread uses only common equity capital, and hence it has no debt outstanding.

a. What is the required rate of return on Goodtread's equity?

b. What discount rate should be used to evaluate capital budgeting projects? Explain your answer fully, and, in the process, illustrate it with a project that costs $160 000, has a 10-year life, and has expected after-tax net cash flows of $30 000 per year.

Integrative Problems

15-14 Risk and return.   Assume that you recently graduated with a major in finance and have landed a job with a large trust company. Your first assignment is to invest $500 000 from an estate for which the company is trustee. Because the estate is expected to be distributed to heirs in about a year, you have been instructed to plan for a 1-year holding period. Further, your boss has restricted you to the following investment alternatives, shown with their probabilities:

State of the Economy	Probability	T-Bills	High Tech	Goldmines	Canadian Brass	Market Portfolio
					Estimated Rate of Return	
Recession	0.1	8.0%	(18.0%)	25.0%	10.0%	(14.0%)
Below average	0.2	8.0	(9.0)	19.5	(10.0)	3.0
Average	0.4	8.0	25.0	(4.0)	7.0	13.0
Above average	0.2	8.0	37.5	(12.0)	45.0	33.0
Boom	0.1	8.0	47.0	(18.0)	30.0	40.0
	1.0					

The trust company's economic and forecasting staff have developed probability estimates for the state of the economy, and a sophisticated computer program has estimated the rate of return on each alternative under each state of the economy. High Tech, Ltd., is an electronics firm; Goldmines Corporation owns gold mines in Canada and the United States; Canadian Brass manufactures pipe, plumbing fixtures, and various other products. The trust company also maintains an "index fund," which owns a market-weighted fraction of all publicly traded securities; you can invest in that fund and thus obtain average stock market results. Given the situation as described, answer the following questions:

a. Why is the T-bill return independent of the state of the economy? Do T-bills promise a completely risk-free return? Why do High Tech's returns move with the economy, whereas Goldmines' are estimated to move counter to the economy?

b. Calculate the expected rate of return on each alternative. Based solely on expected returns, which alternative would you choose?

c. You should recognize that basing a decision solely on expected returns is appropriate only for risk-neutral individuals. Since the beneficiaries of the trust, like virtually everyone, are risk averse, the riskiness of each alternative is an important aspect of the decision. One possible measure of risk is the standard deviation of returns. Calculate this value for each alternative. What type of risk is measured by the standard deviation?

d. Suppose you suddenly remember that the coefficient of variation (CV) is generally regarded as a better measure of total risk than the standard deviation when the alternatives being considered have widely differing expected returns. Calculate the CVs for the different securities. Does the CV produce the same risk rankings as the standard deviation?

e. What would happen if you created a two-security portfolio by investing $250 000 in High Tech and $250 000 in Goldmines? What are the expected return and the standard deviation for this portfolio? How does the riskiness of the portfolio compare to the riskiness of the individual securities?

f. The expected rates of return and the beta coefficients of the alternatives, as supplied by the bank's computer program, are as follows:

Security	Return, $\hat{k}$	Risk (β)
High Tech	18.6%	1.25
Market	15.0	1.00
Canadian Brass	13.8	0.71
T-bills	8.0	0.00
Goldmines	0.6	−0.83

What is a beta coefficient, and how is it used in risk analysis? Do the expected returns appear to be related to each alternative's market risk? Is it possible to choose among the alternatives on the basis of the information developed thus far?

g. Construct a security market line (SML) and use it to calculate the required rate of return on each alternative. How do the expected rates of return compare with the required rates of return? Does the fact that Goldmines has a negative beta make any sense? What are the market risk and the required return of a 50:50 portfolio of High Tech and Goldmines? Of High Tech and Canadian Brass?

h. Suppose investors raised their inflation expectations by 3 percentage points over current estimates as reflected in the 8 percent T-bill rate. What effect would this have on the SML and on the returns of high- and low-risk securities? Suppose instead that investors' risk aversion increased enough to cause the market risk premium to increase by 3 percentage points. What effect would this have on the SML and on returns of high- and low-risk securities?

15-15 Risk analysis in capital budgeting.   You still have the job described in Problem 15-14. For your second assignment, you are asked to evaluate the riskiness of a project by one of the company's long-time clients, South Niagara Ltd. Refer to Chapter 14, Problem 14-8, for a description of the project. It appears to be profitable, but what are the chances that it might be a failure, and how should risk be analyzed and worked into the decision process? You have been asked to discuss risk analysis, both in general terms and as applied to the fruit punch project. To structure the analysis, answer the following questions and perform the following tasks.

a. Why should firms be concerned with the riskiness of individual projects? What are the three types of project risk that are normally considered? Which type is the most relevant? Which type is the easiest to measure? Are the three types of risk generally highly correlated? Would their correlation matter?

b. What is sensitivity analysis? Perform a sensitivity analysis on the project's data, varying net operating revenue, salvage value, and the cost of capital. Assume that each of these variables can deviate from its base case expected value by +10%, by +20%, and by +30%. Prepare sensitivity diagrams, and interpret the results. What is the primary weakness of sensitivity analysis? What is its primary advantage?

c. Assume that you are confident about all of the input estimates in the analysis except gross profits (incremental net revenues). If product acceptance is poor, gross profits will be only $90 000 a year, but a strong consumer response will produce gross profits of $160 000 a year. Assume that there is a 25 percent chance of poor acceptance, a 25 percent chance of excellent acceptance, and a 50 percent chance of average acceptance (the base case). What is the worst case NPV? The best case NPV? Use the worst, base, and best case NPVs and their probabilities of occurrence to find the project's expected NPV, standard deviation, and coefficient of variation.

d. Assume that the company's average project has a coefficient of variation (CV) in the range of 0.4 to 0.6. Would the fruit punch project be classified as high risk, average risk, or low risk? What type of risk is being measured here? What factors would affect the project's within-firm risk?

e. South Niagara Ltd. typically adds or subtracts 3 percentage points to the cost of capital to adjust for risk. Now assume, contrary to the facts as you have developed them, that the fruit punch project has a CV of 1.2 and is judged to be of high risk. Should it be accepted under these modified conditions? What if it had a CV of only 0.15 and was judged to be a low-risk project?

f. What is scenario analysis? What are its primary advantages and disadvantages? What is Monte Carlo simulation, and what are its advantages and disadvantages compared with those of scenario analysis?

g. Assume that the risk-free rate is 8 percent and that the market risk premium is 5 percent. If your estimate of the fruit punch project's beta is 0.6, what is the project's market risk? What is the required rate of return?

h. South Niagara Ltd. is also evaluating two different systems for disposing of wastes associated with another product, fresh pear juice. Plan L would require more workers but less capital, whereas Plan C would require more capital but fewer workers. Both systems have an estimated 3-year life, but the one selected can and will be replicated. Because the waste disposal choice has no effect on revenues, you believe that the decision should be based on the relative present values of future costs of the two systems. The expected net costs are as follows:

Year	Plan L	Plan C
0	($500)	($1000)
1	(500)	(300)
2	(500)	(300)
3	(500)	(300)

Assume initially that the two systems are both of average risk. Which one should be chosen? Now assume that the labour-intensive project, L, is judged to be riskier than an average project because future labour costs are difficult to forecast. Project C, however, is still of average risk. South Niagara Ltd. typically adds 3 percentage points to its cost of capital when evaluating high-risk projects. Now which system should be chosen?

Solutions to Self-Test Problems

ST-1 Refer to the appropriate sections of the text to check your responses.

ST-2 **a.** The average rate of return for each security is calculated by simply averaging the returns over the 5-year period. The average return for each security is 18.90 percent, calculated for Equity A as follows:

$$k_{Avg} = (-10.00\% + 18.50\% + 38.67\% + 14.33\% + 33.00\%)/5$$
$$= 18.90\%.$$

The realized rate of return on a portfolio made up of Securities A and B is calculated by finding the average return in each year as k_A

(% of Security A) + k_B (% of Security B) and then averaging these yearly returns:

Year	Portfolio AB's Return, k_{AB}
1988	(6.50%)
1989	19.89
1990	41.46
1991	9.00
1992	30.65
k_{Avg} =	18.90%

b. The standard deviation of returns is estimated, using the equation in Footnote 3:

$$\text{Estimated } \sigma = S = \sqrt{\frac{\sum_{t=1}^{n} (\bar{k}_t - \bar{k}_{Avg})^2}{n-1}}. \qquad \textbf{(15-3a)}$$

For Security A, the estimated σ is 19.0 percent:

$$\sigma_A = \sqrt{\frac{(-10.00 - 18.9)^2 + (18.50 - 18.9)^2 + \ldots + (33.00 - 18.9)^2}{5-1}}$$

$$= \sqrt{\frac{1445.92}{4}} = 19.0\%.$$

The standard deviation of returns for Security B and for the portfolio are similarly determined. They are as follows:

	Security A	Security B	Portfolio AB
Standard deviation	19.0	19.0	18.6

c. Since the risk reduction from diversification is small (σ_{AB} falls only from 19.0 to 18.6 percent), the most likely value of the correlation coefficient is 0.9. If the correlation coefficient were −0.9, the risk reduction would be much larger. In fact, the correlation coefficient between Securities A and B is 0.93.

d. If more randomly selected securities were added to the portfolio, σ_P would decline to somewhere in the vicinity of 15 percent; see Figure 15-7. σ_P would remain constant only if the correlation coefficient were +1.0, which is most unlikely. σ_P would decline to zero only if the correlation coefficient, r, were equal to zero and a large number of securities were added to the portfolio, or if the proper proportions were held in a two-security portfolio with r = −1.0.

ST-3 **a.** First, find the expected cash flows:

Year	Expected Cash Flow
0	0.2(−$100 000) + 0.6(−$100 000) + 0.2(−$100 000) = ($100 000)
1	0.2($20 000) + 0.6($30 000) + 0.2($40 000) = $ 30 000
2	$ 30 000
3	$ 30 000
4	$ 30 000
5	$ 30 000
5*	0.2($0) + 0.6($20 000) + 0.2($30 000) = $ 18 000

Next, determine the NPV based on the expected cash flows:

$$\text{NPV} = -\$100\,000 + \frac{\$30\,000}{(1.10)^1} + \frac{\$30\,000}{(1.10)^2} + \frac{\$30\,000}{(1.10)^3} + \frac{\$30\,000}{(1.10)^4}$$

$$+ \frac{\$30\,000 + \$18\,000}{(1.10)^5} = \$24\,900.$$

b. For the worst case, the cash flow values from the cash flow column farthest on the left (P = 0.2) are used to calculate NPV:

$$\text{NPV} = -\$100\,000 + \frac{\$20\,000}{(1.10)^1} + \frac{\$20\,000}{(1.10)^2} + \frac{\$20\,000}{(1.10)^3} + \frac{\$20\,000}{(1.10)^4}$$

$$+ \frac{\$20\,000 + \$0}{(1.10)^5} = -\$24\,184.$$

Similarly, for the best case, use the values from the column farthest on the right. Here the NPV is $70 259.

If the cash flows are perfectly dependent, then the low cash flow in the first year will mean a low cash flow in every year. Thus, the probability of the worst case occurring is the probability of getting the $20 000 net cash flow in Year 1, or 20 percent. If the cash flows are independent, the cash flow in each year can be low, high, or average, and the probability of getting all low cash flows will be

$$0.2(0.2)(0.2)(0.2)(0.2) = 0.2^5 = 0.00032 = 0.032\%.$$

c. The base case NPV is found using the most likely cash flows and is equal to $26 142. This value differs from the expected NPV of $24 900 because the Year 5 cash flows are not symmetric. Under these conditions, the NPV distribution is as follows:

P	NPV
0.2	($24 184)
0.6	26 142
0.2	70 259

Thus, the expected NPV is $0.2(-\$24\,184) + 0.6(\$26\,142) + 0.2(\$70\,259) = \$24\,900$. As is generally the case, the expected NPV is the same as the NPV of the expected cash flows found in Part a. The standard deviation is $\$29\,904$:

$$\sigma^2_{NPV} = 0.2(-\$24\,184 - \$24\,900)^2 + 0.6(\$26\,142 - \$24\,900)^2$$
$$+ \ 0.2(\$70\,259 - \$24\,900)^2$$

$$= \$894\,261\,126.$$

$$\sigma_{NPV} = \sqrt{\$894\,261\,126} = \$29\,904.$$

The coefficient of variation, CV, is $\$29\,904/\$24\,900 = 1.20$.

d. Since the project's coefficient of variation is 1.20, the project is riskier than average, and hence the project's risk-adjusted cost of capital is $10\% + 2\% = 12\%$. The project now should be evaluated by finding the NPV of the expected cash flows, as in Part a but using a 12 percent discount rate. The risk-adjusted NPV is $\$18\,357$, and therefore the project should be accepted.

Appendix 15A
Calculating Beta Coefficients

The CAPM is an *ex ante* model, which means that all of the variables represent before-the-fact, *expected* values. In particular, the beta coefficient used in the SML equation should reflect the expected volatility of a given security's return versus the return on the market during some *future* period. However, people generally calculate betas using data from some *past* period and then assume that the security's relative volatility will be the same in the future as it was in the past.

Figure 15A-1 illustrates how betas are calculated. The data tabulated at the bottom of the figure show the historical returns for Security J and for the market over the last five years. We plotted these data points on a scatter diagram and drew a regression line. If all the data points had fallen on a straight line, it would have been easy to draw an accurate line. Since they did not, we had to fit the line by eye as an approximation (we could also have used statistical procedures).

To understand why we need a regression line, recall what the term *regression equation* means. The standard form of a simple linear regression is

$$Y = \alpha + \beta X + e.$$

This equation states that the dependent variable, Y, is equal to a constant, α, plus β times X, where β is the slope coefficient (or parameter) and X is the independent variable, plus an error term, e. Here, the rate of return on a security during a given time period, Y, depends on what happens to the general stock market, which is measured by $X = \bar{k}_M$.

Once the line has been drawn, its intercept and slope, which are the α and β values in $Y = \alpha + \beta X$, can be estimated. The intercept, α, is simply the point at which the line cuts the vertical axis. The slope coefficient, β, can be estimated by the "rise over run" method, which involves calculating the amount by which $\bar{k}_J$ increases for a given increase in $\bar{k}_M$. Observe in Figure 15A-1 that $\bar{k}_J$ increases from -8.9 to $+7.1$ percent (the rise) when $\bar{k}_M$ increases from 0 to 10.0 percent (the run). Thus β, the beta coefficient, can be measured as follows:

$$\beta = \frac{\text{Rise}}{\text{Run}} = \frac{\Delta Y}{\Delta X} = \frac{7.1 - (-8.9)}{10.0 - 0.0} = \frac{16.0}{10.0} = 1.6.$$

Note that rise over run is a ratio, and it would be the same if calculated with any two arbitrarily selected points on the line.

The regression line equation enables us to predict a rate of return for Security J, given a value of $\bar{k}_M$. For example, if $\bar{k}_M = 15$ percent, we can predict $\bar{k}_J = -8.9\% + 1.6(15\%) = 15.1\%$. However, the actual return will probably differ from the predicted return. This deviation is the error term, e_J, for the year, and it varies randomly from year to year depending on company-specific factors.

In actual practice, monthly rather than annual returns are generally used for $\bar{k}_J$ and $\bar{k}_M$, and data for 5 years are employed; thus, there would be

Figure 15A-1
Calculating Beta Coefficients

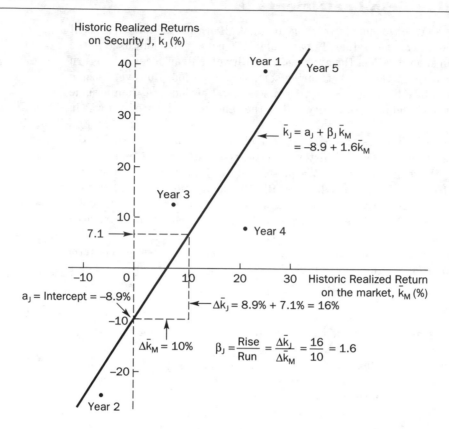

Year	Security J($\bar{k}_J$)	Market ($\bar{k}_M$)
1	38.6%	23.8%
2	(24.7)	(7.2)
3	12.3	6.6
4	8.2	20.5
5	40.1	30.6
Average $\bar{k}$	14.9%	14.9%
$\sigma_{\bar{k}}$	26.5%	15.1%

$5 \times 12 = 60$ dots on the scatter diagram. Also in practice, one would use the *least squares method* for finding the regression coefficients, α and β, a procedure that minimizes the squared values of the error terms. (The method is discussed in statistics courses.)

The least squares value of beta can be obtained quite easily with a computer or even a calculator that has statistical functions.

Appendix Problems

15A-1 Beta coefficients and rates of return.   You are given the following set of data:

	Historic Rates of Return, $\bar{k}$	
Year	Security Y, $\bar{k}_Y$	TSE, $\bar{k}_M$
1	3.0%	4.0%
2	18.2	14.3
3	9.1	19.0
4	(6.0)	(14.7)
5	(15.3)	(26.5)
6	33.1	37.2
7	6.1	23.8
8	3.2	(7.2)
9	14.8	6.6
10	24.1	20.5
11	18.0	30.6
Mean	9.8%	9.8%
σ_k	13.8	19.6

a. Construct a scatter diagram graph (*on graph paper*) showing the relationship between returns on Security Y and the market as in Figure 15A-1; then draw a freehand approximation of the regression line. What is the approximate value of the beta coefficient? (If you have a calculator with statistical functions, use it to calculate beta.)

b. Give a verbal interpretation of what the regression line and the beta coefficient show about Security Y's volatility and relative riskiness as compared with other shares.

c. Suppose the scatter of points had been more spread out but the regression line was exactly where your present graph shows it. How would this affect (i) the firm's risk if the security were held in a one-asset portfolio and (ii) the actual risk premium on the security if the CAPM held exactly? How does the degree of scatter (or the correlation coefficient) affect your confidence that the calculated beta will hold true in the years ahead?

d. Suppose the regression line had been downward sloping and the beta coefficient had been negative. What would this imply about (i) Security Y's relative riskiness and (ii) its probable risk premium?

e. Construct an illustrative probability distribution graph of returns (see Figure 15-6) for portfolios consisting of (i) only Security Y, (ii) 1 percent each of 100 securities with beta coefficients similar to that of Security Y, and (iii) all stocks (that is, the distribution of returns on the market). Use as the expected rate of return the arithmetic mean as given previously for both Security Y and the market, and assume that the distributions are normal. Are the expected returns "reasonable"—that is, is it reasonable that $\hat{k}_Y = \hat{k}_M = 9.8\%$?

f. Now suppose that in the next year, Year 12, the market return was 27 percent but Firm Y increased its use of debt, which raised its perceived risk to investors. Do you think that the return on Security Y in Year 12 could be approximated by this historical characteristic line?

$$\hat{k}_Y = 3.8\% + 0.62(\hat{k}_M) = 3.8\% + 0.62(27\%) = 20.5\%.$$

g. Now suppose $\bar{k}_Y$ in Year 12, after the debt ratio was increased, had actually been 0 percent. What would the new beta be based on the most recent 11 years of data (that is, Years 2 through 12)? Does this beta seem reasonable—that is, is the change in beta consistent with the other facts given in the problem?

15A-2 Security market line.   You are given the following historical data on market returns, $\bar{k}_M$, and the returns on Securities A and B, $\bar{k}_A$ and $\bar{k}_B$:

Year	$\bar{k}_M$	$\bar{k}_A$	$\bar{k}_B$
1	29.00%	29.00%	20.00%
2	15.20	15.20	13.10
3	(10.00)	(10.00)	0.50
4	3.30	3.30	7.15
5	23.00	23.00	17.00
6	31.70	31.70	21.35

k_{RF}, the risk-free rate, is 9 percent. The probability distribution for k_M for next year is as follows:

Probability	k_M
0.1	(14%)
0.2	0
0.4	15
0.2	25
0.1	44

a. Determine graphically the beta coefficients for Securities A and B.
b. Graph the security market line and give its equation.
c. Calculate the required rates of return on Securities A and B.
d. Suppose a new security, C, with $\hat{k}_C = 18$ percent and $\beta_C = 2.0$ becomes available. Is this security in equilibrium; that is, does the required rate of return on Security C equal its expected return? Explain. If the security is not in equilibrium, explain how equilibrium will be restored.

Appendix 15B
Influences on the Security Market Line

The security market line is used to identify the appropriate cost of capital for capital budgeting analysis. There are a number of variables that are important in determining the position and slope of the SML. Changes in these variables have an impact on the cost of capital that should be used. In this appendix, we investigate the impact on the SML of changes in three important variables: inflation, risk aversion, and the firm's beta coefficient.

The Impact of Inflation

As we learned in Chapter 3, interest amounts to "rent" on borrowed money—that is, the price of money. Thus, k_{RF} is the price of money to a riskless borrower. We also learned that the risk-free rate as measured by the rate on Government of Canada securities is called the *nominal rate*, and it consists of two elements: (1) a *real inflation-free rate of return*, k^*, and (2) an *inflation premium, IP*, equal to the anticipated rate of inflation.[19] Thus, $k_{RF} = k^* + IP$. The real rate on long-term Government of Canada bonds has historically ranged from 2 to 4 percent, with a mean of about 3 percent. Therefore, if no inflation were expected, long-term federal government bonds would yield about 3 percent. However, as the expected rate of inflation increases, a premium must be added to the real risk-free rate of return to compensate investors for the loss of purchasing power that results from inflation. Therefore, the 9 percent k_{RF} shown in Figure 15B-1 might be thought of as consisting of a 3 percent real risk-free rate of return plus a 6 percent inflation premium: $k_{RF} = k^* + IP = 3\% + 6\% = 9\%$.

If the expected rate of inflation rose to 8 percent, this would cause k_{RF} to rise to 11 percent. Such a change is shown in Figure 15B-1. Notice that under the CAPM, the increase in k_{RF} also causes an *equal* increase in the rate of return on all risky assets, because the inflation premium is built into the required rate of return of both riskless and risky assets.[20] For example, the rate of return on an average equity security, k_M, increases from 13 to 15 percent. Other risky securities' returns also rise by 2 percentage points.

Changes in Risk Aversion

The slope of the SML reflects the extent to which investors are averse to risk—the steeper the slope of the line, the greater the average investor's risk

---

[19]Long-term Government of Canada bonds also contain a maturity risk premium, MRP. Here we include the MRP in k to simplify the discussion.

[20]Recall that the inflation premium for any asset is equal to the average expected rate of inflation over the life of the asset. Thus, in this analysis we must assume either that all securities plotted on the SML graph have same life or else that the expected rate of future inflation is constant.

Remember that k_{RF} in a CAPM analysis can be proxied by either a long-term rate (the long Canada rate) or a short-term rate (the T-bill rate). Traditionally, the T-bill rate was used, but in recent years there has been a movement toward use of the bond rate because there is a closer relationship between bond yields and equity securities than between T-bill yields and equity securities. See Roger G. Ibbotson and Rex A. Sinquefield, *Stocks, Bonds, Bills, and Inflation; 1988 Yearbook* (Chicago: Ibbotson & Associates, 1988), for a discussion.

Figure 15B-1
Shift in the SML Caused by an Increase in Inflation

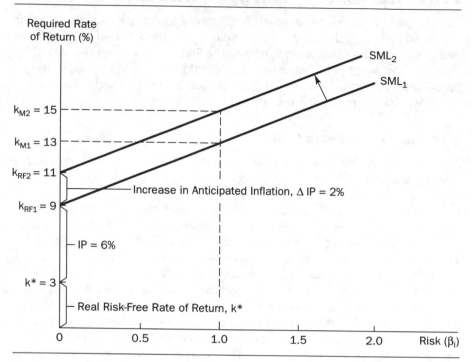

aversion. If investors were indifferent to risk and k_{RF} were 9 percent, then risky assets would also sell to provide an expected return of 9 percent; if there were no risk aversion, there would be no risk premium, so the SML would be horizontal. As risk aversion increases, so does the risk premium and thus the slope of the SML.

Figure 15B-2 illustrates an increase in risk aversion. The market risk premium rises from 4 to 6 percent, and k_M rises from 13 to 15 percent. The returns on other risky assets also rise, with the effect of this shift in risk aversion being more pronounced on riskier securities. For example, the required return on a security with $\beta_i = 0.5$ increases by only 1 percentage point, from 11 to 12 percent, whereas that on a security with $\beta_i = 1.5$ increases by 3 percentage points, from 15 to 18 percent.

Changes in a Security's Beta Coefficient

A firm can affect its market, or beta, risk through changes in the composition of its assets as well as through its use of debt financing. A company's beta may also change as a result of external factors, such as increased competition in its industry, the expiration of basic patents, and the like. When such changes occur, the required rate of return also changes, and, as we shall see in Chapter 16, this will affect the price of the firm's shares. For example, consider Hayes Electronics Corporation, with a beta equal to 1.0. Now suppose something occurs that causes its beta to increase from 1.0 to 1.5. If the conditions depicted in Figure 15B-1 hold, Hayes Electronics's required rate of return will increase from

Figure 15B-2
Shift in the SML Caused by Increased Risk Aversion

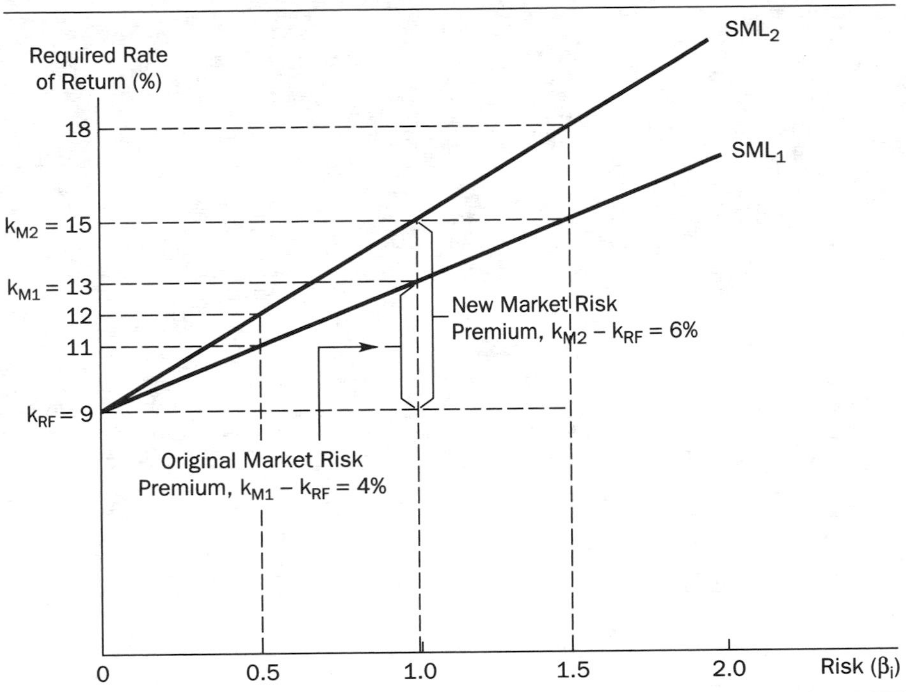

$$k_1 = k_{RF} + (k_M - k_{RF})\beta_i$$
$$= 9\% + (13\% - 9\%)1.0$$
$$= 13\%$$

to

$$k_2 = 9\% + (13\% - 9\%)1.5$$
$$= 15\%.$$

Any change that affects the required rate of return on a security, such as a change in its beta coefficient or in expected inflation, will have an impact on the price of the security unless there are offsetting changes in the expected cash flows. We will examine in detail the relationship between a security's rate of return and its price in Chapter 16.

Concept Review

► What happens to the SML graph (1) when inflation increases and (2) when inflation decreases?
► What happens to the SML graph (1) when risk aversion increases and (2) when risk aversion decreases?
► How can a firm affect its market, or beta, risk?

THE COST OF CAPITAL AND VALUATION

16

▲▲▲

Security Valuation

A MANAGERIAL PERSPECTIVE

The earnings available to common shareholders are an important factor in determining the price per share of the equity of a company. Earnings and their future growth are the base from which current and future dividends can be paid to shareholders, and dividends are the cash flows obtained by investors from their investment in the company's shares.

There are many analysts working in the financial markets who attempt to predict the earnings of various companies in order to make buy–sell recommendations to their clients. It has been observed that large changes in share prices are related to announcements of earnings that differ from their forecasted values. Thus, when announced earnings are greater (less) than expected, the share price will increase (fall). These earnings surprises can occur for a number of reasons including (1) unexpected shifts in the underlying demand for the product or in costs of production and (2) the need for improvement in some analysts' research skills.

Table 16-1 is a newspaper listing of some U.S. examples of deviations of actual from expected profits per share and the associated change in share price. The lesson for financial analysts is obvious—improve your forecasting ability so that you will anticipate what is a surprise for the rest of the market. There are lessons for financial managers as well, and these are considered in this chapter.

In Chapter 1, we noted that financial managers should work to maximize the value of their firms. In Chapters 12, 13, 14, and 15, the chapters on time value of money, capital budgeting, and risk adjustment of discount rates, we saw that the value of any asset—real estate, a factory, machinery, an oil well, a coal mine, or a security such as a share of common equity debt or a bond, and so on—is determined by applying a risk-adjusted discount rate to a stream of future cash flows. In this chapter, we present the general principles of security valuation with an emphasis on how the prices of equity and debt securities are determined. This material is obviously important to investors, and it is equally important to financial managers. Indeed, since all important corporate decisions should be analyzed in terms of how they will affect the price of the firm's common equity, it is essential that managers know how these prices are determined.

Definitions of Value

We can think of assets as being divided into two groups: (1) *real*, or *physical, assets*, such as cars, food, houses, art works, and so on, and (2) *financial assets*,

Table 16-1
Great Expectations

How securities analysts' expectations for certain companies' second-quarter profits compared with the actual profits, and how those companies' stock prices reacted on the day they announced their results. ($U.S.)

	Profit per share		Stock price	
	Expected	Actual	Change	Close
Chrysler	21¢	54¢	−$1.69	$21.75
Compaq Computer	28	35	+3.13	27.75
Computer Associates	8	11	+2.13	13.75
Cray Research	13	5	−4.62	23.87
Fisher Price	20	28	+2.13	21.25
Hewlett-Packard	112	76–87*	−12.62	58.87
Kodak	94	111	+1.12	43.87
Monsanto	127	113	−1.50	54.50
Royal Appliance	21	4	−12.38	8.75
Varian	61	54	−.50	35.75

*The company's projected profits range for its second fiscal quarter ended July 31.

Source: Reprinted from "Great Expectations," *The New York Times Service,* as appearing in *The Globe and Mail.* August 11, 1992. Copyright© 1992 by *The New York Times Company.* Reprinted by permission.

such as corporate shares, bonds, notes, and other securities, which, in general, represent claims on real assets. The values of real assets are set in the marketplace by supply and demand conditions. Automobile prices, for example, depend on how much it costs to build cars, how many people need cars, and so forth. The values of financial assets are also set in the marketplace, but the valuation process is different because financial assets are purchased to provide cash flow, not service as with cars or pleasure as with works of art. For some financial assets, the revenue streams are easy to determine and measure; the interest return on a bond is an example. At other times, the cash flows attributable to the asset can only be approximated, as is true for common shares. Regardless of the difficulties of measuring income flows, it is the prospect of them that gives financial assets value. Of course, since cash flows arise over time and can be risky, the other component of the valuation procedure must include the required return. This concept was discussed in depth in Chapter 15 and is applied in this chapter with specific examples.

Liquidating Value versus Going-Concern Value

Several different definitions of values exist, and different definitions are appropriate at different times. The first distinction that must be made is between liquidating and going-concern value.

Liquidating value is the amount that can be realized if an asset or a group of assets—the entire assets of a firm, for example—is sold separately from the organization that has been using it. If the owner of a machine shop decides to retire, the inventory and equipment may be auctioned off, the receivables collected, and the land and building sold to a grocery wholesaler for use as a warehouse. The sum of the proceeds from each category of assets is the liquidating value of the assets. If the owner's debts are subtracted from this amount, the difference represents the liquidating value of the ownership in the business. In some situations, a division or subsidiary of a firm may be sold. This is termed a *selloff* and is considered in Chapter 24.

The **going-concern value** of a company is its worth as an operating entity under its current management and operating strategy. If this value exceeds the liquidating value, the difference represents the value of the organization as distinct from the value of the assets.[1]

Book Value versus Market Value

Book value, the accounting value at which an asset is carried, must be distinguished from **market value**, the price at which the asset can be sold. If the asset in question is a firm, it actually has two potential market values—a liquidating value and a going-concern value. The higher of these values is generally reflected in the price of its shares. Obviously, if the liquidating value exceeds the going-concern value, the firm is worth more dead than alive, and the share price will reflect the proceeds from the expected liquidation. There are instances in which a firm is taken over and assets or divisions are liquidated. This does not mean that the market price did not reflect the liquidating value properly, but that the going-concern value is based on the decisions and operations of the incumbent management, which does not intend to liquidate these assets.

The *book value* per share of common equity is the firm's total common equity—the sum of common shares, contributed surplus, and accumulated retained earnings—divided by the number of shares outstanding. The market value of the equity, which is what investors will actually pay for a share, can be above or below the book value. As we demonstrate later in this chapter, one important reason for a difference between book and market values is investors' expectations of the future growth of the firm. For example, when it is expected that the firm will make investment decisions for which the NPV is greater than zero, the ratio of price to book value per share will be greater than one. The larger the NPV and the amount invested, the greater the value is above one. Alternatively, if the firm is expected to undertake investment decisions at rates of return less than the cost of capital (negative NPV projects), the price-to-book ratio will be less than one. Since market value depends upon the *future* cash flows while book value reflects the *historic* cost of assets, it is not surprising to find wide deviation between book and market values in a dynamic, uncertain world.

---

[1]Accountants term this difference "good will," but "organization value" would be a more appropriate description.

Bond Valuation

A **bond** is a long-term promissory note (original maturity one year or more) or promise to pay issued by a business or governmental unit. It is issued with a stated face value of **par value**, usually $1000, which is the amount that the company promises to repay at the stated *maturity date* of the bond. The bond also requires the issuer to pay a specified number of dollars of interest every year (or, more typically, every 6 months) until maturity. The **coupon interest rate** is equal to the number of dollars paid per year divided by the face or par value of the bond. Thus, if a bond has a par value of $1000, and interest payments are $120, the coupon interest rate is 12 percent. (Although bond interest payments are referred to as *coupon payments*, there are no coupons to detach from the bond document—as once was the case.)

When first issued, bonds have a market value set very close to the par value. However, once the bonds are issued, they are referred to as *seasoned issues* and their market value can vary widely from their par value. Coupon interest payments are constant, so when there is a change in economic conditions, such as a change in interest rates, or a change in the risk of the company, and hence the risk of the bond, the market value of the bond changes as well.

The Basic Bond Valuation Model

As noted, a bond calls for the payment of a specified amount of interest for a stated number of years and for the repayment of the par value on the stated maturity date. Thus a bond represents an *annuity* plus a lump sum payment (repayment of the *principal*) at the maturity date, and its value is the present value of this payment stream.

The following is the basic model[2] of a bond's value.[3]

$$\text{Value} = V = \sum_{t=1}^{n} I \left(\frac{1}{1 + k_d} \right) + M \left(\frac{1}{1 + k_d} \right)^n \qquad \text{(16-1)}$$

$$= I\,(\text{PVIFA}_{k_d,\,n}) + M\,(\text{PVIF}_{k_d,\,n}).$$

Here

I = dollars or interest paid each year = coupon interest rate × par value.

M = par value, or maturity value, which is typically $1000.

---

[2]In finance, the term *model* refers to an equation or set of equations designed to show how one or more variables affect some other variable. Thus, a bond valuation model shows the mathematical relationship between a bond's price and the set of variables that determine the price.

[3]Actually, since most bonds pay interest semiannually, not annually, it is necessary for us to modify our valuation equation slightly. The modification is discussed later in the chapter. Also, we should note that some bonds pay either no interest during their lives (*zero coupon bonds*) or very low coupon rates. Such bonds are sold at a discount below par and hence are called *original issue discount bonds*. The "interest" earned on a zero coupon bond comes at the end, when the company pays off at par ($1000) a bond that was purchased for, say, $321.97. The discount of $1000 − $321.97 = $678.03 substitutes for interest.

k_d = appropriate rate of interest on the bond.[4]

n = number of years until the bond matures; n declines each year after the bond is issued, so a bond that had a maturity of 30 years when it was issued (original maturity = 30 years) becomes a 29-year bond one year later.

Short-Term Bond

Consider Rock of Gibraltar Ltd., a financially strong company, which issues for $1000 each 1-year bonds that promise to make a $12 interest payment and repay $1000 at the end of the year. The dollar return in this case will be the one interest payment plus the repayment of the maturity value at the end of the year. Using Equation 16-1 and values of n = 1 and a coupon rate of 12 percent, we obtain the current market value of the bond as follows:

$$\text{Value} = V = \frac{I}{1 + k_d} + \frac{M}{1 + k_d} \tag{16-2}$$

$$= (\text{PVIFA}_{12\%,1}) + M(\text{PVIF}_{12\%,1})$$

$$= \$120\ (0.8929) + \$1000(0.8929)$$

$$= \$107.10 + \$892.90$$

$$= \$1000.00.$$

Now suppose that just after the bonds are issued interest rates in the economy rise, and the going rate of interest on similar bonds goes up from 12 to 15 percent. We find the value of the Gibralter bonds at the current interest rate of 15 percent by discounting the future dollar returns at the 15 percent discount rate, using Equation 16-2:

$$\text{Value} = V = \frac{I}{1 + k_d} + \frac{M}{1 + k_d}$$

$$= I\ (\text{PVIFA}_{15\%,1}) + M(\text{PVIF}_{15\%,1}).$$

Substituting the values of our example into Equation 16-2, we find that the value of the 12-percent coupon bond falls to $973.95 when the interest rate rises to 15 percent:

$$V_d = \frac{\$120}{1 + 0.15} + \frac{\$1000}{1 + 0.15}$$

$$= \$120(0.8696) + \$1000(0.8696)$$

$$= \$104.35 + \$869.60$$

$$= \$973.95.$$

---

[4]The appropriate interest rate on debt securities was discussed in Chapter 3. The bond's riskiness, liquidity, and years to maturity, as well as supply and demand conditions in the capital markets, all have an influence.

The value of this bond at different interest rates can be found by applying Equation 16-2 with different interest rates; column 2 of the tabulated part of Figure 16-1 shows the bond's value at interest rates ranging from 0 to 25 percent.

Long-Term Bond

Suppose Rock of Gibraltar also issues 15-year, 12-percent coupon bonds at their $1000 par value. The return in this case is the present value of the interest

---

Figure 16-1
Values of Long- and Short-Term, 12 Percent
Coupon Rate Bonds at Different
Market Interest Rates

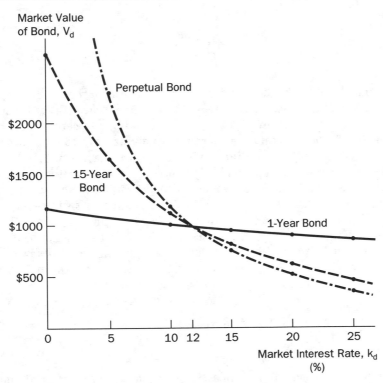

Current Market Interest Rate, k_d (%)	Current Market Value, V		
	1-Year Bond	**15-Year Bond**	**Perpetual Bond**
0	$1120.00	$2800.00	∞
5	1066.67	1726.58	$2400.00
10	1018.18	1152.12	1200.00
12	1000.00	1000.00	1000.00
15	973.91	824.58	800.00
20	933.33	625.96	600.00
25	896.00	498.30	480.00

payments received in each of the 15 years plus the maturity value at the end of that period. To find the value of one of these bonds, we substitute the specific values into Equation 16-1.

$$V = \sum_{t=1}^{15} \frac{I}{(1 + k_d)^t} + \frac{M}{(1 + k_d)^{15}}$$

$$= I(PVIFA_{k_d,15}) + M(PVIF_{k_d,15}).$$

If the going rate of interest is 12 percent, you can confirm that the market value of the 15-year bond is $1000. However, if, as in the previous example, the going interest rate applicable to this bond increases to 15 percent, the value of the 15-year, 12-percent bond is $824.59:

$$V_d = \$120(PVIFA_{15\%,15}) + \$1000(PVIF_{15\%,15})$$

$$= \$120(5.8474) + \$1000(0.1229)$$

$$= \$701.69 + \$122.90$$

$$= \$824.59.$$

The arithmetic of the bond value decrease should be clear, but what is the logic behind it? The fact that k_d has increased to 15 percent means that if you have $1000 to invest, you will invest it in new bonds that pay 15 percent or $150 and will not pay $1000 to obtain the Gibraltar bonds that pay 12 percent or $120. Investors will sell their Gibraltar bonds if the price remains at $1000 and will invest the proceeds in new bonds. This process will drive the price of the existing 12 percent bonds to a level at which the return on the existing bonds equals the return on new bonds. At this point, new investors will be indifferent between investing in the existing Gibraltar bonds or new 15 percent bonds.

If k_d remains constant at 12%, what will be the value of the bond 1 year after it is issued? We can find this value using Equation 16-1, but now the term to maturity is only 14 years—that is, n = 14. We see that V remains at $1000.

$$V = \$120(6.6282) + \$1000(0.2046)$$

$$= \$795.38 + \$204.62$$

$$= \$1000.$$

The value of the bond will remain at $1000 as long as the appropriate interest rate for it remains constant at 12 percent.[5]

---

[5]The bond prices quoted by brokers are calculated as described. However, if you buy a bond between interest payment dates, you have to pay the basic price plus accrued interest. Thus, if you purchase a Gibraltar bond 6 months after it is issued, your broker sends you an invoice stating that you must pay $1000 as the basic price of the bond plus $60 interest, representing one-half the annual interest of $120. The seller of the bond receives $1060. If you buy the bond the day before its interest payment date, you pay $1000 + (364/365)($120) = $1119.67. Of course, you will receive an interest payment of $120 at the end of the next day. See Self-Test Problem 3 for a discussion of bond quotations between interest payment dates.

Throughout the chapter, we assume that the bond is being evaluated immediately after an interest payment date. The better financial calculators have a built-in calendar that permits the calculation of exact values between interest payment dates.

The value of the short- and long-term bonds at different interest rates can be found by using the appropriate values for the PVIFA and PVIF factors in Equation 16-1.

Perpetual Bond

Most bonds have a maturity date, but a few, called *perpetual bonds*, have none; the issuer will never have to repay the principal but promises to pay the stated interest on it in perpetuity. One of the most famous issues of perpetual bonds was sold by the government of England in the early 19th century (see Chapter 12 for details).[6] Although the interest on these bonds was actually stated in pounds, suppose they had promised to pay $120 interest per year in perpetuity. What would they be worth today if the going interest rate is 15 percent?

First, note that any security that promises to pay a constant amount per period forever is a *perpetuity*, and the value of a perpetuity can be expressed as

$$V = \frac{I}{(1 + k_d)^1} + \frac{I}{(1 + k_d)^2} + \ldots + \frac{I}{(1 + k_d)^n} + \ldots$$
$$= \frac{I}{k_d} \tag{16-3}$$

Equation 16-3 is an infinite series of $I a year, and the value of the bond is the discounted sum of the infinite series. Since the market interest rate is 15 percent, then the value of these bonds is $800:

$$V = \frac{\$120}{0.15} = \$800.$$

The value of a perpetual bond at different interest rates is shown in column 3 of the lower part of Figure 16-1.

Interest Rate Risk

As we saw in Chapter 3, market interest rates vary over time, and as interest rates change, the values of the outstanding bonds fluctuate—this point is shown graphically in Figure 16-1. In general, as interest rates rise, bond values decline, and vice versa. Thus, individuals or firms who invest in bonds are exposed to risk from changing interest rates, or *interest rate risk*.

Figure 16-1 shows that the values of bonds with differing maturities have very different responses to changes in the market rate of interest. Note how much less sensitive the short-term bond is to changes in interest rates. At a 12 percent interest rate, all the bonds are valued at $1000. When rates rise to

---

[6]England was not alone in issuing perpetuities. In 1936, the Government of Canada issued a perpetuity with a 3 percent coupon. The issue was not very large ($55 million), and it was callable in 1966. As interest rates increased in the 1970s, the owners of these bonds began to complain about the reduced market values and the low interest payments. In the first quarter of 1975, the government changed some terms of the issue by fixing a maturity date, but maintained the $3 coupon per $100 par value. As would be expected, the price of this "perpetual" increased. Currently, Canadian Pacific Railway (CPR) has a 4 percent perpetual bond outstanding, payable in U.S. dollars. This is the only perpetuity in existence in North America.

20 percent, the perpetuity declines in value to $600 and the 15-year bond falls to $626, but the 1-year bond falls only to $933. The tendency of a bond's price to decline as interest rates rise can be generalized: the longer the maturity of a security, the greater its price change in response to a given change in interest rates. Longer-maturity bonds are generally exposed to more interest rate risk than bonds with shorter maturities. This greater interest rate risk is one factor cited to explain why long-term bonds usually have higher yields, or rates of return, than short-term bonds. It also helps to explain why corporate treasurers are reluctant to hold their near-cash reserves in the form of long-term debt instruments. These reserves are held in short-term securities at moderate interest levels for precautionary purposes, and treasurers are unwilling to sacrifice safety for a little higher yield on a long-term bond.

The logical explanation for the difference in interest rate risk is simple. Suppose you purchased a 14-year bond that yielded 12 percent, or $120 a year, and interest rates on bonds of comparable risk rose to 20 percent. You would be stuck with only $120 of interest for the next 14 years. On the other hand, had you purchased a 1-year bond, you would have a low return for only 1 year. At the end of the year, you would get your $1000 back, and you could then reinvest it and receive 20 percent, or $200 per year, for the next 13 years. Thus, interest rate risk reflects the length of time one is committed to a given investment.

However, even though the 1-year bond has less interest rate risk than a longer term bond, it is exposed to more *reinvestment rate risk*. Suppose that you bought a 1-year bond that yielded 12 percent and then interest rates on bonds of comparable risk fell to 10 percent. After 1 year, when you received your payment, you would have to invest it at only 10 percent, so you would lose $120 − $100 = $20 in annual interest. Had you bought the 14-year bond, you would have continued to receive $120 in annual interest payments even if rates fell. Of course, if you intended to spend the $1000 at the end of the year, investing in a 1-year bond would guarantee (ignoring bankruptcy) that you would get your $1000 back, plus interest, after 1 year. The 14-year bond investment, on the other hand, if sold after 1 year, would return less than $1000 if interest rates had risen.

It has also been observed that the size of the coupon on a bond has an impact on the risk associated with changes in interest rates. The smaller the coupon, the greater is the interest rate risk, assuming all other factors, such as term to maturity and default risk, are held constant. To demonstrate this concept: consider two Government of Canada bonds, each with a 5-year term to maturity and a face value of $1000. Current interest rates are 10 percent per annum. The first bond is issued without any interest payments; this bond is called a *pure discount bond*, or *zero-coupon bond*, and its current value of $620.92 is obtained by finding the present value of the principal repayment, which is to be made in 5 years:[7]

$$V = \frac{\$1000}{(1.1)^5} = \$620.92.$$

---

[7]The zero coupon bond sells at a substantial discount from its face or par value. Bonds that have a small coupon payment—say, 1 or 2 percent—sell at a large discount from their face value and are referred to as *deep-discount bonds*.

The second bond has a coupon rate equal to the current market rate of 10 percent; consequently, the current market value equals the face value of $1000.

Table 16-2 presents the impact on the market value of a change in current interest rates, using 10 percent as the base. As can be observed, a reduction of 1 percentage point in the current interest rate results in a larger increase in the market value of the zero coupon bond than of the 10 percent coupon bond. Similarly, a 1 percentage point increase in the current interest rate has a greater impact on the zero coupon bond.

Bond Valuation with Semiannual Compounding

Although many bonds do pay interest annually, most actually pay interest semiannually. To evaluate bonds with semiannual compounding, we need to modify the basic valuation model (Equation 16-1) as follows:

1. Divide the annual coupon interest payment, I, by 2 to determine the semiannual interest payments.
2. Determine the number of semiannual periods by multiplying the years to maturity, n, by 2.
3. Determine the semiannual interest rate by dividing the annual rate, k_d, by 2.

Once we have made these changes, we can represent the valuation model with semiannual compounding as follows:

$$V = \sum_{t=1}^{2n} \frac{I}{2} \left(\frac{1}{1 + k_d/2} \right)^t + M \left(\frac{1}{1 + k_d/2} \right)^{2n}, \qquad \text{(16-4)}$$

$$= \frac{I}{2}(\text{PVIFA}_{k_d/2, 2n}) + M(\text{PVIF}_{k_d/2, 2n}). \qquad \text{(16-4a)}$$

Table 16-2
Influence of Size of Coupon Payment
on Interest Rate Risk

Current Interest Rate	Zero Coupon Bond		10 Percent Bond	
	Market Value	Percentage Change	Market Value	Percentage Change
9%	$649.93		$1038.90	
		4.67%		3.89%
10%	$620.92		$1000.00	
		−4.42%		−3.70%
11%	$593.45		$963.04	

If the 5-year, 12 percent bond discussed in the last section paid interest semi-annually, then its value at 20 percent interest rate can be found as follows:[8]

$$V_d = \frac{\$120}{2}(9.4269) + \$1000(0.573)$$

$$= \$565.61 + 57.31$$

$$= \$622.92.$$

Students sometimes want to discount the maturity value at 20 percent over 15 years rather than at 10 percent over 30 6-month periods. This is incorrect. Logically, all cash flows in a given contract must be discounted on the same basis, semiannually in this instance. For consistency, bond traders must apply semiannual compounding to the maturity value, and they do.

Time Path of Bond Prices

In the previous sections we considered the impact of a change in interest rates just after the issuance of a bond on bond values. If the new interest rate is expected to remain in effect over the remaining lifetime of the issue, the bond prices are expected to proceed on a particular path over the remaining life of the bond.

Consider a newly issued bond that has a 15 percent coupon and 15 years to maturity and that is issued at par of $1000. Just after the issue, the interest rate on comparable risk bonds falls to 10 percent and is expected to remain at that level over the next 14 years. The value of the bond at the end of Year 1 would be $1368.34:

$$V = \$150(PVIFA_{10\%,\,14}) + \$1000(PVIF_{10\%,\,14})$$

$$= \$150(7.3667) + \$1000(0.2633)$$

$$= \$1105.01 + \$263.31$$

$$= \$1368.34$$

This bond would sell above par, or at a *premium*.

Assuming that interest rates remain constant at 10 percent for the next 14 years, what would happen to the value of this bond? It would fall gradually from $1368.31 at present to $1000 at maturity, when the bond will be redeemed for $1000. This point can be illustrated by calculating the value of the bond 1 year later, when it has 13 years remaining to maturity:

---

[8]Notice that the value of the semiannual bond is slightly less than that of the annual payment bond. At first glance, this seems unreasonable—it would seem that the semiannual bond would have a higher value because its interest payments come in a little more rapidly than do those of the annual payment bond. What is happening is that we are really discounting the cash flows from the two bonds at two different rates. Cash flows from the annual payment bond are being discounted at an effective annual rate, or annual percentage rate (APR), of 20 percent, while those from the semiannual bond are being discounted at an APR of $(1.10)^2 - 1.0 = 21.0$ percent.

$$V = \$150(\text{PVIFA}_{10\%, \ 13 \ years}) + \$1000(\text{PVIF}_{10\%, \ 13 \ years})$$

$$= \$150(7.1034) + \$1000(0.2897) = \$1355.21.$$

Thus, the value of the bond would have fallen from $1368.31 to $1355.21, or by $13.10. If you calculate the value of the bond at other future dates, you can see that the price would continue to fall as the maturity date approached.

Notice that if you purchased the bond at a price of $1368.31 and then sold it 1 year later with k_d still at 10 percent, you would have a capital loss of $13.10, or a total return of $150.00 − $13.10 = $136.90. Your percentage rate of return would consist of an *interest yield*—often called a **current yield**—plus a *capital gains yield*, calculated as follows:

$$
\begin{aligned}
\text{Current, or interest, yield} &= \quad \$150/\$1368.31 = \quad 0.1096 = \quad 10.96\% \\
\text{Capital gains yield} &= -\$13.10/\$1368.31 = -0.0096 = -0.96\% \\
\text{Total rate of return, or yield} &= \quad \$136.90/\$1368.31 = \quad 0.1001 = \underline{\quad 10.00\%}
\end{aligned}
$$

Had interest rates risen from 15 to 20 percent during the first year after issue, rather than fallen, the value of this bond would have declined to $769.49:

$$V = \$150(\text{PVIFA}_{20\%, \ 14 \ years}) + \$1000(\text{PVIF}_{20\%, \ 14 \ years})$$

$$= \$150(4.6106) + \$1000(0.0779)$$

$$= \$691.59 + \$77.90$$

$$= \$769.49.$$

In this case, the bond would sell at a *discount* of $230.51 below its par value:

$$\text{Discount} = \text{Price} - \text{Par value} = \$769.49 - \$1000$$
$$= -\$230.51.$$

The total expected future yield on the bond would again consist of a current yield and a capital gains yield, but now the capital gains yield would be positive. The total yield would be 20 percent. Let's check by calculating the price of the bond with 13 years left to maturity, assuming that interest rates remain at 20 percent.

$$V = \$150(\text{PVIFA}_{20\%, \ 13 \ years}) + \$1000(\text{PVIF}_{20\%, \ 13 \ years})$$

$$= \$150(4.5327) + \$1000(0.0935)$$

$$= \$679.91 + \$93.50$$

$$= \$773.41.$$

Notice that the capital gain for the year is the difference between the bond's value in Year 13 and the bond's value in Year 14, or $773.41 − $769.49 = $3.92. The interest yield, capital gains yield, and total yield are calculated as follows:

$$
\begin{aligned}
\text{Current, or interest, yield} &= \quad \$150/\$769.49 = 0.1949 = 19.49\% \\
\text{Capital gains yield} &= \quad \$3.92 = 0.0051 = \quad 0.51\% \\
\text{Total rate of return, or yield} &= \$153.92/\$769.49 = 0.2000 = \underline{20.00\%}
\end{aligned}
$$

The discount or premium on a bond may also be calculated as follows:

$$\text{Discount or premium} = \left[\begin{array}{c} \text{Interest payment} \\ \text{on the old bond} \end{array} - \begin{array}{c} \text{Interest payment} \\ \text{on a new bond} \end{array} \right] (\text{PVIFA})_{k_d, n},$$

where n = years to maturity on the old bond and k_d = current rate of interest on a new bond. For example, if interest rates had risen to 20 percent 1 year after the old bonds were issued, the discount on them would have been calculated as follows:

$$\text{Discount} = (\$150 - \$200)(4.6106) = -\$230.53.$$

(The minus sign indicates a discount). This value agrees, except for rounding, with the $-\$230.51$ value calculated previously.

From these calculations, we see that the discount is equal to the present value of the interest payments you sacrifice when you buy a low-coupon old bond rather than a high-coupon new bond. The longer the bond has left to maturity, the greater the sacrifice, and hence the greater the discount.

Figure 16-2 graphs the values of the bond over time, assuming that interest rates in the economy (1) remain constant at 15 percent, (2) fall to 10 percent and then remain constant at that level, or (3) rise to 20 percent and remain constant at that level. Of course, if interest rates do *not* remain constant, then the price of the bond will fluctuate. However, regardless of what future interest rates do, the bond's price will approach $1000 as it nears the maturity date (barring bankruptcy, in which case the bond's value might drop to zero).

Figure 16-2 illustrates the following key points:

1. Whenever the going rate of interest, k_d, is equal to the coupon rate, a bond will sell at its par value. Normally, the coupon rate is set at the going interest rate when a bond is issued, so it sells at par initially.
2. Interest rates change over time, but the coupon rate remains fixed after the bond has been issued. Whenever the going rate of interest is *greater than* the coupon rate, a bond will sell *below* its par value. Such a bond is called a **discount bond**.
3. Whenever the going rate of interest is *less than* the coupon rate, a bond will sell *above* its par value. Such a bond is called a **premium bond**.
4. Thus, an *increase* in interest rates will cause the price of an outstanding bond to *fall*, whereas a *decrease* in rates will cause it to *rise*.
5. The market value of a bond will always approach its par value as its maturity date approaches, provided the issuer does not go bankrupt.

These points are very important, for they show that bondholders may suffer capital losses or make capital gains, depending on whether interest rates rise or fall. And, as we saw in Chapter 3, interest rates do indeed change over time.

Finding the Interest Rate on a Bond: Yield to Maturity

Suppose you were offered a 14-year, 15 percent coupon, $1000 par value bond at a price of $1368.31. What rate of interest would you earn on your investment if you bought the bond and held it to maturity? This rate is called the bond's **yield**

Figure 16-2
Time Path of the Value of a 15% Coupon,
$1000 Par Value Bond When Interest Rates
Are 10%, 15%, and 20%

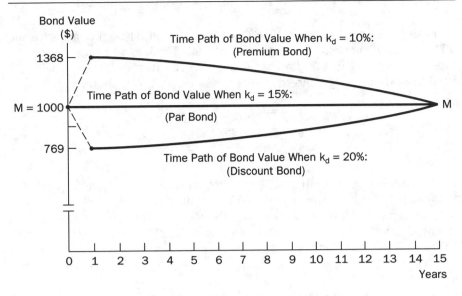

Year	$k_d = 10\%$	$k_d = 15\%$	$k_d = 20\%$
0	—	$1000	—
1	$1368.31	1000	$ 769.49
.	.	.	.
.	.	.	.
.	.	.	.
15	1000	1000	1000

Note: The curves for 10% and 20% have a slight bow.

to maturity (YTM), and it is the interest rate discussed by bond traders when they talk about rates of return. To find the yield to maturity, you could solve Equation 6-1 for k_d:

$$V = \$1368.31 = \frac{\$150}{(1 + k_d)^1} + \cdots + \frac{\$150}{(1 + k_d)^{14}} + \frac{\$1000}{(1 + k_d)^{14}}$$

$$= \$150(\text{PVIFA}_{k_d,14}) + \$1000(\text{PVIF}_{k_d,14}).$$

You can substitute values for PVIFA and PVIF until you find a pair that "works" and forces this equality:

$$\$1368.31 = \$150(\text{PVIFA}_{k_d,14}) + \$1000(\text{PVIF}_{k_d,14}).$$

What would be a good interest rate to use as a starting point? First, you know that because the bond is selling at a premium over its par value ($1368.31

versus $1000.00), its yield to maturity must be less than its 15 percent coupon rate. Therefore, you might try a rate of 12 percent. Substituting factors for 12 percent, you obtain

$$\$150(6.6282) + \$1000(0.2046) = \$1198.83 \neq \$1368.31.$$

The calculated bond value, $1198.83, is below the actual market price, so the YTM is not 12 percent. To raise the calculated value, you must lower the interest rate used in the process, because lower interest rates mean higher bond prices. Inserting interest factors for 10 percent, you obtain

$$
\begin{aligned}
V &= \$150(7.3667) + \$1000(0.2633) \\
&= \$1105.01 + \$263.30 \\
&= \$1368.31.
\end{aligned}
$$

This calculated value is equal to the market price of the bond; thus, 10 percent is the bond's yield to maturity: $k_d = \text{YTM} = 10.0\%$.[9]

As you might guess, by far the easiest way to find the bond's YTM is with a financial calculator. In this example, enter n = 14, PMT = 150, FV = 1000, and PV = 1368.31 (− 1368.31 on some calculators). Now press the i button. The calculator will blink for several seconds, and then the answer, 10 percent, will appear.

The yield to maturity is identical to the *total rate of return* discussed previously. The YTM for a bond that sells at par consists entirely of an interest yield, but if the bond sells at a price other than par value, the YTM consists of the interest yield plus a positive or negative capital gains yield. Note also that a bond's yield to maturity changes whenever interest rates in the economy change, which is almost daily. If you purchase a bond and hold it until it matures, you will receive the YTM that existed on the purchase date, but the bond's calculated YTM will change frequently between the purchase date and the maturity date.

---

[9]A few years ago, bond traders all had specialized tables called *bond tables* that gave yields on bonds of different maturities selling at different premiums and discounts. Because calculators are so much more efficient (and accurate), bond tables are rarely used any more.

R.J. Rodriquez recently developed a formula that can be used to find the *approximate* YTM on a bond:

$$\text{Approximate } k_d = \text{Approximate YTM} \approx \frac{I + (M - V)/n}{(M + 2V)/3}.$$

The numerator gives the average total return (coupon plus capital gain or loss) over the life of the bond, while the denominator is the average price of the bond. In our example, I = $150, M = $1000, V = $1368.31, and n = 14, so

$$\text{Approximate } k_d \approx \frac{\$150 + (\$1000 - \$1368.31)/14}{(\$1000 + \$2736.62)/3} = 0.0993 = 9.93\%.$$

The exact value is 10 percent, so Rodriquez's formula provides a close approximation.

Yield to Call

Most bonds have a provision whereby the issuer may pay them off prior to maturity. This feature, known as a **call provision**, is discussed in some detail in Chapter 21. If a bond is callable and if interest rates in the economy decline or if the interest rate on the debt itself falls since the bond becomes less risky, then the company can sell a new issue of low-interest-rate bonds and use the proceeds to retire the old high-interest-rate issue.

If the bond that you purchased is called by the company, you do not have the option of holding it until it matures so the yield to maturity is not relevant. For example, if the 15 percent coupon bonds we discussed were callable and if interest rates fell from 15 percent to 10 percent, the company could call in the 15 percent bonds, replace them with 10 percent bonds, and save $150 − $100 = $50 interest per bond per year. This would be beneficial to the company as long as it did not have to pay the higher market value of the bonds to the investor to obtain the bonds. Of course, the call provision is not of benefit to the bondholders since the bonds can be redeemed from them at a value less than they could receive if the bonds were sold in the market.

If current interest rates are well below an outstanding bond's coupon rate, then a callable bond is likely to be called, and investors should estimate the expected rate of return on the bond as the **yield to call (YTC)**, rather than as the yield to maturity. To calculate the YTC, solve this equation for k_d:

$$\text{Price of bond} = \sum_{t=1}^{n} \frac{I}{(1 + k_d)^t} + \frac{\text{Call price}}{(1 + k_d)^n}$$

Here n is the number of years until the company can call the bond, call price is the price the company must pay in order to call the bond (it is often set equal to the par value plus 1 year's interest), and k_d is the YTC. In the balance of the chapter, we assume that bonds are not callable unless otherwise noted, but some of the end-of-chapter problems deal with yield to call.

Bond Prices in Recent Years

We know from Chapter 3 that interest rates fluctuate, and we have seen here that the prices of outstanding bonds rise and fall inversely with changes in interest rates. In Figure 16-3 we plot the prices and yields for an index of long-term Canadian bonds, both corporate and government, over the period January 1990 to June 1992. From this figure we observe that bond yields increased over the period January 1990 to October 1990 and then began to fall with dramatic reductions occurring in late 1991 and early 1992 as the recession deepened. That this index covers both corporate and government bonds is important. The recession meant that corporations had an increased risk of default, which should have resulted in an increase in yields, but this effect was offset by the dramatic overall decrease in interest rates in the economy. For example, yields on long-term Government of Canada bonds were 10.02 percent in January 1990 and 10.19 percent in January 1991 but 8.94 percent in January 1992.

Figure 16-3
Long-Term Canadian Bond Index, Prices and Yields

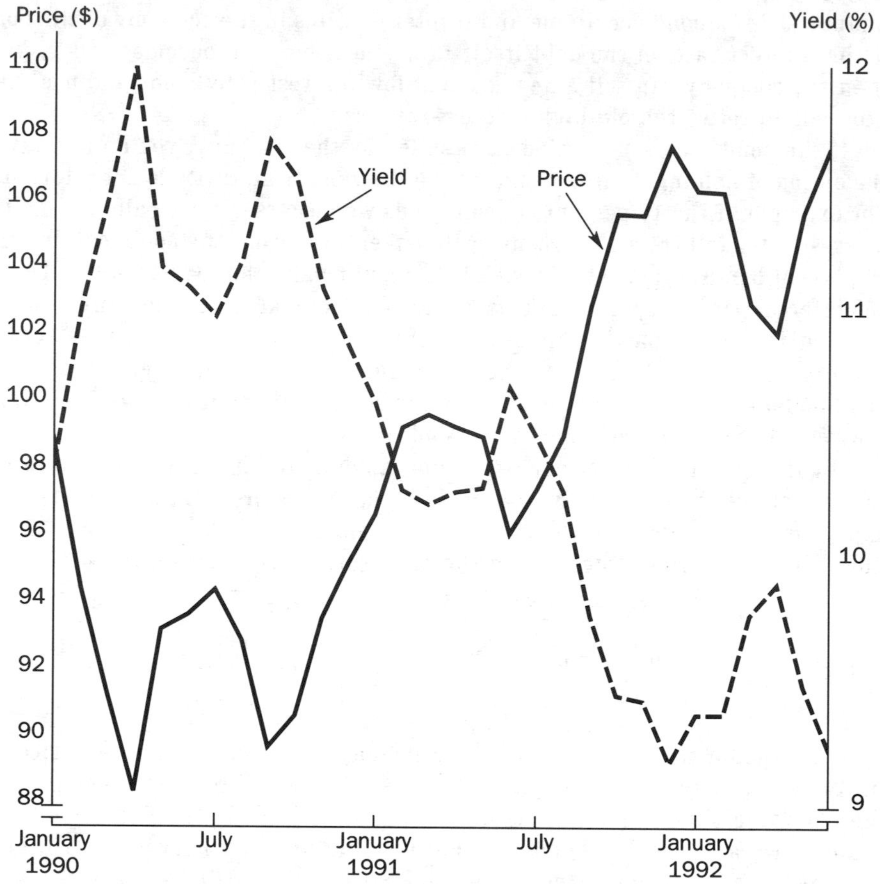

Source: ScotiaMcLeod Inc., *Debt Market Indices.* August 1992.

Bond Markets

Corporate bonds are traded primarily in the *over-the-counter (OTC) market.*
Most bonds are owned by and traded among large financial institutions (for
example, life insurance companies, mutual funds, and pension funds, all of
which deal in very large blocks of securities), and it is relatively easy for
dealers to arrange the transfer of large blocks of bonds among the relatively
few holders. For the vast majority of bonds, there is little trading; they are
kept "locked away" until maturity.

    Information on bond transactions in the over-the-counter market is not
published, but selected quotations on actively traded bond issues in the
Government of Canada, provincial, and corporate segments of the market are
published in the financial papers. Figure 16-4 is *The Globe and Mail's* August 8,
1992 report on the corporate bond segment. The first entry is for a Bell Canada
bond with a coupon of 9.50 percent, maturing June 15, 2002. The price as of

Figure 16-4
Canadian Bond Transactions, August 7, 1992

CANADIAN BONDS

Selected quotations, with changes since the previous day, on actively traded bond issues, provided by RBC Dominion Securities. Yields are calculated to full maturity, unless marked C to indicate callable date. Price is the midpoint between final bid and ask quotations Aug. 7, 1992.

Issuer	Coupon	Maturity	Price	Yield	$ Chg
		Corporate			
BELL CANADA	9.50	15 JUN 02	110.250	7.974	+0.625
BELL CANADA	9.70	15 DEC 32	108.000	8.960	+0.500
BELL CDA ENT	9.00	28 AUG 97	108.250	7.026	+0.500
BC TELEPHONE	9.15	8 APR 02	108.625	7.856	+0.625
BC TELEPHONE	9.65	8 APR 22	107.125	8.958	+0.500
CONSUMER GAS	7.55	15 DEC 97	102.000	7.090	+0.500
CONSUMER GAS	10.80	15 APR 11	115.500	9.061	+0.375
CDN PACIFIC	10.50	30 APR 01	111.375	8.612	+0.500
CDN UTIL	9.92	1 APR 22	109.750	8.973	+0.500
CDN OCC PET	8.40	30 JAN 97	104.125	7.298	+0.375
EATN CR CARD	9.55	2 JUN 97	108.250	7.468	+0.375
IMPERIAL OIL	9.88	15 DEC 99	111.750	7.742	+0.500
IMASCO LTD	9.85	22 APR 02	110.500	8.251	+0.625
JOHN LABATT	9.25	6 MAR 02	107.225	8.146	+0.625
MAR TEL +TEL	9.90	1 MAY 97	111.000	7.108	+0.375
ROYAL BANK	10.50	1 MAR 02	114.075	8.332	+0.500
TD BANK	9.10	*	107.250	7.264C	+0.500
THOMSON CORP	9.15	2 DEC 98	108.375	7.456	+0.500
SEAGRAM CO	9.00	15 DEC 98	108.250	7.345	+0.500

*15 May 02/97

Source: Excerpted from "Canadian Bonds," *The Globe and Mail*, August 7, 1992, Report on Business. Reprinted with permission.

August 7, 1992 was $110.250, which translates to a yield to maturity of 7.974 percent. The price reflects an increase of $0.625 over the price on the previous day. Note that the bonds are listed in alphabetical order by issuer and in the order of the original issue dates beginning with the earliest. Also, although these bonds are issued with $1000 par values, by convention they are quoted on $100 par value basis.

Companies generally set their coupon rates at levels that reflect the going rate of interest on the day of issue. If the rate were set lower, investors simply would not buy the bonds at the $1000 par value, so the company could not borrow the money it needed. Thus, bonds generally sell at their par values on the issue date, but their prices fluctuate thereafter as interest rates change.

Concept Review

► Identify the two primary forms of capital that corporations raise.
► What is meant by the terms *new issue* and *seasoned issue*?
► Explain, verbally, the following equation:

(continued)

(continued)

$$V = I(PVIFA_{k_d,n}), + M(PVIF_{k_d,n}).$$

▶ Write out a formula that can be used to calculate the discount or premium on a bond, and explain it.
▶ Describe how *interest rate risk* and *reinvestment risk* operate.
▶ How does the calculation price differ between a bond that is callable and one that is not?
▶ How is the general bond valuation formula changed to deal with bonds that have semiannual coupons rather than annual coupons?

Preferred Share Valuation

A **preferred equity share** is a long-term equity security that pays a fixed dividend. Preferred equity is a hybrid security, similar to bonds in some respects and to common shares in others. Preferred dividends are similar to interest payments on bonds in that they are fixed in amount and generally must be paid before common equity dividends can be paid. However, like common dividends, preferred dividends can be omitted without bankrupting the firm. In addition, some preferred equity is similar to common equity in that it has no maturity date and is not callable; hence, such issues are *perpetuities*.

Although some preferred issues are eventually retired, the value of a preferred share, V_p, is found as follows:

$$V_p = \frac{D_p}{k_p}, \tag{16-5}$$

where V_p is the value of the preferred share, D_p is the dividend per preferred share, and k_p is the appropriate required rate of return for investments of this degree of risk. For example, suppose Northstar Company pays its preferred shareholders dividends per share of $2.40, and the required rate of return on preferred shares with this degree of risk is 13.5 percent. The value of a share of Northstar preferred can be found by solving Equation 16-5 for V_p as follows:

$$V_p = \frac{\$2.40}{0.135} = \$17.78.$$

As another example, consider the Loblaw Companies Limited preferred share issue that pays a $3.70 annual dividend. The yield on a preferred share, which is similar to that on a perpetual bond, is found by solving Equation 16-5 for k_p. For the Loblaw preferred issue, we observe as of July 28, 1992, that the price per share was $48.00; with the annual dividend of $3.70, the yield can be calculated as follows:

$$k_p = \frac{D_p}{V_p} = \frac{\$3.70}{\$48.00} = 0.771 \text{ or } 7.71\%.$$

Changes in the risk of the preferred shares and the overall level of interest rates will have an impact on the required return or yield on preferred shares.

The analysis has assumed that preferred shares are of the "standard" form. This form, in which there are fixed dividends and perpetual term, is not as common a feature of companies' capital structures as it was in the past. As we shall note in Chapter 21, term preferred shares are more common today, and for some of these securities, the valuation procedure is more closely related to the valuation of debt as presented in Equation 16-1.

> ### *Concept Review*
>
> ▶ In what ways is preferred equity similar to bonds, and in what respects is it similar to common equity?

Common Equity Valuation

Common equity represents the ownership of a corporation, but to the typical investor, a *share* of common equity is simply a piece of paper distinguished by two features:

1. It entitles its owner to dividends, but only if the company has earnings out of which dividends can be paid and only if management chooses to pay dividends rather than to retain all the earnings. Whereas a bond contains a *promise* to pay interest, common equity provides no such promise (in a legal sense) to pay dividends—if you own a share you may *expect* a dividend, but your expectations may not in fact be met. To illustrate, St. Lawrence Cement, the largest cement producer in Eastern Canada, suspended its dividend payments in August 1992, in response to the prevailing economic conditions and the company's expectations of its profitability in the near term. St. Lawrence Cement had been a strong company and had paid dividends since 1970.

2. Shares of equity can be sold at some future date, and the investor hopes the sale price will be greater than the purchase price. If the equity is actually sold at a price per share above its purchase price, the investor will receive a *capital gain*. Generally, at the time people buy common equity, they expect to receive capital gains; otherwise, they would not buy them. However, after the fact they can end up with capital losses rather than capital gains.

The current or actual market price of a share of common equity, P_0, depends upon (1) the cash flow stream an investor expects to receive if he or she buys the share and (2) the riskiness of these expected cash flows. The expected cash flows consist of two elements: (1) the dividend expected in each year, and (2) the price the investor expects to receive when he or she sells the share. The expected final share price includes the return of the original investment plus a capital gain.

Single-Period Share Valuation Model

If an investor expects to hold the share for one year and if the price is expected to grow at the rate g, then the single-period valuation equation is as follows:

$$\hat{P}_0 = \frac{\text{Expected dividend per share for Year 1} + \text{Expected price at end of Year 1}}{1.0 + \text{required rate of return}}$$

$$= \frac{D_1 + \hat{P}_1}{1 + k_s} = \frac{D_1 + P_0(1 + g)}{1 + k_s},$$

which simplifies to

$$\hat{P}_0 = \frac{D_1}{k_s - g}. \tag{16-6}$$

Equation 16-6 represents the present value of the expected dividends and year-end share price, discounted at the required rate of return, k_s. Solving Equation 16-6 gives the **expected** or **intrinsic price** for the common equity. To illustrate, suppose you are thinking of buying a share of Consolidated Wrecking Ltd. and holding it for 1 year. You note that Consolidated earned $2.86 per share last year and paid a dividend of $1.90. Earnings and dividends have been rising at about 5 percent a year, on average, over the last 10 to 15 years, and you expect this growth to continue. Further, if earnings and dividends grow at the expected rate, you think the share price will likewise grow by 5 percent a year.

The next step in obtaining the share price is to determine the **required rate of return** on Consolidated's equity. Suppose the current rate of interest on Government of Canada bonds, k_{RF}, is about 9 percent; Consolidated is clearly more risky than government securities, because competitors could erode the company's market, labour problems could disrupt operations, or an economic recession could cause sales to fall below the breakeven point. Further, even if sales, earnings, and dividends meet projections, the share price could still fall as a result of a generally weak market. Given all these risk factors, you conclude that a 7 percent risk premium, RP, is justified, so you calculate your required rate of return on Consolidated's equity, k_s, as follows:

$$k_s = k_{RF} + RP = 9\% + 7\% = 16\%.$$

Next, you estimate the expected dividend per share for the coming year, D_1, as follows:

$$D_1 = D_0 (1 + g) = \$1.90(1.05) = \$2.00.$$

Now you have the necessary information to estimate the intrinsic value of the share by the use of Equation 16-6:

$$\hat{P}_0 = \frac{D_1}{k_s - g}$$

$$= \frac{\$2}{0.16 - 0.05} = \$18.18.$$

To you, $18.18 represents a reasonable price for Consolidated's equity. If the actual market price, P_a, is less, you should buy it; if the actual price is higher, you should not buy it, or you should sell if you already own it.

Estimating the Expected Rate of Return on a Share

In the preceding section, we calculated the intrinsic value of Consolidated's shares to a given investor. Let us now change the focus somewhat and calculate the rate of return the investor can expect if the common equity is purchased at the current market price per share. The *expected rate of return*, which we denote as $\hat{k}_s$, is analogous to the *internal rate of return* on an investment project. $\hat{k}_s$ is the discount rate that equates the present value of the expected dividends (D_1) and the expected final share price (P_1) to the observed present share price (P_0):[10]

$$P_0 = \frac{D_1 + \hat{P}_1}{(1 + \hat{k}_s)} = \frac{D_1 + P_0(1 + g)}{(1 + \hat{k}_s)}$$

Suppose Consolidated Wrecking is selling for $20 per share. We can calculate $\hat{k}_s$ as follows:

$$\$20 = \frac{\$2 + \$20(1.05)}{(1 + \hat{k}_s)} = \frac{\$2 + \$21}{(1 + \hat{k}_s)} = \frac{\$23}{1 + \hat{k}_s}$$

$$\$20(1 + \hat{k}_s) = \$23$$

$$1 + \hat{k}_s = 1.15$$

$$\hat{k}_s = 0.15 \text{ or } 15\%.$$

Thus, if you the investor expect to receive a $2 dividend and a year-end price of $21, then your expected rate of return on the investment is 15 percent.

Notice that the expected rate of return, $\hat{k}_s$, consists of two components, an expected dividend yield and an expected capital gains yield:

$$\hat{k}_s = \frac{\text{Expected dividend}}{\text{Present price}} + \frac{\text{Expected increase in price}}{\text{Present price}}$$

$$= \frac{D_1}{P_0} + g. \qquad\qquad (16\text{-}7)$$

For Consolidated, if shares are purchased at a price of $20, the expected return must be 15 percent:

$$\hat{k}_s = \frac{\$2}{\$20} + \frac{\$1}{\$20} = 10\% + 5\% = 15\%.$$

Given an expected rate of return of 15 percent, should you purchase the shares of the company? This depends upon how the expected return compares with the

---

[10]The k_s value of Equation 16-6 is a *required* rate of return, but when we transform it below to obtain Equation 16-7, we are finding an *expected* rate of return. The transformation requires that $k_s = \hat{k}_s$. This equality holds if the equity market is in equilibrium, a condition discussed later in the chapter.

required return for a security of this risk. If $\hat{k}_s$ exceeds k_s, buy; if $\hat{k}_s$ is less than k_s, sell; and if $\hat{k}_s$ equals k_s, the share price is in equilibrium and you should be indifferent. In our example, your 16 percent required rate of return for Consolidated Wrecking exceeds the 15 percent expected return, so you should not buy the shares.

Multiperiod Share Valuation Model

So far we have discussed a single-period model of common equity valuation, in which the investor holds the equity for 1 year, receives 1 dividend, and then sells the equity at the end of the year. We now consider multiperiod valuation models.

According to the valuation theory, the value of any financial asset is the present value of the expected cash flows. We used this approach in valuing a bond with the cash flows being the interest payments over the life of the bond plus the repayment of principal at the maturity date. Analogously, a share price is determined as the present value of cash flows that are expected dividends plus the expected sale price of the share when the investor intends to sell the security.

We begin the analysis by assuming that the investor purchases the share with the intention of holding it (within the family) forever. In this case, all that the investor and the heirs will receive is a stream of dividends, and the value of the share of common equity is equal to the present value of an infinite stream of dividends:

$$\text{Value of a share} = \hat{P}_0 = PV(\text{expected dividends})$$

or

$$\hat{P}_0 = \frac{D_1}{(1 + k_s)^1} + \frac{D_2}{(1 + k_s)^2} + \ldots + \frac{D_\infty}{(1 + k_s)^\infty} \qquad \textbf{(16-8)}$$

$$= \sum_{t=1}^{\infty} \frac{D_1}{(1 + k_s)^t}.$$

Of course, individual investors do not normally expect to hold a share forever—they expect to hold it for, say, 5 to 10 years, and then sell it. However, even in this situation, Equation 16-8 will determine the value of the expected price per share. To see this, recognize that for any individual investor, the expected cash flows consist of expected dividends plus the expected sale price of the security. However, the sale price the current investor receives must be equal to the present value of the expected dividends some future investor expects. Therefore, for all present and future investors in total, expected cash flows must be based on expected future dividends. To put this another way, unless a firm is liquidated or sold to another concern, the cash flows it provides to its shareholders is only a stream of dividends; therefore, the value of a share of its common equity must be established as the present value of that expected dividend stream.

The general validity of Equation 16-8 can also be confirmed by the following logic. Suppose you buy a share of common equity and expect to hold it for

1 year. As noted before, you will receive the dividends during the year and the value $\hat{p}_1$ at the end of the year. What determines the value of $\hat{P}_1$? The answer is that it will be determined as the present value of the dividends during Year 2 plus the share price at the end of that year; this in turn will be determined as the present value of another set of future dividends and an even more distant share price. The process can be continued ad infinitum, and the ultimate result is Equation 16-8.

Common Share Valuation under Alternative Growth Patterns

Equation 16-8 as just presented is a generalized equity valuation model in the sense that the time pattern of D_1 can be anything: D_t can rise, fall, remain constant, or even fluctuate randomly, and Equation 16-8 will continue to hold. For many purposes, however, it is useful to estimate a particular time pattern for D_t and then to develop a simplified (that is, easier to evaluate) version of the share valuation model expressed in Equation 16-8. The following sections consider three special cases: zero growth, constant growth, and nonconstant ("supernormal") growth.

Share Values with Zero Growth

Suppose a share's dividends are not expected to grow but, rather, to remain constant. In this case, we have a **zero growth share**—the dividends expected in each future year are equal to some constant amount, $D_1 = D_2 = D_3$ and so on. As we noted earlier in connection with preferred shares, a security that is expected to pay a constant amount each period forever is defined as a *perpetuity*. Therefore, the value of a zero growth share can be calculated using the formula developed for a perpetual bond:

$$\text{Price} \quad = \frac{\text{Dividend}}{\text{Discount rate}}$$

$$\hat{P}_0 = \frac{D_1}{\hat{k}_s}. \quad \text{(16-9)}$$

Solving for $\hat{k}_s$, we obtain

$$\hat{k}_s = \frac{D_1}{P_0}, \quad \text{(16-9a)}$$

which shows that the required rate of return on a share of common equity that has no growth prospects is simply its dividend yield.[11]

---

[11]If you think that having a share pay dividends forever is unrealistic, then think of it as lasting only for 50 years. Here you would have an annuity of 50 years and a terminal value. However, the present value of this terminal value would contribute very little to the present value of the cash flow, so the price would be based almost exclusively on the annuity value.

Consider a company that paid a dividend per share of \$1.82. Assume the required rate of return is 16 percent. The value of the equity is \$11.38:

$$\hat{P}_0 = \frac{\$1.82}{0.16} = \$11.38.$$

Note that if the actual share price is \$11.38, the expected rate of return is equal to 16 percent:

$$\hat{k}_0 = \frac{D_1}{P_0} = \frac{\$1.82}{\$11.38} = 0.16 = 16\%.$$

Normal, or Constant, Growth

Although the zero growth model is applicable to some companies, the earnings and dividends of most companies are expected to increase each year. Expected growth rates vary from company to company; what is called **normal**, or **constant**, **growth** is growth expected to continue into the foreseeable future at about the same rate as that of the economy in general.

The expected growth rate of dividends per share for a specific company depends upon (1) the retention ratio that the company has established and (2) the profitability of the firm's investments. The higher the retention ratio (that is, the lower the payout ratio), the greater the retained earnings invested and hence the higher the expected growth rate in dividends per share. Similarly, if two firms have the same retention ratio, the firm with the greater rate of return on its investments will have the higher expected growth rate in dividends per share. If a company is expected to grow at some constant rate, g, and if its last dividend was D_0, then its dividend in any future year, t, may be forecast as $D_t = D_0(1 + g)^t$. For example, suppose a company just paid a dividend of \$1.82 (that is, $D_0 = \$1.82$); if its investors expected a 10 percent growth rate, then the estimated dividend 1 year hence is $D_1 = (\$1.82)(1.10) = \$2.00$; $D_2 = (\$1.82)(1.10)^2 = \$2.20$; and so forth.

Using this method of estimating future dividends, the current expected price, $\hat{P}_0$, of a constant growth company may be expressed as follows:

$$\hat{P}_0 = \frac{D_1}{(1 + k_s)^1} + \frac{D_2}{(1 + k_s)^2} + \frac{D_3}{(1 + k_s)^3} + \cdots$$

$$= \frac{D_0(1 + g)^1}{(1 + k_s)^1} + \frac{D_0(1 + g)^2}{(1 + k_s)^2} + \frac{D_0(1 + g)^3}{(1 + k_s)^3} + \cdots \qquad \textbf{(16-10)}$$

$$= \sum_{t=1}^{\infty} \frac{D_0(1 + g)^t}{(1 + k_s)^t}.$$

If g is constant, Equation 16-10 can be simplified as follows:[12]

$$\hat{P}_0 = \frac{D_1}{k_s - g}. \qquad \textbf{(16-11)}$$

---

[12]The proof of equation 16-11 is in Eugene Brigham and Louis C. Gapenski, *Intermediate Financial Management*, 3d ed. (Chicago: The Dryden Press, 1990), appendix 3A.

Inserting values into Equation 16-11, we find the value of our illustrative share of common equity to be $33.33:

$$\hat{P}_0 = \frac{\$2.00}{0.16 - 0.10} = \$33.33,$$

where

$$D_1 = \$1.82(1.10) = \$2.00.$$

Notice that the constant growth model expressed in Equation 16-11 is identical to the single-period model, Equation 16-6, developed earlier. Notice also that Equation 16-11 is sufficiently general to encompass the no-growth case. If growth is zero, Equation 16-11 is equal to Equation 16-9. Finally, note that a necessary condition for the derivation of Equation 16-11 is that k_s be greater than g; if the equation is used where k_s is not greater than g, the results are meaningless.

What is $\hat{P}_1$, the price per share of the security expected at the end of Year 1? Using Equation 16-11 and substituting values for k_s, g, and $D_2 = \$2.20$, we obtain a value of $36.67. This price is 10 percent greater than $\hat{P}_0$, the price expected to prevail at the initial period. This confirms the assumption that was made that the share price is expected to grow at rate g.

For the normal growth case, the expected rate of return, $\hat{k}_s$, can be found by solving Equation 16-11 for k:

$$\hat{k}_s = \frac{D_1}{P_0} + g. \qquad\qquad \textbf{(16-12)}$$

This equation has exactly the same form as that used to calculate the expected rate of return with a one-year horizon (Equation 16-7). In our example, if the common equity can be purchased for $33.33 per share, then the expected rate of return is 16 percent.

$$\hat{k}_s = \frac{\$2.00}{\$33.33} + 10\% = 6\% + 10\% = 16\%.$$

If we move the analysis ahead one year, the expected price, calculated as above, is $36.67. The investor thus expects to obtain the dividend yield of $2.00/$33.33 or 6 percent and the expected capital gain yield of $3.33/$33.33 or 10 percent. If we then move ahead one more year, an investor would have invested in the company an amount equal to $36.67 and would expect to obtain a 16 percent return based on a dividend yield of $2.20/$36.67 = 6 percent plus a capital gains yield of 10 percent from the growth in the share price.

Thus for the *constant growth* situation, the following conditions must hold:

1. The dividend is expected to grow forever at a constant rate, g.
2. The share price is expected to grow at this same rate.
3. The expected dividend yield is a constant.
4. The expected capital gains yield is also a constant and equal to g.
5. The expected total rate of return, $\hat{k}_s$, is equal to the expected dividend yield plus the expected growth rate: $\hat{k}_s$ = dividend yield + g.

The word "expected" should be clarified—it means anticipated in a probabilistic sense, as the most likely outcome. Thus, if we say the growth rate is "expected" to remain constant at 10 percent, we mean that we think the most likely growth rate in any future year is 10 percent, not that we literally expect the growth rate to be exactly equal to 10 percent in each future year. In this sense, the constant growth assumption is a reasonable one for many large, mature companies.

Nonconstant, or Supernormal, Growth

Firms typically go through *life cycles* during part of which their growth is much faster than that of the economy as a whole. Automobile manufacturers in the 1920s and computer and office equipment manufacturers in the 1980s are examples. Figure 16-5 illustrates such **nonconstant growth**, also called *supernormal growth*, and compares it with normal growth, zero growth, and negative growth.[13]

Figure 16-5
Illustrative Dividend Growth Rates

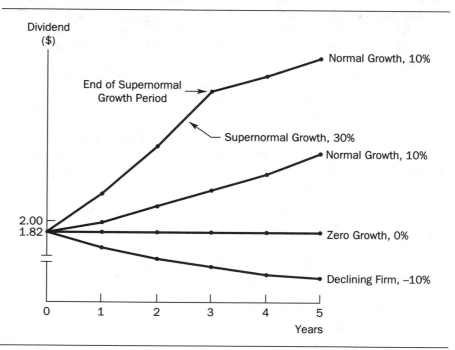

[13]A negative growth rate represents a declining company. A mining company whose profits are falling because of a declining ore body is an example. There is nothing inherently wrong with buying shares of a company whose dividends are expected to decline, although, obviously, you would not pay as much for equity in a company whose current $2 dividend you expect to decrease as you would equity in a company whose dividends you expect to increase.

In the figure, the dividends of the supernormal growth firm are expected to grow at a 30 percent rate for 3 years, after which the growth rate is expected to fall to 10 percent, the assumed average for the economy. The equity value of this firm, like any other, is the present value of its expected dividends. In the case in which D_t is growing at a constant rate, we simplified Equation 16-10 to $\hat{P} = D_1/(k_s-g)$. In the supernormal case, however, the growth rate is not constant—it is very rapid for a time, but then it declines at the end of the period of supernormal growth. To find the value of such a share, we proceed in three steps:

1. Find the PV of the dividends during the period of supernormal growth.
2. Find the price of the equity at the end of the supernormal growth period, and then discount this price back to the present.
3. Add these components to find the present value of the share, P_0.

For an illustration of the process, suppose the following facts exist:

k_s = shareholders' required rate of return = 16%.

n = years to supernormal growth = 3.

g_s = rate of growth in both earnings and dividends during the supernormal growth period = 30%. (Note: The growth rate during the supernormal growth period could vary from year to year. Also, there could be several different supernormal growth periods: for example, 30 percent for 3 years, then 20 percent for 3 years, and then a constant 10 percent.)

g_n = rate of constant growth after the supernormal period = 10%.

D_0 = last dividend the company paid = $1.82.

The valuation process is diagrammed in Figure 16-6, and it is explained in the steps set forth below the time line. The per share value of the equity is calculated to be $53.86.

Comparing Companies with Different Expected Growth Rates

It is useful to summarize our discussion of share valuation models by comparing companies with the four growth situations graphed in Figure 16-5. There we have a zero growth company, one with a constant 10 percent expected growth rate, one whose earnings are expected to decline at a rate of 10 percent a year, and one whose growth rate is not constant.

We can use the valuation equations developed earlier to determine the share prices, dividend yields and price-to-earnings ratios (P/E) for the four companies. These data are shown in Table 16-3. We assume that each firm had earnings per share (EPS) of $3.41 during the preceding reporting period (that is, EPS_0 = $3.41) and that each paid out 53.3 percent of its reported earnings as dividends. Therefore, dividends per share last year, D_0, were $1.82 for each company, but the values of D_1 differ among the firms.

The value of each security equals its market price, and the expected and required term is 16 percent on each; thus $\hat{k}_s = k_s = 16\%$. For the declining firm,

---

Figure 16-6
Process for Finding the Value of a
Supernormal Growth Equity Security

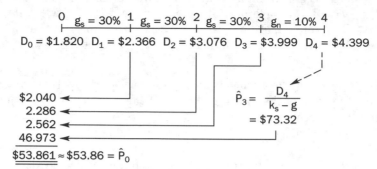

Step 1. Find the dividends paid (D_t) at the end of Years 1 to 3, and then the present values of these dividends, $PV(D_t)$, using the following procedure:

D_0	$\times$	$FVIF_{30\%,t}$	$=$	D_t	$\times$	$PVIF_{16\%,t}$	$=$	$PV(D_t)$
D_1: $1.82	$\times$	1.3000	$=$	$2.366;	$\times$	0.8621	$=$	$2.040
D_2: 1.82	$\times$	1.6900	$=$	3.076;	$\times$	0.7432	$=$	2.286
D_3: 1.82	$\times$	2.1970	$=$	3.999;	$\times$	0.6407	$=$	2.562
				Sum of PVs of supernormal period dividends			$=$	$6.888

Step 2. The share price at the end of Year 3 is the PV of the dividends expected from Year 4 to infinity. To find this, we first (a) find the expected value of the share price at the end of Year 3 and then (b) find the present value of the Year 3 share price:

a.
$$\hat{P}_3 = \frac{D_4}{k_s - g_n} = \frac{D_0(1 + g_s)^3(1 + g_n)}{k_s - g_n} = \frac{D_3(1 + g_n)}{0.16 - 0.10}$$

$$= \frac{\$3.999(1.10)}{0.06} = \frac{\$4.399}{0.06} = \$73.32.$$

b.
$$PV(\hat{P}_s) = \$73.32(PVIF_{16\%,3 \text{ years}}) = \$73.32(0.6407) = \$46.97.$$

Step 3. Find $\hat{P}_0$, the per share value of the equity today:

$$\hat{P}_0 = \$6.89 + \$46.97 = \$53.86.$$

Note: You would normally calculate the stream of dividends and their present values with a financial calculator rather than with FVIF and PVIF factors, but the steps would be the same.

---

this return consists of a high current dividend yield, 26 percent, combined with a capital loss amounting to 10 percent a year. For the no-growth firm, there is neither a capital gain nor a capital loss expectation, so the 16 percent return must be obtained entirely from the dividend yield. The normal growth firm provides a 6 percent current dividend yield plus a 10 percent per year capital gain expectation. Finally, the supernormal growth firm has the lowest current dividend yield but the highest capital gain expectation.

What is expected to happen to the share prices of the four firms' equity over time? Three of the four cases are straightforward. The zero growth firm's share price is expected to remain constant (that is, $\hat{P}_t = \hat{P}_{t+1}$); the declining firm is expected to have a falling share price; and the constant growth firm's share price is expected to grow at a constant rate, 10 percent. The supernormal growth case is more complex, but this firm's share price growth rate starts at 11.6 percent per year and then declines to 10 percent as the supernormal growth period ends.

The relationships among the P/E ratios, shown in the last column of Table 16-3, are similar to what we intuitively expect—the higher the expected growth (all other things being equal), the higher the P/E ratio.[14]

The underlying determinants of growth in earnings, dividends, and share prices that a firm will experience should be noted and related to the observed

Table 16-3
Share Prices, Dividend Yields, and Price/Earnings Ratios for
16 Percent Returns under Different Growth Assumptions

		Price	Current Dividend Yield, D_1/P_0	Capital Gains Yield in Year 1, $(\hat{P}_1 - P_0)/P_0$	Total Expected Return	P/E Ratio[a]
Declining constant growth (−10%)	$\hat{P}_0 = \dfrac{D_1}{k_s - g} = \dfrac{\$1.64}{0.16 - (-0.10)}$	= \$ 6.31	26%	−10.0%	16%	1.85
Zero growth (0%)	$\hat{P}_0 = \dfrac{D}{k_s} = \dfrac{\$1.82}{0.16}$	= 11.38	16	0.0	16	3.34
Normal constant growth (10%)	$\hat{P}_0 = \dfrac{D_1}{k_s - g} = \dfrac{\$2.00}{0.16 - 0.10}$	= 33.33	6	10.0	16	9.77
Supernormal growth $\hat{P}_0$ = (See Steps 1–3, Figure 16-6) =		53.86	4.4	11.6[b]	16	15.79

[a]It is assumed at the beginning of this example that each company is earning \$3.41 initially. This \$3.41, divided into the various prices, gives the indicated P/E ratios.

As the supernormal growth rate declines toward the normal rate (or as the time when this decline will occur becomes more imminent), the high P/E ratio must approach the normal P/E ratio—that is, the P/E of 15.79 will decline year by year and equal 9.77, that of the normal growth company, in Year 3.

Note that D_1 differs for each firm. It is calculated as follows:

$$D_1 = EPS_0(1 + g)(\text{Fraction of earnings paid out}) = \$3.41(1 + g)(0.533).$$

For the declining firm, $D_1 = \$3.41(0.90)(0.533) = \$1.64$.

[b]With $k = 16\%$ and $D_1/P_0 = 4.4\%$, the capital gains yield must be $16.0\% - 4.4\% = 11.6\%$. We could calculate the expected share price at the end of the year, $\hat{P}_1$, using the supernormal growth procedures, to confirm that the capital gains yield in Year 1 is indeed 11.6 percent, but this is not necessary.

[14]Differences in P/E ratios among firms can also arise from differences in the required rates of return, k_s, that investors use in capitalizing the future dividend streams. If one company has a higher P/E ratio than another, the cause could be a higher g, a lower k, or a combination of these two factors.

current share prices in Table 16-3. The key relationship is described in the discussion of capital budgeting in Chapter 13. There it was noted that if the rate of return on new investment is in excess of the firm's cost of capital, the net present value will be positive and this will increase the current share price of the firm and the expected growth rate. For a declining firm, the rate of return is negative. For the normal growth firm, the rate of return on investment is equal to the cost of capital. The supernormal case results from investments in excess of the cost of capital for a fixed period of time. In all of the cases considered in Table 16-3, the reinvestment per share through retained earnings in Year 1 is equal to $1.59 (that is, the earnings per share of $3.41 times the retention ratio of 46.7 percent). In the normal case, the rate of return on the new investment is equal to the required return of 16 percent. This gives the standard or normal case with which the NPV of the new investment is zero.

If the rate of return on the new investment is assumed to be zero, then for every dollar invested, the shareholders lose since they are expected to earn zero percent and they require 16 percent. The price on this share is $11.38 compared to $33.33 for the standard case. The difference of $21.95 in share prices reflects the present value of the expected loss from reinvestment at inadequate rates.[15] The share prices for the first three types of firms in Table 16-2 are specific examples of different values of constant growth obtained by reinvesting funds at a constant rate of return with a specific relationship to the cost of capital.

These relationships between the expected rates of return on new investments and the cost of capital provide one explanation for the difference between the market and the book values of equity. For example, suppose a company beginning its operations issues $1 million of new equity at a price per share equal to $1. The firm intends to pay out all its earnings as dividends. Initially, it is anticipated that the firm will earn a rate of return on this investment equal to the cost of capital. This will result in a share price equal to the book value of equity per share. Owing to an increase in demand for the firm's product, however, the firm is expected to earn in excess of the cost of capital. The share price will increase and exceed the book value of equity per share. Similarly, if the market expects that the firm will earn less than its cost of capital or, equivalently, that the growth rate will fall, the share price can be below the book value of equity. According to this logic, a firm is not undervalued if its share price is below the book value of equity per share, nor is it overvalued if the price per share is greater than the book value of equity. The price per share reflects the present value of the expected earnings, whereas the book value of equity per share measures the historic value of equity committed to the firm.

---

[15]This example presents an extreme. More likely, the firm can reinvest at a rate of return that is positive but less than the cost of capital. For example, if the reinvestment rate is 12 percent, the growth rate is 5.6 percent. The current share price is $18.48. If the reinvestment rate is greater than the cost of capital, the share price is above the price for normal growth. If reinvestment earns 25 percent, growth is 11.68 percent and the current share price is $47.05.

Concept Review

▶ Explain the following statement: "Whereas a bond contains a promise to pay interest, common equity provides an expectation but no promise of dividends."
▶ What are the two elements of a share's expected returns?
▶ How does the general equity valuation model (Equation 16-8) differ from the general bond valuation model (Equation 16-1)?
▶ Write out and explain the valuation model for a zero growth equity security.
▶ Write out and explain the valuation model for a constant growth equity security.
▶ How does one calculate the capital gains yield and the dividend yield of an equity security?

Stock Market Equilibrium

Recall from Chapter 15 that the required return on Share X, k_X, can be found using the *security market line (SML)* equation as it was developed in our discussion of the *capital asset pricing model (CAPM)*:

$$k_X = k_{RF} + (k_M - k_{RF})\, \beta_X.$$

If the risk-free rate of return is 8 percent, the market risk premium is 4 percent, and X, an equity security, has a beta of 2, then the marginal investor will require a return of 16 percent on Share X, calculated as follows:

$$k_X = 8\% + (12\% - 8\%)\, 2.0 = 16\%.$$

This 16 percent required return is shown as a point on the SML in Figure 16-7.

The marginal investor will want to buy Share X if the expected rate of return is more than 16 percent, will want to sell it if the expected rate of return is less than 16 percent, and will be indifferent (hence will hold but not buy or sell) if the expected rate of return is exactly 16 percent. Now suppose the investor's portfolio contains Share X, and after analyzing its prospects he or she concludes that its earnings, dividends, and price can be expected to grow at a constant rate of 5 percent per year. The last dividend was $D_0 = \$2.8571$, so the next expected dividend is

$$D_1 = \$2.8571(1.05) = \$3.$$

Our marginal investor observes that the present share price, P_0, is $30. Should more of Share X be purchased, or should the present holdings be sold, or should the present position be maintained?

The investor can calculate Share X's expected rate of return as follows:

$$\hat{k}_X = \frac{D_1}{P_0} + g = \frac{\$3}{\$30} + 5\% = 15\%.$$

Figure 16-7
Expected and Required Returns on Share X

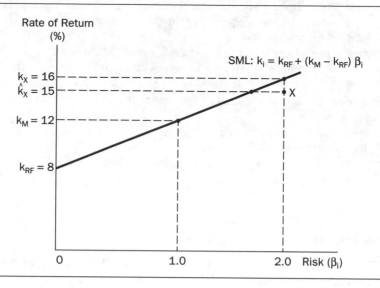

This value is plotted on Figure 16-7 as point X, which is below the SML. Because the expected rate of return is less than the required return, this marginal investor will want to sell the security, as will other holders. However, few people will want to buy at the $30 price, so the present owners will be unable to find buyers unless they cut the price of the security. Thus, the price will decline, and this decline will continue until the share price reaches $27.27. At this point, the market for this security will be in **equilibrium**—that is, there will be no systematic tendency to change—because the expected rate of return, 16 percent, will be equal to the required rate of return:

$$\hat{k}_X = \frac{\$3.00}{\$27.27} + 5\% = 11\% + 5\% = 16\% = k_X.$$

Had the shares initially sold for less than $27.27—say, for $25.00—events would have been reversed. Investors would have wanted to buy the security because its expected rate of return would have exceeded its required rate of return, and buy orders would have driven the share price up to $27.27.

To summarize, in equilibrium these two conditions must hold:

1. The expected rate of return as seen by the marginal investor must equal the required rate of return: $\hat{k}_i = k_i$.
2. The actual market price of the share must equal its intrinsic value as estimated by the marginal investor: $P_0 = \hat{P}_0$.

Of course, some individual investors will believe that $\hat{k}_i > k$ and $\hat{P}_0 > P_0$, and hence they will invest most of their funds in the security. Other investors will have an opposite view and will sell all of their shares. However, it is the *marginal investor* who establishes the actual market price, and for this investor, $k_i = k_i$ and $P_0 = \hat{P}_0$. If these conditions do not hold, trading will occur until they do hold.

Changes in Equilibrium Share Prices

Market share prices are not constant—in fact, they undergo violent changes at times. For example, on October 19, 1987, the Toronto Stock Exchange 300 Index fell by 618 points or 11.28 percent and on October 20, 1987, the drop was 6.71 percent. The impact across segments of the index was varied. On October 19, the shares in the metals and mining segment and the utilities segment lost 15.00 and 7.00 percent, respectively, whereas on October 20, metals lost a further 14.00 percent while utilities gained 2.80 percent!

To see how such changes can occur, let us assume that Share X is in equilibrium, selling at a price of $27.27 per share. If all expectations were exactly met, the price would gradually rise during the next year to $28.63, or by 5 percent. However, many different events could occur to cause a change in the equilibrium price of the security. Consider again the set of inputs used to develop Share X's price of $27.27, along with a new set of assumed input variables:

	Variable Value	
	Original	New
Risk-free rate, k_{RF}	8%	7%
Market risk premium, $k_M - k_{RF}$	4%	3%
Share X's beta coefficient, β_X	2.0	1.0
Share X's expected growth rate, g_X	5%	6%
D_0	$2.8571	$2.8571
Price of Share X	$27.27	?

Now give yourself a test: how will the change in each variable, by itself, affect the price, and what is your guess as to the new share price?

Each change, taken alone, will lead to an increase in the price. The first three variables influence k_X, which declines from 16 to 10 percent:

$$\text{Original } k_X = 8\% + 4\%(2.0) = 16\%.$$

$$\text{New } k_X = 7\% + 3\%(1.0) = 10\%.$$

Using these values, together with the new g value, we find that $\hat{P}_0$, and consequently P_0, rises from $27.27 to $75.71.

$$\text{Original } \hat{P}_0 = \frac{\$2.8571(1.05)}{0.16 - 0.05} = \frac{\$3}{0.11} = \$27.27.$$

$$\text{New } \hat{P}_0 = \frac{\$2.8571(1.06)}{0.10 - 0.06} = \frac{\$3.0285}{0.04} = \$75.71.$$

At the new price, the expected and required rates of return will be equal.

$$\hat{k}_X = \frac{\$3.0285}{\$75.71} + 6\% = 10\% = k_X.$$

Evidence suggests that equity securities, and especially those of large, TSE-listed companies, adjust rapidly to disequilibrium situations. Consequently, equilibrium ordinarily exists for any given security, and, in general, required and expected returns are equal. Share prices certainly change, sometimes violently and rapidly, but this simply reflects changing conditions and expectations. There are, of course, times when a security continues to react for several months to a favourable or unfavourable development, but this does not signify a long adjustment period; rather, it simply illustrates that as more new bits of information about the situation become available, the market adjusts to them. The ability of the market to adjust to new information is discussed in the next section.

The Efficient Markets Hypothesis

A body of theory called the **efficient market hypothesis (EMH)** holds (1) that securities are always in equilibrium and (2) that it is impossible for an investor to "beat the market" consistently. Essentially, those who believe in the EMH note that there are a large number of highly trained professional analysts and traders operating in the market, each of whom tends to specialize in the shares in a specific industry. Further, these analysts work for investment firms and for pension and mutual funds, which have billions of dollars available with which to take advantage of bargains. As a result of provincial securities commissions' disclosure requirements and electronic information networks, as new information about a security becomes available, these analysts all receive and evaluate it at approximately the same time. Therefore, the price of the security adjusts almost immediately to reflect any new developments.

Financial theorists generally define three forms, or levels, of the efficient market hypothesis:

1. The *weak form* of the EMH states that all information contained in past price movements is fully reflected in current market prices. Therefore, information about recent trends in a security's price is of no use in selecting securities—the fact that an equity security price has risen for the past three days, for example, gives no useful clues as to what it will do today or tomorrow. People who believe that weak-form efficiency exists also believe that "tape watchers" and "chartists" are wasting their time.[16]

2. The *semistrong form* of the EMH states that current market prices reflect all *publicly available* information. If this is true, no abnormal returns can be gained by analyzing securities.[17] Thus, if semistrong-form efficiency exists, it does no good to pore over annual reports or other published data, because market prices will have adjusted to any good or bad news contained in such reports as soon as they came out. However, insiders (say,

---

[16]Tape watchers are people who watch the TSE tape, while chartists plot past patterns of share price movements. Both are called "technicians," and both believe that they can see if something is happening to the share that will cause its price to move up or down in the near future.

[17]An "abnormal return" is one that exceeds the return justified by the riskiness of the investment—that is, it is a return that plots above the SML in a graph such as Figure 16-7.

the presidents of companies), even under semistrong-form efficiency, can still make abnormal returns on their own companies' common equity.

3.   The *strong form* of the EMH states that current market prices reflect all pertinent information, whether publicly available or privately held. If this form holds, even insiders will find it impossible to earn abnormal returns in the equity market.[18]

What bearing does the EMH have on financial decisions? Since share prices do reflect public information, most equity securities do seem to be fairly valued. This does not mean that new developments cannot cause an equity security's price to soar or to plummet, but it does mean that securities, in general, are neither overvalued nor undervalued—they are fairly priced and in equilibrium. However, there are cases in which financial managers do have information not known to outsiders.

If the EMH is correct, it is a waste of time for most of us to analyze securities by looking for those that are undervalued. If equity prices already reflect all available information and hence are fairly priced, one can "beat the market" only by luck, and it is difficult, if not impossible, for anyone to outperform the market averages consistently. Empirical tests have shown that the EMH is valid in its weak and semistrong forms. However, people such as corporate officers who have insider information can do better than the averages, and individuals and organizations that are especially good at digging out information on small, new companies also seem to do consistently well. Also, some investors may be able to analyze and react more quickly than others to release of new information, and these investors may have an advantage over others. However, the buy–sell actions of these investors quickly bring market prices into equilibrium. Therefore, it is generally safe to assume that $\hat{k} = k$, that $\hat{P}_0 = P_0$, and that securities plot on the SML.[19]

Actual Share Prices and Returns

Our discussion thus far has focussed on *expected* share prices and *expected* rates of return. Anyone who has ever invested in the stock market knows that there can be and generally are large differences between *expected* and *realized* prices and returns.

We can illustrate this difference by applying the growth model to the following example. The Wood Chips Pulp and Paper Company earned $3.00 per share in 1993

---

[18]Several cases of illegal insider trading in the United States have made the news headlines recently. These cases involved employees of several major investment banking houses, and even an employee of the Securities Exchange Commission (SEC). In the most famous case, Ivan Boesky admitted to making $50 million by purchasing the shares of firms he knew were about to merge. He went to jail and had to pay a large fine, but he helped disprove the strong-form EMH.

[19]Market efficiency also has important implications for managerial decisions, especially those pertaining to common equity issues, share repurchases, and tender offers. Shares appear to be fairly valued, so decisions based on a share's being undervalued or overvalued must be approached with caution. However, managers do have better information about their own companies than outsiders have, and this information can legally be used to the companies' (but not the managers') own advantage.

and has a retention ratio of 50 percent. The company expects to earn a rate of 10 percent on its book value, and its growth rate is expected to be 5 percent for 1994. The growth rate can be estimated by multiplying the retention ratio by the rate of return on book equity: $g = \beta \times ROE = 0.5 \times 0.1 = 0.05$ or 5%. The share price at the beginning of 1994 is $31.50, and this is consistent with a discount rate of 10 percent:

$$\hat{k}_s = \frac{D_1}{P_0} + g = \frac{D_0(1 + g)}{P_0} + g$$

$$= \frac{\$1.50(1 + 0.5)}{\$31.50} + 0.05$$

$$= 0.05 + 0.05 = 0.10.$$

If all expectations are realized, the price at the end of the year will be equal to

$$\hat{P}_1 = \frac{D_2}{(k_s - g)} = \frac{D_0(1 + g)^2}{(k_s - g)}$$

$$= \frac{\$1.50(1.05)^2}{(0.10 - 0.05)}$$

$$= \frac{\$1.6538}{0.05}$$

$$= \$33.08.$$

The realized or actual rate of return over 1994 will be equal to the actual dividend yield received plus the actual capital gain. In this example, the actual rate of return is 10 percent, which is equal to the dividend yield of $1.575/$31.50 = 5% plus the capital gain of ($33.08 − $31.50)/$31.50) = 5%.

However, suppose that at the end of 1994 the firm announces that its earnings will be $3.00 per share and the rate of return on book equity will be reduced to 9.52 percent. This level of earnings is lower than the expected amount of $3.15. The firm decides that it will maintain its payout ratio at 50 percent, so the actual dividend that is paid for 1994 is $1.50, which is less than expected by the market. With the lower rate of return on book equity and the same retention ratio, the growth rate in dividends per share falls to 4.76 percent. What will happen to the price of the security at the end of 1994?

The expected price for the security will be the present value of the future dividends beginning in 1995. The price is written as follows:

$$\hat{P}_1 = \frac{D_1(1 + g_{new})}{(k_s - g_{new})}$$

$$= \frac{\$1.50(1.0476)}{(0.10 - 0.0476)}$$

$$= \frac{\$1.5714}{0.0524}$$

$$= \$30.00.$$

This calculation assumes that the discount rate is unchanged. Assuming that the actual price at the end of 1994 is equal to the expected price calculated above, the actual rate of return over 1994 is equal to 0 percent. This is calculated as the actual dividend yield over the period of $1.50/$31.50 = 0.0476 = 4.76\%$ plus the capital gain over the period of $(\$30.00 - \$31.50)/\$31.50 = -0.0476 = -4.76\%$. Thus even small changes in earnings can generate large changes in prices, leading to wide swings in realized rates of return.

In this example, we have assumed that the overall cost of money, represented by k_s, remains constant. A change in the discount rate for the equity security can occur because of changes internal to the firm that change the risk of the equity or changes in the cost of money for the economy. These changes can be superimposed on changes in expected dividends and profitability, making the price per share fluctuate dramatically.

Figure 16-8 shows how total realized returns for the Toronto Stock Exchange 300 varied over the 1967–92 period. The market trend was strongly up, with an average over the period of 11.55 percent, but it went up in some years and down in others. The shares of individual companies likewise went up and down. This variability is observed in the estimate of the standard deviation of the rates of return, which is equal to 16.4 percent. We know from theory that expected returns as estimated by a marginal investor are always positive, but in some years, as Figure 16-8 shows, negative returns have been realized. Of

Figure 16-8
Toronto Stock Exchange, Total Returns: Dividend
Yield + Capital Gain or Loss, 1967–1992

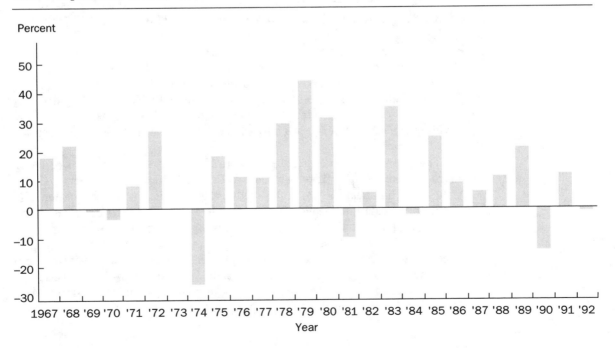

Source: Nominal rates of return data taken from the 1991 Towers Perrin Canadian Economic Tables. Reprinted by permission of Towers Perrin.

course, even in bad years, some individual companies do well, so the "name of the game" in security analysis is picking the winners. Financial managers attempt to take actions that will put their companies into the winners' column, but they do not always succeed. In subsequent chapters, we shall examine the actions that managers can take to increase the odds of their firms doing relatively well in the marketplace.

Stock Market Reporting

Figure 16-9 is taken from the stock market page of the newspaper on July 28, 1992. For each security, the TSE report provides specific data on the trading that took place the prior day, as well as other, more general information. Similar information is available on securities listed on other exchanges and also on shares traded over the counter.

The shares are listed alphabetically, from AGF to Xerox Canada (the data in Figure 16-9 are taken from the top of the listing). Let us consider the information for Alberta Energy common equity shares, found about a third of the way down the figure. The two columns at the left show the highest and lowest prices at which the securities sold during the past 52-week period. Alberta Energy traded between $15 1/8 ($15.125) and $9 3/4 ($9.750). The entry to the right of the abbreviated name, AEC, is the stock exchange trading symbol, which is used by brokers and many computerized information services. The figure just to the right of the ticker symbol is the dividend per share; AEC had a current indicated annual dividend of $0.35 per share.

Next come the high and low prices for the day and then the closing price. On July 27, 1992, AEC traded as high as $13 1/8 ($13.125) and as low as $12 7/8 ($12.875): the last trade was at the daily high value of $13 1/8 ($13.125). Following is the change from the closing price on the previous day. The AEC share price increased by 1/8 of a dollar ($0.125) from the close of the previous day. The next column is the volume of shares traded in hundreds. The final two columns represent the dividend yield and the price-to-earnings ratio (P/E). The dividend yield is expressed as a percentage and is calculated by dividing the indicated annual dividend by the closing price. The P/E is calculated by dividing the current share price by the company's earnings per share for the last 12 months.

There are other points to note in Figure 16-9. First, some entries have one or more suffixes on the ticker symbol. AEC.PR.C indicates a preferred share, "Class C"; WT means a warrant and UN, a unit, which is a combination of a share and a warrant. Second, the lower-case letters to the right of some of the company names indicate special features of the shares; for example, nv indicates a nonvoting class of shares, j indicates that the security is subject to special reporting requirements, and xd signals that the shares went ex-dividend that day (that is, someone who buys these shares will not receive the next dividend). The legend to the tables provides a complete description of these special features.[20] Third, a ↑ preceding the column indicates a new

---

[20]Most of the terms in this paragraph, such as "warrant" and "ex dividend," are explained in Chapters 19 and 22.

Figure 16-9
Stock Market Transactions, July 27, 1992

52-Week high	low	Stock	Sym	Div	High	Low	Close	Chg	Vol (100s)	Yield	P/E ratio
10½	5¼	AGF nv	AGF.PR.B	0.36	9	8⅝	9	−⅛	33	4.00	12.9
2.50	0.25	Aber j	ABZ		1.62	1.55	1.62	+0.04	494		
16¾	13⅞	Abitibi-Price	A	0.50	15½	15¼	15¼		5	3.28	
0.18	0.12	Acadia Minrl j	ALV		0.15	0.15	0.15	+0.01	43		
0.45	0.10	Accugraph j	ACU.A		0.20	0.15	0.15	−0.05	70		
2.23	1.50	Adonos Res	ADS		1.60	1.60	1.60		20		
6¾	3.95	Agnico Eagle	AGE	0.08	6½	6¼	6¼	−⅜	1069		
1.00	0.07	Agnico	AGE.WT.A		0.10	0.10	0.10	−0.01	50		
9	7¼	Agra mv	AGR.B	0.16	7⅜	7⅜	7⅜	+⅛	5	2.17	67.0
9⅛	4.70	Air Canada	AC		5	4.95	4.95	−0.05	142		
15⅛	9¾	Alberta Ener	AEC	0.35	13⅛	12⅞	13⅛	+⅛	182	2.67	93.8
25¾	22	AEC	AEC.PR.C	1.94	25	25	25		8	7.75	
15¾	12	ANG	ANG	0.68	12⅞	12¾	12⅞	+⅛	49	5.28	15.7
26⅜	20⅝	Alcan	AL	0.30	23½	22⅞	23	−⅜	4273		
24½	21½	Alcan C	AL.PR.E	1.85	23	22¾	22¾	−¼	10	8.13	
21¾	16¼	Alcan E	AL.PR.F	1.44	18	18	18	−⅛	1	7.98	
13	5	Allelix	AXB		6¾	6⅝	6⅝	−⅛	12		
0.40	0.13	Alliance	AZR		0.25	0.20	0.25	+0.05	100		
3.45	1.26	Altex	AX		1.38	1.30	1.30	+0.04	59		11.8
2.70	1.15	Amax Gld	AXG.WT		2.60	2.60	2.60		1		
1.85	1.00	Amco.	ACE	0.04	1.55	1.55	1.55	+0.05	4		77.5
35¼	24	Amer Barrick	ABX	0.13	34⅜	33⅞	34⅜	+¼	662		
0.30	0.20	Amer Leduc	ARL		0.22	0.22	0.22	+0.01	100		
13⅜	7	Anderson	AXL		9⅜	9	9	−½	66		150.0
15	10½	Andres nv	ADW.A	0.60	13⅞	13⅞	13⅞	+⅜	1	4.31	13.5
15	11¼	Andres	ADW.B	0.52	13	13	13	+1½	4	4.00	12.6
↑ 31	24⅝	AngCd T	ACT.PR.A	2.25	31	31	31	+2	3	7.26	
36	31¼	AngCd T	ACT.PR.C	2.90	35¼	35¼	35¼	+¼	1	8.23	
41	34	AngCd T	ACT.PR.D	3.15	39	39	39		z10	8.08	
6⅝	0.75	Archer	AAZ		0.95	0.95	0.95	−0.05	15		
5¾	3.25	Arimetco j	ARX		4.20	4.10	4.15	+0.10	2229		
1.95	0.55	Asamera	AUA	1.14	1.35	1.35	1.35		10	84.44	
13¼	10½	Atco nv	ACO.X	0.24	12	12	12	−⅛	90	2.00	9.2
3.90	2.70	Atcor nv	AKR.A		3.75	3.65	3.75		7		31.3
0.40	0.10	Athabaska j	AHB		.175	0.16	.175	+.025	215		
1.80	0.50	Atlanta j	AAG		0.95	0.95	0.95		5		
2.25	0.52	Audrey	AUY		0.70	0.70	0.70	+0.05	50		
3.80	1.93	Aur j	AUR		3.05	2.90	3.05	+0.10	202		
0.39	0.18	Aurizon j	ARZ		0.27	0.25	0.27	+0.01	183		
2.34	1.23	BC Bancorp	BBC		1.29	1.29	1.29	+0.01	10		6.8

Source: Excerpted from *The Globe and Mail*, July 28, 1992, Report on Business. Reprinted with permission.

52-week high whereas ↓ shows a new 52-week low. AngCd T's closing price of $31 was a new 52-week high.

For shares of companies that did not trade on a particular day, the bid and ask prices are provided. The **bid price** is the price at which the shares can be sold. The **ask** or **asked price** is the price at which the shares can be bought. For example, on July 27, 1992, Hy&Zels had bid and ask prices of $1.30 and $1.40 respectively.

Concept Review

▶ When a security is in equilibrium, two conditions must hold. What are they?

▶ What is the difference between the three forms of the EMH: (1) weak form, (2) semistrong form, and (3) strong form?

▶ What is the major conclusion of the Efficient Markets Hypothesis (EMH)?

Summary

Corporate decisions should be analyzed in terms of how alternative courses of action are likely to affect the value of a firm. However, before attempting to measure how a given decision will affect a specific firm's value, it is necessary to know how debt and equity prices are established. Accordingly, this chapter showed how bond and share values are determined, as well as how investors go about estimating the rates of return they expect to earn. The key concepts covered are listed below.

☐ A **bond** is a long-term promissory note issued by a business or governmental unit. The firm receives the selling price of the bond in exchange for a promise to make interest payments and to repay the principal on a specified future date.

☐ The value of a bond is found as the present value of an *annuity* (the *interest payments*) plus the present value of a lump sum (the *principal*). The bond is evaluated at the appropriate periodic interest rate over the number of periods for which interest payments are made.

☐ The equation used to find the value of an annual coupon bond is:

$$V = \sum_{t=1}^{n} \frac{I}{(1 + k_d)^t} + \frac{M}{(1 + k_d)^n}$$

$$= I(\text{PVIFA}_{k_d,n}) + M(\text{PVIF}_{k_d,n}).$$

If the bond pays interest semiannually, the formula must be adjusted: divide I and k_d by 2, and multiply n by 2.

☐ The return earned on a bond held to maturity is defined as the bond's **yield to maturity (YTM)**. If the bond has a **call provision**—the issuer can redeem it before maturity—and if it is called, the return investors will receive is the **yield to call (YTC)**. The YTC is found as the present value of the interest payments received while the bond is outstanding plus the present value of the call price (the par value plus a call premium).

☐ The longer the maturity of a bond, the more its price will change in response to a given change in interest rates; this is called **interest rate risk**. Bonds with short maturities, however, expose the investor to high **reinvestment rate risk**, which is the risk that income will decline because funds received from maturing short-term investments will have to be reinvested at lower interest rates.

☐ Many **preferred shares** are *perpetuities*. The value of a share of perpetual preferred equity is found as the dividend divided by the required rate of return:

$$V_{ps} = \frac{D_{ps}}{k_{ps}}.$$

☐ The value of a share of equity is calculated as the *present value of the stream of dividends* to be received in the future.

☐ The equation used to find the value of a **constant, or normal, growth share of equity** is

$$\hat{P}_0 = \frac{D_1}{(k_s - g)}.$$

☐ The *expected total rate of return* from a share consists of an *expected dividend yield* plus an *expected capital gains yield*. For a constant growth firm, both the expected dividend yield and the expected capital gains yield are constant.

☐ The equation for $\hat{k}_s$, the expected rate of return on a constant growth share, can be expressed as follows:

$$\hat{k}_s = \frac{D_1}{P_0} + g.$$

☐ A **zero growth equity** is one whose future dividends are not expected to grow at all, while a **supernormal growth equity** is one whose earnings and dividends are expected to grow much faster than the economy as a whole over some specified time period.

☐ To find the present value of a supernormal growth share of equity, (1) find the PV of the dividends during the supernormal growth period, (2) find the price per share of the equity at the end of the supernormal growth period, (3) discount this price back to the present, and (4) sum the two components.

☐ The **efficient markets hypothesis (EMH)** holds that securities are always in equilibrium and that it is impossible for an investor to consistently "beat the market." Therefore, according to the EMH, securities are always fairly valued ($\hat{P}_0 = P_0$), the required return on a security is equal to its expected return ($k = \hat{k}$), and all securities' expected returns plot on the SML.

☐ Finally, in this chapter we saw that differences can and do exist between expected and actual returns in the equity and bond markets—only for short-term, risk-free assets are expected and actual (or realized) returns equal.

Questions

16-1 Two investors are evaluating IBM's equity for possible purchase. They agree on the expected value of D_1, on the expected future dividend growth rate, and on the riskiness of the security. However, one investor normally holds equity for 2 years, the other for 10 years. Based on the type of analysis done in this chapter, they should both be willing to pay the same price for IBM's stock. True or false? Explain your answer.

16-2   In what respect is a perpetual bond similar to a zero growth common share and to a preferred share?

16-3   "The values of outstanding bonds change whenever the going rate of interest changes. In general, short-term interest rates are more volatile than long-term rates. Therefore, short-term bond prices are more sensitive to interest rate changes than are long-term bond prices." Is this statement true or false? Explain your answer.

16-4   If you buy a share of common equity, you typically expect to receive dividends plus capital gains. Would you expect the distribution between dividend yield and capital gains to be influenced by a firm's decision to pay more dividends rather than to retain and reinvest more earnings?

16-5   The next expected dividend, D_1, divided by the current price of a share of equity, P_0, is called the share's expected dividend yield. Does the relationship between the dividend yield and the capital gains yield change for a share of a supernormal growth firm as the end of the supernormal growth period approaches? Explain.

16-6   The rate of return you get if you buy a bond and hold it to its maturity date is called the bond's *yield to maturity*. If interest rates in the economy rise after a bond has been issued, what will happen to the bond's price and to its YTM? Does the length of time to maturity affect the extent to which a given change in interest rates will affect the bond price?

16-7   If you buy a callable bond and interest rates decline, will the value of your bond rise by as much as it would have risen if the bond had not been callable?

Self-Test Problems   (solutions appear on page 601)

ST-1   **Key terms.**   Define each of the following terms:
   a. Bond
   b. Par value; maturity date; call provision
   c. Coupon payment; coupon interest rate
   d. Premium bond; discount bond
   e. Current yield (on a bond); yield to maturity (YTM); yield to call (YTC)
   f. Interest rate risk; reinvestment rate risk
   g. Expected value, $\hat{P}_0$; market price, P_0
   h. Required rate of return, k_s; expected rate of return, $\hat{k}_s$; actual, or realized, rate of return, $\bar{k}_s$
   i. Capital gains yield; dividend yield; expected total return
   j. Zero growth stock
   k. Normal, or constant growth; supernormal, or nonconstant, growth

ST-2 Growth rates and valuation. You are considering buying shares of equity of two very similar companies. Both companies are expected to earn $6 per share this year. However, Company D (for "dividend") is expected to pay all of its earnings out as dividends, while Company G (for "growth") is expected to pay out only one-third of its earnings, or $2. D's share price is $40. Which of the following is most likely to be true?

a. Company G will have a faster growth rate than Company D. Therefore, G's share price should be greater than $40.

b. Although G's growth rate should exceed D's, D's current dividend exceeds that of G, and this should cause D's price to exceed G's.

c. Investors in security D will get their money back faster because D pays out more of its earnings as dividends. Thus, in a sense D is like a short-term bond, and G is like a long-term bond. Therefore, if economic shifts cause k_d and k_s to increase and if the expected streams of dividends from D and G remain constant, then Shares D and G will both decline, but D's price will decline further.

d. D's expected and required rate of return is $\hat{k}_s = k_s = 15$ percent. G's expected return will be higher because of its higher expected growth rate.

e. Based on the available information, the best estimate of G's growth rate is 10 percent.

ST-3 Bond valuation. Franklin Limited issued a new series of bonds on January 1, 1967. The bonds were sold at par ($1000), have a 12 percent coupon, and mature in 30 years. Coupon payments are made semiannually (on June 30 and December 31).

a. What was the YTM of the bond on January 1, 1967?

b. What was the price of the bond 5 years after issue—on January 1, 1972—assuming that the level of interest rates had fallen to 10 percent?

c. Find the current yield and capital gains yield on the bond on January 1, 1972, given the price as determined in Part b.

d. On July 1, 1989, the bonds sold for $908.87. What was the YTM at that date?

e. What were the current yield and capital gains yield on July 1, 1989?

f. Now assume that you purchase an outstanding bond on March 1, 1989. The going rate of interest is 15.5 percent. How large a cheque must you write to complete the transaction? (This question provides a challenge!)

ST-4 Constant growth share valuation. You can buy a share of Karp Company's equity today for $36. Karp's last dividend was $2.40. In view of Karp's low risk, its required rate of return is only 12 percent. If dividends are expected to grow at a constant rate, g, in the future and if k is expected to remain at 12 percent, what is the Karp Company's expected share price 5 years from now?

ST-5 Supernormal growth share valuation. Software Systems is experiencing a period of rapid growth. Earnings and dividends are expected to grow at a rate of 15 percent during the next 2 years, 13 percent in the third year, and at a constant rate of 6 percent thereafter. Software's last dividend was $1.15 and the required rate of return on the equity is 12 percent.

   a. Calculate the price per share of equity today.
   b. Calculate $\hat{P}_1$ and $\hat{P}_2$.
   c. Calculate the dividend yield and capital gains yield for Years 1, 2, and 3.

Problems

16-1 Bond valuation.   The Carver Company has two bond issues outstanding. Both bonds pay $100 annual interest plus $1000 at maturity. Bond L has a maturity of 15 years and Bond S a maturity of 1 year.

   a. What will be the value of each of these bonds when the going rate of interest is (i) 5 percent, (ii) 8 percent, and (iii) 12 percent? Assume that there is only one more interest payment to be made on Bond S.
   b. Why does the 15-year bond fluctuate more when interest rates change than does the 1-year bond?

16-2 Bond valuation.   Suppose the Rush Company sold an issue of bonds with a 10-year maturity, a $1000 par value, a 10 percent coupon rate, and semiannual interest payments.

   a. Two years after the bonds were issued, the going rate of interest on bonds such as these fell to 6 percent. At what price would the bonds sell?
   b. Suppose that, 2 years after issue, the going interest rate rose to 12 percent. At what price would the bonds sell?
   c. Suppose the conditions in Part a existed—that is, interest rates fell to 6 percent 2 years after the issue date. Suppose further that the interest rate remained at 6 percent for the next 8 years. What would happen to the price of the Rush bonds over time?

16-3 Perpetual bond valuation.   The bonds of the Stanroy Corporation are perpetuities bearing a 10 percent coupon. Bonds of this type currently yield 8 percent. The par value of the bonds is $1000.

   a. What is the current price of the Stanroy bonds?
   b. Suppose interest rate levels rise to the point at which such bonds now yield 12 percent. What will be the price of the Stanroy bonds?
   c. Suppose interest rate levels drop to 10 percent. At what price will the Stanroy bonds sell?
   d. How would your answers to Parts a, b, and c change if the bonds had a maturity of 20 years?

16-4 Yield to maturity.   The yield to maturity (YTM) is the interest rate earned on a bond that is held to maturity. What will be the yield to maturity of a perpetual bond with a $1000 par value, an 8 percent coupon rate, and a current market price (a) of $600? (b) of $800? (c) of $1000? (d) of $1400? Assume interest is paid annually.

16-5 Yield to maturity.   Assume that a bond has 4 years remaining to maturity and that interest is paid annually.

a. What is the yield to maturity on the bond if it has a $1000 maturity value, a 9 percent coupon rate, and a current market price (1) of $829? (2) of $1104?

b. Would you pay $829 for the bond if your required rate of return for securities in the same risk class were 12 percent (that is, $k_d = 12\%$)? Explain your answer.

16-6 **Constant growth share valuation.**   Your broker offers to sell you some shares of Whistler Gifts Ltd. common equity that paid a dividend of $2 *last year*. You expect the dividend to grow at the rate of 5 percent per year for the next 3 years. If you buy the equity, you plan to hold the shares for 3 years, then sell them.

a. Find the expected dividend of each of the next 3 years—that is, calculate D_1, D_2, and D_3. Note that $D_0 = \$2$.

b. Given that the appropriate discount rate is 12 percent and that the first of the dividend payments will occur 1 year from now, find the present value of the dividend stream—that is, calculate the PV of D_1, D_2, and D_3, and sum these PVs.

c. You expect the price per share 3 years from now to be $34.73—that is, $\hat{P}_3 = \$34.73$. Find the present value of this expected future price given a 12 percent discount rate—that is, calculate the PV of $34.73.

d. If you plan to buy the security, hold it for 3 years, and then sell it for $34.73, what is the most you should pay for it?

e. Use Equation 16-11 to calculate the present value of this equity. Assume that $g = 5\%$ and is a constant.

f. Is the value of this share dependent upon how long you plan to hold it? In other words, if your planned holding period were 2 years or 5 years rather than 3 years, would this affect the value of the equity today, $\hat{P}_0$?

16-7 **Return on common equity.**   You buy a share of equity for $21.40. You expect it to pay dividends of $1.07, $1.1449, and $1.2250 in Years 1, 2, and 3, respectively, and you expect to sell the share at a price of $26.22 at the end of 3 years.

a. Calculate the expected growth rate in dividends.

b. Calculate the expected dividend yield.

c. Assuming the calculated growth rate is expected to continue, you can add the dividend yield to the expected growth rate to get the expected total rate of return. What is this expected total rate of return?

16-8 **Declining growth valuation.**   Kan Mining Company's ore reserves are being depleted, and its costs of recovering a declining quantity of ore are rising each year. As a result, the company's earnings and dividends are declining at a constant rate of 5 percent per year. If $D_0 = \$5$ and $k_s = 15\%$, what is the per share value of Kan Mining's equity?

16-9 **Constant growth valuation.**

a. Investors require a 15 percent return on the common equity of Company M ($k_s = 15\%$). During its most recent complete year, Company M equity earned $4 and paid $2 per share. At what price will the shares sell if investors expect earnings and dividends to grow at a constant rate of (i) −5 percent, (ii) 0 percent, (iii) 5 percent, and (iv) 10 percent?

b. In Part a, what is the constant growth price per share for Company M's equity if the required rate of return is 15 percent and the expected growth rate is (i) 15 percent or (ii) 20 percent? Are these results reasonable? Explain your answer.

16-10 Supernormal growth valuation. It is now January 1, 1994. Prosun Engineering has just developed a solar panel capable of generating 200 percent more electricity than any solar panel currently on the market. As a result, Prosun is expected to experience a 15 percent annual growth rate for the next 5 years. By the end of 5 years, other firms will have developed comparable technology, and Prosun's growth rate will slow to 5 percent per year indefinitely. Shareholders require a return of 12 percent on Prosun equity. The most recent annual dividend, D_0, which was paid yesterday, was $1.75 per share.

a. Calculate the expected dividends for 1994, 1995, 1996, 1997, and 1998.

b. Calculate the share price today, $\hat{P}_0$. Proceed by finding the present value of the dividends expected during 1994, 1995, 1996, 1997, and 1998 plus the present value of the share price at the end of 1998. The year-end 1998 share price can be found by using the constant growth equation. Note that to find the December 31, 1998, price, you use the dividend expected in 1999, which is 5 percent greater than the 1998 dividend.

c. Calculate the current dividend yield, D_1/P_0, the capital gains yield expected in 1994, and the expected total return (dividend yield plus capital gains yield) for 1994. Also, calculate these same three yields for 1998.

16-11 Supernormal growth stock valuation. Koehlman Technologies Corporation (KTC) has been growing at a rate of 20 percent per year in recent years. This same growth rate is expected to last for another 2 years.

a. If $D_0 = $1.60, k = 10\%$, and $g_n = 6\%$, what is a KTC equity share worth today? What are its expected dividend yield and capital gains yield?

b. Now assume that KTC's period of supernormal growth is to last another 5 years rather than 2 years. How does this affect its price, dividend yield, and capital gains yield? Answer in words only.

c. What will be KTC's dividend yield and capital gains yield the year after its period of supernormal growth ends? (Hint: These values will be the same regardless of whether you examine the case of 2 or 5 years of supernormal growth; the calculations are trivial.)

d. Of what interest to investors is the changing relationship between dividend yield and capital gains yield over time?

16-12 Yield to call. It is now January 1, 1994, and you are considering the purchase of an outstanding Sorrell Corporation bond that was issued on January 1, 1992. The Sorrell bond has a 9.5 percent annual coupon and a 30-year original maturity (it matures in 2022). It has a call provision that permits Sorrell to call it anytime after December 31, 1996, at

109 percent of par value, or $1090. Interest rates have declined since the bond was issued, and the bond is now selling at 116.575 percent of par, or $1,165.75. You want to determine both the yield to maturity and the yield to call for this bond. (Note: The yield to call considers the effect of a call provision on the bond's probable yield. In the calculation, we assume that the bond will be called on the first possible date. Thus, the investor will have received interest payments for the period through December 31, 1996, and then will receive the call price on January 1, 1997.)

a. What is the yield to maturity in 1994 for the Sorrell bond? What is its yield to call?

b. If you buy this bond, which return do you think you will actually earn? Explain your reasoning.

c. Suppose the bond had sold at a discount. Would the yield to maturity or the yield to call have been more relevant?

16-13 Equilibrium share price. The risk-free rate of return, k_{RF}, is 11 percent; the required rate of return on the market, k_M, is 14 percent; and Watson Company's equity has a beta coefficient of 1.5.

a. If the dividend expected during the coming year, D_1, is $2.25 and if g = a constant 5%, at what price should Watson's equity sell?

b. Now suppose the Bank of Canada increases the money supply, causing the risk-free rate to drop to 9 percent and k_M to fall to 12 percent. What would this do to the price of the stock?

c. In addition to the change in Part b, suppose investors' risk aversion declines; this fact, combined with the decline in k_{RF}, causes k_M to fall to 11 percent. At what price would Watson's shares sell?

d. Now suppose Watson has a change in management. The new group institutes policies that increase the expected constant growth rate to 6 percent. Also, the new management stabilizes sales and profits and thus causes the beta coefficient to decline from 1.5 to 1.3. After all these changes, what is Watson's new equilibrium price? (Note: D_1 goes to $2.27.)

16-14 Beta coefficients. Suppose Blacksburg Chemical Company's management conducts a study and concludes that if Blacksburg expanded its consumer products division (which is less risky than its primary business, industrial chemicals), the firm's beta would decline from 1.2 to 0.9. However, consumer products have a somewhat lower profit margin, and this would cause Blacksburg's constant growth rate in earnings and dividends to fall from 7 to 5 percent.

a. Should management make the change? Assume the following: k_M = 12%; k_{RF} = 9%; D_0 = $2.

b. Assume all the facts as given above except the change in the beta coefficient. How low would the beta have to fall to cause the expansion to be a good one? (Hint: Set $\hat{P}_0$ under the new policy equal to $\hat{P}_0$ under the old one, and find the new beta that will produce this equality.)

16-15 Expected rate of return. The beta coefficient for the equity of the company C is $\beta_C = 0.4$, whereas that for D is $\beta_D = -0.5$. D's beta is negative, indicating that its rate of return rises whenever returns on most other stocks fall. There are very few negative beta stocks, although gold mining stocks are sometimes cited as an example.

a. If the risk-free rate is 9 percent and the expected rate of return on an average stock is 13 percent, what are the required rates of return on Stock C and D?

b. For Stock C, suppose the current price, P_0, is $25; the next expected dividend, D_1, is $1.50; and the stock's expected constant growth rate is 4 percent. Is the stock in equilibrium? Explain, and describe what will happen if the stock is not in equilibrium.

Integrative Problems

16-16 Bond valuation.   Robert Bellemare and Donna Stead are senior vice presidents of the Energetic Capital Corporation. They are co-directors of the company's pension fund management division, with Bellemare having responsibility for fixed income securities (primarily bonds) and Stead being responsible for equity investments. A major new client has requested that Energetic present an investment seminar to its pension committee. Bellemare and Stead, who will make the actual presentation, have asked you to help them by answering the following questions.

a. How is the value of any asset whose value is based on expected future cash flows determined? How is the discount rate determined?

b. How is the value of a bond determined? What is the value of a 1-year, $1000 par value bond with a 9 percent annual coupon if its required rate of return is 9 percent? What is the value of a similar 10-year bond?

c. What would be the value of the bonds described in Part b if investors required a 12 percent return? a 6 percent return? What would happen to the value of the 10-year bond over time if the required rate of return remained at 12 percent? remained at 6 percent?

d. What is the yield to maturity on a 10-year, 9 percent annual coupon, $1000 par value bond that sells for $739.19? that sells for $1140.47? What is the current yield and capital gains yield in each case?

e. What is interest rate risk? Which bond in Part b has more interest rate risk, the 1-year bond or the 10-year bond? What is reinvestment rate risk? Which bond in Part b has more reinvestment rate risk, assuming a 10-year investment horizon?

f. Redo Parts b and c, assuming that the bonds have semiannual coupons.

g. What is the value of a perpetual bond with an annual coupon of $90 if its required rate of return is 9 percent? 12 percent? 6 percent? Assess the following statement: "Because perpetual bonds match an infinite investment horizon, they have little interest rate risk."

h. Suppose a 10-year, 9 percent, semiannual coupon bond having a par value of $1000 is currently selling for $1142.12, producing a yield to maturity of 7.0 percent. However, the bond can be called after 5 years for a price of $1045. What is the bond's yield to call? If you bought this bond, would you earn the YTM or the YTC?

16-17 Equity valuation.   The seminar-planning continues at Energetic Capital (see Problem 16-16). To illustrate the common equity valuation process, Bellemare and Stead have asked you to analyze the Bon Temps Company, an employment agency that supplies word processor operators and computer programmers to other businesses to help their permanent staff meet temporarily heavy workloads. You are to answer the following questions.

a. What formula can be used to value any share regardless of its dividend pattern? What is a constant growth equity? How are constant growth equities valued? What happens if $g > k_s$? Do many equities have $g > k_s$?

b. Assume that Bon Temps has a beta coefficient of 1.5. Further, assume that the risk-free rate (the yield on long-term Government of Canada bonds) is 11 percent and the required rate of return on the market is 15 percent. What is Bon Temps's required rate of return?

c. Assume that Bon Temps equity has constant growth and its last dividend (D_0, which was paid yesterday) was $2.00. The dividend is expected to grow at a 5 percent rate. What is Bon Temps's expected dividend stream over the next 3 years? What is Bon Temps's current value? What is the equity's expected value in one year? What are the expected dividend yield and the capital gains yield for the first year? What is the expected total yield during the first year?

d. Now assume that Bon Temps's shares are currently selling at $17.50. What is the expected rate of return on the equity?

e. What would Bon Temps's equity be worth if its dividends were expected to have zero growth?

f. Now assume that Bon Temps will experience supernormal growth of 25 percent in the next 3 years and then return to its steady-state constant growth rate of 5 percent. What is its value under these conditions? What are its expected dividend yield and capital gains in Year 1? in Year 4?

g. Suppose Bon Temps is expected to experience no growth during the first 3 years and then to resume its steady-state growth of 5 percent. What is a share's value now? What are its expected dividend yield and capital gains yield in Year 1? In Year 4?

h. Finally, assume that Bon Temps's dividends are expected to grow at a constant −5 percent rate; that is, the dividend is expected to decline by 5 percent each year. What is the current value of a share of Bon Temps's equity? What are the dividend yield and capital gains yield in each year?

Solutions to Self-Test Problems

ST-1   Refer to the appropriate sections of the text to check your responses.

ST-2   a. This is not necessarily true. Since G ploughs back two-thirds of its earnings, its growth rate should exceed that of D, but D pays more dividends ($6 versus $2). We cannot say which company should have the higher share price.

   b. Again, we just do not know which price would be higher.

   c. This is false. The changes in k_d and k_s will have a greater impact on G—its price will decline more.

d. The total expected return for D is

$$\hat{k}_d = \frac{D_1}{P_0} + g = 15\% + 0\% = 15\%.$$

The total expected return for G will have D_1/P_0 less than 15 percent and g greater than 0 percent, but k_G should be neither greater nor smaller than D's total expected return, 15 percent, because the two securities are equally risky.

e. We have eliminated a, b, c, and d, so e must be correct. The information provided suggests that D and G should sell at about the same price, \$40. Thus, $\hat{k}_s = \$6/\$40 = 15\%$ for both D and G. G's current dividend yield is $\$2/\$40 = 5\%$. Therefore, $g = 15\% - 5\% = 10\%$.

ST-3   **a.** The bonds were sold at par. Therefore, the YTM equals the coupon rate; YTM = 12%.

      b. Note that the bonds now have 25 years, or 50 6-month periods, remaining to maturity. Therefore, with $k_d = 10\%$, the value is calculated as

$$V = \sum_{t=1}^{50} \frac{\$120/2}{\left(1 + \dfrac{0.10}{2}\right)^t} + \frac{\$1000}{\left(1 + \dfrac{0.10}{2}\right)^{50}}$$

$$= \$60(\text{PVIFA}_{5\%,50}) + \$1000(\text{PVIF}_{5\%,50})$$

$$= \$60(18.2559) + \$1000(0.0872)$$

$$= \$1095.35 + \$87.20$$

$$= \$1182.55.$$

      c.   Current yield = Annual coupon payment/Price

$$= \$120/\$1182.55$$

$$= 0.101476 = 10.15\%.$$

Capital gains yield = Total yield − Current yield

$$= 10\% - 10.15\% = -0.15\%.$$

      d.

$$\$908.87 = \sum_{t=1}^{15} \frac{\$60}{(1 + k_d/2)^t} + \frac{\$1000}{(1 + k_d/2)^{15}}.$$

The bond sells at a discount; therefore, the YTM must exceed 12 percent.

$$\text{Try } k_d = 14\%:$$

$$V = I(\text{PVIFA}_{7\%,15}) + M(\text{PVIF}_{7\%,15})$$

$$\$908.87 = \$60(9.1079) + \$1000(0.3624)$$

$$= \$546.47 + \$362.40 = \$908.87.$$

Therefore, the YTM on July 31, 1989, was 14 percent.

e.   Current yield = \$120/\$908.87 = 13.20%.

Capital gains yield = 14% − 13.20% = 0.80%.

f. The following time line illustrates the years to maturity of the bond:

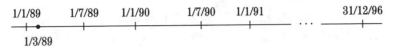

Thus, on March 1, 1989, there are 15 2/3 periods left before the bond matures. Bond traders use the following procedure to determine the price of the bond:

i. Find the price of the bond on the next coupon date, July 1, 1989:

$$V_{1/7/89} = \$60(PVIFA_{7.75\%,\,15}) + \$1000(PVIF_{7.75\%\,,15})$$

$$= \$60(8.6917) + \$1000(0.3264)$$

$$= \$847.90.$$

ii. Add the value of the coupon, \$60, to the bond price to get the total value, TV, of the bond on the next interest payment date:

$$TV = \$847.90 + \$60.00 = \$907.90.$$

iii. Discount this total value back to the purchase date:

$$\text{Value at purchase date (March 1, 1989)} = \$907.90(PVIF_{7.75\%,\,4/6})$$

$$= \$907.90(0.9515)$$

$$= \$863.87.$$

(Note: $PVIF_{7.75\%,\,4/6}$ can be found by substituting k = 7.75% and n = 4/6 periods into the equation for PVIF.)

iv. Therefore, you write a cheque for \$863.87 to complete the transaction. Of this amount, \$20 = (1/3)(\$60) represents accrued interest and \$843.87 represents the bond's basic value. This breakdown will affect your taxes and those of the seller.

ST-4 The first step is to solve for g, the unknown variable, in the constant growth equation. Since D_1 is unknown, substitute $D_0(1 + g)$ as follows:

$$P_0 = \frac{D_0(1 + g)}{k_s - g}$$

$$\$36.00 = \frac{\$2.40(1 + g)}{0.12 - g}$$

Solving for g, we find the growth rate to be 5 percent. The next step is to use the growth rate to project the share price 5 years hence:

$$P_5 = \frac{D_0(1 + g)^6}{k_s - g}$$

$$= \frac{\$2.10(1.05)^6}{0.12 - 0.05} = \$45.95.$$

Therefore, the Karp Company's expected share price 5 years from now, P_5, is $45.95.

ST-5   **a.**   **i.**   Calculate the PV of the dividends paid during the supernormal growth period.

$$D_1 = \$1.1500(1.15) = \$1.3225.$$
$$D_2 = \$1.3225(1.15) = \$1.5209.$$
$$D_3 = \$1.5209(1.13) = \$1.7186.$$

$$PV\ (D) = \$1.3225(0.8929) + \$1.5209(0.7972) + \$1.7186(0.7118)$$
$$= \$1.1809 + \$1.2125 + \$1.2233$$
$$= \$3.6166 \approx \$3.62.$$

ii. Find the PV of the share price at the end of Year 3:

$$\hat{P}_3 = \frac{D_4}{k_s - g} = \frac{D_3(1 + g)}{k_s - g}$$

$$= \frac{\$1.7186(1.06)}{0.12 - 0.06}$$

$$= \$30.36.$$

$$PV\ (\hat{P}_3) = \$30.36(0.7118) = \$21.61.$$

iii. Sum the two components to find the value of the share today:

$$\hat{P}_0 = \$3.62 + \$21.61 = \$25.23.$$

b. $\hat{P}_1 = \$1.5209(0.8929) + \$1.7186(0.7972) + \$30.36(0.7972)$
$= \$1.3580 + \$1.3701 + \$24.2030$
$= \$26.9311 \approx \$26.93.$
$\hat{P}_2 = \$1.7186(0.8929) + \$30.36(0.8929)$
$= \$1.5345 + \$27.1084$
$= \$28.6430 \approx \$28.64.$

c.

Year	Dividend yield	+	Capital gains yield	=	Total return
1	$\dfrac{\$1.3225}{\$25.23} = 5.24\%$		$\dfrac{\$26.93 - \$25.23}{\$25.23} = 6.74\%$		$\approx 12\%$
2	$\dfrac{\$1.5209}{\$26.93} = 5.65\%$		$\dfrac{\$28.64 - \$26.93}{\$26.93} = 6.35\%$		$\approx 12\%$
3	$\dfrac{\$1.7186}{\$28.64} = 6.00\%$		$\dfrac{\$30.36 - \$28.64}{\$28.64} = 6.00\%$		$\approx 12\%$

17

The Cost of Capital

Electric utilities, natural gas pipelines, and telephone companies are, to a large extent, *natural monopolies*, which means that one firm can serve customers in a given area at a lower cost than could two or more firms. Therefore, utilities have been granted legal monopoly status in their service areas. Although monopoly status does improve operating efficiency, it also creates a problem: monopolists have the power to raise prices, to exploit their customers, and to earn unreasonably high rates of return on their invested capital. So public utility commissions regulate the public utilities to ensure, among other things, that they charge consumers "fair" prices.

What constitutes a fair price for a utility's service? To oversimplify from the many issues involved in this determination, the generally accepted answer is: "The price that a utility is allowed to charge should be sufficient to cover all reasonable operating costs and to leave a profit which is just large enough to cover the cost of the capital investors have supplied to make it possible for the company to operate." Operationally, this means that a utility commission must examine each company under its jurisdiction to ensure that its operating costs are reasonable, to ascertain how much capital investors have supplied, to determine the cost of that capital, to multiply the dollars of capital times the cost of capital to determine the company's target profit level, and then to set utility service rates that will produce that target profit level.

By far the most difficult part of this process is determining the cost of capital. That determination is made in rate cases, in which utilities present evidence as to what their cost of capital is, and then other parties, especially consumer representatives, present their own counterevidence. The commissioners must decide whose story to buy or how to reach a compromise. The decision is important, for if the cost of capital is underestimated, then the companies will not be allowed to earn their true capital cost, the industry will not be able to attract sufficient capital in the long run, and, eventually, there will be hydro or gas shortages or poor telephone service. On the other hand, if the cost of capital is overestimated, utility customers will be charged too much, and there will be a transfer of wealth from utility customers to utility investors.

The procedures covered in this chapter are, with some modifications, the same ones that are used in utility rate cases, so if you understand the chapter, you will be in a good position to go to work for a utility, a consumer advocacy group, or a regulatory commission. You will also be in a better position to understand the issues when you read about a utility rate case in the newspaper, and, if you become involved with investments, to understand why some hydro, gas, and telephone companies' shares go up while others go down.

Utilities are not the only firms interested in the cost of capital. The topic is critically important throughout the business world for three main reasons: (1) to maximize a firm's value, its managers must minimize the costs of all inputs, including capital, and to minimize the cost of capital, the managers must be able to measure it; (2) financial managers require an estimate of the cost of capital if they are to make correct capital budgeting decisions; and (3) many other types of decisions made by financial managers, including those related to leasing, to bond refunding, and to working capital policy, require estimates of the cost of capital.

Our first topic in this chapter is the logic of the weighted average cost of capital. Next, we consider the costs of the major types of capital, after which we see how the costs of the individual components of the capital structure are brought together to form a weighted average cost of capital. Finally, we examine the relationship between capital budgeting and the cost of capital.

It should be noted that the cost of capital models and formulas used in this chapter are the same ones we developed in Chapter 16, where we were concerned with the rates of return investors require on different securities. Now we use those same models and formulas to estimate the firm's cost of capital. Indeed, the rate of return on a security to an investor is the same as the cost of capital to a firm, and exactly the same models are used by investors and by corporate treasurers.

The Logic of the Weighted Average Cost of Capital

Suppose a particular firm's cost of debt is estimated to be 8 percent, its cost of equity is 12 percent, and the decision has been made to finance next year's projects by selling debt. The argument is sometimes advanced that the cost of capital for these projects is 8 percent because debt is being used to finance them. However, this position is incorrect. To finance a particular set of projects with debt implies that the firm is using up some of its potential for obtaining new low-cost debt in the future. As expansion occurs in subsequent years, the firm will find it necessary at some point to use additional equity financing to prevent the debt ratio from becoming too large.

To illustrate, suppose the firm borrows heavily at 8 percent during 1993, using up its debt capacity in the process, to finance projects yielding 9 percent. In 1994 it has projects available that would yield 11 percent, well above the return on 1993 projects, but it cannot accept these new projects because they would have to be financed with 12 percent equity money. To avoid this problem, the firm should view itself as an ongoing concern; the cost of capital used in capital budgeting should be calculated as a *weighted average, or composite of the various types of funds it generally uses,* regardless of the specific financing used to fund a particular project.

Concept Review

▶ Why should the cost of capital used in capital budgeting be calculated as a weighted average of the various types of funds the firm generally uses, regardless of the specific financing used to fund a particular project?

Basic Definitions

The items on the right-hand side of a firm's balance sheet—various types of debt, preferred shares, and common equity—are called its *capital components*. A firm's **capital structure** is the mix of capital components it uses: for example, 20 percent debt and 80 percent common equity, or 40 percent debt, 10 percent preferred equity and 50 percent common equity. Any increase in total assets must be financed by an increase in one or more capital components.

Capital is a necessary factor of production, and like any other factor, it has a cost. The cost of each component is called the *component cost* of that particular type of capital. For example, if a firm can borrow money at 8 percent, its before-tax component cost of debt is stated as 8 percent. In this chapter, we concentrate primarily on debt, preferred shares, retained earnings, and new issues of common equity, which are the four major capital structure components. Their costs are identified by the following symbols:[1]

k_d = interest rate on the firm's new debt = *component cost of debt, before tax.*

$k_d (1 - T)$ = *component cost of debt, after tax*, where T is the firm's marginal tax rate. $k_d (1 - T)$ is the debt cost used to calculate the weighted average cost of capital.

k_p = *component cost of preferred shares.*

k_s = *component cost of retained earnings* (or internal equity). This is identical to the k_s developed in Chapter 16 and defined there as the *required rate of return on common equity.*

k_e = component cost of external capital obtained by issuing new common equity, as opposed to retaining earnings. As we shall see, it is necessary to distinguish between equity raised by retained earnings and that raised by selling new shares. That is why we distinguish between k_s and k_e. Further, k_e is always greater than k_s.

k_a = WACC = the *weighted average cost of capital*, also called the *composite* cost of capital. When a firm raises new capital to finance asset expansion if it is to keep its capital structure in balance (that is, if it is to keep the same percentages of debt, preferred shares, and common equity), then it must raise part of the new funds as debt, part as preferred shares, and part as common equity (with equity coming either from retained earnings or from the sale of new common shares).[2] It must be emphasized that these are long-run or target proportions. Financing is typically lumpy, and any particular project may be financed with one source of funds which moves the capital structure away from the target proportions; this will necessitate that subsequent projects be financed with a different source of funds. Also, k_a is a marginal cost of capital since it relates to the incremental or marginal cost of funds needed to finance an investment program.

The fact that the composite cost of capital, k_a, is referred to as both a marginal and an average cost is not inconsistent with economic theory. The composite cost of capital

---

[1]The literature also refers to these component costs as *required yields*. That terminology is actually more precise, as the investor in preferred, common equity, or debt has an opportunity cost or yield requirement. For the sake of convenience and custom we continue, however, to refer to the required yields on a source of capital as the cost of that source of capital.

[2]Firms do try to keep their debt, preferred shares, and common equity in balance; they do not try to maintain any proportional relationship between the common equity and retained earnings accounts as shown on the balance sheet. For capital structure purposes, common equity is common equity, whether it is represented by common shares or by retained earnings.

reflects the current opportunity cost or marginal cost of each specific source of funds used by the company. Thus, it is a marginal concept. Because the firm uses these funds in long-run proportions to finance investments, however, the calculation of the composite cost of capital requires a weighted average of the specific marginal costs to be utilized. Since the composite cost is a weighted average of the marginal costs of each source of financing, it is itself a marginal cost.

These definitions and concepts are explained in detail in the remainder of this chapter, where we develop a marginal cost of capital schedule (MCC) that can be used in capital budgeting. Then in Chapter 18 we shall extend the analysis to determine the mix of types of capital that will minimize the MCC schedule. If the firm finances so as to minimize its MCC, uses this MCC to calculate NPVs, and makes capital budgeting decisions on the basis of the NPV method, this will lead to a maximization of the common equity share price.

The significance of the marginal cost of capital concept is demonstrated in the following simplified example. Assume that a company has two sources of financing: debt with a current interest rate of 8 percent and common equity with a required yield or cost of equity of 15 percent. The total amount of debt plus equity is $100 million, of which 70 percent is equity and 30 percent is debt; these capital structure proportions are the target values. The firm has invested the full amount of capital and expects to earn a rate of return of 12.9 percent. It pays out as dividends all earnings after interest payments; there is no corporate income tax.

The management of the company is contemplating an investment of $10 million, which is to be financed in the current proportions of debt and equity; new debt can be issued at 8 percent.

What is the minimum rate of return on the investment that will leave the market value of the existing equity holders unchanged? This rate of return is the *marginal cost of capital*.

The analysis is presented in Table 17-1. Column 1 lists the capital structure and cash flows existing before the investment. The equity holder obtained a rate of return of 15 percent—dividends divided by the value of equity = $10 500 000/$70 000 000 = 0.15, or 15 percent.

In order to determine the cost of capital, we must identify the incremental impact of the investment decision on the equity holder. Since the firm will issue an additional $3 000 000 of debt at 8 percent, it is obvious that the project must earn at least the incremental interest payments of $240 000. But the project must also earn enough to ensure that existing equity holders are not harmed. In column 2 of Table 17-1, we observe that if the earnings before interest on the project are $1 290 000, there is enough to pay the incremental interest and have $1 050 000 left over to pay the new equity holder a 15 percent rate of return without impairing the dividends to the old shareholders. The overall rate of return on investment that meets these constraints is 12.9 percent—$1 290 000/$10 000 000—and this is the firm's cost of capital. Note that the rate of return on equity to all shareholders after the investment decision (see column 3) is also 15 percent—$11 550 000/$77 000 000.

Suppose the firm's new investment is expected to earn 10 percent. This will leave incremental earnings after interest of $760 000, instead of $1 050 000; the total earnings (dividends) after the investment will be $11 260 000. The rate of

Table 17-1
Incremental Impact of Investment Decision

	Before Investment Decision (1)	Incremental Impact of Investment Decision (2)	After the Investment Decision (3)
Capital structure			
Debt (8%)	$ 30 000 000	$ 3 000 000	$ 33 000 000
Equity	70 000 000	7 000 000	77 000 000
Total capital	$100 000 000	$10 000 000	$110 000 000
Earnings before interest	12 900 000	1 290 000	14 190 000
Interest (at 8%)	2 400 000	240 000	2 640 000
Dividends (earnings available to common equity)	$ 10 500 000	$ 1 050 000	$ 11 550 000

return on equity after the investment will be 14.6 percent, a reduction from the preinvestment return on equity of 15 percent. If the project is undertaken, the shareholders will experience a reduction in share price. Conversely, if the project earns in excess of the cost of capital, then the postinvestment rate of return on equity will be greater than 15 percent—a clear gain to current shareholders.

Suppose the firm decides to finance this project by issuing $5 000 000 of debt instead of $3 000 000. As long as the firm intends to maintain its target capital structure at 30 percent debt and 70 percent equity, it will have to finance subsequent investment opportunities with an equity component in excess of 70 percent. But as long as the capital structure targets are unchanged, the marginal cost of capital remains at 12.9 percent. If, however, the firm decides to alter its capital structure targets, the marginal costs of capital can be altered to reflect the new targets as well as any changes in the costs of capital for specific sources of funds induced by the change in capital structure.

Concept Review

▶ Identify the firm's four major capital structure components and give their respective component cost symbols.

Cost of Debt, k_d (1−T)

The **after-tax cost of debt**, $k_d(1-T)$, is used to calculate the weighted average cost of capital. It is the interest rate on debt, k_d, less the tax savings that result because interest is a tax deductible expense. This is the same as k_d multiplied by $(1-T)$ where T is the firm's marginal tax rate.[3]

$$\text{After-tax component cost of debt} = \text{Interest rate} - \text{Tax savings}$$
$$= k_d - k_d T$$
$$= k_d (1 - T) \qquad \qquad \textbf{(17-1)}$$

In effect, the government pays part of the cost of debt because interest is tax deductible. Therefore, if a firm can borrow at an interest rate of 10 percent, and if it has a marginal tax rate of 40 percent, then its after-tax cost of debt is 6 percent.

$$k_d (1 - T) = 10\%(1.0 - 0.4) = 10\%(0.6)$$
$$= 6.0\%.$$

The reason for making the tax adjustment is as follows. The value of the firm's equity, which we want to maximize, depends on *after-tax* income, and interest is a deductible expense. To put the costs of debt and equity on a comparable basis, we adjust the interest rate downward to take account of the preferential tax treatment of debt.[4]

Note that the cost of debt is the interest rate on *new* debt, not the interest rate on debt that was issued in the past and is still outstanding. In other words, we are interested in the *marginal* cost of debt. Our primary concern with the cost of capital is to use it in deciding whether to obtain capital to make new investments. Whether the firm has borrowed at high or at low rates in the past has created a sunk cost that is irrelevant for cost of capital purposes.

---

[3]Note that the cost of debt is considered in isolation. We consider the impact of debt on the cost of equity, as well as on future increments of debt, when we derive the weighted cost of a combination of debt and equity. Also, we ignore *issue costs*, or the costs of selling the debt, since issue costs for debt issues are generally quite low—in fact, most debt is placed directly with banks, insurance companies, pension funds, and the like and involves no issue costs.

If bonds are publicly placed and do involve issue costs, the solution value of k_d in the following formula is used as the after-tax cost of debt:

$$M(1 - F) = \sum_{t=1}^{n} \frac{I (1 - T)}{(1 + k_d)^t} + \frac{M}{(1 + k_d)^n},$$

where F is the percentage amount of the bond issue cost, n is the number of periods to maturity, I is the dollars of interest per period, T is the corporate tax rate, M is the maturity value of the bond, and k_d is the after-tax cost of debt adjusted to reflect issue costs. If we assume that the bond in the example calls for annual payments, that it has a 20 year maturity, and that F = 2%, then the after-tax cost of debt adjusted for issue cost is 6.18 percent, versus 6.00 percent before the issue cost adjustment.

[4]It should also be noted that the tax rate is zero for a firm with losses. Therefore, for a company that does not pay taxes, the cost of debt is not reduced—that is, in Equation 17-1 the tax rate equals zero, so the after-tax cost of debt is equal to the interest rate.

Cost of Preferred Shares, k_p

Preferred shares, which will be described in detail in Chapter 21, are a hybrid between debt and common equity. Like debt, preferred shares carry a fixed commitment on the part of the corporation to make periodic payments, and, in liquidation, the claims of the preferred shareholders normally take precedence over those of the common shareholders. Failure to make the preferred dividend payments does not result in bankruptcy, however, as does nonpayment of interest on bonds. Thus, to the firm, preferred shares are somewhat riskier than common equity but less risky than bonds.

The component **cost of preferred shares, k_p,** used to calculate the weighted cost of capital is the preferred dividend, D_p, divided by the net issuing price, P_p, or the price the firm receives after deducting issue costs:

$$\text{Component cost of preferred shares} = k_p = \frac{D_p}{P_p}. \qquad (17\text{-}2)$$

For example, suppose a firm has preferred shares that pay a $12 dividend per share and sell for $100 per share in the market. If it issues new preferred shares, it will incur an underwriting (or issue) cost of 2.5 percent, or $2.50 per share, so it will net $97.50 per share. Therefore, the cost of preferred shares will be 12.31 percent:[5]

---

[5]The cost of preferred shares can also be written as the yield on preferred shares excluding issue costs and an adjustment factor to reflect these costs. The cost of preferred capital can be written as

$$k_p = \frac{D_p}{P_n} = \frac{D_p}{P_p(1 - F)} = \frac{\text{Yield on preferred shares}}{1 - F},$$

where P_p is the price of the preferred share before issue costs and F is the issue cost as a proportion of the price.

In the example, the yield on preferred shares before issue cost $12/$100 = 12%. Since F = 0.025, the component cost is

$$k_p = \frac{0.12}{1 - 0.025} = 0.1231 \text{ or } 12.31\%.$$

This formulation is useful when the preferred yield excluding issue costs is estimated from capital market data.

$$k_p = \frac{\$12.00}{\$97.50} = 12.31\%.$$

This estimated value is the before-personal-tax cost of preferred equity. Note that no corporate tax adjustments are made when calculating k_p because, unlike interest expense on debt, dividend payments on preferred shares are *not* tax deductible.

Because of their hybrid nature, preferred shares are less risky than common equity but riskier than bonds to the investor. Thus, an investor who is willing to buy a firm's bonds at a 10 percent yield might, because of risk aversion, be unwilling to purchase the same firm's preferred shares at a yield of less than 11 percent. This would be the case in a taxation system in which interest payments and preferred dividends received equivalent tax treatment in the hands of the investor. However, Canada has two tax provisions that result in a favourable tax treatment for preferred dividends relative to interest. First, intercorporate dividend payments on some preferred shares are tax free; second, individual investors can take advantage of the dividend tax credit on preferred dividends.

Both of these factors are important in determining the yield differentials between the bonds and preferred shares of the same company. It is certainly true that the higher risk of preferreds should result in investors' requiring a higher *after-personal-tax* rate of return on preferreds than on bonds. This would refer to the 10 percent yield on debt and the minimum 11 percent yield on preferred shares noted above. With the application of the dividend tax credit, it is possible to obtain this higher after-personal-tax rate of return from a lower before-personal-tax yield on preferreds. In fact, the before-personal-tax yields on preferreds are less than on bonds of the same company. For example, on July 27, 1992, the yield on a B.C. Telephone bond maturing in 2022 was 9.65 percent while the yield on the same company's preferred shares, series F, was 7.74 percent.

Note, however, that the component cost of preferred shares is the *before-personal-tax* yield.

Concept Review

► Does the component cost of preferred equity include or exclude issue costs? Explain your answer.

► Is a tax adjustment made to the cost of preferred equity? Why or why not?

► Is the yield calculated from market prices published in the newspaper the before- or after-personal tax component cost?

Cost of Retained Earnings, k_s

The costs of debt and preferred shares are based on the return investors require on these securities. Similarly, the **cost of retained earnings, k_s,** is the rate of return shareholders require on equity capital that the firm obtains by retaining and reinvesting earnings.[6]

The reason we must assign a cost of capital to retained earnings involves the *opportunity cost principle*. The firm's after-tax earnings literally belong to the shareholders. Bondholders are compensated by interest payments, while earnings belong to the common equity holders and serve to compensate them for the use of their capital. Management may either pay out earnings in the form of dividends or retain earnings and reinvest them in the business. If management decides to retain earnings, there is an opportunity cost involved— shareholders could have received the earnings as dividends and invested this money in other shares, in bonds, in real estate, or in anything else. Thus, the firm should earn on the retained earnings at least as much as shareholders themselves could earn in alternative investments of comparable risk.

What rate of return can shareholders expect to earn on equivalent risk investments? First, recall from Chapter 16 that securities are normally in equilibrium, with the expected and required rates of return being equal: $\hat{k}_s = k_s$. Therefore, the firm's shareholders expect to earn a return of k_s on their money. If the firm cannot invest retained earnings and earn at least k_s, then it should pay these funds to its shareholders and let them invest directly in other assets that do provide this return.[7] To the extent that management retains funds and invests them to earn an expected return of less than k_s, the current share price will fall.

Whereas debt and preferred shares are contractual obligations that have easily determined costs, it is not at all easy to measure k_s. However, we can employ the principles developed in Chapters 15 and 16 to produce reasonably good cost of equity estimates. To begin, recall that in equilibrium (which is the typical situation), the required rate of return, k_s, is equal to the expected rate of return, $\hat{k}_s$. Further, the required return is equal to a riskless rate, k_{RF}, plus a risk premium, RP, while the expected return on a constant growth equity security is equal to a dividend yield, D_1/P_0, plus an expected growth rate, g:

$$\text{Required rate of return} = \text{Expect rate of return.}$$
$$k_s = k_{RF} + RP = D_1/P_0 + g = \hat{k}_s. \qquad \textbf{(17-3)}$$

Therefore, we can estimate k_s either as $k_s = k_{RF} + RP$ or as $k_s = \hat{k}_s = D_1/P_0 + g$.

Actually, three methods are commonly used for the estimation of the cost of retained earnings: (1) the capital assets pricing model (CAPM) approach, (2) the bond yield-plus-risk-premium approach, and (3) the discounted cash flow

---

[6]The term *retained earnings* can be interpreted to mean the balance sheet item "retained earnings," which consists of all the earnings retained in the business throughout its history, or it can mean the income statement item "additions to retained earnings." The income statement definition is used in this chapter. For our purpose, **retained earnings** refers to that part of current earnings not paid out in dividends but retained and reinvested in the business. Recall that *equity* is defined in this chapter to exclude preferred shares. Equity is the sum of stated capital, contributed surplus, and accumulated retained earnings.

[7]One complexity in estimating the cost of retained earnings deals with the fact that dividends and capital gains are taxed differently. Retaining earnings rather than paying them out as dividends can convert dividend income to capital gains. This point is discussed in Chapters 19 and 20.

(DCF) approach. These three approaches are discussed in the following sections.

The CAPM Approach

To use the capital asset pricing model (CAPM) as developed in Chapter 15, we proceed as follows:

Step 1. Estimate the riskless rate, k_{RF}, over the holding period required. For example, if a 1-year horizon is used and the cost of equity is being evaluated at the beginning of 1993, the riskless rate is the interest rate prevailing at the evaluation date on Government of Canada bonds outstanding with 1 year to maturity.[8] If the horizon is a shorter term—say, 30 days—the 30-day treasury bill rate is used.

Step 2. Estimate the equity's beta coefficient, β, and use this as an index of the equity's risk.

Step 3. Estimate the expected rate of return on "the market," or on an "average" share. Designate this return k_M.

Step 4. Estimate the required rate of return on the firm's equity as follows:

$$k_s = k_{RF} + \beta(k_M - k_{RF}). \qquad (17\text{-}4)$$

$k_M - k_{RF}$ is the risk premium[9] on the average share, while β is an index of the particular share's own risk. For an illustration of the CAPM approach, assume that $k_{RF} = 8\%$, $k_M = 13\%$, and $\beta = 0.7$ for a given security. The security's k_s is calculated as follows:

$$k_s = 8\% + 0.7(13\% - 8\%) = 8\% + 3.5\% = 11.5\%.$$

Had β been 1.8, indicating that the security was riskier than average, k_s would have been

$$k_s = 8\% + 1.8(5\%) = 8\% + 9\% = 17.0\%.$$

For an average security,

$$k_s = k_M = 8\% + (1.0)(5\%) = 13\%.$$

It should be noted that although the CAPM approach appears to yield accurate, precise estimates of k_s, there are actually several problems with it. First, if a

---

[8]If the government bond used has a term to maturity that is greater than the horizon, it is not riskless. At the end of the horizon, the bond would have to be liquidated, and its value at that time will depend upon what has happened to interest rates. Thus, the return earned over the year will not be riskless since it is not known with certainty at the start of the period. Similarly, investing in a bond with a maturity less than the horizon is also risky since reinvestment at future uncertain interest rates will be necessary to obtain a value at the horizon date.

[9]Instead of obtaining an estimate of the rate of return on the market (step 3) and then an estimate of the risk premium, analysts often use a direct estimate of the risk premium. A reasonable estimate of this risk premium is between 4 and 5 percent on an annual basis; however, the risk premium does vary and depends upon macroeconomic variables.

firm's shareholders are not well diversified, then they may be concerned with *total risk*, rather than market risk only; in this case the firm's true investment risk will not be measured by beta, and the CAPM procedure will understate the correct value of k_s. Further, even if the CAPM method is valid, it is hard to obtain correct estimates of the inputs required to make it operational: (1) there is uncertainty over whether to use long-term or short-term government bond rates for k_{RF}; (2) it is hard to estimate the beta that investors expect the company to have in the future; and (3) it is hard to estimate the market risk premium. This last problem was especially vexing in the 1980s, because the riskiness of equities versus bonds was changing, making the market risk premium unstable.

Bond-Yield-plus-Risk-Premium Approach

Although it is essentially an ad hoc, subjective procedure, analysts often estimate a firm's cost of common equity simply by adding a risk premium of 2 to 4 percentage points to the interest rate on its own long-term debt. It is logical to think that firms with risky, low-rated, and consequently high-interest-rate debt will also have risky, higher-cost equity, and the procedure of basing the cost of equity on readily observable debt cost utilizes this precept. For example, if an AAA-rated firm's bonds yield 9 percent, then its cost of equity might be estimated as follows:

$$k_s = \text{Bond rate} + \text{Risk premium} = 9\% + 3\% = 12\%.$$

A BAA firm's debt might carry a yield of 12 percent, making its estimated cost of equity 16 percent:

$$k_s = 12\% + 3\% = 15\%.$$

Because the 3 percent risk premium is a judgement-based estimate, the estimated value of k_s is also judgement-based. Also, studies show that the equity-over-bond risk premium is not stable, so this method is not likely to produce a very accurate cost of equity—about all it can do is get us "into the right ballpark."

Dividend-Yield-plus-Growth-Rate, or Discounted Cash Flow (DCF) Approach

In Chapter 16 we saw that the expected rate of return on a share of common equity depends ultimately on the dividends it is expected to pay:

$$P_0 = \frac{D_1}{(1 + k_s)^1} + \frac{D_2}{(1 + k_s)^2} + \ldots \qquad \text{(17-5)}$$

$$= \sum_{t=1}^{\infty} \frac{D_t}{(1 + k_s)^t}.$$

Here P_0 is the current price per share of the equity; D_t is the dividend per share expected to be paid at the end of Year t; and k_s is the required rate of return. If dividends are expected to grow at a constant rate, then, as we saw in Chapter 16, Equation 17-5 reduces to the following expression:

$$P_0 = \frac{D_1}{k_s - g}. \tag{17-6}$$

We can solve for k_s to obtain the required rate of return on common equity, which in equilibrium is also the expected rate of return:

$$k_s = \hat{k}_s = \frac{D_1}{P_0} + \text{expected } g. \tag{17-7}$$

Thus, investors expect to receive a dividend yield, D_1/P_0, plus a capital gain, g, for a total expected return of $\hat{k}_s$, and in equilibrium this expected return is also the required return. This method of estimating the cost of equity is called the *discounted cash flow, or DCF, method*. Henceforth in this chapter, we assume that equilibrium exists, so we shall use the terms k_s and $\hat{k}_s$ interchangeably.

To illustrate the DCF approach: suppose a share of the firm's equity sells for $20.00; its next expected dividend is $1.60; and its expected growth rate is 7 percent. The firm's expected and required rate of return, and hence its cost of retained earnings, is 15 percent:

$$k_s = \hat{k}_s = \frac{\$1.60}{\$20.00} + 7\% = 8\% + 7\% = 15\%.$$

This 15 percent is the minimum rate of return that management must expect to earn to justify retaining earnings and ploughing them back into the business rather than paying them out to shareholders as dividends.

It is relatively easy to determine the dividend yield, but it is difficult to establish the proper expected growth rate. Yet success in using this model depends on the estimate of the expected growth rate. Three measurement techniques are widely used: historic growth rates, estimates of the components of growth, and outside estimates of growth.

Historic Growth Rates.   The growth rate used in the calculation of the cost of equity should reflect investors' expectations. In many instances, these estimates of growth can be based on growth rates derived from past data.[10]

The theoretical literature on the dividend-yield-plus-growth model notes that, under certain conditions, the expected growth rate refers to growth in per share dividends and earnings; the growth rates should be the same for both. Therefore, the analyst can use historical growth rates in earnings or dividends per share as a proxy for the expected growth rate. Even though the growth rates should be the same from a theoretical point of view, the estimated growth

---

[10]Although theoretically equivalent to growth rates in per share dividends and earnings, growth rates derived from historical share price performance do not provide good estimates of expected growth. Since the share price reflects not only the present value of firm's earnings and dividends but also economy-wide influences, the estimated growth rates are extremely variable.

rates using historical dividend and earnings data will differ. The analyst must use judgement to choose the appropriate growth rate. If past growth rates in earnings and dividends have been relatively stable and if investors appear to be projecting a continuation of past trends, then g may be based on the firm's historic growth rate. However, if the company's growth has been abnormally high or low, either because of its own unique situation or because of general economic conditions, or if there have been significant changes in historic profitability, leverage and/or dividend policies, then investors will not project the past growth rate into the future. In this case, g must be estimated in some other manner.

Estimates of the Components of Growth.   The expected growth rate can be decomposed into its underlying components. We begin the discussion by assuming that the firm has no debt and intends to finance all of its new investments from retained earnings. Therefore, the new investment per share is equal to the amount of retained earnings per share during Year t; investment per share in Year t is denoted as N_t. Earnings per share in Year t are equal to the sum of dividends per share and retained earnings per share. We now define the *retention ratio*, which is denoted as γ, as the proportion of total earnings that are retained (and hence reinvested). For example, if earnings per share (EPS) are $3 and dividends per share are D_t, $2, retained earnings per share are $1 and the retention ratio is 0.33 (that is, $\gamma = \$1/\$3 = 0.33$).

Therefore, we can write the components of earnings per share as follows:

$$
\begin{aligned}
\text{EPS}_t &= D_t + \text{Retained earnings per share}_t \\
&= (1 - \gamma)\text{EPS}_t + \gamma\text{EPS}_t \\
&= (1 - \gamma)\text{EPS}_t + N_t.
\end{aligned}
$$

Investment in Year t is equal to the retention ratio times the earnings per share in Year t.

What is the level of earnings per share in Year t + 1? Assume that the investment in Year t is expected to earn a rate of return equal to the internal rate of return (IRR). Thus, the earnings per share are written as the sum of the earnings per share from the existing assets plus earnings expected from the new investment:

$$
\begin{aligned}
\text{EPS}_{t+1} &= \text{EPS (old assets)} + \text{EPS (new investment)} \\
&= \text{EPS}_t + (N_t \times \text{IRR}).
\end{aligned}
\tag{17-8}
$$

By substituting the definition of N_t into Equation 17-8, we obtain

$$
\begin{aligned}
\text{EPS}_{t+1} &= \text{EPS}_t + (\gamma\text{EPS}_t \times \text{IRR}) \\
&= \text{EPS}_t (1 + \gamma \times \text{IRR}) \\
&= \text{EPS}_t (1 + g),
\end{aligned}
\tag{17-9}
$$

where $g = \gamma \times \text{IRR}$. Therefore, we observe the earnings per share grow at a rate of g, which is the product of two components: (1) the expected retention ratio of the firm, γ, and (2) the rate of return expected to be earned on these retained earnings.

A simple numerical example will demonstrate this measure of expected growth. Consider a company that has current earnings per share of $10 out of which it has paid a current dividend per share of $4. Therefore, the retention ratio is 0.60. Investors expect that the firm will earn 20 percent on its new investments, in the future—that is, IRR = 0.20. Also, investors expect that the firm will continue to retain 60 percent of its earnings in the future.

Using Equation 17-8:

$$
\begin{aligned}
EPS_t + 1 &= EPS_t + (N_t \times IRR) \\
&= \$10.00 + \$6.00 \times 0.20 \\
&= \$10.00 + \$1.20 \\
&= \$11.20.
\end{aligned}
$$

As current earnings per share are $10.00, the expected growth in earnings per share is 12 percent—that is, ($11.20 − $10)/$10.00. Alternatively, the expected growth in EPS can be written as

$$
\begin{aligned}
g &= \gamma(IRR) \\
&= 0.60 \times (0.20) \\
&= 0.12, \text{ or } 12 \text{ percent.}
\end{aligned}
$$

The growth rate that is required in the dividend growth model should reflect expected growth in dividends per share. If we continue to assume that the firm is expected to have a constant retention ratio, then we have the following relationship:

$$
D_t = (1 - \gamma) \, EPS_t.
$$

If EPS are expected to grow at rate g, then dividends per share, which are proportional to EPS, must also be expected to grow at the same rate, g. Thus, the components of growth technique can be used to estimate the expected growth rate in dividends per share as well. Therefore, the required rate of return on common equity is equal to:

$$
\hat{k}_s = \frac{D_1}{P_0} + \gamma(IRR).
$$

To this point we have discussed the cost of equity by referring to the expected rate of return on the new investment. Since there is no information on this quantity, the analyst assumes that the expected return on the overall equity of the company is a good proxy for the return on the new project. The former is measured by the expected return on equity (ROE). Therefore, when estimating the cost of equity using this approach, the expected ROE is substituted for the expected IRR. The required rate of return on equity is thus estimated using the following equation:

$$
\hat{k}_s = \frac{D_1}{P_0} + \gamma(ROE).
$$

This decomposition of the growth term is intuitively appealing. For example, suppose the company decides to increase the retention ratio by paying less in the way of dividends. This increase in γ will result in an increase in the expected growth rate. In addition, it will reduce the dividend term D, in the dividend yield component.

Also, if γ remains constant and the profitability of retained earnings reinvestment increases—that is, if IRR increases—the growth rate will increase. From our discussion of valuation theory, we can anticipate that this will result in an increase in the share price, P_0, and hence an offsetting reduction in the dividend yield component in the required rate of return on equity.

There are a number of techniques used to estimate the retention ratio and the rate of return on the retention financing. The former is measured either as the most recent retention ratio or an average of past ratios. The rate of return on investment can be measured as the most current rate of return on book equity (ROE), or an average of these rates of return over a historical period. Whatever the technique chosen, it should reflect the investors' most current expectations of these variables. This approach is particularly useful if the historical growth experience in earnings or dividends has been unstable.

In the discussion to this point we have assumed an all-equity company that finances new investment through retained earnings. We now relax this requirement and assume that the firm maintains a constant debt-to-equity ratio. Thus, for every dollar retained, a certain amount of debt must be issued to keep the ratio at its target value. In this case, the same formula holds:

$$\text{Expected } g = \gamma(\text{ROE}).$$

As we shall see in Chapter 18 on financial leverage, the presence of *leverage* (debt financing) increases the variability of the rate of return on equity and increases the expected rate of return on equity. Since IRR is equal to the expected rate of return on new equity investment, an increase in leverage will increase IRR, and if the retention ratio remains constant, there will be an increase in the expected growth rate.

Outside Estimates of Growth.   Security analysts regularly make earnings and dividends growth forecasts, looking at such factors as projected sales, profit margins, and competitive factors. Someone making a cost of capital estimate can obtain such analysts' forecasts and use them as a proxy for the growth expectations of investors in general, then combine g with the current dividend yield, and estimate $\hat{k}_s$ as follows:

$$\hat{k}_s = \frac{D_1}{P_0} + \text{Growth rate as projected by security analysts.}$$

[11]Analysts' growth rate forecasts are usually for 5 years into the future, and the rates provided represent the average growth rate over that 5-year period. Studies have shown that analysts' forecasts represent a good source of growth rate data for DCF cost of capital estimates. See Robert Harris, "Using Analysts' Growth Rate Forecasts To Estimate Shareholder Required Rates of Return," *Financial Management*, Spring 1986.

Again, note that this estimate of $\hat{k}_s$ is based upon the assumption that g is expected to remain constant in the future.[11]

In summary, when estimating the cost of equity capital for a firm using the dividend growth model, the difficult problem is estimating the expected growth rate. The use of growth rates estimated from historical data is appropriate only when there are no unusual influences on the company. The second procedure, which breaks growth into its components, permits a financial analyst to relate expected growth to the most recent experience of the company. The reliability of the growth rates derived by outside sources, such as security analysts, depends on the forecasting techniques they chose. In the end, the estimated growth rate may reflect combinations of the results from the three growth measurement techniques presented.

People experienced in estimating equity capital costs recognize that both careful analysis and some very fine judgements are required. It would be nice to pretend that these judgements are unnecessary and to specify an easy, precise way of determining the exact cost of equity capital. Unfortunately, this is not possible. Finance is in large part a matter of judgement, and we simply must face that fact.

Concept Review

▶ Why must a cost be assigned to retained earnings?
▶ What are the three approaches to estimating the cost of retained earnings?
▶ Identify some problems with the CAPM approach.
▶ What is the reasoning behind the bond-yield-plus-risk-premium approach?
▶ Which of the components of the DCF formula—dividend yield or the growth rate—is more difficult to estimate? Why?
▶ What are the three methods to estimate the expected growth rate?

Cost of Newly Issued Common Shares, or External Equity, k_e

The **cost of new common equity, k_e**—external equity capital—is higher than the cost of retained earnings, k_s, because of *issue costs* involved in selling new common equity. What rate of return must be earned on funds raised by selling new equity in order to make the new issue worthwhile? To put it another way, what is the cost of new common equity?

For a firm with a constant growth rate, the answer is found by applying the following formula:

$$k_e = \frac{D_1}{P_0(1 - F)} + g. \qquad (17\text{-}10)$$

Here F is the percentage issue cost incurred in selling the issue, so $P_0(1 - F)$ is the net price per share received by the company when it sells a new equity issue.[12]

Suppose that the illustrative firm has an issue cost of 10 percent. Its cost of new outside equity is computed as follows:

$$k_e = \frac{\$1.60}{\$20.00(1 - 0.10)} + 7.0\% = \frac{\$1.60}{\$18.00} + 7.0\%$$
$$= 8.9\% + 7.0\%$$
$$= 15.9\%.$$

Investors require a return of $k_s = 15.0\%$ on the equity. However, because of issue costs, the company must earn *more* than 15.0 percent on funds obtained by selling shares in order to provide this 15.0 percent. Specifically, if the firm earns 15.9 percent of funds obtained from new common equity issues, then earnings per share will not fall below previously expected earnings; the firm's expected dividend can be maintained, and as a result, the price per share will not decline. If the firm earns less than 15.9 percent, then earnings, dividends, and growth will fall below expectations, causing the share price to decline; if it earns more than 15.9 percent, the share price will rise.

The reason for the issue adjustment can perhaps be made clear by a simple example. Suppose Weaver Realty Company has $100 000 of assets and no debt, it earns a 15 percent return (or $15 000) on its assets, and it pays all earnings out as dividends, so its growth rate is zero. The company has 1000 shares of equity outstanding, so EPS = DPS = $15.00, and $P_0 = \$100.00$. the firm's cost of equity is thus $k_s = \$15.00/\$100.00 + 0 = 15\%$. Now suppose Weaver can get a return of 15 percent on new assets. Should it sell new equity to acquire new assets? If it sells 1000 new shares to the public for $100.00 per share but incurs

---

[12]Equation 17-10 is derived as follows:

1. The old shareholders expect the firm to pay a stream of dividends, D_t. This dividend stream will be derived from existing assets. New investors will likewise expect to receive the same stream of dividends, D_t. For new investors to obtain this stream *without impairing the D_t stream of the old investors*, the new funds obtained from the sale of equity must be invested at a return high enough to provide a dividend stream whose present value is equal to the price the firm receives:

$$P_n = \sum_{t=1}^{\infty} \frac{D_t}{(1 + k_e)^t}.$$

Here P_n is the net price to the firm, $P_n = P_0(1 - F)$; D_t is the dividend stream to new shareholders, and k_e is the cost of new outside equity.

2. When growth is a constant, this equation reduces to

$$P_n = P_0(1 - F) = \frac{D_1}{k_e - g}.$$

3. Solve for k_e:

$$k_e = \frac{D_1}{P_0(1 - F)} + g.$$

a 10 percent issue cost on the issue, it will net $100.00 − 0.10($100) = $90.00 per share, or $90 000 in total. It can then invest this $90 000 and earn 15 percent, or $13 500. Its new total earnings will be $15 000 from the old assets plus $13 500 from the new, or $28 500 in total, but it will now have 2000 common shares outstanding. Therefore, its EPS and DPS will decline from $15.00 to $14.25:

$$\text{New EPS and DPS} = \frac{\$28\,500}{2000} = \$14.25.$$

Because its EPS and DPS will fall, the share price also will fall, from $P_0 = \$100.00$ to $P_1 = \$14.25/0.15 = \$95.00$. This result occurs because investors have put up $100.00 per share but the company has received and invested only $90.00 per share. Thus, we see that the $90.00 must earn more than 15 percent to provide investors with a 15 percent return on the $100.00 they put up.

Now suppose Weaver earns a return of k_e based on Equation 17-10 on the $90 000 of new assets:

$$k_e = \frac{D_1}{P_0(1 - F)} + g$$

$$= \frac{\$15}{\$100(0.90)} + 0 = 16.667\%.$$

Here is the new situation:

$$\text{New total earnings} = \$15\,000 + \$90\,000(0.1667)$$
$$= \$15\,000 + \$15\,000$$
$$= \$30\,000.$$
$$\text{New EPS and DPS} = \$30\,000/2000 = \$15.00.$$
$$\text{New price} = \$15.00/0.15 = \$100.$$

Thus, if the return on the new assets is equal to k_e as calculated by Equation 17-10, then EPS, DPS, and the share price will all remain constant. If the return on the new assets exceeds k_e, then EPS, DPS, and P_0 will rise. This confirms the fact that because of issue costs, the cost of external equity exceeds the cost of equity raised internally from retained earnings.

Concept Review

► Why is the cost of external equity capital higher than the cost of retained earnings?
► How can the DCF model be changed to incorporate issue costs?

The Weighted Average, or Composite, Cost of Capital, WACC = k_a

As we shall see in Chapter 18, each firm has an *optimal capital structure*, which is that mix of debt, preferred shares, and common equity that causes its share price to be maximized. Therefore, a rational, value-maximizing firm will establish its *target* (optimal) capital structure and raise new capital in a manner that will keep the actual capital structure on target over time. In this chapter, we assume that the firm has identified its optimal capital structure, uses this optimum as the target, and finances so as to remain constantly on target. How the target is established will be examined in Chapter 18.

The target proportions of debt, preferred, and common equity, along with the component costs of capital, are used to calculate the firm's overall, or **weighted average, cost of capital, WACC = k_a**, which is also called the *composite cost of capital*.

If we return to Table 17-1, we can see the calculation of the cost of capital in a highly simplified, no-corporate-tax situation. Before undertaking the investment decision, the company has interest payments of \$2 400 000 and equity requirements of \$10 500 000. The cost of capital is the total required earnings divided by the total capital or 12.9 percent.

By a very simple derivation, the composite cost of capital is measured as a weighted average of the component marginal costs of funds; the weights are the proportion of the total capital structure made up by each type of capital.[13] In the simple example in Table 17-1, debt has a weight of 30 percent and a marginal cost of 8 percent. Equity has a weight of 70 percent and marginal cost of 8 percent. Equity has a weight of 70 percent and marginal cost of 15 percent. The cost of capital is a weighted average and is equal to 12.9 percent.

$$
\begin{aligned}
k_a &= (k_d \times w_d) + (k_s \times w_s) \\
&= k_d (0.3) + k_s(0.7) \\
&= (0.08)(0.3) + (0.15)(0.7) \\
&= 0.129, \text{ or } 12.9 \text{ percent,}
\end{aligned}
$$

where w_d and w_s are capital structure weights associated with debt and equity, respectively.

When we introduce corporate taxes, the appropriate marginal component costs are measured after corporate tax. Thus, the relevant cost of debt required in an after-tax composite cost of capital calculation is $k_d(1 - T)$, not k_d. However, the capital structure weights are not altered.

To illustrate: suppose Universal Machine Company has a target capital structure calling for 30 percent debt, 10 percent preferred shares, and 60 percent common equity (retained earnings plus common shares). Its before-tax cost of debt, k_d, is 10.0 percent; its after-tax cost of debt is $k_d(1 - T) = 10\%(0.6)$

---

[13] $k_a = \text{Cost of capital} = \dfrac{\text{Interest} + \text{Equity requirement}}{\text{Total capital}} = \dfrac{\text{Interest} + \text{Equity requirement}}{\text{Outstanding Debt} + \text{Equity}}$

$= \dfrac{k_d \left(\dfrac{\text{Debt}}{\text{outstanding}}\right) + k_s \left(\dfrac{\text{Equity}}{\text{outstanding}}\right)}{\text{Total capital}}$

$= k_d \left(\dfrac{\text{Debt}}{\text{Total capital}}\right) + k_s \left(\dfrac{\text{Equity}}{\text{Total Capital}}\right)$

$= k_d \times w_d + k_s \times w_s.$

= 0.06 or 6 percent; its cost of preferred shares, k_p, is 12.0 percent; its cost of common equity from retained earnings, k_s, is 15.0 percent; and its marginal tax rate is 40 percent.

Now suppose the firm needs to raise $100. In order to keep its capital structure on target, it must obtain $30 as debt, $10 as preferred, and $60 as common equity. (Common equity can come either from retained earnings or from the sale of new shares.) The weighted average cost of the $100, assuming the equity portion is from retained earnings, is calculated as follows:

Component	Weight	Component Cost	Product
Debt	0.30	6.0%[a]	1.8%
Preferred shares	0.10	12.0	1.2
Common equity	0.60	15.0	9.0
		Weighted average cost = k_a =	12.0%

[a]After-tax cost of debt = $k_d(1 - T)$ = 10%(0.6) = 6.0%.

We can represent the generalized equation for the weighted average cost of capital, k_a, as follows:

$$\text{WACC} = k_a = w_d k_d(1 - T) + w_p k_p + w_s k_s \qquad (17\text{-}11)$$
$$= 0.3(10\%)(0.6) + 0.1(12\%) + 0.6(15\%) = 12\%.$$

Here, w_d, w_p, and w_s are the weights used for debt, preferred shares, and common equity, respectively.

Every dollar of new capital that Universal Machine Company obtains consists of 30 cents of debt with an after-tax cost of 6 percent, 10 cents of preferred shares with a cost of 12 percent, and 60 cents of common equity with a cost of 15 percent. The average cost of each whole dollar, k_a, is 12.0 percent.

The weights can be based either on the accounting values shown in the firm's balance sheet (book values) or on the market values of the different securities. Theoretically, the weights should be based on market values, but if a firm's book value weights are reasonably close to its market value weights, book value weights can be used as a proxy for market value weights. This point is discussed further in Chapter 18, but in the remainder of this chapter we shall assume that the firm's market values are approximately equal to its book values and then use book value capital structure weights.

Concept Review

▶ How do you calculate the weighted average cost of capital?

The Marginal Cost of Capital (MCC)

The *marginal cost* of any item is the cost of another unit of that item. For example, the marginal cost of labour is defined as the cost of adding one additional worker. The marginal cost of labour might be $25 per person if 10 workers are added but $35 per person if the firm tries to hire 100 new workers, because it would be harder to find that many people willing and able to do the work. The same concept applies to capital. As the firm tries to attract more new dollars, the cost of each dollar will, at some point, rise. Thus, the **marginal cost of capital (MCC)**, is defined as the cost of obtaining another dollar of new capital, and it rises as more and more capital is raised.

We can use Universal Machine to illustrate the marginal cost of capital concept. The company's target capital structure and other data follow:[14]

Debt	$3 000 000	30%
Preferred shares	1 000 000	10
Common equity	6 000 000	60
Total capital	$10 000 000	100%

$P_0 = \$20.00$.

$D_0 = \$1.495 =$ dividends per share in the *last* period. D_0 has already been paid, so someone purchasing this equity today would *not* receive D_0 but would receive D_1, the *next* dividend.

$g = 7\%$, and it is expected to remain constant.

$$k_s = \frac{D_1}{P_0} + g = \frac{D_0(1 + g)}{P_0} + g = \frac{\$1.495(1.07)}{\$20.00} + 0.07$$

$$= \frac{\$1.60}{\$20.00} + 0.07 = 0.08 + 0.07 = 0.15 = 15\%.$$

$k_d = 10\%$.

$k_p = 12\%$.

$T = 40\%$.

Based on these data, the weighted average cost of capital, WACC = k_a, is 12 percent:

$$k_a = \left(\begin{array}{c}\text{Fraction of}\\ \text{debt}\end{array}\right)\left(\begin{array}{c}\text{Interest}\\ \text{rate}\end{array}\right)(1 - T) + \left(\begin{array}{c}\text{Fraction of}\\ \text{preferred}\end{array}\right)\left(\begin{array}{c}\text{Cost of}\\ \text{preferred}\end{array}\right) + \left(\begin{array}{c}\text{Fraction of}\\ \text{common}\\ \text{equity}\end{array}\right)\left(\begin{array}{c}\text{Cost of}\\ \text{equity}\end{array}\right)$$

$$\begin{array}{lll} = 0.3(10\%)(0.6) & + 0.1(12\%) & + 0.6(15\%) \\ = 1.8\% & + 1.2\% & + 9.0\% \\ = 12\%. & & \end{array}$$

Since the firm's optimal capital structure calls for 30 percent debt, 10 percent preferred, and 60 percent equity, each new (or marginal) dollar will be raised as 30 cents of debt, 10 cents of preferred, and 60 cents of common equity—

---

[14]Because we assume that Universal has only a negligible amount of payables and accruals, which have no explicit cost, these items are ignored. For a discussion of how these items are handled, see Eugene F. Brigham and Louis C. Gapenski, *Intermediate Financial Management*, 3d ed. (Chicago: Dryden Press, 1990), chap. 4. In general, though, they are ignored.

otherwise, the capital structure would not stay on target. As long as Universal keeps its capital structure on target and its debt has an after-tax cost of 6 percent, its preferred equity has a cost of 12 percent, and its common equity has a cost of 15 percent, then its weighted average cost of capital will be 12 percent.

The graph shown in Figure 17-1 is Universal's **marginal cost of capital (MCC) schedule**. Here the dots represent dollars raised. Since each dollar of new capital has a cost of 12 percent, the MCC for Universal is constant at 12 percent under the assumptions we have used thus far.[15]

Breaks in the MCC Schedule

Can Universal raise an unlimited amount of new capital at the 12 percent cost? The answer is no. As a practical matter, as a company raises larger and larger

Figure 17-1
Marginal Cost of Capital (MCC) Schedule for
Universal Machine Company

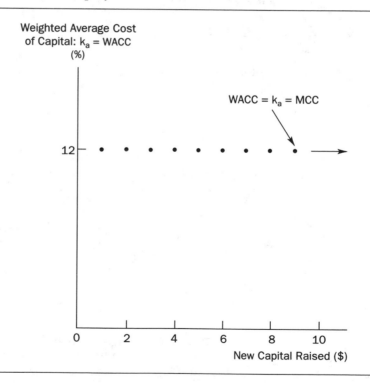

---

[15]Universal's MCC schedule in Figure 17-1 would be different if the company used any capital structure other than 30 percent debt, 10 percent preferred, and 60 percent equity. This point will be developed in Chapter 18, but as a general rule, a different MCC schedule exists for every possible capital structure, and the optional structure is the one that produces the lowest MCC schedule.

sums during a given time period, the costs of both the debt and the equity components begin to rise, and as this occurs, the weighted average cost of each new dollar also rises. Thus, just as corporations cannot hire unlimited numbers of workers at a constant wage, neither can they raise unlimited amounts of capital at a constant cost. At some point, the cost of each new dollar will increase.

Where will this point occur for Universal? As a first step to determining the answer, recognize that although the company has total long-term capital (at market value) of $10 million, all of this capital was raised in the past and has been invested in assets that are being used in operations. New (or marginal) capital will presumably be raised so as to maintain the 30:10:60 debt:preferred:common relationship. Therefore, if Universal wants to raise $1 million in new capital, it will obtain $300 000 of debt, $100 000 of preferred shares, and $600 000 of common equity. The new equity can come from either of two sources: (1) retained earnings, defined as the part of this year's profits that management decides to retain in the business rather than use for dividends (but not earnings retained in the past, for these have already been invested in plant, equipment, inventories, and so on), and (2) the sale of new common equity.

The debt will have an interest rate of 10 percent, or an after-tax cost of 6 percent, while the preferred shares will have a cost of 12 percent. The cost of common equity will be $k_s = 15.0\%$ as long as the equity is obtained by retained earnings, but it will jump to $k_e = 15.9\%$ once the company uses up all of its retained earnings and is thus forced to sell new common equity.

Consider first the case in which all the new equity comes from retained earnings. Universal's equity now sells for $20 per share; its last dividend, D_0, was $1.495; its expected growth rate is 7 percent; and its next expected dividend is $1.60. Thus, we estimate the expected and required rate of return on common equity, k_s, to be 15 percent:

$$k_s = \frac{D_1}{P_0} + g = \frac{\$1.60}{\$20} + 7\% = 8\% + 7\% = 15\%.$$

Now suppose the company expands so rapidly that its retained earnings for the year are not sufficient to meet its needs for new equity, forcing it to sell new common shares. If the issue cost on new equity, F, is 10.0 percent, then Universal's cost of equity will rise to 15.9 percent:

$$k_e = \frac{D_1}{P_0(1 - F)} + g = \frac{\$1.60}{\$20(0.9)} + 7\% = 15.9\%.$$

The company will net $18 per share when it sells new equity, and it must earn 15.9 percent on this $18 in order to provide all of its equity investors with a 15.0 percent return on the $20 they actually put up.

Universal's weighted average cost of capital, using first new retained earnings (earnings retained this year, not in the past) and then new common equity, is shown in Table 17-2. We see that the weighted average cost of each dollar, or the marginal cost of capital, is 12.0 percent so long as retained

Table 17-2
Universal's Marginal Cost of Capital Using (I) New
Retained Earnings and (II) New Common Equity

I. MCC when equity is from new retained earnings

Component	Weight	Component Cost	Product
Debt	0.3	6.0%	1.8%
Preferred shares	0.1	12.0	1.2
Common equity (retained earnings)	0.6	15.0	9.0
	1.0	$WACC_1 =$	12.0%

II. MCC when equity is from sale of new common shares

Component	Weight	Component Cost	Product
Debt	0.3	6.0%	1.8%
Preferred shares	0.1	12.0	1.2
Common equity (new common shares)	0.6	15.9	9.5
	1.0	$WACC_2 =$	12.5%

earnings are used, but the average cost jumps to 12.5 percent as soon as the firm exhausts its retained earnings and is forced to sell new common equity.[16]

How much new capital can Universal raise before it exhausts its retained earnings and is forced to sell new common shares? That is, where will the break point in the MCC occur? We find this point as follows:

1. The company expects to have total earnings of $840 000 for the year, and it has a policy of paying out half of its earnings as dividends. Thus, the addition to retained earnings will be $420 000 during the year.

2. If the company is to remain at its optimal capital structure, it must raise each dollar as 30 cents of debt, 10 cents of preferred shares, and 60 cents of common equity. Therefore, each 60 cents of retained earnings will support $1 of capital, and the $420 000 of retained earnings will not be exhausted—and hence the WACC will not rise—until $420 000 of retained earnings plus the proportionate amounts of debt and preferred shares have been used up.

3. We now want to know how much *total financing*—from debt, preferred shares, and retained earnings—can be done before the $420 000 of retained earnings is exhausted and the firm is forced to sell new common equity. In effect, we are seeking some amount of capital, X, which is called a *break point (BP)* and which represents the total financing that can be done before Universal is forced to sell new common equity.

---

[16]At relatively low growth rates, expansion could be financed by spontaneously generated debt and retained earnings, but at higher growth rates, external capital is needed. If Universal needs no external equity, its marginal cost of capital will be 12 percent. However, if its growth rate is rapid enough to require it to sell new common equity, then its marginal cost of capital will rise to 12.5 percent.

4. We know that 60 percent, or 0.6, of X, the total capital raised, will be retained earnings, while 40 percent will be debt plus preferred shares. We also know that retained earnings will amount to $420 000. Therefore,

$$\text{Retained earnings} = 0.6X = \$420\,000.$$

5. Solving for X, we obtain $BP_{RE} = \$700\,000$:

$$X = BP_{RE} = \frac{\text{Retained earnings}}{\text{Equity fraction}} = \frac{\$420\,000}{0.6} = \$700\,000.$$

6. Thus, Universal can raise a total of $700 000, consisting of 0.6($700 000) = $420 000 of retained earnings plus 0.10($700 000) = $70 000 of preferred equity and 0.30($700 000) = $210 000 of new debt supported by these new retained earnings, without altering its capital structure. In summary:

New debt supported by retained earnings	$210 000	30%
Preferred equity supported by retained earnings	70 000	10
Retained earnings	420 000	60
Total expansion supported by retained earnings, or break point for retained earnings	$700 000	100%

7. The value of X, or $BP_{RE} = \$700\,000$, is called the *retained earnings break point* and is the amount of total capital at which a break, or jump, occurs in the MCC schedule.

Figure 17-2 graphs Universal's marginal cost of capital schedule with the retained earnings break point. Each dollar has a weighted average cost of 12 percent until the company has raised a total of $700 000. This $700 000 will consist of $210 000 of new debt with an after-tax cost of 6 percent, $70 000 of preferred shares with a cost of 12.0 percent, and $420 000 of retained earnings with a cost of 15.0 percent. However, if Universal raises $700 001, the last dollar will contain 60 cents of equity obtained by selling new common equity at a cost of 15.9 percent; therefore WACC = k_a jumps from 12.0 percent to 12.5 percent as calculated in Table 17-2.

Other Breaks in the MCC Schedule

There is a jump, or break, in Universal's MCC schedule at $700 000 of new capital. Could there be other breaks in the schedule? Yes, there could. For example, suppose Universal could obtain only $300 000 of debt at a 10 percent interest rate, with additional debt costing 12 percent. This would result in a second break point in the MCC schedule at the point where the $300 000 of 10 percent debt is exhausted. At what amount of *total financing* will the 10 percent debt be used up? We know that this total financing will amount to $300 000 of debt plus some amount of preferred and common equity. If we let BP_{debt} represent the total financing at this second break point, then we know that 30 percent, or 0.3, of BP_{debt} will be debt, so

Figure 17-2
Marginal Cost of Capital Schedule for
Universal Machine Company Using Both
Retained Earnings and New Common Equity

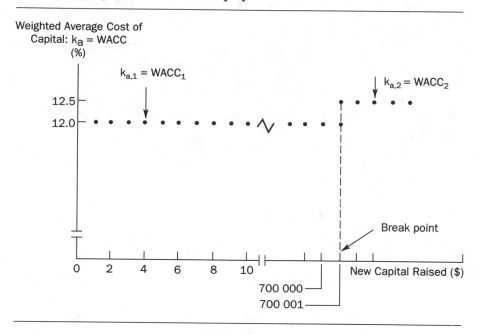

$$0.3(\text{BP}_{\text{debt}}) = \$300\,000,$$

and solving for BP_{debt}, we obtain

$$\text{BP}_{\text{debt}} = \frac{\text{Amount of 10\% debt}}{\text{Debt fraction}} = \frac{\$300\,000}{0.3} = \$1\,000\,000.$$

Thus, there will be another break in the MCC schedule after Universal has raised a total of $1 million. This second break results from a jump in the cost of debt.

As we have seen, for $0 to $700 000 of new capital, the WACC is 12.0 percent, and just beyond $700 000 the WACC rises to 12.5 percent. Then, as a result of the increase in k_d from 10 percent to 12 percent, the WACC rises again, at $1 000 000, to 12.9 percent:

WACC above $1 Million

Component	Weight		Component Cost		Product
Debt	0.3	×	7.2ᵃ	=	2.2%
Preferred shares	0.1	×	12.0	=	1.2
Common equity	0.6	×	15.9	=	9.5
				WACC = k_{a3} =	12.9%

ᵃ12%(1 − T) = 12%(0.6) = 7.2%, up from 6%.

In other words, the next dollar beyond $1 million will consist of 30 cents of 12.0 percent debt (7.2 percent after taxes), 10 cents of 12.0 percent preferred, and 60 cents of new common equity at a cost of 15.9 percent (retained earnings were used up much earlier), and this marginal dollar will have a cost of $WACC_3$ = 12.9 percent.

The effect of this new MCC increase is shown in Figure 17-3. We now have two break points, one caused by using up all the retained earnings and the other caused by using up all the 10 percent debt. With the two breaks, there are three different WACCs: $WACC_1$ = 12.0% for the first $700 000 of new capital; $WACC_2$ = 12.5% in the interval between $700 000 and $1 million; and $WACC_3$ = 12.9% for all new capital beyond $1 million.[17]

Figure 17-3
Marginal Cost of Capital Schedule for Universal Machine Company Using Retained Earnings, New Common Equity, and Higher-Cost Debt

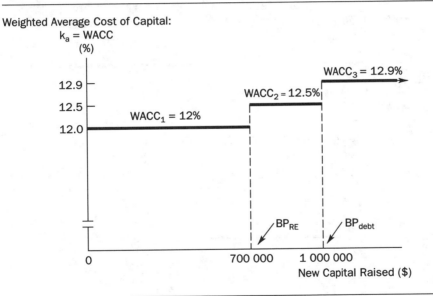

[17]When we use the term *weighted average cost of capital*, we are referring to k_a, which is the cost of $1 raised partly as debt, partly as preferred shares, and partly as common equity. We could also calculate the average cost of *all* the capital the firm raises during a given year. For example, if Universal raises $2 million, then the first $700 000 will have a cost of 12.0 percent, the next $300 000 will have a cost of 12.5 percent, and the last $1 million will have a cost of 12.9 percent. The entire $2 million will have an average cost of

$$\left(\frac{0.7}{2}\right)(12.00\%) + \left(\frac{0.3}{2}\right)(12.50\%) + \left(\frac{1}{2}\right)(12.90\%) = 12.53\%.$$

In general, this particular cost of capital should *not* be used for financial decisions — it usually has no relevance in finance. The only exception to this rule occurs when the firm is considering a very large asset that must be accepted in total or else rejected, and the capital required for it includes capital with different WACCs. For example, if Universal was considering one $2 million project, that project should be evaluated with a 12.53 percent cost.

There could of course be still more break points; they would occur if the interest rate continued to rise, if the cost of preferred shares rose, or if the cost of common equity rose.[18] In general, a break point will occur whenever the cost of one of the capital components rises. The break point can be determined by the following equation:

$$\text{Break point} = \frac{\text{Total amount of lower-cost capital of a given type}}{\text{Fraction of this type of capital in the capital structure}}.$$

$$(17\text{-}12)$$

We see, then, that numerous break points can occur. At the limit, we can even think of an MCC schedule with so many break points that it rises almost continuously beyond some given level of new financing. Such an MCC schedule is shown in Figure 17-4.

The easiest sequence for calculating an MCC schedule is as follows:

1. Use Equation 17-12 to determine each point at which a break occurs. A break will occur any time the cost of one of the capital components rises.

Figure 17-4
Smoothed, or Continuous, Marginal Cost
of Capital Schedule

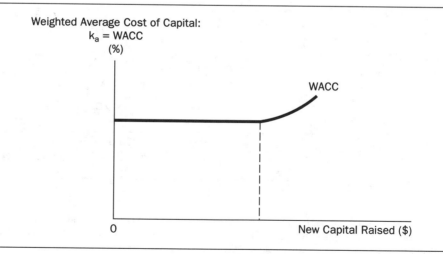

---

[18]The first break point is not necessarily the point at which retained earnings are used up—it is possible for low-cost debt to be exhausted *before* retained earnings have been used up. For example, if Universal had available only $150 000 of 10 percent debt, BP$_{debt}$ would occur at $500 000:

$$BP_{debt} = \frac{\$150\,000}{0.3} = \$500\,000.$$

This is well before the break point for retained earnings, which occurs at $700 000.

(It is possible that two capital components will both increase at the same point.) After determining the exact break points, make a list of them.

2. Determine the cost of capital for each component in the intervals between breaks.

3. Calculate the weighted averages of these component costs to obtain the WACCs for each interval, as we did in Table 17-2. The WACC is constant within each interval, but it rises at each break point. (Notice that if there are n separate breaks, there will be n + 1 different WACCs. For example, in Figure 17-3 we see two breaks and three different WACCs.)

Before closing this section, we should note again that a different MCC schedule would result if a different capital structure were used. As we will show in Chapter 18, the optimal capital structure produces the lowest MCC.

Concept Review

▶ What are break points? Why do they occur in MCC schedules?

▶ How can a break point be determined?

▶ How does one calculate a firm's MCC schedule?

▶ If there are n breaks in the MCC schedule, how many different WACCs are there?

Combining the MCC and the Investment Opportunity Schedules

Now that we have calculated the MCC schedule, we can use it to determine the *discount rate* used in the capital budgeting process—that is, we can use the MCC schedule to find the *cost of capital for use in determining projects' net present values (NPVs)* as discussed in Chapter 13.

To understand how the MCC schedule is used in capital budgeting, assume that Universal has three financial executives: a financial vice president (VP), a treasurer, and a director of capital budgeting (DCB). The financial VP asks the treasurer to develop the firm's MCC schedule, and the treasurer produces the schedule shown earlier in Figure 17-3. At the same time, the financial VP asks the DCB to determine the dollar amounts of all projects that are potentially acceptable. The DCB then lists all of the firm's potential projects with the cost of each and its projected annual net cash inflows, life, and IRR. These data are presented at the bottom of Figure 17-5. For example, Project A has a cost of $200 000 and is expected to produce inflows of $55 757 per year for 5 years, so its IRR is 12.2 percent. Project B, which has a cost of $150 000, is expected to produce inflows of $33 917 per year for 7 years and has an IRR of 13.0 percent. (NPVs and MIRRs cannot be shown yet, because we do not yet know the marginal cost of capital.) For simplicity, we assume now that all projects are independent, that they are equally risky, and that their risk is equal to that of the average existing asset in the firm.

The DCB then plots the IRR data as the **investment opportunity schedule (IOS)** shown in Figure 17-5. The IOS schedule shows in rank order how much

Figure 17-5
Combining Universal Machine Company's
MCC and IOS Curves To Determine Its
Optimal Capital Budget

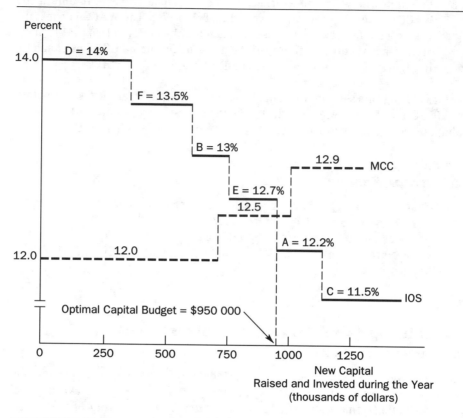

Potential Capital Budgeting Projects Available to Universal Machine Company

Project	Cost	Annual Inflows	Project Life (years)	IRR, or Discount Rate at Which NPV = 0
A	$200 000	$ 55 757	5	12.2%
B	150 000	33 917	7	13.0
C	250 000	43 344	10	11.5
D	350 000	90 005	6	14.0
E	200 000	41 250	8	12.7
F	250 000	106 781	3	13.5

money Universal could invest at different rates of return. Figure 17-5 also shows Universal's MCC schedule as it was developed by the treasurer and plotted in Figure 17-3. Now consider Project D: its IRR is 14 percent, and it can be financed with capital that costs only 12 percent; consequently, it should be accepted. Recall from Chapter 13 that if a project's IRR exceeds its cost of capital, its NPV will also be positive; therefore, Project D must also be acceptable based on the NPV criterion. Projects F, B, and E can be analyzed similarly; they are all acceptable because IRR > MCC and hence NPV > 0. Projects A and C, on the other hand, should be rejected because for them IRR < MCC and NPV < 0.

Notice that if the cost of capital had started at a point above 14 percent, none of the available projects would have positive NPVs; hence, none of them should be accepted. In that case, Universal should simply not expand. However, in the actual situation, where the MCC starts at 12 percent and then rises, Universal should accept the four projects (D, F, B, and E) that have rates of return in excess of the cost of the capital that would be used to finance them, ending up with a capital budget of $950 000.

People sometimes ask this question: "If we took Project A first, it would be acceptable, because its 12.2 percent return would exceed the 12.0 percent cost of money used to finance it. Why couldn't we do this?" The answer is that we are seeking, in effect, to maximize the *excess of returns over costs*, or the area that is above the WACC but below the IOS. We accomplish this by graphing (and accepting) the most profitable projects first.

Another question that sometimes arises is this: "What would happen if the MCC cut through one of the projects? For example, suppose the second break point in the MCC schedule occurred at $900 000 rather than at $1 million so that the MCC cut through Project E. Should we then accept Project E?" If Project E could be accepted in part, then the firm should take on only part of it. Otherwise, the answer is determined by (1) finding the average cost of the funds needed to finance Project E (some of the money would cost 12.5 percent and some would cost 12.9 percent) and then (2) comparing the average cost of this money to the 12.7 percent return on the project. The firm should accept Project E if its return exceeds the average cost of the $200 000 needed to finance it.

The preceding analysis as summarized in Figure 17-5 reveals a very important point: the *cost of capital* used in the capital budgeting process as discussed in Chapter 13 is actually determined at the *intersection of the IOS and MCC schedules*. If this intersection rate (WACC$_2$ = 12.5% in Figure 17-5) is used, then the firm will make correct accept–reject decisions, and its level of financing and investment will be optimal. If it uses any other rate, its capital budget will not be optimal.

If Universal had fewer good investment opportunities, then its IOS schedule would be shifted to the left, causing the intersection to occur at a lower level on the MCC curve. Conversely, if the firm had more and better investment opportunities, the IOS would be shifted to the right, and the intersection would occur at a higher WACC. In either event, the WACC at the intersection could change. Thus, we see that the cost of capital used in capital budgeting is influenced *both* by *the set of projects that is available* and by *the shape of the MCC curve*.

We have, of course, abstracted from differential project riskiness in this chapter; for simplicity, we have assumed that all projects are equally risky. As noted in Chapter 15, the cost of capital used to evaluate riskier projects should be adjusted upward, and a lower rate should be used for projects with below-average risk. The intersection WACC as determined in Figure 17-5 should be used to find the NPVs of new projects that are about as risky as the firm's existing assets, but this corporate cost of capital should be adjusted up or down to find NPVs for projects with higher or lower risk than the average project.

Some Problem Areas in Cost of Capital

A number of difficult issues relating to the cost of capital either have not been mentioned or have been glossed over in this chapter. These topics are covered in advanced courses, but they deserve some mention now so that the reader may be alerted to potential dangers as well as provided with a preview of some of the matters considered in advance finance courses.

The effects of personal income taxes.   Our discussion of the cost of capital dealt with *corporate* income taxes, but apart from the cost of preferred equity, we did not consider the impact of *personal* taxes. When we use the equation $k_s = D_1/P_0 + g$, the share price will reflect the personal income tax treatment of dividends and capital gains. Under Canadian income tax provisions, if we assume common shares are sold and not held indefinitely, the tax rate applied to realized capital gains is never less than the rate of dividends. The result is measured costs of equity that reflect the payout policy of the firm. Thus, the cost of retained earnings, k_s, and the cost of new common shares, k_e, may diverge by an amount that is different from issue costs.

Depreciation-Generated Funds.   The largest single source of capital for many firms is depreciation, yet we did not discuss the cost of funds from this source. In brief, depreciation cash flows can be either reinvested or returned to investors (shareholders *and* creditors). The cost of depreciation-generated funds is approximately equal to the weighted average cost of capital in the interval in which capital comes from retained earnings and low-cost debt.

Deferred Taxes.   The balance sheets of most companies show, as a liability, an item called "deferred taxes." Deferred taxes arise principally from the difference between depreciation for book purposes and delays in payments of regular taxes. These tax differences arise from "timing" differences. Deferrals can constitute an important source of funds for many companies. Since deferred taxes are, in effect, an interest-free loan from the federal government, they have a zero cost. Some companies include deferred taxes in the weighted average cost of capital calculation but give the item a zero cost. If deferred taxes are material for a given company, some care should be exercised in how this issue is handled.

Privately Owned Firms.   Our whole discussion of the cost of equity was related to publicly owned corporations, and we concentrated on the rate of return required by public shareholders. There is a serious question as to how one should measure the cost of equity for a firm whose shares are not traded. Tax issues also become especially important in these cases. As a general rule, most authorities feel that the same principles of cost of capital estimation apply to both privately held and publicly owned firms, but the problems of obtaining input data are somewhat different for each.

Small Businesses.   Small businesses are generally privately owned, making it difficult to estimate their cost of equity. Debt financing is obtained either from government sources (sometimes at subsidized rates) or from financial institutions but with the use of personal guarantees and/or substantial collateral. However, the same theoretical principles apply to both large and small firms.

Measurement Problems.   We cannot overemphasize the practical difficulties encountered in actually estimating the cost of equity. It is very difficult to obtain good input data for the CAPM, for g in the formula $k_s = D_1/P_0 + g$, and for the risk premium in the formula k_s = bond yield + risk premium. As a result, one can never be sure of the accuracy of the estimated cost of capital.

Costs of Capital for Projects of Differing Riskiness.   As noted in Chapter 15, care must be taken to assign different risk-adjusted discount rates to capital budgeting projects of differing degrees of riskiness.

Capital Structure Weights.   In this chapter, we simply took as given the target capital structure and used it to obtain the weights needed to calculate k_a. Since these are target weights, the financing mix utilized in any one year need not correspond exactly. Deviations from the target in a particular year will require offsetting future financings. As we shall see in Chapter 18, establishing the target capital structure is a major task in itself.

Dynamic Considerations.   Capital budgeting and cost of capital estimates are a part of the *planning process*—they deal with ex ante, or estimated, data rather than ex post, or historical, data. Hence, one can be wrong about the location of the IOS and the MCC. For example, a manager can underestimate the MCC and hence accept projects that, with 20:20 hindsight, should have been rejected. In a dynamic, changing world, this is a real problem. For example, interest rates and money costs may be low at the time plans are being laid and contracts to build plants are being finalized, but 6 or 8 months later these capital costs may have risen substantially. Thus, a project that once looked good could now look bad because the MCC schedule was wrongly forecasted.

Although the listing of problem areas may appear formidable, the state of the art in cost of capital estimation is really not in bad shape. The procedures outlined in this chapter can be used to obtain cost of capital estimates that are sufficiently accurate for practical purposes, and the problems listed here merely indicate the desirability of certain refinements. The refinements are not unimportant, but the problems identified certainly do not invalidate the usefulness of the procedures outlined in the chapter.

Concept Review

▶ Differentiate between the MCC and the IOS schedules.
▶ How do you find the corporate cost of capital, which is used to evaluate average risk projects to determine their NPVs?
▶ How should the corporate cost of capital be adjusted for projects that are more risky or less risky than average?

Summary

This chapter showed how the MCC schedule is developed and then used in the capital budgeting process. The key concepts covered are listed below.

☐ The cost of capital to be used in capital budgeting decisions is the *weighted average* of the costs of various types of capital the firm uses: typically, debt, preferred equity, and common equity.

☐ The component **cost of debt** is the *after-tax* cost of new debt. It is found by multiplying the cost of new debt by $(1 - T)$, where T is the firm's marginal tax rate: $k_d(1 - T)$.

☐ The component **cost of preferred equity** is calculated as the preferred dividend divided by the net issuing price, where the net issuing price is the price the firm receives after deducting issue costs: $k_p = D_p/P_p$.

☐ The **cost of common equity** is the cost of retained earnings as long as the firm has retained earnings; it becomes the cost of new common equity once the firm has exhausted its retained earnings.

☐ The **cost of retained earnings** is the rate of return required by shareholders on the firm's common equity. It can be estimated using one of three methods: (1) the CAPM approach, (2) the bond-yield-plus-risk-premium approach, and (3) the dividend-yield-plus-growth-rate, or DCF, approach.

☐ To use the *CAPM approach*, one (1) estimates the firm's beta, (2) multiplies this beta by the market risk premium to determine the firm's risk premium, and (3) adds the firm's risk premium to the risk-free rate to obtain the firm's cost of retained earnings: $k_s = k_{RF} + (k_M - k_{RF})B_i$.

☐ The *bond-yield-plus-risk-premium approach* requires one to add a risk premium of from 2 to 4 percentage points to the firm's interest rate on long-term debt: $k_s = $ Bond rate $+$ RP.

☐ To use the *dividend-yield-plus-growth-rate approach*, also called the *DCF approach*, one adds the firm's expected growth rate to its expected dividend yield: $k_s = D_1/P_0 + g$.

☐ The cost of new common equity is higher than the cost of retained earnings because the firm must incur *issue expenses* to sell equity. To find the *cost of new common equity*, the share price is first reduced by the issue expense, then the dividend yield is calculated on the basis of the price the firm will actually receive, and then the expected growth rate is added to this *adjusted dividend yield*: $k_e = D_1/[P_0(1 - F)] + g$.

☐ Each firm has an *optimal capital structure*, defined as the mix of debt, preferred shares, and common equity that minimizes the firm's **weighted average cost of capital (WACC)**:

$$k_a = \text{WACC} = w_d k_d (1 - T) + w_p k_p + w_e (k_s \text{ or } k_e).$$

☐ The **marginal cost of capital (MCC)** is defined as the cost of the last dollar of new capital that the firm raises. The MCC increases as the firm raises more and more capital during a given period. A graph of the MCC plotted against dollars raised is the **MCC schedule**.

☐ A *break point (BP)* will occur in the MCC schedule each time the cost of one of the capital components increases.

☐ The **investment opportunity schedule (IOS)** is a graph of the firm's investment opportunities, with the project having the highest returns plotted first.

□ The MCC schedule is combined with the IOS schedule, and the intersection defines the **corporate cost of capital**, which is used to evaluate average risk capital budgeting projects.

The concepts developed in this chapter are extended in Chapter 18, where we consider the effect of the capital structure on the cost of capital.

Questions

17-1   In what sense does the marginal cost of capital schedule represent a series of average costs?

17-2   How would each of the following affect a firm's cost of debt, $k_d(1 - T)$; its cost of equity, k_s; and its average cost of capital, k_a? Indicate by a plus ($+$), a minus ($-$), or a zero (0) if the change would raise, lower, or have an indeterminate effect on each of the items in question. Assume other things are held constant. Be prepared to justify your answer, but recognize that several of the parts probably have no single correct answer; these questions are designed to stimulate thought and discussion.

	Effect on		
	$k_d(1 - T)$	k_s	k_a
a. The corporate tax rate is lowered.	_____	_____	_____
b. The Bank of Canada tightens credit.	_____	_____	_____
c. The firm uses more debt—that is, it increases the debt-to-assets ratio.	_____	_____	_____
d. The dividend payout ratio is increased.	_____	_____	_____
e. The firm doubles the amount of capital it raises during the year.	_____	_____	_____
f. The firm expands into a risky new area.	_____	_____	_____
g. The firm merges with another firm whose earnings are countercyclical to those of the first firm and to the equity market.	_____	_____	_____
h. The equity market falls drastically, and our firm's share price falls along with the rest.	_____	_____	_____
i. Investors become more risk averse.	_____	_____	_____
j. The firm is an electric utility with a large investment in nuclear plants. A ban on nuclear power generation is proposed.	_____	_____	_____

17-3   Suppose a firm estimates its MCC and IOS schedules for the coming year and finds that they intersect at the point (10%, $10 million). What cost of capital should be used to evaluate average projects, high-risk projects, and low-risk projects?

17-4   The shares of XYZ Company are currently selling at their low for the year, but management feels that the share price is only temporarily depressed because of investor pessimism. The firm's capital budget this year is so large that the use of new outside equity is contemplated. Management does not want to sell new equity at the current low price, however, and is therefore considering a departure from its "optimal" capital structure by borrowing the funds it would otherwise have raised in the equity markets. Does this seem to be a wise move? Explain your answer.

Self-Test Problems   (solutions appear on page 647)

ST-1   **Key terms.**   Define each of the following terms:
a. Weighted average cost of capital, k_a
b. Cost of debt after-tax, $k_d(1 - T)$
c. Cost of preferred shares, k_p
d. Cost of retained earnings, k_s
e. Cost of new common equity, k_e
f. Issue cost, F
g. Target capital structure
h. Marginal cost of capital, MCC
i. MCC schedule; break in the MCC schedule; break point
j. IOS schedule; intersection of the IOS and MCC schedules

ST-2   **Optimal capital budget.**   Lancaster Engineering, Inc. (LEI), has the following capital structure, which it considers to be optimal:

Debt	25%
Preferred shares	15
Common equity	60
	100%

LEI's expected net income this year is $34 285.72; its established dividend payout ratio is 30 percent; its tax rate is 40 percent; and investors expect earnings and dividends to grow at a constant rate of 9 percent in the future. LEI paid a dividend of $3.60 per share last year, and its common equity currently sells at a price of $60.00 per share. (Note: All dollars except per share figures are in thousands.)
     LEI can obtain new capital in the following ways:
• *Issuing common shares.* The issue costs will be 10 percent for up to $12 000 of new common equity and 20 percent for all new common shares over $12 000.
• *Issuing preferred shares.* New preferred shares can be sold at a price of $100 per share, with a dividend of $11. The issue costs will be $5 per

share for up to $7500 of preferred equity and $10, or 10 percent, per share on all preferred equity over $7500.

- *Selling debt.* Up to $5000 of debt can be sold at an interest rate of 12 percent; debt in the range of $5001 to $10 000 will carry an interest rate of 14 percent; and all debt over $10 000 will have a rate of 16 percent.

LEI has the following investment opportunities:

Project	Cost at t = 0	Annual Net Cash Flow	Project Life	IRR
A	$10 000	$2919.20	7 years	12.0%
B	10 000	3154.42	5 years	17.4
C	10 000	2170.18	8 years	14.2
D	20 000	3789.48	10 years	13.7
E	20 000	5427.84	6 years	

a. Find the break points in the MCC schedule.
b. Determine the component costs of capital for each capital structure component.
c. Calculate the weighted cost of capital in the interval between each break in the MCC schedule.
d. Calculate the IRR for Project E.
e. Construct a graph showing the MCC and IOS schedules.
f. Which projects should LEI accept?

Problems

17-1   After-tax cost of debt.   Calculate the after-tax cost of debt under each of the following conditions:
a. Interest rate, 13 percent; tax rate, 0 percent.
b. Interest rate, 13 percent; tax rate, 40 percent.
c. Interest rate, 13 percent; tax rate, 60 percent.

17-2   After-tax cost of debt.   The Graham Company's financing plans for next year include the sale of long-term bonds with a 10 percent coupon. The company believes it can sell the bonds at a price that will give a yield to maturity of 12 percent. If the tax rate is 40 percent, what is Graham's after-tax cost of debt?

17-3   Cost of preferred equity.   Infinity Industries has just issued some $100 par preferred shares with an 11 percent dividend. The shares are selling on the market for $97, and Infinity must pay issue costs of 5 percent of the market price. What is the cost of the preferred shares for Infinity?

17-4   Cost of retained earnings.   The earnings, dividends, and share price of Barry Technologies, Inc. are all expected to grow at 7 percent per year after this year. Barry's common equity sells for $23.00 per share, its last dividend was $2.00, and the company will pay a dividend of $2.14 at the end of the current year.

a. Using the discounted cash flow approach, calculate Barry's cost of retained earnings.

b. If the firm's beta is 1.6, the risk-free rate is 9 percent, and the average return on the market is 13 percent, what will be the firm's cost of equity using the CAPM approach?

c. If the firm's bonds earn a return of 13 percent, what will k_s be using the bond-yield-plus-risk-premium approach?

d. Given your results for parts a through c, what would you estimate Barry's cost of retained earnings to be?

17-5   Estimating growth rate.   The Iversen Company's EPS in 1994 was $6.50. Its EPS in 1989 was $4.42. The company pays out 40 percent of its earnings as dividends, and a share sells for $36.

a. Calculate the growth rate in earnings per share. (Hint: This is a 5-year growth period.)

b. Calculate the *next* expected dividend per share, D_1. ($D_0 = 0.4(\$6.50) = \$2.60$.) Assume the past growth rate will continue.

c. What is the cost of retained earnings, k_s, for the Iversen Company?

17-6   Break point calculations.   The Devine Corp. expects earnings of $30 million next year. Its dividend payout ratio is 40 percent, and its debt-to-assets ratio is 50 percent. Devine uses no preferred shares.

a. What amount of retained earnings does Devine expect next year?

b. At what amount of financing will there be a break point in the MCC schedule?

c. If Devine can borrow $12 million at an interest rate of 11 percent, another $12 million at a rate of 12 percent, and an additional amount at a rate of 13 percent, at what points will rising debt costs cause breaks in the MCC schedule?

17-7   Cost of new common equity.   Booth Bridges Ltd.'s next expected dividend, D_1, is $3.18; its growth rate is 6 percent; and the share price is now $36.00. New common equity can be sold to net the firm $32.40 per share.

a. What is Booth's percentage issue cost, F?

b. What is Booth's cost of new common equity, k_e?

17-8   Weighted average cost of capital.   The Renoir Company's cost of equity is 16 percent. Renoir's before-tax cost of debt is 13 percent, and its tax rate is 40 percent. Using the following balance sheet (in thousands of dollars), calculate Renoir's after-tax weighted average cost of capital.

Assets		Liabilities	
Cash	$ 120		
Accounts receivable	240		
Inventories	360	Long-term debt	$1152
Plant and equipment, net	2160	Equity	1728
Total assets	$2880	Total liabilities and equity	$2880

17-9 Return on common equity. Parnelli Products' equity is currently selling for $60.00 a share. The firm is earning $5.40 per share, and it is expected to pay a year-end dividend of $3.60.

    a. If investors require a 9 percent return, what rate of growth must be expected for Parnelli?

    b. If Parnelli reinvests retained earnings to yield the expected rate of return, what will be next year's EPS?

17-10 Optimal capital budget. On January 1, 1994, the total assets of the Burton Company are $270 million. During the year, the company plans to raise and invest $135 million. The firm's present capital structure, shown below, is considered to be optimal. Assume there is no short-term debt.

Debt	$135 000 000
Common equity	135 000 000
Total liabilities and capital	$270 000 000

New bonds will have a 10 percent coupon rate and will be sold at par. Common shares, currently selling at $60 a share, can be sold to net the company $54 a share. Shareholders' required rate of return is estimated to be 12 percent, consisting of a dividend yield of 4 percent and expected growth of 8 percent. (The next expected dividend is $2.40, so $2.40/$60.00 = 4%.) Retained earnings are estimated to be $13.5 million. The marginal corporate tax rate is 40 percent. All asset expansion (gross expenditures for fixed assets plus related working capital) is included in the capital budget; the dollar amount, ignoring depreciation, is $135 million.

    a. To maintain the present capital structure, how much of the capital budget must be financed by equity?

    b. How much of the new equity funds needed must be generated internally? externally?

    c. Calculate the cost of each of the equity components.

    d. At what level of capital expenditure will there be a break in the MCC schedule?

    e. Calculate the WACC (i) below and (ii) above the break in the MCC schedule.

    f. Plot the MCC schedule. Also, draw in an IOS schedule that is consistent with the MCC schedule and the projected capital budget. (Any IOS schedule that is consistent will do.)

17-11 Marginal cost of capital. The following tabulation gives earnings per share figures for the Riley Company during the preceding 10 years. The firm has 7.8 million common shares outstanding. They are now selling for $65 per share, and the expected dividend for the current year (1994) is 55 percent of the 1993 EPS. Investors expect past trends to continue, so g may be based on the earnings growth rate.

Year	EPS	Year	EPS
1984	$3.90	1986	$4.55
1985	4.21	1987	4.91

Year	EPS	Year	EPS
1988	$5.31	1991	$6.68
1989	5.73	1992	7.22
1990	6.19	1993	7.80

The current interest rate on new debt is 9 percent. The firm's marginal tax rate is 40 percent. The firm's capital structure, considered to be optimal, is as follows:

Debt	$104 000 000
Common equity	156 000 000
Total liabilities and capital	$260 000 000

a. Calculate the after-tax cost of new debt and of common equity, assuming new equity comes only from retained earnings. Calculate the cost of equity as $k_s = D_1/P_0 + g$.

b. Find the weighted average cost of capital, assuming that no new common equity is sold and that all debt costs 9 percent.

c. How much can be spent for capital investments before external equity must be sold? (Assume that retained earnings available for 1994 are 45 percent of 1993 earnings. Obtain 1993 earnings by multiplying 1993 EPS by the shares outstanding.)

d. What is the weighted average cost of capital (the cost of funds raised in excess of the amount calculated in Part c) if new common shares can be sold to the public at $65.00 a share to net the firm $58.50 a share? The cost of debt is constant.

17-12 Optimal capital budget. Austen Enterprises has the following capital structure, which it considers to be optimal under the present and forecasted conditions:

Debt (long-term only)	45%
Common equity	55
Total liabilities and capital	100%

For the coming year, management expects to realize net earnings of $2.5 million. The past dividend policy of paying out 60 percent of earnings will continue. Present commitments from its banker will allow Austen to borrow according to the following schedule:

Loan Amount	Interest Rate
$0 to $500 000	9% on this increment of debt
$500 001 to $900 000	11% on this increment
$900 001 and above	13% on this increment

The company's tax rate is 40 percent, the current market price of its equity is $22 per share, its *last* dividend was $2.20 per share, and the expected growth rate is 5 percent. External equity (new common shares) can be sold at an issue cost of 10 percent.

The firm has the following investment opportunities for the next year:

Project	Cost	Annual Cash Flows	Project Life	IRR Schedule
1	$675 000	$155 401	8 years	
2	900 000	268 484	5 years	15.0%
3	375 000	161 524	3 years	
4	562 500	185 194	4 years	12.0
5	750 000	127 351	10 years	11.0

Management asks you to help to determine what projects (if any) should be undertaken. You proceed with this analysis by answering the following questions (or performing the tasks) as posed in a logical sequence:

a. How many breaks are there in the MCC schedule? At what dollar amounts do the breaks occur, and what causes them?

b. What is the weighted average cost of capital, k_a, in each of the intervals between the breaks?

c. What are the IRR values for Projects 1 and 3?

d. Graph the IOS and MCC schedules.

e. Which projects should Austen's management accept?

f. What assumptions about project risk are implicit in this problem? If you learned that Project 1, 2, and 3 were of above-average risk yet Austen chose the projects that you indicated in Part e, how would this affect the situation?

g. The problem stated that Austen pays out 60 percent of its earnings as dividends. Explain in words how the analysis would change if the payout ratio were zero, 100 percent, or somewhere in between. (No calculations are necessary.)

Integrative Problem

17-13 Cost of capital.   Assume that you were recently hired as an analyst by Mitchell Technologies, and you have been asked by the firm's financial vice president, Connie Smith, to estimate Mitchell's cost of capital. You are provided with the following data, which Smith believes may be relevant to your task:

- The firm's tax rate is 40 percent.
- The current price of Mitchell's 12 percent semiannual coupon bonds with 15 years remaining to maturity is $1153.72. Mitchell does not use short-term interest-bearing debt on a permanent basis.
- The current price of the firm's 10 percent, $100 par value, quarterly dividend, perpetual preferred equity is $113.10. Mitchell would incur issue costs of $2.00 per share on a new issue.
- The common equity is currently selling at $50.00 per share. Its last dividend, D_0, was $4.19, and dividends are expected to grow at a constant rate of 5 percent in the foreseeable future. Mitchell's beta is 1.2; the current yield on long-term Government of Canada bonds is 7 percent; and the market risk premium is 6 percent. Using the

bond-yield-plus-risk-premium approach, the firm has estimated the risk premium at 4 percentage points.

- Up to $300 000 of new common equity can be sold at an issue cost of 15 percent. Above $300 000, the issue cost will be 25 percent.
- Mitchell's target capital structure is 30 percent long-term debt, 10 percent preferred equity, and 60 percent common equity.
- The firm is forecasting retained earnings of $300 000 for the coming year.

To structure the task somewhat, Smith has asked you to answer the following questions:

a. i. What sources of capital should be included in the estimate of the overall cost of capital? Explain your answer.

   ii. Should the component cost estimates be before-tax or after-tax costs? Explain.

   iii. Should the costs used in calculations be historical (embedded) costs or new (marginal) costs? Explain.

b. What is Mitchell's component cost of debt?

c. i. What is the firm's cost of preferred equity?

   ii. Mitchell's preferred equity is riskier to investors than its debt, yet the yield to preferred investors is lower than the yield to maturity on the debt. Does this suggest that you have made a mistake?

d. i. Why is there a cost associated with retained earnings?

   ii. What is Mitchell's estimated cost of retained earnings if you use the CAPM approach?

   iii. Why is the Canada bond rate a better estimate of the risk-free rate for our purposes than the short-term treasury bill rate?

e. What is the estimated cost of retained earnings if you use the discounted cash flow (DCF) approach?

f. What is the bond-yield-plus-risk-premium estimate for Mitchell's cost of retained earnings?

g. What is your final estimate for k_s?

h. What is Mitchell's cost for up to $300 000 of newly issued common equity, k_{e1}? What happens to the cost of equity if Mitchell sells more than $300 000 of new common equity?

i. i. What is the firm's overall, or weighted average, cost of capital (WACC) when retained earnings are used as the equity component?

   ii. What is the firm's WACC when up to $300 000 of new common equity with a 15 percent issue cost is used?

   iii. What is the WACC if more than $300 000 of new common equity is sold?

   iv. Would Mitchell prefer to use retained earnings or new common shares as the common equity component? Does it have a choice? Explain your answers.

j. i. At what amount of new investment will Mitchell be forced to issue new common equity?

   ii. At what amount of new investment will Mitchell be forced to issue new common equity with a 25 percent issue cost?

   iii. What is a marginal cost of capital (MCC) schedule? Construct Mitchell's MCC schedule.

iv. Will Mitchell's MCC schedule remain constant at 12.8 percent beyond $2 million regardless of the amount of capital required?

k. Mitchell's director of capital budgeting has identified the four following potential projects:

Project	Cost	Life	Cash Flow	IRR
A	$700 000	5 years	$218 795	17.0%
B	500 000	5	152 705	16.0
B′	500 000	20	79 881	15.0
C	800 000	5	219 185	11.5

Projects B and B′ are mutually exclusive, whereas the remainder are independent. All of the projects are equally risky.

i. Plot the IOS schedule on the same graph that contains your MCC schedule. What is the firm's marginal cost of capital?

ii. What is Mitchell's optimal capital budget? Explain your answer fully.

iii. If WACC$_3$ had been 18.5 percent rather than 12.8 percent, but its break point had still occurred at $1 000 000, how would that have affected the analysis?

iv. If the four projects had differential riskiness, how would that have affected the analysis?

Solutions to Self-Test Problems

ST-1   Refer to the appropriate sections of the text to check your responses.

ST-2   **a.** A break point will occur each time a low-cost type of capital is used up. We establish the break points as follows, after first noting that LEI has $24 000 of retained earnings:

$$\text{Retained earnings} = (\text{total earnings})(1.0 - \text{payout})$$
$$= \$34\,285.72(0.7) = \$24\,000.$$

$$\text{Break point} = \frac{\text{total amount of low-cost capital of a given type}}{\text{fraction of this type of capital in the capital structure}}.$$

Capital Used Up	Break Point Calculation	Number
Retained earnings	$BP_{RE} = \dfrac{\$24\,000}{0.60} = \$40\,000.$	2
10% issue cost common	$BP_{10\%E} = \dfrac{\$24\,000 + \$12\,000}{0.60} = \$60\,000.$	4
5% issue cost preferred	$BP_{5\%P} = \dfrac{\$7500}{0.15} = \$50\,000.$	3
12% debt	$BP_{12\%D} = \dfrac{\$5000}{0.25} = \$20\,000.$	1
14% debt	$BP_{14\%D} = \dfrac{\$5000 + \$5000}{0.25} = \$40\,000.$	2

Summary of Break Points

i. There are three common equity costs, and hence two changes (and two equity-induced breaks) in the MCC. There are two preferred equity costs and hence one preferred equity break. There are three debt costs and hence two debt breaks.

ii. The numbers in the right column of the table designate the sequence of the breaks. They were determined after the break points were calculated. Note that the second debt break and the break for retained earnings both occur at $40 000.

iii. The first break point occurs at $20 000, when the 12 percent debt is used up. The second break point, $40 000, results from using up both the retained earnings and the 14 percent debt. The MCC curve also rises at $50 000 and $60 000 as preferred shares with a 5 percent issue cost and common equity with a 10 percent issue cost, respectively, are used up.

b. Component costs within indicated total capital intervals:

Retained earnings ($0 to $40 000):

$$k_s = \frac{D_1}{P_0} + g = \frac{D_0(1 + g)}{P_0} + g$$

$$= \frac{\$3.60(1.09)}{\$60} + 0.09 = 0.0654 + 0.09 = 15.54\%.$$

Common equity with $F = 10\%$ ($40 001 to $60 000):

$$k_e = \frac{D_1}{P_0(1.0 - F)} + g = \frac{\$3.924}{\$60(0.9)} + 9\% = 16.27\%.$$

Common equity with $F = 20\%$ (Over $60 000):

$$k_e = \frac{\$3.924}{\$60(0.8)} + 9\% = 17.18\%.$$

Preferred shares with $F = 5\%$ ($0 to $50 000):

$$k_p = \frac{\text{Preferred dividend}}{P_p} = \frac{\$11}{\$100(0.95)} = 11.58\%.$$

Preferred shares with $F = 10\%$ (Over $50 000):

$$k_p = \frac{\$11}{\$100(0.9)} = 12.22\%.$$

Debt at $k_d = 12\%$ ($0 to $20 000):

$$k_d(1 - T) = 12\%(0.6) = 7.20\%.$$

Debt at $k_d = 14\%$ ($20 001 to $40 000):

$$k_d(1 - T) = 14\%(0.6) = 8.40\%.$$

Debt at $k_d = 16\%$ (Over \$40 000):

$$k_d(1 - T) = 16\%(0.6) = 9.60\%.$$

c. WACC calculations within indicated total capital intervals:
  i. \$0 to \$20 000 (debt = 7.20%, preferred = 11.58%, and RE = 15.54%):

$$
\begin{aligned}
WACC_1 &= w_d k_d(1 - T) + w_p k_p + w_s k_s \\
&= 0.25(7.20\%) + 0.15(11.58\%) + 0.60(15.54\%) \\
&= 12.86\%.
\end{aligned}
$$

  ii. \$20 001 to \$40 000 (debt = 8.4%, preferred = 11.58%, and RE = 15.54%):

$$
\begin{aligned}
WACC_2 &= 0.25(8.4\%) + 0.15(11.58\%) + 0.60(15.54\%) \\
&= 13.16\%.
\end{aligned}
$$

  iii. \$40 001 to \$50 000 (debt = 9.6%, preferred = 11.58%, and equity = 16.27%):

$$
\begin{aligned}
WACC_3 &= 0.25(9.6\%) + 0.15(11.58\%) + 0.60(16.27\%) \\
&= 13.90\%.
\end{aligned}
$$

  iv. \$50 001 to \$60 000 (debt = 9.6%, preferred = 12.22%, and equity = 16.27%):

$$
\begin{aligned}
WACC_4 &= 0.25(9.6\%) + 0.15(12.22\%) + 0.60(16.27\%) \\
&= 14.00\%.
\end{aligned}
$$

  v. Over \$60 000 (debt = 9.6%, preferred = 12.22%, and equity = 17.18%):

$$
\begin{aligned}
WACC_5 &= 0.25(9.6\%) + 0.15(12.22\%) + 0.60(17.18\%) \\
&= 14.54\%.
\end{aligned}
$$

d. IRR calculation for Project E:

$$PVIFA_{k,6} = \frac{\$20\,000}{\$5\,427.84} = 3.6847.$$

This is the factor for 16 percent, so $IRR_E = 16\%$.
e. See the graph of the MCC and IOS schedules for LEI on the following page.
f. LEI clearly should accept Projects B, E, and C. It should reject Projects A and D because their IRRs do not exceed the marginal costs of funds needed to finance them.

   The firm's capital budget would total \$40 000.

**MCC and IOS Schedules for
Lancaster Engineering, Inc.**

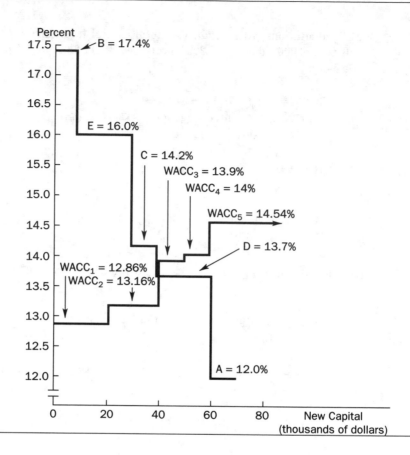

18

▲▲

Capital Structure and Leverage

A MANAGERIAL PERSPECTIVE

The time period from 1984 to 1989 was one of significant growth in the Canadian economy. Growth occurred not only from mergers and acquisitions but also from expansion of internal corporate operations. The financing of this activity had a significant debt component, supported by strong cash flows from operations. Then the recession that began in 1990 and its lengthy continuation had a significant impact on cash flows and on the ability of companies to maintain their prerecession debt levels. Many companies were forced to take a hard look at their operations and identify the amount of debt that could be supported under the existing and near-term forecasted cash flows. Based on this analysis, some companies concluded that their leverage ratios should be reduced; this was accomplished either through the sale of assets or divisions that did not fit with the corporate objectives and the application of the proceeds to pay down debt or through the issuance of new equity and the use of the funds to repay some portion of the outstanding debt. An example of the latter approach was provided by Sears Canada, which issued 10.5 million common shares in August 1992 and used the proceeds to reduce its debt by $76 million.

In this chapter, we analyze the determinants of the company's optimal capital structure. An understanding of these determinants helps to explain how optimal capital structures for firms can change over time.

The Importance of Capital Structure

In Chapter 17, when we calculated the weighted average cost of capital for use in capital budgeting, we took as given the capital structure weights, or the mix of securities the firm uses to finance its assets. However, changing the weights can have an effect on the calculated cost of capital and consequently can change the set of acceptable projects. Also, changing the capital structure can affect the riskiness inherent in the firm's common shares and thus affect k_s and P_0. Therefore, the choice of a capital structure is important.

As we shall see, the firm analyzes a number of factors and then establishes a **target capital structure**, which is the mix of debt, preferred shares, and common equity the firm would like to use for capital financing. This target may change over time as conditions vary, but at any given moment the firm's management does have a specific capital structure in mind, and individual financing decisions should be consistent with this target. If the actual debt ratio is below the target ratio, expansion capital will probably be raised by issuing debt, whereas common equity will probably be sold if the debt ratio is above the target level.

Capital structure policy involves a trade off between risk and expected returns. Using more debt raises the riskiness of the firm's earnings stream, but a higher debt ratio generally means a higher expected rate of return. Higher risk associated with greater debt tends to lower the share price, but a higher expected rate of return raises it. The **optimal capital structure** is the one that strikes a balance between these risks and expected returns and thus maximizes the price of the company's common equity.

Several factors influence capital structure decisions. The first is the firm's *business risk*, or the riskiness that would be inherent in the firm's assets if it used no debt. The greater the firm's business risk, the lower its optimal debt ratio. A second key factor is the firm's *tax position*. A major reason for using debt is that interest is a tax-deductible expense, which lowers the effective cost of debt. However, if much of a firm's income is already sheltered from taxes by capital cost allowances or tax-loss carryforwards, its tax rate will be low, and in this case debt will not be as advantageous as it would be to a firm with a higher effective tax rate. A third important consideration is *financial flexibility*, or the ability to raise capital on reasonable terms under adverse conditions. Corporate treasurers know that a steady supply of capital is necessary for stable operations, which in turn are vital for long-run success. They also know that when money is tight in the economy or when a firm is experiencing operating difficulties, suppliers of capital prefer to advance funds to companies with strong balance sheets. Therefore, the potential future availability of funds and the consequences of a funds shortage have a major influence on the target capital structure.

Business Risk and Financial Risk

In Chapter 15, when we examined risk from the viewpoint of the individual investor, we distinguished between *market risk*, which is measured by the firm's beta coefficient, and *total risk*, which includes both beta risk and a type of risk that can be eliminated by diversification. Then, we examined risk from the viewpoint of the corporation, and we considered how capital budgeting decisions affect the riskiness of the firm. There again we distinguished between *beta risk* (the effect of a project on the firm's beta) and *corporate risk* (the effect of the project on the firm's total risk).

Now we introduce two new dimensions of risk: (1) *business risk*, which is the riskiness of the firm's operations if it uses no debt, and (2) *financial risk*, which is the additional risk placed on the common equityholders as a result of the firm's decision to use debt. Conceptually, the firm has a certain amount of risk inherent in its operations; this is its business risk. When it uses debt, it partitions this risk and concentrates most of it on one class of investors—the common shareholders.[1]

---

[1]Using preferred shares also adds to financial risk. But to simplify matters somewhat in this chapter, we consider only debt and common equity. Also, if a firm uses an especially large amount of debt in a leveraged buyout (LBO), as RJR Nabisco Ltd. did, then its debt will be classified as "junk bonds," and the bondholders will also be exposed to financial risk. Some junk bonds practically amount to equity.

Business Risk

Business risk is defined as the uncertainty inherent in projections of future returns on assets (ROA)—or returns on equity (ROE) if the firm uses no debt financing. It is the single most important determinant of a firm's capital structure. Consider Bigbee Electronics Company, a firm that currently uses 100 percent equity financing. Figure 18-1 gives some clues about Bigbee's business risk. Panel a shows the trend in ROE from 1983 through 1993; this graph gives both security analysts and Bigbee's management an idea of the degree to which ROE has varied in the past and might vary in the future.[2] Panel b shows the beginning-of-year probability distribution of Bigbee's ROE for 1993, subjectively estimated on the basis of the trend line in Panel a. The estimate was made at the beginning of 1993, and the expected value of 12 percent was read from the trend line. As the graphs indicate, actual ROE in 1993 (8 percent) fell below the expected value (12 percent).

Bigbee's past fluctuations in ROE were caused by many factors—booms and recessions in the national economy, successful new products introduced both by Bigbee and by its competitors, labour strikes, a fire in Bigbee's major plant, and so on. Similar events will doubtless occur in the future, and when they do, ROE will rise or fall. Further, there is always the possibility that a long-term disaster might strike, permanently depressing the company's earning power. For example, a competitor could introduce a new product that would permanently lower Bigbee's earnings. This element of uncertainty about Bigbee's future ROE is the company's *basic business risk*.

Business risk varies from one industry to another and also among firms in a given industry. Further, business risk can change over time because of changes in the competitive structure of the industry, technological change, or shifts in the nature of society and the economy.[3] Today food processors and grocery retailers are frequently given as examples of industries with low business risk, whereas cyclical manufacturing industries, such as steel, are regarded as having especially high business risk. Smaller companies and single-product firms also have a relatively high degree of business risk.[4]

Business risk depends on a number of factors, the more important of which are the following:

1. *Demand variability.* The more stable the demand for a firm's products, other things held constant, the lower the firm's business risk.

2. *Sales price variability.* Firms whose products are sold in highly volatile markets are exposed to more business risk than are similar firms whose output prices are relatively stable.

---

[2]The degree of business risk is reflected in the variability of the realized ROE about the trend value. This provides an indication of the deviation of the actual from the expected values of ROE.

[3]Two examples of "safe" industries that turned out to be risky are the railways just before automobiles, airplanes, and trucks took away most of their business and the telegraph business just before telephones came on the scene. Also, numerous individual companies have been hurt, if not destroyed, by fraud or just plain bad management.

[4]We avoid any discussion of market versus company-specific risk in this section. We note, however, (1) that any action that increases business risk will generally increase a firm's beta coefficient, but (2) that a part of business risk as we define it is generally company-specific and hence subject to elimination through diversification by the firm's shareholders.

Figure 18-1
Bigbee Electronics Company:
Trend in ROE, 1983–1993, and
Subjective Probability Distribution of ROE, 1993

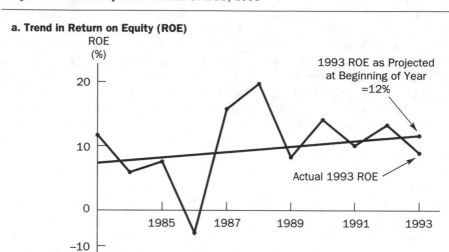

a. Trend in Return on Equity (ROE)

1993 ROE as Projected at Beginning of Year =12%

Actual 1993 ROE

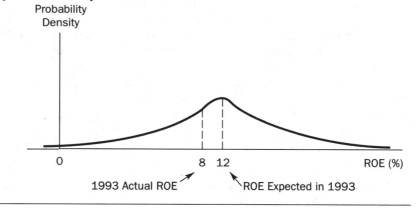

b. Subjective Probability Distribution of ROE

1993 Actual ROE

ROE Expected in 1993

3. *Input price variability.*   Firms whose input prices are highly uncertain are exposed to a high degree of business risk.

4. *Ability to adjust output prices for changes in input prices.*   Some firms have little difficulty in raising their own output prices when input costs rise, and the greater the ability to adjust output prices, the lower the degree of business risk. This factor is especially important during periods of high inflation.

5. *The extent to which costs are fixed: operating leverage.*   If a high percentage of a firm's costs are fixed and hence do not decline when demand falls off, this increases the company's business risk. This factor is called *operating leverage*, and it was discussed at length in Chapter 6.

Each of these factors is determined partly by the firm's industry characteristics, but each is also controllable to some extent by management. For example, most firms can, through their marketing policies, take actions to stabilize both unit sales and sales prices; however, this stabilization may require either large expenditures on advertising or price concessions to induce customers to commit to purchasing fixed quantities at fixed prices in the future. Similarly, firms like Bigbee Electronics can reduce the volatility of future input costs by negotiating long-term labour and materials supply contracts, but they may have to agree to pay prices above the current spot price level to obtain these contracts.

Financial Risk

Financial leverage refers to the use of fixed-income securities—debt and preferred shares—that have claims on corporate cash flows prior to equity, and **financial risk** is the additional risk placed on the common shareholders as a result of using financial leverage. Conceptually, the firm has a certain amount of risk inherent in its operations; this is its business risk, which is defined as the uncertainty inherent in projections of future ROA. By financing with debt and preferred equity (financial leverage), the firm concentrates its business risk on the common shareholders. To illustrate: suppose ten people decide to form a corporation to manufacture running shoes. There is a certain amount of business risk in the operation. If the firm is capitalized only with common equity and if each person buys 10 percent of the equity, then each investor will bear an equal share of the business risk. However, suppose the firm is capitalized with 50 percent debt and 50 percent equity, with five of the investors putting up their capital as debt and the other five putting up their money as equity. In this case, the investors who put up the equity have to bear essentially all of the business risk, so their common shares are twice as risky as they would have been had the firm been financed only with equity. Thus, the use of debt concentrates the firm's business risk on its shareholders.

In the next section, we shall learn how financial leverage affects a firm's expected earnings per share, the riskiness of those earnings, and, consequently, the price of the firm's equity. As we shall see, the value of a firm that has no debt first rises as it substitutes debt for equity, then hits a peak, and finally declines as the use of debt becomes excessive. The objective of our analysis is to determine the capital structure at which value is maximized; this point is then used as the *target capital structure*.[5]

---

[5]In this chapter, we examine capital structures on a *book value* (or *balance sheet*) *basis*. An alternative approach is to calculate the market values of debt, preferred shares, and common equity and then to reconstruct the balance sheet on a *market value basis*. Although the market value approach is more consistent with financial theory, bond rating agencies and most financial executives focus their attention on book values. Moreover, the conversion from book to market values is a complicated process, and market value capital structures are thought by many to be too unstable to serve as operationally useful targets. Finally, exactly the same insights are gained from the book value and market value analyses. For all these reasons, the market value analysis of capital structure is better suited for advanced than for introductory finance courses.

Determining the Optimal Capital Structure

We can illustrate the effects of financial leverage with the data for an illustrative company that we call Firm B. As shown in Part I of Table 18-1, the company now has no debt. Should it continue the policy of using no debt, or should it start using financial leverage? If it does decide to substitute debt for equity, how far should it go? As in all such decisions, the correct answer is that it should choose *the capital structure that maximizes the price per share of its common equity.*

Since the price of a share of equity is the present value of its expected future dividends, if the use of financial leverage is to affect the share's price, it

---

Table 18-1
Data on Firm B

I. Balance Sheet on 12/31/93

Current assets	$100 000	Debt		$ 0
Net fixed assets	100 000	Common equity (10 000 shares)		200 000
Total assets	$200 000	Total claims		$200 000

II. Income Statement for 1993

Sales		$200 000
Fixed operating costs	$ 40 000	
Variable operating costs	120 000	160 000
Earnings before interest and taxes (EBIT)		$ 40 000
Interest		0
Taxable income		$ 40 000
Taxes (40%)		16 000
Net income after taxes		$ 24 000

(continued)

Table 18-1 *(continued)*

III. Other Data

1. Earnings per share = EPS = \$24 000/10 000 shares = \$2.40.
2. Dividends per share = DPS = \$24 000/10 000 shares = \$2.40. (Firm B pays all of its earnings out as dividends.)
3. Book value per share = BVS = \$200 000/10 000 shares = \$20.
4. Market price per share = P_0 = \$20. (The equity sells at its book value, so M/B = 1.0)
5. Price-to-earnings ratio = P/E = \$20/\$2.40 = 8.33 times.
6. Return on (book) equity (ROE) = EPS/BVS = \$2.40/\$20.00 = 0.12 or 12%.
7. Return on (book) assets (ROA) = EBIT/Assets = \$40 000/\$200 000 = 0.20 or 20%.

must do so by changing either the expected dividend stream or the required rate of return on equity, k_s, or both. We first consider the effect of capital structure on earnings and dividends; then we examine its effect on k_s.

EBIT-EPS Analysis of the Effects of Financial Leverage

Changes in the use of debt will cause changes in earnings per share (EPS) and consequently in the share price. To understand the relationship between financial leverage and EPS, consider first Table 18-2, which shows how Firm B's cost of debt will vary if it uses various percentages of debt in its capital structure. Naturally, the higher the percentage of debt, the riskier the debt and hence the higher the interest rate lenders will charge.

Now consider Table 18-3, which shows how expected EPS varies with changes in financial leverage. Part I of the table begins with a probability distribution of sales; we assume for simplicity that sales can take on only three values, \$100 000, \$200 000, or \$300 000. In the remainder of Part I, we calculate

Table 18-2
Interest Rates for Firm B with
Different Debt-to-Assets Ratios

Amount Borrowed	Debt-to-Assets Ratio[a]	Interest Rate, k_d, on All Debt
\$ 20 000	10%	8.0%
40 000	20	8.3
60 000	30	9.0
80 000	40	10.0
100 000	50	12.0
120 000	60	15.0

[a]We assume that the firm must borrow in increments of \$20 000. Also, we assume that Firm B is unable to borrow more than \$120 000, or 60 percent of assets because of restrictions in its existing contracts.

Table 18-3

Firm B: EPS with Different Amounts of Financial Leverage (thousands of dollars, except per share figures)

I. Calculation of EBIT

Probability of Indicated Sales	0.20	0.60	0.20
Sales	$100.00	$200.00	$300.00
Fixed costs	40.00	40.00	40.00
Variable costs (60% of sales)	60.00	120.00	180.00
Total costs (except interest)	$100.00	$160.00	$220.00
Earnings before interest and taxes (EBIT)	$ 0.00	$ 40.00	$ 80.00
Return on assets (ROA)	0%	20%	40%

II. Situation If Debt-to-Assets Ratio (D/A) = 0%

EBIT (from Part I)	$ 0.00	$ 40.00	$ 80.00
Less: Interest	0.00	0.00	0.00
Earnings before taxes	$ 0.00	$ 40.00	$ 80.00
Taxes (40%)[a]	0.00	(16.00)	(32.00)
Net income after taxes	$ 0.00	$ 24.00	$ 48.00
Earnings per share on 10 000 shares (EPS)[b]	$ 0.00	$ 2.40	$ 4.80
Expected EPS		$ 2.40	
Standard deviation of EPS		$ 1.52	
Coefficient of variation		0.63	
Return on equity (ROE)	0%	12%	24%

III. Situation If Debt-to-Assets Ratio (D/A) = 50%

EBIT (from Part I)	$ 0.00	$ 40.00	$ 80.00
Less: Interest (0.12 × $100 000)	12.00	12.00	12.00
Earnings before taxes	($ 12.00)	$ 28.00	$ 68.00
Taxes (40%)[a]	4.80	(11.20)	(27.20)
Net income after taxes	($ 7.20)	$ 16.80	$ 40.80
Earnings per share on 5000 shares (EPS)[b]	($ 1.144)	$ 3.36	$ 8.16
Expected EPS		$ 3.36	
Standard deviation of EPS		$ 3.04	
Coefficient of variation		0.90	
Return on equity	−7.2%	16.8%	40.8%

[a]Assumes tax credit on losses.

[b]The EPS figures can also be obtained using the following formula, where the numerator amounts to an income statement at a given sales level laid out horizontally:

$$\text{EPS} = \frac{(\text{Sales} - \text{Fixed costs} - \text{Variable costs} - \text{Interest})(1 - \text{Tax rate})}{\text{Shares outstanding}} = \frac{(\text{EBIT} - I)(1 - T)}{\text{Shares outstanding}}$$

For example, at sales (S) = $200 000 and D = 0, $\text{EPS}_{D/A=0} = \dfrac{(\$200\,000 - \$40\,000 - \$120\,000 - 0)(0.6)}{10\,000} = \$2.40.$

And at S = $200 000 and D = 50%, $\text{EPS}_{D/A=0.5} = \dfrac{(\$200\,000 - \$40\,000 - \$120\,000 - \$12\,000)(0.6)}{5000} = \$3.36.$

Since the equation is linear, the sales level at which EPS will be equal under the two financing policies, or the indifference level of sales, S_1, can be found by setting $\text{EPS}_{D/A=0}$ equal to $\text{EPS}_{D/A=0.5}$ and solving for S_1:

$$\text{EPS}_{D/A=0} = \frac{(S_1 - \$40\,000 - 0.6S_1 - 0)(0.6)}{10\,000} = \frac{(S_1 - \$40\,000 - 0.6S_1 - \$12\,000)(0.6)}{5000} = \text{EPS}_{D/A=0.5}. \ S_1 = \$160\,000.$$

By substituting this value of sales, we can find EPS_1, the earning per share at this indifference point, as $\text{EPS}_1 = \$1.44.$

earnings before interest and taxes (EBIT) at each of the three sales levels. Note that we assume here that both sales and operating costs are independent of financial leverage. Therefore, the three EBIT figures ($0, $40 000, and $80 000) will always remain the same, no matter how much debt Firm B uses.[6]

Part II of Table 18-3 goes on to show the situation if Firm B continues to use no debt. Net income after taxes is divided by the 10 000 shares outstanding to obtain EPS. If sales are as low as $100 000, EPS will be zero, but it will rise to $4.80 at sales of $300 000. The EPS at each sales level is then multiplied by the probability of that sales level to calculate the expected EPS, which is $2.40 if Firm B uses no debt. We also calculate the standard deviation and the coefficient of variation of EPS as indicators of the firm's risk at a zero debt ratio: $\sigma_{EPS} = \$1.52$ and $CV_{EPS} = 0.63$.[7]

Part III of the table shows the financial results that can be expected if Firm B is financed with a debt-to-assets ratio of 50 percent. In this situation, $100 000 of the $200 000 total capital is debt. The interest rate on debt, 12 percent, is taken from Table 18-2. With $100 000 of 12 percent debt outstanding, the company's interest expense, as shown in Table 18-3, is $12 000 per year. This is a fixed cost—it is the same regardless of the level of sales—and it is from EBIT as calculated in the top deducted section. Next, taxes are taken out to derive total net income. EPS is then calculated as net income after taxes divided by shares outstanding. With debt = 0, there are 10 000 shares outstanding. However, if half the equity is replaced by debt (debt = $100 000), then there will be only 5000 shares outstanding, and we use this fact to determine the EPS figures that will result at each sales level.[8] With a debt-to-assets ratio of 50 percent, EPS will be −$1.44 if sales are as low as

---

[6]In the real world, capital structure *does* at times affect EBIT. First, if debt levels are excessive, the firm will probably not be able to finance at all if its earnings are low at a time when interest rates are high. This could lead to a stop-and-start construction program and/or to the necessity of passing up good investment opportunities. Second, a weak financial situation brought on by having too much debt can cause a firm to lose contracts. For example, companies such as General Motors examine closely the financial strength of potential suppliers, and if they are so weak that they might not be able to deliver materials as called for in the contract, they simply will not get the business. Third, financially strong companies are able to bargain hard with unions as well as with their suppliers, while weaker companies may have to give in simply because they do not have the financial resources to carry on the fight. Finally, a company with so much debt that bankruptcy is a serious threat will have difficulty attracting and retaining managers and employees or will have to pay them premium salaries. People value job security, and financially weak companies simply cannot provide such protection. For all these reasons, it is not totally correct to say that a firm's financial policy has no effect on its operating income.

Note also that EBIT is dependent on operating (but not financial) leverage. If we were analyzing a firm with either more or less operating leverage, Part I of Table 18-3 would be quite different. The range of EBIT over the different sales levels would be narrower if a lower degree of operating leverage were used but wider if more operating leverage were employed.

[7]See Chapter 15 for a review of procedures for calculating standard deviations and coefficients of variation. The advantage of the coefficient of variation is that it permits better comparisons when the mean values of EPS vary, as they do here in the 50 percent and zero debt situations.

[8]We assume in this example that the firm could change its capital structure by repurchasing some of its common equity at its book value of $100 000/5000 shares = $20 per share. However, the firm may actually have to pay a higher price to repurchase its equity. If Firm B has to pay $22 per share, then it can repurchase only $100 000/$22 = 4545 shares; in this case, expected EPS will be only $16 800/(10 000 − 4545) = $16 800/5455 = $3.08.

$100 000; it will rise to $3.36 if sales are $200 000; and it will soar to $8.16 if sales are as high as $300 000.

The EPS probability distributions under the two financial structures are graphed in Figure 18-2, where we use the continuous distributions rather than the discrete distributions contained in Table 18-3. Although expected EPS is much higher if financial leverage is employed, the graph makes it clear that the risk of low or even negative EPS is higher if debt is used.

Another view of the relationships among expected EPS, risk, and financial leverage is presented in Figure 18-3. The tabular data in the lower section were calculated in the manner set forth in Table 18-3, and the graphs plot the data. Here we see the expected EPS rises for a while as the use of debt increases—interest charges rise, but the declining number of shares outstanding as debt is substituted for equity still causes EPS to increase. However, EPS peaks at a debt ratio of 50 percent. Beyond this ratio, interest rates rise so rapidly that EPS is depressed in spite of the falling number of shares outstanding. Risk, as measured by the standard deviation or coefficient of variation of EPS, rises continuously, and at an increasing rate, as debt is substituted for equity.

We see then that using leverage involves a risk–return tradeoff: higher leverage increases expected earnings per share (in the example, until the D/A ratio equals 50 percent), but it also increases the firm's risk. Before discussing how this tradeoff can be resolved and where in the range of 0 to 50 percent the D/A ratio should be set, we pause to emphasize the risk aspect of leverage by demonstrating directly its influence on the variability of returns on equity.

In Table 18-4 (see page 663) we have collected information concerning the returns on assets and equity for Firm B at various leverage ratios.

How do the different leverage ratios affect shareholder returns (ROE)? The answer depends partly on the impact of the economy on the firm's net operating income. When the economy is depressed, sales and profit margins are

Figure 18-2

Firm B: Probability Distribution of EPS with Different Amounts of Financial Leverage

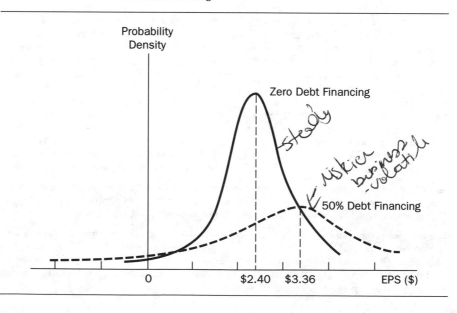

Figure 18-3
Firm B: Relationships among Expected EPS,
Risk, and Financial Leverage

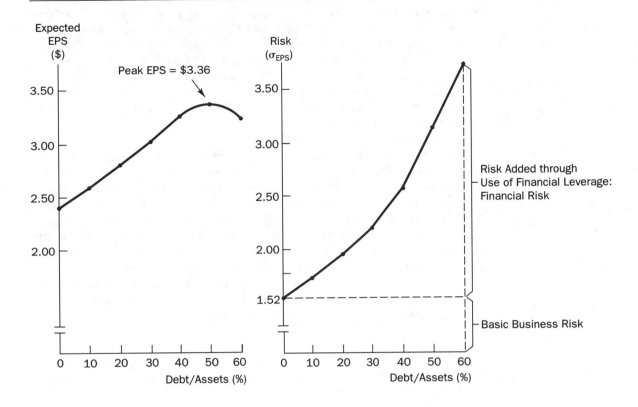

Debt-to-Assets Ratio	Expected EPS	Standard Deviation of EPS	Coefficient of Variation
0%[a]	$2.40[a]	$1.52[a]	0.63[a]
10	2.56	1.69	0.66
20	2.75	1.90	0.69
30	2.97	2.17	0.73
40	3.20	2.53	0.79
50[a]	3.36[a] peak	3.04[a]	0.90[a]
60	3.30	3.79	1.15

[a]Values for D/A = 0 and 50 percent are taken from Table 18-3. Values at other D/A ratios were calculated similarly.

depressed and the firm earns a 0 percent return on assets. Under normal economic conditions, the return on assets for the firm is 20 percent. Finally, under very good conditions, the rate of return on assets is 40 percent.

The remainder of Table 18-4 demonstrates how the use of financial leverage magnifies the impact of fluctuations in the rate of return on assets on shareholders' returns. With zero leverage, the after-tax return on total assets is equal to the rate of return on shareholders' equity (ROE); there is no amplification of the underlying variability of the return on assets. As debt is used, the amount of interest paid affects the relation between the after-tax return on total assets and the return on equity.

Consider a change in economic conditions from normal to very good: there is a twofold increase of the rate of return on assets—from 20 percent to 40 percent. With no leverage, there is also a twofold increase in ROE; no amplification of the economic condition has occurred. As leverage increases, amplification occurs and increases with the increasing leverage. With the 50 percent debt ratio, the ROE has increased 2.43 times. Thus, the presence of leverage amplifies the increase in the rate of return on assets.

Amplification also operates when the economy turns down, and poor economic results are translated into rates of return on equity that depend on the leverage ratio.

Table 18-4 also demonstrates that the higher the ratio of financial leverage employed, the greater the dispersion of returns. With no leverage, the range for the ROE is 24 percentage points; with a 50 percent leverage factor, the range is 48 percentage points. Financial leverage magnifies the volatility of returns whether measured by net income, return on equity, or earnings per share.

These results are depicted in Figure 18-4. When all the total assets are financed by equity, the relationship of the return on shareholders' equity (ROE) to the return on total assets is a relatively flat line.[9] For the leverage ratio equal to 50 percent, the line becomes steeper. This means that a small change in the ratio of EBIT to total assets produces a very large change in the rate of return on shareholders' equity. Thus, greater financial leverage produces greater volatility in the rate of return on equity.

---

[9]The relationship between the return on equity and the return on assets can be presented algebraically. Let ROA be the return on assets and ROE be the return on equity. By definition we have the following relationships:

$$ROA = \frac{EBIT}{Assets} \tag{1}$$

$$ROE = \frac{After\text{-}tax\ net\ income}{Equity} \tag{2}$$

$$But\ Assets = Debt + Equity \tag{3}$$

$$and\ After\text{-}tax\ net\ income = (EBIT - Interest)(1 - T) \tag{4}$$

where T is the tax rate.
We can expand Equation (2) as follows:

$$ROE = \frac{(EBIT - Interest)(1 - T)}{Equity} = \frac{EBIT\ (1 - T)}{Equity} - \frac{Interest(1 - T)}{Equity} \tag{5}$$

But from (1), EBIT = ROA × assets; substituting into (5) to obtain:

$$ROE = -Interest(1 - T)/Equity + (Assets/Equity(1 - T))ROA \tag{6}$$

This is a straight-line equation with an intercept equal to Interest $(1 - T)$/Equity and a slope equal to Assets$(1 - T)$/Equity. As leverage increases, the ratio of assets to equity becomes larger and the slope of the line is steeper. Thus, a given change in ROA leads to a larger change in ROE as leverage increases. In addition, as leverage increases, interest payments increase owing to an increase in both the interest rate and the amount of debt outstanding; thus, the intercept becomes a larger negative number. The curves will intersect at an ROA equal to the before-tax interest rate on debt. If the firm earns this ROA, the ROE equals the after-tax interest rate.

**Table 18-4
Firm B: Returns on Assets and Common Equity
(at Book Values) with Different Amounts
of Financial Leverage**

Probability of indicated sales	0.2	0.6	0.2
Sales	$100	$200	$300
Return on assets (before tax)	0%	20%	40%
Return on assets (after tax)[a]	0%	12%	24%
Return on equity when D/A = 0%	0%	12%	24%
Return on equity when D/A = 50%	−7.2%	16.8%	40.8%

[a]After-tax return on assets = Before-tax return × (1 − T).

**Figure 18-4
Leverage and Return on Equity**

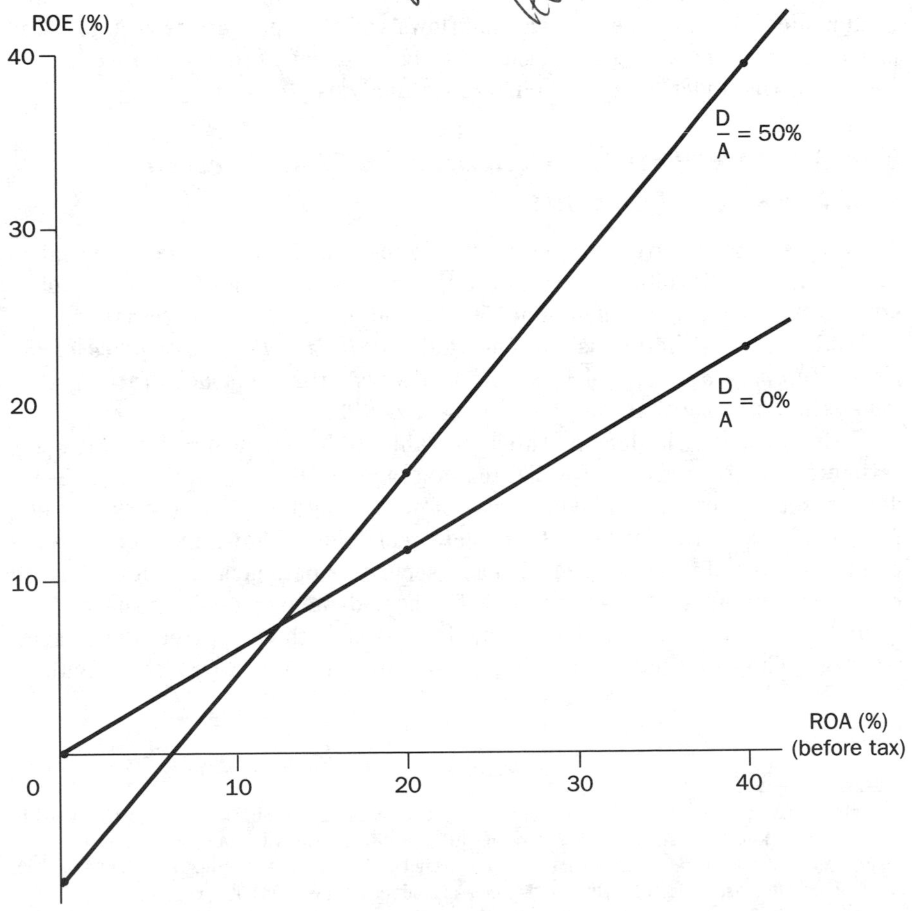

EPS Indifference Analysis

Another way of presenting the data on Firm B's two financing methods is shown in Figure 18-5, which depicts the **EPS indifference point**—the point of indifference between the use of debt and common equity. At a low level of sales, EPS is much higher if common equity rather than debt is used. The debt line has a steeper slope and rises faster, however, showing that earnings per share will go up faster with increases in sales if debt is used. The two lines cross at sales of $160 000. Below that sales volume, EPS will be higher if the firm issues common shares; above $160 000, debt financing will produce higher earnings per share.[10]

If the managers of Firm B knew with certainty that sales would never again fall below $160 000, bonds would be the preferred method of financing the asset increase, as EPS would always be higher for every possible sales outcome. But they cannot know this for certain—in fact, investors know that in a number of previous years sales have fallen below this critical level and if any of several detrimental events should occur in the future, sales would again fall below $160 000. On the other hand, if sales continue to expand, higher earnings per share would result from the use of bonds, an advantage that no investor would want to forego.

EPS indifference analysis should be used not for capital budgeting decisions but only for financing decisions. The capital budgeting decision has already been made based on the expected cash flows and the appropriate risk-adjusted discount rate. The assets acquired (or to be acquired) provide the basic cash flow patterns underlying the indifference analysis.

The Effect of Capital Structure on Share Prices and the Cost of Capital

As we saw in Figure 18-3, Firm B's expected EPS is maximized at a debt-to-assets ratio of 50 percent. Does this mean that Firm B's optimal captial structure is 50 percent debt and 50 percent equity? Not necessarily. The optimal capital structure is the one that *maximizes the share price of the firm's common equity*, and this almost always calls for a debt ratio that is lower than the one that maximizes expected EPS.

This statement is demonstrated in Table 18-5, which develops Firm B's estimated share price and weighted average cost of capital at different debt/assets ratios. The EPS and debt cost data in columns 1, 2, and 3 are taken from Table 18-2 and Figure 18-3. The beta coefficients shown in column 4 were estimated. Recall from Chapter 15 that a security's beta measures its volatility relative to that of an average share. It has been demonstrated both theoretically and empirically that a firm's beta increases with its degree of financial leverage. The exact nature of this relationship for a given firm is difficult to

---

[10]An alternative presentation of indifference analysis relates EPS to EBIT. There is a relationship between sales and EBIT since these two values differ by fixed and variable costs. Therefore, the result based on sales can be transformed into one based on EBIT. For example, at sales of $160 000, EBIT is $24 000; that is, $160 000 − $40 000 (fixed costs) − $96 000 (variable costs). The indifference EPS must remain at $1.44.

Figure 18-5
Earnings per Share for Equity and Debt Financing

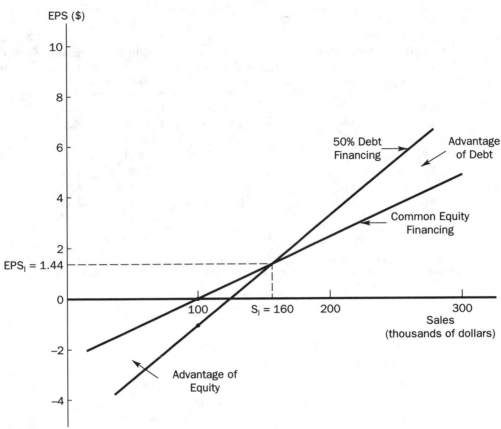

1. These values of the indifference level of sales, S_I and EPS_I, are the same as those obtained algebraically in Table 18-3. These relationships would be somewhat different if we did not assume that common shares can be repurchased at book value.

2. For those who like math, we can develop an equation to find the sales level at which EPS is the same under different degrees of financial leverage:

$$EPS_1 = \frac{S_{BE} - F - V - I_1}{Shares_1} = \frac{S_{BE} - F - V - I_2}{Shares_2} = EPS_2.$$

Here, EPS_1 and EPS_2 are the EPSs at two debt levels; S_{BE} is the sales breakeven (or indifference) level at which $EPS_1 = EPS_2$; I_1 and I_2 are interest charges at the two debt levels; $Shares_1$ and $Shares_2$ are shares outstanding at the two debt levels; F is the fixed costs; and V = variable costs = Sales × v, where v is the variable cost percentage. Solving for S_{SE}, we obtain this expression:

$$S_{BE} = \left(\frac{(Shares_2)(I_1) - (Shares_1)(I_2)}{Shares_2 - Shares_1} + F \right) \left(\frac{1}{1 - v} \right)$$

In our example,

$$S_{SB} = \left(\frac{(5000)(0) - (10\,000)(\$12\,000)}{-5000} + \$40\,000 \right) \left(\frac{1}{0.4} \right) = \$160\,000.$$

It should be noted that in our example we assume that the price at which shares are issued is $20, regardless of the amount of leverage employed.

Table 18-5
Share Price and Cost of Capital Estimates for Firm B with Different Debt-to-Assets Ratios

D/A (1)	k_d (2)	Expected EPS (and DPS)[a] (3)	Estimated Beta (4)	$k_s = [k_{RF} + b(k_M - k_{RF})]$[b] (5)	Implied Price[c] (6)	Resulting P/E Ratio (7)	Weighted Average Cost of Capital,[d] WACC (8)
0%	—	$2.40	1.50	12.0%	$20.00	8.33	12.00%
10	8.0%	2.56	1.55	12.2	20.98	8.20	11.46
20	8.3	2.75	1.65	12.6	21.83	7.94	11.08
30	9.0	2.97	1.80	13.2	22.50	7.58	10.86
40	10.0	3.20	2.00	14.0	22.86	7.14	10.80
50	12.0	3.36	2.30	15.2	22.11	6.58	11.20
60	15.0	3.30	2.70	16.8	19.64	5.95	12.12

[a]Firm B pays all of its earnings out as dividends, so EPS = DPS.
[b]We assume that $k_{RF} = 6\%$ and $k_M = 10\%$. Therefore, at D/A = 0, $k_s = 6\% + 1.5 (10\% - 6\%) = 6\% + 6\% = 12\%$.
Other values of k_s are calculated similarly.
[c]Since all earnings are paid out as dividends, no retained earnings will be ploughed back into the business, and growth in EPS and DPS will be zero. Hence, the zero growth model developed in Chapter 16 can be used to estimate the share price of Firm B's equity at D/A = 0:

$$P_0 = \frac{DPS}{k_s} = \frac{\$2.40}{0.12} = \$20.$$

Other prices were calculated similarly.
[d]Column 8 is found by use of the weighted average cost of capital equation developed in Chapter 17:

$$WACC = k_a = w_d k_d (1 - T) + w_s k_s = (D/A)(k_d)(1 - T) + (1 - D/A)k_s.$$

For example, at D/A = 40%,

$$k_a = 0.4(10\%)(0.6) + 0.6(14.0\%) = 10.80\%.$$

estimate, but the values given in column 4 are assumed to show the approximate nature of the relationship for Firm B.

Assuming that the risk-free rate of return, k_{RF}, is 6 percent and that the required rate on an average share, k_M, is 10 percent, we can use the CAPM equation to develop estimates of the required rates of return, k_s, for Firm B as shown in column 5. Here we see that k_s is 12.0 percent if no financial leverage is used, but that k_s rises to 16.8 percent if the company finances with 60 percent debt. The relationship of k_s with different levels of leverage reflects the influence of leverage on the beta of the equity of the firm.

The zero growth valuation model developed in Chapter 16 is used, with the column 3 values of DPS and the column 5 values of k_s, to develop the implied share prices shown in column 6. Here we see that the expected share price first rises with financial leverage, hits a peak of $22.86 at a debt-to-assets ratio of 40 percent, and then begins to decline. Thus, we can conclude that Firm B's optimal capital structure calls for 40 percent debt.

The price-to-earnings ratios shown in column 7 were calculated by dividing the implied price in column 6 by the expected earnings given in column 3. We use the pattern of P/E ratios as a check on the "reasonableness" of the other data. As a rule, P/E ratios should decline as the riskiness of a firm increases. Also, at the time the example was developed, the P/Es shown here were generally consistent with those of zero growth companies with varying amounts of financial leverage. Thus, the data in column 7 reinforce our confidence that the implied prices shown in column 6 are reasonable.

Finally, column 8 shows Firm B's weighted average cost of capital, k_a, calculated as described in Chapter 17, at the different capital structures. If the company uses zero debt, its capital is all equity; hence, WACC = k_s = 12%. As the firm begins to use debt, its weighted average cost of capital declines. However, as the debt ratio increases, the costs of both debt and equity rise, and the increasing costs of the two components begin to offset the fact that larger amounts of the debt component are being used. At 40 percent debt, WACC hits a minimum, and it rises after that as the debt ratio is increased.

The EPS, cost of capital, and share price data shown in Table 18-5 are plotted in Figure 18-6. As the graph shows, the debt-to-assets ratio that maximizes Firm B's expected EPS is 50 percent, but the cost of capital is minimized with 40 percent debt, and the expected share price is also maximized at a 40 percent debt ratio. Thus, the optimal capital structure calls for 40 percent debt and 60 percent equity. Management should set its target capital structure at these ratios, and, if the present ratios are off target, should move toward the target when new security offerings are made.

Concept Review

▶ Explain the following statement: "Using leverage has both good and bad effects."

▶ What does the EPS indifference point show? What occurs at sales below this point? What occurs at sales above this point?

▶ Is the optimal capital structure the one that maximizes expected EPS? Explain your answer.

Degree of Leverage

In our discussion of operating leverage in Chapter 6, we made no mention of financial leverage, and when we discussed financial leverage, operating leverage was assumed to be given. Actually, the two types of leverage are interrelated. For example, if Firm B *reduces* its degree of operating leverage, this will probably lead to an *increase* in its use of financial leverage. On the other hand, if it decides to use more operating leverage, its optimal capital structure will probably call for a lower debt ratio.

The theory of finance has not been developed to the point at which one can simultaneously determine the optimal levels of operating and financial leverage. However, we can gain a better understanding of how operating and financial leverage interact through an analysis of the *degree of leverage concept.*

Figure 18-6
Relationship between Firm B's Capital Structure
and Its EPS, Cost of Capital, and Share Price

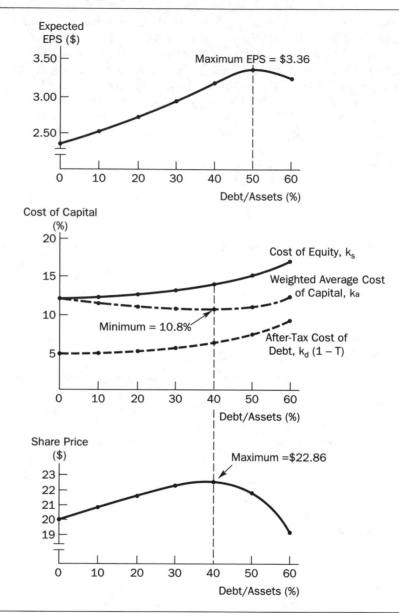

Degree of Operating Leverage (DOL)

The *degree of operating leverage (DOL)* is defined as the percentage change in operating income (or EBIT) associated with a given percentage change in sales volume:

$$DOL = \frac{\text{Percentage change in EBIT}}{\text{Percentage change in sales}} = \frac{\frac{\Delta EBIT}{EBIT}}{\frac{\Delta Q}{Q}}. \qquad \textbf{(18-1)}$$

In effect, the DOL is an index number that measures the effect of a change in sales from a given output level, Q, on operating income, or EBIT. DOL can be calculated by using Equation 18-2, which is derived from Equation 18-1:[11]

$$DOL_Q = \text{Degree of operating leverage at Point Q} = \frac{Q(P - V)}{Q(P - V) - F} \qquad \textbf{(18-2)}$$

or, based on dollar sales, rather than units,

$$DOL_S = \frac{S - VC}{S - VC - F}. \qquad \textbf{(18-2a)}$$

Here Q is units of output, P is the average sales price per unit of output, V is the variable cost per unit, F is fixed operating costs, S is sales in dollars, and VC is total variable cost. Equation 18-2 is normally used to analyze a single product, such as IBM's PC, whereas Equation 18-2a is used to evaluate an entire firm with many types of products, a situation in which "quantity in units" and "sales price" are not meaningful phrases.

Applying Equation 18-2a to data for Firm B at a sales level of $200 000, as shown in Table 18-3, we find its degree of operating leverage to be 2.0, so an x percent increase in sales will produce a 2x percent increase in EBIT:

$$DOL_{\$200\,000} = \frac{\$200\,000 - \$120\,000}{\$200\,000 - \$120\,000 - \$40\,000}$$

$$= \frac{\$80\,000}{\$40\,000} = 2.0.$$

---

[11]For those interested in proofs, Equation 18-2 is developed from 18-1 as follows. The change in units of output is defined as ΔQ. In equation form, EBIT = $Q(P - V) - F$, where Q is units sold, P is the price per unit, V is the variable cost per unit, and F is the total fixed cost. Since both price and fixed costs are constant, the change in EBIT is $\Delta EBIT = \Delta Q(P - V)$. The initial EBIT is $Q(P - V) - F$, so the percentage change in EBIT is

$$\%\,\Delta EBIT = \frac{\Delta Q(P - V)}{Q(P - V) - F}.$$

The percentage change in output is $\Delta Q/Q$, so the ratio of the percentage change in EBIT to the percentage change in output is

$$DOL = \frac{\frac{\Delta Q(P - V)}{Q(P - V) - F}}{\frac{\Delta Q}{Q}} = \left(\frac{\Delta Q(P - V)}{Q(P - V) - F}\right)\left(\frac{Q}{\Delta Q}\right) = \frac{Q(P - V)}{Q(P - V) - F}. \qquad \textbf{(18-2)}$$

For example, a 50 percent increase in sales, starting from sales of $200 000, will result in a 50%(2.0) = 100% increase in EBIT. This situation is confirmed by examining Part I of Table 18-3, where we see that a 50 percent increase in sales, from $200 000 to $300 000, causes EBIT to double. Notice also that the DOL is specific to the initial sales level; thus, if we evaluated the equation from a sales base of $300 000, there will be a different DOL.

$$DOL_{\$300\,000} = \frac{\$300\,000 - \$180\,000}{\$300\,000 - \$180\,000 - \$40\,000}$$

$$= \frac{\$120\,000}{\$80\,000} = 1.5.$$

In general, if a firm is operating close to its breakeven level, the degree of operating leverage will be high, but DOL declines the higher the base level of sales is above breakeven sales. Looking back at Part I of Table 18-3, we see that the company's breakeven point (before consideration of financial leverage) is at sales of $100 000. At that level, DOL is infinite:

$$DOL_{\$100\,000} = \frac{\$100\,000 - \$60\,000}{\$100\,000 - \$60\,000 - \$40\,000}$$

$$= \frac{\$40\,000}{0} = \text{undefined but} \approx \text{infinity}.$$

When evaluated at higher and higher sales levels, DOL progressively declines.

Degree of Financing Leverage (DFL)

Operating leverage affects earnings before interest and taxes (EBIT), whereas financial leverage affects earnings after interest and taxes, or the earnings available to common shareholders. In terms of Table 18-3, operating leverage affects Part I, whereas financial leverage affects Parts II and III. Thus, if Firm B decided to use more operating leverage, its fixed costs would be higher than $40 000, its variable cost ratio would be lower than 60 percent of sales, and its EBIT would be more sensitive to changes in sales. Financial leverage takes over where operating leverage leaves off, further magnifying the effect on earnings per share of a change in the level of sales. For this reason, operating leverage is sometimes referred to as *first-stage leverage* and financial leverage as *second-stage leverage*.

The *degree of financial leverage (DFL)* is defined as the percentage change in earnings per share that is associated with a given percentage change in earnings before interest and taxes (EBIT), and it may be calculated as follows:[12]

$$DFL = \frac{\% \, \Delta \, EPS}{\% \, \Delta \, EBIT}$$

$$= \frac{EBIT}{EBIT - I}. \qquad\qquad (18\text{-}3)$$

For Firm B at sales of $200 000 and an EBIT of $40 000, the degree of financial leverage with a 50 percent debt ratio is

$$\text{DFL}_{S \,=\, \$200\,000,\ D/A \,=\, 50\%} = \frac{\$40\,000}{\$40\,000 - \$12\,000}$$

$$= 1.43.$$

Therefore, a 100 percent increase in EBIT will result in a $100(1.43) = 143$ percent increase in earnings per share. This may be confirmed by reference to Part III of Table 18-3, where we see that a 100 percent increase in EBIT, from $40 000 to $80 000, produces a 143 percent increase in EPS.

$$\% \,\Delta\, \text{EPS} = \frac{\Delta\,\text{EPS}}{\text{EPS}_0} = \frac{\$8.16 - \$3.36}{\$3.36} = \frac{\$4.80}{\$3.36} = 1.43 = 143\%$$

If no debt is used, the degree of financial leverage is 1.0, so a 100 percent increase in EBIT will produce exactly a 100 percent increase in EPS. This can be confirmed from the data in Part II of Table 18-3.

Combining Operating and Financial Leverage: Degree of Total Leverage (DTL)

We have seen that the greater the degree of operating leverage (or fixed costs), the more sensitive EBIT is to changes in sales, and that the greater the degree

---

[12]Equation 18-3 is developed as follows:

1. Notice that $\text{EBIT} = Q(P - V) - F$.
2. Earnings per share (EPS) = $(\text{EBIT} - I)(1 - T)/N$, where EBIT is earnings before interest and taxes, I is interest paid, T is the corporate tax rate, and N is the number of shares outstanding.
3. I is a constant, so ΔEPS, the change in EPS, is

$$\Delta\text{EPS} = \frac{(\Delta\text{EBIT} - \Delta I)(1 - T)}{N} = \frac{\Delta\text{EBIT}(1 - T)}{N}.$$

4. The percentage change in EPS is the change in EPS over the original EPS:

$$\frac{\dfrac{\Delta\text{EBIT}(1 - T)}{N}}{\dfrac{(\text{EBIT} - I)(1 - T)}{N}} = \frac{\Delta\text{EBIT}}{\text{EBIT} - I}.$$

5. The degree of financial leverage is the percentage change in EPS over the percentage change in EBIT:

$$\text{Degree of financial leverage (DFL)} = \frac{\dfrac{\Delta\text{EBIT}}{\text{EBIT} - I}}{\dfrac{\Delta\text{EBIT}}{\text{EBIT}}} = \frac{\text{EBIT}}{\text{EBIT} - I}.$$

6. This equation must be modified if the firm has preferred shares outstanding.

of financial leverage, the more sensitive EPS is to changes in EBIT. Therefore, if a firm uses a considerable amount of both operating and financial leverage, even small changes in the level of sales will produce wide fluctuations in EPS.

Equation 18-2 for the degree of operating leverage can be combined with Equation 18-3 for the degree of financial leverage to produce the total leveraging effect, or the *degree of total leverage (DTL)*, which shows how a given change in sales will affect earnings per share. Here are three equivalent equations for DTL:[13]

$$DTL = \frac{Q(P - V)}{Q(P - V) - F - I}. \tag{18-4a}$$

$$DTL = \frac{S - VC}{S - VC - F - I}. \tag{18-4b}$$

$$DTL = DOL \times DFL. \tag{18-4c}$$

For firm B at sales of $200 000, the degree of total leverage, using 50 percent debt, is

$$\text{Degree of total leverage (DTL)} = \frac{\$200\,000 - \$120\,000}{\$200\,000 - \$120\,000 - \$40\,000 - \$12\,000}$$

$$= \frac{\$80\,000}{\$28\,000} = 2.86$$

$$\text{or DTL} = 2.00 \times 1.43 = 2.86.$$

We can also use the degree of total leverage (DTL) to find the new earnings per share (EPS$_1$) for any given percentage increase in sales (%Δ Sales), proceeding as follows:

---

[13]Equations 18-4a and 18-4b are developed as follows:

1. Recognize that EBIT = Q(P − V) − F; then rewrite Equation 18-3 as follows:

$$\frac{EBIT}{EBIT - I} = \frac{Q(P - V) - F}{Q(P - V) - F - I} = \frac{S - VC - F}{S - VC - F - I} \tag{18-3a}$$

2. The degree of total leverage is defined as the degree of operating leverage times the degree of financial leverage, or Equation 18-2 times Equation 18-3a:

Degree of total leverage = DOL × DFL   (18-4c)

$$DTL = (\text{Equation 18-2})(\text{Equation 18-3a})$$

$$= \left[\frac{Q(P - V)}{Q(P - V) - F} \right] \left[\frac{Q(P - V) - F}{Q(P - V) - F - I} \right]$$

$$= \frac{Q(P - V)}{Q(P - V) - F - I} \tag{18-4a}$$

$$= \frac{S - VC}{S - VC - F - I}. \tag{18-4b}$$

$$EPS_1 = EPS_0 + EPS_0[(DTL)(\% \Delta \text{ Sales})]$$

$$= EPS_0[1.0 + (DTL)(\% \Delta \text{ Sales})]. \qquad (18\text{-}5)$$

For example, a 50 percent (or 0.5) increase in sales, from \$200 000 to \$300 000, would cause EPS_0 (\$3.36 as shown in Part III of Table 18-3) to increase to \$8.16:

$$EPS_1 = \$3.36 [1.0 + (2.86)(0.5)]$$

$$= \$3.36(2.43)$$

$$= \$8.16.$$

This figure agrees with the one for EPS shown in Table 18-3.

The degree of leverage concept is useful primarily for the insights it provides regarding the joint effects of operating and financial leverage on earnings per share. The concept could be used to show the management of a business, for example, that a decision to automate a plant and to finance the new equipment with debt would result in a situation wherein a 10 percent decline in sales would produce a 50 percent decline in earnings, whereas with a different operating and financial leverage package a 10 percent sales decline would cause earnings to decline by only 20 percent. Having the alternatives stated in this manner might give the decision-makers a better idea of the ramifications of alternative actions.[14]

Concept Review

▶ Give the formula for calculating the degree of operating leverage (DOL), and explain what DOL is.

▶ Why is the DOL different at various sales levels?

▶ What is the value of the DOL at the company's breakeven point?

▶ Give the formula for calculating the degree of financial leverage (DFL), and explain what this calculation means.

▶ Give the formula for calculating the degree of total leverage (DTL), and explain what DTL is.

▶ Why is the degree of leverage concept useful?

---

[14]The degree of leverage concept is also useful for investors. If firms in an industry are classified as to their degrees of total leverage, an investor who is optimistic about prospects for the industry might favour those firms with high leverage, and vice versa if industry sales are expected to decline. However, it is very difficult to separate fixed from variable costs. Accounting statements simply do not make this breakdown, so the analyst must make the separation on a judgement basis. Note that costs are really fixed, variable, and "semivariable," for if times get tough enough, firms will sell off depreciable assets and thus reduce depreciation charges (a fixed cost), lay off "permanent" employees, reduce salaries of the remaining personnel, and so on. For this reason, the degree of leverage concept is generally more useful in explaining the general nature of the relationship than in developing precise numbers, and any numbers developed should be thought of as approximations rather than as exact specifications.

Liquidity and Cash Flow Analysis

There are some practical difficulties with the types of analyses described thus far in the chapter, including the following:

1. It is virtually impossible to determine exactly how either P/E ratios or equity capitalization rates (k_s values) are affected by different degrees of financial leverage. The best we can do is make educated guesses as to these relationships. Therefore, management rarely, if ever, has sufficient confidence in the type of analysis set forth in Table 18-3 and Figure 18-6 to use it as the sole determinant of the target capital structure.

2. Many firms are not publicly owned. If the owners do not plan to ever have the firm go public, then potential market value data may not be deemed to be important. However, (a) an analysis based on implied market values for a privately owned firm is useful if the owner is interested in knowing how the market value of the firm would be affected by leverage should the decision be made to go public, and (b) when the owner dies, the firm's market value must be determined in order to establish the capital gains tax liability.

3. The managers may be more or less "conservative" than the average shareholder and hence may set a somewhat different target capital structure than the one that would maximize the share price. The managers of a publicly owned firm would never admit this for, unless they owned voting control, they would quickly be removed from office. However, in view of the uncertainties about what constitutes the value-maximizing structure, managers can always say that the target capital structure employed is, in their judgement, the value-maximizing structure, and it is difficult to prove otherwise. Still, if management is far off target, especially on the low side, then chances are very high that some other firm or management group will effect a takeover, increase leverage, and thereby raise the value of the firm. This point is discussed in more detail later in the chapter.

4. Managers of large firms, especially those providing vital services such as natural gas distribution or telephone communications, have a responsibility to provide *continuous* service; therefore, they must refrain from using leverage to the point at which the firm's long-run viability is endangered. Long-run viability may conflict with short-run share price maximization.[15]

For all of these reasons, managers are very much concerned with the effects of financial leverage on the risk of bankruptcy, so an analysis of this factor is an

---

[15]Recognizing this fact, some regulatory commissions require utilities to obtain their approval before issuing long-term securities. However, in addition to concern over the firms' safety, which suggests low debt ratios, both managers and regulators recognize a need to keep all costs as low as possible, including the cost of capital. A firm's capital structure affects its cost of capital, so regulatory commissions and utility managers try to select capital structures that will minimize the cost of capital, subject to the constraint that the firm's solvency not be endangered. Under certain circumstances, regulatory authorities have used a capital structure that is different from the firm's actual capital structure to obtain the weights for the cost of capital calculation.

important input in all capital structure decisions. Accordingly, managements give considerable weight to such ratios as the *times-interest-earned (TIE) ratio*. The lower the ratio, the higher the probability that a firm will default on its debt and be forced into bankruptcy.

The tabular material in Figure 18-7 shows Firm B's expected TIE ratio at several debt-to-assets ratios. If the debt-to-assets ratio is only 10 percent, the expected TIE is a high 25 times, but the interest coverage ratio declines rapidly as the debt ratio is increased. Note, however, that these coverages are expected values at different debt ratios—the actual TIE will be higher if sales exceed the expected $200 000 level but lower if sales fall below $200 000.

The variability of the TIE ratio is highlighted in the graph in Figure 18-7, which shows the probability distributions of the TIEs at debt-to-assets ratios of 40 percent and 60 percent. The expected TIE is much higher if only 40 percent debt is used. (The relationship between actual companies' TIEs and debt ratios

Figure 18-7
Firm B: Probability Distributions of
Times-Interest-Earned Ratios with
Different Capital Structures

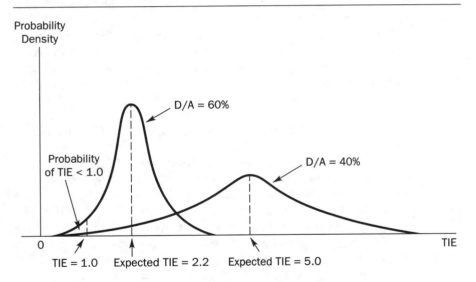

Debt-to-Assets Ratio	Expected TIE[a]
0%	Undefined
10	25.0
20	12.0
30	7.4
40	5.0
50	3.3
60	2.2

[a]TIE = EBIT/Interest. For example, when Debt/Assets = 50%, TIE = $40 000/$12 000 = 3.3. Data are from Tables 18-2 and 18-3.

will be examined later.) Even more important, with less debt, there is a much lower probability of a TIE of less than 1.0, the level at which the firm is not earning enough to meet its required interest payment and thus is seriously exposed to the threat of bankruptcy.[16]

Concept Review

▶ Why do managers give considerable weight to the TIE ratio when they make capital structure decisions? Why don't they just use the capital structure that maximizes the share price?

Capital Structure and Mergers

One of the most exciting developments in the financial world during the 1980s was the high level of merger activity, especially hostile takeovers. Although this activity was most prominent in the United States, it occurred in Canada and in all developed countries. This takeover activity has left as a legacy a large number of bankruptcies among the companies that engaged in it. In order to understand the current problems, we must first understand the rationale and mechanics of the takeover market.

Underlying the takeover activity was the belief that the target firm's shares were undervalued, so the acquiring company was willing to pay a significant premium over the prevailing market price in order to obtain control. The premiums ranged from 40 percent to 100 percent. For example, Kohlberg Kravis paid $106.00 per share in its leveraged buyout (LBO) of RJR Nabisco's shares; RJR's preannouncement price was $55.00. Campeau Corporation paid $73.50 per share for Federated Stores, whose share price was $32.87 before the announcement.

Very often the acquisitions were financed with substantial amounts of debt, the riskiest of which was raised in the form of "*junk bonds*," whose high interest rates included a substantial risk premium. However, the large increase in the debt ratio was not expected to remain in place over the long period. The target firms were frequently in mature industries with large and stable cash flows. This made the payment of large amounts of interest possible. In addition, the new managements usually engaged in restructuring of the target firms by streamlining operations, selling assets not used in the core business, and reducing investments. All of these changes were used to repay large amounts of debt in a short period of time. However, the new managers understood that debt brought a benefit in its tax treatment. In those companies that were successful

---

[16]Note that cash flows, which include depreciation, can be sufficient to cover required interest payments even though the TIE is less than 1.0. Thus, a firm can avoid bankruptcy, at least for a while, even though its operating income is less than its interest charges. Note also, though, that most firms' debt contracts stipulate that they must maintain the TIE ratio above some minimum level, say 2.0 or 2.5, or else they cannot borrow any additional funds, which severely constrains operations. This point, as much as the threat of actual bankruptcy, constrains the use of debt.

Finally, the actual TIE ratio for a company will reflect the interest payments made at interest rates established when the debt was issued. Thus, in a period of falling interest rates, the actual TIE ratio will fall over time as old debt is replaced by new, lower-cost issues.

in paying off their debt quickly, the resulting capital structure was more debt-intensive than it had been prior to the takeover.

There were also significant risks in these highly levered transactions. First, even though the firms involved were primarily in industries with relatively stable cash flows—such as broadcasting, foods, electronic equipment, and department stores—those cash flows were still sensitive to the state of the economy. In addition, some acquiring firms planned to sell assets that, under poor economic conditions, would not generate the expected cash flows and thus repayment of large debt would be delayed. At the end of the 1980s, the recession began, and cash flows from operations as well as from asset sales were reduced; this left many of the highly levered companies vulnerable since they could not make payments on their debt and were bankrupt. However, it is important to stress that not all of these transactions were unsuccessful. It appears that the problems occurred in companies for which the cash flows were less stable than expected, for which the price paid was very high, and for which the debt financing was substantial. For example, in the Campeau acquisition of Federated Stores, the financing of the takeover was accomplished with approximately 97 percent debt.

During the takeover period, the managements of firms with lower leverage ratios that did not want to be taken over reacted by attempting to find their optimal debt levels and then issuing debt and repurchasing equity. Thus they brought their firms' actual debt ratios up to the levels that would maximize the prices of their securities. This made these companies less attractive acquisition targets.

The bankruptcies observed in the early 1990s in some companies with high leverage do not negate the validity of the analyses described in this chapter. First, the high leverage ratios were not intended to be permanent but to facilitate the transactions and be paid off as soon as possible. Second, the industries in which these transactions occurred were, by and large, those in which a high target leverage ratio would be expected.

Concept Review

▶ Why does capital structure sometimes provide an incentive for one firm to take over another?

▶ Does the failure of many of the acquiring companies in highly leveraged transactions suggest that we can not identify an optimal capital structure?

Checklist for Capital Structure Decisions

In addition to the points discussed previously, firms that are making decisions about capital financing generally consider the following factors, which have an important, though difficult to measure, bearing on the optimal capital structure:

1. *Sales stability.* A firm whose sales are relatively stable can safely take on more debt and incur higher fixed charges than can a company with

unstable sales. An additional consideration is the probability of bankruptcy and its associated costs. As leverage ratios increase, the probability of bankruptcy increases. Bankruptcy is costly, and increases in leverage increase the expected value of bankruptcy costs (the sum of the probability of bankruptcy times the bankruptcy costs), which will have a depressing impact on the value of the firm. Financial managers, in attempting to maximize the market value of the firm, will choose the leverage rate that includes all factors, including the expected value of bankruptcy costs. Companies with very stable sales may have high bankruptcy costs; as the probability of bankruptcy is low, however, the *expected* costs of bankruptcy are low. Thus, these firms can handle high leverage ratios. For example, the stability of sales for regulated utilities—natural gas pipelines, gas distributors, telecommunications companies, and so on—has permitted these companies to make use of large amounts of debt and preferred shares.

2. *Competitive structure.*   Debt-servicing ability depends upon the profitability, as well as the volume, of sales. Hence, the stability of profit margins is as important as the stability of sales. The ease with which new firms can enter the industry and the ability of competing firms to expand capacity influence profit margins. A growth industry promises higher profit margins; such margins are likely to narrow, however, if the industry is one in which the number of firms can be easily increased through additional entry. For example, franchised fast food was a very profitable industry in the early 1960s, but it was relatively easy for new firms to enter this business and compete with older firms. As the industry matured during the late 1960s and early 1970s, the capacity of the old and the new firms grew at an increased rate. Consequently, profit margins declined.

   Other firms in other industries are better able to resist competitive pressures. For example, some firms have technical, service, and distribution facilities that are difficult to duplicate. This suggests that profit margins for these firms are less subject to erosion.

3. *Asset structure.*   Firms whose assets are suitable as security for loans tend to use debt rather heavily. Thus, firms with long-lived fixed assets, such as utilities, use long-term mortgage debt extensively. General-purpose assets, which can be used by many businesses and hence have a liquid market, make good collateral, whereas special-purpose assets do not. Thus, real estate companies tend to be heavily leveraged, but growth and high technology companies employ less debt.

4. *Operating leverage.*   Other things being equal, a firm with less operating leverage is better able to employ financial leverage because, as we have seen, the interaction of operating and financial leverage determines the overall impact of a decline in sales on operating income and net cash flows.

5. *Growth rate.*   Other things being the same, faster-growing firms must rely more heavily on external capital (see Chapter 5). Further, the issue costs involved in selling common equity exceed those incurred when selling debt. Thus, rapidly growing firms tend to use somewhat more debt than do slower-growth companies.

6. *Profitability.* One often observes that firms with very high rates of return on investment use relatively little debt. Although there is no theoretical justification for this fact, the practical reason seems to be that very profitable firms simply do not need to do much debt financing—their high rates of return enable them to do most of their financing with retained earnings.

7. *Taxes.* Interest is a tax-deductible expense, and deductions are most valued by firms with high tax rates. Hence, the higher a firm's corporate tax rate, the greater the advantage of using debt.

8. *Nondebt tax shield.* For some firms, substantial tax savings are generated by other forms of tax-deductible expenses, the obvious one being the capital cost allowance (CCA). Firms that are highly capital-intensive and have a high rate of growth in assets may already be sheltering substantial amounts of earnings. Hence, the impact of the tax savings from interest deductibility is small, which leads them to decide on a low ratio of debt to total capital.

9. *Control.* The effect that debt or equity financing might have on a management's control position may influence its capital structure decision. If management has voting control (more than 50 percent of the equity) but is not in a position to buy any more shares, it may choose debt for new financings. On the other hand, a management group that is not concerned about voting control may decide to use equity rather than debt if the firm's financial situation is so weak that the use of debt might subject the firm to serious risk of default because if the firm goes into default, the managers will almost surely lose their jobs. However, if too little debt is used, management runs the risk of a takeover. In general, control considerations do not necessarily suggest whether to use debt or equity because the type of capital financing that best protects management will vary from situation to situation. However, if management is at all insecure, the effects of capital structure on control will certainly be taken into account.

10. *Management attitudes.* In the absence of proof that one capital structure will lead to higher share prices than another, management can exercise its own judgement about a proper capital structure. Some managements tend to be more conservative than others and thus use less debt than the average firm in their industry; the reverse is true for other managements.

11. *Lender and rating agency attitudes.* Regardless of managers' own analyses of the proper leverage factors for their firms, there is no question that lenders' and rating agencies' attitudes frequently influence financial structure decisions. In the majority of cases, the corporation discusses its financial structure with lenders and rating agencies and gives much weight to their advice. But when management is so confident of the future that it seeks to use leverage beyond the norms for its industry, lenders may be unwilling to accept such debt increases or may do so only at a high price.

As we have observed, when the leverage ratio increases, the interest rate on debt increases to compensate the lender for the added risk. If bankruptcy is costly, the lenders will also require higher interest rates to cover the expected cost of bankruptcy. The lenders may decide that it is counterproductive to require progressively higher interest rates, as this will almost guarantee that the company becomes bankrupt. Therefore, lenders may impose a credit limit, which is equivalent to rationing credit.

12. *Market conditions.*   Conditions in the equity and bond markets undergo both long- and short-run changes that can have an important bearing on a firm's optimal capital structure. For example, during the credit crunch in the second half of 1982, there was simply no market at any "reasonable" interest rate for new long-term bonds rated below A. Therefore, low-rated companies that needed capital were forced to go to the equity market or to the short-term debt market, regardless of their target capital structure. When conditions eased, however, these companies were able to bring their capital structures back to their target levels.

13. *The firm's internal condition.*   A firm's own internal condition can also have a bearing on its target capital structure. For example, suppose a firm has just successfully completed a research and development (R&D) program and projects higher earnings in the immediate future, but the new earnings are not yet anticipated by investors and hence are not reflected in the price of the equity. This company would not want to issue shares. It would prefer to finance with debt until the higher earnings materialize and are reflected in the share price, at which time it could sell an issue of common equity, retire the debt, and return to its target capital structure.

14. *Financial flexibility.*   An astute corporate treasurer made this statement to the authors:

"Our company can earn a lot more money from good capital budgeting and operating decisions than from good financing decisions. Indeed, we are not sure exactly how financing decisions affect our stock price, but we do know that having to turn down a promising venture because funds are not available will reduce our long-run profitability. For this reason, my primary goal as treasurer is to always be in a position to raise the capital needed to support operations.

"We also know that when times are good, we can raise capital with either stocks or bonds, but when times are bad, suppliers of capital are much more willing to make funds available if they are given a secured position, and this means bonds. Further, when we sell a new issue of stock, this sends a negative signal to investors, so stock sales by a mature company such as ours are not generally desirable."

Putting these thoughts together gives rise to the goal of *maintaining financial flexibility*, which, from an operational viewpoint, means *maintaining adequate reserve borrowing capacity*. Determining an "adequate" reserve borrowing capacity is a matter of judgement, but it clearly depends on the factors mentioned previously in the chapter, including the firm's forecasted need for funds, predicted capital market conditions, management's confidence in its forecasts, and the consequences of a capital shortage.

Concept Review

▶ How does sales stability affect capital structure?
▶ How does asset structure affect capital structure?
▶ How does growth rate affect capital structure?
▶ How do tax considerations affect capital structure?
▶ How do lender and rating agency attitudes affect capital structure?
▶ How does the firm's internal condition affect capital structure?
▶ What is *financial flexibility*? Is it increased or decreased by having a high debt ratio?

Variations in Capital Structures among Firms

As might be expected from our discussion in this chapter, wide variations in the use of financial leverage occur among industries and even among firms within the same industry. Table 18-6 illustrates the first point. To interpret this table, we assume that the observations for 1990 are representative of the target capital structure for the average company in the industry. When we consider long-term sources of funds, we see that the communications industry has the most intensive use of long-term debt; its ratio of long-term debt to total long-term sources (debt and net equity) is 47 percent. The lowest value of this leverage ratio is found for department stores followed closely by chemicals (26 and 28 percent respectively). One important difference among these industries that leads to the different debt ratios is the debt capacity generated by the assets through the possibility of their use as collateral. In addition, the variability of cash flow is likely to be lower for the communications industry than the chemical industry, for example; this would also lead to a higher debt ratio for the communications industry.

Table 18-6
Capital Components as a Percentage of Total Capital, 1990
(firms with over $1 million in assets)

Industry	Current Liabilities	Long-Term Debt	Total Liabilities	Net Equity
Printing and publishing	38.0	25.1	63.1	36.9
Chemicals	33.3	18.4	51.7	48.3
Machinery	39.5	20.2	59.7	40.3
Communications	28.8	33.3	62.1	37.9
Retail—department stores	32.0	18.0	50.0	50.1

Source: Dun and Bradstreet Canada. "Industry Norms and Key Business Ratios."
Copyright 1992 Dun and Bradstreet Canada Limited. Reprinted by permission.

For short-term debt, all of the industries listed except communications make heavy use of current liabilities. This reflects the nature of the product or service provided by the industries. In the retail industry, inventories are financed by short-term debt, whereas in the communications industry, this reason for the use of short-term debt does not exist.

Summary

In this chapter we examined the effects of financial leverage on share prices, earnings per share, and the cost of capital. The key concepts covered are listed below:

- A firm's **optimal capital structure** is that mix of debt and equity which maximizes the price of the firm's shares. At any point in time, the firm's management has a specific **target capital structure** in mind, presumably the optimal one, although this target may change over time.
- Several factors influence a firm's capital structure decisions. These factors include (1) the firm's *business risk*, (2) its *tax position*, and (3) its need for *financial flexibility*.
- **Business risk** is the uncertainty associated with a firm's projections of its future returns on equity. A firm will tend to have low business risk if the demand for its products is stable, if the prices of its inputs and products remain relatively constant, if it can adjust its prices freely as its costs increase, and if a high percentage of its costs are variable and hence decrease as its output and sales decrease. Other things being the same, the lower a firm's business risk, the higher its optimal debt ratio.
- **Financial leverage** is the extent to which fixed-income securities (debt and preferred shares) are used in a firm's capital structure. **Financial risk** is the added risk to shareholders that results from financial leverage.
- The **EPS indifference point** is the level of sales at which EPS will be the same whether the firm uses debt or common equity financing. Equity financing will be better if the firm's sales end up below the EPS indifference point, whereas debt financing will be better at higher sales levels.
- The *degree of operating leverage (DOL)* shows how changes in sales affect operating income, whereas the *degree of financial leverage (DFL)* shows how changes in operating income affect earnings per share. The *degree of total leverage (DTL)* shows the percentage change in EPS resulting from a given percentage change in sales: DTL = DOL × DFL.

Although it is theoretically possible to determine the optimal capital structure, as a practical matter we cannot estimate this structure with precision. Accordingly, financial executives generally treat the optimal structure as a range—for example, 40 to 50 percent debt—rather than as a precise point, such as 45 percent. The concepts discussed in this chapter help managers understand the factors they should consider when they set the optimal capital structure ranges for their firms.

Questions

 18-1 "One type of leverage affects both EBIT and EPS. The other type affects only EPS." Explain what this statement means.

18-2 What is the relationship between market (or beta) risk and leverage?

18-3 Explain why the following statement is true: "Other things being the same, firms with relatively stable sales are able to carry relatively high debt ratios."

18-4 Why do public utility companies usually pursue a financial policy different from that of retail firms?

18-5 Why is EBIT generally considered to be independent of financial leverage? Why might EBIT actually be influenced by financial leverage at high debt levels?

18-6 If a firm went from zero debt to successively higher levels of debt, why would you expect its share price first to rise, then to hit a peak, and then to begin to decline?

18-7 Why is the debt level that maximizes a firm's expected EPS generally higher than the debt level that maximizes its share price?

18-8 Assume that you are advising the management of a firm that is about to double its assets to serve its rapidly growing market. It must choose between a highly automated production process and a less automated one, and it must also choose a capital structure for financing the expansion. Should the asset investment and financing decisions be jointly determined, or should each decision be made separately? How would these decisions affect one another? How could the degree of leverage concept be used to help management analyze the situation?

18-9 Your firm's R&D department has been working on a new process that, if it works, can produce oil from coal at a cost of about $5 per barrel versus a current market price of $20 per barrel. The company needs $10 million of external funds at this time to complete the research. The results of the research will be known in about a year, and there is about a 50:50 chance of success. If the research is successful, your company will need to raise a substantial amount of new money to put the idea into production. Your economists forecast that although the economy will be depressed next year, interest rates will be high because of international monetary problems. You must recommend how the currently needed $10 million should be raised—as debt or as equity. How would the potential impact of the project influence your decision?

Self-Test Problems   (solutions appear on page 689)

ST-1 **Key terms.**   Define each of the following terms:
    a. Target capital structure; optimal capital structure; target range
    b. Business risk; financial risk
    c. Financial leverage; total leverage
    d. EPS indifference point
    e. Degree of operating leverage (DOL)
    f. Degree of financial leverage (DFL)
    g. Degree of total leverage (DTL)
    h. Times-interest-earned (TIE) ratio

ST-2   Financial leverage.   Jog Motors, Ltd., a producer of turbine generators, is in this situation:

EBIT = $4 million.
Tax rate = T = 35%.
Debt outstanding = D = $2 million.
k_d = 10%.
k_s = 15%.
Shares outstanding = N_0 = 600 000.
Book value per share = $10.

Jog's product market is stable, and it expects no growth, so all earnings
are paid out as dividends. The debt consists of perpetual bonds.

a. What are Jog's earnings per share (EPS) and its price per share
(P_0)?

b. What is Jog's weighted average cost of capital (WACC)?

c. Jog can increase its debt by $8 million, to a total of $10 million, using
the new debt to buy back and retire some of its shares at the current
price. Its interest rate on debt will be 12 percent (it will have to call
and refund the old debt), and its cost of equity will rise from
15 percent to 17 percent. EBIT will remain constant. Should Jog
change its capital structure?

d. If Jog did not have to refund the $2 million of old debt, how would
this affect things? Assume the new and the still outstanding debt
are equally risky, with k_d = 12 percent, but the coupon rate on the
old debt is 10 percent.

e. What is Jog's TIE coverage ratio under the original situation and
under the conditions in Part c?

Problems

 Risk analysis.

a. Given the following information, calculate the expected value for
Firm C's EPS: EPS_A = $5.10, and σ_A = $3.61; EPS_B = $4.20, and σ_B =
$2.96; and σ_C = $4.11.

	Probability				
	0.1	**0.2**	**0.4**	**0.2**	**0.1**
Firm A: EPS_A	($1.50)	$1.80	$5.10	$8.40	$11.70
Firm B: EPS_B	(1.20)	1.50	4.20	6.90	9.60
Firm C: EPS_C	(2.40)	1.35	5.10	8.85	12.60

b. Discuss the relative riskiness of the earnings of the three firms (A,
B, and C).

18-2 **Financial leverage effects.**   Firms HL and LL are identical except for
their leverage ratios and interest rate on debt. Each has $20 million in
assets, each earned $4 million before interest and taxes in 1992, and

each has a 40 percent corporate tax rate. Firm HL, however, has a leverage ratio (D/A) of 50 percent and pays 12 percent interest on its debt, while Firm LL has a 30 percent leverage ratio and pays only 10 percent interest on debt.

a. Calculate the rate of return on equity (net income/equity) for each firm.

b. Observing that HL has a higher return on equity, LL's treasurer decides to raise the leverage ratio from 30 to 60 percent, which will increase Firm LL's interest rate on debt to 15 percent. Calculate the new rate of return on equity for LL.

18-3 **Effects of financial leverage on ROE.** Tanner Company Ltd. wishes to calculate next year's return on equity under different leverage ratios. Tanner's total assets are $14 million, and its average tax rate is 40 percent. The company is able to estimate next year's earnings for three possible states of the world. It estimates that 1993 earnings before interest and taxes will be $4.2 million with a 0.2 probability, $2.8 million with a 0.5 probability, and $700 000 with a 0.3 probability. Calculate Tanner's expected return on equity, the standard deviation, and the coefficient of variation for each of the following leverage ratios, and evaluate the results.

Leverage (Debt/Total Assets)	Interest Rate
0%	—
10	9%
50	11
60	14

18-4 The Nordlund Company plans to raise a net amount of $270 million to finance new equipment and working capital. Two alternatives are being considered: common equity may be sold to net $60 per share, or debentures yielding 12 percent may be issued. The balance sheet and income statement of the Nordlund Company prior to financing are as follows:

The Nordlund Company
Balance Sheet as of December 31, 1993
(millions of dollars)

Current assets	$ 900.00	Accounts payable	$ 172.50
Net fixed assets	450.00	Notes payable to bank	255.00
		Other current liabilities	225.00
		Total current liabilities	$ 652.50
		Long-term debt (10%)	300.00
		Common equity	60.00
		Retained earnings	337.50
Total assets	$1350.00	Total claims	$1350.00

**The Nordlund Company
Income Statement for Year Ended
December 31, 1993
(millions of dollars)**

Sales	$2475.00
Earnings before interest and taxes (10%)	247.50
Interest on short-term debt	(15.00)
Interest on long-term debt	(30.00)
Earnings before taxes	202.50
Tax (40%)	(81.00)
Net income after tax	$ 121.50

The probability distribution for annual sales is as follows:

Annual Sales	Probability
$2250	0.30
2700	0.40
3150	0.30

a. Assuming that EBIT is equal to 10 percent of sales, calculate earnings per share under both the equity financing and the debt financing alternatives at each possible level of sales.

b. Calculate expected earnings per share and σ_{EPS} under both debt and equity financing.

c. Calculate the debt ratio and the times-interest-earned (TIE) ratio at the expected sales level under each alternative. The old debt will remain outstanding.

d. Which financing method do you recommend?

18-5 **Operating leverage effects.**   Drake Corporation will begin operations next year to produce a single product at a price of $12 per unit. Drake has a choice of two methods of production: Method A, with variable costs of $6.75 per unit and fixed operating costs of $675 000; and Method B, with variable costs of $8.25 per unit and fixed operating costs of $401 250. To support operations under either production method, the firm requires $2 250 000 in assets, and it has established a debt ratio of 40 percent. The cost of debt is $k_d = 10$ percent. The tax rate is irrelevant for the problem, and fixed *operating* costs do not include interest.

a. The sales forecast for the coming year is 200 000 units. Under which method would EBIT be most adversely affected if sales did not reach the expected levels? (Hint: Compare DOLs under the two production methods.)

b. Given the firm's present debt, which method would produce the greatest percentage increase in earnings per share for a given increase in EBIT? (Hint: Compare DFLs under the two methods.)

c. Calculate DTL under each method, and then evaluate the firm's total risk under each method.

d. Is there some debt ratio under Method A that would produce the same DTL_A as the DTL_B that you calculated in Part c? (Hint: Let $DTL_A = DTL_B$ as calculated in Part c, solve for I, and then determine the amount of debt that is consistent with this level of I. Conceivably, debt could be *negative*, which implies holding liquid assets rather than borrowing. Also, you should have found $DTL_B = 2.90$ in Part c.)

18-6 **Degree of leverage.** Astrocom Corporation supplies headphones to airlines for use with movie and stereo programs. The headphones sell for $288 per set, and this year's sales are expected to be 45 000 units. Variable production costs for the expected sales under present production methods are estimated at $10 200 000, and fixed production (operating) costs at present are $1 560 000. Astrocom has $4 800 000 of debt outstanding at an interest rate of 8 percent. There are 240 000 shares of common equity outstanding; there are no preferred shares. The dividend payout ratio is 70 percent, and the tax rate is 40 percent.

The company is considering investing $7 200 000 in new equipment. Sales would not increase, but variable costs per unit would decline by 20 percent. Also, fixed operating costs would increase from $1 560 000 to $1 800 000. Astrocom could raise the required capital by borrowing $7 200 000 at 10 percent or by selling 240 000 additional shares at $30 per share.

a. What would be Astrocom's EPS (i) under the old production process, (ii) under the new process if it uses debt financing, and (iii) under the new process if it uses common shares?

b. Calculate DOL, DFL, and DTL under the existing setup and under the new setup with each type of financing. Assume that the expected sales level is 45 000 units, or $12 960 000.

c. At what unit sales level would Astrocom have the same EPS, assuming it undertakes the investment and finances it with debt or with equity? (Hint: V = variable cost per unit = $8 160 000/45 000, and EPS = [(PQ − VQ − F − I)(1 − T)]/N. Set $EPS_{Stock} = EPS_{Debt}$ and solve for Q.)

d. At what unit sales level would EPS = 0 under each of the three production-financing setups—that is, under the old plan, the new plan with debt financing, and the new plan with equity financing? (Hint: Note that $V_{old} = $10 200 000/45 000$, and use the hints for Part c, setting the EPS equation equal to zero.)

e. Given your analysis in Parts a through d, which plan is the riskiest, which has the highest expected EPS, and which would you recommend? Assume here that there is a fairly high probability of sales falling as low as 25 000 units, and determine EPS_{Debt} and EPS_{Stock} at that sales level to help assess the riskiness of the two financing plans.

Integrative Problem

18-7 **Optimal capital structure.** Assume that you have just been hired as night manager of Campus Deli and Sub Shop (CDSS), which is located adjacent to the campus. Last year sales were $700 000, variable costs were 60 percent of sales, and fixed costs were $40 000. Therefore, EBIT totalled $240 000. Because the university's enrolment is steady, EBIT is expected to be constant over time. Since no expansion capital is required, CDSS pays out all earnings as dividends.

CDSS is currently all equity financed, and its 80 000 shares outstanding sell at a price of $10 per share. The firm's tax rate is 34 percent. On the basis of discussions in your finance course, you believe that the firm's shareholders would be better off if some debt financing were used. When you suggested this to the principal shareholder, who is also your uncle, you were encouraged to pursue the idea but asked to provide justification for the suggestion.

You, along with your finance professor, have developed the following estimates of the costs of debt and equity at different debt levels (in thousands of dollars):

Amount Borrowed	k_d	k_s
$ 0	—	15.0%
160	10.0%	15.5
320	11.0	16.5
400	13.0	18.0
480	16.0	20.0

If the firm were recapitalized, the borrowed funds would be used to repurchase equity. Shareholders, in turn, would use funds provided by the repurchase to buy equities in other fast food companies similar to CDSS. You plan to conduct your analysis by asking and then answering the following questions.

a. What is *business risk*? What factors affect the amount of business risk inherent in a firm?

b. What is meant by the term *financial leverage*? What is *financial risk*? How does financial risk differ from business risk?

c. Consider two hypothetical firms, Firm U, with zero debt financing, and Firm L, with $8000 of 12 percent debt. Both firms have $16 000 in total assets and a 40 percent tax rate, and they face the following EBIT distribution for next year:

Probability	EBIT
0.25	$1600
0.50	2400
0.25	3200

    i. Construct partial income statements for the two firms at each level of EBIT.

    ii. Now calculate the ratio of EBIT to total assets and the ROE for each firm at each EBIT level.

    iii. What does this example illustrate concerning the impact of financial leverage on expected return and risk?

d. With the preceding points in mind, you now begin to consider the optimal capital structure for CDSS.

    i. Define the term *optimal capital structure.*

    ii. Describe briefly, without using numbers, the sequence of events that will occur if CDSS recapitalizes.

    iii. Calculate CDSS's expected EPS at debt levels of \$0, \$160 000, \$320 000, \$400 000, and \$480 000. How many shares would remain after recapitalization under each scenario? Assume that shares could be repurchased at the current market price of \$10 per share. Is a \$10 repurchase price reasonable?

    iv. What would be the new share price if CDSS recapitalizes at \$160 000 of debt? \$320 000? \$400 000? \$480 000?

    v. Considering only the levels of debt discussed, what is CDSS's optimal capital structure?

    vi. Is EPS maximized at the debt level that maximizes share price?

  e. **i.** What is meant by the *degree of operating leverage*? If CDSS's fixed cost total \$40 000, what is its degree of operating leverage?

    ii. What is the *degree of financial leverage*? What would be CDSS's degree of financial leverage if it increased its debt to the optimal level of \$400 000?

    iii. What is the *degree of total leverage*? What would be CDSS's degree of total leverage with EBIT of \$240 000 and \$400 000 of debt?

  f. What are some factors managers should consider when determining the optimal capital structures for their firms?

Solutions to Self-Test Problems

ST-1   Refer to the appropriate sections of the text to check your responses.

ST-2 **a.**

EBIT	\$4 000 000
Interest (\$2 000 000 × 0.10)	200 000
Net income before taxes	\$3 800 000
Taxes (35%)	1 330 000
Net income after taxes	\$2 470 000

$$\text{EPS} = \$2\,470\,000/600\,000 = \$4.12.$$
$$P_0 = \$4.12/0.15 = \$27.47.$$

  b.

Equity   = 600 000 × \$10 = \$6 000 000.
Debt   = \$2 000 000.
Total Capital = \$8 000 000.
WACC   = $w_d k_d (1 - T) + w_s k_s$
          = (2/8)(10%)(1 − 0.35) + (6/8)(15%)
          = 1.63% + 11.25%
          = 12.88%.

  c.

EBIT	\$4 000 000
Interest (\$10 000 000 × 0.12)	1 200 000
Net income before taxes	\$2 800 000
Taxes (35%)	980 000
Net income after taxes	\$1 820 000

Shares bought and retired:

$$\Delta N = \Delta Debt/P_0 = \$8\,000\,000/\$27.47 = \$291\,227.$$

New outstanding shares:

$$N_1 = N_0 - \Delta N = 600\,000 - 291\,227 = 308\,773.$$

New EPS:

$$EPS = \$1\,820\,000/308\,773 = \$5.89.$$

New price per share:

$$P_0 = \$5.89/0.17 = \$34.65 \text{ versus } \$27.47.$$

Therefore, Jog Motors should change its capital structure.

d. In this case, the company's net income after taxes would be higher by $(0.12 - 0.10)(\$2\,000\,000)(1 - 0.35) = \$26\,000$, because its interest charges would be lower. The new price would be

$$P_0 = \frac{(\$1\,820\,000 + \$26\,000)/308\,773}{0.17} = \$35.18.$$

In the first case, in which the debt had to be refunded, the bondholders were compensated for the increased risk of the higher debt position. In the second case, the old bondholders were not compensated; their 10 percent coupon perpetual bonds would now be worth

$$\$100/0.12 = \$833.33,$$

or $\$1\,666\,667$ in total, down from the old $2 million, or a loss of $\$333\,333$. The shareholders would have a gain of

$$(\$35.18 - \$35.65)(308\,773) = \$163\,650.$$

This gain would, of course, be at the expense of the old bondholders. (There is no reason to think that bondholders' losses would exactly offset shareholders' gains.)

e.
$$TIE = \frac{EBIT}{I}.$$

$$\text{Original TIE} = \frac{\$4\,000\,000}{\$200\,000} = 20 \text{ times.}$$

$$\text{New TIE} = \frac{\$4\,000\,000}{\$1\,200\,000} = 3.33 \text{ times.}$$

Appendix 18A
Capital Structure Theory

Modern capital structure theory began in 1958, when Professors Franco Modigliani and Merton Miller (hereafter MM) published what has been called the most influential finance article ever written.[17] MM proved, under a very restrictive set of assumptions, that because of the tax deductibility of interest on debt, a firm's value rises continuously as it uses more debt, and hence its value will be maximized by financing almost entirely with debt. MM's assumptions included the following:

1. There are no brokerage costs.
2. There are no personal taxes.
3. Investors can borrow at the same rate as corporations.
4. Investors have the same information as management about the firm's future investment opportunities.
5. All the firm's debt is riskless, regardless of how much debt it uses.
6. EBIT is not affected by the use of debt.

Since several of these assumptions were obviously unrealistic, MM's position was only a beginning.

Subsequent researchers and MM themselves extended the basic theory by relaxing the assumptions. Other researchers attempted to test the various theoretical models with empirical data to see exactly how share prices and capital costs are affected by capital structure. Both the theoretical and the empirical results have added to our understanding of capital structure, but none of these studies has produced results that can be used to precisely identify a firm's optimal capital structure. A summary of the theoretical and empirical research to date is expressed graphically in Figure 18A-1. Here are the key points about the figure:

1. The fact that interest is a tax-deductible expense makes debt less expensive than common or preferred shares. In effect, the government pays part of the cost of debt capital, or, to put it another way, debt provides tax shelter benefits. As a result, more of the firm's operating income (EBIT) flows through to investors, so the more debt a company uses, the higher its value and the higher the price of its shares. Under the assumptions of the original paper, Modigliani and Miller concluded that the firm's share price will be maximized if it uses virtually 100 percent debt; the line labelled "Pure MM Result" in Figure 18A-1 expresses this relationship between share prices and debt.
2. The MM assumptions do not hold in the real world. First, interest rates rise as the debt ratio rises. Second, EBIT declines at extreme levels of leverage. Third, expected tax rates fall, thus reducing the value of the debt tax shelter. And, fourth, the probability of bankruptcy, which brings with it lawyers' fees and other costs, increases as the debt ratio rises.

---

[17]Franco Modigliani and Merton H. Miller, "The Cost of Capital, Corporation Finance, and the Theory of Investment," *American Economic Review*, June 1958.

Figure 18A-1
Effect of Leverage on the Value of Firm B's Equity

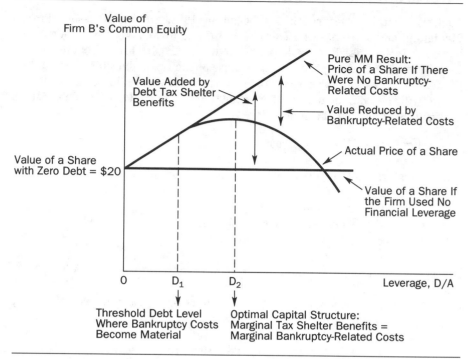

3. At low levels of leverage, there is a low probability of bankruptcy; hence, the influence of bankruptcy costs is minimal. The important influence is not just bankruptcy costs that would occur in the event of a bankruptcy but also the probability of a bankruptcy. The product of bankruptcy costs and the probability of bankruptcy result in *expected bankruptcy costs*. For a given firm, bankruptcy costs are independent of leverage, but the probability of bankruptcy and thus the expected bankruptcy costs increase with an increase in the ratio of debt to equity. Bankruptcy costs include loss of customers and hence reduction of net operating income. Also, money that would have been used to pay the claims of bondholders is given to nonfinancial claimants such as lawyers and trustees. The present value of the *expected* bankruptcy costs reduces the value of the levered firm and the price per share below what it would have been in the absence of these costs. As the amount of leverage increases, there is a higher probability of bankruptcy and a higher value of expected bankruptcy costs. Deducting the expected bankruptcy costs from the value of the leveraged firm in which there was costless bankruptcy will result in a reduction in the value of the leveraged firm and the price per share.

4. There is some threshold level of debt, labelled D_1 in Figure 18A-1, below which the effects noted in Point 3 are immaterial. Beyond D_1, however, the expected bankruptcy-related costs become increasingly important, and they reduce the tax benefits of debt at an increasing rate. In the

range from D_1 to D_2, expected bankruptcy-related costs reduce but do not completely offset the tax benefits of debt, so the firm's share price rises (but at a decreasing rate) as the debt ratio increases. However, beyond D_2 expected bankruptcy-related costs exceed the tax benefits, so from this point on increasing the debt ratio lowers the share value. Therefore, D_2 denotes the optimal capital structure.

5. Both theory and empirical evidence support the preceding discussion. However, statistical problems prevent researchers from identifying points D_1 and D_2, either for firms in general or for any given firm.

6. Although theoretical and empirical work supports the general shape of the curves in Figures 18-6 and 18A-1, these graphs must be taken as approximations, not as precisely defined functions. The numbers in Figure 18-6 are shown to one and two decimal places, but that is merely for illustrative purposes—the numbers are not nearly that accurate since the data with which the graph was constructed are judgement-based estimates.

Asymmetric Informational Effects

MM assumed that investors have the same information about a firm's prospects as its managers—that there is *symmetric information*. However, we know that in fact managers often have better information about their firms than do outside investors. The existence of such *asymmetric information* has an important effect on the optimal capital structure. To see why, consider two situations, one in which the company's prospects are extremely favourable (Firm F) and one in which they are very unfavourable (Firm U). Suppose, for example, that Firm F's R&D labs have just discovered a cure for the common cold that cannot be patented. Firm F's managers want to keep the new product a secret for as long as possible to delay competitors' entry into the market. New plants and distribution facilities must be built to exploit the new product, so capital must be raised. How should Firm F raise this capital? If the firm sells equity, then, when profits from the new product start flowing in (really, when the new product is announced), the share price will rise sharply, and the purchasers of the new shares will have made a bonanza. The current shareholders (including the managers) will also do well, but not as well as they would have done if the company had not sold shares before the price increased, because then they would not have had to share the benefits of the new product with new shareholders. Therefore, one would expect a firm with very favourable prospects to try to avoid selling equity and, rather, to attempt to raise any required new capital by other means, including using debt beyond the normal target capital structure. (Note: It would be illegal for Firm F's managers to purchase more shares on the basis of their inside knowledge of the new product. They could be sent to jail if they did.)

Now let's consider Firm U. Suppose its managers have information that new orders are off sharply because a competitor has installed new technology that has improved its products' quality. Firm U must upgrade its own facilities, at a high cost, just to maintain its recent sales level. As a result, its return on investment will fall (but not by as much as if it took no action, which would lead to a 100 percent loss through bankruptcy). How should Firm U raise the needed capital? Here the situation is just the reverse of that facing Firm F, which did not want to sell equity so as to avoid having to share the benefits of future developments. A firm with unfavourable prospects should sell equity, which would mean bringing in new investors to share the losses![18]

The conclusions from all this are that firms with extremely bright prospects prefer not to finance through new common equity offerings, whereas firms with poor prospects do like to finance with outside equity. How should you, as an investor, react to this conclusion? You ought to say, "If I see that a company plans to issue new equity, this should worry me, because I know that management would not want to issue common equity if future prospects looked good, but it would want to issue equity if things looked bad. Therefore, I will lower my estimate of the firm's value, other things held constant, if I read an announcement of a new equity offering. Of course, my negative reaction would be stronger if the sale of new common equity was by a large, established company that surely has many financing options, than if it was by a small company. For the latter company, a new equity issue might mean truly extraordinary investment opportunities that were so large that they just could not be financed without an equity issue."

If you gave that answer, your views are completely consistent with those of sophisticated portfolio managers of major institutions. So, in a nutshell, the announcement of an equity offering by a mature firm that seems to have financing alternatives is taken as a signal that the firm's prospects as seen by its management are not bright. This, in turn, suggests that when a mature firm announces a new equity offering, its share price will decline. Empirical studies have shown that this situation does indeed exist.[19]

What are the implications of all this for capital structure decisions? The answer is that firms should, in normal times, maintain a *reserve borrowing capacity* which can be used in the event that some especially good investment opportunities come along. This means that firms should, in normal times, carry less debt than would be suggested by the tax-benefit–bankruptcy-cost tradeoff expressed in Figure 18A-1.

The concepts of signalling and asymmetric information also have implications for the marginal cost of capital (MCC) curve as discussed in Chapter 17. There we saw that the weighted average cost of capital (WACC) jumps when retained earnings are exhausted and the firm is forced to sell new common shares to raise equity. The jump in the WACC, or the break in the MCC schedule, was attributed in Chapter 17 only to issue costs. However, if the announcement of an equity issue causes a decline in the share price, then k_s as measured by $k_s = D_1/P_0 + g$ will rise because of the decline in P_0. This factor reinforces the effects of issue costs; perhaps it is an even more important explanation for the break in the MCC schedule at the point at which new equity must be issued. For example, suppose that $P_0 = \$10$, $D_1 = \$1$, $g = 5\%$, and

---

[18]Of course, Firm U would have to make certain disclosures when it offered new shares to the public, but it could probably meet the legal requirements without fully disclosing management's worst fears.

[19]Paul Asquith and David W. Mullins, Jr., "The Impact of Initiating Dividend Payments on Shareholders' Wealth," *Journal of Business*, January 1983: 77–96.

F = 10%. Therefore, $k_s = 10\% + 5\% = 15\%$, and k_e, the cost of external equity, is 16.1 percent:

$$k_e = \frac{D_1}{P_0(1 - F)} + g = \frac{\$1}{\$10(1.0 - 0.10)} + 5\% = 16.1\%.$$

Suppose, however, that the announcement of the share issue causes the market price to fall from $P_0 = \$10$ to $P_0 = \$8$. This will produce an increase in the costs of both retained earnings (k_s) and external equity:

$$k_s = \frac{D_1}{P_0} + g = \frac{\$1}{\$8} + 5\% = 17.5\%.$$

$$k_e = \frac{D_1}{P_0(1 - F)} + g = \frac{\$1}{\$8(0.9)} + 5\% = 18.9\%.$$

This will, of course, have further implications for capital budgeting. Specifically, it will make it even more difficult for a marginal project to show a positive NPV (or IRR > WACC) if the project requires the firm to sell common equity to raise capital.

Free Cash Flow

It is frequently the case that mature companies have annual cash flows that are relatively stable and exceed the amount of investment indicated by their capital budgeting analysis. This excess, called *free cash flow (FCF)* in the finance literature, can be distributed to the common shareholders as dividends, held in the company as cash or marketable securities awaiting good investment projects, or invested in projects for which the net present value is negative. If management is interested in maximizing shareholder wealth, the second and third choices are not appropriate. Although these choices may benefit managers who want to manage a large firm or have pools of marketable securities available to make discretionary investments, they leave the shareholders worse off. Thus, if significant amounts of funds are left in the firm, the share price may fall, reflecting expectations of this suboptimal behaviour.

To avoid this price impact on share price, managers must make a credible promise to pay out free cash flow to the shareholders rather than to keep it in the firm. One way of achieving this is to promise to pay out the funds as dividends, but since dividend payments are only a promise and not a binding commitment, management may not be believed by shareholders. An alternative method of handling a free cash flow is to increase the debt ratio and pay out the FCF as interest payments. Unlike dividends, interest payments are enforceable since nonpayment will result in default. Thus, by increasing the debt ratio, the share price will increase, reflecting removal of the expectation that management will make suboptimal use of the free cash flow. Note that this increase in share price is independent of the tax effect.

The implication of the free cash flow argument is that mature firms with cash flows that are stable and large relative to their investment opportunities should have a high debt ratio. This will eliminate any discount in the share price reflecting the potential of suboptimal investment decisions by management.

Conclusion

If you find the discussion of capital structure theory somewhat confusing or at least imprecise, you are not alone. In truth, no one knows how to identify precisely the optimal capital structure for a firm or how to measure precisely the effect of the firm's capital structure on either its value or its cost of capital. In real life, capital structure decisions must be made more on the basis of judgement than numerical analysis. Still, an understanding of the theoretical issues as presented in this appendix is essential to making sound judgements on capital structure issues.

19

Dividend Policy

The beginning of the 1990s brought a recession and an end to the high growth in earnings and dividends per share. Companies had to rethink their dividend policy. Many introduced dividend decreases or even stopped payment of dividends entirely. For example, a number of companies that were part of the Bronfman group—Carena Developments, Trizec, Bramalea, and Royal Trustco Ltd.—reduced their dividends in July 1992. The reaction as summed up by one financial analyst was: "Companies that cut dividends to live within their means are viewed by investors as sensible."

In this chapter, we discuss dividend policy in theory and practice and the factors that influence it. The object is to clarify why some companies retain all of their earnings while others pay out most of their earnings as dividends and to make students aware of the effects of these choices on equity prices.

We begin with a general discussion of dividend policy and some important institutional background on dividend payment procedures, then examine factors that affect the optimal dividend policy, and conclude with a discussion of share repurchases as an alternative to cash dividends.

Dividend Payments and Procedures

Dividend policy determines the division of earnings between payments to shareholders and reinvestment in the firm. Retained earnings are one of the most significant sources of funds for financing corporate growth, but dividends constitute the cash flows that accrue to shareholders. Although both growth and dividends are desirable, these two goals can be in conflict. For example, suppose a firm limits its investment budget in a given year to the amount of retained earnings for that year. An increase in the dividend **payout ratio**—the percentage of earnings paid out as dividends—will result in lower retained earnings and hence a reduced amount of investment. In this instance, dividend policy is equivalent to investment policy, and by reducing the amount of retained earnings, the firm may be forced to reject profitable investment opportunities. A more reasonable approach is for the firm to determine its investment budget in advance. The dividend decision then has an impact on the amount of new, outside funds that must be raised. A higher dividend rate means lower retained earnings and hence a heavier reliance on new outside equity. The increased cash flow to the shareholder through the higher dividend per share will, at the same time, result in lower expected growth in per share dividends and earnings. Thus, dividend policy has two opposing effect. The **optimal dividend policy** for a firm strikes a balance between current dividends and future growth that maximizes the price of the firm's shares.

Payment Procedure

Dividends are normally paid quarterly, and, if conditions warrant, the dividend is increased once each year. For example, Imasco paid a quarterly dividend of $0.32 per share for 1991, which is an annual rate of $1.28. In common financial parlance, we say that Imasco's *regular quarterly dividend* was 32 cents, or that its annual dividend was $1.28.

The actual payment procedure for dividends is as follows:

1. *Declaration date.*   The directors meet, say, on November 17 and declare the regular dividend. On this date, they issue a statement similar to the following: "On November 17, 1992, the directors of XYZ Company met and declared the regular quarterly dividend of 50 cents a share, payable to holders of record on December 18, payment to be made on January 15, 1993." For accounting purposes, the declared dividend becomes an actual liability on the *declaration date*, and if a balance sheet were constructed, the amount—$0.50 × number of shares outstanding—would appear as a current liability, and retained earnings would be reduced by a like amount.

2. *Holder-of-record date.*   On December 18, the *holder-of-record date*, the company closes its share transfer books and makes up a list of the shareholders as of that date. If XYZ Company is notified of the sale and transfer of some shares before 5:00 P.M. on December 18, the new owner receives the dividend. If notification is received on or after December 19, the previous owner of the shares gets the dividend cheque.

3. *Ex-dividend date.*   Suppose Jean Buyer buys 100 shares of common equity from John Seller on December 15. Will the company be notified of the transfer in time to list her as the new owner and thus pay her the dividend? To avoid conflict, the brokerage business has set a convention of declaring that the right to the dividend remains with the share until four business days prior to the holder-of-record date; on the fourth day before the record date, the right to the dividend no longer goes with the shares. The date when the right to the dividend leaves the shares is called the *ex-dividend date.* In this case, the ex-dividend date is four business days prior to December 18, or December 14. Therefore, if Buyer is to receive the dividend, she must buy the shares before December 14. If she buys it on December 14 or later, Seller will receive the dividend since he is the holder of record. The following is a picture of the process:

	December 13	Buyer receives dividend
Ex-dividend date	December 14	Seller receives dividend
	December 15	
	December 16	
	December 17	
Holder-of-record date	December 18	

The total dividend amounts to $0.50, so the ex-dividend date is important. Barring fluctuations in the stock market, we normally expect the price per share to drop by approximately the amount of the dividend on the ex-dividend date. Thus if XYZ closed at $30 1/2 on Friday, December 11, 1992, it probably opened at about $30 on Monday, December 14.[1]

4. *Payment date.* The company actually mails the cheques to the holders of record on January 15, the *payment date*.

Here is an example of this procedure. On July 30, 1992, Imasco Ltd. declared a $0.34 dividend per share on its common equity to holders of record on August 31, 1992 and payable, September 31, 1992. This was an increase of 2 cents per share over the quarterly dividend paid during 1991.

Dividend Reinvestment Plans

During the 1970s, most of the larger companies instituted **dividend reinvestment plans (DRPs)**, whereby shareholders can automatically reinvest all dividends received from a company back into its shares. A DRP allows a firm to maintain its dividend policy while giving shareholders the opportunity to increase their investment in the corporation. Companies with DRPs include BCE, Bank of Montreal, and TransCanada Pipelines.

There are two basic types of DRPs: (1) plans that involve only shares that are already outstanding and (2) plans that involve newly issued shares. In either case, the shareholder must pay income taxes on the amount of the dividends even though equity rather than cash is received.

Under the "old shares" type of plan, the shareholder elects either to continue receiving dividend cheques or, alternatively, to have the dividends

---

[1]Tax effects cause the price decline on average to be less than the full amount of the dividend. Suppose you were an investor in a 40 percent tax bracket. If you bought XYZ's shares on December 11, you would receive the dividend, but you would almost immediately pay 40 percent of it out in taxes. Thus, you would want to wait until December 14 to buy the shares if you thought you could get them for $0.50 less per share. Your reaction, and that of others, would influence equity prices around dividend payment dates. Here is what would happen:

1. Other things held constant, the share price should rise during the quarter, with the daily price increase for XYZ equal to $0.50/90 = $0.005556. Therefore, if the price started at $30.00 just after its last ex-dividend date, it would have risen to $30.50 on December 11.

2. In the absence of taxes, the share price would fall to $30.00 on December 11 and then start up as the next dividend accrual period began. Thus, over time, if everything else were held constant, the share price would follow a sawtooth pattern if it were plotted on a graph.

3. Because of taxes, the share price would neither rise by the full amount of the dividend nor fall by the full dividend amount when it went ex-dividend.

4. The amount of the rise and subsequent fall would depend on the average investor's marginal tax rate.

See Edwin J. Elton and Martin J. Gruber, "Marginal Stockholder Tax Rates and the Clientele Effect," *Review of Economics and Statistics*, February 1970: 68–74, for an interesting discussion of all this.

A paper entitled "The Ex-Dividend Day Behaviour of Canadian Stock Prices: Tax Changes and Clientele Effects" by L.D. Booth and D.J. Johnston in the June 1984 edition of the *Journal of Finance* observed that the ratio of the price drop on the ex-dividend day to the dividend paid increased from 0.27 in 1970–71 to 0.62 in 1978–80. This time period covered changes in the *Income Tax Act* that introduced taxation of capital gains and reduced the effective tax rate on dividends.

used to buy more shares in the corporation. If the shareholder elects reinvestment, a trust company or broker, acting as trustee, takes the total funds available for reinvestment (less a fee), purchases the corporation's shares on the open market, and allocates the shares purchased to the participating shareholders' accounts on a pro rata basis. The transactions costs of buying shares (brokerage costs) are low because of volume purchases, so these plans benefit small shareholders who do not need cash dividends for current consumption.

The "new shares" type of DRP provides for dividends to be invested in *newly issued* equity. Hence, such a plan raises new capital for the firm. BCE and many other companies had such plans in effect in 1991, using them to raise substantial amounts of new equity capital. No fees are charged to shareholders, and many companies offer shares at a discount of 5 percent below the actual market price. The companies absorb these costs as a tradeoff against issue costs that would be incurred on equity sold through investment dealers rather than through the dividend reinvestment plans. Companies use the new share plans only if they need more equity capital than retained earnings can provide.

Dividend Policy Theories

Dividend policy is influenced by a number of factors, including the investment opportunities available to the firm, alternative sources of capital, and shareholders' preferences for current versus future income. Our major goal in this chapter is to show how these factors interact to determine a firm's optimal dividend policy. We begin by examining two theories of dividend policy: (1) the dividend irrelevance theory and (2) the "bird-in-the-hand" theory.

Dividend Irrelevance Theory

It has been argued that dividend policy has no effect on either the firm's share price or its cost of capital—that is, that dividend policy is *irrelevant*. The principal proponents of the **dividend irrelevance theory** are Merton Miller and Franco Modigliani (MM).[2] In the early 1960s, they wrote that the value of the firm is determined only by its basic earning power and its business risk; in other words, MM argued that the value of the firm depends only on the income produced by its assets, not on how this income is split between dividends and retained earnings (and hence growth). MM concluded that an increase in dividends requires the firm to issue more equity in order to finance the previously determined investment budget. This results in more shares outstanding and a reduction in the growth rate of dividend per share to existing shareholders. The increased dividend is just offset by the lower expected growth, leaving the share price unchanged.

MM based their proposition on theoretical grounds. As in all theoretical work, they had to make some assumptions in order to develop a manageable theory. Specifically, they assumed (1) that there are no personal or corporate income taxes, (2) there are no issue costs or transactions costs, (3) that financial leverage has no effect on the cost of capital, (4) that investors and

---

[2]Merton H. Miller and Franco Modigliani, "Dividend Policy, Growth, and the Valuation of Shares," *Journal of Business*, October 1961: 411–33.

managers have the same information about the firm's future prospects, (5) that the distribution of income between dividends and retained earnings has no effect on the firm's cost of equity, k_s, and (6) that a firm's capital budgeting policy is independent of its dividend policy. Obviously these assumptions do not hold in the real world. Firms and investors do pay income taxes; firms do incur issue costs; managers often know more about the firm's future prospects than outside investors; investors do incur transactions costs; and both taxes and transactions costs may cause k_s to be affected by dividend policy. MM argued (correctly) that all economic theories are based on simplifying assumptions and that the validity of a theory must be judged on empirical tests, not on the realism of its assumptions. We shall discuss empirical tests of the MM dividend theory shortly.

Bird-in-the-Hand Theory

The fifth assumption in MM's dividend irrelevance theory is that dividend policy does not affect investors' required rate of return on equity, k_s. This particular assumption has been hotly debated in academic circles. For example, Myron Gordon and John Lintner argued that k_s increases as the dividend payout is reduced, because investors are less certain of receiving the capital gains that should result from retained earnings than they are of receiving dividend payments.[3] Gordon and Lintner said, in effect, that investors should value a dollar of expected dividends more highly than a dollar of expected capital gains because the dividend yield component, D_1/P_0, is less risky than the g component in the total expected return equation, $\hat{k}_s = D_1/P_0 + g$.

MM disagreed. They argued that k_s is independent of dividend policy, which implies that investors are indifferent between D_1/P_0 and g, and hence between dividends and capital gains. They called the Gordon–Lintner argument the **bird-in-the-hand** fallacy because, in MM's view, most investors plan to reinvest their dividends in the shares of the same or similar firms anyway, and, in any event, the riskiness of the firm's cash flows to investors in the long run is determined only by the riskiness of its *operating cash flows* and not by its dividend payout policy.

Figure 19-1 presents two graphs that highlight the MM versus Gordon–Lintner arguments. Panel a shows the Miller–Modigliani position. Here the graph shows $k_s = D_1/P_0 + g = $ a constant 13.3 percent for any dividend policy. Thus, the required return on the security, k_s, is assumed to be a constant 13.3 percent regardless of whether it comes entirely as a dividend yield (the vertical axis intercept, 13.3 percent), entirely as expected capital gains (the horizontal axis intercept, also 13.3 percent), or as any combination of the two. For example, MM believed that a representative investor would be indifferent between a 13.3 percent dividend yield with zero expected capital gains, a 10 percent dividend yield plus a 3.3 percent expected capital gain, a 3.3 percent dividend yield and 10 percent expected capital gain, and a zero dividend yield with a 13.3 percent expected capital gains return.

---

[3]Myron J. Gordon, "Optimal Investment and Financing Policy," *Journal of Finance*, May 1963: 264–72; and John Lintner, "Dividends, Earnings, Leverage, Stock Prices, and the Supply of Capital to Corporations," *Review of Economics and Statistics*, August 1962: 243–69.

Figure 19-1
The Miller–Modigliani and
Gordon–Lintner Dividend Hypotheses

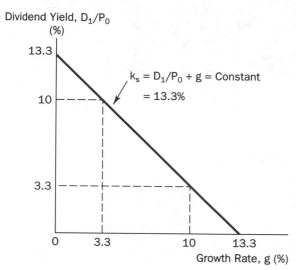

a. Dividends Are Irrelevant (MM)

Dividend Yield, D_1/P_0 (%)

$k_s = D_1/P_0 + g = $ Constant

$= 13.3\%$

Growth Rate, g (%)

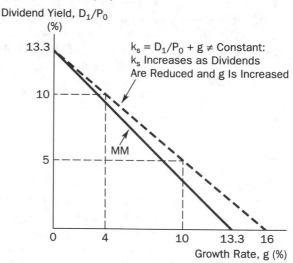

b. Dividends Are Relevant: Investors Like Dividends (GL)

Dividend Yield, D_1/P_0 (%)

$k_s = D_1/P_0 + g \neq $ Constant: k_s Increases as Dividends Are Reduced and g Is Increased

MM

Growth Rate, g (%)

Panel b repeats the MM relationship, but it also shows, as the dashed line, the Gordon–Lintner view. Gordon–Lintner argued that a dividend "in the hand" is less risky than a possible capital gain "in the bush," so investors require a larger total return if that return has a larger capital gains component than dividend yield. In other words, Gordon–Lintner argued that *more than 1 percent* of additional growth is required to offset a 1 percent reduction in dividend yield. Thus, the required rate of return or cost of equity is, say, 13.3 percent if the firm pays all of its earnings out in dividends, but as it lowers the payout and hence the dividend portion of the total return, the cost of equity increases. In our example, k_s would be 16 percent at a zero payout, the point at which the dividend yield is zero.

At this time, we are not prepared to say which of these two positions is more correct. Before reaching any conclusions, we must examine the empirical evidence.

Concept Review

► Differentiate between the dividend irrelevance theory and the bird-in-the-hand theory. Use a graph such as Figure 19-1 to illustrate your answer.
► List the assumptions of Modigliani and Miller concerning the dividend irrelevance theory.
► How did the bird-in-the-hand theory get its name?
► Describe the two different types of dividend reinvestment plans.

Tests of Dividend Theories

In the preceding section, we presented two dividend theories:

1. MM argued that dividend policy is irrelevant; that is, it does not affect a firm's value or its cost of capital. Thus, according to MM, there is no optimal dividend policy—one dividend policy is as good as any other.
2. Gordon and Lintner disagreed with MM, arguing that dividends are less risky than capital gains, so a firm should set a high dividend payout ratio and offer a high dividend yield in order to minimize its cost of capital. MM called this the bird-in-the-hand fallacy.

These two theories offer contradictory advice to corporate managers. Which one should we believe? The most logical way to proceed is to test the theories empirically. Actually, many empirical tests have been used in attempts to determine the true relationship between dividend yield and required return. The earliest type of test was designed along the lines set forth in Figure 19-1. In theory, we could take a sample of companies that have different dividend policies, and hence different dividend yields and growth rate components, and plot them in graphs such as those shown in Figure 19-1. If all the points fell on the line labelled MM in Panel b, this would support the MM irrelevance hypothesis. If all the points fell on the dashed line, this would support the Gordon–Lintner hypothesis.

Such tests have been conducted, but the results have been unclear. Indeed, the empirical tests suggest that either of the theories could be correct, or that they could both be incorrect. There are two reasons for this situation: (1) for a valid statistical test, things other than dividend policy must be held constant—that is, the sample companies must differ only in their dividend policies—and (2) we must be able to measure with a high degree of accuracy the expected growth rates for the sample firms. Neither of these two conditions actually holds. We can neither find a set of publicly owned firms that differ only in their dividend policies nor obtain precise estimates of investors' expected growth rates. Therefore, we cannot determine with much precision what effect dividend policy has on the cost of equity. Hence, this particular type of test has been unable to solve the dividend policy puzzle.

Academic researchers have also studied the dividend yield effect from a CAPM perspective. These studies hypothesize that required returns are a function of both market risk, as measured by beta, and dividend yield. Like studies of the Figure 19-1 type, the CAPM studies have given mixed results, and they suffer from empirical problems. The major problem is that they generally used historic earned rates of return as proxies for required returns, and with such a poor proxy, the tests were almost bound to have mixed results. Thus, the CAPM-based empirical tests, like the others, have not led to definitive conclusions about which dividend theory is more correct. As a result, the issue is still unresolved; researchers at this time simply cannot tell corporate decision-makers how dividend policy affects share prices and capital costs.

Concept Review

▶ What have been the results of empirical tests of the MM versus Gordon–Lintner dividend theories?

Other Dividend Policy Issues

Before discussing dividend policy in practice, we must examine two other theoretical issues that could affect our views toward dividend policy: (1) the information content, or signalling, hypothesis and (2) the clientele effect.

Information Content, or Signalling, Hypothesis

If investors expect a company's dividend to increase by 5 percent per year and if the dividend is in fact increased by 5 percent, then the share price generally will not change significantly on the day the dividend increase is announced. In financial parlance, such a dividend increase is "discounted," or anticipated, by the market. However, if investors expect a 5 percent increase but the company actually increases the dividend by 25 percent—say, from $2 to $2.50—this change is generally accompanied by an increase in the share price. Conversely, a less-than-expected dividend increase or a reduction generally results in a price decline.

The fact that large dividend increases generally cause share price increases suggests to some that investors in the aggregate prefer dividends to capital gains. However, MM argued differently. They noted the well-established fact that corporations are always reluctant to cut dividends, and, consequently, that managers do not raise dividends unless they anticipate higher, or at least stable, earnings in the future. Therefore, according to MM (and many others), a larger-than-expected dividend increase is taken by investors as a "signal" that the firm's management forecasts improved future earnings, whereas a dividend reduction signals a forecast of poor earnings. Thus, MM claimed that investors' reactions to changes in dividend payments do not show that investors prefer dividends to retained earnings; rather, the share price changes simply indicate that important information concerning future earnings is contained in dividend announcements. This theory is referred to as the **information content**, or **signalling, hypothesis**.

There is some empirical evidence relating to the information effects of changes in dividends on the firm's share prices. One study investigated the impact on announcements of initiating dividends for firms that either had never paid a dividend or had not paid one over the last 10 years. The dividend payment was totally unanticipated and hence any impact on share prices had to result solely from the announcement. By removing the impact of other events from the rates of return on the company's equity over the two days surrounding the announcements, the authors identified a rate of return of 3.7 percent over 2 days. They explained this result as either information about the size of future cash flows or a potential benefit to shareholders since dividends could now be used as a signalling device. In the first explanation, the signal is informative to shareholders since it is based on the obvious condition that dividends must be paid out of cash flow and the dividend is initiated only if the cash flow is expected to be available in the future to support the dividend.

Researchers also looked at dividend increases and decreases that were greater than expected; these expectations were based on existing and historical levels of dividends and earnings. The unexpected dividend changes were "surprises" to the market, and any impact on share prices had to come from the information content in the dividend change. The empirical results were consistent with the information content in dividend "surprises." For dividend reductions, there was a negative rate of return on equity of 3.6 percent around the announcement period. For dividend increases, the rate of return was approximately 1 percent over the same period. These rates of return are called *excess returns* because they are in excess of the rate of return attributable to general market movements, which typically affect all securities in the same direction.

Clientele Effect

MM suggested that a **clientele effect** might exist, and, if so, this might help explain why share prices change after announced changes in dividend policy. Their argument went like this: a firm sets a particular dividend payout policy, which then attracts a "clientele" consisting of those investors who like this particular dividend policy. For example, some shareholders, such as university endowment funds and retired individuals, prefer current income to future capital gains, so they want the firm to pay out a high percentage of its earnings. Other shareholders have no need for current investment income—they simply reinvest any dividend income received, after first paying income taxes on it, so they favour a low payout. The Canadian tax system may induce a preference for dividends since the marginal tax rate on dividends is less than on capital gains if the shares are sold after 1 year and the capital gains tax is paid at that time. To the extent that investors hold the securities and delay the payment of the capital gains tax, however, the effective tax rate on capital gains is less than on dividends.

If the firm retains and reinvests income rather than paying dividends, those shareholders who need current income will be disadvantaged. They can presumably receive capital gains, but they have to go to the trouble and expense of selling some of their shares to obtain cash. Since brokerage costs are quite high on small transactions, selling a few shares to obtain periodic income is expensive and inefficient. Also, some institutional investors (and trustees for individuals) are precluded from selling shares and then "spending capital." However, if the firm pays out most of its income, other shareholders who do not need current cash income are forced to receive such income, pay taxes on it, and then go to the trouble and expense of reinvesting what's left of their dividends after taxes. MM concluded from all this that those investors who desire current investment income will own shares in high-dividend-payout firms, whereas those who do not need current cash income will invest in low-payout firms.

This suggests that each firm should establish the specific policy that its management deems most appropriate and then have shareholders who do not like this policy sell their shares to other investors who do. However, investor switching is costly because of (1) brokerage costs, (2) the likelihood that selling shareholders will have to pay taxes on their capital gains, and (3) a possible shortage of investors in the aggregate who like the firm's newly stated dividend policy. This means that firms should not change dividend policies frequently, because such changes will result in net losses to their shareholders from brokerage costs and capital gains taxes. If there are enough investors in the economy who favour the new policy, however, then their demand for the shares could more than offset the costs associated with a given change and lead to an increase in the share price.

Several studies have investigated the importance of the clientele effect.[4] Like most other issues in the dividend arena, the implications of the clientele effect are still up in the air.

Concept Review

▶ Define (1) the *information content hypothesis* and (2) the *clientele effect*, and explain how they affect dividend policy.

Dividend Policy in Practice

We noted earlier that there are two conflicting theories as to what dividend policy firms should follow: (1) Miller and Modigliani's theory that dividend policy is irrelevant, or (2) the bird-in-the-hand theory that dividends are less risky than capital gains and hence k_s rises as dividend payments are reduced. We also saw that dividend payments send signals to investors—an unexpectedly large dividend increase conveys management optimism, whereas a cut conveys pessimism—and that companies' dividend policies attract clienteles of shareholders who prefer a dividend policy similar to the one the company is following. All of this provides insights that aid corporate decision-makers. However, no one has been able to develop a formula that can be used to tell management how a given dividend policy will affect a firm's share price.

Even though no dividend policy formula exists, management must still establish dividend policies. This section discusses several alternative policies that are used in practice.

Residual Dividend Policy

In practice, dividend policy is very much influenced by investment opportunities and by the availability of funds with which to finance new investments. This fact has led to the development of a **residual dividend policy**, which states that a firm should follow these four steps when deciding on its payout ratio: (1) determine the optimal capital budget, (2) determine the amount of capital needed to finance that budget, (3) use retained earnings to supply the equity component to the extent possible, and (4) pay dividends only if more earnings are available than are needed to support the capital budget. The word

---

[4]For example, see R. Richardson Pettit, "Taxes, Transactions Costs, and the Clientele Effect of Dividends," *Journal of Financial Economics*, December 1977: 419–36.

residual means "left over," and the residual policy implies that dividends should be paid only out of "leftover" earnings.

The basis of the theory is that investors prefer to have the firm retain and reinvest earnings rather than pay them out in dividends if the rate of return the firm can earn on reinvested earnings exceeds the rate of return the investors could obtain on other investments of comparable risk. If the corporation can reinvest retained earnings at a 20 percent rate of return, while the best rate of return shareholders can obtain if they receive earnings in the form of dividends is 10 percent, then shareholders prefer to have the firm retain the profits.

We saw in Chapter 17 that the cost of retained earnings is an *opportunity cost* that reflects rates of return available to equity investors. If a firm's shareholders can buy other securities of equal risk and obtain a 10 percent dividend-plus-capital-gain yield, then 10 percent is the firm's cost of retained earnings. The cost of new outside equity raised by selling common shares is higher because of the costs of floating the issue.

Most firms have a *target capital structure* that calls for at least some debt, so new financing is done partly with debt and partly with equity. Debt has a different, and generally lower, component cost than equity, so the two forms of capital must be combined to find the *weighted average cost of capital*. As long as the firm finances at the optimum point, using the proper amounts of debt and equity, and provided it intends to use only internally generated equity (retained earnings), its marginal cost of each new dollar of capital will be minimized. Internally generated equity is available for financing a certain amount of new investment; beyond this amount, the firm must turn to more expensive new common equity. At the point at which new equity must be sold, the cost of equity, and consequently the marginal cost of capital, rises.

These concepts, which were developed in Chapter 17, are illustrated in Figure 19-2 for Atlantic Mining Limited. Atlantic has a marginal cost of capital of 10 percent so long as retained earnings are available, but the marginal cost of capital begins to rise when new equity must be sold. Atlantic has $60 million of net income and a 40 percent optimum debt ratio (that is, ratio of debt to total assets). Provided it does not pay cash dividends, Atlantic can make net investments (investments in addition to asset replacements financed from depreciation) of up to $100 million financed with $60 million from retained earnings and $40 million in new debt supported by the retained earnings, at a 10 percent marginal cost of capital. Therefore, its MCC is constant at 10 percent for up to $100 million of capital. Beyond $100 million, the marginal cost of capital rises as the firm begins to use more expensive new common equity.

Of course, if Atlantic does not retain all of its earnings, the MCC will begin to rise before $100 million. For example, if Atlantic retains only $30 million, then the MCC will begin to rise at $50 million: $30 million of retained earnings + $20 million debt = $50 million.

Now suppose Atlantic's director of capital budgeting constructs an investment opportunity schedule and plots it on a graph. The investment opportunity schedules for three different years—one for a good year (IOS_G), one for a normal year (IOS_N), and one for a bad year (IOS_B)—are shown in Figure 19-3. Atlantic can invest the most money, and earn the highest rates of return, when the investment opportunities are given as IOS_G.

Figure 19-2
Atlantic Mining Limited:
Marginal Cost of Capital

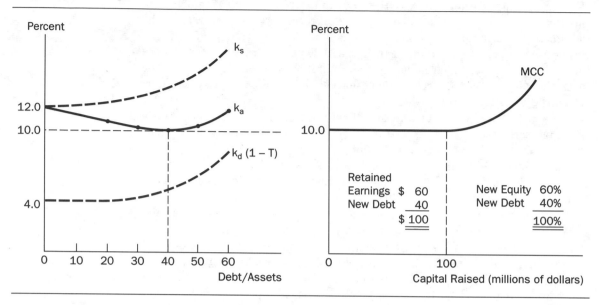

In Figure 19-4, we combine these investment opportunity schedules with the cost of capital schedule that would exist if the company retained all of its earnings. The point at which the relevant IOS curve cuts the MCC curve defines the proper level of new investment. When investment opportunities are

Figure 19-3
Atlantic Mining Limited:
Investment Opportunity (or IRR) Schedules

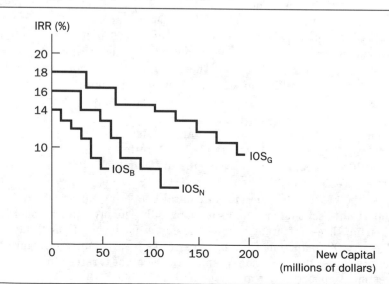

Figure 19-4
Atlantic Mining Limited:
Interrelationships among Cost of Capital,
Investment Opportunities, and New Investment

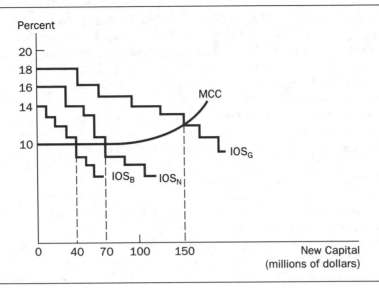

relatively bad (IOS$_B$), the optimum level of investment is $40 million; when opportunities are normal (IOS$_N$), $70 million should be invested; and when opportunities are relatively good (IOS$_G$), Atlantic should make new investments in the amount of $150 million.[5]

Consider the situation in which IOS$_G$ is the appropriate schedule. Atlantic should raise and invest $150 million. It has $60 million in earnings and a 40 percent target debt ratio. Thus it can finance $100 million, consisting of $60 million of retained earnings plus $40 million of new debt, at an average cost of 10 percent. The remaining $50 million would include external equity and thus would have a higher cost. If Atlantic paid out part of its earnings in dividends, it would have to begin using expensive new common equity sooner, so its MCC curve would rise sooner than it otherwise would. This suggests that under the conditions of IOS$_G$, Atlantic should retain all its earnings and actually sell some new common shares in order to take advantage of its investment opportunities. According to the residual theory, Atlantic's payout ratio should be zero if IOS$_G$ applies.

Under the conditions of IOS$_N$, however, Atlantic should invest only $70 million. How should this investment be financed? First, notice that if it retained the full amount of its earnings, $60 million, it would need to sell only $10 million of new debt. However, by doing this, the firm would move away

---

[5]Figure 19-4 shows one MCC schedule and three IOS schedules for three possible sets of investment opportunities. Actually, both the MCC and the IOS schedules would normally change from year to year as interest rates and share prices change. Figure 19-4 is designated to illustrate a point, not to duplicate reality. In reality, there would be one MCC and one IOS for each year, but those schedules would change from year to year.

from its target capital structure. To stay on target, Atlantic must finance the required $70 million as 60 percent equity—retained earnings—and 40 percent debt: that is, $42 million by retained earnings and $28 million by debt. If Atlantic has $60 million in total earnings and retains only $42 million, it would have to distribute the residual $18 million to its shareholders. In this case, the optimal payout ratio is 30 percent ($18 million divided by $60 million).

Finally, under the conditions of IOS_B, Atlantic should invest only $40 million. Because it has $60 million in earnings, it could finance the entire $40 million out of retained earnings and still have $20 million available for dividends. Should this be done? Under our assumption, this would not be a good decision, because Atlantic would move away from its target debt ratio. To hold to the 40 percent target debt-to-assets ratio, Atlantic must retain $24 million and sell $16 million of debt. When the $24 million of retained earnings is subtracted from the $60 million of earnings, the firm is left with a residual of $36 million—the amount that should be paid out in dividends. In this case, the payout ratio as prescribed by the residual theory is 60 percent.

Since both the IOS schedule and earnings levels vary from year to year, strict adherence to the residual dividend policy would result in dividend variability—one year the firm might declare zero dividends because investment opportunities were good, but the next year it might pay a large dividend because investment opportunities were poor. Similarly, fluctuating earnings would also lead to variable dividends even if investment opportunities were stable over time. Thus, following the residual dividend policy is optimal only if investors are not bothered by fluctuating dividends. However, if investors prefer stable, dependable dividends, k_s will be higher and the share price lower than if the firm follows the residual theory in a strict sense.

Constant, or Steadily Increasing, Dividends

In the past, many firms set a specific annual dollar dividend per share and then maintained it, increasing the annual dividend only if it seemed clear that future earnings would be sufficient to allow the new dividend to be maintained. A corollary of that policy was this rule: *never reduce the annual dividend.*

For several decades through the mid-1980s, inflation tended to push earnings up, so many firms that would otherwise have followed the *stable dividend payment policy* switched over to what is called the *stable growth rate policy.* Here the firm sets a target growth rate for dividends (for example, 4 to 6 percent per year, which was close to the long-run average inflation rate) and strives to increase dividends by this amount each year. Obviously, earnings must be growing at about the same rate for this policy to be feasible, but such a policy provides investors with a stable income.[6]

There are a number of sound reasons for paying a stable, predictable dividend, rather than following the residual dividend policy. First, investors may value more

---

[6]Beginning in the late 1980s, the recession became manifest in a slow growth in corporate profits, and firms were forced to move away from a stable growth policy to one that reflected both the stability and quantity of earnings. The poor earnings resulted at first in a no-growth dividend policy, but as the recession deepened, some firms reduced their dividend or even eliminated it entirely. An example is provided by Dofasco, which eliminated its dividend as a result of continuing poor earnings.

highly dividends they are more sure of receiving: fluctuating dividends are riskier than stable dividends. Accordingly, the same average amount of dividends received under a fluctuating-dividend policy could have a higher k_s applied to it than is applied to dividends under a stable-dividend policy, and hence a lower share price.

Second, many shareholders use dividends for current consumption, and they are put to trouble and expense if they have to sell some of their shares to obtain cash because the company cuts the dividend. In addition, a dividend cut causes them anxiety.

Third, a stable dividend is consistent with the requirement of legal listing. **Legal lists** are lists of securities in which pension funds and insurance companies are permitted to invest. The requirements to be included in the legal list for insurance companies have been amended to include companies that pay dividends or have the ability to pay dividends; insurance companies can invest only limited amounts in the shares of companies that do not pay dividends. Therefore, even though a stable dividend is not essential for a company to be included on a legal list, the existence of a stable dividend makes it more likely that the company will be included. Therefore, legal listing may encourage the pursuit of a stable-dividend policy.

Fourth, stable dividends permit management to use the dividend as a signal of the underlying profitability of the company. Although the reported profit figures can be altered by means of creative accounting, manipulations of the dividend are less likely to occur since the dividend payment is a cash outflow from the corporation. Moreover, for this signal to be of any use, the dividend must be stable so that any changes in the dividend will be quickly interpreted by investors as a signal of improved future profitability.

Even though the optimal dividend as prescribed by the residual policy may vary somewhat from year to year, actions such as delaying some investment projects, departing from the target capital structure during a particular year or even issuing new common equity make it possible for a company to avoid the problems associated with unstable dividends.

Constant Payout Ratio

It would be possible for a firm to maintain a dividend policy of a *constant payout ratio*—that is, to pay out a constant percentage of earnings. However, since earnings will surely fluctuate, this policy would necessarily mean that the dollar amount of dividends would vary. For example, if the firm's earnings fall, a strict adherence to this policy would result in a decrease in dividends, even if the earnings decrease were transitory. Thus, for reasons discussed in the preceding section, a constant ratio policy is unlikely to maximize the value of the firm's shares.

Many firms do, however, conduct an analysis similar to the residual analysis set forth earlier in the chapter and then establish a *target* payout ratio based on the most likely set of conditions. The target is not hit in every year, but over time the average payout is close to the target level. Of course, the target must be changed if fundamental changes in the company's position occur.

Low Regular Dividend plus Extras

A compromise between a stable (or stable growth rate) dividend and a constant payout rate is a policy of paying a *low regular dividend plus a year-end extra*. Such a policy gives the firm flexibility, yet investors can count on receiving at least a minimum dividend. The directors can set a relatively low regular dividend—low enough so that it can be maintained even in low-profit years or in years when a considerable amount of retained earnings is needed—and then supplement it with an extra dividend in years when excess funds are available. By labelling the additional dividend payment as an extra, the company is informing the shareholders that it is transitory. If a firm's earnings and cash flows are volatile, this policy may well be its best choice. However, if the company pays an extra dividend year after year, then it becomes expected by investors. Reducing or eliminating it then has the same effect as a similar change in the regular dividend.

Dividend Policy in Practice

Managements of major Canadian companies have stated in surveys that the most important factors in determining the dividend payment are current and expected earnings, the target payout ratio, and last year's dividend payment. When asked about the impact of an increase in dividends on their share price, two-thirds agreed that an increase in dividends signals increased future profitability leading to a share price increase; they did not believe that investors interpret such an increase as a signal of poor investment opportunities to the firm and thus there will not be a reduction in share price.

As we can see from the previous discussion, dividend policies are established to provide stable dividends but include considerations of cash availability, investment needs, and target payout ratios.

Dividend Policy Decisions

Most corporations identify a target payout ratio. However, this payout ratio is not achieved every year because the corporation increases (decreases) dividends, with a lag, after earnings increase (decrease). Dividends are increased only after an increase in earnings appears clearly sustainable and relatively permanent. Once dividends have been increased, strenuous efforts are made to maintain them at the new level. If earnings decline, the existing dividend will usually be maintained, and the observed payout ratio will be above its target, until it is clear to management that an earnings recovery will not take place.

Figure 19-5 identifies the per share dividends (DPS) and earnings (EPS) for firms that have listed equity on the Toronto Stock Exchange 300 index over the period 1973 to 1991. The patterns of dividends and earnings confirm the dividend policy conclusions we have made. First, the variability in earnings is not replicated in the dividend payouts. Over the growth period 1973 to 1980, dividends per share grew but at a much slower rate than earnings per share. This resulted in payout ratios in the range of 30 to 40 percent. The recession of 1981–82 found a modest reduction of dividends in the face of a substantial reduction in earnings. This resulted in very large payout ratios of 80 percent. The growth period from 1983 to 1988 found steady but slow growth in dividends

Figure 19-5
Dividends and Earnings per Share
for Companies on the TSE 300 Index

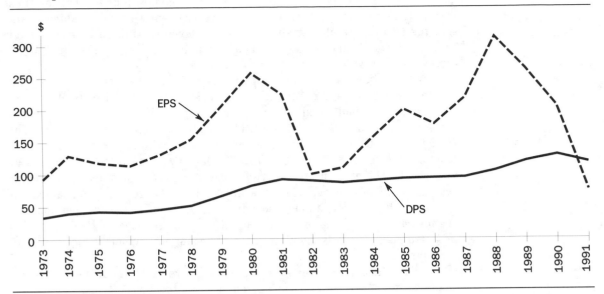

per share. The beginning of the recession in 1989 was accompanied by a levelling off of DPS payouts and resulted in higher payout ratios. In 1991, DPS and EPS fell with the earnings decrease being substantial. This resulted in an average payout ratio of 1.54!

The relationship between DPS and EPS that is graphed in Figure 19-5 is consistent with the proposition that firms adjust slowly to changes in earnings and are concerned with the negative implications of dividend decreases. However, as seen for 1981 and 1982 and for the recession that began in 1989, firms do decrease dividends when necessary.

The stability of the earnings of the company will have an impact on the speed with which dividends change after a change in earnings. If the company—for example, a regulated utility—has stable earnings, then the permanence of an observed earnings change can be determined quickly, and an appropriate change in dividends will follow the change in earnings with very little lag. If the earnings of the company are volatile, however, it is more difficult for management to determine within a short space of time whether the increase is permanent or transitory. Therefore, management will delay a change in dividends or make a small change until more observations of earnings are available and the permanence of the earnings change can be established.

This dividend policy behaviour has been modelled by J. Lintner.[7] Lintner hypothesized that firms have a *target* payout ratio that, when applied to the level of earnings in a particular year, generates the target level of dividends to

[7]J. Lintner, "Distribution of Incomes of Corporations Among Dividends, Retained Earnings, and Taxes," *American Economic Review*, May 5, 1956: 97–113.

be paid out. The most recent level of earnings, however, may not allow a firm to set its new dividend equal to the target dividend. There is, in fact, an adjustment toward the target dividend over a number of years, since management is not certain that earnings will remain at the new higher level and thus sustain the dividend at its target level. If management were reasonably certain that the earnings would remain at their new level, the full adjustment would occur immediately and the new dividend would immediately be set equal to the target dividend value.

This behaviour is consistent with the relationship between dividends and earnings per share for companies on the TSE index. As an example of the behaviour for an individual company, consider Royal Trustco Ltd. From 1982 to 1989, the earnings per share increased by 19 percent per annum from a value of $0.40 to $1.70. Over the same period, dividends grew by 14 percent per annum, reaching a level of $0.70 in 1989. In 1990, earnings per share fell to a loss of $1.20, while the dividend per share increased to $0.74. Earnings recovered in 1991 to $0.25 per share, while the dividend per share was maintained. In July 1992, the company announced a dividend decrease to 10 cents per quarter; in November 1992, the quarterly dividend was reduced to 5 cents. This reflected management's view that earnings could not support a high dividend per share.

In 1992, the earnings per share were a negative $1.93. In March 1993, some of the assets of Royal Trustco were acquired by the Royal Bank.

Concept Review

▶ Explain the logic of the residual dividend policy, the steps a firm would take to implement it, and why it is more likely to be used to establish a long-run payout target than a strict year-by-year payout ratio.

▶ Describe the constant, or steadily increasing, dividend policy, and give three reasons why a firm might follow such a policy.

▶ Explain what a low-regular-dividend-plus-extras policy is, and why a firm might follow such a policy.

▶ Describe the Lintner model, and relate it to the different dividend policies discussed.

Summary of Factors Influencing Dividend Policy

Thus far in the chapter, we have described the major theories that deal with the effects of dividend policy on the value of a firm, and we have discussed alternative payment policies. Firms choose a particular policy based on managements' beliefs concerning the dividend theories plus a host of other factors as described below.

1. *Legal rules.*   The legal rules provide that dividends must be paid from earnings—either from the current year's earnings or from past years' earnings as reflected in the balance sheet account "retained earnings."

   Legislation emphasizes three rules: the net profits rule, the capital impairment rule, and the insolvency rule. The *net profits rule* provides that dividends can be paid from past and present earnings. The *capital impairment rule* protects creditors by forbidding the payment of dividends from paid-in capital, which would amount to distributing the investment in a company rather than its earnings. The *insolvency rule* provides that a corporation may not pay dividends while insolvent and may not pay dividends if the result is to make the company insolvent. (*Insolvency* can be defined either as the company's having liabilities that exceed assets or its failure to meet current obligations as they fall due.) The payment of dividends under such conditions would mean giving shareholders funds that rightfully belong to the creditors.

Legal aspects are significant in that they provide the framework within which dividend policies can be formulated.[8] Within their boundaries, however, financial and economic factors have a major influence on policy.

2. *Availability of cash.*   Cash dividends can be paid only with cash. Thus, a shortage of cash in the bank can restrict dividend payments. However, the ability to borrow can offset this factor.

3. *Need to repay debt.*   When a firm has sold debt to finance expansion or to substitute for other forms of financing, it is faced with two alternatives: it can refund the debt at maturity by replacing it with another form of security, or it can make provisions for paying off the debt. If the decision is to retire the debt, the firm will generally be forced to retain earnings.

4. *Restrictions in debt contracts.*   Debt contracts, particularly those involving long-term debt, frequently restrict a firm's ability to pay cash dividends. Such restrictions, which are designed to protect the position of the lender, usually state (a) that future dividends can be paid only out of earnings generated *after* the signing of the loan agreement—that is, they cannot be paid out of past retained earnings—and (b) that dividends cannot be paid when net working capital is below a specified amount. Similarly, preferred share agreements generally state that no cash dividends can be paid on the common shares until all accrued preferred dividends have been paid.

5. *Location of the IOS schedule.*   If a firm's "typical" IOS schedule, as shown earlier in Figure 19-4, is far to the right, this will tend to produce a low target payout ratio, and vice versa if the IOS is far to the left.

6. *Possibility of accelerating or delaying projects.*   The ability to accelerate or to postpone projects will permit a firm to adhere more closely to its target dividend policy.

7. *Access to capital markets.*   If a firm needs to finance a given level of investment, it can obtain equity by retaining earnings or by selling new common shares. If issue costs (including any negative signalling effects of a share offering) are high, k_e will be well above k_s, making it better to set a

---

[8]It is possible, of course, to return shareholders' capital, but when this is done, the procedure must be clearly stated as such. A dividend paid out of capital is called a *liquidating dividend*.

low payout ratio and to finance through retention rather than through the sale of new common shares. On the other hand, a high dividend payout ratio is more feasible for a firm whose issue costs are low. Issue costs differ among firms—for example, the issue cost percentage is generally higher for small firms and for firms with unstable earnings, so they tend to set low payout ratios.

8. *Ability to substitute debt for equity.*   A firm can finance a given level of investment with either debt or equity. As noted above, low equity issue costs permit a more flexible dividend policy because equity can be raised either by retaining earnings or by selling new shares. A similar situation holds for debt policy: if the firm can adjust its debt ratio without raising costs sharply, it can maintain a constant dollar dividend, even if earnings fluctuate, by using a variable debt ratio. The shape of the average cost of capital curve (in Panel a of Figure 19-2 above) determines the practical extent to which the debt ratio can be varied. If the average cost of capital curve is relatively flat over a wide range, then a higher payout ratio is more feasible than it would be if the curve had a V shape.

9. *Control.*   If managers are concerned about maintaining control, they may be reluctant to sell new equity and thereby dilute the control of the dominant group in the company. Hence the company may retain more earnings than it otherwise would. However, if shareholders want higher dividends and a proxy fight looms, then the dividend will be increased.

10. *Taxation.*   Bonds, preferred shares, and common equity have various tax effects for issuing firms. The tax effects for investors also differ. (See Chapter 2.)

11. *Effects of dividend policy on k_s.*   The effects of dividend policy on k_s may be considered in terms of three factors: (1) shareholders' desire for current versus future income, (2) perceived riskiness of dividends versus capital gains, and (3) the information content of dividends (signalling). Since we discussed each of these factors in detail earlier, we need only note here that the importance of each factor in terms of its effect on k_s varies from firm to firm depending on the makeup of its current and possible future shareholders.

It should be apparent from our discussion thus far that dividend policy decisions are truly exercises in informed judgement, not decisions that can be quantified precisely. Even so, to make rational dividend decisions, financial managers must take account of all the points discussed in the preceding sections.

Concept Review

▶ Identify the factors that affect dividend policy.
▶ List the three factors that should be considered when assessing the effects of dividend policy on the cost of equity, k_s.

Stock Dividends and Stock Splits

Stock dividends and stock splits are related to the firm's cash dividend policy. The rationale for stock dividends and splits can best be explained through an example. We shall use Porter Electronic Controls, Ltd., a $700 million electronic components manufacturer, for this purpose. Since its inception, Porter's markets have been expanding, and the company has enjoyed growth in sales and earnings. Some of the earnings were paid out in dividends, but some were also retained each year, causing earnings per share and market price per share to grow. The company began its life with only a few thousand shares outstanding, and, after some years of growth, each of Porter's shares had a very high EPS and DPS. When a "normal" price-to-earnings (P/E) ratio was applied, the derived market price was so high that few people could afford to buy a "round lot" of 100 shares. This limited the demand for the shares and thus kept the total market value of the firm below what it would have been if more shares, at a lower price, had been outstanding. To correct this situation, Porter can "split its stock," as described in the next section.

Stock Splits

Although there is little empirical evidence to support the contention, there is nevertheless a widespread belief in financial circles that an *optimal price range* exists for securities. "Optimal" means that if the price is within this range, the P/E ratio, and hence the value of the firm, will be maximized. Many observers, including Porter's management, believe that the best range for most equity securities is $20 to $80 per share. Accordingly, if the price of Porter's shares rises to $80, management will probably declare a two-for-one **stock split**, thus doubling the number of shares outstanding, halving the earnings and dividends per share, and thereby lowering the share price. Each shareholder will have more shares, but each share will be worth less. If the price after the split is $40, Porter's shareholders will be exactly as well off as they were before the split. However, if the share price stabilizes above $40, shareholders will be better off. Stock splits can be of any size—for example, the shares can be split two-for-one, three-for-one, one-and-a-half-for-one, or in any other way.[9]

Stock Dividends

Stock dividends are similar to stock splits in that they "divide the pie into smaller slices" without affecting the fundamental position of the current shareholders. On a 5 percent stock dividend, the holder of 100 shares receives an additional 5 shares (without cost); on a 20 percent stock dividend, the same holder receives 20 new shares; and so on. Again, the total number of shares is increased, so earnings, dividends, and price per share all decline.

---

[9]*Reverse splits*, which reduce the shares outstanding, can even be used. For example, a company whose equity sells for $5 per share might employ a one-for-five reverse split, exchanging 1 new share for 5 old ones and raising the value of the shares to about $25, which is within the optimal range. Companies usually engage in reverse splits after years of poor performance have driven the share price below what is believed to be the optimal range.

If a firm wants to reduce its share price, should it use a stock split or a stock dividend? Stock splits are generally used to produce a large price reduction after a sharp price run-up. Stock dividends are frequently used on a regular annual basis to keep the share price more or less constrained. For example, if a firm's earnings and dividends are growing at about 10 percent per year, the share price will tend to go up at about that same rate, and it will soon be outside the desired trading range. An annual 10 percent stock dividend will maintain the share price within the optimal trading range.

Balance Sheet Effects

Although the economic effects of stock splits and stock dividends are virtually identical, accountants treat them somewhat differently. On a two-for-one split, the shares outstanding are doubled and each share's book value is halved. This treatment is shown in Part II of Table 19-1 for Porter Electronic Controls, using a pro forma balance sheet.

Part III of Table 19-1 shows the effect of a 20 percent stock dividend. With a stock dividend, an accounting entry is made transferring capital from the retained earnings account to the common equity account. The transfer from retained earnings is calculated as follows:

Table 19-1
Porter Electronic Controls, Ltd.: Shareholders'
Equity Accounts, Pro Forma, December 31, 1993

I. Before a Stock Split or Stock Dividend	
Common equity (6 million shares authorized, 5 million outstanding)	$ 15 000 000
Retained earnings	155 000 000
Total common equity	$170 000 000
Book value per share	$34.00
II. After a Two-for-One Stock Split	
Common equity (12 million shares authorized, 10 million outstanding)	$ 15 000 000
Retained earnings	155 000 000
Total common equity	$170 000 000
Book value per share	$17.00
III. After a 20 Percent Stock Dividend	
Common equity (6 million shares authorized, 6 million outstanding)[a]	$ 95 000 000
Retained earnings[b]	75 000 000
Total common equity	$170 000 000
Book value per share	$28.33

[a]Shares outstanding are increased by 20 percent, from 5 million to 6 million.

[b]A transfer equal to the market value of the new shares is made from the retained earnings account to the equity account.

$$\text{Transfer} = (5\,000\,000 \text{ shares})(0.2)(\$80) = \$80\,000\,000.$$

$$\begin{matrix} \text{Dollars} \\ \text{transferred from} \\ \text{retained earnings} \end{matrix} = \begin{pmatrix} \text{Number} \\ \text{of shares} \\ \text{outstanding} \end{pmatrix} \begin{pmatrix} \text{Percentage} \\ \text{of the} \\ \text{stock dividend} \end{pmatrix} \begin{pmatrix} \text{Market} \\ \text{share} \\ \text{price} \end{pmatrix}.$$

Porter has 5 million shares outstanding, and they sell for $80 each, so a 20 percent stock dividend would require the transfer of $80 million:

$$\text{Dollars transferred} = (5\,000\,000)(0.2)(\$80) = \$80\,000\,000.$$

As shown in the table, $80 million is added to the common equity account, and the retained earnings account is reduced from $155 million to $75 million.[10]

Price Effects

Several empirical studies have examined the effects of stock splits and stock dividends on share prices. The findings of a study by Barker are presented in Table 19-2.[11] When stock dividends were associated with a cash dividend increase, the value of the company's shares 6 months after the ex-dividend date (ex of the stock dividend) had risen by 8 percent. On the other hand, when stock dividends were not accompanied by cash dividend increases, share prices fell by 12 percent during the subsequent 6-month period, which approximated the percentage amount of the average stock dividend.

Another empirical study,[12] using a more sophisticated analysis, investigated the impact of stock splits and stock dividends (of 25 percent or more) on rates of return to common equity holders—dividends plus capital gains, measured

Table 19-2
Price Effects of Stock Dividends

	Prices at Selected Dates (Percentages)		
	6 Months Prior to Ex-Dividend Date	At Ex-Dividend Date	6 Months after Ex-Dividend Date
Cash dividend increase	100	109	108
No cash dividend increase	100	99	88

[10]Note that Porter could not pay a stock dividend that exceeded 38.75 percent; a stock dividend of that percentage would exhaust the retained earnings. Thus, a firm's ability to declare stock dividends is constrained by the amount of its retained earnings. Of course, if Porter had wanted to pay a 50 percent stock dividend, it could have just switched to one-and-a-half-for-one stock split and accomplished the same thing.

[11]C. Austin Barker, "Evaluation of Stock Dividends," *Harvard Business Review*, July-August 1958: 99–114. Barker's study has been replicated several times in recent years, and his results are still valid—they have withstood the test of time.

[12]Eugene Fama, Lawrence Fisher, Michael Jensen, and Richard Roll, "The Adjustment of Stock Prices to New Information," *International Economic Review* 10, no. 1 (February 1969): 1–21.

relative to an equity market index. One finding of this study was that companies that engaged in stock splits had rates of return, before the split date, that were high relative to the market. This reflected dramatic increases in expected earnings and dividends. The authors then examined the rate of return on the shares after the split date. The overall sample was divided into two subgroups: those companies with dividend increases after the stock split and those with dividend decreases. The increases and decreases were measured relative to the change in the dividends on the market index. It was found that for the first set of companies, the rates of return after the split were marginally better than the index for approximately 1 year. For the second group, however, the rates of return were below the index.

The explanation of this differential behaviour is straightforward. It appears that, on average, stock splits are followed by increases in dividends per share: of the 940 splits considered, 672 had dividend increases. It is not the increased dividend per se that affects the rate of return, but the information that the increased dividend conveys. As noted before, because managements are averse to reducing dividends, the increased dividend conveys information about future earnings. Thus, an increased dividend after a split confirms the market's expectations, and there is no significant impact on the rate of return. A decrease in dividends, however, is completely new and unexpected information, and the rate of return falls.

Both of these studies suggest that stock dividends are seen for what they are—simply additional pieces of paper—and they do not represent true income. When they are accompanied by higher cash dividends, the information in the increased dividends is reflected in the share price. But when stock dividends are not accompanied by an increase in cash dividends, the share price falls to reflect the new information that earnings are not expected to be higher in the future. Therefore, the fundamental determinant of share price is the underlying expected profitability of the company.

Finally, another study[13] has shown that relative to a set of control companies (matched by size and industry), companies that split their shares had, on average, significantly higher growth in earnings and dividends per share beginning 5 years before the split. After the split, earnings per share grew at higher rates, on average, over the first year and dividends per share over the first and second years. Finally, the average price per share of the splitting firms after the split was not different from the average share price of the control companies.

For the stock dividend sample, earnings per share grew at a faster rate than for the control group in the 1-to-2-year period before the stock dividend, but there was no difference in dividend per share growth in the same period. Two years after the stock dividend, there was only a slight excess growth in dividends per share.

The results for the stock split sample are consistent with the idea that the event provides investors with information about future earnings and dividends. However, stock dividends appear to provide little or no information.

---

[13]J. Lakonishok and B. Lev, "Stock Splits and Stock Dividends: Why, Who and When," *Journal of Finance*, September 1987: 913–32.

> ### Concept Review
>
> ► What is the rationale for a stock split? What economic conditions might suggest that a series of stock dividends be used rather than a stock split?
>
> ► Differentiate between the accounting treatments for stock splits and stock dividends.
>
> ► What have been the results of studies concerning the effect of stock dividends on share prices? What difference does it make if a cash dividend does or does not accompany the stock dividend?

Share Repurchases

In a **share repurchase**, a firm buys back some of the outstanding shares of its own equity. The stated reasons and the true motivation (they need not be identical) for share repurchases are varied. One reason may be an attempt to consolidate control in management's hands to prevent a hostile takeover. Other reasons include the following: (1) the firm had excess cash; (2) management felt that the company's shares were undervalued; and (3) management felt that the shareholders would be served better by having the company repurchase shares rather than having the excess funds paid out as a cash dividend.

An analysis of the repurchase decision begins with the recognition that if some of the outstanding shares are repurchased,[14] fewer shares will remain outstanding. Assuming that the repurchase does not adversely affect the firm's earning power, the earnings per share of the remaining shares will increase. This increase in EPS should result in a higher market price per share. Thus, capital gains will have been substituted for dividends. These effects are illustrated in the following subsection. However, as will be noted, the repurchase need not be financed only through cash balances accumulated for dividend payments.

---

[14]Share repurchases are commonly made in three ways. First, a publicly owned firm can simply buy its own shares through a broker on the open market. Second, it can issue a *tender*, under which it permits shareholders to send in (that is, "tender") their shares to the firm in exchange for a specified price per share. When tender offers are made, the firm generally indicates that it will buy up to a specified number of shares within a specified time period (usually about 2 weeks); if more shares are tendered than the company wishes to purchase, then purchases are made on a pro rata basis. Finally, the firm can purchase a block of shares from one larger holder on a negotiated basis.

Also, note that repurchased shares held by the firm are called *treasury stock*. They are not included in "shares outstanding" and hence do not enter into the calculation of earnings per share. Note also that treasury stock can be reissued should the company choose to do so. Such reissues are often made (1) to pay for the acquisition of another company, (2) to issue shares when convertible securities are converted or warrants exercised, (3) to issue shares when executive stock options are exercised, and (4) to raise capital to expand operations.

The Effects of Share Repurchases

Many companies have been repurchasing their shares in recent years.[15] The decision to engage in a share repurchase is followed by an announcement in the financial press and the filing of documents with the appropriate securities commission. For example, Imasco Ltd's board authorized a share repurchase through the market (which is referred to as a "normal course issuer bid") representing about 1 percent of its shares outstanding. The time period for the repurchase was August 6, 1992 to, at the latest, August 6, 1993. This authorization followed the repurchase of 372 000 common shares over the previous 12 months.

The effects of a repurchase can be illustrated with data on Canadian MultiMinerals Ltd. (CMM). The company earned $4.4 million last year; of this amount, 50 percent, or $2.2 million, has been allocated for distribution to common shareholders. There are currently 1.1 million shares outstanding, and the market value is $22 a share. This price, which is measured before the annual dividend is declared and thus reflects the earnings that have not yet been paid out, is referred to as the *cum-dividend price*. CMM can use the $2.2 million to repurchase 100 000 of its shares through a tender offer of $22 a share, or it can pay a cash dividend of $2 per share. If the latter alternative is chosen, the share price will fall to $20 when the shares go *ex dividend*; the ex-dividend price is thus $20.

The market value of the equity before the repurchase is composed of two parts: the first is the present value of the earnings generated from the existing assets; the second reflects the earnings retained as cash. When the repurchase is undertaken, the second part is removed from the firm's value and only the first is left.

Thus, the current market value of the CMM before the repurchase is written as follows:

$$\begin{pmatrix} \text{Market value} \\ \text{CMM} \end{pmatrix} = \begin{pmatrix} \text{Market value,} \\ \text{based on} \\ \text{expected} \\ \text{earnings} \end{pmatrix} + \begin{pmatrix} \text{Cash to be paid} \\ \text{out as dividends,} \\ \text{or to finance} \\ \text{repurchase} \end{pmatrix},$$

where

$$\begin{pmatrix} \text{Market value} \\ \text{CMM} \end{pmatrix} = \text{1.1 million shares} \times \$22 \text{ per share}$$
$$= \$24.2 \text{ million}$$

$$\begin{pmatrix} \text{Market value,} \\ \text{based on} \\ \text{expected} \\ \text{earnings} \end{pmatrix} = \$1.1 \text{ million shares} \times \$20 \text{ per share}$$
$$= \$22 \text{ million (ex-divided price).}$$

$$\begin{matrix} \text{Cash to be} \\ \text{paid out} \end{matrix} = \$2.2 \text{ million.}$$

---

[15]Share repurchase plans were given extra prominence after the market crash in October 1987, when many companies announced share repurchase programs in an attempt to support their share prices. Ironically, only a small proportion went through with the transactions.

The effect of the repurchase on the EPS and market price per share of the remaining shares is determined as follows:

1. Current EPS $= \dfrac{\text{Total earnings}}{\text{Number of shares}} = \dfrac{\$4.4 \text{ million}}{1.1 \text{ million}}$
$= \$4$ per share.

2. Ex-dividend P/E ratio $= \dfrac{\text{Ex-dividend price}}{\text{Earnings per share}} = \dfrac{\$20}{\$4} = 5$ times.

3. EPS after repurchase of 100 000 shares $= \dfrac{\$4.4 \text{ million}}{1 \text{ million}} = \$4.40$ per share.

4. Expected market price after repurchase $= (P/E)(EPS) = (5)(\$4.40) = \$22$ per share.

It should be noted from this example that, ignoring tax differences on dividends and capital gains, investors should be indifferent to the method by which the dividend is paid. The wealth of an equity investor is equal under two methods: the per share wealth under the repurchase scheme is $22 whether or not the investor sells the shares. If the investor does not sell, his or her wealth equals the share price of $22 after the repurchase; if the investor sells, he or she receives $22. Under the cash dividend option, the investor's wealth is also $22; this is obtained as the sum of the dividend per share of $2 plus the ex-dividend share price of $20. In this example, under the share repurchase, the firm pays out the funds and the shareholders whose shares are repurchased receive the $2 per share dividend as a realized capital gain; those investors who do not sell receive a $2 unrealized capital gain—that is, the share price remains at its current value of $22, which is $2 above its value if the dividend is paid.

The equality of shareholder wealth under the share repurchase and cash dividend alternatives occurs because we have assumed (1) that the P/E ratio will remain constant, (2) that there is no impact of differential taxes on capital gains and dividends, and (3) that the shares can be repurchased at exactly $22 per share. The P/E ratio might change as a result of the repurchase operation, rising if investors view it favourably and falling if they view it unfavourably.[16] One important factor that could have an impact on the P/E ratio is the difference in taxes on capital gains and on dividends. If all investors defer the realization of the capital gain, then the effective tax rate on dividends can exceed that on capital gains and the share repurchase is preferred. Conversely, the dividend payment is preferred if the effective tax rate on dividends is less than the tax rate on capital gain. The problem that the company faces is that its investors have different marginal tax rates, and thus, unless the company can discern where the majority of effective tax rates are located, it does not know whether to repurchase or pay cash dividends.

---

[16]An increasing P/E multiple suggests that new value has been created through the share repurchase. Since the components that affect the P/E multiple (risk and expected earnings) do not appear to be altered by a repurchase, an increase in the P/E multiple is a puzzle that will be addressed in a subsequent section.

Finally, the example assumes that a repurchase can be undertaken at the current market price. Suppose, for some reason, that the repurchase price is set at a price above \$22. This operation will benefit the tendering shareholders at the expense of the nontendering shareholders. Also, the size of the impact on the remaining shareholders will depend on the number of shares repurchased relative to the number of shares outstanding before the repurchase.

To illustrate these relationships: consider first the case in which the repurchase or tender price, P_T, is set above the share price before the repurchase is undertaken, P_0. Let the tender price per share be \$30. At a price of \$30 per share, 73 333 shares will be repurchased (2.2 million shares/\$30). Therefore there will be 1 026 667 shares outstanding. The share price after the repurchase is consummated is determined as follows:

$$\text{EPS after repurchase of 73 333 shares} = \frac{\$4.4 \text{ million}}{1\,026\,667} = \$4.286.$$

$$\begin{aligned}\text{Expected market price after repurchase, } P_E &= (P/E)(EPS) \\ &= 5 \times \$4.286 = \$21.43.\end{aligned}$$

In this example, the shareholders who do not tender will have a share price after the repurchase that is less than the value before the repurchase. These nontendering shareholders will lose \$0.571 per share or \$586 227 in total (\$0.571 × 1 026 667). The shareholders who tender at \$30 per share will gain \$8 per share, or, in aggregate, \$586 664 (\$8 × 73 333). Therefore, the gain to tendering shareholders is equal to the loss to those who do not tender (up to a rounding error).

If the firm decided to use more of its earnings in the repurchase, this could have an impact on the P/E multiple; the retained earnings available for investment might be lower, which would affect the price per share.

One final implication to be gleaned from this example is that there is no increase in value to the firm from the repurchase itself. The market value of the firm's equity after the repurchase is the same as its value before the repurchase after removing the payment of \$2.2 million. Regardless of the tender price, the product of the value of P_E times the number of shares outstanding based on a particular tender price is equal to \$22 million. This is the market value of CMM based on expected earnings. Further, the fact that in all the examples the gains and losses to parties in the repurchase net out to zero implies that no value is created in this example of a repurchase.

Considerable research has been conducted into the impact on share prices of repurchase through the use of tender offers. The evidence presented in these studies is that the average tender price is approximately 20 percent in excess of the market price prevailing prior to the repurchase. From the previous discussion, we would anticipate that $P_E < P_0$ (that is, that the price after the offer is completed would be below the pre-offer price). This, however, is *not* the case—the price reported by empirical researchers was approximately 12 percent above the pre-offer price (after removing the impact of general stock market movements). The gains, as measured by the relationship of P_E and P_0, were largest for repurchases financed by a debt issue and smallest for repurchases effected through open market repurchases.

Since $P_E > P_0$ even though $P_T > P_0$, there must be a gain in value to the firm from a repurchase. The average gain in value as a percentage of the prepurchase market value was 15.7 percent; only 11.0 percent of the repurchases had a wealth decrease.[17]

The final observation from the empirical literature is that the gain in value from the repurchase depends directly on the proportion of shares repurchased, the size of the tender price, and the proportion of shares held by insiders.

The empirical regularities reported in the share repurchase literature pose the following questions. What explains the gain in total value of equity compared to its prepurchase level? Why should the dollar value of this gain depend upon the proportion of shares repurchased, F; the tender price, P_T; the fraction of shares held by insiders; and the method by which the repurchase is financed?

A number of explanations have been put forward; these are described and evaluated below.

1. *Leverage increases and tax benefits.*   The repurchase may result in an increase in the debt-to-equity ratio. By issuing debt and repurchasing equity, a firm obtains an instantaneous change in the leverage ratio, which, as noted in Chapter 18, can be of benefit to existing equity holders. Hence there is an overall gain, since debt is a tax-deductible expense and the tax savings are of benefit to equity holders. (This assumes that the firm does not go beyond the debt ratio at which the increased probability of bankruptcy, with its associated costs, offsets the expected tax savings.)

2. *Expropriate wealth of bondholders.*   To the extent that the company can facilitate an unexpected increase in the risk to existing bondholders by a share repurchase, there will be a gain to shareholders. This is an unlikely explanation for the gain in the value of the firm, however, since bondholders, in an attempt to protect themselves from this behaviour of equity holders, generally introduce bond covenants limiting the shareholders' decision-making flexibility. In addition, the studies on share repurchase found an insignificant impact on the prices of preferred shares and straight debt for those companies engaged in share repurchases. If risk did increase, the values of these securities should fall.

3. *Reduction in the agency costs of equity.*   The agency cost of equity reflects the decrease in share price required to induce a shareholder to purchase a share of a company in which management owns a proportion of the equity. The smaller the proportion of equity held by managers, the greater the agency cost of equity. Existing and potential shareholders' anticipation that managers will consume perquisites and shirk must be reflected in the share price. However, the cost to a manager of this behaviour, and hence the incentive to engage in it, depends upon the proportion of equity owned by the manager. For example, if the manager owns 80 percent of a firm, for every dollar of perquisites consumed, he or she bears 80 cents of the cost; the gain to the manager is 20 cents. If the proportion is 20 percent, then the

---

[17]An example of the price behaviour of share prices in a share repurchase is presented in the appendix to this chapter.

manager bears 20 cents of the cost and the gain is 80 cents. Clearly, agency costs are higher in the latter case.

In a share repurchase, managers typically do not tender their shares. Therefore, their proportionate interest in the equity of the firm after the share repurchase will increase. This should lead to an expected reduction in agency costs and hence an increase in share price upon the announcement of the repurchase.[18]

4. *Information, or signalling argument.*   When questioned about their motives in a share repurchase, managers often state that they feel that the repurchase is the best investment they can undertake with the firm's funds. One interpretation of this statement is that there exist informational asymmetries: management has more information than shareholders about the future cash flows of the company. The share repurchase is a signal to the market that the market value of the equity does not reflect the higher cash flows that management believes will arise.

For a signal to be credible to the market, a number of elements must be present. First, the signal must be amenable to corroboration from observed data subsequent to the repurchase. In the repurchase research, it has been observed that the per-share earnings of these firms after the repurchase were above the values that could have been predicted by pre-announcement earnings data. Second and most important, there should be no incentive for management to lie; thus, false signals must result in true wealth losses for those who made the false signal.

The structure of the share repurchase leads to a penalty for false signals as long as management owns some of the shares. Since any false signal will ultimately result in a reduction in share price and managers do not tender, they will ultimately bear the cost of a false signal. The greater the proportion of shares they currently own and the greater the proportion of shares repurchased, the greater the managers' ultimate liability for a false signal will be, since they will end up holding a greater proportion of the equity in the firm. In addition, a high tender premium implies that managers believe that there are gains sufficiently large for the gain to nontenderers to be positive. If a false signal is sent, the larger the tender premium, the greater the loss to nontenderers will be when the share price reacts. Finally, the use of debt to finance the repurchase reinforces the credibility of the signal. With greater debt, there is a higher interest component, which can be serviced only out of higher cash flows. If a false signal is sent and cash flows will not be higher, the probability of default increases, and management, being an equity holder, will incur a loss as share prices fall to reflect the potential for default and its associated costs. Therefore, all the signs point to the share repurchase signal as being credible; hence, the gain reflects the market's evaluation of the signal concerning expected future cash flows.

---

[18]There is an offsetting element if share ownership becomes too concentrated in management's hands; this concentration could lead to a reduction in the probability of the firm's being a takeover target. The implication of this result is discussed in Chapter 24.

The Advantages and Disadvantages of Repurchases

Advantages from the Shareholders' Viewpoint.   A number of advantages to shareholders may accrue from share repurchase.

1. Repurchase announcements are often viewed as positive signals by investors because the repurchase is often motivated by management's belief that the firm's shares are undervalued.
2. The shareholder has a choice: to sell or not to sell. On the other hand, the person who receives a dividend has to accept the payment and pay the tax.
3. A qualitative advantage advanced by market practitioners is that a repurchase can often remove a large block of shares overhanging the market.

Advantages from Management's Viewpoint.   Advantages to management of repurchases include the following:

1. Dividends are sticky in the short run, because managements are reluctant to raise dividends if the new dividend cannot be maintained in the future. Hence, if an excess cash flow is thought to be only temporary, management may prefer to make the distribution in the form of a share repurchase rather than to declare a cash dividend that it believes cannot be maintained.
2. Repurchased shares can be used for acquisitions or released when stock options are exercised, when convertibles are converted, or when warrants are exercised. Discussions with financial managers indicate that it is frequently more convenient and less expensive to use repurchased shares rather than newly issued shares for these purposes.
3. With informational asymmetries, management may be able to signal, in a credible manner, that cash flows of the firm are expected to increase.
4. Repurchases can be used to effect large-scale changes in capital structure. For example, suppose a company has very little long-term debt outstanding. The company decides that its optimal capital structure calls for the use of considerably more debt, but even if it finances only with debt it will take years to get the debt ratio up to the newly defined optimal level. The company can, however, sell long-term debt and use the proceeds to repurchase its common shares, thereby producing an instant change in its capital structure.
5. If directors are wealthy and have large holdings themselves, they may have especially strong preferences for repurchases rather than dividend payments because of the tax factor.
6. In order to retain control in a takeover bid, management can repurchase shares at a price in excess of the price in the takeover bid.

Disadvantages from the Shareholders' Viewpoint.   Disadvantages to shareholders of repurchases include the following:

1. Shareholders may not be indifferent between dividends and capital gains, and the price of the shares may benefit more from cash dividends than

from repurchases. Cash dividends are generally thought of as relatively dependable, but repurchases are not. Further, if a firm announces a regular, dependable repurchase program, the likelihood increases that the repurchase will be interpreted by the income tax authorities as a dividend distribution.

2. The *selling* shareholders may not be fully aware of all the implications of a repurchase or may not have all the pertinent information about the corporation's present and future activities. For this reason, firms generally announce a repurchase program before embarking on it.

3. The corporation may pay too high a price for the repurchased shares, to the disadvantage of remaining shareholders. If the shares are inactively traded and if the firm seeks to acquire a relatively large number of its shares, the price may be bid above its equilibrium value and then fall after the firm has ceased its repurchase operation. To minimize this impact, the repurchases in the market will be undertaken slowly.

Disadvantage from Management's Viewpoint. From management's viewpoint, the chief disadvantage of repurchases is that some investors feel that announcing a repurchase program is like announcing that management cannot locate good investment projects. One could argue that instituting a repurchase program should be regarded in the same manner as announcing a higher dividend payout, but if repurchases are regarded as indicating especially unfavourable growth opportunities, they can have an adverse impact on the firm's image and on the market price of its shares.

Reporting Requirements in Share Repurchase

The Ontario Securities Commission (OSC) and the Toronto Stock Exchange have requirements dealing with share repurchases, which are referred to as *issuer bids*.

There are also a number of specific provisions that are included in the Ontario *Securities Act*; we will consider a few of the more important ones. First, the act does not apply to federally incorporated companies, private companies, or companies that intend to repurchase the shares through the stock exchange. In addition, the provisions do not apply to open market purchases to a limit of 5 percent of the shares outstanding of a particular class of equity over a period of 12 consecutive months.

If the issuer bid does not fall within one of the exemptions noted above, then it must meet certain information provision requirements. First, a directors' circular must be distributed within 10 days of the commencement of the bid; the circular must include recommendations of the directors to shareholders whether or not to tender—or, if no recommendation is made, the reasons must be given. Any changes in information that would affect the directors' circular require a notice of change to be sent to all shareholders.

An issuer bid circular must be sent to all shareholders. The purpose of the information included in this circular is to get "hidden" information into the market. The information to be provided is substantial and includes reasons for the bid, volume of trading in the security for the previous 12 months, and beneficial interest in the company by insiders. The required information is very detailed and can be costly to prepare.

Under some circumstances, a valuation of the company must be undertaken, and this information, along with any prior valuations, must be included in the issuer bid circular.

If the tender offer is made through the TSE, there are still information provision requirements. For purchases over a 12-month period of less than 5 percent of the shares outstanding, a notice of intention must be filed with the TSE, sent to the shareholders, and released to the press prior to the commencement of the bid. For more substantial bids, the firm must distribute an issuer bid circular that conforms to disclosure rules required by the OSC.

Conclusion on Share Repurchases

When all the pros and cons on share repurchases have been totalled, where do we stand? Our own conclusions can be summarized as follows:

1. Repurchases on a regular, systematic, dependable basis—like quarterly dividends—may not be feasible because of uncertainties about the tax treatment of such a program and about the market price of the shares, how many shares will be tendered, and so on.
2. However, repurchases may offer some significant advantages over dividends to some investors, so the procedure should be given careful consideration.
3. Repurchases can be especially valuable in effecting a significant shift in capital structure within a short period.
4. Repurchases appear to be a credible method for management to signal higher expected cash flows for the firm.

Repurchases to Go Private

So far we have considered only repurchase situations in which the company's shares will continue to be traded on a securities exchange. Alternatively, a share repurchase can be structured so that a firm with publicly traded equity will eliminate its publicly traded securities by going *private*. This development is not new, but it has become prominent since 1976.

The "going private" phenomenon received attention in the United States in the mid-1970s. The common scenario is that a junior industrial firm that went public in a boom capital market at a high market price is faced with a relatively low share price. The management decides that the disadvantages of having the shares listed on an exchange outweigh the advantages, and the company repurchases its shares to become private again.

The Ontario Securities Commission is concerned about a problem associated with a company's returning to private status. This problem, referred to as a *squeeze-out*, occurs when the majority shareholders attempt to eliminate or reduce the importance of the minority interests. There are a number of ways to effect a squeeze-out, but the OSC is concerned about the repurchase technique. The minority shareholders may be bought out at a price per share that is less than the issue price when the firm went public, is less than the current appraised value, but is in excess of the prevailing market price.

There are a number of examples of going-private attempts. For example, Sifton Properties Limited made a share repurchase bid at $12.00 per share, and through other financial arrangements, any remaining public shareholders would have been squeezed out. An independent valuation of the adjusted book value per share was $20.25. The squeeze-out was conditional upon the approval of a majority of the minority shareholders. Sifton Properties Limited ultimately abandoned the plans for a squeeze-out.

There is some empirical evidence concerning the impact on share prices of the announcement of a company that it is going private. One study found that over 2 days the announcement of a going-private transaction provided shareholders a rate of return of 22 percent over and above the return on the market! If the return was computed over the 40 days before the date of the announcement, the excess return earned was 30 percent. (This longer period incorporated the anticipation of the announcement and/or leakage of information.) Therefore, going private appears to provide enough expected gains to management that it can offer premiums to acquire the shares. In fact, for 57 companies in which there was a pure cash transaction, the average premium of the offer price over the market price 40 days prior to the announcement was 56 percent!

There can be a number of benefits to the firm in going private; these benefits can be the source of the large premiums paid to shareholders. The first such benefit is the reduction of shareholder servicing costs; these include direct costs, such as registration, listing, legal and accounting services, annual report preparation, mailing, proxy statements, and the maintenance of a public relations department for dealing with shareholders, plus indirect (but significant) costs such as the time spent by the chief executive officer on public relations. One study estimated the value of these costs to be $100 000 per year. When capitalized, they can be a significant amount for a small firm. The second benefit is in managerial incentives. With managers having higher ownership levels in the new firm, there is less incentive to shirk, and the improved performance will increase the value of the firm. Moreover, it is easier to write compensation contracts tied to profitability when there are no outside shareholders. Thus, if managers have to spend a disproportionate share of their time on a particular project, compensation contracts recognizing this can be structured more easily. This, too, improves performance.

Although these benefits may be substantial, they are not important for all companies, because only a small proportion of firms undertake repurchases to go private. There are companies for which the benefits of public ownership exceed the benefits of going private. The benefits from public ownership include access to equity markets and the ability afforded owners of equity to diversify risk.

Concept Review

▶ Explain how repurchases can (1) help shareholders reduce taxes and (2) help firms change their capital structures.
▶ What are the three ways a firm can make repurchases?
▶ What are the advantages of repurchases from both a shareholder's and management's viewpoints? What are the disadvantages?
▶ Describe a "going private" transaction and its benefits.

Summary

Dividend policy involves the decision to pay out earnings versus retaining them for reinvestment in the firm. If dividends are to be paid, a decision must be made as to the percentage of earnings to pay out. This percentage is known as the **payout ratio**. Dividend policy decisions can have either favourable or unfavourable effects on the price of the firm's shares. The key concepts covered are listed below.

☐ The **optimal dividend policy** is the policy that strikes the exact balance between current dividends and future growth that maximizes the share price of the firm's common equity.

☐ Miller and Modigliani developed the **dividend irrelevance theory**, which holds that a firm's dividend policy has no effect either on the value of the firm or on its cost of capital.

☐ The **bird-in-the-hand theory**, advocated by Gordon and Lintner, holds that the value of the firm will be maximized by a high dividend payout ratio because investors regard actual dividends as being less risky than potential capital gains.

☐ Because empirical tests of the two theories have been inconclusive, academicians simply cannot tell corporate managers with any degree of precision how a change in dividend policy will affect share prices and capital costs. Thus, actually determining the optimal dividend policy is extremely difficult.

☐ Dividend policy should also reflect the information content of dividends (signalling) and the clientele effect. The **information content**, or **signalling, hypothesis** states that investors regard dividend changes as a signal of management's forecast of future earnings. The **clientele effect** suggests that a firm will attract investors who like the firm's dividend policy.

☐ In practice, most firms try to follow a *stable dividend payment policy* or a *stable growth rate policy*—paying a constant, or steadily increasing, dividend. This policy provides investors with a stable, dependable income, and, if the signalling theory is correct, it also gives investors information about management's expectations for earnings growth.

☐ Other dividend policies used include: (1) the **residual dividend policy**, in which dividends are paid out of earnings left over after the capital budget has been financed; (2) the *constant payout ratio policy*, in which a constant percentage of earnings is targeted to be paid out; and (3) the *low-regular-dividend-plus-extras policy*, in which the firm pays a constant, low dividend that can be maintained even in bad years, and then pays an extra dividend in good years.

☐ A **dividend reinvestment plan (DRP)** allows shareholders to have the company automatically use their dividends to purchase additional shares of the firm's equity. DRPs are popular with investors who do not need current income because the plans allow shareholders to acquire additional shares without incurring normal brokerage fees.

☐ Other factors, such as legal constraints, investment opportunities, and the availability and cost of funds from other sources, and taxes, are considered by managers when they establish dividend policies.

□ A **stock split** increases all the shares of a class by some multiple. The action is taken by a firm to increase the number of shares outstanding. Normally, splits reduce the price per share in proportion to the increase in shares because splits merely "divide the pie into smaller slices." A **stock dividend** is a dividend paid in additional shares of stock rather than in cash. Both stock dividends and stock splits are used to keep stock prices within an "optimal" range.

□ Under a **share repurchase plan**, a firm buys back some of its outstanding shares, thereby decreasing the number of shares, which in turn increases both EPS and the share price. Repurchases are useful for making major changes in a firm's capital structure, as well as for allowing shareholders to delay paying taxes on their share of the firm's profits. It is also viewed as a signal by management that it believes the firm is undervalued. If all the common shares are purchased, the firm is said to be engaged in a going private transaction. For certain companies, the costs of having publicly traded shares exceed the benefits and a going private share repurchase removes the company's shares from the market.

Questions

19-1 As an investor, would you rather invest in a firm that has a policy of maintaining (a) a constant payout ratio, (b) a constant dollar dividend per share, (c) a target dividend growth rate, or (d) a constant regular quarterly dividend plus a year-end extra when earnings are sufficiently high or corporate investment needs are sufficiently low? Explain your answer, stating how these policies would affect your k_s. Discuss how your answer might change if you were a student, a 50-year-old professional with peak earnings, or a retiree.

19-2 How would each of the following changes probably affect aggregate (or average for all corporations) payout ratios, other things held constant? Explain your answers.
   a. An increase in the personal income tax rate.
   b. An increase in the capital cost allowance (CCA) rates for all classes.
   c. An increase in the dividend tax credit (assume that the gross-up proportion remains unchanged).
   d. A rise in interest rates.
   e. An increase in corporate profits.
   f. A decline in investment opportunities.
   g. A change in the *Income Tax Act* so that corporations can deduct dividends for tax purposes as they now do interest charges.

19-3 Discuss the pros and cons of having the directors formally announce what a firm's dividend policy will be in the future.

19-4 "The cost of retained earnings is less than the cost of new outside equity capital. Consequently, it is totally irrational for a firm to sell a new issue of equity and to pay dividends during the same year." Discuss this statement.

19-5 Would it ever be rational for a firm to borrow money in order to pay dividends? Explain your answer.

19-6   What is the difference between a *stock dividend* and a *stock split*? As a shareholder, would you prefer to see your company declare a 100 percent stock dividend or a two-for-one split? Assume that either action is feasible.

19-7   In theory, if we had perfect capital markets, we would expect investors to be indifferent between cash dividends or an equivalent repurchase of shares outstanding. What factors might in practice cause investors to value one over the other?

19-8   Evaluate the benefits and costs to the shareholders of repurchases to go private. In your analysis, be sure to include the possibility that the majority shareholders have inside information concerning the future profitability of the firm.

19-9   Most firms would like to have their shares selling at a high P/E ratio, and they would also like to have extensive public ownership (many different shareholders). Explain how stock dividends or stock splits may help achieve these goals.

19-10   "Executive salaries have been shown to be more closely correlated to the size of the firm than to its profitability. If a firm's board of directors is controlled by management instead of by outside directors, this might result in the firm's retaining more earnings than can be justified from the shareholders' point of view." Discuss the statement, being sure (a) to use Figure 19-4 in your answer and (b) to explain the implied relationship between dividend policy and share prices.

19-11   Modigliani and Miller (MM) on the one hand and Gordon and Lintner (GL) on the other have expressed strong views regarding the effect of dividend policy on a firm's cost of capital and value.
   a. In essence, what are the MM and GL views regarding the effect of dividend policy on the cost of capital and share prices?
   b. According to the text, which of these theories, if any, has received statistical confirmation from empirical tests?
   c. How could MM use the information content (signalling) hypothesis to counter their opponents' arguments? If you were debating MM, how would you counter them?
   d. How could MM use the clientele effect concept to counter their opponents' arguments? If you were debating MM, how would you counter them?

19-12   One position expressed in the financial literature is that firms set their dividends as a residual after using income to support new investment.
   a. Explain what a residual dividend policy implies, illustrating your answer with a graph showing how different conditions could lead to different dividend payout ratios.
   b. Could the residual dividend policy be consistent with (i) a constant growth-rate policy, (ii) a constant payout policy, and/or (iii) a low-regular-dividend-plus-extras policy? Answer in terms of both year-to-year consistency and longer-run consistency.
   c. Think back to Chapter 18, in which we considered the relationship between capital structure and the cost of capital. Imagine a graph in

which the plot of k_a versus the debt ratio is shaped like a sharp V. Now imagine one in which the plot is shaped like a shallow bowl (or a flattened U). Would the two situations have different implications for the importance of setting dividends according to the residual policy?

d. Assume that Companies A and B both have IOS schedules that intersect their MCC schedules at a point that, under the residual policy, calls for a 30 percent payout. In both cases, a 30 percent payout requires a cut in the annual dividend from $3.00 to $1.50. One company cuts its dividend, whereas the other does not. One company has a relatively steep IOS curve, whereas the other has a relatively flat one. Explain which company probably has the steeper curve.

Self-Test Problems   (solutions appear on page 738)

ST-1   Key terms.   Define each of the following terms:
   a. Optimal dividend policy; payout ratio
   b. Declaration date; holder of record date; ex-dividend date; payment date
   c. Dividend irrelevance theory; bird-in-the-hand theory
   d. Information content, or signalling, hypothesis; clientele effect
   e. Residual dividend policy
   f. Extra dividend
   g. Dividend reinvestment plan (DRP); legal list
   h. Stock split; stock dividend
   i. Share repurchase

ST-2   Alternative dividend policies.   Canadian Manufacturing Company Ltd. (CMC) has an all-equity capital structure. It has 200 000 shares of $2 par value common equity outstanding.

When CMC's founder, who was the company's research director and most successful inventor, retired unexpectedly in late 1992, CMC was left suddenly and permanently with materially lower growth expectations and relatively few attractive, new investment opportunities. Unfortunately, there was no way to replace the founder's contributions to CMC. Previously, CMC found it necessary to plough back most of its earnings to finance growth, which had been averaging 12 percent per year. Future growth at a 6 percent rate is considered realistic, but that would require an increase in the dividend payout. Further, it now appears that new investment projects with at least the 14 percent rate of return required by CMC's shareholders ($k_s = 14\%$) would amount to only $800 000 for 1993 in comparison to a projected $2 million of net income after taxes. If the existing 20 percent dividend payout were continued, retained earnings would be $1.6 million in 1993, but, as noted, investments that yield the 14 percent cost of capital would amount to only $800 000.

The one encouraging thing is that high cash inflows from existing long-term contracts are expected to continue, and net income of $2 million is still expected for 1993.

Given the dramatically changed circumstances, CMC's management is undertaking a review of the firm's dividend policy.

a. Assume that the acceptable 1993 investment projects would be financed entirely by earnings retained during the year and that CMC uses the residual payment policy. Calculate DPS in 1993.

b. What payout ratio does this imply for 1993?

c. If a 60 percent payout ratio is maintained for the foreseeable future, what is your estimate of the present market price of CMC's common equity? How does this compare with the market price that should have prevailed under the assumptions existing just prior to the news about the retirement of the founder? If the two values of P_0 are different, comment on why.

d. What are the implications of continuing the existing 20 percent payout on the price per share? Assume that, if this payout is maintained, the rate of return on the retained earnings would be 7.5 percent, and the new growth rate would be

$$g = (1.0 - \text{Payout ratio})(\text{ROE})$$
$$= (1.0 - 0.2)(7.5\%)$$
$$= (0.8)(7.5\%) = 6.0\%.$$

Problems

19-1 External equity financing. Quebec Heating and Cooling has a 6-month backlog of orders for its patented solar heating system. Management plans to expand production capacity by 40 percent with a $10 million investment in plant machinery to meet this demand. The firm wants to maintain a 40 percent debt-to-total-assets ratio in its capital structure; it also wants to maintain its past dividend policy of distributing 45 percent of last year's after-tax earnings. In 1992, after-tax earnings were $5 million. How much external equity must the firm seek at the beginning of 1993 in order to expand capacity as desired?

19-2 Dividend payout. Divine Systems expects next year's after-tax income to be $15 million. The firm's current debt ratio is 40 percent. Divine has $12 million of profitable investment opportunities and wishes to maintain its current debt ratio. According to the residual theory of dividends, how large should the firm's dividend payout ratio be next year?

19-3 Stock split. After a five-for-one stock split, the Walker Company paid a dividend of $0.75 per new share, which was a 9 percent increase over last year's presplit dividend. What was last year's dividend per share?

19-4 Stock dividend. Butler Corporation declared a 6 percent stock dividend plus a cash dividend of $0.90 per share. The cash dividend was paid on both the old shares and the new shares received from the stock dividend. Construct a pro forma balance sheet showing the effect of these actions; use one new balance sheet that incorporates both actions. The equity was selling for $37.50 per share. A condensed version of

Butler's balance sheet as of December 31, 1993, before the dividends, follows (in millions of dollars):

Cash	$ 112.5	Debt	$1500
Other assets	2887.5	Common equity (90 million shares authorized, 75 million shares outstanding)	75
		Retained earnings	1125
Total assets	$3000.0	Total liabilities and equity	$3000

19-5   **Alternative dividend policies.** In 1993, the Lansing Company paid dividends totalling $3 600 000 on after-tax income of $10.8 million. For the past 10 years, earnings have grown at a constant rate of 10 percent, and 1993 was a normal year. However, in 1994, earnings are expected to jump to $14.4 million, and the firm expects to have profitable investment opportunities of $8.4 million. It is predicted that Lansing will not be able to maintain the 1994 level of earnings growth—the high forecast earnings level is attributable to an exceptionally profitable new product line that is being introduced—and the company will return to its previous 10 percent growth rate. Lansing's target debt ratio is 40 percent.

   a. Calculate Lansing's total dividends for 1994 if it follows each of the following policies:

     i. Its 1994 dividend payment is set to force dividends to grow at the long-run growth rate in earnings.

     ii. It continues the 1993 dividend payout ratio.

     iii. It uses a pure residual dividend policy (40 percent of the $8.4 million investment is financed with debt).

     iv. It employs a regular-dividend-plus-extras policy, with the regular dividend based on the long-run growth rate and the extra dividend set according to the residual policy.

   b. Which of the preceding policies would you recommend? Restrict your choices to the ones listed, but justify your answer.

   c. Assume that investors expect Lansing to pay total dividends of $9 000 000 in 1994 and to have the dividend grow at 10 percent after 1994. The total market value of the equity is $180 million. What is the company's cost of equity?

   d. What is Lansing's long-run average return on equity? (Hint: Recall that $g = (1 -$ Payout rate$)($ROE$)$. This formula can be applied using estimates of average long-run rates.)

   e. Does a 1994 dividend of $9 000 000 seem reasonable in view of your answers to Parts c and d? If not, should the dividend be higher or lower?

19-6   **Dividend policy and capital structure.** Tillsonburg Tobacco Company (TTC) has for many years enjoyed a moderate but stable growth in sales and earnings. However, cigar consumption and consequently TTC's sales have been falling recently, primarily because of an increasing awareness of the dangers of smoking to health. Anticipating further declines in tobacco sales, TTC's management hopes eventually to move almost entirely out of the tobacco business and into a newly developed, diversified product line in a growth-oriented industry. The company is especially interested in the prospects for pollution-control devices, because its research department has already done much work on the problems of filtering smoke. Right now the company estimates that an investment of $15 million is necessary to purchase new facilities and to begin operations on these products, but the investment could be earning a return of about 18 percent within a short time. The only other available investment opportunity totals $6 million and is expected to return about 10.4 percent.

The company is expected to pay a $3.00 dividend on its 3 million outstanding shares, the same as its dividend last year. The directors might, however, change the dividend if there are good reasons for doing so. Total earnings for the year are expected to be $14.25 million; the common equity is currently selling for $56.25 per share; the firm's target debt-to-assets ratio is 45 percent; and its tax rate is 40 percent. The costs of various forms of financing are as follows:

New bonds, $k_d = 11\%$. This is a before-tax rate.

New common equity sold at $56.25 per share will net $51.25.

Required rate of return on retained earnings, $k_s = 14\%$.

a. Calculate TTC's expected payout ratio, the break point at which MCC rises, and its marginal cost of capital above and below the point of exhaustion of retained earnings at the current payout. (Hint: k_s is given, and D_1/P_0 can be found. Then, knowing k_s and D_1/P_0, you can determine g.)

b. How large should TTC's capital budget be for the year?

c. What is an appropriate dividend policy for TTC? How should the capital budget be financed?

d. How might risk factors influence TTC's cost of capital, capital structure, and dividend policy?

e. What assumptions, if any, do your answers to the preceding parts make about investors' preferences for dividends versus capital gains (in other words, their preferences regarding the D_1/P_0 and g components of k_s)?

Integrative Problem

19-7 Dividend policy. Computer Systems, Inc., (CSI) was founded 5 years ago by Donald Brown and Margaret Clark, who are still its only shareholders. CSI has now reached the stage at which outside equity capital is necessary to maintain its optimal capital structure of 60 percent equity and 40 percent debt. Therefore, Brown and Clark have decided to take the company public. Up to this point, Brown and Clark have routinely reinvested all earnings in the firm and hence dividend policy has not been an issue, but now they must decide on a dividend policy.

Assume that you were recently hired by Arthur Adamson & Company, a consulting firm that has been asked to help CSI prepare for its public offering. Martha Millon, the senior consultant in your group, has asked you to make a presentation to Brown and Clark in which you review some basic dividend policy issues by discussing the following questions:

a. i. What is meant by a firm's *dividend policy*?

ii. What are the two major theories regarding dividend policy's effect on a firm's value? Briefly describe each theory.

iii. What do the two theories indicate regarding an optimal dividend policy?

iv. Construct a graph with dividend yield on the Y axis and capital gains yield on the X axis. Now assume that if the company paid out all earnings as dividends, it would have a required rate of return of 14 percent. Plot the dividend yield versus the capital gains yield for different payout ratios under each dividend policy theory. Explain your plots.

v. Have empirical tests been able to prove which theory, if any, is correct? How does this affect managers?

b. Discuss the information content, or signalling, hypothesis and the clientele effect, and their effects on dividend policy.

c. i. Explain in general terms what the residual dividend policy is.

ii. Assume that CSI has a $1 000 000 capital budget planned for the coming year. You have determined that its present capital structure (60 percent equity and 40 percent debt) is optimal, and its net income is forecasted at $750 000. What would be the total dollar dividend and the payout ratio if the firm used the residual policy? What if net income were forecasted at $500 000? $1 000 000?

iii. How would a change in investment opportunities affect the residual payment policy?

iv. What are the advantages and disadvantages of the residual policy? (Hint: Don't neglect signalling and the clientele effect.)

d. What are three other commonly used dividend payment policies? What are their advantages and disadvantages?

e. Briefly describe what a dividend reinvestment plan is, and give the two ways of operating such a plan.

f. Briefly describe how most firms set their dividend policy in practice.

g. What are share repurchases? Discuss the advantages and disadvantages of share repurchases.

h. What are stock dividends and stock splits? When should a firm consider using a stock dividend? When should a firm consider splitting its stock?

Solutions to Self-Test Problems

ST-1   Refer to the appropriate sections of the text to check your responses.

ST-2   a.

Net income	$2 000 000
Less: Capital project investments	800 000
Available residual	$1 200 000
Shares outstanding	200 000

DPS = $1 200 000/200 000 shares = $6 = D_1.

b. EPS = $2 000 000/200 000$ shares = $10.

$$\text{Payout ratio} = \text{DPS}/\text{EPS} = \$6/\$10 = 60\%.$$
$$\text{Total dividends}/\text{NI} = \$1\,200\,000/\$2\,000\,000 = 60\%.$$

c. Currently,
$$P_0 = \frac{D_1}{k_s - g} = \frac{\$6}{0.14 - 0.06} = \frac{\$6}{0.08} = \$75.00.$$

Under the former circumstances, D_1 would be based on a 20 percent payout on $10 EPS, or $2. With $k_s = 14\%$ and $g = 12\%$, we solve for P_0.

$$P_0 = \frac{D_1}{k_s - g} = \frac{\$2}{0.14 - 0.12} = \frac{\$2}{0.02} = \$100.00.$$

Although CMC has suffered a severe setback, its operations are well protected with long-term contracts. The cash generated by operations should be passed on to the shareholders, as the slowed internal growth will reduce the need for funds. The net result is to decrease the value of those shares by 25 percent, given that the required rate of return, k_s, is assumed to be constant.

d. If the payout ratio remained at 20 percent, the share price would decline to $2/(0.14 - 0.06) = \$25.00$, rather than to $75.00. Therefore, the present value of the increased dividend payment to the shareholders will reduce the decline in the market price of the equity. The increase in dividend payout is consistent with maximizing shareholder wealth.

Because of the downward-sloping IOS curve (see Figure 19-4), the greater the firm's level of investment, the lower the average ROE. Thus, if CMC retains and invests more money, its average ROE should decline. We can determine the average ROE under different conditions as follows:

Old situation (founder active and a 20% payout)

$$g = (1.0 - \text{payout})\text{ROE}$$
$$12\% = (1.0 - 0.2)\text{ROE}$$
$$\text{ROE} = 12\%/0.8 = 15\% > k_s = 14\%.$$

Note that the *average* ROE is 15 percent, whereas the *marginal* ROE is presumably equal to 14 percent. In terms of a graph like Figure 19-4, the intersection of the MCC and IOS curves is at 14 percent, and the average of the IOS curve, above the intersection, is 15 percent. *New situation (founder retired and a 60% payout)*

$$g = 6\% = (1.0 - 0.6)\text{ROE}$$
$$\text{ROE} = 6\%/0.4 = 15.0\% > k_s = 14\%.$$

This suggests that the new payout is appropriate and that the firm is taking on investments down to the point at which marginal return is equal to the cost of capital. In terms of a graph like Figure 19-4, the IOS curve shifted to the left after the founder retired. Note that if the 20 percent payout was maintained, the average ROE would be only 7.5 percent, which would imply a marginal ROE far below the 14 percent cost of capital.

Appendix 19A
Gains and Losses in Share Repurchase

This appendix presents an example constructed to aid the student in understanding the firm's share price behaviour during a cash tender offer for a share repurchase and the resulting gains to the various parties. The relationships between the pre-announcement price and the subsequent prices until the expiration date are based on empirical evidence from a number of studies investigating the excess rates of return at various points in time during a repurchase offer. The evidence is restricted to U.S. companies.

In our example, the price before a share repurchase, P_0, has an assumed value of $100. There are 10 000 shares outstanding: $n_0 = 10\,000$. The firm states that shares will be repurchased at a tender price, P_T, of $123 per share. Management specifies the proportion of shares that will be repurchased. F represents this proportion and has a value of 0.27—that is, 27 percent of the outstanding shares will be repurchased. Thus, on the expiration date, 2700 shares will have been repurchased, leaving 7300 shares outstanding. The symbol n_E represents the number of shares outstanding after the expiration date.

In the majority of share repurchases, the tender offer is oversubscribed, and the firm takes up the tendered shares on a pro rata basis; thus, each shareholder has the same proportion of shares tendered taken up by the company.

Upon expiration of the offer, the share price, P_E, is observed to be approximately 12 percent above the pre-announcement price of $100: that is, $P_E = \$112$. This price is the present value of the expected per-share earnings of the firm as a going concern subsequent to the completion of the repurchase.

Following the discussion in Chapter 19, the overall gain in wealth to the firm is equal to the gain to the tendering shareholders plus the gain to those who did not tender—including the existing management (who typically do not tender). The total increase in wealth is written as

$$\Delta\text{Wealth} = \text{Gain to tendering shareholders} + \\ \text{Gain to nontendering shareholders} \\ = (n_0 - n_E)(P_T - P_0) + n_E(P_E - P_0). \quad \text{(19A-1)}$$

In this example, the change in wealth is

$$\Delta W = (10\,000 - 7300)(\$123 - \$100) + 7300(\$112 - \$100) \\ = 2700(\$23) + 7300(\$12) \\ = \$62\,100 + \$87\,600 \\ = \$149\,700.$$

Given that the initial value of the firm is $1 000 000, the gain in value is approximately 15 percent of the initial value.

In this example, there is a positive gain to both sets of shareholders from the sharing of the overall increase in value of the firm.

The particular split of the total value gain in this example depends upon the tender price selected by management as well as the share price after the share repurchase is complete, P_E. For example, suppose the tender price, instead of being \$123, is \$140 per share. If the total gain remains constant and no new information is provided by the higher bid, then the expiration-day share price must fall. This fall is explained by the fact that those shareholders who tender are taking more per share out of the existing firm.

The new post-expiration day price in the revised example is obtained by solving Equation 19A-1 for P_E.

$$
\begin{aligned}
\$149\,700 &= 2700(P_T - P_0) + 7300(P_E - P_0) \\
&= 2700(\$140 - \$100) + 7300(P_E - \$100) \\
&= \$108\,000 + 7300P_E - \$730\,000. \\
P_E &\approx \$105.70.
\end{aligned}
$$

These prices result in a gain to tenderers of \$108 000, an increase over the previous example of \$45 900 and a gain to those who do not tender of \$41 700, a decrease of \$45 900 from the previous example. However, the tender price was still selected to provide a gain for those who remain with the firm. It is possible for the tender price to be set so high that any increase in firm value accrues totally to the tendering shareholders. For example, at a tender price of approximately \$155, there is no gain to nontendering shareholders, since $P_E = P_0$.[19]

The relationship between the observed prices during the course of the repurchase is presented in Figure 19A-1. On the announcement of the share repurchase, the share price increases to a value of \$115: $P_A = \$115$. If all shares tendered were to be accepted, the share price after the announcement would be equal to the tender price: that is, $P_A = P_T$. But since the repurchase proportion, F, is less than 100 percent and repurchases are oversubscribed, the market price after the announcement must be less than the tender price.

At the announcement date, only the terms of the share repurchase are available; how does the market determine the value of P_A? This price can be thought of as a weighted average of the tender price, P_T, and the price expected after the expiration date, P_E. This latter price will be referred to as the equilibrium price. The weights are related to the proportion of shares that will be taken up in the tender offer.

The actual equation representing the derivation of P_A is presented below, where it is applied to the numbers in our example.

$$
\begin{aligned}
P_A &= F \times P_T + (1 - F)P_E \qquad\qquad \textbf{(19A-2)} \\
&= 0.27 \times \$123 + 0.73 \times \$112 \\
&= \$115.
\end{aligned}
$$

---

[19]It is possible for the tender price to be set so high that all value gains to the firm are captured by the tendering shareholders and there is in addition a wealth redistribution from nontenderers to tendering shareholders. In this case P_E is less than P_0—the gain to nontenderers is negative. For example, if the tender price were \$160 per share, the total gain would remain \$149 700 but the gain to tenderers would be \$162 000 and to nontenderers −\$12 300. The tenderers gain wealth over and above the overall value increase—at the expense of the nontenderers. The value of P_E is \$98.32. The management of a firm would not have undertaken this repurchase with this expectation. The market's estimation of the value gain and the tender price chosen actually resulted in a loss to nontenderers!

Figure 19A-1
Share Price Movements During
A Share Repurchase

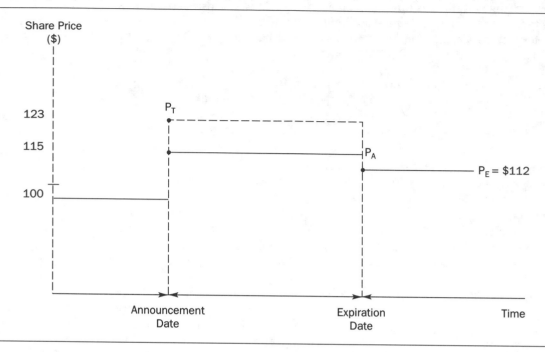

Notice that, in this example, the market expected an equilibrium price of $112, and this translated into a value for P_A of $115. Of course, if the market expected a different value for P_E, the weighted average price would differ.

To convince yourself that P_A must be an average price, consider the total value of equity after the share repurchase has been announced. This equity value is equal to the number of shares outstanding, 10 000, times the market price. This market value is divided among those shares that are tendered and those that are not. In our example, the former is equal to 2700 × $123 or $332 100, and the latter, 7300 × $112 or $817 600. The sum of these is equal to the market value of equity, or $1 149 700:

$$10\ 000P_A = (2700 \times P_T) + (7300 \times P_E).$$

Dividing both sides by 10 000 shares provides a weight applied to P_T of 0.27 and to P_E of 0.73 and provides a value of $115 for P_A.

The relationship identified above can be used to extract the market's estimate of the share price after the expiration date, P_E, at any point in time after the announcement date of the repurchase until the expiration of the bid. For example, a company has announced a share repurchase for 10 percent of the shares of the company at a tender price of $30.00 per share. After the announcement, the share price of the company becomes $26.50. Rearranging Equation 19A-2, the expected price after the expiration day is written as

$$P_E = \frac{P_A - F \times P_T}{1 - F}$$

$$= \frac{\$26.50 - 0.1 \times \$30.00}{0.9} = \$26.11.$$

Comparing this price to the pre-announcement price (P_0) lets us determine if the nontendering shareholders obtain any gain. If P_0 is greater than P_E, then nontendering shareholders expected to lose, but these shareholders are expected to gain if P_0 is less than P_E.

Appendix Problem

19A-1 The Careful Tile Company Ltd (CTC) currently has 1 million shares outstanding at a price per share of $25. The firm has no debt in its capital structure. The company decides to repurchase 20 percent of its shares at a tender price of $30 per share. The share repurchase will be financed with a debt issue of $6 million.

Upon announcement of the repurchase and method of finance, the share price increases to $29.20 ($P_A$).

a. Calculate: (i) the dollar gain to tendering shareholders, (ii) the dollar gain to nontendering shareholders, and (iii) the total dollar gain in value to the equity from the repurchase.

b. Explain your observation of the total gain from the repurchase.

LONG-TERM FINANCING

20

Capital Markets, Common Equity Financing, and the Underwriting Process

A MANAGERIAL PERSPECTIVE

With the significant reductions in interest rates in 1992 and 1993 came renewed interest on the part of corporations in issuing equity, rather than debt, securities. During the first 5 months of 1992 alone, firms undertook new equity issues of $5.2 billion, compared with approximately $1 billion over the same period in 1991. On the debt side, with reduced interest by investors because of low interest rates, debt issues over the period in 1992 were $3.1 billion, compared with $4.4 billion in 1991.

In this chapter we consider the capital markets in which these securities are issued and then focus specifically on the decisions firms make regarding common equity financing. We begin with an overview of the main sources of funds used by business corporations. We then examine the general process by which firms raise new long-term capital, the *underwriting process*, including an analysis of the relative costs of different methods of sale of new issues. In the final part of the chapter, we examine the characteristics of common equity and the decisions involved in common equity financing.

Sources of Business Financing

Business corporations use three primary sources of funds: (1) internal cash flows, which are long term in nature and consist primarily of capital cost allowances and retained earnings, (2) long-term external funds, and (3) short-term external funds.

In making decisions about where and how to raise long-term funds, an important choice is between private sources and the public markets. *Direct financing*, or *private placement*, represents funds obtained directly from one or a few individuals or financial institutions such as banks, insurance companies, or pension funds. *Public financing* uses investment dealers to sell securities to a large number of investors—both individuals and financial institutions.[1] Before the development of broad financial markets, business firms were necessarily financed by a relatively few wealthy individuals. However, in the

---

[1]As we shall see later in this chapter, a type of public financing for equity securities called the *bought deal* results in a narrow distribution of securities. The purchasers of a new issue distributed this way are large financial institutions; each purchases a large block of the issue.

last century, income taxes, inheritance taxes, labour unions, increased education, and a number of other social changes have served to create a more wealthy middle class, one with savings to invest. Also, the shift from farms to urban centres and from small, family-owned businesses to large corporations meant that more people were forced to invest savings indirectly rather than in their own farm or business. In the meantime, industrialization meant that companies needed capital for investment. Because of the increased needs of savers for a place to invest money and the increased needs of business for outside capital, the *investment dealer industry* was created: it enabled the general public to participate in financing arrangements by assembling small amounts of funds from a large number of sources and making the entire amount available to business firms.

By the 1930s, savings were being automatically channelled from the public into financial intermediaries, and large pools of funds had been accumulated in insurance companies and banks. This made possible an increase in direct financing that bypassed to some degree the investment dealers. We shall discuss both public and direct financing.

Investment Dealers

In our economy, saving is usually done by one group of people and investing to purchase plant, equipment, and inventory by another. Mechanisms have evolved to assist in the efficient transfer of funds between savers and investors. Basically, the investor issues a financial instrument that is purchased by savers. In the banking system, this transfer of funds is indirect, as the money used to purchase the financial instruments (demand loans or notes) has been deposited by savers. This is not, however, the only mechanism by which savers' funds can be channelled to firms wishing to acquire plant and equipment and to hold inventories. The firm could issue securities, either debt or equity, and sell them directly to savers. But this requires that a firm has well-organized selling organization and knowledge of the current conditions in the securities markets. It is more efficient for investment dealers to perform these functions, and thus the distribution of new securities issues is performed by this group. In this section, we are interested in how investment dealers assist in the channelling of funds. The new securities of individual companies are purchased by the investment dealer and then sold to the savers. The **investment dealer** performs the functions of underwriting, advising, and distributing securities.

A note about vocabulary is in order here. In the United States, the term "investment banker" is used to designate an individual or company that performs the functions noted above. This term is misleading, for an investment banker is neither a long-term investor nor a banker who takes deposits.[2] In

---

[2]The investment dealer may unintentionally become a short-term investor if in performing its underwriting duties it is unable to sell to investors all of the issue it has purchased from the issuer. The investment dealer, however, *intends* to sell these securities in the future. In the process of making a firm purchase of the issue from the company, the investment dealer is taking on a risky position. This function is different from a merchant banker such as Hees International Corp. A *merchant banking firm* is highly entrepreneurial and provides the following functions: advising management, arranging financing, and taking a long-term risk position, usually through holding common equity or warrants.

Canada, the term "investment banker" is not used. We refer to these securities firms as *investment dealers*; this is a general term that includes firms that trade securities, provide research, underwrite and distribute securities, and operate as fiscal agents by providing advice and counsel. (For this discussion, however, we are not interested in the first two functions.)

Alternatively, we could refer to these firms as *underwriters*. An underwriter need not, however, be an investment dealer and does not provide the other functions associated with the investment dealer function. Given the lack of a generally accepted descriptive title, we shall use the terms "investment dealer" and "underwriter" interchangably.

Underwriting

Underwriting is the insurance function of bearing the risks of adverse price fluctuations during the period in which a new issue of securities is being distributed. The nature of the underwriting function of the investment dealer can best be conveyed by an example. (This example describes a conventional underwriting of a bond issue; the purpose of the underwriting and the procedures followed are similar for preferred and common equity issues.)

Suppose a business firm needs $10 million. It selects an investment dealer, conferences are held, and the decision is made to issue $10 million of bonds. A legal contract called an *underwriting agreement* is drawn up. On a specific day, called the *closing date*, the investment dealer presents the company with a cheque for $10 million (less commission). In return, the investment dealer receives bonds in denominations of $1000 each, which it then sells to the public.

The company receives its funds about 3 to 4 weeks after the issue's **prospectus**—the document describing the new security issue and the issuing firm's financial status—has been cleared through all of the relevant provincial securities commissions. Often the investment dealer has sold the issue by this time. It can, however, take the investment dealer 6 weeks or longer to sell the bonds. If, in the interim, the bond market collapses, the investment dealer will be carrying the risk of loss on the sale of the bonds. The issuing firm, however, need not be concerned about the risk of market price fluctuations while the investment dealer is selling the bonds. The firm has received its money. Therefore, we can say that one economic function of the investment dealer is to underwrite the risk of a decline in the market price between the time the issue is cleared through all the securities commissions and is ready to be sold and the time the bonds are placed in the hands of their ultimate buyers. For this reason, the investment dealer is often called an *underwriter*: it "underwrites" the risk during the distribution period.

Certain events can occur that will relieve the underwriter of its insurance function; these events can trigger a clause in an underwriting contract called a *disaster out* or *market out* clause, which terminates the liability of the underwriter to purchase the issue. When these clauses exist, the underwriter does not provide full insurance; the issuing company is bearing part of the risk. These "escape" clauses are discussed in more depth in a subsequent section.

Because of the increase in competition in the investment business, there have been some recent, significant changes in the underwriting process. First, there are instances in which the right to underwrite an issue is put up for auction; the underwriter or underwriting group willing to provide the company the highest net proceeds per share wins the auction. An example of an auction was the TransCanada Pipeline (TCPL) equity issue in February and March of 1988. The winning bidder was an underwriting group composed of Merrill Lynch Canada Inc. and Gordon Capital Corp. Another innovation is the *bought deal*, in which the underwriter purchases the issue from the issuing company and has no recourse to the issuer if the issue remains unsold. There are no "escape" clauses in the contract; the underwriter bears the full risk. Such an issue is sold to large institutions in order to remove the securities from the underwriter's portfolio quickly.

A vivid example of the risk borne by underwriters was provided by the British Petroleum privatization issue of $770 million underwritten by Wood Gundy (50 percent), McLeod Young Weir (25 percent), and Dominion Securities Inc. (25 percent). The underwriting contract had an escape clause, but it could be activated only by the British government. Between the time the agreement to underwrite and deliver a certain price to the British government was signed and the closing date of the deal, there was a massive fall in the stock market. Black Monday (October 19, 1987) resulted in a dramatic drop in the share price of British Petroleum. The issue had to be sold at the 'post-collapse' price, yet the payment to the issuer was based on pre-collapse prices. The Canadian underwriters faced massive losses, but they could not tear up the deal without losing credibility. The deal went through (with some assistance from the British government to reduce the underwriters' losses). Wood Gundy, for example, was reported to have lost $20 million.

Advising

When a firm decides to issue securities to provide new capital, it usually begins by selecting as an investment dealer an expert on the terms and characteristics of securities that will appeal to investors and, therefore, can provide valuable advice. The investment dealer may recommend a direct placement with a financial institution, in which case it will help design the issue, locate potential investors, and negotiate the final terms. If the best choice is a public offering, the investment dealer will again advise on the planning, then help with the sale, and often, after the sale, sit on the board of the issuing firm.[3] Thus, the investment dealer provides continuing financial counselling in order to increase the issuing firm's probability of success and to protect its own reputation as a seller of quality securities.

Distribution

The third function of the investment dealer is to market the new issue of securities. The investment dealer has the capacity to perform the physical distribution function more efficiently and economically than could an

---

[3]It has been suggested that an underwriter who accepts a seat on the board of directors may be faced with a conflict of interest. First, any new security issue will go to the existing underwriter even though it may be to the company's advantage to search for a new underwriter. Second, the firm and the underwriter will encounter some very hard negotiating on the terms of new security issues. The underwriter who is also a member of the board of the company cannot serve both parties. Therefore, many underwriters decline direct involvement in a board of directors but continue to provide advice.

individual corporation. The investment dealer has a permanent, trained staff and dealer organization available to distribute securities. In addition, the investment dealer's reputation for selecting good companies and for pricing securities fairly enables it to build up a broad clientele over time, and this increases the efficiency with which it can sell securities.

Underwriting Operations

Probably the best way to gain a clear understanding of the investment dealer function is to trace the history of a new issue of securities.[4] Accordingly, this section describes the steps necessary for issuing new securities.

Pre-Underwriting Conferences

The first step involved in issuing new securities is for representatives of the issuing firm and the underwriter(s) to hold a series of pre-underwriting conferences to discuss the amount of capital to be raised, the type of security to be issued, and the terms of the underwriting agreement.

Memoranda will be written by the treasurer of the issuing company to the firm's directors and other officers, describing alternative proposals suggested at the conferences. Meetings of the board of directors of the issuing company will be held to discuss the alternatives and to attempt to reach a decision.

A number of meetings are required to prepare the preliminary prospectus, which must be filed with the appropriate provincial securities commission — for example, the *Ontario Securities Commission (OSC)*. This prospectus must give full disclosure of all important developments that will materially affect the company. In addition, all the covenants, if it is a bond issue, are presented. The *preliminary prospectus* reflects the agreement of all parties on the terms of the issue; it is a draft of the final prospectus with only the size of the issue, price, underwriter commission, and, if a bond issue, the sinking fund requirements omitted. A public accounting firm will provide an audit of the issuing firm's financial situation and assist in the preparation of the financial statements for the preliminary prospectus. From the start of the process to the signing of the final draft of the preliminary prospectus takes approximately 4 weeks. During this period, the underwriter and the issuer have not signed a contract.

Preliminary Prospectus

When the preliminary prospectus has been signed, it is filed with the appropriate provincial securities commission. A preliminary prospectus must be filed in each province in which the underwriter intends to sell the securities. Ontario's statutes, for example, set a 21-day or 15-business-day waiting period (which, in practice, may be lengthened or shortened by the securities commission) during which the commission staff analyzes the

---

[4]The process described here relates primarily to situations in which the firm doing the financing picks an investment dealer and then negotiates the terms of the issue. This is called a *negotiated underwriting.*

preliminary prospectus to determine if there are any omissions or misrepresentations of fact. Each commission may file deficiencies to the preliminary prospectus or ask for additional information from the issuing company or the underwriter.

After all the deficiencies have been received, the underwriter attempts to satisfy the requested changes. This usually takes about 2 days, but in some cases the deficiencies are complex so the time required to amend the prospectus is longer. Once these deficiencies are satisfied, the underwriter is ready to prepare the final draft of the prospectus and submit it for final clearance by the securities commission(s). The final draft includes all pricing information and the size of the underwriter's discount. Only after each provincial securities commission has cleared the final prospectus can the underwriter offer the securities for sale in the various provinces.

Waiting Period

The *waiting period* for a new security issue runs from the time that the preliminary prospectus has been filed with the securities commissions to the time that the final prospectus has been cleared and the underwriter can offer the securities for sale. The length of the waiting period varies widely, depending on the particulars of the issue. Ideally, it should take approximately 4 weeks.

Final Prospectus and Final Clearance

After all deficiencies noted by the securities commissions have been resolved, the final prospectus is prepared. The underwriters and the issuing company meet late in the business day and reach a final decision on the price of the issue. This pricing decision is based on the closing market for the day. The next morning, the final prospectus is signed and filed with the various securities commissions. Ideally, on the same day, final clearance is given by the commission and the company can begin to sell the securities.

In addition to signing the prospectus, the parties sign the **underwriting agreement**; this document specifies the terms and conditions under which the issue will be purchased from the company by the underwriters. Any breach or failure to comply with the terms and conditions permits the underwriter to terminate its obligation to purchase the security issue.

Finally, the underwriting agreement specifies the date on which the underwriter must purchase the security issue from the issuer. This date is referred to as the *closing date* and is approximately 3 to 4 weeks after final clearance.

The type of underwriting described here is referred to as a *firm underwriting*; the company receives a firm commitment from the underwriter to a predetermined amount of money. This is not the only method that investment dealers use to distribute new securities. For high-risk companies, the underwriter may act only as an agent for the company; the underwriter does not insure the company against market fluctuation risk but contracts to use its best efforts to sell the issue. This method of selling new securities is *best efforts underwriting*. In this chapter, however, we consider firm underwriting exclusively.

The sequence and timing of the events in the preparation of the final prospectus are presented in Figure 20-1.

Figure 20-1
Preparation of a Prospectus for an Issue of
Securities in Ontario

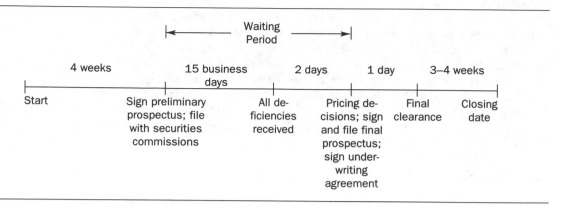

Streamlining the Process

The deregulated atmosphere of the European financial markets permits corporations to issue securities quickly and at a minimal cost. The U.S. markets responded to this competition by streamlining their procedures. These events put pressure on the regulators in Canada to follow suit if they intended to maintain viable markets.

One area in which the streamlining has occurred is the prospectus system. Each issuer used to be required to incur the costs and delay of filing a prospectus for each offering. This often required up to 75 days to get an issue to market. The response was the development of the *Prompt Offering Qualification System (POP)*. Under this system, firms that meet certain size and reporting requirements can use a short-form version of a prospectus. The prospectus is abbreviated since the issuers have been submitting financial information on a current basis. The short-form prospectus is submitted to the securities commission, and upon approval, which is granted quickly to qualified issuers, the issue can proceed. As a result, the processing time has been reduced to less than 1 week.

The benefits of the POP system include (1) reduced costs, including paperwork and time, and (2) increased flexibility to respond to market opportunities for a share issue. The POP system, however, is not available to all issuers, but only to senior issuers who have a history of publicly traded securities and meet a minimum size constraint.

Pricing the Issue

The actual price that the underwriter pays the issuer is not usually determined until the final clearance of the prospectus. Speed of clearance is crucial in this phase; the longer the period between setting the price and the final clearance, the greater the probability that the market will change.

In a new issue of bonds or preferred shares, the price is based on the closing yields in the market. On an issue of common shares for a company with shares outstanding, the price is based on the closing share price on the final clearance date. On the closing date, the issuing firm receives an amount equal to this price, less the underwriter's commission.

The preceding pricing arrangements hold, of course, only for additional offerings of the shares of firms whose existing stock is currently traded. When a company "goes public" for the first time, the underwriter and the firm negotiate a price in accordance with the valuation principles described in Chapter 16.

Distribution: Underwriting Syndicates

It is unusual for a security issue to have only a single underwriter. The common pattern is for two or three investment dealers to act as underwriters, with one of them being the lead, or the managing underwriter. The *lead underwriter* is the one most heavily involved in the negotiations leading to the preliminary and final prospectuses. The other underwriters are kept abreast of the negotiations and may attend meetings and make suggestions concerning the various terms of the issue. For some issues, two underwriters operate as *co-managers*; they both attend meetings and assist in the drafting of the preliminary and final prospectuses.

The impetus to have more than one underwriter originates from the issuing company. For a number of reasons, ranging from repayment for past services rendered to the introduction of a little rivalry among the underwriters, companies feel they are better served by more than one underwriter. Because the underwriting group splits a commission that is independent of the number of underwriters, it is to their monetary advantage to be a sole underwriter.

If the issue is large and there is a risk of price fluctuations, the underwriter(s) do not want to accept the full liability to purchase and sell the whole issue. The usual situation is for the managing underwriter to form an **underwriting syndicate** to spread the underwriting risk. (A "syndicate" is a temporary association for the purpose of carrying out a specific objective.) During the preparation of the preliminary prospectus, the lead underwriter invites investment dealers to express interest in joining a **banking group**. The banking group accepts some of the risk of the issue by agreeing to purchase from the underwriting group a certain proportion of the issue. The composition of the banking group is not firm until the banking group agreement is signed on the day of the final clearance. The dealers' expression of strong interest, however, is usually a clear indication of their ultimate participation. The underwriters do not sell the total issue to the banking group but keep a portion for themselves. Thus, the underwriters are members of the banking group.

During the waiting period, the underwriters and the other members of the banking group are not allowed to sell the securities. Expressions of interest may be obtained from potential purchasers of the issue, however. To prevent duplication of selling effort, the lead underwriter will approach a group of institutions on the *exempt list*, which includes banks, life insurance companies, pension funds, and investment counsellors.[5] Armed with the preliminary

---

[5]The exempt list is described in detail later in the chapter. In brief, it is a list of potential investors who are regarded as so knowledgeable or so sophisticated that they do not need all the protections required by provincial regulatory authorities.

prospectus, the lead underwriter determines the interest of the members of the exempt list. At the same time, the banking group is contacting retail institutions for expressions of interest.

Although the expressions of interest are not commitments to purchase the issue, this canvassing permits the underwriter to gauge the acceptability of the terms of the issue. When the issue obtains final clearance, the banking group and lead underwriter check with their clients to determine if, based on the final terms, their interest still exists. A firm sale is not made until the final prospectus is delivered to the client (usually 2 days after final clearance), and a 2-day period elapses during which the purchasers may re-evaluate their decision.

The final group in the underwriting syndicate is the **selling group**. Invitations to join the selling group are made by the banking group, although both underwriters and banking group members can sell the securities to the ultimate purchasers. Members of the selling group purchase the securities from members of the banking group and are expected to resell the securities at the issue price. As of the date of the final clearance, the selling group members sign a selling group agreement that lasts 30 to 90 days.

The purpose of forming a selling group is to encourage a rapid and, if required, widely distributed sale of the securities. For some issues, there is no selling group. Sales are made by the banking group, and any sales to exempt institutions by the lead underwriter are made on behalf of the whole banking group. Finally, even though the selling group buys the securities from the banking group, the selling group does not accept any liability for the issue. Thus, if the issue is unsold, the liability rests with the banking group.

Escape Clauses

The **underwriting agreement** specifies the conditions under which the underwriters are no longer bound to take the issue and, hence, when they are protected from unexpected events. The first condition is concerned with an order issued that restricts the trading or distribution of the issue. The second occurs if, before the fourth day after final clearance, there is a change that seriously affects or will affect the financial markets or the company's business. This is called the *market out* or *disaster out clause*. Finally, if during the distribution period there is any material change that makes the final prospectus incorrect or misleading, then a new filing is required and the market out clause again becomes applicable.

An example of the use of the disaster out clause occurred on the $100 million issue of a convertible debentures for Cambridge Shopping Centres Ltd., a real estate investment firm. Even though the issue was a *bought deal*, the underwriter pulled out of its commitment to purchase the entire issue after Black Monday of October 1987. In February 1988, the company again tried to issue the securities through a bought deal that included a disaster out clause specifing that the event permitting the underwriter to rely on this clause would be a specific point drop in the Dow Jones industrial average. This objective measure gave the company more assurance of the conditions under which it would bear the risk of market movements.[6]

---

[6]It is somewhat incongruous to negotiate a bought deal, which is intended to remove all risk to the issuer, and introduce a disaster out clause, which makes the company bear some risk.

Price Restrictions

Both the banking and the selling group agree to sell to the ultimate purchasers at the issue price. The lead underwriter may break these price restrictions at any time after the distribution period begins. Typically, price restrictions are maintained for 2 to 4 days. In addition, the lead underwriter has the right to look at the records of the banking group to determine if the price restrictions are being maintained.

The purpose of the price restriction is to protect the members of the banking group against a member that sells all its allotment below the issue price. For example, suppose the issue price on a bond is $100, but, during the distribution period, an increase in interest rates has lowered the bond price below $100—say, to $98. The lead underwriter does not want to be placed in a position in which the members of the banking group cannot sell any securities at the issue price because one of them is selling its allotment below the issue price. But if all the members adhere to the price restrictions, they may be saddled with a stagnant issue. In this instance, the price restrictions will be lifted; the price will fall below the issue price, and the issue will be sold. In this case, the commission to the banking group will be reduced; the market may even have fallen enough to force the banking group to incur a loss—the issue is sold on the market at a price that is less than the price at which the buying group purchased the securities from the underwriters.

Commissions

Commissions are specified in the banking group and selling group agreements. The gross underwriting spread, per bond, is the difference between the issue price and the proceeds to the company. The banking group purchases its allotment from the underwriting group at a specified price; this gives the underwriters their commission. The banking group then sells to the exempt list, to the selling group, and to its own customers at set prices; this determines the banking group commission. Finally, the sale of the issue by the selling group at the issue price results in the selling group commission.

As an example, consider a $50 million bond issue selling at par $100 with a gross underwriting spread of $2. The total commission to be spread among the participants in the underwriting group is $1 million, as shown in Table 20-1.

From this table, we can estimate the size of the commissions to each group. The underwriters obtain a commission of $0.40 per bond sold to the banking group, or a total of $200 000. This commission is split among the underwriting group on the basis of a negotiated agreement. The lead underwriter will obtain a larger share in compensation for the additional duties performed. Next, the banking group as a whole obtains a commission equal to the difference between the price at which the bonds were purchased from the underwriter and the prices at which they are sold. A full commission of $1.60 per bond ($100.00 − $98.40) is obtained from sales to exempt-list clients and their own customers. On sales to the selling group, the commission is $0.60 per bond ($99.00 − $98.40). The total commission to the banking group is $775 000. Finally, the commission to the selling group is $1.00 per bond (they buy the bonds at $99 and sell them at $100), or $25 000 in total.

The distribution of the total commission is presented in Table 20-2.

Table 20-1
Commission Structure on a Bond Issue[a]

	Face Value ($ million)	Number of Bonds (thousands)	Amount Paid ($ million)	Price per Bond
1. Underwriter obtains securities from company	$50.0	500	$49.000	$ 98.00
2. Issue sold to banking group	50.0	500	49.200	98.40
3. Banking group sells to				
Exempt list	24.0	240	24.000	100.00
Selling group	2.5	25	2.475	99.00
Own customers	23.5	235	23.500	100.00
4. Selling group sells to own customers	2.5	25	2.500	100.00

[a]This example is taken from *Canadian Investment Finance—Part I Corporate Finance*. Canadian Securities Institute, 1976.

The amount allocated to each member of the banking group, including the underwriters, depends on the proportion of the issue sold by each member. To determine the actual commission to each member, the net proceeds on hand, after all issue expenses are removed, are multiplied by participation of each banking group member.

It must be emphasized that the commission structure in this example is based on sales of the issue to the ultimate purchaser at the issue price. If the issue is sold at a price below the issue price, the commissions are reduced.

Table 20-2
Distribution of Total Commission

	Commission per Bond	Number of Bonds Sold (thousands)		Commission
Underwriter	$0.40	500		$ 200 000
Banking group on sales to				
Exempt list	1.60	240	$384 000	
Selling group	0.60	25	15 000	
Own customers	1.60	235	376 000	
Total				775 000
Selling group				
Sales to own customers	1.00	25		25 000
Total commission				$1 000 000

Market Stabilization

During the period of distribution, the lead underwriter is authorized, through the banking group agreement, to stabilize the price of the issue by placing orders to buy the securities of the issue in the open market. The duration of this "price pegging" operation is usually limited to 30 days. The pegging operation is designed to prevent a large cumulative downward movement in the price of the security, which would result in losses for all members of the underwriting group.

It has been charged that pegging the price during the offering period constitutes a monopolistic price-fixing arrangement. The investment dealer would reply that not to stabilize the price would increase underwriters' risk, and hence the underwriting commission would have to increase accordingly.

Issue Costs

Issue costs[7] are the costs associated with issuing, or "floating," a new issue of financial instruments. Although there are some data on issue costs in the U.S. capital market, there are few current Canadian data. Feedback from investment dealers in Canada suggests, however, that the relationships observed in the United States are also found in Canada, but the level of issue costs appears to be higher north of the border.

When issue costs are stated in dollars, they are usually measured as the *gross underwriting spread*, which is defined as the difference between the issue price and the proceeds of the issue to the company; this difference goes to the underwriter to cover out-of-pocket costs as well as compensation for underwriting risk.

Frequently, issue costs are stated not in dollars but as a percentage of either the gross or the net proceeds of the issue. In the United States, the issue costs for underwritten issues have been found to range from 4.0 percent of the net proceeds for large issues to 17.0 percent for small ones with an average of 6.0 percent.[8] For bonds, the issue costs ranged from 1.1 percent to 14.0 percent, expressed as a percentage of gross proceeds, and again depending on the size of the issue.[9]

Two generalizations about issue costs can be made from the available data:

1. Issue costs for common shares are greater than those for preferred shares, and the costs for both are greater than the issue costs for bonds.
2. Issues costs as a percentage of the net proceeds are greater for small issues than for large ones.

What are the reasons for these relationships? The explanations are found in the amount of underwriting risk involved in the issue and the complexity of physical distribution. Bonds are usually bought in large blocks by a relatively

---

[7] The costs associated with a new issue of securities are also referred to as *flotation costs.*

[8] C.W. Smith, "Alternative Methods for Raising Capital: Rights versus Underwritten Offerings," *Journal of Financial Economics*, December 1977.

[9] J. Weston and E. Brigham, *Essentials of Managerial Finance,* 9th ed., (Hinsdale, IL: Dryden Press, 1990), Table 20-4, p. 791

few institutional investors, whereas common shares are bought by a large number of individuals. For this reason, the distribution and marketing expenses for shares are greater. As the gross underwriting spread must cover these expenses, the spreads are higher for a share issue than a bond issue. Similarly, because share prices are, in general, more volatile than bond prices, underwriting risks are larger for share than for bond issues, and the underwriting spreads reflect the added risk.

The explanation for the variation in cost with the size of issue is also easily found. First, certain fixed expenses are associated with any distribution of securities: the underwriting investigation, the preparation of the prospectuses, and legal fees. These expenses are relatively large and fixed, so their percentage of the total cost of an issue runs high on small issues. Second, small issues are typically those of relatively less well-known firms, so underwriting expenses may be larger than usual because the danger of omitting vital information is greater. Furthermore, the selling job is more difficult: sales representatives must exert greater effort to sell the securities of a less well-known firm. Finally, small firms tend to be riskier in terms of price volatility, and thus a large underwriting spread is required. For these reasons, issue costs are relatively high for small issues.

Suppose that a particular company makes a number of common share issues of the same size over a given time period. Even if the risk characteristics of the security remain constant, there is no reason to believe that the gross underwriting spread will be identical for each issue. The size of this spread will depend on the state of the stock market at the time of the issue. If the market is extremely volatile, then the underwriting risk will be greater, and therefore the underwriting spread will be larger. Conversely, a stable market will result in a smaller spread.

Initial Public Offerings. To this point we have considered issue costs for companies that already have issued equity and wish to make another issue, which is called a *seasoned issue* or *offering*. However, other companies seek to raise funds through a first or *initial public offering (IPO)* on the equity markets. These companies were private in the past, and the market usually has only limited recognition of the names. An initial public offering tends to have large issue costs. One reason is that the issue size is usually small. In addition, there is more risk to the underwriter in the transaction, so higher compensation is required. The underwriting fees range from 6 to 10 percent of the net proceeds. To this must be added the out-of-pocket costs, which, in dollars, are very close to a fixed cost and hence for a small issue will be a large percentage of the net proceeds.[10]

Underwriting Existing Shares

The underwriting process can also be used for the distribution of large blocks of existing shares. The two largest bought deals in Canadian history occurred during the week of February 8-13, 1993. On February 9, Noranda Forest Inc., a public company in the Hees-Edper group, sold its 49 percent stake in

---

[10]J. Zeidenberg, *The Globe and Mail*, Report on Business, April 27, 1993.

MacMillan-Bloedel to a group of underwriters co-led by Burns Fry and RBC Dominion Securities. The 55.5 million shares were resold by the syndicate, with installment receipts, for $17.50 each. MacMillan-Bloedel had been trading at $17.50 on February 8 and closed at $17.00 on the day of the sale. On February 12, Brascan Ltd., another Hees-Edper company, sold its 37 percent stake of John Labatt Ltd. to a group of underwriters co-led by Wood Gundy Inc. and Gordon Capital Corp. These shares were also resold in installment receipts, for $28.25 each. Labatt's had closed at $28.50 on February 11 but fell $1.875 on the day of the sale to close at $26.625. The investment dealers were reported to have earned $78.6 million in commission fees for the transactions.

With an *installment receipt*, the buyer makes a partial or down payment on the shares and pays the balance later, usually in a year. The MacMillan-Bloedel installment receipts called for an initial payment of $6.00, with two later payments of $5.75 in 1994 and 1995. The Labatt issue also had three installment payments. The receipts receive the full amount of dividends, making the yield very attractive until the subsequent installments are due. The receipts can be traded and are listed on the TSE.

Private Placement Market (Direct Financing)

Private placement, also called *direct financing*, occurs any time a business firm obtains capital directly from a financial institution such as a bank, insurance company, pension fund, mutual fund, individual, or even a nonfinancial corporation. The security used can be a bond, preferred or common equity, or a short-term loan. In most instances, the private placement is sold through an underwriter, which acts only as an agent and does not guarantee to underwrite the securities. One investment very frequently used in direct placements is the *term loan*. Term loans are negotiated directly between the borrowing firm and a financial institution, and they generally have maturities of 1 to 15 years. In addition, a number of government agencies, such as the Ontario Development Corporation and the Federal Business Development Bank, provide term loans.

In this section we consider privately placed equity and term loans in more detail.

Advantages of Direct Financing

Direct financing offers firms three major advantages over publicly issued securities—speed, flexibility, and low issue costs. Since an underwriter is involved only as an agent, the underwriting fees are relatively low. Because term loans are negotiated directly between the lender and the borrower, formal procedures are minimized. The key provisions of the loan can be worked out more quickly and with greater flexibility than can those for a public issue, and it is not necessary to go through the provincial regulatory registration process. Because of this flexibility, a number of provisions in financial instruments were first used in the private placement market but are now found in public issues. An example is the *floating-rate preferred share*, whose dividend payment is set a fixed number of percentage points above an interest rate (say, the prime rate) and is changed in response to changes in the underlying series.

A further advantage of direct financing over publicly held debt securities has to do with future flexibility. If a bond issue is held by many different bondholders, it is difficult to obtain permission to alter the terms of the agreement, even though new economic conditions may make such changes desirable. With a private placement, the borrower generally can sit down with the lender and work out modifications in the contract. Direct financing is also an important source of funds for small and medium-sized companies because their opportunities for financing with internal funds and access to capital markets are somewhat limited.

The benefits generated through privately placed equity are similar to those of privately placed debt. Since the issue is offered to exempt-list purchasers, who are considered to be sophisticated and knowledgeable investors, no involved prospectus is required. The *offering memorandum* that substitutes for the prospectus is much less comprehensive than the prospectus required for a public issue. Also, like privately placed debt, the equity does not have to meet registration requirements of the applicable provincial securities legislation.

Characteristics of Privately Placed Equity

Privately placed equity has become an important source of equity capital, especially for smaller resource companies. During the 1980s, privately placed equity was approximately 13 percent of total new equity issues.

An offering memorandum is prepared and distributed to a number of exempt purchasers; this distribution can be done through an investment dealer. In some cases, this "shopping" of the offer is not necessary because there is already a buyer (for example, the firm's parent company).

Exempt-list purchasers include financial institutions and three other categories: (1) senior officers (and their close relatives) of the company making the issue; (2) buyers of an issue purchased by fewer than 25 investors who are acting as principals; and (3) individual investors who purchase at least $150 000. All of these exempt purchasers are considered "knowledgeable" investors who are sophisticated enough not to need the regular protection of the securities commissions.

Since the private placement circumvents the reporting requirements of a new issue, regulators are concerned that the shares not be resold immediately to the marketplace. If this occurs, the private placement turns out to be a public issue with exempt purchasers acting as underwriters. Therefore, the purchasers of an exempt issue must hold it for a minimum of 6 months (for companies licensed under the Ontario *Insurance Act*) to 18 months. The normal required holding period is 1 year.

Concept Review

▶ What is the sequence of events when a firm decides to issue new securities?
▶ What are the functions performed by an investment dealer?
▶ What type of firm would use a POP? a bought deal? Explain your answers.
▶ Describe the differences between a public issue and a private placement.

Emerging Trends

Important developments are taking place in the financial markets; these developments affect participants such as chartered banks and investment dealers. Some of these developments result from regulatory and legislative changes and others from fundamental shifts in the nature of economic and financial relationships.

One important catalyst in promoting these developments has been the increasing importance of international financial markets. Canadian investment dealers, to compete on a world scale, need access to adequate capital. The capital base needed to finance larger underwriting deals, both domestically and internationally, is much larger than the amount that can be generated internally. In response, some investment dealers have obtained new equity capital by going public and issuing shares that are traded on a stock exchange. Other companies merged so as to rationalize some of their operations and generate the needed capital. This merger activity actually resulted from the deregulation of fixed commission rates for security trading in equity securities.

Beginning in the 1990s, both the Ontario and federal regulators recognized that enabling Canadian underwriters to compete internationally and to maintain or improve the Canadian securities market would require significant deregulation. As noted in Chapter 3, deregulation is requiring disintegration of the artificial barriers among the four pillars—chartered banks, trust companies, life insurance companies, and investment dealers—in favour of increased competition among these participants in the financial industry. The mergers of investment dealers and chartered banks are providing the needed capital base. Also, the entry of foreign investment dealers, either directly or indirectly through the acquisition of a Canadian dealer, benefits the domestic financial markets and allows Canadian underwriters access to foreign markets.

Institutional investors, especially pension funds, are continuing to replace the individual retail investor on the buying side, and competition for institutional business has changed the way both brokerage and investment dealer companies operate. Institutional investors, such as pension plans, may have a significant stake in a firm. They can be active investors, attempting to influence directors to undertake or reject certain courses of action. However, this introduces the risk that they may be considered insiders, which will impose constraints on their trading of shares. Alternatively, they can be passive investors, staying out of day-to-day management and investing simply for profit.

Two of Canada's largest institutional investors, the Ontario Municipal Employees' Retirement System (OMERS) and the Caisse de dépôt et placement du Québec, have opted for the activist role. OMERS has challenged Xerox Canada Inc. in court over the way the company swapped voting shares for nonvoting shares that were convertible into shares of the company's U.S. parent. The Caisse, owner of 13.5 percent of the shares of Univa, announced in March 1993 that it was opposed to a proposed leveraged buyout of the firm by U.S. investment banker Blackstone Group and Unigesco Inc. Its statement that it viewed the bid as illegal was seen as an indication that it would challenge Blackstone in court. The Caisse also thought that the $11 per share offer was too low and that Univa would have too much debt after the buyout. Blackstone subsequently withdrew its offer, even before Univa's board had finished considering it.

What is happening is that the financial markets are experiencing fundamental changes. Regulations are changing, but, more important, the underlying economic and financial forces are exploding in many different directions. From the standpoint of managerial finance, these changes profoundly influence the investment and financing decisions of business firms. Many firms have become financial institutions. The range and types of investments made by manufacturing firms have greatly multiplied. In addition, the forms and sources of financing of business firms have also changed greatly in their variety and complexity.

Concept Review

▶ What are some important new developments that are taking place in the financial markets?

Financing with Common Shares

Any decision to acquire new assets necessitates the raising of new capital, and, generally, long-term assets are financed with long-term capital. Since equity financing constitutes the first source of funds to a new business and equity provides the base of support for borrowing by existing firms, we discuss equity financing before analyzing the other forms of long-term financing.

The nature of equity ownership depends on the form of the business or organization. The central issue in such ownership revolves around an apportionment of certain rights and responsibilities among those who have provided the funds necessary for the operation of the business. The rights and responsibilities attached to equity ownership consist of positive considerations (income potential and control of the firm) and negative considerations (loss potential, legal responsibility, and personal liability).

Figure 20-2 presents a copy of a share certificate for—evidence of ownership in—The Molson Companies Limited. The share certificate identifies (1) that the firm is incorporated federally—under the *Canadian Business Corporations Act* and (2) the share class, which is class A, nonvoting. Left blank are the number of shares that this certificate represents and the identity of the registered owner. (Investors in the market normally never see such a share certificate since they hold their securities through a broker in a "street name.")

General Rights of Holders of Common Shares

A business in Canada can be incorporated either provincially or federally. The decision depends on the relative severity of the requirements for incorporation and, more important, whether the firm intends to operate in more than one province. For multiprovince operations, federal incorporation is usual although not necessary.

Figure 20-2
A Sample Share Certificate

SHARES · ACTIONS

NUMBER · NUMÉRO

N AB232804

CUSIP 608710 30 7

INCORPORATED UNDER THE CANADA BUSINESS CORPORATIONS ACT

CONSTITUÉE EN VERTU DE LA LOI SUR LES SOCIÉTÉS COMMERCIALES CANADIENNES

THE MOLSON COMPANIES LIMITED
LES COMPAGNIES MOLSON LIMITÉE

THIS CERTIFIES THAT· CECI ATTESTE QUE

SPECIMEN

FULLY PAID AND NON-ASSESSABLE CLASS "A" NON-VOTING SHARES OF

THE MOLSON COMPANIES LIMITED

ACTIONS DE CATÉGORIE "A" SANS DROIT DE VOTE, ENTIÈREMENT LIBÉRÉES ET NON SUSCEPTIBLES
D'APPELS DE FONDS, DE

LES COMPAGNIES MOLSON LIMITÉE

LE SECRÉTAIRE,   LE PRÉSIDENT DU CONSEIL,

SECRETARY   CHAIRMAN OF THE BOARD

COUNTERSIGNED AND REGISTERED
CONTRESIGNÉ ET ENREGISTRÉ
THE R-M TRUST COMPANY
COMPAGNIE T
TRANSFER AGENT
AGENT DES TRAN

BY
PAR   AUTHORIZED OFFICER · DIRIGEANT AUTORISÉ

TRANSFERABLE AT HALIFAX, MONTREAL, TORONTO, WINNIPEG,
REGINA, CALGARY AND VANCOUVER.
TRANSFÉRABLES À HALIFAX, MONTRÉAL, TORONTO, WINNIPEG,
REGINA, CALGARY ET VANCOUVER.

Source: The Molson Companies Limited share certificate is used with the permission.

The rights of the holders of common shares in a business corporation are established by the requirements in the jurisdiction in which the company is incorporated. In the following discussion, we present the rights that are common to all jurisdictions. Where there are important differences, they are noted.

Collective Rights.   Certain collective rights are usually given to the holders of common shares. Some of the more important rights allow shareholders (1) to amend the articles of incorporation; (2) to adopt and amend bylaws; (3) to elect the directors of the corporation; (4) to authorize the sale of fixed assets; (5) to enter into mergers and amalgamations; (6) to change the amount of authorized common and preferred shares; (7) to alter the rights and restrictions attached to the common shares; and (8) to create a right of exchange of other shares into common shares.

Specific Rights.   Holders of common shares also have specific rights as individual owners. (1) They have the right to vote in the manner prescribed by the corporate charter. (2) They may sell their share certificates and in this way transfer their ownership interest to other persons. (3) They have the right to inspect the corporate books.[11] (4) They have the right to require the company to purchase their shares at an appraised price if the company takes certain prescribed actions. This *appraisal right* protects dissenting shareholders from decisions of the majority in instances in which, for example, amendments of some of the articles of incorporation will alter the rights of common shareholders and/or the business itself. (5) They have the right to share the residual assets of the corporation on dissolution; however, the holders of common shares are the last set of claimants to the assets of the corporation.

Apportionment of Income

Two important positive considerations are involved in equity ownership: income and control. The right to income carries risk of loss. Control also involves responsibility and liability. In an individual proprietorship that uses only funds supplied by the owner, the owner has a 100 percent right to income and control but also bears total responsibility for losses. As soon as the proprietor incurs debt, however, he or she has entered into contracts that limit that individual's complete freedom to control the firm and to apportion its income.

In a partnership, these rights are apportioned among the partners in an agreed-upon manner. In the absence of a formal agreement, a division is made by law. In a corporation, more significant issues arise concerning the rights of the owners.

---

[11]There must be, and there are, practical limitations to this right. Obviously, a corporation cannot have its business affairs disturbed by allowing every shareholder to go through any record that he or she would like to inspect. A corporation could not wisely permit a competitor who happened to buy shares to look at all the corporate records.

Apportionment of Control

Through the right to vote, the holders of common shares have legal control of the corporation. As a practical matter, the principal officers of many corporations constitute all or a majority of the members of the board of directors. In such circumstances, the board of directors may be controlled by the management rather than the owners. Numerous examples demonstrate, however, that in this situation shareholders can reassert their control if they are dissatisfied with the policies of the corporation. Proxy battles, with the aim of altering corporate policies, have occurred; firms whose managers are unresponsive to shareholders' desires may be subject to takeover bids by other firms.[12]

As the residual income claimant, the holders of common shares are the owners and ultimately have control of the company. Presumably, the firm is managed on behalf of the owners, but there has been much dispute about the actual situation. The view has been expressed that the corporation is an institution with an existence separate from the owners, and that the corporation exists to fulfil certain functions for shareholders as only one among other important groups, such as workers, consumers, and the economy as a whole. This view may have some validity, but it should also be noted that in some instances the officers of a firm have significant shareholdings. In addition, more and more firms are relating officers' compensation to the firm's profit performance, either by granting executives share purchase options or by giving bonuses. Finally, officers of the company want to maintain their mobility and marketability. They will be able to do this only if they are successful in their existing jobs; success is measured in terms of corporate earnings and share prices. By means of direct and indirect pressures, therefore, managers' personal goals are aligned with those of the owners. To the extent that the two diverge, the market for corporate control may provide the necessary constraint on managerial behaviour.

Apportionment of Risk

Another consideration involved in equity ownership is risk. Upon liquidation, holders of common shares are last in the priority of claims. Thus, the portion of capital they contribute provides a cushion for creditors if losses occur on dissolution. The ratio of equity to total assets indicates the percentage by which assets may shrink in value on liquidation before creditors will incur losses.

For example, compare two corporations, A and B, whose balance sheets are shown in Table 20-3. The ratio of equity to total assets in Corporation A is 80 percent. Total assets would, therefore, have to shrink by 80 percent before creditors would lose money. By contrast, the extent to which Corporation B

---

[12]Early in 1992, Gordon Capital, a Bay Street brokerage firm, launched a proxy fight against the then president and chairman of the board of Teleglobe Inc. The fight reflected shareholder discontent that the company had invested too many resources in money-losing computer and software operations to the detriment of its wholly owned, regulated, international telecommunications carrier, Teleglobe Canada. This fight was supported by a number of shareholders, including BCE Inc. and the Caisse de dépôt et placement du Québec. Ultimately, the dissident shareholders prevailed, the firm restructured its operations toward the regulated sector, and many of the previous members of the board left.

Table 20-3
Balance Sheets for Corporations A and B

		Corporation A				Corporation B	
		Debt	$ 20			Debt	$ 60
		Equity	80			Equity	40
Total assets	$100	Total claims	$100	Total assets	$100	Total claims	$100

assets may shrink in value on liquidation before creditors lose money is only 40 percent.

Nature of Voting Rights

For each common share owned, the holder has the right to cast one vote at the annual meeting of shareholders of the corporation or at such special meetings as may be called. In general, decisions are decided by majority vote.

Proxies.   Corporations acts make provision for the temporary transfer of the right to vote by an instrument known as a **proxy**, which is a legal document giving one person the right to act for another. The transfer of corporate voting rights is limited in its duration, typically for a specific occasion, such as the annual meeting of shareholders. At the time of the solicitation of the proxy, the management must supply to the shareholders a circular that contains specified information; this circular must be filed with the provincial securities commission. Specific forms for the proxy and disclosure requirements are stated by provincial legislation for a number of reasons. First, if the proxy machinery is left wholly in the hands of management, there is a danger that the incumbent management will be self-perpetuated. Second, if it is made easy for minority groups of shareholders and opposition shareholders to oust management, there is the danger that they could gain control of the corporation for temporary advantages or to place their friends in management positions.

Empirical evidence has been collected in the United States on the impact of proxy contests for control on the prices of the company's common shares. It was found that there was an 8 percent increase in the share price of the company upon the announcement of the proxy contest. Shareholders appeared to believe that a proxy contest either would lead to a change in control or would be an indication to incumbent management of the disquiet among existing shareholders.

Cumulative Voting.   In voting for directors, the usual rule is a majority vote. Some jurisdictions, however, provide for the use of a device called *cumulative voting*, which is designed to enable a minority group of shareholders to obtain some voice in the control of the company by electing at least one director to the board.

Cumulative voting permits multiple votes for a single director. For example, suppose six directors are to be elected. The owner of 100 shares can cast 100 votes for each of the six openings. Cumulatively, she has 600 votes. When cumulative voting is permitted, the shareholder may accumulate her votes and cast 600 votes for *one* director, instead of 100 each for *six* directors.

The Ontario and federal acts permit the use of cumulative voting as long as there are specific provisions in the articles or bylaws. The Alberta and British Columbia acts do not mention cumulative voting specifically, but this voting would be allowed if included in the articles.

Pre-emptive Right

The **pre-emptive right** gives the existing holders of common shares the first option to purchase additional issues of common shares in proportion to their existing holdings. There is no pre-emptive right unless specified in the articles of incorporation. The pre-emptive right is permitted by the Alberta, Ontario, and federal acts. The British Columbia act permits the pre-emptive right for public companies and requires it for private companies. Under the federal *Bank Act*, banks must include the pre-emptive right in their articles of incorporation.

The purpose of this right is twofold. First, it protects the control position of present shareholders. If it were not for this safeguard, the management of a corporation under criticism from shareholders could prevent shareholders from removing it from the office by issuing a large number of additional shares at a very low price and purchasing those shares itself. Management would thereby secure control of the corporation to frustrate the will of the current shareholders.

The second and by far the more important reason for the pre-emptive right is that it protects shareholders against a dilution of value. For example, assume that 1000 common shares, each with a price of $100, are outstanding, making the total market value of the firm $100 000. An additional 1000 shares are sold to new shareholders at $50 a share; the proceeds of the sale are $50 000, and the total market value of the firm becomes $150 000. When this total market value is divided by the new total shares outstanding, a value of $75 a share is obtained. The old shareholders thus lose $25 per share, and the new shareholders have an instant profit of $25 per share. Thus, selling common equity at a price below the market value dilutes its share price and transfers wealth from the present shareholders to those who are allowed to purchase the new shares. The pre-emptive right prevents such occurrences; the new shares must be sold to all existing shareholders at the $50 price and their position will not be diluted. (This point is further discussed in the appendix to this chapter.)

Authorized, Issued, and Outstanding Shares

The company's articles of incorporation specify the *authorized* number of shares; this is the maximum number of shares that can be issued. The articles can be amended so as to increase the authorized number of shares, but this requires a vote. To add flexibility, most companies set the authorized number of shares in excess of the amount needed in the short run. As the shares are sold, they become *issued*. The *outstanding* shares reflect the number of shares actually held by shareholders. This will be less than the number of issued shares only if the company has repurchased shares.

For companies incorporated under the *Canada Business Corporations Act* it is not necessary to limit or authorize the number of shares, but the company may, if it so desires, specify in the articles of incorporation an authorized number of shares.

Concept Review

▶ Give some examples of collective and specific rights of common shareholders.

▶ Describe a proxy and how it is used in corporate governance.

▶ What are the two primary reasons for the existence of the pre-emptive right?

Classes of Common Shares

Up to this point, we have considered common equity as a homogeneous class. Common shares, however, can be separated into different classes, each having different rights and privileges. Generally, when special classifications are used, one type is designated *class A*, another *class B*, and so on. One example of this distinction is the use of two classes of shares with different voting rights. One class has normal voting rights and the other has restricted voting rights. The restrictions are set up so that the holders of the securities either cannot vote or have diminished votes compared to holders of the voting class. This classification of equity has achieved a great degree of popularity and notoriety in recent years. In a number of instances, restricted or **nonvoting shares** have a **coattail provision**, which gives their holders a vote in the event of a takeover bid for the company. Also, the restricted shares may have a higher dividend in an attempt to compensate for the absence of a vote. In all other ways, however, the voting and nonvoting shares are identical.

The primary purpose of creating nonvoting shares is to consolidate the voting control of the company in the hands of a particular group, which currently has control, but at the same time reduce the investment by this group in the company. The normal procedure for creating nonvoting shares is to split each original voting share into a new voting share and a nonvoting share. The voting shares are normally convertible into nonvoting, but the converse is not the case. This situation permits controlling shareholders who own the voting shares to issue new nonvoting common equity without diluting their control position. Further, by selling the nonvoting shares, the members of the group can maintain their voting control and at the same time reduce their investment in the equity of the company.

Both voting and nonvoting shares trade on the stock exchange, but normally the latter, which are more numerous, trade more frequently than the former. A company's voting shares sell for a premium over its nonvoting shares. This premium depends on a number of variables, one of which is the protection afforded to holders of the restricted shares in the event of a takeover. If nonvoting shares become voting shares upon the acquisition by another company of a small number or proportion of the voting shares, then nonvoting shareholders will share in any premium paid to shareholders to acquire control. In this case, the discount on nonvoting shares will be small. Alternatively, if a change in control can be accomplished without triggering the coattail, the protection is minimal, and there will be a large discount on the nonvoting shares' price.

Concept Review

▶ Define a *"coattail" provision*, and explain why its existence results in a higher share price for a nonvoting share.

▶ What are some justifications for the use of shares classified as to voting rights?

Evaluation of Common Shares as a Source of Funds

Thus far, the chapter has covered the main characteristics of *common shares*, frequently referred to as *equity shares*. Now we appraise this type of financing from the viewpoint of the issuing corporation and from a social perspective.

From the Corporation's Viewpoint

Advantages.   There are several advantages to the corporation associated with common equity financing:

1. Common shares do not obligate the firm to make fixed payments to shareholders. If the company generates earnings and has no pressing internal need for them, it can pay common equity dividends. Had it used debt for financing, it would have incurred a legal obligation to pay interest on that debt regardless of its operational conditions and cash flows.

2. Common shares carry no fixed maturity date—they never have to be repaid, as would a debt issue.

3. Since common shares provide a cushion against losses on the part of creditors, the sale of common shares increases the creditworthiness of the firm. This, in turn, improves its bond rating, lowers its cost of debt, and provides flexibility for its future long-term financing choices. The firm will have the base on which to issue more debt if needed or equity if this is the appropriate source of funds to use.

4. If a company's prospects look bright, then common equity can often be sold on better terms than debt. Common equity appeals to certain groups of investors because (a) it typically carries a higher expected total return (dividends plus capital gains) than does preferred equity or debt, and (b) it represents the ownership of the firm and so provides the investor with a better hedge against unanticipated inflation than do preferred shares or bonds. Ordinarily, common equity increases in value and dividends also rise during inflationary periods.

5. When a company is having operating problems, it often needs new funds to overcome its problems. Investors, however, are reluctant to supply capital to a troubled company, and if they do, they generally require some type of security. From a practical standpoint, this often means that a firm that is experiencing problems can obtain new capital only by issuing debt, which is safer from the investor's standpoint. Because corporate treasurers are well aware of this, they often opt to finance with common equity during good times in order to maintain some reserve borrowing capacity. Indeed, surveys have indicated that maintenance of an adequate reserve of borrowing capacity is the primary consideration in most financing decisions.

Disadvantages. Disadvantages to a company that issues common shares include the following:

1. The sale of common shares extends voting rights—control—to new share owners. For this reason, additional equity financing is often avoided by small firms and new firms, whose owner-managers may be unwilling to share control of their companies with outsiders.
2. Common equity gives new owners the right to share in the income of the firm; if profits soar, then new shareholders will share in this bonanza, whereas if debt had been used, new investors would receive only a fixed return, no matter how profitable the company has been.[13]
3. As we saw earlier in this chapter, the costs of underwriting and distributing common shares are usually higher than those for underwriting and distributing preferred shares or debt. Issue costs associated with the sale of common equity are characteristically higher because (a) the costs of investigating an equity security investment are higher than on a comparable debt security and (b) equities are riskier than debt, which means investors must diversify their equity holdings, which in turn means that a given dollar amount of new shares must be sold to a greater number of purchasers than the same amount of debt.
4. If the firm has more equity or less debt than is called for in its optimal capital structure, the average cost of capital will be higher than necessary. Therefore, a firm would not want to sell equity to the point at which its equity ratio exceeds the optimal level.
5. Common share dividends are not deductible as an expense in calculating the corporation's income subject to the federal income tax, but bond interest is deductible. The impact of this factor is reflected in the relative cost of equity capital vis-à-vis debt capital.
6. The empirical evidence is that upon the announcement of an equity issue, there is a reduction in the share price of approximately 3 percent for industrial companies and a much smaller percentage loss for utility issues (the figures are net of overall market movements). The reason for this

---

[13]This point has given rise to this interesting new theory: "If a firm makes a large bond issue, this is a signal that management expects the company to earn high profits on investments financed by the new capital, and that it does not wish to share these profits with the new shareholders. On the other hand, if the firm issues common equity, this is a signal that its prospects are not so bright."

loss in value is that investors believe that management is timing its common equity sales so as to issue equity when it is overpriced. This hypothesis is based on management's having better information about the company's future cash flows and hence the true value of its share price than do outsiders.

7.   If the issue is an *initial public offering (IPO)*, the issue most likely has been underpriced—that is, issued at too low a price. Thus, if original owners continue to hold securities in the firm, they absorb a loss in value. If the securities had been issued at a higher price, fewer securities would have been sold and the owners would have maintained a higher percentage ownership. Empirical research on Canadian IPOs has observed a (net of market) underpricing of approximately 11 percent—that is, from the issue date to 5 days later, there is an 11 percent increase in the share price.

From a Social Viewpoint

From a social viewpoint, common equity is a desirable form of financing because it renders business firms less vulnerable to the consequences of declines in sales and earnings. Common equity financing involves no fixed charges, the payment of which might force a faltering firm into reorganization or bankruptcy. From the standpoint of the economy as a whole, if too many firms use too much debt, business fluctuations can be amplified and minor recessions can turn into major ones.

Concept Review

▶ What are the major advantages of common equity financing to a corporation? The major disadvantages?

▶ From a social viewpoint, why may common equity be considered a desirable form of financing?

The Market for Common Shares

Some companies are so small that their common shares are not actively traded—they are owned by only a few people, usually the companies' managers. Such firms are said to be **closely held companies** or *privately owned*, and the equity is said to be *closely held equity*. On the other hand, the shares of many larger companies are owned by a fairly large number of investors, most of whom are not active in management. Such companies are said to be **publicly owned companies** and their equity is said to be *publicly held equity*.

As we saw in Chapter 3, the shares of smaller publicly owned firms are not listed on an exchange; they trade in the *over-the-counter (OTC)* market, and the companies and their shares are said to be *unlisted*. A larger, publicly owned company generally applies for listing on an organized exchange, and these companies and their shares are said to be *listed*.

Companies generally trade over the counter at first and later apply for listing on the Toronto Stock Exchange (TSE) and/or The Montreal Exchange. If the company is a junior resource or high technology company, the issue could be listed on the Vancouver Stock Exchange (VSE).

Institutional investors, such as pension trusts, insurance companies, and mutual funds, own approximately 30 percent of all common shares. But because the institutions buy and sell relatively actively, they account for approximately 65 percent of all transactions. Thus, the institutions have a heavy influence on the prices of individual securities.

Types of Stock Market Transactions

We can classify market transactions into three distinct types:

1. *Trading in the outstanding shares of established, publicly owned companies: the secondary market.*   Suppose Carter Chemical Company has 50 million shares of stock outstanding. If the owner of 100 shares sells his or her stock, the trade is said to occur in the **secondary market**. Thus, the market for outstanding shares, or *used shares*, is defined as the secondary market. The company itself receives no new money when sales occur in the market. If the sale is of a substantial block of shares, it is called a *secondary offering*. Once again, the company receives no new money from this block transaction.

2. *Purchasing of new, additional shares sold by established, publicly owned companies: the primary market.*   If Carter Chemical decides to sell (or issue) an additional 1 million shares to raise new equity capital, this transaction is said to occur in the **primary market**.[14]

3. *Purchasing of new public offerings floated by privately held firms: the primary market.*   In 1993, Second Cup Ltd., a chain of specialty coffee shops, sold one-third of its equity, or 2 million shares, at $7 per share. Of the total $14 million paid by investors, Second Cup received $13.2 million. Second Cup stated that it planned to use the proceeds to pay off long-term debt and to expand into Quebec, where the company had no stores, and into the United States. This type of transaction is called **going public**. Whenever shares in a closely held corporation are offered to the public for the first time, the company is said to be going public. The market for equity that has recently gone public is referred to as the **new issue market**. The securities involved in the market are often called *initial public offerings (IPOs)*. Firms can go public without raising any additional capital. For example, in a *spinoff*, the shares of a subsidiary of a parent company are given to the outstanding shareholders of the parent company as a dividend. The subsidiary becomes a new firm with new equity, yet neither the parent firm nor the new firm receive any funds from the issue.

---

[14]Provided that the number of authorized shares exceeds the number of shares outstanding by more than the size of the issue, the issue can proceed. If this excess does not exist, Carter's management will have to obtain shareholder approval to increase the number of authorized shares.

The Decision to Go Public

Most businesses begin life as proprietorships or partnerships, and the more successful ones, as they grow, at some point find it desirable to convert into corporations. Initially, these new corporations' shares are generally owned by their officers, key employees, and/or a very few investors who are not actively involved in management. If growth continues, at some point the company may decide to go public. The advantages and disadvantages of going public are discussed next.

Advantages of Going Public

1. *Shareholder diversification.* As a company grows and becomes more valuable, its founders often have most of their wealth tied up in the company. By selling some of their shares in a public offering, the founders can diversify their holdings and thereby reduce somewhat the riskiness of their personal portfolios.

2. *Increased liquidity.* The equity of a closely held firm is very illiquid; no ready market exists for it. If one of the owners wants to sell some shares to raise cash, it is hard to find potential buyers, and even if a buyer is located, there is no established price at which to complete the transaction. These problems do not exist with publicly owned firms.

3. *Increased ease of raising new corporate cash.* If a privately held company wants to raise cash by a sale of new equity, then it must go to its existing owners, who may have no money or not want to put any more eggs in this particular basket, or it must shop around for wealthy investors willing to make an investment in the company. However, it is usually difficult to get outsiders to put money into a closely held company, because if they do not have voting control (more than 50 percent) of the shares, then the inside shareholders-managers can run roughshod over them. The insiders can pay or not pay dividends, have private deals with the company, and so on. For example, the president might buy a warehouse and lease it to the company or get use of an automobile and "all-the-frills" travel to conventions. The insiders can even keep the outsiders from truly knowing what the company's earnings are or what it is really worth. There are few positions more vulnerable than that of an outside shareholder in a closely held company, and for this reason it is hard for closely held companies to raise new equity capital. Going public, which brings with it disclosure and regulation by the appropriate securities commission, greatly reduces these problems and thus makes people more willing to invest in the company.

4. *An established value for the firm.* For a number of reasons, it is often useful for a closely held firm to establish its value in the marketplace. For one thing, when the owner of a privately owned business dies, the capital property of the taxpayer is deemed to have been disposed of immediately prior to death at fair market value. Setting this amount will require the estate to use appraisers, who could set too high a value. To circumvent this problem, a clause is inserted in the shareholders' agreement requiring the remaining shareholders to purchase the shares of the deceased taxpayer at book value. Although this approach avoids the valuation problem for tax

fairly low but accurate

purposes, book value does not generally represent a market value. A company that is publicly owned, however, has its value established with little room for argument. Similarly, if a company wants to give incentive stock options to key employees, it is useful to know the exact value of these options. In addition, employees much prefer to own equity or options on common equity that is publicly traded because public trading increase liquidity.

Disadvantages of Going Public

1. *Cost of reporting.* A publicly owned company must file quarterly and annual reports with the stock exchange it is listed on and with the appropriate securities commission. These reports can be costly, especially for small firms.

2. *Disclosure.* Management may not like the idea of reporting operating data because such data are then available to competitors. Similarly, the owners of the company may not want people to know their net worth. Since publicly owned companies must disclose the number of shares owned by officers, directors, and major shareholders, it is easy enough for anyone to multiply shares held by price per share to estimate the net worth of any insider.

3. *Self-dealing.* The owners-managers of closely held companies have many opportunities for questionable but legal self-dealings, including the payment of high salaries, nepotism, personal transactions with the business (such as a leasing arrangement), extravagant retirement programs, and not-truly-necessary fringe benefits. Such self-dealing is much harder to arrange and/or justify if the company is publicly owned—it must be disclosed, and the managers are also subject to shareholder suits.

4. *Possibility of inactive market and low price.* If a firm is very small and its shares are not traded with much frequency, then its shares will not really be liquid and the market price may not really be representative of the shares' true value. Security analysts and brokers simply will not follow the security because there will not be enough activity to generate enough sales commissions to cover their costs of keeping up with it.

5. *Shareholder relations.* Once the firm is publicly traded, the management must spend time dealing with shareholders and potential investors. This includes not only annual meetings but also calls and visits by shareholders. These activities take time away from the managerial function.

The disadvantages of being a publicly held company occasionally lead a firm's managers and/or principal owner to attempt to repurchase its outstanding shares and establish (or re-establish) the business as a closely held company. This process, which is called **going private**, was described in Chapter 19.

Conclusions on Going Public

It should be obvious from this discussion that no hard-and-fast rules can be laid down regarding whether or when a company should go public. This is an individual decision that should be made on the basis of the company's and its shareholders' own unique circumstances.

If a company does decide to go public, either by the sale of newly issued equity to raise new capital for use by the corporation or by the sale of shares by the current owners, setting the price at which shares will be offered to the public is a key issue. The company and its current owners want to set the price as high as possible—the higher the offering price, the smaller the fraction of the company the current owners will have to give up to obtain any specified amount of money. On the other hand, potential buyers will want to buy the shares at as low a price as possible.

The Decision To List Shares

The decision to go public, as discussed previously, is a truly significant event in a company's life; it marks a major transition in the relationship between the firm and its owners. The decision to list, on the other hand, is not a major event. The company will have to file a few new reports with an exchange, it will have to abide by the rules of the exchange, and the share price will be quoted in the newspaper under a stock exchange rather than in the over-the-counter section. These are not very important differences.

In order to have its shares listed, a company must apply to an exchange, pay a fee, and meet the exchange's minimum requirements. Assuming that a company qualifies, many people believe that listing is beneficial both to it and to its shareholders. Listed companies receive a certain amount of free advertising and publicity, and the listed status enhances their prestige and reputation. This may have a beneficial effect on the sales of the firm's products, and it is probably advantageous in terms of lowering the required rate of return on its common equity. Investors respond favourably to increased information, increased liquidity, and confidence that the quoted price is not being manipulated. By providing investors with these benefits in the form of listing their companies' shares, financial managers may lower their firms' costs of capital and increase the value of their equity shares.

Reverse Takeover

An alternative for obtaining a stock exchange listing has been used by a number of companies, primarily glamorous ventures such as film, real estate, and high technology. This approach requires that the company desiring a listing on the stock exchange engage in a reverse takeover with a company that already has a listing in the exchange. This latter company, however, has few or no ongoing operations and its sole asset is its exchange listing. This company is referred to as a *shell company*, and its market value on the exchange reflects its possible use in the reverse takeover.

A *reverse takeover* is a transaction in which the control of the surviving firm resides in the hands of shareholders of the nonsurviving firm, which is the target of the takeover.

In the context of the listing issue, a reverse takeover occurs when the shell company "takes over" the private company by issuing a large number of shares to the owners of the private company, and the shell company takes over the assets. The net result is that the private company shareholders control the shell company.

Under the reverse takeover alternative, the once-private company obtains a listing but avoids listing costs—both time and money—and the full disclosure required in a prospectus when it first issues shares. The disclosure in the reverse takeover usually takes the form of a press release describing some current operating and financial statistics of the company; there is no historical data presented. This procedure has been criticized by some regulators, who suggest that it is a "back-door" method of obtaining a listing. They have also criticized the fact that the valuation of the shell company will be based on the limited financial information for the private company. Not all securities exchanges permit this type of listing. The Montreal Exchange, for example, considers the reverse takeover with a shell company to be a new listing, thus carrying with it the prospectus requirements.

A recent example of a reverse takeover was given by HCI Holdings Ltd., the shell and surviving company, which was originally in the resources and investments area. It issued 105 million shares for a real estate company. The share price after the reverse takeover was approximately $1.60; its low, before the reverse takeover, was about 30 cents.

Concept Review

► Differentiate between a closely held corporation and a publicly owned corporation.
► Differentiate between a listed and an unlisted equity security.
► Differentiate between the primary and secondary markets.
► What are the major advantages and disadvantages of going public?
► Which is more significant: the decision to list or the decision to go public? Why?

Regulation of Security Markets

The operations of investment dealers, securities exchanges, and over-the-counter markets described in the previous sections of this chapter are influenced to a high degree by securities regulation. In the United States, securities regulation is a federal matter administered by a federal agency known as the Securities and Exchange Commission (SEC). The situation in Canada, however, is very different. Securities regulation is a provincial responsibility, and when a security issue is to be sold in a number of provinces, a regulatory body of each must review the issue. The existence of a number of regulatory bodies can cause problems, especially if the regulations differ among provinces. For regulatory issues that are common to all regulatory regimes, there is a body called the Canadian Securities Regulators, which is composed of provincial regulators. This group identifies issues of common concern and releases policy statements describing the regulatory approach to these issues.

In our brief discussion of securities regulation, we concentrate on the regulations in Ontario, because the TSE is the major exchange in Canada; in addition, the four western provinces have followed the lead of the Ontario Securities Commission (OSC). Securities issued in Ontario must meet the requirements of the Ontario *Securities Act*. The western provinces have generally the same provisions in their securities acts.

The financial manager is affected by these securities acts in several ways: (1) corporate officers can be subject to personal liability; (2) the laws affect the ease and costs of financing, as well as the behaviour of the money and capital markets in which the corporation's securities are sold and traded; and (3) investors' willingness to buy securities may be influenced by the existence of safeguards provided by these laws.

The two basic reasons for securities regulation are the protection of the individual investor and the efficient allocation of capital by means of capital markets. Both of these goals are achieved through the requirements of full, continuing, and timely disclosure and of control of individuals who are permitted to operate in the securities industry.

Disclosure Requirements

Full Disclosure.   The purpose of *full disclosure* is to assist an individual investor in making a well-informed decision. This requirement is primarily intended to assist individual investors. The disclosure requirements on issues directed to the institutional investor with access to professional advice are much less onerous. For example, a private placement issue requires minimal disclosure.

A securities commission can take two approaches to the full disclosure requirement. The first approach is to require disclosure of all material information but not to comment on the quality of the issue. In other words, with full disclosure, the investor is considered sufficiently informed to make an investment decision on his or her own. The Ontario *Securities Act* also has a withdrawal provision consistent with its full disclosure provisions. The purchaser can rescind the contract to purchase up to 90 days after the date of receipt of the prospectus or the contract date, whichever is later, if there were material errors or omissions in the prospectus.

The alternative approach is to argue that full disclosure is not sufficient— the commission may simply refuse the prospectus or lay down severe conditions that must be met. This paternalistic attitude is a remnant of the repealed "blue sky" laws that once required new issues to be approved by a government official. Such paternalism has been found in the handling of new issues of penny mining shares.

The fact that a purchaser has up to 2 business days after the receipt of the prospectus to withdraw from the purchase contract without needing *any* reason is another example of individual investor protection.

Continuing Disclosure.   *Continuing disclosure* is required to keep investors informed about events concerning the company. This is reflected in reporting requirements for insider trading, regular financial reporting, mandatory solicitation of proxies, and provision of information circulars to shareholders prior to the annual meeting. This continuing disclosure should improve efficiency in the capital markets.

Timely Disclosure.   The requirement of *timely disclosure* focuses on the availability of information in the case of unusual or episodic events. An example introduced in 1968 concerns timely disclosure to prevent insiders from making trading profits from their access to private information. In a recent development, the OSC emphasized the stipulation by requiring companies to disclose to the chairman of the commission, on a confidential basis, future developments that may have an impact on their securities. The purpose of this policy is to assist the commission in its monitoring of market trading.

Control of Participants

In 1928, Ontario passed an act that dealt mainly with the control of individuals trading in securities. This act required registration of brokers and dealers. The attorney general had broad discretion to deny registration, and somewhat more limited discretion to cancel existing registration. Conduct that was deemed to be fraudulent was identified and penalties for fraudulent acts were specified.

Currently, registration conditions are quite detailed. In addition, supervision of those registered to trade in securities has increased.

Concept Review

▶ What are the two methods used to achieve the goals of security regulation?
▶ Distinguish between continuous and timely disclosure.

Summary

This chapter is more descriptive than analytical, but a knowledge of the issues discussed here is essential to an understanding of finance. The key concepts covered are listed below.

□ An **investment dealer** assists in the issuing of securities by helping the firm determine the size of the issue and the type of securities to be used, by establishing the selling price, by selling the issue, and, in some cases, by maintaining an after-market for the securities.

□ **Underwriting** is the process through which an investment dealer or dealers remove the risk to the issuing company that all of a new issue of securities will not be sold and the required funds will not be obtained by the firm. This is accomplished by the underwriter purchasing the issue from the issuing company.

□ An important part of the new issue process is the preparation and dissemination of the **prospectus**. This document provides information to the potential purchaser of the security about the specifics of the issue and information on the issuing company itself.

□ The *net proceeds* from an issue are equal to the total amount raised less the *issue costs*; these costs reflect compensation to the underwriter for bearing risk, and their amount will depend upon the type of security being issued—debt or equity.

□ In some instances, securities are issued directly to a large financial institution or small group of investors through a **private placement**. This type of issue has lower issue costs and is more flexible in terms of the prospectus requirements.

☐ A **proxy** is a document that gives one person the power to act for another person—typically, the power to vote shares of common stock. A *proxy fight* occurs when an outside group solicits shareholders' proxies in order to vote a new management team into office.

☐ Shareholders often have the right to purchase any additional shares sold by the firm. This right, called the **pre-emptive right**, protects the control of the present shareholders and prevents dilution of the value of their stock.

☐ The major advantages of common equity financing are as follows: (1) there is no obligation to make fixed payments, (2) common equity never matures, (3) the use of common equity increases the creditworthiness of the firm, (4) shares can often be sold on better terms than debt, and (5) using equity helps the firm maintain its reserve borrowing capacity.

☐ The major disadvantages of common equity financing are (1) it extends voting privileges to new shareholders, (2) new shareholders share in the firm's profits, (3) the costs of equity financings are high, (4) using equity can raise the firm's cost of capital, and (5) dividends paid on common equity are not tax deductible.

☐ A **closely held corporation** is one that is owned by a few individuals who are typically associated with the firm's management.

☐ A **publicly owned corporation** is one that is owned by a relatively large number of individuals who are not actively involved in its management.

☐ **Going public** facilitates shareholder diversification, increases liquidity of the firm's equity, makes it easier for the firm to raise capital, and establishes a value for the firm. However, reporting costs are high, operating data must be disclosed, management self-dealings are harder to arrange, and public ownership may make it harder for management to maintain control of the firm.

Questions

20-1 Before entering a formal agreement, investment dealers carefully investigate the companies whose securities they underwrite; this is especially true of the issues of firms going public for the first time. Since the dealers do not themselves plan to hold the securities but intend to sell them to others as soon as possible, why are they so concerned about making careful investigations?

20-2 Company A has assets of $40 million and a net income after taxes of $2 million, manufactures widgets, and is publicly owned. Company B is identical to A in every respect except that B's shares are all owned by its founder. If each firm sells shares to the public to raise $10 million of new money for corporate purposes, which will probably have the higher issue cost? Why?

20-3 By what percentage could total assets shrink in value upon liquidation before creditors would incur losses in each of the following cases:
a. Equity-to-total-assets ratio of 50 percent?
b. Debt-to-equity ratio of 50 percent?
c. Debt-to-total-assets ratio of 40 percent?

20-4 It is frequently stated that the primary purpose of the pre-emptive right is to allow individuals to maintain their proportionate share of the ownership and control of a corporation.

    a. How important do you suppose this consideration is for the average shareholder of a firm whose shares are traded on the Toronto Stock Exchange?

    b. Is the pre-emptive right likely to be of more importance to shareholders of closely held firms? Explain your answer.

20-5 **a.** Is a firm likely to get a wider distribution of shares if it sells new shares through a pre-emptive rights offering to existing shareholders or directly to underwriters?

    b. Why would a company be interested in getting a wider distribution of shares?

20-6 What are the advantages that accrue to a firm that lists its shares on a major stock exchange?

20-7 Evaluate the following statement: "The fundamental purpose of the provincial security laws dealing with new issues is to prevent investors, principally small ones, from sustaining losses on the purchase of shares."

20-8 The OSC attempts to protect investors who are purchasing newly issued securities by making sure that the information put out by a company and its investment dealers is correct and not misleading. However, the OSC *does not* provide any information about the real value of the securities; hence, an investor might pay too much for some new shares and consequently lose heavily. Do you think the OSC should, as a part of every new share or bond offering, render an opinion to investors as to the proper value of the securities being offered? Explain your answer.

20-9 Each month the Ontario Securities Commission publishes a report on the transactions made by the insiders of listed firms in their own companies' equity securities. Why do you suppose the OSC makes this report?

20-10 Two large companies just received the net proceeds from their equity issues. One of the companies is in the steel industry, and the issue costs were 8 percent of the gross proceeds. These costs are less than those on an issue of comparable size undertaken 5 years before. The second company is a regulated utility and had issue costs of 5 percent of the gross proceeds.

    Discuss the factors that could explain why (a) the issue costs are different for the two firms, and (b) why the current issue costs for the first firm are less than they were 5 years ago.

20-11 Because investment dealers price new issues in relation to outstanding issues, should a spread exist between the yields on the new and the outstanding issues? Discuss this matter separately for share issues and for bond issues.

Self-Test Problem   (solution appears on page 785)

ST-1 **Key terms.**   Define each of the following terms:

a. Private placement; public financing

b. Underwriting agreement

c. Underwriting syndicate; lead underwriter; banking group; selling group

d. Issue costs

e. Cumulative voting

f. Proxy; proxy fight

g. Pre-emptive right

h. Voting shares; nonvoting shares

i. Closely held corporations versus publicly held corporations

j. Organized exchanges; over-the-counter (OTC) market

k. Listed security; unlisted security

l. Secondary market; primary market; secondary offering

m. Going public

n. New issue market

o. Registration with securities commissions; OSC

p. Prospectus; preliminary prospectus

q. Bought deal

r. POP system

s. Market out clause

Problems

20-1 **Profit (loss) on new equity issue.**   Security Brokers Ltd. specializes in underwriting new issues by small firms. On a recent offering of Meran, Ltd., the terms were as follows:

Price to public	$7.50 per share
Number of shares	3 million
Proceeds to Meran	$21 000 000

The out-of-pocket expenses incurred by Security Brokers in the design and distribution of the issue were $450 000. What profit or loss did Security Brokers incur if the issue sold to the public at an average price of

a. $7.50 per share?

b. $9.00 per share?

c. $6.00 per share?

20-2 **Cost of preferred shares.**   As the chief financial officer of Leisure Goods, Inc., you are planning to sell $100 million of 10-year bonds to finance the construction of a giant hot-tub factory. The market rate of interest on debt of this quality and maturity is 11.7 percent. However, the total costs of the underwriting have been estimated to be 1.7 percent of the gross proceeds. Calculate the effective cost of this debt to your firm, before taxes. (Hint: Let the coupon rate be 11.7 percent so that the bonds will sell at face value; then solve for the IRR that will make the future payments on the bond equal to the face value less 1.7 percent— that is, to $983 per bond.)

20-3 **Underwriting and issue expenses.** The Amelia Candy Co. Ltd., whose share price is now $30.00, needs to raise $15 million in common equity. Underwriters have informed Amelia's management that it must price the new issue to the public at $27.53 per share because of a downward-sloping demand curve. The underwriters' compensation will be 7 percent of the issue price, so Amelia will net $25.60 per share. Amelia will also incur expenses in the amount of $360 000. How many shares must Amelia sell to net $15 million after underwriting and issue expenses?

20-4 **Book value per share.** Atlantic Resources Ltd. had the following balance sheet at the end of 1993:

Atlantic Resources Company: Balance Sheet
December 31, 1993

		Accounts payable	$ 64 400
		Notes payable	71 400
		Long-term debt	151 200
		Common equity (20,000 shares outstanding)	364 000
		Retained earnings	336 000
Total assets	$987 000	Total liabilities and equity	$987 000

a. What is the book value per share of Atlantic's common equity?
b. Suppose the firm sold 10 000 new shares and netted $32.55 per share from the sale. What would be the new book value per share?

20-5 **Setting the price of a new share issue.** U-Fix-It, a small home improvement building supplier, has been successful and has enjoyed a good growth trend. Now U-Fix-It is planning to go public with an issue of common shares, and it faces the problem of setting an appropriate share price. The company's management and its investment dealers believe that the proper procedure is to select several familiar firms with publicly traded common shares and to make relevant comparisons.

Several home improvement building suppliers are reasonably similar to U-Fix-It with respect to product mix, size, asset composition, and debt-to-equity proportions. Of these companies, Home Headquarters and Smitty's are most similar. When analyzing the following data, assume that 1988 and 1993 were reasonably normal years for all three companies; that is, these years were neither especially good nor especially bad in terms of sales, earnings, and dividends. At the time of the analysis, k_{RF} was 10 percent and k_M was 15 percent. Home Headquarters and Smitty's are listed on the TSE, while U-Fix-It will be traded in the OTC market.

	Home Headquarters	**Smitty's**	**U-Fix-It (totals)**
Earnings per share			
1993	$ 3.60	$ 6.00	$ 960 000
1988	2.40	4.40	652 800
Price per share			
1993	28.80	52.00	—
Dividends per share			
1993	1.80	3.00	480 000
1988	1.20	2.20	336 000
Book value per share, 1993	24.00	44.00	7 200 000
Market-to-book ratio, 1993	120%	118%	—
Total assets, 1993	$22.4 million	$65.6 million	$16 million
Total debt, 1993	$9.6 million	$24 million	$8.8 million
Sales, 1993	$32.8 million	$112 million	$29.6 million

a. Assume that U-Fix-It has 100 shares outstanding. Use this information to calculate earnings per share (EPS), dividends per share (DPS), and book value per share for U-Fix-It. (Hint: U-Fix-It's 1993 EPS = $9600.)

b. Calculate earnings and dividend growth rates for the three companies. (Hint: U-Fix-It's EPS g = 8%.)

c. Given your answer to Part a, do you think U-Fix-It's equity would sell at a price "in the same ballpark" as that of Home Headquarters and Smitty's—that is, in the range of $25 to $100 per share?

d. Assuming that U-Fix-It's management can split the shares so that the 100 shares could be changed to 1000 shares, 100 000 shares, or any other number, would such an action make sense in this case? Why?

e. Now assume that U-Fix-It did split its shares and has 400 000 shares. Calculate new values for EPS, DPS, and book value per share. (Hint: U-Fix-It's new 1993 EPS is $2.40.)

f. Return on equity (ROE) can be measured as EPS/(book value) per share or as (total earnings)/(total equity). Calculate ROEs for the three companies for 1993. (Hint: U-Fix-It's 1993 ROE = 13.3%.)

g. Calculate dividend payout ratios for the three companies. (Hint: U-Fix-It's 1993 payout ratio = 50%.)

h. Calculate debt/total assets ratio for the three companies. (Hint: U-Fix-It's 1993 debt ratio = 55%.)

i. Calculate the P/E ratios for Home Headquarters and Smitty's. Are these P/E ratios reasonable in view of relative growth, payout, and ROE data? If not, what other factors might explain them? (Hint: Home Headquarters's P/E = 8 ×.)

j. Now determine a range of values for U-Fix-It's share price, with 400 000 shares outstanding, by applying Home Headquarters's and Smitty's P/E ratios, price-to-dividends ratios, and price-to-book value ratios to your data for U-Fix-It. For example, one possible price for U-Fix-It's equity is (P/E Home Headquarters)(EPS U-Fix-It) = 8($2.40) = $19.20 per share. Similar calculations would produce a range of prices based on both Home Headquarters's and Smitty's data. (Hint: Our range was $19.20 to $21.60.)

k. Using the equation $k = D_1/P_0 + g$, find approximate k values for Home Headquarters and Smitty's. Then use these values in the constant growth share price model to find a price for U-Fix-It's stock. (Hint: We averaged the EPS g and the DPS g for U-Fix-It.)

l. At what price do you think U-Fix-It's shares should be offered to the public? You will want to select a price that will be low enough to induce investors to buy the share but not so low that it will rise sharply immediately after it is issued. Think about relative growth rates, ROEs, dividend yields, and total returns ($k = D_1/P_0 + g$).

Integrative Problem

20-6   **Investment banking process.** Allen Food Stores, a family-owned grocery store chain headquartered in Waterloo, has grown to the point at which it would like to expand its operations throughout southwestern Ontario. The proposed expansion would require Allen to raise $15 million in additional capital. Because Allen currently has a debt ratio of 50 percent and because the family members already have all their funds tied up in the business, the owners would like to sell shares to the public. However, they want to ensure that they retain control of the company. This would be Allen's first equity sale, and the owners are not sure just what would be involved. Therefore, they have asked you to research the process and to help them decide exactly how to raise the needed capital. In doing so, you should answer the following questions.

a. What are the advantages to Allen of financing with equity rather than bonds? What are the disadvantages of using equity?

b. Are the shares of Allen Food Stores currently publicly held or privately owned? If the firm sells shares to the public, will it then be publicly held or privately owned?

c. What type of common shares should Allen sell to the public to allow the family to retain control over the operations of the business? What would be the drawbacks of such shares?

d. What is meant when a firm is said to be *going public*? What would be the advantages to the Allen family of having the firm go public? What would be the disadvantages?

e. What does it mean for shares to be *listed*? Do you think that Allen's shares would be listed as soon as it goes public? If not, where would the shares trade?

f. Suppose the firm has decided to issue $15 million of class A nonvoting shares. Without doing any calculations, describe the procedure by which Allen and its investment dealer will determine the price at which the shares will be offered to the public.

g. What is a *prospectus*? What is the difference between a preliminary and final prospectus? Why do provincial securities commissions require firms to file a preliminary prospectus before selling shares?

What steps do the securities commissions take to ensure that the information in the prospectus presents a fair and accurate portrayal of the issuing firms's financial position? Would Allen Food Stores be able to use the Prompt Offering Qualification System for their prospectus?

h. If Allen goes public and sells equity that the public buys at a price of $11 per share, what will be the approximate percentage cost, including both underwriting costs and other costs? Assume the company sells 1.5 million shares. Would the cost be higher or lower if the company were already publicly owned?

i. Would you recommend that Allen have the issue underwritten or sold on a best efforts basis? Why? What would be the difference in costs between the two procedures?

j. Suppose some of the Allen family members wanted to sell some of their own shares, in order to diversify, at the same time the company was selling new shares to raise expansion capital. Would this be feasible?

k. Would it be a good idea to use a rights offering for the issue? Why or why not?

Solution to Self-Test Problem

ST-1   Refer to the appropriate sections of the text to check your responses.

Appendix 20A
Use of Rights in Financing

If the pre-emptive right is contained in the articles of a firm, then it must offer any new common shares to existing shareholders. If the articles do not prescribe a pre-emptive right, the firm has a choice of making the sale to its existing shareholders or to an entirely new set of investors. If the sale is to the existing shareholders, the share issue is called a **rights offering**. Each shareholder is issued an option to buy a certain number of the new shares, and the terms of the option are contained on a piece of paper called a **right**. The terms of the option specify the number of rights and the cash payment necessary to purchase one new share. Each shareholder receives one right for each share of equity he or she owns. The advantages and disadvantages of rights offerings are described in this appendix.

Theoretical Relationships

Several issues confront the financial manager who is deciding on the details of a rights offering. The various considerations can be made clear by the use of illustrative data on Canadian Maritime Company Limited, whose balance sheet and income statement are given in Table 20A-1.

Maritime earns $4 million after taxes and has 1 million shares outstanding, so earnings per share are $4. The common equity sells at 25 times earnings, or $100 a share. The company plans to raise $10 million in new equity funds through a rights offering and decides to sell the new equity to existing shareholders for $80 a share. The questions now facing the financial manager are the following:

Table 20A-1
Canadian Maritime Company Ltd.:
Financial Statements before Rights Offering

I. Partial balance sheet

		Total debt (at 10%)	$ 40 000 000
		Common shares	10 000 000
		Retained earnings	50 000 000
Total assets	$100 000 000	Total liabilities and capital	$100 000 000

II. Partial income statement

Total earnings	$12 000 000
Interest on debt	4 000 000
Income before taxes	$ 8 000 000
Taxes (50% assumed)	4 000 000
Earnings after taxes	$ 4 000 000
Earnings per share (1 million shares)	$4
Market price of stock (price-to-earnings ratio of 25 percent assumed)	$100

---

1. How many rights will be required to purchase a share of the newly issued equity?
2. What is the value of each right?
3. What effect will the rights offering have on the price of the existing equity?

Number of Rights Needed to Purchase a New Share.   Maritime plans to raise $10 million in new equity funds and to sell the new shares at a subscription price of $80 per share. Dividing the subscription price into the total funds to be raised gives the number of shares to be issued:

$$\text{Number of new shares} = \frac{\text{Funds to be raised}}{\text{Subscription price}} = \frac{\$10\,000\,000}{\$80}$$

$$= 125\,000 \text{ shares.}$$

The next step is to divide the number of new shares into the number of previously outstanding shares to get the number of rights required to subscribe to one share of the new equity. Note that shareholders always get one right for each share they currently own:

$$\frac{\text{Number of rights needed}}{\text{to buy a new share}} = \frac{\text{Number of old shares}}{\text{Number of new shares}} = \frac{1\,000\,000}{125\,000} = 8 \text{ rights.}$$

Therefore, a shareholder will have to surrender 8.0 rights plus $80 to receive one of the newly issued shares. Had the subscription price been set at $95 a share, 9.5 rights would have been required to subscribe to each new share; if the price had been set at $10 a share, only 1.0 right would have been needed. Notice that given the total amount of funds to be raised, the higher the subscription price, the larger the number of rights needed to purchase a new share. Equivalently, the higher the subscription price, the fewer the number of new shares that will be issued.

Value of a Right.   It is clearly worth something to be able to buy, for less than $100, a share selling for $100. The right provides this privilege, so the right must have a value. To see how the theoretical value of a right is established, we continue with the example of Canadian Maritime, assuming that it will raise $10 million by selling 125 000 new shares at $80 a share.

First, notice that the *market value* of the old shares was $100 million: $100 a share times 1 million shares. (The book value is irrelevant.) When the firm sells the new equity, it brings in an additional $10 million. As a first approximation, we assume that the market value of the common shares increases by exactly this $10 million.[15]

Assume that all rights will be exercised and that the market value reflects the new funds brought in. The total market value of the common shares after the new issue will be $110 million. Dividing this new value by the new total

---

[15]In fact, the share price falls after the announcement of a rights issue. This may reflect the market's evaluation of the information inherent in a new equity issue; this information could be that management believes that the equity is overpriced and it is a good time to issue equity.

number of shares outstanding, 1.125 million, we obtain a new market value of $97.78 a share. Therefore, after the financing has been completed, the price of a common share will have fallen from $100.00 to $97.78.

Because the rights give the shareholders the privilege of buying for only $80.00 a share that will end up being worth $97.78, thus saving $17.78, is $17.78 the value of each right? The answer is no, because eight rights are required to buy one new share; we must divide $17.78 by 8 to get the value of each right. In the example, each one is worth $2.22.

Ex Rights.   Maritime's rights have a value that accrues to the holders of the common shares. But what happens if the shares are traded during the offering period? Who will receive the rights, the old owners or the new? The standard procedure calls for the company to set a *holder-of-record date* and for the shares to go *ex rights* 5 business days prior to the holder-of-record date. If a share is sold prior to the ex rights date, the new owner will receive the rights; if it is sold on or after the ex rights date, the old owner will receive them. For example, on October 15, Maritime might announce the terms of the new financing, stating the rights will be mailed out on December 1 to shareholders of record as of the close of business on November 15. Anyone buying the old shares on or before November 9 will receive the rights; anyone buying the equity on or after November 10 will *not* receive the rights. Thus, November 10 is the *ex rights date*; before November 13, the shares sell *rights on*. In the case of Maritime, the *rights-on price* is $100.00, and the *ex-rights price* is $97.78.

Theoretical Value of a Right.   Equations have been developed to determine the value of rights without going through all the procedures described above. We develop and illustrate these equations next.

1. *Rights on.*   While the equity is still selling rights on, the value at which the rights will sell when they are issued can be found by use of the following formula:

$$\text{Value of one right} = \frac{\text{Market value of a share, rights on} - \text{Subscription price}}{\text{Number of rights required to purchase one share} + 1}$$

$$V_r = \frac{P_0 - P_s}{N + 1} \tag{20A-1}$$

P_0 = rights-on price of the equity.
P_s = subscription price.
N = number of rights required to purchase a new share of equity.
V_r = theoretical value of one right.

Substituting the appropriate values for Canadian Maritime, we obtain:

$$V_r = \frac{\$100 - \$80}{8 + 1} = \frac{\$20}{9} = \$2.22.$$

This agrees with the value of the rights we found by the step-by-step analysis.

2. *Ex Rights.* Suppose you are a shareholder in Canadian Maritime and the equity is selling ex rights for $97.78 a share. How can you calculate the theoretical value of a right? Simply by using the following formula, which follows the logic described in preceding sections, you can determine the value of each right to be $2.22:

$$\frac{\text{Value of}}{\text{one right}} = \frac{\text{Market value of a share, ex rights} - \text{Subscription price}}{\text{Number of rights required to purchase one share}}$$

$$V_r = \frac{P_e - P_s}{N} \hspace{4cm} \textbf{(20A-2)}$$

$$V_r = \frac{\$97.78 - \$80}{8} = \frac{\$17.78}{8} = \$2.22$$

P_e is the ex rights price of the equity.[16]

Instead of holding the rights and exercising them to purchase new shares, the investor can sell the rights through the stock exchange. Rights are traded on the exchange, and published quotations of the trading activity are readily available. The market value of a right exceeds the theoretical value as calculated by Equation 20A-2. The difference between the market and theoretical values of the right narrows as the final date to exercise the rights approaches. The reason for this difference in market and theoretical values is that when purchasing a right, the investor obtains an option to purchase a security at a fixed price. If the market price of the security increases, the price of that right increases as well. The percentage increase in the value of the right, however, is much larger than the percentage increase in the value of the security. Thus, the investor, when purchasing a right, is buying the chance to have a very large percentage increase in his or her investment.

As an example of the difference in market and theoretical values for a right, consider the rights issue of Algonquin Mercantile Corporation. This issue permitted the shareholder to purchase 1 new share for $9.50 and 5 rights. Each existing share was entitled to 1 right. The theoretical value of this right as of

---

[16]Equation 20A-2 is developed directly from the verbal explanation given in the earlier subsection "Value of a Right." Equation 20A-1 can then be derived from Equation 20A-2 as follows:

1. Note that

$$P_e = P_0 - V_r. \hspace{4cm} \textbf{(20A-3)}$$

2. Substitute Equation 20A-3 into Equation 20A-2, obtaining

$$V_r = \frac{P_0 - V_r - P_s}{N}. \hspace{4cm} \textbf{(20A-4)}$$

3. Simplify Equation 20A-4 as follows, ending with Equation 20A-1.

$$V_r N = P_0 - V_r - P_s$$

$$V_r(N + 1) = P_0 - P_s$$

$$V_r = \frac{P_0 - P_s}{N + 1}. \hspace{4cm} \textbf{(20A-1)}$$

July 20, 1987, was $0.60, and the market value was $0.70. The theoretical value, with the share selling ex rights, is calculated using Equation 20A-2 with the following data:

$$P_e = \$12.50 \qquad P_s = \$9.50 \qquad N = 5$$

$$V_r = \frac{\$12.50 - \$9.50}{5} = \$0.60.$$

Effects on Position of Shareholders

A shareholder has the choice of exercising rights or selling them. If the shareholder has sufficient funds and desires to buy more shares of the company's equity, the shareholder will exercise the rights. If he or she does not have the money or does not want to buy more shares, then the rights can be sold. In either case, provided the formula value of the rights holds true, the shareholder will neither benefit nor lose by the rights offering. This statement can be made clear by considering the position of an individual shareholder in Canadian Maritime.

Assume the shareholder had 8 shares before the rights offering. The 8 shares had a market value of $100.00 each, so the shareholder's wealth in the equity of Canadian Maritime was $800.00. If he or she exercised the right, the owner now has 9 shares of Maritime equity, which, after the rights offer, has a value of $97.78 per share. The market value of the holdings is now $880.00. To purchase the additional share, however, the investor had to exercise the right at $80.00. Thus, the wealth of the investor is $800.00, which is equal to the market value of the equity after the rights issue less the investment to purchase the new share. Therefore, if the investor exercises the right, the investor's wealth is not impaired.

Alternatively, if the 8 rights were sold and each right had a value of $2.22, the investor received $17.78 in cash. But the original 8 shares now have a market price of $97.78 a share. The $782.22 market value of the stock plus the $17.78 in cash is same as the original $800.00 market value of the 8 shares of stock. Thus, if the investor sold the rights, his or her wealth is not affected by a rights issue.

Therefore, from a theoretical point of view, the shareholder neither benefits nor loses from the sale of additional shares of equity through rights. In fact, since the market value of a right exceeds the theoretical value, it is obvious that an investor cannot be hurt by the rights issue if the investor sells the rights. If the rights are not sold, a decision has been made to forego the added income from selling them at above their theoretical value for the chance to play the option. Of course, if the owner forgets to exercise or sell the rights, then he or she can suffer a loss. But, in general, adequate time is given to enable the shareholder to take some action, so losses are minimal.

Stock Split Effect

We have demonstrated that the investor is not hurt in a rights issue, even though the share price falls when the share sells ex rights. The decrease in the ex rights price will depend on the difference between the current market price and the subscription price. For example, in the Canadian Maritime example, where the subscription price was set at $80.00, the ex rights price was $97.78. If the subscription price was set at $10.00, the theoretical value of a right would be $45.00, and the ex rights price, $55.00. In both instances, the funds obtained total $10 000 000, so the impact on the value of the equity must be identical. The different ex rights prices have no effect on the wealth of the investor but are a result of dividing the pie into more pieces, as in a stock split.

For example, at a subscription price of $80 there will be 125 000 new shares issued, but at a $10 subscription price, 1 000 000 new shares are needed to raise $10 million. The latter issue divides the pie into more pieces, so the value per piece is lower. The stock split effect is related directly to the difference between the share price and the subscription price. When the two are equal, there is no stock split effect.

There is a common error, made by some financial writers, that a rights issue is detrimental to existing shareholders because the share price falls, ex rights. We can see that this conclusion is false and that the rights issue is not more detrimental than a stock split.[17]

Market Price and Subscription Price

Setting the subscription price is an important consideration; this gives value to the rights. The subscription price must be set so that, even with a fall in the share price of the company on the expiry date of the rights issue, the rights will still be exercised; consequently, the firm will receive its funds only if the market price exceeds the subscription price. To increase the probability that this will happen, the subscription price is set well below the current market price.

Measured from the registration date for the new issue of the security, the average percentage by which the subscription prices of new issues were below their market prices has been approximately 15 percent in recent years. Examples of price concessions of 40 percent or more were observed in a small percentage of issues; the most frequently encountered discounts, however, were from 10 to 20 percent. The larger price concessions are given on issues that have very volatile share prices. Conversely, regulated utilities and banks have much more stable shares prices, and the discounts on issues by these types of companies are much lower.

Effect on Subsequent Behaviour of Market Price of Equity.   It is often stated that issues of new shares through rights will depress the price of the existing common shares of the company. To the extent that a subscription price in connection with the rights offering is lower than the market price, there will be a stock-split effect on the market price of the common shares. With the prevailing market price of Maritime's shares at $100 and a $10 subscription price, the new market price will probably drop to approximately $55. As we have seen, however, this is not an important issue.

---

[17]One interesting complication is the impact on the dividends and earnings per share. Just as an adjustment is made in the per-share financial variables for a stock split, the same adjustment for the stock-split effect should be made for a rights issue.

The crucial question is whether, because of the rights offering, the actual new market price will be $55, lower, or higher. Again, empirical analysis of the movement in share prices during rights offerings indicates that generalization is not practical. What happens to the market price of the equity ex rights and after the rights trading period depends upon the prospects of the issuing company.

Concept Review

▶ Distinguish between the value of a right measured *ex rights* and *rights on*.
▶ Explain why the reduction in share price after a rights offer is not detrimental to current shareholders.

Appendix Problems

20A-1 **Rights offering.**   Canadian Cabinet (CC) wants to sell shares via a rights offering. CC has 2 million shares outstanding at a per share market price of $45. The new issue will be used to raise $16 million of new equity for the firm. Existing shareholders will receive 1 right per share held.
   a. If the subscription price is $40, how many new shares must be sold? How many rights per share of new equity will be required? What will be the value of a right?
   b. If the subscription price is $32, how many new shares must be sold? How many rights per share of new equity will be required? What will be the value of a right?

20A-2 **Subscription price.**   The Berry Real Estate Company's common equity now sells for $37 per share. There are 13 000 000 shares outstanding. The company plans to raise $65 million of new equity by selling more shares. Since the pre-emptive right is contained in the corporate charter, rights will be used. Management has decided that the rights will be worth $1 each. Such a price will ensure that most shareholders will either exercise or sell their rights rather than just let them expire, yet a careless failure to use the rights would not impose too severe a hardship on anyone.
   a. What subscription price should Berry set for its offering?
   b. What will be the final share price, assuming that the theoretical relationships hold?

21

Debt and Preferred Shares

A MANAGERIAL PERSPECTIVE

Different groups of investors prefer different types of securities, and investors' tastes can change over time. Thus, astute financial managers seek to package securities with characteristics that will make them attractive to a wide range of investors. By offering those securities that best match the tastes and needs of potential investors, financial managers can hold the firm's costs of financing to the lowest possible levels. These financing costs may also be minimized by issuing debt in foreign markets, either in foreign currencies or in Canadian dollars. Minimizing financing costs results in a gain in value to current common shareholders. In this chapter, we consider two important types of fixed-income securities—bonds and preferred shares.

Traditional Debt Instruments

There are many types of long-term debt instruments: term loans, bonds, secured and unsecured notes, marketable and nonmarketable debt, and so on. In this section, we discuss briefly the traditional long-term debt instruments, and in the next we identify some important features of debt contracts. Later, we consider recent innovations in long-term debt financing.

An understanding of long-term forms of financing requires a familiarity with several important terms and definitions.

Funded Debt. Long-term debt is often called **funded debt**. When a firm "funds" its short-term debt, it replaces short-term debt with securities of longer maturity. "Funding" does not imply that the firm places money with a trustee or other repository; it is simply part of the jargon of finance. This replacement is often done after a certain amount of financing corporate activities with short-term debt; when the outstanding amount is large enough a share or bond issue is sold with the proceeds used to pay off (or fund) its outstanding bank loans. Since there is a fixed cost involved in selling common shares or bonds, it is very expensive to issue small amounts of these securities and the periodic funding used by companies is sensible.

Term Loans. A *term loan*, as described in Chapter 11, is a contract under which a borrower agrees to make a series of interest and principal payments on specific dates to the lender. Term loans are usually negotiated directly between the borrowing firm and a financial institution—generally a bank, an insurance company, or a pension fund—and their maturities range from 3 to 15 years. In addition, a number of government agencies, such as the Ontario Development Corporation and the Federal Business Development Bank, provide term loans. The variation in the maturity of the term loan is related to the type of lender. Chartered banks, which have short-term liabilities, lend at the short end of the maturity range, and insurance companies and pension funds, which have long-term liabilities, lend at long maturities. Banks and insurance companies may co-operate in their term lending; for example, a firm wishing a 15-year term loan may find a bank as the lender for the first 5 years and an insurance company for the last 10 years of the loan.

Most term loans are repayable on an amortized basis (see Chapter 12 for a discussion of *amortization*). Amortization protects the lender against the possibility that the borrower will not make adequate provision for the loan's retirement during the life of the loan. Amortization is especially important when the loan is for the purpose of purchasing a specific item or equipment; the amortization schedule should be geared to the productive life of the equipment, and the payments should be made from the cash flows that result from the use of the asset.

Term loans have three major advantages over public offerings of securities —*speed*, *flexibility*, and *low issuance costs*. Because term loans are negotiated directly between the lender and the borrower, formal documentation is minimized. The key provisions of a term loan can be worked out much more quickly than those for a public issue, and it is not necessary for the loan to go through a provincial securities registration process.

The interest rate on a term loan can either be fixed for the life of the loan or be variable. If a fixed rate is used, it is generally set close to the rate on bonds of equivalent maturity and risk. If the rate is variable, it is usually set at a certain number of percentage points over the prime rate, the commercial paper rate, the treasury-bill rate, the banker's acceptance rate, or the London Inter-Bank Offered Rate (LIBOR). Then, when the index rate goes up or down, so does the rate charged on the outstanding balance of the term loan. Rates may be adjusted annually, semiannually, quarterly, monthly, or on some other basis, depending on what the contract specifies.

In recent years, institutional investors have increasingly required compensation over and above the fixed interest payments on directly negotiated loans. The most popular form of additional compensation is an *option to purchase* common shares, with the option being in the form of detachable *warrants* permitting the purchase of the shares at specified prices over a designated period. The option-related elements in term loans are normally found in the high-risk segment of the market.

Bonds. A *bond*, as described in Chapter 16, is a long-term contract under which a borrower agrees to make payments of principal and interest, on specific dates, to the holder of the bond. Although bonds have traditionally been issued at fixed interest rates with maturities in excess of 15 years, in recent years bonds with shorter maturities and variable (*floating*) interest rates have been used to an increasing extent. Bonds are similar to term loans, but a bond issue is generally advertised, offered to the public, and actually sold to many different investors. Indeed, many individual and institutional investors may purchase bonds when a firm sells a bond issue, whereas there is generally only one lender in the case of a term loan.[1] There are a number of different types of bonds. We discuss the most important next.

Mortgage Bonds.   Under a **mortgage bond**, the company pledges designated property as security for the bond.[2] The pledge is a condition of the loan. In the event that the company defaults on the loan, the bondholders can foreclose on the pledged property and sell it to satisfy their claims. The company can also issue *second mortgage bonds* secured by the same property. In the event of liquidation, the holders of these second mortgage bonds have a claim against the property, but only after the first mortgage bondholders have been paid in full. Thus, second mortgages are sometimes called *junior mortgages*, because they are junior in priority to the claims of *senior mortgages*, or *first mortgage bonds*. Even though both bonds are "secured" by claims on assets, the degree of security is not the same. Note that the security of mortgage bonds is found not only in the first claim to liquidate the asset, but also in the earning power of the asset.

All mortgage bonds are written subject to an *indenture*, which is a legal document (further described later in the chapter) that spells out in detail the rights of both the bondholders and the company. The indentures of most major companies were written 20 or more years ago. These indentures were generally *open ended*, meaning that new bonds may be issued from time to time under the existing indenture. However, the amount of new bonds that can be issued is virtually always limited to a specified percentage of the firm's total "bondable property," which generally includes all plant and equipment. In some instances, the indentures limit the flexibility of the company to issue new debt. Changing the provisions of an indenture is very difficult since the holders of the outstanding bonds have to approve any changes; many companies now close old indentures and do not issue new debt under its provisions.

Debentures.   A **debenture** is an *unsecured* bond and, as such, provides no lien on specific property as security for the obligation. Debenture holders are therefore general creditors whose claim is protected by property not otherwise pledged. In essence, debentures rely upon the earning power of the company's assets alone. The advantage of debentures from the standpoint of the issuer is that property is left unencumbered for subsequent financing. In practice, however, the use of debentures depends on the nature of the firm's assets and its general credit strength.

If the credit position of a firm is exceptionally strong, the firm can issue debentures—it simply does not need specific security. Currently, Bell Canada issues debentures to obtain the debt financing it requires. Bell Canada does, however, have first-mortgage bonds outstanding that are secured by a first

---

[1]However, for very large term loans, a number of financial institutions may form a syndicate to grant the credit. Also, a bond issue can be sold to one lender (or to just a few); in this case, the issue is said to be *privately placed*. Companies that place bonds privately do so for the same reasons that they use term loans—speed, flexibility, and low issuance costs.

[2]There is also the *chattel mortgage*, which is secured by personal property, but this is generally an intermediate-term instrument. *Real property* is defined as real estate—land and buildings. *Personal property* is defined as any other kind of physical property, including equipment, inventories, and furniture. *Intangible property* includes patents, goodwill, and the like.

mortgage and a floating charge. Because some covenants in the first-mortgage bond indenture restricted Bell's flexibility to issue new first-mortgage bonds, Bell closed the first-mortgage indenture and now issues only debentures under a more flexible trust indenture. Bell is a company strong enough not to have to provide specific security for its debt issues.

Debentures are also issued by companies in industries in which it would not be practical to provide security through a mortgage on fixed assets. Examples of such companies are large mail-order houses and finance companies, whose fixed assets are not large in relation to their total assets. The bulk of their assets is in the form of inventories or receivables, neither of which is satisfactory security for a mortgage bond.

Subordinated Debentures.   The term *subordinate* means "below" or "inferior to." In the event of bankruptcy, subordinated debt has claims on assets only after senior debt. **Subordinated debentures** may be subordinated either to designated notes payable (usually bank loans) or to all other debt. In the event of liquidation or reorganization, holders of subordinated debentures cannot be paid until senior debt as named in the trust indenture has been paid in full. Senior debt typically does not include trade accounts payable. The way in which the subordination provision works and how it strengthens the position of senior debtholders is shown in Table 21.1. In Part I of the table, we assume that $200 is available for distribution on liquidation, and the subordinated debt has a claim on 25 percent of $200, or $50. However, this claim is subordinated to the bank debt (the only senior debt), so the $50 initially allocated to the subordinated debt is added to the $100 claim of the bank. As a consequence, 75 percent of the bank's original claim is satisfied. If $300 is available for distribution, the $75 initially allocated to the subordinated debt is divided into two parts: $50 goes to the bank and the other $25 remains for the subordinated debtholders. In this situation, the senior bank debtholders are fully paid off, 75 percent of other debt is paid, and holders of the subordinated debt receive only 25 percent of their claim.

The use of subordinated debentures rises during periods of tight money when financial institutions require more security for short-term financing. Subordinated debentures provide an additional cushion for loans from chartered banks and other providers of senior debt.

Serial Bonds and Debentures.   For a regular bond, the principal normally comes due at the maturity date of the bond. However, in a **serial bond** issue, part of the principal comes due and is paid off each year. Normally, the bonds that are paid off are identified through a lottery, and the investor is not aware in advance that her bonds will be paid off. Thus the bond issue is equivalent to a number of separate bond issues, each with different maturity dates but all issued at the same time.[3] As the bonds are paid off, the interest burden to the company diminishes and the security to the bonds increases, and thus the quality of the remaining bonds in the issue increases.

---

[3]Municipalities also issue serial bonds, but unlike the corporate variety, they are issued with different maturities. Investors receive a yield equivalent to the maturity of the bond. In the normal serial bond with random payoff, each investor obtains the same yield when the bond is purchased, but those whose bonds are paid off before maturity can receive a yield different from that expected at the date of purchase.

Table 21-1

Illustration of Bankruptcy Payments to Senior Debt, Other Debt, and Subordinated Debt

Financial Structure	Stated Value (1)	Percentage of Total Debt (2)	Initial Allocation[a] (3)	Actual Payment[b] (4)	Percentage of Original Claim Satisfied (5)
I. $200 available for claims on liquidation					
Bank debt	$200	50%	$100	$150	75%
Other debt	100	25	50	50	50
Subordinated debt	100	25	50	0	0
Total debt	$400	100%	$200	$200	50%
Common equity	300				0
Total claims[c]	$700				29%
II. $300 available for claims on liquidation					
Bank debt	$200	50%	$150	$200	100%
Other debt	100	25	75	75	75
Subordinated debt	100	25	75	25	25
Total debt	$400	100%	$300	$300	75%
Common equity	300				0
Total claims[c]	$700				43%

[a]Each type of debt is expressed as a percentage of total debt (Column 2). That percentage is then multiplied by the amount available to obtain the initial allocation (Column 3).

[b]The subordinated debt is subordinate to bank debt. Therefore, the initial allocation to subordinate debt is added to the bank debt allocation until it has been exhausted or until the bank debt is paid in full.

[c]The common shares will be wiped out in both situations, because debt exceeds available funds. Note also that if mortgage bonds were present, then (1) the mortgage bondholders would have first claim on proceeds from the sale of the securing property, up to the amount of the mortgage bonds, and (2) if the proceeds from the sale of the securing property were insufficient to pay off the mortgage bonds, then the unsatisifed portion of the claim would be treated as a general creditor claim. These points and others are discussed in Chaper 25.

Income Bonds. Typically arising from corporate reorganizations, **income bonds** pay interest only if there is sufficient net income or profit to meet the obligation. Because the company has been in difficult financial circumstances, interest is not set as a fixed charge; the principal, however, must be paid when due. Income bonds are not very common in Canada or in the United States.

Although management is not required to pay the interest if it is not earned, it is required to pay interest if profits are sufficient. Because the interest payment is out of profits and is not a fixed charge, the payment is treated as a dividend payment and is *not* deductible for income tax purposes. In order to qualify as an income bond, a bond must have no fixed element in the interest payment.

The income bond is basically a risky obligation from the point of view of the investor; therefore, it is usually issued on a secured basis. This security can cover either just the principal repayment or the interest as well.

One important benefit that accrues to the company from the use of income bonds is that they do not have the same expected bankruptcy costs as does straight debt. With the latter, default or bankruptcy can occur if the interest or principal is not paid as promised in the bond contract. The occurrence of default or bankruptcy has direct and indirect costs that affect the value of the company.[4] For an income bond, however, interest is not a fixed commitment, so failure to pay it does not result in default with its associated costs. There is, however, a fixed term to maturity on an income bond and a commitment to repay principal by the maturity date. The failure to meet this requirement can result in bankruptcy. The company can minimize this problem by increasing the term to maturity of the income bond. For example, of 42 income bonds issued during the period 1955 to 1976 in the United States, 37 had terms to maturity in excess of 50 years; an income bond issued by Elmyra and Williamsport Railroad has a maturity of 1000 years! (Of the 37 bonds noted previously, 23 were issued as a result of a corporate reorganization.)

Some income bonds are convertible into shares of common equity at a fixed price. There are sound reasons for the convertible feature when the bonds arise out of a reorganization. Creditors who receive income bonds in exchange for defaulted obligations have a less desirable position than they had previously. Since they have received something based on an adverse and problematical forecast of the future of the company, it is appropriate that if the company should prosper, they should be entitled to participate.

Even though income bonds have a smaller expected bankruptcy cost potential than does straight debt, this benefit must be weighed against the nondeductibility of the interest payments for corporate income tax purposes. The limited use of this financial instrument implies that the lost tax savings from the nondeductibility of interest more than offsets the gain owing to lower expected bankruptcy costs.

Retractable Bonds.   A **retractable bond** provides the bondholder with an opportunity to sell the bond back to the issuer at *par value* at a specified time before the maturity. Normally, the retraction feature is found on long-term debt, and the specifics of the issue are identified in the bond contract. The holder's decision to exercise this retraction option must be provided to the company during the *election period*, which usually occurs 6 months to a year before the earlier maturity date. If notice is not given, the debt automatically remains long term. Therefore, the retractable feature permits a bondholder to purchase a long-term bond and convert it to a short-term one. As an example, Trizec Corporation Limited issued $25 million, 10.5 percent senior debentures on April 5, 1978, to mature June 1, 1998. The bonds include a retraction feature that permitted the bondholder to sell the bond back to Trizec on June 1, 1988, at the par value of the bond. If the bondholder exercised this option, the maturity of the bond was reduced. The election period extended from September 1, 1987 to December 1, 1987.

This retractable feature is of benefit to bondholders if interest rates are above the coupon rate during the election period. In the Trizec case, for example, if before December 1, 1987, interest rates exceeded the 10.5 percent yield, the price of the bond would have been below par. But bondholders selling

---

[4]The direct and indirect costs of bankruptcy were considered in Chapters 17 and 18. These costs may influence the debt vs. equity choice and the overall cost of capital.

in the market would have had to suffer a capital loss. By exercising the retraction option, the bondholder could sell the bonds without incurring a capital loss and use the proceeds to invest in higher yielding bonds. As of the election period, interest rates were in fact above the 10.5 percent level, so investors used the retraction feature. As of October 30, 1991, only $3.2 million of these bonds were outstanding.

The retraction feature is the bondholder's analogue to the corporation's inclusion of a *call feature*, which is described later in the chapter.[5] As the option is of value to the bondholder, the interest rate on newly issued retractable bonds should be less than that on newly issued nonretractable bonds. The value of the option, and hence the saving in interest cost to the corporation, depends on the expected volatility of interest rates.[6] The retraction feature is just one of many possible "bells and whistles" that are included in bond issues as "sweeteners" for the bond investor.

Extendible Bonds. An **extendible bond** is a short-term bond that provides the holder with the option to exchange it for a similar amount of long-term debt, on or before a specified date, at an interest rate determined at the date of the original issue. The interest rate on the new debt is either the same or slightly higher than the interest rate on the original issue. The original debt issue usually has a maturity of 5 years and the new debt issued is longer term, usually for 10 years. Thus, the extendible bond provides the bondholder with the option of increasing the maturity of the debt. This option will be exercised only if, during the election period, the interest rate on new debt is less than the interest rate on the debt that could be obtained from using the extendible feature. Like the retraction feature, this option has the potential of being of value to the bondholder; thus, the yield on an extendible bond should be lower than on a similar bond without the extendible feature.

International Bonds. For a number of Canadian corporations and all levels of government, the capital market in which bonds can be issued has expanded beyond the geographical boundaries of the country. The bond market has become international, and a Canadian corporation can now issue debt in capital markets outside Canada in currencies of the company's choice. This leads to two different types of international bonds.

1. *Foreign Bonds.* Canadian companies sometimes raise long-term debt capital in the domestic capital market of a foreign country. For example, suppose Bell Canada requires U.S. dollars and it decides to raise the needed capital in the U.S. bond market. The bond issue is denominated in (that is, pays interest and principal in) U.S. dollars and sold to investors in the United States. A **foreign bond** from the viewpoint of the Canadian corporation is one that is issued to investors in a foreign country in the

---

[5]The Trizec bond permitted the company to increase the rate of interest payable after June 1, 1988, provided notice of the increase had been given on or before December 15, 1987. Such a provision gives the company the option of increasing the interest rate on its debt, if it so desires, so as to prevent the investors from exercising their retraction option.

[6]A discussion of the variables that are important in determining the value of an option is presented in Chapter 22.

currency of that country. The bulk of Canadian foreign borrowings are placed in the United States capital market. Federal and provincial governments are very active in this market; Canadian corporate debt sold in the United States has been issued primarily, but not exclusively, by regulated utilities.

2. *Eurobonds.*   The second type of international bond is the **Eurobond**, which is denominated in a currency *other than* that of the country in which it is sold. For example, a Canadian company can sell Eurobonds denominated in U.S. dollars to investors in Germany. The principal and interest payments are made in U.S. dollars, which the investor can convert to domestic currency if so desired. The EuroCanadian market includes bonds denominated in Canadian dollars, which are issued by companies from all over the world and not just from Canada. To a company issuing a Eurobond, one important feature of the process is a far lower level of required disclosure than for bonds issued domestically; this provides companies with more rapid access to the capital markets and lower transaction costs given the lower regulatory burden.

Eurobonds generally are issued as *bearer bonds*, rather than as *registered* bonds, which means the names and nationalities of investors are not recorded. They appeal to two classes of investors: retail and institutional. In the retail side of the market, individuals who desire anonymity, whether for privacy reasons or for tax avoidance, find Eurobonds to their liking. (The beginnings of the market can be traced to Luxembourg and the investment practices of Belgian dentists.) In addition, most governments do not withhold taxes on interest payments associated with Eurobonds. If the investor requires an effective yield of 10 percent, a bond that is exempt from withholding tax needs a coupon rate of 10 percent, in contrast, if tax is withheld on the same bond at a rate of, say, 30 percent, a coupon rate of 14.3 percent is required to obtain the 10 percent yield.[7] Foreign investors who desire secrecy do not want to file for a refund of the tax, so they prefer

---

[7]Suppose the bond is issued at 10 percent with a face value of $1000. The interest payment every year is $100 (= 10% × $1000). However, with a withholding tax, w, of 30 percent, the interest payment received is $70: that is, $100 × (1 − w) = $100 × 0.7 = $70. In order for the earnings to be 10 percent on this bond, the price must fall below its face value. Using a perpetuity equation, we can write the price of the bond as

$$100 \times \frac{(1 - w)}{k} = \frac{\$70}{0.10} = \$700.$$

Given a $700 price and a coupon rate of $100, the yield on the bond is k^*, the internal rate of return of the following equations:

$$\text{Price} = \frac{\text{Interest Payment}}{k^*} = \frac{\$100}{k^*} = \$700,$$

$$k^* = 1.43 \text{ or } 14.3\%.$$

In general,

$$k^* = \frac{k}{1 - w}.$$

Eurobonds to domestic bonds. Because of this tax advantage, the yields on Eurobonds can be lower than on domestic issues.

More than half of all Eurobonds are denominated in U.S. dollars; bonds in Japanese yen, German marks, and Dutch guilders account for most of the remainder. The Canadian dollar segment is small. Although the market is centred in Europe, Eurobonds are truly international. Their underwriting syndicates include investment bankers from all parts of the world, and the bonds are sold to investors not only in Europe but also in such faraway places as Bahrain and Singapore.

Until a few years ago, Eurobonds were issued solely by multinational firms, international financial institutions, and national governments. Today, however, the Eurobond market is being tapped by domestic Canadian companies. However, the investors place a significant amount of importance on name recognition of issuing companies, so only the largest and best known of the Canadian firms can utilize this market to reduce their debt costs.

Other Types of Bonds.   Several other types of bonds are used sufficiently often to warrant mention. First, **convertible bonds** are securities that are convertible into common shares at a fixed price at the option of the bondholder. Convertibles have a lower coupon rate than does nonconvertible debt, but they offer investors a chance for capital gains in exchange for the lower coupon rate.

Bonds issued with warrants are similar to convertibles. **Warrants** are options that permit the holder to buy shares for a stated price, thereby providing a capital gain if the price of the common equity rises. Like convertibles, bonds that are issued with warrants carry lower coupon rates than do straight bonds; both types of bonds are discussed in detail in the following chapter.

Putable bonds (also referred to as "bonds with a poison put") may be turned in and exchanged for cash at the *holder's* option; generally, the put option can be exercised only if the issuer takes some specified action, such as being taken over by a weaker company or increasing the outstanding debt by a large amount. In either case, the existing bondholders would be worse off, and without the put option, the value of the debt would fall. However, their position is protected since they can put the bonds back to the company at a price that does not reflect the increased risk.

A new type of bond first issued in November 1991 is the **purchasing power** (*indexed* or *real return*) bond. This type of bond is popular in countries plagued by high rates of inflation, such as Brazil and Israel among others. The British government issued an indexed bond whose interest rate is set equal to the British inflation rate plus 3 percent. Thus, these bonds provide a "real return" of 3 percent. A Government of Canada bond is similar in design to the British bond; $700 million was issued at par and a maturity date of December 2021 to yield a real return of 4.5 percent. The bond immediately fell in price to yield 4.75 percent. More bonds were reissued in September 1992 to yield the 4.75 percent real return. Since the bonds generate a taxable capital gain, they are held by non-tax-paying investors, such as registered retirement savings plans (RRSPs) and pension funds.

Concept Review

▶ Describe the differences between a foreign bond and a Eurobond.
▶ What are the benefits of issuing a Eurobond?

Features of Debt Contracts

A firm's managers are concerned about both the effective cost of debt and any restrictions in debt contracts that might limit the firm's flexibility in undertaking future financing or investment decisions. In this section, we discuss features that could affect either the cost of the firm's debt or the firm's flexibility.

Trust Indentures

A bond is a long-term promissory note; thus, a long-term relation between the borrower and lender is established in a document called an **indenture**, also termed a *trust indenture* or a *trust deed*. Over the term of an ordinary 60- or 90-day promissory note, few new developments are likely to occur in the life or affairs of the borrower that might endanger repayment. (The lender looks closely at the would-be borrower's current position because current assets are the main source of repayment.) A bond, however, is a long-term contractual relationship between the corporation and the bondholders, and for a lengthy period the bondholder has cause to worry about a number of issues that relate to the *agency problems* discussed in Chapter 1. Conflicts among the corporate stakeholders can lead to decisions undertaken by management that will benefit shareholders at the expense of bondholders. Examples of these decisions include the following: new bond issues with a priority of interest and principal payments equal to, or higher than, those of the outstanding bonds; a reduction in the value of the security pledged for outstanding bonds; and changes in the risk characteristics of the firm's assets. The trust indenture specifies terms and conditions that are attached to the bond to mitigate agency problems and protect the bondholders against decisions by the company that would cause the quality of the debt to deteriorate after it has been issued.

In the ordinary common share or preferred share certificate, the details of the contractual relationship can be summarized in a few paragraphs. The trust indenture, however, may be a document of several hundred pages covering a large number of factors important to the contracting parties, such as (1) the form of the bond and the instrument; (2) a complete description of property pledged, if any; (3) the authorized amount of the bond issue; (4) detailed protective clauses that usually include limits on indebtedness, restrictions on dividends, a *sinking fund* provision, and a minimum *current ratio requirement*; and (5) provisions for redemption or *call privileges*.

Trustee. To facilitate communication between the issuer and the numerous bondholders, a mechanism for representing the bondholders was created; a representative, called the **trustee**, is appointed and presumed to act at all times for the protection of the bondholders and on their behalf. The trustee is chosen by the bondholders and is usually a department of a trust company. The trustee has the responsibility of ensuring that the borrowing corporation lives up to the obligations it has assumed under the terms of the trust deed. If the borrower fails to meet the conditions in the trust deed, the trustee must exercise the rights given to it under the provisions of that deed. Thus, the trustee is responsible for taking appropriate action on behalf of the bondholders if the corporation defaults on the payment of principal or interest, for example.

Restrictive Covenants.   A **restrictive covenant**, often simply called a **covenant**, is a provision in a bond indenture or term loan agreement that requires the issuer of the bond to meet certain stated conditions. Typical provisions include requirements that debt not exceed a specific percentage of total capital, that the current ratio be maintained above a specific level, that dividends not be paid on common shares unless earnings are maintained at a given level, and so on. Overall, these covenants are designed to ensure, insofar as possible, that the firm does nothing to cause the quality of its debts to deteriorate after they have been issued.

The importance of the restrictive covenants is magnified as the firm approaches financial distress; at this point, the firm may be unable to meet its interest payments on debt as they fall due. The managers, in the best interests of the shareholders, may make certain decisions that will result in an increase in value to the equity holders and an equal loss in value to the bondholders. An example is the payment of a large dividend to shareholders. This will reduce the cash available to pay bondholders in the event of a default and improve the wealth of the equity holders. Another decision that shifts wealth to the equity holders is an increase in the risk of the assets. Since the company is near default, riskier assets imply that there can be a large loss or a large gain. If the former occurs, the firm will be bankrupt, an event that was likely to occur anyway; if the latter occurs, the payoff will be sufficient to meet the debt service requirement, and there will be money left over for the equity holders. This "risk-shifting" strategy reduces the market value of debt and increases the market value of equity.

Bondholders are aware that managers may engage in this behaviour, so to protect themselves, they ask for a higher interest rate on debt. This higher interest rate results in a lower share price. In order to minimize the interest rate charged on the debt, the corporation wishes to have restrictions on managers' decisions that are credible to bondholders: restrictive covenants provide credible restraints, and thus the interest rate need not be increased. Under this analysis, the shareholders, through the management, will even request that restrictive covenants be inserted in trust indentures.

The trustee is responsible for making sure the covenants are not violated and for taking appropriate action if a violation occurs. What constitutes "appropriate action" varies with the circumstances. In some situations, insisting on a firm's immediate compliance may result in bankruptcy and possibly large losses on the bonds; in such a case, the trustee may decide that the bondholders will be better served by giving the company a chance to work out its problems and thus avoid bankruptcy.

Call Provision.   A **call provision** gives the issuing corporation the right to call the bond for redemption. The bonds may be callable immediately after issue or after a predetermined number of years, as set out in the bond contract. The call provision generally states that the company must pay an amount greater than the par value of the bond when it is called; this additional sum, known as the **call premium**, is typically equal to 1 year's interest if the bond is called during the first year after it becomes callable, and the premium declines at a constant rate of I/n each year thereafter, where I = annual interest rate, and n = original maturity in years. For example, the call premium on a $1000 par value, 10-year, 10 percent bond may be $100 if called during the first year, $90 if called during the second year (calculated by reducing the $100, or 10 percent, premium by one-tenth), and so on.

The *call privilege* is valuable to the firm. As interest rates decrease, the market value of the outstanding bonds will increase. If the firm wants to refinance some of its outstanding high-coupon interest rate debt, it can use the call provision. The bonds can be repurchased at the call price, which is less than the current market value, and new debt can be issued at the lower interest rate. In effect, the firm is able to substitute bonds paying lower interest rates for bonds on which higher interest rates are being paid. This process is called a **refunding** operation and can be undertaken for debt and for preferred shares. A numerical example of the refunding process is presented in Appendix 21A.

The call feature is potentially of negative value to the investor, especially if the bond is issued in a period when interest rates are cyclically high. Accordingly, the interest rate on a new issue of callable bonds will exceed that on a new issue of bonds of the same company that are alike in all features except in being noncallable.

The difference in interest rates on a callable and noncallable bond depends on the probability the bond will be called and on the expected life of the bond until it is called. The probability that the bond will be called depends on the variability of interest rates in the capital market. If interest rates are not expected to fluctuate very much during the life of the bond, then it is unlikely that there will be a decrease in interest rates of a magnitude large enough to make it profitable for the company to invoke the call feature. Alternatively, if interest rates are expected to be volatile, then the call feature has more potential use to the corporation, and interest rates on callable bonds therefore increase.

The expected life of the bond until it is called depends on the volatility of interest rates and on the number of years specified from the date of the bond issue to the date when the securities first become callable. Thus, a company can issue debt that has a *deferred call* feature whereby the bonds are not callable before, say, 10 years. With this *call protection* for the investor, the call feature is worth less to the company or, to say the same thing, provides less risk (or cost) to the bond investor. Thus, the interest rate on a bond with a deferred call will be less than the rate on an identical bond that is immediately callable.

The number of years in the deferral of the call is a variable that management changes in response to the expected volatility of interest rates; this change affects the risk facing the investor and hence the interest rate on callable debt. Thus, in capital markets when the expected volatility in interest rates is very high, a large proportion of bonds issued with a call feature may have a 10-year deferral of the date to first call. In fact, some bonds will be issued without a call feature.

Sinking Fund. A **sinking fund** is a provision that facilitates the orderly retirement of all or part of a bond (or in some instances, an issue of preferred shares). Typically, this provision requires the firm to set aside sufficient funds to retire a portion of the bond issue each year. The amount to be retired is specified in the bond indenture. Usually the firm is required to retire either a stipulated percentage of the issue or a fixed dollar amount. Under some bond contracts, the company has the option of retiring a specified amount in excess of the normal sinking fund requirement.

If the sinking fund payments are mandatory, a failure to meet the payment causes the bond issue to be in default, which may force the company into bankruptcy. Obviously, then, a sinking fund can constitute a dangerous cash drain on the firm. Alternatively, without an arrangement for the orderly repayment of the debt issue, the firm must face the risk that at maturity it may not be in a position to retire the debt either by refinancing through a new debt issue or by a new issue of equity. The bondholders thus face a lower risk of nonrepayment of principal at maturity if a sinking fund is present.

Under most corporate bond or debenture contracts, a trustee is appointed to administer the sinking fund. At a fixed date during the year, the company is obliged to forward the sinking fund payment to the trustee. The payment can be made either in cash or in bonds of the issue itself. In the latter case, the company may have obtained the securities either by purchases of the debt in the open market or by exercising a call provision unassociated with the sinking fund itself. If cash is delivered to the trustee, it has the following options:

1. Invest the payment in securities, usually riskless bonds that will mature at the same time as the bond issue; the proceeds of investment will be used to refund the debt.
2. Call in for redemption, usually at par value plus accrued interest, an amount of bonds equivalent to the dollar payment. For example, the trustee may be able to redeem an amount equal to 2 percent of the total original amount of the issue at a price of $1000 plus accrued interest. The bonds are numbered serially and those called for redemption are determined by a lottery. Thus, the bondholders who expected to hold the debt to maturity may have their holdings called before their expected maturity date.

Since the firm has the option of delivering cash or bonds to the trustee, it will choose the least cost alternative. If interest rates have risen, causing bond prices to fall, the firm will choose to deliver bonds that have been purchased on the open market at a discount to face value. If interest rates have fallen, the company will deliver cash to the trustee, who in turn will use the sinking fund call provision. Note that a call for sinking fund purposes is quite different from a refunding call as discussed above. A sinking fund call requires no call premium, but only a small percentage of the issue is normally callable in any one year. The payment of par value plus accrued interest in the sinking fund call just reflects the fact that the par amount does not include any interest that is payable. A refunding call is at a premium to any accrued interest that was outstanding.

Although sinking funds are designed to protect bondholders by ensuring that an issue is retired in an orderly fashion, it must be recognized that at times they work to the detriment of bondholders. For example, suppose the bond carries a 15 percent interest rate and yields on similar bonds have fallen to 10.5 percent. A sinking fund call at par will require an investor to give up $150 of interest and then to reinvest in a bond that pays only $105 per year. This obviously disadvantages those bondholders whose bonds are called. On balance, however, securities that provide for a sinking fund are regarded as being safer than those without such a provision, so at the time they are issued they have lower coupon rates than otherwise similar bonds without sinking funds.

Purchase Fund. A **purchase fund** is a fund established to permit the company to purchase and retire through the market a specified amount of bonds or debentures. The purchases can only be made if the bond price is not above a specified price. The purchase fund does not have a call feature and normally retires a smaller proportion of the issue than does a sinking fund.

In some bond issues, there is a combination of a purchase fund and a sinking fund. For example, Trizec Corporation debentures due June 1, 1998, had a purchase fund for $750 000 in each of the years 1979 through 1987. The sinking fund was established in 1989 to retire 5 percent per year of the debt outstanding on June 2, 1988.

New Developments in the Long-Term Corporate Bond Market

The discussion to this point has revolved around conventional forms of debt—long-term instruments with fixed interest rates. Some innovations ("bells and whistles"), such as retractable and extendable features, have been described, but by and large the types of securities available were very standard for many years.

During the early and mid-1980s, however, interest rate volatility increased dramatically, and there were pressures on both the supply and demand sides of the bond market for changes in the form of the bond contract. On the demand side, investors were concerned about volatile interest rates and the market values of their debt holdings. To the extent that the investor's time horizon was shorter than the maturity of the bond, the investor was exposed to potential loss from selling debt at depressed market prices. This led to a preference for short-term debt and even to debt with a variable interest rate.

On the supply side, some corporations were interested in issuing long-term debt to lock in an interest rate. On the other hand, many felt that interest rates were transitorily high, and therefore they utilized either shorter-term debt or variable-rate debt.

The uncertainty in interest rates and corporations' desire to choose debt instruments based on their expectations concerning the course of future interest rates led to an explosion of financial innovation in the bond market. This financial innovation has had an important impact on corporations' decisions on the type of debt to issue.

For example, in time periods before the financial innovation explosion, companies interested in hedging business risks through financial strategies chose debt characteristics such as maturity of debt and fixed or variable interest rates based on the maturity of the assets and the interest sensitivity of the company's cash flows. In addition, the currency in which the cash flows were generated often led to the issuance of debt denominated in a foreign currency.

Financial innovation has changed some of the rules and in many situations has disconnected the relationship between the form of the debt issued and the characteristics of the company's assets and their cash flows. Under the new regime, companies can now go to any market to raise debt through the most inexpensive means and then make adjustments in the debt's characteristics to reflect their preferred strategies. In addition, it is now easier to incorporate expectations of future interest rates in the choice of fixed or variable interest rates, and, if the latter is chosen, to constrain the risk. In this section we describe a number of financial innovations at an intuitive level.

Commodity-Backed Bonds

A number of bonds have been issued that are **commodity bonds**: that is, the interest and/or principal are payable in a commodity that is produced by the company. For example, Sunshine Mining of Dallas issued a silver-backed bond in which the interest is payable in silver, and the bond is exchangeable at maturity, or redeemable, for the cash value of 50 ounces of silver, if this value is greater than the face value of the security. This latter condition is an option to the investors since the minimum cash payment they can receive at maturity is the face value of the debt. If silver prices increase to an extent that the 50 ounces of silver times the price per ounce is above the face value of the debt, the bondholder gains. As this option has value to the investor, the yield on the silver bonds is reduced accordingly.

Another example is a gold bond issued by a European subsidiary of RMI Refinery Inc., a U.S.-based precious-metal company. For this bond, both principal and interest are payable in fine gold, and the bondholder receives an option of obtaining U.S. dollars based on the price of gold at the London afternoon fixing on the payment date.

Both these bonds were priced to yield low interest rates—8.5 percent for the silver bond and 4 percent for the gold bond. The yields are low relative to yields on debt of comparable risk to reflect the options available to the bondholder.

Some commodity-backed bonds have been issued or considered in the Canadian oil and gas industry. For example, Dome Petroleum, which was in financial trouble, negotiated with some of its unsecured debtholders to convert some of its outstanding debt to notes that have interest rates linked to oil prices. Another example is the issuance of an oil-linked debenture by IPL in the purchase of the oil and gas assets owned by Walker and Home. The debenture has no sinking fund, and interest payments are indexed to the price of a barrel of oil, with a minimum or floor rate of 5 percent. These issues reflect a hedging strategy for the issuing companies, since an increase (reduction) in oil prices will be associated with increased (decreased) revenues and an unimpaired ability of the company to service the debt.

Floating-Rate Bonds

With the increase in volatility in interest rates during the early 1980s, the floating-rate bond became a popular financial instrument. The **floating-rate**

bond has a fixed maturity but the interest rate charged on the bond is changed every 6 months based on the level of an underlying interest rate series. Some corporate issues have been tied to longer-term Government of Canada bond rates, while other issues have been tied to short-term rates, such as the bank prime rate. The majority of Eurobonds issued are of the floating-rate variety, and they are tied to the short-term London interbank offered rate (LIBOR). Many additional provisions can be included in floating rate issues; for example, the Bank of Montreal issued floating rate debentures tied to the 3-month treasury bill rate with a minimum rate of 7 percent. The *floor* rate of 7 percent provides some protection to the investor if interest rates should fall precipitously. Another provision is a *cap*, which is the maximum interest rate that will be paid. The cap is of benefit to the issuing company if interest rates increase dramatically. A floating rate bond that includes both a floor and a cap is called a *collar* bond. The yields on these bonds reflect the existence of the caps and floors and the volatility of interest rates, since the volatility influences the probability that the cap or floor will be invoked.

Floating-rate debt is advantageous to investors because the interest rate moves up if market rates rise, thereby stabilizing the market value of the debt. It also provides lenders who have obligations that are interest-sensitive with a way to obtain income to meet these obligations. For example, a bank that owns floating-rate debt can use the interest it earns to pay interest on its own deposits. Floating rate debt, moreover, is advantageous to corporations, because by using it, firms can issue debt with a long maturity without committing themselves to paying an interest rate that they consider to be too high for the entire life of the loan.

Of course, if interest rates move even higher after a floating rate note has been signed, the borrower would have been better off issuing conventional fixed-rate debt. This interest rate risk faced by the borrower is minimized if the cash flows of the firm that are available to pay the floating rate interest payments move in a direct relationship with the interest rate.

Junk Bonds

Another new type of bond is the **junk bond** or highly subordinated bond, a high-risk, high-yield bond issued to finance a buyout, a merger, or a troubled company. In junk bond deals, the debt ratio is generally extremely high, so the bondholders must bear as much risk as shareholders normally would. Normally, the term to maturity on the deeply subordinated debt is greater than that on the senior debt, there are few covenants, and interest cannot be paid if payment would cause a default on senior debt. The bonds' yields are very high, reflecting the strong possibility of default. An example of deeply subordinated debt is found in some of the debt securities issued in the Campeau acquisition of Allied stores.

The emergence of junk bonds as an important type of debt is another example of how the investment banking industry adjusts to and facilitates new developments in capital markets. In the 1980s, mergers and takeovers increased dramatically. People like T. Boone Pickens in the United States thought that certain old-line, established companies were run inefficiently and were financed too conservatively. They wanted to take over the companies and restructure them both financially and operationally. To help finance these takeovers, the investment banking firm of Drexel Burnham Lambert began an active campaign to persuade financial institutions to purchase high-yield, high-risk subordinated debt. Drexel developed an expertise in structuring deals that were attractive to institutions and yet feasible in the sense that the projected cash flows from operations and the sale of assets of the firm were sufficient to meet the required interest payments and reduce the originally high levels of debt to more manageable levels. In addition, the firm was instrumental in establishing a market in which junk bonds could be traded. Drexel, along with many other specialty investment banking firms, was instrumental in changing the shape of the U.S. financial scene.

The indictment of Michael Milken of Drexel for a number of charges, including insider trading and parking securities, and the resulting illiquidity of the high-yield bonds resulted in large losses in the value of the bonds; in addition, with the recession, some of the junk bonds went into default. Although the concept of high-yield, deeply subordinated bonds is still a reasonable one for certain companies, its re-emergence to its previous level of importance in the U.S. economy is unlikely. However, junk bonds increased in use in 1992.

The junk bond market has not been frequently used in Canada. First, the merger and takeover market, both friendly and hostile, was less active here than in the United States, so the demand for this financing vehicle was negligible. Second, the high-risk segment of the market was being serviced for some companies through normal financing relationships of corporations and banks. Currently, there are some institutions that have pools of funds available to invest in situations that require the issuance of deeply subordinated debt.

Interest Rate Swaps

A corporation decides on the characteristics of the debt that it will issue on the basis of the cash flow characteristics of the firm and of its asset structure. Suppose, for example, a firm with long-lived assets and cash flows that are not sensitive to interest rates normally issues long-term fixed-rate debt. In reviewing the yields necessary to issue various debt instruments, the company treasurer notes that if floating-rate debt is issued, the cost will be lower than if fixed-rate debt is issued. In times past, if by issuing floating-rate debt the treasurer wanted fixed-rate debt, the alternative of reducing financing costs would not be used. However, within the last 10 years a market has developed in which corporations **swap** their debt payments, either directly or through a financial intermediary, thereby converting fixed-rate debt to floating-rate or vice versa. A company can now canvass all possible markets and calculate the cheapest cost to obtain the debt obligations with the required interest rate pattern. With an active swap market, a firm that wants fixed-rate debt can issue floating-rate debt in a particular market and swap the interest payments to obtain fixed-rate debt. The total cost of the swap-related transaction, including the cost of the swap itself, is less than the cost of a direct issue of fixed-rate debt.

The basis of swap-related transactions is to take advantage of an arbitrage opportunity since the capital markets have not priced the floating- and fixed-rate debt properly. If the pricing were correct, the straight debt issue could not be more expensive than the 'floating swapped to fixed' transaction.

In addition to the interest rate swaps just discussed, there are *currency swaps* in which a company desiring Canadian dollar debt can issue debt denominated in, say, Dutch guilders in the Euromarket and swap the guilders for Canadian dollars. This transaction is used by companies to achieve their desired foreign currency exposure.

There are many reasons for engaging in a swap to obtain the desired interest rate or currency exposure, rather than issuing debt to obtain that exposure directly. Usually the swap transaction provides one or both parties with lower-cost access to specific debt markets, and the risk premiums assessed by the parties in the transaction are different from the market's assessment. The net result is a cheaper source of financing, including any transactions costs necessary to achieve the swap.

The markets for currency and interest rate swaps are well developed and accessible by most medium to large size companies. The mechanics underlying the swap transactions are described in Appendix 21B.

Bond Ratings

An important element in determining the yield on bonds is the risk of default. The term *default risk* covers more than the extreme case of bankruptcy; it also includes instances in which interest payments are not met in full as they come due. In deciding whether or not to purchase a debt instrument, the potential bondholder evaluates the risk of default and decides whether the promised yield on the bond is sufficient to compensate for the risk.

In Canada, the Canadian Bond Rating Service (CBRS) and the Dominion Bond Rating Service (DBRS) evaluate the risk on bonds of Canadian issuers and assign quality ratings to reflect their perceptions of this risk. In the United States, Moody's and Standard & Poors perform this service. All the **bond rating** services include as factors in determining their rates liquidity, earnings (both historical and expected), and the bond covenants. In addition, qualitative or subjective factors enter into the rating decision. These include an assessment of management's abilities and the potential for growth in earnings. The CBRS and DBRS rating designations are shown in Table 21-2.

The Canadian and American rating agencies have three general categories: A, B, and C. As the protection afforded the bondholder falls, the rating falls.

Table 21-2

Ratings Used by Canadian Bond Rating Service and Dominion Bond Rating Service

	High Quality		Investment Grade		Speculative		Default
CBRS	A^{++}	A^{+}	A	B^{++}	B^{+}	C	D
DBRS	AAA	AA	A	BBB	BB	C	CC

Note: Both services modify their ratings by the designation of "high" or "low"; this fine tuning indicates the relative position of the bond issue quality within the given rating classification.

Bonds in the A category have a long history of earnings and asset protection, and it is expected that the protection afforded to the bondholder will be maintained in the future. Within this A category, the three CBRS rankings are A^{++}, A^+, and A (the DBRS equivalent rankings are AAA, AA, and A). The first category represents the highest quality. The top CBRS rating in the B category, B^{++} (the DBRS equivalent is BBB), is given to bonds that are of medium or average creditworthiness. "Single A" and "triple B" bonds are strong enough to be considered *investment-grade bonds*, and they are the lowest-rated bonds that many life insurance companies and institutional investors are permitted by law to hold. The B^+ (BB) rating reflects protection to bondholders that is modest or unstable. The lowest rate in this category, B, is given to companies that lack most qualities for long-term investment: protection to bondholders is poor and the operating conditions of the companies are volatile. Finally, both rating services give a C rating to speculative bonds. In extreme cases, the bonds may be in default and the rating assigned is a D. For a firm that is experiencing severe financial and operating problems, a "suspended" rating is assigned to the bonds.[8]

As an illustration of the relationship of bond rating to protection afforded investors, consider the ratings for the bonds of TransCanada Pipelines Ltd., which owns and operates a natural gas distribution pipeline from Alberta to Quebec and markets natural gas to Canadian and U.S. distribution companies. The company has four classes of debt. The first, mortgage bonds, with the greatest protection to the bondholder, have a CBRS rating of A (high); the sinking fund debentures (with somewhat lower protection) and the term notes have a rating of A (low); the riskiest of TransCanada's debt instruments, the subordinated debentures, have a rating of B^{++}.

Bond Rating Criteria

Although the rating assignments are judgement-based, they rest on both qualitative and quantitative factors, some of which are listed below:

1. Debt-to-assets ratio.
2. Times-interest-earned ratio.
3. Fixed-charge coverage ratio.
4. Current ratio.
5. Mortgage provisions. Is the bond secured by a mortgage? If it is and if the property has a high value in relation to the amount of bonded debt, the bond's rating is enhanced.
6. Subordination provisions. Is the bond subordinated to other debts? If so, it will be rated at least one notch below the rating it would have if it were not subordinated. Conversely, a bond with other debt subordinated to it will have a somewhat higher rating.
7. Guarantee provisions. Some bonds are guaranteed by other firms. If a weak company's debt is guaranteed by a strong company (usually the

---

[8]The description of the protection from default and the investment quality of the bonds classified in the different categories is based on the discussion in the CBRS manual; these descriptions are generally equivalent to those found in the DBRS manual.

     weak company's parent), then the bond will be given the strong company's rating.

8.   Sinking fund. Does the bond have a sinking fund to ensure systematic repayment? This feature is a plus factor to the rating agencies.

9.   Maturity. Other things being the same, a bond with a shorter maturity will be judged less risky than a longer-term bond, and this will be reflected in the rating.

10.   Indenture provisions. Are there covenants in the bond indenture that constrain management's ability to alter the operations of the firm or remove liquid assets from the company? With covenants in place, the ability of management to reduce the wealth of bondholders is reduced and the bond rating is higher.

11.   Stability. Are the issuer's sales and earnings stable?

12.   Regulation. Is the company regulated, and could an adverse regulatory climate cause its economic position to decline? Regulation is especially important for electric and gas utilities and telephone companies.

13.   Overseas operations. What percentage of the firm's sales, assets, and profits are from overseas operations, and what is the political climate in the host countries?

14.   Environmental factors. Is the firm likely to face heavy expenditures for pollution control equipment?

15.   Pension liabilities. Does the firm have unfunded pension liabilities that could pose a future problem?

16.   Labour unrest. Are there potential labour problems on the horizon that could weaken the firm's position?

17.   Accounting policies. If a firm uses relatively conservative accounting policies, then its reported earnings will be judged to be of higher quality than if it uses less conservative accounting procedures. Thus, conservative accounting policies are a plus factor in bond ratings.

Representatives of the rating agencies have consistently stated that no precise formula is used when setting a firm's rating; all the factors listed, plus others, are taken into account, but not in a mathematically precise manner. Statistical studies bear out this contention. Researchers who have tried to predict bond ratings on the basis of quantitative data have had only limited success, which indicates that the agencies use judgement when establishing a firm's rating.[9]

Importance of Bond Ratings

Bond ratings are very important both to firms and to investors for several reasons. First, a bond's rating is an indicator of its default risk; hence, the rating has a direct, measurable influence on the bond's interest rate and the firm's cost of debt capital. Second, most bonds are purchased by institutional investors, not by individuals, and these institutions are generally restricted to investment-grade securities. Thus, if a firm's bonds fall below B^{++}, it will have

---

[9]See Ahmed Belkaoui, *Industrial Bonds and the Rating Process* (Westport, Conn.: Quorum Books, 1983).

a difficult time selling new bonds, as most of the potential purchasers will not be allowed to buy them.

Ratings also have an effect on the availability of debt capital. If an institutional investor buys B^{++} bonds and these bonds are subsequently downgraded to B^+ or lower, then the institution may face problems from regulators if it continues to hold the security and problems of marketability in the face of diminished demand if it attempts to liquidate the downgraded bonds. Because of this fear of downgrading, many institutions restrict their bond portfolios to A or even A^+ bonds. Thus, the lower a firm's bond rating, the smaller the group of available purchasers for its new issues.

As a result of their higher risk and more restricted market, lower-grade bonds have much higher required rates of return, k_d, than do high-grade bonds. Figure 21-1 illustrates this point. In each of the years shown on the graph, Government of Canada bonds have always had the lowest yields, A^{++} bonds have been next, and the B^{++} bonds have had the highest yields. The Figure also shows that the gaps between yields on the three types of bonds vary over time, indicating that the cost differentials, or risk premiums, fluctuate from year to year. This point is highlighted in Figure 21-2, which gives the yields on the three types of bonds and the risk premiums for A^{++} and B^{++} bonds in June 1982, in June 1987, and in June 1991. In 1982, interest rates for all risk categories were extremely high, reflecting the high expected rates of inflation and the variability in the inflation rate. The risk premium[10] that reflected investors' risk aversion and can be observed in the slope of the line was 0.81 percent on the top-rated corporate bonds but rose dramatically to 2.93 percent on the BBB bonds, reflecting investors' uncertainty concerning the state of the economy and the uncertain inflation impacts. The fall in yields and risk premiums from 1982 to 1987 mirrors the reduction in the inflation rate and the strengthening of the economy; this confidence is reflected in the reduction in the risk premium on BBB bonds to 1.31 percent. Over the period 1987 to 1991, although the inflation uncertainty was diminished, the economy entered a recession. As of June 1991, the risk premium on BBB bonds increased from its value in 1987 but actually fell for AAA bonds. This reflected investors' flight to quality as

---

[10]The term *risk premium* ought to reflect only the difference in required returns between two securities that results from differences in their risk. However, the differences among *yields to maturities* on different types of bonds consist of (1) a true risk premium; (2) a liquidity premium, which reflects the fact that Government of Canada bonds generally are more readily marketable than corporates; (3) a call premium, if corporate bonds are callable while long-term government bonds are not; and (4) a yield differential that incorporates the probability of loss on the corporate bond. The yield to maturity on a bond is the promised yield. If there is no probability of default, the promised yield equals the required return. If there is risk of default, the promised yield exceeds the required yield. Given some probability of default and losses in the event of default, the bondholder expects to earn the *required yield,* on average. The required yield is based on the risk of the bond and increases with the risk of debt. To illustrate the relationship between promised and required yields and the risk premium, consider the following example. Suppose the yield to maturity (the promised yield) on a BBB bond is 10 percent versus 7 percent on government bonds, but there is a 5 percent probability of default loss on the corporate bond. In this case, the expected rate of return (required yield) on the BBB bond is 9.5 percent, and the risk premium is 2.5 percent, not the full 3 percentage point difference on promised yields to maturity. In fact, the yield differential between the promised and required yields is a "default" premium. Therefore, the risk premiums given in Figure 21-2 overstate somewhat the true (but unobservable) risk premiums.

Figure 21-1
Yields on Long Term Government of Canada Bonds, A⁺⁺
Corporates and B⁺⁺ Corporates, 1982–1992ᵃ

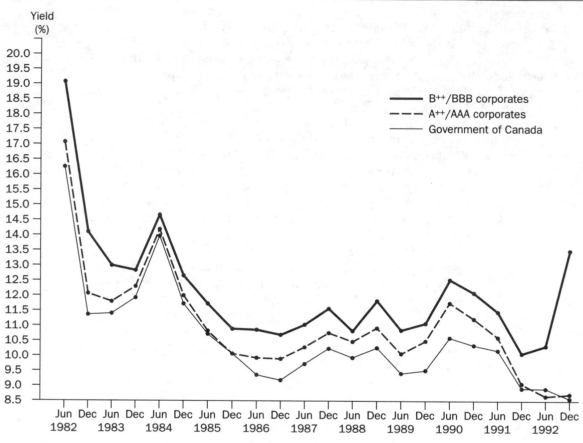

ᵃYield Reported.

Source: Canadian Bond Rating Service, Long-Term Monthly Bond Yield Averages, 1982–1992.

the economy entered the recession, reducing yields on safe securities and increasing them on risky securities.

Changes in Ratings

Changes in a firm's rating may have notable effects both on its ability to borrow long-term capital and on the cost of that capital. Rating agencies review outstanding bonds on a periodic basis, occasionally upgrading or downgrading a bond as a result of its issuer's changed circumstances. Also, an announcement of a new issue will trigger agency reviews and possibly lead to rating changes.[11]

---

[11]Rating agencies do review ratings without being prompted by the company, but many reviews are associated with new issues and are actually requested by the company. The investment dealers will make this a condition of the offering. A company must pay the agency to have its bonds rated.

Figure 21-2
Relationships between Bond Ratings and Bond
Yields, 1982, 1987, 1991

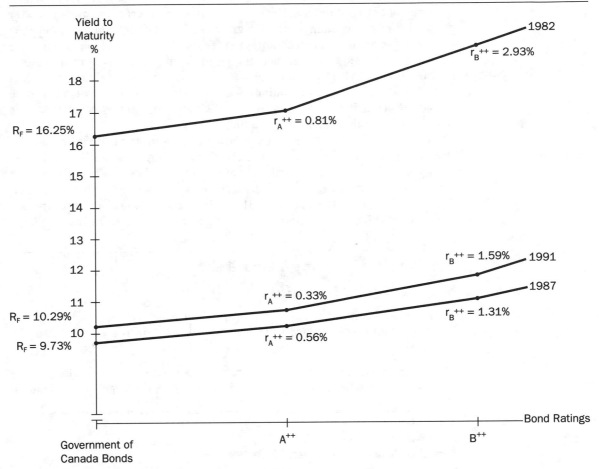

r_{A++} = risk premium on A++ bonds
r_{B++} = risk premium on B++ bonds

	Long-Term Government Bonds (Default-Free) (1)	A++ Corporate Bonds (2)	B++ Corporate Bonds (3)	Risk Premiums	
				A++ (4) = (2) − (1)	B++ (5) = (3) − (1)
June 1982	16.25%	17.06%	19.18%	0.81%	2.93%
June 1987	9.73	10.29	11.04	0.56	1.31
June 1991	10.29	10.62	11.88	0.33	1.59

Source: Canadian Bond Rating Service, Long-Term Monthly Bond Yield Averages, 1982–1991.

In 1991, the medium-term notes of Southam Inc. were downgraded to A (low) from A. Southam is involved in the communications and media industry; it publishes newspapers in Canada, retails books and magazines, operates commercial printing businesses, and provides information services. The reasons for the downgrading were related to the slump in retail and classified advertising resulting from the recession and the increased debt load resulting from the company's acquisition and capital expenditures.

Table 21-3 summarizes DBRS rating changes from 1982 to 1990. Over the whole period, the number of rating changes averaged 44 per year, approximately 22 percent of the total number of issues rated. Downgradings were a greater proportion of rating changes than upgradings. For the recession years of 1982 and 1990, the number of downgradings exceeded the number of upgradings by a substantial amount, and the percentage of rating changes were above the average for the whole period. The weak earnings associated with high debt levels resulted in the downgradings. The 1987–89 period was associated with an improvement in the economy and the reduction of debt by companies. The result was a large number of upgradings.

A bond's yield can change even before a change in its rating is announced; this can lead to an observation that the rating change had no impact on the bond yield. Since the creditworthiness of a company's bonds is being evaluated continually by investors in the marketplace, when the probability of default changes, the market does not need the rating agency to provide this information. Therefore, changes in yields often precede a change in rating category.

Evaluation of Long-Term Debt

Debtholder's Viewpoint

From the viewpoint of a holder, long-term debt is good in regard to risk, has limited advantages in regard to income, and is weak in regard to control. To elaborate:

1. In the area of risk, debt is favourable because it gives the holder priority with respect both to earnings and to assets in the event of liquidation.

Table 21-3
Bond Rating Changes:
Dominion Bond Rating Service, 1982–1990

	Total Number	Upgrades		Downgrades		Rating Changes as % of Total Rated Issues
		No.	%	No.	%	
1982	54	6	11	48	9	36%
1983	23	10	44	13	56	15
1984	26	17	65	9	35	15
1985	39	20	51	19	49	21
1986	50	12	24	38	76	25
1987	43	30	70	13	30	19
1988	47	30	64	17	36	20
1989	50	30	60	20	40	20
1990	67	6	9	61	91	26
Average	44	18	44	26	56	22

Source: W. Schroeder, "Rating Debt in Canada: The Issues," in R. Rupert, *The Canadian Investment Banking Review* (Toronto: McGraw-Hill Ryerson Limited, 1991).

Debt also has a definite maturity, and it is protected by the covenants of the indenture.

2. Regarding income, the bondholder generally receives a fixed return, for, except in the case of income bonds, interest payments are not contingent upon the company's level of earnings. However, debt does not participate in any superior earnings of the company, and capital gains are limited by call provisions. Moreover, the interest payments on bonds, except in the case of indexed bonds and floating rate bonds, do not adjust to change in inflation. Thus, bondholders can actually suffer real losses during periods of *unanticipated* inflation. A 20-year, 14 percent bond pays $140 of interest (per $1000 of par value) each year. Because investors attempt to protect their investment from expected inflation, the 14 percent coupon includes the market's expectation of the inflation rate. If inflation is greater than expected, then the purchasing power of the $140 payment is eroded more than expected, causing a loss in real value to the bondholder. Also, if inflation increases, then so will interest rates, and that will drive the value of the bond down and cause its owner to suffer a capital loss.

3. As for control, the bondholder usually does not have the right to vote. However, if the bonds go into default, then bondholders may actually take control of the company.

Corporation's Viewpoint

From the viewpoint of the issuing corporation, bonds have both advantages and disadvantages. The advantages include the following:

1. The cost of debt is definitely limited, and bondholders do not share in the rising profits if the firm is highly successful.
2. The owners of the corporation do not have to share control when debt financing is used.
3. The required rate of return is lower than that of common equity.
4. Except in the case of income bonds, the interest payment on debt is a tax-deductible expense, which further reduces its relative cost.
5. By inserting a call provision into the bond indenture, the firm can reduce its fixed charges if interest rates decline.

The disadvantages of bonds are as follows:

1. Debt is a fixed charge; if the earnings of the company fluctuate, it may be unable to meet the charge, and at the very least, the use of debt will cause net income available to common shareholders to be more volatile than sales and operating income.
2. As we saw in Chapters 17 and 18, higher risk leads to a higher cost of equity capital. In addition, the increasing debt levels may increase the probability of default with the associated costs of bankruptcy. Thus, even though leverage raises earnings per share, the increased probability of default, along with the higher capitalization rate, may drive down the value of the common shares.
3. Debt usually has a fixed maturity date, and the financial officer must make provisions for repayment of the debt at that time.
4. Since long-term debt involves a commitment for a long period, it also involves risk. The expectations and plans on which the debt was issued

may not materialize, and the debt may prove to be a burden. For example, if national income, employment, the general price level, and interest rates all fall greatly, then the prior assumption of a large amount of long-term, fixed-rate debt may turn out to be a disastrous financial policy. An example in this regard comes from the oil and gas industry, where major expansions were predicated on continuing high energy fuel prices, and financed with debt at high interest rates. The fall in energy prices left many companies unable to meet the heavy financial charges that they had undertaken earlier when the future looked rosier than it turned out to be.

5. The long-term contractual relationship inherent in a bond requires the indenture provisions to be much more stringent than would be true of a short-term credit agreement. Therefore, a firm that uses long-term debt may find itself subject to much more disturbing and crippling restrictions than if it had borrowed on a short-term basis or had issued common equity.

6. There is a limit on the extent to which funds can be raised through long-term debt. Generally accepted standards of financial policy dictate that the debt ratio should not exceed certain limits. When debt goes beyond these limits, (1) its cost rises rapidly and (2) indenture provisions become even more restrictive.

Preferred Shares

As explained in Chapter 16, *preferred shares* are equity securities that pay a stated dividend. They have claims and rights ahead of common shares—a preference—but behind all bonds. The preference relative to common shares may be a prior claim on earnings, a prior claim on assets in the event of liquidation, or preferential position with regard to both earnings and assets.[12]

The hybrid nature of preferred shares becomes apparent when we try to classify them in relation to bonds and common shares. The priority feature and the (generally) fixed dividend indicate that preferred shares are similar to bonds. Payments to the preferred shareholders are limited in amount so that the common shareholders receive the advantages (or disadvantages) of leverage for their use. However, if the preferred dividends are not earned, the directors can "pass" (not pay) them without putting the company into bankruptcy. In this regard, preferred shares are similar to common shares; failure to pay the stipulated dividend does not cause default of the obligation, as does failure to pay bond interest.

Accountants classify preferred shares as equity and report it in the equity portion of the balance sheet under "preferred equity." However, financial analysts sometimes treat preferred equity as debt and sometimes treat it as

---

[12]The term *preferred share* is not used in either the Ontario or the Canada business corporation acts. In the former, corporations can have a number of different classes of shares, one of which must be voting common shares. The other classes can be called preference shares if they have some preference or right over common shares. Note that this "preference" is broader than just a prior claim over dividends or assets in the event of liquidation. In the *Canada Business Corporations Act*, the same concept of preference shares is used. In this section, we specialize the preference to consider shares that are nonvoting, have preference on dividends and/or assets (in liquidation) over common shares, and have claims junior to all bondholders.

equity, depending on the type of analysis being made. If the analysis is being made by a common shareholder, the key consideration is the fact that the preferred dividend is a fixed charge, which reduces earnings on the common, so from the common shareholder's point of view preferred shares are similar to debt. Suppose, however, that the analysis is being made by a bondholder who is studying the firm's vulnerability to failure brought on by declines in sales and income. If the firm's income declines, the debtholders have a claim to the available income ahead of preferred shareholders, and if the firm fails, debtholders have a prior claim to assets when the firm is liquidated. Thus, to a bondholder, preferred equity is similar to common equity.

From management's perspective, preferred equity lies between debt and common equity. Since failure to pay dividends on preferred shares will not force the firm into bankruptcy, preferred equity is safer to use than debt. At the same time, if the firm is highly successful, the common shareholders will not have to share that success with the preferred shareholders, because preferred dividends are fixed. Remember, however, that the preferred shareholders do have a higher priority claim than the common shareholders.

We see, then, that preferred shares have some of the characteristics of debt and some of the characteristics of common shares, and they are used in situations in which conditions are such that neither debt nor common shares are entirely appropriate. For shareholders, preferred shares are a leverage-inducing instrument much like debt. For creditors, they constitute an additional equity cushion. Preferred shares can therefore be treated either as debt or as equity, depending on the nature of the problem under consideration.

Major Provisions of Preferred Share Issues

As we have already observed, changes in economic circumstances lead to the introduction of new kinds of securities. The varieties of securities are limited chiefly by the imagination and ingenuity of the investment dealers formulating the terms of the security issues. It is not surprising, then, that preferred shares can be found in a variety of forms. We now look at the main terms and characteristics and examine the possible variations in relation to the kinds of situations or circumstances in which they could occur.

Priority to Assets and Earnings

Many provisions in a preferred share certificate are designed to reduce risk to the purchaser in relation to the risk carried by the holder of common shares. Preferred shares usually have priority with regard to earnings and assets, and two provisions designed to prevent undermining this priority are often found. The first states that, without the consent of the holders of the preferred shares, there can be no subsequent sale of securities having a prior or equal claim on earnings, and no conversion of shares from a class with a lower priority to a class with priority equal to or greater than the priority on the preferred shares. The second provision is an attempt to prevent the company from dissipating the assets through dividend payments to common equity. These negative covenants on dividend distribution require a minimum level of retained earnings before common share dividends are permitted to be paid. In order to assure the availability of liquid assets that may be converted into cash for the payment of preferred dividends, the maintenance of a minimum current ratio may also be required.

Par Value

Unlike common shares, preferred shares usually have a par value (or its equivalent under some other name), and this value is a meaningful quantity. First, the par value establishes the amount owing to the preferred shareholders in the event of liquidation. Second, the preferred dividend is frequently stated as a percentage of the par value. For example, British Columbia Telephone has a 6.80 percent preferred share with a par value of $25.00. The annual dividend to be paid on the preferred share is $1.70. On other preferred shares, dividends are stated in dollar amounts rather than as a percentage of par value.

Cumulative Dividends

Unless the indenture includes an explicit statement to the contrary, dividends on preferred shares are **cumulative dividends**—that is, all preferred dividends in arrears must be paid before common dividends can be paid. The cumulative feature is a protective device; if the preferred shares were not cumulative, preferred and common share dividends could be "passed" for a number of years, and the directors of the company could then vote a large dividend on the common shares, but only the stipulated annual dividend to the preferred. Obviously, such an action would negate the preferred position that the holders of preferred shares have tried to obtain. The cumulative feature prevents such evasion.[13]

Large arrears on preferred shares make it difficult to resume dividend payments on common shares. To avoid delays in beginning common share dividend payments again, a compromise arrangement with the holders of preferred shares is likely to be worked out. A package offer is one possibility; for example, a recapitalization plan may provide for an exchange of shares. The arrearage will be wiped out by the donation of common shares with a value equal to the amount of the preferred dividend arrearage; this provides the preferred holders with a direct ownership share in the corporation. In addition, resumption of current dividends on the preferred shares may be promised. The advantage to the company of substituting common shares for dividends in arrears is that it can start again with a clean balance sheet. If earnings recover, dividends can be paid to the holders of the common shares without having to make up arrearages to the holders of preferred shares. The original common shareholders, of course, will have given up a portion of their ownership of the corporation.

At the beginning of December 1991, Crownx proposed a restructuring plan to address its unpaid preferred dividends, which were accruing at a rate of $34 million per year. The company proposed to offer nonvoting common shares to the preferred shareholders and the warrant holders (the latter securities were

---

[13]Note, however, that compounding is absent in the cumulative plans. In other words, the arrearages themselves earn no return.

convertible, starting January 1992, into preferred shares with a dividend tied to the prime rate). If the reorganization plan had gone through, the controlling family would have continued to have a 48.0 percent stake in the voting shares and only a 4.2 percent holding in the total equity of the company. A reorganization of this type must be approved by all shareholders, including the warrant holders. On December 6, 1991, the warrant holders defeated the proposed reorganization plan. A number of reasons were put forward. The strongest was that the warrant holders wanted to have voting and not nonvoting shares. Given the poor performance of the company, there was some indication that warrant and preferred holders who obtained voting common shares could be a threat to the existing management since the control position of the family would be eroded. It was suggested that the warrant and preferred holders would wait out the arrearages since the family members obtained their cash flow from common dividends and that the longer that there was no deal on the preferred dividend arrearages, the more expensive it would be to re-establish the dividend.

Convertibility

A substantial proportion of the preferred shares issued in recent years are convertible into common shares. For example, one share of a particular preferred may be convertible into two and a half shares of the firm's common shares at the option of the preferred shareholder. (The nature of convertibility is discussed in Chapter 22).

Use of Series

The company may from time to time want to issue more preferred shares. With changing conditions in the capital market, both the preferences and the dividend rate required on these subsequent issues of preferred shares may differ from those of the original issue. To eliminate the costs of calling a shareholders' meeting to ratify the terms of the new issue, the company can make use of a *series provision*. For a given class of shares, there can be either a maximum amount or an unlimited amount of shares authorized to be issued. If the company requires new issues within a particular class, each issue will be designated as a series. Each series issue may differ with respect to the dividend payment and certain preferences—for example, conversion, retraction, and compulsory redemption. All series within a class, however, must have the same overall creditor position. If the company wishes to issue a preferred share with a higher priority than the existing preferreds, it must create a new class of shares, which requires the vote of the classes junior to this class.

For example, as of October 30, 1990, Trizec Corporation Ltd. had two classes of preferred shares outstanding, each with a number of series. The senior preferred class B shares were issued in five series, 1 through 4 and 6. Each series had the same general preferences but the five differed in the dividend payments. All class B shares were junior to those of the senior preferred class A in terms of dividend and liquidation distributions.

Other Provisions

Some other provisions one occasionally encounters in preferred shares include the following:

1. *Sinking fund.*   Some preferred issues have a sinking fund requirement, which generally calls for the purchase and retirement of a given percentage of the preferred shares each year. The mechanics of the sinking fund are identical to those used in sinking funds for bonds.

2. *Purchase fund.*   Many preferred shares have a purchase fund that permits the retirement of a portion of the issue each year through direct purchases by the company in the open market.

3. *Voting rights.*   Preferred shares generally carry the right to vote for directors if the company has not paid preferred dividends and/or made purchase or sinking fund payments for a specified number of quarters. This feature permits the preferred shareholders to elect a specified number of directors, usually providing the preferred shareholders with minority representation on the board of directors.

4. *Maturity.*   Generally, preferred shares do not have maturity dates on which they must be retired. If the issue has a sinking fund, this effectively creates a maturity date, as some of the shares are retired under the sinking fund provision. Many preferred shares issued recently have specified maturity dates.

5. *Participation.*   The conditions on a preferred share may provide for participation with the common shares in any dividend payments after there has been a dividend payment to the common shareholders equal to that paid to the preferred shareholders. The terms under which this participation takes place must be specified in the articles of incorporation. In addition, there may be participation with the common shareholders in the liquidation of a company.

6. *Call or redemption.*   The issuing corporation has the right, if specified, to call in the preferred shares for redemption; this provision is the same as a call for bonds. If the preferred share has a par value, the redemption terms are set as a premium above par value. For some issues, this *call premium* decreases over time. For example, a $25 par value share might be redeemable at the option of the company at $26.75 during 1995 and at a price decreasing by 25 cents per year until 1999. From 2000 and on, the redemption price will be $25.00. If the preferred shares have no par value, the terms under which they can be redeemed must be written into the contract. Before redemption can occur, all current dividends and those in arrears must be paid.

7. *Purchase for cancellation.*   To add flexibility to its financing plans, the company may add a provision permitting the purchase of shares for cancellation directly from the shareholders. The maximum prices for these purchases are set equal to the redemption price (or prices). Unlike the redemption provision, the company does not have the power to force the sale; shareholders need not accept the offer.

Recent Innovations in Preferred Shares

Increases in interest rate volatility and changes in the income tax provisions concerning the treatment of dividends in the hands of investors have led to financial innovations in the preferred share market. The new preferred shares are often referred to as *term preferred shares*, and they have a number of unique features or terms. The thrust of many of the financial innovations is to reduce the maturity of the preferred share, usually as a right given to the holder to require redemption, acquisition, or cancellation of the shares. This is of benefit to the holder of the shares and hence results in lower yields.

1. *Retractable preferreds.*   Just as it does for a bond, a retraction feature on a preferred share provides an option to the holder to force the company to redeem the security on a specified date (or series of dates) at a specified price. In some preferred share issues, the retraction feature is combined with others, such as a conversion option or an option given to the firm to increase the preferred dividend, to prevent the exercise of the retraction feature on all of the preferred shares.

2. *Variable- or floating-rate preferreds.*   Variable-rate preferred shares have dividend payments that fluctuate with changes in an underlying interest rate series. The relationship of dividend payments to the interest rate series and the actual interest rate series to be used are identified in the preferred share contract. In most of these preferred issues, there is a floor or minimum dividend payment; issuers either expect that interest rates are not going to go higher or are able to hedge any increase in dividend payments induced by increases in interest rates by the interest-sensitive cash flows from their operations. For example, the Toronto-Dominion Bank's variable rate class A cumulative preferred shares series D has a par value of $25 per share. The quarterly dividends are set at a variable rate, on an annual basis, equal to 71 percent of the bank's average daily prime rate for the immediately preceding 3-month period. Thus, the dividend payments are partially hedged, since increases in the prime rate reflect higher cash flows, which are available to pay the higher dividend.

Quality Ratings

There are quality ratings for preferred shares, just as there are for bonds, and the factors underlying the quality ratings are similar, reflecting the debt characteristics of preferred shares.

CBRS has six ranking categories for preferred shares. The highest rating of $P-1^+$ is given to securitized preferred shares; these are preferred shares that are guaranteed by a company with superior financial strength. The ratings then range from highest quality, P-1, to speculative, poor quality, P-5. As with the debt ratings, the designations "high" and "low" are used to indicate an issuer's relative strength within a rating category.[14]

Evaluation of Preferred Shares

Before we consider the pros and cons of issuing and purchasing preferred shares, it is useful to review some important tax consequences of preferred

---

[14]DBRS also rates preferred shares; their highest category is Pfd-1 and generally includes companies whose bonds are rated AA (low) or higher. The lowest category, Pfd-5, reflects speculative preferred shares and coincides with bonds rated in the B category or lower. They also utilize the high/low designation.

shares. From the corporation's point of view, dividends on preferred shares are *not* a tax-deductible expense. From the investor's perspective, the dividends are eligible for the dividend tax credit. Thus, if the current yield on preferred shares is approximately 8 percent, this is equivalent on an after-personal-tax basis to an interest rate on debt, which is taxed differently, of approximately 10 percent. Another income tax wrinkle is that under normal circumstances intercorporate dividends are tax free. However, the *Income Tax Act* requires that dividends received by another company on term preferred shares be taxed as regular income. Only if the term preferred shares are issued in circumstances of financial difficulty for a term of 5 years or less will the dividend payments be tax free to other corporations. The implications of these income tax treatments are considered below.

Corporation's Viewpoint

There are both advantages and disadvantages to a corporation's financing with preferred shares.

1. In contrast to bonds, preferred shares let the firm avoid the obligation of making fixed interest payments.
2. A firm wishing to expand its use of financial leverage can do so without running the risk of bankruptcy.
3. By selling preferred shares, the financial manager avoids the provision of equal participation by new shareholders in higher future earnings of the firm, which the sale of new additional common shares would require.
4. Preferred shares financing also permits a company to avoid sharing control through participation in voting.
5. In contrast to bonds, preferred shares enable the firm to conserve mortgageable assets for use in an emergency. Alternatively, they permit the raising of funds when such assets are already heavily mortgaged.
6. For preferred shares with no maturity and no sinking fund, there are fewer cash flow problems than with bonds.
7. Preferred shares are considered as equity for many bond trust indenture provisions. If any of these constraints are close to being breached, an issue of preferred shares instead of common equity will remove the problem.
8. Some firms have a number of tax shields available through capital cost allowances; this results in an effective tax rate that is very low. Therefore, the deductibility of interest payments on debt may not be very appealing. Even though preferred dividends are not tax deductible, the out-of-pocket cost (that is, the dividend rate) may be less than the interest rate on debt. (In this scenario, both financing sources are paid out of after-tax cash flow.)[15]

The primary disadvantage of preferred equity financing is cost. Since preferred share dividends are not deductible as a tax expense, their component cost is

---

[15]The existence of the dividend tax credit makes preferred shares attractive to investors, and hence yields on preferreds have fallen. In recent years, high-grade preferreds have actually sold with a lower pre-personal-tax yield than the bonds of the same company. The after-personal-tax yield to investors, however, was greater on the preferred shares than on the bonds. Also, if the company has taxable income, the after-tax cost of the debt is less than the after-tax cost of the preferred shares.

much greater than that of bonds. As noted in Chapter 18, the after-tax cost of debt is roughly half the stated coupon rate for profitable firms. The cost of preferred shares, however, is the full percentage amount of the preferred dividend.[16]

Shareholder's Viewpoint

In designing securities, the financial manager must consider the corporation's point of view. Frequently, it is asserted that preferred shares have so many disadvantages both to the issuer and to the investor that they should never be issued. Nevertheless, preferred shares are issued in substantial quantities. Preferred shares provide the following advantages to the investor:

1. They provide reasonably steady income.
2. Preferred shareholders have a preference over common shareholders in liquidation; numerous examples can be cited in which the senior position of holders of preferred shares saved them from losses incurred by holders of common shares.
3. Many corporations like to hold preferred shares as investments because dividends received by a corporation from taxable Canadian corporations are tax free.
4. The dividend tax credit can be applied to the dividends on preferred shares, thereby reducing the effective tax rate. This increases the attractiveness of preferred shares among investors. For example, for an investor in the 29 percent federal tax bracket, living in a province with a 50 percent rate, a bond with a 7.5 percent yield gives an after-tax return of 5.4 percent, whereas a preferred share with the same pretax yield generates 6.9 percent after tax.

Preferred shares also have some disadvantages to investors:

1. Although the holders of preferred shares bear a substantial portion of ownership risk, their returns are limited.
2. The shares have no legally enforceable right to dividends, even if the company earns a profit.
3. Accrued dividend arrearages are seldom settled in cash comparable to the amount of the obligation that has been incurred.
4. Price fluctuations in preferred shares are greater than those in bonds with maturities less than or equal to the preferreds since (a) the longer maturity of the preferred makes their prices highly sensitive to changes in underlying yields and (b) prices move up and down with changes in both interest rates and the company's fortunes. Nevertheless pre-tax yields on bonds are frequently higher than those on preferred shares.[17]

---

[16]It must be remembered, however, that the purchaser of debt must pay taxes on the interest payments at regular income tax rates, which are higher than the effective tax rates for dividends and capital gains. This higher tax liability should be reflected in a higher before-tax interest rate on debt. This will offset, somewhat, the benefit obtained through the deductibility of interest payments in the calculation of corporate tax liability.

[17]Is this observation consistent with the basic finance concept that higher risks require higher returns? As expected, the answer is yes. Investors are interested in after-tax yield, and the risk-return relationship will hold for after-tax yields. Since preferred dividends result in a lower tax liability to investors (due to the dividend tax credit or to tax-free status of intercorporate dividends) than do interest payments on debt, the before-tax yields can easily have the observed relationship, whereas the after-tax yields have the relationship consistent with the risk-return tradeoff.

Decisions on the Use of Preferred Shares

We can now distill the circumstances favouring the use of preferred shares from the foregoing analysis. As a hybrid security, preferred shares are favoured by conditions that fall between those favouring the use of common shares and those favouring the use of debt. When a firm's profit margin is high enough to more than cover preferred share dividends, it will be advantageous to employ leverage. If the firm's sales and profits are subject to considerable fluctuations, however, the use of debt with fixed interest charges may be unduly risky. Preferred shares can offer a happy compromise. Their use is strongly favoured if the firm already has a debt ratio that is high in relation to the other firms in its line of business.

The relative costs of alternative sources of financing are always important considerations. When the capital market is operating efficiently, there is a relationship between risk and expected return on all types of securities that is determined by investors when making capital structure decisions. Thus, there are no bargains to be obtained by issuing one form of security if its cost is low relative to other securities. All yield differences are related to investors' evaluations of the differences in risk. Management may believe, however, that the yields (or costs) of one of the security types is out of line and that the firm should, therefore, issue a particular type of security. Thus, if management and its underwriters believe, for example, that the market has overreacted in its evaluation of the dividend tax credit and that yields on preferreds are transitorily low, then the firm should issue preferred shares on the basis of relative cost.

Preferred shares may also be the desired form of financing whenever the use of debt would involve excessive risk but the issuance of common shares would result in problems of control for the dominant ownership group in the company. These noncost considerations are often particularly important in determining how many preferred shares a firm should have in its capital structure.

Rationale for Different Classes of Securities

Why are there so many different forms of long-term securities? Why is anybody ever willing to purchase subordinated bonds or income bonds? The answers to both questions can be made clear by reference to Figure 21-3, which depicts the now familiar risk–return tradeoff function drawn to show the risk and the expected after-personal-tax rates of return to an investor for the various securities of Longstaff Co. Ltd. for a particular holding period—say, 1 year. First, 1-year Government of Canada treasury bills, which represent the risk-free rate, are shown for reference. Longer-term Government of Canada bonds, although free of default risk, expose an investor with a 1-year horizon to risk; they are plotted at a higher risk and expected return point of the diagram. The company's lowest-risk long-term securities are its floating rate bonds; these securities are free of interest rate risk but are exposed to some default risk. Longstaff's first mortgage bonds are slightly more risky than its floating rate notes since they are exposed to interest rate risk, so they sell at a slightly higher required and expected after-tax return. The second mortgage bonds are even more risky and have a still higher expected return. Subordinated debentures, income bonds, and preferred shares are increasingly risky and

Figure 21-3
The Longstaff Co. Ltd.: Risk and Expected
Returns on Different Classes of Securities

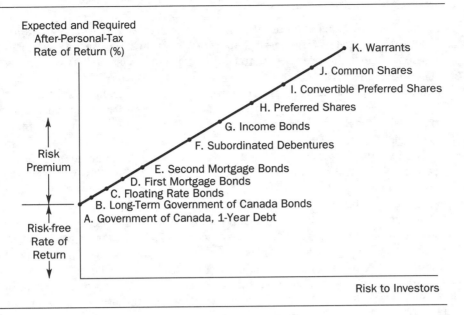

have increasingly higher expected returns. Longstaff warrants, the riskiest security the firm issues, have the highest expected return of any of its offerings. (Warrants and convertibles will be discussed in the next chapter.)

Why does Longstaff issue so many different classes of securities? Why doesn't it offer just one type of bond plus common shares? The answer lies in the fact that different investors have different risk–return tradeoff preferences. To appeal to the broadest possible market, Longstaff must offer securities that attract as many different types of investors as possible. Also, certain securities are more popular at different points in time, and firms tend to issue whatever is popular at the time they need money as long as it remains consistent with their overall financing targets. Used wisely, a policy of selling differentiated securities to take advantage of market conditions may lower a firm's overall cost of capital below what it would be if it issued only one class of debt and common shares.

Concept Review

▶ List some different types of securities in order of highest to lowest risk.
▶ Why do corporations issue so many different classes of securities?

Factors Influencing Long-Term Financing Decisions

Many factors influence a firm's long-term financing decisions. The factors' relative importance varies among firms at any point in time and for any given firm over time, but any company planning to raise new long-term capital should consider each of the points discussed below.

Target Capital Structure

As we discussed in Chapter 18, firms typically establish target capital structures, and one of the most important considerations in any financing decision is how the firm's actual capital structure compares to its target structure. However, few firms finance in any one year exactly in accordance with their target structure, primarily because exact adherence would increase their issue costs: since smaller issues of new securities have proportionally larger issue costs, firms tend to use debt financing one year and equity financing the next.

For example, Regional Drilling, Ltd., a Halifax machine tool manufacturer, needs $15 million of new external capital in each of the next 2 years. Its target capital structure calls for 40 percent debt, so if Regional raises debt in both years, it will issue $6 million of new bonds in each, with issue costs of 3.2 percent of each $6 million issue. To net $6 million, Regional will have to sell $6 000 000/0.968 = $6 198 347 each year and pay $198 347 in issue costs on each issue, for a total of $396 694 in issue costs over the 2 years. Alternatively, Regional can raise the total $12 million of debt in 1 year. The issue cost for a $12 million issue will be about 1.9 percent, so the firm can float an issue for $12 000 000/0.981 = $12 232 416 and pay $232 416 in total issue costs. By issuing debt only once, Regional can cut its debt issue costs by more than 40 percent. The same relationship applies to sales of preferred shares and to new common equity issues.

Making fewer but larger security offerings will cause Regional's capital structure to fluctuate about its optimal level rather than stay right on target. However, as we discussed in Chapter 18, small fluctuations about the optimal capital structure have little effect either on a firm's cost of debt and equity or on its overall cost of capital. Also, investors recognize that such issues are prudent and that the firm can save substantial amounts of issue costs by financing in this manner. Therefore, even though firms such as Regional do tend to finance over the long haul in accordance with their target capital structures, issue costs plus the other factors discussed in the following sections have a definite influence on the specific financing decisions in any given year.

Maturity Matching

Assume that Regional decides to float a single $12 million nonconvertible bond issue with a sinking fund. It must next choose a maturity for the issue, taking into consideration the shape of the yield curve, management's own expectations about future interest rates, and the maturity of the assets being financed. In the case at hand, Regional's capital projects during the next 2 years consist primarily of new automated milling and stamping machinery for its Halifax plant. This machinery has an expected economic life of 10 years. Should Regional finance the debt portion of the capital raised for this equipment with 5-year, 10-year, 20-year, or 30-year debt or with debt of some other maturity? One approach is to *match* the maturity of the liabilities with the maturity of the assets being financed.

Note that some of the new capital for the machinery will come from common equity, which is generally considered to be a perpetual security with an infinite maturity. (Of course, common equity can always be repurchased on the open market or by a tender offer, so its effective maturity can be reduced significantly.)

Debt maturities, however, are specified at the time of issue. If Regional finances its capital budgets over the next 2 years with 10-year sinking fund bonds, it will be matching its asset and liability maturities. The cash flows resulting from the new machinery should be sufficient to make the interest and sinking fund payments on the issue, and the bonds will be retired as the machinery wore out. If Regional uses 1-year debt, it will have to pay off the loan with cash flows derived from assets other than the machinery in question. If its operations are stable, the company can probably roll over the 1-year debt, but if it plans to do so and interest rates rise, then it will have to pay a higher rate. And if Regional subsequently experiences difficulties, its lenders may be hesitant to extend the loan, and the company may be unable to obtain new short-term debt at any reasonable rate. On the other hand, if it uses 20-year or 30-year debt, Regional will have to service that debt long after the assets that were purchased with it have been scrapped and have ceased providing cash flows. This is likely to worry potential lenders.

For all these reasons, one commonly used financing strategy is to match debt maturities with asset maturities. In recognition of this fact, firms do consider maturity relationships, and this factor has a major influence on the type of debt securities used.

Interest Rate Levels

Financial managers also consider interest rate levels, both absolute and relative, when making financing decisions. For example, long-term interest rates were high by historic standards in 1981 and 1982, so many managers were reluctant to issue long-term debt and thus lock in those high costs for long periods. We already know that one solution to this problem is to use long-term debt with a call provision. Callability permits the company to refund the issue should interest rates drop, but there is a cost, because firms must pay more if they make their debt callable. Alternatively, a firm may finance with short-term debt whenever long-term rates are historically high, and then, assuming that interest rates subsequently fall, sell a long-term issue to replace the short-term debt. Of course, this strategy has its risks. If interest rates move even higher, the firm will be forced to renew the short-term debt at higher and higher rates or to replace the short-term debt with a long-term bond that costs more than it would have when the original decision was made.

Firms often base their financing decisions on expectations about future interest rates. The success of such a strategy requires interest rate forecasts to be right more often than they are wrong, and it is very difficult to find someone with a long-term forecasting record better than 50:50.

The Firm's Current and Forecasted Conditions

If a firm's current financial condition is poor, its managers may be reluctant to issue new long-term debt because (1) a new bond issue would probably trigger a review by the rating agencies, and (2) long-term debt issued when a firm is in poor financial condition costs more and is subject to more severe restrictive covenants than debt issued from a strong position. Thus, a firm that is in a weakened condition but that is forecasting a better situation in the future is inclined to delay permanent financing until things improve. Conversely, a firm that is strong now but whose forecasts indicate a potentially bad time in the period just ahead is motivated to finance long term now rather than to wait.

These scenarios imply that the capital markets are inefficient in the sense that investors do not have as much information about the firm's future as does its management. Although this situation is undoubtedly true at times, the choice of maturity may give a signal to the market about management's expectation of the company's future performance.

The firm's earnings outlook and the extent to which forecasted higher earnings per share are reflected in share prices also have an effect on the choice of securities. If a successful R&D program has just been concluded and, consequently, management forecasts higher earnings than do most investors, the firm will not want to issue common equity. It will use debt, and then, after earnings had risen and pushed up the share price, it will sell common equity to restore the capital structure to its target level.

Restrictions in Existing Debt Contracts

There are situations in which companies are restricted from issuing new first mortgage bonds by indenture coverage requirements. This is just one example of how indenture covenants can influence a firm's financing decisions. Restrictions on the current ratio, the debt ratio, and so on can also restrict a firm's ability to use different types of financing at a given time.

Availability of Collateral

Generally, secured long-term debt is less costly than unsecured debt. Thus, firms with large amounts of general-purpose (as opposed to specialized) fixed assets that have a ready resale value are likely to use a relatively large amount of debt, especially mortgage bonds. Additionally, each year's financing decision is influenced by the amount of newly acquired assets that are available as security for new bonds.

Concept Review

► Do most firms finance each year exactly in accordance with their target capital structures? Why or why not?
► Why is the matching of debt maturities with asset maturities a commonly used financing strategy?
► If a firm's current financial condition is expected to improve shortly, why might its managers be reluctant to issue new long-term debt?
► Which type of firm is more likely to use a relatively large amount of debt, a firm with general-purpose fixed assets or one with specialized fixed assets? Explain your answer.

Summary

This chapter described the characteristics, advantages, and disadvantages of the major types of long-term debt and preferred equity securities. The key concepts covered are listed below.

☐ **Term loans** and **bonds** are long-term debt contracts under which a borrower agrees to make a series of interest and principal payments on specific dates to the lender. A term loan is generally sold to one (or a few) lenders, while a bond is typically offered to the public and sold to many different investors.

☐ There are many different types of bonds. They include **mortgage bonds**, **debentures**, **convertibles**, bonds with **warrants**, **income bonds**, **putable bonds**, and **purchasing power (indexed) bonds**. The return required on each type of bond is determined by the bond's riskiness.

☐ A bond's **indenture** is a legal document that spells out the rights of the issuing corporation and of the bondholders. The latter include **covenants** that restrict the borrower's total indebtedness and payments of dividends, limit the current ratio, and so on. A **trustee** is assigned to make sure that the terms of the indenture are carried out.

☐ A **call provision** gives the issuing corporation the right to redeem the bonds prior to maturity under specified terms, usually at a price greater than the maturity value (the difference is a **call premium**). A firm will typically call a bond and **refund** it if interest rates fall substantially.

☐ A **sinking fund** is a provision that requires the corporation to retire a portion of the bond issue each year. The purpose of the sinking fund is to provide for the orderly retirement of the issue. No call premium is paid to the holders of bonds called for sinking fund purposes.

☐ Some recent innovations in long-term financing include **floating-rate debt**, whose interest payments fluctuate with changes in the general level of interest rates; highly subordinated **junk bonds**, which are high-risk, high-yield instruments issued by firms that use a great deal of financial leverage; **commodity bonds** in which the interest and/or principal is payable in a commodity the company produces; and **swaps,** which permit a company to alter the interest rate or currency of the debt.

☐ Bonds and preferred shares are assigned **ratings** that reflect the probability of their going into default. The higher a bond's rating, the lower its interest rate.

☐ A firm's long-term financing decisions are influenced by its *target capital structure*, the *maturity of its assets*, current and forecasted *interest rate levels*, the firm's current and forecasted *financial condition*, *restrictions* in its existing debt contracts, and the suitability of its *assets for use as collateral*.

☐ Canadian firms often find that they can raise long-term capital at a lower cost outside the country by selling bonds in the international capital markets. International bonds may be either **foreign bonds**, which are exactly like regular domestic bonds except that the issuer is a foreign company, or **Eurobonds**, which are bonds sold in a foreign company but denominated in the currency of the issuing company's home country, or any other currency desired.

☐ **Preferred shares** are a hybrid security with some characteristics of debt and some of equity. Equity holders view preferred shares as being similar to debt because they have a claim on the firm's earnings ahead of the claim of the common shareholders. Bondholders, however, view preferred shares as equity because debtholders have a prior claim on the firm's income and, in the event of bankruptcy, on the firm's assets.

☐ The primary advantages of preferred shares to the issuer are (1) that preferred dividends are limited and (2) that failure to pay them will not bankrupt the firm. The primary disadvantage to the issuer is that the cost of preferred is higher than that of debt because preferred dividend payments are not tax deductible.

☐ To the holder, preferred equity offers the advantage of more dependable income than common shares, and, under certain circumstances, such dividends are not taxable for a corporation. The principal disadvantages are that the returns are limited and that the holder has no legally enforceable right to a dividend.

Appendix 21A discusses bond refundings—or paying off high interest rate debt with new, lower-cost debt—an important consideration, especially today because many firms that issued long-term debt in the early 1980s at rates of 18 percent or more now have an opportunity to refund this debt at a much lower cost. Appendix 21B describes the interest rate swap. This is a technique used by firms to obtain their preferred financing—fixed or floating rate—with the lowest possible interest cost.

Questions

21-1   What effect would each of the following items have on the interest rate a firm must pay on a new issue of long-term debt? Indicate whether the factor will tend to raise, lower, or have an indeterminate effect on the interest rate, and explain why.

    a. The firm uses bonds rather than a term loan.

    b. The firm makes its bonds convertible into common equity.

    c. The firm uses nonsubordinated debentures rather than first mortgage bonds.

    d. The firm makes its debentures subordinated to its bank debt. What will the effect be (i) on the debentures? (ii) on the bank debt? (iii) on the average cost of total debt?

    e. The firm sells income bonds rather than debentures.

    f. The firm must raise $100 million, all of which will be used to construct a new plant, and it is debating the sale of mortgage bonds or debentures. If it decides to issue $50 million of each type, as opposed to $75 million of mortgage bonds and $25 million of debentures, how will this affect (i) the cost of the debentures? (ii) the cost of the mortgage bonds? (iii) the average cost of the $100 million?

    g. The firm is planning to raise $25 million of long-term capital. Its outstanding bonds yield 9 percent. If it sells preferred shares, how will this affect the yield on the outstanding debt?

    h. The firm puts a call provision on its new issue of bonds.

    i. The firm includes a sinking fund on its new issue of bonds.

    j. The firm's bonds are downgraded from A to B++.

    k. The firm sells Eurobonds rather than Canadian domestic bonds.

21-2   Rank the following securities from lowest (1) to highest (8) in terms of their riskiness for an investor. All the securities except the government bond are for a given firm. If you think two or more securities are equally risky, indicate so.

		Rank **(8 = Highest Risk)**
a.	Income bond	_____
b.	Subordinated debentures, noncallable	_____
c.	First mortgage bond, no sinking fund	_____
d.	Preferred shares	_____
e.	Common shares	_____
f.	Government of Canada bond	_____
g.	First mortgage bond with sinking fund	_____
h.	Subordinated debentures, callable	_____

21-3   A sinking fund is set up in one of two ways:
- The corporation makes annual payments to the trustee, who invests the proceeds in securities (frequently government bonds) and uses the accumulated total to retire the bond issue on maturity.
- The trustee uses the annual payments to retire a portion of the issue each year, either calling a given percentage of the issue by a lottery and paying a specified price per bond or buying bonds on the open market, whichever is cheaper.

Discuss the advantages and disadvantages of each procedure from the viewpoint of both the firm and the bondholders.

21-4   Since a corporation often has the right to call bonds at will, do you believe individuals should be able to demand repayment at any time they so desire? Explain.

21-5   For purposes of measuring a firm's leverage, should preferred shares be classified as debt or as equity? Does it make a difference if the classification is being made (a) by the firm's management, (b) by creditors, or (c) by equity investors?

21-6   If preferred share dividends are passed over for several years, the preferred shareholders are frequently given the right to elect several members of the board of directors. In the case of bonds that are in default on interest payments, this procedure is not followed. Why does this difference exist?

21-7   It was noted that some of the important variables in determining bond ratings are size, earnings instability, leverage, interest coverage, and subordination. Describe how these variables should affect default risk and hence bond ratings.

21-8   You are told that one corporation just issued $100 million of preferred equity and another purchased $100 million of preferred shares as an investment. You are also told that one firm has an effective tax rate of 20 percent whereas the other is in the 34 percent bracket. Which firm is more likely to have bought the preferred? Explain.

21-9 One often finds that a company's bonds have a higher yield than its preferred shares, even though the bonds are considered to be less risky than the preferred to a buyer. What causes this yield differential?

21-10 Why would a company choose to issue floating-rate as opposed to fixed-rate preferred shares?

21-11 Draw an SML graph (security market line—risk versus return). Put dots on the graph to show (approximately) where you think a particular company's (a) common shares and (b) bonds would lie. Now put on dots to represent a riskier company's shares and bonds.

Self-Test Problems   (solutions appear on page 838)

ST-1   Key terms.   Define each of the following terms:
a. Funded debt
b. Term loan; bond
c. Mortgage bond
d. Debenture; subordinated debenture
e. Serial bond; convertible bond; warrant; income bond; putable bond; purchasing power (indexed) bond
f. Retractable bond; extendible bond
g. Indenture; covenant
h. Trustee
i. Call provision; sinking fund; purchase fund
j. Floating-rate bond
k. Junk bond
l. Investment grade bond
m. Foreign bond; Eurobond
n. Preferred shares
o. Cumulative dividends
p. Variable-rate preferred shares
q. Interest rate swap

ST-2   Sinking fund.   The Vancouver Development Company has just issued a $100 million, 10-year, 12 percent bond. A sinking fund will retire the issue over its life. Sinking fund payments of equal amounts will be made *semiannually*, and the proceeds will be used to retire bonds immediately. Bonds can be called at par for sinking fund purposes, or the funds paid into the sinking fund can be used to buy bonds in the open market.
a. How large must each semiannual sinking fund payment be?
b. What will happen, under the conditions of the problem so far, to the company's debt service requirements per year for this issue over time?
c. Now suppose that Vancouver Development had set up its sinking fund so that equal *annual* amounts, payable at the end of each year, were being used to buy government bonds that paid 9 percent interest. The payments, plus accumulated interest, will total $100 million at the end of 10 years, and the proceeds will be used to retire

the bonds at that time. How large will the annual sinking fund payment have to be?

d. What will be the annual cash requirements for covering bond service costs under the procedure described in Part c? (Note: interest must be paid on Vancouver's outstanding bonds but not on the bonds that have been retired.)

e. What would have to happen to interest rates to cause the company to buy bonds on the open market rather than call them under the original sinking fund plan?

Problems

21-1   Yield to call.   Six years ago your company sold a 20-year bond issue with a 14 percent annual coupon rate and a 9 percent call premium. Today your firm called the bonds. The bonds originally were sold at their face value of $1000. Compute the realized rate of return for investors who purchased the bonds when they were issued and will surrender them today in exchange for the call price.

21-2   Distribution in liquidation.   On January 1, 1994, the loan officer of the Confederation Bank agreed to make a $1 500 000, 5-year term loan to the Camping Company on the condition that any new debt issued by Camping during the next 5 years must be subordinated to the Confederation loan. On June 1, 1994, Camping sold $700 000 in subordinated debentures.

In spite of these two infusions of capital, the Camping Company was forced into bankruptcy on September 12, 1994. Camping's financial structure as of September 12 is given below:

Accounts payable	$ 300 000
Bank debt	1 500 000
Subordinated debentures	700 000
Total debt	$2 500 000
Equity	1 950 000
Total claims	$4 450 000

a. What dollar amount and percentage of Confederation's claim will be paid off if $1 200 000 is available for claims after liquidation of Camping's assets?

b. What dollar amount and percentage of Confederation's claim will be paid off if $2 000 000 is available for claims upon liquidation?

c. What is the minimum amount that must be available for claims to completely pay off the bank debt?

21-3   Cumulative preferred dividends.   Net losses for the past 3 years have prevented the Finan Company from paying the 9 percent dividend on its cumulative preferred share issue. There are 20 000 shares of the $100 par preferred equity and 350 000 shares of common equity outstanding. This year Finan has after-tax profits of $1 400 000, and the board of directors would like to declare a dividend on common equity. What is the largest dividend per share that can be declared on the common?

21-4   Financing alternatives. David Electronics is planning an expansion program. It estimates that it will need to raise an additional $400 million. David is discussing with its investment dealer whether to raise the $400 million through debt financing, or by selling additional shares of common equity.

The underwriter's recommendation will be based on the following background information. The cost of debt is 10 percent and the cost of equity is 16 percent. If the additional funds are raised by debt, the cost of debt will increase to 12 percent, and the cost of equity will rise to 19 percent. If the additional funds are raised by common equity, the cost of debt will remain at 10 percent, and the cost of common equity will fall to 13 percent. New shares can be sold at $5.75 per share. David's dividend payout ratio has averaged 30 percent of net income and it is expected to continue at this rate. The risk-free rate, R_F, is 6 percent, and the expected return on the market, $\hat{k}_M$, is 12 percent.

Average financial ratios for the electronics industry and David's financial statements follow.

Electronics Industry Standards

Long-term-debt-to-shareholders'-equity ratio	30%
Shareholders'-equity-to-total-assets	55%
Fixed-charge coverage	7 ×
Current ratio	2.1 ×
Return on equity	11%

a. Make a financial risk analysis using the financial structure ratios.

b. Calculate the effect of each financing alternative on the firm's beta.

c. Complete the pro forma income statements under the two forms of financing. Compare fixed-charge coverage under the two alternatives.

d. Calculate the market value of equity and the indicated market price per share before and after financing by the two methods.

David Electronics
Balance Sheet as of December 31, 1993
(millions of dollars)

Assets		Liabilities	
Total current assets	$ 900	Notes payable (10%)	$ 150
Net fixed assets	1800	Other current liabilities	150
		Total current liabilities	$ 300
		Long-term debt (10%)	750
		Other liabilities	450
		Total debt	$1500
		Common equity, $1 par value	150
		Paid-in capital	450
		Retained earnings	600
Total assets	$2700	Total claims on assets	$2700

David Electronics
Income Statement for Year Ended
December 31, 1993
(millions of dollars)

	Current Year	With Expansion, Equity Financing, Pro Forma	With Expansion, Debt Financing, Pro Forma
Total Revenues	$3000	$3600	$3600
New operating income	347	420	420
Interest expense	(90)	____	____
Net income before taxes	$ 257	____	____
Income taxes (46%)	(118)	____	____
Net income	$ 139	====	====

   e. Calculate the weighted cost of capital at present and under the two financing alternatives. Use book value weights.
   f. Recommend the best form of financing for David.

Integrative Problem

21-5 **Debt/Preferred share financing.** Eastern Automotive Sales Ltd. (Eastern) needs $15 million to build a new regional warehouse in Fredericton. The warehouse will take six months to construct and is expected to have a 15 year operational life. Eastern plans to raise the $15 million by selling long-term fixed income securities. Its underwriters have stated that Eastern could sell 15 year bonds or preferred shares. Bonds would require annual interest payments of 10 percent and would be callable after 5 years. If called, the bonds would be redeemed on the anniversary date of the issue at a premium of 6 months' interest. The preferred shares would be issued to yield 8 percent. The company's tax rate is 40 percent.
   You have been assigned the task of making a report to Eastern's management regarding the type of financing to use. As part of your report, you must answer the following questions:
   a. What is the difference between a bond and a term loan? What are the advantages of a term loan over a bond?
   b. Suppose Eastern issues bonds and uses the warehouse as collateral for the issue. What type of bond would this be? Suppose, instead of using this type of bond, that Eastern decided to sell debentures. Would this affect the interest rate that it would have to pay on the debt?
   c. What is a bond indenture? What are some examples of provisions the bondholders would require Eastern to include in its indenture?
   d. Eastern's bonds will be callable after 5 years. If the bonds were not callable, would the interest rate required be higher or lower than 10 percent? What would be the effect if the bonds were callable

immediately? What are the advantages to Eastern of making the bonds callable?

e. If Eastern's indenture included a sinking fund provision that required it to retire one fifteenth of the bonds each year, would this provision raise or lower the interest rate required on the bonds? How would the sinking fund operate? Why might Eastern's investors require it to use a sinking fund? For this particular issue, would it make sense to include a sinking fund?

f. Would the impact of the introduction of a call provision on preferred shares have the same impact as found for the debt issue?

g. What would be the after-tax cost of debt and preferred shares to Eastern?

h. Eastern is an A-rated firm. Suppose its bond rating was (i) lowered to triple-B or (ii) raised to double-A. What would be the effect of these changes on the interest rate required on Eastern's new long-term debt and on the market value of its outstanding debt?

i. If prior to the issue, Eastern's bond rating was reduced to a triple-B, due to a high equity ratio, would this influence the decision to issue debt or preferred shares?

j. What are some of the factors a firm like Eastern should consider when deciding whether to issue long-term debt or preferred shares?

Solutions to Self-Test Problems

ST-1 Refer to the appropriate sections of the text to check your responses.

ST-2 a. $100 000 000/10 = $10 000 000 per year, or $5 million every 6 months. Since the $5 million will be used to retire bonds immediately, no interest will be earned on it.

b. The debt service requirements will decline. As the amount of bonds outstanding declines, so will the interest requirements, as follows (in millions of dollars):

Semiannual Payment Period (1)	Sinking Fund Payment (2)	Outstanding Bonds on Which Interest Is Paid (3)	Interest Payments[a] (4)	Total Bond Service (2) + (4) = (5)
1	$5	$100	$6.0	$11.0
2	5	95	5.7	10.7
3	5	90	5.4	10.4
.	.	.	.	.
.	.	.	.	.
.	.	.	.	.
20	5	5	0.3	5.3

[a]Interest is calculated as (0.5)(0.12)(column 3); for example, interest in Period 2 = (0.5)(0.12)($95) = $5.7.

The company's total cash bond service requirement will be $21.7 million per year for the first year. The requirement will decline by 0.12 ($10 000 000) = $1 200 000 per year for the remaining years.

c. Here we have a 10-year, 9 percent annuity whose compound value is $100 million, and we are seeking the annual payment, PMT, in this equation:

$$\$100\,000\,000 = \sum_{t=1}^{10} PMT(1 + k)^t$$

$$= PMT(FVIFA_{9\%,\,10})$$

$$= PMT(15.193).$$

$$PMT = \$6\,581\,979 = \text{Sinking fund payment.}$$

The solution can also be obtained with a financial calculator. Input FV = 100 000 000, n = 10, and i = 9, and press the PMT key to obtain $6 582 009. The difference results from rounding the FVIFA to 3 decimal places.

d. Annual debt service costs will be $100 000 000(0.12) + $6 582 009 = $18 582 009.

e. If interest rates rise, causing the bond's price to fall, the company will use open market purchases. This will reduce its debt service requirements.

Appendix 21A
Refunding a Bond or a Preferred Share Issue

Suppose a company sells bonds or preferred shares at a time when interest rates are relatively high. Provided the issue is callable, the company can sell a new issue of low-yielding securities if and when interest rates drop and use the proceeds to retire the high-rate issue. This is called a *refunding operation*. Refunding decisions actually involve two separate questions: (1) is it profitable to recall an outstanding bond in the current period and to replace it with a new issue? and (2) even if refunding is currently profitable, will the expected value of the firm be increased even more if refunding is postponed to a later date? We consider both these questions in this appendix.

The decision to refund a security issue is analyzed in much the same manner as a capital budgeting expenditure. The costs of refunding (the investment outlay) are (1) the call premium paid for the privilege of calling the old issue, (2) the issue costs incurred in selling the new issue, and (3) the net interest that must be paid while both issues are outstanding (the new issue is often sold 1 month before the refunding to ensure that the funds will be available). The annual receipts, in the capital budgeting sense, are the interest payments saved each year; for example, if the interest expense on the old issue is $1 million while that on the new issue is $700 000, the $300 000 savings constitutes the annual benefit.

The net present value method is used to analyze the advantages of refunding. The future interest savings are discounted back to the present and compared with the discounted value of the cash outlays associated with the refunding. The firm should refund the bond only if the present value of the savings exceeds the cost—that is, if the NPV of the refunding operation is positive.

In the discounting process, the *after-tax* cost of the new debt should be used as the discount rate. The reason is that there is relatively little risk to the savings; their value is known with relative certainty, which is quite unlike the situation in most capital budgeting decisions. The following example illustrates the calculations needed in a refunding decision.

Becker Brass Works Limited has outstanding a $60 million, 25-year bond issue carrying a 15 percent annual coupon rate. This issue, which was sold 5 years ago, had issue costs of $3 million. The bond indenture includes a call provision, making it possible for the company to retire the bonds by calling them in at a 10 percent call premium. Investment dealers have assured the company that it can sell an additional $60 million to $70 million worth of 20-year bonds at an interest rate of 12 percent. To ensure that the funds required to pay off the old debt will be available, the new bonds will be sold 1 month before the old issue is called, so for 1 month, interest must be paid on two issues. Current short-term rates are 11 percent. Predictions are that long-term interest rates are unlikely to fall below 12 percent. Issue costs on the new issue will amount to $2.65 million. Becker's effective tax rate is 40 percent. Should the company refund the $60 million of 15 percent bonds? The following steps outline the decision process; they are summarized in worksheet form in Table 21A-1.

Table 21A-1
Worksheet for the Bond Refunding Decision

	Amount before Tax	Amount after Tax
1. Cost of Refunding at t = 0		
a. Call premium outflow	$ 6 000 000	$ 6 000 000
b. Issue costs on new issue	2 650 000	2 650 000
c. Extra interest on old issue	750 000	450 000
d. Interest earned on short-term investment	(550 000)	(330 000)
e. Total after-tax investment		8 770 000
2. Annual savings		
Refunding from t = 1 to 20		
a. Interest on old bond	$9 000 000	$ 5 400 000
b. Interest on new bond	(7 200 000)	(4 320 000)
c. Net savings on interest	$1 800 000	$ 1 080 000
d. PV of interest savings		$11 265 804
3. PV of tax savings on amortized issue costs		$ 864 607
4. Refunding NPV		

NPV = PV of interest savings + PV of tax savings on amortized
      issue costs − PV of investment
  = $11 265 804 + $ 864 607 − $8 770 000
  = $3 360 411.

Step 1. Determine the investment outlay required to refund the issue.
   a.   Start with the call premium on the old issue.

$$0.10 \ (\$60\ 000\ 000) = \$6\ 000\ 000.$$

Be aware that the call premium of $6 000 000 is *not* a tax-deductible expense.[18]

   b.   State the issue costs on the new issue.
        Total issue costs are $2.65 million. For tax purposes, these issue costs are tax deductible, amortized on a straight line basis over 5 years. Tax savings will occur over this time period, not at period 0. Therefore, the investment outlay at time 0 is $2.65 million.

   c.   and d. Calculate the net additional interest.
        One month's "extra" interest on old issue, after taxes, is

$$(\text{Dollar amount}) \ 1/12 \ \text{of} \ 15\%(1 - T) = \text{Interest cost}$$
$$\$60\ 000\ 000(0.0125)(0.6) = \$450\ 000.$$

---

[18]In the United States, the call premium is a tax-deductible expense. Thus the after-tax cost of the call premium here would be $6 000 000 × 0.6 = $3 600 000.

However, the proceeds from the new issue can be invested in short-term securities for 1 month. Thus, $60 million invested at a rate of 11 percent will return $330 000 in after-tax interest:

$$(\$60\,000\,000)(1/12 \text{ of } 11\%)(1 - T) = \text{Interest earned}$$
$$(\$60\,000\,000)(0.009167)(0.6) = \$330\,000.$$

The net after-tax additional interest cost is thus $120 000:

Interest paid on old issue	$ 450 000
Interest earned on short-term securities	(330 000)
Net additional interest	$120 000

These figures are reflected on lines 1c and 1d of Table 21A-1.

e. Find the total after-tax investment.

The total investment outlay required to refund the bond issue, which will be financed by debt, is thus $8 770 000:

Call premium	$6 000 000
Issue costs, new	2 650 000
Net additional interest	120 000
Total investment	$8 770 000

This total is found on line 1e of Table 21A-1.

Step 2. Calculate the annual savings.

a. State the interest on old bonds, after tax:

$$\$60\,000\,000(0.15)(0.6) = \$5\,400\,000.$$

b. State the new bond interest, after tax:[19]

$$\$60\,000\,000(0.12)(0.6) = \$4\,320\,000.$$

c. Calculate the net annual interest savings:

The net annual interest savings would be $1 080 000.

Interest on old bonds, after tax	$5 400 000
Interest on new bonds, after tax	(4 320 000)
Annual interest savings	$1 080 000

---

[19]The investment outlay (in this case, the $8 770 000) is usually obtained by increasing the amount of the new bond issue. In the example given, the new issue would be $68 770 000. However, the interest on the additional $8 770 000 of debt *should not* be deducted at Step 2, because the $8 770 000 itself is deducted at Step 4. If additional interest were deducted at Step 4, then interest would, in effect, be deducted twice. The situation here is exactly like that in regular capital budgeting decisions. Even though some debt may be used to finance a capital project, interest on that debt is not subtracted when developing the annual cash flows. Rather, the annual cash flows are discounted by the project's cost of capital.

d. Find the present value of the annual savings.

The PV of $1 080 000 per year for 20 years is $11 265 804:[20]

$$PV = \$1\,080\,000(PVIFA_{7.2\%})$$
$$= \$1\,080\,000(10.4313) = \$11\,265\,804.$$

These values are used in step 4, for finding the NPV of the refunding operation.

Step 3. Determine the PV of the issue cost tax effects.

Total issue costs are $2.65 million, and for tax purposes, are amortized over five years. Therefore, the annual tax deduction is

$$\frac{\$2\,650\,000}{5} = \$530\,000.$$

Because Becker is in a 40 percent tax bracket, it has a tax savings of ($530 000) (0.4) = $212 000 per year. This is an annuity for 5 years discounted at 7.2 percent (the after-tax cost of debt), for a total value of $864 607.

Step 4. Determine the NPV of the refunding.

Interest savings	$11 265 804
Tax savings on amortized issue costs	864 607
Net investment outlay	(8 770 000)
NPV from refunding	$ 3 360 411

Because the net present value of the refunding is positive, it will be profitable to refund the old bond issue.

Several other points are significant. First, since the $1 080 000 annual savings is an essentially riskless after-tax return, its present value is found by discounting at the firm's least risky after-tax rate—its after-tax cost of debt. Second, since the refunding operation is advantageous to the firm, it must be disadvantageous to bondholders; they must give up their 15 percent bonds and reinvest in new ones yielding 12 percent. This points out the danger of the call provision to bondholders and explains why bonds with call protection (without a call feature) command higher prices than immediately callable bonds. Third, although it is not emphasized in the example, we assume that the firm raises the investment required to undertake the refunding operation (the $8 770 000) as debt. This should be feasible, as the refunding operation will improve the interest coverage ratio even though a larger amount of debt is outstanding.[21]

---

[20]The PVIFA for 7.2 percent over 20 years is 10.4313, found with a financial calculator.

[21]For a discussion of how the method of financing the refunding affects the analysis, see Ahron R. Ofer and Robert A. Taggart, Jr., "Bond Refunding: A Clarifying Analysis," *Journal of Finance*, March 1977: 21–30. Ofer and Taggart prove that if the refunding investment outlay is to be raised as debt, then the after-tax cost of debt is the proper discount rate, while if these funds are to be raised as common equity, then the before-tax cost of debt is the proper rate. Since a profitable refunding will virtually always raise the firm's debt-carrying capacity (because total interest charges after the refunding will be lower than before the refunding), it is more logical to use debt than either equity or a combination of debt and equity to finance the operation. Therefore, the after-tax cost of debt is the proper discount rate for a refunding analysis.

Fourth, we set up our example in such a way that the new issue has the same maturity as the remaining life of the old issue. Often the old bond has a relatively short time to maturity (say, 5 to 10 years), while the new bond has a much longer maturity (say, 25 to 30 years). In such a situation, the analysis should be set up like a replacement chain analysis in capital budgeting. Fifth, refunding decisions are well suited for analysis with a computer spreadsheet such as *Lotus 1-2-3* or *Excel*. The spreadsheet is simple to set up, and once the model has been constructed, it is easy to vary the assumptions (especially the assumption about the interest rate on the refunding issue) and to see how such changes affect the NPV.

One final point should be addressed: Although our analysis shows that the refunding will increase the value of the firm, will refunding *at this time* truly maximize the firm's expected value? If interest rates continue to fall, the company might be better off waiting, for this could increase the NPV of the refunding operation even more. The mechanics of calculating the NPV in a refunding are easy, but the decision of *when* to refund is not at all easy because it requires a forecast of future interest rates. Thus, the final decision on refunding now versus waiting for a possibly more favourable time is a matter of judgement.

Preferred Share Refunding

The analysis of a preferred share refunding is similar to that of the bond refunding operation. The tax provisions for the call premium, underwriting discount, and issue costs are identical. In calculating the annual savings from the preferred share refunding operation, remember that the dividends are not tax deductible. Associated with the tax treatment of dividends is the choice of the discount rate to calculate the present value of the dividend savings. In the bond refunding example, the after-tax cost of new debt was used to capture the impact of the tax savings generated from financing the investment with debt. But if the investment in the preferred share refunding operation is financed with new preferred shares—which is most likely—there are no tax savings generated. Therefore, the discount rate to be used is the before-tax yield on new preferred shares.

Appendix Problems

21A-1 Refunding analysis.   Goulbourne Technologies is considering whether or not to refund a $75 million, 15 percent coupon, 30-year bond issue that was sold 5 years ago. Goulbourne's investment bankers have indicated that the company could sell a new 25-year issue at an interest rate of 12 percent in today's market. Neither they nor Goulbourne's management anticipate that interest rates will fall below 12 percent any time soon, but there is a chance that rates will increase.

A call premium of 15 percent would be required to retire the old bonds, and flotation costs on the new issue would amount to $3 million. Goulbourne's marginal tax rate is 40 percent. The new bonds would be issued 1 month before the old bonds were called, with the proceeds being invested in short-term government securities returning 11 percent annually during the interim period.

a. Perform a complete bond refunding analysis. What would be the bond refunding's NPV?

b. What factors would influence Goulbourne's decision to refund now rather than later?

21A-2 Preferred share refunding. Newfoundland Off-Shore Oil Ltd. has outstanding $160 million of callable preferred shares. The par value share is $50 and the dividend paid on the shares is 13 percent. The preferred shares are callable at $56 per share (that is, a 12 percent call premium). Current yields on preferred shares are 10 percent, and the company's underwriters have told the company that an underwriter's discount of 2 percent of the face value of the issue will be required. The company intends to issue new preferred shares to finance the call premium. There will be no overlapping period when the new and the old issue are both outstanding. Assume the corporate tax rate is 45 percent. Should the preferred share issue be refunded?

Integrative Problem

21A-3 Bond refunding. Robert Hollinger, financial manager of Montreal Transport Company Limited (MTL), has been asked by his boss to review MTL's outstanding debt issues for possible bond refunding. Five years ago, MTL issued $40 000 000 of 13 percent, 25-year debt. The issue, with semiannual coupons, is currently callable at a premium of 11 percent, or $110 for each $1000 par value bond. Issue costs on this issue were 3 percent, or $1 200 000.

Hollinger believes that MTL could issue 20-year debt today with a coupon rate of 11 percent. The firm has placed many issues in the capital markets during the last 10 years, and its debt issue costs are currently estimated to be 2 percent of the issue's value. MTL's tax rate is 40 percent.

Help Hollinger conduct the refunding analysis by answering the following questions:

a. What is the total dollar call premium required to call the old issue? Is it tax deductible? What is the next after-tax cost of the call?

b. What is the dollar issue cost on the new issue? Is it immediately tax deductible? What is the after-tax issue cost?

c. What is the net after-tax cash outlay required to refund the old issue?

d. What is the semiannual after-tax interest savings that would result from the refunding?

e. Thus far, Hollinger has identified two future cash flows: (i) the net of new-issue issue cost tax savings, and (ii) after-tax interest savings. What is the sum of these two semiannual cash flows? What is the appropriate discount rate to apply to these future cash flows? What is the present value of these cash flows? (Hint: $PVIFA_{3.33\%, 40} = 22.0336$).

f. What is the NPV of refunding? Should MTL refund now or wait until later?

Appendix 21B
Interest Rate Swaps

Interest rate swaps occur in a variety of degrees of complexity. Here we consider the simplest of the swap transactions, the plain vanilla interest rate swap. Other transactions are variations of this basic design.

Consider two firms of different risk that are considering a debt issue of $100 million Canadian. The rating services give Firm X an AA rating, whereas Company Y has a BB. Based on their firm-specific characteristics, Company X wants to issue floating-rate debt and Y fixed-rate debt. We assume for expositional purposes that the two companies have identified each other and are approaching the markets in a co-ordinated way. (In the real world, one or both of the companies could have already issued debt and be interested in a swap to alter the interest rate characteristics.)

Table 21B-1 identifies the annual interest rate that each of the companies must pay if it issues either fixed- or floating-rate debt. The less risky company has an absolute cost advantage in issuing both fixed- and floating-rate debt. However, what is important is the relative cost advantages, since the total cost of Company X's issuing one type of security and Company Y's the other may differ.

If Company X issues fixed-rate debt and Company Y floating-rate debt, the total cost will be 10.8 percent plus the banker's acceptance (BA) rate plus 0.75 percent or BA + 11.55%.[22] Alternatively, if Y issues fixed-rate debt and X floating-rate debt, the total cost will be 12 percent plus BA plus 0.25 percent or BA + 12.25%. Clearly the total cost is less when X issues fixed rate debt and Y issues floating-rate debt, even though these are not the preferred types of debt for each company. The saving of total cost is 70 basis points (0.70 percent), which can be shared by the two companies.

Therefore Company Y will issue floating-rate debt and be responsible for the interest payment to the lender. In order to obtain its preferred fixed-rate debt position, it must make a payment of a fixed amount. But it will receive an amount from the other company that covers the floating-rate element in its cost. Similarly, Company X will issue fixed-rate debt, but to be in its preferred position, it will pay a floating rate and receive a fixed-rate payment to offset the fixed payments it must make to its lender.

Table 21B-1
Interest Cost for Companies A and B

Company	Rating	Fixed rate	Floating rate
X	AA	10.8%	BA + 0.25%
Y	BB	12.0%	BA + 0.75%

---

[22]In a Canadian swap, the base rate may be prime instead of the BA rate. However, this alternative is used rarely since the BA rate is determined in a competitive market whereas prime is not. In a Eurobond financing, the floating-rate base would be LIBOR.

In Figure 21B-1, the cash flow patterns basic to the swap are displayed. Company Y makes fixed-rate payments to Company X equal to 10.9 percent and Company X makes floating-rate payments equal to BA to Company Y. How does this pattern of payments lead to the desired result? Consider Company X first. Its net cost position is a payment of 10.8 percent to its lender, a payment of the banker's acceptance rate to Y and a receipt of 10.9 percent from Y. The net position is BA − 0.1, which is a floating rate and is cheaper than a direct issue of floating-rate debt at a rate of BA plus 0.25 percent. The saving for X is 35 basis points. For Y, the net cost is 11.65 percent and is composed of a payment to lenders of BA plus 0.75, a payment to X of 10.9 percent and the receipt from X of BA. Through this swap arrangement, Y has converted its floating-rate debt to a fixed cost, at a saving of 35 basis points from a direct issue of fixed-rate debt at 12 percent. The total cost saving in this example of 70 basis points is shared equally among the two firms. Note that in a swap transaction, only the interest payments are swapped and not the principal. The swap contract specifies a notional amount of debt, and it is this notional amount on which the interest payments are transferred. The notional amount of debt need not be the amount that has been issued by either company.

From the above description, it appears that the settlement of the interest payments is very complex, requiring cross-payments from each company. However, the reality is different. All that is required is one net payment from X to Y or vice versa depending on the level of the BA rate relative to the fixed rate for the flows transferred between X and Y. For example, suppose that the BA rate equals 10.9 percent. In this case, the difference in the yields on the transferred flows is equal to zero and no net payment is required. To convince yourself of this, consider that the net payment for X is 10.8 percent, which is equal to BA minus 0.1 percent, and the net payment to Y is BA plus 0.75 percent, which is equal to 11.65 percent, the amount originally set in the contract.

If the BA rate is 10.0 percent at the settlement date, then a transfer will be required. Since Firm X has, in effect, issued floating-rate debt, a transfer should go to this company so that its interest payments are equal to BA minus 0.1 percent as contracted. The method of achieving this is to transfer to Firm X a dollar amount equal to the difference in yields on the transferred flows times the notional amount of the debt. The difference in yields is equal to

Figure 21B-1
Cash Flow Transfers in a Swap

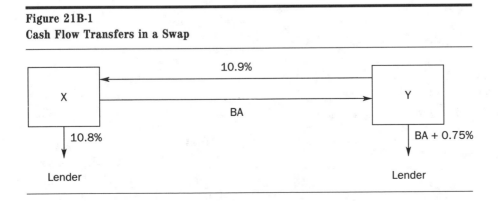

10.9 percent minus BA or 0.9 percent. With a notional debt of $100 million, the transferred dollar amount is $900 000. With this amount transferred, Company Y's total payments equal the amount paid to its lender at 10.75 percent (BA + 0.75%) plus the transfer of 0.9 percent for a total of 11.65 percent, the fixed rate amount. Company X pays its lender 10.8 percent minus the transfer of 0.9 percent for a net amount of 9.9 percent, which is the contractual yield amount of BA less 10 basis points. If the BA rate were 12 percent, then X would have to make a net payment of 1.1 percent times $100 million or $1.1 million to Y.[23]

Introducing a Financial Intermediary

In the discussion above, we assumed that the two parties to the swap transaction, the *counterparties,* were aware of each other and thus no costs were incurred to find a counterparty for the swap transaction. Unfortunately, the reality is a costly search and delays in obtaining the desired financing position. However, the process can be expedited by the introduction of a financial intermediary, which can be the counterparty to each side of the transaction and need not have both principals enter at the same time.

In Figure 21B-2, we picture the introduction of a bank into the process. The companies and the borrowing rates they face remain the same. Company Y transacts with the bank, receiving the floating rate at BA and paying a fixed rate of 11 percent. The net cost is 11.75 percent, which is a savings of 25 basis points over the rate if fixed-rate debt had been issued directly. At the settlement dates, the company or the bank makes a payment based on the net position of the BA compared to 11 percent; if BA is above 11 percent, the bank makes a payment to the company. If this were the only transaction that the bank entered, it would be exposed to a floating-rate position. However, it also enters a transaction with Company X in which it receives the floating rate at

Figure 21B-2
Swap Flows with Bank as Intermediary

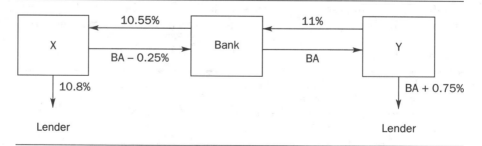

---

[23]Since the payment is semiannual, the actual dollar payments transferred are calculated slightly differently than in this example. Take the case in which the BA rate is 10 percent. The net payment is 0.90 percent per annum. With a notional amount of debt of $100 million, the semiannual dollar payment is as follows:

$$\text{Payment} = (\text{Net payment}) \, (6/12)(100 \text{ million})$$
$$= (0.1090 - 0.10) \, (0.5)(\$100 \text{ million})$$
$$= \$450\,000.$$

BA minus 0.25% from X and pays a fixed rate of 10.55 percent to X. Company X's net cost for the floating-rate debt is BA and represents a saving of 25 basis points from the direct issue of floating-rate debt.

How does the bank fare in this process? On the fixed-rate side, it receives 11.0 percent and pays out 10.55 percent, leaving a gain of 45 basis points. On the floating-rate side, it receives BA minus 0.25 percent and pays out BA, leaving a loss of 25 basis points. Over the combined transaction, the bank nets 20 basis points with certainty; this is the payment for its services. Therefore, the 70 basis points gain we observed from the swap transaction has been apportioned among the three parties to the transaction: 25 basis points to each company and 20 to the bank. With a competitive swap market, the gains from arbitrage will become smaller along with the fees charged by intermediaries.

Currency Swaps

To this point, the focus has been on an interest rate swap; however, in their pursuit of the minimization of debt cost, corporations may issue debt in foreign currencies and then swap to the currency of preference. The mechanics of the currency swap are very similar to those of an interest rate swap. The one difference is that the counterparties actually swap the principal as well as the interest payments. The principal is swapped at the start of the contract at the prevailing foreign exchange spot rate; at its maturity, it is swapped back at an exchange rate agreed upon at the initiation date. In the interest rate swap, no principal is swapped; the principal amount is notional and established to identify the interest rate payments.

Appendix Problem

21B-1 Interest rate swap.   Assume that Company A can borrow at a fixed rate of 11 percent or a floating rate of prime plus 0.2%. Company B can borrow at a fixed rate of 15 percent or a floating rate of prime plus 3.0 percent. Company A would like to borrow at a fixed rate and Company B would like to borrow at a floating rate. Assume the principal amount they wish to borrow is the same.

   a. If the two companies agree to a swap, what total interest rate savings are available?

   b. Design a swap to allocate the savings equally to the two parties.

22

▲▲

Options and Option-Related Securities

A MANAGERIAL PERSPECTIVE

In our discussion of long-term financing in previous chapters, we examined the use of shares, preferred shares, and various types of debt. In this chapter, we show how the financial manager, through the use of option-based securities, such as warrants and convertibles, can make a company's securities attractive to an even broader range of investors. Because option-based securities are being used more frequently, it is important to understand the characteristics of these securities and the conditions under which their use is most beneficial to the company. We also examine the rapidly growing options market, which is attractive to many investors.

Options

An **option** is a contract that gives its holder the right to buy or sell an asset at some predetermined price, called the *strike price*, within a specified period of time.

There are many types of options. *Pure options* are instruments that are created by outsiders rather than the firm itself. They are bought and sold by investors (or speculators), and the exchange of funds is between the investors; no new funds enter or leave the firm. *Executive stock options* provided by the company as incentives to key executives are also options: the contract provides a time limit and a price at which the company's shares can be bought. These options, however, are created by the company and are given to the executive in exchange for something of value—improved executive performance. The cost to the shareholders of providing these options is that the executives can purchase shares at the strike price, which is below the actual share price at the time of exercising the option. *Warrants* and *convertible financings* are also options created and issued by the firm.

An understanding of the nature of options will permit the financial manager to understand the role of option-related securities in the financing plans of the company.

Option Types and Markets

To understand how options work, consider the following situation. Suppose on November 1, 1993 you owned 100 shares of Placer Dome equity, which were selling for $31.125 per share. You could create an option by selling to someone else the right to buy your 100 shares at any time during, say, the next 2 months at a price of, say, $35 per share. The $35 price is called the **strike** or **exercise price** and the amount paid for the contract is called the *premium*. Such options exist and are traded through Trans Canada Options, a clearing house for Canadian option contracts. This type of option is known as a **call option**, since the purchaser has a "call" on 100 shares of equity. The seller of a call option receives the premium and is known as a *option writer*. An investor who writes a call option against shares held in his or her portfolio is said to be writing a *covered call*. Options sold without the shares to back them up are called *naked options*.

On November 1, 1993, Placer Dome's 3-month, $35 option sold for $1.00. Thus, for $1.00(100) = $100 you could buy an option contract giving you the right to purchase 100 shares of Placer Dome at a price of $35 per share anytime during the next 3 months. If the share price stayed below $35 during that period, you would lose your $100, but if it rose to $50, then your $100 investment would be worth ($50 − $35)(100) = $1500. That translates into a very healthy rate of return. Incidentally, if the share price did go up, you would probably not actually exercise your options and buy the shares; rather, you would sell the options, which would then each have a price of at least $15.00 versus the $1.00 you had paid, to another buyer.

You can also buy an option that gives you the right to *sell* an asset at a specified price at some time in the future—this is called a **put option**. For example, suppose on November 1, 1993, you expected Placer Dome's share price to decline sometime during the next month. For $90, you could buy a 1-month put option giving you the right to sell 100 shares (which you would not necessarily own) at a price of $30.00 per share ($30.00 is the put option strike price). If you bought a 100 share put option contract for $90 and Placer Dome's share price fell to $25.00, you would have made ($30.00 − $25.00)(100) = $500 minus the $90 you paid for the put option, for a net profit before taxes and commissions of $410.

Option Markets

Options trading is one of the "hottest" financial activities in the financial markets today. The leverage involved makes it possible for speculators with just a few dollars to make a fortune almost overnight. Also, investors with sizable portfolios can sell options on their equity and earn the premium on them (less brokerage commissions) even if the share price remains constant. Still, those who have profited most from the development of options trading are security firms, which earn commission income on such trades.

Corporations, such as Placer Dome, on whose equity options are written have nothing to do with the options market. The corporations do not raise money in the options market, nor do they have any direct transactions in it. Option holders do not receive dividends and do not vote for corporate directors (unless they exercise their options to purchase the shares, which few actually do). There have been studies by the Securities and Exchange Commission in the United States and others as to whether options trading stabilizes or destabilizes the stock market and whether it helps or hinders corporations seeking to raise new capital. The studies have not been conclusive, but options trading is here to stay, and many regard it as the most exciting game in town.

Theoretical Value versus Option Price

How is the actual price of an option determined in the market? For the valuation concept, consider the following simple example of a call option for New Technologies Ltd. (NTL). The company has recently gone public, and its share price has had significant fluctuations. The current price is $50. The option has a strike price of $20 and a 6-month maturity. In order to value the option, consider the value of the option at the expiration date. If the shares are selling above the strike price (that is, selling "in the money"), the value of the call option per share of common equity is equal to the actual price per share minus the exercise price. If the share price at expiration is less than the exercise price (that is, the option is "out of the money"), then the option has a zero value.

The theoretical value of the option estimated at the expiration date is as follows:

If the share price is above the strike price,

$$\text{Theoretical value} = \text{Current share price} - \text{Strike price.}$$

However, if the share price is below the strike price,

$$\text{Theoretical value} = 0.$$

The crucial element in the value of the option is that it can never have a negative value. Thus, when the share price is less than the exercise price, the value of the option at expiration is zero since the contract does not force the individual to exercise the option at the expiration date.

The theoretical option values are identified as at the expiration date. Earlier, option values are above their theoretical values, as can be seen by observing prices prior to the expiration dates. We now examine why this arises.

Consider Figure 22-1, which presents some data for NTL for a particular time period before expiration. In the lower section of the figure, column 1 shows the trading range of share prices; column 2 shows the strike price of the option; column 3 shows the theoretical value of the option as at the expiration date for the different market prices for the shares: and column 5 shows the excess of the actual option price over its theoretical value. These data are plotted in the graph.

In this example, for any share price below $20, the theoretical value is zero; as the options begin to trade in the money—that is, as the share price rises above the exercise price—each $1 increase in the share price brings with it a $1 increase in the option's theoretical value. Note that the actual market price of the option lies above the theoretical value at all prices of the common shares, but that the excess of the option value over the theoretical value declines as the price of the shares increase. For example, when the shares sell for $20 and the option has a zero theoretical value, its actual price and the excess are $9. Then, as the price of the shares rises, the theoretical value matches the share price increase dollar for dollar but the market price of the option climbs less rapidly, causing the excess to decline. Thus, the excess is $9 when the shares sell for $20, but it declines to $1 by the time the share price reach $73, and beyond that point the excess virtually disappears.

Figure 22-1
New Technologies Ltd. (NTL):
Option Price and Theoretical Value

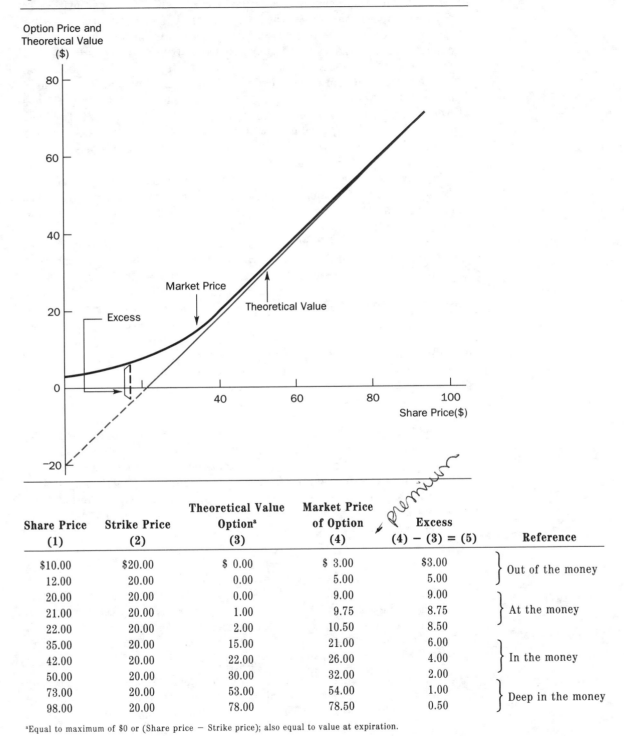

Option Price and
Theoretical Value
($)

Share Price (1)	Strike Price (2)	Theoretical Value Option[a] (3)	Market Price of Option (4)	Excess (4) − (3) = (5)	Reference
$10.00	$20.00	$ 0.00	$ 3.00	$3.00	} Out of the money
12.00	20.00	0.00	5.00	5.00	
20.00	20.00	0.00	9.00	9.00	
21.00	20.00	1.00	9.75	8.75	} At the money
22.00	20.00	2.00	10.50	8.50	
35.00	20.00	15.00	21.00	6.00	
42.00	20.00	22.00	26.00	4.00	} In the money
50.00	20.00	30.00	32.00	2.00	
73.00	20.00	53.00	54.00	1.00	} Deep in the money
98.00	20.00	78.00	78.50	0.50	

[a]Equal to maximum of $0 or (Share price − Strike price); also equal to value at expiration.

Why does this pattern exist? Why should an option ever sell for more than its theoretical value, and why does the excess decline as the price of the share increases? The answer lies in the speculative appeal of options; they enable an investor to gain a high degree of personal leverage when buying securities. To illustrate: suppose that NTL's price per share is $21 and its options sell for exactly their theoretical value, $1. Suppose you are thinking of investing in the company's common shares. If you buy a share and the price rises to $42 in a year, you will have made a 100 percent capital gain. If you purchased the option at its theoretical value of $1, your capital gain will be $21 on a $1 investment, a 2100 percent gain. At the same time, your total loss potential with the option is $1, whereas the potential loss from the purchase of the shares is $21. The huge capital gains potential, combined with the loss limitation, is clearly worth something; the exact amount it is worth to investors is the amount of the excess.

Why does the excess decline as the share price rises? The answer is that both the leverage effect and the loss protection feature decline at high share prices. For example, if you are thinking of buying shares at $73 a share, the theoretical value of the option is $53. If the share price doubles to $146, the theoretical value of the option goes from $53 to $126. Although the capital gain on both the shares and the option is $73, the percentage gain on the shares is 100 percent and on the option, 138 percent; this is a substantial reduction from the 2100 percent gain on the option associated with the doubling in share price from $21. Notice that the loss potential on the options is much greater when the option is selling at high prices. These two factors—the declining leverage impact and the increasing danger of losses—help explain why the excess diminishes as the price of the common shares rises.

In addition to the share price and the strike price, the value of an option depends on (1) the option's time to maturity and (2) the variability of the underlying share price, as explained below:

1. The longer an option has to run, the greater its value and the larger the excess of its price over the theoretical value. If an option expires at 4:00 P.M. today, there is not much chance that the share price will go way up before expiry. Therefore, the option will sell at close to its formula value, and the excess will be small. On the other hand, if the option has a year to go, the share price could rise sharply in that period, pulling the option's value with it.

   To demonstrate the impact of term to maturity and strike price on the value of an option, we offer Table 22-1, which presents the option values for a number of Placer Dome options as at November 1, 1993. The share price was $31.125. For the $32.00 strike price, the options were trading just in the money with a theoretical price of $1.13. As the strike price increased, the value of the option decreased. Looking at the options with the $32.00 strike price, we see that the value of the option increased as the term to maturity of the option increased.

2. An option on a company's equity for which the share prices are extremely volatile is worth more than one on common equity that is very stable. We know that an option whose price rarely moves does not offer much chance for a large gain. On the other hand, an option on shares that have a highly

Table 22-1
Option Values for Placer Dome Options,
November 1, 1993

Strike Price	Theoretical Value	Maturity Date: End of January	April
$30.00	$1.13	$3.45	[a]
32.50	0	2.00	3.55
35.00	0	1.00	[a]

[a]Options with this characteristic not outstanding.

volatile price could provide a large gain, so such an option is valuable. Note also that because losses on options are limited, large declines in a company's share price do not have a corresponding bad effect on option holders. Therefore, share price volatility can only enhance the value of an option.[1]

If everything else were held constant, then in a graph like Figure 22-1, the longer an option's life, the higher its market price line would be above the theoretical value line. In fact, there would be a separate option market price line for each term to maturity. Also, the more volatile the price of the underlying shares, the higher the market price line would be.

Concept Review

▶ Differentiate between a *call option* and a *put option*.
▶ Do the corporations on whose securities options are written raise money in the options market? Explain your answer.

(continued)

[1]To illustrate this point, suppose that for $2 you could buy an option on a share of common equity now selling for $20. The strike price is also $20. Now suppose the equity is highly volatile, and you think it has a 50 percent probability of selling for either $10 or $30 when the option expires in one month. What is the expected value of the option? If the shares sell for $30, the option will be worth $30 − $20 = $10. Since there is a 50–50 chance that a share will be worth $10 or $30, the expected value of the option is $5:

$$\text{Expected value of option} = 0.5(0) + 0.5(\$10) = \$5.$$

To be exactly correct, we would have to discount the $5 back for 1 month. Now suppose the equity was more volatile, with a 50–50 chance of being worth zero or $40. Here the option would be worth

$$\text{Expected value of option} = 0.5(0) + 0.5(\$20) = \$10.$$

This demonstrates that the higher the volatility, the greater the value of the option. The reason this result occurs is that the large loss on the equity ($20) has no more of an adverse effect on the option holder than the small loss ($10). Thus, option holders benefit greatly if the share goes way up, but they do not lose too badly if it drops all the way to zero. These concepts have been used to develop formulas for pricing options, with the most widely used formula being the Black–Scholes model, which is discussed in most investment texts.

(continued)
▶ How does one calculate the theoretical value of an option? How is the premium on the option calculated?
▶ Why does the premium on the option decline as the price of the underlying security increases?
▶ Explain how these factors affect the premium on an option: (1) the time remaining before the option expires, and (2) the volatility of the underlying security.

Warrants

A **warrant** is an option issued by a corporation that gives the holder the right to purchase a stated number of shares of the company's equity at a specified price. Generally, warrants are attached to an issue of debt, preferred shares, or common shares. The warrants are detachable from their associated security issue and can be traded separately or exercised by the investor.

When the warrants are attached to an issue of either debt or preferred shares, they are an inducement to investors to purchase the associated security at a lower interest rate than would otherwise be required. For example, when NTL wanted to sell $50 million of 20-year bonds in 1991, the company's investment dealers informed the financial vice president that with their lack of operating information and the riskiness of the company, straight bonds would be difficult to sell and an interest rate of 14 percent would be required. However, the investment dealers suggested as an alternative that investors would be willing to buy bonds with a coupon rate as low as 10.375 percent if the company could offer 30 warrants with each $1000 bond, each warrant entitling the holder to buy one share of common equity at a price of $22 per share. The common equity was selling for $20 per share at the time, and the warrants would expire in 1996 if they had not been exercised previously.

Why would investors be willing to buy NTL's bonds at a yield of only 10.375 percent in a 14.000 percent market just because warrants were offered as part of the package? The answer is that warrants are *long-term options,* and they have a value for the reasons set forth in the previous section. In the NTL case, this value offsets the low interest rate on the bonds and makes the entire package of low-interest bonds plus warrants at least as attractive as the straight 14 percent debt issue. There is a potential cost to the company from this transaction as well. If the share price increases so much that exercise of the warrants is undertaken, then the company will receive $22 per share issued when the prevailing price is greater than $22. This results in dilution of the equity, but the premium on the warrant—the lower coupon rate—is the offsetting benefit to the firm.

When a warrant and common shares are issued as a unit,[2] the value of the package should be equal to the value of the common shares plus the value of

---

[2] A *unit* need not refer exclusively to a warrant and common equity issue. Other combinations of financial securities can also be issued as a unit.

the warrant. On a specified number of days after the issue, called the *separation date*, the warrants may be detached from the shares and traded separately. An example of a unit offering: Dofasco issued 9.6 million units at $20.00 per unit for trading on September 30, 1991, with a separation date on October 7, 1991. Each unit consisted of a common share plus half a share purchase warrant; one full warrant entitled the holder to purchase one Dofasco common share at $20.50 on or before April 1, 1994. Just before the sale of the unit, the common equity was selling in the $17.38 to $17.88 range. After the first day of trading, the unit traded for approximately $18.50 and the shares for $17.70. The value of the half-a-share purchase warrant was equal to the difference between the unit price and the share price or $0.80; a full warrant sold for $1.60. The value of the half-a-share purchase warrant accrued to Dofasco as compensation for writing the warrant. If these warrants were exercised, the result would be equivalent to a new common equity issue with the per share proceeds of the issue equal to the exercise price. On November 1, 1993, well after the separation date, the shares were trading for $19.63 and a full warrant for $2.00. Although this warrant had a specified exercise date, some have perpetual lives.

Initial Price of Bonds with Warrants

If the NTL bonds had been issued as straight debt, the interest rate would have been 14.000 percent. However, with warrants attached, the debt could be sold to yield 10.375 percent. The terms of the issue are 30 warrants with each $1000 par value bond; each warrant entitles the holder to purchase one common share at $22 per share. The maturity on the bond is 20 years.

Since the going interest rate on bonds as risky as this company's is 14 percent, we can find the straight debt value of the bond, assuming an annual coupon, as follows:

$$\text{Straight debt value} = \sum_{t=1}^{20} \frac{\$103.75}{(1.14)^t} + \frac{\$1000}{(1.14)^{20}}$$

$$= \$103.75(\text{PVIFA}_{14\%,\,20}) + \$1000(\text{PVIF}_{14\%,\,20})$$

$$= \$103.75(6.6231) + \$1000(0.0728)$$

$$= \$687.15 + \$72.80 = \$759.95 \approx \$760.$$

Thus, an investor purchasing the bonds in the initial underwriting would pay $1000 and would receive in exchange a straight bond worth about $760 plus warrants worth $1000 − $760 = $240:

$$\begin{array}{ccc} \text{Price paid for bond} \\ \text{with warrants} \end{array} = \begin{array}{c} \text{Straight debt} \\ \text{value of bond} \end{array} + \begin{array}{c} \text{Value of} \\ \text{warrants} \end{array}$$

or

$$\$1000 \quad = \quad \$760 \quad + \quad 240.$$

Because investors receive 30 warrants with each bond, each warrant has an implied value of $240/30 = $8. Since the warrant is an option, we can obtain the theoretical value of the warrant by using the same approach as in the option analysis. The theoretical value of the warrant is written as follows:

$$\begin{matrix} \text{Theoretical} \\ \text{value} \end{matrix} = \begin{pmatrix} \text{Market price of} \\ \text{common shares} \end{pmatrix} - \begin{pmatrix} \text{Exercise} \\ \text{price} \end{pmatrix} \begin{pmatrix} \text{Number of shares} \\ \text{per warrant} \end{pmatrix}.$$

For the NTL example, at the issue date, the option is selling out of the money since the current price is below the exercise price and the theoretical value is zero. The actual value of the option reflects the volatility of the shares and the long term to maturity. Subsequent to the issue, if the share price increases, the theoretical value of the warrant will increase.

Why would an investor prefer the package of a bond with a warrant to a debt instrument with a higher interest rate if both securities have the same present value of $1000? The investor who chooses the bond-warrant combination must believe that the price of the shares of the company will increase faster than other market participants expect. If the investor's expectation was the same as the rest of the market's, he or she would be indifferent to the alternative packages.

The key issue in setting the terms of a bond-with-warrants offering is finding the value of the warrants. The straight debt value of the bond can be estimated quite accurately. However, even though there are mathematical models available, it is much more difficult to estimate the value of the warrants. If their value is overestimated relative to their true market value, it will be difficult to sell the issue at its par value. Conversely, if the warrants' value is underestimated, investors in the issue will receive a windfall profit, because they can sell the warrants in the market for more than they implicitly paid for them, and this windfall profit would come out of the pockets of NTL's current shareholders.

Use of Warrants in Financing

In the past, warrants have generally but not exclusively been used by small, rapidly growing firms as *sweeteners* when selling debt, preferred shares, or common equity. Since potential investors frequently regard these firms as being highly risky, their bonds can be sold only if they are willing to pay extremely high rates of interest and to accept very restrictive indenture provisions. To avoid this, firms often offer warrants along with bonds. The use of warrants is very widespread, and there are a large number of them listed and traded on the Toronto Stock Exchange.

Getting warrants along with bonds (and preferred shares) enables investors to share in the company's growth—if it does in fact grow and prosper. Therefore, they are willing to accept a lower bond interest rate and less restrictive indenture provisions. A bond with warrants has some characteristics of debt and some characteristics of equity. It is a hybrid security that provides the financial manager with an opportunity to expand the firm's mix of securities and to appeal to a broader group of investors.

Virtually all warrants today are *detachable warrants*. When these warrants are exercised, the bonds themselves (with their low coupon rate) will remain outstanding. Thus, the warrants will bring in additional equity while leaving low interest rate debt on the books.

The exercise price is usually set 10 to 30 percent above the market price of the firm's shares on the date when the bond is issued. For example, if the shares sell for $10, the exercise price will probably be set in the $11 to $13 range. If the firm does grow and prosper and if its share price rises above the exercise price, warrant holders will turn in their warrants, along with cash equal to the stated exercise price, in exchange for shares. Without some incentive, however, many warrants will never be exercised prior to maturity. Their value in the market will always be greater than their value if exercised (the *theoretical value*), and hence holders will sell warrants rather than exercise them.

There are three situations that encourage holders to exercise their warrants. (1) Warrant holders will *surely* surrender warrants and buy shares if the warrants are about to expire with the market price of the shares above the exercise price. This implies that if a firm wants its warrants exercised soon in order to raise capital, it should set a relatively short expiration date. However, this will also lead to a lower value for the warrant and a smaller "sweetener" impact. (2) Warrant holders will tend to surrender options and buy shares if the company raises the dividend on the common shares by a sufficient amount. Since no dividend is earned on the warrant, investors receive no current income. However, if the common shares pay a high dividend, it provides an attractive dividend yield, thereby inducing warrant holders to exercise their option to buy the shares. Thus, if a firm wants its warrants exercised, it can raise the dividends on its common shares. (3) Warrants sometimes have *stepped-up exercise prices*, which prod holders into exercising them. For example, La Fosse Platinum Group warrants were issued with an exercise price of $5.00 per share until August 18, 1988, at which time the exercise price became $5.50 per share. If the price of the common share was a little more than $5.00 just before August 18, 1988, many warrant holders would exercise their options before the stepped-up price took effect.

Another useful feature of warrants is that they generally bring in funds only if such funds are needed. If the company grows and prospers, it will probably need new equity capital. At the same time, growth will cause the price of the common shares to rise and lead to the exercise of the warrants and thereby provide the firm with additional cash. If the company is not successful and cannot profitably employ additional money, the price of its shares will probably not rise sufficiently to induce exercise of the warrants.

Other Types of Warrants

In the examples considered to this point, although the warrant was combined in a package with different securities of the company, the value of the warrant depended upon the share price of the issuing company. However, warrants need not be restricted in this way; their value may depend upon other securities. For example, a common warrant issued by gold companies is the gold purchase warrant. Here, the warrant provides the option to purchase a specified amount of gold at a particular price. For example, the gold purchase warrants issued by Golden Rule Resources Ltd. stated that one ounce of gold could be purchased from the company on or before July 1, 1992 in exchange for 50 warrants and

$425. The value of this warrant depended upon the price of gold. Companies in the gold mining business issue these warrants because they are able to pay off the warrant, if exercised, with their output, thereby providing a natural hedge.

Another type of warrant permits the holder to purchase the equity of a company that is not that of the company issuing the warrant. For example, Oakwood Petroleum issued a warrant that permitted a holder to purchase three common shares of Alberta Natural Gas, owned by Oakwood, at $8.83 per share on or before March 31, 1988. In this example, the warrants permitted Oakwood Petroleum to sell its shareholdings in Alberta Natural Gas for a value that was greater than the share price at the date of issue of the warrant.

Convertibles

Convertible securities are bonds or preferred shares that can be exchanged under specified terms and conditions into common shares at the option of the holder. Unlike the exercise of warrants associated with a debt issue, which brings an additional capital but maintains debt in the firm's capital structure, the exercise of a convertible bond (or preferred share) simply replaces debt (or preferred equity) with common equity. Thus, a convertible issue is often referred to as a delayed equity issue because the conversion of the convertibles results in an increase in equity in the capital structure and the removal of the debt (or preferred shares), thereby strengthening the firm's balance sheet and making it easier to raise additional capital in a separate action.

Conversion Ratio and Conversion Price

One of the most important provisions of a convertible security is the number of shares of common equity a bondholder receives upon conversion, which is called the **conversion ratio**, CR. Related to the conversion ratio is the **conversion price**, P_c, which is the effective price paid for the common shares when conversion occurs. The relationship between the conversion ratio and conversion price is illustrated by Morgan Hydrocarbons' 9.5 percent convertible preferred shares. On or before July 1, 1996, the preferred shareholder can turn in one preferred share and receive in its place five shares of common equity; therefore, shares received upon conversion = CR = 5. The preferred share has a par value of $25, so the holder is giving up this amount on conversion. Dividing the par value of $25 by the five shares received gives a conversion price, P_c, of $5 a share.

$$\text{Conversion price} = P_c = \frac{\text{Par value of convertible security}}{\text{Shares received, CR}} = \frac{\$25}{5} = \$5.$$

Similarly, if we know the conversion price, we can find the conversion ratio, CR:

$$CR = \frac{\$25}{P_c} = \frac{\$25}{\$5} = 5 \text{ shares.}$$

Once CR is set, the value of P_c is established, and vice versa.

Like a warrant's exercise price, the conversion price is characteristically set 10 to 30 percent above the prevailing market price of the common shares at the time the convertible issue is sold. Generally, the conversion price and ratio are fixed for the life of the preferred equity or debenture, although sometimes a stepped-up conversion price is used. The Inter-City Gas convertible preferred, although no longer outstanding, provides a good example. The security had a conversion ratio that declined after May 2, 1988. Prior to this date, the conversion ratio was 1.74 common shares, and based on a $25.00 par value, the conversion price was $14.37. From this date to the expiration date of May 2, 1990, the conversion ratio was 1.64 common shares with a conversion price of $15.25. The declining conversion ratio and hence increasing conversion price is a method of inducing investors to convert their securities early.

Another factor that may cause a change in the conversion price and ratio is a standard feature of almost all convertibles—a clause protecting the convertible against dilution from stock splits, stock dividends, and the sale of common shares at prices below the conversion price. The typical provision states that if common shares are sold at a price below the conversion price, the conversion price must be lowered (and the conversion ratio raised) to the price at which the new shares were issued. Also, if the shares are split or a stock dividend is declared, the conversion price must be lowered by the percentage amount of the stock split or dividend. For example, if Morgan Hydrocarbons had a two-for-one split, the conversion ratio would automatically be adjusted to 10 and the conversion price lowered to $2.50. If this protection were not contained in the contract, a company could completely thwart conversion by the use of stock splits and dividends. Warrants are similarly protected against dilution.

This standard protection against dilution from selling new shares at prices below the conversion price can, however, get a company into trouble. For example, Morgan Hydrocarbon's shares were selling for only $4 in 1993, versus the conversion price of $5. Thus, Morgan would have had to give its preferred shareholders some compensation if it had wanted to sell new common shares. Problems like this must be kept in mind by firms considering the use of convertibles or bonds with warrants.

Convertible Bond Analysis

Suppose Adam's Electric Ltd. (AEL) is thinking of issuing 20-year convertible bonds at a price of $1000 per bond; this $1000 would also be the maturity and the par value. The bonds would pay a 10 percent annual coupon interest rate, or $100 per year. Each bond could be converted into 20 shares of common equity, so the conversion price is $P_c = \$1000/20 = \$50$. If the bonds did not have the conversion feature, investors would require a yield of 12 percent, because $k_d = 12\%$. Knowing k_d, the coupon rate, and the maturity, we can find the straight debt value of the convertibles at the time of issue, B_0, using the bond valuation model developed back in Chapter 16. The bonds would initially sell at a price of $851:

$$\text{Straight debt value at time of issue} = B_0 = \sum_{t=1}^{20} \frac{\$100}{(1.12)^t} + \frac{\$1000}{(1.12)^{20}} = \$851.$$

Adam's shares are expected to pay a dividend of $2.80 per share for the coming year. The current share price is $35, and this price and the dividend per share

are expected to grow at a constant rate of 8 percent per year. Thus, the share price expected in each future year t is $P_t = P_0(1 + g)^t = \$35(1.08)^t$. Further, since Adam's convertibles would permit their holders to convert them into 20 shares of common equity, the value a bondholder would expect to receive if he or she converted, denoted as C_t, would be $C_t = \$35(1.08)^t(20)$.

The convertible bonds would not be callable for 10 years, after which they would be called at a price of $1000, with this price declining by $5 per year. If after 10 years, the conversion value exceeded the call price by at least 20 percent, management has indicated that it would call the bonds.

Figure 22-2 shows the expectations of both the average investor and the company.

1. The horizontal line at M = $1000 represents the par (and maturity) value. Also, $1000 is the price at which the bond is initially offered to the public.

2. Since the convertible has a 10 percent coupon rate and since the yield on a nonconvertible bond of similar risk was stated to be 12 percent, the straight debt value of the convertible, B_t, must be less than par. At the time of issue, it is actually $851. Note, however, that the bond's straight debt value must be $1000 just prior to maturity, so the bond value rises over time. B_t follows the line B_0M'' in the graph.

3. The bond's initial *conversion value*, C_t, or the value of the shares the investor would receive if the bond were converted at t = 0, is $700:

$$\text{Conversion value} = P_0CR = \$35(20 \text{ shares}) = \$700.$$

Since the share price is expected to grow at an 8 percent rate, $P_t = \$35(1.08)^t$. If the share price rises over time, so will the conversion value of the bond. For example, in Year 3 the conversion value should be $C_3 = P_3(CR) = \$35(1.08)^3(20) = \$882$. The expected conversion value, over time, is given by the line C_t in Figure 22-2.

4. The actual market price of the bond must always be equal to or greater than the *higher* of its straight debt value or its conversion value. If the market price were below the straight bond value, people who wanted bonds would recognize this one as a bargain and buy it as a bond. If the market price were below the conversion value, people would buy the bond, convert it to shares, and sell the shares at a profit. Therefore, the higher of the bond value and conversion value curves in the graph represents a "floor price" for the bond. In Figure 22-2, the floor price is represented by the heavy line B_0XC_t.

5. The market value of a convertible generally exceeds the floor price for the same reasons that an option's or a warrant's price exceeds its theoretical value. Investors are willing to pay a premium over the straight debt value (which establishes the initial floor) because of the possibility of earning large capital gains if the share price shoots up. After Year 3, when the conversion value exceeds the straight bond value and thus establishes the floor, the market price will still exceed the floor. This is because the convertible is safer than the shares, for even if profits decline and the share price falls, the bond's value will never fall below its straight debt value.[3]

---

[3]Note, however, that the bond value line, B_0M'', would fall if interest rates rose in the economy or if the company's credit risk deteriorated, both of which would cause k_d to rise.

Figure 22-2
Model of a Convertible Bond

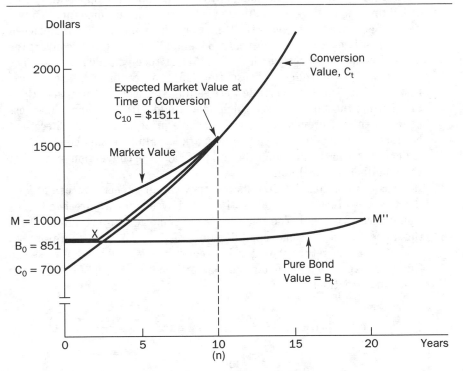

Year	Pure Bond Value, B_t	Conversion Value, C_t	Maturity Value, M	Market Value
0	$ 851	$ 700	$1000	$1000
1	853	756	1000	1042
2	855	816	1000	1086
3	858	882	1000	1132
4	861	952	1000	1180
5	864	1029	1000	1229
6	867	1111	1000	1281
7	872	1200	1000	1335
8	876	1296	1000	1391
9	881	1399	1000	1450
10	887	1511	1000	1511
11	893	1632	1000	1632
.	.	.	.	.
.	.	.	.	.
.	.	.	.	.
20	1000	3263	1000	3263

6. The gap between the market price of the convertible and the floor
declines over time and is zero in Year 10. This convergence will occur for
two reasons. First, the dividends received on the shares presumably are
growing at 8 percent a year, whereas the interest on the bond is fixed at

$100 annually. After 8 years, the dividends that would be received from 20 shares of common equity, $2.80(1.08)^8(20) = 103.65, would exceed the $100 of interest paid by the bond; beyond that point, the opportunity cost of holding the bond rather than converting it would become increasingly heavy. Second, after 10 years the bond would become callable at a price of $1000. If Adam's called the issue, the bondholder could either convert the bond to common shares worth $C_{10} = 1511 or receive $1000 in cash. The holder would, of course, choose the $1511 of common shares. Note, however, that if the convertible were selling at a price greater than $C_{10} = 1511 when the call occurred, the holder would suffer an immediate loss equal to the difference between the bond's price and $1511. Therefore, because of the call provision, the market value of the bond cannot logically exceed the higher of the call price and the conversion price after the bond becomes callable.[4]

7. If investors purchased AEL's shares, they would expect a return of $k_s = D_1/P_0 + g = $2.80/$35 + 8\% = 16\%$. If they bought a pure bond, they would earn 12 percent. The convertible has some guaranteed interest plus the expectation of some capital gains, so its risk and therefore its expected rate of return should be between $k_d = 12\%$ and $k_s = 16\%$. We can find the expected return on the convertible by solving for k_c in the following equation:

$$\text{Initial price} = \sum_{t=1}^{10} \frac{\text{Interest}}{(1 + k_c)^t} + \frac{\text{Conversion value}}{(1 + k_c)^{10}}$$

$$\$1000 = \sum_{t=1}^{10} \frac{\$100}{(1 + k_c)^t} + \frac{\$1511}{(1 + k_c)^{10}}.$$

Using a financial calculator, we find $k_c = 12.8\%$. Therefore, under the assumptions of this example, an investor who purchased the convertible at its initial $1000 offering price could expect to earn a rate of return of 12.8 percent.

Use of Convertibles in Financing

Convertibles offer two important advantages from the issuer's standpoint. First, convertibles, like bonds with warrants, permit a company to sell debt with a lower interest rate and with less-restrictive covenants than straight bonds. Second, convertibles provide a way of selling common equity at prices higher than those currently prevailing. Many companies actually want to sell common equity and not debt, but they believe that the price of their shares is temporarily depressed. The financial manager may know, for example, that earnings are depressed because of startup costs associated with a new project, but he or she may expect earnings to rise sharply during the next year or so, pulling the price of the shares along. In this case, if the company sells equity now, it will be giving up too many shares to raise a given amount of money. However, if it sets the conversion price at 20 to 30 percent above the present market price of the equity, then 20 to 30 percent fewer shares will have to be

---

[4]The assumption is that the firm will always call the bond when it is in a position to do so. This is not always the case; many firms do not call their debt.

given up when the bonds are converted. Notice, however, that management is counting on the share price's rising sufficiently above the conversion price to make the bonds attractive in conversion. If earnings do not rise and pull the share price up and hence conversion does not occur, the company will be saddled with debt in the face of low earnings, which could be disastrous.

How can the company be sure that conversion will occur if the price of the shares rises above the conversion period? Typically, convertibles contain a call provision that enables the issuing firm to force bondholders to convert. Suppose the conversion price is $50, the conversion ratio is 20, the market price of the common equity has risen to $60, and the call price on the convertible bond is $1050. If the company calls the bond, bondholders can either convert into common shares with a market value of $1200 or allow the company to redeem the bond for $1050. Naturally, bondholders prefer $1200 to $1050, so conversion will occur. The call provision thus gives the company a means of forcing conversion, but only if the share price is greater than the conversion price.

Convertibles are useful, but they do have three important disadvantages. (1) The use of a convertible security may in effect give the issuer the opportunity to sell common shares at a price higher than it could sell shares otherwise. However, if the share price increases greatly, the company would probably have been better off if it had used straight debt in spite of its higher interest rate and then later sold common equity to refund the debt. (2) If the company truly wants to raise equtiy capital and if its share price does not rise sufficiently after the bond is issued, then the firm will be stuck with debt, although at low interest rates. (3) Convertibles typically have a low coupon interest rate, an advantage that will be lost when conversion occurs. Warrant financings, on the other hand, permit the company to continue to use the low-coupon debt for a longer period.

Concept Review

▶ Does the exchange of convertible securities for common stock bring in additional funds to the firm? Explain.

▶ How do you calculate (1) the conversion price, P_c, and (2) the conversion ratio, CR?

▶ How is a convertible bond's initial conversion value, C_t, calculated? How does this value change over time?

▶ Why does the premium (the excess of the market value of a convertible over either the conversion value or the straight bond value) decline over time and eventually go to zero?

▶ What are the key advantages and disadvantages of convertibles?

Reporting Earnings If Convertibles or Warrants Are Outstanding

Firms with convertibles or warrants outstanding are required to report earnings per share (EPS) in two ways: (1) *basic EPS*, which in essence is earnings available to common shares divided by the number of shares actually outstanding, and (2) *fully diluted EPS*, which shows what EPS would be if all warrants had been exercised or convertibles converted prior to the reporting data. For firms with large amounts of option-based securities outstanding, there can be a substantial difference between the two EPS figures. The purpose of the provision is, of course, to give investors more information on the firm's profit position.

Summary

The key concepts in this chapter are listed below.

☐ An **option** is a contract that gives its holder the right to buy or sell an asset at some predetermined price within a specified period of time. Option features are used by firms to *"sweeten"* debt offerings.

☐ A **warrant** is an option issued along with a bond that gives the holder the right to purchase a stated number of shares of equity at a specified price within a specified period. A warrant will surely be exercised if it is about to expire and the equity price is above the exercise price.

☐ A **convertible security** is a bond or preferred share that can be exchanged for common equity at the option of the holder. When the security is converted, it is replaced with common equity, and no money changes hands.

☐ The conversion of bonds or preferred shares by their holders does not provide additional funds to the company, but it does result in a lower debt ratio. The exercise of warrants does provide additional funds, which strengthens the firm's equity position, but it still leaves the debt or preferred equity on the balance sheet. Low interest rate debt remains outstanding when warrants are exercised, but the firm loses this advantage when convertibles are converted.

Questions

22-1 Why do options typically sell at prices greater than their theoretical values?

22-2 What effect does the expected growth rate in a firm's share price (subsequent to issue) have on its ability to raise funds (a) through convertibles and (b) through warrants?

22-3 If a firm expects to have additional financial requirements in the future, would you recommend that it use convertibles or bonds with warrants? What factors would influence your decision?

22-4 How does a firm's decision to pay out a higher percentage of its earnings as dividends affect each of the following?
  a. The value of long-term warrants.
  b. The likelihood that convertible bonds will be converted.
  c. The likelihood that warrants will be exercised.

22-5 Evaluate the following statement: "Issuing convertible securities represents a means by which a firm can sell common equity at a price above the existing market."

22-6 Why do corporations often sell convertibles on a rights basis?

22-7 Why might an investor prefer a bond with a warrant attached over a convertible bond?

22-8 Suppose a company simultaneously issues $50 million of convertible bonds with a coupon rate of 9 percent and $50 million of straight bonds with a coupon rate of 12 percent. Both bonds have the same maturity. Does the fact that the convertible issue has a lower coupon rate suggest that it is less risky than the straight bond issue? Explain your answer.

22-9 Suppose a company has a capital structure containing $50 million of 9 percent convertible bonds and $50 million of common equity with k_s of 15 percent. Its tax rate is 40 percent. Is the firm's weighted average cost of equity $k_a = 0.5(9\%)(0.6) + 0.5(15\%) = 10.2\%$? Explain your answer.

Self-Test Problems (solutions appear on pages 873)

ST-1 Key terms. Define each of the following terms:
  a. Warrant; detachable warrant
  b. Theoretical value; exercise value
  c. Stepped-up price
  d. Convertible security
  e. Conversion ratio; conversion price; conversion value
  f. "Sweetener"
  g. Primary EPS; basic EPS; fully diluted EPS
  h. Option; call option; put option
  i. Strike price

ST-2 Option price. On June 15, 1992, the share price of the Toronto-Dominion Bank closed at $17.125. The following table shows prices of options traded on the bank on the same day. What is the theoretical value of these options? Why are they trading above their theoretical value? Why do the longer-dated options have higher premiums? (Hint: Consider actual price versus theoretical value.)

Date	Strike Price	Option Price
June	$16	$1.15
	$17	0.25
July	$17	0.40
September	$17	0.75
	$18	0.30

ST-3 Convertible bonds. FutureTel Ltd. needs to raise $35 million to begin producing a new compact personal telephone. FutureTel's straight, nonconvertible debentures currently yield 12 percent. Its common equity sells for $38 per share; the last dividend was $2.46; and the expected growth rate is a constant 8 percent. Investment dealers tentatively propose that FutureTel raise the $35 million by issuing convertible debentures. Each convertible will have a $1000 face value, carry a coupon rate of 10 percent, have a 20-year maturity, and be convertible into 20 common shares. The bonds will be sold at par. They will be noncallable for 5 years, after which they will be callable at a price of $1075; this call price will decline by $5 per year in Year 6 and each year thereafter. FutureTel has issued convertibles in the past, and once they were eligible for call, management has called them (and presumably will call them again in the future) as soon as their conversion value was about 20 percent above their par value (not their call price).

a. What is the conversion price?

b. Given FutureTel's growth prospects, how many years will it be before the convertible debenture holders will consider converting?

c. Given FutureTel's growth prospects, what will the conversion value be in 5 years when the debentures first becomes callable? What will the debenture holders do if FutureTel calls the debentures?

d. Given FutureTel's growth prospects and past management behaviour, when will the debentures be called?

e. If the debentures are called as predicted in Part d, what return will a debenture holder have had? What would the return over the same period have been on purchasing shares of common equity?

f. What is the pure bond price of the debentures when issued? in 5 years?

g. Prepare a table showing the pure bond price, conversion value, and value of the debenture under the given assumptions. Draw a graph similar to Figure 22-2 showing the price of the debenture over time.

h. What is the value of k_s, the cost of equity capital, for FutureTel?

i. Now suppose that 2 years from now a U.S. company comes out with an even smaller personal telephone, with more features, and FutureTel's expected growth rate drops to zero. Assume that the dividend at the time of the drop is $2.87. The company's credit strength is not impaired, and its value of k_s is also unchanged. What will happen to (i) the stock price and (ii) the price of the convertible debenture?

Problems

22-1 **Options.**   Shares of the Bank of Vancouver are selling for $53 per share. Call options that expire in 1 month and have a strike (exercise) price of $50 are selling for $3.875. Put options that expire in 1 month and have a strike price of $50 are selling for $0.125. What will the value of your holdings and your profit be, per share, if the price goes to (i) $55 (ii) $50 (iii) $45 on the share? on the call option? on the put option?

22-2 **Options leverage.**   Shares of company XYZ are selling for $20 per share. Call options with a strike (exercise) price of $20 that expire in 1 month are selling for 50¢. (Note that when you buy options, each contract is for 100 shares; therefore, you'd need to pay $50 to buy an option contract on 100 shares of XYZ.) You have $1000 to invest.

Compute your payoff in dollars and as a percentage from buying the shares and from buying the call options if the price of XYZ in 1 month is (i) $20, (ii) $21, (iii) $30, (iv) $15. Ignore transactions costs.

22-3 Warrants. Flin Flon Industries has warrants outstanding that permit the holder to purchase one share of equity per warrant at $21 per share.

a. Calculate the theoretical value of Flin Flon's warrants if the common shares sell at the following prices: (i) $18, (ii) $21, (iii) $25, and (iv) $70.

b. At what approximate price do you think the warrants would actually sell under each condition indicated in Part a? What excess is implied in your price? Your answer is a guess, but your prices and excesses should bear reasonable relationships to one another.

c. How would each of the following affect your estimates of the warrants' prices and excesses in Part b?

  i. The life of the warrant is lengthened.

  ii. Expected variability, σ_p, in the share's price decreases.

  iii. The expected growth rate in the share's EPS increases.

  iv. The company announces the following change in dividend policy: whereas it formerly paid no dividends, henceforth it will pay out *all* earnings as dividends.

d. Assume Flin Flon's shares now sell for $18 per share. The company wants to sell some 20-year, annual interest, $1000 par value bonds. Each bond will have attached 50 warrants, each exercisable into one share of equity at an exercise price of $21. Flin Flon's straight bonds yield 10 percent. Regardless of your answer to Part b, assume that the warrants will have a market value of $1.50 when the shares sell at $18. What coupon interest rate and dollar coupon must the company set on the bonds with warrants if they are to clear the market? Round to the nearest dollar or percentage point.

22-4 Convertibles. It is the summer of 1994, and Moosonee Manufacturing Company Ltd. is planning to finance an expansion. The principal executives have agreed that an industrial company such as theirs should finance growth by means of common equity rather than debt. However, they feel the price of the company's equity does not reflect its true worth, so they have decided to sell a convertible security. They consider a convertible debenture but fear the burden of fixed interest charges if the common shares does not rise in price sufficiently to make conversion attractive. They settle on an issue of convertible preferred shares, which will pay a dividend of $1.05 per share.

The common equity is selling at $21 per share. Management projects earnings for 1994 at $1.50 a share, and it expects a future growth rate of 10 percent a year in 1995 and beyond. It is agreed by the investment dealers and management that the common equity will sell at 14 times earnings, the current price-to-earnings ratio.

a. What conversion price should be set by the issuer? The conversion ratio will be 1.0—that is, each share of convertible preferred can be converted into one share of common. Therefore, the convertible's par value (and also the issue price) will equal the conversion price, which in turn will be determined as a percentage over the current market price of the common. Your answer will be a guess, but make it a reasonable one.

b. Should the preferred shares include a call provision? Why or why not?

22-5   Convertibles.   Vaught Engineering, Ltd., has outstanding a convertible bond with a face value of $1000 and an 8 percent coupon rate. The bond is convertible into common equity at $40—that is, each bond can be exchanged for 25 shares. The current share price is $32.

a. If the price per share grows at 8 percent per year for 5 years, what will the approximate conversion value be at the end of 5 years?

b. If dividends on the equity are now $1.80 per share, and if these also grow at 8 percent per year, will bondholders convert after 5 years or will they tend to hold onto their bonds? Explain your answer.

c. If the bonds are callable at a 10 percent premium, about how much would you lose per bond if they were called before you converted? (Assume the same conversion value as in Part a, at the end of 5 years.)

22-6   Convertibles.   On July 2, 1993, it was announced that Dana Instruments was issuing $180 million face amount of bonds at $750 for each $1000 face amount of securities. The bonds carry a 7 percent coupon and mature in 2016. They are convertible until December 15, 2001, at $125 face amount of bonds for each common share. The share price closed on July 2, 1993, at $85.

a. How many shares of common equity will be received upon conversion?

b. What is the conversion price, given the $750 issue price of the bonds?

c. What premium percentage does this represent over the $85 common share price?

d. Using the data given, calculate the yield to maturity of the bonds. (Assume semiannual compounding.)

e. Assume that the common equity of Dana increases in price by 10 percent per year and that the bonds sell at the higher of 12 percent above their conversion value or at their "intermediate face value," which is the $750 issue price increased by 4 percent per year. Assume that for personal reasons a purchaser of the bonds sells them at the end of 8 years. Based on the higher of the two prices, what return has the investor earned?

22-7   Financing alternatives.   National Tech Ltd. has grown rapidly during the past 5 years. Recently its bank has urged the company to consider increasing its permanent financing. Its bank loan under a line of credit has risen to $150 000, carrying a 10 percent interest rate. National has been 30 to 60 days late in paying trade creditors.

Discussions with an investment dealer have resulted in the suggestion to raise $250 000 at this time. Investment dealers have assured the company that the following alternatives will be feasible (ignoring issue costs):

- Sell common equity at $8 per share.
- Sell convertible bonds at a 10 percent coupon, convertible into 100/10 shares of common equity for each $1000 bond (the conversion price is $10 per share).
- Sell debentures with a 10 percent coupon, each $1000 bond carrying 100 warrants to buy one share of common equity at $10.

Additional information is given in the company's balance sheet and income statement, which follow.

National Tech Ltd.
Balance Sheet

		Current liabilities	$200 000
		Common equity	50 000
		Retained earnings	25 000
Total assets	$275 000	Total liabilities and capital	$275 000

National Tech Ltd.
Income Statement

Sales	$550 000
All costs except interest	(495 000)
Gross profit	$ 55 000
Interest	(15 000)
EBT	$ 40 000
Taxes (at 40%)	(16 000)
Net income	$ 24 000
Shares outstanding	50 000
Earnings per share	$ 0.48
P/E ratio	18×
Market price of common equity	$ 8.64

Wendy Cukier, the president, owns 80 percent of National's common equity and wishes to maintain control of the company; 50 000 shares are outstanding.

a. Show the new balance sheet under each alternative. For alternatives 2 and 3, show the balance sheet after conversion of the debentures or exercise of warrants. Assume that $150 000 will be used to pay off the bank loan and the rest to increase total assets.
b. Show Cukier's control position under each alternative, assuming that she does not purchase additional shares.
c. What is the effect on earnings per share of each alternative if it is assumed that profits before interest and taxes will be 20 percent of total assets?
d. What will be the debt ratio under each alternative?
e. Which of the three alternatives would you recommend to Cukier? Explain.

Integrative Problem

22-8   Warrants and convertibles. Kathy Allen, financial manager of MicroEd, Ltd., is facing a dilemma. The firm was founded 5 years ago to provide educational software for the rapidly expanding primary and secondary school markets. Although MicroEd has done well, the firm's founder and chairman believes that an industry shake-out is imminent. To survive, the firm must capture market share now, and this requires a large infusion of new capital.

Because the share price may rise rapidly, Allen does not want to issue new common equity. On the other hand, interest rates are currently very high by historical standards, and with the firm's B debt rating, the interest payments on a new debt issue would be too much to handle if sales took a downturn. Thus, Allen has narrowed her choice of securities to bonds with warrants or convertible bonds. She has asked you to help in the decision process by answering the following questions:

a. What is a call option? Why does a knowledge of call options help one understand warrants and convertibles?

b. Computerized Teaching Aids, Ltd. (CTAL) has options listed on the Toronto Stock Exchange. The following table gives the option price for its 6-month, $10 call option at 3 different share prices:

Share Price	Option Price
$10	$ 2
15	6
20	10

i. What is the option's theoretical value and premium at each share price? Why do call options sell for more than their theoretical value?

ii. Assume that CTAL's share price increased from $10 to $15. What rate of return would this provide to an equity investor? An option investor? What is the loss potential on the stock? On the option?

iii. Now assume that CTAL's share price increased from $15 to $20. What would be the rate of return to an equity investor? To an option investor? What is the loss potential on the equity? On the option? Why does the premium over the theoretical value decline as the share price increases?

c. One of Allen's alternatives is to issue a bond with warrants attached. MicroEd's current share price is $10, and its cost of 20-year, annual coupon debt without warrants is estimated by its underwriters to be 12 percent. They suggest attaching 50 warrants per bond, with each having an exercise price of $12.50. It is estimated that each warrant, when detached and traded separately, will have a value of $1.50.

i. What coupon rate should be set on the bond with warrants if the total package is to sell for $1000?

ii. Suppose that the bonds are issued and the warrants immediately trade for $2.50 each. What does this imply about the terms of the issue?

      iii. When will the warrants be exercised?

      iv. Will the warrants bring in additional capital when exercised? If so, what type of capital?

      v. Because warrants lower the cost of the accompanying debt issue, why shouldn't all debt be issued with warrants? What is the expected cost of the bond with warrants if the warrants are expected to be exercised in 5 years, when MicroEd's share price is expected to be $17.50?

d. As an alternative to the bond with warrants, Allen is considering convertible bonds. The firm's underwriters estimate that MicroEd could sell a 20-year, 10 percent annual coupon, callable convertible bond for its $1000 par value, whereas a straight debt issue would require a 12 percent coupon. MicroEd's current share price is $10, its last dividend was $0.74, and the dividend is expected to grow at a constant 8 percent. The convertible could be converted into 80 shares of MicroEd common equity at the owner's option.

      i. What conversion price, P_c, is implied in the convertible's terms?

      ii. What is the straight debt value of the convertible? What is the implied value of the convertibility feature?

      iii. What is the formula for the bond's conversion value in any year? Its value at Year 0? At Year 10?

      iv. What is meant by the "floor value" of a convertible? What is the convertible's expected floor value at Year 0? At Year 10?

      v. Assume that MicroEd intends to force conversion by calling the bond when its conversion value is 20 percent above its par value, or at 1.2($1000) = $1200. When is the issue expected to be called? Answer to the closest year.

      vi. What is the expected cost of the convertible to MicroEd? Does this cost appear consistent with the riskiness of the issue? Assume conversion in Year 5 at a conversion value of $1 200.

e. Allen believes that the costs of both the bond with warrants and the convertible bond are essentially equal, so her decision must be based on other factors. What are some of the factors that she should consider in making her decision?

Solutions to Self-Test Problems

ST-1 Refer to the appropriate sections of the text to check your responses.

ST-2

Date	Strike Price	Option Price	Theoretical Value
June	$16	$1.15	$1.125
	$17	0.25	0.125
July	$17	0.40	0.125
September	$17	0.75	0.125
	$18	0.30	0

As long as an option has some time left before maturity, there is some chance the share price will rise further, thus making the theoretical value of the option greater. This is why options trade above their theoretical values—investors are paying for this possible future gain. The longer the option has until maturity, the greater the chance of the share price rising.

ST-3   **a.** The conversion price is $1000/20 = $50 per share.

     b.
$$\$50 = (\$38)(1.08)^n = (\$38)(FVIF_{8\%, \, n}).$$

$$FVIF_{8\%, \, n} = \frac{\$50}{\$38} = 1.3158.$$

From Table A-3 on the insert card you know n must be between 3 and 4 years. The actual answer is 3.565, or slightly more than 3½ years.

     c. In 5 years, the conversion value will be $(\$38)(1.08)^5(20) = \$1116.69$. If FutureTel calls the debentures, the holders will have to choose between converting the option into 20 shares, each worth $55.835, for a total of $1116.69, or turning in the debenture for $1075. They will convert.

     d. FutureTel will call when the debenture is 20 percent above its par value, or $(\$1000)(1.20) = \$1200$. Therefore, the debenture is called when $(\$38)(1.08)^n(20) > \$1200$. This occurs at n = 6, when the conversion value is $1206.02.

     e. The investor who buys the debenture pays $1000 in Year 0, receives $100 in coupon payments for 6 years, and then converts in Year 6 when the debenture is called. Assume that she immediately sells her 20 shares for $1206.02.

$$\$1000 = (\$100)(PVIFA_{r\%, \, 6}) + (\$1206.02)(PVIF_{r\%, \, 6}).$$

Using the internal rate of return (IRR) function on a financial calculator or spreadsheet gives r = 12.5 percent.

     Someone who bought a share at $38 would have received 6 years of dividends and sold at $55.83.

$$\$38 = \frac{\$2.66}{1 + r} + \frac{\$2.87}{(1 + r)^2} + \frac{\$3.10}{(1 + r)^3} + \frac{\$3.35}{(1 + r)^4} + \frac{\$3.61}{(1 + r)^5} +$$

$$\frac{\$3.90}{(1 + r)^6} + \frac{\$55.83}{(1 + r)^6}.$$

Use of the IRR function gives r = 13.83 percent.

     f. The pure bond price is given by discounting the cash flows from the bond at the yield of FutureTel's nonconvertible debentures.

$$P_0 = \sum_{t = 1}^{20} \frac{Coupon_t}{(1 + Yield)^t} + \frac{Face \; value}{(1 + Yield)^{20}}$$

or

$$P_0 = \$100(PVIFA_{12\%, \, 20}) + \$1000(PVIF_{12\%, \, 20})$$

$$= \$100(7.4694) + \$1000(0.1037)$$

$$= \$850.64.$$

After 5 years, $P_5 = \sum_{t=1}^{15} \dfrac{\text{Coupon}_t}{(1 + \text{yield})^t} + \dfrac{\text{Face value}}{(1 + \text{yield})^{15}}.$

$$P_5 = \$100(\text{PVIFA}_{12\%,\,15}) + \$1000(\text{PVIF}_{12\%,\,15})$$

$$= \$100(6.8109) + \$1000(0.1827)$$

$$= \$863.79.$$

g.

Year	Share Price ($38)(1.08)^n	Conversion Value 20S	Bond Value	Theoretical Value max[CV, bond]
0	$38.00	$ 760.00	$850.61	$ 850.61
1	41.04	820.80	852.68	852.68
2	44.32	886.46	855.01	886.46
3	47.87	957.38	857.61	957.38
4	51.70	1033.97	860.52	1033.97
5	55.83	1116.69	863.78	1116.69
6	60.30	1206.02	867.44	1206.02[a]
7	65.13	1302.51	871.53	1302.51
8	70.34	1406.71	876.11	1406.71
9	75.96	1519.24	881.25	1519.24
10	82.04	1640.78	887.00	1640.78

[a]Debenture will be called at this price.

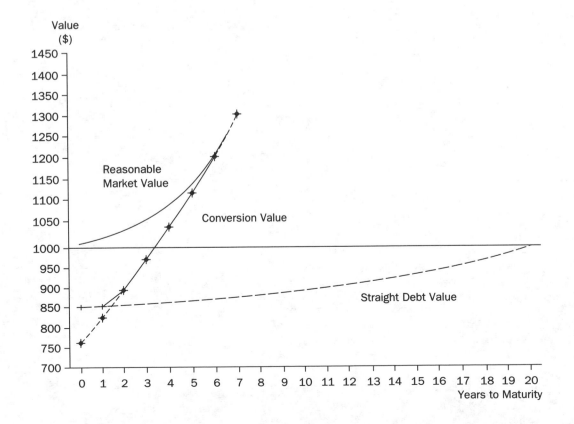

h. $P_0 = DIV_1/(k_s - g)$

$$\$38 = \frac{(\$2.46)(1.08)}{k_s - 0.08}$$

$$k_s = \frac{(\$2.46)(1.08)}{\$38} + 0.08 = 0.15 = 15\%.$$

i.   Before the change in growth,

$$P_2 = DIV_3/(k_s - g)$$
$$= (\$2.87)(1.08)/0.15 - 0.08) = \$44.27.$$

Now $g = 0$.

$$P_2 = DIV_3/(k_s - g)$$
$$= \$2.87/0.15 - 0) = \$19.13.$$

This is a drop of 57 percent in the share price.

At this price, the conversion price of the debenture will be ($19.13)(20) = $382.60, so conversion will never occur. The price of the debenture will be determined by its bond value. From the table in Part g, we see that the bond price is $855.01. From the graph in Part g, the price of the debenture would have been about $1025. This is a drop of 17 percent, only about 30 percent of the drop in the share price.

23

‍‍‍

Lease Financing

A Managerial Perspective

Firms generally own fixed assets and report the investment on their balance sheets. However, it is the *use* of the buildings and equipment that is important, not the ownership per se. One way to obtain the use of assets is to buy them; an alternative is to lease them. The decision will determine the importance of lease payments in the financial statements of a company. In some companies—for example, institutional caterers—equipment is leased with a term equal to the term of the contract. In this way, the company does not have to purchase specific assets, and with each new contract, new and perhaps customer-specific assets are leased and put to use.

Under the lease alternative, a contractual arrangement is established under which the owner of the asset (the *lessor*) permits a second party (the *lessee*) to use the services of the asset for a specified period of time in exchange for a series of payments. Ownership of the leased asset remains with the lessor, and the lessee can purchase the asset at the expiry of the lease only if that option was specified in the lease contract.

Leasing first came to prominence with real estate assets—land and buildings. Currently, it is possible to lease virtually any kind of fixed asset. Examples of assets that are leased include airplanes, shopping centres, shoe manufacturing equipment, and even cranes for construction purposes.

It may appear from the discussion to follow that "lessors" are a homogeneous group. This impression is useful for describing the techniques of leasing, but in fact the leasing "industry" is composed of a large number of very different participants. Financial institutions are the major group involved in this industry. Life insurance companies, trust companies, and some pension funds are heavily involved as lessors.

In Chapters 13 and 14, we evaluated the acquisition of an asset separately from its financing; we assume that once it was decided that a particular asset should be purchased, the required cash was obtained by using the sources of funds available to the firm. Leasing, on the other hand, provides for the simultaneous acquisition of assets and their financing. The financing is quite similar to borrowing; each requires a set of fixed contractual payments over a stated term. The advantage of a lease over debt is that the lessor is in a better position than a creditor if the user firm experiences financial difficulties. If the lessee does not meet the lease obligations, the lessor has a stronger legal right to take back the asset because the lessor still owns it. A creditor, even a secured one, may encounter costs and delays in recovering assets that have been directly or indirectly financed. Since the lessor has less risk than other financing sources used in acquiring assets, the riskier the firm seeking financing, the greater the reason for the supplier of financing to formulate a leasing arrangement rather than a loan. Because leasing can be viewed as a form of debt financing, however, it provides financial leverage, thereby increasing both the risk and expected return to the equity investor. The presence of the fixed lease payments also adds risk to those creditors whose claims are subordinate to the lease payments.

Types of Leases

Leases take three forms: (1) operating or service leases, (2) straight financial or capital leases; and (3) sale-and-leaseback arrangements.

Operating Leases

Operating leases, sometimes called *service leases*, provide for both *financing* and *maintenance* services. IBM is one of the pioneers of the operating lease contract, and computers and office copying machines, together with automobiles and trucks, are still the primary types of equipment involved. Ordinarily these leases call for the lessor to maintain and service the leased equipment, and the cost of providing this maintenance is built into the lease payments.

Another important characteristic of operating leases is the fact that they are frequently *not fully amortized*. In other words, the payments required under the lease contract are not sufficient to recover the full cost of the equipment. However, the lease contract is written for a period shorter than the expected economic life of the leased equipment, and the lessor expects to recover all investment costs in subsequent renewal payments, through subsequent leases to other lessees, or by selling the leased equipment.

A final feature of operating leases is that they frequently contain a *cancellation clause* giving the lessee the right to cancel the lease and return the equipment before the expiration of the basic arrangement. This is an important consideration for the lessee, since the equipment can be returned if it is rendered obsolete by technological developments or if it is no longer needed because of a decline in the lessee's business. This flexibility benefits lessees because it lowers their risk, but the lessors face correspondingly higher risk.

Financial or Capital Leases

Financial leases, sometimes called *capital leases*, differ from operating leases in three respects: (1) they do not provide for maintenance service, (2) they are *not cancellable*, and (3) they are *fully amortized* (that is, the lessor receives rental payments that are equal to the full price of the leased equipment plus a return on the investment). In a typical financial lease arrangement, the firm that will use the equipment (the lessee) selects the specific items it requires and negotiates the price and delivery terms with the manufacturer or the distributor. The user firm then negotiates terms with a leasing company or financial institution and, once the lease terms are set, arranges to have the lessor buy the equipment from the manufacturer or the distributor. When the equipment is purchased, the user firm simultaneously executes an agreement to lease the equipment from the financial institution.

The lease contract specifies the terms and conditions of the lease. The length of the lease will depend upon the expected economic life of the asset. In most instances, the rate of return to the lessor is close to the percentage rate the lessee would have to pay on a secured term loan. For example, if the lessee would have to pay 10 percent for a term loan, then a rate of close to 10 percent will be built into the lease contract. The lessee is generally given an option either to renew the lease at a reduced rental on expiration of the original lease or to purchase the asset from the lessor at a stated price.[1] Finally, the contract specifies which of the parties has the responsibility to pay for repairs and maintenance, taxes, insurance, and other expenses. If the lessee is responsible for these costs, the lease is called a *net-net lease*. If the lessor maintains the asset and pays the insurance, it is called a *maintenance lease*.

Financial leases are almost the same as sale-and-leaseback arrangements; the major difference is that the leased equipment is new and the lessor buys it from a manufacturer or a distributor instead of from the user-lessee. A sale and leaseback may be thought of as a special type of financial lease. Both sale-and-leaseback arrangements and financial leases are analyzed in the same manner.

Sale and Leaseback

Under a **sale and leaseback**, a firm owning land, buildings, or equipment sells the property at approximately market value to a financial institution, independent leasing company, or even an individual investor and simultaneously executes an agreement to lease the property back for a specified period under specific terms. The sale-and-leaseback plan is an alternative to a mortgage.

The seller-lessee immediately receives the purchase price put up by the buyer-lessor. At the same time, the seller-lessee retains the use of the property just as if it had borrowed and mortgaged the property to secure the loan; the buyer-lessor retains ownership, and hence a claim on the residual value of the asset. This parallel to borrowing is carried over to the lease payment schedule. Under a mortgage loan agreement, the lessor would normally receive a series of equal payments just sufficient to amortize the loan and provide a specified rate of return on the outstanding balance. Under a sale-and-leaseback arrangement, the lease payments are set up in exactly the same way; the payments are sufficient to return the full purchase price to the lessor while providing a specified rate of return on the lessor's outstanding investment.

---

[1]Other provisions may be written into the lease contract: for example, that (1) the lessee has the right to purchase the asset at the maturity date of the contract at its fair market value; (2) the lessee has the right to purchase the asset at any time during the life of the contract, usually at specified prices that vary through time; and (3) the lessee has the right to cancel the lease at any time after a stated period of time.

Tax Implications of a Lease

The full amount of annual lease payments is deductible for federal income tax purposes *provided* that the tax authorities agree that a particular contract is a genuine lease and not simply an installment loan called a lease (that is, a disguised sale). This is particularly important for a lease that provides an option to the lessee to purchase the leased equipment for a specified amount at the end of the lease period. There are instances in which a very low option price resulted in an interpretation of the contract as a time-payment purchase and not a lease.[2]

One purported benefit of a lease is that the cost of land can be amortized in lease payments. This permits the amortization of this cost for federal income tax purposes. (This benefit would not be available if the asset were purchased because land cannot be depreciated for tax purposes.) Of course, there are a number of impacts offsetting this "benefit." First, the firm that leases does not own the land and hence gives up the value at the end of the lease. Second, competition among potential lessors and lessees can result in a sharing of these tax benefits.

Financial Statement Effects

Lease payments are shown as operating expenses on a firm's income statement, but under certain conditions, neither the leased assets nor the liabilities under the lease contract appear on a firm's balance sheet. For this reason, leasing is often called *off balance sheet financing*. This point is illustrated in Table 23-1 by the balance sheets of two hypothetical firms, B (for buy) and L (for lease). Initially, the balance sheets of both firms are identical, and they both have debt ratios of 50 percent. Each firm decides to acquire an asset that costs $100. Firm B borrows $100 to buy the asset, so both an asset and a liability are recorded on its balance sheet, and its debt ratio is increased to 75 percent. Firm L leases the equipment, so its balance sheet is unchanged. The lease may call for fixed charges as high as or even higher than those on the loan, and the obligations assumed under the lease may be equally or more dangerous from the standpoint of financial safety, but the firm's debt ratio remains at 50 percent.

To correct this anomaly, the Canadian Institute of Chartered Accountants (CICA) requires firms entering into financial (or capital) leases to restate their balance sheets to report leased asset under "fixed assets" and the present value of the future lease payments as a debt. This process is called *capitalizing the lease*, and its net effect is to cause Firms B and L to have similar balance sheets, both of which will, in essence, resemble the one shown for Firm B after the asset increase.

---

[2]If the option is exercised, the exercise price becomes the capital cost of the asset and the lessee is permitted to claim capital cost allowances on that amount. If the lease permits the application of the lease payments as partial payment of the cost of the assets, the resulting capital cost of the asset to the lessee is the purchase price less the partial payments.

Table 23-1
Balance Sheet Effects of Leasing

Before Asset Increase				After Asset Increase							
Firms B and L				Firm B				Firm L			
Current assets	$ 50	Debt	$ 50	Current assets	$ 50	Debt	$150	Current assets	$ 50	Debt	$ $50
Fixed assets	50	Equity	50	Fixed assets	150	Equity	50	Fixed assets	50	Equity	50
Total assets	$100		$100	Total assets	$200		$200	Total assets	$100		$100

The logic behind this provision is as follows. If a firm signs a lease contract, its obligation to make lease payments is just as binding as if it had signed a loan agreement. The failure to make lease payments can bankrupt a firm just as surely as the failure to make principal and interest payments on a loan. Therefore, for all intents and purposes, a financial lease is identical to a loan.[3] This being the case, the signing of a lease agreement has, in effect, raised the firm's "true" debt ratio and thereby has changed its "true" capital structure. Accordingly, if the firm has previously established a target capital structure and if there is no reason to think that the optimal capital structure has changed, then using lease financing requires additional equity support in exactly the same manner as does the use of debt financing.

If disclosure of the lease were not made in the Table 23-1 example, then Firm L's investors could be deceived into thinking that its financial position is stronger than it actually is. Even if the lease were disclosed in a footnote to the balance sheet, investors might not fully recognize its impact and might not see that Firms B and L are in essentially the same financial position. If this were the case, Firm L would have increased its true amount of debt through a lease arrangement but its required return on debt, k_d, its required return on equity, k_s, and consequently its average required rate of return, would have increased less than those required returns for Firm B, which borrowed directly. Thus, investors would be willing to accept a lower return from Firm L because they would view it as being in a stronger financial position than Firm B. These benefits of leasing would accrue to shareholders at the expense of new investors, who were, in effect, being deceived by the fact that the firm's balance sheet did not fully reflect its true liability situation.

---

[3]There are, however, certain legal differences between loans and leases. In the event of liquidation in bankruptcy, a lessor is entitled to take possession of the leased asset, and if the value of the asset is less than the required payments under the lease, the lessor can enter a claim (as a general creditor) for 1 year's rental payments. In a reorganization, the lessor receives the asset plus 3 years' rentals if needed to cover the value of the lease. In contrast, the lender under a secured loan arrangement has a security interest in the asset, meaning that if the asset is sold, the lender will be given the proceeds, and the full unsatisfied portion of the lender's claim will be treated as a general credit obligation (see Chapter 25). It is not possible to state, as a general rule, whether a supplier of capital is in a stronger position as a secured creditor or as a lessor. Since one position is regarded as being about as good as the other at the time the financial arrangements are being made, a lease is about as risky as a secured term loan from both the lessor-lender's and the lessee-borrower's viewpoint.

The question of whether investors would truly be deceived has been debated but never resolved. Those who believe strongly in efficient markets think that investors would not be fooled and that footnotes to balance sheets are sufficient, while those who question market efficiency think that leases should be capitalized. The solution represents a compromise between the two positions, though one that is tilted heavily toward those who favour capitalization.

A lease is classified as a *capital lease* and hence capitalized and shown directly on the balance sheet if any one of the following conditions exists:

1. Under the terms of the lease, ownership of the property is effectively transferred from the lessor to the lessee at the end of the lease term.
2. The lease runs for a period equal to or greater than 75 percent of the asset's life. Thus, if an asset has a 10-year life and the lease is written for 8 years, the lease must be capitalized.
3. The present value of the lease payments is equal to or greater than 90 percent of the initial value of the asset less any tax credit taken by the lessor.[4]

These rules, together with strong footnote disclosure rules for operating leases, should certainly be sufficient to ensure that no one is fooled by lease financing. Thus, leases are recognized to be essentially the same as debt, and they have the same effects as debt on the firm's required rate of return. Therefore, leasing does not generally permit a firm to use more financial leverage than could be obtained with conventional debt.

Evaluation by the Lessee

Any prospective lease must be evaluated by both the lessee and lessor. The lessee must determine whether leasing an asset is less costly than buying it and financing the purchase with a debt issue; the lessor must decide what lease payment is required to provide a reasonable rate of return. Since our focus in this book is primarily on financial management, as opposed to investments, we restrict our analysis to that conducted by the lessee.

In the typical case, the events leading to a lease arrangement follow the sequence described in the following list. We should note that a great deal of literature exists about the theoretically correct way to evaluate lease-versus-purchase decisions, and some very complex decision models have been developed to aid in the analysis. The analysis given here, however, leads to the correct decision in every case we have encountered.

1. The firm decides to acquire a particular building or piece of equipment; this decision is based on regular capital budgeting procedures and is not at issue in the typical lease analysis. In a lease analysis, the firm is concerned simply with whether to finance the machine by a lease or by a loan. However, if the effective cost of the lease is substantially lower

---

[4]The discount rate used to calculate the present value of the lease payments must be the lower of (1) the rate used by the lessor to establish the lease payments and (2) the rate of interest the lessee would have paid for new debt with a maturity equal to that of the lease.

than the cost of debt—and this could occur for several reasons, including the situation in which the lessor is able to utilize the CCA tax shelters but the lessee is not—then the capital budgeting decision should be re-evaluated, and projects formerly deemed unacceptable may become acceptable.

2. Once the firm has decided to acquire the asset, the next question is how to finance its acquisition. Well-run businesses do not have excess cash lying around, so new assets must be financed in some manner.

3. Funds to purchase the asset could be obtained by borrowing, by retaining earnings, by selling new equity, or by some combination of these sources. Alternatively, the asset could be leased. Because of the capitalization-disclosure provision for leases, we assume that a lease would have the same capital structure effect as a loan.

As indicated earlier, a lease is comparable to a loan in the sense that the firm is required to make a specified series of payments, and failure to meet these payments can result in bankruptcy. Thus, the most appropriate comparison is the cost of lease financing versus the cost of debt financing.[5]

Concept Review

▶ Define each of these terms: (1) *operating lease*, (2) *financial*, or *capital lease*, and (3) *sale-and-leaseback*.

▶ What are the conditions in which a lease must be considered a capital lease?

▶ What is *off balance sheet financing*? Can it cause any problems in interpreting a company's financial position? What is the accounting convention to resolve any problem?

NPV Analysis

The lease versus borrow-and-purchase analysis is illustrated with data on the Monroe Manufacturing Company Limited. The following conditions are assumed:

1. Monroe plans to acquire equipment with a 5-year life at a cost of $10 million, delivered and installed.

2. Monroe can borrow the required $10 million, using a 10 percent loan to be amortized over 5 years. Therefore, the loan will call for payments of $2 637 965.60 per year, calculated as follows:

$$\text{Payment} = \frac{\$10\,000\,000}{\text{PVIFA}_{10\%,\,5}} = \frac{\$10\,000\,000}{3.7908} = \$2\,637\,965.60.$$

---

[5]The analysis should compare the cost of leasing to the cost of debt financing *regardless* of how the asset is actually financed. The asset may actually be purchased with available cash if it is not leased, but because leasing is a substitute for debt financing, a comparison between the two is still appropriate.

3. Monroe can lease the equipment for 5 years at a rental charge of $2 791 670 per year payable at the end of the year, but the lessor will own it at the expiration of the lease. (The lease payment schedule is established by the potential lessor, and Monroe can accept it, reject it, or negotiate.)

4. The equipment will definitely be used for 5 years, at the end of which time its estimated net salvage value will be $715 000. Monroe plans to continue to use the equipment, so (1) if it purchases the equipment, the company will keep it, and (2) if it leases the equipment, the company will exercise an option to buy it at its estimated salvage value of $715 000.

5. The lease contract stipulates that the lessor will maintain the equipment. However, if Monroe borrows and buys, it will have to bear the cost of maintenance, which will be performed by the equipment manufacturer at a fixed contract rate of $500 000 per year, payable at year-end.

6. The equipment falls into a class in which the capital cost allowance (CCA) rate is 30 percent. The effective tax rate for Monroe is 40 percent.

Table 23-2 shows the outflows that will be incurred in each year under each of the two financing plans, and is set up to produce a time line of cash flows.

Year	1	2	3	4	5
Cash flows	CF_1	CF_2	CF_3	CF_4	CF_5

Table 23-2
Monroe Manufacturing Company Limited:
Lease versus Purchase Analysis
(thousands of dollars)

	Year				
	1	2	3	4	5
I. Borrow and Purchase Plan					
Loan amortization schedule					
1. Loan payment	$2638	$2638	$2638	$2638	$2638
2. Interest	1000	836	656	458	240
3. Principal payment (1) − (3)	1638	1802	1982	2180	2398
4. Remaining balance	8362	6560	4578	2398	0
Cash outflows					
5. Loan payment	$2638	$2638	$2638	$2638	$2638
6. Interest tax saving	(400)	(334)	(262)	(183)	(96)
7. Maintenance (after tax)	300	300	300	300	300
8. Net cash outflows (buy) (5) + (6) + (7)	2538	2604	2676	2755	2842
9. PVIF at 6%	0.9434	0.8900	0.8396	0.7921	0.7473
10. PV of owning cash flows (8) × (9)	$2394	$2317	$2246	$2182	$2124
11. PV tax savings from CCA	(3239)	—	—	—	—
12. Total PV cost of owning (10 in each year) + (11)	8025				

(continued)

Table 23-2 (*continued*)

	Year				
	1	**2**	**3**	**4**	**5**
II. Lease Plan					
13. Net cash outflows (lease)	$ 1675	$ 1675	$ 1675	$ 1675	$ 1675
14. PVIF at 6%	0.9434	0.8900	0.8396	0.7921	0.7473
15. PV of leasing cash flows (13) × (14)	$ 1580	$ 1491	$ 1406	$ 1327	$ 1252
16. Purchase option price	—	—	—	—	715
17. PV tax savings from purchase	—	—	—	—	(238)
18. Net impact from purchase option	356	—	—	—	—
19. Total PV cost of leasing	7412				

III. Cost Comparison

Net advantage to leasing: Total PV cost of owning − Total PV cost of leasing = $8025 − $7412 = $613.

Line-by-Line Explanation of Lines

1. Determined as explained in the text.
2. Calculated as 10 percent of the prior year's remaining balance. Initially, the remaining balance (at Year 0) is $10 million, so the first year's interest is 0.1($10 000 000) = $1 000 000, written here as $1000.
3. The loan payment minus the interest component; for example, $2 638 000 − $1 000 000 = $1 638 000 in Year 1.
4. Calculated as the remaining balance from the prior year minus the principal repayment: for example, $10 000 000 − $1 638 000 = $8 632 000 in Year 1.
5. From line 1; this represents a cash flow.
6. Calculated as Interest(Tax rate) = Interest(0.40). This amount is shown as a negative because it reduces outflows. To look at the point another way: the after-tax cost of interest in Year 1 is $1 000 000 − $400 000 = $600 000. We included the $1 000 000 on line 2, so we must subtract the $400 000 here.
7. Pretax maintenance costs are $500 000 per year, so after-tax costs are $500 000(1 − T) = $500 000(0.60) = $300 000 per year.
8. Calculated as line 5 + line 6 + line 7. Notice these amounts do not reflect CCA.
9. Values, based on the 6 percent after-tax cost of debt, taken from Table A-1 of the insert card.
10. Calculated as line 8 times line 9.
11. The tax savings, assuming that the purchased asset will not be sold. The value has a negative sign (it is a cash inflow) because it reduces the taxes that have to be paid by the firm.
12. Calculated as the sum of the items on line 10 (that is, the cash flow for each year) plus line 11.
13. After-tax value, calculated as in text.
14. Same as in Line 9.
15. Calculated as line 13 times line 14.
16. As stated in the text. The amount is a cash outflow in Year 5 since the firm plans to exercise its option to purchase the asset.
17. Tax savings from future CCA charges after Year 5. The value in the table is measured at the end of Year 5 (or the beginning of Year 6).
18. Calculated as the present value of the sum of the entries in Line 16 and Line 17: ($715 000 $PVIF_{6\%, 5}$) − ($238 000 $PVIF_{6\%, 5}$) = [($715 000)(0.7473)] − [($238 000)(0.7473)] = $534 320 − $177 857 = $356 463, which is rounded and represented as $356.
19. Calculated as the sum of the entries in line 15 (that is, the PV of the leasing cash flow in each year) plus line 18.

All cash flows occur at the end of the year, and the CF$_t$ values are shown on lines 10 and 11 for borrowing to purchase and line 17 for leasing respectively.

Section I of the table is devoted to the costs of borrowing and buying. This section identifies not only the cost of financing the acquisition but also the interest payments, which generate a tax saving. Lines 1 to 4 provide the loan amortization schedule. Lines 5 to 7 show the individual cash outflow items; note that the interest tax savings are shown as negative values, because they are actually cash inflows savings resulting from the deductibility of interest expense. Line 8 summarizes the annual net cash outflows, except CCA expenses, that Monroe will incur if it finances the equipment with a loan. The present values of these outflows are found by multiplying each cash flow by the appropriate present value interest factor shown on line 9. The annual present values are given in line 10.

To completely specify all cash flows associated with the purchase, the tax savings associated with the CCA charges must be identified. Since it is anticipated that Monroe will continue to use the machine beyond the 5 years and there will be no salvage value when it is finally sold, the present value of the tax savings from the purchase, as at Year 1, is calculated and presented in line 11 under the Year 1 column. The value is estimated from the present value of tax savings formula:

$$\text{PVTS} = \left(\frac{tdC_0}{k + d}\right) \left(\frac{2 + k}{2(1 + k)}\right)$$

Substituting in the values for the variables and using a value for k equal to the after-tax cost of debt of 6 percent, we estimate an amount of \$3 239 000. Note that since this is a tax saving (a cash inflow), it is identified as a negative amount. The sum of the annual present values of all non-CCA cash flows plus the present value of the tax savings in line 12 equals the present value of the cost of owning, which is shown on line 12 in the Year 1 column.

Section II of the table calculates the present value of the cost of leasing. The lease payments are \$2 791 670 per year; this amount, which in this example but not in all cases includes maintenance, was established by the prospective lessor and offered to Monroe Manufacturing. If Monroe accepts the lease, the full \$2 791 670 will be a tax-deductible expense, so the after-tax cost of the lease can be calculated as follows:

$$
\begin{aligned}
\text{After-tax cost} &= \text{Lease payment} - \text{Tax savings} \\
&= \text{Lease payment} - (\text{Tax rate})(\text{Lease payment}) \\
&= \text{Lease payment}(1 - \text{Tax rate}) \\
&= \$2\,791\,670(1 - 0.4) \\
&= \$1\,675\,002.
\end{aligned}
$$

This amount is shown on line 13.

Line 14 in the lease section presents the present value factors, and the present values of the lease payments are shown in line 15. Line 16 shows the \$715 000 that Monroe Manufacturing would pay in Year 5 to purchase the equipment. We include this amount as a cost of leasing because Monroe will almost certainly want to continue the operation and thus will be forced to purchase the equipment from the lessor. This will generate tax savings based on CCA charges beginning in Year 6. The present value of the tax savings generated from the purchase are included in the leasing option cash flow in line 17 for Year 5. The calculation of this value is demonstrated below.

If we had assumed that the operation would not be continued, then no entry would appear in lines 16 and 17. However, in that case, we would have included the $715 000 as a Year 5 inflow (that is, as a negative value) in the purchase analysis because if the asset were purchased originally, it would be sold after 5 years. (It would be subtracted because it would then be an inflow, whereas all other cash flows are outflows.) In addition, the present value of tax savings in line 11, Year 1 would have to be reduced by the present value of the lost tax savings from the sale of the asset in Year 5. Line 17 shows the present value of the CCA tax savings as *at the end of Year 5* based on the cost of the acquisition in Year 5.

The net impact on the cash flows from the purchase option is presented in line 18 and is equal to the sum of the present value of the effects in lines 16 and 17. Line 19 is the PV cost of leasing and is equal to the sum of the present values of leasing cash flows in line 15 plus the net impact from the purchase option.

The present value of the tax savings at the end of Year 5 is equal to the present value of the CCA tax savings based on the purchase price in Year 5. The formula used is as follows:

$$\text{PV tax savings} = \frac{tdS}{k + d}$$

$$= \frac{(0.4)(0.3)(\$715\,000)}{0.6 + 0.30}$$

$$= \$238\,000.$$

The net impact value is the present value of the Year 5 cash flows in lines 16 and 17. This is the net impact from the purchase option and is equal to:

$$\$715\,000 \times \frac{1}{(1.06)^5} - 238\,000 \times \frac{1}{(1.06)^5} = \$356\,453.$$

The rate used to discount the cash flows is a critical issue. In Chapter 15 we saw that the riskier the cash flow, the higher the discount rate used to find its present value. This same principle was observed in our discussion of capital budgeting, and it also applies in lease analysis. Just how risky are the cash flows under consideration here? Most of them are relatively certain, at least when compared with the types of cash flow estimates that were developed in capital budgeting. For example, the loan payment schedule is set by contract, as is the lease payment schedule. The capital cost allowance charges are also established by law and are not subject to change, and the $500 000 annual maintenance cost is fixed by contract as well. The tax savings are somewhat uncertain, but they will be as projected so long as Monroe's effective tax rate remains at 40 percent. The residual value is the least certain of the cash flows, but even here Monroe's management is fairly confident that it will want to acquire the property and also that the cost of doing so will be close to $715 000.

Since the cash flows under both the lease and the borrow-and-purchase alternatives are all relatively certain, they can be discounted at a relatively low rate. Most analysts recommend that the company's cost of debt be used, and this rate seems reasonable in our example. Further, since all the cash flows are on an after-tax basis, the *after-tax* cost of debt, which is 6 percent, should be used. The financing method that produces the smaller present value of costs is the one that should be selected. For our example, Table 23-2 indicates that leasing has a net advantage over buying. The present value of the costs of leasing is $613 000 less than that of buying. In this instance, it is to Monroe Manufacturing's advantage to lease.

Additional Influences on the Leasing versus Owning Decision

A number of other factors can influence the user firm's costs of leasing versus owning capital assets. These include: (1) different costs of capital for the lessor versus the user firm, (2) higher financing costs in leasing, (3) differences in maintenance costs, (4) the benefits of residual values to the owner of the assets, (5) the possibility of reducing obsolescence costs by the leasing firms, and (6) the possibility of increased credit availability under leasing. A number of arguments exist with respect to the advantages and disadvantages of leasing, given these factors. Many of the arguments carry with them implicit assumptions that are not reasonable in a competitive leasing market.

Different Costs of Capital. If the lessor has a lower cost of capital than the user, the cost of leasing is likely to be lower than the cost of owning, and vice versa. It is difficult, however, to formulate the conditions under which the cost of capital would be different except for differential tax effects. Since it is the risk of the project in which the asset is used that determines the applicable cost of capital, why should the risk be different if the owner is a lessor rather than a user?

Financing Costs Higher in Leasing. A similar view is that leasing always involves higher implicit financing costs than owning. This argument is also of doubtful validity. It is difficult to separate the money costs of leasing from the other services embodied in a leasing contract. If, because of its specialized operations, the leasing company can perform nonfinancial services (such as maintenance of the equipment) at a lower cost than either the lessee or some other institution can perform them, then the effective cost of leasing may be lower than the cost of funds obtained from borrowing or other sources. The efficiencies of performing specialized services may thus enable the leasing company to operate by charging a lower total cost than the lessee would have to pay for the package of money plus services on any other basis.

Differences in Maintenance Costs. Another argument frequently encountered is that because leasing involves no explicit maintenance costs it may be less expensive than owning. However, maintenance costs are included in the lease-rental rate. The key question is whether the maintenance can be performed at a lower cost by the lessor or by an independent firm that specializes in performing maintenance on capital assets of the type involved. Whether the costs will differ depends on the industries and particular firms involved.

Residual Values. The lessor owns the property at the expiration of the lease. The estimated value of the property when the lease expires is called the

residual value. Superficially, it seems that if residual values are large, owning should have an advantage over leasing. However, if expected residual values are large, then competition among leasing companies will force leasing rates down to the point at which potential residual values are fully recognized in the lease contract rates. Thus, the existence of residual values on equipment is not likely to bias the decision against leasing.

In decisions about whether to lease or to own land, however, the obsolescence factor is involved only to the extent of deterioration in areas with changing population or use patterns. In a period of optimistic expectations about land values, there may be a tendency to overestimate their rates of increase. As a consequence, the current purchase of land may involve a price so high that the probable rate of return on owned land will be relatively small. Under this condition, leasing may well represent the more economical way of obtaining the use of land. Conversely, if the probable increase in land values is not fully reflected in current prices, it will be advantageous to own the land.

It is difficult to generalize about whether residual value considerations are likely to make the effective cost of leasing higher or lower than the cost of owning. The results depend on whether the individual firm has opportunities to take advantage of optimistic or pessimistic evaluations of future value changes by the market as a whole and whether the firm or market is correct on average.

Obsolescence Costs. Another popular notion is that leasing costs will be lower than buying costs because of the rapid obsolescence of some kinds of equipment. It is argued that by having a lease with a very short life, the risk of obsolescence can be shifted to the lessor—the lessee does not have to bear the risk of holding an obsolete asset. Unfortunately, this argument is not very persuasive. The lessor will not bear this obsolescence risk without appropriate compensation through a higher rate of return. Thus, the lease payments will reflect the high rate of obsolescence, and the lessee pays for this risk. In general, it might be argued that obsolescence rates do not affect the cost of owning versus leasing.

It is possible, however, that leasing companies may be better equipped than the lessee to handle the obsolescence problem. If the leased equipment becomes obsolete to one user, the leasing company may find other companies for which this equipment is still useful. The lessor is equipped to engage in this redirection of assets among user companies. If the user company purchased the asset and it became obsolete, it might be very costly to find other companies that could make use of the equipment. The lessor company reduces the economic cost of obsolescence by increasing the effective residual value of the equipment. Part of this benefit will be passed along to the lessee by means of reduced lease payments. Therefore, leasing may be preferred to an outright purchase because the economic costs of obsolescence are lower.

Increased Credit Availability. As noted earlier, leasing is sometimes said to have an advantage for firms seeking the maximum degree of financial leverage. First, it is sometimes argued that firms can obtain more money and for a longer period under a lease arrangement than under a loan secured by the asset. Second, since some leases do not appear on the balance sheet, lease financing has been said to give the firm a stronger appearance in a *superficial* credit analysis, thus permitting it to use more leverage than it could if it did not lease. There may be some truth to these claims for smaller firms. However, now that larger firms are required to capitalize major leases and report them on their balance sheets, this point is of questionable validity.

Concept Review

▶ Why is it appropriate to compare the cost of lease financing with that of debt financing?

▶ Why does the comparison above not depend on how the asset will actually be financed if it is not leased?

▶ List six additional factors that are often identified as relevant to a leasing decision. Briefly evaluate the impact, if any, each should have on the leasing decision.

Summary

The key concepts covered in this chapter are listed below.

□ Leasing is a means of obtaining the use of an asset without purchasing that asset. The three most important forms of leasing are: (1) **sale-and-leaseback arrangements**, under which a firm sells an asset to another party and leases the asset back for a specified period under specific terms, (2) **operating leases**, under which the lessor both maintains and finances the asset, and (3) **financial leases** or *capital leases*, under which the asset is fully amortized over the life of the lease, the lessor does not normally provide maintenance, and the lease is not cancelable.

□ Leasing sometimes represents *off balance sheet* financing, which permits firms to obtain more financial leverage if they employ leasing than if they use straight debt to finance the purchase of the asset. With the requirement to *capitalize* financial or capital leases and show their values on the firm's balance sheets, this justification for leasing has less force.

□ The *decision whether to lease or to buy an asset* is made by comparing the financing costs of the two alternatives and choosing the financing method with the lower cost. All cash flows should be discounted at the *after-tax cost of debt*, because lease analysis cash flows are relatively certain and are on an after-tax basis.

Questions

23-1 Distinguish between *operating leases* and *financial leases*. Would you be more likely to find an operating lease employed for a fleet of trucks or for a manufacturing plant?

23-2 Are lessees likely to be in higher or lower income tax brackets than lessors?

23-3 Leasing is often called a hedge against obsolescence. Under what conditions is this actually true?

23-4 One alleged advantage of leasing voiced in the past was that it kept liabilities off the balance sheet, thus making it possible for a firm to obtain more leverage than it otherwise could have. This raised the question of whether both the lease obligation and the asset involved should be capitalized and shown on the balance sheet. Discuss the pros and cons of capitalizing leases and related assets.

23-5   Suppose there were no income tax restrictions on what constituted a valid lease. Explain, in a manner a legislator might understand, why some restrictions should be imposed.

23-6   Suppose new tax laws were enacted that would (a) permit equipment to be depreciated for tax purposes over a shorter period, (b) lower corporate tax rates, and (c) reinstate the investment tax credit. Discuss how each of these potential changes would affect the relative volume of leasing (versus conventional debt) in the Canadian economy.

Self-Test Problems   (solutions appear on page 895)

ST-1   **Key terms.**   Define each of the following terms:
   a. Lessee; lessor
   b. Operating lease; financial lease; capital lease; sale and leaseback
   c. "Off balance sheet" financing; lease capitalization
   d. Residual value; salvage value
   e. Lease analysis

ST-2   **Lease or buy.**   The Nelson Company has decided to acquire a new truck. One alternative is to lease the truck on a 4-year contract for a lease payment of $9600 per year, with payments to be made at the end of each year. The lease includes maintenance, which would cost $1000 per year, payable at year-end, if contracted separately. Alternatively, Nelson can purchase the truck outright for $40 000, financing the purchase by a bank loan for the full purchase price. The loan would be amortized over the 4-year period at an interest rate of 10 percent per year, with payments to be made at the end of the year. The truck has a CCA rate of 30 percent, and it has a salvage value of $10 000, which is the expected market value after 4 years. Nelson intends to replace the truck regardless of whether it leases or buys. Nelson has a tax rate of 40 percent.
   a. What is Nelson's present value cost of leasing?
   b. What is Nelson's present value cost of owning? Should the truck be leased or purchased?
   c. Typically, lease payments are made at the *beginning* of the year. Redo Part a assuming that Nelson would have to make them at the beginning of the year. Does this affect the lease–buy decision?
   d. The appropriate discount rate for use in Nelson's analysis is the firm's after-tax cost of debt. Why?
   e. The salvage value is the least certain cash flow in the analysis. How might Nelson incorporate its higher riskiness into the analysis?

Problems

23-1   **Determining lease payment.**   Sunspot Leasing, Ltd., which specializes in business financing in the Vancouver area, is setting up a financial lease with Park Stadium, Ltd. The lease will cover ice machines, pizza ovens, popcorn poppers, and cola dispensers that have a total cost of $350 000. The lease runs for 5 years. What is the annual lease payment based on a 10 percent interest rate? (Ten percent is simply the rate used to establish the lease payments; it is not the rate of return to the lessor.)

23-2 **Impact on financial statements.** Two industrial machine manufacturing companies, Clark Machinery and Stockton Machine Shop, began operations with identical balance sheets. A year later, both required additional manufacturing capacity at a cost of $200 000. Clark Machinery obtained a 5-year, $200 000 loan at an 8 percent interest rate from its bank. Stockton decided to lease the required $200 000 capacity from Leasing Canada for 5 years; an 8 percent return was built into the lease. The balance sheet for each company, before the asset increases, is as follows:

	Debt	$200 000
	Equity	200 000
Total assets $400 000	Total claims	$400 000

a. Show the balance sheets for both firms after the asset increase, and calculate each firm's debt ratio.
b. Show how Stockton's balance sheet will look immediately after the financing if it capitalizes the lease.
c. Is the rate of return on (i) assets and (ii) equity affected by the choice of financing? How?

23-3 **Lease or buy.** Bradley Steel Company Ltd. must install $1.5 million of new machinery in its Hamilton steel plant. It can obtain a bank loan for 100 percent of the required amount. Alternatively, a Toronto investment firm, which represents a group of dentists, believes that it can arrange for a lease financing plan. Assume that these facts apply:
- The equipment falls in a class for which the applicable CCA rate is 30 percent.
- Estimated maintenance expenses are $75 000 per year.
- Bradley's tax rate is 40 percent.
- If the money is borrowed, the bank loan will be at a rate of 15 percent, amortized in three equal installments, each payable at the end of the year.
- The tentative lease terms call for payments of $480 000 per year for 3 years.
- Under the proposed lease terms, the lessee must pay for insurance, property taxes, and maintenance.
- Bradley must use the equipment if it is to continue in business, so it will almost certainly want to acquire the property at the end of the lease. If it does, then under the lease terms it can purchase the machinery at its fair market value at that time. The best estimate of this market value is the $325 000 salvage value, but it could be much higher or lower under certain circumstances.

To assist management in making the proper lease-versus-buy decision, you are asked to answer the following questions:

a. Assuming that the lease can be arranged, should Bradley lease or borrow and buy the equipment? Explain your answer.

b. Consider the $325 000 estimated salvage value. Is it appropriate to discount it at the same rate as the other cash flows? What about the other cash flows—are they all equally risky? (Hint: Riskier cash flows are normally discounted at higher rates, but when the cash flows are *costs* rather than *inflows*, the normal procedure must be reversed.)

23-4 Lease or buy. As part of its overall plant modernization and cost reduction program, Quebec Mills' management has decided to install a new automated weaving loom. In the capital budgeting analysis of this potential equipment, the IRR of the project was found to be 20 percent versus a required return for the project of 12 percent.

The loom has an invoice price of $250 000, including delivery and installation charges. The net financing requirement, if Quebec Mills borrows the funds, will be the purchase price. The funds needed can be borrowed from the bank on a 4-year amortized loan at a 10 percent interest rate, with payments to be made at the end of each year. The manufacturer will maintain and service the loom, in the event that it is purchased, for a fee of $20 000 per year payable at the end of each year. The loom has a CCA rate of 10 percent, and Quebec Mills' marginal tax rate is 40 percent.

Simard Automation, Ltd., maker of the loom, has offered to lease the loom to Quebec Mills for $50 000 upon delivery and installation (at t = 0) plus 4 additional annual lease payments of $50 000 to be made at the end of Years 1 through 4. (Note that there are 5 lease payments in total.) The lease agreement includes maintenance and servicing. Actually, the loom has an expected life of 8 years, at which time its expected salvage value is zero. However, after 4 years, its expected market value equals its undepreciated capital cost. Quebec Mills plans to build an entire new plant in 4 years, so it has no interest in either leasing or owning Simard's loom for more than that period.

a. Should the loom be leased or purchased?

b. The salvage value is clearly the most uncertain cash flow in the analysis. What effect would a salvage value risk adjustment have on the decision? (Assume that the appropriate salvage value discount rate is 15 percent.)

c. The original analysis assumed that Quebec Mills will not need the loom after 4 years. Now assume that the firm will continue to use the loom after the lease expires. Thus, if it leases, Quebec Mills will have to buy the asset after 4 years at the then-existing market value, which is assumed to equal the undepreciated capital cost. What effect would this requirement have on the basic analysis?

Integrative Problem

23-5 Lease or buy. Martha Millon, capital acquisitions manager for Heath Financial Services, Inc., has been asked to perform a lease-versus-buy analysis on a new share price quotation system for Heath's Regina branch office. The system would receive current prices, record the information for retrieval by the branch's brokers, and display current prices in the lobby.

The equipment costs $1 200 000, and, if it is purchased, Heath could obtain a term loan for the full amount at a 10 percent cost. The loan would be amortized over the 4-year life of the equipment, with payments made at the end of each year. The equipment falls into CCA class 10, with a rate of 30 percent. If the equipment is purchased, a maintenance contract must be obtained at a cost of $25 000, payable at the end of each year.

After 4 years the equipment will be sold, and Millon's best estimate of its residual value at that time is $125 000. Because technology is changing rapidly in real-time display systems, however, the residual value is very uncertain.

As an alternative, National Leasing is willing to write a 4-year lease on the equipment, including maintenance, for payments of $340 000 at the end of each year. Heath's marginal tax rate is 40 percent. Help Millon conduct her analysis by answering the following questions:

a. i. Why is leasing sometimes referred to as *off balance sheet* financing?
  ii. What effect does leasing have on a firm's capital structure?
b. i. What is Heath's present value cost of owning the equipment?
  ii. Explain the rationale for the discount rate you used.
c. i. What is Heath's present value cost of leasing the equipment?
  ii. What is the net advantage to leasing? Should Heath buy or lease the equipment?
d. What would be the impact on the lease-versus-buy decision if the maintenance payments and lease payments had to be made at the *beginning* of the year?
e. Now assume that Millon believes the equipment's residual value could be as low as $0 or as high as $250 000, but she stands by $125 000 as her expected value. She concludes that the residual value is riskier than the other cash flows in the analysis, and she wants to incorporate this differential risk into her analysis. Describe how this can be accomplished. What effect will it have on Heath's lease decision?
f. Millon knows that her firm has been considering moving to a new downtown location for some time, and she is concerned that these plans may come to fruition prior to the expiration of the lease. If the move occurs, the company will obtain completely new equipment. Hence Millon would like to include a cancellation clause in the lease contract. What effect would a cancellation clause have on the riskiness of the lease?

Solutions to Self-Test Problems

ST-1   Refer to the appropriate sections of the text to check your responses.

ST-2 $k_d = (1 - 0.4)(10) = 6\%$.

    a. The cost of leasing is calculated as follows. Note that, according to the problem, the payments will be due at the year-end. The tax shields will be realized at the same time.

Year	Payment	Tax Savings	Total	PVIF	PV
1	$9600	$3840	$5760	0.9434	$5 434
2	9600	3840	5760	0.8900	5 126
3	9600	3840	5760	0.8396	4 836
4	9600	3840	5760	0.7921	4 562
					$19 959

    The PV of leasing is $19 959.

    b. The PV of owning is calculated as

$$PV \text{ to own} = C_0 + \sum_{t=1}^{n} \frac{\text{Additional expense after tax}}{(1+k)^t} - PV_{\text{tax saving}}$$

$$PV_{\text{tax saving}} = \frac{TC_0 d}{k+d} \cdot \frac{2+k}{2(1+k)} + \frac{S}{(1+k)^n} \left[1 - \frac{Td}{k+d} \right]$$

$$PV \text{ of owning} = \$40000 + \sum_{t=1}^{4} \frac{1000(1-0.4)}{1.06^t} - \left[\frac{0.4(0.30)(\$40000)}{0.06+0.30} \left(\frac{2.06}{2.12} \right) \right]$$

$$- \frac{\$10000}{(1.06)^4} \left[1 - \frac{0.4(0.30)}{0.06+0.30} \right]$$

$$= \$40000 + \$2179 - \$12\,956 - \$5281$$

$$= \$23\,842.$$

    The present value of owning is $23 842. The present value of leasing is the lesser amount, so Nelson should lease.

    c. In this scenario, although the tax savings are still realized at year-end, the lease payments are made at the beginning of each year. Thus, the calculation is:

Year	Payment	Tax Savings	Total	PVIF	PV
0	$9600		$9600	1.0000	$9 600
1	9600	$3840	5760	0.9434	5 434
2	9600	3840	5760	0.8900	5 126
3	9600	3840	5760	0.8396	4 836
4		3840	(3840)	0.7921	(3 042)
					$21 955

    The PV of leasing is $21955. This amount is higher than the one found in Part a. It is still cheaper to lease, however.

d. Because the decision to buy the truck has already been made, we are really only looking at how to finance it. Since the certainty of the lease payment tax shields is equivalent to the interest tax shields, we use the after-tax cost of debt as the discount rate when comparing the alternatives.

e. Adjust the salvage value to reflect its certainty equivalent *or* adjust the discount rate upward to reflect the added risk. (Adjust only the discount rate for the salvage value, not the other cash flows.)

VII

INTEGRATED TOPICS IN MANAGERIAL FINANCE

24

Corporate Restructurings: Mergers, Takeovers, and Divestitures

A Managerial Perspective

Over the period 1983 to 1989, many companies in North America were actively engaged in the merger and takeover market at both the domestic and international levels. In Canada and to a greater extent in the United States, these transactions were often financed with a significant amount of debt. In fact, the availability of highly leveraged financing permitted a relatively small company to take over a much larger one. The onset of the recession has dramatically slowed merger and acquisition activity and changed its characteristics. Whereas prior to the recession the key to these transactions was profitable growth opportunities, now they are often the result of bankruptcy or serious financial problems. Companies are now concerned with their financial viability, and part of this concern is reflected in their attempts to reduce the debt in their capital structure. The focus of corporate transactions is now on the dismantling of corporate asset structures, frequently to generate cash to pay down debt. (An associated benefit is that managerial interest tends to focus on the remaining operations.) Daily the newspapers report this activity, which has affected even the largest companies: for example, BCE, John Labatt, and Southam, among others, have been involved in asset restructurings.

In this chapter we examine the rationale for mergers and other business combinations and emphasize the importance of making a thorough analysis before the combination takes place. In addition, we discuss asset restructurings, including mergers, tender offers, divestitures, and leveraged buyouts.

Mergers and Takeovers

Technically, a **merger** is a business combination that creates one economic unit from two or more previously independent ones; the managements of all participating companies approve the arrangement. A **takeover** accomplishes the same end, but the management of one or more participants may be hostile to the change. Following contemporary practice, we use the term *merger* for both situations throughout most of the chapter. Takeovers are, however, discussed specifically in one section.

Mergers and takeovers, as methods of reorganizing industrial structure, are important economic events. Table 24-1 summarizes merger activity in Canada

Table 24-1
Mergers in Canada, 1985–1990

Date	Announcements (number) (1)	Completed Transactions ($ billions) (2)	Median Value ($ millions) (3)
1985	1042	15	8.3
1986	1198	19	10.0
1987	1363	28	8.8
1988	1301	24	6.4
1989	1208	30	10.3
1990	828	20	9.0

Source: *Directory of Mergers and Acquisitions in Canada: 1990* (Toronto: Crosbie & Company Inc., 1990). Used with permission.

over the period 1985 to 1990. The number of merger announcements (column 1) peaked in 1987, and there was sharp decline in 1990, reflecting the beginning of the recession. Column 2 lists the total dollar value of completed deals; this figure is sensitive to the number of large deals that are actually undertaken in any one year since the median value of deals (column 3) is usually low. In 1990, by far the largest number of deals were in the less than $5 million category (132 deals) and the $5 to $10 million category (55 deals). However, these two categories accounted for less than 5 percent of the value of merger transactions in that year; 7 large deals (more than $5 million) accounted for approximately 50 percent of the value.

The recession has reduced but not eliminated mergers and acquisitions in the economy. The transactions reflect mergers of bankrupt companies, sales of divisions of firms that require cash to pay down debt, and an increasing number of *management buyouts,* in which the incumbent management of a division buys the division from the parent company.

There has been some research to explain the observed cyclical pattern of mergers over time and why certain industries are affected more than others. It has been suggested that the reorganization activities reflect: (1) withdrawal of resources from industries that are shrinking or growing more slowly than the economy, (2) deregulation in financial services, (3) improvements in takeover technology, and (4) changes in technology within the industry. Thus the different restructuring activity observed by industry category reflects the importance of these elements.

Types of Mergers

Economists classify mergers into four groups: (1) horizontal, (2) vertical, (3) congeneric, and (4) conglomerate. A **horizontal merger** occurs when one firm combines with another in the same line of business; Westcoast Energy Inc.'s proposed acquisition of Union Energy Inc. is an example of a horizontal merger. A **vertical merger** occurs when a company acquires either one of its own suppliers or a user of its product; a steel producer may acquire an iron or coal mining firm, and an oil producer may acquire a petrochemical company. An example of a vertical merger in the second category is the acquisition by PetroCanada, which produces gas, of the distribution network of Gulf Canada. Congeneric means "allied in nature or action"; hence, a **congeneric merger** involves enterprises that are related but are not producers of the same product (as in a horizontal merger) or firms in a producer-supplier relationship (as in a vertical merger). An example of a congeneric merger is the Royal Bank's acquisition of Dominion Securities. A **conglomerate merger** occurs when unrelated enterprises combine; the merger of Onex and Beatrice Foods, Canada illustrates a conglomerate merger.

Operating economies (and anticompetitive effects) are at least partially dependent on the type of merger involved. Vertical and horizontal mergers generally provide the greatest operating benefits, but they are also the ones most likely to be attacked by the Bureau of Competition Policy under the provisions of the *Competition Act*. (The Bureau of Competition Policy is part of Consumer and Corporate Affairs Canada.) In any event, it is useful to think of these economic categories when analyzing the feasibility of a prospective merger.

Concept Review

▶ Explain briefly the four economic classifications of mergers.

Procedures for Combining Firms

In the vast majority of merger situations, one firm (generally the larger of the two) simply decides to buy another company, negotiates a price, and then acquires that target company. Occasionally the acquired firm will initiate the action, but it is much more common for a firm to seek acquisitions than to seek to be acquired.[1] Following convention, we shall call a company that seeks to acquire another the *acquiring company* and the one that it seeks to acquire the *target company*.

Once an acquiring company has identified a potential target, it must establish a suitable price, or range of prices, that it is willing to pay. With this in mind, the acquiring firm's managers must decide how to approach the target company's managers. If the acquiring firm has reason to believe the target company's management will approve the merger, then it simply proposes a merger and tries to work out suitable terms. If an agreement can be reached, the two management groups issue statements to their shareholders recommending that they approve the merger. Assuming that the shareholders do approve, the acquiring firm simply buys the target company's shares from its shareholders, paying with its own shares (in which case the target company's

---

[1]However, if a firm is in financial difficulty, if the managers are elderly and do not feel that suitable replacements to run the company are on hand, or if the firm needs the support (often the capital) of a larger company, then it may seek to be acquired.

shareholders become shareholders of the acquiring company), with cash, or with a combination of the two. Such a transaction is called a **friendly merger** and is by far the most frequent type of merger transaction.

Under other circumstances, the target company's management may resist the merger. Perhaps the managers believe that the price offered for the shares is too low, or perhaps they simply want to keep their jobs. In either case, the target firm's management is said to be hostile rather than friendly, and in a **hostile merger**, the acquiring firm must make a direct appeal to the target firm's shareholders. In a hostile merger, the acquiring company generally makes a *tender offer*, in which it asks the shareholders of the firm it is seeking to control to submit ("tender") their shares in exchange for a specified price. The price is generally stated as so many dollars per share of the shares to be acquired, although it can be stated in terms of shares of equity of the acquiring firm. Since this tender offer is a direct appeal to shareholders, it permits the acquirer to purchase the company even if the incumbent management is hostile to the offer. The tender is often called a *takeover bid*.[2]

Concept Review

▶ Differentiate between the *acquiring company* and the *target company* in a merger situation.

▶ How do the acquiring firm's actions in a hostile merger attempt differ from those in a friendly merger attempt?

Techniques of Completing a Merger

The choice of technique used in the merger will depend upon the impact of a number of legal and tax issues on the merging firms. In this section, we describe the merger techniques available.

1. *Acquisition of the Assets.*   The acquired company's assets, both fixed and current, are purchased for either cash or shares. The acquired company does not disappear as a result of the acquisition, but it is left with a considerable amount of cash as its only asset. The company then decides whether to pay its shareholders a liquidating dividend and wind up operations or to use the cash to purchase shares in a number of corporations —that is, to become a holding company. Under the federal and most provincial corporations acts, the shareholders of the acquired company must vote on the terms of the purchase. The terms are the result of involved negotiations between the managements of the merging firms. If there are any dissenting shareholders, they have an *appraisal right*; this provides them with the right to have the acquiring company purchase their shares at an appraised price.

---

[2]Tender offers can also be friendly, with the target firm's management recommending that the shareholder tender their shares. They are discussed in more detail in a subsequent section of this chapter.

2. *Acquisition of the shares.*   The most common technique to effect a merger is through the acquisition of shares. The method of payment for them can be cash, shares of the acquiring company, or a combination. When purchasing the shares, the acquiring company obtains not only the assets but also all the liabilities.

3. *Amalgamation.*   An amalgamation occurs when two or more companies form one corporate entity based on statutory provisions of the appropriate corporations act. The terms of the amalgamation must be voted on by shareholders of all companies in the amalgamation. The terms are determined by negotiations of the managements involved. Finally, an appraisal right for dissenting shareholders also exists under this technique.

Concept Review

▶ Describe the three methods by which a merger can be completed.

Motivations for Merger

A merger can be considered as a value-maximizing decision for the acquiring company; therefore, the acquirer must identify those potential merger partners whose acquisition would result in an increase in earnings (or cash flows) over and above those that derive from the acquired company as an independent entity. In this section, we describe the conditions under which these incremental earnings are most likely to occur. In the next section, we shall investigate the price that will be paid for the acquired firm.

Economic Motivations

A substantial amount of financial literature has been written on mergers, and many aspects of mergers have been studied. The studies have identified four general motivations for mergers.

Synergy.   The primary motivation for most mergers is to increase the value of the combined enterprise. If Companies A and B merge to form Company C and if C's value exceeds that of A and B taken separately, then **synergy** is said to exist.[3] Synergistic influences arise in two general ways. First, as the firm grows in size, its costs grow less than proportionally. This is referred to as *operating economies of scale* in management, production, and/or distribution and results in increased cash flows. An example of this benefit the increased efficiency derived from integrating small plants. This type of synergistic effect occurs predominantly in horizontal mergers.[4] Second, there may be imperfect markets

---

[3] If synergy exists, the whole is greater than the sum of the parts. Synergy is also referred to as the "2 plus 2 equals 5 effect." The distribution of the synergistic gain between A's and B's shareholders is determined by negotiation, a point to be discussed later in the chapter.

[4] Another possible benefit from horizontal mergers is the acquisition of monopoly power. If this type of merger is not stopped by anticombines legislation, then postmerger profits will be higher than the sum of premerger profits. This is not a result of synergy.

in the purchase and sale of certain assets, such as management expertise, personnel, production facilities, and marketing. A merger may permit a more efficient use of such an asset and hence result in higher profits. For example, suppose Company A hires a management team that turns out to be so efficient that there is excess capacity. Company A would have preferred to pay only for the services needed to run its company, but the market is imperfect—Company A had to buy all of the management services or none. In this case, a merger will permit fuller use of the services of the management team without any increase in cost. This will result in an increase in profits to the acquirer in excess of the profits of the acquired firm. Of course, the excess capacity in the specialized assets may be found in the acquired company. For example, a merger may result in the acquisition of a technically competent scientific or engineering staff that is required by the acquiring company. Or the acquirer may need to develop an effective sales organization to make up for a lack of an industrial sales organization and find that merger is a solution to this problem.[5]

Purchase of Assets below Their Replacement Cost.   Sometimes a firm becomes an acquisition candidate because the replacement value of its assets is considerably higher than its market value. For example, in the 1980s oil companies could acquire reserves more cheaply by buying out other oil companies than by exploratory drilling.

The acquisition of Federated Department Stores by Campeau Corporation, a Toronto-based real estate development firm, is another illustration of an acquisition that took place because the share price of the company being acquired (Federated) did not reflect its true market value. Federated at the time was the largest department store chain in the United States, but its performance had been lacklustre in recent years, and its share price had fallen by more than 50 percent. However, steps taken by Federated were finally beginning to pay off, and earnings were rising. Federated had some of the best-known names in retailing, and it had acquired its buildings years before at low prices. Thus, the company was an attractive takeover target. As a result, Campeau Corporation and R.H. Macy & Company (a long-time rival of Federated) made separate bids for control of Federated. Campeau was primarily interested in acquiring Federated's undervalued real estate assets, while Macy saw the situation as an opportunity to merge the operations of the two retailing chains to gain economies of scale in purchasing and operations. Eventually, Campeau and Macy joined forces, and their plan was to acquire Federated and then split up the company. This merger was highly leveraged: it was financed using 97 percent debt. Campeau sold off approximately 50 percent of the assets for an amount equal to approximately 90 percent of the value of the company before the acquisition was announced. Subsequent economic events and the inability to meet the large payments required on its loans resulted in bankruptcy. At the end of 1993, there was still litigation by creditors over some of Robert Campeau's personal assets.

---

[5]If the managers of the target or acquired firm agree to the terms of the merger, it is unlikely that they will lose their jobs after the merger. Thus, any gains that might have arisen by replacing inefficient management will not be available. Alternatively, the acquired firm's managers may have been given a large settlement to remove their hostility to the merger.

Financial Motivations

Diversification.   Managers often claim that diversification helps to stabilize the firm's earnings stream and thus to reduce corporate risk. Therefore, diversification is often given as a reason for mergers. Stabilization of earnings is certainly beneficial to a firm's employees, suppliers, customers, and managers, but its value to shareholders is less clear. If an investor is worried about earnings variability, he or she can diversify through equity purchases for a portfolio more easily and certainly more cheaply than the firms can through acquisitions. Therefore, why should Firms A and B merge to stabilize earnings when shareholders in Firm A could sell half of their equity in it and use the proceeds to purchase equity in Firm B? In fact, if the company pays a premium to acquire companies, there could be a negative impact on the share price of the acquirer. The risk reduction will reduce the default risk on the company's debt, however, and this will be of benefit to the existing bondholders. With the lower default risk, interest rates on the company's debt will be lower and the maximum amount of debt that the firm can issue (the firm's debt capacity) will increase. Since interest payments on debt are a tax-deductible expense, there is therefore a benefit from the higher leverage that accrues to current shareholders.[6]

Changing Financial Variables.   Suppose an existing independent company has a very low leverage rate or is paying out very little in dividends and investing the retained earnings in cash or marketable securities. If the acquiring company intends to change the leverage rate and thus obtain the benefits of the tax subsidy on debt, then the market value of the equity of the acquiring company will increase. If the acquiring company believes that a suboptimal dividend policy of the acquired firm has depressed its share price, then an acquisition will be of benefit. If, however, investors realize that the leverage or dividend policies of a company are inappropriate, they also recognize that the company is a merger candidate. Thus, the current share prices of these firms will reflect some part of the potential merger gains that will be obtained when these policies are changed and the potential benefits to the acquiring companies are reduced but not eliminated.

Increased Growth.   It has been argued that growth, either in earnings per share or in sales, is an important motivation for mergers. This argument is based on the desire of the acquiring company's management to maintain an historic, or target, level of growth. To the extent that investors value growth per se or if growth and profitability are correlated, then growth can be a legitimate motivation for mergers. If, however, growth is desired only by the

---

[6]In a pure conglomerate merger, the reduction of default risk will reduce the interest rate on new debt and thus increase the market value of debt. Since the merger has no synergistic effects, the increased market value of debt is matched by a reduction in the market value of equity. Thus, this pure financial effect will hurt existing shareholders. This effect is known as the *co-insurance effect*. Co-insurance occurs as follows. When two companies are separate entities, their bondholders face a certain risk of default. When the companies are merged, it is possible that poor earnings in one company, which would have resulted in default had it been independent, will be offset by good earnings in the other company in the merged entity. The risk of default has thus been reduced.

management of the acquiring company, its impact on the market value of the acquiring firm will not be positive.

Financing.   Sometimes it is possible to finance an acquisition when it is not possible to finance internal growth. Building a large steel plant, for example, involves a sizable investment. Steel manufacturing capacity can be acquired more cheaply in a merger through an exchange of shares than by buying the facilities outright. Sellers are often more willing to accept the purchaser's shares in payment for the facilities sold than are the investors in a public offering, and the use of shares reduces cash requirements for the acquisition of assets. In addition, merger activity has been supported by financing from commercial and merchant banking sources.

Tax Considerations

Tax considerations have stimulated a number of mergers. For example, a firm that is highly profitable and in the highest corporate tax bracket may acquire a company with large accumulated tax losses and then use those losses to shelter its own income.[7] Similarly, a company with large losses may acquire a profitable firm. Also, tax considerations may result in mergers' being a desirable use for excess cash. For example, if a firm has a shortage of internal investment opportunities compared to its cash flows, it has excess cash, and its options for disposing of it are (1) paying an extra dividend, (2) investing in marketable securities, (3) repurchasing its own shares, or (4) purchasing another firm. If the firm pays an extra dividend, its shareholders will have to pay taxes on the distribution. Marketable securities such as Treasury bills provide a good temporary parking place for money, but the rate of return on such securities is less than that required by shareholders. A share repurchase might result in a capital gain for the remaining shareholders, but it could be disadvantageous if the company has to pay a high price to acquire the shares; moreover, if the repurchase is designed solely to avoid paying dividends, it may be challenged by Revenue Canada. However, using surplus cash to acquire another firm has no immediate tax consequences for either the acquiring firm or its shareholders, and this fact has motivated a number of mergers.

Maintenance Control

In a hostile merger or takeover, the managers of the acquired companies generally lose their jobs or at least their autonomy. Therefore, managers who own less than 51 percent of the equity in their firms look to devices that will lessen the chances of their firms' being taken over. Mergers can serve as such a device. For example, when a firm is under attack or expects to be a target, it can purchase a firm and finance the cost by issuing debt. By increasing its size, it can make it harder for any potential acquirer to digest the company. Also,

---

[7]A merger undertaken only to use accumulated tax losses would probably be challenged by Revenue Canada. There are specific requirements that have to be met in order to be able to use the tax losses. However, because many factors are present in any given merger, it is hard to prove that a merger was motivated only, or even primarily, by tax considerations.

the much higher debt level resulting from the merger will make it hard for any acquiring company to use debt to finance the acquisition.

Such defensive mergers are difficult to defend on economic grounds. The managers involved invariably argue that synergy, not a desire to protect their own jobs, motivated the acquisition. However, there can be no question that mergers can be designed more for the benefit of managers than for that of shareholders.

Concept Review

▶ What are the four primary motives behind most mergers?
▶ From what sources do synergistic effects arise?
▶ How have tax considerations stimulated mergers?
▶ Is diversification to reduce shareholder risk a valid motive for mergers?

Merger Analysis

In theory, merger analysis is quite simple. The acquiring firm simply performs a capital budgeting analysis to determine whether the present value of the cash flows expected from the merger exceed the price that must be paid for the target company. The expected postmerger cash flows are based on the cash flows from the acquired company under revised management plus any increased operating income (or reduced costs) to be derived from merging the two firms. If the net present value is positive, the acquiring firm should take steps to acquire the target firm. The target company shareholders, on the other hand, should accept the proposal if the price offered exceeds the present value of the cash flows they expect to receive in the future if the firm continues to operate independently. (Note that the threat of a takeover may result in more efficient operations by incumbent management and thus the present value of the expected cash flows may be greater than the current market price of the target firm.)

Theory aside, however, some difficult issues are involved: (1) the acquiring company must estimate the cash flows that will result from the acquisition; (2) it must also determine what effect, if any, the merger will have on its own required rate of return on equity; (3) it must decide how to pay for the merger—with cash, with its own equity, or with some other type of package of securities; and (4) having estimated the benefits of the merger, the acquiring and target firms' managers and shareholders must bargain (or fight) over how to share these benefits. The required analysis can be extremely complex, and the end result may be less a result of financial analysis and more the consequence of ego and blind commitment to the goal of acquiring the firm.

Finally, the decision whether to merge or to grow internally (given that the growth will be profitable) is also an investment decision. If the internal growth route is used, it will take longer for earnings to be realized and there may be startup problems, such as finding managerial talent. If the merger route is taken, there may be problems of integrating the new company's operations into the existing company. In addition, the cost of merger may be higher than the cost of internal growth. An example of this decision was the entry by the chartered banks into the underwriting and investment dealer business. Some banks acquired an investment dealer; for example, the Canadian Imperial Bank of Commerce acquired Wood Gundy. Other banks, such as the Toronto-Dominion Bank, decided to establish an investment dealer subsidiary through internal growth. There is no one correct answer to the decision whether to "make or buy"; it depends upon the specifics of the companies in the transaction.

Operating Mergers versus Financial Mergers

From the standpoint of financial analysis, there are two basic types of merger: operating mergers and financial mergers.

1. An **operating merger** is one in which the operations of two companies are integrated with the expectation of obtaining synergistic effects.
2. A **financial merger** is one in which the merged companies will not be operated as a single unit and from which no significant operating economies are expected. The acquisition of Purolator Courier by Onex is an example of a financial merger.

Of course, mergers may actually combine these two features.

Merger Terms

The terms of a merger include two important questions: (1) who will control the combined enterprise? (2) how much will the acquiring firm pay for the acquired company? These points are discussed next.

Postmerger Control

The employment and control situation is of vital interest in a merger. First, consider the situation in which a small, owner-managed firm sells out to a larger concern. The owner-manager may be anxious to retain a high status position and may also be concerned about keeping operating control of the organization after the merger. Thus, these points are likely to be stressed during the merger negotiations.[8] When a publicly owned firm not controlled by its managers is merged into another company, the acquired firm's management also is worried about its postmerger position. If the acquiring firm agrees to retain the incumbent management, then the target firm's management may be willing to support the merger and to recommend its acceptance to the

---

[8]The acquiring firm may also be concerned about these points, especially if the acquired firm's management is quite good. A condition of the merger may be that the management team agree to stay on for a period such as 5 years after the merger. Also, the price paid may be contingent on the acquired firm's performance subsequent to the merger. If the managers of the target company are highly competent but do not wish to remain on after the merger, the acquiring firm may build into the merger contract a noncompetition agreement whereby they agree not to start or affiliate with a business that would be in competition with their former company.

shareholders. If the old management is to be removed, then it will probably resist the merger.[9]

The Price Paid

The second key element in a merger agreement is the price to be paid for the acquired company—the cash or shares of equity to be given to the target firm's shareholders. The analysis is similar to a regular capital budgeting analysis: the incremental earnings are estimated; a discount rate is applied to find the present value of these earnings; and, if the present value of the future incremental earnings exceeds the price to be paid for the acquired firm, then the merger is approved. Thus, only if the target firm is worth more to the acquiring firm than its market value as a separate entity will the merger be feasible. Obviously, the acquiring firm tries to buy at as low a price as possible, while the acquired firm tries to sell out at the highest possible price. The final price is determined by negotiations, with the side that negotiates better capturing most of the incremental value. The larger the synergistic benefits, the more room there is for bargaining and the higher the probability that the merger will actually be consummated.[10]

If the merger is for cash, the cost to the acquiring firm is very easy to calculate: it is the price per share offered times the number of shares acquired. If the merger calls for an exchange of shares, then the cost of the merger is equal to the dollar equivalent of the shares exchanged, based on the price per share of the acquiring company's shares, and the *share exchange* terms. For example, suppose the acquiring company has a price per share of $50 as of the merger date, and the share exchange terms are one share of the acquiring firm in exchange for two shares of the target firm. This means that the acquiring firm will have paid $25 per share to acquire the shares of the target firm. The total cost of the merger will equal the price per share of the target company paid by the acquiring company times the number of target shares outstanding.

Empirical Results: Mergers

The merger motivations identified in a previous section have implications for the impact of the merger announcement on the share prices of the participating firms. If the acquisition is based on profit-maximizing motivations, then there should be a gain in value, which is split among the acquiring and the target firms. Not unexpectedly, the announcement will always bring a gain to the seller's share price (since the acquisition price must be in excess of the prevailing market price); the buyer's share price may increase or decrease, depending upon whether the price paid is too high or too low.

---

[9]Managements of firms that are thought to be attractive merger candidates occasionally arrange *golden parachutes* for themselves—extremely lucrative retirement plans that take effect if a merger is consummated. The existence of a golden parachute may make incumbent management less eager to contest a merger.

[10]It has been estimated that of all merger negotiations seriously begun, only about one-third actually result in a merger. Also, in contested merger situations, the company that offers the most will usually make the acquisition, and the company that stands to gain the greatest synergistic benefits can generally bid the most.

Empirical studies in the United States using data up to the end of 1979 have identified an increase in total dollar value to both firms' equity resulting from the merger announcement. In successful mergers, sellers had a premium of approximately 20 percent over the preannouncement share price.[11] In the same example, buyers did not lose (that is, the net of market rate of return was approximately zero). This suggests that the merger was expected to be a zero net present value transaction and that the shareholders of the buying firm do earn their opportunity cost. Studies using more recent time periods for their samples (1979 to 1982 and 1979 to 1984) found a higher premium to selling firms and a slightly negative return to buyers. This observation suggests that investors in the stock market believe that the price paid in some acquisitions was too high.

Another interesting empirical observation is that the premiums to targets and losses to bidders increase if the original merger offer is revised because of management intransigence or a competing offer.[12] This suggests that managements of bidding firms, once engaged in a bidding contest, pay too much for the target.

The evidence in Canada is generally similar, but, because of data limitations, the results cannot be compared directly to the U.S. results.[13] Combining both takeovers and mergers, this study observed net of market returns, over the 10 months to the month of the announcement, of approximately 10 percent to targets and 4 percent to bidders. This appears to result in a more even distribution of the gains from the merger among the participants.

Concept Review

▶ What, in theory, is involved in a merger analysis?

▶ What is the essential difference between an operating merger and a pure financial merger?

▶ In analyzing a proposed operating merger, what is the single most important factor?

▶ When negotiating a friendly merger, what are the two most important considerations?

▶ If mergers are value-maximizing investments, what would you expect to happen to the share price of the acquiring firm?

▶ What determines the split of the gains in the merger among the participants?

---

[11]This percentage rate of return is measured net of overall stock market movements.

[12]There is evidence that a management veto of a merger proposal results in no reduction in share price of the target firm. The reason is that investors anticipate that there will be a takeover bid to counter the hostile reaction of incumbent management.

[13]See E. Eckbo, "Mergers and the Market for Corporate Control," *Canadian Journal of Economics* 19: 236–60. This paper reports 1683 bidder observations and 413 target firms. Unlike the U.S. studies, this study did not match the bidders and targets; many targets in the Canadian sample did not have publicly traded common equity.

Valuing the Target Firm

To determine the value of the target firm, two key items are needed: (1) a set of pro forma financial statements that develop the expected cash flows, and (2) a discount rate, or cost of capital, to apply to the projected cash flows.

Pro Forma Income Statements

Table 24-2 contains the projected income statements for CompuEd Corporation, which is being considered for acquisition by Canadian Technologies Ltd. (CTL), a large conglomerate. The projected data are postmerger, so all synergistic effects are included. CompuEd currently uses 30 percent debt, but if it were acquired, CTL would increase CompuEd's debt ratio to 50 percent. Both CTL and CompuEd have a 34 percent marginal tax rate.

Table 24-2
CompuEd Corporation:
Projected Postmerger Income Statements
as of December 31
(millions of dollars)

	1993	1994	1995	1996	1997
Net sales	$105	$126	$151	$174	$191
Cost of goods sold	80	94	111	127	137
Selling and administrative expenses	10	12	13	15	16
EBIT	$ 15	$ 20	$ 27	$ 32	$ 38
Interest[a]	3	4	5	6	6
EBT	$ 12	$ 16	$ 22	$ 26	$ 32
Taxes[b]	4	5	7	9	11
Net income	$ 8	$ 11	$ 15	$ 17	$ 21
Retentions for growth[c]	4	4	7	9	12
Cash available to CTL	$ 4	$ 7	$ 8	$ 8	$ 9
Terminal value[d]					121
Net cash flow[e]	$ 4	$ 7	$ 8	$ 8	$130

[a]Interest payment estimates are based on CompuEd's existing debt plus additional debt to increase the debt ratio to 50 percent, plus additional debt after the merger to finance asset expansion but subject to the 50 percent target capital structure.

[b]CTL will file a consolidated tax return after the merger. Thus, the taxes shown here are the full corporate taxes attributable to CompuEd's operations; there will be no additional taxes on the cash flowing from CompuEd to CTL.

[c]Some of the net income generated by CompuEd after the merger will be retained to finance its own asset growth, and some will be transferred to CTL for payment of dividends on its equity or for redeployment within the corporation. It is assumed that CompuEd's depreciation-generated funds are used to replace its wornout and obsolete plant and equipment.

[d]CompuEd's available cash flows are expected to grow at a constant 10 percent after 1995. The value of all post-1995 cash flows to CTL, as of December 31, 1997, is estimated by use of the constant growth model to be $121 million:

$$V_{1997} = \$9(1.10)/(0.1815 - 0.10) = \$121 \text{ million}.$$

In the next section, we discuss the estimation of the 18.15 percent cost of equity.

[e]These are the net cash flows available to CTL from the acquisition of CompuEd. They may be used for dividend payments to CTL shareholders or for financing asset expansion in CTL's other divisions and subsidiaries.

The net cash flows shown in Table 24-2 are the flows that would be available to CTL's shareholders, and these are the basis of the valuation.[14] Of course, the postmerger cash flows attributable to the target firm are extremely difficult to estimate. In a complete merger valuation, just as in a complete capital budgeting analysis, the component cash flow probability distributions would be specified, and sensitivity, scenario, and simulation analyses would be conducted. Indeed, in a friendly merger, the acquiring firm would send a team, consisting of literally dozens of accountants, engineers, and finance people, to the target firm's headquarters to go over its books, to estimate required maintenance expenditures, to set values on assets such as petroleum reserves, and the like.

Estimating the Discount Rate

Because the bottom line net cash flows shown in Table 24-2 are equity flows, they should be discounted at the cost of equity rather than at the overall cost of capital. Further, the cost of equity used must reflect the riskiness of the net cash flows in the table; thus, the appropriate discount rate is CompuEd's cost of equity, not that of CTL or the consolidated postmerger firm. CompuEd's market-determined premerger beta was 1.30; however, this reflects its premerger 30 percent debt ratio, whereas its postmerger debt ratio will increase to 50 percent. CTL's financial advisors estimate that CompuEd's beta will rise to 1.63 if its debt ratio is increased to 50 percent.

We can use the security market line to determine CompuEd's approximate cost of equity. If the risk-free rate is 10 percent and the market risk premium is 5 percent, then CompuEd's cost of equity, k_s, after the merger would be 18.15 percent:

$$k_s = k_{RF} + (RP_M)\beta$$
$$= 10\% + (5\%)1.63$$
$$= 18.15\%.$$

Valuing the Cash Flows

The value of CompuEd to CTL is the present value of the cash flows expected to accrue to CTL, discounted at 18.15 percent. In millions of dollars:

$$\text{Value} = \frac{\$4}{(1.1815)^1} + \frac{\$7}{(1.1815)^2} + \frac{\$8}{(1.1815)^3} + \frac{\$8}{(1.1815)^4} + \frac{\$130}{(1.1815)^5}$$
$$= \$74.$$

Thus, if CTL can acquire CompuEd for $74 million or less, the merger appears to be acceptable from CTL's standpoint.

---

[14]We purposely kept the cash flows simple to help focus on the key issues of the valuation process. In an actual merger valuation, the cash flows would be much more complex, normally including such items as additional capital furnished by the acquiring firm, tax loss carryforwards, tax effects of plant and equipment valuation adjustments, and inflows expected from planned asset sales.

Tender Offers

If one firm wishes to gain control over another, it typically approaches the other firm's management to seek its approval of the merger. The shareholders of the acquired firm are then asked to vote in favour of the merger. In a takeover bid, the process is different. The acquiring company, called the *bidder*, offers to purchase the shares of the target company at a stated price that is in excess of the prevailing market price. The offer is sent to shareholders, and they in turn may send their agreement to sell their shares to the agent for the bidder; this agent is typically a trust company. The consideration involved can be cash, shares, or other securities. The offer may be conditional on obtaining a certain percentage of the outstanding shares.

What we have described above is called a **tender offer**: the bidder has asked the shareholders of the target firm to submit, or tender, their shares. A **takeover bid** is a tender offer that, if successful, will result in the acquiring company's obtaining a given percentage of the target firm's shares. This percentage is identified in legislation. Most of the provincial securities acts also include regulations about the form of the offer and the notification requirements. In Ontario, for example, the bidder must file with the Ontario Securities Commission (OSC) a *takeover bid circular*, which is equivalent in form to a prospectus. All shares must be treated equally. Therefore, if a takeover bid is for 40 percent of the shares and 50 percent are tendered, then the acquiring company must prorate its acceptances—that is, each shareholder who tendered shares will have 80 percent of his or her offer accepted.

Because the takeover bid is a direct appeal to the shareholders, it need not be approved by the management of the target firm. Thus a tender offer is an alternative means of obtaining control of a firm when the incumbent management is hostile. OSC regulations, however, require the management of the target company to send to its shareholders a circular that recommends either acceptance or rejection of the bid.

The regulatory provisions have been introduced to (1) increase the information available to target company shareholders, (2) provide all shareholders with fair and equitable treatment, and (3) permit shareholders time to evaluate the bid. One result of these regulations has been to increase the likelihood that there will be a competing bid in the takeover. This will initiate an auction process in which the target firm's shareholders gain and bidding firms' shareholders have an equivalent reduction in wealth.

Empirical Evidence: Takeover Bids

Like any merger offer, a takeover bid is an attempt by one managerial team to acquire the control of a set of assets (a firm) from another managerial team. If the purpose of the takeover is to improve operations in the target or to achieve economies of scale, there should be a total gain from the takeover that can be shared between target and bidder. The premium paid to the target firm as a percentage of the premerger market price is approximately 53 percent; it is slightly higher (56 percent) for an initial hostile bid and 51 percent for an initial friendly bid.

One look at successful takeover bids using data prior to the end of 1980 shows that, over a 2-month period up to and including the announcement date of the bid, there was a net market percentage change on the target firm's share price of 30 percent; the rate of return for the bidder over the same time period was 4 percent. Thus, the price paid for the takeover was sufficient to provide a gain to the target as well as to the bidder. Studies using data subsequent to 1980 show that the targets had a net of market rate of return of 39 percent, whereas bidders lost approximately 1 percent. It appears that targets are obtaining a greater benefit at the expense of bidder firms' shareholders. This could be a result of the existence of auctions.[15]

Defensive Tactics and Takeover Bids

Existing management of a company can introduce provisions, some with shareholder approval, to make takeover bids more difficult and/or expensive. These provisions can be introduced either before a takeover bid has been made—prebid provisions—or after a bid has been made. Any provision that is introduced must be consistent with the managers' (and board of directors') fiduciary responsibilities.

Managers, in introducing these antitakeover provisions (also called "shark repellents"), face a serious conflict of interest. On the one hand, management should make all decisions consistent with shareholder wealth maximization. Thus, any defensive or antitakeover provisions should increase the company's share price. On the other hand, management has a strong incentive to defeat the takeover bid, because a successful tender offer usually means a new management team will be put in place. Thus, antitakeover provisions will provide management with job security. If this is the purpose of the antitakeover provisions, then the share price of the firm should fall upon the announcement of these provisions, because there will never be a successful hostile bid with its associated high premium for existing shareholders.

We now consider the defensive tactics used both before and during a bid, along with some empirical evidence on the impact of the announcement of antitakeover provisions on the share price of the firm.

Prebid Tactics.   Prebid tactics are intended to achieve three purposes: (1) to avoid the firm's having characteristics of a typical target, (2) to make it difficult to acquire control without board approval, and (3) to increase the cost of a hostile change in control.

---

[15]There was a similar observation using more recent data on mergers as well. One argument to explain this is the "winner's curse," which states that in an auction the winning bidder is most likely the one who has overpaid the most. Thus, when a bidding contest arises in a hostile tender offer or contested merger, the winner is the company that overpays the most. This would explain why there is a negative net of market rate of return on the bidder firm's shares; the decision is viewed by the market as a negative net present value transaction.

To avoid having the characteristics of a typical target, the firm will reduce its liquid assets and identify and sell off undervalued assets. These are characteristics consistent with a poorly managed firm. Another benefit is that these changes remove some assets that a bidding firm might use to pay off debt issued to finance an offer.

A number of techniques have been used to improve management's position in the event of a hostile offer. These include issuing nonvoting shares to the public with or without coattail provisions (this route has been taken by Crownx, Seagram, and Maclean Hunter, among others); swapping voting shares with a friendly corporation (Southam-Torstar used this technique)[16]; and issuing voting shares to a pension fund or ally. These changes permit the management either to make a tender offer impossible or to thwart a hostile offer.

The final tactic is to increase the cost of any hostile takeover. One way to achieve this result is to introduce delaying tactics that will give the management time to find other companies that are willing to enter an auction process. Another technique is a *golden parachute*, which is a substantial payment to the incumbent managers in the event of a takeover. Finally, the firm can introduce a *poison pill* provision. A poison pill is special right that can be exercised when one of several triggering events occurs. The usual triggering event is the acquisition by an individual or company of a certain percentage of the firm's voting shares; the percentage is usually in the 10 to 15 percent range. If an acquiring company exceeds this threshold value, all shareholders *except* the acquiring company have the right to purchase new shares at a discount of 50 percent from the current price. If the pill is activated, the value of the acquiring company's holdings are diluted significantly and its voting position is diminished since new shares have been issued to all the other shareholders. The poison pill makes a takeover so costly to the acquiring firm that no offer will be made. Shareholders must vote on the pill within 6 months of its introduction. The poison pill can be made inoperative only with the agreement of the incumbent management. Approximately 20 companies have introduced poison pills in Canada. In general, they have been introduced by widely held companies that, in some cases, have major holdings in the United States. The first pill in Canada was introduced by Inco in association with a $10 per share dividend. Other companies with pills include Canadian Pacific and Moore Corp.

If these tactics are undertaken with shareholder approval, it is difficult to argue that they are not in the shareholders' best interests. However, there are instances in which the introduction of antitakeover provisions has reduced the share price. In the United States, a study investigated antitakeover amendments introduced during the period 1979 to 1985. For all forms of amendments, it was observed that the share prices fell about 1.25 percent (net of market movements) over a 30-day period surrounding the proxy statement signing date. It was also observed that the largest negative impact on share prices was for provisions that (1) gave management control over whether the

---

[16]In this swap, Southam was afraid of a hostile takeover. It negotiated a swap in which Torstar received a new issue of Southam equity (20 percent of the amount outstanding) and issued to Southam nonvoting common shares. Torstar also agreed to vote in favour of Southam's management.

shareholders had to approve any takeover with a supermajority and (2) established authorized preferred shares (which could be used as poison pills).

During-Bid Tactics.   Once a takeover bid has been made, there is a fine line between management activities that entrench incumbent managers and those that are intended to obtain the highest price for the shares.

The following are some of the techniques that have been used:

1. Find another corporation that management would prefer as the bidder. These corporations are called *white knights* and are often paid to become involved. Because the number of companies in Canada that could be white knights is small, foreign companies may be approached; an example was Allied-Lyons in the Gulf–Hiram Walker takeover.

2. Issue a tender offer for the firm's own shares financed either with the firm's liquid assets or through an investment dealer that provides funds to the company by purchasing a new issue of voting preferred shares.

3. Sell the "crown jewels." If the bidder is particularly interested in a particular division of the firm (the crown jewels), then its sale to a third party will quickly remove the incentive for the takeover. For example, Hiram Walker sold its distilling division to Allied-Lyons so as to defuse the Gulf bid.

4. Purchase a company that is unprofitable, pay a very high price for an acquisition, or buy a firm that is a poor fit with the operations of the bidding firm. This will decrease the attractiveness of the target. Whether this is a good decision from the viewpoint of the shareholders of the target firm is debatable. An example of this tactic was the acquisition of Burns Foods by Union Gas as a defence against the Unicorp bid.

5. Use a poison pill provision.

Since these tactics are usually introduced without shareholder approval, they are very questionable. An empirical study of U.S. data investigating the introduction of poison pills during a takeover bid (or during speculation about an impending bid) found that the share price of the target firm lost approximately 2.4 percent over the day before and the day of an announcement of the introduction of the poison pill. This is a substantial reduction in the market value of the equity of the target firm.

Conclusion on Defensive Tactics.   The most frequent result of a tender offer, even when defensive tactics are introduced, is that it is successful. Defensive strategies appear to enrich investment dealers, white knights, incumbent management, and target shareholders at the expense of the shareholders of bidding firms.

Commentators on the takeover market usually split over the proper role of management in a takeover bid. If there is a belief that takeovers are beneficial to the economy, then management should be constrained in its response. Some researchers argue that management should be required to do nothing once a bid is made! On the other side of the debate are researchers who believe that takeovers have costs that outweigh their benefits and that defensive tactics by managers are therefore acceptable.

Takeover Bids: Voting and Nonvoting Shares   As noted in Chapter 20, some companies undergo a reorganization of their share capital such that each old share of equity is converted into one voting and one or more nonvoting shares. These arrangements are normally undertaken by companies that are controlled by a single shareholder or a family. The majority shareholders are interested in obtaining some capital from the firm but do not want to diminish their control position. By issuing nonvoting shares, the controlling shareholders can sell the nonvoting shares, retain the voting shares, and thereby obtain cash without diluting their control.

In a company with a majority owner, a merger or tender offer cannot be accepted without the agreement of the controlling shareholders. If there are voting and nonvoting shares in the capital structure, any takeover bid is directed only to the holders of voting shares, since it is they who are required under law to complete the change in control. Therefore, the holders of nonvoting shares obtain none of the premiums associated with takeover bids.

Some nonvoting shares are created, however, with a *coattail* provision to ensure that both voting and nonvoting shares are eligible for premiums under a takeover bid. For example, under circumstances specified in the issuing documents, the nonvoting shares have a vote and hence will obtain the premium. Although there are still nonvoting shares that do not have coattail provisions, Toronto Stock Exchange regulations now require that any new issues of restricted (nonvoting) shares must be given coattails in order to be listed. Further, if any securities are issued by a firm with restricted voting shares in its capital structure, the restricted voting shares must be provided a coattail in order for the securities of the firm to be listed on the exchange.

An example of coattail provisions and their efficiency was the bid by the dealers of Canadian Tire for the voting shares of Canadian Tire. In 1983, there was a reorganization of the firm's share structure. The result was a class of voting shares that represented only 4 percent of the equity of Canadian Tire. These voting shares were held by the Billes family (60.9 percent), the dealers of Canadian Tire (17.4 percent), and the public. The nonvoting shares were held by the public, including some large blocks held by institutional investors. Under this structure, the Billes family was able to control the company with approximately 2.5 percent of the total equity of the company.

At the time of the reorganization, takeover protection was afforded the nonvoting shares by a coattail provision to the effect that a takeover bid in which the majority of the common shares issued and outstanding had been tendered and taken up would result in each nonvoting share's being given a vote.

On December 9, 1986, the dealers (through a holding company) made an offer to purchase 49 percent of the outstanding voting shares at $160.24 per share, a 400 percent premium over the prevailing market price at that time. Since the dealers already held 17.4 percent of the voting shares, a successful bid would have resulted in their holding approximately 66 percent of the voting stock—provided the coattail was not triggered. If the coattail were triggered, the dealers would have had to purchase a majority of the nonvoting shares as well in order to obtain control.

The dealers argued that their takeover bid should not trigger the coattail because they were bidding for only 49 percent of the voting shares—less than the 50 percent trigger stated in the coattail. They interpreted the coattail to exclude their current holdings from the calculation. The effect of their bid was to deny the nonvoting shares any portion of the takeover premium.

On December 19, 1986, the Ontario Securities Commission (OSC) issued a cease-trading order against the dealers' offer, arguing that the bid was abusive of capital markets and contrary to the public interest. The cease-trading order was upheld in the subsequent appeals by the dealers.

The decision appeared to be based on a different interpretation of the coattail provision—that the trigger was "pulled" when the total holding subsequent to the bid would exceed 50 percent. The OSC argued that it was this latter interpretation on which the market was valuing the nonvoting shares and that the dealers' offer was an attempt to circumvent the coattail provisions.

This bid generated substantial debate and activity in the investment and regulatory communities. The prices of nonvoting shares fluctuated as investors attempted to determine the strength of their coattail provision.

The Canadian Tire bid and its aftermath have raised many interesting questions regarding the role of the OSC, the sanctity of contracts, and the problems associated with the nonvoting shares. For investors, the crucial issue is the strength of coattails and the protection they afford against unfair treatment of the nonvoting shareholders compared to the voting shareholders in the event of a takeover bid.

Leveraged Buyouts and Associated Transactions

The term **leveraged buyout (LBO)** is a general one identifying any takeover bid that is financed with a high proportion of debt. In many instances the acquiring party is a consortium of individuals or groups. These include the primary acquirer, which takes the majority of the equity of the target firm; an investment dealer or merchant banker, which may take an equity position and usually arranges for the debt financing; and a third party (often a pension fund), which also takes an equity interest. Not all LBOs involve all three parties. For smaller companies where the primary party has limited experience in raising debt, the merchant banker plays an important role in the issuance of debt, called *junk bonds*; this term reflects the high debt ratio and consequent high risk to the debt holder.

When the primary party to the takeover is the incumbent management, the transaction is called a *management buyout (MBO)*. The result of a successful offer is that the company goes private (that is, the company no longer has any publicly traded equity). The reasons for engaging in going-private transactions are discussed in more detail in a subsequent section.

Since the LBO infuses substantial debt into the company, it would be expected that the characteristics of the target company would be conducive to maintaining high leverage ratios. Alternatively, if the debt is not anticipated to be maintained in the capital structure, the assets should be sufficiently marketable to assist in extinguishing the debt quickly.

The characteristics of companies heavily involved in LBOs are as follows:

1. *Stability of cash flows.* The company is established, with a visible and dependable record of cash flows and good prospects for continued profitability. Little research and development is required, and there are no growth

opportunities. The company has a strong presence in the market and substantial customer loyalty.

2. *Low risk.*   The company has a valuable asset base, which can be sold easily if necessary. Also, there is a low debt ratio and noncyclical cash flows; this results in a low level of systematic risk—the average beta of companies involved in LBOs has been approximately equal to 0.7.

3. *Management control.*   There is an experienced management that already holds a significant percentage of the outstanding equity.

All three characteristics permit a large infusion of debt because they are related to the debt capacity of the company.

Industries that have had substantial activity in the LBO market in the United States include retailing, fabricated metals, electrical and electronic machinery, distribution and wholesale trade, food and allied products, and printing and publishing. All of these industries certainly exhibit many of the characteristics identified as necessary for an LBO.

A good example of a Canadian company that has grown through the use of leveraged buyouts is Onex Corp., which at the end of 1987 following a series of LBO transactions had total assets of approximately $2.1 billion; at the end of 1991 assets were $1.3 billion. Under its LBOs, the acquired companies assumed the long-term debt load associated with the acquisition. Thus, creditors of the company had no recourse to Onex's other assets in the event of a default of one company.

The Onex LBO that took place in August 1987 was its biggest to that date. Onex purchased Beatrice Foods Canada Ltd. for $300 million; at the date of acquisition, Beatrice Canada had no debt of its own. The financing of the acquisition illustrates the LBO principle. Onex put up equity of $50 million for 60 percent of the company. The other equity was owned by management (20 percent) and TLC Group L.P., a New York investment firm that purchased the Canadian subsidiary from the parent and then resold it to Onex. The remainder of the purchase price was financed with debt. In 1991 Onex sold its equity position in Beatrice Foods for a net after-tax cash profit to Onex of $73.8 million.

Other companies acquired by Onex in 1987 and financed in a similar manner included the following:

- American Can Canada Inc. (now Onex Packaging Inc.), acquired for $220 million; 43 percent ownership.
- Citibank Leasing Canada, acquired for $270 million; 65 percent ownership (now Norex Leasing Inc. and sold to a chartered bank in 1990).
- Purolator Courier Ltd., acquired by auction for $225 million; 68 percent ownership.
- Sky-Chefs Inc. of Dallas, acquired for $153 million U.S.; 59 percent ownership.
- Freight Car, manufacturing division of Bethlehem Steel, acquired from that company for $63 million in 1991.
- Burger King Distribution, acquired from its parent in 1992.

Given the stable cash flows and strong assets of some of the companies, acquisition by LBO was feasible. However, with the high levels of debt within each company, reductions in operating cash flows could lead to severe reductions in the earnings available to common shareholders. This, in fact, occurred in 1991 and 1992 as a result of the recession.

Going-Private Transactions

In a *going-private tender offer*, the distinguishing feature is that a company, through its management, purchases all of the outstanding common shares. The financing of the going-private transaction is similar to that in the normal LBO case; thus, the company characteristics will be very similar.

There has been some controversy over going-private transactions; it is alleged that managers who instigate such transactions have better information concerning the true value of the company than do the shareholders. Thus, the tender offer price, although it is at a premium to the prevailing price (typically, more than 50 percent), may not reflect the true value of the company. Hence, it is said, managements take firms private in order to capture "hidden values."[17]

There are, however, many reasons aside from capturing hidden values for taking a firm private. They include the following:

1. *Avoidance of shareholder servicing costs.*   The direct costs of shareholder servicing include fees for registration, listing, legal and accounting services, annual report preparation, and mailings of various documents. One U.S. study concluded that these costs had a capitalized value of $1 million. This may not be a significant amount for large firms, but for small firms (which make up the majority of companies going private), these savings are not necessarily trivial.

2. *Improved efficiency.*   The improved efficiency in operations comes from both internal and external forces. For the former, the managers now have a higher proportion of the equity of the company, and any shirking or nonoptimal decision-making is a direct cost to them. In addition, with a high debt ratio, any inefficiencies will result in a default and a loss in wealth to managers. These internal forces are powerful incentives to efficient actions. On the external side, the merchant banker and the third party in the LBO are interested in the efficient operations of the firm. It will be easier for them to monitor management's decisions because they will have ready access to the firm and expertise to evaluate the actions.

3. *Tax benefits.*   Tax benefits[18] come from two sources. First, the significant increase in leverage will generate tax savings from the interest deductibility provisions. Second, becoming a Canadian-controlled private corporation can provide tax benefits.

---

[17]This argument might have some force if the companies taken private had growth opportunities or were in markets in which there could be an increase in future demand. But the characteristics of the companies involved in going-private transactions suggest that hidden values are unlikely; the companies are very stable.

[18]The gain based on this factor is not a gain to society. If the tax burden of one firm is reduced by a going-private transaction, there must be an offsetting increase in taxes for other parties, assuming that government expenditures remain constant.

Thus, there are economic gains from going-private transactions. Not all firms, however, will find it advantageous to go private. If a company requires access to the equity market, going private is inappropriate. Firms that are going private expect to be able to meet all of their financing needs either internally or through new debt issues.

Corporate Alliances

Mergers are not the only way in which the resources of two firms can be combined. In fact, many companies are striking co-operative deals that fall far short of merging. Such co-operative deals are called **corporate alliances**, and they take many forms, from marketing agreements to joint ownership of world-scale operations. One form of corporate alliance is the **joint venture**, which involves the joining together of parts of two or more companies to accomplish a specific, limited objective. Joint ventures are controlled by the combined management of the parent companies.

An example of a corporate alliance is the "strategic partnership" established by Crosbie & Company Inc. (C&CO) and Houlihan Lokey Howard & Zukin (HLHK). The former company is a Canadian merchant bank based in Toronto, involved in mergers, acquisitions, and restructurings; the latter company, based in major cities in the United States, is among that country's leading firms in firm valuations and reorganizations. The partnership results in joint marketing, joint resources, and shared knowledge and products and will generate economies of scale, build cross-border and international representation, and provide access to capital resources both internal and external. Through the partnership, HLHK obtains a Canadian presence and instant Canadian credibility.

Concept Review

► What is the difference between a merger and a joint venture?

Divestitures

A corporation can be viewed as a portfolio of productive assets. For most companies, the portfolio is a set of assets that generate cash flows. For some companies, one can view the assets as divisions or subsidiaries in related and unrelated businesses. In an acquisition, productive assets are added to the portfolio; in a **divestiture**, assets are removed from the company. Divestitures can be accomplished through either a selloff or a spinoff. In this section, we consider each of these strategies and provide illustrations.

Selloffs

In a *selloff*, the company sells some of its assets, usually a subsidiary or a division, for cash and/or marketable securities. In the usual case, the assets are sold to an independent company. Alternatively, the assets—for example, a division of the firm—are sold to management of the company. The latter case is referred to as a *divisional buyout* and is similar to a management or leveraged buyout. Since the assets are sold, the company will pay tax on the proceeds, and thus the tax-paying position of the company is an important input in the analysis.

Since the management of the divesting company should make decisions to maximize the market value of the equity of the company, the selloff transaction should result in a positive net present value. Therefore, the announcement that a selloff is to take place should be associated with an increase in the share price of the divesting (selling) company.

After some successful acquisitions, either through merger or a takeover bid, there is a selloff of a number of divisions of the acquired firm. The acquiring firm may have wanted only a particular segment of the target firm's operations. In addition, the acquirer may have financed the operation through a large debt issue. The selloff of the "unwanted" operations provides funds to pay off some or all of the debt used. A good example of this approach is found in the Imasco acquisition of Genstar; the latter firm was a conglomerate with operations in such disparate areas as waste management, building materials, and financial services. Imasco sold off the nonfinancial services operations and was left with Canada Trust, which was the target when it bid for Genstar. Other examples of selloffs after acquisitions include Gulf and Hiram Walker in Canada, Campeau and Allied Stores and Campeau and Federated in the United States.

There are a number of arguments that have been presented to explain why a selloff is a good thing for current shareholders:

1. *Removing an unprofitable unit.* Removing an unprofitable element from the firm will increase the share price. This is not a very convincing argument. The current share price of the firm can be viewed as a weighted average of the implicit market values for each division (that is, the market value of the division if it were independent, or stand-alone). The contribution to the share price of the unit involved in the selloff is equal to the present value of its cash flows. A gain to the divesting firm will occur only if the price paid for the division was in excess of its contribution to the overall value of the firm. If the acquirer of the division recognizes that the division is losing money, why should it pay anything above its current going-concern implicit value, as reflected in the firm's current share price, unless perhaps the purchaser believes that it will be able to run it more efficiently than the current management?

   However, a benefit can be found if the unprofitable unit of the firm is creating *negative synergies*. This may arise if management is devoting substantial amounts of time to this unit to the detriment of the operations of the other parts of the operations. By removing the unprofitable unit, the value of the remaining operations will increase.

2. *Paying a premium price.* There may be instances in which the acquirer firm will pay a premium over the price of the unit implicit in the valuation of the firm. If the acquiring firm is more efficient at operating the unit than is the current management, then the former can pay a higher price since the expected cash flows under the new management will be greater than

under current management. There are a number of reasons to believe this argument is true. The current management may have a number of divisions or subsidiaries to manage and therefore may not be able to focus enough attention on a particular division. In addition, the division may be in a business unrelated to the other activities of the company; hence, effective management of the division is hampered. Finally, it may be difficult to structure management compensation schemes that focus on the profitability of the division; thus, incentives for effective management are blunted. The management of the sold-off unit will not be faced with these problems and may be able to improve the unit's cash flow.

3. *Focussing activities.*   By removing the division or subsidiary, the firm may benefit in its remaining operations through increased efficiency. First, some of the head office expenses may be eliminated as the company is reduced in size. Second, by removing a division, management can focus its attention on the remaining operations. If the division that was sold off is in another line of business, management can now focus on activities that are the firm's core operations. This leads to an expectation in the market of increased cash flows and thereby an increase in share price.

4. *Raising funds for internal purposes.*   In the early 1990s, with the onset of the recession, many companies found that their debt ratios were too high, given the reduced cash flows from their operations. By selling off divisions of subsidiaries for cash, they were able to reduce their leverage ratio. In addition, if funds were needed for internal purposes, the equity market was not receptive to a new issue, and the firm did not want to borrow any more, a selloff could generate needed cash. This strategy, however, only makes sense if there are reasons for the selloff beyond raising cash. If the division is making a contribution to the firm and none of the benefits already noted would arise from selling it, then a selloff will be a zero or negative net present value transaction.

A combination of more effective management of the remaining operations and a premium price paid by the acquirer of the sold-off division should result in an increase in share prices when the company announces the selloff.

There have been a number of examples of selloffs recently. A current example is the sale by Southam Inc. of its Canadian and U.S. business forms operations to Maclean Hunter Ltd. This selloff is just the latest example of sales by Southam of printing operations in an attempt to return to its core business of newspaper operations. Maclean Hunter stated that the acquisition would permit it to take advantage of economies of scale and improve the efficiency of its operations.

The empirical evidence is consistent with these arguments. During the period beginning 2 or 3 days prior to the announcement of a selloff and ending with the actual announcement date, there is a cumulative increase in share price of about 1 to 2 percent. This increase is measured so as to remove the impact of general market movements over this period; hence, it reflects only the impact of this event. In addition, the research found that over the month before the selloff there was an additional increase in share price (net of market movements) of approximately 2 percent. Therefore, selloffs are positive net present value transactions. (These results are based on U.S. evidence only.)

One interesting empirical observation is that if the selloff is cancelled, the increase in share price is lost. This suggests that a change in control of the division is necessary for there to be any gains to shareholders. Therefore, the selloff announcement provides more than just a signal that the division is available for sale.

Spinoffs

In a *spinoff*, the shares of a subsidiary or division are distributed to the shareholders of the firm. The distribution is either as a dividend or more likely through a complex transaction known as a plan of arrangement. (This latter route is often chosen since the transaction results in a tax-deferred transfer to shareholders.) Each shareholder ends up with shares of the new company and those of the remaining company. As a result of this transaction, a new equity security is traded on the market. However, no funds flow to the company in exchange for the loss of the assets.

The main argument in favour of a spinoff is similar to that for a selloff. The management of the remaining entity can now focus its attention on a less diverse portfolio of assets. This should result in more effective management and thus higher expected cash flows. This argument is consistent with some of the characteristics of companies undertaking spinoffs and subsidiaries being spun off. It was observed that for the 5 years prior to the spinoff, companies had about a 20 percent per annum growth rate in assets and employees. In addition, in approximately 80 percent of the spinoffs, the subsidiary and the company were in different industries. Both of these observations suggest that difficulties in managing the overall operations led to the spinoff of the subsidiaries.

Additional arguments about why a spinoff should result in a gain to the shareholders of the firm include:

1. *Shifted risk.* Removing some assets from the firm means reducing the collateral for the outstanding debt, which then, according to this theory, becomes riskier. This unanticipated increase in risk reduces the market value of debt and results in an increase in shareholders' wealth. This wealth transfer is unlikely to occur for a number of reasons. First, debt is often spun off with the equity so that there is no wealth loss to the remaining debtholders. Second, the spinoff is accomplished through a dividend payment, and bondholders, through covenants, can limit the extent of dividend payments.

2. *Optimal management contracts.* The share price of the new, spunoff company can be used as a basis for compensation contracts that include stock options for management. This will align the interests of management and shareholders of the new firm. This alignment was impossible before since the operations of the management of the specific subsidiary could not be identified in changes in the share price of the overall firm.

3. *Clarity premium.* When the subsidiary was part of an overall operation, it may have been difficult to obtain information on it and on other subsidiaries

of the firm; the result was a security price that was not representative of the true value of the operating entities. When the subsidiary is removed from overall operations, more information is made available on its operations and performance and the share price can reflect its true value. This can result in an increase in its share price above its value as part of the overall entity.

Spinoffs have become an increasingly frequent restructuring event in the past few years. Recently, John Labatt Ltd. announced a spinoff of Ault Foods Ltd. in Canada and Johanna Dairies Inc. in the United States into a separate entity with its own management. This was the latest of a series of Labatt restructurings, which included a selloff of JL Foods to Heinz Company. Labatt's management stated that the purpose behind the restructuring was to return to its core business: beer and entertainment. At the same time as the announcement of the spinoff, Labatt also announced a $3 per share dividend.

The empirical evidence has shown that there is a gain to shareholders when a subsidiary is spun off. The net of market percentage increase in share prices over the period 1 day before the announcement date of the spinoff to the announcement date is 2.8 percent.

Concept Review

▶ What are the major types of divestitures?
▶ Differentiate between spinoffs and selloffs.
▶ What are some reasons for divestitures?

Summary

This chapter discussed mergers, divestitures, and LBOs. The key concepts covered are listed below:

☐ A **merger** occurs when two firms combine to form a single company. The primary motives for mergers are (1) synergy, (2) tax considerations, (3) purchase of assets below their replacement costs, (4) diversification, and (5) gaining control over a large enterprise.

☐ Mergers can provide economic benefits through *economies of scale* or through the *concentration of assets* in the hands of more efficient managers. However, mergers also have the potential for reducing competition, and for this reason they are carefully regulated by governmental agencies.

☐ In most mergers, one company (the *acquiring firm*) initiates action to take over another (the *target firm*).

☐ A **horizontal merger** occurs when two firms in the same line of business combine.

☐ A **vertical merger** is the combination of a firm with one of its customers or suppliers.

☐ A **congeneric merger** involves firms in related industries, but for which no customer–supplier relationship exists.

☐ A **conglomerate merger** occurs when firms in totally different industries combine.

☐ In a **friendly merger**, the managements of both firms approve the merger, while in a **hostile merger** the target firm's management opposes the merger.

☐ An **operating merger** is one in which the operations of the two firms are combined. A **financial merger** is one in which the firms continue to operate separately, and hence no operating economies are expected.

☐ In a *merger analysis*, (1) the price to be paid for the target firm and (2) the employment/control situation are the key issues to be resolved.

☐ To determine the *value of the target firm*, the acquiring firm must (1) forecast the cash flows that will result after the merger and (2) develop a discount rate to apply to the projected cash flows.

☐ *Poison pills* are actions a firm can take that will make the firm less valuable if it is acquired in a hostile takeover. *Golden parachutes* are large payments made to a firm's managers if it is acquired.

☐ A **joint venture** is a **corporate alliance** in which two or more companies combine some of their resources to achieve a specific, limited objective.

☐ A **divestiture** is the sale of some of a company's operating assets. A divestiture may involve (1) *selling off* an operating unit to another firm or to that unit's managers or (2) *spinning off* a unit as a separate company.

☐ The reasons for divestitures include the clarification of what a company actually does, the raising of capital needed to strengthen the corporation's core business, and the improvement of compensation schemes.

☐ A **leveraged buyout (LBO)** is a takeover financed with a high proportion of debt. If the primary acquirer is the firm's own management, the transaction is called a *management buyout (MBO)*.

Questions

24-1 Four economic classifications of mergers are horizontal, vertical, conglomerate, and congeneric. Explain the significance of these terms in merger analysis with regard to (a) the likelihood of governmental intervention and (b) the possibilities for operating synergy.

24-2 Firm A wants to acquire Firm B. Firm B's management agrees that the merger is a good idea. Might a tender offer be used?

24-3 Distinguish between *operating mergers* and *financial mergers*.

24-4 Two large, publicly owned firms are contemplating a merger. No operating synergy is expected. However, since returns on the two firms are not perfectly positively correlated, the standard deviation of earnings would be reduced for the combined corporation. One group of consultants argues that this risk reduction is sufficient grounds for the merger. Another group thinks this type of risk reduction is irrelevant because shareholders can themselves hold the shares of both companies and thus gain the risk reduction benefits without all the hassles and expenses of the merger. Whose position is correct?

24-5 Is the book value of a company's assets considered the absolute minimum price to be paid for that firm? Is there any value that qualifies as an absolute minimum? Explain.

Self-Test Problem   (solution appears on page 929)

ST-1 **Key terms.** Define each of the following terms:
  a. Synergy; merger; takeover
  b. Horizontal merger; vertical merger; congeneric merger; conglomerate merger
  c. Friendly merger; hostile merger; defensive merger; tender offer; acquiring company; target company
  d. Operating merger; financial merger
  e. White knight; poison pill; golden parachute
  f. Joint venture; corporate alliance
  g. Divestiture; spinoff; selloff
  h. Leveraged buyout (LBO); management buyout (MBO)

Problems

24-1 **Capital budgeting analysis.** Denning Gifts & Stationery Shoppe wishes to acquire Carol's Card Gallery for $400 000. Denning expects the merger to provide incremental earnings of about $64 000 a year for 10 years. Karl Denning has calculated the marginal cost of capital for this investment to be 10 percent. Conduct a capital budgeting analysis for Denning to determine whether or not he should purchase Carol's Card Gallery.

24-2 **Merger analysis.** Calgary Appliance Corporation is considering a merger with the Edmonton Vacuum Company. Edmonton is a publicly traded company, and its current beta is 1.30. Edmonton has been barely profitable, so it has paid an average of only 20 percent in taxes during the last several years. In addition, it uses little debt, having a market value debt ratio of just 25 percent.

   If the acquisition is made, Calgary would operate Edmonton as a separate, wholly owned subsidiary. Calgary would pay taxes on a consolidated basis, and the tax rate would therefore increase to 34 percent. Calgary also would increase the debt capitalization in the Edmonton subsidiary on a market value basis to 40 percent of assets, which would increase its beta to 1.50. Calgary's acquisition department estimates that Edmonton, if acquired, would produce the following net cash flows to Calgary's shareholders (in millions of dollars):

Year	Net Cash Flow
1	$1.30
2	1.50
3	1.75
4	2.00
5 and beyond	Constant growth at 6%

These cash flows include all acquisition effects. Calgary's cost of equity is 14 percent, its beta is 1.0, and its cost of debt is 10 percent. The risk-free rate is 8 percent.

  a. What discount rate should be used to discount the estimated cash flows? (Hint: Use Calgary's k_s to determine the market risk premium.)

  b. What is the dollar value of Edmonton to Calgary?

  c. Edmonton has 1.2 million common shares outstanding. What is the maximum price per share that Calgary should offer for Edmonton? If the tender offer is accepted at this price, what will happen to Calgary's share price?

24-3 **Merger analysis.**   TransWorld Products, Ltd., a large conglomerate, is evaluating the possible acquisition of London Siding Company (LSC), a small aluminum siding manufacturer. TransWorld's analysts project the following postmerger data for LSC (in thousands of dollars):

	1994	1995	1996	1997
Net sales	$450	$518	$555	$600
Selling and administrative expense	45	53	60	68
Interest	18	21	24	27
Tax rate after merger	34%			
Cost of goods sold				
(as a percentage of sales)	65%			
Beta after merger	1.50			
Risk-free rate	8%			
Market risk premium	4%			
Terminal growth rate of cash flow				
available to TransWorld	7%			

If the acquisition is made, it will occur on January 1, 1994. All cash flows shown in the income statements are assumed to occur at the end of the year. LSC currently has a market value capital structure of 40 percent debt, but TransWorld would increase that to 50 percent if the acquisition were made. LSC, if independent, would pay taxes at 20 percent, but its income would be taxed at 34 percent if it were consolidated. LSC's current market-determined beta is 1.40, and its investment advisers think that its beta would rise to 1.50 if the debt ratio were increased to 50 percent. The cost of goods sold is expected to be 65 percent of sales, but it could vary somewhat. Depreciation-generated funds would be used to replace wornout equipment, so they would not be available to TransWorld's shareholders. The risk-free rate is 8 percent, and the market risk premium is 4 percent.

  a. What is the appropriate discount rate for valuing the acquisition?

  b. What is the terminal value? What is the value of LSC to TransWorld?

Integrative Problem

24-4 **Merger analysis.** Smitty's Home Repair Company, a regional hardware chain that specializes in materials and equipment rentals for "do-it-yourself" projects, is cash rich because of several consecutive good years. One of the alternative uses for the excess funds is an acquisition. Linda Wade, Smitty's treasurer and your boss, has been asked to place a value on a potential target, Hill's Hardware, a small chain that operates in an adjacent province, and she has enlisted your help.

The following are Wade's estimates of Hill's earnings potential if it came under Smitty's management (in millions of dollars):

	1993	1994	1995	1996
Net sales	$60.0	$90.0	$112.5	$127.5
Cost of goods sold (60%)	36.0	54.0	67.5	76.5
Selling, administrative expense	4.5	6.0	7.5	9.0
Interest expense	3.0	4.5	4.5	6.0
Necessary earnings retentions	0.0	7.5	6.0	4.5

The interest expense listed here includes the interest on Hill's existing debt, on new debt that Smitty's would issue to help finance the acquisition, and on new debt expected to be issued over time to help finance expansion within the new "H division," the code name given to the target firm. The retentions represent earnings that would be reinvested within the H division to help finance its growth.

Hill's Hardware currently uses 40 percent debt financing, and it pays taxes at a 30 percent rate. Security analysts estimate Hill's beta to be 1.2. If the acquisition takes place, Smitty's would increase Hill's debt ratio to 50 percent, which would increase its beta to 1.3. Further, because Smitty's is highly profitable, taxes on the consolidated firm would be 40 percent. Wade realizes that Hill's Hardware also generates depreciation cash flows, but she believes that these funds would have to be reinvested within the division to replace wornout equipment.

Wade estimates the risk-free rate to be 9 percent and the market risk premium to be 4 percent. She also estimates that net cash flows after 1993 would grow at a constant rate of 6 percent.

Smitty's management is new to the merger game, so Wade has been asked to answer some basic questions about mergers as well as to perform the merger analysis. To structure the task, Wade has developed the following questions; you must provide answers and then defend them to Smitty's board.

a. Several reasons have been proposed to justify mergers. Among the more prominent are (i) tax considerations, (ii) Diversification, (iii) control, (iv) purchase of assets at below replacement cost, and (v) synergy. Which of the reasons are economically justifiable? Which are not? Explain.

b. Briefly describe the differences between a hostile merger and a friendly merger.

c. Use the data in the table to construct the H division's cash flow statements for 1993 through 1996. Why is interest expense deducted in merger cash flow statements, whereas it is not normally deducted in a capital budgeting cash flow analysis? Why are retentions deducted in the cash flow statement?

d. Conceptually, what is the appropriate discount rate to apply to the cash flows developed in Part c? What is your estimate of the actual value of this discount rate?

e. What is the terminal value of the acquisition; that is, what is the value of the H division's cash flows beyond 1996? What is Hill's value to Smitty's? Suppose another firm were evaluating Hill's as an acquisition candidate. Would it obtain the same value? Explain.

f. Assume that Hill's has 10 million shares outstanding. These shares are traded relatively infrequently, but the last trade, made several weeks ago, was at a price of $9 per share. Should Smitty's make an offer for Hill's? If so, how much should it offer per share?

Solution to Self-Test Problem

ST-1   Refer to the relevant sections of the text to check your responses.

25

▲▲

Bankruptcy and Reorganization

A Managerial Perspective

With the impact of the Canada-U.S. Free Trade Agreement and the onset of the recession late in the 1980s, a number of companies in the Canadian economy faced financial distress. No industry was spared these problems, and large size was not an effective deterrent. An example was PWA Corporation at the beginning of December 1992. After a series of significant losses, PWA had entered discussions with Air Canada concerning a merger, but they faltered. In an attempt to improve its operations and financial performance, the company then undertook a number of restructuring and other changes, including pay cuts for executives and directors, salary cuts under negotiations with employees, bailout financing from the federal government, and the sale of aircraft. In addition, the company altered its capital structure by converting its 7.875 percent convertible debentures to common shares and negotiating to convert preferred shares to common shares.

Each of these moves had saved the company a substantial amount in interest and dividend payments, but the changes were insufficient. At the end of November 1992, PWA announced that it would not make payments on its debt or leases, although it would continue to pay its operating expenses. In addition, it announced that it would meet with its creditors to discuss means through which the company could restructure its financial structure and operating assets. The nonpayment of interest is a technical default. Both the company and the creditors now could undertake further responses to protect the firm's continuing operations or to precipitate liquidation. The options are discussed in this chapter, along with the conditions under which one may be preferred to others.

Many firms encounter financial difficulties, and some actually fail. The financial manager of a firm in financial distress must know how to ward off the firm's total collapse and thereby reduce potential losses to shareholders. In addition, financial managers of successful firms must know their rights and how to enforce them when one of their customers fails.

We now examine issues facing unsuccessful firms and those who must deal with them. We consider the extent of business failures, and the legal and informal remedies available both to creditors and debtors in the event of financial distress.[1]

---

[1]Bankruptcy, reorganization, and liquidation is a very involved subject. The purpose of this chapter is to provide some general guidelines and not to analyze specific provisions or techniques.

Failure

Failure can be interpreted in several ways, depending on the problems involved or the situation facing the firm. As will become clear subsequently, failure does not necessarily imply the collapse and dissolution of a firm with an associated loss of the total investment of creditors. For the sake of clarity, it is necessary to define some terms:

Economic failure.   An economic failure signifies that a firm's revenues do not cover its total costs, including its cost of capital.

Business failure.   The term *business failure* includes any business that has terminated with a resultant loss to creditors.[2]

Technical insolvency.   A firm is considered to be *technically insolvent* if it cannot meet its current obligations as they fall due. Another way to describe this situation is to say that the company is in *technical default* on its obligations. Technical insolvency or default denotes a lack of liquidity, and it may be only temporary. However, it provides a signal to the creditors that there is a potential problem, and they will react based on their perception of the extent of financial difficulty.

Insolvency in bankruptcy.   In contrast, a firm is *insolvent in bankruptcy* when its total liabilities exceed the true valuation of its assets. This condition, which is more serious than technical insolvency, often leads to liquidation of the firm.

Financial distress.   The term *financial distress* is frequently used to cover all instances in which the firm has not met all the conditions of the contracts under which creditors have advanced funds or goods to the firm. Thus, it encompasses both technical insolvency and insolvency in bankruptcy.

Legal bankruptcy.   Although many people use the term *bankrupt* to refer to any firm that has failed, a firm is not *legally bankrupt* unless (1) it has failed according to criteria established by the *Bankruptcy and Insolvency Act* and (2) it has been declared bankrupt by a court. **Bankruptcy** is a legal procedure for liquidating or reorganizing a business, with the liquidation or reorganization being carried out under special courts of law. Bankruptcy can be either *voluntary*, with the failing firm petitioning the court, or *involuntary*, with the firm's creditors petitioning the court and proving that the debtor is not meeting its debt payments as they fall due.

Liquidation.   The dissolving of a firm through selling of its assets is called **liquidation**.

---

[2]Failure statistics are available in the *Annual Statistical Summary* of the Office of the Superintendent of Bankruptcy.

Receivership.   When a firm cannot meet its financial obligations, its affairs are put into the hands of a *receiver*, who is appointed either by a court or by a secured creditor under provisions of a debt contract. The firm is then said to be in **receivership**. The receiver will either liquidate the firm or continue it—and even manage it—with liquidation as the goal. If new funds are to be raised to facilitate operations in the short run, the receiver will approach the secured creditor for the funds. (Clearly no other party would provide funds if it could not have a position under liquidation senior to secured creditors.) Although most receiverships lead to a liquidation of the assets of the firm, some can lead to a sale of the assets as a going concern and then to a **reorganization**. In a reorganization (also called a *workout*), the firm continues its existence but its liabilities are restructured with creditors receiving new financial securities whose market value reflects the current risk of the firm. Equity holders' securities may be worthless. This is an alternative procedure to actions under the *Bankruptcy and Insolvency Act*.

Sequence of Events

In order to place the definitions in context, we present the events that arise in the process of the liquidation or rehabilitation of a company in financial distress. The signal to the creditors of a company that their investment is in jeopardy occurs when the firm does not make its contractual payments as stipulated. Of course, this is not the first sign that the company is in trouble, but it is the event that permits creditors to take action to minimize the loss of their investment.

At this point, the creditors must make a decision whether to dissolve the company through *liquidation* procedures or to keep it alive through a *reorganization*. Fundamentally, this decision depends on a determination of the value of the firm if it is *rehabilitated* versus the value of its assets if they are sold off individually. The procedure that promises higher returns to the creditors and owners will be adopted. If rehabilitation is the appropriate economic choice, the total value that can be divided among the creditors and perhaps the owners of the company is fixed. Therefore, intense negotiations on the position of each creditor in the reorganized firm will be undertaken, since what one creditor or class of creditors receives will result in a compensating reduction in the value received by another creditor, creditor class, or the owners of the firm.

The creditors have three options available to them; their choice will depend upon the severity of the financial distress, the complexity of the financial structure that is in place, and the size of the firm.

1. Under the first option, the creditors, upon negotiations with the firm, either extend the time period for the payment of interest and/or principal or reduce the interest rate on the outstanding debt. Both procedures effectively reduce the financial burden on the firm and permit it to continue operating, and the creditors incur minimal transactions and legal costs. This option is chosen when the financial distress is perceived to be transitory: the firm is economically sound, and creditors still have confidence in the existing management. The transitory financial distress may arise from a temporary shift in demand for the product

or from debt issues at high interest rates. Typically, this option is used for firms with simple capital structures or a few large creditors and some smaller ones. This option may result in a voluntary reorganization of the debt payments.

2. The second option is a receivership. This is a more expensive procedure than the first option and is used in more severe cases of financial distress. Once the receiver is installed, the creditors must decide whether the firm is "worth more dead than alive." If the expected market value of the firm under continued operation is less than its liquidation value, the firm should be liquidated and the proceeds distributed according to a prearranged formula. If the converse is true, then a reorganization or workout must be structured in which the financial burden of the firm is reduced and each creditor class loses some of its original investment. The resulting financial structure is the product of complex negotiations. In many cases, conditions for a successful workout involve the replacement of existing management, the liquidation of some of the assets, and the issue to creditors of new financial securities whose payoffs are contingent on the success of the company.

3. The final option is to utilize the legal remedy of the **Bankruptcy and Insolvency Act**, under which the firm is declared bankrupt and ultimately liquidated using the rules specified in the act. If creditors have chosen this option first, then it is possible the owners of the firm may present them with a proposal for a reorganization that they must evaluate. If they conclude the firm is worth more dead than alive, the proposal is rejected and the firm liquidated. This option is used most frequently for small firms. Alternatively, the creditors may have tried either options 1 or 2 and after being unable to arrive at an acceptable deal use the *Bankruptcy and Insolvency Act* for the liquidation.

Existing owners do have some influence on the process. Large companies with the financial resources to hire legal and accounting assistance may apply to the court for protection under the *Companies Creditors Arrangement Act (CCAA)*. (This act is described in more detail later in the chapter. The essence of it is to provide time for the owners of the firm to develop a reorganization plan, which must be submitted for approval to all creditors and ultimately the court.) Also, under the new *Bankruptcy and Insolvency Act* secured creditors must give a 10-day notice if they intend to claim the security on a loan. This provides time for management to apply under provisions of this act to stop all actions against the firm by creditors and to prepare a reorganization proposal, which has to be approved by creditors. During the time the proposal is being prepared, the creditors cannot take any action against the company. If this proposal is rejected, the firm is bankrupt and liquidation follows.

The options considered and the management responses are very important in ensuring that the economy's resources are allocated to their most efficient use through their redeployment from unprofitable to profitable firms. Profits, defined in economic terms, are opportunity costs adjusted for risk. By having mechanisms in place in which long-run viable firms facing financial distress are rehabilitated and all others liquidated, resources are not being wasted.

Concept Review

► Distinguish between *economic* and *business failure* and between *insolvency* and *bankruptcy*.

► Provide a definition of a *receiver* and describe its responsibilities.

► Identify the options available to creditors in the event of a technical default.

► Identify the options available to the management of companies in default.

► What is the underlying financial rationale that creditors should use in evaluating the potential liquidation of a firm?

The Failure Record

How widespread is business failure in Canada? In Table 25-1, we see that a fairly large number of businesses do fail each year and that the liabilities per failure are substantial. For example, in 1982, which was the height of the previous recession, there were 10 265 business failures and the average liability per failure was $187 266. In 1991, which was in the midst of the most recent recession, there were 12 952 failures and the liabilities per failure increased to $377 211. Part of the increase in dollars per failure reflects the impact of inflation over the period. However, the severity of the most recent recession is reflected in the liabilities per failure figure.

The failure statistics are further subdivided into a number of industrial categories. The liabilities per failure are very different for each industry. The information for 1991 is presented in Table 25-2. As can be observed there, the

Table 25-1
Business Bankruptcies in Canada, 1981–1991

Year	Number of Failures	Average Liabilities per Failure
1981	7 708	$ 133 568
1982	10 265	187 266
1983	9 826	192 505
1984	9 258	238 053
1985	8 314	218 675
1986	8 143	191 960
1987	7 371	211 309
1988	7 721	326 506
1989	8 314	229 415
1990	11 180	254 280
1991	12 952	377 211

Note: "Businesses" here include proprietorships, partnerships, and limited companies.
Source: Consumer and Corporate Affairs Canada, *Insolvency Bulletin*, various issues.

Table 25-2
Selected Statistics on
Business Bankruptcies in Canada, 1991

| Industry | Failures | | Average Liabilities | Average Deficiency (assets − liabilities) |
	Number	% of Total		
Primary industries	859	6.4%	$261 832	$154 366
All manufacturing	1100	8.2	547 938	319 433
All construction	2012	15.0	258 759	157 244
Transport	966	7.2	429 044	290 603
All trade	3952	29.2	417 344	182 156
Finance and insurance	166	1.2	2 928 056	2 413 580
All services	3900	28.9	385 950	279 114
Communications and utilities	97	0.7	153 008	95 276
Real estate and insurance agencies	434	3.2	1 720 266	1 277 112
Total	13 496	—	457 191	285 778

Source: Office of the Superintendent of Bankruptcy. *Annual Statistical Summary,* 1991.
The same information appears in the *Insolvency Bulletin,* Consumer and Corporate Affairs Canada, March 1992, vol. 12, no. 3, p. 147.

major areas in which failures occurred were the trade sector (29.2 percent of total failures) and services (28.9 percent). The smallest percentages were observed in the communication area (0.7 percent) and the finance and insurance area (1.2 percent). However, the proportion of failures in each industry category does not give the complete picture. The average liability and average deficit give information on the amount of creditor claims per failure and the extent to which liabilities exceeded assets per failure. It is the latter statistic that indicates the potential loss for creditors. The "winner" in the failure statistics is the finance area: although it had few bankruptcies, the average deficiency was over $2 million. And the average deficiency in the real estate industry was $1.3 million. These observations reflect the severity of the recession in these two areas. Well down in terms of dollar losses but still above the overall values for all failures were the manufacturing industry (an average deficiency of $319 433) and transport industry (an average deficiency of $290 603).

Although it appears that most failures occur in smaller establishments, large firms are not immune to failure. There are, however, a number of offsetting factors that keep the failure rate of large companies lower. These factors include government intervention (referred to as a *bailout*) to keep the firm in operation, merger of a failing firm with a solvent one, and the desire by creditors to reorganize rather than force a liquidation of a large company with significant amounts of loans outstanding. Both federal and provincial governments in Canada have been active in the "financial assistance business," providing loan insurance and loan guarantees to a number of large companies.

These include Massey-Ferguson and PWA. Preferred equity guarantees were provided for Massey-Ferguson. These guarantees (or insurance), although requiring no out-of-pocket expense for the government, are not riskless to the government! The failure of a company and the exercise of the guarantee can be a major financial burden for the government.[3]

It should be noted that the failure statistics referred to in Table 25-1 do not provide a complete picture of the true financial failures in the economy. The statistics refer only to bankruptcy, but a large number of companies fail and go into receivership or are wound up by means other than bankruptcy and thus do not show up in these statistics. In a number of instances, firms are not liquidated but are reorganized and continue operations.

Restructuring Outside the Provisions of the *Bankruptcy and Insolvency Act*

In the case of a fundamentally sound company whose financial difficulties appear to be temporary, the creditors generally prefer to work directly with the company and help it recover and re-establish itself on a sound financial basis. This procedure is accomplished outside the *Bankruptcy and Insolvency Act* so as to maintain flexibility and minimize costs. Such voluntary plans usually require some type of **restructuring** of the firm's debt. This restructuring involves either **extension**, which postpones the date of required payment of past-due obligations, or **composition**, by which the creditors voluntarily reduce their claims on the debtor. Both procedures are designed to keep the debtor in business and to avoid court costs. Although creditors do not obtain immediate payment and may still suffer losses, they often recover more money, and sooner, than if one of the formal procedures had been followed.

The start of a voluntary debt restructuring is a filing by a debtor of a restructuring proposal. Subsequently, a meeting of the debtor and the creditors is held. The creditors appoint a committee consisting of some of the largest creditors and perhaps one or two of the smaller ones. The purpose of the meeting, and of any subsequent meetings, is to work out a proposal that is acceptable to all parties. Usually a vote with a two-thirds majority of each creditor class is required to have the proposal accepted and binding on all creditors.

An extension is preferred by creditors because it provides for payment in full. The debtor makes current purchases on a cash basis and pays off its past balance over an extended time. In some cases, creditors may agree not only to extend the time of payment but also to subordinate existing claims to new debts incurred in favour of vendors extending credit during the period of the extension. The creditors must have faith that the debtor will solve its problems.

Because of the uncertainties involved, however, creditors will want to exercise some control over the debtor while waiting for their claims to be paid. For a control mechanism, the committee may, for example, insist that an

---

[3]This subject is analyzed in depth in M.J. Trebilcock et al., *The Political Economy of Corporate Bailouts* (Toronto: Ontario Economic Council, 1986).

assignment (turnover of assets to the creditors' committee) be executed, to be held in case of default. The committee may obtain security in the form of notes, mortgages, or assignment of accounts receivable.

In a composition, a pro rata cash settlement is made. Creditors in the same class receive in cash from the debtor a uniform percentage of the obligations. The cash received, which may be as low as 10 cents on the dollar, is taken as full settlement of the debt. Bargaining will take place between the debtor and the creditors over the savings that result from avoiding certain costs associated with the bankruptcy: costs of administration, legal fees, expenses of outside experts. In addition to avoiding such costs, the debtor gains in that the stigma of bankruptcy may be avoided; as a result, the debtor may be induced to part with most of the savings that result from avoiding bankruptcy.

Often the bargaining process will result in a compromise involving both an extension and a composition. For example, the settlement may provide for a cash payment of 25 percent of the debt and six future installments of 10 percent each for a total payment of 85 percent. Installment payments are usually evidenced by notes, and creditors will also seek protective controls.

Voluntary settlements are informal and simple. They are also relatively inexpensive, because legal and administrative expenses are held to a minimum. Thus, voluntary procedures result in the largest return to creditors. In addition, an almost-bankrupt business may be saved to continue as a future customer. One possible disadvantage is that the debtor may be left to manage the business. This situation may result in an erosion of assets, but there are numerous controls available to protect the creditors. It should also be noted that small creditors may play a nuisance role by insisting on payment in full. As a consequence, settlements typically provide for payment in full for claims under $500 or $1000. If a composition is involved and all claims under $500 are paid, all creditors will receive a base of $500 plus the agreed-upon percentage for the balance of their claims.

An example of a voluntary restructuring is provided by Fleet Aerospace Corp. This company supplies sophisticated products to the aerospace and defence industries. With the reduction in defence spending in the United States and the onset of the recession, Fleet's earnings fell dramatically, and the firm was in technical default to its bank, which was owed approximately $40 million on demand loans. Provincial and federal loan guarantees of approximately $20 million were available to Fleet provided it was able to undertake a successful restructuring. Finally, it was agreed that if the bank satisfied its claim and forced the company into bankruptcy there would be little left for any other creditors or equity holders. Moreover, the costs of liquidation would be high and the time period over which the bank would finally receive any payments would be extended. Given that a loan guarantee was in the offing, the value of Fleet would be enhanced if it were able to reorganize.

The reorganization, which was approved by all classes of creditors and shareholders, had the following structure.

- The bank agreed to convert $25 million of its outstanding debt to distress preferred shares. The dividends on these shares are tax free to the bank and thus the interest rate is low. The remainder of the loan was still repayable.

- The preferred shareholders had not received dividends since 1989 and the total amount in arrears was $1.65 per share. The preferred shareholders would receive 3.5 new common shares for each outstanding preferred share; this was to compensate the preferred shareholders for the value of their share including the passed dividends.
- Each holder of common shares and of class A nonvoting common shares was to receive one new share for each old share.

The financial structure of the reorganized firm was as follows:

Loans	$16 million
Preferred shares	$25 million to bank
Common equity	14.0 million shares to holders of old preferred shares
	3.7 million shares to holders of old common shares
	4.5 million shares to holders old class A nonvoting shares
	22.2 million

Reorganizations: More Complex Situations

Under more complex situations, reorganizations or workouts can involve very complicated negotiations in an attempt to keep a company alive by changing its capital structure and perhaps altering its asset structure; this will reduce its interest expense and its debt repayment schedules. Many larger companies that have been in technical default have used this mechanism. Examples include Algoma Steel, Bramalea Ltd., and Olympia & York. Reorganizations have certain features in common.[4]

1. The firm is insolvent either because it is unable to meet cash obligations as they come due or because claims on the firm exceed the value of its assets. Hence, some modifications in the nature or the amount of the firm's obligations must be made—fixed charges must be reduced or at least stretched out. The procedure may include scaling down interest charges, converting short-term debt into long-term debt, converting debt into common shares, or simply writing off some claims against the company.

2. Firms in financial trouble almost always let their properties run down, and they generally deplete their liquid assets. Therefore, in most reorganizations, new funds must be raised to increase working capital and to rehabilitate property.

3. The operating and managerial causes of the difficulty must be identified and eliminated.

---

[4]In some instances, the creditors put pressure on the company to change management and bring in someone who will be able to negotiate with all of the creditors and effect the voluntary reorganization. For example, the president of Dome Petroleum was brought in to engage in very complex negotiations with the purpose of restructuring the company and preventing any creditor from forcing the company into the procedures under the *Bankruptcy Act*. In other instances, the secured creditors can put in a receiver who gets involved in a restructuring of the debt.

Although the form of the reorganization will differ depending on the specifics of the company, there are some general principles with which all financial managers should be familiar. As has been noted, a reorganization requires a scaling down of claims, and in any reorganization two conditions must be met: (1) the scaling down must be fair to all parties, and (2) there must be a reasonably high probability of successful rehabilitation and profitable future operations.

Although it is often most cost effective to have a voluntary reorganization, there are situations in which a legal proceeding is required. When the negotiations are quarrelsome, when the number of creditors is large and co-ordination is very difficult, and when the issues are very complex, a legal proceeding can impose order on chaos. For example, consider the situation of Olympia & York: there were more than 100 lenders, not including the holders of outstanding commercial paper, there were properties in three countries, and there were a number of relatively small creditors that could, by demanding payment, force the company into bankruptcy, which no one really wanted. In this situation, a court procedure was the only possible way of resolving the issues.

The legislation used in these situations is the *Companies Creditors Arrangement Act* (CCAA), which was introduced during the Depression but was little used until the spate of defaults beginning in 1990. The CCAA is very flexible since there are very few rules spelled out. The law is made through the interpretations of judges in specific situations, and it could be biassed toward reorganizations and the continued existence of companies since judges do not want to take the responsibility for putting down large companies. With the flexibility comes the problem of uncertainty faced by creditors and the significant cost of professional assistance. Therefore, the use of the CCAA is reserved for large companies.

Under the CCAA, the company is protected from its creditors and can continue to operate for a specified period. During this period, the company is overseen by a receiver and is required to submit a restructuring plan to its creditors, suppliers, and shareholders for approval by a date determined in the original filing or as amended with court approval. Agreement by these groups will permit a renewed company to continue operations.

An example of a reorganization under the CCAA has been the attempt by Steinberg Inc. to prepare a reorganization plan. The assets of Steinberg were acquired by Socanov Inc. in 1989. Early in 1992, Steinberg sold off its core Quebec supermarket chain. This left 107 Valdi stores in Quebec and Ontario, and 24 Smitty's Super Valu Inc. stores in Arizona. On May 19, 1992, Steinberg filed for protection under the CCAA and prepared a reorganization plan, proposing the following arrangements for the company's creditors:

- A 14-member banking syndicate was owed approximately $80 million. The loans would be paid in full on a schedule to be worked out with the banks and the company.
- Suppliers were owed approximately $72 million, and about $62 million of it would be paid, with the money coming from the proceeds of a pending law suit. The payouts to the suppliers would depend upon the size of the claim. Those with claims of less than $1000—34 percent of the total—would be

paid in full. With an increased dollar claim, the payout per dollar claim diminished. For example, of the more than 600 creditors who were owed more than $40 000, the payout was 14¢ per dollar of claim.

- Both the Caisse de dépôt et placement du Québec and the Société de developpement industriel du Québec (SDI) had financed the operations of Socanov in its acquisition of Steinberg. In the plan, both agencies would take a back seat to the suppliers. The Caisse, which was owed $90 million, would receive shares and 30 percent of the discretionary cash flow for 5 years. SDI, which was owed $72 million, would receive a $10 million up-front cash payment and shares providing for 50 percent of the discretionary cash flow over 5 years.

This plan was to go forward to a vote by the creditors. However, late in November 1992, the Caisse and the SDI rejected the deal, arguing that they did not want shares in lieu of cash. They said they would expect a better deal to be forthcoming or they would vote against the plan. Whether they will follow through on their threat must be evaluated by the company. In any restructuring there is a fixed pie available for allocation and a claim by one party for an increased payout can be met only at the expense of another party. Therefore, it may be very difficult to meet the objections, and no enhancement of terms may be made before the vote. Note that a failure of the plan could lead to bankruptcy and ultimately liquidation of the company—a situation that would likely result in no payout to the Caisse or to the SDI. In January 1993 a proposal was accepted by the creditors; there were minor changes from the original proposal described above.

Concept Review

▶ Describe the process underlying a voluntary restructuring.

▶ Define an *extension* and a *composition* in the context of a restructuring.

▶ Review the voluntary restructuring example in the text, and describe how the final result reflects the priority of each financial claimant to the earnings stream.

▶ Under what conditions would a company choose to file under the CCAA?

The *Bankruptcy and Insolvency Act*

The old *Bankruptcy Act*, a federal statute dating from 1949, provided for an orderly and equitable distribution of the assets of an insolvent company to its creditors. It was also supposed to provide an opportunity for a debtor to reorganize its debts to avoid bankruptcy with the permission of its creditors. Although the act was successful in its first goal, it was unsuccessful in the second. Very few plans of arrangement (reorganizations) were undertaken under the act. In fact, if possible, companies preferred to operate outside of the act, usually through private arrangements or more recently the CCAA.

In recognition of this problem, there were six reform bills introduced after 1975, but none of them was enacted by Parliament. Finally in 1991, a bill to amend the act was introduced and passed. The new act, referred to as the

Bankruptcy and Insolvency Act, became effective at the beginning of December 1992. The changes in the act are intended to make it easier for companies to avoid bankruptcy by reorganizing their operations and financial claims and to continue operations by obtaining needed inputs. Whether the revisions to the act are successful in achieving this goal will be seen only with the passage of time.

Bankruptcy proceedings begin when a debtor is unable to meet, or can forecast an inability to meet, scheduled payments to its creditors. At that time, these central issues arise:

1. Is the inability to meet scheduled debt payments a temporary cash flow problem (technical insolvency), or is it a permanent problem caused by a decline in asset values and earning power below debt obligations (insolvency in bankruptcy)?

2. If the problem is temporary, then a simple extension, which enables the firm to recover and to satisfy everyone, will be worked out. However, if basic long-run assets values have truly declined, then economic losses have occurred. In this event, who should bear the losses? Two theories exist: (a) the **absolute priority doctrine**, which states that claims must be paid in strict accordance with the priority of each claim, regardless of the consequence to other claimants, and (2) the **relative priority doctrine**, which is more flexible and gives a more balanced consideration to all claimants. The pricing of the securities of the various creditors will depend upon which of these rules is expected to be operational in the event of a bankruptcy. The *Bankruptcy and Insolvency Act* specifies that the absolute priority rule must be followed in either a liquidation or a rehabilitation undertaken under its provisions.

3. Is the company "worth more dead than alive"—that is, will the business be more valuable if it is maintained and continued in operation or if it is liquidated and sold off in pieces? Under the absolute priority doctrine, unless specific provisions are found in the act to make it easier to reorganize and continue operations, liquidations are more likely, because liquidations generally permit senior creditors to be paid off sooner, but often at the expense of junior creditors and shareholders. Under the relative priority doctrine, senior creditors are more likely to be required to wait for payment in order to increase the chances of providing some returns to junior creditors and shareholders.

4. Who should control the firm while it is being liquidated or rehabilitated? Should the existing management be left in control, or should a *trustee* be placed in charge of operations?

Prerequisites for Bankruptcy

A voluntary petition of bankruptcy (or assignment) may be filed by the debtor. Creditors may petition for an involuntary bankruptcy if the following two conditions are met.

1. Creditor(s) must have $1000 or more owing.

2. Within the 6 months preceding the filing of a creditor's petition, the debtor must have committed one or more acts of bankruptcy. These acts of bankruptcy raise the presupposition that the debtor is either unable to pay the debts or is attempting to avoid payment.

Acts of Bankruptcy

The ten acts of bankruptcy can be summarized briefly.

1. *Fraudulent conveyance.*   Fraudulent conveyance is a transfer of property to a third party without adequate consideration and with intent to defraud creditors.

2. *Preferential transfer.*   A preferential transfer is the transfer of money or assets by an insolvent debtor to a creditor, giving the creditor a greater portion of his or her claim than other creditors would receive on liquidation. This is also referred to as a *fraudulent preference.*

3. *Concealment or removal.*   Concealment constitutes hiding of property with the intent to defraud creditors. Removal refers to the removal of property with the same intent.

4. *Assignment.*   If a debtor makes a general assignment for the benefit of creditors, an act of bankruptcy exists. This enables creditors who have become distrustful of the debtor in the process of assignment to transfer the proceedings to an involuntary bankruptcy.

5. *Sudden departure.*   If the debtor absconds in order to defeat or delay the creditors, then a petition for bankruptcy can be filed.

6. *Admission at creditors' meeting.*   The debtor commits an act of bankruptcy if, at a meeting of the creditors, he or she either presents a statement of assets and liabilities showing that he or she is insolvent or admits, in writing, that he or she is unable to pay debts.

7. *Default on a proposal.*   In order to prevent bankruptcy, the debtor may have presented a proposal for a commercial arrangement under the *Bankruptcy and Insolvency Act.* Any default on such a proposal is an act of bankruptcy.

8. *Notice to creditors.*   If the debtor presents notice to any creditor that he or she has suspended or will suspend payments on the debt, then an act of bankruptcy has occurred.

9. *Execution order.*   An act of bankruptcy occurs if the debtor fails to redeem goods that have been seized under an execution issued against the debtor.

10. *Technical insolvency.*   The most common act of bankruptcy occurs when the debtor is unable to meet liabilities generally as they become due.

After a petition for involuntary bankruptcy has been filed, the court may appoint a trustee to be an *interim receiver*. The purpose of the interim receiver is to protect the estate for the creditors. If the receiving order is issued by the court and bankruptcy procedures continue, the interim receiver is usually appointed as the trustee of the estate.

In a voluntary bankruptcy, there is no petition or receiving order, and the trustee is appointed directly. After appointment of the trustee, however, the procedures for an involuntary and a voluntary bankruptcy are identical.

Upon the appointment of the trustee, the date of the creditor's meeting is determined. The trustee is very important in the procedure under the *Bankruptcy and Insolvency Act*. The functions performed include calling the creditors' meeting and preparing a report on the debtor company. This report usually outlines the historical background of the firm, its financial position, the cause of its financial difficulties, the conduct of the debtor, evaluation of assets both as a going concern and in liquidation, and the difference between declared liabilities and the claims produced by creditors for payment.

Proposal for Reorganization

A *proposal for reorganization* is a form of extension or composition of the firm's obligations and has the following features that are similar to those found under a voluntary reorganization:

1. The firm is insolvent either because it is unable to meet cash obligations as they come due or because claims on the firm exceed its assets. Hence, some modifications in the nature or amount of the firm's obligations must be made. A scaling down of terms or amounts must be formulated. This procedure may be based on decreasing fixed charges or converting short-term debt into long-term debt.
2. New funds may have to be raised for working capital and for property rehabilitation.
3. The operating and managerial causes of difficulty must be eliminated.

The filing of a notice of intention to file a proposal by the bankrupt or insolvent debtor effectively freezes the enforcement remedies of the creditors during the period while the proposal is being prepared. The notice of intention can be a reaction to secured creditors' filing a notice to take possession of the security for their loan or it may be a pre-emptive move by the debtor.[5] The proposal must be filed within 30 days of the filing of the intention. Extensions are possible in increments of (maximum) 45 days, not to exceed in aggregate 5 months. The extensions must approved by the court, and creditors may oppose them under certain conditions. The proposal must provide that the claims of creditors having a priority under the act be paid along with trustees. If there is no proposal within the time period permitted, the debtor company is declared bankrupt and liquidation follows.

The proposal must cover unsecured creditors and can include secured creditors. After it is filed, the affected creditors vote on its terms. If the secured creditors are included in the proposal, they vote first as a class. If they vote against, the proposal can still go forward subject to the unsecured creditors' approval, but it will not apply to the secured creditors and they can seize the security for their loans. The unsecured creditors vote as a class and if they defeat the proposal, the firm is bankrupt. This provision ensures that no single unsecured creditor can defeat the proposal.

If the proposal is approved by the creditors, then it must be approved by the court: this is usually automatic since the court is unlikely to overturn a voluntary agreement between the debtor and its creditors.

---

[5]The secured creditors must give 10 days' notice before seizing the security for their loan.

Example of Proposal

Under the previous bankruptcy act, business proposals were rare events since the companies involved were typically small and the creditors were worried about a loss in value under a proposal that would permit them to continue to operate. Larger firms were normally dealt with under the CCAA or through voluntary arrangements. However, if the new act is successful, more proposals will be forthcoming for smaller firms, although it is likely that larger firms will continue to use the current techniques.

To highlight the important concerns in a proposal, we use a simple, hypothetical example. Many of the principles observed here are similar to those identified under the voluntary reorganization route. To illustrate the characteristics of proposals, we then review a simplified version of a successful proposal.

Table 25-3 presents the balance sheet, as of December 31, 1993, for New-Life Furniture Company, Limited. The company is a medium-sized manufacturer of furniture and has been suffering substantial losses for the past two years. In March 1994, the company filed a proposal for a reorganization.

In preparing the proposal, the company provided an evaluation of its prospective value as a viable concern. After a survey and discussions with various experts, an estimate of future earnings was formulated. Based on a reasonable price-earnings multiple for furniture manufacturers, a valuation of New-Life as a viable business was $750 000.

The proposal required the company to issue new debt and new common equity for the outstanding claims of New-Life. The new company would issue $500 000 of 20-year, 12 percent debentures in exchange for the existing first-mortgage bonds. This would provide for the payment in full of the first priority claims and result in a net value available to ordinary unsecured creditors of $250 000. Their claims, however, totalled $480 000. With only

---

Table 25-3
New-Life Furniture Company, Limited
Balance Sheet as of December 31, 1993
(thousands of dollars)

Assets		
Current assets	$ 200	
Net property	800	
Total assets	$1000	
Liabilities and capital		
Accounts payable	$ 80	
Notes payable	100	
8% first-mortgage bonds	500	
8½% sinking fund debentures	300	
Common shares	120	
Retained earnings	(100)	
Total liabilities	$1000	

$250 000 available, each claimant would be entitled to 52 percent of its claim. The proposal provided for the ordinary unsecured creditors to receive, in aggregate, 100 000 shares of the new company as settlement for their claims in full. The claims and settlement are shown in Table 25-4.

Of course, any proposal must also include payment of the trustee's costs and of any outstanding taxes.

Notice that in New-Life's proposal, the common shareholders of the firm do not receive anything. Under the absolute priority rule, the highest-priority claim must be settled in full before the claim of any lower-priority class can be considered. This rule does not imply that the first mortgage bondholders must receive securities of the same class in the reorganized company. In fact, if the valuation of the company were much lower, the first mortgage bondholders could have received common shares. The absolute priority rule specifies the order in which claims must be settled in full.

Clearly, the larger the valuation of the company, the more likely it is that the original common shareholders will receive something in the proposal. If the valuation of New-Life's common equity were in excess of $980 000, the claims of the ordinary, unsecured creditors could be settled in full and the shareholders would receive some new shares.

In addition to satisfying the priority claims of the creditors, the proposal must present a new financial structure that is feasible, given the forecasted earnings for the company. It is essential that the new capital structure be determined so that the firm is not forced into bankruptcy again because of earnings that are not adequate to service a very large debt component.

A Real-World Example.   Up to this point, we have considered the concept of a proposal in general terms with reference to an artificial example. We now present an actual commercial arrangement to demonstrate the absolute priority rule and the types of securities that are given to creditors in an arrangement. The arrangement concerns Rideau Carleton Raceway Investments Limited (hereafter called Investments) and a wholly owned subsidiary, Rideau Carleton Raceway Holdings Limited (hereafter called Holdings). Both

Table 25-4
New-Life Furniture Company: Proposal for Reorganization

Prior Claims	Amount	Receives	
First mortgage bonds	$500 000	$500 000 in debentures of new company	

Ordinary Unsecured Creditors	Amount	52 Percent of Claim	Number of Common Shares
Notes payable	$100 000	$ 52 000	20 800
Sinking fund debentures	300 000	156 000	62 400
Accounts payable	80 000	42 000	16 800
	$480 000	$250 000	100 000

companies had head offices in Ottawa. The first company was incorporated under federal jurisdiction and the second in the province of Ontario.[6]

On April 2, 1962, Investments had issued $1 million of 6.75 percent first mortgage bonds secured by the outstanding shares of Holdings. In addition, $1 million of 6.50 percent sinking fund debentures were also issued and secured by a floating charge on the assets of Investments; interest had not been paid on these bonds since November 15, 1962. There was also a mechanic's lien of $897 621 on the real property of Holdings; this lien had been outstanding since March 5, 1966. On May 19, 1962, Investments had issued 100 000 preferred shares with a par value of $5 per share. The preferred shares were entitled to a dividend only if the consolidated net income of Investments was in excess of $30 000. As net earnings never exceeded this value, no dividends were paid. Upon liquidation, the preferred holders were entitled to the paid-up value of the shares. Finally, Investments had issued 250 000 common shares of no par value in 1962. The aggregate consideration for the shares was $112 500. The company had been in financial distress for many years but it was not until 1971 that a proposal was actually devised. Table 25-5 sets out the creditors' claims.

The proposal, dated August 9, 1971, was somewhat complicated. In essence, Holdings was to take over all obligations of Investments, and any shares issued by Investments were convertible into shares of Holdings on a one-for-one basis. In the following evaluation, we assume that all shares issued by Investments were converted into Holdings so that only the shares of Holdings were outstanding.

The first mortgage bondholders received $900 000 in 12 percent, first mortgage bonds of Holdings plus 200 000 common shares. In addition, for each $1000 of principal amount of existing bonds, a cash payment of $100 was made in respect of the accrued interest. The holders of the sinking fund debentures received 500 000 common shares in settlement of their claim. The holders of the mechanic's lien received $500 000 worth of 8 percent secured-income bonds, which were subordinated to the 12 percent first mortgage bonds. In addition,

---

Table 25-5

Proposed Compensation in Reorganization of "Investments" and "Holdings"

Creditors	Claims	Proposed Compensation
First mortgage bonds	$1 000 000	$900 000 + 200 000 common shares
Sinking fund debentures	1 000 000	500 000 common shares
Mechanic's lien	897 621	$500 000 + 750 000 common shares (income bonds)
Preferred shares; 100 000 shares	500 000	100 000 common shares
Common shares; 250 000 shares	112 500	25 000 common shares
	$3 510 121	

---

[6]Although the example is from 1971, it illustrates the issues that are addressed in a proposal for a reorganization. Since there are so few proposals and restructurings usually proceed outside the bankruptcy act, this example was one of the few available.

the lien holders received 750 000 common shares of Holdings. The holders of preferred shares received 1 new share of Holdings for every preferred share. Finally, the common shareholders received 1 new share for every 10 shares of Investments held. This resulted in the issuance of 25 000 common shares.

One way of evaluating this plan is to assume that the payment given to the old first mortgage bonds equalled $1 million. Thus, the implicit price per common share was $0.50. The preferred share claim of $500 000 was therefore settled for $50 000, and the holders of the old common shares received $12 500 in new common shares of Holdings.

Included in the proposal was the payment in cash for the fees, costs, and expenses of the receiver and the trustee. The acceptance of the proposal by the creditors was equivalent to creditors' granting of a complete and full discharge of all claims against Holdings and Investments.

Concept Review

▶ Describe firm actions that will result in bankruptcy under the *Bankruptcy and Insolvency Act.*
▶ How does the act assist in the rehabilitation of companies rather than in their liquidation?
▶ Describe the operation of the absolute priority rule in the design of proposals.

Liquidation Procedures

If a company is too far gone to be rehabilitated, then it must be liquidated. Liquidation should occur when the business is worth more dead than alive or when the possibilities of restoring profitability are so remote that the creditors run a high risk of loss if operations are continued.

Liquidations can occur either outside the provisions of the *Bankruptcy and Insolvency Act* or through a formal *bankruptcy procedure* carried out under the jurisdiction of a bankruptcy court.

Outside the Bankruptcy and Insolvency Act

In order to avoid the costs of the bankruptcy procedures and to gain flexibility, many liquidations occur outside of the *Bankruptcy and Insolvency Act.* We shall consider two procedures: (1) assignment and (2) voluntary liquidation.

Assignment.   Assignment is an informal procedure for liquidating debts, and it usually yields creditors a larger amount than they would receive in a formal bankruptcy.[7] An **assignment** calls for title to the debtor's assets to be transferred to a third person, known as an *assignee* or *trustee.* The assignee is

---

[7]The description refers to common law assignment. A statutory assignment is similar in concept to the common law assignment but is carried out under statutes relating to assignment and proceeds under court order and supervision.

instructed to liquidate the assets through a private sale or a public auction and then to distribute the proceeds among the creditors on a pro rata basis.

The assignment does not automatically discharge the debtor's obligations. If a corporation goes out of business and does not satisfy all its claims, there will still be claims against it; in effect, however, the corporation has ceased to exist. The people who have been associated with the company can then proceed to organize another corporation free of the debts and obligations of the previous corporation. There is always the danger, however, that the court may hold the individuals responsible; therefore, it is usually important to obtain a statement from creditors that claims have been completely settled. Such a statement is, of course, even more important for an unincorporated business. Alternatively, the assignment may take place with the creditors' agreeing beforehand that the assignment will represent a complete discharge of the debtor's obligations.

Assignment has some advantages over bankruptcy through the courts, which involves more time, legal formality, and expense. The assignee has more flexibility in disposing of property than does a bankruptcy trustee. Action can be taken sooner, before the inventory becomes obsolete or the machinery rusts; also, since the assignee is often familiar with the channels of trade in the debtor's business, better results may be achieved.

Voluntary Liquidation.   When a firm approaches bankruptcy, a number of decisions can be made. One choice is to engage in a *voluntary liquidation* and hence not be involved in the bankruptcy process with the bankruptcy costs and an involuntary liquidation. By taking the voluntary route, management makes a deliberate decision to sell the firm either to another firm or piecemeal to a number of firms. If managers make decisions that are in the best interest of shareholders, then the voluntary decision should provide shareholders with the largest possible payoff from the set of decisions available. If, as is often the case, managers own some of the shares, the alignment of their interests with other shareholders of the firm is complete. Therefore, when we observe a voluntary liquidation, we would expect that the liquidating dividend from this strategy is greater than the market value of the equity as a going concern.

If liquidations provide the best results for common shareholders, then the share price should increase upon the announcement of a liquidation. Since there are often information leaks concerning the liquidation and rumours concerning potential mergers, share prices may even increase before the announcement date. One researcher found that the share price increased approximately 21 percent, net of overall market movements, over the 1-month period before the announcement date. Hence, voluntary liquidations are wealth-increasing activities.

Liquidation under the Bankruptcy and Insolvency Act

The *Bankruptcy and Insolvency Act* serves three important functions during a liquidation: (1) it provides safeguards against fraud by the debtor; (2) it provides for an equitable distribution of the debtor's assets among the creditors; and (3) it allows insolvent debtors to discharge all their obligations and to start new businesses unhampered by a burden of prior debt. However, liquidation is time-consuming, it can be costly, and it results in the extinction of the business.

The distribution of assets in a liquidation is governed by the following priority of claims:

1. *Secured creditors who are entitled to the proceeds of the sale of specific property pledged for a lien or a mortgage.*   If the proceeds from the sale of property do not fully satisfy the secured creditors' claims, the remaining balance is treated as a general creditor claim. (See Item 9.)[8]

2. *Trustee's costs to administer and operate the bankrupt firm.*

3. *Expenses incurred after an involuntary case has begun but before a trustee has been appointed.*

4. *Wages due workers if earned within 3 months prior to the filing of the petition in bankruptcy.*   The amount of wages is not to exceed $2000 per person.

5. *Claims for unpaid contributions to employee benefit plans that were to be paid within 6 months prior to filing.*   These claims, together with wages in Item 4, are not in total to exceed the $2000-per-wage-earner limit.

6. *Claims for unpaid goods shipped within 30 days of a purchaser's declaring bankruptcy.*

7. *Taxes due the federal, provincial, and municipal governments and any other government agency.*

8. *General or unsecured creditors.*   Trade credit in excess of amount in Item 6, unsecured loans, the unsatisfied portion of secured loans, and debenture bonds are classified as general creditor claims. Holders of subordinated debt also fall into this category, but they must turn over required amounts to the holders of senior debt.

9. *Preferred shareholders, who can receive an amount up to the par value of the issue.*

10. *Common shareholders, who receive any remaining funds on an equal, pro rata basis.*

Claimants described under Items 2 through 5 are generally referred to as *preferred creditors*. All creditors in a specific class, except for the secured creditors, are paid on a pro rata basis. Absolute priority is followed: no

---

[8]When a firm (or an individual) goes bankrupt with a bank loan outstanding, the bank will attach the firm's deposit balances and use them to offset the loan balances. This is called, in legal terms, *the right of offset.* The loan agreement may stipulate that the bank has a first-priority claim against any deposits. If so, the deposits are used to offset all or part of the bank loan. In this case, the bank will not have to share the deposits with other creditors. Compensating balances are often designated as security against a loan. If the bank has no explicit claim against deposits, it will attach the deposits and hold them for the general body of creditors, including itself. Without an explicit statement in the loan agreement, the bank does not receive preferential treatment with regard to attached deposits.

payment is made to a class of a lower priority until all claims of a higher priority are paid in full.

To illustrate how this priority of claims works out, here is a specific example. The balance sheet of a bankrupt firm is shown in Table 25-6. Assets total $91 million. The claims are those indicated on the right-hand side of the balance sheet. Notice that the subordinated debentures are subordinated to the first and second mortgage bonds.

Now assume that the assets of the firm are sold. These assets are greatly overstated in the balance sheet in Table 25-6; they are, in fact, worth much less than the $91 million at which they are carried. The following amounts are realized on liquidation:

Current assets	$28 000 000
Net property	5 000 000
Total assets	$33 000 000

The order of priority of payment of claims is shown in Table 25-7. Fees and expenses of administration are assumed to be $6 million. Next in priority are wages owed to workers, which total $1 million, and trade credit for goods shipped within 30 days of the date of bankruptcy, which amounts to $5 million. The bank and the holder of the first mortgage are secured creditors; the bank is able to obtain the full amount of its claim from the assets not pledged to specific debt, and the first mortgage is then paid from the net proceeds of $5 million from the sale of fixed property. This leaves $6 million available to the unsecured creditors.

Table 25-6
Bankrupt Firm
Balance Sheet

Current assets	$80 000 000	Accounts payable	$20 000 000
Net property	$11 000 000	Notes payable (due bank)	10 000 000
		Accrued wages, 1000 @ 1000	1 000 000
		Federal taxes	1 000 000
		Provincial taxes	1 000 000
		Current debt	$33 000 000
		First mortgage	$ 6 000 000
		Second mortgage	1 000 000
		Subordinated debentures[a]	8 000 000
		Long-term debt	$15 000 000
		Preferred shares	2 000 000
		Common equity	26 000 000
		Contributed surplus	4 000 000
		Retained earnings	11 000 000
		Net worth	$43 000 000
Total assets	$91 000 000	Total claims	$91 000 000

[a]Subordinated to unsatisfied portions of first or second mortgage bonds.

Table 25-7
Bankrupt Firm
Order of Priority of Claims

Distribution of Proceeds on Liquidation	
1. Proceeds of sale of assets	$33 000 000
2. Fees and expenses of administration of bankruptcy	6 000 000
3. Wages owed to workers	1 000 000
4. Trade credit for goods sold within 30 days	5 000 000
5. Notes payable to bank	10 000 000
6. First mortgage, paid from sale of net property	5 000 000
7. Available to ordinary unsecured creditors	$ 6 000 000

Type of General Creditor	Amount of Claim[a] (1)	Application of 22 Percent[b] (2)	After Subordination Adjustment[c] (3)	Percentage of Original Claim Received[d] (4)
Taxes	$ 2 000 000	$ 444 400	$ 444 400	22
Unsatisfied portion of first mortgage	1 000 000	222 200	1 000 000	100
Unsatisfied portion of second mortgage	1 000 000	222 200	1 000 000	100
Accounts payable	15 000 000	3 333 300	3 333 300	42
Subordinated debentures	8 000 000	1 777 700	222 100	3
	$27 000 000	$ 5 999 800	$ 5 999 800	43

[a] Column 1 is the claim of each type of creditor. Total claims equal $27 million.

[b] From Line 7 in the upper section of the table we see that $6 million is available. This sum, divided by the $27 million of claims, indicates that general creditors will receive 22 percent of their claims. This is shown in column 2.

[c] The debentures are subordinated to the first and second mortgage bonds. So $1 555 600 must be transferred from debentures to first and second mortgage bonds, as shown in column 3.

[d] Column 4 shows the results of dividing the column 3 figure by the original amount given in Table 25-6 except for first mortgage, where $5 million paid on the sale of property is included, and accounts payable, where the $5 million received is included. The 43 percent total includes the first mortgage and accounts payable transactions: ($5 999 800 + $5 000 000 + $5 000 000) ÷ ($27 000 000 + $5 000 000 + $5 000 000) = 43%.

The claims of the unsecured creditors total $27 million. As $6 million is available, each claimant is scheduled to receive approximately 22 percent of its claim before the subordination adjustment. This adjustment requires that the holders of the subordinated debentures turn over to the holders of the first and second mortgage bonds all amounts received, in equal amounts, until the bonds are satisfied. In this situation, the claim for both mortgage bonds is $2 million but only $444 400 is available; the deficiency is therefore $1 555 600. After transfer by the subordinated debentures of this amount, the mortgage bond holders are paid in full whereas the subordinated debenture holders receive only 3 percent of their claim. These figures illustrate the usefulness of the subordination provision.

Concept Review

▶ What procedures can be used outside of the *Bankruptcy and Insolvency Act* to effect a liquidation?

▶ What are the differences between general, preferred, and secured creditors?

▶ Why would subordinated debentures have a lower interest rate than nonsubordinated debentures?

Summary

This chapter described the remedies available to creditors and owners in the event of default. The key concepts covered are listed below:

☐ **Financial distress** is the formal signal to creditors that they can take actions to protect their investment. **Technical default** occurs when the creditor does not meet a condition of a loan such as paying interest.

☐ Creditors must evaluate whether the firm is worth more to them dead or alive; this will determine their behaviour in the event of a **reorganization** of assets and financial claims.

☐ In any reorganization of financial claims under the *Bankruptcy and Insolvency Act*, the **absolute priority rule** is followed in which creditors of higher priority must have their financial claims settled in full before creditors (or owners) of lower priority can receive any payout. If the reorganization is undertaken outside of the Act, the priority rule used will depend on the bargaining power of the debt and equity holders.

☐ Possible changes included in a reorganization include an **extension**, which postpones the date of any payments to the creditors, a **composition**, which reduces the amount owed, or a combination of both.

☐ To prevent the secured creditors from removing their security in the event of a default, management can apply for a stay of proceedings either under the *Companies Creditors Arrangement Act* (CCAA) or the *Bankruptcy and Insolvency Act* (BIA). If the stay is granted, the creditors must give the company a specified amount of time to prepare a *proposal for a restructuring*. This proposal must be presented to creditors for their acceptance and then be approved by the court.

☐ Rejection of the proposal under the BIA results in automatic liquidation; rejection under the CCAA can lead to bankruptcy and, ultimately, liquidation.

☐ Under a liquidation, proceeds are applied to creditors in the following order: *secured* creditors, *preferred* creditors, and *general* creditors.

Questions

25-1 "A certain number of business failures is a healthy sign. If there are no failures, this is an indication (a) that entrepreneurs are overly cautious and hence not as inventive and as willing to take risks as a healthy, growing economy requires; (b) that competition is not functioning to weed out inefficient producers; or (c) that both situations exist.'' Discuss this statement.

25-2 Distinguish between a *receivership* and a *bankruptcy.*

25-3 Would it be a sound rule to liquidate whenever the liquidation value is above the value of the corporation as a going concern? Discuss.

25-4 Why do liquidations usually result in losses for the creditors, the owners, or both? Would partial liquidation or liquidation over a period limit their losses? Explain your answer.

25-5 Are liquidations likely to be more common for public utilities or industrial corporations? Why?

25-6 One of the recent amendments to the *Bankruptcy and Insolvency Act* permits trade creditors to claim goods sold to companies within 30 days of the date of bankruptcy. How does this affect (a) the interest rate charged by banks on loans and (b) the amount of credit provided by banks to companies?

25-7 It has been suggested that with the new *Bankruptcy and Insolvency Act*, the CCAA will be used for large company reorganizations and the new BIA will be used for small and medium-sized firms. Explain whether you agree or disagree.

Self-Test Problems   (solutions appear on page 957)

ST-1 **Key terms.**   Define each of the following terms:
   a. Business failure; technical insolvency; legal bankruptcy
   b. Debt restructuring; extension; composition
   c. Reorganization; liquidation
   d. Receivership
   e. Absolute priority doctrine; relative priority doctrine
   f. Assignment
   g. Proposal

ST-2 **Liquidation.**   At the time it defaulted, Scotshop Discount Stores Ltd. had net current assets valued on its books at $12 million and net fixed assets of $15 million. At the time of final settlement, its debts were as follows:

Current liabilities	$8 million
First mortgage bonds	6 million
Second mortgage bonds	3 million
Debentures	2 million

None of the current liabilities has preferences in liquidation as provided in the *Bankruptcy and Insolvency Act*, and none has been secured by pledge of assets.

   Assume that the amount shown for each of the four classes of liabilities includes all unpaid interest to the date of settlement. The fixed assets were pledged as security for the first mortgage bonds and repledged for the second mortgage bonds. Determine the appropriate distribution of the proceeds under the following conditions:

a. Liquidation of current assets realizes $10.5 million, and $5 million is obtained from fixed assets.

b. Liquidation of current assets realizes $6 million, and $3 million is obtained from fixed assets.

Problems

25-1   Recapitalization.   The 1993 financial statements of the Pegasus Printing Ltd. follow.

Pegasus Printing Ltd.
Balance Sheet as of December 31, 1993
(millions of dollars)

Current assets	$135	Current liabilities	$ 52
Investments	50	Prepaid orders	82
Net fixed assets	200	Reserves	8
Goodwill	15	$10 preferred shares, $100 par (1 500 000 shares)	150
		$17 preferred shares, no par (100 000 shares, callable at $180)	18
		Common equity, $1.50 par (10 000 000 shares outstanding)	15
		Retained earnings	75
Total assets	$400	Total claims	$400

Pegasus Printing Ltd.
Income Statement for Year Ended
December 31, 1993
(millions of dollars)

Operating income		$650.0
Operating expense		(608.7)
Net operating income		$ 41.3
Other income		3.0
Other expense		0.0
Earnings before income tax		$ 44.3
Income tax (46%)		(20.4)
Income after taxes		$ 23.9
Dividends on $10 preferred shares	15.0	
Dividends on $17 preferred shares	1.7	(16.7)
Income available for common equity		$ 7.2

A recapitalization plan is proposed in which each share of the $10 preferred will be exchanged for one share of $5 preferred (stated value: $33) plus one 10 percent subordinated income debenture (stated principal: $67). The $17 preferred shares will be retired from cash.

a. Show the pro forma balance sheet (in millions of dollars) giving effect to the recapitalization and showing the new preferred shares at their stated value and the common equity at its par value.

b. Present the pro forma income statement (in millions of dollars carried to two decimal places).

c. How much does the income available to common shares increase as a result of the recapitalization?

d. How much smaller are the required pretax earnings after the recapitalization than before the change? (Hint: Required earnings are the amount that is just enough to meet fixed charges—debenture interest and/or preferred dividends.)

e. How is the debt-to-assets ratio affected by the recapitalization? (Hint: Debt includes prepaid orders.)

f. Would you vote for recapitalization if you were a holder of the $10 preferred shares?

25-2 Reorganization vs. liquidation. The PosiTech Company Ltd. produces precision instruments. The company's products, designed and manufactured according to specifications set out by its customers, are highly specialized. Declines in sales and increases in development expenses in recent years have resulted in a large deficit at the end of 1993, as shown by the balance sheet and sales and net income data that follow.

PosiTech Company Ltd.
Balance Sheet as of December 31, 1993
(millions of dollars)

Current assets	$1.5	Current liabilities	$1.8
Fixed assets	1.5	Long-term debt (unsecured)	0.9
		Common equity	0.6
		Retained earnings (deficit)	(0.3)
Total assets	$3.0	Total claims	$3.0

PosiTech Company Ltd.
Sales and Net Income, 1989–1993
(millions of dollars)

Year	Sales	Net Income after Tax before Fixed Charges
1989	$10.5	$1.05
1990	10.0	1.00
1991	9.6	0.90
1992	5.7	(0.30)
1993	5.4	(0.45)

Independent assessment has led the firm's management to the conclusion that PosiTech would have a liquidation value of about $2 400 000. As an alternative to liquidation, management has concluded that a

reorganization is possible with the investment of an additional
$1 200 000. Management is confident of the company's eventual success
and has stated that the additional investment would restore earnings to
about $500 000 a year after taxes and before fixed charges. The
appropriate capitalization multiplier is 8 times. Management is negotiating with a local investment group to obtain the additional $1 200 000.
If the funds are obtained, the holders of the long-term debt will be given
half the common equity in the reorganized firm in place of their present
claims.

Should the creditors agree to the reorganization, or should they
force liquidation of the firm?

25-3   Proceeds from liquidation.   The Puffin Fish Company has the following balance sheet (in thousands of dollars):

Current assets	$5040	Accounts payable	$1080
Fixed assets	2700	Notes payable (to bank)	540
		Accrued taxes	180
		Accrued wages	180
		Total current liabilities	$1980
		First mortgage bonds	$ 900
		Second mortgage bonds	900
		Total mortgage bonds	$1800
		Subordinated debentures	1080
		Total debt	$4860
		Preferred shares	360
		Common shares	2520
Total assets	$7740	Total liabilities and equity	$7740

The debentures are subordinated only to first mortgage bonds and $80 of
the accounts payable are less than 30 days old. Suppose Puffin goes
bankrupt and is liquidated, with $1800 being received from the sale of
the fixed assets, which were pledged as security for the first and second
mortgage bonds, and $2880 received from the sale of current assets. The
trustee's costs total $480. How much will each class of investors receive?

25-4   Bankruptcy distributions.   Waterloo Furniture Ltd. has the following
balance sheet:

Current assets	$1 875 000	Accounts payable	$ 375 000
Fixed assets	1 875 000	Notes Payable (to bank)	750 000
		Debentures	750 000
		Total debt	$1 875 000
		Common equity	1 875 000
Total assets	$3 750 000	Total liabilities and equity	$3 750 000

The trustee's costs total $281 250, and Waterloo has no accrued taxes or
wages and all accounts payable are greater than 30 days. If the firm
goes bankrupt, how much will each class of investors receive under each
of the following conditions?
a. A total of $2.5 million is received from sale of the assets.
b. A total of $1.875 million is received from sale of the assets.

Solutions to Self-Test Problems

ST-1   Refer to the appropriate sections of the text to check your response.

ST-2   **a.**   Since the claims of the first mortgage holders amount to $6 million and only $5 million is realized from liquidation of fixed assets, the balance of $1 million reverts to the status of a general, unsecured liability. The breakdown of general claims is

Current liabilities	$ 8 000 000
First mortgage (residual)	1 000 000
Second mortgage	3 000 000
Debenture bonds	2 000 000
Total	$14 000 000

Proceeds of liquidation of current assets = $10 500 000.

$$\text{Distribution ratio} = \frac{\$10\,500\,000}{\$14\,000\,000} = 75\%.$$

The distribution summary is

Current liabilities: 0.75 ($8 000 000)	$ 6 000 000
First mortgage: 0.75 ($1 000 000) +	
$5 000 000 from fixed assets	5 750 000
Second mortgage: 0.75 ($3 000 000)	2 250 000
Debenture bonds: 0.75 ($2 000 000)	1 500 000
	$15 500 000

b.   The claims of the first mortgage holders total $6 million and only $3 million is realized from liquidation of fixed assets; therefore the balance of $3 million reverts to the status of a general unsecured liability. The breakdown of general claims is

Current liabilities	$8 000 000
First mortgage (residual)	3 000 000
Second mortgage	3 000 000
Debenture bonds	2 000 000
Total	$16 000 000

Proceeds of liquidation of current assets = $6 000 000.

Distribution ratio = $6 000 000/$16 000 000 = 37.5%.

The distribution summary is

Current liabilities: 0.375 ($8 000 000)	$3 000 000
First mortgage: 0.375 ($3 000 000) +	
$3 000 000 from fixed assets	4 125 000
Second mortgage: 0.375 ($3 000 000)	1 125 000
Debenture bonds: 0.375 ($2 000 000)	750 000
	$9 000 000

A

Answers to Selected
End-of-Chapter Problems

2-2   at 20%, UCC = $23 593

2-4   tax payable $1 540 000

2-6 $ 240.66

2-7   **i.** $297.66   **ii.** $ 440.80   **iii.** $330.60

3-3   15%, IP_2 = 11%

4-1   Profit Margin = 2%; Debt Ratio = 40%

4-3   Quick Ratio = 1.19

4-4   Sales = $2 592 000; DSO = 36.3

4-5   Sales = $ 450 000; Cost of Goods Sold = $337 500

4-8   **a.** 16%

5-1   **b.** $ 1 820 000

5-2   **a.** $ 480 000   **b.** $ 18 750

5-3   **a.** $ 13 300 000   **c.** Current Ratio = 2.00   **d.** Current Ratio = 4.25

5-4   **a.** Total Assets = $ 29 160 000

5-5   **b.** 33%

5-6   **a.** Total Assets = $ 2 700 000   **d.** 3.45%

5-7   **b.** Notes Payable = $ 51 000

6-1   **b.** 140 000 units   **c.** $DOL_{125\,000}$ = −8.3

6-2   **a.** Gain at 18 000 units = $ 40 000
   b. $ 350 000   **c.** $DOL_{18\,000}$ = 4.5
   d. Breakeven quantity = 8750 units
   e. Breakeven sales = $ 542 500

6-3   **b.** 7000 units   **c.** 2600 units

6-4   **a.** Fixed costs = $ 80 000   **c.** $ 400 000

6-6   **b.** Surplus in July = $ 111 300; Loan in October = $ 22 800

7-1   **a.** 83 days   **c.** 4.9

7-2   **a.** ROE = 14.35%, 13.05%, 10.80%

7-5   **b.** $ 288 000

8-1   EOQ = 110

8-2   **a.** EOQ = 3873   **c.** $12 544

8-3   **b.** 65   **c.** 14 600   **d.** @ 4000 units = $ 20 856

8-4   **a.** EOQ = 13 200; Total Cost = $ 5220
   b. 42   **c.** 20 800   **d.** 41.67%
   f. −83.33%

8-5   **a.** EOQ = 100 000   **c.** $56 250

9-1   **a.** DSO = 28 days   **b.** $ 69 048

9-2   **a.** DSO_o = 27 days; DSO_N = 22.5 days
   b. D_o = $15 680; D_N = $ 38 220   **c.** C_o = $ 9986; C_N = $ 10 818

9-3   Category 3: Change in gross profits = $ 112 500; Change in net income = $ 59 714

9-4   **a.** Change in net income = −$ 60 735

9-5   **b.** DSO_{30} = 28.6; DSO_{90} = 35.1
   e. October 31 balance = $12 650; November 30 balance = $ 2600

9-6   Change in net income = $ 13 430

10-1   **a.** 18.43%

10-2   **a.** $ 4264;   **b.** h = $ 52 793; 1 = $40 000

10-3 $ 19 315

10-4 **a.** C* = $ 45 000   **b.** $ 22 500   **c.** 100

11-1 **a.** 73.74%   **d.** 21.28%

11-2 45.15%

11-3 **a.** $ 98 630   **c.** Average payables = $295 890; Approximate cost = 37.24%

11-4 **1.** 16%   **2.** 11.25%   **3.** 13.92% **4.** Approximate rate = 20%

11-6 **a.** $ 300 000

11-8 **a.** **1.** $ 5104   **2.** $ 10 500

11-9 **a.** $ 386 930 **b.** Monthly savings = $12 808

11-10 **a.** Total assets = $ 1 852 565; Accounts payable = $ 230 565   **b.** EAR = 20.86%

11-11 $ 72 998

11-12 **a.** 55 150

12-1 **a.** $530.00   **c.** $471.70

12-2 **a.** $895.40   **b.** $ 1552.90

12-3 **a.** $ 6374.96; **d.** $ 7012.46; $ 1160.38; $ 2000.00

12-5 **a.** Stream A = $ 1251.21

12-6 $ 3078.51

12-8 11.2208 million tonnes

12-9 **b.** 7 years

12-10 14%

12-11 9%

12-12 $ 27 311.43

12-13 **a.** $ 7298.27   **b.** $ 54 999.60

12-15 9%

12-17 **b.** 7%   **c.** 9%   **d.** 15%

12-18 **a.** $ 881.15   **b.** $ 895.40   **c.** $ 903.05 **d.** $ 563.40

12-19 **a.** $ 279.20   **b.** $ 276.85   **c.** $ 443.70

12-20 **a.** $ 1979.50   **b.** $ 2512.22

12-22 **a.** $750.77

12-23 **b.** $748.51   **c.** $906.15

13-1 **b.** $ 7486.20   **d.** 6.51 years

13-2 NPV_T = $ 409; IRR_T = 15%; Accept; NPV_P = $ 3318; IRR_P = 20%; Accept

13-3 NPV_E = $ 3861; IRR_E = 18%; NPV_G = $ 3057; IRR_G = 18%; Purchase electric powered forklift; it has higher NPV

13-4 NPV_S = $448.86; NPV_L = $607.20; IRR_S = 15.24%; IRR_L = 14.67%; $MIRR_S$ = 14.67%; $MIRR_L$ = 14.37%

13-5 **b.** IRR_A = 18.1%; IRR_B = 24.0%   **d.** at 12% $MIRR_A$ = 15.10%; $MIRR_B$ = 17.03%; at 18% $MIRR_A$ = 18.05%; $MIRR_B$ = 20.49%

13-6 **b.** 16.0665%   **d.** IRR_A = 20.0%; IRR_B = 16.7%; Crossover rate = 16.07%

13-7 **a.** NPV_A = $ 14 486 808; NPV_B = $ 11 156 893; IRR_A = 15.03%; IRR_B = 22.26%   **b.** NPV_Δ = $ 3 329 914; IRR_Δ = 11.71%

13-10 **b.** PV_c = −$ 556 717; PV_F = −$ 493 407; Forklift should be chosen

14-1 NPV = $62 727

14-2 **b.** NPV = −$ 23 777   **c.** IRR = 5.3%; MIRR = 6.8%

14-3 **b.** NPV = $ 9366   **c.** IRR = 15.6%; MIRR = 14.7%

14-4 NPV = −$ 564

15-1 **a.** $\hat{k}_M$ = 13.5%; $\hat{k}_j$ = 11.6% **b.** σ_M = 3.85%; σ_j = 6.22% **c.** CV_M = 0.29; CV_j = 0.54

15-2 **a.** $\hat{k}_Y$ = 14%   **b.** σ_X = 12.20%

15-3 **a.** b_A = 2   **b.** k_A = 12.5 %

15-4 **a.** k_I = 15.5%   **b.** **1.** k_M = 15%; k_I = 14.5%;   **c.** **1.** k_M = 16%; k_I = 18.1%

15-5 b_N = 1.16

15-6 b_P = 0.7625; k_P = 12.1%

15-7 **a.** k_i = 8% + (5.5%)b_i **b.** 17.90% **c.** Indifference rate = 19%

15-8 **a.** $\bar{k}_A$ = 11.30%   **c.** σ_A = 20.8%; σ_P = 20.1%

15-9 **a.** 16%   **b.** NPV = $ 411; Accept.

15-10 **a.** Expected CF_A = $ 6750; Expected CF_B = $ 7650; CV_A = 0.0703; CV_B = 0.7579

15-11 NPV_5 = $ 2212; NPV_4 = −$ 2081; NPV_8 = $ 13 329

15-12 **a.** 15%   **b.** 1.48; 15.4%; 17%.

15-13 **a.** 14%

16-1 **a.** V_L at 5% = $ 1518.97; V_L at 8% = $ 1171.15; V_L at 12% = $ 863.79

16-2 **a.** $ 1251.26;   **b.** $ 898.90

16-3 **b.** $ 833.33

16-4 **a.** 13.3%   **c.** 8%

16-5 **a.** YTM at $ 829 = 15%

16-6 **b.** $ 5.29   **d.** $ 30.01

16-8 $23.75

16-9   **a. 1.** $9.50   **2.** $13.33
    b. 1. Undefined

16-10   **a.** Div. for 1995 = $2.66   **b.** $39.42
    c. Div. yield for 1993 = 5.10%; for 1997
    = 7.00%

16-11   **a.** $54.11

16-12   **a.** YTM = 8%; YTC = 6.1%

16-13   **a.** $21.43   **b.** $26.47   **d.** $40.54

16-14   **a.** New price = $31.34   **b.** beta =
    0.49865

16-15   **a.** k_C = 10.6%; k_D = 7%

17-1   **a.** 13%   **b.** 7.80%   **c.** 5.20%

17-2   7.20%

17-3   11.94%

17-4   **a.** 16.3%   **b.** 15.4%   **c.** 16%

17-5   **a.** 8%   **b.** $2.81   **c.** 15.81%

17-6   **a.** $18 million   **b.** BP = $36 million
    c. BP_1 = $24 million; BP_2 = $48 million

17-7   **a.** F = 10%   **b.** k_e = 15.8%

17-8 k_a = 12.72%

17-9   **a.** g = 3%   **b.** EPS = $5.562

17-10   **a.** $67 500 000   **c.** k_s = 12%; k_e =
    12.4%   **d.** $27 000 000   **e.** $WACC_1$ =
    9%; $WACC_2$ = 9.2%

17-11   **a.** $k_d(1-T)$ = 5.4%; k_s = 14.6%
    b. k_a = 10.92%;   **d.** k_a = 11.36%

17-12   **a.** 3 breaks; BP_1 = $1 111 111; BP_2 =
    $1 818 182; BP_3 = $2 000 000   **b.** k_{a_1} =
    10.96%; k_{a_2}; = 11.50%; k_{a_3} = 12.14%; k_{a_4}
    = 12.68%   **c.** IRR_1 = 16%; IRR_3 = 14%

18-1   **a.** $5.10

18-2   **a.** ROE_{LL} = 14.6%; ROE_{HL} = 16.8%
    b. ROE_{LL} = 16.5%

18-3   No leverage: ROE = 10.5%; σ = 5.4%;
    CV = 0.51; 60% leverage: ROE = 13.7%;
    σ = 13.5%; CV = 0.99

18-5   **a.** DOL_A = 2.80; DOL_B = 2.15;
    Method A   **b.** DFL_A = 1.32;
    DFL_B = 1.35; Method B
    d. Debt = $129 310; D/A = 5.75%

18-6   **a.** EPS_{Old} = $2.04; New: EPS_D = $4.74;
    EPS_S = $3.27   **b.** DOL_{Old} = 2.30;
    DOL_{New} = 1.60; DFL_{Old} = 1.47;
    $DFL_{New, Stock}$ = 1.15; $DTL_{New, Debt}$ = 2.53
    c. 33 975 units   **d.** $Q_{New, Debt}$ = 27 225
    units

19-1 $3 250 000

19-2   52%

19-3 $3.44

19-5   **a. 1.** $3 960 000   **2.** $4 800 000
    3. $9 360 000   **4.** Regular =
    $3 960 000; Extra = $5 400 000   **c.** 15%
    d. 15%

19-6   **a.** PO = 63.16%; BP = $9.55 million;
    MCC_1 = 10.67%; MCC_2 = 10.96%

19A-1   **a. i.** $1 000 000

20-1   **a.** $1 050 000   **b.** $5 550 000
    c. −$3 450 000

20-2   12%

20-3   600 000 shares

20-4   **a.** $35.00;   **b.** $34.18

20-5   **a.** EPS_{1993} = $9600; DPS_{1993} = $4800;
    BV_{1993} = $72 000 per share   **b.** g_{EPS}: HH
    = 8.4%; S = 6.4%; U = 8%; g_{DPS}: HH =
    8.4%; S = 6.4%; U = 7.4%   **e.** EPS_{1993} =
    $2.40; DPS_{1993} = $1.20; BV_{1993} = $18 per
    share   **f.** ROE_{HH} = 15.00%; ROE_S =
    13.64%; ROE_U = 13.33%   **i.** P/E_{HH} = 8;
    P/E_S = 8.67   **k.** k_{HH} = 15.2%; k_S =
    12.5%; U-Fix-It's price; $P_0(HH)$ =
    $17.23; $P_0(S)$ = $26.93

20A-1   **a.** Value of a right = $0.83

21-1   15.03%

21-2   **c.** $1 704 545

21-3 $1.94

21-4   **b.** Current beta = 1.67; Beta with debt
    = 2.17   **d.** Debt price per share =
    $5.06; Equity price per share = $5.78
    e. Debt k_a = 11.2%

22-1   S = $55: value of call option = $5;
    profit on call option = $1.125; value of
    put option = $0; profit on put option
    = −$0.125

22-3   **a.** Theoretical value = −$3; $0; $4;
    $49   **d.** 9%; $90

22-5   **a.** $1175.46   **b.** Dividends in year 5 =
    $2.64   **c.** $75.46

22-6   **b.** $93.75   **c.** 10.3%   **d.** 9.7%
    e. 16.8%

22-7 **b.** Percentage ownership: original = 80%; Plan 1 = 53%; Plans 2 and 3 = 57%   **c.** $EPS_0 = \$0.48$; $EPS_1 = \$0.60$; $EPS_2 = \$0.64$; $EPS_3 = \$0.86$ **d.** $D/A_1 = 13\%$; $D/A_2 = 13\%$; $D/A_3 = 48\%$

23-1 $\$92\,328.80$
23-2 **a.** $D/A_C = 66.7\%$; $D/A_S = 50\%$
23-3 PV Cost of Owning = $\$1\,057\,506$
23-4 PV Cost of Owning = $\$127\,994$; PV Cost of Leasing = $\$139\,008$; Purchase loom.

24-1 NPV = $-\$6746$; do not purchase
24-2 **a.** 17% **b.** V = $\$14.65$ million
24-3 **a.** 14% **b.** T.V. = $\$1160$; V = $\$890.1$

25-1 **a.** Total assets = $\$382$ **b.** Income available for common shareholders = $\$10.99$ million **c.** $\$3.79$ million **e.** New debt ratio = 61.4%

B

Selected Equations

Chapter 2

$$UCC_t = \begin{cases} C_0 & \text{for } t = 1 \\ C_0(1 - (d/2))(1 - d)^{t-1} & \text{for } t \geq 2 \end{cases}$$

$$CCA_t = \begin{cases} d/2 * UCC_1 & \text{for } t = 1 \\ d * UCC_1 & \text{for } t \geq 2 \end{cases}$$

Chapter 4

$$\text{Current ratio} = \frac{\text{Current assets}}{\text{Current liabilities}}.$$

$$\text{Quick ratio} = \frac{\text{Current assets} - \text{Inventory}}{\text{Current liabilities}}.$$

$$\text{Debt ratio} = \frac{\text{Total debt}}{\text{Total assets}}.$$

$$\text{TIE} = \frac{\text{EBIT}}{\text{Interest charges}}.$$

$$\text{FCC} = \frac{\text{EBT} + \text{Interest charges} + \text{Lease obligations}}{\text{Interest charges} + \text{Lease obligations}}.$$

$$\text{Cash flow coverage} = \frac{\text{Cash inflows}}{\text{Interest charges} + \text{Lease obligations} + \dfrac{\text{Preferred dividends}}{(1 - T)} + \dfrac{\text{Debt repayment}}{(1 - T)}}.$$

$$\text{Inventory turnover} = \frac{\text{Sales}}{\text{Inventory}}.$$

$$\text{DSO} = \frac{\text{Receivables}}{\text{Sales per day}} = \frac{\text{A/R}}{\text{Sales}/365}.$$

$$\text{Fixed turnover assets} = \frac{\text{Sales}}{\text{Net fixed assets}}.$$

$$\text{Total turnover assets} = \frac{\text{Sales}}{\text{Total assets}}.$$

$$\text{Profit margin} = \frac{\text{Net income}}{\text{Sales}}.$$

$$\text{BEP} = \frac{\text{EBIT}}{\text{Total assets}}.$$

$$\text{ROA} = \frac{\text{Net income after taxes}}{\text{Total assets}} = \frac{\text{Net income}}{\text{Sales}} \times \frac{\text{Sales}}{\text{Total assets}} \qquad \text{ROE} = \frac{\text{Net income}}{\text{Common equity}}.$$

$$\text{P/E ratio} = \frac{\text{Price per share}}{\text{Earnings per share}}. \qquad \text{M/B Ratio} = \frac{\text{Market value}}{\text{Book value per share}}.$$

Chapter 5

$$\text{AFN} = A/S(\Delta S) - L_s/S(\Delta S) - Mb(S_1).$$

Chapter 6

$$\text{Breakeven quantity } Q_{BE} = \frac{F}{P - V}.$$

$$\text{Breakeven sales} = PQ_{BE}.$$

$$\text{DOL} = \frac{\dfrac{\Delta \text{EBIT}}{\text{EBIT}}}{\dfrac{\Delta Q}{Q}}.$$

Chapter 8

$$\text{TIC} = CP\left(\frac{Q}{2}\right) + F\left(\frac{S}{Q}\right).$$

$$\text{EOQ} = \sqrt{\frac{2FS}{CP}}.$$

Chapter 10

$$C^* = \sqrt{\frac{2FT}{k}}.$$

$$\text{TC} = F(T/C^*) + k(C^*/2).$$

Chapter 11

$$\text{Percentage cost} = \frac{\text{Discount percent}}{100 - \text{Discount percent}} \times \frac{360}{\text{Final due date} - \text{Discount period}}.$$

$$\text{Effective rate of interest on simple interest loan} = \frac{\text{Interest}}{\text{Borrowed amount}}.$$

Effective rate of interest on discounted interest loan $= \dfrac{\text{Interest}}{\dfrac{\text{Borrowed}}{\text{amount}} - \text{Interest}}$

$$= \frac{\text{Nominal interest rate}}{1.0 - \text{Nominal interest rate}}.$$

Approximate rate on installment loan $= \dfrac{\text{Annual interest}}{\text{Borrowed amount}/2}$.

$\begin{array}{c}\text{Effective rate of interest on} \\ \text{compensating balance loan}\end{array} = \dfrac{\text{Nominal interest rate}}{1.0 - \dfrac{\text{Compensating}}{\text{balance fraction}}}$.

Discount loan with compensating balance $= \dfrac{\text{Nominal interest rate}}{1.0 - \dfrac{\text{Compensating}}{\text{balance fraction}} - \dfrac{\text{Nominal interest}}{\text{rate}}}$.

Chapter 12

$$FV_n = PV(1 + k)^n$$
$$= PV(FVIF_{k,n}).$$

$$FVIFA_{k,n} = \frac{(1 + k)^n - 1}{k}.$$

$$PV = FV_n[1/(1 + k)]^n$$
$$= FV_n(PVIF_{k,n}).$$

$$PVIFA_{k,n} = \frac{1 - \dfrac{1}{(1 + k)^n}}{k}.$$

$$PVIF_{k,n} = \frac{1}{FVIF_{k,n}} = \frac{1}{(1 + k)^n}$$

$$EAR = \left(1 + \frac{k_{nom}}{m}\right)^m - 1.0.$$

$$PV = FV_n\left(\frac{1}{1 + \dfrac{k_{nom}}{m}}\right)^{mn}$$

$$FV_n = PV\left(1 + \frac{k_{nom}}{m}\right)^{mn}.$$

$$PV(\text{Perpetuity}) = \frac{PMT}{k}.$$

$$FVA_n = PMT \sum_{t=1}^{n} (1 + k)^{n-t}$$

$$PVA_n = PMT \sum_{t=1}^{n} \left(\frac{1}{1 + k}\right)^t$$

$$= PMT\left[\frac{(1 + k)^n - 1}{k}\right]$$

$$= PMT\left[\frac{1 - \dfrac{1}{(1 + k)^n}}{k}\right]$$

$$= PMT(FVIFA_{k,n}).$$

$$= PMT(PVIFA_{k,n}).$$

$$FVA_n \text{ (Annuity due)} = PMT(FVIFA_{k,n})(1 + k).$$
$$PVA_n \text{ (Annuity due)} = PMT(PVIFA_{k,n})(1 + k).$$

Chapter 13

$$NPV = \sum_{t=1}^{n} \frac{CF_t}{(1 + k)^t} - I.$$

$$IRR: \sum_{t=1}^{n} \frac{CF_t}{(1 + IRR)^t} - I = 0.$$

$$MIRR: \frac{TV}{(1 + MIRR)^n} - I = 0.$$

Chapter 14

$$PV_{\text{tax saving}} = \frac{TC_0 d}{k + d} \cdot \frac{2 + k}{2(1 + k)} + \frac{S}{(1 + k)^n}\left[1 - \frac{Td}{k + d}\right]$$

Chapter 15

$$\hat{k}_A = \sum_{i=1}^{S} P_i \tilde{k}_A.$$

$$\sigma_A^2 = \sum_{i=1}^{S} P_i(\tilde{k}_i - \tilde{k}_A)^2.$$

$$\sigma_A = \sqrt{\sum_{i=1}^{S} P_i(\tilde{k}_i - \tilde{k}_A)^2}.$$

$$CV_j = \frac{\sigma_j}{\tilde{k}_j}.$$

$$\hat{k}_P = \sum_{j=1}^{n} w_j \tilde{k}_j.$$

$$k_j = k_{RF} + \beta_j(\hat{k}_M - k_{RF}).$$

→ ## Chapter 16 _(13 mks)_

$$V_d = \sum_{t=1}^{n} \frac{I}{(1 + k_d)^t} + \frac{M}{(1 + k_d)^n} = I(PVIFA_{k_d,n}) + M(PVIF_{k_d,n}).$$

$$V_p = \frac{D_p}{k_p}.$$

$$P_0 = \frac{D_1}{k_s - g}.$$

$$k_s = \frac{D_1}{P_0} + g.$$

$$P_0 = \sum_{t=1}^{n} \frac{D_0(1 + g_s)^t}{(1 + k_s)^t} + \left(\frac{D_{n+1}}{k_s - g}\right)\left[\frac{1}{(1 + k_s)^n}\right].$$

Chapter 17   (17 mks)

k_d After-tax $= k_d(1 - T)$.

$$k_p = \frac{D_p}{P_p}.$$

$$k_e = \frac{D_1}{P_0(1 - F)} + g.$$

$$k_s = \frac{D_1}{P_0} + g.$$

$$k_a = w_d k_d(1 - T) + w_p k_p + w_s(k_s \text{ or } k_e).$$

$$\text{Break point} = \frac{\begin{array}{c}\text{Total amount of lower-cost}\\ \text{capital of a given type}\end{array}}{\begin{array}{c}\text{Fraction of this type of capital}\\ \text{in the capital structure}\end{array}}.$$

Chapter 18   (30 mks.

$$\text{EPS} = \frac{(\text{EBIT} - \text{I})(1 - T)}{\text{Shares outstanding}}.$$

$$\text{DOL} = \frac{Q(P - V)}{Q(P - V) - F} = \frac{S - VC}{S - VC - F}.$$

$$\text{DFL} = \frac{\text{EBIT}}{\text{EBIT} - \text{I}}.$$

$$\text{DTL} = \frac{Q(P - V)}{Q(P - V) - F - I} = (\text{DOL})(\text{DFL}).$$

$$\text{EPS}_1 = \text{EPS}_0[1 + (\text{DTL})(\% \Delta\text{Sales})].$$

Appendix 20A

$$\frac{\text{Number of}}{\text{new shares}} = \frac{\text{Funds to be raised}}{\text{Subscription price}}.$$

$$\frac{\text{Number of rights needed}}{\text{to buy a share of equity}} = \frac{\text{Old shares}}{\text{New shares}}.$$

$$V_r = \frac{P_0 - P_s}{N + 1} = \frac{P_e - P_s}{N}.$$

Chapter 22

$$P_c = \frac{\text{Par value of bond}}{\text{Shares received}}.$$

GLOSSARY

Absolute Priority Rule In bankruptcy proceedings, the doctrine that states that claims must be paid in strict accordance with the priority of each claim, regardless of the consequence to other claimants.

Accounting Beta Method A method to estimate the beta of a project by running a linear regression of the company's return on assets and the average ROA for a large sample of firms. ROA is based on accounting data, hence the name.

Accruals Continually recurring short-term liabilities. Examples are accrued wages, accrued taxes, and accrued interest.

Additional Funds Needed (AFN) Funds that a firm must acquire externally by borrowing or selling new common or preferred equity. This is in contrast to spontaneously generated funds, which are obtained automatically by normal business operations.

Adjusted Dividend Yield The dividend yield when the denominator is the share price less issue costs.

Ageing Schedule A report showing how long accounts receivable have been outstanding. It gives the percentage of receivables now past due and the percentage past due by, for example, one month, two months, or other periods.

Agency Costs The costs associated with monitoring management's actions to ensure that these actions are consistent with contractual agreements among management, shareholders, and debtholders.

Agency Problem A potential conflict of interest between the shareholders of a firm and the firm's management, or between the bondholders and the shareholders.

Amortization Schedule A schedule that shows precisely how a loan will be repaid. It gives the required payment on each specific date and a breakdown of the payment showing how much of it constitutes interest and how much constitutes repayment of principal.

Amortize To liquidate on an installment basis. An amortized loan is one in which the principal amount of the loan is repaid in installments during the life of the loan.

Annual Report A report, issued annually by corporations to their shareholders, which contains basic financial statements as well as management's opinion of the past year's operations and prospects for the future. *See also* Balance Sheet, Income Statement, Statement of Retained Earnings, Statement of Cash Flows, and Statement of Changes in Financial Position.

Annuity A series of payments of a fixed amount for a specified number of years.

Annuity, Ordinary A series of payments of a fixed amount for a specified number of periods, with the payments occurring at the end of the period. Sometimes called deferred payment.

Annuity Due A series of payments of a fixed amount for a specified number of periods, with the payments occurring at the beginning of the period.

Arbitrage The process of selling overvalued and buying undervalued equivalent assets so as to bring about an equilibrium in which all equivalent assets are properly valued.

Arrearage An overdue payment; frequently, an omitted dividend on preferred stock.

Asset Management Ratios Ratios that show how effectively a firm is managing its assets. *See also* Inventory Turnover Ratio, Days Sales Outstanding, Total Assets Turnover.

Ask Price The price at which a dealer or specialist in securities will sell shares of stock out of inventory.

Assignment A relatively inexpensive way of liquidating a failing firm that does not involve going through the courts.

Average Collection Period (ACP) Accounts receivable divided by credit sales per day. It represents the average length of time a firm must wait after making a sale before receiving cash. *See also* Days Sales Outstanding (DSO).

Balance Sheet A financial statement that shows the total assets, liabilities, and equity of a firm at a specific point in time. The assets and liabilities are in order of maturity, with the current assets at the top and fixed assets at the bottom. Current liabilities are at the top of the liability side of the balance sheet, with permanent capital or owners' equity at the bottom.

Banker's Acceptance (BA) A short-term promissory note issued by a company and guaranteed by a chartered bank. The guarantee fee is charged to the issuing company and the interest rate on the BA reflects the risk of the bank providing the guarantee.

Bankruptcy A legal procedure in which a business is either reorganized or is liquidated.

Basic Earning Power Ratio Operating income, or EBIT, divided by assets. This ratio indicates the power of the firm's assets to generate operating income.

Basis Point Percentage point times 100; for example, 2.5 percentage points equals 250 basis points.

Baumol Model An economic model which determines the optimal cash balance by using economic ordering quantity (EOQ) concepts.

Bearer Bond Possession of a bearer bond is primary evidence of its ownership; opposite of "registered bond."

Benefit/Cost Ratio Equals the present value of benefits divided by the present value of costs. Also known as *Profitability Index*.

Beta Coefficient A measurement of the extent to which the rate of return on the equity of a company moves with the rate of return on the overall stock market index.

Bid Price The price a dealer or specialist in securities will pay for a stock.

Bird-in-the-Hand Theory A theory that says investors prefer the certainty of dividends to the uncertainty of reinvesting retained earnings for future capital gains; therefore a firm's value will be maximized by a high dividend payout ratio.

Bond A long-term debt instrument.

Bond Rating A rating assigned to bonds based on the probability of their firms' default. Those bonds with the smallest default probability are rated AAA (or A^{++}) and carry the lowest interest rates.

Book Value The accounting value of an asset. The book value of a share of common equity is equal to the common equity (common shares plus paid-in capital plus retained earnings) of the corporation divided by the number of shares of equity outstanding.

Breakeven Analysis An analytical technique for studying the relationships among fixed cost, variable cost, and profits. A breakeven *chart* graphically depicts the nature of breakeven analysis. The breakeven *point* represents the volume of sales at which total costs equal total revenues (that is, profits equal zero).

Break Point (BP) A break point occurs in the MCC (marginal cost of capital) schedule where the amount of capital represents the total financing that can be done before a company is forced to sell new common equity. In general, a break point will occur whenever the cost of one of the capital components (cost of debt, preferred shares, or common equity) rises.

Bridge Loan A loan that permits the use of funds from some source, such as the sale of an asset, a bond issue, or a share issue, before they are actually received. A bridge loan "bridges" the period during which the funds are needed to be used and when they are received, and is normally outstanding for a very short term. Also called "interim financing."

Budget A plan stated in terms of specific revenues and expenditures for specific purposes. It is used both for planning and control. Projected, or *pro forma,* financial statements are used to report a budget.

Business Failure The condition of a business when it has terminated with a loss to creditors.

Business Risk The basic risk inherent in a firm's operations. Business risk plus financial risk resulting from the use of debt equals total equity risk.

Call (1) An option to buy (or "call") a share of stock at a specified price within a specified period. (2) The process of redeeming a bond or preferred stock issue before its normal maturity.

Call Premium The amount in excess of par value that a company must pay when it calls a security.

Call Price The price that must be paid when a security is called. The call price is equal to the par value plus the call premium.

Call Privilege A provision incorporated into a bond or a share of preferred stock that gives the issuer the right to redeem (call) the security at a specified price.

Call Provision A provision in a bond contract that gives the issuer the right to redeem the bonds under specified terms prior to the normal maturity date.

Capital Asset An asset with a life of more than one year that is not bought and sold in the ordinary course of business.

Capital Asset Pricing Model (CAPM) A model based on the proposition that any stock's required rate of return is equal to the riskless rate of return plus its risk premium: $k_i = k_{RF} + \beta_i (k_M - k_{RF})$. *See also* Security Market Line.

Capital Budgeting The process of planning expenditures on assets whose returns are expected to extend beyond one year.

Capital Cost Allowance (CCA) The depreciation expense for tax purposes. The charge in any year is equal to a capital cost rate for the pool in which the asset belongs times the underpreciated capital cost of the asset at the start of the year. Generally, the assets fit into a pool and the total CCA charge for the pool is obtained.

Capital Gains Profits on capital assets.

Capital Gains Yield A yield on an investment that, in any year, is equal to the capital gain during the year divided by the beginning price.

Capital Intensity The amount of assets required to produce a dollar of sales.

Capital Losses Losses on the sale of capital assets.

Capital Market Line A graphical representation of the relationship between risk and the required rate of return.

Capital Markets Financial markets involving instruments with maturities greater than one year.

Capital Rationing A situation where a constraint is placed on the total size of the capital investment during a particular period.

Capital Structure The percentage of each type of capital used by the firm—debt, preferred shares, and common equity. (Common equity consists of common shares, paid-in capital, and retained earnings.)

Capital Tax In Canada, large corporations and financial institutions pay a tax which is a percentage of their total asset base. This is in addition to income and other taxes.

Capitalization Rate A discount rate used to find the present value of a series of future cash receipts; sometimes called *Discount Rate*.

Capitalize In finance: to find the present value of a stream of cash flows. In accounting: to reflect costs on the balance sheet rather than charging them off through the income statement, as to capitalize major repairs to a fixed asset.

Carryback; Carryforward For income tax purposes, losses that can be carried backward or forward to reduce federal income taxes.

Carrying Costs The cost of tying up funds to finance the maintenance of inventory; that is, the foregone earnings on the money invested in the inventory.

Cash Breakeven Point The breakeven point when noncash items (such as depreciation) are subtracted from fixed costs.

Cash Budget A schedule showing cash flows (receipts, disbursements, and net cash) for a firm over a specified period.

Cash Conversion Cycle The length of time between the purchase of raw materials and the collection of accounts receivable generated in the sale of the final product.

Cash Discount An element of credit policy designed to encourage early payment. Customers are offered a percentage discount on the stated sales price if payment is made within a specified number of days. Also called a "trade discount."

Cash Flow The actual net cash, as opposed to accounting net income, that flows into (or out of) a firm during some specified period. Cash flow is equal to net income after taxes plus non-cash expenses, usually depreciation.

CCA rate The maximum percentage that can be applied to the undepreciated capital cost (UCC) in a particular CCA class. The *Income Tax Act* specifies the CCA rates for each asset class. The product of the CCA rate and the UCC is a tax-deductible expense.

Certainty Equivalent The amount of cash (or rate of return) that someone would require *with certainty* in order to be indifferent between this certain sum (or rate of return) and a risky sum (or rate of return).

Charter A formal legal document that describes the scope and nature of a corporation and defines the rights and duties of its shareholders and managers.

Chattel Mortgage A mortgage on personal property (not real estate). For example, a mortgage on equipment would be a chattel mortgage.

Clientele Effect The tendency of a firm to attract a certain type of investor according to its dividend policy.

Closely Held Corporation A corporation that is not publicly owned; a corporation owned by a few individuals who are typically associated with the management of the firm. Also called a *Closed Corporation.*

Coefficient of Variation The standard deviation divided by the mean.

Collateral Assets that are used to secure a loan.

Commercial Paper Unsecured, short-term promissory notes of large firms. The rate of interest on commercial paper is typically somewhat below the prime rate of interest.

Commitment Fee The fee paid to a lender for a formal line of credit.

Common-Size Statement A type of financial statement in which each balance sheet item is expressed as a percentage of total assets, and each income statement item is stated as a percentage of total sales.

Company-Specific Risk That part of a security's risk associated with random events; such risk, also referred to as non-systematic, can be eliminated by proper diversification.

Compensating Balance A required minimum chequing account balance that a firm must maintain with a commercial bank. The balance is generally equal to a percentage of the amount of loans outstanding to the firm. Compensating balances can raise the effective rate of interest on bank loans.

Composition An informal method of reorganization in which creditors voluntarily reduce their claims on the debtor firm.

Compound Interest An interest rate that is applicable when interest in succeeding periods is earned not only on the initial principal but also on the accumulated interest of prior periods.

Compounding The arithmetic process of determining the final value of a payment or series of payments when compound interest is applied.

Congeneric Merger A merger among firms in the same general industry in which the merger partners are neither customers nor suppliers of one another. The term was first used in connection with mergers between financial institutions, as, for example, when a bank holding company acquired a mortgage service company or a leasing company.

Conglomerate Merger A merger among companies in different industries. For example, if a grocery chain acquired a steel company, then a conglomerate corporation would result.

Consol Bond A perpetual bond issued by England to consolidate past debts; in general, any perpetual bond.

Continuous Compounding (Discounting) As opposed to discrete compounding, a situation where interest is added continuously rather than at discrete points in time.

Conversion Price The effective price paid for common shares when they are obtained by converting either convertible preferred shares or convertible bonds. For example, if a $1000 bond is convertible into 20 common shares, the conversion price is $1000/20 = $50.

Conversion Ratio or Conversion Rate The number of shares of common equity that may be obtained by converting a convertible bond or share of convertible preferred equity.

Convertible Securities Bonds or preferred shares that are exchangeable at the option of the holder for common shares of the issuing firm.

Corporate Risk In capital budgeting, this reflects the effects of a project on the firm's risk, as measured by the effect on the firm's earnings variability. In the worst case, a project could incur losses that would destabilize profits or even cause bankruptcy.

Corporation A legal entity or "person" that can enter contracts and own property. A corporation is separate and distinct from its owners and managers, and thus has the advantages of unlimited life, easy transferability of ownership interests, and limited liability.

Correlation Coefficient A measurement of the degree of relationship between two variables.

Cost of Capital The discount rate that should be used in the capital budgeting process.

Cost of Debt The interest rate on a new debt issue. The after-tax cost of debt is the interest rate on debt less the tax savings resulting from interest tax deductibility.

Cost of New Common Equity The rate of return that must be earned on funds raised by selling new equity; this cost is greater than the cost of retained earnings in order to cover the issue costs involved in selling new common equity.

Cost of Preferred Shares The preferred dividend per share divided by the share price. For a new preferred share issue, the cost is calculated as the preferred dividend per share divided by the net issue price.

Cost of Retained Earnings The rate of return that shareholders require on equity capital obtained by the firm by retaining and reinvesting earnings.

Coupon Rate The stated rate of interest on a bond.

Covenant A detailed clause in term loan agreements and bond indentures, designed to protect lenders. It includes such items as limits on total indebtedness, restrictions on dividends, minimum current ratio, and similar provisions.

Covered Options Options sold by an investor against shares held in his or her portfolio.

Credit Period The length of time for which credit is granted.

Credit Standards Standards that stipulate the minimum financial strength of acceptable credit customers.

Credit Terms The combination of the credit period and cash discount allowed to a company's credit customer.

Creditors Every stakeholder to whom the firm owes money; can include suppliers and debtholders.

Cumulative Dividends A protective feature of preferred shares that requires all past preferred dividends to be paid before any common dividends are paid.

Cumulative Voting A method of voting for corporate directors that permits multiple votes for a single director. This can enable a minority group of shareholders to obtain some voice in the control of the company.

Current Ratio Current assets divided by current liabilities. This ratio indicates the extent to which the claims of short-term creditors are covered by assets expected to be converted to cash in the near future.

Current Yield (of a Bond) The internal rate of return that equates the future cash flows on a bond, interest, and repayment of principal to the current price of a bond.

Days Sales Outstanding (DSO) An asset management ratio; total receivables divided by average daily sales. Also called *Average Collection Period.*

Debenture A long-term debt instrument that is not secured by a mortgage on specific property.

Debt Management Ratios Ratios that reflect the use of financial leverage in the firm. *See also* Financial Leverage, Debt Ratio, Times Interest Earned.

Debt Ratio Total debt divided by total assets.

Debtholders Investors who have purchased the debt securities of a firm; also called bondholders.

Decision Tree A device for setting forth graphically the pattern of relationship among decisions and probability factors.

Default The failure to fulfill a contract; generally, the failure to pay interest or principal on debt obligations.

Default Risk Risk that an issuer of securities will not be able to make interest payments or repay the principal amount on schedule.

Default Risk Premium The difference between the interest rate on a government of Canada bond and a corporate bond of equal maturity and marketability.

Degree of Financial Leverage (DFL) The percentage increase in earnings available to common resulting from a given percentage increase in operating income.

Degree of Operating Leverage (DOL) The percentage increase in operating income resulting from a given percentage increase in sales.

Degree of Total Leverage (DTL) The percentage change in profits resulting from a given percentage increase in sales; it is the product of DFL * DOL.

Devaluation The process of reducing the value of a country's currency stated in terms of other currencies; for example, the British pound might be devalued from $2.25 for £1 to $2.00 for £1.

Discount Rate The interest rate used in the discounting process; sometimes called the *Capitalization Rate.*

Discount Interest Interest that is calculated on the face amount of a loan but is deducted in advance.

Discounted Cash Flow (DCF) Techniques Methods of ranking investment proposals, including the internal rate of return method and the net present value method.

Discounted Payback Period The length of time required for discounted cash flows from a project to match the project's cost.

Discounting The process of finding the present value of a series of future cash flows. Discounting is the reverse of compounding.

Divestiture The removal of some of a firm's operating assets either through a sale to another company (selloff) or the issue to existing equity holders of securities in a new firm composed of the removed assets (spinoff).

Dividend Irrelevance Theory The theory that a firm's dividend policy has no effect on its value or cost of capital. The principal proponents are Modigliani and Miller.

Dividend Payout Ratio The percentage of earnings paid out in dividends.

Dividend Reinvestment Plan (DRP) A plan that enables a shareholder to automatically reinvest dividends received back into the shares of the paying corporation.

Dividend Tax Credit The adjustment to some preferred and all common share dividends received from Canadian sources that reduces the amount of federal, and hence provincial, tax payable.

Dividend Yield The ratio of the current dividend to the current price of a share of stock.

Dividend-Yield-Plus-Growth-Rate Approach An ad hoc method of estimating the firm's cost of equity using its current dividend yield and an estimate of the growth rate of future dividends. Also called the *Discounted Cash Flow (DCF) method*.

Du Pont System A system of analysis designed to show the relationships among asset turnover, the profit margin, the use of debt, and the return on equity.

$$\text{ROA} = \text{Profit Margins} \times \text{Total Assets Turnover}$$

$$= \frac{\text{Net Income}}{\text{Sales}} = \frac{\text{Sales}}{\text{Total Assets}}$$

Earnings Retention Ratio This represents the amount of earnings returned as a proportion of net income. It is calculated as net income less common dividends divided by net income.

EBIT Abbreviation for *Earnings Before Interest and Taxes*.

Economic Ordering Quantity (EOQ) The optimum (least cost) quantity of inventory that should be ordered.

Effective Annual Rate (EAR) The interest rate that, under annual compounding, would give the same results as a given periodic rate with m compounding periods per year. If k_{nom} is the nominal rate, then $\text{EAR} = \left(1 + \frac{k_{nom}}{m}\right)^m - 1$.

Efficient Markets Hypothesis The hypothesis that securities are typically in equilibrium—that they are fairly priced in the sense that the price reflects all publicly available information on each security.

Efficient Portfolio The portfolio of securities that provides the highest possible expected return for any degree of risk or the lowest degree of risk for any expected return.

Electronic data interchange (EDI) An application of computer and telecommunications technology that enables the order entry system of the customer to interface directly with the purchase order system of the supplier. Ordering goods is faster and less error-prone with this method.

EPS Abbreviation for *Earnings Per Share.*

Equilibrium A situation in which there is no systematic tendency for change. If a security is in equilibrium, then there is no pressure for its price to change.

Equity The net worth of a business, consisting of capital stock, capital surplus (or paid-in capital), earned surplus (or retained earnings), and, occasionally, certain net worth reserves. *Common equity* is that part of the total net worth belonging to the common shareholders. *Total equity* includes that held by preferred shareholders. The terms *Common Shares, Net Worth,* and *Common Equity* are frequently used interchangeably.

Escape Clause In an underwriting the escape clauses permit the underwriter to be relieved of responsibility to purchase and distribute the shares of the company. The situations in which the escape clauses are used reflect dramatic reductions in prices of the financial securities or fundamental changes in the operations of the company.

Eurobond A bond sold in a country other than the one in whose currency the bond is denominated.

Eurodollar A U.S. dollar on deposit in a foreign bank—generally, but not necessarily, a European bank.

Ex Ante Before the fact; opposite of ex post.

Ex-Dividend Date The date on which the right to the current dividend no longer accompanies a share of common equity. (For a listed share, the ex-dividend date is four working days prior to the date of record.)

Ex Post After the fact; opposite of ex ante.

Ex Rights The date on which share purchase rights are no longer transferred to the purchaser of the shares.

Exchange Rate The number of units of a given currency that can be purchased for one unit of another currency.

Exchange Ratio In mergers, the number of shares the acquiring firm must give for each of the acquired firm's shares.

Excise Tax A tax on the manufacture, sale, or consumption of specified commodities.

Exercise Price The price that must be paid for a share of common equity when it is bought by exercising a warrant.

Expectations Theory The theory that long-term interest rates are determined by investors' expectations about future short-term rates.

Expected Return The return that is expected to be realized from an investment. The expected return is the mean value of the probability distribution of possible returns.

Expected Value The weighted average of all possible outcomes, where the weights are the probabilities of all expected outcomes.

Extendible Bond A short-term bond that allows the bondholder the option of exchanging it for a similar amount of long-term debt, on or before a specified date, at an interest rate determined at the date of original issue.

Extension An informal method of reorganization in which a firm's creditors voluntarily postpone the date of required payment on past-due obligations.

External Funds Funds acquired through borrowing or by selling new common or preferred shares.

Factoring A method of financing accounts receivable under which a firm sells its accounts receivable (generally without recourse) to a company (the "factor").

Feasible Set A hypothetical set of all possible portfolios; also known as the *attainable set.*

Field Warehousing A method of financing inventories in which a "warehouse" is established at the place of business of the borrowing firm.

Financial Control The feedback and adjustment process required during implementation of a financial plan to ensure adherence to the plan or to make modifications to the plan.

Financial Distress A situation in which a firm is having trouble meeting its fixed obligations as they come due.

Financial Institutions Establishments that handle monetary affairs, including insurance companies, chartered banks, savings and loans companies, leasing companies, and institutional investors.

Financial Intermediation Financial transactions conducted through a financial institution that bring together savers and those who need capital so that savings can be redistributed into their most productive uses.

Financial Lease A lease that does not provide for maintenance services, is not cancelable, and is fully amortized over its life. Also called a *Capital Lease.*

Financial Leverage The ratio of total debt to total assets. There are other measures of financial leverage, including ones that relate cash inflows to required cash outflows. In this book, either the debt/total assets ratio or the debt/total market value ratio is generally used to measure leverage. In situations where preferred shares are outstanding, since they are fixed claims, they are included with debt.

Financial Markets Markets involving transactions in which the creation and transfer of financial liabilities take place.

Financial Planning The projection of sales, income, and assets based on alternative marketing or production strategies, and the determination of the resources needed to achieve these projects.

Financial Risk The portion of total corporate risk over and above basic business risk, resulting from using debt.

Financial Structure The entire right-hand side of the balance sheet—the way a firm is financed.

Five C's of Credit Five factors traditionally used to measure the credit quality of potential credit customers: Character, Capacity, Capital, Collateral, and Conditions.

Fixed Assets Turnover The ratio of sales to fixed assets. This ratio measures the utilization of plant and equipment.

Fixed Charges Costs that do not vary with the level of output, especially fixed financial costs such as interest, lease payments, and sinking fund payments.

Floating Rate Bond A bond whose interest rate fluctuates with shifts in the general level of interest rates.

Flotation Cost The cost of issuing new financial instruments.

Foreign Bond A bond sold by a foreign borrower but denominated in the currency of the country in which it is sold.

Foreign Exchange Exposure Exposure to losses due to fluctuating exchange rates.

Fully Diluted EPS Earnings available to common shareholders divided by the average number of shares that would have been outstanding if all warrants and convertibles had been exercised or converted regardless of the likelihood of their exercise or conversion.

Funded Debt Long-term debt.

Funding The process of replacing short-term debt with long-term securities (shares or bonds).

Future Value (FV) The amount to which a payment or series of payments will grow by a given future date when compounded by a given interest rate. FVIF = future value interest factor.

Futures Markets Markets in which assets are bought or sold for delivery at some future date, such as six months or one year in the future.

GIGO One of the fundamental laws of computer science, this stands for "garbage in, garbage out." The term has now been broadened and applied to all aspects of financial analysis.

Going Private A tender offer in which all of the outstanding common shares of the company are purchased by the management.

Going Public The sale of shares by a closely held corporation (or its principal shareholders) to the public at large; also called an *Initial Public Offer (IPO)*.

Goods in Transit Goods that have been ordered but have not yet arrived.

Goodwill Intangible assets of a firm established by the excess of the price paid for the going concern over the value of its assets.

Half-Year Rule In calculating the capital cost allowance, when an asset is purchased only one half of the value is eligible for CCA charges. In the second and subsequent years, the ineligible half of the asset value is added back to the base. In the formulas the equivalent result is obtained by using one half of the CCA rate for the first year only.

Hedging The process of protecting oneself against loss due to future price changes.

Historic Rate of Return The dividend yield plus capital gain or minus capital loss that actually occurred for a given security in a given year.

Holder-of-Record Date The date on which registered security owners are entitled to receive the forthcoming cash or stock dividend.

Holding Company A corporation that owns the common shares of other corporations; can also be called a management company.

Horizontal Merger The combination of two firms that produce the same type of goods or services, for example, a merger between two shoe retailing chains or two shoe manufacturers.

Hurdle Rate In capital budgeting, the minimum acceptable rate of return on a project. If the expected rate of return is below the hurdle rate, the project is not acceptable. The hurdle rate should be the marginal cost of capital, adjusted for the project's risk.

Impairment of Capital A legal restriction to protect creditors. It limits dividend payments to retained earnings.

Income Bond A bond that pays interest to bondholders only if the interest due is earned.

Income Statement A financial report showing the results of an entity's operations in terms of revenue, expenses, and net income during an interval of time.

Incremental Cash Flow The net cash flow attributable to an investment project.

Incremental Cost of Capital The average cost of the increment of capital raised during a given year.

Indenture A formal agreement between the issuer of a bond and the bondholders.

Independent Project A project whose cash flows are unaffected by the decision to accept or reject some other project.

Inflation Premium A premium for anticipated or expected inflation that investors add to the pure rate of return.

Installment Interest Interest calculated and added to funds received to determine the face amount of the loan. Typically used for consumer loans such as car loans.

Insolvency The inability to meet maturing debt obligations.

Interest Factor (IF) Numbers found in compound interest and annuity tables. Usually called the FVIF or PVIF.

Interest Rate Risk Risk to which investors are exposed due to changing interest rates.

Internal Financing Funds made available for capital budgeting and working capital expansion through the normal operations of the firm. Internal financing is approximately equal to retained earnings plus depreciation.

Internal Rate of Return (IRR) The rate of return on an asset investment, calculated by finding the discount rate that equates the present value of future cash flows to the cost of the investment.

Intrinsic Value The value of an asset that, in the mind of the analyst, is justified by the facts, often as distinguished from the asset's current market price and/or its book value.

Inventory Conversion Period The average length of time required to convert raw materials into finished goods and to sell them.

Inventory Turnover Ratio The ratio of sales divided by inventories. Inventory turnover is sometimes known as *Inventory Utilization.*

Inverted Yield Curve A yield curve that is downward-sloping; that is, interest rates on longer maturity securities are lower than rates on shorter maturity securities of equal risk.

Investment Dealer One who underwrites and distributes new investment securities.

Investment Opportunity Schedule (IOS) A listing, or graph, of the firm's investment opportunities ranked in order of the projects' rates of return.

Investment Tax Credit A specified percentage of the dollar amount of new investments in each of certain categories of assets that business firms can deduct as a credit against their income taxes.

Issue Cost The cost of issuing new financial instruments; also called *Flotation Cost.*

Joint Venture A corporate alliance in which two or more firms combine their resources to achieve a specific, limited objective.

Junior Securities Securities that have a lower priority in claims on assets and income than do other, senior securities. For example, preferred equity is junior to debentures, but debentures are junior to mortgage bonds. Common equity is the most junior of all corporate securities.

Just-in-Time (JIT) An inventory control method in which goods are ordered to arrive at the production plant just at the moment they are required. This reduces the need for the manufacturer to hold inventories of parts.

Legal List A list of securities in which pension funds, insurance companies, and other fiduciary institutions are permitted to invest. Also referred to as "legal for life."

Leverage Factor The ratio of debt to total assets.

Leveraged Buyout (LBO) A takeover bid financed with a high proportion of debt. The acquisition is financed through a consortium of investment dealers or merchant bankers, pension funds, and the primary acquirer who is responsible for the bulk of the equity. If the primary acquirer is the incumbent management, the transaction is called a *Management Buyout (MBO)*.

Lien A lender's claim on assets that are pledged for a loan.

Line of Credit An arrangement whereby a financial institution commits itself to lend up to a specified maximum amount of funds during a designated period. Sometimes the interest rate on the loan is specified; at other times, it is not. Sometimes a commitment fee is imposed for obtaining the line of credit.

Liquidation The dissolving of a firm through the sale of its assets.

Liquidity A firm's position with respect to cash and marketable securities versus its short-term debt, reflecting its ability to meet maturing obligations. For an individual asset, it is how easily the asset may be sold at a reasonable price on short notice.

Liquidity Preference Theory The theory which states that investors generally prefer short-term to long-term debt and, therefore, must be compensated by a premium (called a "liquidity" or "maturity" premium) for investing in long-term bonds.

Liquidity Premium A premium added to the expected return on investments that are difficult or time-consuming to sell, to compensate investors for a possible loss if the asset must be sold quickly at 'fire-sale' prices.

Liquidity Ratios Ratios that show the relationship of a firm's cash and other current assets to its current liabilities. *See also* Current Ratio, Quick Ratio.

Listed Securities Securities traded on an organized security exchange.

Lockbox Plan A procedure used to speed up collections and reduce float.

Mail Float The float caused by the delay between the time a cheque is mailed and received. Also called *Disbursement Float*.

Managerial Compensation Corporate executives can be compensated, or paid, for their work by a combination of salary, bonuses and stock options. One of the objectives of managerial compensation is to align the goals of the executive with those of the shareholders.

Margin—Profit on Sales The *Profit Margin* is the percentage of profit after tax to sales.

Margin—Securities Business The buying of equities or bonds on credit, known as *Buying on Margin*.

Marginal Cost The cost of an additional unit. The marginal cost of capital is the cost of an additional dollar of new funds.

Marginal Cost of Capital (MCC) Schedule A table or graph that shows how a firm's weighted average cost of capital changes as additional dollars of new capital are raised.

Marginal Efficiency of Capital A schedule showing the internal rate of return on investment opportunities.

Marginal Revenue The additional gross revenue produced by selling one additional unit of output.

Marginal Tax Rate The tax rate applicable to the last unit of income.

Market Portfolio The portfolio of all investment opportunities available.

Market Risk The part of a security's risk that cannot be eliminated by diversification. It is measured by the beta coefficient.

Market Risk Premium The additional return over the risk-free rate that is required to compensate an investor for assuming an average amount of risk. Market risk premium depends on the aversion that investors in the aggregate have to risk.

Market Segmentation Theory The theory that capital markets are segmented and that the yield curve is determined by the relative supply and demand for short- and long-term funds.

Market-to-Book Ratio The market value per share divided by the book value per share. Market-to-book ratio depends on both industry (or economy) influences and individual firm influences, and indicates the value that the financial markets attach to the management and the organization of the company as a going concern.

Market Value The price at which an asset can be sold.

Market Value Ratios Ratios that relate the firm's share price to various accounting measures. *See also* Price/Earnings Ratio, Market-to-Book Ratio.

Marketable Securities Securities that can be sold on short notice for close to their quoted market prices; examples are government of Canada Treasury bills, Bankers' Acceptances, and commercial paper.

Marketability Premium A premium that investors add to the interest rate of a security to compensate for the security's lack of marketability; often called a *Liquidity Premium.*

Maturity Risk Premium A premium to compensate investors for interest rate risk. Longer maturity bonds are more exposed to interest rate risk, or changes in value when interest rates change.

Merchant Banker A financial company that takes an equity or investment position in another firm and attempts to reorganize or restructure the company so as to improve its profitability.

Merger Any combination that forms one company from two or more previously existing companies.

Miller–Orr Model A cash management model based on inventory management that incorporates ordering and holding costs and sets an upper and lower limit for cash balances.

Modified IRR (MIRR) The discount rate at which the present value of a project's cost is equal to the present value of its terminal value. The terminal value is found as the sum of the future values of the cash inflows, compounded at the firm's cost of capital.

Money Market A financial market in which funds are borrowed or lent for short periods. (The money market is distinguished from the capital market, which is the market for long-term funds.)

Monte Carlo Simulation A sensitivity technique in which a computer generates possible future outcomes for a project, using random probabilities. The outcomes are weighted by the probabilities to get the most likely outcome, and hence the most likely NPV.

Mortgage A pledge of designated property as security for a loan.

Mutual Funds Organizations that invest the pooled funds of many savers, thus obtaining economies of scale in investing and reducing risk by diversification. There are many types of mutual funds, each with different objectives designed to suit different savers' needs.

Mutually Exclusive Projects A set of projects out of which only one project can be accepted.

Naked Options Options sold by an investor without any shares of equity to back them up.

Net Present Value (NPV) Method A method of ranking investment proposals. The NPV is equal to the present value of future returns, discounted at the marginal cost of capital, minus the present value of the cost of the investment. If the NPV of a project is positive, and the projects under consideration are independent, it should be accepted. If the NPV is positive, and the projects under consideration are mutually exclusive, the one with the highest NPV should be accepted.

Net Worth The capital and surplus of a firm—capital stock, capital surplus (paid-in capital), earned surplus (retained earnings), and, occasionally, certain reserves. For some purposes, preferred shares are included; generally, *Net Worth* refers only to the common shareholders' position.

New Issue Market The market that consists of stocks of companies that have just gone public.

Nominal Interest Rate The contracted, or stated, interest rate, undeflated for price level changes.

Nonvoting Shares Shares that have no voting rights. Nonvoting shares may have a higher dividend to compensate for the absence of a vote. Nonvoting shares are a specific example of *restricted shares,* which may have diminished voting rights.

Normal Yield Curve The usual, or normal, shape of the yield curve is upward-sloping. Interest rates on longer maturity securities are higher than interest rates on shorter maturity securities of equal default risk.

Offering Price The price at which common equity is sold to the public.

Operating Company A subsidiary of a holding company.

Operating Cycle A measure of the amount of time that elapses between the purchase of raw materials to produce goods, and the collection of cash in payment for those goods after they have been sold.

Operating Lease A lease in which the lessor both maintains and finances the asset. The lease can be cancelled by the lessee.

Operating Leverage The extent to which fixed costs are used in a firm's operation. Breakeven analysis is used to measure the extent to which operating leverage is employed.

Operating Merger A merger in which the operations of two companies are integrated with the expectation of achieving synergistic benefits.

Opportunity Cost The rate of return on the best *alternative* investment available—the highest return that will *not* be earned if the funds are invested in a particular project. For example, the opportunity cost of *not* investing in Bond A (which yields 8 percent) might be 7.99 percent, which could be earned on Bond B.

Option A contract giving the holder the right to buy or sell an asset at some predetermined price within a specified period of time.

Ordering Costs The costs associated with keeping only a small inventory and ordering day-to-day; that is, clerical and administrative costs, as well as the cost of lost current sales (in the event of the company being unable to meet requirements due to lack of inventory) and lost future sales (through a negative reputation effect).

Ordinary Income Income from normal operations but specifically excluding income from the sale of capital assets.

Organized Security Exchanges Formal organizations having tangible, physical locations and conducting auction markets in designated ("listed") investment securities. The Toronto Stock Exchange is an organized security exchange.

Over-the-Counter (OTC) Market All facilities that provide for trading in unlisted securities—those not listed on organized exchanges. The over-the-counter market is typically viewed as a "telephone market," since most business is conducted by telephone.

Paid-in Capital The funds received in excess of par value when a firm sells stock. Paid-in capital can also be increased when a company declares a stock dividend.

Par Value The nominal or face value of a share equity or bond; for equity, most firms no longer issue par value shares.

Partnership An unincorporated business owned by two or more persons.

Payables Deferral Period The average length of time between receipt of raw materials and payment of their associated account payable.

Payback Period The length of time required for the net revenues of an investment to return the cost of the investment.

Payment Patterns Approach A method for monitoring accounts receivable where accounts receivable are related to sales in the month of origin, rather than to the average over some longer period. This method has an advantage over DSO (Days Sales Outstanding) and the Ageing Schedules methods in that the payment pattern is not affected by the averaging period chosen or by increasing or decreasing sales.

Payout Ratio The percentage of earnings paid out in the form of dividends.

Percentage-of-Sales Method A method of forecasting financial requirements by expressing various balance sheet items as a percentage of sales and then multiplying these percentages by expected future sales to construct pro forma balance sheets.

Perpetual Bond A bond that pays interest annually (or semi-annually) into perpetuity.

Perpetuity A stream of equal future payments expected to continue forever.

Pledging of Accounts Receivable Short-term borrowing from financial institutions where the loan is secured by accounts receivable. Under pledging, the lender has recourse to the borrower. Also called *Discounting of Accounts Receivable.*

Pooling of Interests An accounting method for combining the financial statements of two firms that merge. Under the pooling of interests procedure, the assets of the merged firms are simply added to form the balance sheet of the resulting corporation. This method is different from the "purchase" method, where goodwill is put on the balance sheet to reflect a premium (or discount) paid in excess of book value.

Portfolio A collection or combination of assets.

Portfolio Effect The extent to which the variation in returns on a combination of assets (a "portfolio") is smaller than the sum of the variations of the individual assets.

Portfolio Theory The theory that deals with the selection of optimal portfolios—portfolios that provide the highest possible return for any specified degree of risk.

Post-Audit A comparison of the expected and actual results for a given capital project.

Precautionary Balance A cash balance held in reserve for random, unforeseen fluctuations in inflows and outflows.

Preemptive Right A provision contained in the corporate charter and bylaws that gives common shareholders the right to purchase on a *pro rata* basis new issues of common shares (or securities convertible into common shares).

Preferred Equity A long-term equity security paying a fixed dividend.

Present Value (PV) The value today of a future payment, or stream of payments, discounted at the appropriate discount rate.

Pressure The effect on the share price when a company sells a substantial block of new equity. The sale may tend to temporarily depress the price of outstanding shares.

Price/Earnings (P/E) Ratio The ratio of price to earnings; it shows the dollar amount investors will pay for $1 of current earnings. Faster-growing or less risky firms typically have higher P/E ratios than either slower-growing or more risky firms.

Primary EPS The earnings available to common shareholders divided by the average number of shares that would have been outstanding if warrants and convertibles likely to be converted in the near future had actually been exercised or converted.

Primary Markets The markets in which newly issued securities are bought and sold for the first time.

Prime Rate A published rate of interest charged by chartered banks on short-term loans to very large, stable corporations and their most creditworthy customers.

Private Placement Financing directly from the source of funds without the use of an intermediary such as an investment dealer.

Processing Float The float caused by delays within the firm between receipt of a cheque and depositing it in the bank. Also called *Processing Float.*

Profitability Ratios Ratios that show the combined effect of liquidity, asset management, and debt management on operating profits. *See also* Basic Earning Power, Return on Assets, Return on Equity.

Pro Forma A financial statement that shows how an actual statement will look if certain specified assumptions are realized. Pro forma statements may be either future or past projections. A backward pro forma statement may be used in a merger.

Probability Distribution A listing of all possible outcomes or events, with a probability (the change of the event's occurrence) assigned to each outcome.

Profit Centre A unit of a large, decentralized firm that has its own investments and for which a rate of return on investment can be calculated.

Profit Margin The ratio of profits after taxes to sales.

Progressive Tax A tax that requires a higher percentage payment on higher incomes. The personal income tax in Canada is progressive.

Promissory Note A document specifying the amount, percentage interest rate, repayment schedule, and other terms and conditions of a loan.

Proprietorship An unincorporated business owned by one individual.

Prospectus A document issued for the purpose of describing a new security issue. The securities commission in each province in which the securities will be issued examines prospectuses to ensure that statements contained in them are not false or misleading.

Proxy A document giving one person the authority or power to act for another. Typically, the authority in question is the power to vote shares of common equity.

Proxy Fight An attempt by a person, group, or company to gain control of a company by getting the shareholders to vote a new management into office.

Pure Play Method A method to estimate the beta of a project by determining the beta of firms whose only business in the product or project in question.

Purchase In mergers, the situation in which a large firm acquires a smaller one.

Purchasing Power Risk The risk that inflation will reduce the purchasing power of a given sum of money.

Put An option to sell a specific security at a specified price within a designated period; it is the opposite of a call.

Quick Ratio Current assets minus inventory, divided by current liabilities; it is sometimes called the *Acid Test Ratio.*

Rate of Return The internal rate of return on an investment.

Ratio Analysis A type of financial analysis making use of the relationships between the various items in financial statements. These relationships can be expressed in the form of ratios, and the comparison of these ratios, over time and with other companies or benchmarks, form the basis of financial decisions that are made.

Real Risk-Free Rate of Interest The rate of interest on default-free government of Canada bonds less the expected inflation rate.

Receivables Conversion Period The average length of time required to convert receivables into cash; it equals days sales outstanding.

Receivership A firm is in receivership when it cannot meet its financial obligations as they come due. Its affairs are put into the hands of a receiver, who is appointed either by a court or by a secured creditor under the provisions of a debt contract.

Recourse Arrangement A term used in connection with accounts receivable financing. A firm may sell its accounts receivable to a financial company under a recourse agreement. If the accounts receivable cannot be collected, the selling firm must repurchase them from the company.

Refunding The sale of new debt securities to replace an old debt issue.

Regression Analysis A statistical procedure for predicting the value of one (dependent) variable on the basis of knowledge about one or more other (independent) variables.

Reinvestment Rate The rate of return at which cash flows from an investment are reinvested. The reinvestment rate may or may not be constant from year to year.

Reinvestment Rate Risk The risk that a decline in interest rates will lead to lower income when funds from maturing bonds or intermediate cash flows such as coupons are reinvested.

Relative Priority In bankruptcy proceedings, a flexible approach to the priority of creditors' claims, which gives balanced consideration to all claimants.

Reorder Point The inventory level at which goods must be reordered.

Reorganization The situation in which the assets of a financially troubled firm are restated to reflect their current market value and the firm's financial structure is restated to reflect any changes on the asset side of the statement. This is also known as a *Workout*. Under a reorganization the firm continues in existence.

Retractable Bond A bond that allows the holder the option of selling it back to the issuer at par value at a specified time before the maturity date.

Return on Investment (ROI) The return on all capital invested in the firm is measured as the ratio of net operating income after taxes to total assets. Also called *Returned on Total Assets (ROA)*.

Required Rate of Return The rate of return that shareholders expect to receive on common equity investments.

Residual Theory of Dividends The theory that dividends paid should equal the excess of earnings over retained earnings necessary to finance the optimal capital budget.

Residual Value The value of leased property at the end of the lease term.

Restricted Voting Shares Common equity that has restricted voting rights compared to the remaining equity. The dividends on the restricted shares are often higher than on the unrestricted shares. In Canada, the restriction on the shares results in *no* voting rights and the restricted shares are called nonvoting shares. In other countries, the restriction diminishes the voting rights but does not remove them.

Restrictive Covenant A provision in debt contracts, including bond indentures, that constrains the actions of a borrower.

Retained Earnings That portion of earnings not paid out in dividends. The figure that appears on the balance sheet is the sum of retained earnings for all the years throughout the company's history.

Retention Ratio The proportion of earnings retained in the company.

Return on Assets (ROA) The ratio of net income after taxes to total assets—sometimes defined as earnings before interest and taxes (EBIT) divided by total assets, which is also called the *Basic Earning Power Ratio*.

Return on Common Equity Income available to common shareholders divided by common equity.

Revolving Credit Agreement A formal line of credit extended to a firm by a bank.

Right A short-term option to buy a specified number of shares of a new issue of securities at a designated "subscription" price.

Rights Offering A securities flotation offered to existing shareholders.

Risk The probability that actual future returns will be below expected returns. Risk is measured by the standard deviation of expected returns, the coefficient of variation of earnings, or the beta coefficient.

Risk-Adjusted Discount Rate The discount rate that applies to a particular risky (uncertain) stream of income; the riskless rate of interest plus a risk premium appropriate to the level of risk attached to the particular income stream.

Risk Aversion A dislike for risk. Investors who are averse to risk have higher required rates of return for securities with higher risk.

Risk-Free Rate of Interest The rate of interest on default-free government of Canada bonds or Treasury bills. If the planning horizon is relatively short, the rate of interest on Treasury bills should be used; for longer time frames, the rate on longer maturity bonds should be used. Also called the *Riskless Rate of Interest*. Since it is a nominal rate, it includes an inflation premium: $k_{RF} = k^* + IP$, where k^* is the real risk-free rate and IP is the inflation premium.

Risk Premium The difference between the required rate of return on a given risky asset and the rate of return on a riskless asset with the same expected life. *See also* Inflation Premium, Default Risk Premium, Liquidity Premium, Maturity Risk Premium.

Risk, Relevant The risk of a security that cannot be diversified away, or market risk. In theory, risk premiums should apply only to relevant risk.

Risk/Return Trade-off Function *See* Capital Market Line.

Risk, Total The total of market and nonmarket risk of a security.

Safety Stock Additional inventories carried to guard against changes in sales rates or production/shipping delays.

Sale and Leaseback An operation whereby a firm sells land, buildings, or equipment to a leasing firm and simultaneously leases the property back for a specified period under specific terms.

Salvage Value The value of a capital asset at the end of a specified period. In a capital budgeting problem, it is the current market price of an asset being considered for replacement.

Scenario Analysis A short version of simulation, where bad and good sets of financial circumstances are compared with a most likely, or base, case NPV.

Seasoned Issue Outstanding bonds, or bonds that have been on the market for a while.

Secondary Market In investment terminology, the "market" in which stocks are traded after they have been issued by corporations. When a company sells a new issue of company equity, the transaction is considered a "primary market transaction."

Security Market Line The line that shows the relationship between risk and rates of return for individual securities.

Self-Liquidating A financing technique that matches the maturity of assets and liabilities; thus a short-term loan to finance inventory will be paid off when the inventory is sold.

Selling Group A group of brokerage firms formed for the purpose of distributing a new issue of securities; it is part of the underwriting process.

Sell-off A divestiture or sale of a subsidiary or division of a company for cash or marketable securities.

Senior Securities Securities having claims on assets and income that rank higher than certain other securities (junior securities). For example, mortgage bonds are senior to debentures, but debentures are senior to common shares.

Sensitivity Analysis Simulation analysis in which key variables are changed one at a time and the resulting change in the rate of return is observed. Typically, the rate of return is more sensitive to changes in some variables than to changes in others.

Shark Repellent A set of transactions that can be undertaken by the management of the target firm in a hostile takeover to reduce the probability of an offer being successful. The techniques have been the subject of debate concerning whether they are in the shareholder's or manager's best interests.

Share Repurchase A means by which a firm distributes income to shareholders by buying back its own shares, thereby decreasing shares outstanding, increasing EPS, and increasing the price of the shares.

Short Selling The selling of a security that is not owned by the seller at the time of the sale. The seller borrows the security from a brokerage firm and must at some point repay the brokerage firm by buying the security on the open market.

Simulation A technique whereby probable future events are simulated on a computer. Estimated rates of return and risk indexes can be generated.

Sinking Fund A required annual payment designed to amortize a bond or a preferred share issue. The sinking fund may be held in the form of cash or marketable securities but, more generally, the money put into the fund is used to retire some of the securities in question each year.

Social Responsibility The idea that businesses should be partly responsible for the welfare of society at large.

Sovereign Risk The risk of expropriation of a foreign subsidiary's assets by the host country or of unanticipated restrictions on cash flows to the parent.

Specific Item Forecasting If a specific revenue item or expense is known, that item can be forecast specifically. For instance, if it is known that the expected increase in sales will require hiring additional staff in the accounts receivable department, their salaries can be specifically forecast.

Specialists Members of stock exchanges who facilitate the trading process by keeping an inventory of shares of the stocks in which they specialize.

Speculative Balance A cash balance that is held to enable the firm to take advantage of any bargain purchases that might arise.

Spinoff A divestiture of a subsidiary where the shares of the subsidiary are distributed as a dividend to current shareholders. No cash or equivalent is obtained for the assets.

Spontaneous Financing Financing (for example, trade credit) that arises from ordinary business transactions.

Spontaneously Generated Funds Funds from sources such as accounts payable and accruals, which rise spontaneously with sales.

Spot Market A market in which assets are bought and sold for delivery "on the spot."

Spot Rate The effective exchange rate for a foreign currency for delivery on (approximately) the current day.

Spread The difference between the price a security dealer offers to pay for securities (the "bid" price) and the price at which the dealer offers to sell them (the "asked" price).

Stand-Alone Risk The risk of undertaking a capital project, disregarding the fact that it is but one asset within the firm's portfolio of assets, and that the firm in question is but one security in most investors' portfolios. Stand-alone risk is measured with respect to the project's cash flow risk and not the risk of the overall company.

Standard Deviation A statistical measurement of the variability of a set of observations.

Statement of Cash Flows A financial statement that shows the sources and uses of cash for a specific period. Operating, investing, and financing activities all impact cash flows. Also called the *Statement of Changes in Financial Position*.

Statement of Changes in Financial Position A financial statement that shows the sources and uses of cash for a specific period. Operating, investing and financing activities all impact cash flows. Also called the *Statement of Cash Flows*.

Statement of Retained Earnings A financial statement that shows how much of a firm's earnings were retained, or not paid out as dividends.

Stay of Proceedings A legal term meaning a firm is given some time to prepare a proposal for restructuring; during the stay its creditors cannot remove their security.

Stock Dividend A dividend paid in additional shares of equity rather than cash. It involves a transfer from retained earnings to the capital stock account; therefore, stock dividends are limited by the amount of retained earnings.

Stock Split An accounting action to increase the number of shares outstanding; for example, in a three-for-one split, shares outstanding are tripled and each shareholder receives three new shares for each one formerly held. Stock splits involve no transfer from retained earnings to the capital account.

Strike Price The price that must be paid for a share of common equity when it is bought by exercising a warrant. See also *Exercise Price*.

Subordinated Debenture A bond having a claim on assets only after the senior debt has been paid off in the event of liquidation.

Subscription Price The price at which a security may be purchased in a rights offering.

Sunk Cost An outlay of funds that has already been committed, or that has already occurred and hence is not affected by the accept–reject decision under consideration.

Supernormal Growth The part of the life cycle of a firm in which the firm's growth is much faster than that of the economy as a whole.

Sustainable Growth Rate The growth in sales that can be financed without recourse to the outside capital markets.

Swap A financial arrangement between a company and a chartered bank or second company in which the current interest payments on the company's debt can be exchanged with the other party. The purpose of this transaction is to convert either floating rate debt to fixed or fixed to floating.

Synergy A situation in which the whole is greater than the sum of its parts. In a synergistic merger, the postmerger earnings exceed the sum of the individual companies' premerger earnings.

Systematic Risk Also called *Market Risk,* this is the part of a security's risk that results from broad swings in the stock market and that cannot be eliminated by diversification.

Takeover The acquisition of one firm by another, sometimes over the opposition of the target firm's management.

Tangible Assets Physical assets as opposed to intangible assets such as goodwill and the stated value of patents.

Target Firm A company that another firm, generally a larger one, wants to acquire through merger.

Technical Default A situation in which a firm violates a bond covenant; it may be as simple as having a current ratio below a specified level.

Temporary Current Assets Current assets that fluctuate seasonally or cyclically.

Tender Offer A situation in which one firm offers to buy the shares of another by going directly to the shareholders, frequently over the opposition of the target company's management.

Term Loan A loan, generally obtained from a bank or insurance company, with a maturity greater than one year. Term loans are generally amortized.

Term Structure of Interest Rates The relationship between yields and maturities of securities.

Time Line A tool in value-of-money analysis to aid in visualizing the timing of events in a particular financial situation.

Times Interest Earned A ratio measuring earnings before interest and taxes divided by interest charges. It measures the ability of the firm to meet its annual interest charges.

Total Assets Turnover The ratio of sales divided by total assets, which measures the utilization, or turnover, of all of the firm's assets.

Total Carrying Costs (TCC) The costs of carrying inventory; includes the rent and utilities for the warehouse, cost of capital tied up, and obsolescence. Carrying costs generally increase with the average amount of inventory held.

Total Inventory Costs (TIC) The sum of total carrying costs and total ordering costs.

Total Ordering Costs (TOC) The cost of placing an order; includes setup of production runs, long-distance telephone or fax charges, and taking delivery of the goods. Ordering costs are assumed to be independent of the average size of inventory.

Trade Credit Interfirm debt arising through credit sales and recorded as an account receivable by the seller and as an account payable by the buyer.

Transactions Balance A cash balance associated with payments and collections; the balance necessary to conduct day-to-day business.

Translation Loss The loss resulting from translating financial statements from a foreign subsidiary's currency into the parent's currency.

Treasury Shares Common shares that have been repurchased by the issuing firm.

Trend Analysis An analysis of a firm's financial ratios over time in order to determine the improvement or deterioration of its financial situation.

Trust Receipt An instrument acknowledging that the borrower holds certain goods in trust for the lender. Trust receipt financing is used in financing inventories for automobile dealers, construction equipment dealers, appliance dealers, and other dealers in expensive durable goods.

Trustee The representative of bondholders who acts in their interest and facilitates communication between them and the issuer. Typically these duties are handled by a department of a trust company.

Undepreciated Capital Cost (UCC) In the Canadian tax system, assets are grouped into classes and depreciated as a group. The amount of depreciation that can be deducted in any year for tax purposes is specified by the *Income Tax Act* as the product of the CCA rate for that particular class times the undepreciated capital cost. The UCC must then be decremented by that amount. Purchases of assets increase the UCC, and sales decrease it.

Underwriting (1) The entire process of issuing new corporate securities. (2) The insurance function of bearing the risk of adverse price fluctuations during the period in which a new issue of shares or bonds is being distributed.

Underwriting Syndicate A syndicate of investment firms formed to spread the risk associated with the purchase and distribution of a new issue of securities. The larger the issue, the greater the number of firms typically involved in the syndicate.

Unlisted Securities Securities that are traded in the over-the-counter market.

Unsystematic Risk The diversifiable or company-specific risk, which is caused by factors unique to the company and which can be eliminated when the equity of a company is held in a well-diversified portfolio.

Venture Capital Risk capital supplied to small companies by wealthy individuals, partnerships, or corporations, usually in return for an equity position in the firms.

Vertical Merger A company's acquisition of one of its suppliers or one of its customers.

Warehouse Receipt Financing A form of inventory financing in which the lending institution employs a third party to exercise control over the borrower's inventory and to act as the lender's agent.

Warrant A long-term option to buy a stated number of shares of common equity at a specified price. The specified price is generally called the *Exercise Price*.

Weighted Average Cost of Capital (WACC) A weighted average of the component costs of debt, preferred shares, and common equity; also called the *Composite Cost of Capital*.

Within-Firm Risk In capital budgeting, this reflects the effects of a project on the firm's risk, as measured by the effect on the firm's earning variability. In the worst case, a project could incur losses that would destabilize profits or even cause bankruptcy. Also called *Corporate Risk*.

Working Capital A firm's investment in short-term assets—cash, short-term securities, accounts receivable, and inventories. *Gross working capital* is a firm's total current assets. *Net working capital* is its current assets minus current liabilities. If the term *working capital* is used without further qualification, it generally refers to gross working capital.

Working Capital Policy Basic policy decisions regarding target levels for each category of current assets and for the financing of these assets.

Yield The rate of return on an investment; the internal rate of return.

Yield to Call The rate of return earned on a bond if it is held until its expected call date, and redeemed for its expected call price.

Yield Curve The graph of the relationship between the yields and maturities for various issues of a security.

Yield to Maturity (YTM) The rate of interest earned on a bond if it is held to maturity.

INDEX

READER REPLY CARD

We are interested in your reaction to the fourth edition of *Canadian Managerial Finance,* by Halpern, Weston, and Brigham. With your comments, we can improve this book in future editions. Please help us by completing this questionnaire.

1. What was your reason for using this book?
   _____ university course
   _____ college course
   _____ continuing education courses
   _____ professional development
   _____ personal interest
   _____ other (please specify)

2. If you are a student, please identify your school and course. If you used this text for a program, what was the name of that program?

3. Approximately how much of the book did you use?
   _____ all   _____ 3/4   _____ 1/2   _____ 1/4

4. Which chapters or sections were omitted from your course?

5. What is the best aspect of this book?

6. Is there anything that should be added?

7. Were the Concept Review summary boxes a helpful review of each section?

8. Was the information in this text presented in an interesting manner?

9. Was there enough problem material to support the level of difficulty in the text?

10. Please add any comments or suggestions.

(fold here and tape shut)

0116870399-M8Z4X6-BR01

Scott Duncan
Publisher, College Division
HARCOURT BRACE & COMPANY, CANADA
55 HORNER AVENUE
TORONTO, ONTARIO
M8Z 9Z9

Frequently Used Symbols

APR   Annual percentage rate

A/R   Accounts receivable

b   The fraction of a firm's earnings retained rather than paid out as dividends (in percent)

β Beta coefficient, a measure of an asset's riskiness

C   Coupon payment for a bond

CAPM   Capital asset pricing model

CF   Cash flow; CF_t is the cash flow in Period t

CR   Conversion ratio

CV   Coefficient of variation

D   (1) Dividend per share (DPS); D_t is the dividend in Period t
(2) Total market value of debt

DCF   Discounted cash flow

Dep   Depreciation

DSO   Days sales outstanding

EBIT   Earnings before interest and taxes = net operating income (NOI)

EOQ   Economic ordering quantity

EPS   Earnings per share

F   (1) Fixed operating costs
(2) Percentage issue cost

FCC   Fixed-charge coverage ratio

FV   Future value

FVA_n Future value of an annuity for n years

FVIF   Future value interest factor for a lump sum

FVIFA   Future value interest factor for an annuity

g   Growth rate in earnings, dividends, and share prices

I   (1) Interest payment in dollars
(2) Rate of inflation

IRR   Internal rate of return

k   (1) A percentage discount rate, or cost of capital
(2) A required rate of return

$\bar{k}$ "k bar," historic, or realized, rate of return

$\hat{k}$ "k hat," an expected rate of return

k_a Weighted average cost of capital (WACC)

k_d Cost of debt

k_e Cost of new common shares (equity)

k_j Cost of capital for an individual firm or security

k_M Cost of capital for "the market," or an "average" share

k_{nom} Nominal risk-free rate of interest

k_p Cost of preferred share

k^*_{RF} Real risk-free rate of interest

k_{RF} Rate of return on a risk-free security

k_s (1) Cost of retained earnings
(2) Required rate of return on equity

M   Maturity value of a bond

M/B   Market-to-book ratio

MCC   Marginal cost of capital

MIRR   Modified internal rate of return